Gateway to the West

GATEWAY

to the

W·E·S·T

Volume 1

Compiled by

Ruth Bowers and Anita Short

Genealogical Publishing Co., Inc.

Gateway to the West was published quarterly between 1967 and 1978
as follows:
September 1967: Vol. 1, No. 1-A (trial issue)
1968-1977: Vol. 1, No. 1-Vol. 10, No. 4 (40 issues total)
1978: Vol. 11 (single, large issue)

This edition of *Gateway to the West* has been excerpted from the ori-
ginal numbers, consolidated, and reprinted in two volumes, with added
Publisher's Note, Tables of Contents, and Indexes, by Genealogical
Publishing Co., Inc. Baltimore, 1989.
Library of Congress Catalogue Card Number 88-82636
International Standard Book Number, Volume 1: 0-8063-1237-8
Set Number: 0-8063-1236-X
Made in the United States of America

Note

Gateway to the West had a short but spectacular life as a periodical. In slightly more than ten years, from 1967 to 1978, it managed to cover some of the least accessible yet most important genealogical records of 76 of Ohio's 88 counties. From common pleas court records, guardianships, naturalizations, and deed abstracts to the more conventional births, marriages, deaths, cemetery records, and wills, *Gateway* offered a range of genealogical source materials unmatched by any other Ohio publication. At its peak it had a circulation of nearly 2,000, and when it ceased publication with Volume 11 in 1978, its fame had surpassed even that of the *Old Northwest Genealogical Quarterly*.

Ever since it ceased publication interest in the periodical has continued unabated, and demand for back issues has now so far outstripped availability that it is a rare thing to find a single issue anywhere on the market. For that matter, it is a rare thing to find a complete set even in a library. What is almost as bad, those libraries and individuals lucky enough to own a complete set have found that it is almost unusable without an index to the concentrated mass of material locked within its pages. Owing to the continuing demand for the work and the lack of a comprehensive index, it seemed a reasonable object to gather all the articles together and to bring them out in a reprint edition, complete with index.

Accordingly, the principal articles, arranged under their respective counties, have been consolidated into two large volumes—each with its own index—and reprinted under their original banner—*Gateway to the West*. Altogether, in nearly 2,000 pages, in some 350 articles naming more than 95,000 persons, in records ranging from Adams County to Wood County, from court records to church records, from township records to cemetery records, the researcher now has permanent access to a priceless body of material.

Genealogical Publishing Company

Contents

Will Abstracts

Clark County

Clermont County

Clinton County

Cemetery Records

Licking County

ADAMS COUNTY, OHIO - ADMINISTRATORS AND EXECUTORS DOCKET RECORDS 1836-1841

The following records were taken from the Administrators and Executors Docket which is located in the basement vault Archives Section of the Adams County Court House at West Union. Due to the court house fire in 1910 few of the Probate Record exist, that this one does is remarkable. All information given in the record has been included. These records essentially will prove only that a person died in this county near the time of the date of the record. However, the deeds records for this county are complete through 1797 and it may be possible to prove heirs through deeds. Page on which record is found in book is given in parenthesis.

FULTON, Rachel - #1; 3-20-1837; David Fulton, adms.; Bond $400.; Enos Gore and James P. Lovett, securities; settled. (1)

BAUGHMAN, John - #2; 3-20-1837; John Cappel, adms.; Bond $4500.; Thomas Hale and Robert Morrison, securities; settled. (1)

LOVETT, Daniel - #1; 3-20-1837; Daniel Lovell and Edmund O. Lovell, executors; Bond $10,000.; Enos Gore, David Fulton and James P. Lovett, securities. (1)

OSMAN, Charles - #2; 3-20-1837; Simon Osman, executor; Bond $400.; Jonathan Hughes and Jacob Easter, securities; Settled Oct Term 1828, Order Book 12, page 89.(1)

CARRIGAN, Andrew - #3; 3-22-1837; Will, no executors. (1)

BURKETT, Thomas - #4; 3-24-1837; John Collier, executor; Bond $3500.; Kennard Norford and Michael Collier, securities. (1)

ANDERSON, William - #5; 3-25-1837; Richard H. Anderson, executor; Bond $700.; Isaac Foster and Robert List, security. (1)

ROUSH, Dobbins - #6; 5-9-1837; Wm T. Smith, adms. Bond $600.; John Bryant and Parmunius Roush, security; settled Sept. 1843. (1)

GIBSON, Thomas - #7; 7-17-1837; James Truitt, adms.; Bond $100. William Parker and William Dryden, security; settled Sept 1840, Court Order Book 12, page 385. (1)

MORRISON, Archibald F. - #10; 7-18-1837; James E. Morrison, adms.; Bond $700.; Jacob N. Murphy and David W. Murphy, security. (1)

COLLIER, Joseph - #11; 7-18-1837; Gabriel D. Darlinton, adms.; Bond $300.; Isaac Aerl and John Bratton, security; settled. (1)

MARQUIS, Joseph - #12 #6 (Marked out); 7-20-1837; Moris McMeekin, adms.; Bond $1000.; William Robbison and James Doyl, security; final settlement 4-7-1853. (1)

STEEN, Alexander - $24; 7-20-1837; Josiah Y. Steen, executor; Bond $500.; Samuel Dryden and Henry Sharp, security; settled 3-11-1844 Order Book 13, page 490. (2)

ELLISON, Robert - #14; 7-21-1837; Moris Ellison, adms. Bond $500.; James Hood and Wm. Kirker, security; settled Apr. 1841, O.B. 12, page 458. (2)

CHIPPS, John - #15; 7-21-1837; John Patterson, adms.; Bond $400.; James Finley and Henry Rape, security. (2)

MEANS, John - #16; 7-21-1837; Hugh Menas, adms.; Bond $6000.; John Sparks and James Hood, security; settled Oct. Term 1838, Order Book 12, page 2. (2)

KIRKER, Thomas - #7; 2-25-1837; Wm Kirker, executor; Bond $4500.; John Sparks, James Hood and John McCullough, security; executor settled within court. (2)

TESTER, Conrod - #8; 2-9-1836; Richard Noleman, executor; Bond $3500.; James M. Governey and Thomas Governey, security. (2)

CLARK, John - #9; 4-7-1836; George Clark. executor; Bond $800.; Archibald Carothers and Samuel Clark, security; settled July Term 1838, O.B. 12, page 41. (2)

BAILEY, Joel - #10; 10-5-1836; Lemuel Lindsey, executor; Bond $400.; John
Sparks and John Bailey, security. Adms with will annexed settled Aug. 1842.(2)

LEWIS, James - #11; 10-7-1836; Edward Easton and Jacob Zile, executors; Bond
$400.; John Patterson and Wm Kisling, security. (2)

DINNING, Job - #12; 12-29-1836; Daniel Dinning and Wm Henry Harrison Dinning
executors; Bond $800.; George Sparks and Gabriel O. Darlinton, security;
settled. (2)

RHOADS, Thomas - #23; 2-9-1836; Samuel Rhoads, adms.; Bond $500.; Wm Carson and
James Carson, security. (2)

RADER, Martin - #24; 3-26-1837; Wm. W. Carpenter, adms.; Bond $400.; Oliver Smith
and Jedediah Foster, security. (2)

PAUL, James - #25; 4-7-1836; Samuel McClelland, adms.; Bond $500.; Jane Paul
and George Sparks, security; settled. (3)

PRISS (or PRICE?), Isaac H. - #26; 7-18-1836; Robt. C. Jones, adms.; Bond $1000.;
John Marker and John Anderson, security. (3)

PENCE, Robert - #27; 10-8-1836; Samuel Ellis, adms.; Bond $800.; Henry Rape and
Robert McDavid (or McDaniel) Jr., security; settled Apr. Term 1838, Order
Book 1, page 502. (3)

WADE, Alras - #28; 11-3-1836; James Pixley, adms.; Bond $800.; Hosea Moore and
David Carr, security; settled Order Book #12, page 380. (3)

KENDALL, John - #29; 2-25-1837; Samuel Kendall, adms.; Bond $700.; Amos Rees
and Christian Bottleman, security, settled Oct. Term 1838, Order Book 12,
page 90. (3)

FOSTER, Hiram - #30; 9-16-1837; Thomas Foster, adms.; Bond $1000.; Samuel Foster
and Boone Montgomery, security; settled Oct. Term 1839. (3)

ELLISON, John son of Arthur Ellison - #31; 9-16-1837; William Ellison, adms.;
Bond $300.; Arthur Ellison and Aaron Rawbuck, security; settled. (3)

CARL, Joseph - #32; 9-16-1837; Andrew B. Carl. adms.; Bond $350.; Wm Shepherd
and Daniel John, security; settled. (3)

FURNIER, Henry - #33; 10-6-1836; David Furnier, adms.; Bond $500.; Wm T. Reynolds
and James Cole, security. (3)

ADAIR, Joseph - #34; 10-17-1837; Edward Moore, adms.; Bond $2600.; Alexander
Woodrow, Wm W. Carpenter and Samuel G. Bradford, security. (3)

WADE, Zephaniah - #35; 1-9-1838; Elijah Wade, adms.; Bond $800.; Joseph Wade
and John Wear, security; settled order Book No. 12, page 456. (3)

McCUTCHEN, John - #13; 1-16-1838; Nathaniel McCutchen, executor; Bond $300.;
John Anderson and James Smith, security; settled Order Book 12, page 458. (3)

EDGINGTON, Isaac - #14; 3-21-1836; no executor, no bond given. (3)

WEAR, Elizabeth - #15; 12-29-1836; no executor; no bond given. (3)

ELLISON, Andrew Jr. - #16; copy of will certified from Lawrence Co.; admitted Adams
Co. Mar. 1836; Jane G. Ellison, Dyer Burgess and Joseph Riggs, executors. (4)

McCLELLAND, Thomas - #17; 3-16-1838; James B. McClelland, adms. with will annexed;
Bond $400.; William McCormick and James Burns, security; settled. (4)

SECHRIST, George - #18; 3-16-1838; Asa Williamson adms. de bonis non with will
annexed; Bond $2000.; George Sparks, Samuel Foster and James Smith, security.(4)

FINLEY, Samuel S. - #19; 4-27-1838; Andrew McIntire and Robert B. Glasgow,
executors; Bond $2500.; Wm McIntire and John S. Patton, security; settled. (4)

ARMSTRONG, Jane #20; 4-24-1838; John Paul, executor; Bond $400.; Thomas McGovern
and Elijah Baldwin, security. (4)

2

McDANIEL, William - #44 (marked out) #21; 4-23-1838; Hannah McDaniel, executor; no bond. (4)

BLACK, Thomas - #45 (marked out) #22; 4-27-1838; William Black, executor; no bond.(4)

WALKER, James - #46 (marked out) #23; 4-27-1838; Joseph Walker and Alexander Walker, executors; no bond; settled July 1843. (4)

MURFIN, Samuel - #47; 4-23-1838; Thomas I. Murphy and Craven Phillips, adms.; Bond $800.; John Sinter and John Wright, security; settled Order Book 13, page 376. (4)

LEECH, James - #48; 4-27-1838; Thomas Huston, adms.; Bond $500.; David Leech and Archibald Leech, security; settled. (5)

SPARKS, Solomon - #49; 4-23-1838; James Sparks, adms.; Bond $3200.; Hiram Burnett and Milton Gassett, security. (5)

ROBINSON, Andrew - $50; 4-27-1838; James Querry, adms.; Bond $800.; Wm Thompson and Joseph Walker, security; settled Order Book 13, page 375. (5)

OLDSON, Samuel - #51; 4-24-1838; Samuel Harlan, adms.; Bond $150.; Zlex'r Woodrow and Joseph W. Lafferty, security. (5)

BRYAN, Thomas - #52; 5-11-1838; Daniel M. Bryan, adms.; Bo nld $2500.; Thomas Buck and Thomas J. Bradney, security. (5)

(note: at this point in the record a notation is entered that from this point on the executor and adms. case numbers will be numbered separate with adms. to begin with #52 and executors to begin with #25.)

BOYLES, William - #53; 9-19-1838; Robert Storey, adms.; Bond $1000.; Van S. Brady and William Ellison, security; settled Aug. Term 1842. (5)

McCLURE, Holbert - #25; 10-22-1838; Samuel McClure adms. with will annexed; Bond $400.; Asa Williamson and James McNeil, security. (5)

SMITH, Levi - #26; 11-23-1838; David D. Smith, executor; Bond $6000.; David Doak and John Criswell, security; settled. (5)

CORYELL, Salathiel - #54; 11-23-1838; Archibald Coryell, adms.; Bond $500.; Daniel V. Coryell and Fields Marlatt, security; settled. (5)

PAGE, John - #55; 11-23-1838; Joseph C. Page, adms.; Bond $900.; James Hood and Edward S. Moore, security; settled. (5)

KING, Nancy - #27; 11-23-1838; Laban Parks, adms. with will annexed; Bond $500.; John Warmsley and John Puntenney, security. (5)

NEWMAN, William - #56; 12-13-1838; James Puntenney, adms.; Bond $2600.; Laban Parks and John Puntenney, security. (6)

PHILLIPS, Henry - #57; 12-13-1838; John Phillips, adms.; Bond $700.; Zechariah Black and George Sparks, security. (6)

DUZAN, Abraham - #28; 4-2-1839; John Campbell, executor; no bond. (6)

BECK, Alexander - #29; 4-5-1839; Eli Grooms, executor; Bond $1000.; Adam McCoonsy(?) and Zachariah Grooms, security. (6)

LATHROP, James - #58; 4-4-1839; James Stout, adms.; Bond $800.; Wm Stout Sr. and James Puntenney, security. (6)

GUTRIDGE, Andrew - #59; 4-5-1839; Elijah Leedom, adms. ; Bond $400.; Azariah Egington and John Smith, security. (6)

VEACH, Edward - #60; 4-6-1839; Henry G. Hook, adms.; Bond $500.; John Hook and Wm Hook, security; settled O.B. 13, page 61. (6)

KEYS, John - #61; 4-6-1839; John Oliver, adms.; Bond $800.; Jesse Smalley and John Hull, security; settled O.B. 12, page 531. (6)

GLASGOW, Robert - #30; 8-5-1839; James Glasgow, executor; Bond $4000.; James McNeil and Samuel Foster, security; settled. (6)

FINLEY, Joseph S. - #31; Aug 1839; John Patterson and James Finley, executors; Bond $2000.; Field Marlatt, Samuel G. Bradford and Thomas M. Goveny, security. (6)

CAMPBELL, James - #62; 8-6-1839; Robert K. Campbell, adms.; Bond $5000.; Sam'l Campbell and Wm McCormick. security. (7)

McMAHAN, Joseph - #63; 8-8-1839; Robert McMahan, adms.; Bond $300.; John Collier and John H. Piatt, security. (7)

McHENRY, John - #64; 8-10-1839; Joshua McHenry, adms. de bonis non; Bond $300.; Wm Stevenson and James V. Willman, security. (7)

McINTIRE, Robert S. - #65; 10-22-1839; Jacob Wickersham, adms.; Bond $4000.; John Wickersham and John Davis, security; settled 9-13-1844. (7)

SHELTON, Thomas - #66; 9-25-1839; Jeremiah Shelton, adms.; Bond $800.; Hudson Low and Robert Shelton, security. (7)

VINSONHALER, George - #32; 9-27-1839; Flavius Josephus Vinsonhaler, executor; Bond $1000.; Asa Williamson and John Gustin, security. (7)

GUTHRIE, Henry - #33; 9-28-1839; Elizabeth Guthrie and John Burnside, executors; Copy of will from Mason Co., Ky; Bond $6000.; Hugh McCullough and William Thompson, security. (7)

CANNON, Jeremiah A.M. - #34; 11-8-1839; Edward C. Cannon, executor; Bond 1200.; Andrew Davidson and William Gore, security. (7)

BURGESS, Isabella - #35; 11-8-1839; Dyer Burgess, John McClanahan and Joseph Riggs, executors; Bond $50,000.; Gabtiel D. Darlinton, John Sparks, Samuel McClanahan, Addison McCullough and James Hood, security; settled. (7)

WILLIAMSON, Rev'd William - #67; 11-23-1839; Wm Kirker, adms.; Bond $500.; John McCullough and Bazaleel Gordon, security; settled. (8)

HALL, Benjamin #68; 11-23-1839; James H. Hall, adms.; Bond $700.; James Puntany and Hosea Cordry, security; settled 7-24-1852. (8)

LOCKHART, Robert - #36; copy of will from Frederick Co., Va.; (no date 1839-40); Josiah Lockhart, Joseph Baker and John Wright, executors; Baker refused to serve. (8)

ARCHER, George - #37; 1-9-1840; Mary Archer, executrix; Bond $8000.; Amos Dixon and John Anderson, security. (8)

SPARKS, George - #69; 1-9-1840; John Sparks, adms.; Bond $9000.; Dyer Burgess and James Hood, security. (8)

SYMONDS, John - #70; 1-9-1840; James Hood, adms.; Bond (no amount given); Dyer Burgess and John Sparks, security; settled. (8)

McNARY, John - #71; 1-9-1840; Thomas R. Tucker, adms.; Bond $2200.; Isaac Foster, G. D. Darlinton and James Smith, security. (8)

SPARKS, Margaret - #72; 2-13-1840; Mary T. Sparks, adms.; Bond $20,000.; Gabriel D. Darlinton and Joseph D. Darlinton, security. (8)

GRAHAM, James - #38; 2-13-1840; John Moore, executor; Bond $1000.; Leonard Phillips and Samuel R. Wood, security. (8)

DAVIS, Josiah - #39; 3-2-1840; Youphamy Davis, executor; Bond $2000.; John Bailey and Nathan D. Thompson, security. (9)

MOROMAN, Thomas Senior - #73; 3-2-1840; Thomas Moroman Jr., adms.; Bond $400.; Wm. Metz and Isaac Smalley, security; settled Order Book 13, page 489. (9)

ROBINSON, Andrew - #74; 3-7-1840; William Querry, adms. de bonis non; Bond $7000.; Wm Thompson and Joseph Walker, security; settled. (9)

4

LOWREY, Peter - #75; 3-7-1840; Wm Thompson, adms.; Bond $400.; Wm McVey and John
Thompson, security; settled. (9)
GROOMS, Abraham - #40; 3-3-1840; no executor; no bond. (9)
KINCAID, Margaret Jane - #41; 4-8-1840; Thomas Kincaid, executor; Bond $700.; Wm
McClanahan, Arch'd J. Coryell and John H. Kincaid, security. (9)
BURBBAGE, Levin D. #42; 6-1-1840; Sarah Burbbage, executrix; Bond $800.; John
Cropper and Handy Cropper, security. (9)
COMPTON, George L. - #43; 6-13-1840; Alexander Compton, executor; Bond $7000.;
Adam M. Govney, Andrew Jack and Wm W. Carpenter, security. (9)
PENNIWIT, Mark - #76; 6-6-1840; John Penniwit, adms.; Bond $1200.; Charles
Stevenson and Jonathan Wamsley, security. (9)
PATTON, Thomas - #77; 6-4-1840; Robert G. Patton, adms.; Bond $400.; Wm. McIntire
and Robt. Sproull, security; settled O.B. 13, page 560. (9)
WALLACE, John - #78; 6-1-1840; John Wallace, adms.; Bond $1000.; Asa Williamson
and Thomas Buck, security. (10)
WILLSON, Doct. Wm B. - #79; 8-8-1840; Addison McCullough, adms.; Bond $8000.;
Wm Kirker and John Sparks, security. (10)
BALDWIN, Stephen - #80; 8-15-1840; Joseph G. Baldwin, adms.; Bond $800.; Wm.
Mahaffey and James Miller, security; settled O.B. 13, page 490. (10)
VORIS, Ralph - #44; 8-15-1840; Samuel Voris, executor; Bond $1500.; Wm Ellison
and Wm Baird, security. (10)
SATTERFIELD, Benjamin - #81; 9-24-1840; Van R. McCarty, adms.; Bond $500.; Wesly
Satterfield and Jacob Hunpleman, security; settled. (10)
SATTERFIELD, James - #82; 9-18-1840; Wesley Satterfield, adms.; Bond $800.; Daniel
Dinning and Jonathan Ralston, security; settled. (10)
CAMPBELL, George - #83; 9-22-1840; Mary Jane Campbell, adms.; Bond $400.; Joseph
W. Lafferty and Wm W. Carpenter, security. (10)
BOWMAN, Philip - #84; 9-16-1840; John Bryan, adms. ; Bond $1200.; Major V. Cropper
and Wm. Rickards, security. (10)
WAITE, Jonathan - #85; 9-14-1840; James Puntany, adms.; Bond $6000.; Laban Parks,
Wm Stout Sr. and Geo. H. Puntany, security. (10)
SILCUTT, Valentine - #86; 9-21-1840; Wm Baird, adms.; Bond $3000.; John Morrison
and Wm Stevenson, security. (10)
GROOMS, Zachariah - #87; 9-21-1840; Zachariah Grooms Jr., adms; Bond $600.; Job
Dinning and John Grooms, security. (11)
BEATTY, Robert #88; 9-16-1840; Rhynard C. Beatty, adms.; Bond $800.; Josiah L.
Mathenny and James M. Bradney. security. (11)
DUNRETH, David - #89; 9-16-1840; Robert Dunreth and James W. Dunreth, adms.; Bond
$700.; Joseph W. Lafferty and Joseph Brewer, security; settled. (11)
BAIRD, James A. - #90; 9-14-1840; John H. Baird, adms.; Bond $4500.; Robert Baird
and Wm Stout Jr., security. (11)
DRYDEN, Isaac - #91; 9-14-1840; James Conner, adms.; Bond $200.; Wm Drydin and
Thomas Boyle, security; settled. (11)
WIKOFF, William - #92; 10-6-1840; Jesse Wikoff, adms.; Bond $1500.; Nathan Foster
and Andrew Jack, security. (11)
NEWKIRK, Abraham - #45; certified copy (not stated where from); 10-6-1840; Cyrus
Newkirk, executor; Bond $400.; Amos Dunkin and Adam McGovney, security. (11)
BLAIR, George - #93; 11-10-1840; Andrew Young, adms.; Bond $600.; Wm McIntire
and David Leech, security. (11)

5

WAITE, Sarah - #94; 11-10-1840; Wm Leech, adms.; Bond $400.; David Leech and Wm
McIntire, security; settled. (11)
GREEN, Doct. Triplet C. - #95; 11-25-1840; E.L.O. Lovett, adms.; Bond $2000.;
Thomas A. Lovett and Jacob Summers, security; settled O.B. 13, page 489. (11)
WALKUP, Samuel - #96; 12-5-1840; James Smith Sr., adms.; Bond $1000.; Wm T. Smith
and John Smith, security. (12)
HERD, William - #97; 2-12-1841; Henry Hutson, adms.; Bond $2500.; Asa Leedom and
Azariah Edginton, security; settled 7-11-1845. (12)
LANG, James - #46; 2-12-1841; Barton S. Lang, executor; Bond $1500.; Henry Hutson
and Asa Leedom, security; settled 7-24-1843. (12)
LEECH, Jane - #47; 3-12-1841; David Leech, executor; Bond $400.; John McCullough
and John Caraway, security. (12)
HANNAH, John - #98; 3-12-1841; Sarah Hannah, adms.; Bond $1200.; W S. Ellison
and Wm Rabe, security; settled 7-13-1844, O.B. 13, page 560. (12)
BENTLEY, John - #99; 3-12-1841; John Caraway, adms.; Bond $400.; Jacob Pile and
David Leech, security. (12)
SMITH, Reubin - #100; 4-7-1841; Joel Smith, adms.; Leonard Cole and Jacob Trever,
security; settled 3-6-1846. (12)
PITTINGER, William - #48; 4-5-1841; Wm Pittinger Jr., _adms._; Bond $2000.; Robert
Stevenson and Wesly Pittinger, security. (13)
COMPTON, George - #49; 4-9-1841; Abraham Hollingsworth and Adam McGovney, executors;
Bond $500.; John Sparks and Thomas McGovney, security. (13)
THOMAS, David - #50; 4-6-1841; Rebecca Thomas, executrix; Bond $500.; Samuel S.
Mason and John Hamilton, security. (13)
ARMSTRONG, Mary - #51; 4-8-1841; Wm Armstrong, executor; Bond $200.; Jonathan
Yankey and John Armstrong, security; settled 10-22-1842. (13)
JONES, Andrew - #52; 8-10-1841; Hiram Jones and Oliver Jones, executors; Bond $700.;
Laban Parks and Joseph M. Walden, security; settled July 1845. (13)
STORER, James - #53; 8-10-1841; Campbell G. Dick and Henry H. Storer, executors;
Bond #1800.; Robert B. Glasgow and James Glasgow, security; settled O.B. 13,
page 489. (13)
WRIGHT, Samuel - #54; 8-13-1841; Thomas Ralston, executor; Bond $200.; Thomas C.
Kirkpatrick and Robert Ralston, security. (13)
FOSTER, Nathaniel - #55; 8-12-1841; James Smith, executor; no bond. (14)
McCOY, Alexander - #56; 8-12-1841; George McCoy, executor; no bond. (14)
DUNBAR, James #57; 8-13-1841; Isabella Dunbar and Samuel R. Wood, executors;
Bond $9000.; John Moore, John Oliver, Richard Fristoe, George Sample and
Samuel G. Bradford, security; settled 6-14-1852. (14)
ALEXANDER, Andrew - #58; 8-12-1841; Hamilton Alexander, executor; no bond. (14)
STEVENSON, Charles - #101; 8-13-1841; Wm Stevenson, adms.; Bond $600.; Elijah
Lowe and Wm Miller, security. (14)
STRUDE, John S. - #102; 8-9-1841; David W. Murphy, adms.; Bond (not given);
Recompence S. Murphy and Israel Earley, security. (14)
BURBAGE, Sarah - #103; 10-18-1841; Jacob Lawrence, adms.; Bond $1200.; J.P.
Bloomhuff and John Kincaid, security; settled 7-24-1843. (14)
BAIRD, William - #104; 10-18-1841; John Moore, adms.; Bond $3000.; Silas Thomas
and Wesley Lee. security. (15)
HAYSLIP, John - #105; 10-23-1841; Samuel Foster, adms.; Bond $1000.; John Osman
and Samuel C. Wason (or Mason?), security. (15)

6

SILCUT, Valentine - #106; 10-22-1841; Aaron Pence, adms. de bonis non; Bond $2600.;
John Sparks and Wm Stevenson, security. (15)

FRY, George - #107; 10-21-1841; Charles McCoprty, adms.; Bond $250.; Wm Thompson
and Wm McVey Jr., security. (15)

FENTON, Jeremiah - #59; 10-18-1841; George Fenton and Benjamin Fenton, executors;
Bond $4400.; Jeremiah Fenton and Barnet Horner, security. (15)

WICKERHAM, Peter - #60; 10-23-1841; Jacob Wickersham, executor; Bond (not given);
Andrew McIntire and John Davis, security; settled 7-11-1845. (15)

EAKINS, William - #61; 11-2-1841; Elizabeth Eakins and James Eakins, executors;
Bond $1000; Wm Smalley and Wm. Nesbit, security. (15)

HOWELL, William - #208; 11-2-1841; Thankful Howell and Hugh Means, adms.; Bond $800.;
John Spark and John McCullough, security. (16)

BAIRD, Moses (Judge) - #62; 12-3-1841; Robert Baird and Chambers Baird, executors;
Bond $7000.; Joshua Truitt and Jacob N. Murphy, security. (16)

MITCHELL, Andrew - #109; 12-3-1841; Andrew M. Mitchell, adms.; Bond $1000.; Wm
Kirker and John H. Kincais, security. (16)

ADAMS COUNTY, OHIO - McHENRY CEMETERY

Contributed by: Col. & Mrs. J.C. McHenry, 1055 Westbridge Ave., Danville, Cal.94526
Cemetery located one mile north of State Route #52 on Brush Creek Rd. across from
the Joe Reynolds farmhouse. All inscriptions taken for all stones found.
POOL, Infant son of Wm. S. Pool and died July 7, 1873 (same stone as below)
    Infant son of Wm. W. Pool and died May 19, 1873
McHENRY, Susan died in the year 1831, aged 30 years
    Joshua born Sept. 12, 1800, died Feb. 18, 1871
    Andrew 1841-1900; Anna M. his wife 1855-------(not engraved)
    John born July 1, 1822, died June 15, 1874
    Margaret born 1813 died Feb. 17, 1871
    Johnny son of L.D. & M.M. born Oct. 6, 1875, died April 1, 1876
    L.D. born July 1, 1827, died Mar. 3, 1884
    Mary S. dau. of J.W. McH & Jennie Howe born March 27, 1872, died 7 months,
       21 days
Small stones (possibly either Head or Foot Stones) found with the following initials:
  A.M.   J.P.   I.P.I.P.   M.M.   S.M.   M.S.H.   J.M.   J.M.

ADAMS COUNTY, OHIO - CEMETERY

This cemetery is located on State Route 125 about three miles east of West Union
and one-fourth mile east of Poplar Ridge Road. All inscriptions were taken.
KRATZER, Roy and Ray (no dates given)
McCARTY, Mattie wife of J.A. McCarty Jan. 24, 1874 - April 16, 1892
    Robert L. died Dec. 29, 1890 aged 25 years and 12 days
(note: two graves marked only by field stones)
BALDWIN, Christena 1858-1943
JACKSON, Lettie 1835-1897
    Eloner(?) died Oct. 22, 1889 aged 88 yrs. 4 mos. 10 ds.
    William died Aug. 15, 1881 aged 89 years
STEWARD, Russell 1877-----(not engraved) Lillie his wife 1882-1915
McCARTY, Wesley 1852-1928 Alice 1862-1943
BALDWIN, Willard K. July 26, 1941 - June 20, 1968
McCARTY, E.C. Dec. 27, 1884 - Mar. 27, 1962
    Louella Rader his wife June 18, 1891 - Oct. 20, 1915
    Their children: Alta Pearl Oct. 24, 1911 - Jan. 17, 1912
               Paul Forest Aug. 12, 1914 - Aug. 17, 1915
JACKSON, G. W. 1841-1940 Rebecca his wife 1844-1916

ADAMS COUNTY, OHIO - MARRIAGES 1798-1803

The following marriages were found in "Deed Book 1-2-3" in the Recorder's Office at the court house in West Union. Page on which record may be found is given in parenthesis.

ABRITT, Joseph to Ann Nelue	11-26-1801 by Noble Grimes, J.P.	(211)
ARMSTRONG, Aaron to Nancy Robertson	2-11-1802 by Jos. Moore, J.P.	(208)
BARRET, James to Sarah Snodgrass	8-27-1802 by John Gutridge, J.P.	(261)
BARSMAN (BOUSMAN?), William to Sarah Whalley	1-22-1801 by Noble Grimes, J.P.	(154)
BARTERS, Alexander to Becky Dennis	8-25-1799 by Noble Grimes	(116)
BAULDRIDGE, Sam'l to Polly Maggarrey	7-25-1802 by Thos. Kirker, Esq.	(261)
BEEKMAN, Gabriel to Margaret Mirew	3-23-1802 by Jos. Moore, J.P.	(240)
BELLI, Jno. to Cynthia Harrison	3-21-1800 by Samuel Jackson, M.G.	(132)
BERTRONE, John Baptist to Sectoque Dugles	4-12-1802 by Kimber Barton, J.P.	(240)
BIBBY, Abraham to Susanna Saltsburry	8-8-1800 by Wm Jackson, J.P.	(143)
BILBE, Peter to Isabel Morrison	1-22-1799 by Thos. Kirker	(185-6)
BRAIN, John to Nancy Keith	12-9-1802 by John Gutridge, Esq.	(292)
BRAWCLES, Frederick to Nancy Erls	11-26-1798 by Thos. Kirker	(185-6)
BRIGGS, John to Polly Smith	3-18-1800 by Noble Grimes	(128)
BRIYAN, George to Memcy Notas (Nolas)	1-6-1801	(185-6)
BROWMLEY, John of Kentucky to Elisabeth Wycoff of this county	6-15-1800 by Thos. W. Swinny,MG	(135)
BROWN, Henry to Elizabeth Lower	12-29-1801 by Thos. W. Swinny, MG	(197)
BROWN, Thomas to Sally Smith	10-23-1800 by Noble Grimes, J.P.	(153)
BURNSIDE, Alexander to Margareti Martin, widow of Beatty	12-20-1798 by Jno. Belli, Justice	(92)
BURT, Thos. to M. Rudebeauch	2-17-1801 by Wm Jacison, MG	(156)
CAMPBELL, William to Polly Smart	12-20-1801 by Thos. Kirker, Esq. Manchester twp.	(207)
CARL, Sanford to Jane Byar residents of Kentucky	6-25-1801 by John Gutridge, Esq.	(185)
CARRIGAIN, Mark to Sarah Roys	7-23-1802 by JohnGutridge, J.P.	(261)
CARRINGTON, Jesse to Elisabeth Talbourt	7-7-1802 by Moses Baird	(261)
CHAMBERS, Benjamine to Mary Reed	1-4-1803 (1802?) rec, 3-9-1802 by Jno. Russill	(207)
CORN, John to Ann Goheen.	9-18-1800 by Wm Jackson, J.P.	(143)
CORNS, Joseph to Ann Frausdalee(Truasdale)	10-23-1799 by Jno. Belli	(119)
CORNS, William to Nancy Meyers	3-8-1802 by William Jackson, MG	(244 & 265)
CRACRAFT, Joseph to Mrs. Manly, widow	7-8-1800 by Jno. Russell	(141)
CRAWFORD, William to Elisabeth Peterson	6-7-1800 by Wm Jackson, J.P.	(143)
CRAYCRAFT, John to Sally Meek	8-17-1802 by Kimber Barton, J.P.	(261)
CROSBY, William to Elaseph Morris	9-4-1802 by John Gutridge, J.P.	(261)
DAVIS, John to Nancy Actkin	1-10-1799 by Moses Baird	(116)
DAVIS, Turner to Elizabat Vance	8-9-1798 by Jno. Belli	(77)
DRAGGUE, Andrew to Mary Hardeste	6-23-1803 by John Gutridge, Esq.	(319)
DUNLAP, William to Sarah Shepherd	4-21-1801 by John Dunlavy	(185)
EDGINTON, Abesam to Jeaney Kincaid	3-18-1802 by Jno. Dunleavy	(239)
EDGAR, Andrew to Nancy Brooks	6-12-1798 by James Scott, Esq.	(59)
ELLISON, Robert to Rebeca Lockhart	10-11-1802 by Jno. Russell	(292)
EVANS, Benjamine to Mary Gragray	1-29-1801 by Mills Stephenson	(155)

9

FOLSUM, James to Elisabeth Martin both of Mason County (Ky.)	10-31-1798 by Jno. Russel, JP	(91)
FOSTER, Nathaniel to Hester Smith	2-24-1802 by Jos. Moore, J.P.	(208)
FOSTER, Thomas to Jenny McGoveney	4-4-1799 by Jno. Dunlavy, MG of Presbyterian denomination	(133)
FRANKLIN, George to Phebe Precket	6-27-1803 by John Gutridge, Esq.	(319)
FRIZELL, John to El. Wordley	2-3-1801 by Wm Jackson, M.G.	(156)
GIFFORD, Timothy to Iossebeeth Frizel	9-5-1800 by Noble Grimes, J.P.	(153)
GRAGER, Jonathan to Rache Evans residents of Kentucky	2-5-1801 by John Gutridge, Esq.	(155)
GRANT, William to Peggy Shunkwiler	1-10-1801 by Jno. Belli, J.P.	(151)
GRIMES, Thomas to Betsey Brown	2-10-1801 by Jno. Russel	(156)
GUTHRIE, Robert to Mary Galaspy residents of Kentucky	7-29-1801 by John Gutridge, Esq.	(185)
HAMBLETON, (James?) to Agnes Corns both of Union twp.	7-12-1802 by Jos. Moore, J.P.	(261)
HARROD, Thomas to Esther Tomplin	6-5-1798 by James Scott, Esq.	(59)
HESLER, John to Elizabeth Watt	8-3-1802 by Wm Jackson, M.G.	(244 & 265)
HOOD, Thomas to Sarah Picket	6-28-1801 by Kimber Barton, J.P.	(185)
HUMBERSON, Thomas to Ann Stevenson	3-30-1801 by John. Gutridge, Esq.	(168)
HUTTON, James to Elizabeth Harmon	5-18-1802 by William Jackson, MG	(244 & 265)
IRVIN, James to Rachel Swala	3-8-1803 by John Gutridge, Esq.	(307)
JOHN, Thomas to Nancy Art residents of this territory	7-9-1801 by John Gutridge, Esq.	(185)
JOHNSTON, George to Catherine Manley	5-21-1801 by Moses Baird	(168)
JONES, John to Jane Mitchell	12-30-1799 by Jno. Belli	(123)
KELLY, James to Sarah McFerson	12-3-1801 by Jno. Dunlavy	(207)
KEMPSON, Mathew to Salley Basset	4-3-1803 by Moses Baird	(319)
KIBBY, Moses to Sally Everman	4-13-1802 by Kimber Barton, J.P.	(240)
KILGORE, George to Elizabeth Cochran	4-17-1798 by James Scott, Esq.	(59)
KILLEN, John to Rachel Harper	11-19-1801 by Noble Grimes, J.P.	(211)
KINCAID, John to Sarah Hannah	3-27-1800 by John Dunlavy, MG of Presbyterian denomination	(133)
KNOWL, John to Mary Dysand	9-2-1801 by Will Jackson, M.G.	(197)
LAKE, Thomas to Elisabeth Pary	1-13-1803 by John Gutridge, Esq.	(307)
LANE, Joseph to Mary Hartley	4-17-1798 by James Scott, Esq.	(59)
LEE, Allen to Mary Bilby	3-19-1801 by George Rogers	(173)
LENSEY, Oliver to Polley Naylor	3-14-1802 by Thos. Kirker, Esq.	(239)
LIMING, Jonathan to Jane Liming	9-17-1799 by Jno. Dunlavay, MG of Presbyterian denomination	(133)
LINDSAY, John to Mary Marshall	1-8-1800 by Jno. Belli, Justice	(123)
LITTLE JOHN, Aaron to Margaret Cracraft	1-1-1799 by Moses Baird	(116)
LODWICK, John to Hannaw Filbley	7-13-1802 by Thos. Kirker, Esq.	(261)
LYTLE, John to Elizabeth Crane	12-30-1801 by Jno. Gutridge	(208)
McCONNELL, Arthur to Nancy Miller	2-7-1798 by Jno. Belli	(9)
McGEEGUS (McGREGOR?), Barne to Hannah Howard	11-23-1802 by John Gutridge, Esq.	(292)
McGLAUGHLIN, William to Priscilla Murris	4-23-1800 by George Rogers, VDM	(133)
McGOVENY, Johon to Peggie McGoveny	4-29-1802 by Thos. Kirker, Esq.	(239)

10

MACRE, Wm to Kezua Baldwin	7-15-1801 by Thos. Kirker	(185-6)
MAGINS, Wm to Sarah Morris	2-14-1803 by John Gutridge, Esq.	(307)
MASSIE, Benjamine to Elizabeth Lougay	4-3-1801 by Thos. Kirker	(185-6)
(Lovejoy?)		
MENEXS, James to Jane Upson	3-4-1802 by Noble Grimes, J.P.	(211)
MIDDLETON, John to Elisabeth	3-20-1801 by John Gutridge, Esq.	(168)
MIDDLETON, Thomas Jr. to Elizabeth Swisher	6-12-1802 by Mills Stephenson	(261)
MILLER, David to Catherine Studdybaker	1-3-1799 by Moses Baird	(116)
MILLER, George F. to Sarah Hutchason	1-6-1802 by Mills Stephenson	(307)
residents of Kentucky		
MILLER, James to Elizabeth Murphy	6-9-1798 by John Belli, Justice	(39)
MITCHELL, D'd (David) to Mary Stockham	2-14-1801 by Wm Jackson, M.G.	(156)
MULLIN, Charles to Jane Smith	7-31-1800 by Jo. Moore	(141)
MUNROE, George to Anna Brownfield	4-5-1800 by George Rodgers VDM	(132)
NELSON, Jesse to Martha Wilson	3-5-1799 by Moses Baird	(116)
NICKLESON, Thomas to An Boon	6-17-1802 by John Gutridge, J.P.	(261)
NOLAS, George to Poley Edgerton	1-22-1799 by Thos. Kirker	(185-6)
NOLAS, John to Margery Yarden	7-9-1801 by Thos. Kirker	(185-6)
NUSTARD (MUSTARD?), Samuel of Ross Co. to	4-29-1802 by Wm Tolbot	(261)
Catheren Boydston of Adams Co.		
OPPY, David to Elisabeth Edwards	10-21-1802 by Jos. Moore	(291)
both of Springhill twp.		
OURSLER, Joseph to Juday McDonal	2-23-1801 by Mills Stephenson	(155)
PAXTON, Eli to Sarah Grimes	11-26-1801 by Jno. Russill	(207)
PENCE, John to Prisela Tumelston	10-5-1800 by Thos. Kirker	(185-6)
PICKELSOMON, Joseph to Nance Donnehue	6-14-1803 by John Gutridge, Esq.	(319)
PIPER, Robert to Katthran Swearingen	11-22-1800 by Noble Grimes, J.P.	(153)
PORTER, John to Releran Kester	5-7-1801 by Thos. Kirker	(185-6)
ROSS, James to Elisabeth Farrow (or Farron)	4-6-1802 by John Gutridge, Esq.	(239)
RALSTONE, Robert to Ally Chaste (or Charte)	12-29-1801 by Jno. Russill	(207)
REDMAN, Daniel to Prudence Tyler	1-15-1801 by Mills Stephenson	(155)
RICE, Wm to Jean Morgan	8-26-1801 by John Gutridge, Esq.	(185)
residents of Kentucky		
ROBINSON, William to Mary Barr	1-1-1801 --------------------	(156)
both of this territory		
RUGLES, Thomas to Rachael Freeland	5-30-1801 by John Gutridge, Esq.	(168
residents of Kentucky		& 185)
RUPE, David to Margaret Knowl	9-2-1801 by Will Jackson, M.G.	(197)
RUSSEL, Wm to Ruth Hineman	8-7-1798 by Jno. Belli	(77)
RYAN, Thomas to Polly Tumelston	2-30-1802 by Thos. Kirker, Esq.	(207)
SHANNON, John to Mary Thirn	3-4-1801 by Mills Stephenson	(155)
SHAW, Sanuel to Saley McBride	4-8-1802 by Thos. Kirker, Esq.	(239)
SHEPHERD, Abraham to Peggy Moore	9-12-1799 by Jno. Dunlavy, MG	(133)
	of Presbyterian denomination	
SHEPHERD, Eliah (or Eliak) to Hannah Rogers	8-20-1799 by Jno. Belli	(116)
SHEPHERD, Icabe (isaac) to Nancy Jansten	6-3-1802 by Jno. Dunleavy	(239)
(or Zansten)		
SMALLEY, Isaac of Union twp. to	12-2-1802 by Jos. Moore	(291)
Nancy Wikoff of Springhill twp.		
SMALLEY, Thomas to Dockey Bagbey	3-10-1801 by Wm Jackson, M.G.	(156)
SMITH, John to Nancy Dennis	7-25-1799 by Noble Grimes	(116)

11

SMITH, John to Elizabeth McCowmes	10-4-1801 by Noble Grimes, J.P.	(211)
SRICKLEY, Jacob to Margaret Coxe	10-31-1798 by Jno. Russel, J.P.	(91)
both of Mason County (ky.)		
STEEL, Solomon to Nancy Lee	2-11-1802 by Noble Grimes, J.P.	(211)
STOCKAM, John to Frances Kahan	8-15-1799 by Moses Baird	(116)
STORER, David to Ruth Hutton	3-5-1801 by Moses Baird	(155)
STOUT, Isaac to Ann Snodgrass	7-11-1800 by Jno. Russell	(141)
STOUT, Wm to Margaret Benet	5-16-1799 by Jno. Russell	(141)
SWIM, Samuel to Susannah Edwards	4-1-1800 by Joseph Moore	(132)
THOMAS, Abraham to Margaret Baker	8-8-1799 by Jno. Dunlavy, M.G.	(133)
	of Presbyterian denomination	
THOMAS, Mordekoy to Rachel Armstrong	2-11-1802 by Jos. Moore, J.P.	(208)
TRAICHLER, Daniel to Mary Notgrass	4-29-1802 by Jos. Moore, J.P.	(240)
TRAVIS, Asa of Adams Co. to	6-15-1800 by Thos. W. Swinny, M.G.	(135)
Sophia Howard of Ross Co.		
TUMELSTON, Samuel to Sally Edgington	12-10-1800 by Thos. Kirker	(185-6)
TWEED, Samuel to Sarah Evans	3-17-1801 by John Dunlavy	(185)
ULET, Thomas to Catherine Smith	3-3-1803 by Jos. Moore	(319)
WADE, Joseph to Poley Baldwin	12-12-1800 by Joseph Kerr	(151)
WALLINGSFORD, Joseph to Jean Thorn	7-29-1801 by John Gutridge, Esq.	(185)
residents of Kentucky		
WARNOCK, James to Rebeckah Howe	8-12-1802 by K. Barton, J.P.	(261)
WESTBROOK, Joseph to Elizabeth Wright	1-21-1802 by Jno. Russill	(207)
WEVER, John to Tency Moss	3-2-1803 by John Gutridge, Esq.	(307)
WHITE, Alexander to Mary Wheals(or Whealer)	3-9-1802 by Jno. Russill	(207)
WHITE, Jas. to Larence Barber	9-26-1802 by Jno. Russell	(292)
WHITE, Joseph to Elizabeth McHenry	6-14-1799 by Noble Grimes	(113)
WOOD, David to Ache Anderson	6-4-1803 by Gutridge, Esq.	(319)
WOOLSEY, Joseph to Jane Logan	8-14-1800 by Jno. Belli, Justice	(135)
WORSTELL, Joseph to Nancy Gin	4--10-1800 by Joseph Moore	(132)
WRIGHT, John to Jemima Thomas	3-13-1801 by Thos. Kirker	(185-6)
WYKOFF, John to Catherine Blain (or Blair)	9-18-1800 by Jos. Moore	(151)
YOUNG, David to Poley Morrison	8-12-1801 by Thos. Kirker	(185-6)

ADAMS COUNTY, OHIO - DEED BOOK 1-2-3, 1797-1803

The following records were abstracted from "Deed Book 1-2-3" found in the Recorder's
Office at the court house at West Union. This is the first three deed books of
the county in one combined volume. At this early period, Adams County covered an
area later formed into numerous other counties. Page on which record may be found
in the original book is given in parenthesis.

3-13-1797 - Nathan'l MASSIE of Hamilton Co., NW Territory to Hose MOORE of same
place; 30 pds. Kentucky money; Ironridge twp., part 400a tract patented to Massie
as assignee of Robert Jowitt on upper side Brush Creek containing 200a; lines-- Thos.
Burkett, Williamson. Wit: Jn. Wilson, Wm George Wilson. Rec. 9-12-1797. (1)

2-1-1797 - Henry CLARK of Ohio Co., Virginia to John SHARPE of NW Territory; land
warrant containing 200a by military warrant for Clark's own services as a Sgt. in
8th Va. Regt; consideration of 100 pds. Pa. money. Wit: Walter Denny, John Burns.
Rec. 9-12-1797. (2)

8-29-1797 - Nath'l MASSIE of Adams Co., NW Territory to Thomas BURKETT of same;
15 pds. Ky. money; 100a East side Brush Creek; lines--Moore's. Wit: John Beasley.
Rec. 9-13-1797. (2)

8-16-1797 - Nath'l MASSIE of Adams Co., NW Territory to Thomas WORTHINGTON of same;
$50.00 Ky. money; in-lots 1,2,5,6,26, & 28 and out-lots 38 & 39 containing 4 acres
each in the last two in Chillicothe. Wit: John Beasley. Recorded 9-13-1797. (3)

8-30-1797 - Winthrop SARGENT, Esq. acting as Governor to Joseph DARLINGTON of Adams
Co., ferry license; to run ferry on the Ohio opposite Cabin Creek for one year
to transfer all persons, horses, carriages, cattle, etc. at such rates now used
and to provide good and sufficient boates and skillful persons to run same. Rec.
9-14-1797. (4)

6-24-1797 - Nath'l MASSIE of Adams Co., NW Territory to Joseph DARLINTON of Mason
Co., Ky.; 120 pds. Ky. money; 400 acres; lines--James Lawson. Wit: Benj. Goodin.
Rec. 9-14-1797. (4)

9-1-1797 - Nath'l MASSIE of Adams Co., NW Territory to Henry SHELY of same; 6 pds.
Ky. money; in-lots 33 & 208 in Chillicothe. Wit: T. Worthington. Rec. 11-6-1797.
(5)

10-20-1797 - Alexander SCOTT of Lancaster Co., Pa. to John BELLI of NW Territory;
Power of Attorney to sell all tract land containing 615a, tract 445a;tract 490a;
tract 450a, all surveys dated 4-10-1796. Wit: Jno. Henry. Rec. 11-20-1797. (6)

11-30-1797 - John CRAWFORD of Adams Co., NW Territory to Moses CRAWFORD; consideration of personal regard for my son Moses and sum of 5 shillings; 5 cows and calves,
1 bay mare, 20 hogs and all my farming utensils. Wit: John Beasley. Rec. 12-13-
1797. (7)

13

11-30-1797 - John CRAWFORD of Adams Co., NW Territory to Sarah CRAWFORD; consid-
ation of personal regard for my daughter Sarah and 4 shillings; 5 beds and furniture, 6 chairs, one table, 12 Pewter plates and 1 chest drawers. Wit: Jno.
Beasley. Rec. 12-13-1797. (7)

9-26-1797 - Major General Charles SCOTT of Woodford Co., Ky. to Nath'l MASSIE of
Adams Co., NW Territory; $1666. and 2/3rds dollars Ky money; NW of Ohio on Scioto
River being 833 1/3rd acres Survey No. 1455; lines--John Sinton survey 614; said
tract conveyed being granted to Scott by patent from United States 5-4-1796 for
military service in the Va. line on the Cont'l Establishment. Wit: Thomas Bodley.
Rec. 12-13-1797. (8)

6-29-1797 - Nath'l MASSIE of Hamilton Co., NW Territory to Benjamin MUNSTON of same;
·3 pds. Ky money; in-lot 134 in Chillicothe. Wit: T. Worthington. Rec. 12-13-1797,
(9)

7-1-1797 - George PORTER of Baltimore, Md. to John BISHONG of Bourbon Co., Ky.;
7 pds. 10 shillings Ky money; in-lot 15 in Chillicothe. Wit: John Beasley. Rec.
2-11-1798. (10)

3-13-1797 - Nath'l MASSIE of Hamilton Co., NW Territory to Peter WICKERHAN of same;
225 pds. Ky money; tract land in Hamilton Co., Ironbridge twp. on waters of Brush
Creek being 600a part 1000a patent to Massie as assignee of Leven Powell; lines--
Massie, line between Wickerhan and Peter Platter. Wit: John McDonald, Daniel
Sherrod. Rec. 2-26-1798. (10)

3-13-1797 - Nath'l MASSIE of Hamilton Co., NW Territory to Peter PLATTER of same;
150 pds. Ky money; tract land in Iron Bridge twp., Hamilton Co. on waters of Brush
Creek being 400a part tract of 1000a survey patented to said Massie as assignee of
Levin Powell; lines--old line between Peter Platter and Peter Wickerhan. Wit: John
McDonald, Daniel Sherrod. Rec. 2-26-1798. (11)

9-1-1797 - Nath'l MASSIE of Adams Co., NW Territory to William LUCAS of same; 3 pds.
in-lot 169 in Chillicothe. Wit: T. Worthington. Rec. 3-8-1798. (12)

9-1-1797 - Nathal MASSIE of Adams Co., NW Territory to Samuel HARRIS of same; 3 pds.
Ky money; in-lot 133 & out lot 25, the latter containing 4 acres, in Chillicothe.
Wit: James Scott. Rec. 3-13-1798. (13)

9-1-1797 - Nath'l MASSIE of Adams Co., NW Territory to Hugh COCHRAN of same; 3 pds.
Ky money; in-lot 10 in Chillicothe. Wit: T. Worthington. Rec. 3-13-1798. (14)

9-1-1797 - Nath'l MASSIE of Adams Co., NW Territory to Abraham MILLER of same; 7pds.
Ky money; in-lot 99 also out-lot 52 containing 4 acres in Chillicothe. Wit: T.
Worthington. Rec. 3-12-1798. (15)

9-1-1797 - Nath'l MASSIE of Adams Co., NW Territory to Joseph LAMON of same; 10 pds.
Ky money; in-lots 176,179 & 223 Chillicothe. Wit: T. Worthington. Red. 3-13-1798.
(16)

7-6-1797 - Nath'l MASSIE of Hamilton Co., NW Territory to John WILLSON of same; 3 pds. Ky money; in-lot 195 in Chillicothe. Wit: James Scott. Rec. 3-13-1798. (17)

9-2-1797 - Nath'l MASSIE of Adams Co., NW Territory to William Craig of same; 3 pds.; in-lot 160 in Chillicothe. Wit: T. Worthington. Rec. 3-13-1798. (18)

9-2-1797 - Nath'l MASSIE of Adams Co., NW Territory to Thomas DICK of same; 13 pds. Ky money; in-lots 74, 196 & 240, also out-lot 12 in Chillicothe. Wit: T. Worthington. Rec. 3-13-1798. (19)

9-2-1797 - Nath'l MASSIE of Adams Co., NW Territory to Wm CRAIG of same; $10.00; in-lot 213 in Chillicothe. Wit: James Scott. Rec. 3-13-1798. (20)

11-22-1797 - Roger BRIGGS of Adams Co., NW Territory to William SNELL of same; 47 pds.; in-lot 175 in Chillicothe. Wit: John Biswell, Benjamin Rogers, Ephraim Baits. Rec. 3-13-1798. (20)

7-21-1797 - Joseph C. VANCE and Sarah (mark) wife to John WEBB, all of Mason Co., Ky.; 20 pds.; 100a NW side Ohio River about 1 mile below the mouth of Salt Lick Creek; lines--James Morrison's Lower corner. Wit: Jno. Wilson, Joseph Kerr. Rec. 3-13-1798. (21)

3-2-1798 - John (mark) WEBB and Rachel (mark) wife of Hamilton Co., NW Territory to James MORRISON of Adams Co.; $331.00; 100a NW Bank Ohio; lines--tract of said Morrison purchased from said Vance. Wit: Joseph Kerr, Benj. Goodin. Rec. 3-13-1798. (22)

9-1-1797 - Nath'l MASSIE of Adams Co., NW Territory to Forgus MOORE of same; 3 pds. Ky money; in-lot 241, also out-lot 241 containing 4 acres in Chillicothe. Wit: T. Worthington. Rec. 3-13-1798. (23)

9-1-1797 - Nath'l MASSIE of Adams Co., NW Territory to James ARMSTRONG of same; 3 pds. Ky money; in-lot 42; also out-lot 8 containing 4 acres in Chillicothe. Wit: T. Worthington. Rec. 3-13-1798. (24)

9-101797 - Nath'l MASSIE of Adams Co., NW Territory to Elijah KIRKPATRICK of same; 3 pds. Ky money; in-lot 210 in Chillicothe. Wit: James Scott. Rec. 3-13-1798. (25)

9-1-1797 - Nath'l MASSIE of Adams Co., NW Territory to Adam GILFILIN of same; 3 pds. Ky money; in-lots 222 & 206 in Chillicothe. Wit: James Scott. Rec. 3-13-1798. (26)

9-1-1797 - Nath'l MASSIE of Adams Co., NW Territory to James McCRARY of same; 3pds. Ky money; in-lot 265 in Chillicothe. Wit: T. Worthington. Rec. 3-13-1798. (26)

9-1-1797 - Nath'l MASSIE of Adams Co., NW Territory to James MORE of same; 3 pds. Ky money; in-lot 228 in Chillicothe. Wit: T. Worthington. Rec. 3-13-1798. (27)

15

10-10-1797 - James EDWARDS of Hamilton Co., NW Territory to Nathan ELLIS of same; 206 pds. Ky money; 227 and 3/4th acres part tract granted to Philip Slaughter by Virginia patent 2-10-1789 and also part granted James Edwards by Robert Coleman for said Slaughter 8-6-1796; lines--Miles Connaway, Nathan Ellis, survey made for Philip Slaughter. Wit: Edward Martin, John Rains, John Stark. Rec. 3-14-1798.(28)

11-18-1797 - Nathan ELLIS and Mary Ann wife of Adams Co., NW Territory to Abraham EVANS of same; 50 pds. 6 shillings; Iron Ridge twp. being 50a & 20 poles part of tract granted Philip Slaughter by Virginia on 2-10-1789 and sold by Slaughter to Robt. Coleman and by him to James Edwards 8-6-1796 and by Edwards on 10-10-1797 to Ellis; lines--Land of Nathan Ellis, Backline of Philip Slaughter original assignee. Wit: Jas. Lawson, John (mark) Penticost. Rec. 3-14-1798. (30)

9-1-1797 - Nath'l MASSIE of Adams Co., NW Territory to Bazel ABRAMS of same; 3 pds. Ky money; in-lots 150,135,215,231 & 114; also out-lots 10 & 32 containing 4 acres each. Wit: James Scott. Rec. 3-20-1798. (31)

9-1-1797 - Nath'l MASSIE of Adams Co., NW Territory to James MITCHEL of same; 3pds. Ky money; in-lot 73 Chillicothe. Wit: T. Worthington. Rec. 3-20-1798. (32)

7-28-1795 - Joseph C. VANCE and Sarah (mark) wife of Mason Co., Ky. to John HEATH of same; 53 pds. 18 shillings Ky money; 217a part of a 1000a survey on NW side of the Ohio opposite mouth of Salt Lick Creek patented to Mayo Carrington 3-21-1791 and by Carrington sold to Joseph C. Vance. Wit: John Wilson, John Gutridge. Rec. 3-21-1798. (33)

7-1-1797 - George PORTER of Baltimore, Md. to David POWELL of Hamilton Co., NW Territory; 9 pds. Ky money; in-lot 200 in Chillicothe. Wit: John Beasley. Rec. 4-26-1798. (34)

9-2-1797 - Nath'l MASSIE of Adams Co., NW Territory to Daniel POWELL of same; $33.00; in-lot 185 in Chillicothe. Wit: T. Worthington. Rec. 4-26-1798. (35)

5-12-1797 - Nath'l MASSIE of Hamilton Co., NW Territory to Reuben ADAMS of same; 16 pds. Ky money; in-lots 36,161, & 283; also out-lot 22 containing 4 acres all in Chillicothe. Wit: John Beasley. Rec. 5-9-1798. (36)

8-22-1797 - Nath'l MASSIE of Adams Co., NW Territory to William SAWYER of same; $10.00; in-lot 65 in Chillicothe. Wit: Benj. Goodin. Rec. 5-17-1798. (37)

3-1-1798 - Wm SAWYER of Adams Co., NW Territory to William PARKESON; 12 pds.; in-lot 65 in Chillicothe. Wit: John Taylor, John Craighead. Rec. 5-13-1798. (38)

5-24-1798 - Nath'l MASSIE of Adams Co., NW Territory to Samuel HARRIS of same; 3 pds. Ky money; in-lot 263 Chillicothe. Wit: T. Worthington. Rec. 6-12-1798. (39)

9-26-1797 - Henry SHEELY of Adams Co., NW Territory to Samuel JACKSON of same; 9 pds. Ky money; in-lot 208 in Chillicothe which Sheely purchased from N. Massie. Wit: James Scott. Rec. 6-12-1798. (40)

9-1-1797 - Nath'l MASSIE of Adams Co., NW Territory to Joseph McCOY of same; 7 pds. Ky money; in-lot 132, also out-lot 1 containing 4 acres in Chillicothe. Wit: James Scott. Rec. 6-12-1798. (41)

7-5-1797 - Nath'l MASSIE of Hamilton Co., NW Territory to S amuel HENDERSON of same; 17 pds. Ky money; in-lots 23,80 & 180, also out-lots 20 & 56 containing 4 acres each in Chillicothe. Wit: Hugh Cochran, Jas. Scott. Rec. 6-12-1797. (42)

9-1-1797 - Nath'l MASSIE of Adams Co., NW Territory to James FERGUSON of same; 3 pds. Ky money; in-lot 86 and out-lot 21 in Chillicothe. Wit: T. Worthington. Rec. 6-12-1798. (44)

10-17-1797 - Robert SMITH of Adams Co., NW Territory to James FURGUSON of same; $80.00; in-lot 60 in Chillicothe. Wit: Jno. Sharp, Thos. McCoy. Rec. 6-12-1798. (45)

10-17-1997 - Reuben ABRAMS and Rachel (mark) wife of Adams Co., NW Territory to Mathew FORGUSON of Franklin Co., Pa.; $80.00; out-lot 22 containing 4 acres in Chillicothe. Wit: John Sharp, James Ferguson. Rec. 6-12-1798. (46)

10-4-1796 - Nath'l MASSIE of Hamilton Co., NW Territory to William JOHNSON and James LAWSON of same; 80 pds. Ky money; 266 and 2/3rds acres part Archilles Perkins survey NW bank of Ohio River; lines--Upper corner Nath'l Fox survey, old survey line, Massies corner. Wit: John Beasley, Benj. Goodin. Rec. 6-12-1798. (47)

7-18-1797 - Nath'l MASSIE of Adams Co., NW Territory to Benjamin ROGERS of same; 14 pds. Ky money; in-lots 77 & 117, also out-lots 27 & 96 containing 4 acres each. Wit: Benj. Goodin. Rec. 6-12-1798. (48)

9-2-1797 - Nath'l MASSIE of Adams Co., NW Territory to John McCOY of same; 14 pds. Ky money; in-lots 101 & 58, also out-lots 2 & 37 containing 4 acres each in Chillicothe. Wit: James Scott. Rec. 6-12-1798. (49)

7-18-1797 - Nath'l MASSIE of Adams Co., NW Territory to Samuel GIBSON of Bourbon Co., Ky; 1- pds. Ky money; in-lots 157 & 205, also out-lots 45 containing 4 acres in Chillicothe. Wit: John Rodgers, Mary Rogers. Rec. 6-12-1798. (50)

9-1-1797 - Nath'l MASSIE of Adams Co., NW Territory to Joseph LANE of same; 3pds. Ky money; in-lot 174 in Chillicothe. Wit: James Scott. Rec. 6-12-1798. (51)

8-20-1797 - Nath'l MASSIE of Adams Co., NW Territory to Isaac WAMSLEY Sr. of same; $500.00; 279a on Brush Creek granted to Massie by patent dated 2-20-1796; lines-- Thomas Barkers survey No. 933, John Jewitt's survey No. 1633. Wit: Benj. Goodin. (52)

9-1-1797 - Nath'l MASSIE of Adams Co., NW Territory to Daniel HAMILTON of same; 11 pds. Ky money; in-lot 92 and out-lots 140 & 143 the last two containing 4 acres each, all in Chillicothe. Wit: T. Worthington. Rec. 6-16-1798. (53)

9-1-1797 - Nath'l MASSIE of Adams Co., NW Territory to David SHELLY of same; 10 pds.; in-lots 191 & 224, also out-lot 163 containing 4 acres in Chillicothe. Wit: T. Worthington. Rec. 6-16-1798. (54)

7-18-1797 - Nath'l MASSIE of Adams Co. NW Territory to Daniel HAMILTON of same; 4 pds Ky money; lot 89 in Chillicothe. Wit: John Rogers, Benj. Rogers. Rec. 6-16-1798. (55)

1-20-1798 - John Lewis MALDEN of Adams Co., NW Territory to Samuel Thomas of Green Co. (no state given); lot 77 containing 217a being portion granted to me by Congress to French Inhabitants of Gallipolis. Wit: Robert Worst, James Burson. 6-21-1798 - Ane Malden for herself and as adms. of John Lewis Maldan quit claims all right in lot 77 which her late husband sold Samuel Thomas being land granted to France settlers opposite Little Sandy. (Signed) Ane Malden adms. of J. L. Maldan. Wit: John B. Ginats, Joseph Woolsey. Rec. 6-21-1798. (56)

7-6-1797 - Nath'l MASSIE of Hamilton Co., NW Territory to Benjamine KIRKPATRICK of same; 10 pds. Ky money; in-lots 116,217 & 233, also out-lot 24 containing 4 acres in Chillicothe. Wit: James Scott, Duncan McArthur. Rec. 7-3-1797. (56)

7-6-1797 - Nath'l MASSIE of Hamilton Co., NW Territory to Joseph Kirkpatrick of Bourbon Co., Ky; 100 pds Ky money; 400a on upper side of Paint Creek; lines -- Hugh Crochran, Henry Abrams, Robt. Finley, line of out-lots of town of Chillicothe. Wit: Jas. Scott, Duncan McArthur. Rec. 7-3-1797. (57)

7-9-1797 - Nath'l MASSIE of Adams Co., NW Territory to William MONTGOMERY of same; 337 pds.; 374 acres; lines--Upper corner Genl Chas. Scott survey on Scioto River. Wit: John Barritt, James Collings. Rec. 7-20-1798. (59)

9-2-1797 - Nath'l MASSIE of Adams Co., NW Territory to Elijah FULTON of same; 18 pds. Ky money; in-lots 225 & 243, also out-lots 165,128 & 168 the last three each containing 4 acres, all in Chillicothe. Wit: James Scott. Rec. 7-25-1798. (60)

9-2-1797 - Nath'l MASSIE of Adams Co., NW Territory to William CARR of same; 7 pds. Ky money; in-lot 64, also out-lot 28 cont. 4 acres, in Chillicothe. Wit: James Scott. Rec. 8-13-1798. (61)

9-28-1797 - John ROGERS of Adams Co., NW Territory to Joseph POTTER of same; 14 pds. 8 shillings Ky money; in-lot 49 in Chillicothe. Wit: James Scott. Rec. 8-13-1798. (62)

9-1-1797 - Nath'l MASSIE of Adams Co., NW Territory to Jeremiah McCLAIN of same; 3 pds. Ky money; in-lot 51 in Chillicothe. Wit: James Scott. Rec. 8-13-1798. (63)

9-2-1797 - Nath'l MASSIE of Adams Co., NW Territory to James HAYS of same; 10 pds. Ky money; in-lots 175 & 143, also out-lot 142 cont. 4 acres in Chillicothe. Wit: T. Worthington. Rec. 8-13-1798. (64)

18

9-1-1797 - Nath'l MASSIE of Adams Co., NW Territory to Solomon SALMAN of same; 3 pds Ky money; in-lot 244 in Chillicothe. Wit: James Scott. Rec. 8-13-1798. (65)

6-23-1798 - Nath'l MASSIE of Adams Co., NW Territory to James HAYS of same; 3 pds. Ky money; in-lot 44 in Chillicothe. Wit: T. Worthington. Rec. 8-13-1798. (66)

9-1-1797 - Nath'l MASSIE of Adams Co., NW Territory to James ROGERS of same; 18 pds. Ky money; in-lots 42 & 50; also out-lots 50,49 & 57, all in Chillicothe. Wit: James Scott. Rec. 8-13-1798. (67)

9-1-1797 - Nath'l MASSIE of Adams Co., NW Territory to Robert MITCHELL of same; 6 pds.; in-lot 145 & 211 in Chillicothe. Wit: James Scott. Rec. 8-13-1798. (68)

5-25-1798 - Nath'l MASSIE of Adams Co., NW Territory to Robert MITCHELL of Bourbon Co., Ky.; 3 pds. Ky money; in-lot 209 Chillicothe. Wit: James Scott. Rec. 8-13-1798. (69)

10-13-1797 - Henry ABRAMS Sr. of Adams Co., NW Territory to George HILL of Westmoreland Co., Pa.; $50.00; in-lot 248 in Chillicothe. Wit: James Scott. Rec. 8-13-1798. (70)

9-1-1797 - Nath'l MASSIE of Adams Co., NW Territory to William MITCHELL of Bourbon Co., Ky.; 7 pds. Ky money; in-lot 98, also out-lot 90 cont. 4 acres all in Chillicothe. Wit: James Scott. Rec. 8-13-1798. (71)

9-1-1797 - Nath'l MASSIE of Adams Co., NW Territory to James BROWN of same; 18 pds. Ky money; in-lots 113 & 166, also out-lots 56, 62 & 38 the last three containing 4 acres each, all in Chillicothe. Wit: James Scott. Rec. 8-13-1798. (72)

9-1-1797 - Nath'l MASSIE of Adams Co., NW Territory to James MANARY of same; 3 pds.; in-lot 197 in Chillicothe. Wit: T. Worthington. Rec. 8-13-1798. (73)

9-23-1797 - William McDONALD and Effie (mark) his wife of Adams Co., NW Territory to Samuel ROBERTSON of Ohio Co., Va.; $65.00; lot 53 in Chillicothe conveyed by N. Massie to Thompson Smith 9-1-1797 and by Smith to McDonald 9-20-1797. Wit: James Scott. Rec. 8-13-1798. (74)

9-23-1797 - William McDONALD and Effie (mark) his wife of Adams Co., NW Territory to John COFFEY of Ohio Co., Va.; $60.00; in-lot 54 in Chillicothe conveyed by N. Massie to Thos. Writehouse 9-2-1797 and by him to McDonald 9-20-1797. Wit: James Scott. Rec. 8-13-1798. (75)

4-14-1798 - William PARKESON of Washington, Mason Co., Ky. to Sam'l and James BALDWIN of same; $130.00 Ky money; in-lot 65 in Chillicothe. Wit: Nathan Ellis. Rec. 8-15-1798. (76)

9-__-1797(no day given) - John ROSE of Westmoreland Co., Va. to Christian RICHARD of Shanandoah Co., Va.; Whereas John Rose in Nov. last contracted to convey to Christian Richard part of military warrant No. 1850 on west side Scioto; lines-- Archibald Blair; containing as by patent issued by Secretary of War on 5-13-1797, 100 acres; that representatives of Doctor Robert Rose conveyed their claims to said John Rose as recorded in deeds in Fairfax County, Va. Wit: Francis Peyton, Henry Rose, Jacob Richard, Thomas Richard. Rec. 9-11-1798. (77)

5-16-1798 - Joseph C. VANCE and Sarah wife of Mason Co., Ky. to John ADAMS of same; $100.00; 83 acres & 4 poles NW side of the Ohio opposite mouth of Salt Lick Creek part of large tract Vance purchased from Mayo Carrington; lines--Webb. Wit: Henry Prather, John Heath, Wm Falkner. Rec. 9-11-1798. (79)

6-23-1797 - Nath'l MASSIE of Adams Co., NW Territory to Robert FULTON of Westmore-land Co., Pa.; 3 pds. Ky money; in-lot 242 in Chillicothe. Wit: T. Worthington. Rec. 9-11-1798. (80)

6-23-1797 - Nath'l MASSIE of Hamilton Co., NW Territory to Forgus MOORE of same; 7 pds. in-lot 46, also out-lot 103 cont. 4 acres, all in Chillicothe. Wit: John Beasley. Rec. 9-11-1798. (81)

9-3-1798 - Forgus MOOR and Elizabeth wife of Adams Co., NW Territory to James ARMSTRONG of same; $11.00; in-lot 46 in Chillicothe. Wit: T. Worthington. Rec. 9-11-1798. (82)

3-17-1798 - John Peter Romain BUREAU of Gallipolis, Washington Co., NW Territory to Peter Bacus; $330.00; lot 80 consisting of 217 acres granted by Congress to Anthony Francis Saugrin late of Gallipolis who sold same to Bureau by deed dated 9-15-1796, as one of French inhabitants of Gallipolis. Wit: John Belli. Rec. 9-15-1798. (83)

9-14-1798 - John Peter Romain BUREAU of Gallipolis, Washington Co., NW Territory to Francis PEURT of Adams Co., NW Territory; $780.00; 325 acres being lot 18 and half of lot 19, granted by Congress to the French Inhabitants of Gallipolis which Bureau purchased lot 18 from Anthony Bartholemew and 19 from Phillip August Pithoud. Wit: John Belli. Recorded 9-15-1798. (84)

9-14-1798 - Nath'l MASSIE of Adams Co., NW Territory to Michael THOMS of same; 50 pds. Ky money; 66 and 3/4th acres on waters of Scioto being tract town of Chilli-cothe is situated on, lines--Machirs tract, Wm Robertson; also in-lots 45 & 258 and out-lot 9 cont. 4 acres in Chillicothe. Wit: Benj. Goddin. Rec. 9-22-1798.(84)

8-27-1798 - John Gilbert PETTIT of Harrison Co., Va. only executor of Francis DUSERGE dec'd to Francis DEHERBCOURT of Marietta, NW Territory; $200.00; lot 27 in tract granted by Congress to French settlers and granted in name of Francis Dewerge. Deed dated, Belpre Island. Wit: Rich'd Lee, Henry Washburn, Har. B. Hassett. Recorded in Washington County, vol. 5, page 511. Rec. 10-20-1798. (85)

1-1-1798 - John S. WILLS to Wintrop SARGENT; consideration of Wills being indebted to Sargent for $1500.00 and in consideration of said debt; one undivided one-fourth part of 2000 acres between Churchill Jones Survey No. 459 and Mayo Carrington survey No. 436 to include one-fourth part of town laid out on same. Wit: John Belli, Thos. Gibson. Grantor attested to in Hamilton Co. Rec. 10-20-1798. (86)

11-12-1797 - Alexander SCOTT of Lancaster, Pa, by his attorney in fact, John BELLI
of Adams Co., NW Territory to Winthrop SARGENT of Hamilton Co., NW Territory;
$6000.00; several tracts: 615a NW side Ohio, lines--Churchill Jones survey No. 459
on Brush Creek; 490a NW side Ohio, lines--upper corner of above tract, on Stout's
Run; 450a NW side Ohio, lines--upper corner of last tract, on Long Lick Creek; 445a
NW side of Ohio, lines--upper corner of last tract, lower corner Mayo Carrington
survey no. 436; all surveyed for Charles Scottin four surveys and in four patents,
said Alexander Scott as assignee by United States 3-3-1797. Wit: Thos. Gibson,
J. L. Willis. Rec. 10-20-1798. (87)

1-2-1798 - Winthrop SARGENT of Cincinnati, Hamilton Co., NW Territory to John BELLI
of Adams Co., NW Territory; $1500.00; one undivided one-fourth part of 2000 acres on
Ohio River between Churchill Jones survey no. 459 and Mayo Carrington survey no. 436
including one-fourth part of town laid out on tract and which land was conveyed to
Sargent by Jno. Belli as attorney for Alexander Scott and originally surveyed for
Charles Scott and patented to Alexander Scott his assignee. Wit: Jno. S. Wills,
Thos. Gibson. Rec. 10-20-1798. (89)

9-22-1798 - John BELLI of Adams Co., NW Territory to Joseph WOOLSEY of same; $400.00;
100a part of survey of 1000a originally surveyed in name of Larkin Smith no. 175 and
patented to Smith 8-13-1789 and sold by said Larkin Smith 4-13-1795 to John Brown
and Jno. Belli with Brown selling his part to Belli 7-29-1796. Wit: Jas. Ediaon.
Rec. 11-12-1798. (90)

11-8-1798 - James MORRISON and Sarah wife of Adams Co., NW Territory to Archibald
MORRISON of same; $133.40; 40a part tract 1000a patented to Mayo Carrington 3-21-
1791 and conveyed by Carrington to Joseph C. Vance and by Vance to James Morrison,
lines--survey formerly belonging to John Webb. Wit: Moses Baird. Rec. 12-16-1798.
(91)

10-3-1798 - Nath'l MASSIE of Adams Co., NW Territory to Joseph DARLINTON of same;
120 pds. Ky money; 400a on the Ohio, lines--James Lawson tract. Wit: Jeremiah
Young, Jacob (mark) Pickett. Rec. 3-12-1799. (93)

10-11-1798 - Article of Agreement. James LAWSON of Adams Co., NW Territory and
Joseph DARLINGTON of same; that controversey has long existed between parties res-
pecting the establishment of their ferries across the Ohio from land on which they
now live and agreeing to submit this dispute to a jury of twelve men who according
to agreement entered upon business yesterday they have this day agreed the ferry's
shall be jointed into one from this day forward and kept by the two parties--that
Darlington to keep ferry the first year and Lawson the second year and in like
manner hereafter with license for the ferry to be issued in names of both parties
and both parties to share expenses and income. Wit: Ric'd Bounsaville, Chas.
Carmay, Nathan Rogers. Rec. 3-12-1799. (94)

1-11-1799 - Peter MATRIE (MATRY) of Gallipolis, Washington Co., NW Territory to John
Gabriel GERVAIS; $550.00; lot 16 containing 217a part tract land granted by Congress
3-3-1795 to French inhabitants of Gallipolis and conveyed to Matrie by John Baptist
Bertrand it being his portion of said grant. Wit: Ft. Loclercq, C. Menage. Rec.
3-30-1799. (95)

21

6-14-1799 - Nath'l MASSIE of Adams Co., NW Territory to William CAMPBELL of same; 131 pds. 14 shillings Ky money; 2931 west side River Scioto, lines--Henry Utts tract. Wit: T. Worthington. Rec. 6-1-1799. (96)

5-29-1799 - William (mark) CAMPBELL and Mary (mark) wife of Adams Co., NW Territory to Dennis MURPHY of same; 67 pds 15 shillings Ky money; 135½ acres west side Scioto, lines--Campbell. Wit: Jno. Belli. Rec. 6-1-1799. (97)

3-30-1799 - Thomas PARKER and Sally wife of Frecerick Co., Va. to Alexander PARKER, Esq.; Power of Attorney to lease or sell all lands in their name on NW side Ohio River. Wit: Raleigh Colston, Adam Douglass. Rec. 6-4-1799. (99)

6-3-1799 - Alex PARKER of Westmoreland Co., Va. to Elias LANGHAN, Esq.; Power of Attorney to convey lands NW of Ohio River. Wit: Jno. Belli. Rec. 6-4-1799. (101)

6-3-1799 - Thomas PARKER and Sarah wife of Frederick Co., Va. to John MOORE of Adams Co., NW Territory; $50.50; lot (9?0 in Alexandria.) Wit: Jno. Belli. Rec. 6-4-1799. (102)

6-3-1799 - Thomas PARKER and Sarah wife of Frederick Co., Va. to James EDISON of Adams Co., NW Territory; $62.00; lot 10 in Alexandria. Wit: Jno. Belli. Rec. 6-4-1799. (102)

6-3-1799 - Thomas PARKER and Sarah wife of Frederick Co., Va. to John HESTLER of Adams Co., NW Territory; $110.00; lots 11 & 12 in Alexandria. Wit: Jno. Belli. Rec. 6-4-1799. (103)

6-3-1799 - Thomas PARKER and Sarah wife of Frederick Co., Va. to Christian PORTLEMAN of Adams Co., NW Territory; $51.00; lot 13 in Alexandria. Wit: Jno. Belli. Rec. 6-4-1799. (104)

6-3-1799 - Thomas PARKER and Sarah wife of Frederick Co., Va. to William RUSSEL of Adams Co., NW Territory; $61.50; lot 14 in Alexandria. Wit: Jno. Belli. Rec. 6-4-1799. (105)

6-3-1799 - Thomas PARKER and Sarah wife of Frederick Co., Va. to William RICBY of Adams Co., NW Territory; $51.00; lot 16 in Alexandria. Wit: Jno. Belli. Rec. 6-4-1799. (106)

6-3-1799 - Thomas PARKER and Sarah wife of Frederick Co., Va. to Philip MOORE of Adams Co., NW Territory; $51.00; lot 17 (or 19?) in Alexandria on Ohio St. Wit: Jno. Belli. Rec. 6-4-1799. (106)

6-3-1799 - Thomas PARKER and Sarah wife of Frederick Co., Va. to John COLLINS of Adams Co., NW Territory; $72.00; lot 18 in Alexandria on Ohio St. Wit: Jno. Belli. Rec. 6-4-1799. (107)

6-3-1799 - Thomas PARKER and Sarah wife of Frederick Co., Va. to Lewis ROGERS and Emanuel TRAXLER of Adams Co., NW Territory; $77.00; lot 20 in Alexandria. Wit: E. Laughman, Wm Russel. Rec. 6-4-1799. (108)

6-3-1799 - Thomas PARKER and Sarah wife of Frederick Co., Va. to Elias LAUGHAM of Ross Co., NW Territory; $100.00; lot 20 in Alexandria. Wit: Jno. Belli. Rec. 6-4-1799. (108)

6-3-1799 - Thomas PARKER and Sarah wife of Frederick Co., Va. to William SALESBERRY of Adams Co., NW Territory; $45.00; lot 88 in Alexandria on High St. Wit: Jno. Belli. Rec. 6-4-1799. (109)

6-3-1799 - Robert BEADLE of Madison Co., Va. to Elias LANGHAM, Esq.; Power of Attorney to sell and convey Beadle's lands on NW side of River Ohio. Wit: Jno. Belli. Rec. 6-4-1799. (110)

6-3-1799 - Alexander PARKER and Sarah wife of Westmoreland Co., Va. by Power of Attorney to Thomas PARKER and Sarah wife of Frederick Co., Va. to John BELLI of Adams Co., NW Territory; $100.00; in-lot 8 and out-lots 2 & 3 in Alexandria. Wit: P. Moore, Jno. Pollock, Wm Russel. (111)

7-10-1798 - Nath'l MASSIE of Adams Co., NW Territory to James COLLINS of same; 60 pds. Ky money; 400 acres, lines--Jno. Fitzgerald's survey no. 1581. Wit: Benj. Goodin. Rec. 6-12-1799. (111)

4-8-1799 - Alexander SCOTT of Lancaster, Pa. to Jno. WILKINS of Pittsburgh, Pa.; power of attorney to receive all sums of money due Scott from Joh Belli, Esq. of NW Territory and to convey any lands from Belli. Wit: R. Alden, Chas. Taylor. Rec. 4-8-1799. (113)

6-3-1799 - Thomas PARKER and Sarah wife of Frederick Co. Va. to Andrew COLLINS of Adams Co., NW Territory; $61.00; lot 15 in Alexandria on Ohio St. Wit: Wm Russell, John Collins. Rec. 8-2-1799. (114)

9-14-1798 - John GRAHAM of Richmond, Va. by Nath'l MASSIE his attorney in fact of Adams Co., NW Territory to David MITCHELL of Adams Co., same; 80 pds.; tract land on Ohio River, lines--Abner N. Dunn survey of 270a. Wit: Wm Geo. Wilson, Wm Crawford, Isaac Collins. Rec. 8-17-1799. (114)

12-22-1795 - William REYNOLDS of Henrico Co., Va. to Nath'l MASSIE of Hamilton Co., NW Territory; power of attorney to convey to Robert Pollard of Richmond, Va. full title to military land warrant for 6262 acres issued by Register of State of Va. to Mose Fauntleroy a Major in the Va. Cont'l line in the late War with Great Britian and assigned by Fauntlaroy to Richard Smith and by Smith to said Reynolds. Wit: Miles Selden, Chas. R. Arthur. Rec. 9-8-1799. (116)

6-19-1799 - Nath'l MASSIE of Adams Co., NW Territory to Peter SHOEMAKER of same; 75 pds. Ky money; 200a east side Brush Creek part of a tract of 1666a surveyed in name of John Taylor Griffin and by him assigned to Robert Morris, Esq. of Philadelphia and Morris to Nath'l Massie by a patent by president. Wit: Thomas Massie. Rec. 9-10-1799. (117)

9-16-1799 - AMY formerly a slave to Nathaniel MASSIE of Adams Co., NW Territory; that Amay voluntarily binds herself for term of 8 years to Massie to serve with obediance during said time for which Massie pays $250.00 to Amay for her said services. Wit: Peter Lee, Jno. Belli. Rec. 9-16-1799. (118)

10-13-1798 - John B. GENET of Adams Co., NW Territory to David McKIBBON of Charleston, Brooke Co., Va.; $332.00; lot 13 on plan of donation lands being 217a part of tract of said donation land opposite Little Sandy River which was given to the French settlers of Gallipolis. Wit: J. G. Gervais, John Gobeau. Rec. 10-5-1799.(118)

12-6-1798 - John Baptist BERTRAND of Gallipolis, Washington Co., NW Territory, yeoman to Peter MATRY of Gallipolis, same, yeoman; $600.00; lot 16 being 217.39 acres in plat of 24,000 acres directed by Congress 3-3-1795 to French inhabitants of Gallipolis. Wit: J. LeClercq, C. Manager. Rec. 11-5-1799. (119)

8-30-1799 - John Peter Romain BUREAU of Gallipolis, Washington Co., NW Territory to Kimber BARTON of Adams Co., NW Territory; $650.00; lot 20 being 217.39a in plat of tract of 24,000 acres directed by Congress 3-3-1795 to the French inhabitants of Gallipolis; also 217.39a half of lot 19 being half adjoining lot 20; said lot 20 purchased by Bureau 5-23-1799 from Stephen Bastide and lot 19 purchased from Philip August Pithoud by deed dated Baersburgh 5-22-1797. Wit: J. Leclercq, Robt. Safford, J. G. Gervais. Rec. 11-5-1799. (120)

9-6-1799 - Claudius BERTHELOT of Gallipolis, Washington Co., NW Territory, yeoman to Thomas PATTON of Adams Co., same; $434.00; lot 31 being 270.39a in plat directed by Congress 3-3-1795 to French inhabitants of Gallipolis, being "my portion" of said grant. Wit: J. Gervais, C. Maneger. Rec. 11-5-1799. (120)

10-27-1799 - John HESLER and Catherine wife of Adams Co., NW Territory to Joshua PARISH of same; $60.00; lot 12 on Water St. in town of Alexandria. Wit: Wm Russel, Jno. Collins, Wm Robey. Rec. 11-8-1799. (121)

7-29-1799 - Nath'l MASSIE of Adams Co., NW Territory to Joseph COLLIER of same; 15 pds.; 100a east side Brush Creek pt. 400a tract granted N. Massie assignee of George Nicholass assignee of Robert Lautt (or Truitt) by United States. Wit: Joseph Kerr. Rec. 7-19-1799. (122)

6-3-1799 - Thomas PARKER and Sarah wife of Frederick Co., Va. to Joseph MOORE of Adams Co., NW Territory; $50.50; lot 45 in Alexandria. Wit: Wm Russell, And'w Collins. Rec. 2-5-1800. (123)

11-19-1799 - John HESLER of Juings(?) twp., Adams Co., NW Territory to George BOWER of same; Hesler gave bond 11-19-1799 to Bower on contract to sell to Bower lot 7 including farm house, gardens, stables, outhouses in town of Elicsanter. Wit: Peter Kester. Rec. 2-17-1800. (124)

12-25-1799 - Abraham SHEPHERD of Berkley Co. Va. to John ARMSTRONG; $450.00; 500a part 1000a granted to Shepherd by patent 6-12-1798, lines--mouth of Bakear Fork of Ohio. Wit: John Beasley. Rec. 3-12-1800. (125)

2-19-1800 - James EDWARDS and Sarah wife of Adams Co., NW Territory to Charles OURSLER of same; 120 pds. Ky money; 206a on waters of Ohio, lines--NW side of Three Mile Creek. Wit: James Stevenson, Wm Rains, Wm Hamilton. Rec. 3-12-1800. (126)

3-17-1800 - Nicholas THEVENIN of Gallipolis, Washington Co., NW Territory to Peter
BACKUS of Adams Co., same; $350.; one-half of lot 14 containing about 108½ acres,
said lot conveyed to Thevenin by Francis Valodin 5-9-1796, being part of tract
granted to French inhabitants opposite mouth of Little Sandy. Wit: And'w Collins,
Robt. Crane. Rec. 3-17-1800. (127)

12-29-1799 - Abraham SHEPERD of Berkley Co., Va. to John SHEPHERD of Adams Co., NW
Territory; 154 pds. Va. money; tract on Red Oak Creek granted to Abraham Sheperd by
patent dated 6-12-1798 being 1000 acres. Wit: Andrew Moore, Amos Moore, Isaac
Shepherd, Moses Moore. Rec. 3-17-1800. (127)

3-21-1800 - Cathrine HESLER of Juings(?) twp., Adams Co., NW Territory and John
HESLER of same place; whereas unhappiness has arisen between Cathrina and her hus-
band John Hesler and they have mutually agreed to live separate and apart, that John
Hesler discharges his wife Cathrina from him as if never married and allows her to
work and give house to travel as if she was alone and never married to him. Wit:
William Corn, John Moore. Rec. 4-8-1800. (128)

9-30-1799 - John Peter Romain BUREAU of Gallipolis, Washington Co., NW Territory to
Stephen BASTIDE of Gallipolis, same; $400.00; lot 33 being 217.39 acres part of plat
or tract of 24,000 acres granted by Congress of United States 3-3-1795 to French
inhabitants of Gallipolis and patented to Bureau 3-7-1799. Rec. 4-10-1800. (129)

12-28-1799 - Abraham SHEPHERD of Berkley Co., Va. to Abraham, Isaac and Jacob
SHEPHERD of Adams Co., NW Territory; 150 pds.; 1000 acres being land granted to
Abraham Shepherd by patent dated 6-12-1798 on Brush Creek, lines--Bakers fork.
Wit: Andrew Moore, Moses Moore. Rec. 6-10-1800. (130)

10-12-1799 - A. ST CLAIR to Joseph DARLINGTON; Ferry license; to keep ferry opposite
Waughs Ferry in Kentucky in Adams Co., to transfer all persons, cattle, wagons
and other moveables for reasonable and customary compensation until ferriage rates
can be established and to provide boats and skillful men to run same. Rec. 6-10-
1800. (131)

12-3-1799 - A. ST CLAIR to Nathan ELLIS of Hamilton Co., NW Territory; ferry license;
to keep ferry on Ohio River landing nearly opposite mouth of Limestone Creek to
opposite side of said river, to transfer all persons, cattle, wagons and moveables
for reasonable and customary compensation until ferriage rates can be established
and and to provide boats and skillful men to run same. Rec. 6-10-1800. (132)

2-14-1797 - Certificate of Samuel Vance, Lieut. and Pay Master, 3d Sub-legion,
United States certifying that William LITTLE was a Pvt. in late Capt. Reads Co.
of said Sub-legion and was discharged for disability 12-31-1794 and is entitled
(on surgeon's certificate) to pension equal to one-half allowed for highest disability at rate of 2.50 per month, given at the War Office. Rec. 6-10-1800. (133)

3-1-1800 - Thomas PARKER and Sarah wife of Frederick Co., Va. by Elias LANGHAN their
agent to Robert GREER of Adams Co., NW Territory; $50.00; lot 7 in Alexandria on
Water St. Wit: Jno. L. Wills, Wm Creighton. Rec. 6-10-1800. (133)

6-7-1800 - Robert GREER of Adams Co., NW Territory to Jno. BELLI of same; $16.66 and 2/3rds; 1/3rd part of Lot 7 in town (not stated--Alexandria) on Water St., originally conveyed to Greer by Thos. and Sarah Parker. Wit: Daniel Mullins, Thomas Hart. Ree. 6-10-1800. (134)

10-1-1799 - Arthur ST CLAIR, Governor of the Territory to James EDWARDS; Ferry license; since a ferry is necessary at the mouth of a gut in Adams Co. nearly opposite Limestone and said Edwards has requested permission to erect said ferry license is granted to ransport persons, horses, cattle and other moveables with Edwards to receive the customary compensation until rates of ferriage shall be settled at the Gen'l Quarter Session of Court, that Edwards is to provide one suitable boat and more if necessary and to have a sufficient number of able and skillful ment to navigate same. Rec. 7-22-1800. (135)

4-8-1800 - John GRAHAM of Richmond, Va. to Nathaniel MASSIE of NW Territory; 100 pds.; 1000a on Eagle Creek patented to Graham as assignee of Philip Slaughter dated 8-22-1799. Wit: John Robinson. Rec. 8-14-1800. (136)

------- - Charles JOHNSTON of Richmond, Va. to Nathaniel MASSIE, Esq. of NW Territory; power of attorney to sell in his name to the legal represenatives of Edmond Lyne, dec'd 2000 acres as per contract entered by Lyne and the late Gen. Charles Harrison part 5466 and 2/3ds acres military land surveyed in name of Harrison and patented as follows--2-4-1800, 2/3 acres, two tracts patented Feb. 5 of same year for 1200a each, one other tract patented Feb. 7 same year for 1200a, all NW Ohio River. Wit: Henry S. Shore, John Fox, Thomas Nelson. Rec. 8-14-1800. (137)

12-20-1798 + Hastings MARKS of Albemarle Co., Va. by John W. HINDE of Clark Co., Ky. his attorney to James EUBANK of Fayette Co., Ky.; 80 pds.; all the undivided interest of Marks in two tracts--one being 1906a surveyed for John Marks part military warrant No. 7 on Elk run a branch of Brush Creek; tract two being 2000a surveyed for John Marks part military warrant No. 7 on waters of east fork of Brush Creek. Wit: D. Bullock. Rec. 8-14-1800. (138)

8-24-1799 - James ASKEW of Mercer Co., Ky. to Ree THOMAS of Adams Co., NW Territory; $125.00; 100a as by survey of 11-20-1787 first granted to said James Askey by patent dated 1-1-1797 on military warrant No. 1 on waters of Eagle Creek. Wit: Jos. Kerr, Jno. Barret. Rec. 8-18-1800. (140)

7-17-1800 - Charles JOHNSTON of Richmond, Va. by Nat'l MASSIE of Adams Co., NW Territory, his attorney to William PITENGER of last named place; 570 pds. Ky money; 800a part of tract of 1200a surveyed in name of Charles Harrison and patented by United States to Charles Johnston 2-5-1800, lines--Samuel Hopkins survey No. 641. Wit: Jos. Kerr, Benj. Goodin. Rec. 9-10-1800. (141)

1-23-1800 - Thomas PARKER and Sarah wife of Frederick Co., Va. to Stephen SMITH of Adams Co., NW Territory; $40.00; lot 43 in Alexandria. Wit: E. Langham, Wm Russell, Ruben Smith. Rec. 9-13-1800. (143)

8-8-1800 - Joseph FEURT of Adams Co., NW Territory to Benjamin FEURT of Montgomery Co., Caintucke; 2 milk cows, 2 heifers, one bull calf, nine head of sheep, 15 head of hogs, 60 fowels, 3 cittles, 2 pots, one bake oven, 3 beds and bedding, 38 of puter, one set tea ware, 2 spinning wheels, a half dosin chairs, one churn, 2 culars, 4 buckets, a half bushel sowing flax, 30 bushels corn, 1 plow, 2 sets geers, 3 axes, 5 hoes, 4 draw knives, 4 bushel flax ceed, 2 saws. Wit: Gabriel Feurt, Stephen Carey. Rec. 11-17-1800. (144)

12-28-1799 - Abraham SHEPHERD of Berkely Co., Va. to Abraham SHEPHERD, Isaac SHEP-HERD and Jacob SHEPHERD of Adams Co., NW Territory; 150 pds. Va. money; 1000a on Brush Creek patented to Abraham Shepherd 6-12-1798. Wit: Andrew Moore, Amos Moore and Moses Moore. Rec. 11-24-1800. (144)

5-4-1799 - Alexander SCOTT of Lancaster, Pa. to Henry MILLER, Esq. of York Town, Pa.; $3000.00; undivided one-half part 12 tracts of land situated in Washington Co., NW Territory conveyed to me by Peregine Foster, Esq. by power of attorney of John Davis of Morgan Town, Va. Wit: Benj. Joes. Gilman, Jno. Jos. Henry. Recorded in Washington Co., Ohio 5-20-1799 in Volume 6. Rec. 12-17-1800. (145)

8-16-1800 - John Baptiste GINAT of Gallipolis, Adams Co., NW Territory to Nicholas THEVENIN of Washington Co., NW Territory; $200.00; lot 12(13?) of 217a being "my share" in land granted by Congress to the French inhabitants of Gallipolis. Wit: John B. Ferard, Francis (mark) Marien. Rec. 12-25-1800. (146)

5-27-1800 - Samuel HOPKINS and Betty wife of Henderson Co., Ky. to the Heirs of Arthur FOX, dec'd of Mason Co., Ky.; for consideration of locating 5600a military land warrants in NW Territory by said Arthur Fox, dec'd, do convey to his heirs on waters of Eagle and Straight Creek 1400a. Wit: Mathew Campbell, Emanuel Dixon. Rec. 12-25-1800. (146)

5-27-1800 - Samuel HOPKINS and Betty wife of Henderson Co., Ky. to Bazil DUKE and John COBURN of Mason Co., Ky.; $5600.00; 2800a in forks of Eagle Creek being two surveys made in name of Samuel Hopkins known by Nos. 641 & 99. Wit: Mathew Campbell, Emanuel Dixon. Rec. 12-25-1800. (147)

7-5-1800 - Noble GRIMES, Thomas GRIMES and Richard GRIMES of Washington, Adams Co., NW Territory to George GORDON; $198.00; lots 5,15,106,92,30,32,88,43,3 & 18 in Washington. Wit: David Bradford, Samuel Bradford. Rec. 12-25-1800. (148)

6-6-1800 - Noble GRIMES, Thomas GRIMES, Richard GRIMES of Washington, Adams Co., NW Territory to John GRAHAM, Esq., of Mason Co., Ky.; $30.00; in-lot 87 in Washington. Wit.: David Bradford, Samuel Bradford. Rec. 12-25-1800. (150)

1-29-1801 - Phillip DYER of Alexandria, Adams Co., NW Territory to Chrisley BOTTLE-MAN of same; $30.00; lot 21 in Alexandria. Wit: Benj. Tupper, Robt. Russell, Joshua Parrish. Rec. 1-29-1801. (151)

1-30-1801 - John BELLI of Adams Co., NW Territory to John WILKINS Jr. of Pittsburgh, Pa.; in consequence of power of attorney of Alexander Scott of Lancaster, Pa. dated 4-8-1799 to said Wilkins to receive and obtain of Belli all money on account of Scott and deed by Belli on behalf of Scott; 1/4th part of 2000a between Churchill Jones survey 459 and Mayo Carringtons survey 436 including in said 1/4th part the town laid out on tract as conveyed by Winthrop Sargent 1-2-1798 to said Belli and belonging to Jno. Wilkins Jr. Wit: Noble Grimes. Rec. 1-30-1801. (152)

--------- - John Adams, President of United States in consideration of military services performed by Churchill Jones a Captain for 3 years in Va. Line on Cont'l Establishment and by act of Congress passed 8-10-1790 entitling officers and soldiers of the Va. Line on said establishment to obtain land in NW Territory and also by act of Congress passed 6-9-1795 do grant to Noble GRIMES assignee of Churchill Jones 100a being survey dated 11-17-1787 on military warrant 2311 (for 4000a this being part) on Brush Creek. Recorded War Dept. Vol. 1, page 466. Rec. 2-9-1801. (152)

1-14-1801 - Nicholas TREVENIN and Hannah Mein his wife of Gallipolis, Washington Co., NW Territory, as admsx. as ordered by probate of Adams Co. dated 4-2-1798 to Ellis CHANDLER of Mason Co., Ky; $201.00; lot 22 being 217 acres property of Nicholas Prionse Deglement, dec'd and sold at public sale 12-1-1800 by order of court of Adams Co. dated 11-12-1798 which lot P. Priome purchased from Martinas Vandenbonden as per deed dated 1-30-1797 being part of land granted by Congress to the French inhabitants of Gallipolis. Wit: Claudius R. Manage, Anselem Tupper. Rec. 2-10-1801. (154)

1-25-1801 - Francis D'HEBECOURT of Marietta, Washington Co., NW Territory to David KINKEID of Mason Co., Ky.; $350.00; lot 27 being 217a part of 24,000a granted by Congress 3-4-1795 which said lot 27 was drawn in name of Francis Duvarge and patented to him and sold to D'Hebecourt by John Gilbert Pettit executor of estate of Francis Duverge. Wit: Eli Barton, W. Diduit. Rec. 3-7-1801. (154)

3-16-1801 - Stephen MONOT (MOROT) of Gallipolis, Washington Co., NW Territory to Anthony Claudius VINCENT of Marretta, NW Territory; whereas by act of Congress dated 6-25-1798 Monot (Morot) was granted lot 6 being 150a part of tract of 1200a do now for consideration of $25.00 sell 4 acres in upper corner part of said lot 6. Wit: F. LeClerqc, J. Bureau. Rec. 4-21-1801. (156)

-------- - Surveyed for Larkin SMITH 1000a part of military warrant No. 619 on River Ohio, NW side. (Signed) John O. Bannon, 11-21-1787. Copy of survey in Va. land office 4-14-1795 said land being due to Larkin Smith for service of 3 years as Capt. in Va. Cont'l Line and that on 4-13-1795 in Richmond, Va. Larkin Smith sold said land to John BROWN and John BELLI and that on 7-29-1796 in Frankfort, Ky. John Brown sold his interest to John Belli. Rec. (not given). (157)

6-19-1799 - John Waller JOHNSTON of Lexington, Ky. to John JORDON Jr. of same; 700 pds. Ky money; 700a patented 6-28-1798 by survey 11-20-1792 made to Jno. W. Johnston on several Cont'l military warrants: No. 69 to Hamilton Cole for 200a, No. 1778 to Robt. Scott for 200a, No. 2051 to George Bond for 100a and No. 4076 to Coledrop Freeman for 200a, lying on west side of Brush Creek. Wit: Cuthbert Banks, J.P. Rec. 6-10-1801. (158)

6-8-1801 - Andrew ELLISON and Mary wife of Adams Co., NW Territory to Samuel STARRET
of same; $888.00; 209½a on waters of Three Mile Creek, lines--corner of Abraham
Kirkpatricks survey No. 912. Wit: Joseph Kerr, Jno. Collings. Rec. 6-10-1801.(160)

4-6-1801 - Nath'l MASSIE and Susan wire of Adams Co., NW Territory to Amos GUSTIN;
45 pds. Ky money; 100a on waters of Brush Creek, part of 1000a granted by United
States to Massie assignee of Leven Powell 5-13-1796, lines--Peter Wickams. Rec.
6-10-1801. (161)

11-8-1800 - Nath'l MASSIE and Susan wife of Adams Co., NW Territory to James CARSON
of same; 200a on Soldiers Run branch of Brush Creek part of tract of 720a granted
to Massie by United States 2-20-1796, lines--Alexander Dunlaps 200a, Isaac Wamsleys
line, Thomas Barbee's tract and Rankins tract. Wit: Jos. Moore, Geo. Gordon. Rec.
6-10-1801. (162)

6-9-1801 - John BEASLEY and Sally wife of Adams Co., NW Territory to Joseph McNEAL
of same; $66.00; part of tract of 200a by United States to Jno. Beasley by patent
dated 6-8-1798 on waters of Cherry fork of Brush Creek, being 137a. Wit: Samuel
Wright. Rec. 6-10-1801. (164)

6-11-1801 - Noble GRIMES, Thomas GRIMES and Richard GRIMES and Mary wife of Washington, Adams Co., NW Territory to Moses CRAWFORD of same; $1000.00; 210a part of sur-
vey of 1000a made in name of Churchill Jones. Wit: Moses Baird. Rec. 6-11-1801.(165)

8-9-1800 - George GORDON and Sally W. wife of Washington, Adams Co., NW Territory to
David BRADFORD of same; $150.00; lots 3 & 8 in town of Washington. Wit: Noble
Grimes. Rec. 6-11-1801. (166)

8-24-1791 - Alexander McINTIRE of Mason Co., Va. in the District of Ky to Belteshazer
DRAGOO; bond of 200 pds.; condition of obligation that McIntire to make to Dragoo a
deed for 450a land on both sides Eagle Creek for a mill seat and to be within 10
miles of river. Wit: Stephen Tracy. Rec. 6-15-1801. (168)

5-4-1801 - Peter HEATH of Chillicothe, Ross Co., NW Territory to Thomas SHAIN of
Mason Co., Ky.; power of attorney to sell Heath's plantation in Adams Co. on the
Ohio river opposite the mouth of Salt Lick Creek adjoining lands of Moses Baird
and others. Wit: Moses Baird, Simon Rains. Rec. 6-18-1801. (168)

6-5-1801 - Thomas SHANE of Mason Co., Ky attorney for Peter HEATH of Ross Co., NW
Territory to John G. McDOWELL of Mason Co., Ky.; $1000.00; tract of land being 217
acres. Wit: Andrew Smith, James Davis. Rec. 6-18-1801. (169)

6-9-1801 - Noble GRIMES, Richard GRIMES and Thomas GRIMES of Adams Co., NW Territory
to Jno. BELLI of same; $50.00; lot 7 on Front or Waters Sts. and fronting Ohio at
mouth of Brush Creek in town of Washington. Wit: Moses Baird. Rec. 6-22-1801. (170)

-------- - Francis D'HEBECOURT of Marietta, Washington Co., NW Territory to Eli
BARTON residing in the French Grant, Adams Co., NW Territory; by power of attorney of
Peter Maret Sr. dated Gallipolis 7-17-1799 sell lot 9 being 217.39 acres part of tract
of 24,000 acres granted by Congress to the French Settlers of Gallipolis 3-3-1795,
said lot 9 being shown on map made by Abslom Martin, surveyer and entered in the name
of Peter Maret. Wit: Elias Chandler, J.G. Gervais. Rec. 6-30-1801. (171)

7-31-1801 - John KILLEN of Adams Co., NW Territory to Nathan ELLIS of same; $56.50; in-lot 28 containing 1/3rd acre and out-lot 33 containing 4 acres in Killenstown. Wit: Wm Stuart, David Bradford. Rec. 8-1-1801. (171)

6-6-1800 - Andrew COLLINS and Margaret wife of Adams Co., NW Territory to John BOYLE of same; $22.00; lot 15 in town of Alexandria. Wit: Jno. Belli. Rec. 8-3-1801.(172)

8-1-1807 - Plat of town of St. Clairsville (Decatur) by Bazil DAKE and John CORBURN, joint proprietors. Rec. 8-10-1801. (174)

4-4-1797 - Lenday HEWEY to George MITCHELL, both of Mason Co., Ky.; that Lendy Hewey has placed and bound her daughter, Ruth LEWIS to serve as a servant apprentice to said Mitchell for 13 years from 1-1-1797 and which will end 1-1-1800. That George Mitchell for $50.00 makes over his right of indenture of Ruth LEWIS to John BELLI. 3-20-1801. Approved by Lendy Hewey. Wit: Arthur Mitchell. Rec. 8-11-1801. (175)

5-29-1797 - Robert BARTON of Greenville Co., North Carolina acting as executor of Jno. BARTON, dec'd to Eli WILLIAMS of Washington Co., Maryland; being two tracts of military land lying NW of the Ohio belonging to the estate of John Burton, one tract containing 1333 and 1/3rd acres on lower side of Indian Creek and the other tract containing 1333 and 1/3rd acres on White Oak Creek; also grant power of attorney to said Williams to apply to Surveyor General of military lands to have survey made in his name. Rec. 9-10-1801. (176)

6-28-1783 - Land Office. Military Warrant No. 1273 in land set aside for Officers and soldiers of Virginia said warrant surveyed and laid off for John BARTON heir at law of Hutchins Barton, dec'd; 2666 and 2/3rds acres granted unto John Barton in consideration of Hutchins Barton's services for 3 years as Lieut. in Virginia Cont'l Line, (Signed) John Harvie, Land office. Land laid off in two surveys of 1333 and 1/3rd acres in each as follows: No. 1213 being 1333 and 1/3rd acres, No. 761 being 1333 and 1/3rd acres. Rec. 9-10-1801. (177)

7-25-1801 - Nath'l MASSIE and Susan wife of Adams Co., NW Territory to John ELLISON of same; $80.00; in-lots 15,17,44 & 45, also out-lots 12,13,19,25 & 33 the last containing 4 acres each, all in town of Manchester. Wit: Joseph Kerr. Rec. 9-10-1801. (177)

8-5-1801 - John KILLEN of Adams Co., NW Territory to John MEGGET of same; $66.76; in-lot 15 and out-lot 2 in Killingstown. Wit: Jos. Kerr, D'd. Decamps. Rec. 9-10-1801. (178)

9-9-1801 - John KILLEN of Adams Co., NW Territory to James W. BEASLEY of same; $108.00; in-lots 5 & 32, out-lots 3 & 23 Killens Town. Wit: J. Darlinton. Rec. 9-10-1801. (179)

8-13-1801 - Nath'l MASSIE and Susan wife of Adams Co., NW Territory to Thomas KIRKER of same; 30 pds. Ky money; 690a on Beasleys fork of Brush Creek, lines--tract of Massie. Wit: John Briggs, Thos. Massie. Rec. 9-10-1801. (180)

9-3-1801 - George TONNER (TANNER) and Hannah wife of Adams Co., NW Territory to John SHURLEY of same; $500.00; 102a on west side of Brush Creek. Wit: Geo. Gordon, Rich'd Grimes. Rec. 9-10-1801. (181)

1-20-1801 - Peter FERARD of Gallipolis, Washington Co., NW Territory to Thomas
THOMPSON of Adams Co., same; $13.33 and 1/3rd and also for $186.66 and 2/3rds to be
paid by Thompson afterwards; lot 92 of 217.39 acres in plat of 24,000 acres granted
by Congress to French Inhabitants of Gallipolis on 3-3-1795, said lot being Perard's
portion of said grant. Wit: P. Bureau, Minguay. Rec. 9-10-1801. (183)

7-14-1801 - Nath'l MASSIE and Susan wife of Adams Co., NW Territory to George TANNER
of same; 45 pds. Ky money; 312a on west side of Brush Creek being tract surveyed in
name of Massie and a part entered and surveyed in name of John J. Griffin and patented to Massie as assignee of Griffin. Wit: Adam Renerd, Jos. Kerr. Rec. 9-10-
1801. (184)

11-1-1800 - Thomas PARKER and Sarah wife of Virginia to John COLLINS of Alexandria,
NW Territory; $100.00; lots 17 & 18 adjoining town of Alexandria. Wit: Thomas Hart,
Wm Rusel, And. Collins. Rec. 11-5-1801. (186)

5-16-1801 - Nath'l MASSIE and Susan wife of Adams Co., NW Territory to William
CRAWFORD of same; 146 pds. 13 shillings Ky money; 838a on Hills fork of Eagle Creek,
lines--John Baldwin, Nathan Parry, James Megoveny. Wit: Needham Perry, Thomas
Perry. Rec. 12-8-1801. (186)

6-6-1801 - William CRAWFORD and Martha wife of Adams Co., NW Territory to David ROBE
of Mason Co., Ky.; $430.00; 200a on waters of Hills fork of Eagle Creek being part
of entries 3052 & 3571 containing 2800a and part of 3 Virginia Military Warrants
Nos. 815,1730 & 4722, entered and surveyed in name of Nath'l Massie, lines--James
McGoveney, Stephen Baldwin. Wit: William Knox. Rec. 12-8-1801. (188)

8-19-1801 - Nath'l MASSIE and Susan E. wife of Adams Co., NW Territory to John KITE
of Ross Co., same; $186.40; 466a south side of East fork of Eagle Creek part of
entries 3052 * 351 containing 2800a surveyed and patented to said Massie. Wit:
Joseph Kerr. Rec. 12-8-1801. (189)

6-24-1800 - Dudley WOODBRIDGE Jr. to Francis D'HERBECOURT, both of Marietta, Washington Co., NW Territory; consideration of obligation dated 5-14-1800 for $727.75; do-
nation lot 26 in bottom of Meigs Creek on Muskingum cont. 100a said lot drawn by
Nathan Goddale late of Belprie, Washington Co. and conveyed by Isaac Pierce adms.
of said estate 4-3-1798; also 3 acre lot 480 one mile north of Campius Martius, also
13 acres No. 347 about 1 mile northeast from stockade to Marietta also drawn by
Nathan Goddale of Bellpre and conveyed by Isaac Pierce adms. of estate; also 100
acres lot 89 in 3rd twp., 8th range drawn by John Lathbee of Belprie, Washington Co.
conveyed 9-20-1797; also lot 48 of 217 acres in tract of land granted by Congress to
French settlers of Gallipolis 3-4-1795, drawn by Lewis LeClercq of Gallipolis and
conveyed by deed dated 7-7-1797, as shown in map by Absalom Martin. Wit: Mathew
Bachus, John Woodbridge. Rec. 12-21-1801. (193) (note: deed states Dudley Woodbridge Jr. to Francis D'HEBECOURT, but indications are it should read, "Francis
D'Hebecourt to Dudley Woodbridge, Jr.")

31

7-7-1797 - Lewis LECLERC of Gallipolis, Washington Co., NW Territory, husbandman
to Francis D'HEBECOURT of same; $300.00; lot 48 containing 217 acres as shown on map
made by Absalom Martin, part of tract of 24,000 acres lying on northerly bank of Ohio
River being 2 miles by straight line above mouth of Little Sandy (then down course
of river 8 miles to include the entire 24,000 acres), as granted in March 1795 by
Congress to the French inhabitants of Gallipolis. Wit: Petit P. Marret. Rec.
12-21-1801. (193)

2-6-1801.- Joseph KERR and Nancy wife of Adams Co., NW Territory to William McCLARRAN
of same; 500 pds. Ky money; 100a on waters of Brush Creek, lines--Joseph Hoofmans
survey of 100a, being tract granted to said Joseph Kerr by patent dated 2-1-1800.
Rec. 1-1-1802. (194)

9-8-1785 - John BELLIS and Andrew CRAWFORD of Washington Co., Maryland, shopkeepers
to Samuel PURVIANCE, Robert PURVIANCE and William KNOX of Baltimore, Md., merchants;
bond of 498 pounds 2 shillings 5 pence Maryland money; whereas John Belli and Andrew
Crawford are indebted to parties of second part. Release whereas on 7-7-1801 John
Belli paid $1546.68 in principal and interest on said bond. (Signed) A. St. Clair
attorney for Henry Purviance. Wit: Jos. Woolsey, Wm Corn. Rec. 1-6-1802. (195)

10-1-1801 - Edward BROWN of Maryland now of this Territory to John BELLI of Adams
Co., NW Territory; bond of $1000.00 condition of obligation that Brown to pay Belli
by 10-1-1807 600 silver dollars and interest from 10-1-1802 and Belli to deliver to
Brown deed for 100a land on Ohio River adjoining Joseph Woolsey's 100a. Rec. 1-14-
1802. (196)

8-19-1801 - Nath'l MASSIE and Susan wife of Adams Co., NW Territory to Dunkin
MACKINZIE of same; 23 pds; in-lots 26 & 67, also out-lots 5,7,35,41,44,51 & 52,
all in town of Manchester. Wit: Joseph Kerr. Rec. 3-9-1802. (198)

7-14-1801 - Nath'l MASSIE and Susan wife of Adams Co., NW Territory to Adam PENNYWIT
of same; 345a granted by U.S. to Massie as assignee of David O'Bannon, lines--mouth
of Donaldsons Creek, Wm Markland. Wit: Joseph Kerr. Rec. 3-9-1802. (199)

7-14-1801 - Nath'l MASSIE and Susan wife of Adams Co., NW Territory to Adam PENNYWIT
of same; 37 pds. 10 shillings; in-lots 35,19,46 & 48 in Manchester. Wit: Joseph Kerr.
Rec. 3-9-1802. (200)

5-27-1801 - Andrew ELLISON and Mary wife of Adams Co., NW Territory to Gabriel GLEN
of Fiatta (Fayette?) Co., Pa.; $600.00; part of tract of 1000a to Andrew Ellison
by Chas. Johnston assignee of Charles Harrison patented 2-1-1800, lines--Abraham
Shepherd survey of 1200a. Wit: Wm Black, W. Mahffey. Rec. 3-9-1802. (202)

11-3-1801 - Hervy HEATH and Rebecca wife of Brooke Co., Va. to Ralph PETERSON of
Adams Co., NW Territory; $400.00; 202a part of tract patented to Hervy Heath cont.
1000a 4-20-1792 on Eagle Creek. Wit: James Clark, Thomas Fawcett, Evan Shelly.
Rec. 3-9-1802. (203)

12-16-1801 - William STARLING and Susanna wife of Kentucky and said Starling as
attorney for William LYNE, Henry LINE, Edward Howe and Ann his wife, legatees and
devisees of Edward LYNE, dec'd to Igntius MITCHELL of Mason Co., Ky.; $2000.00;
1000a NW side of Ohio River opposite Charleston, lines--Mace Clements survey. Wit:
Lucas Sullivant, Jno. Holloway, Wm Starling Jr. Rec. 3-9-1802. (204)

2-16-1802 - William LUCAS and Elizabeth wife to John WHITE, all of Adams Co., NW Territory; $100.00; 110a on waters of Scioto part of tract granted by United States to Lucas for 360a patented 8-18-1801. Wit: Jno. Beasley. Rec. 3-9-1802. (206)

3-9--1802 - Plat of town of Killenstown. John Killen, proprietor. Rec. 3-10-1802. (209)

3-10-1802 - Plat of town of Watterford. And'w Ellison, proprietor. Rec. 3-10-1802. (210)

3-10-1802 - Noble GRIMES of Adams Co., NW Territory to Peter NOEL of same; $30.00; lot 91 in town of Washington. Wit: Mills Stephenson. Rec. 4-10-1802. (211)

4-14-1802 - Ellias LANGHAM and Mary wife of Ross Co., NW Territory to William RUSSEL of Adams Co., same; $60.00; lot 1 in town of Alexandria. Wit: Jno. Carlisle, Abner Meeker, Wm Rector. Rec. 4-24-1802. (212)

4-15-1802 - Plat of town of Washington. Noble Grimes, proprietor. Rec. 4-27-1802. (213)

4-18-1802 - Plat of town of Manchester. Nath'l Massie, original proprietor, Rec. 4-29-1802. (214)

6-10--1801 - Peter HEATH and Mary wife of Ross Co., NW Territory to John HEATH of Mason Co., Ky.; 300 pds.; 217a on Bank of Ohio River nearly opposite mouth of Salt Lick Creek part of survey patented to Mayo Carrington 3-21-1791 and by Carrington to Joseph C. Vance to conveyed to Peter Heath. Wit: Moses Baird, Mary Baird. Rec. 5-16-1802. (216)

10-15-1801 - Nicholas THEVENIN and Hannah Mien wife of Gallipolis, Washington Co., NW Territory by power of administration to Ellis CHANDLER of Mason Co., Ky.; $201.00; lot 22 containing 217a which lot was property of Nicholas Prioux Deglement, dec'd and sold at public sale on Oct. 13 by order of Court of Adams Co. dated 9-8-1801, situated on bank of Ohio being land granted to French inhabitants of Gallipolis. Wit: Kimber Barton, M. Barton. Rec. 5-23-1802. (217)

8-5-1801 - John HEATH and Margaret wife of Mason Co., Ky. to Elijah CREWS of same; 300 pds. by Ky money; on bank of Ohio opposite mouth of Salt Lick Creek part of survey patented to Mayo Carrington 3-21-1791 and by Carrington conveyed to Joseph C. Vance who conveyed to Peter Heath who conveyed to John Heath, being 217a. Wit: John Nottproth, James Dozer. Rec. 6-2-1802. (218)

6-14-1801 - Nathan Ellis Sheriff of Adams Co., NW Territory to John STEPHENSON of same; said sheriff by order of court sold at open market lots 89 & 90 in town of Washington for $32.50 to said Stephenson. Wit: Noble Grimes, Rich'd Grimes. Rec. 6-9-1802. (219)

3-9-1802 - John KILLEN of Adams Co., NW Territory to Samuel BALDRIDGE of same; $35.00; in-lot 18, also out-lot 31 containing 4 acres on waters of Brush Creek, in Killinstown. Wit: Noble Grimes. Rec. 6-9-1802. (220)

9-14-1801 - John BEASLEY and Salley wife of Adams Co., NW Territory to Joseph
ILEAR of same; $500.00; land on waters of Brush Creek part of tract of 2866 and
2/3rds acres patented to Robt. Rankin 10-28-1799. Wit: Joseph Kerr. Rec.
6-9-1802. (221)

2-26-1802 - Robert RANKINS and Peggy wife of Mation Co., Ky. to John BEASLY of Adams
Co., NW Territory; $700a on waters of Brush Creek part of tract granted
Robt Rankins patented 10-28-1799, lines--Rankins survey of 866 and 2/3rds acres.
Wit: Tho. Massie, Nath'l Collins, Wm Perry. Rec. 6-9-1802. (222)

6-11-1801 - Noble GRIMES, Thomas GRIMES and Rich'd GRIMES of Washington town in
NW Territory to John Stephenson; $100.00; lots 38,39, & 95 in town of Washington.
Wit: Moses Baird. Rec. 6--9-1802. (223)

4-13-1802 - Ignatius MITCHELL and Mille wife of Mason Co., Ky. to Joseph SHAW of
same; $1350.00; 450a part of tract of 1000a opposite Charlestown, being survey
patented in name of Edmond Lyne and adjoining Mace Clements survey at mouth of
Eagle Creek on upper side. Wit: Thomas Foote, Thomas Foote Jr., Mills Stephenson.
Rec. 6-9-1802. (224)

6-10-1801 - Andrew ELLISON and Mary wife of Adams Co., NW Territory to William
MAHAFFEY of Fayette Co., Pa.; $300.00; 150a part tract of 1000a deeded to Andrew
Ellison by Charles Johnson and entered in name of Charles Harrison on waters of
Eagle Creek, lines--Gabriel Glenn tract of 300a. Wit: Jno. Ellison.
Rec. 6-9-1802. (226)

12-11-1802 - John BEASLEY and Sally wife of Adams Co., NW Territory to Obediah STOUT
of same; $200.00; 200a part of survey in name of John Beasley, lines--Stouts run,
creek. Wit: Thos. Kirker. Rec. 6-9-1802. (227)

1-13-1802 - John GRAHAM of Virginia, Nath'l MASSIE and Susan wife of Ross Co., NW
Territory to William LEEDOM of Adams Co., same; $260; 130a on Three Mile Creek
part of survey of 1000a in name of Callhill Mines (or Mires), lines--Samuel Hopkins
old survey, John Bryan tract. Wit: Jno. Beasley, Jno. Bryan. Rec. 6-9-1802. (229)

1-30-1802 - John GRAHAM of Richmond, Va. and Nath'l MASSIE and Susan wife of Ross
Co., NW Territory to Joseph EDENTIN of Adams Co., NW Territory; $652.00; 326a on
Three Mile Creek part of Callehill Mins (or Mirs) survey, lines--George Wilsons
tract, Jno. Bryans tract, Wm Leedoms tract. Wit: Jno. Beasley, Wm Leedom. Rec.
6-9-1802. (230)

1-30-1802 - Jno. GRAHAM of Virginia and Nath'l MASSIE and Susan wife of Ross Co.,
NW Territory to Isaac ENGINTON of Adams Co., NW Territory; $642.00; 321a on Three
Mile Creek part of Mines (or Mires) Survey, lines--Collohill Mins (or Mirs) old
survey, Joseph Edgenton corner. Wit: Jno. Beasley, Will Leedom. Rec.6-9-1802.(232)

1-30-1802 - John GRAHAM of Richmond, Va. and Nath'l MASSIE and Susan wife of Ross Co.,
NW Territory to John BRYAN of Adams Co., NW Territory; $200.00; 200a on waters of
Three Mile creek part of tract patented to Minnis and assigned to Wm Reynolds who
conveyed same to Robert Means who conveyed same to Jno. Graham, lines--survey in name
of Cullhill Minnis No. 660. Wit: Jno. Beasley, Wm Leedom. Rec. 6-9-1802. (234)

4-8-1802 - Nath'l MASSIE and Susan wife of Ross Co., NW Territory to Peter SHOEMAKER of Adams Co., NW Territory; 34 pds.; 200a on Beasleys fork of Brush Creek part of tract of 690a patented to said Massie. Wit.: D'd Massie, Jno. Ellison. Rec. 6-9-1802. (236)

2-23-1802 - Nath'l MASSIE and Susan wife of Ross Co., NW Territory to James HEMPHILL of Adams Co., same; 27 pds.; 180a on Beasleys fork of Brush Creek part of tract of 690a patented to said Massie. Wit: John Brown. Rec. 6-9-1802. (237)

3-1-1802 - John SHEPHERD of Adams Co., NW Territory to Antony DUNLAVEY of same; $200.00; 100a on Red Oak, granted to Abraham Shepherd by patent dated 6-20-1798 and conveyed by him to said John Shepherd. Wit.: W. Kinkead, Wm Dunlap, Isaac Shepperd. Rec. 6-9-1802. (238)

4--21-1802 - Elias LANGHAM and Mary wife of Ross Co., NW Territory to William D. THORP of Adams Co., same; $150.00; lot 20 in town of Alexandria. Wit: Abriah Springer, Thos. Scott, Benj. Miller. Rec. 7-3-1802. (240)

3-5-1802 - John BEASLEY and Sally wife of Adams Co., NW Territory to William LUCAS of same; $200.00; 400a on Scioto Brush Creek patented to Beasley by United States, lines--Benjamin Selars survey 1583. Wit: Thos. Kirker. Rec. 7-2-1802. (241)

3-__-1802 (no day given) - William LUCAS and Elizabeth wife of Adams Co., NW Territory to John BEASLEY; $300.00; land on Lick fork of Brush Creek granted by United States patent to Wm Lucas 8-18-1802, lines--Joseph Bauses survey 3729. Wit: Jno. Belli. Rec. 7-21-1802. (242)

--------- - Nicholas THEVENIN of Gallipolis, Washington Co., NW Territory to Vincent FERGESON of same; $450.00; lot 2 being 217a above and opposite mouth of Little Sandy being my portion of land granted by Congress to the French inhabitants of Gallipolis. Wit: Duduit L. Charpentier. Rec. 7-23-1802. (243)

6-4-1802 - Nathaniel MASSIE and Susan wife of Ross Co., NW Territory to Alexander SMITH of Adams Co., same; 72 pds.; 110a NW bank of Ohio river part of survey of 490a in name of David O'Bannon patented by United States to Nath'l Massie assignee of O'Bannon, lines Donaldsons Creek. Wit: Thos. Massie, Jno. Brown. Rec. 9-14-1802. (244)

4--8-1802 - Nath'l MASSIE and Susan wife of Ross Co., NW Territory to Needham PERRY of Adams Co., same; 45 pds. Ky money; 200a N side of East fork of Eagle Creek part of tract of 2800a survey in name of Massie, also 14a part of above mentioned tract. Wit: D'd Massie, Jno Ellison. Rec. 9-14-1802. (245)

6-4-1802 - Nath'l MASSIE and Susan E. wife of Adams Co., NW Territory to Aron MOORE of same; $100.00; 200a South side East fork of Eagle Creek. Wit: Thomas MASSIE, Jno. Brown. Rec. 9-14-1802. (247)

4-8-1802 - Charles JOHNSTON of Richmond, Va. by his attorney Nath'l MASSIE of Ross Co., NW Territory to Joseph WASHBURN of Adams Co., NW Territory; $600.00; 300a on waters of East fork of Eagle Creek being part of survey in name of Chas. Harrison and patented to Chas. Johnson, lines--Chas. Harrison survey of 1200a, Samuel Hopkins survey of 1400a. Wit: D'd Massie, Jno. Ellison. Rec. 9-14-1802. (248)

1-2-1802 - John EVANS of Adams Co., NW Territory to Rhoads SHANKLAND of Sussex Co., Delaware; $2000.00 title to two lots (numbers not given) in Manchester which were given for services by Robert Ellison to defend the iphabitants of said town from the savages and their accomplices with improvements placed on lost by Benj. Goodin and have now become thepropperty of John Evans. Wit: Mary Cook, Josiah H. Stanbury. Rec. 9-14-1802. (249)

8-11-1802 - William LYTLE and Eliza N. wife of Clermont Co., NW Territory to Daniel COLIER of Adams Co., same; $666.66 and 2/3rds; 500s on Waters of Brush Creek, lines-- Truitts survey 1630, Mountjoy's survey 1567. Wit: Owen Todd. (251)

8-16-1802 - Joseph EILAR and Molly wife of Adams Co., NW Territory to Adam HEMPLE-MAN of same; $100.00; 100a on waters of Brush Creek part of tract of 866a granted by United States to Robert Rankins 10-28-1799. Wit: John Beasley. Rec. 9-14-1802.(252)

6-11-1802 - Nathan ELLIS, Sheriff of Adams Co. to David (also called Robert) KINKAD; by order of Common Pleas Court of Washington Co. in Marietta judgement was rendered against Francis Dehebecourt in behalf of John Husman of Pa. dated 12-11-1800 and have sold at open marked land in Adams County 15 miles above mouth of Big Scioto in French Grant, Upper twp. lot 27 for $90.00. Wit: joshua Parris, Isaac Collins, Jane Thompson. Rec. 9-14-1802. (253)

8-28-1802 - Saray VINEDINE of Brook Co., Va. quit claim to my coloured slave know by the name of Bendine his freedom from service or slavery of myself, my heirs and assigns forever on condition of his good behavior. Wit: Wm(mark) Noler, Samuel Kinkaid. Rec. 9-14-1802. (254)

7-12-1802 - Lewis/VONSCHRILTZ and Mary Margaret wife of Gallipolis, Washington Co., NW Territory to Mitchall BACCUS of Adams Co., same; $100.00; lot 90 containing 117a granted by Congress to French inhabitants of Gallipolis 3-3-1795 and joines 100 acres Vonschriltz sold to August Philip Pitoud. Wit: C. Etienne, P. Bureau. Rec. 9-14-1802. (255)

4-7-1802 - Lewis Anthony CHARPENTER (signed: Antoine Louis Charpenter) of Adams Co., NW Territory to Peter Bachus; $300.00; lot 87 being 150a on banks of Ohio River lying on French Grant being tract of land granted by congress to Stephen Marmot. Wit: Bareau J. Gervais, A. Lovrouin, Rec. 9-14-1802. (256)

9-12-1802 - Andrew ELLISON and Mary wife of Adams Co., NW Territory to Robert BALSTON (RALSTON?) of same; $50.00; 50a on Stouts Run & branch of Ohio being patented in name of said Ellison, lines--John Beasleys survey No. 2024. Wit: Benj. Bowman, John Eakine. Rec. 9-14-1802. (257)

7-12-1802 - John BEASLLEY and Sally wife of Adams Co., NW Territory to James HAMILTON; $400.00; 88a on Turkey Creek. Wit: John Collins, John Worley, Thomas Philips. Rec. 9-14-1802. (259)

10-10-1800 - Byrd HENDRICK of Scott Co., Ky. to Thomas MASSIE of Adams Co., NW Territory; power of attorney to sell lands northwest of the Ohio. Grantor attested to in Franklin Co. (Ohio). Rec. 9-14-1802. (260)

8-31-1802 - John COLLINS of Adams Co., NW Territory to Samuel THOMAS; $275.40; lot 18 and dwelling house in Alexandria, deeded to said Collins by Thomas Parker. Wit: Jno. Belli. Rec. 9-14-1802. (260)

7-23-1802 - John COLLINS of Adams Co., NW Territory to Thomas PARKER of Frederick Co. Va.; $79.26; lots 17 & 18 in Alexandria. Wit: Jno. Belli. Rec. 9-14-1802. (262)

7-1-1802 - Thomas PARKER and Sally wife of Virginia by their power of attorney to JohnBELLI of Adams Co., NW Territory to Cristian BOTTLEMAN of same; $80.; lots 29 & 30 in Alexandria. Rec. 9-14-1802. (262)

8--18-1802 - Isaac WANSLEY Sr. of Adams Co., NW Territory to Isaac WAMSLEY Jr. of same; consideration of "ninety-three French Crowns"; land on Brush Creek. Wit: Sally W. Gordon, Geo. Gordon. Rec. 9-15-1802. (263)

2-17-1801 - Robert POLLARD and Joel his wife of Richmond, Va. to George PICKET of same; whereas Robert Pollard and and George Picket have been purchasing military lands and patents usually taken by Pollards in his name for their joint use, now partition and divide said lands...(note: goes on to give very extensive descriptions of many tracts--did not copy). Wit: Jno. Staples, Chas. Johnston, James Camp, John Fox, Hugh Moss, Jos. Jefferson. Rec. 9-15-1802. (265)

10-7-1802 - James NORRIS of Adams Co., NW Territory to Philip MOORE of same; $50.00; personal property consisting of cattle, pewter, dishes, etc. Wit: Wm Russell, S.T. Carey. Rec. 10-13-1802. (269)

10--14-1802 - Elijah GLOVER of Adams Co.. NW Territory to Thomas PARKER of Frederick Co., Va.; $65.82; lot 15 in town of Alexrndria, sold to Glover by Andrew Collins. Wit: Jno. Belli. Rec. 10-16-1802. (269)

2-19-1801 - Thomas PARKER and Sally wife of Frederick Co., Va. (attested to in Northumberland Co., Va.) to John BELLI, Esq. of NW Territory; Power of Attorney to lease and sell in their names tract of land in Ohio. Rec. 10-16-1802. (270)

10-6-1802 - Richard WOOD of Mason Co,, Ky. to Robert McCALEMAN of Adams Co., NW Territory; $300.00; 100a part of 1000a surveyed for Walter Ashmore and Richard Wood assignees of Alesander Door (D. Orr), lines--Nath'l Massie survey 2465. Wit: Joseph Beam, John Miggit. Rec. 11-9-1802. (271)

11-22-1802 - Plat of town of Edwardsville located at mouth of Little Scioto River. Jno. Edwards, proprietor. Rec. 11-22-1802. (273)

9-22-1802 - George ROGERS and Susannah wife of Adams Co., NW Territory to Richard ROUNSAVILLE of same; $100.00; 50a on Ohio River in Manchester twp. Wit: J. Darlington. Rec. 11-22-1802. (274)

4-19-1802 - Lucas SULLIVANT attorney in fact for Rueben ZIMMERMAN and Mary wife of Culpepper Co., Va. to Henry KNAUSE of Washington, Ky.; $670.00; tract of land on waters of Scioto; lines--John Sintons survey 614, Tylers survey. Wit: James Scott. Rec. 11-23-1802. (275)

5-7-1802 - Deposition of Lucas SULLIVANT stating that he sold Henry KNOWS as attorney for Reuben ZIMMERMAN and Mary his wife, 336a on Scioto River NW of Ohio river for $2.00 per. Wit: A. D. Orr, Jno. Macher. Rec. 11-23-1802. (276)

9-20-1802 - John EDWARDS Sr. of Mason Co., Ky. to Archibald BEALL of Bourbon Co., Ky.; $332.00; 300a part of 3338a granted to Edwards on waters of Straight and Red Oak in Adams and Clermont Counties, dated 4-22-1800; lines--William Bauses, Thomases line. Wit: John Walker, John Ellis, Patrick (mark) Higgins. Rec. 11-8-1802. (276)

12-2-1802 - John EDWARDS Sr. of Mason Co., Ky. to Robert McPHERSON of Adams Co., NW Territory; $333.00; 200a & 70 rods part of tract no. 3338 granted by U. S. to John Edwards assignee of Col. Josiah Parker patented 4-22-1800, lines--Williams. Wit: John Walker, John Ellis, Patrick (mark) Higgins. Rec. 12-8-1802. (278)

------1802 (no mo. or day given) - Winne (mark) JASSON to John EDWARDS; that Winne Jasson has bound herself to said Edwards to perform work and labor for 5 years as a servant. Wit: John Ellison, Robert McFerson. Rec. 12-1802. (279)

6-4-1802 - Nath'l MASSIE and Susan wife of Ross Co., NW Territory to Samuel SHEREWOOD of Adams Co., same; 25 pds Ky money; 105a part survey of 490a in name of Wm Davis and John O'Bannon patented by United States to Nath'l Massie assignee of same being on NW bank of the Ohio. Wit: Jno. Brown, Thos Massie. Rec. 12-14-1802. (279)

11-13-1802 - Nath'l ELLIS and Mary Ann wife of Adams Co., NW Territory to John SEWART of same; $100.00; tract of land on waters of Ohio, lines--Philip Slaughter survey no. 396. Wit: Abraham Evans, James Stevenson. Rec. 12-14-1802. (281)

9-8-1802 - John SHEPHERD of Adams Co., NW Territory to Jacob SHEPHERD of same; $1000.00; 225a on waters of Red Oak Creek part of tract granted Abraham Shepherd 6-12-1798 and conveyed to John Shepherd 12-29-1799. Wit: Isaac Shepherd, Wm Dunlap. Rec. 12-14-1802. (282)

9-6-1802 - John SHEPHERD and Martha wife of Adams Co., NW Territory to Isaac SHEPHERD of same; $1000.00; 200a on waters of Red Oak Creek part of tract patented to Abraham Shepherd 6-12-1798 and conveyed to John Shepherd and Martha his wife 12-29-1799, lines--David Worshell. Wit: Wm Kinkead, Jacob Shepherd. Rec. 12-14-1802.(283)

9-6-1802 - John SHEPHERD and Martha wife of Adams Co., NW Territory to David WORSTELL of same; $208.00; tract of land on waters of Red Oak Creek part of grant to Abraham Shepherd patented 6-12-1798 and conveyed to John and Martha Shepherd 12-29-1799. Wit: Wm Kinkead, Isaac Shepherd. Rec. 12-14-1802. (284)

--------- - Henry MOORE of Adams Co., NW Territory of full age has sworn and deposeth that about the month of June 1797, Col. Nath'l Massie gave to him bond for conveyance of tract of 683a on Upper side of Brush Creek in Ironbridge twp. on which deponent now lives and that he has mislaid same. Wit: Geo. Gordon. Rec. 12-14-1802. (285)

12-3-1802 - Ignatius MITCHELL and Milly wife of Mason Co., Ky. to Ann HARDESTY of Adams Co., NW Territory; $500.00; 190a part of Lynes survey; lines--Eagle Creek, Brun Branch. Wit: Mill Stephenson, Forgus McLean. Rec. 12-14-1802. (285)

38

9-8-1802 - John SHEPHERD of Adams Co., NW Territory to William DUNLAP of same;
$1000.00; 172a on waters of Red Oak Creek part of tract granted Abraham Shepherd
by patent 6-2-1798 and conveyed to John Shepherd 12-29-1799. Wit: Isaac Shepherd,
Jacob Shepherd. Rec. 12-14-1802. (287)

10-14-1802 - John KITE and Elisabeth wife of Adams Co., NW Territory to Seth FOSTER
of same; $148.00; 213a South side East fork of Eagle Creek, lines--Aaron Moore. Wit:
Thos. Kirker. Rec. 12-14-1802. (288)

10-23-1802 - John KILLEN and Rachel wife of Adams Co., NW Territory to Job DEMMING
of same; $215.00; in-lots 1,6,&9, also four out-lots (numbers not given) containing
3 acres & 150 poles each and half of out-lot 4 all in Killen's Town on waters of
Brush Creek said town being part of tract patented to Robert Rankin. Wit: John
Lodwick. Rec. 12-14-1802. (289)

8-16-1802 - Joseph EILAR and Mally wife of Adams Co. NW Territory to Stephen
BALEY of same/ $100.00; 100a on waters of Brush Creek part of tract of 2826 and 2/3rds
acres granted by United States to Robert Rankins by patent dated 10-28-1799. Wit:
JnoBeasley. Rec. 12-14-1802. (290)

1-14-1803 - Wm D. THORP of Alexandria, Adams County, NW Territory to Richard GAMMOND
of Mason Co., Ky.; $100.00; lot 20 and house in Alexandria. Wit: Will Russell,Ruth
Russell. Rec. 1-14-1803. (292)

1-1-1803 - John BELLI and Cynthia wife of Adams Co., NW Territory to William RUSSELL
of same; $180.00; out-lots 2 & 3 in town of Alexandria. Wit: Evan Frizell. Rec.
2-19-1803. (293)

1-16-1803 - Thomas PARKER and Sarah wife of Frederick Co., Va. by their power of
attorney to John BELLI of Adams Co., NW Territory to William JACKSON of Adams Co.,
same; $77.00; in-lot 1 in town of Alexandria. Wit: Joseph Lucas. Rec. 2-26-
1803. (294)

2-23/-1803 William RUSSELL of Adams Co., NW Territory to David JOHNSTON of Mason Co.Ky.;
power of attorney to sue and recover from David and Hannah Hindman of Chester Co.,
Pa. whatever sums of money are now due and owing the legal heirs of John Hindman,
dec'd. Wit: John Belli. Rec. 2-26-1803. (295)

1-27-1803 - William LEEDOM and Elizabeth wife of Adams Co., NW Territory to James
GUTRIDGE of same; $650.00; 130a on Three Mile Creek, lines--John Bryan, Samuel
Hopkins, Isaac Edgenton.,Wit: James Lowry, Robt. Miller, Moses Gutridge. Rec.
3-9-1803. (296)

12-25-1802 - Nath'l MASSIE and Susan wife of Ross Co., Ohio to Hugh SHANNON of Scott
Co., Ky.; 100 pds Ky money; 400a on waters of Brush Creek. Grantors attested to in
Jessemine Co., Ky. Rec. 3-9-1803. (297)

10-6-1802 - Richard WOOD of Mason Co., Ky. to Salethial SPARKS of Adams Co., NW
Territory; $300.00; 100a part 1000a survey made for Walter Ashmore and Richard Wood
as assignees of Alexander Dorr; lines--Joseph Lovejoy, Sparks. Wit: Robt. McClenahan, James Ellison. Rec. 3-9-1803. (298)

8-13-1801 - Nathaniel MASSIE and Susan E. wife of Adams Co., NW Territory to William PETERSON of same; $115.00; 231a on west side of Ohio on Brush Creek, lines--Wm Peterson, Creek. Wit: John Briggs, Thos. Kirker. Rec. 3-9-1803. (300)

1-24-1803 - James EDWARDS of Adams Co., NW Territory to William PATTERSON of same; $500.; 105a on Ohio River part of land deed by Philip Slaughter to James Edwards, lines--Geo. Mefford corner. Wit: William Rains, John West, John Lawill. Rec. 3-9-1803. (301)

2-9-1803 - Will of James EDWARDS of Adams Co., Ohio - dated 2-9-1803; recorded 3-9-1803. Son, George Edwards 10 acres on lower side of Fishing gut to include house, also 10 acres around mill on same gut--lines--Scotts garden, uphill, also land now called Aberdeen part of survey in name of Philip Slaughter to be divided between his two sons--William and James. Grand-daughter, Elenor Edwards. Thirty pounds to Sinci Furr. Son, William to have 4 pounds. Two daughters: Janet Rains and Elenor West. Executor: son, George. Signed: James (his mark) Edwards. Wit: Geo. Mitchell, Robert West, Mitchall McDonald. (303)

11-13-1802 - Nathan ELLIS and Mary Ann wife of Adams Co., NW Territory to William HUTCHENSON of same; $150.00; 60a on waters of Ohio, lines--Philip Slaughter, Joseph Stuart. Wit: Abraham Evans, James Stevenson. Rec. 3-9-1803. (303)

1-23-1803 - Hugh SHANNON and____(left blank) wife of Scott Co., Ky. to Jacob FRY of Harrison Co., Ky.; $1200.00; 400a on waters of Brush Creek. Wit: John Hawkins. Rec. 3-9-1803. (304)

1-8-1803 - Charles OURSLER and Martha wife of Adams Co., NW Territory to Ezekiel BEASLEY of Mason Co., Ky.; $10.00; 5 acres, lines--Whites upper corner upon bank of river. Wit: William Middleton, George Swisher, Archable Oursler. Rec. 3-9-1803.(306)

11-5-1802 - John STEPHENSON adms. of Ann STEPHENSON, dec'd paid 60 pds Pa. currency to Hugh Stephenson, it being his share of whole amount of sales, also 51 pds. Pa. currency the property coming from his brother, Richard, for lands sold to John Fisher, also 349 pds. Pa. currency and 100 pds. Pa. currency being his part of land his mother owned at her death in Fayette Co., Tyrone twp., Pa. (signed) Hugh Stephenson. Wit: Geo. Gordon, David Bradford, Henry Aldric. Rec. 3-14-1803. (307)

9-15-1802 - Lawrence BUTLER of Frederick Co., Va. makes deposition that he has given power of attorney to Major John BELLI of NW Territory to dispose of all lands. Wit: Wm. H. Powell, Thomas Parker. Rec. 3-15-1803. (308)

1-31-1801 - J. WILKINS by power of attorney for Alexander SCOTT has settled all accounts for said Scott on one-half tract land on White Oak Creek conveyed by Wilkins to Belli. Wit: Jno. Boyle. Rec. 4-4-1803. (308)

--------- - Plat of town of Portsmouth. Henry Massie of Ross Co., Proprieter. Two squares containing 4 lots each marked A & B to be for public use. Rec. 4-1-1803. (308 & 309)

11-25-1802 - Nathan RANDOLPH of Mercer Co., Ky. to Peter CAREY of same; 1300 pds.; 1000a on waters of Brush Creek. Wit: Tho. Allen, James Slaughter, Sam'l Gray. Rec. 4-3-1803. (310)

12-3-1802 - Peter CASEY (or CAREY) of Mercer Co., Ky. to Peter MUGHLEN BURG of Philadelphia; 300 pds.; 2000a on waters of Brush Creek. Wit: James Slaughter, Sam'l Gray. Rec. 4-13-1803. (311)

4-15-1803 - Lawrence BUTLER of Frederick Co., Va. to John BELLI of Ohio; power of attorney to enter lands in his name and procure title. Wit: Thos. Smith, Thomas Parker. Rec. 4-29-1803. (312)

6-23-1803 - Robert HIGGINS and Mary wife of Clermont Co., Ohio to John SHROPH of same; $158.00; 79a on waters of Straight Creek. Wit: John Gutridge, Mills Stephenson. Rec. 8-3-1803. (313)

7--29-1803 - Ignatius MITCHELL and Milly wife of Mason Co., Ky. to Thomas FOOTE of Adams Co., Ohio; $305.00; 1221 on Eagle Creek, lines--Logan gap. Wit: Elisabeth Findley, Mills Stephenson. Rec. 8-3-1803. (314)

6-23-1803 - Robert HIGGINS and Mary wife of Clermont Co., Ohio to Nicholas WASHBURN; $250.00; 125a on Straight Creek. Wit: John Gutridge Sr., Mills Stephenson. Rec. 8-3-1803. (316)

6-23-1803 - Robert HIGGINS and Mary wife of Clermont Co., Ohio to Nehemiah HAYS of Adams Co., Ohio; $1200.00; 100a on waters of Straight Creek. Wit: Jno. Gutridge Sr., Mills Stevenson. Rec. 8-3-1803. (316)

2-4-1803 - Abraham SHEPHERD and Margaret wife of Adams Co., Ohio to Isaac EARLES of Ross Co., Ohio; $50.00; 70a on waters of Brush Creek part of survey entered in name of Abraham Shepherd Sr. conveyed to Abraham Shepherd as reference to record. Wit: John Armstrong, Sarah (mark) Shepherd. Rec. 8-3-1803. (317)

The State of Ohio, Adams County. We the subscribers Associate Judges of the Court of Common Pleas in and for county aforesaid pursuant to the provisions of an act entitled, "An act to authorize the judges of the Court of Common Pleas of Adams County to cause to be transcribed a part of the records of deeds in said county" have carefully examined and compared the foregoing transcribed record containing on 319 pages with the original record from which they were taken kept by John Belli when recorder of Adams County under the Territorial Government which said original records are contained in three small volumes marked A, B & C. And we do hereby certify that the foregoing contained as aforesid on 319 pages are tirely transcribed and are a true and perfect Transcript of the original books aforesaid from which they were taken. Given under our hands and seals 28th day October in year of our Lord one thousand eight hundred and twenty. (Sighed) Moses Baird, Andrew Livingston, Job Dinning.(319)

6-3-1799 - Plat of town of Alexandria. Col. Thomas Parker of Frederick Co., Va., proprietor. (Signed) E. Langham. (320)

The following records were taken from "Inventory Book No. 10" as found in the court house at West Union. Page on which record may be found in the original book is given in parenthesis.

William PENCE, dec'd of Sprigg twp. - 8-7-1849 - Widow (not named) received family Bible, picture and three school books. Inventory by James Conner, Handy Cropper and Thornton Shelton, appraisers. (1)

George W. LOWE, dec'd of Sprigg twp. - 10-25-1849 - mentions widow and three children (not named) under seven years. Widow received spinning wheel, looms, one Bible, etc. Inventory by James Truit, Joseph Britingham and Wm Greenlee. (3)

Leaman GIFFORD, dec'd - 11-1-1849 - John W. Gifford, adms. Allowance made for maintenance and schooling of minor heirs (not named). Inventory by Robert McMahan, James W. Adams and John McKinly. Public sale held 11-19-1849 with some of the persons purchasing items being: John H. Gifford, Wm W. Gifford, John Bennington, James Fitzpatrick, Mary Ann Gifford, Timothy Gifford and Gerusha Brown. (5)

William PARKS, dec'd - 10-10-1849 - Inventory by James Freeman, J. M. Walden and Isaac N. Williams, appraisers. Public sale held 10-30-1849 with some of the persons purchasing items being: Thomas Evans, Keziah Parks, Henry Willman, Alfred Aldridge, George Newman, Henry Zortman, Elizabeth Waters, Wm Brooks, A. J. Waters, John Scott, James Willman, George Mustard, Jonathan Ralston, John Parks and Wilson Copus. (8)

David COX, dec'd - 5-29-1849 - Inventory by R. N. Edgington, Barton S. Long and Azariah Edgington, appraisers. (12)

Philip ROUSH, dec'd, of Sprigg twp. - 8-2-1849 - Michael Roush, adms. $40.00 appropriated for keeping youngest child for one year from death of her father (not named). Inventory by Henry Hutson, James Kirker and Ismay Munford, appraisers. Public sale of personal property held 8-17-1849 with some of the persons purchasing items being: Robert Roush, Wm Roush, Wm Clark, Moses Roush, Thompson Shelton, B. Dragoo, Permenius Roush, Wm T. Smith, Wm Swearingen, Lewis Rape, Michael Roush Jr., Wm Thompson, Wm E. Hopkins, Mrs. Moses Roush, Harrison Pence, James Hook, Mrs. Washburn, John T. Wright, Wesly Pence, Michael Pence, JohnHutson, Nathan Roush, James P. Matheney, Jacob Ebright, Wm Clark, John Roush, Thos Moore, Ezekiel Edgington, Mrs. Michael Roush, Absolem Roush, David McDaniel, Mrs. Absolem Roush, L. L. Conner, Lucinda Moore, Betsy Ann Roush, Catharine Roush, P. O. Philips, Moses Matheny, Mary Sevilla Roush, Lewis Hawk, Samuel Roush, Samuel Neal, Catharine Smith, John Gutridge, Solomon White. (13)

Samuel McCULLOUGH, dec'd of Scott twp. - 10-16-1849 - Archibald McCullough, adms. Property set off for support of widow and children (not named). Inventory by John McIntire, John Milligan and Alexander W. Cavin. Public sale held 10-18-1849 with some of the person purchasing items being: John McIntire, Wm R. McCreight, Wm Riley, Mahlon Fulton, Jacob Owen, Wm McIntire, Andrew Morrison, Henry Debolt, Robert F. Glasgow, Samuel H. Williamson, Wm Montgomery, George Cornelius, Jesse McCreight, Wm O. McCreight, John A. Smiley, Joseph A. McIntire, Robert Right, A. B. McCullough, John Wickersham, David Gaston, Stephen Wright, John Milligan, Wm Dryden and David Steel. (22)

Hudson LOW, dec'd late of Sprigg twp. - 10-1-1849. Estate with will annexed. Widow (not named) allowed personal property. Inventory by Thos. G. Dryden, Wm Greenlee and Robert Shelton, appraisers. Public sale held 10-2-1849 with some of the persons purchasing items being: Thomas Lowe, Wm J. Low, Abraham Teeters, John Brittenham, Harrison Warner, Elijah Starrit, Smith Hutson, Robert Shelton Sr., Labina Low, G. D. Darlinton and W. H. Dryden. (26)

John JONES, dec'd - 11-3-1849 - Wm Morrison and John Jones, executors. Inventory
by Samuel Thoroman, Luther Collier, appraisers. Persons purchasing items
at public sale were: Samuel Thoroman, Josiah Hull, Jefferson Toll, Elijah
Waldron, Luther Collier, Jefferson Treber, John Jones, Hercules Dunkin,
James Smith, John Hamilton, William Harrison, William Morrison, John Collier,
Daniel Thompson, Nathaniel McGown, Thomas McClanahan, John Spurgen, Calvin
R. Bradney, Wm Cummins and James Daugherty. (29)
Jesse SWIM, dec'd - 1849 - Jesse Wikoff, adms. Property set off to four minor
children included Family Bible, wearing apparel, etc. (33)
William FRYER, dec'd late of Sprigg twp. - 8-7-1849 - Inventory by Robert Shelton,
James Truit, Lemuel Dryden, appraisers. Purchasing items at public sale
being: Alex Fryer, John Teetees, J. M. Palmer, Jeremiah Paul, A. J. Greenlee,
A. S. Teeters, Wm Fryer, Kindle Low, Wm Bolin, Alex Shelton, John Blythe. (40)
Alfred MOWRER a minor-9-8-1849 - Account filed by Christian Mowrer, Guardian. (43)
Hester and Nathaniel SMITH minor heirs of Wm SMITH, dec'd - 1849 - account filed
by Hosea Moore, guardian for period from 3-24-1846 to 9-21-1848. (44)
John PATTON, dec'd - 1849 - Nancy W. Patton, admsrx. filed account. (44)
Margaret J. KINCAID, dec'd - 1849 - Thomas Kincaid, executor filed accounty. (46)
Thomas Methias CANNON and Martha CANNON - 1849 - Levin M. Cannon, guardian filed
accornt. Account shows $558.86 received from sale of real estate by
executor of J. A. B. Cannon, dec'd on 3-1-1847. (46)
James GRAHAM, dec'd - 1849 - Jno. Moore, executor files account which includes
payment to him for trips to Greenup, Kentucky, Maysville, Kentucky and
Lawrence Co., Ohio. (48)
Nancy Jane DRYDEN child of Isaac N. Dryden, dec'ed - 8-16-1849 - Martha Dryden ,
guardian files accounty. James Conner adms. of estate of Isaac N. Dryden.(48)
Heirs of Valentine FEAR, dec'd - 11-20-1849 - Peter Fear, guardian files account.
Accounts begin in 8-14-1841 and separate accounts are given for Sarah
Goodwin, Mary Ann Fear, Francis A. Fear and Margaret Cluxton, heirs of
Valentine Fear, dec'd. (50)
David BRADFORD, DEC'd - 1849 - Samuel G. Bradford, adms. files account. (54)
Robert ANDERSON, dec'd - 1849 - James Anderson adms. filed account. Account
shows $250.00 paid to widow (not named). (56)
Reuben(?) SMYTH, dec'd - 1849 - Account filed by Joel Smith, adms. Account shows
John T. Smith, Clarinda Smith, John M. Smith and Joel Smith received money
from estate possibly for services, all were small amounts except for amount
paid Clarinda Smith which was $185.00. (58)
E. C. CANNON, dec'd - 1849 - Byas N. Cannon, adms. filled account. Account shows
$100.00 paid to Mary Cannon. (60)
Andrew J. MANNON - 1849 - Robert Mannon, guardian files account. Account shows
received $96.00 from executor of Mary Mannon, dec'd and sheriff of Adams
County as part of the estate of William Mannon, dec'd. Account runs from
1842 to 1849. (62)
Sarah J. KIRKPATRICK, Nathaniel R. KIRKPATRICK and Mary T. KIRKPATRICK - 11-13-1849 -
Joseph P. Kirkpatrick, guardian files account. Account shows that on
8-17-1847 cash was received from Wm McIntire adms. of D. D. Finley, dec'd in
amount of $94.95 and that on 9-25-1847 cash in the amount of $42.94 was received from A. C. Kirkpatrick adms. of Mary Kirkpatrick, dec'd; also on 1-12-
1848 and 6-13-1848 cash in the amounts of $10.00. $25.25,$47.00 and $70.82
was received from John Kirkpatrick adms. of Thomas C. Kirkpatrick, dec'd.(64)

Elizabeth GLASGOW aged 5 yrs., Robert GLASGOW aged 3 yrs., minor children of William
Glasgow, dec'd - 1849 - John Thompson, guardian files account. Account shows in
Dec. 1848 cash received in amount of $35.83 from adms. of estate of Elizabeth
A. Glasgow and cash received in amount of $35.83 from adms. of estate of Robert
Glasgow. (66)
Peter WICKERSHAM, dec'd - 1849 - Jonathan Tener, adms. files account. Mentions
judgement paid Copeland and Davis executors of Jacob Wickersham, dec'd. (68)
Abraham EVANS, an insane person - 1849 - Account filed by W. G. Gilbert, guardian.(70)
John BIERLEY, dec'd - 1-30-1850 - John Crisswell, Joseph McCreight and John Milligan,
appraisers. Personal property sold at public auction 2-5-1850 with some of the
persons purchasing items being: James Williams, Frederick Mathews, Malon Kirk-
patrick, John Wiskersham, John Criswell, James W. Bierly, Robert Ralston,
Mathew Williams, Malon Fulton, Alfred Lovet, John Milligan, James McCreight,
James Gaston, John McCullough, J. R. Scott, Eliza Elliot, Milton Kirkpatrick,
Alexander Cavin, John McIntyre. (72)
Samuel ALLISON, dec'd - 8-21-1849 - Thomas Thoreman, John Oliver and John Fristoe,
appraisers. (77)
Ephriam WHEATON, dec'd - 9-21-1849 - from numerous accounts due estate and from
inventory it would be indicated that Wheaton may have been a physician. (87)
Thomas RALSTON, dec'd. - 2-6-1850 - Joseph Criswell, Joseph McCright and Milton
Kirkpatrick, appraisers. Property set off to widow (not named). Public sale
of personal property held 2-7-1850 with some of the persons purchasing items
being: Robert Ralston, Wm McIntire, Rebecca Ralston, Rebecca M. Ralston,
Daniel Cockerill, Glasgow Finly, Mahon Fulton, John Wickersham, Wm Seaton,
Thomas Cane, Anderson Glasgow, John B. Campbell, Wm Steele, Mathew Hamphill,
John McMillan, Archibald McCullough and John Wagoner. (94)
John WEAVER, dec'd - 1849 - Property set off to widow (not named) included bible.
John Oliver, George W. Sample, and W. F. Dunbar, appraisers. Public sale
held 9-4-1849 with the following persons being some of the purchasers:
Catherine Weaver, John Wright, Henry Weaver, Joseph Eakins, John W. Weaver,
George Thomas, Aquila Purtee and Capt. John Wright. (100)
Balsor ZINKHORN, dec'd - 12-4-1849 - Allowance set off to widow (not named).
I. N. Williams, Leonard Brooks and Jacob Shively, appraisers. (102)
William HANNAH, dec'd - 12-14-1849 - Aaron Hannah, executor. Thomas M. Gorney,
James Miller and Robert Patton, appraisers. (103)
William ALLEN, dec'd - 1849 - property set off to widow, Matilda Allen and to
minor child, John Clark Allen. (105)
Alleniah BALDRIDGE, dec'd - 3-1-1850 - John Baldridge Jr., adms. Samuel S. Mason,
F. Teaman, and James Reed, appraisers. (108)
Griffeth EVANS, dec'd - 12-24-1849 - Silas Thomas, Adms. Property set off for
support of widow and nine children (not named). John Vance, Andrew Rea
and John Swearingen, appraisers. (109)
S. B. PERRY, dec'd late of Winchester - 4-10-1850 - J. O. Sparks, adms. W. Robbins,
J. H. Delrein and Tom A. Black, appraisers. Inventory includes merchandise
that would be found in a general store. (110)
William WILLIAMS, dec'd, late of Scott twp. - 4-9-1850 - A. M. Kirkpatrick, adms.
John Criswell, John McIntire and Joseph McCright, appraisers. Public sale
of personal property held 4-10-1850 with some of the persons purchasing
items being: Mahlon Fulton, John Wickersham, A. M. Kirkpatrick, James Williams,
James Williams, Sr., Nancy Williams, Ebenezer Williams, John Williams, David
McCright, Jane Cunningham, Angeline Cunningham, A.W. Carson and George W.
Marsh. (181)

William GAGGIN, dec'd - 5-4-1850 - John S. Adamson, adms. Property set off for
support of widow, Mary Gaffin. Eligah Leedom, O. M. Stewart and W P.
Cliveton, appraisers. (185)
Heirs of Samuel MURPHIN - 1850 - Accounty filed by Joseph Rogers, guardian. (188)
Duncan McKINZEE, dec'd - 4-18-1850 - John Spurgeon, executor. Samuel S. Mason,
Samuel Thoroman and Luther Colier, appraisers. (188)
Thomas COPUS, dec'd - 1850 - Account filed by John Copus, adms. (189)
McGovney VANCE, dec'd - 7-22-1850 - personal property of one family Bible, three
family pictures, etc. set off to widow, Ann E. Vance and minor children;
Amanda I. Vance, Ann E. Vance, Arrabelle Vance, Louisa E. Vance, Cary Allen
Vance and Artimotia Vance. Public Sale of personal property held 8-10-1850
with some of the persons purchasing items being; Eliza Vance, W. B. Jones,
W. M. Janes, W. T. Reynolds, W. B. Baird, J. K. Billings and Melissa Vance.(190)
Joseph BEEVERS, dec'd - 6-3-1850 - Jonathan Tener, Wm Dunlap and J. R. Copeland,
apprajsers, Public sale of personal property held 6-4-1850 with the following
persons among those purchasing items: Thomas Beevers, James Folis, Silas
Courtwright, W. Beevers, I. M. Beevers, J. R. Copeland, Madison Beevers, Binsen
(Vinsen) Beevers, Lorenzo Grooms, James Johnson, Stephen Hughes, Jacob Tenor,
A. Young, Wn Jenkins, J. B. Downing, Enos Nichols, James Sutterfield, Isaac
Newland, Hamilton Crab, Julis Tracy, Isiah Jenkins, James Horn and George
Dunlap. (193)
John POWERS, dec'd - 4-29-1850 - Widow, Louesa Powers also serves as admsrx. James
Truitt, Thos. G. Dryden and Robert Shelton, appraisers. (196)
Wm H. DRYDEN, heir of Isaac Dryden, dec'd - 3-12-1850 - Wm H. C. Dryden, guardian
files account. (198)
Samuel THOMAS, dec'd - 3-28-1850 - mentions family Bible among personal property
set off to widow and one child, a minor (not named). Isaac Wittemyer, Saml
R. Wood and G. W. Sample, appraisers. Public sale of personal property held
6-20-1850 with the following among the persons purchasing items: Elizabeth
Thomas, Wm Thoroman, Wm Metz, George Thomas, John McMillen, T. Metz, A.
Wiscop, W. Thomas, J. Whitlock, W. Graves, W. Anderson, Wm Robinson, Saml.
Thoroman, W. A. Sample, E. Philips, John Wright and J. Bowers. (200)
Ephriam JONES, dec'd - 12-26-1850 - Family Bible and other goods set off for widow
and minor children (not named). James Freeman, Jonathan Hughs, and I. D.
Thompson, appraisers. Public sale held 12-30-1850 with some of the persons
purchasing items being: Wm F. Jones, Roxy Ann Jones, John M. Jones, J. Hughs,
J. Abbott. (205)
Samuel STARRETT, dec'd - 10-11-1850 - John Starrett, adms. James Truitt, John
Brookover and Joseph Brittenhan, appraisers. Public sale of personal property
with some of the persons purchasing items being: Asariah Edington, Harrison
Warner, D. Glasscock, Wm Roush, A. J. Greenlee, B. E. Gilbert, John Hudson,
Thos. Low, T. R. Leedon, E. Starrett, Daniel Starrett, Samuel Starrett, C.
Robbins, Aley Shelton, T. J. McClelland, Alex Shelton, Jas. Greenlee, John
Edgington, N. S. Hewel, P. Brittingham, Peter Pence, A. Teeters, John Pence
and D. Montague. (211)
Benjamin WASHBURN, dec'd - 9-5-1850 - John Cline, Richard Frister and John Fristor,
appraisers. Public sale of personal property held with the following persons
being among some of those purchasing items: Mary Ann Washburn, Westley
Thoroman, Wm Z. Thoroman, Thomas Thoroman, Washington Thoroman, John Fristor,
D. D. Linch, Daniel Galespy, Joseph Fry, G. W. Sample, John Wright and Richard
Fristor. Property set off to widow (not named) for support. (225)

Daniel H. BUCHANAN, dec'd - 11-20-1850 - John Patton, John Wasson and Thomas Kain, appraisers. Widow, Elizabeth Buchanan. Minor children, William Buchanan, Daniel H. Buchanan, Mary Isabel Elizabeth I. Buchanan and Thomas R. Buchanan. (228)

Robert ASKREN, dec'd - 1850 - James McNeil, James M. Taylor and Wm McIntire, appraisers. (234)

James McCANLESS, dec'd - 1850 - Saml. G. Jackson, adms. I. M. Stewart, Jason McDermed and John Watson. (237)

Hosea CORDREY, dec'd - 10-26-1850 - John H. Baird, John Sparks and John R. Stout, appraisers. Widow, Sarah Cordrey. Public sale of personal property held 10-26-1850 with some of the persons purchasing items being: Sarah Cordrey, James Cordrey, Robert B. Stout, Thomas G. Hening, T. G. Lewis, John Little, Samuel Montgomery, John Beech, T. G. Henise and R. B. Sterret. (238)

Zachariah LEATHERWOOD, dec'd late of Franklin twp. - 10-17-1850. William Hamilton, William Dunlap and John Reynolds, appraisers. Property set off for support of widow (not named) included a Bible. Public sale of Personal property with some of the persons purchasing items being: Aaren Leatherwood, Meranda Leatherwood, Lewis Hunt, Thomas H. Ralley, Cornelius Palmer, John Buners, Philly Zink, W. T. McClure, George Jenkins, Wm Tarlton, T. B. Ridwell, John Butters, John D. Reynolds, Bransan Ridwell and Wm Dunlap. (242)

John JAMES, dec'd - 8-16-1850 - Samuel McClure and Nancy James, adms. George Campbell, J. T. Willson and Robert B. Glassgow, appraisers. Widow, Nancy Janes. Public sale of personal property with the following persons among those purchasing items: J. R. Janes, Charles Bruce, L. M. Atwell, Evi Janes, Ben Hook, Jesse Thompson, Jacob Hart, James Stewart and Wm. Cohen. (247)

Silas MOSMAN, dec'd of Jefferson twp. - 1850 - Jacob Shiveley, John Ellis and Jonathan Hughs, appraisers. Public sale with some of those purchasing items being: Jemima Mosman, Joseph M. Cay, Jacob Shively, John Scott, Joseph McKee, John Zartman, Joseph Taylor, William Taylor, Henry Wiltman, Charles Osman, John Miller, Henry Eastin, John Balden, John Ellis. (250)

James CAMPBELL, dec'd - 1850 - Robert R. Campbell, adms. filed account. (252)

James LEE, dec'd - 3-18-1850 - Alex Woodson, adms. filed account. (256)

Parker TRUITT, dec'd - 1850 - Samuel S. Mason, executor filed account. (258)

Elizabeth CAMPBELL, dec'd - 1850 - Samuel Campbell adms. de bonis non files account. Former adms. was John Kirkpatrick. (260)

John M. COMPTON - 1850 - Johnson Ellison, guardian files account. (262)

Heirs of Wm THOMPSON - 1850 - John Morrison, guardian files account. Mary Thompson is only name mentioned, not stated as to who she is. (264)

James S. McCREIGHT, dec'd - 12-19-1850 - Joseph McCreight, adms. James Criswell, Samuel Ross and John McCreight, appraisers. Property set off for widow's (not named) support. Public sale held 2-13-1851 with the following persons being some who purchased items: Joseph McCreight, James McCreight, Jonathan McCreight, Elizabeth McCreight and William McCreight. (266)

David McCREIGHT, dec'd - 12-13-1850 - Joseph McCreight, executor. John T. Willson, Archibald McCullough and John M. McCreight, appraisers. Pualic sale of personal property held 2-13-1851 with the following being some of those purchasing items: David McCreight, Jonathan McCreight, John Creight, Wm McCreight, Jesse McCreight, Joseph McCreight and James McCreight. (272)

William B. WILLSON, dec'd - 10-12-1849 - Account filed by Adison McCullough, adms.
Distribution to heirs: Widow, Ann N. Willson $1194.94, $34.02 & $84.00;
William W. Willson $335.45 & $15.00; Amanda J. Willson $397.88 & $55.00;
John M. Willson $365.27 & $26.00; Sophronia H. Willson $117.63 & $35.00. (278)
David Robe, dec'd - 1850 - Thomas McGoveney surviving executor files account. (283)
Robert ADAMS, dec'd - 1850 - John McKinly, adms. files account. Widow (not named)
received $188.29 in personal property. (284)
Elizabeth CAMPBELL, dec'd - 1850 - Samuel Campbell, adms. de bonis non files
account. (286)
Nancy KING, dec'd - 1850 - Laban Parke, adms. with will annexed files account. (288)
Heirs of George L. COMPTON - 1850 - A. McGovney, guardian files account. Names
of Mary Ann Compton and John M. Compton are mentioned. (290)
William RAMSEY, dec'd late of Meigs twp.- 12-28-1850 - Henry Phillips, Wm G. Powel
and James Clark, appraisers. Property set off for support of widow and minor
children (not named). Public sale of personal property held 1-4-1851 with
some of the persons purchasing items being: Wm Ramsey, Letty Ramsey, Robert
Ramsey, David Gardner, George Marsh, Ralph W. Petterson, Edward G. Peterson,
Charles R. Hedges, John Mercer, Cornelius Peterson, H. H. Pinkerton, Wm Metz,
Henry Philips, Abraham Wisecup, Joseph Spurgeon, James Cox, Oliver Eakins,
Alvin Moore, David German, Mathew German and John German. (292)
Robert WILLIAMS, Dec'd - 1850 - James M. Taylor and Samuel Foster, appraisers.
Public sale of personal property held 12-18-1850 with some of the persons
purchasing items being: Jane Williams, John Baylis, Elene Williams, Robert
A. Glassgow, David McCreight, James Montgomery, J. T. Montgomery, Andrew
Young, A. C. Kirkpatrick, Wm Morrison, John Williams, Wm McIntire, N.C. Patton,
and James Ellison. (296)
Robert THOMPSON, dec'd - 6-6-1831 - John Patton, J. M. Taylor and H. McSneely,
appraisers. Public sale of personal property held 6-14-1851 with some of
the persons purchasing items being: James Thompson, John Grooms, John L.
Wasson, Thomas Thompson, Israel Thompson and Nathaniel Kirkpatrick. (299)
Casse Ann CANNEN and J. A. B. CANNEN, children of J. A. B. Cannen, dec'd - 7-4-1851 -
J. P. Cockerell, guardian, files account. (301)
Jacob DILLING - 1851 - N. Parry, guardian file account. D. Gorden paid for
boarding ward to 12-2-1850. (301)
Robert JACKSON, dec'd - 10-23-1851 - Alex Woodson, John P. Hood and James R. Oldsen,
appraisers. Among personal property set off to widow was Bible and 57 volumes
of books. Widow, Elizabeth Jackson. Minor children: Theodore H. Jackman,
Henrietta F. Jackman, and George William Jackman, (302)
Henry CLEMMERS, dec'd - 8-7-1851 - Wm Robbins, James Dozer and C. Bottleman,
appraisers. Bible included in personal property set off to widow. Widow,
Nancy Clemmers. Minor children: Wm S. Clemmers, Lucinda Clemmers, Rebecca
Clemmers, Henry W. Clemmers, Laura V. Clemmers and Eva Clemmers. (308)
Joseph McNEILL, dec'd - 9-29-1851 - John Patton, Silas Marlatt and T. W. Baldridge,
appraisers. Family Bible among personal property set off to widow and minor
children. Public sale of personal property held 9-30-1851 with some of the
persons purchasing items being: Joseph McNeil, Jonathan McNeil, Robert
Glassgow, Frederick Shuster and Samuel McCormick. (323)
Joseph EYLER Sr., dec'd - 6-2-1851 - E. E. Willkins and Elizabeth Eyler, adms.
Wm Robins, John Grossman and George A. Dixon, Appriasers. Widow, Elizabeth
Eyler. Minor children: Samuel H. Eyler, James M. Eyler, Elizabeth V. Eyler,
Emaline A. Eyler, Madison F. Eyler, Aaron R. Eyler and Charles E. Eyler. (326)

Joseph DARLINGTON, dec'd - 9-22-1851 - G. D. Darlington and M. A. Darlington,
   Executors, George N. McFarland, Adam McCoveny and D. A. McFarland,
   a;;raksers . (360)
Steven CLARK, dec'd late of Scott twp. - 10-16-1851 - George Campbell, Assa F.
   Philips and Em. R. A. Altman, appraisers. Personal property set off to
   support widow included family Bible. (373)
Thomas WASON, dec'd - 1-1-1852 - John Patton, A. D. Kirkpatrick and D. C. Sample,
   appraisers. (375)
(note: from this point on numbering is not in order, it reverts back to smaller
   numbers several times, duplicating other numbers.)
Willson PRATHER, dec'd - 12-27-1851 - Property set off for support of widow included
   Family Bible. Widow, Mary Ann Prather. Minor children: Rebecca Jane Bell
   Prather, Walter Wirt Prather and Mary Elizabeth Prather. (367)
George GRANT, dec'd - 11-15-1851 - J. R. Cockerelle and F. Marlatt, executors.
   E. P. Evans, Wm Robe and J. W. Lafferty, appraisers. (370)
Frances SHINN, dec'd late of Tiffin twp. - 9-5-1851 - E. P. Evans, adms. James
   C. Fink and Joseph W. Lafferty, appraisers. Mentions widow and three
   children under the age of 15 yrs. (does not name). (377)
Arthur McFARLAND, dec'd, late of Tiffin twp. - 10-27-1851 - John Holmes, C. D.
   Darlinton and James Anderson, appraisers. Puglic sale of personal property
   held 10-29-1851 with some of the persons purchasing items being Arthur
   McFarland, Eliza McFarland, George N. McFarland, David McFarland, Jacob
   McFarland, Edward Clark, Christian Helmley, James Holmes, Alex Compton,
   Joel Traber, Beam Howland and James Wilson. (372)
Jonathan WAITE, dec'd - 8-26-1851 - Alexander Morrison, R. J. Daggett and J. S.
   Patton, appraisers. Widow, Isabella Waite. Son, Jonathan White. (379)
Joseph MASSIE, dec'd - 8-26-1851 - Noval Osburn, Christian Battlman and Wm Robbins,
   appraisers. Erastus Massie, Adms. Family Bible and family pictures set
   off to widow and minor children. Widow, Martha Massie. Minor children:
   John Massie, Harrison T. Massie, Samuel G. Massie, Catharine Massie and
   Martha J. Massie. (386)
Joseph CURRY, dec'd late of Meigs twp. - 8-16-1851 - John Oliver, Henry Phillips
   and J. M. Bryan, appraisers. Widow (not named) given year's support. (403)
Thomas KANE, dec'd - 8-13-1851 - Alexander Morrison, James McNeill and John Wason,
   appraisers. Widow and minor children (not named) given family Bible. (408)
John PRATHER, dec'd - 6-7-1851 - Alex'r Woodrow, W. Mulern and J. Hempleman,
   appraisers. (411)
N. D. THOMPSON, dec'd - 11-28-1851 - James Sparks, James Doyle (or Dayle) and
   A. C. Lewis, appraisers. Widow, Nancy Thompson. (313)
William LAUGHRIDGE, dec'd of Tiffin twp. - 12-5-1851 - J. A. Laughridge, executor.
   Robert Ellison, N. Cutchon and M. Keller, appraisers. (314)
Thornton SHELTON, dec'd - 7-19-1851 - Thomas Shelton, adms. (317)
William M. REED, dec'd, late of Franklin twp. - 1-11 -1852 - David Fulton, Jam s P.
   Lovett and D. M. Sechler, appraisers. Widow and minor children granted
   support (not named). (319)
Adam McCORMICK, dec'd - 10-9-1849 - George Collings, executor. Wilson Prother,
   Robert Buck and Sam'l G. Bradford, appraisers. Public sale of personal
   property held 10-10-1849 with the following persons purchasing items:
   William Killin, James Moore, James Dement, Perry Chambers. Robert Buck,
   Ebenezer Hanes, Frederick Myer, H. N. Cole and Jas. McCormick. (322)

48

Copied and contributed by: Barbara Adams, 21674 Dingman-Slagle Rd.,
Sidney, Ohio 45365
Marriages were taken from Book I.

Page	Groom	Bride	Marriage Date 1831	Married by
1	Bailey, David	Daniels, Rhoda	June 23	Rev. Isaac McHenry
	of Champaign Co.			
1	Harter, Henry	Bryant, Sarah	Sept 2	John Ireland
1	Cochrane, Wm.	Hire, Catherine	Sept 22	John Ireland, JP
1	Lippincott	Wood, Samiramas	Nov 6	Lewis Srouge, JP
1	Wood, Albert G.	Burtch, Emily	Dec 25	Lewis Srouge, JP
		dau of Sanford Burtch		
			1832	
2	Daniels, James H.	Lippincott, Hariet Ann	Jan 26	L. Sroufe, JP
	Consents by James Daniels & Wm. Lippincott			
2	Stevenson, Jesse Leo	Ridenour, Hannah	Mar 11	Lewis Stroufe
2	Saxton, James	Jones, Nancy	Apr 15	Lewis Sroufe
2	Clark, Fleet	Enslen, Mary	May 6	Lewis Sroufe
3	Enslen, Abraham	McCoy, Nancy	May 6	Lewis Sroufe, JP
3	Hanthorn, Thomas	Daniels, Myra S.	May 14	Silas Faurot, JP
3	Spurrier, Beal	Van Blaricum, Julian	July 15	Lewis Sroufe
4	Devore, Felix	Sutton, Eliza	Aug. 26	John Ireland, JP
3	Carback, W. M.	Osborn, Elizabeth	Aug. 30	Silas Faurot
5	Opdyche, Henry C.	Sunderland, Eleanor	Sept 9	John Ireland, JP
4	Daniels, Benjamin M.	Hanthorn, Martha	Nov 22	Silas Faurot
3	Hall, Anthony	Chandler, Mary	Dec 23	Silas Faurot
			1833	
4	Hall, Wm. M.	Walton, Lydia	Jan 3	Tolson Ford
3	Chenoweth, John	Hanthorn, Eliza	Jan 22	Wm. Chaffee, MG
5	Martin, Dan	Vaughn, Eliza	Feb 3	Adriel Hursey, MG
4	Osborn, Barzilla	Chenoweth, Martha	Feb 7	Wm Chaffee
5	Vance, Benj. W.	Taylor, Susanna	Mar 12	Wm Chaffee
5	Ward, Wm.	Ridenour, Eliza	Apr 14	Peter Ridenour, JP
6	Culison, Jesse	Ward, Sarah	Apr 4	Nathan Daniels, JP
6	Hall, Abraham H.	Walton, Arvilla	Apr 23	Silas Faurot, JP
6	Strickell, John	Walton, Harriet E.	May 14	Silas Faurot, JP
6	Hering, Philip	Hartman, Elizabeth	July 21	P. Ridenour
5	Osborn, Ebenezer	Hanson, Mahala	Mar 8	Nathan Daniels, JP
7	Cochrane, Andrew	Cannon, Nancy	Aug 22	Wm. Chaffee, EBC
7	Martin, Archelaus	Russell, Catherine	Aug 29	Wm. Chaffee, EBC
7	Shellenbarger, Jos.	Bresler, Elizabeth	Sept 15	Jos. G. Walton
121	Mayberry, William	Shannon, Hannah	Sept 26	John Alexander,Jr.MG
10	Church, David G.	Saxton, Mary	Oct 31	J. P. Walton, JP
8	Earll, Alanson	Day, Rachel	Nov 21	Tolson Ford, JP
8	Sutton, Thomas	Kephart, Susan	Nov 24	Wm. Berryman, JP
9	Stow, Edward	Morecraft, Esther	Nov 24	Tolson Ford
9	Clawson, Josiah	Higher, Elizabeth	Dec 9	Wm. Berryman, JP
9	Reece, David	Nichols, Priscilla	Dec 24	Nathan Daniels, JP
			1834	
10	Hoffman, Geo. M.	Nichols, Hannah	*Jan 4	Wm. Chaffee
11	Miller, Jacob	Moore, Elizabeth	Feb 9	Wm. Berryman, JP

* Date marriage was reported.

Page	Groom	Bride	Marriage Date 1834	Married by
12	O'Ferrell, John	Yasell, Sarah	Mar 9	Tolson Ford, JP
17	Stukey, Enos	Ehreman, Hester	Apr 3	Peter Ridenour, JP
11	Casebolt, William	Sligley, Tamer	*Apr 17	Wm. Chaffee
14	Whetstone, Abraham	Berryman, Eliza	Apr 17	Wm. Berryman, JP
16	Alfred, Ames	Hover, Sarah A.	*June 5	Wm. Chaffee
17	Petty, Jos. N.	Prosser, Nancy	June 19	Silas Faurot
18	Musser, Martin	Clark, Augusta	June 27	Rev. James W. Finley
17	Carlisle, Hector	Woods, Elizabeth	July 1	L. Sroufe
18	McPherrin, J.	Crossley, Huldah	Aug 2	Nathan Daniels
18	Harter, Charles	Carr, Susan	Aug 14	Wm. Berryman, JP
19	Maltbie, Harrison	Dowling, Susan	*Sept 11	Wm. Chaffee
19	Keller, John	McCoy, Sarah	*Sept 11	Wm. Chaffee
23	Morecraft, John	Witham, Lodesa	Sept 14	James Mahin, JP
21	Smith, William	Neely, Elizabeth	Oct 12	John Jameson
20	Fisher, William	Coleman, Martha	Oct 14	Lewis Sroufe, JP
20	Edgecomb, Ezra	Woods, Sarah Ann	Oct 21	John Jameson, JP
20	Adgate, James	Fleming, Sallie	Oct 22	Nathan Daniels
24	Fisher, Andrew	France, Mary	Nov 8	James Spray, JP
24	Ryan, Zechariah	Montgomery, Elizabeth	Nov 13	James Spray, JP
24	Trebein, William	Sneider, Matilda	Nov 20	Rev. FerdinandYoesting
22	Patterson, Moses	Hawk, Mary	Nov 25	John Jameson, JP
21	Alexander, John	Hover, Eliza M.	Nov 25	Peter Sharp, MG
23	Helm, Isaac	Patton, Jane M.	Dec 4	George Sheldon, MG
30	Corder, Elias	Howell, Eleanor	Dec 4	John Morris, JP
29	Friar, Henry	Deal, Catherine	Dec 7	Rev. Ferd.Yoesting
28	Franklin, James	Hanthorn, Sarah	Dec 11	Wm. Chaffee
27	Hanson, James A.	Ward, Rebecca C.	Dec 13	Nathan Daniels, JP
40	Anderson, John	Cannon, Esther	Dec 14	Simeon Cochran, JP
30	Patterson, John	Coon, Catherine	Dec 16	John Morris, JP
25	Rupert, John	Monger, Margaret	Dec 17	James Spray, JP
25	Shimmel, Conrad	Full, Katherine	Dec 17	James Spray, JP
26	Margandall, Gasper	Full, Magdalene	Dec 17	James Spray, JP
29	Spees, Mathias E.	Jones, Sarah	Dec 18	John Morris, JP
27	Evick, Absalom	Staley, Mahala	Dec 23	John Jameson, JP
26	Miller, John	Williams, Katherine	Dec 23	James Spray, JP
26	Williams, Columban	Full, Katherine	Dec 23 1835	James Spray, JP
28	Baker, Alfred	Gant, Mary	Jan 1	Rev. Wm. Chaffee
29	Shermer, John Leonhard	Vitedom, Mary	Jan 4	Rev. H.F. Yoesting
32	Howell, John M.	Spray, Abigail	Jan 8	James Spray
32	Northup, Levi D.	Ryan, Susan	Jan 15	James Spray
27	Moore, Robert	Creek, Lydia	Jan 22	Peter Sharp, MG
31	Mahlin, James	Call, Mary	Feb 5	James Mahin, JP
30	Pangle, Vance B.	Jacobs, Flaville	Feb 26	Rev. Wm. Chaffee
40	Wright, Elias	Bowman, Sarah A.	Mar 2	Rev. Simon Cochran
33	Bryan, James	Stukey, Dinah	Mar 5	Benj. F. Cochran, JP
33	Valentine, Cram	Musser, Nancy	Mar 10	Rev. Geo. Sheldon

* Date marriage was reported.

Page	Groom	Bride	Marriage Date	Married by
			1835	
31	Pearce, Richard	Coon, Maria	Mar 18	Tolson Ford, JP
32	Meyers, George	Ford, Nancy	Apr 14	Tolson Ford, JP
31	Purdy, Daniel	Kill, Mary	Apr 26	Lewis Sroufe, JP
34	Hering, Lewis	Shope, Elizabeth	Apr 28	Peter Ridenour, JP
34	North, Thomas	Stukey, Susanna	May 3	Benj. F. Cochran, JP
42	Keck, John	Rohrbacker, Mary	May 12	Rev. H.F. Yoesting
39	Warner, Joseph	Clifford, Catherine	June 8	James Spray
35	Shockey, William	Hardesty, Mary	June 11	Peter Sharp, MG
34	Jameston, Samuel H.	McCluer, Sarah Ann	June 18	John Jameson, JP
40	Bowman, John C.	Johnston, Ellen	June 25	Rev. Simon Cochran
35	Lindsley, William B.	Curtiss, Sabra	July 7	Lewis Sroufe, JP
35	Osburn, Wm. C.	Tunget, Mary	July 22	Rev. Peter Sharp
36	Heater, Henry A.	Cowan, Rachel Ann	July 26	Rev. Peter Sharp
36	McFheron, Wm.	Logan, Lydia	Aug 6	Rev. Wm. Chaffee
37	Coleman, Henry	Mars, Mary	Aug 6	John Morris, JP
37	Coon, Asa	Coon, Hannah	Aug 9	Rev. Wm. Chaffee
37	Bailey, John	Osborn, Rhoda	Aug 13	Rev. Wm. Chaffee
38	Sever, George	Casto, Elizabeth	Aug 13	Tolson Ford, JP
36	Coon, Alexander	Mills, Delilah Affaline	Aug 19	Benj. F. Cochran, JP
39	Stevenson, Elias	Howell, Rebecca	*Aug 31	James Spray, JP
38	Williams, James	Balsigner, Elizabeth	Sept 10	Lewis Sroufe, JP
38	Mattox, Moses	Van Nortwick, Hester	Sept 17	John Morris, JP
42	Rumbaugh, Morris	Hanson, Mary	Sept 22	Nathan Daniels, JP
39	Stevenson, Joseph F.	Bowyer, Adeline	Oct 8	Tolson Ford, JP
41	Boman, Alexander S.C.	Baxter, Rachel	Oct 9	Rev. Simon Cochran
41	Graham, Charles	Carter, Rachel	Oct 9	John Morris, JP
41	Grapner, John Jacob	Altin,Hannah Appalonia	Oct 11	Rev. J.H.F. Yoesting
43	Cotrell, Samuel	Baker, Phoebe	Oct 25	James Mahin, JP
48	Reed, Manuel	O'Harra, Elizabeth	Nov 17	Rev. Wm. Chaffee
44	Ellsworth, Joseph C.	Shigley, Sarah	Nov 22	James Mahin, JP
47	Birk, Erhard	Rohrback, Louisa	*Nov 24	Rev. J.H.F. Yoesting
42	Black, Joseph	Mosher, Wealthy	Nov 26	David Reece, JP
43	Sprague, Joshua	Provinmire, Sarah	Dec 13	Asa Wright, JP
48	McHenry, William	Tompkins, Malvina	Dec 17	Rev. Wm. Chaffee
45	Leist, Elias	Baxter, Maria	Dec 31	Benj. F. Cochran, JP
46	Coon, George W.	Williams, Elizabeth	Dec 31	Rev.JamesCunningham
			1836	
44	Wollet, Solomon	Ridenour, Rebecca	Jan 7	Adam White, JP
45	Cutler, Daniel	Welsh, Marcissa A.	Jan 10	Rev. David Burns
45	Elliott, James	Stockdale	Jan 17	Rev. David Burns
47	Vitzedom, Wunnabald	George, Catharine	Jan 19	Rev. J.H.F. Yoesting
46	Cochran, George W.	Sunderland, Mary	Jan 21	Benj. F. Cochran
49	Ward, Rauzewed	Rhodes, Harriet	Jan 30	Wm. Reece, JP
49	Lusk, Joseph	Waggoner, Julian	Jan 31	John Morris, JP
44	Musser, Daniel	Mitchell, Maria	Jan 31	David Burns, MG
48	Reesbarger, Jacob	Wymott, Catherine	Feb 2	James H. Coleman
47	Yacobe, John	Sammetinger,Barbara	Feb 9	Rev. Yoesting

*Date marriage was reported.

51

Page	Groom	Bride	Marriage Date 1836	Married by
50	Candler, John W.	Swaim, Sarah	Feb 9	John Jameson
49	Logan, Alfred	Jones, Elizabeth	Feb 14	John Morris, JP
51	Bowyer, Madison	Largent, Rachel	Mar 1	Tolson Ford
50	Kidd, Nathaniel G.	Meek, Jane	Mar 17	John Jameson
51	Irvin, John	Robertson, Lavina	Mar 20	Tolson Ford
50	Landramer, Mathias	Krentznerr, Christina	*Mar 21	Rev. Yoesting
50	Koennacher, Joseph	Sabaugher, Marianna	*Mar 21	Rev. Yoesting
51	Church, Reuben W.	Reece, Mary	May 5	John Jameson
52	Faurot, David	Rumbaugh, Hannah	Apr 7	Adam White, JP
52	Ramey, David	Higher, Nancy	Apr 24	RichardMetheany, JP
52	Wilhelm, George	Altin, Maria Anna Margaretta	*Apr 25	Rev. Yoesting
53	Hathaway, Daniel F.	Musser, Frances	May 10	Rev. D. Burns
53	Mans, George	Rumbaugh, Jane	May 12	Adam White, JP
54	Spitler, Daniel	Weller, Margaret	May 22	Joseph Conger, JP
91	Binkey, Ferdinand	Poage, Malinda	June 1	Albert Helfenstein
53	Gant, George W.	Plummer, Rachel	June 14	David Reece, JP
65	Bowyer, Alphonsey	Stevens, Elizabeth	June 16	Tolson Ford, JP
54	Metheany, Richard	Levering, Hester Ann	June 16	Rev. Wm. Chaffee
66	Beachdolt, Peter	Gruber, Susanna	June 23	John Morris, JP
54	Lanning, Benjamin	Bobb, Anna	July 3	Beal Sperrier, JP
53	Stone, Joseph	Lindsley, Sarah	July 10	Louis Sroufe, JP
66	Loomis, Aaron	Pennington, Elisabeth C.	Aug 11	John Jameson
55	Sunderland, Wm.	Johnson, Elizabeth	Aug 12	Benj. Cochran
66	Stevanson, John	Brentlinger, Susanna	Aug 14	David Reece, JP
69	Allen, Warren C.	Coleman, Mary	Aug 18	James H. Coleman, JP
65	Kreidler, Samuel	Reed, Amelia Ann	*Aug 18	Rev. D. Burns
91	Hutt, Wm. T.	Finley, Elizabeth P.	Aug 23	Rev. A. Halfenstein
55	Dillow, Frederick	Bareter, Jane	Aug 24	Benj. Cochran
69	Lucas, Isaac	Nickles, Elizabeth	Aug 24	Samuel Bleakley, JP
67	Lusk, Charles	Mix Lucinda	Sept 15	John Morris, JP
67	Devore, Felix	Berryman, Adaline	Sept 18	Wm. Berryman, JP
55	Card, Richard	Ridenour, Sarah	Sept 29	Lewis Sroufe, JP
68	Coy, Isaac	Watt, Sarah Jane	Oct 11	J. H. Coleman, JP
65	Fisher, Peter	Kook, Maria	*Aug 23	Rev. Yoesting
68	Harshe, David	Candler, Martha Jane	Oct 13	Wm. Reece, JP
56	Berden, James	Wright, Sarah	Oct 17	John Morris, JP
57	Snyder, Daniel	Styles, Demar's	Oct 18	Rev. Wm. Chaffee
67	Bolsinger, George	Hall, Mary	Oct 20	John Jameson, JP
56	Harter, Elias	Harter, Sarah	Oct 27	Benj. F. Cochran, JP
56	Jackson, John	Chambers, Rachel	Nov 6	James Spray, JP
68	Beaty, Alexander	Vance, Eliza	Nov 10	Rev. Wm. Gray
57	Shuckleton, John P.	Levering, Melinda M.	Nov 22	Rev. Wm. Chaffee
57	Copner, Justice D.	Myers, Elisabeth	Nov 24	J. H. Coleman, JP
61	Leatherman, Daniel	Swain, Rachel	Nov 24	John Jameson, JP
60	Kentner, Emanuel	Bopp, Susanna	Dec 1	Rev. Yoesting
63	Beekamp, Silas	Jodhunter, Clarenda	Dec 1	John W. Starr
59	Elsworth, David	Shigley, Elizabeth	Dec 2	James Mahin, JP

*Date marriage was reported.

52

Page	Groom	Bride	Marriage Date	Married by
			1836	
60	Maderis, Oliver	Princehouse, Sally	Dec 4	Rev. Alden Besse
63	Bodkin, William	Clawson, Maria	Dec 8	Richard Metheany, JP
			1837	
61	Cremean, Edward	Povemire, Mary	Jan 15	John Ireland, JP
61	Povemire, Isaac	Cremean, Maria	Jan 15	John Ireland, JP
91	Chenoweth, James	Skilling, Nancy	Jan 16	Rev. A. Halfenstein
91	Meyers, Samuel	Delong, Catherine	Jan 17	Rev. A. Halfenstein
59	Smith, John	Hulson, Sarah	Jan 24	Samuel Bleakley, JP
64	Cunningham, James	Kennedy, Martha	Feb 1	Rev. Geo. D. Poague
63	Barton, William	Devolt, Nancy	Feb 9	Daniel Reece, JP
64	Shockey, Abraham	Smith, Rachel D.	Feb 12	Tolson Ford, JP
70	Woodley, Robert	Payne, Hannah	Feb 14	James Mahin, JP
71	Shaw, William H.	Turton, Elizabeth	Feb 16	Rev. Alden Besse
60	Buck, Ebenezer	Thompson, Margaret	Feb 23	Thomas D. Furrness
70	Hawk, John	Gilbert, Achsah	Feb 26	John Jameson, JP
59	Lucas, Ebenezer	Nichols, Mary	Mar 7	Samuel Bleakley
64	Boyd, Abraham	Hover, Maria B.	Mar 9	Rev. Geo. B. Poague
70	Miller, John	Bowers, Matilda	Mar 21	Asa Wright, JP
69	Wollet, Samuel	Ridenour, Phoebe	Mar 30	Adam White, JP
73	Graham, Charles G.	Logan, Keziah Ann	Apr 3	Rev. John W. Starr
76	Bowdle, Thomas	McCoy, Miram	Apr 11	Rev. Jesse Bowdle
74	Baxter, James	John, Melissa	Apr 20	Benj. F. Cochran, JP
71	Wolary, Casper	Hester, Elizabeth	Apr 20	John Morris, JP
71	Plummer, Calahan	Ashing, Sarah Jane	Apr 27	Tolson Ford, JP
74	Fischer, Blasius	Wiemann, Anna Marie	Apr 29	Rev. J. W. Horstman
75	Zanglain, Nicholas	Waltz, Susanna	May 4	James Spray, JP
71	Ferguson, Elijah	Cramer, Rosanna	May 11	Lewis Sroufe, JP
72	Boyer, Daniel	Hughes, Sarah G.	May 16	Rev. James A. Kellam
72	Smith, John	Shaffer, Rachel	May 21	Adam White, JP
72	Stiles, Newell B.	Patterson, Nancy	May 25	Rev. Geo. G. Poague
76	Smith, John	Mayberry, Elizabeth	May 25	Isaac Bennett
73	Stukey, Daniel H.	Van Dalsem, Susanna Van Norst	June 1	Rev. Geo. G. Poague
76	Bush, Joseph	Craft, Elizabeth	June 1	James Elliott, JP
77	Burke, William	Parlot, Mary	June 1	John Morris, JP
72	Wamsley, John B.	Boman, Sarah R.	June 6	Rev. James A. Kellam
77	Mix, Uri	Bayliff, Margaret	June 22	"a J.P."
73	Berryman, Russell	Slane, Margaret	June 29	Daniel Gregory, JP
73	Stemen, John	Herring, Mary Jane	July 4	Asa Wright
78	Lusk, Isaac	Lusk, Elizabeth	July 13	John Corder, JP
74	Bob, Charles	Tobias, Elizabeth	*July 14	Rev. Yoesting
75	Knerr, Adam	Albrand, Mina	*Aug 1	Rev. Yoesting
74	Yeazel, Solomon	Weaver, Elizabeth	Aug 2	Rev. James A. Kellam
77	Church, Walton	Reece, Elizabeth	Aug 17	Adam White, JP
80	Skillings, Charles	Richie, Lucinda	Aug 17	James Mahin, JP
91	Reichelderfer, Wm.	Stebeltan, Sarah	Aug 28	Rev. A. Halfenstein
78	Van Nuys, John	Wilson, Katherine	Sept 8	Rev. Enos French
78	Sunderland, Daniel	Dubois, Frances Maria	Sept 12	Daniel Hoak, JP

*Date marriage was reported.

Page	Groom	Bride	Marriage Date 1837	Married by
79	Reece, William	Reynolds, Mary	Sept 13	Adams White, JP
78	Lonas, John	Baker, Elizabeth	Sept 14	John M. Wilson, JP
115	Bodkin, George	Manier, Charity	Sept 16	Daniel Gregory, JP
78	Zanglein, Andrew	Waltz, Mary	Sept 19	James Spray, JP
80	Sanford, Michael	Klickard, Barbara	Oct 1	James Elliott, JP
79	Baker, Henry	Parlet, Diana	Oct 6	John Morris, JP
79	Peterson, Levi	------	Oct 8	Isaac Bowyer, JP
79	Bazzle, James	Lusk, Elizabeth	Oct 15	John Morris, JP
80	Berry, Henry	McCoy, Matilda	Oct 19	Rev. Jesse Bowdle
80	Kaylor, Samuel	Eich, Mary Magdalene	Nov 5	Adam White, Jp
82	Hanson, Hollis	Shaw, Sarah	Nov 9	H. C. V. Williams
83	Ream, John	Bresler, Lydia A.	Nov 19	Adam White
81	Taylor, William	Buck, Mary	Nov 19	Daniel Hoak, JP
81	Heindel, Jacob	Dewey, Elizabeth	*Nov 28	Rev. Wm. Chaffee
81	Miller, Joseph	Raderer, Barbara	Nov 28	Lewis Sroufe
82	Looney, Steve	Bitter, Louisana	Nov 30	John Morris, JP
84	Whetstone, Samuel	Berryman, Anna Marie	Dec 9	Daniel Hoak, JP
70	Watson, William	Scott, Rachel Ann	Dec 20	H. D. V. Williams
81	Skinner, Joseph J.	Hoyt, Susan	Dec 24	Lewis Sroufe, JP

*Date marriage was reported.

ALLEN COUNTY, OHIO - WILL ABSTRACTS 1836-1844

The following wills were abstracted from "Will Book A2", page on which will is found is given in parenthesis.

DEVER, Abraham - Highland Co., Ohio - dated 5-2-1836; recorded 7-28-1836 - Wife: Elizabeth - Children: Mary McFadden, John J. Dever, Mariah Perkins, Evan Dever, Louisa Woolman, Elizabeth Harper, Lucinda Johnson, James B. Dever, William S. Dever, Abraham Dever, David H. Dever and Jonathan T. Dever - Executors: Wife, Elizabeth Dever; James E. Johnson and Jesse Harper - Signed: Abraham (mark) Dever - Witnesses: Jacob Horton, Robert Elwood and Isaac McKay. (2)

WOLLET, Philip - dated 9-3-1835; recorded 10-21-1836 - Wife: Mary - Sons: Michael, deceased, his heirs; Solomon; Samuel; Daniel - Daughters: Lydia wife of George Leach; Mary wife of Harmon Webb; Rebekah wife of Solomon Donoven; Saloma Christena "in Dutch, in English generally called Sally"; Catharine wife of Henry Shenk; Nancy; Elizabeth, deceased, late wife of David Rowland - grandchildren: Samuel, Henry, Philip, Daniel, Lydia and Margaret, heirs of daughter Elizabeth Rowland, deceased - Executors: Adam White and Solomon Wollet - Signed: Philip Wollet - Witnesses: James Daniels, Benjamin Hanson and Aaron Osmun. (5)

FRENCH, William - dated 10-11-1836; recorded 5-27-1837 - wife: Elizabeth - Eight children: Samuel D., David Carlile, William J., George, Newton, Ann B., Elizabeth and Mary Jane French - Executors: Wife, Elizabeth and James Davisson - Signed: Wm. French - Witnesses: James Daniels, Matthew Dobbins and Peter Tunget. (9)

ICE, Solomon - dated 3-26-1837; recorded (not given) - Wife: Elizabeth - Children: Samuel and Mary Ellen Ice, not of age - Executors: Moses McCoy and Nicholas D. Mares - Signed: Solomon (mark) Ice - Witnesses: Nicholas D. Mares and Moses McCoy. (12)

JILLIAMS, John - dated 7-1-1837; recorded 4-30-1838 - Wife: Margaret - Sons: John W., George Washington, Elias Nelson Delashmont, Lewis Jackson and Philemon Beecher Williams - Daughters: Rebecca Millegan and Comfort - Executors: Wife, Margaret and son, George - Signed: John Williams - Witnesses: Perry Oliphant and John Lowry.(13)

LONG, Abraham - Mercer Co., Ohio - dated 8-13-1838; recorded 9-17-1838 - Father: Jacob Long, also to serve as executor - Mother: Elizabeth Long - Signed: Abraham Long - Witnesses: Rich'd R. Barrington, Aaron C. Badgley and Ephraim McKay. (15)

KEITH, Elizabeth - dated 10-16-1837; recorded (not given 1838) - Heirs: Sarah Keith, Elizabeth Beauddle, Hannah Valentine and Mary Hullenbarger wife of John Hullenbarger - Mentions: Title bond on William Keith for 40 acres of land SE¼ NE¼ Section 9, Township 4 south (Note: No range given.)--Executor: William Keith - Signed: Elizabeth (mark) Keith - Witnesses: Tolsen (or Tolser) Ford and George Ford. (17)

MYERS, Jacob - Moulton Twp. - (original will in German) - dated 4-28-1838; recorded August 1838 - Wife: Mary Ann - Mentions:; Martin Myers is to care for and to support Mary Ann - Signed: Jacob Myers - Witnesses: John George Fryman, John Waite and Nathaniel Bonsen. (22)

CHENOWETH, William - dated 8-6-1832; recorded 10-11-1838 - Wife: Ann - Five youngest children: John Chenoweth, Nelly Franklin, Martha Chenoweth, Lewis Chenoweth
and Mason Chenoweth - Children by first wife: John, deceased, "land sold in Virginia
which came by his grandfather Rinker", (Note: In other estate papers it is stated
land was in Frederick Co., Va.); Mary Chriswell; Eleanor Chenoweth, Elizabeth Chenoweth; Catharine Chenoweth; Jacob Chenoweth, deceased, his heirs; William Chenoweth,
deceased, his heirs; Casper Chenoweth; Barbary Martindale; Sarah Franklin; last nine
named received $200 each from plantation given to first wife by her father -
Executors: Wife, Ann and son, John - Signed: William Chenoweth - Witnesses:
Robert Terry, James Daniels and Phebe (mark) Homan. (19)

McCOY, Andrew - dated 6-24-1838; recorded 4-3-1839 - Wife: Sarah - Sons: Elisha
(Elijah), David and Moses - Daughters: Mary W. Stevenson; Elizabeth Bowile; Matilda
Berry; Mirian Bowdle; Jane, Malinda and Letitia McCoy; last three not of age -
Executors: Eli Stevenson and Frederick Rudy - Signed: Andrew McCoy - Witnesses:
William Gilmer and Samuel Ashing. (23)

MILLER, Isaac - Verbal Will made 6-10-1839; recorded 6-15-1839 - Son: William -
Daughter: Sarah Anna - Executor: Brother, George Miller - Witnesses: Thomas
Coleman and Warren C. Allen. (26)

WRIGHT, Asa - dated 8-13-1839; recorded (not given) - Wife: Jane, also to serve as
executor - Signed: Asa Wright - Witnesses: Isaac Bowyer and David Beeler. (27)

WILLIAMS, Jacob - Wayne Twp. - dated 8-5-1839; recorded (not given) - Sons: Samuel,
eldest son; Lenuel; Lewis E.; William E.; Thomas - Daughters: Lydia Ann, eldest
daughter, Rebecca Maria; Ethaline - Executor; Son, Samuel - Signed: Jacob Williams
- Witnesses: Moses Ross, Jesse L. Bowdle and Nathan Woodbury. (28)

STOCKDALE, William - dated 10-6-1838; recorded 8-22-1840 - Children: Mary Middleton;
Ellen Elliott; Jane; Joseph; George and William Stockdale- Mentions: That money
is to go to the "Quaker establishment lying in Allen County" - Executors: Lemuel
Hyde and son, Joseph Stockdale - Signed: William Stockdale - Witnesses: William
Jackson and Elias Horner. (31)

DENISON, James - dated 3-9-1841; recorded (not given) - Son: James Denison Jr.,
with John Brandstretter to be his guardian - Daughters: Agnis and Martha Denison -
Executor: Alexander Cress - Signed: James (mark) Denison - Witnesses: Jacob L.
Baker, Wm. Keith and Alexander Cress. (33)

FISHER, Michael - dated 3-22-1841; recorded (not given) - Wife: Barbara - Son: John,
not of age - Brothers: Andrew and John - Mentions: That money is to go to the Catholic Church in Fryburg - Executors: Wife, Barbara; Gervasy Seiter and Joseph Busch
- Signed: Michael (mark) Fisher - Witnesses: Kolbhon Wilhelm and Katharine Fall. (36)

NEHER, David - Clark Co., Ohio - dated 7-13-184?; recorded (not given) - Wife: Anna
- Mentions land in Butler Twp., Allen County; personal property in Clark County -
Executor: Father-in-law, Abraham Miller - Signed; David (mark) Neher -
Witnesses: Daniel Miller and John Dickey. (37)

WELINER, Francis - Pusheta Twp. - Verbal Will made 10-19-1841, died 10-21-1841; recorded 10-28-1841 - Leaves all of estate to Catholic Church of St. Peter and Paul in Pusheta Twp. and to the School District Fund - Executors: Joseph Wehner and Andrew Schaup - Witnesses: Andrew J. Schaup and Joseph Wehner. (39)

SPEES, Matthias - Union Twp. - dated 3-30-1842; recorded 5-6-1842 - Wife: Mentioned but not named - Sons: John, Matthias E., Samuel, Daniel and Andrew - Daughter: Eve Bartan- Grandson: George Hook, not of age - Mentions: Mary Studling as an heir, but no relationship given - Signed: Matthias (mark) Spees - Witnesses: William Shaw and Robert C. Layton. (40)

WHETSTONE, Michael - dated 3-26-1842; recorded 5-7-1842 - wife: Margaret - Four sons: Henry, John, William and James - Daughters: Elizabeth Hipperds, Margaret Colwell and Sarah Bennet - Executors: Sons, Henry and John - Signed: Michael Whetstone - Witnesses: Joseph (mark) Brown and Amos S. Bennet. (43)

BOWMAN, Joseph - dated 5-31-1842; recorded 6-29-1842 - Wife, Frances - Four children: Mary, Elizabeth, Catharine and John Bowman - Executors: John and Joseph Byerstaffer - Signed: Joseph Bowman - Witnesses: Peter Bower and John Sheff. (44)

SAUM, Matthias - dated 10-29-1841; recorded (not given-1842) - Wife: Elizabeth - Sons: Matthias, Solomon, Jonathan, John and Jacob - Daughters: Susanna Weller, Catharine Macklin, Mary Fansler, Magdalene Pence and Eve Arnatt - Executors: William Pence and Jacob Arnett - Signed: Matthias (mark) Saum - Witnesses: Atcheson Blakeley and Samuel Blakeley. (46)

FAUSOT, Silas - Lima - dated 12-9-1842; recorded 12-29-1842 - Wife: mentioned but not named - Son: Charles F. Fausot, also to serve as executor - Signed: Silas Fausot - Witnesses: John Ward and John P. Fay. (47)

STANDIFORD, Elijah - dated 9-8-1840; recorded (not given) - Wife: Rebecca - Son: John F. - Daughter: Provy Black - Signed: E. Standeford - Witnesses: John Alexander, Jr. and T. K. Jacobs. (51)

BUSH, Joseph Sr. - Persheta Twp. - dated 4-16-1843; recorded 5-8-1843 - Wife: Elizabeth - Daughter: Susanna - Son: Peter, not of age - Mentions: Michael Bush and William Bush but does not state relationship, may be sons - Signed: Joseph Bush - Witnesses: William Craft, Sr. and Andrew Werst. (52)

REIER, Philip - Clay Twp. - dated 10-14-1842; recorded 5-11-1843 - Wife: Elizabeth, also to serve as guardian of minor children - Five children: Falleathine, Adam, Margaret, Joseph and Philip - Executor: Michael Bush - Sighed: Phillip Reier - Witnesses: James Linff(?), Adam Catzenberger and Michael Bush. (53)

VANTRESS, Benjamin - Clay Twp. - dated 4-27-1843; recorded 7-8-1843 - Wife: Mentioned but not named - Children: Sylvester Vantress, Mary Burden, Lydia Rees, Sarah Jane Bitler, Thomas, Ann Eliza, Almira, Benjamin Jr., Abigail, Elizabeth and Clarender Vantress - executors: John Morris and Sylvester Vantress - Signed: Benjamin Vantress - Witnesses: Charles Martin and John M. Shaw. (56)

EDMINSTON, David - dated (not given); recorded 10-7-1843 - Wife: Jane - Sons: Joseph P., Andrew S. and John R. - Mentions: "remainder of heirs including one not yet born" - Mentions: Land in Dushequet and Union Townships - Executor: John Lowery - Signed: David Edmiston - Witnesses: John Lowry and Joseph Lowry. (58)

STRICKLER, John J. - dated 7-1-1843; recorded 10-7-1843 - Wife: Sarah - Signed: John J. (mark) Strickler - Witnesses: Eli Logan, Andrew Moore and S. W. Slater. (60)

HOVER, Julius A. - dated 5-28-18 '; recorded 5-5-1843 - Sister: Eliza Alexander - Mentions: Mother and brothers, but does not name - Executor: Father, Joseph Hover - Signed: Julius A. Hover - Witnesses: Nathan Daniels and Manuel Hover. (61)

YOUNG, Joseph M. - dated 11-29-1843; recorded 1-2-1844 - Wife: Mary - Mentions: "all my children", but does not name - Executors: Job Throg and Richard Melheny - Signed: Joseph M. Young - Witnesses: Charles Levering and Oliver Smith. (62)

HENRY, Robinson - dated 8-3-1843; recorded 5-13-1844 - Appoints Joseph M. Irwin administrator to pay all debts, no heirs named - Signed: Robinson Henry - Witnesses: C. H. Williams; G. G. Poage of Logan County, Ohio. (65)

RAYL, George - dated 1-11-1844; recorded 5-14-1844 - Wife: Prudence - Two sons: George and Daniel - Four daughters: Prudence Dearth, Hannah and Susan (Note: Fourth daughter not named) - Signed: George Rayl - Witnesses: William Hedges and George McCaskey. (67)

SAUM, Elizabeth - dated 12-20-1842; recorded 5-14-1844 - Sons: Solomon and Matthias - Signed: Elizabeth (mark) Saum - Witnesses: Daniel Rankins and William M. Crane.(70)

HOVER, Joseph - dated 6-14-1844; recorded 9-10-1844 - Wife: Caroline - Six children: Eliza Matilda Alexander; Joshua B., Cyrus H., William Ulysses, James A. and Joseph O. Hover - Mentions: "sons are to remember widowed sister" - Executors: Sons, Joshua B., Cyrus H. and William U. Hover - Signed: Joseph Hover - Witnesses: Lester Bliss and Nathan Daniels. (72)

SHOCKEY, Isaac - dated 8-29-1844; recorded 10-2-1844 - Wife: Hannah, Also to serve as executrix - sons: Henry and Isaac - Two sons-in-law: Philip Kiblinger and Robert Underwood - Mentions: "that the above heirs are to be made equal with John Shockey, Samuel Shockey, William Shockey and Abram Shockey; Johmas Crooks, Abraham Fitchpatrick and Charles Rector who have each received $100." - Heirs: Joseph Titsworth and Frederick Rector - Signed Isaac Shockey - Witnesses: James Watts and David Gilmer. (74)

WILLIAMS, James - dated 12-1-1837; recorded 4-4-1844 - Wife: Sarah - Sons: William and John - Daughter: Elizabeth Coon - Grandson: James Williams - Executors: Wife, Sarah Williams and James Watts - Signed: James Williams - Witnesses: John Ward and Samuel Watt. (77)

TISSUE, Edward - dated 9-24-1843; recorded 10-1-1844 - Wife: Esther - Two youngest sons: Jackson and Isaac - Daughter: Esther - Signed: Edward (mark) Tissue - Witnesses: James H. Coleman and John Morris. (82)

KEITH, William - dated 2-17-1843; recorded 10-1-1844 - Wife: Sarah - Sons: James T. and William - Mentions: Minor heirs of Elizabeth Russel, deceased; does not name - Mentions: "money to be divided equal among all my children" - Executor: Son, James T. Keith - Signed: Wm. Keith - Witnesses: William H. Valentine, Thomas Guthrie and John Smith. (79)

MERGENTHAL, Casper - dated 7-18-1841; recorded 11-16-1841 (or 1844?) - Wife: Mentioned but not named - Daughter: Ana Maria, not of age, wife to serve as guardian - Executors: Conrad Schemmel and Michael Dumbroff - Signed: Casper Mergenthal - Witnesses: Conrad Schemmel, Michael Franz and John Manger. (83)

CAMPBELL, Malcom - Washington Township - dated 10-25-1844; recorded 11-13-1844 - Wife: Mentioned but not named - Brothers: William, Thomas and John - Sisters: Abbegale Wilson and Isabella Hughy - Executor: Samuel Blakely - Signed: Malcom (mark) Campbell - Witnesses: Thomas H. Standish and Jacob Arnet. (85)

JONES CEMETERY - DELPOS, ALLEN COUNTY, OHIO

Contributed by: Lucy Bloomquist, 1156 Briarcliff Dr., Rantoul, Ill. 61866
Cemetery located short distance west of the town of Delphos. Copied in full.

WILLIAMS.... Jonah d. July 7, 1850 ae 58y 8m 19d
            Mariah d. Sep. 6, 1862 ae 72y
GLEASON..... Magy E. JONES w/o Peter d Jan. 30, 1855 ae 22y 2d
JONES....... Melanchloe S. d June 21, 1847 ae 26y 11m 10d
            Lucy w/o Selden d Oct. 7, 1880 ae 93y 2m 24d
GREEN....... Mary C. WESTON w/o Isaac d Feb. 5, 1858 ae 59y
JONES....... Lucy Ann d/o S. M. & P. d Sept. 2, 1861 ae 18y 1m 5d
            Charles M. s/o S. M. & P. d Dec. 24, 1861 ae 18y 1m 5d
            Flavel B. s/o S. M. & P., Co. D, 101 Ohio Vols., d at Chickamauga
            Sept. 19, 1865 ae 23y 5m 22d. His remains lie in Tenn.
            Semantha R. d/o S. M. & P. d Apr. 10, 1869 ae 26y 21d
            Stirling M. d Apr. 24, 1880 ae 71y 4m 25d
            Patience d Apr. 14, 1884 ae 72y 5m 7d
            Elizabeth A. 1839-1913
BOWLBY...... Samuel d Sep. 10, 1850 ae 72y 11m 18d
ALLEN ...... William W., 1847-1929
            James M. d July 22, 1871 ae 63y 3m 19d
            Jane d Apr. 9, 1886 ae 69y 6m 23d
TRUXELL .... Jacob d Oct. 12, 1882 ae 91y
            Rebecca w/o Jacob d June 25, 1880 ae 81y

59

The following records were taken from "Journal B", the page on which each record is found is given in parenthesis.

4-30-1838 - Susannah JULIEN, etal - In Chancery - J. S. UPDEGRAFF appointed guardian of Stephen, John, Susan, Rachal, and Rebecca JULIEN minor defendants.(2)

4-30-1838 - Naturalization - Joseph KELLER, a native of France produced a certificate dated 10-2-1834 by the Common Pleas Court of Montgomery Co., Ohio; court certifies. (2)

4-30-1838 - William STOCKDALE, guardian vs. Thomas MIDDLETON, etal. - Petition to sell land. (2)

4-30-1838 - Will of John WILLIAMS, deceased, presented to court - Executors, Margaret Williams and George Williams - Margaret Williams, widow, relinquishes her right to administer estate in favor of John LOWRY. (3)

4-30-1838 - David CAMPBELL, an ordained minister of the Regular Baptist Church granted right to solemnize marriages. (3)

4-30-1838 - Will of Elizabeth KEITH presented to court - William KEATH, Executor(4)

5-1-1838 - Margaret WILLIAMS appointed guardian of Lewis WILLIAMS, aged 19 years; Philemon B. WILLIAMS, aged 17 years and Comfort WILLIAMS, aged 12 years - Bond $300. with Perry OLIPHANT and John WILLIAMS, securities. (5)

5-1-1838 - Naturalization - David MORGAN, a native of Wales in Great Britain presented certificate of intention dated 11-11-1833. (8)

5-2-1838 - Susannah JULIEN, admsx. of estate of William JULIEN, deceased, filed account. (9)

5-2-1838 - Peter HAMMELL vs. Henry STODDARD, Rachel SMITH, John J. SMITH, Jane SMITH, James SMITH and Nicholas SMITH - In Chancery. (11)

5-2-1838 - George WOLLET, etal. vs. Heirs of Philip WOLLET, deceased - In Chancery - land described as northwest quarter, Section 34, Township 3 south, Range 7 east. (12)

5-2-1838 - Adms. of estate of Abraham WARD, deceased vs. Heirs - Petition to sell land. (13)

5-3-1838 - Elizabeth LIPPINCOTT vs. Samiramis, Mary Jane, Henrietta, Samuel B. LIPPINCOTT and William SCOT - Ill in Chancery - Christopher WOOD appointed guardian of Mary Jane and Henrietta LIPPINCOTT, minors - Samiramis LIPPINCOTT by Curtis BATES along with William SCOTT and Samuel B. LIPPINCOTT waive process(14)

5-3-1838 - Naturalization - John Leonard SHERMER, a native of Germany makes his declaration to become citizen. (14)

5-3-1838 - William LIPPINCOTT vs. Samuel and George LIPPINCOTT - In Chancery.(15)

5-3-1838 - Adms. of James A. ANDERSON vs. Widow and Heirs of Decedent -
Petition to sell real estate described as In-lot number 124 in Lima. (15)

5-3-1838 - John KELLER, guardian vs Mary Elizabeth McCOY - Petition to sell
land. (15)

5-3-1838 - Estate of Joseph SCOTT - Deceased left no widow and kin - On motion
of court, Samuel WATT appointed adms. and gave bond of $600 - Appraisors:
Abraham BOWERS, Crain VALENTINE and Samuel BLACK. (18)

6-22-1838 - David McMULLEN appointed adms. of estate of William McCARTNEY -
Mary McCARTNEY, widow relinquishes her right to administer estate - Bond .
$1400. (20)

8-13-1838 - Naturalization - Leonard AUSTIN, native of the Province of Lower
Canada makes his declaration to become citizen. Michael SCIFERT, a native of
Baiern, Germany makes his declaration to become citizen. John MILLER and Henry
MILLER, natives of Hanover, Germany make their declaration to become citizens.(22)

8-13-1838 - Naturalization - John JACKSON and Joseph JACKSON, natives of England
make their declaration to become citizens. (23)

8-13-1838 - Naturalization - Matthias LEBAL, a native of Baden, Germany produced
a certificate of intention from the Common Pleas Court of Butler Co., Ohio dated
Sept. 1833. (23)

8-13-1838 - John MILLER appointed guardian of Henry MILLER, aged about 15 months,
heir of Girard MILLER, deceased. (23)

8-13-1838 - Benjamin DAVISON appointed guardian of Genvenies H. NELSON, aged
19 years, heir of Joshua NELSON. (24)

8-13-1838 - Adms. of John P. STRICKLE vs. Susannah STRICKLE - Petition to sell
real estate. (25)

8-13-1838 - John BRAND vs. Thomas J. MOORE. - In Chancery - Defendants, Thomas J.,
Sarah and Jeremiah MOORE convey all their interest to John BRAND. (25)

8-14-1838 - Henry MILLER appointed adms. of the Estate of Gerard MILLER -
Widos (not named) relinquishes her right to adms. estate - Bond $150 by Henry
MILLER with James SPRAY as security. (28)

8-15-1838 - Lewis SROUFE, adms. of David BELLENGER, deceased vs. Heirs -
Petition to sell land - Curtis BATES appointed guardian of minor defendants;
Louisa, William, Bethuel, Hester Ann and Lewis BELLINGER. (33)

8-15-1838 - Samuel WATT and Joshua McFARLAND license to keep tavern. (34)

8-15-1838 - Will of Jacob MYERS presented - Mary Ann MYERS, widow appointed
adms. - Bond $500. (39)

61

10-11-1838 - Will of William CHENOWETH presented - Ann CHENOWETH and John CHENOWETH, executors - Bond $1400. (40)

11-5-1838 - Ann CHENOWETH, widow of William CHENOWETH, deceased, relinquishes her dower in favor of provisions under her husband's will. (43)

11-5-1838 - William BERRYMAN, license to keep tavern. (44)

11-5-1838 - Arba ALEXANDER appointed guardian of Emelia JACKSON aged 11 years and Darius JACKSON aged 7 years, minor children of John JACKSON, deceased - Bond $400. (45)

11-5-1838 - David PERKINS, license to keep tavern. (45)

11-5-1838 - Naturalization - Michael FORRIS, a native of Biern, Germany makes his declaration to become citizen. Nicholas FAEZ, a native of France makes his declaration to become citizen. (46)

11-6-1838 - Henry B. THOMAS, license to keep tavern. (53)

11-6-1838 - Aaron OSMON appointed guardian of Mason CHENOWETH, aged 17 years on the 4th day of May, 1838, son of William CHENOWETH, deceased - Bond $1400. (53)

11-6-1838 - Jeremiah AYERS, license to keep tavern. (54)

11-6-1838 - Adms. of estate granted to Catharine KEPHART, widow of George KEPHART, deceased and James STEWART - Bond $200. (54)

11-6-1838 - Margaret KELLER late widow of Adam BACH, deceased, relinquishes her right to administer estate in favor of Adam SNYDER - Bond $300. (55)

12-5-1838 - Estate of Jesse J. HUDSON, deceased - Mary HUDSON appointed adms. - Bond $600. (64)

1-14-1839 - John WATT aged 17 years on 30 March 1839, Susan WATT aged 15 years on 7th July 1838, Mary WATT aged 14 years on 13 Jan. 1839 chose Elizabeth WATT as their guardian. The court thereupon appointed said Elizabeth as guardian of Sarah WATT aged 12 years on 9 Sept. 1838, Willis Watt aged 9 years on 10 Oct. 1838, Elspy WATT aged 8 years on 30 May 1839, Margaret WATT aged 6 years on 25 Jan. 1839, Samuel WATT aged 5 years on 1 May 1839, Eliza Jane WATT aged 2 years on 6 Sept, 1838; all above named children are minor heirs of William WATT, deceased. (65)

1-14-1839 - Samuel COBEAN appointed adms. of Estate of John COBEAN, deceased - Bond $600. (65)

2-1-1839 - Adam FOCHT appointed adms. of Estate of John LANDICKS, late of Union Twp. - Elicabeth LANDICK relinquishes her right to adms. estate. (66)

4-22-1839 – William BITLER appointed guardian of Ludwick LAWTIGH aged 9 years and Leah LAWTIGH aged 7 years, minor children of John LAWTIGH, deceased – Bond $300. (68)

4-22-1839 – James P. HARRIS, aged 17 years, chose Moses McCLUER his guardian – Bond $800. (72)

4-22-1839 – Will of Andrew McCOY presented – Eli STEVENSON and Frederick RUDY, executors. (73)

4-22-1839 – Adms. of Lee TURNER, deceased vs. Widow and Heirs – Petition to sell land – William J. THOMAS appointed guardian of minor defendants; Nancy, John and Lee TURNER – land described as northwest quarter Section 12, Township 5 South, Range 8 east. (73)

4-22-1839 – Moses PATTERSON appointed guardian of Mariah CUNNINGHAM aged 13 years – Bond $600. (75)

4-22-1839 – Josiah DELONG – license to keep tavern. (75)

4-22-1839 – Emelia and Darius JACKSON by guardian Arba ALEXANDER vs. James JACKSON and others – Partition – Rachel ALEXANDER assigned dower portion, 1/10th part to Emelia JACKSON, 1/10th part to Darius JACKSON, 1/10th part to James JACKSON, 1/10th part to Rebecca JACKSON, 1/10th part part to Jesse JACKSON, 1/10th part to John JACKSON, 1/10th part to Polly JACKSON, 1/10th part to Methenia RILEY and Nathan RILEY and 1/10th part to James JACKSON. (81)

4-22-1839 – William McGOOKIN, minister of the Gospel in the Presbyterian church; license to solemnize marriages. (81)

4-22-1839 – Crain VALENTINE – license to keep tavern. (86)

4-22-1839 – John HULLENBARGER and wife vs. William KEITH and others – In chancery. (86)

4-22-1839 – George CRIST – license to keep tavern. (87)

4-22-1839 – Eliza BRITTAIN widow of Joseph BRITTAIN relinquishes her right to adms.estate in favor of George RUMBAUGH – Bond $400. (87)

4-22-1839 – Naturalization – Flarance HEISTMAN a native of Baden in Europe makes declaration to become citizen. (87)

4-22-1839 – Naturalization – Adam MILLER a native of Bavaria makes declaration to become citizen. George SNEIDER a native of Hesse Cassel makes declaration to become citizen. Antonie ROTT a native of Prussia makes declaration to become citizen. John RUPPERT a native of Bavaria filed his certificate of intention dated 4-28-1834. (88)

63

4-22-1839 - Naturalization - George GUYER, Stephen VALLING and Charles LOWER natives of France make their declaration to become citizens. George Frederick ROTH a native of Biern makes his declaration to become citizen. William DAUCH a native of Saxony makes his declaration to become citizen. Earl LONG a native of Saxony makes his declaration to become a citizen. Joseph STOCKDALE a native of Great Britian makes his declaration to become citizen. (89)

4-22-1839 - Naturalization - George BERWIND, Peter ROHRBACKER, Michael BAERINEL and Michael KEIFER natives of Bavaria make their declaration to become citizen.(90)

6-15-1839 - Will of Isaac MILLER presented - George MILLER, executor - Bond $1400. (91)

6-29-1839 - Roxanna A. HARSHE and Andrew HARSHE appointed adms. of the Estate of James R. HARSHE, deceased - Bond $1000. (92)

8-9-1839 - Estate of Samuel H. JAMESON, deceased - Susanna JAMESON relinquishes right to adms. estate of her husband in favor of John JAMESON - Bond $600. (93)

8-24-1839 - Estate of William WELLER, deceased - Widow (not named) relinquishes her right to administer estate in favor of Jonathan DUTTON and Daniel C. TOMPKINS - Bond $700. (94)

9-23-1839 - Hannah RIDENOUR widow of Michael RIDENOUR, deceased, relinquishes her right to administer estate in favor of Samuel RIDENOUR and Richard VARD. (96)

9-23-1839 - Will of Asa WRIGHT presented - Jane WRIGHT, executor - Bond $600. (98)

9-23-1839 - James BRYAN appointed guardian of William H., Frances N. and Stephen T. DILTS minor heirs and children of John DILTS, deceased - Bond $400. (99)

9-23-1839 - Josiah C. COCHRUN appointed guardian of Benjamin L. COCHRUN aged 7 years and Leah Jane COCHRUN aged 6 years minor children of said Josiah C. COCHRUN. (99)

9-23-1839 - William STOCKSDALE appointed guardian of Thomas MIDDLETON aged 8 years, John MIDDLETON aged 6 years and Christopher MIDDLETON aged 4 years minor children of Christopher MIDDLETON, deceased. (99)

9-23-1839 - Jane WRIGHT, widow of Asa WRIGHT, deceased, elects to relinquish her dower right in favor of provisions under will. (99)

9-23-1839 - Marilla ALLEN widow of Harvey P. ALLEN, deceased, relinquishes her right to administer estate in favor of Edward HARTSBORN - Bond $160. (100)

9-23-1839 - William NEAL appointed adms. of the Estate of John D. WILLIAMS, deceased. (100)

9-23-1839 - Andrias MOUTER vs. Barbary KOLPH and others - In Chancery - Barbary, Michael, John and Martha KOLPH minor heirs of Martin KOLPH, deceased by Loren KENNEDY their guardian - Barbary KLOPH widow of Martin KLOPH, deceased. (103)

9-23-1839 - James McCULLOUGH and Mary CAMPBELL, executors of John CAMPBELL, deceased vs. Henry TRAEBING - In Chancery - Land described as southwest quarter of northwest quarter, Section 3, Township 3 south, Range 6 east. (106)

9-23-1839 - Rufus W. STEARNS, adms. of Samuel STATLER, deceased vs. Nancy STATLER and others - Petition to complete real contract - Petitioner asks that deed be made by him as adms. of deceased to Jacob LONG for life estate and to heirs of Abraham LONG in accordance to the last will of Abraham LONG, deceased. (107)

0-23-1839 - Estate of James A. ANDERSON, deceased - Charles BAKER appointed adms. (109)

9-23-1839 - Joseph KELLER, license to keep tavern - Samuel L. WATT license to keep tavern in town of Lafayette. - Jeremiah AYLRS, license to keep tavvern in Wapakoneta. (115)

9-23-1839 - William G. WOOLERY, license to keep tavern in Galliton - John BASE-HORE, license to keep tavern in Lima. (116)

9-23-1839 - Naturalization - Frederick MITTENDORF a native of Hanover, Germany makes his declaration to become citizen - Michael DUMBROFF a native of Bavaria, Germany makes his declaration to become citizen. (116)

9-23-1839 - Naturalization - Lewis STEIN a native of Prussia makes his declaration to become citizen - Bernard ROESSING a native of Hesse Cassel, Germany makes his declaration to become citizen - John HOFFMAN, Jr. a native of Holland makes his declaration to become citizen - Kolibahn WILHELM a native of Bayern, Germany makes his declaration to become citizen - Conrad HILL a native of Hesse Cassel, Germany makes his declaration to become citizen. (117)

9-23-1839 - Naturalization - Anthony MILLER and Henry HASENEYER natives of Hesse Cassel, Germany make their declaration to become citizens - Matthias LANAKAMMER a native of Austria makes his declaration to become citizen - Samuel LYNCH a native of Ireland makes his declaration to become citizen. (118)

9-23-1839 - Jesse HUFFMAN vs. Abner SMITH and Isaac SMITH - Petition for Partition - Jesse HUFFMAN to have five equal 1/8ths parts - Abner SMITH to have three equal 1/8th parts - (119)

9-23-1839 - Joseph CROSLEY appointed guardian of Julian LANE aged 11 years and 10 months, Samuel LANE aged 9 years and 10 months, Joseph LANE aged 8 years, Ross LANE aged 6 years, minor children of John LANE, deceased - Bond $200. (120)

9-23-1839 - Alexander COON appointed guardian of Nathan COON aged 3 years, minor son of Alexander COON and heir at law of Nathan MILLS, deceased. (122)

9-23-1839 - George COON appointed guardian of Squire MILLS aged 15 years, son of Nathan MILLS, deceased. (122)

9-23-1839 - Fanny LITTLE widow of George LITTLE, deceased relinquishes right to administer estate to Elmer HARTSBORN. (122)

10-10-1839 - Will of Jacob WILLIAMS presented with Samuel WILLIAMS, executor - Sarah WILLIAMS, widow of Jacob, relinquishes her dower in favor of provisions under will. (124)

10-10-1839 - William E. WILLIAMS aged 17 years and Lydia Ann WILLIAMS aged 15 years chose Sarah WILLIAMS their guardian and Sarah WILLIAMS was also appointed guardian of Thomas WILLIAMS aged 11 years on 26 August last, Rebecca M. Williams aged 9 years on 10 August last and Ethaline WILLIAMS aged 7 years on 19 July last, minor children and heirs of Jacob WILLIAMS, deceased. (124)

ASHLAND COUNTY, OHIO - DEATH RECORDS 1867-1869

The following records were copied from "Death Record 1." Pages on which record may
be found are given in parenthesis. An asterisk(*) denotes duplicated record. Records
were often duplicated because they were reported by doctors, ministers and assessors;
and also reported by a family member. Abbreviations used are:-
d-died; a-age; m-married; s-single; w-widow/widower; pd-place of death; r-residence;
pb-place of birth; rep-reported by. If residence and place of death were the same,
only place of death has been given. Persons 40 yrs. of age and over.

WARNER, John - d 5-22-1867; a 67-7-5; m; pd Lake twp.; pd -----(2)
SCHUMUKER, Magdalena - d 9-25-1867; a 88y 22d; m; pd Montgomery twp.; pd Pa.(2)
McGUIRE, Mary - d 9-10-1867; a 71y; m; pd Montgomery twp.; pb ----(2)
McGUIRE, Hugh - d 9-13-1867; a 82y; w; pd Montgomery twp.; pb ----(2)
STAFFORD, Samuel - d ---1867; a 53y; pd----; pb----(2)
TILKINS, Mrs. - d 8-29-1867; a 83y; w; pd Ashland Co. Infirmary; pb-----(2)
HEARST, John - d 9-19-1867; a 73-7-5; m; pd Ruggles twp; pb Cumberland Co. Pa. (2)
RUSEH, Maria - d 9-17-1867; a 61y; m; pd Lake twp.; pb German. (2)
MYERS, Mary - d 8-8-1867; a 63-2-15; m; pd Montgomery twp.; pb Lancaster Co. Pa.(2)
BECHTEL, Martin - d 8-4-1867; a 80-10-8; m; pd Green twp.; pb Lakes twp. (2)
BARNHART, George - d 8-21-1867; a 81-5-14; w; pd Loudenville; pb Bavaria; r Madison
          Co., Ohio. (2)
HOY, Charles - d 9-20-1867; a 78-6-12; m; pd Stephenson Co., Ill; pb Washington Co.,
          Pa; r Jackson twp.; rep. Dawson Hoy. (2)
PHELPS, Elisha - d 11-5-1867; a 63-6-6; m; pd Troy twp; pb New York. (2)
BONEBRIGHT, Mariah D. - d 9-18-1867; a 79y 8d; w; pd Mifflin twp.; pb Adams Co., Pa.;
          rep. Wm. Bonebright. (2)
BOWERMASTER, Frederick - d 12-24-1867; a 87-6-8; w; pd Mifflin twp.; pb-----(2)
SMILIE, John A. - d 12-1-1867; a 62-3-20; m; pd Vermillion twp.; pb Washington Co.,
          Pa.; rep. Richard Smilie. (2)
McKINLEY, Samuel - d 12-13-1867; a 71y 2m; w; pd Mohecan twp.; pb Washington Co.,
          Pa.; rep. Benj. McKinley. (2)
HEFFNER, Henry - d 12-14-1867; a 75-2-7; m; pd Montgomery twp.; pb-----(4)
FULLER, Ephraim B. - 12-23-1867; a 68y 5m; m; pd Loudenville; pb Ashland Co. (4)
LYBOLT, Mary Ann - d 12-24-1867; a 56y; m; pd Hanover twp.; pb Ashland Co. (4)
GRAHAM, M - d 10-7-1867; a 70y; w; pd Perrysville; pb Ashland Co. (4)
O'HARROW, Mary - d 11-1-1867; a 72y; w; pd McCay; pb Ashland Co. (4)
SIMPSON, Samuel - d 11-28-1867; a 74y 2d; m; pd Richland Co., Ohio; pb Beaver Co.,
          Pa. (4)
SANDERS, Mary - d 8-12-1867; a 64y; m; pd Lake twp.; pb Pa. (4)
GUYER, Mary - d 12-19-1867; a 75-1-5; w; pd Sullivan O.; pd Greensburg, Pa. (4)
HOUSER, Jacob - d 10-31-1867; a 77-10-25; m; pd Ashland Co.; pb Pa.; r. Mohecan
          twp. (4)
HOUSER, Sarah - d 11-25-1867; a 62-11-26; w; pd Ashland Co.; pb Pa.; r. Mohecan
          twp. (4)
VAN NIMAN, Jemima - d 12-18-1867; a 74-3-10; w; pd Ashland Co.; pb New Jersey;
          r. Defiance Co., Ohio. (4)
SMITH, _____(not given) - d 12-1-1867; a 68-3-7; s; pd Green twp.; pb Pa.;
          r. Perrysville, Ohio. (4)
FORNEY, Catharine - d 12-16-1867; a 69y; 2; pd Orange twp,; pb Pa. (6)
KIBLER, George - d 10-22-1867; a 72-5-19; m; pd Hanover twp.; pb Pa.; rep. Adam
          Kibler. (8)

RICKETS, Christopher - d 1-26-1868; a 76-7-6; m; pd Orange twp.; pb Washington Co.,
         Pa. (4)
NORRIS, Coffman - d 2-4-1868; a 60-9-26; m; pd Milton twp.; pb Pa. (4)
SHISLER, Henry - d 2-8-1868; a 83-5-23; m; pd Jackson twp.; pb New Jersey. (4)
TREEBORN, John - d 2-16-1868; a 90y; pd Clear Creek twp.; pb Donegal, Ireland. (4)
BOWMAN, Catherine - d 2-27-1868; a 71-2-9; pb Pa.; r. Clear Creek twp. (4)
HEFFNER, Jacob - d 3-14-1868; a 82-5-20; m; pd Orange twp.; pb Pa. (6)
SNYDER, Mary - d 3-10-1868; a 77-2-15; w; pd Orange twp.; pb Pa. (6)
COFFIN, James Parker - d 3-23-1868; a 79y; m; pd Milton twp.; pb ----(6)
FIKE, Elizabeth - d 1-1-1868; a 76y 11m; m; pd Milton twp.; pb Pa. (6)
OFFINEER, James - d 3-29-1868; a 71-4-10; m; pd Mohecan twp.; pb Hardy Co., Va. (6)
SIGLER, Sarah - d 3-1-1868; a 75y; pd Vermillion twp.; pb Pa. (6)
SLOCUM, Mary - d 1-6-1868; a 76y 7m; w; pd Ashland; pb Hartford. (6)
COFFIN, J. B. - d 3-22-1868; a 61y 3m; pd Ashland; pb Troy, N. Y. (6)
YEAMAN, Ann - d 3-3-1868; a 80-1-1; w; pd Richland Co.; pb Pa. (6)
WICKS, Joseph - d 5-5-1868; a 42y 28d; m; pd Jackson twp.; pb Ohio. (8)
STOCKMAN, Sarah - d 2-16-1868; a 71-6-19; s; pd Loudonville; pb New Jersey. (8)
LUCAS, John - d 4-18-1868; a 62-8-2; m; pd Perry twp.; pb ----(8)
LAIRD, Mathew - d 5-17-1868; a 67-10-13; m; pd Hayesville; pb Ireland. (8)
EIGHINGER, Phillip - d 6-9-1868; a 81-8-27; m; pd Vermillion twp.; pd Pa.; rep.
         Benj. Eighlinger. (8)
MY ERS, Jane - d 6-30-1868; a 57-7-27; m; pd Jackson; pb Ohio; rep. Jno Myers. (8)
MARTIN, Phillip - d 3-5-1868; a 48y; m; pd Ashland Co.; pb Pa. (8)
BUCHANAN, Rebecca - d 4-9-1868; a 50y; pd Albion; pb Pa. (8)
EHERHART, Joshua - d 8-4-1868; a 52-3-20; m; pd Lake twp.; pb Huntington, Pa. (8)
BIDDLE, Martha - d 9-5-1868; a 81y; w; pd Mohecan twp.; pb New Jersey. (8)
CULLER, Joseph - d 6-25-1868; a 41-5-16; m; pd Ashland Co.; pb Ashland Co. (8)
ROY, William d 4-24-1868; a 61-2-14; pd Richland Co.; pb Richland Co. (8)
GLENN, John - d 5-14-1868; a 73-6-10; w; pd Mohecan twp. pb ----- (8)
GLENN, John S. - d 6-1-1868; a 47-6-22; s; pd Mohecan twp.; pb ----(8)
MOULTRIP, ___(not given) - d. 6-25-1868; a 70y; pd Perrysville; pb New York. (8)
BOYD, Margaret - d 6-14-1868; a 62-11-11; w; pd Savannah; pb Beaver Co., Pa.;
         r. Darlington, Pa. (8)
GROSSCUP, Paul - d 9-17-1868; a 84-7-22; m; pd Milton twp.; pb Berks Co., Pa. (8)
SILL, Jacob - d 9-27-1868; a 45-7-4; m; pd Milton twp.; pb Bedford Co., Pa.;
         parents, Samuel Sill; rep. Mrs. Elizabeth Sill. (8)
SHEMSHIMER, Jacob - d 7-14-1868; a 60y; m; pd Ashland, O.; pb ----(8)
FIGLEY, Nancy - d 7-21-1868; a 84y; w; pd Montgomery twp.; pb ----(10)
CLARK, George - d 9-17-1868; a 68-5-29; w; pd Montgomery twp.; pb ---- (10)
BACON, Comfort - d 9-23-1868; a 89y 2m; w; pd Milton twp.; pb Hartford, Ct. (10)
SCOTT, Eliza - d 7-28-1868; a 60y; w; pd Loudenville; pb Pa. (10)
SWANGER, Jacob d 8-7-1868; a 50y; s; pd Co. Infirmary; pb ------- (10)
SWINEBARGER, Catharine - d 9-5-1868; a 43y 5d; m; pd Perry twp; pb Perry twp. (10)
CUMMINGS, Jno. - d 8-24-1868; a 52y 7m; m; pd Sullivan twp.; pb New York. (10)
YATES, Joseph - d 8-6-1868; a 48y 15d; m; pd Richland Co.; pb Jefferson Co., Pa.(10)
SELBY, Thomas - d 9-20-1868; a 86y; m; pd Ashland; pb ---- (10)
WREFF, Rebecca - d 8-13-1868; a 67-8-10; w; pd Perrysville; pb Pa. (10)
SHARR, Robt. - d 6-16-1868; a 50-4-16; m; pd Ruggles twp.; pb Richland Co.;
         r. Clear Creek twp. (10)

EBERHART, Joshua - d 8-4-1868; a 52-3-18; m; pd Lake twp.; pb Huntinton Co. Pa.(10)*
RHAMY, Mary - d 8-8-1868; a 52-9-13; m; pd Mohecan twp.; pb Va. (10)
MORRER, Sarah - d 9-12-1868; a 75-9-5; m; pd Mohecan twp.; pb Bedford Co. Pa. (10)
McKIBBEN, Hugh Baird - d 9-26-1868; a 64-4-18; m: pd Clear Creek twp.; pb Beaver Co.
    Pa. (10)*
RUPERT, John Adam - d 10-23-1868; a 74y 22d; m; pd Jackson twp.; pb Germany; rep.
    Adam Rupert. (10)
KRABILL, Samuel - d Oct. 1868; a 82y; m; pd Milton twp.; pb ----(10)
FULMER, John - d 11-9-1868; a 83y 5d; m; pd Orange twp.; pb Northampton Co. Pa.(10)
HUNTER, Catharine - d 9-13-1868; a 60y; m; pd Green twp.; pb not known. (12)
BOON, Daniel - d 11-26-1868; a 75y 2m; w; pd Lake twp.; pb Maryland. (12)
McKIBBEN, Hugh B. - d 9-26-1868; a 64y 4m; m; pd Clear Creek twp.; pb Beaver Co.,
    Pa.; rep. Robt. McKibben. (12)*
RIBLET, Henry - d 11-24-1868; a76-4-8; pd Hanover twp.; pb Pa.; rep. Levi Riblet.(12)
MYERS, John - d 12-3-1868; a 74-4-15; m; pd Orange twp.; pb Carrol Co. Md. (12)
HOKE, Catharine - d 9-26-1868; a 70y; s; pd Ashland Co.; pb Pa. (12)
ZIMMERMAN, Elisabeth - d 5-7-1868; a 41-3-28; m; pd Montgomery twp; pb Ashland Co.(12)
GAVER, Adam - d 12-21-1868; a 80-4-2; m; pd Mohecan twp.; pb Ashland Co.; rep.
    Jacob Gaver. (12)
SIGLER, John - d 9-10-1868; a 72-6-14; w; pd Vermillion twp.; pb Maryland. (12)
STAHL, Adam - d 12-14-1868; a 55y 3m; pd Milton twp.; pb Ashland Co. (12)
MYKRANTZ, Susan - d 11-26-1868; a 48-8-12; m; pd Clear Creek twp.; pb---- (12)
GRABILL, John - d 10-11-1868; a 82-7-4; m; pd Milton twp.; pb Bavaria. (12)
BRUBAKER, John - d 10-11-1868; a 75-11-10; m; pd Ashland Co.; pb Pa. (12)
RILEY, Levi - d. 12-21-1868; a 46y 8m; m; pd Hayesville, O.; pb Perrsville, O.(12)
STEPHENS, George - d 12-17-1868; a 42y; s; pd Green twp.; pb ------ (12)
BAIN, Anna - d 12-17-1868; a 68-6-24; w; pd Clear Creek twp.; pb Scotland. (14)
CLARK, Mary Ann - d 9-27-1868; a 53-3-10; m; pd Sullivan twp.; pb Winchester, Va.(14)
PRESTON, Samith - d 8-20-1868; a 55y 6m; pd Huntington; pb New York. (14)
WHEELER, Sarah - d 12-24-1868; a 43y 8m; m; pd Rochester; pb Michigan. (14)
BACHELDOR, Mrs. - d. 8-23-1868; a 64y; m; pd Ashland Co.; pb ------ (16)
FRETZ, Catharine - d 2-28-1868; a 64-1-28; m; pd Green twp.; pb Berks Co. Pa.(16)
LEPLE, Henry - d 8-6-1868; a 78-9-24; m; pd Monroe twp.; pd Pa. (16)
PECK, Martin - d 1-12-1869; a 73y 6m; m; pd Ashland Co.; pb Lancaster Co. Pa.;
    r. Troy twp. (12)
KOSHT, Margaret B . - d 1-14-1869; a 69y 3m; m; pd Montgomery twp.; pb Cumberland
    Co., Pa. (12)
GREGG, John - d 1-15-1869; a 59y; m; pd Clear Creek twp.; pb Ireland; r. Ill. (14)
BAKER, Andrew - d 2-7-1869; a 44-6-9; s; pd Orange twp.; pb German; r. Mansfield.(14)
MURRAY, Sarah - d 2-14-1869; a 64y; s; pd----; pb Westmoreland Co., Pa. (14)
CAMPBELL, Ann - d 2-7-1869; a 77y; m; pd Vermillion twp.; pb Ireland. (14)
CAMPBELL, James - d 2-17-1869; a 87y; m; pd Vermillion twp.; pb Ireland, (14)
WALTERS, George W. - d 2-13-1869; a 62-11-7; m; pd Clear Creek twp.; pb Lancaster
    Co., Pa.; rep. George W. Walters, Jr. (14)
KEISTER, Samuel - d 2-24-1869; a 58y; s; pd Hayesville; pb ------ (14)
GREINER, Elizabeth - d 2-13-1869; a 62-1-28; pd Ashland; pb Lancaster Co., Pa.;
    rep. Jno. Greiner. (14)
STEM (or STEIN), Elizabeth - d 3-21-1869; a 71-5-15; pd Savannah; pb Pa. rep.
    E. A. Stein (?). (14)

STEM (or STEIN), David - d 3-18-1869; a 80y 18d; m; pd Savannah; pb Westmoreland
    Co. Pa. (14)
METCALF, Sarah - d 3-13-1869; a 49-1-4; m; pd Mohecan twp.; pb Carlyle, Pa. (14)
WOODRED, John - d 3-1-1869; a 64y 8d; m; pd Hanover twp.; pb N.Y. State. (14)
STUMP, Francis - d 1-23-1869; a 65y 5m; m; pd Ashland Co.; pb Berks Co., Pa.;
    r. Perry twp. (14)
BAUM, Adam - d 3-21-1869; a 54-11-28; m; pd Ashland; pb ---- (16)
RYALL, Phebe - d 4-5-1869; a 71y(?); w; pd Ashland; pb Pa. (16)
OGDEN, Rebecca - d 3-17-1869; a 79-6-3; s; pd Troy twp.; pb Lancaster Co. Pa. (16)
NELSON, Robert - d 6-7-1869; a 56-4-7; m; pd Milton twp.; pb Northampton Co. Pa.(16)
JOHNSON, James - d 6-13-1869; a 61y; s; pd Clear Creek twp.; pb Ohio. (16)
KAGEY, Nancy - d 3-16-1869; a 68-3-1; m; pd Mifflin twp.; pb Pa. (16)
KARGER, Catharine - d 4-11-1869; a 79-8-13; w; pd Milton twp.; pb Pa. (16)
BAUM, Mary - d 3-9-1869; a 67-8-8; m; pd Vermillion twp.; pb Pa. (16)
STANFER, Abraham - d 3-24-1869; a 79-4-24; m; pd Vermillion twp.; pb ----(16)
COFFMAN, John - d 8-4-1869; a 56y; m; pd Jackson twp.; pb Pa. (16)
COWIE, Christina - d May 1869; a 45y; m; pd Savannah; pb ---- (16)
STAHL, Catharine - d 9-6-1869; a 80-1-8; w; pd Clear Creek twp.; pb Pa.; rep.
    Dan'l Stahl. (18)
YOUNG, Michael - d 9-20-1869; a 69-6-18; m; pd Vermillion twp.; pb Pa. (18)
FRANTZ, George - d 7-3-1869; a 87y 6m; pd ----; pb Lancaster Co., Pa. (18)
GRENDLE, George - d 7-22-1869; a 60y; m; pd Perry twp.; pb Lancaster Co. Pa. (18)
SIMELTON(?), Sarah - d 10-4-1869; a 65-4-7; w; pd Decalb Co. Ia.; pb Pa.;
    r. Ashland Co. (18)
FOSS, Samuel - d 10-11-1869; a 81-9-5; m; pd Ashland Co.; pb Lancaster Co., Pa.(18)
HESS, Charity - d 11-3-1869; a 51-7-16; m; pd Ashland Co.; pb Lancaster Co.,Pa.(18)
STAUFER, Barbara - d 11-3-1869; a 46-9-16; w; pd Hayesville; pb Tuerkheim, Germany.
    (18)
INHOFF, John - d 11-11-1869; a 71y 5d; m; pd Milton twp.; pb Switzerland. (18)
WOODBURN, John - d 3-25-1869; a 76-8-8; m; pd Milton twp.; pb Washington Co.,Pa.(18)
ANDERSON, James - d 12-6-1869; a 67y 2m; m; pd Milton twp.; pb Washington Co.Pa.(18)
WEDDELL, Daniel - d 11-3-1869; a 62-2-22; m; pd Milton twp.; pb Westermoreland Co.,
    Pa. (18)
BAUM, Samuel - d 4-16-1869; a 64-7-18; m; pd Milton twp.; pb Lancaster Co., Pa.(18)
BAUM, Catharine - d. 2-29-1869; a 64y 8m; m; pd Milton twp.; pb Lancaster Co., Pa.(18)
HAZLETTE, Mary - d 4-12-1869; a 62y; m; pd Milton twp.; pb Maryland. (18)
SNYDER, Lydia - d 5-18-1869; a 57-1-2; m; pd Ruggles twp.; pb Northunberland Co.
    Pa. (18)
KIRKTON, Jane - d 8-16-1869; a 57y; m; pd Ruggles twp.; pb Scotland. (18)
BOYD, Thomas - d 6-18-1869; a 82y 8m; m; pd Vermillion twp.; pb Cumberland Co. Pa.
    (20)
YOUNG, Michael - d 10-20-1869; a 62y; m; pd Vermillion twp.; pb Union Co. Pa.(20)*
SHENBARGER, Baltzer - d 11-28-1869; a 90-4-8; m; pd Vermillion twp.; pb York Co. Pa.
    (20)
PETERS, Rebecca - d 7-20-1869; a 42y; m; pd Orange twp.; pb Orange twp. (20)
BURTON, Andrew W. - d - 7-12-1869; a 49-3-28; m; pd Montgomery twp.; pb------
    parents Jacob Burton and Hannah Perrywell (or Peny well); (note:
    notation "taken from tombstone"). (20)

70

JOHNSON, James - d 6-13-1869; a 61y; s; pd Savannah; pb Ireland. (20)*
PAXTON, Andrew - d 3-18-1869; a 64y; m; pd Savannah; pb Washington Co., Pa. (20)
SWASICK, James - d 12-16-1869; a 97y 9m; w; pd Green twp.; pb Pa. (20)
CASTOR, Anna - d. 8-18-1869; a 73y 10m; m; pd Green twp.; pb Pa. (20)
MOULTRIP, Rosannah - d 7-24-1869; a 42-3-20; m; pd Loudenville; pb New York. (22)
RUST, Stephen - d 9-20-1869; a 73y; w; pd Loudenville; pb New York. (22)
BURD, Catharine - d 10-18-1869; a 71y; w; pd Lake twp.; pb Tenn. (22)
REINHART, John G. - d 8-16-1869; a 82y; m; pd Lake twp.; pb Germany. (22)
WOLF, Mary - d 8-1-1869; ae 46-2-25; m; pd Lake twp. - pb Germany. (22)
DOOR, Valentine - d 12-30-1869; a 72y; m; pd Hanover twp.; pb Germany. (22)
SIMONTON, Benjamin - d 11-19-1869; a 43y; m; pd Montgomery twp.; pb Pa. (22)
YEATER, Samuel - d 11-10-1869; a 48-5-16; m; pd Montgomery twp.; pb Mifflin Co.,
          Pa. (22)
HESS, Charity - d 11-3-1869; a 51-7-16; m; pd Montgomery twp.; pb Pa. (22)*

NOTE:- ASHLAND COUNTY, OHIO, formed 1846 from WAYNE COUNTY, OHIO.

Persons 50 years of age and over. m-married; w-widow(er); s-single; c-colored

Name	Date of Death	Age	Marital Status	Place of Death	Place of Birth
WATT, George	8-16-1867	63-10-20	m.	Ames twp.	Ames twp.
RANDALL, Ann Celia	11-17-1867	69y 5m	m.	Athens twp.	Providence, R. I.
SILVUS, Mary	11-20-1867	52-4-16	m.	Alexander twp.	Boston, Mass.
	Father: Leonard JARVIS				
WITHIM, Martha	12-19-1867	70y 6m	m.	Lodi twp.	Washington Co., O.
	Father: Manul SERRLIN				
CANNY, John	1-2-1868	54y 2m	m.	Lee twp.	Lee twp.
	Parents: George CANNY & Polly BOMAN				
WILKS, Farmer	11-8-1867	88-11-18	w.	Waterloo twp.	Fairfield Co.Ct.
FOX, Mickiel	2-5-1868	50y	m.	Infirmary	Ireland
SHANON, Nuton	11-27-1867	50y	m.	Infirmary	Ohio
STEVENS, Thomas	12-13-1867	96y	m.	Infirmary	Main(e)
TIPPE, Susan	11-28-1867	81y	w.	Infirmary	Ames twp.
FULLER, Jedadiah	1-7-1868	79y 3m	m.	Coolville	Middletown,Mass.
	Parents: David & Debby FULLER				
BARTLETT, Francis	3-10-1868	71y 13d	m.	Coolville	Plymouth, Mass.
BERRY, Sarah	3-14-1868	71-11-11	w.	New England	Winchester, Va.
FROST, Heman	6-7-1868	73y	m.	Rome twp.	New York
	Parents: Abner & Bulah FROST				
MICKEL, Andrew	7-25-1868	50-11-1	m.	Troy twp.	Cohara, N. York
WOODARD, Ichabord Sr.	6-2-1868	85-7-20	m.	Hocking Co.O.	New York
	Parents: William & Martha WOODARD				
PERRY, William	4-21-1868	73y	m.	York twp.	Delaware
	Parents: John & Mary Perry				
PRINDLE, Daniel	9-8-1868	83-3-16	m.	Hocking Co.O.	Connecticut
	Parents: David & Jemima PRINDLE				
LAMB, Nancy	9-27-1868	72-7-18	w.	Athens twp	Huntington, Pa.
	Parents: John & Nancy ARMITAGE				
FRENCH, John	10-7-1868	94-9-18	m.	Waterloo twp	Fauquier Co. Va.
WILSON, Barbara	11-16-1868	55-10-14	m.	Athens twp	Washington Co.Pa.
	Parents: Daniel & Catharine HERROLD				
WALDEN, John O.	12-8-1868	61y 5m	-	Troy twp.	Jefferson Co. O.
	Parents: Francis & Mary WALDEN				
GOODSPEAD, Clarrissa	2-1-1869	64-1-9	m.	Athens	Barnstable, Mass.
BRADFORD, Clara	11-18-1868	50y 9m	m.(c)	Columbus	Fauquier Co. Va.
TUBBS, Laura	9-26-1869	66-8-25	w.	Troy twp.	New York
GROCE, Lewis Sr.	2-7-1869	93-9-4	m.	Waterloo twp.	Germany
SPURBACK, Eleanor	4-3-1869	88-4-8	m.	Dover twp.	Bedford Co. Pa.
	Father: John SMITH				
SMITH, William	8-18-1869	66y	w.	York twp.	Virginia
	Parents: Daniel & Mary SMITH				
BROWN, Alexander	8-5-1869	66y 6m	m.	Vinton Co. O.	- - - - - -
	Parents: William & Sarah BROWN				
PICKETT, Elizabeth	11-16-1869	70-7-16	m.	York twp.	Virginia
	Parents: Nathan & Mary BENJAMIN				
DEAN, Mariah	7-15-1869	66-3-19	m.	Athens	- - - - - -
	Parents: G. & Sarah FOSTER				

Persons 50 years of age and over. m–married; w–widow(er); s–single; c–colored

Name	Date of Death	Age	Marital Status	Place of Death	Place of Birth
HOPPER, Morris	11-19-1869	54y 4m	m.	Athens	Cincinnati
Parents: Aaron & Mary HOPPER					
SMITH, Lucy P.	4-20-1869	55y 7m	m.	Athens	Athens
Parents: A. & Sally STEDMAN					
GREEN, Mary R.	3-27-1869	75y	s.	Athens	Providence, R. I.
Parents: Malachi & C. GREEN					
WILSON, John	11-11-1869	67-5-16	m.	Athens	Eart, Virginia
Parents: Thomas & Sarah WILSON					
DRAKE, Daniel	6-1-1869	64-1-5	m.	Alexander twp.	Athens twp.
DILLINGER, Thomas	9-28-1869	54-5-11	s.	Lodi twp.	New Jersey
DILLINGER, Mathias	9-27-1867	84-8-22	m.	Lodi twp.	Pennsylvania
FROST, Leonard	9-28-1869	52-1-16	–	Lodi twp.	Meigs Co. Ohio
COLE, Elizabeth	11-22-1869	60y	w.	Carthage	Pennsylvania
LOTTRIDGE, Abigail	10-28-1869	88-4-9	w.	Carthage	New York
JEFFERS, Eleva	8-12-1869	57-4-28	m.	Wert, Va.	Pennsylvania
STOUT, Elvina	8-17-1869	71-8-20	w.	Carthage	—————
DEAN, Jeptha	12-2-1869	84y	w.	Carthage	Connecticut
PLACE, Sarah	11-22-1869	72y	w.	Decatur twp.	Virginia
WINDSOR, Joseph	8-11-1869	50-1-15	m.	Rome twp.	Athens Co.
DENTON, John	7-26-1869	60y 4m	w.	Lee twp.	Lee twp.
GARDNER, Mary	11-13-1869	75-7-11	m.	Trimble	Germany
JUNIPER, George	8-23-1869	69-5-11	m.	Trimble	Maryland
WILSON, Henry	11-13-1869	72y	w.	- - - -	Pennsylvania
WATERMAN,,Betsey	9-16-1869	64y 4m	s.	Troy twp.	New York
Parents: Samuel & Lydia WATERMAN					
COOLY, Abigail	5-17-1869	72-3-20	m.	Troy twp.	Vermont
Parents: Jacob & Abigail COOLY					
TUBBS, Laura**	9-27-1869	66-9-27	w.	Troy twp.	State of N.
JONES, William	10-26-1869	78-8-26	w.	Troy twp.	Massachusetts
Parents: Jacob & Sophia JONES					
DAVIS, David	12-20-1869	72-9-12	m.	Troy twp.	Virginia
Parents: Cornelius & Margaret DAVIS					
PICKETT, Elizabeth**	11-16-1869	69-7-28	m.	York twp.	Wheeling, Va.
TREMAIN, Susan	5-10-1869	(Supposed	m.	York twp.	- - - - -
		(to be 105 years old			
WOLLETT, Ann Eliza	12-16-1869	59-6-6	m.	York twp.	Bedford, Pa.
Parents: J. & Mary DAVIS					
ALLEN, David	5-25-1869	64y	w.	York twp.	Columbiana, Ohio
Parents: James & Orpha ALLEN					
WASHBURN, Erastus	1-8-1869	77y	m.	Infirmary	New York
DORRIS, Mary	1-11-1869	70y	m.	Dover twp.	Millfield, Ohio
CLESTER, Samuel N.	8-14-1869	54y	m.	Dover twp.	- - - - -
WIRT, Frederick	5-16-1869	78y 8m	m.	Waterloo	Germany
ELLIOTT, John	9-30-1869	51y	m.	- - - -	- - - - -
SHANNON, Charles	6-1-1869	84y 7m	w.	Waterloo	Pennsylvania
NINNEGAR, Martha	Oct. 1869	76y	w.	Canann twp.	Switzerland

**Repeated in original records

73

ATHENS COUNTY, OHIO - DEATH RECORDS 1870-1871

The following records were taken from Death Record 1 as found in the Probate Court at the court house in Athens (1969). They include only records for persons 40 years and over. Residence is same as place of death unless stated. Abbreviations: d=died; a=age; m=married; w=widow or widower; s=single; pd=place of death; pb= place of birth; res=residence.

WALKER, Mary - d 1-20-1870; a 85-2-4; w; pd Athens; pb Tennessee; parents C. & Mary Lotspeach

PALMER, Nathaniel - d 5-15-1870; a 53y; m; pd Carthage; pb Jefferson Co., Ohio.

YEARGER, James - d 2-1-1870; a 74y 1m; w; pd Rome; pb Pennsylvania.

CRAMPTON, Robert - d 3-5-1870; a 75y; w; pd Rome twp.; pb Pennsylvania.

MOSS, Matilda - d 2-19-1870; a 69y 10m; w; pd Rome twp.; pb Athens Co.

BEAN, Biscoe - d 3-11-1870; a 83-11-19; m; pd Rome twp.; pb Hardy Co., Virginia.

KING, Elizabeth - d 3-30-1870; a 61y 7m; w; pd (not given) pb Pennsylvania; father, _____ Knight.

BROWN, Polly - d 4-25-1870; a 90-6-7; w; pd Ames twp.; pb Mass.; father, Noah Farem.

JONSTON, Henry - d 4-29-1870; a 90y 10m; m; pd Ames twp.; pb Pennsylvania parents, Thomas and Nancy Jonston.

GOENS, Wilson - d 4-19-1870; a 75y; s; colored; pd Ames twp.; pb Virginia; parents, Joshua and Winny Goens.

MOORE, Mordica - d 1-28-1870; a 81-5-19; w; pd Trimble; pb Maryland.

FEATHERSTON, Joseph - d 4-7-1870; a 85-2-13; m; pd Troy twp.; pb Maryland, parents, Thomas and Margaret Fetherston.

KNOWLES, William - d 1-21-1870; a 80-9-18; m; pd Troy twp.; pb Connecticut; parents, James and Martha Knowles.

THOMPSON, Elizabeth - d 4-16-1870; a 62-11-22; w; pd York twp.; pb Athens Co.; parents, Joseph and Sarah Carpenter.

DAVIS, Elnor E. - d 2-28-1870; a 85y; w; pd Canaan twp.; pb Maryland.

FUNK, Adam - d 1-2-1871; a 50-11-14; m; pd Bern twp.; pb Westmoreland, Pa.

EVMER, John - d 2-18-1871; a 85-3-8; m; pd Ames twp.; pb New York.

BROWN, Mary E. - d 11-26-1870; a 61-11-26; m; pd Ames twp.; pb Mass.; parents, Nathan Dean and Mary Thoyer.

BETHEL, Nancy - d 7-13-1870; a 75y; m; pd Trimble twp.; pb Hampshire Co., Va.

McVAY, Elizabeth - d 8-24-1870; a 82y 6m; w; pd Lee twp.; pb Washington Co.; father, _____ Mackey.

ROBINSON, John - d 2-27-1871; a 77y; w; pd Albany; pb-----(not given)

KNOWLTON, Sidney - d 10-7-1870; a 59y; m; pd Lee twp.; pb Athens.

BODWELL, Enoch - d 12-3-1870; a 77-1-3; w; pd Lodi twp.; pb------(not given).

BLAZIER, Susan - d 12-9-1870; a 65y 21d; m; pd Lodi twp.; pb Pennsylvania.

BURSON, James C. - d 12-2-1870; a 68-11-15; m; pd Lodi twp.; pb Virginia.

RICHEY, Benjamine - d 8-20-1870; a 81-6-7; m; pd Lodi twp.; pb Pennsylvania.

RUSSEL, Ann H. - d 9-6-1870; a 71y; m; pd Troy twp.; pb Jefferson Co., Ohio.

ELRED, Ann - d 7-4-1870; a 74y; m; pd Troy twp.; pb Pennsylvania.

GRIFFIN, Daniel - d 3-8-1871; a 55y 1m; m; pd Troy twp.; pb Athens.

HAWK, Susan E. - d 12-20-1870; a 62-3-20; m; pd Waterloo twp.; pb New Jersey.

WERT, Anna M. - d 2-25-1871; a 70y 10d; w; pd Waterloo twp.; pb Germany.

BROOKS, Joseph - d 2-5-1871; a 61y; m; pd Waterloo twp.; pb Waterloo twp.

McCOY, Daniel - d 4-17-1871; a 58-3-25; w; pd Waterloo twp.; pb Washington Co., Pennsylvania.

MINEAR, Philip - d 8-2-1870; a 51y; m; pd Waterloo twp.; pb Virginia.

ALEY, Fanny - d 9-14-1870; a 68-11-22; w; pd Yellow Springs; pb Delaware Co.,
    N.Y.; father, _____ Beardsley.
HIGGINS, Michael - d 6-28-1870; a 74-8-9; m; pd Athens; pb Westmoreland, Penn.;
    parents, Andrew and Sarah Higgins.
SHERIDAN, Nancy - d 10-5-1870; a 60-2-14; m; pd Cannan twp.; pb Ireland.
SANDERSON, Margaret - d 9-7-1870; a 64-6-1; m; pd Athens; pb Scotland.
BARROWS, Orange - d 9-27-1870; a 65-7-27; m; pd Rome twp.; pb Rome twp.
SMITH, Margaret - d 1-2-1871; a 59-4-7; w; pd Rome twp.; pb Rome twp.
FULLER, Nancy - d 10-27-1870; a 73y; pd Dover twp.; pb Maine.
GREEN, Caroline - d 5-29-1871; a 59y; pd Infirmary; pb Mass.
MORGAN, Benjamine - d 2-21-1871; a 108 years; pd Infirmary; pb Pennsylvania.
CANFIELD, Wm - d 7-6-1870; a 66y; pd Infirmary; pb Pennsylvania.
CAGG, John - d 4-29-1870; a 81y; pd Infirmary; pb Pennsylvania.
JANER, John - d 5-27-1871; a 67y; pd Infirmary; pb Ohio.
DUNCAN, Mary - d 3-25-1871; a 84y; pd Infirmary; pb Ireland.
ADAMS, Catharine - d 9-30-1870; a 53y; pd Infirmary; pb Virginia.
SIX, Deborah - d 1-2-1871; a 65y; pd Dover twp.; pb ------(not given).
SOUTH, Martha - d 7-20-1870; a 51y; pd Dover twp.; pb------(not given).
HARRISON, John - d 10-16-1870; a 53y 7m; m; pd Nelsonville; pb England.
THOMPSON, Mary N. - d 7-25-1870; a 54-7-4; m; pd York twp.; pb-------(not given)
SACIA, Modisto - d 2-28-1871; a 58y; m; pd Nelsonville; pb France.

ATHENS COUNTY, OHIO - POWER OF ATTORNEYS

Sept. 18, 1810 - Stephen Dean, Samuel Adams and Elexth Adams of Whitestown in
the County of Oneida, State of New York, Brethren and Sister of Silas Dean late
of the town of Ames, supposed to be heirs of one-half of estate left by said
Silas Dean, dec'd, do make constitute and grant Reuben Moore of the town of
Chathan, County of Columbia, State of New York, our true and lawful attorney.
(Deed Book 1, page 240)

Sept. 14, 1810 - Joseph Penney and Lydia Penney of the town of Galway, County
of Saratoga, State of New York, brother and sister of Silas Dean late of Ames,
deceased, supposed to be heirs of the one-fourth part of the estate left by
Silas Dean, dec'd, appoint Reuben Moor of the town of Chathan, County of Columbia, State of New York, our true and lawful attorney. (Deed Book 1, page 241)

Sept. 5, 1809 - Lucy Ensworth of Windham County, Connecticut, widow of Jediah
Ensworth, dec'd, Sophia F. Ensworth, Lucy A. Ensworth, David A. A. Ensowrth,
children and heirs-at-law of the estate of said Jediah Ensworth, dec'd, appoint
Daniel Stewart of Troy, State of Ohio, our true and lawful attorney.
(Deed Book 1, page 232)

May 23, 1810 - Lucy Adams of Sturbridge, County of Worcester, Commonwealth of
Massachusetts, widow of David Adams, dec'd, constitute and appoint Daniel
Stewart of Troy, Athens County, my factor, agent, trustee and lawful attorney.
(Deed Book 1, page 231)

The majority of the dates in the following records consist of the date the license was issued, as the marriage returns do not begin until 1820 and then they were few. The dates preceded by (M) denote actual marriage date. Spelling was exceedingly poor.

ALLEN, Phineas to Rachel FULTON	11-17-1817
AUSTIN, Thomas to Sally HOLBERT	3-16-1820
BALLARD, Jesse Jr. to Sally ANDERSON	7-20-1820
BARHELDER, Daniel to Polly SPENCER	1-1-1819
BARROWS, Jacob to Anna FAULK	4-30-1818
BARROWS, Wm. Jr. to Eve PETTY	11-20-1819
BATTERSON, Lewis to Betsey DAVIS	4-10-1820
BEAN, McCraven to Jemima BOBO	2-2-1820
BEAN, Wm. 2nd to Esther MANSFIELD	2-14-1820
BEARDSLEY, Francis to Elisa CULVER	1-15-1818
BEEBE, Charles to Sally STARR	12-16-1817
BEEBE, Peter to Melissa COOK	9-3-1819
BIERCE, Wm. W. to Lucinda CULVER	2-19-1818
BING, George to Jane JOHNSON	3-12-1819
BLACKMAN, Nathaniel to Molly SMITH - Oath N. Blackman	8-7-1818
BOBO, Joshua to Sally REYNOLDS	3-2-1819
BOWMAN, Jabez to Philadelphia CASE	4-1-1819
BOYLES, George to Martha SPROAT	3-3-1820
BRADLEY, Wm. to Deborah RICHARDSON	10-7-1818
BREWER, Alex'r to Rachel PHILLIPS	6-11-1818
BRINE, Jonathan to Betsey BOBO	6-6-1820
BROOKS, Jno. Jr. to Marcia Irwin	1-1-1818
BROOKS, Thomas 2nd to Sally SNOWDON	6-30-1818
BROWN, David to Hannah THOMPSON	8-25-1819
BROWN, Pearly to Eliza HULBERT	6-16-1819
BUCKINGHAM, Isaac to Ora MORSE (M)	12-14-1820
BUCKLEY, Aratus to Margaret LONG	9-18-1819
BURCHET, Jonah to Lucinda GREEN	8-30-1817
CALDWELL, Alex'r to Margaret FESTER	1-26-1819
CALDWELL, Charles to Rachel WASHBURN	10-12-1820
CAMP, Jesse to Betsey BROWN	1-8-1820
CAMPBELL, Charles to Peggy THOMASON	12-17-1819
CAMPBELL, Thomas L. to Sally JOHNSON	1-4-1820
CARTER, Harley to Zimrod BIGNELL	9-21-1818
CARTER, John to Mary THOMAS	3-2-1819
CATLIN, Daniel to Anna BROWN	3-14-1817
CATLIN, William to Miriam PARSONS	7-25-1818
CHAMBERLAIN, Jno. D. to Thirza GROW	8-8-1817
CHANDLER, Jno. to Nancy BINGHAM	11-11-1817
CHANDWICK, Thomas to Margaret FONCANNON	10-19-1819
CLARK, Aaron B. to Mary RANDOLPH	7-5-1819
CLEVELAND, Asahel to Margaret CALKINS	11-4-1817
COE, Beach to Anna DEW	4-20-1819
COE, Jno. to Nancy ARMITAGE	6-11-1817
COE, Josiah to Emily CODNER	6-11-1818

```
COGSWELL, Solomon F. to Polly CULVER                          2-25-1819
COLUMBIA, John to Lucy B. CLARK                              12-31-1819
COLVERT, William to Polly JACKSON                            6-14-1819
CONN, Robert to Elizabeth MANSFIELD                          7-20-1819
CONNER, John to Ady OGDEN                                    5-13-1817
CONNETT, Isaac to Sarah MANSFIELD                            4-30-1817
CONWELL, Joseph to Sally OSBORNE - oath of Aaron Osborn      2-18-1818
COOPER, Cornelius to Keziah SWETT - oath of Caleb Johnson    3-17-1819
COURTNEY, Alanson to Nancy CAMBY                             5-18-1818
CRIPPEN, Thaddeus to Betsey HATCH                           12-12-1817
CROCKER, Samuel S. to Phebe BALLARD                          5-24-1819
CUTLER, Charles to Maria WALKER                              3-27-1819
DANA, Joseph to Anna LYONS                                   1-13-1819
DAWLEY, Nathan to Anna . . .                                 7-15-1820
DAYTON, Hezekiah to Cynthia CROSLEY (CROSBY)                 6-16-1818
DESHLER, Christopher to Nancy PHILLIPS                       9-22-1817
DEVORE, Benjamin to Fanny COLLUM                             2-5-1819
DEWITT, James to Mille LEVETT                               10-7-1818
DICKEY, John to Margaret LONCOR                             11-2-1819
DOBSON, James to Jane COWELL                                12-31-1819
DONALDSON, William to Margt. C. BRAWLEY                     12-13-1817
DUNBAUGH, Jacob to Polly BOBO                                3-5-1818
EUTSLER, Henry to Jane KIRKENDALL                            8-16-1817
EUTSLER, Jno. Jr. to Elizabeth EUTSLER                       4-2-1817
EVERTS, Ambrose to Amelia EVERTS                             5-15-1819
EVERTS, Eheelock to Ruth MITCHELL                            2-3-1820
FISH, Nathaniel to Eliza BUZZARD                             5-9-1818
FISH, Nath'l to Deidamia EASTERMAN (EASTMAN)                 8-8-1820
FLOWERS, Jno. to Nancy SPACEY                                4-7-1817
FOX, James to Jane DUDDER                                    2-13-1818
FRANCIS, Daniel to Martha PHILLIPS                          11-12-1818
FRANCIS, Nicholas to Thankful PHILLIPS                       8-23-1817
FRANCIS, Thomas to Polly FULTON                             12-31-1819
FRAZEE, Hezekiah Jr. to Sarah EUTSLER - oat of C. Eutsler    3-8-1819
FROST, Heman to Susannah BARROWS                             9-12-1818
FULLER, James to Mrs. Nelly BROWN             (M)            8-7-1820
FULTON, John to Elizabeth NEAL                               2-15-1817
FULTON, Loammi to Polly TOMPKINS                             1-31-1818
FULTON, Samuel to Ann SIMONTON                               5-10-1820
GAMBLE, Wm. to Catharine LONG                                3-23-1818
GLASS, Andrew to Tryphena HEWITT                             9-12-1818
GLASS, Andrew to Rhoda WARD                                  2-5-1820
GLASS, James to Ann KIRKLAND                                 6-13-1820
GLAZIER, Loring B. to Jane HENRY                             2-16-1820
GRAHAM, Samuel to Sarah LOWRY                               11-22-1819
GRAHAM, William to Hannah BUCK                (M)            8-24-1820
GREENLEAF, Elias to Sarah TWITCHEL                           7-8-1818
GREY, Combs to Elizabeth BARKER (BAKER)                     11-7-1820
GUTHRIE, Stephen to Mariam ACKLEY                           11-9-1819
HALSEY, Charles to Hannah WILEY                              9-8-1818
HALSEY, Jarvis to Sally HENRY                                3-12-1819
```

```
HANING, Isaac to Polly BROOKS                                    11-18-1817
HARPER, Wm to Persatia MANOR                          (M)       8-2-1820
HAWK, Conrad to Rachel CABLE                                    4-6-1820
HAWLEY, Isaac to Lucina STANCLIFF                              2-21-1820
HECOX, Sylvester to Rebecca HUGT                               5-7-1818
HERROLD, Daniel to Elizabeth HARPER                           8-30-1820
HEWITT, Aaron to Mary LOWRY                                    4-6-1819
HEWITT, Joseph to Ruth CRANSTON                               6-4-1818
HEWITT, Moses 2nd to Sally MARKHAM                            9-29-1819
HIGGINS, Michael to Polly McCLENTICK                          5-12-1819
HILL, Jonathan to Nancy ARNOLD                               12-15-1818
HOPKINS, Luther to Mary DICKEY                                1-23-1817
HULL, Ezra to Polly BEGGERSTAFF                               2-18-1817
HUMPHREY, Isaac to Harriet SAWYER                            12-16-1817
HUMPHREY, Stephen to Hannah BARROWS                           4-30-1818
HUSTON, Moses to Betsey STANLEY                              12-20-1819
HYDE, Wm. to Achsah WYATT                                     3-20-1818
JAMES, Jno. to Minerva WHEELER                               4-14-1818
JEFFERS, Geo. to Abigail MILLAR                              1-29-1818
JOHNSON, Abraham to Clarinda EDDY                             8-5-1817
JOHNSON, Henry to Sally LINSCOTT                             11-22-1819
JOHNSON, James to Matilda DAVIS                               4-25-1820
JOHNSON, Peter to Anna CONNER                                2-15-1817
JOHNSON, Walter to Roxanna BALLARD                          11-27-1819
JONES, Wm. to Susanna MORROW - dau. of Jas. Morrow           8-9-1820
KEARNES, David to Mrs. Sarah SCOT                            5-30-1817
KESTERSON, Meredy to Polly ERWIN                             6-2-1820
KING, Lucius to Margaret DUNKET                              2-1-1819
KIRBY, Wm. Harrison to Fanny FULLER                          5-3-1819
KNAPP, Cyrus to Kirenhappuch PHILLIPS                        12-8-1819
LENTNER, Jacob to Elizabeth BROOKS                           8-31-1819
LINDLEY, Ziba Jr. to Polly M. BARTLETT                      12-31-1819
LOVE, Thos. L. to Comfort PUGSLEY                            4-17-1818
LOVELESS, Nathan to Hannah STANCLIFF                         9-10-1819
LOWRY, James to Rosanna TEETS                                8-14-1819
LUDLOW, Joseph to Harriet CLAPP                              1-5-1818
McAFEE, Mark to Margaret WEATHERBY                           9-18-1818
McDONALD, David to Betsey WILSON - oath of Jno. Furst        1-15-1817
McEVERS, Elisha to Sally KNAPP                               6-22-1818
McEVERS, Wm. to Mary A. D. COLENY                           11-2-1819
McKEE, David to Polly CHADWICK                              11-24-1820
McKEE, Robert to Nancy FIERCE                               11-27-1820
MATHENY, James to Jemima MITCHELL                            1-4-1820
MATHENY, John to Rebecca BENJAMIN                            5-15-1819
MANSFIELD, Simeon to Roxanna PHILLIPS                       11-15-1819
MANSFIELD, Thomas Jr. to Hannah WATSON                       1-13-1819
MARTEN, Samuel to Hetty MERRITT - oath of James Magee       10-30-1817
MILES, Benajah to Catharine DUNKELL                         10-20-1818
MINTON, Jonathan to Peggy FURST                              5-13-1818
MONTGOMERY, Thos. to Catharine DUNKELL                       3-25-1818
```

78

```
MOORE, John to Polly ROSS                                    9-6-1819
MOORE, Matthew to Maria SHIDLER                              12-31-1819
MOREY, Jonathan to Margret COLUMBIA                          9-23-1818
NORRIS, Calvary to Polly JEWETT                              3-3-1818
MORRISON, Calvin to Sarah HAWK                               6-19-1820
MORSE, James to Sally SPACHT                                 3-8-1820
MOSS, Thomas to Arey Ann PETTY                               4-17-1819
NEVILL; Robert to Betsey C. BARTLETT                         6-8-1817
NORRIS, Aaron to Widow GOULD                                 2-13-1818
NORRIS, Isaac to Hannah ADAMS                                10-19-1818
OTTO, James to Mehitable FIELD                               4-26-1820
PARKER, Thomas to Eliza STEPHENS                             2-25-1818
PARKS, Jehiel to Mary FULLER                                 11-19-1818
PARSONS, Horace to Abigail FROST                             2-25-1818
PAULK, Hexxes Jr. to Miranda BARROWS                         6-6-1818
PERKINS, Eliphas Jr. to Zipporah PORTER                      1-12-1818
PERKINS, Zabez to Electa REYNOLDS                            1-4-1820
PETTIS, David to Eunice COREY                                12-5-1818
PHILLIPS, Jno. to Esther BACHELDER                           4-17-1820
PHILLIPS, Solomon to Sally BROOKS - oath of John Brooks      12-29-1817
PICKET, James Jr. to Anna MANSFIELD                          12-29-1817
PICKETT, Heathcoat to Betsey BENJAMIN                        6-8-1818
PICKETT, John to Jane CONNETT                                10-15-1819
PILCHER, John to Laura WARREN                                4-20-1819
POLLY, Amos to Sally BUCK                                    11-12-1819
PORTER, Solomon to Phebe BURNHAM                             5-25-1820
REED, Whittemore to Polly STOUT                              9-10-1817
REYNOLDS, Edward to Mary SIMMONS                             8-14-1819
* RICE, Asa to Therisa M. BARTLETT                           6-1-1820
ROBINETT, Lemuel to Anna MOORE                               2-2-1820
ROWELL, William to Lucia PORTER                              1-23-1818
RUE; Henry to Elizabeth THOMAS                               12-30-1818
RUE, Russell to Nancy FIRST                                  8-22-1818
SAGE, James to Nancy LAMPHER                                 5-20-1819
SAUNDERS, Benjamin to Hannah HUNTLEY                         8-15-1820
SAUNDERS, Stephen R. to Sally BARROWS                        5-24-1817
SEVERLY, John to Nancy MANN                                  11-4-1818
SHATTRECK, Samuel to Sally RITCHY                            3-12-1819
SHERRADEN, Abram to Catharine YOUNG                          2-1-1820
SHIPMAN, Dan'l to Vina WINSETT                               4-20-1818
SHUINES, John to Rhoda WEBLE                                 7-25-1820
SIBLEY, Jno. to Susannah WEIR                                9-26-1818
SIMPSON, Lyman to Sarah ROBINSON                             9-10-1819
SMART, Charles Jr. to Ruth HOIT                              2-2-1819
SMITH, Abner to Elizabeth MARTIN                             3-17-1818
SMITH; Francis to Mary ASHTON                                9-1-1819
SMITH, Thomas to Catharine GILBERT                           10-30-1818
SPEED, George to Mary ROBINETT                               1-14-1818
SPENCER, Alvan to Sally FAULK                                7-13-1818
SPERRY, Joab to Sina PALMER                                  9-8-1819
```

79

```
*  STANCLIFF, David to Amy MILES                                      7-4-1820
   STANLEY, Archelaus to Jenny BOWERS                                 11-27-1819
   STEWART, Garrett to Evelina WALKER                                 9-4-1819
   STEWART, Levi to Frances SAWYER                                    3-4-1819
   STOUT, George to Eliza BUZZARD                                     3-22-1820
   STRAIGHT, Jno. to Polly WOODBURY                                   12-20-1819
   SWAIM, Jno. Alex'r to Susannah WILKINSON                           9-10-1819
   TALBOT, Welcome to Susan AUCKER                                    6-3-1819
   TAYLOR, Philo to Orabel M. KENT                                    11-12-1818
   TAYLOR, Samuel to Abigail SPENCER                                  11-20-1819
   TEEBLES, Reuben to Betsey BUFFINGTON                               7-31-1818
   THOMAS, Eliphabet to Nancy COPP                                    11-14-1820
   THOMPSON, William to Esther RUSSELL                                2-11-1817
   TIBBLES, John to Jane CALDWELL                                     9-8-1818
   TRIPP, Russ to Nancy EATON                                         1-29-1820
   TRYON, Elijah to _____BUZZARD (no first name given)             3-19-1818
   TUCKER, Jno. 2nd to Damius CONE                                    8-4-1819
   WALKER, Thomas to Drusilla TUCKER                                  11-14-1820
   WALTON, Isaac to Pamela GOULD                                      1-29-1818
   WASHBURN, Eleazer Jr. to Sophia McAFEE                             9-10-1819
   WATERMAN, Eusebuius to Sally McAFEE                                7-24-1819
   WATKINS, David to Betsy ARNOLD                                     5-17-1820
   WATKINS, Matthew to Lucy ALDERMAN                                  3-21-1817
   WEISS, Jacob to Rosanna STALDUT                                    5-11-1820
   WELD, Alfred to Magdalena DIXON                                    3-10-1817
   WELDON, Richard to Sally STEDMAN                                   11-1-1817
   WEST, Isaac to Elizabeth KENDRICK                                  5-3-1820
   WHALEY, David W. to Polly WICKHAM                                  1-22-1818
   WHITE, Isaac to Mary DUNKELL                                       12-15-1818
   WILLIAMS, William to Abigail LOWRY                                 10-22-1817
   WILSON, Ezekiel to Nancy MORY                                      11-14-1823
   WOODWARD, Elooman to Lavina DECKER - oath of Moses Decker 1-5-1818
   WOODWARD, Oliver A. to Sarah TERRY                                 11-4-1817
   WYATT, John to Emily CARPENTER                                     4-26-1819
   WYCKIFF, John to Anna CLAYPOOL - oath of Jas. Claypool  4-26-1819
   YOUNG, Ephrain to Drusilla BEAN                                    5-31-1819
   ZIN, Abram to Eliza BROOKS                                         2-7-1818


   *RICE, Jonas to Tamar CULVER                                       12-14-1820
   *STAGE, John to Betsey MINOR                                       12-18-1820
```

The majority of the dates given in the following, are the dates the licenses were issued. The marriage returns do not begin until 1820 and then there are very few. Dates preceded by (M) denot actual marriage date.

ALLEN, Andrew to Fanny Boyles		2-14-1822
ARLINGTON, Bazzava to Mahala Staler (Stater)		4-11-1822
ARNOLD, Welcome to Sylvia Howard		1-22-1821
AUSTIN, Andrew to Betsey Burch		7-29-1822
AUSTIN, Nathan to Delia Goraline	(M)	1-29-1821
BAKER, Nicholas, Jr. to Clarinda White		12-25-1822
BARKER, Timothy to Eleanor Parker	(M)	1-1-1822
BARROWS, Parker to Jane Doane		3-3-1821
BARTLETT, Cophas to Louisa Everts		3-29-1821
BATES, Nicholas to Eunice Coe		7-9-1821
BEAN, Wm. to Sarah Austin		5-31-1822
BEEBE, Peter to Betsey Vaughn		6-21-1822
BIGGERSTAF, Wm. 2nd to Polly Robinett - oath of Kerregan		5-29-1821
BIGGS, Ira to Nancy Zane		1-1-1822
BODWELL, Jno. to Mrs. Elizabeth Decker		10-11-1822
BOLE, Wm. to Loley Rood		12-23-1822
BOWMAN, Jno. Jr. to Elizabeth Jacks		4-14-1821
BOYLES, Absalom to Nancy Henry		10-1-1822
BRADLEY, Wm. to Hannah ROWELL		3-8-1822
BRIDGE, Bazelul to Phebe Lyon		4-13-1822
BROOKS, Sam'l to Elizabeth Gates		4-5-1821
CHILDS, Oliver to Nancy Olney		4-5-1822
CLARK, Elias to Nancy Sweary	(M)	1-19-1822
COE, James to Catharine Hulbert		6-17-1822
CONEY, John to Lois Eastman		6-8-1822
CONNER, Nathan to Sally Bennett		8-27-1821
CORNER, George L. to Sally Hart		11-25-1822
CROSS, Daniel D. to Jane Decker		8-25-1821
CRUTCHFIELD, Arthur to Elizabeth Rogers	(M)	2-7-1821
DAUGHERTY, Hugh to Delilah Lowther		12-10-1821
DAWES, William to Sally Rice		11-17-1821
DAWLEY, Nathan to Anna ____(not given)		7-15-1820
DEAN, George L. to Irena Wheeler		5-5-1821
DEAN, Jno. N. to Mariah Foster		12-31-1822
DENNIS, Joseph to Deborah Casper		6-21-1822
DOWD, Jesse to Delilah Dawson		3-28-1821
DRIGGS, George to Abigail Conant		6-4-1821
DRIGGS, Seth to Hannah Whaley		2-24-1821
DUFFY, Daniel to Margaret Donahue		11-20-1821
DUTTON, Kinsman to Nancy Faulk		3-13-1822
DUTTON, Samuel to Nancy Brookhart		1-12-1821
EARHART, Samuel to Dorcas Gabill		12-27-1821
EDWARDS, Jno. to Anna Pugsley		11-7-1822

81

EVANS, Joshua to Polly Aucker   9-25-1821
EVERTS, Milo to Polly B. Pruden   1-14-1822
FENY, George to Clarissa Jordan   7-8-1822
FERRIS, Zina to Alma Morse   12-16-1822
FOSTER, Eben to Achsah Culber   1-30-1822
FOSTER, Hull to Orinda L. Carpenter   4-26-1821
FRENCH, George to Rachel Biggerstaff   4-3-1822
FULLER, Samuel to Huldah Catlin   12-8-1821
GABILL, Bazel to Ruth Bobo   1-16-1822
GIBBS, Simeon to Simanthey Westcoat   1-26-1822
GIBSON, Herman to Hannah Brooks   4-27-1821
GILLMORE, Harvey R. to Lucy Curtiss   2-18-1822
GLEASON, Wm. to Jean Biggerstaff   4-29-1822
GRAHAM, Thomas to Mary Ann Coates   (M)   2-26-1822
GRANT, Landers to Hannah Catlin   1-4-1822
HAGERMAN, John to Eliza Harris   3-23-1811
HERROLD, Daniel, Jr. to Fanny Fierce   11-16-1822
HERROLD, Jno. to Clarissa Allen   4-10-1821
HICKS, Sam'l to Rebekah Fish   9-27-1822
HILL, Samuel to Harriet Hatch   7-30-1821
HOPKINS, James H. to Jane Alderman   (M)   8-28-1822
HOSKINSON, Andrew to Eliza Pilcher   12-27-1822
HOWARD, Samuel to Anna Alderman   6-30-1821
HUDSON, James to Polly Dunbaugh   10-10-1821
HUNTLEY, Joseph Jr. to Jane Douglas   12-20-1822
HYDE, Oliver Jr. to Polly Wyatt   5-4-1821
JACKSON, Isaac to Clarissa Buckley   5-27-1822
JOHNSON, Samuel to Hannah Clark   6-11-1822
KEATON, Jno. to Elizabeth Ross   4-2-1822
LINZEE, Robert to Electa Reynolds   3-15-1821
LIVINGSTON, John to Christiana Hawk   5-1-1821
LONCOR, Leonard to Martha Chivington   1-8-1822
LOTTRIDGE, Isaac B. to Experience Cross   4-3-1822
LOWRY, Daniel to Deborah Allen   2-6-1821
McKEE, Samuel to Rachel Linzee   2-14-1821
McKENZIE, Donald to Polly Dunkle   7-4-1821
MANN, David to Sally Sickles   6-4-1821
MANN, Isaac to Betsey Bullard   7-23-1821
MARTIN, Cornelius to Elizabeth Aucker   5-11-1822
MARTIN, Stephen to Polly Colvin   8-6-1821
MARTIN, William to Isabel McClelland   2-10-1822
MARTIN, Wm. to Sarah Wilson   (M)   9-4-1822
MATHENY, Richard to Mary Young   9-25-1821
MILES, J. B. to Betsey Fulton   4-11-1822
MILES, S. S. to Eliza Gillmore   7-5-1821
MILLAR, Jno. B. to Rebecca Posten   12-28-1821
MILLAR, Wm. B. to Mary D. Copp   7-18-1821
MUNROE, Albert to Sarah Conrow   4-6-1822
MYRICK, Elias to Lydia Jackson   12-24-1822

82

NANNA, James to Esther Shepherd		12-24-1821
NASH, Samuel to Lucy Goodno	(M)	1-1-1822
NICHOLS, Elias N. to Sally Hewitt		11-20-1822
NORTHROP, Amos to Mary Collins		3-28-1821
NORTON, Isaac N. to Harriet Carpenter		2-20-1822
OGG, Andrew to Lucy Munsell		7-17-1822
OGG, Richard to Sally Sweatt		5-13-1822
PARSONS, Sylvester to Nancy King		10-3-1821
PAULK, Hexxes to Elizabeth Bayless		2-11-1822
PHILLIPS, Evert V. to Tacy Hopkins	(M)	8-28-1822
PRICE, Jno. to Polly Jones		2-19-1822
PRUDEN, S. R. to Olly Cranston		7-23-1821
PUGSLEY, Francis to Elizabeth Green	(M)	12-25-1821
REED, Downie to Phebe Gillespie		11-26-1821
REEVES, David to Matilda Woodyard		4-30-1821
ROBERTS, Joseph to Sally Hewitt		1-14-1822
ROBINETT, Nathan to Drusilla Robinett		3-7-1821
ROSS, Calvin to Elizabeth Bennet		10-30-1822
ROWELL, William to Hester Lentner		1-26-1822
SAMSON, Jacob to Rachel Hull		3-26-1822
SECOY, Wm. M. to Catharine Draper		5-14-1822
SELBY, Joseph to Betsy Simmons		10-22-1822
SIMMONS, Jonathan to Betsey Beckley		12-28-1821
SIMMONS, Jonathan to Nancy Colvert		2-28-1822
SIX, Nathaniel to Lydia Lewis	(M)	2-1-1821
SMITH, Isaac to Sally Thomas		10-5-1821
SNOW, Lovil to Freelove Dulcher	(M)	1-28-1821
SNOW, Robert to Lucy Atwood		11-10-1821
STEWART, Jno. to Sally Long		8-18-1821
STRINGER, Daniel to Sally Johnson		1-7-1822
TANNEHILL, John to Peggy Fulton		7-25-1821
THOMAS, John to Rachel Witteington		5-25-1822
THOMAS, Major to Elizabeth Houser		1-1-1822
THOMPSON, Jno. W. to Nancy Loncor		8-17-1821
THOMPSON, Wm. P. to Peggy Keiterson		2-14-1822
TUTTLE, Cyrus to Sarah Seamans		3-10-1821
WADE, Asa to Sally Lowther		5-8-1822
WADE, Joseph to Live Conner		5-14-1822
WARREN, Michael to Mary Cee		8-24-1821
WEATHERBY, Jno. to Eunice Woodward		12-11-1822
WHALEY, Arden to Betsy Hewitt		8-13-1822
WHALEY, David to Cynthiann Arnold		12-7-1821
WHITE, Horace to Ann Walker		4-25-1821

The following is the complete contents of Will Book 1. Wills and estates are given in the order in which they are listed in the book, as no dates of recording are given. Page on which record is listed is given in parenthesis.

HEWITT, Moses - Will - Wife, mentioned but not named. Sons: Moses, Aaron, Joseph, Pardon, George and Ephram. Brother: Ephraim Hewitt to serve as guardian of son Moses. Daughters: mentioned but not named. Mentions: land deeded to him by Rev. Wm. Woodbridge and also by John Lowry; town lots in Athens and lot in Hockhocking; tract of college land. Executors: Silas Bingham and Henry Barlett. Dated 2-24-1814. Signed Moses Hewitt. Witnesses: Jacob Lindly, Wm. Beebe and Henry Bartlett. (1)

JEWETT, Doct. Leonard - Inventory of Estate - July 1816. (13)
PIERCE, William - Orange Twp. - Inventory of Estate - 4-23-1814. (20)

HULBERT, Elisha - Appraisal of personal property. No date given. Appraised by Peter Bailes, John Bailes and John C. Carrico. (23)

CONNET, Abner - Dover - Appraisal of personal property. No date given. Appraised by Resolve Fuller, Rosewell Culver and Joseph Fuller. (25)

_____, Samuel (page torn) - Orange - Inventory and Appraisal - no date given. Appraised by Nathaniel Williams, Jacob Humphry and Samuel Coleman. (27)

ROGERS, Joseph - Elk Twp. - Inventory of Estate. No date given. Appraised by Levi Johnson, John Philips and James Bothwell. (28)

ACKLEY, George - Athens - Inventory of Estate. No date given. Appraised by Silas Bingham, Charles Shipman and Jacob Lindly. (29)

GUILE, Benjamin - Troy - Will. Wife: Lucy. Children: James, Hannah, Polly, Benjamin Jr. and Lucy Guile. Executor: Joseph Guthrie. Dated 5-10-1813. Signed: Benjamin Guile. Witnesses: Jacob Humphrey, Alphews Cross and Joseph Gutharie.(32)

DEAN, Silas - Ames Twp. - Inventory of estate. August 1810. Appraised by Joshua Wyatt, Ezra Greene and John Brown. Adms.: Zebulon Griffin. (35)

THOMPSON, John - Alexander Twp. - Inventory of Estate - 2-14-1815 - Appraised by Joseph McMahan, John Brooks and Jesse Camp, Jr. (38)

SAWYER, Nathaniel - Rome Twp. - Inventory of Estate - 5-5-1813 - Daniel Stewart, adms. Appraised by Elijah Rowell, George Barrows and James Crippen. (42)

HEWITT, John - Inventory of Estate. No date given. Appraised by Nehemiah Davis, Nathan Nye and Isaac Stephens. (45)

MUNROE, Solomon - Orange - Inventory of Estate. 7-4-1814. Appraised by Benj. Stout, Truman Hecox and Joel Cowdery. (46)

84

BURRILL, Widow Abigail - Orange - Inventory of Estate, No date given. Peter Grow, adms. (48)

BOWERS, Michael - Inventory of Estate - No date given. Appraised by Robert McKinstry, William McKinstry and James Gibson. (49)

JELLY, Hugh - Athens - Will. Wife: mentioned but not named. Sons: James and Andrew. Daughters: Polly Mulford; Anna; Elizabeth; Jane Jelly. Grandson: Hugh Mulford son of Daniel and Polly Mulford Executor: son, James Jelly and Silas Bingham. Dated 7-17-1809. Signed: Hugh (mark) Jelly. Witnesses: Arthur Coats, Daniel Mulford and Hugh Bartlett. (52)

JONES, Jarret - Urbana, Champaign Co., Ohio - Will. Sisters: Sarah Stedman, Casander More and Mary Miller. Nephew: Jarret More son of Samuel Moore. Executors: Alexander Steadman and Edmund Dorr. Dated 3-9-1813. Signed: Jarret Jones. Witnesses: Jonas Smith; Asher Waterman and James Davisson. (56)

FULTON, Alexander - Athens - Inventory of Estate. No date given. William Lowry and Rachel Fulton, adms. Apprised by Wm. Harper, Abel Man and Michael Barker.(60)

PUGSLEY, Abram - Inventory of Estate. No date given. Appraised by Daniel Weether, Nathan Woodbury and Josiah True. (62)

McDONALD, Kennet - Athens - Inventory of Estate. No date given. Appraised by Edmond Dorr, Peter Phillips and Nicholas Phillips. (64)

DUNBAUGH, Jacob - Inventory of Estate. No date given. Polly Dunbaugh, widow.(66)

SHEPARD, Daniel - Inventory of Estate. 2-23-1825. Appraised by Elias Spencer and James Knight. (73)

The following records were taken from "Chancery Record 1" located in the Common Pleas Court (Clerk of Court's Office) in the court house at Wapakoneta. Page on which record may be found in the original book is given in parenthesis.

Nov. 1848 - Israel GATES vs. Fanny GATES. Divorce. Filed 8-24-1848. Married 7-21-1841 Van Wert Co., Ohio where resided until March 1845 when moved to Mercer Co., Ohio. There Fanny left petitioner on 7-28-1845 to visit Van Wert Co., but instead went to State of Indiana leaving petitioner with small children. (1)

Nov. 1848 - Nancy BATES vs. Sarah J. Bates, et al. Petition for Dower. Filed 4-24-1848. Theodore Bates, dec'd, late of Mercer Co., Ohio departed life about year 1848. Widow, Nancy Bat4s of Auglaize Co., Ohio. Land, Theodore died seized of an estate of inheritance in SE¼ Section 5, Township 6 South, Range 4 East and fractional quarter Section 34, Township 5 South, Range 4 East and also one undivided half of lot 78 in north addition to St. Marys. Robert Girdon is entitled to next estate of inheritance in first mentioned tract. Heir: Sarah Jane Bates. (2)

July 1848 - James LOWERY vs. Margaret Lowery, et al. Petition for Partition. Filed 5-24-1848. Land, 240 acres SE¼ and S½NE¼ Section 1, Township 5 South, Range 6 East. John Lowery, dec'd. Widow, Margaret Lowery entitled to dower. Heirs: 1/5th part, James Lowery; 1/5th part, Lydia Ann wife of George Hook; 1/5th part, Samuel Lowery; 1/5th part, Nancy Lowery; 1/5th part, Miles B. Lowery; all of Auglaize Co., Ohio. (5)

July 1848 - Ohio Life and Insurance Trust Co. vs. Isaac Helm, adms. of John Helm, dec'd. To foreclose mortgage. Filed 5-24-1849. John Helm, dec'd, late of Auglaize County, but died in Indiana died seized of E½ SW¼ Section 5, Township 6 South, Range 4 East and out-lot 17 in St. Marys. (8)

July 1848 - Rubin MILLER vs. Sarah MILLER. Divorce. Filed 5-15-1848. Married 8-11-1844 in Delaware Co., Ohio to Sarah Woocock and moved to Allen Co., Ohio now in the bounds of Auglaize Co and lived together until 11-1-1844. (13)

Apr. 1849 - Joseph KOKINGE vs. Catharine KOKINGE and others. In Partition. Filed 8-28-1848. Land, 40 acres NE¼ SE¼ Section 26, Township 7 South, Range 4 East. John B. Kokinge, dec'd. Widow, Katharine Kokinge entitled to dower. Heirs: 1/4th part, Joseph Kokinge of Auglaize Co.; 1/4th part, Elizabeth wife of Bernard Pluns; 1/4th part, Dina wife of Henry Aufderhane; 1/4th part, Henry Kokinge. (18)

July 1849 - Bernard H. KOOP vs. John F. BOSCHE and others. Petition to compel performance of real contract. Filed 8-28-1848. John B. Koop, dec'd then of Mercer Co., Ohio died intestate in August 1839. On petition of John F. Bosche and Sophia F. D. his wife a daughter of John B. Koop partition was confered at Sept. term 1849 of Mercer Co., Ohio court and by partition, William Koop and John F. Bosche and Sophia D. F. his wife became joint owners of NW corner E½ NE¼ Section 15 and SW¼ Section 15, Township 7, Range 4 and lots 49,50,51,52,45,48,38,39,6,7,8 in South addition of Bremen. That Bernhard H. Koop was to have lot 3 in same. That Sophia D. F. Bosche died before deed could be made. (22)

July 1849 - Benjamin RIDLEY vs. Sarah RIDLEY, et al. In Chancery. Filed 4-5-1849.
Land, Benjamin Ridley son of John Ridley now dec'd purchased in 1847 from John 40
acres NW¼ NW¼ Section 17, Township 5 South, Range 8 East for which he was to pay by
services and $200.00 and receive deed when he reached his majority. John Ridley,
dec'd. Widow, Sarah Ridley. Heirs: Benjamin Ridley, Barbara wife of ____ (not given)
Blain, Esther Ridley, Mary Ridley, Sarah Ridley Jr., Matthias Ridley, Abigail Ridley,
Eliza Ridley, Amanda Ridley and Juda Ridley, the last five named being minors. (26)

July 1849 - F. L. LANGLEY and wife vs. Samuel DEWEESE, et al. Petition for
Partition. Filed 9-25-1848. Land, 80 acres W½ SE¼ Section 22, Township 7 South,
Range 4 East. Moses Connell (or Cornell), dec'd. Heirs: 1/5th part, Susannah wife
of Fielding L. Langley of Miami Co., Ohio; 1/5th part, Rachel wife of Samuel Deweese;
1/5th part, Samuel Cornell of Kentucky; 1/5th part, James Cornell, dec'd, his heirs
--James and Samuel Cornell both minors of Kentucky; 1/5th part Elizabeth Oldham, her
heirs--Joseph B. and Margaret Ann Oldham of Indiana. (28)

Oct. 1849 - Jabez CRETCHER vs Heirs of Matthew CRETCHER, dec'd. In Chancery.
Filed 5-12-1849. Jabez Cretcher states that Matthew Cretcher on 10-15-1836 for
natural love and affection and $500.00 contracted with said Jabez to deliver within
two years from 10-15-1836 lands in Allen Co., Ohio now in Auglaize County as follows:
107 acres off west side NW¼ Section 28, 24 acres off east side NE¼ Section 29, 24
acres off east side SE¼ Section 20, W½ SW¼ Section 20 and 13½ acres off west side
SE¼ SW¼ Section 21, all in Township 5 south, Range 7 east. Children: Jabez Cretcher
of Logan Co., Ohio; Nathan Cretcher of Shelby Co., Ohio; John Cretcher of Kentucky;
Sarah formerly Cretcher wife of Samuel Ireland of Kentucky; Matthew Cretcher, dec'd,
his children--John Cretcher of Indiana, Jane formerly Cretcher wife of John Leonard
of Champaign Co. Ohio, Sarah Cretcher, Matthew Cretcher, Nancy Cretcher, Elizabeth
Cretcher and Thomas Cretcher, the last four being minors and who all with their mother
Nancy Cretcher reside in Champaign Co., Ohio; Peter Cretcher, dec'd, his children--
David Cretcher of Champaign Co., Ohio and Sarah late Cretcher wife of Thomas Naylor
of Auglazie Co., Ohio. (31)

Oct. 1849 - Herman H. BOSCHE adms. (states also executor) of John Gerard SCHUMILLN
vs. Catherine M. ACA and others. Petition to sell land. Filed8-28-1848. Land, 40
acres NE¼ SE¼ Section 20, Township 7 South, Range 4 East in German twp. No widow.
Heirs: Catherine Mary wife of John Aca, Elizabeth wife of John G. Hagstey and Mary
Anna Schmilln, all of Germany. That Henry Deweese has next estate of inheritance.(40)

Oct. 1849 - Herman H. and Anna LANDEVER vs. John H. BATH, et al. Petition for
partition. Filed 5-21-1849; one half of S½ NW¼ Section 3, Township 7 south, Range
4 east of which John H. Bath owns other half. Partition: 1/2 part, Anna Maria
wife of Herman H. Landever. Widow, Maria Engel now the wife of Gerhard Hehman
has dower interest. (42)

Apr. 1850 - John H. KRUSE vs. H. B. KRUSE, et al. Partition. Filed 5-21-1849.
Land, 40 acres NE¼ SW¼ Section 12, Township 7 South, Range 4 East. Herman Rodolf
Kruse, dec'd. Widow, Katharine Mary Kruse entitled to dower. Partition 1/8th part
Jon H. Kruse; 1/8th part, Herman Roldolf Kruse; 1/8 part, Anna Mary Kruse; 1/8th
part, Catharine Mary Kruse; 1/8th part, Ana Regina Kruse; 1/8th part, Herman Henry
Kruse; 1/8th part, Henry Wilbrant Kruse; 1/8th part, Sophia Eliza Kruse; all of
Hamilton Co., Ohio. (50)

Apr. 1830 - Gerhard H. WEHREYER vs. Ann Maria WEHRMEYER. Partition. Filed 5-21-1849. Land, 40 acres SE¼ SW¼ Section 36, Township 6 South, Range 4 East. Partition: 1/4th part, Gerhard H. Wehrmeyer; 1/4th part, Anna Maria Wehrmeyer; 1/4th part, Ernest August Wehrmeyer; 1/4th part, Frederick Wehrmeyer; all of Auglaize Co. Oh.(54)

Apr. 1850 - C. W. COWAN adms. of Robert HOUSTAN, dec'd vs. Nancy MEWHORTER, et al. Petition to sell lands. Filed 6-11-1849. Land, lot 18 of subdivision of Wm A. Houston's estate south addition St. Marys being 1/3rd part. William Houstan a minor heir of Robert Houston has 1/3rd interest mentioned above. The remaining 2/3rds interest belong to John Houstan of Shelby Co., Ohio and to Nancy wife of Thomas Newhorter of Indiana. (57)

Apr. 1850 - Wm CRAFT Jr. and Theresa CRAFT vs. Joseph NEFF, et al. In Chancery. Filed 3-31-1849. Land, 34 acres NW fraction NW¼ Section 31, Township 5 South, Range 6 East. Peter Hammel, dec'd late of Auglaize Co. Heirs: Theresa wife of William Craft Jr., Parmelia wife of Joseph Neff, Eleanor Jane Hammel and Joseph Hammel, the last two named being minors. (60&102)

Apr. 1850 - Robert C. RUSSELL adms. of John MELLINGER, dec'd vs Widow and Heirs. In Chancery. Filed 4-16-1850. John Mellinger, dec'd late of Shelby Co., Ohio. Widow, Martha Mellinger. Heirs: Jasper Mellinger, Colin Mellinger, Florence Mellinger and Leonora Mellinger, all minors. That John Mellinaer, dec'd in his lifetime on 1-28-1848 in Auglaize Co. for $267.69 sold Francis M. Trentman of Auglaize County 53.93 acres NE fraction N½ Section 22, Township 6 South, Range 6 East and died without executing deed. (62)

Apr. 1850 - Herman Frederick WELLMAN vs. Elizabeth SCHARDLEMAN, et al. In Chancery. Filed 7-17-1849. Herman F. Wellman represents that about 11-12-1841 by descent from his infant daughter Sophia Margaret Wellman under the will of Henrietta Wellman 40 acrew SE¼ SE¼ Section 3, Township 7 South, Range 4 East came in his possession and has been in same for seventeen years since, that said land was originally purchased from United States by John Henry Shardleman as part of entry of 160 acres SE¼ Section 3, Township 7 South, Range 4 East in his own name but paid for by funds of John Henry Pangel and by agreement Pangel was put in possession of NE¼ SE¼ Section 3 with reference made to Common Pleas Court of Mercer County, Ohio to Chancery suit at July term 1841 entitled Henry Pengel vs. widow and heirs of John Henry Schardelman. That Elizabeth Schardelman of Germany was widow of John Henry Schardelman, dec'd and other heirs are unknown. Now petition to clear title. (68)

July 1850 - John H. SHULTE vs. Sophia SHULTE, et al. Partition. Filed 2-8-1850. Land, 40 acres NW¼ SE¼ Section 35, Township 6 South, Range 4 East. Partition: 1/4th part, John Henry Shulte of Auglaize Co.; 1/4th part, Sophia Shulte; 1/4th part, Gerhard H. Shulte; 1/4th part, Maria A. Shulte. (74)

July 1850 - Thomas L. ALLEN and John ALLEN adms. of estate of Larew ALLEN, dec'd vs. Widow and Heirs. Petitition to sell land. Filed 1-28-1850. Land, 80 acres S½ NW¼ Section 23, Township 5 South, Range 6 East. Widow, Mary Allen entitled to dower. Heirs: Sarah Ann wife of Alexander S. Anderson, Martha Allen, William J. Allen, Caroline Allen, Mary Jane Allen, Rebecca Allen and Henry Clay Allen. (77)

July 1850 - John Henry NEIBERG vs. Catharine NEIBERG. Divorce. Filled 2-8-1850. Married 7-2-1846 to Catharine Donnesburg. That Catharine is now believed to live in Baltimore, Md. (81)

July 1850 - Geo. KLINGMANN, et al. vs. Elizabeth KLINGMANN, et al. Petition for Partition. Filed 4-3-1849. Land 80 acres E½ NW¼ and 160 acres NE¼ Section 24, Township 5 South, Range 6 East. John Tam, dec'd late of Duchouquet twp. Widow, Elizabeth Klingamann. Partition: 1/4th part, Mary wife of George Klingamann; 1/4th part, Milton Tam; 1/4th part, Celia Tam; 1/4th part, Elizabeth Tam; the last three named being minors. (83)

July 1850 - Frederick KUHLHORST adms. of Frederick SHULENBURG, dec'd vs. William SHULENBURG, et al. Petition to sell land. Filed 3-28-1850. Land, lots 21,40 & 72 in New Bremen. No widow. Children, William Shulenburg, Frederick Shulenburg, Wilhelmine Shulenburg, Henry Shulenburg, Bernard Shulenburg, and Caroline Shulenburg. (90)

July 1850 - John W. WIERMEYER vs. Adam H. BRUGGERMAN, et al. Petition for Partition. Filed 3-20-1850. Land, lots 32,33,37 & 76 in Koops addition to town of New Bremen originally in Mercer County now in Auglaize County owned jointly by John William Wiemeyer and Christopher H. Wiemeyer now dec'd by deed of purchase 8-21-1847, with each owning half--that John William Wiemeyer is now possessed of his original one half and also 1/6 of 1/2. That Christopher H. Wiemeyer, dec'd died intestate in 1850 leaving widow, Adelheit now the wife of Henry Kuncel who is entitled to dower in one-half, but that he died without issue leaving the following heirs: John W. Wiemeyer, Mary Engel Bruggaman, Maria Margaretta Henefelt, Catharine Maria Schmitt , Catharine Klefoth, Maria Klefoth, Henry Schmidt, Louisa Schmidt and Catharine Schmidt. (106 & 147)

July 1850 - Thomas S. Sturgeon adms. of George BURK vs. Margaret BURK, et al. Petition to sell land. Filed 3-30-1850. Land, lot 6 in Block 9 of East addition of St. Marys and also lot 195 north addition of St. Marys. Widow, Margaret Burk entitled to dower. Heirs: Robert Burk, John Burk, Sarah Burk, and Exabel Burk. (110 & 159)

Apr 1850 - Jesse WAMPLER guardian vs. his wards and others. Petition to sell land. Filed 3-19-1850. Land, 28 acres part Sections 31 & 32, Township 4 south, Range 6 East. Frederick Crider, dec'd. Widow, (name not stated) now wife of Richard Sandliam. Heirs: Ann Crider, Elizabeth Crider, Mary Crider and Catharine Crider, minors by Jesse Wampler their guardian. (121)

Oct. 1850 - William FINK adms. of Hiram GILLE, dec'd vs. Henry BRUGGERMAN. Petition to see land. Filed 3-28-1850. Land 20 acres E½ NE¼ NW¼ Section 14, Township 7 South, Range 4 East. Hiram (also given as Haman) H. Gille, dec'd late of Auglaize Co. Heirs: Mary late Gille wife of Henry Bruggerman and Henry Gilly. (131)

Oct. 1850 - B. A. WENDELIN adms. of Casper UNTIET, dec'd vs. Mary UNTIET, et al. Petition to sell lands. Filed 4-1-1850. Land, 50.94 acres NE¼ NW¼ Section 30, Township 7 South, Range 5 East in Shelby Co., Ohio. Heirs: Maria Untiet aged 13 yrs. and Clara Untiet aged 9 yrs. by John B. Frederick their guardian. (134 & 136)

Oct. 1850 - Thomas BEER vs Nancy BEER. Divorce. Filed 8-27-1849. Divorce. Filed 8-27-1849. Married 12-4-1845. Lived together until 4-7-1846 when Nancy left and has lived in parts unknown. (139)

Oct. 1850 - Charles MARTIN and Mary VANTRESS adms. of Sylvester VANTRESS, dec'd vs. Widow and Heirs. Petition to sell land. Filed 4-17-1849. Land, 1 acre adjoining lot 9 in town of St. John's, being pt SE corner W½ Section 32, Township 5 South, Range 7 east and also lots 1 & 9 in town of St. Johns. Widow, Mary Vantress. Heirs: Eli Vantress, Harriet Vantress, George Vantress and Thomas Vantress. (141)

April 1850 - Bernard H. LOHMAN vs. Bernard BRAMBRINK and others. Petition for Partition. Filed 4-1-1850. Land, 80 acres W½ SE¼ Section 33, Township 7 South, Range 4 East. 1/2 part, Bernard Henry Lohman of German twp., Auglaize Co.; 1/2 part, Bernard Brambrink aged 15 yrs., Henry Brambrink aged 12 yrs. and Elizabeth Brambrink aged 9 yrs., children of Anna Mary Margaret Elizabeth formerly named Brambrink and after death of her husband she obtained by marriage the name A.M.M.E _____(left blank) and conveyed unto Bernard, Henry and Elizabeth the undivided 1/2 of above premises. (154)

Oct. 1850 - Leonard PLACE vs. Caroline E. MEDBERRY, et al. In Chancery. Filed 11-3-1848. Land, Nathaniel Medberry late Franklin Co., Ohio, dec'd on 3-7-1845 entered at Receiver's office Upper Sandusky, Ohio tract land South fraction NW fractional quarter Section 7, Township 4 South Range 4 East being80.34 acres and Place contracted with Medberry to buy land on 6-25-1845 but Medberry died before deed was made. Nathaniel Medberry late of Franklin Co., Ohio, dec'd. Widow, Caroline E. Medberry of Franklin Co., Ohio. Heirs: Arnold Medberry, Hezekiah Medberry Jr., Annis Medberry, Jacob Medberry, Sylvester Medberry, Hezekiah Medberry, Henry A. Field, Arthur Field and Polly Cleveland, all of Franklin Co., Ohio. (156)

Oct. 1850 - Henry MEYROSE and others vs. Gertrude MENKE, et al. In Chancery. Filed 7-17-1850. Henry Boerger late of German twp., dec'd. Daughters: Elizabeth Menke, dec'd late wife of John William Menke, also dec'd, her only child--William Menke, a minor; and Agnes wife of Henry Meyrose. Land, Lots 3 & 58 in Minster with Agnes to have lot 58 and Elizabeth to have lot 3, that Elizabeth and her husband John W. Menke sold lot 3 to Henry Calvelage, now also dec'd who left widow, Catharine Gertrude Calvalege. (162)

Oct. 1850 - Clemens STÜEVE vs. Bernard STÜEVE, et al. In Chancery. Filed 4-3-1850. That Clement StÜeve on or about 4-7-1849 and Henry StÜeve formed a partnership for the purpose of building a steam saw mill and carring on a sawmill business, that they purchased so much of lot 18 as lies between Hanover St. and the canal and so much of lot 7 as lies between Hanover St. and the canal, all in Minster from Bernard von Handorf and Caroline his wife from said Clemens StÜeve and Mary Elizabeth his wife and went on making preparations to build and construct the steam sawmill, that the frame for the sawmill was raised and then his partner and father, Herman H. StÜeve died on or about7-28-1849 andpetitioner states that he managed the whole partnership and paid all expenses with his own money and that he is liable for purchase money on lot 17. Herman H. StÜeve, dec'd. Children: Clemens StÜeve, the petitioner; Bernard StÜeve aged 20 yrs., residence not known; and Herman H. StÜeve aged 8 yrs. (165)

Oct. 1850 - Hannah CONKLIN vs. John CONKLIN. Divorce. Filed 10-8-1849. Married in 1819. Lived together until Sept. 1849 when John took money and went to parts unknown. Six children, all minors living with petitioner. Petition dismissed.(172)

Oct. 1850 - James H. SKINNER vs. John HUTZEN, et al. In Chancery. Filed 2-26-1850. Land, lot 13 Wapakoneta sold to John Hutzen but mistake made and called lot 12, the correct error. Robert J. Skinner, dec'd. Heirs: James H. Skinner of Auglaize Co.; Phebe Eliza wife of Julius C. Curtis of Montgomery Co., Ohio; Harriet wife of David Morrison of Montgomery Co., Ohio. (175)

Oct. 1850 - John H. BUDDA adms. of Joseph BUDDA, dec'd vs Mary Ann BUDDA. Petition to complete real contract. Filed 10-11-1850. Land, Juseph Budda in his lifetime on 5-1-1850 contracted to sell to Henry Gaehr 40 acres NE¼NE¼ Section 36, Township 7 South, Range 4 East for $150.00 with $35.00 being paid. Only daughter, Mary Ann Budda. (182)

Oct. 1850 - Gerhard SIVERIN adms. of John H. TIMMERMAN, dec'd vs. Heirs. Petition to sell land. Filed 3-20-1850. Land, 120 acres SE¼ SW¼ and W½ SE¼ Section 29, Township 7 South, Range 4 East. No widow. Heirs: Henry Timmerman, Harm H. Timmerman, Caroline Timmerman, Mary Ann Timmerman and Catharine Timmerman. (184)

Oct. 1850 - Richard R. Barrington adms. of John POP, dec'd vs. George POP, et al. Petition to sell land. Filed 4-2-1850. Land, 80 acres W½ SW¼ Section 8, Township 5 South, Range 3 East. No widow. Children: George Pop, Mary Ann Pop, Barbary Jane Pop, and Catharine Pop. (187)

Apr. 1851 - Christian HEINE vs. Albert LEMKUHL, et al. Bill in Chancery. Filed 6-3-1850. Christian Hein of Auglaize County states that on 4-6-1847 one John Philip Rothaas became indebted for $650.00 on a promissary note on land then in Mercer County now in Auglaize Co. described as 20 acres W½ NW¼ Section (not stated), Township 7 South, Range 4 East and that said note was sold to Lemkuhl. Johan Philip Rothass, dec'd died intestate leaving no property. Heirs Fredericka wife of Albert Lemkuhl, Louisa Rothaas, Caroline Rothaas and August Rothaas. (189)

Apr. 1851 - William FINKE adms. of Carl P. COLERT, dec'd vs. Catherena COLERT, et al. Petition to sell land. Filed 3-21-1850. Land, 80 acres NW¼ NE¼ & NW¼ NW¼ Section 9, Township 7 South, Range 5 East in Shelby Co., Ohio. Widow, Catherina Colert entitled to dower. Heirs: Catherena Colert Jr. and Palina Colert. (193)

Apr. 1851 - E.C. STANCLIFT adms. of John DAVIDSON, dec'd vs. Widow and Heirs. Petition to sell land. Filed 3-30-1850. Land, lots 4 & 5 in Block 7 in East addition of town of St. Marys. Widow, Elizabeth L. Davidson. No children. Heirs are brothers and sisters who reside in Massachusetts their names and exact residence not known. (196)

Apr. 1851 - J. H. STINEMAN adms. of Herman HOLTFOGHT, dec'd vs. Widow and Heirs. Petition to sell land. Filed 3-20-1850. Land, E½ NW¼ Section 29, Township 7 South, Range 4 East. Widow , Mareanna Holtfoght now the wife of Albert Schmut, entitled to dower. Heirs: Elizabeth Holtfoght, Henry Holtfoght and Caroline Holtfoght.(199)

Apr. 1851 - John L. CAMPBELL adms. of Archibald CAMPBELL, dec'd vs. Archibald CAMPBELL. Petition to sell land. Filed 3-19-1850. Land, 40 acres NW¼SE¼ Section 15, Township 6 South, Range 5 East. Widow, Julia Ann Campbell entitled to dower, but has quit claimed dower to petitioner. Heir: Archibald Campbell, a minor. (202)

Apr. 1851 - Courd TANGEMAN adms. of Henry KUKENMILLER, dec'd vs. Widow and Heirs. Petition to sell land. Filed 9-24-1850. Land, 80 acres W½ SE¼ Section 31, Township 6 South, Range 4 East. Widow, Caroline Kukenmiller. Heirs: Henryietta late Kukenmiller wife of Conrad Rüsse of Ohio; Maria C. Kukenmiller of Ohio; and Fritz Kukemiller of Philadelphia, Pa. (205)

Apr. 1851 - Nicholas ZANGLINE surviving adms. of Matthias SAUM, dec'd vs. Catharine SAUM, et al. Petition to sell land. Filed 10-6-1851 (1850). Land, SW¼ NW¼ Section 9, SE¼ NE¼ Section 8 and SE¼ Section 5 all in Township 6 South, Range 5 East, the last tract in Section 5 having an exception of 40 acres conveyed by Matthias Samum Sr. in his lifetime to Solomon Saum as per deed recorded in Allen Co., Ohio Deed Book C, page 532 & 533. Widow, Catharine Saum entitled to dower. Heirs: Hannah Copsy, Eva Saum, John Saum, Catharine Saum, Matthias Saum, William Saum, Solomon Saum, Simon Saum, Amos Saum and Richard Saum. (209)

Apr. 1851 - John H. STEIMAN adms. of Phillip LONGE, dec'd vs. Widow and Heirs. Petition to sell land. Filed 3-20-1850. Land, located in both Auglaize and Mercer Counties--W½ SE¼ Section 9 and W½ NW¼ and E½ and W½ SE¼ Section 4, all in Township 13, Range 2 east; also E½ NW¼ Section 30 and E½ W½ NE¼ and W½ E½ NE¼ Section 33 all in Township 7 South, Range 4 East. Widow, (not given) Long entitled to dower. Heirs: William Ruther, Jacob Longe, Elizabeth Longe, Lydia A. Longe, Susanna Longe, Nancy Longe, Phillip Longe and Mary Longe. (221)

Apr. 1851 - Anthony HAVENRBACK adms. of Detrick OLDEGES, dec'd vs. Widow and Heirs. Petition to sell land. Filed 4-3-1850. 18 2/3 acres par SE corner Section 34, Township 7 South, Range 4 East in Auglaize County and 26 2/3 acres lot 3 (no further description given) in Shelby Co., Ohio in plat of lots made by Common Pleas Court of Shelby County at April term 1836. Widow, Catharine Oldeges. Posthumous made child name Theodore. (226)

Apr. 1851 - Nicholas ZANGLINE adms. of Solomon SAUM, dec'd vs. Heirs. Petition to sell land. Filed 7-30-1850. Land, 50 acres NW¼ NW¼ Section 20 and south end SE¼ Section 17 (no township and range given); also 50 acres SW corner SE¼ Section 5, Township 6 South, Range 5 East. Heirs: Mahala Saum, Mary Ann Saumn and Jacob Saum, minor children of dec'd. (230)

AUGLAIZE COUNTY, OHIO - SHANAHAN CEMETERY
(Also known as SCOTT'S)
Pusheta Township - SE cor. SE¼ S19 -   Cox Farm

HOWELL, George W. d. 12-22-1887 ae 42-8-5
SHINN, Thomas E. d. 6-17-1855 ae 37 y
        Rebecca 4-11-1889 ae 80y 4m - ss
CORNELL, N. T. 1809-1843
        Cora S. d/o N.T.&M.E. Cornell d. 1-21-1883 ae 5-9-20
HOWELL, John M. d. 9-22-1878 ae 64-9-6
        Abigail w/o J.M. Howell d. 12-5-1869 ae 51-5-10 - ss
JACKSON, John d. 4-4-1871 ae 58-8-5
        Rachel w/o John Jackson d. 1-27-1876 ae 55-11-13 - ss
PARR, Rachel d/o J.W. & E. Parr d. 10-22-1869 ae 1-8-17
        William A. s/o - same - d. 10-8-1869 ae 2-9-13
COTTRELL,. Sarah L. d. 11-6-1878 ae 78-9-6
RITTER, Abraham d. 1-11-1844 ae 37-11-10
COTTRELL, Job d. 6-6-1856 ae ??y 8m 8d (Broken)
        Theodore s/o Job & E Cottrell d. 6-(6?)-1854 ae 8m
        Aaron L. d. July . . . . ?
COTTREL, Nancy w/o J. Cottrel d. 5-25-1862 ae 23y
        John d. at Lake Pr...? La. 3-10-1863 ae 24-2-28 Co F - 20R ss
VANDERVEER, Reuhama d/o Wm. & Synthia d. 11-20-1863 ae 16-5-4
JELLEY, Mary E. w/o James b. Shelby Co., O. 4-4-1839;d.12-8-1893 (Stone
        has "Father and Mother" but no Father inscription.
ABBOTT, Mary E. w/o J. M. (d/o J.&M.E.JELLEY)d.1-24-1887-ae 29-11-20
JONES, Inf. s/o J.M. & P. Jones d. 2-3-1860
SHANAHAN, George s/o J.&Mary A. d. 7-22-186(?)(chipped) ae 10m. 20d
CAMPBELL, John L. d. 9-5-1859 ae 80y
        Robert H. s/o J.&E. Campbell d. 12-12-1849 ae 13y 25d
        Elizabeth w/o J. Campbell d. 1-27-1866 ae (Broken)
SHANAHAN, Mary d/o H. & J. d. 8-17-1850 ae 5y 6m
FRAME, Nath- d. 1-5-1853 ae 79-4-9
SHANAHAN, Robert M. s/o H. & J. d. 8-11-1850 ae 11m
CAMPBELL, Archibald s/o A. & J. Campbell d. 4-16-1850 ae 8m 19d
CAMPBELL (?) - Christopher C. d. 5-26-1838
HARNER, Isabell w/o Francis Harner d. 8-31-1843 ae 21-3-27
        Doratha d/o F. & I. Harner d. July 1845 ae 2y 10m
CAMPBELL, Archibald d. July . . . . ? (Broken)
SPRAY, Jane w/o James Spray d. 9-20-1842 ae 26y 9m
BOWLAN, Levi s/o P. & S. Bowlan d. 1-19-1850 ae 17 y
VANDERVEER, Geo. W. s/o W.&C. Vanderveer d. 9-20-1850 ae 11m 10d
CAMPBELL, Melcom d. 10-29-1844 in 61st year of his age
VANDERVEER, Bency s/o Wm. & S. b. 8-23-1856 d. June 1861
CAMPBELL, Rachel J. d. Jan. 1838 ae. ????
HOWELL, Children of J.M.&A. - ss:- James P. d. 1-2-1851 ae 1m
        Inf. dau., Mary J., d. 1-25-1839 ae 6m;Sarah d.6-14-1843-7y 6m
SHINN, George W. s/o Thos. & R. Shinn d. 7-7-1841 ae 4m 21d
STOCKSDALE, William, Sen. d. 8-7-1840 ae 56-3-12
        George, Sen. d. Aug. 1832 ae about 56 years
        George d. 2-22-1841 ae 16-6-22 - ss
MIDLETON, C d. Sept. 1835 ae 30th yr. of his age - ss Stocksdales

Inscriptions on broken pieces:-
        d. 8-3-1855 ae 1 da
        3-10-1847

Auglaize County was formed in 1848 from portions of Allen, Logan, Darke, Mercer
and Shelby. The following records concern land which is now in the bounds of
Auglaize county prior to its formation. They were copied from Volume 5, pages
given in parenthesis.

George BORTON and others by Eli GASKILL their attorney to James WIMART - 3-31-1845 -
part SW¼ Section 31, Township 5, Range 7, 90 acres - George Borton and Mary his wife;
Josiah Borton and Lydia his wife; John Borton and Elizabeth his wife; Mahson Borton
and Rachel his wife; Isaac Borton; Job Borton and Elizabeth his wife; Henry Borton
and Rachel Ann his wife; Jeremiah Rakestraw and Margaret his wife formerly Borton;
Jacob Burden and Rebecca his wife formerly Borton; Job Rakestraw and Pheby his wife
formerly Borton; John S. Peacock and Jane his wife formerly Borton; Japheth Pricket
and Phebe his wife formerly Borton; legal heirs, devisees and legatees of Josiah
BORTON, dec'd late of Clinton County, Ohio.   (5)

Isaac W. Meason and others to John Meason - 3-17-1845 - Quit Claim - $120. -
40 acres SE¼ NW¼ Section 6, Township 5, Range 6 - Isaac W. Meason and Emily his
wife, George W. Meason and Catharine J. his wife of Fairfield Co., Ohio; S. A.
Baxter and Nancy M. his wife of Pickaway County, Ohio.   (23)

James COOK adms. of Charles HANKINSON, dec'd to John HINHSLEY - 9-6-1845 - NE¼ &
NW¼ NE¼ Section 13, Township 6, Range 6 - Sept. Term 1842 Butler County, Ohio.
Petition for sale of real estate. James Cook adms. of Charles Hankinson, dec'd,
late of Butler Co. vs. Elleanor Wicoff late Eleanor Hankinson, Rebecca Hankinson
and female name unknown; all daughters and heirs of deceased.   (..)

Beverley SHAW and others to Michael BOBP - 1-29-1842 - S½ W½ NE¼ Section .., Township 6, Range 6, 40 acres - Beverly Shaw, Julian Shaw, Jacob Bub, Elizabeth Bub,
John Sanduskey, Charles Bub, Elizabeth Bub and Mary Dover all of Allen Co., Ohio(53)

Executor and Heirs of Simon PERKINS, dec'd, to Jacob PERKINS - 11-8-1845 - 150 acres
S½ Section 6, Township 4, Range 5; 180 acres N½ Section 6, Township 5, Range 5;
80 acres N½ SE¼ Section 6, Township 6, Range 5; 162 acres S½ Section 18, Township 5,
Range 5; 160 acres SW¼ Section 8, Township 3, Range 5; and 80 acres W½ SE¼ Section
30, Township 3, Range 5 - Frederick Kinsman of Trumbull Co., Ohio; Simon Perkins
and Grace J. his wife of Summit Co., Ohio; Joseph Perkins and Martha E. his wife,
Henry B. Perkins and Jacob Perkins of Trumbull Co., Ohio; devisees under the will
of Simon Perkins, dec'd late of Trumbull Co., Ohio.   (56)

William BITLER and others to John M. SHAW - 9-22-1845 - pt. NW¼ Section 5 and part
NE¼ Section 5, Township 6, Range 7 and SE¼ Section 32, Township 5, Range 7; being
part of land which was by partition set off to Eli Bitler heir of D. Bitler Sr.,
dec'd. - Signed: William Bitler and Rebecca his wife, John F. Neil and Catharine
his wife, Henry Bitler and Margaret his wife, Daniel Bitler and Sarah Jane his wife,
Stephen Looney and Lucy Ann his wife, Elizabeth Bitler guardian of Samuel Bitler
all of Allen Co. and Lincoln G. Morehead and Justina his wife of Franklin Co., Ohio
(83)

John MONROE and Mary his wife of Shelby Co., Indiana by Power of Attorney to David
STEBLETON to John Schooler and Simon Bob Sr. - 12-13-1845 - E½ NE fractional quarter
Section 3, Township 5, Range 6, 77 acres. (71)

Richard BROWN, adms. to Hamilton DAVISON - 12-29-1845 - West middle fraction of
Section 30, Township 5, Range 6, 64 acres and NE fraction NE¼ Section 25, Township
5, Range 5, 46 acres - George Burnass of Montgomery Co., Illinois adms. of
Richard Brown, dec'd, late of Montgomery County, Illinois.   (89)

William CAZAD of Greene Co., Ohio to Mary HALL and Heirs - 4-18-1846(?) - 160 acres
SE¼ Section 11, Township 6, Range 5 - Consideration "Natural love and affection
for my daughter Mary Hall wife of Moses Hall, Jr." - Signed; William Cazad (no
co-signer). (119)

Lemuel H. IDE and Mary his wife, Joseph STOCKDALE and Melissa E. his wife of
Sangamon Co., Illinois to James ELLIOTT of Allen Co., Ohio - Quit Claim - $400.
- 5-5-1846 - NE fraction Section 19, SE¼ Section 19, N½ SW¼ Section 10, S½ SW¼,
W½ SE¼ Section 20 N½ NE¼ and E½ NW¼ Section 30 all in Township 6, Range 6 -
"interest in the estate of William Stockdale and George Stockdale, dec'd, of
Allen Co., Ohio.   (153)

Samuel MYERS and others to Conrad ROTH - 10-13-1846 - $150. -SW¼ NW¼ Section 14,
Township 6, Range 6 - Samuel Myers and Hannah, John Fouts and Elizabeth, John
Pownell and Catharine, John D. Copner and Elizabeth; their interest as heirs of
Joseph Myers, dec'd.   (194)

Jonathan A. MYERS and other to Conrad ROTH - 7-18-1846 - $75. - 40 acrew SW¼ SW¼
Section 14, Township 6, Range 6 - Jonathan A. Myers and Mary, Joseph Myers and
Mary A. of Butler and Montgomery Cos., Ohio; heirs of Joseph Myer... dec'd.   (   )

Margaret WISE widow of Charles WISE, dec'd to Conrad ROTH - 3-9-1846 - $75. -
Quit Claim - lots 23-33 Fryburgh. (196)

Henry CULBY and Mary his wife of Allen Co. to Conrad ROTH - 2-19-1846 -- In-lot 32
in Fryburgh, Pusheta Twp. - $400.   (197)

Peter F. DEMOSS and wife Lovina formerly Lovina Myers both of Cass County, Indiana
to Conrad ROTH - 8-11-1846 - $38. - 40 acres NW¼ Section 14, Township 6, Range 6
with "exception of family graveyard so long as heirs of Myers keep said graveyard
enclosed with sufficient fence".   (198)

Margaret BEEVER of North Lebanon Twp., Lebanon Co., Pa. Power of Attorney to
Phillip AMENTZ of Mexea Lumeto, Lebanon Co., Pa. - 5-13-1847. Interest in 80
acres (no further description of land given).   (262)

Augustus BEAVER and Samuel BEAVER adms. of Elias BEAVER, dec'd late of Allen Co.
to Philip K. ARENTZ of Juniata Co., Pa. - 6-30-1847 - 120 acres E½ NE¼ & E½ W½ NE¼
Section 14, Township 5, Range 5.   (272)

Grover AYERS and Jane his wife of Sangamon Co., Illinois to George W. Trumbull of
Allen Co. - 11-17-1846 - lots 1 & 42 in Wapokeneta. (282)

John BLUEST and Catharine his wife of Gasconade Co., Missouri to John BOP
- 7-9-1847 - $500. - NW¼ SW¼ Section 15, Township 6, Range 6.   (292)

Elizabeth BOB to John WALK - 1-16-1847 - $100. - Quit Claim - NW¼ Section 4, Township 6, Range 7, 48 acres - Elizabeth Bob now widow of John Bob, dec'd, formerly widow of John Londing - "land which belonged to my former deceased husband John Londing". (287)

Charles RAKESTRAW and Mary his wife of Madison Co., Ohio to George W. HOLBROOK - 8-28-1847 - Quit Claim - $300. - One-sixth part E½ NE¼ Section 23, Township 5, Range 6. (333)

Josiah BORTON and Lydia his wife of Allen Co., Ohio to George W. HOLBROOK - 6-14-1847 - Quit Claim - $38. - one-sixth part E½ NE¼ Section 23, Township 5, Range 6. (334)

John RAKESTRAW and Ann his wife of Allen Co. to George W. HOLBROOK - 5-29-1847 - Quit Claim - $35. - one-sixth part E½ NE¼ Section 23, Township 5, Range 6. (334)
Joshua RAKESTRAW and Nancy Ann his wife of Allen Co. to George W. HOLBROOK - 3-30-1847 - Quit Claim - one-sixth part E½ NE¼ Section 23, Township 5, Range 6. (335)

Jeremiah RAKESTRAW and wife Margaret of Clinton Co., Ohio to George W. HOLBROOK - 9-27-1847 - Quit Claim - interest in E½ NE¼ Section 23, Township 5, Range 6. (336)

Samuel RAKESTRAW and Margaret his wife of Warren Co., Indiana to George W. HOLBROOK - 1847 - Quit Claim - interest E½ NE¼ Section 23, Township 5, Range 6. (337)

Charles C. MARSHALL, et al to Daniel RICHARDSON - 8-25-1847 - SW Fraction Section 26, Township 4, Range 5 town of Amanda - Jinkey Berryman, Charles C. Marshall and Susan his wife, Freeman Bell and Handa his wife, Archelias Martin and Catharine, his wife, William Harter and Jinkey his wife and William Cochran of Allen, Mercer and Putnam Counties, Ohio. (344)

Aaron RICHARDSON and Ann his wife of Washington Co., Iowa, to Heirs of Abraham RICHARDSON - 4-27-1847 - $320. - SE¼ SW¼ Section 6, Township 6, Range 8 - Abraham Richardson, dec'd, late of Clark Co., Ohio. (354)

N. F. BRODRICK and others to David HENRY of Shelby Co., Ohio - 2-18-1839 - $300. - 40 acres NE¼ NE¼ Section 30, Township 5, Range 7 - N. F. Brodrick and Margaret S. his wife of Elkhart Co., Indiana; John H. Henry and Isabel his wife of Hardin Co., Ohio; Robert Henry and Barbary his wife, Eleazer Hathaway and Sally his wife, Joseph Henry, Robinson Henry, William Henry, Betsy R. Henry and Jane Henry all of Shelby Co., Ohio. (546)

AUGLAIZE COUNTY, OHIO - LAND GRANTS

Auglaize County was formed in 1848 from portions of Allen, Logan, Darke, Mercer and Shelby Counties. It should be noted that the following land was granted prior to formation of the county. Records are from Deed Book 5. f denotes fractional quarter and pt denotes part.

Name and Place	Description	Section-Twp. & Range	Acres	Date	Page
NIPGEN, John of Allen Co.	ne pt ne f$\frac{1}{4}$	26-6-7	55	9-4-1838	1
NIPGEN, John of Allen Co.	w pt w$\frac{1}{2}$ n f$\frac{1}{4}$	25-6-7	39	9-4-1838	2
NIPGEN, Casper of Allen Co.	e pt ne$\frac{1}{4}$	4-6-6	64	3-15-1837	3
NIPGEN, Michael of Clark Co.	nw f$\frac{1}{4}$	19-6-7	97	3-16-1837	4
RICE, William of Logan Co.	w$\frac{1}{2}$ sw$\frac{1}{4}$	23-5-5		3-20-1837	13
WILLIAMS, Edw. of Allen Co.	nw$\frac{1}{4}$ ne$\frac{1}{4}$	13-6-6	40	10-16-1835	26
OVERHALSER, Adam of Clark Co.	w$\frac{1}{2}$ nw$\frac{1}{4}$	33-4-6	80	12-24-1835	46
PRITCHARD, John of Coshocton Co.	sw$\frac{1}{4}$	36-5-7		8-21-1837	46
VOORHIS, Jacob of Warren Co.	sw$\frac{1}{4}$	11-6-6	160	10-8-1835	116
SWICKARD, George of Franklin Co.	nw$\frac{1}{2}$ sw$\frac{1}{4}$	2-6-7		8-21-1837	127
SWICKARD, George of Franklin Co.	ne$\frac{1}{4}$ se$\frac{1}{4}$	3-6-7	40	8-21-1837	128
STILLWAY, Philip of Butler Co.	se$\frac{1}{4}$ ne$\frac{1}{4}$	15-6-5	40	10-10-1840	172
CROZIER, James of Ross Co.	se pt n$\frac{1}{2}$	27-4-5	77	5-10-1826	181
CROZIER, James of Ross Co.	e pt s$\frac{1}{2}$	27-4-5		5-10-1826	182
NAUMBUGER, Sophia Dorothea Magdalene of Allen Co.	sw$\frac{1}{4}$ se$\frac{1}{4}$	7-6-6	40	10-10-1840	204
BAILY, Richard of Allen Co.	sw$\frac{1}{2}$ & sw$\frac{1}{2}$ nw$\frac{1}{4}$	11-6-7	80	3-15-1837	210
MILLER, John of Miami Co.	se$\frac{1}{4}$	29-5-7	60	10-16-1835	219
MARSHALL, Samuel of Shelby Co.	sw pt nw$\frac{1}{4}$	14-5-5	35	10-8-1835	221
MARSHALL, Samuel of Shelby Co.	ne pt	15-5-5	29	10-8-1835	222
BLUEST, John of Montgomery Co.	sw$\frac{1}{4}$	15-6-6	160	10-9-1834	291
FULLER, Joel of Onondaga Co., New York	sw$\frac{1}{4}$ nw f$\frac{1}{4}$ & nw$\frac{1}{4}$ sw f$\frac{1}{4}$	15-6-5		3-20-1837	321
FULLER, Joel of Onondaga Co., New York	e$\frac{1}{2}$ nw$\frac{1}{4}$	15-6-5	80	3-20-1837	321
RUSSEL, Andrew of Amanda	sw f$\frac{1}{4}$	26-4-6	23	8-6-1822	343
CODDINGTON, William of Allen Co.	s$\frac{1}{2}$ se$\frac{1}{4}$	5-6-8	80	9-16-1835	351
NASON, John Wesly of Champaign Co.	se$\frac{1}{4}$ nw$\frac{1}{4}$	22-5-8	40	3-18-1837	444
MILLER, George of Pickaway Co.	nw$\frac{1}{4}$ nw$\frac{1}{4}$	23-5-7	40	10-7-1835	459
MILLER, George of Pickaway Co.	e$\frac{1}{2}$ nw$\frac{1}{4}$	32-5-7	80	10-7-1835	460
McCONNELL, John of Logan Co.	se$\frac{1}{4}$ se$\frac{1}{4}$	1-5-7	40	3-15-1837	466
ARNETT, John of Montgomery Co.	nw pt nw$\frac{1}{4}$	22-6-5	54	10-16-1835	468
WELLS, Harris of Allen Co.	nw$\frac{1}{4}$ nw$\frac{1}{4}$	21-5-8	40	3-16-1837	476
ELLIS, John of Portage Co.	w$\frac{1}{2}$ se$\frac{1}{4}$	3-5-5	80	8-21-1837	480
WOODBURY, Nathan of Allen Co.	nw$\frac{1}{4}$ ne$\frac{1}{4}$	22-5-8	40	3-16-1837	486
McCARTNEY, William of Philadelphia Co., Pa.	nw & sw pt nw$\frac{1}{4}$	7-5-6	75	3-20-1837	491
CHRISTIAN, Henry & Gottlieb NIETERT of Montgomery Co.	w$\frac{1}{2}$ se$\frac{1}{4}$	6-6-6	80	10-8-1835	512
SMITH, Casper of Miami Co.	e$\frac{1}{2}$ nw$\frac{1}{4}$	20-5-7	80	9-15-1835	513
SPEES, Matthias E. of Allen Co.	ne$\frac{1}{4}$	17-5-7	40	10-17-1834	519
NEAL, St. Seger of Perry Co.	s$\frac{1}{2}$ se$\frac{1}{4}$	2-5-8	80	3-16-1837	520
ZINN, Jacob of Butler Co.	se$\frac{1}{4}$ sw$\frac{1}{4}$	24-5-6	40	2-15-1836	541

Name and Place	Description	Section Twp. & Range	Acres	Date	Page
CONKEL, John of Allen Co.	w½ sw¼	34-4-6	80	3-13-1837	564
HEIL, Conrad of Allen Co.	ne¼ sw¼	26-5-6		8-21-1837	582
MILLER, Anton of Allen Co.	w½ se¼	26-5-6	80	8-21-1837	583
TEMPLETON, Daniel Gooden of Washington Co., Pa.	sw¼ nw¼	5-5-6		9-15-1835	586
COPELAND, John of Green Co.	nw¼ se¼	5-6-7	40	3-16-1837	589
BLACK, Daniel of Allen Co.	w pt	35-5-8	80	2-15-1836	596
BLACK, Daniel of Allen Co.	nw¼ se¼	27-5-8	40	2-5-1836	597
BLACK, Daniel of Allen Co.	w½ ne¼	34-5-8	80	3-3-1832	598
BLACK, Daniel of Allen Co.	sw¼ ne¼	27-5-8	40	3-16-1837	599
WILLIAMS, Jacob of Allen Co.	sw½ se¼	14-5-8	40	3-16-1837	615
WILLIAMS, Jacob of Allen Co.	se¼ ne¼	23-5-8	40	3-16-1837	616
HARROD, Levi of Allen Co.	n pt sw f¼	15-5-7	42	3-15-1837	623
HARROD, Elijah of Knox Co.	sw f¼	19-5-8	140	3-16-1837	624
HARROD, Martha of Knox Co.	w½ nw f¼	19-5-8	24	3-16-1837	625
BECKDOLT, Peter	s½ nw½	7-6-7	77	7-2-1839(?)	633
WALTER, George Jr. of Putnam Co.	sw¼ se¼	14-5-5	40	3-20-1837	648
WALTER, George of Hocking Co.	ne¼ se¼	14-5-5	40	3-20-1837	649

AUGLAIZE COUNTY, OHIO - MINISTERS' LICENSES

Name	Church	License Granted	County Granted	Recorded Auglaize Co.
MILLER, Rev. William	U. B.	10-30-1845	Allen	4-7-1848
REIMENSCHNIDER, Engehart	Germ. Meth. E.	11-17-1845	Allen	4-10-1848
SPRAY, Rev. James	U. B.	10-19-1847	Allen	4-25-1848
BOBST, Martin	Catholic	10-2-1844	Allen	4-17-1848
BRANDEBERRY, Chas. B.	M. E.	5-28-1841	Wayne	5-4-1848
THOMAS, Rev. Daniel	Baptist	10-25-1845	Knox	5-11-1848
HAUCK, Rev. Peter	Germ. E. Luth.	6-19-1843	Erie	5-15-1848
FAUT, Stephen	M. E.	10-27-1846	Sandusky	5-24-1848
KREVSH, Matthias	Catholic	10-3-1846	Huron	6-7-1848
COURADI, Rev. Adolph	Germ. E. Luth.	2-20-1845	Butler	6-9-1848
CAMERON, Rev. James	Presbyterian	8-29-1844	- - -	- - 1848
RICHARDSON, Daniel	Christian	11-19-1848	Franklin	7-28-1848
BORTON, Joshua	Meth. Prot.	5-3-1845	Wood	9-1-1848
WILSON, Samuel	M. E.	5-5-1842	Allen	9-8-1848
MARTZ, Michael	Christian	11-16-1840	Putnam	9-25-1848
HEOLETHNEEL, Andrew	Catholic	4-19-1848	Seneca	11-7-1848
WHITMORE, Rev. John	Catholic	6-21-1845	Huron	11-7-1848
BOWDLE, Jesse	M. E.-Deacon	9-23-1829	Ross	11-14-1848
YOURTEE, Samuel L.	M. E.	11-14-1842	Lucas	1-20-1849
EANMIGER, Rev. Lymen	Meth. Prot.	7-16-1845	Highland	3-10-1849
CARPENTER, Rev. Peter A.	Catholic	6-21-1845	Huron	- - 1849
KEMPLIN, Andrew	Catholic	4-19-1848	Seneca	5-22-1849
HAINBURGER, Maxamillian	Catholic	4-19-1848	Seneca	5-22-1849
GRIFFITH, Rev. Thomas	Presbyterian	5-17-1843	Montgomery	5-30-1849
BORHENS, Rev. H.	- - - - -	9-15-1843	Fairfield	- - 1849
SRECKNESS, John George	Evan. Luth.	10-13-1847	Van Wert	9-30-1849
DONER, Abrehan	Germ. E. Luth.	5-5-1842	Allen	10-12-1849
BESSE, Alden	Meth Prot.	3-7-1836	Fairfield	10-19-1849
GIBSON, Samuel B.	M.E.-Deacon	11-12-1840	Licking	11-3-1849
BOGGS, Rev. James	Presbyterian	7-20-1838	Crawford	12-24-1849

AUGLAIZE COUNTY, OHIO - MARRIAGES 1848-1849

Auglaize County was formed in 1848 from portions of Allen, Logan, Darke, Mercer and Shelby.

AWALT, John to Barbery Coon	10-22-1849
AYERS, Jermiah to Rachael Baker	2-11-1849
BADGLEY, George to Martha Watkins-Consent; Jane Watkins(mother)	11-18-1849
BAILEY, Perry T. to Sarah Ridley	4-1-1849
BAILY, Andrew Green to Alanda Hammock	4-22-1849
BAKER, John to Sarah Miller	3-22-1849
BALGENORT, William (Wilhelm) to Mary Agnes Kruse	6-5-1849
BARRINGTON, John to Mary Ann Watkins	9-12-1848
BAUGHMAN, David to Rebecca Beaver	lic. 8-15-1848
BENSMAN, John Wilhelm to Catharina Danzig	11-27-1849
BENSMANN, Hennamnus to Anna Maria Barger	5-28-1848
BERTING, Joseph to Elizabeth Hukenburg Nodna	8-8-1848
BIGLER, John to Mary Ann Tester	9-22-1849
BITLER, Henry to Keziah Hires	8-15-1849
BITLER, Samuel to Susanah Coleman	6-8-1848
BITMAN, George to Gertrude Mellerarned	11-28-1849
BIXLER, Michael to Chaterin Oswalts	3-12-1848
BLANK, Jacob to Sarah Justice	8-24-1848
BODA, Henry to Sarah Pernel	10-24-1849
BODKIN, Lewis to Levina Doute	11-22-1849
BOKRATH, Henry to Bermardina Luhman	11-6-1849
BORTON, Josiah to Mahala Noggle	2-23-1849
BRADFORD, N. T. to Aurelia Dennison	6-7-1849
BRESLER, Peter to Sarah Ashburn - both of Union Twp.	5-23-1848
BRINKLINGER, William to Marinda Gardner	3-29-1849
BRYANT, James to Ann Maria Smith	8-29-1849
BRYANT, William to Maria Elizabeth Smith	10-23-1849
BRUGANSHIMID, John Bernard to Anna Mary Clara Ruhe	5-22-1849
BUCHMAN, David to Rebecca Beber (Note: See BAUGHMAN, David)	8-16-1848
BUDDE, Joseph to Maria Elizabeth Guartmann	5-28-1848
BUDDE, Theodore to Mary Gertrud Elizabeth Alkenburg	10-16-1849
BÜKER, Henry to Clara Brugenschmid	10-23-1849
BUP, Seckueal to Magdalene Dearbaugh	12-12-1848
BURMIESTER, Carl to Charlotte Koch	11-2-1849
BURTON, Joshua U. to Mary Giberson	4-15-1848
CAIN, John B. to Barbra Ridley	4-20-1848
CAMPELL, Archibal to Julia Ann Long	4-13-1848
CARTER, Samuel to Lucy Gardner	3-8-1849
CEPERSON, Zacariah to Sidney Tilberry	7-20-1848
CHAMBERLIN, Thomas T. to Elizabeth Young	11-12-1848
CHURCH, James P. to Mary M. Shaw	3-1-1849
CLARK, Samuel B. to Hester Ann Benner	lic. 5-10-1848
CLARK, William Hamilton to Martha Barrington	lic. 7-24-1848
CLAWSON, Isaih to Lydia Ann Cochran	lic. 5-7-1849
CLINGAMON, Hirom to Sophrona Kent	7-6-1848
COLEMAN, James H. to Polly Miller	6-24-1849
COMPTON, Isaac R. to Sarah Brentlinger	8-9-1849
COOK, Lewis to Catherin Groshauts	lic. 5-7-1849
COOK, William to Mary Elizabeth Brunsman	10-14-1849

COON, Samuel to Phebe Jane Bramblet	8-16-1849
COOPER, Alexander to Julia Dennison	1-18-1849
COPSAY (COPEY), Philip G. to Elizabeth Holbrook	8-20-1849
COPSEY, Richard to Hannah Saum	8-1-1848
COWAN, Calvert W. to Martha J. McCune	6-30-1849
CRAFT, Charles to Christine Lorar	7-1-1848
CROW, Richard to Elizabeth Moorcraft	4-26-1849
DENNEY, John to Susan Jacobs	7-2-1848
DENNY, Jorden to Sally Daniels	9-6-1849
DORSTON, John Henry to Mary Kath. Osterfeld	11-22-1849
DRAHMAN, John Henry to Anna Mary Volting	11-21-1849
DREES, John Michael to Mary Cath. Wellerding	11-8-1849
DRESSE, Richard to Maria Angelan Elson	11-16-1848
EILERMANN, Joseph to Ana Maria Helensing	9-28-1848
EITINK, John to Katharina Firing	9-17-1849
ELLIOTT, Alexander to Elizabeth Deed	5-24-1849
ELLIOTT, Alexander to Ency Beardsley Ellis	10-11-1849
ELLIS, David to Caroline Teeman	8-9-1849
ELLSWORTH, George to Martha Jane Constant	6-18-1848
EMERSON, Adams to Nancy Jane Corder	4-13-1848
EVANS, William to Anna Coil	4-13-1848
FARLMAN, Haniz to Elizabeth Dickson	4-24-1849
FAY, Stephen B. to Cassann Call	10-4-1849
FINKE, William to Catherin Kunzel	5-22-1848
FISBACH, Michael to Elizabeth Young	6-1-1848
FISHBACK, Michael to Bena Gipe	12-24-1848
FORTMAN, Heinrich to Elizabeth Penna	10-9-1849
FRANK, Peter to Charlotte Shaeffer	11-29-1849
FRAUTWAIN, T. F. to Chi Reinacher	6-21-1849
FRITZ, Daniel to Maria Leever	12-25-1848 (1849)
GISH, John to Rachael Kern	4-26-1849
GOODMAN, Nicholas to Mary E. Munger	lic. 1-24-1849
GRAHAM, Christopher to Mary T. Cowan	6-22-1848
GUARTMANN, Maria Elizabetha to Joseph Budde	5-28-1848
HADIN, Isaac to Ester Ridley	4-5-1849
HAMILTON, David J. to Mary Jane Miller	8-9-1849
HAMILTON, Samuel to Rebeca Ann Davis	10-12-1848
HARPS, William to Barbra Bearlin	3-28-1848
HAWTHORN, John to Melinda Haines	8-23-1849
HECKFORT, Bernard Henry to Clara Elizabeth Huchtscheiper	10-16-1849
HECKFOUT, Bernard Herr to Anna Maria Scheber	11-14-1848
HEID, Paulus to Catharine Birk	10-15-1849
HERSHFIELD, George to Mary Engel Louisa Woodmeyer	8-27-1849
HESTER, David to Rachael Woolrey	11-29-1849
HEZEKER, Charles A. to Catharine Engel Wisman	6-28-1849
HORBERKAY, Adolph to Christine Elizabeth Shear	7-16-1848
HOWEL, Samuel Jackson to Sarah M. Adney	4-1-1849
HUCKRIEDE, Henry W. to Anna M. Smith	11-15-1849
HUDSON, Elijah to Margaret Combs	4-19-1849
HUNTER, William to Mary Agnes Barrington	10-25-1849
HUTSON, Solomon to Elizabeth Combs	2-1-1849
JAKWITH, Anton to Anna Maria Rathwer	5-28-1848

100

```
JULIAN, Isaac to Cornelia Young                                  10-7-1849
JULIN, John to Ellen Kisaman                                     5-30-1849
KATHARENAM, Josephus Tabbens to Agnes Neeman                     10-2-1849
KEARNS, William to Ellen Newland - Consent: Martin Newland       6-10-1849
KEYSER, John F. to Barbary Baughman                              5-17-1849
KING, Aaron to Margaret Ann Hammon                          lic.7-6-1848
KIZER, Joseph to Elizabeth Brown                                12-13-1849
KNOESEL, George to Elizabeth Bup                                 12-21-1848
KNOST, John H. to Wilhelmine Muller                             12-21-1849
KNOSTMAN, Heinicus to Elizabeth Willowh                          9-24-1849
KOHLER, Frederick Wilhelm to Katharine Zorn                      8-1-1849
KRAUND, JOHN to Anna Mary Holtfogt                               11-5-1849
KREITZER, David to Rachael Markly                                1-1-1849
KREMER, Henry to Sophia Nieter - New Bremen                      8-6-1848
LAMPING, Frederick to Anna Wehrman                               9-19-1849
LAMPING, John F. to Mary Wehrmann                           lic. 6-13-1848
LECKLENBURG, Frederick to Catharine Lamping                      12-13-1849
LIPPERT, William to Christena Fisher                             4-29-1849
LOCKARD, James to Mary Jane Whetstone                            5-1-1849
LOHMAN, Henry to Katharina Raw                                  10-16-1849
LONGWORTH, Cyrus to Eliza Jane Rout                             12-12-1849
LOONEY, Jonathan to Rebecca Childs                               4-23-1848
LUTTRELL, John L. to Charlotte Holbrook                          3-29-1849
LYNCH, James F. to Sarah Jane Bannum                        lic. 3-19-1849
LYONS, Washington to Hannah Mariah Clark                         5-15-1849
McFARLAND, Robert to Margaret Cox                           lic. 11-12-1849
MACHETAUZ, Gotleip to Catherin Frymore                           5-11-1848
MERTZ, Casper to Catharine Keller                                1-5-1849
METZ, Casper to Phillips Metz                                   10-16-1849
METZ, William to Eliza Bassel                                    5-24-1849
MÖNKWITH, Wilhelm to Gertrude Gävels                            11-28-1849
MONTGOMERY, David to Sarah Jane Branum                           4-18-1849
MOORE, George G. to Elizabeth Hullinger                          6-7-1849
MORGAN, George to Rachael Bartlett                              12-8-1848
NELSON, William S. to Elizabeth Fairfield                       11-8-1849
NICHOLS, William H. to Mary Crozier                             10-24-1849
NIEMAN, John B. to Arolina Louisa Hezeker                        6-24-1849
NOGLE, G. C. to Mary Ann Brewer                                  9-2-1848
NORTHOF, Stephen to Catharena Ceiese                             4-23-1849
NOXEL, henry to Catharine Bahlman                               10-30-1849
OAKLEY, Thomas A. to Mary Jane Atkinson                         12-31-1849
OCRMANN, Joseph to Maria (Mary) Dickson                          8-28-1849
ODLE, Benjamin F. to Martha Ann Overly                           7-15-1848
OLDIGER, Wilhelm to Catharine Elizabeth Lehster                 11-20-1849
ORR, John to Nancy E. Shaw                                      11-1-1849
OSBORN, John F. to Melzena Liggot                                9-14-1848
PEARCE, William to Sarah Ann Ream                                4-12-1849
PERKINS, Elias to Elizabeth Beers                                4-25-1849
POBENMIRE, George to Nancy Jane Bowersock                       10-26-1848
RAKESTRAW, Joshua to Elizabeth Walters                           8-10-1848
REES, William to Margaret Cooper                                12-13-1849
RICHARDSON, Perry to Elizabeth Harris                    12-15-1849(1848)
```

RICHARDSON, William to Catherin Schoonover

(lic. gives Catherin Keath)   10-8-1848

RICHTER, John Heineicus to Anna Maria Hinders   2-15-1849

RONEL, Mathias to Elizabetha Grubli   9-5-1848

ROTHAUSE, Henrich to Catharine Klikhammer   9-1-1848

RUDY, Aaron to Malinda McCoy   12-14-1848

ROTHSHULLING, Joseph Herr to Anna Maria Blanke   11-12-1848

SCHEBEL, Tynatz to Megdildis Schell   1-10-1849

SCHEMEL, Heinricus to Anna Mary Eitert   9-24-1849

SCHNEIDER, Nicholas to Margarethree Nippichen   5-9-1848

SCHNIDER, John Paul to Mariah Anna Franzisca Dorsten   2-15-1849

SCHROEDER, Frederick to Henrietta Freverd   2-16-1849

SEITER, John to Nietoria Grof   9-5-1848

SELLINGER, Michael to Barbara Fahr   11-7-1848

SHIELDS, John M. to Orpha Mead   12-25-1849

SMITH, James T. to Susan C. R. Corder   5-15-1848

SMITH, John Frederick to Wilhelmine Draganfuller   9-30-1849

SMITH, Marmaduke W. to Rosanna McConell   8-27-1849

SMITH, Richard to Mary Ann Barrington   10-3-1849

SPRAGUE, John to Ann Elizabeth Blake   9-29-1849

STEINK, George to Mary Catharine Mayers   5-29-1848

STINE, Lewis to Mathilda Sophia Dicker   lic. 8-16-1849

STRATTON, Minard F. to Mary Ann Newland   1-17-1849

SUNDERLAND, James to Jemima Baker   3-16-1848

SUTTON, Thomas H. to Mary Wagner   10-8-1849

TACKLENBURY, Henry to Catherin Henders   8-3-1848

TANGEMANN, John Albert to Ana Catherin Mary Harus   9-18-1848

TAYLOR, James to Lydia Mariah Voorhis   6-1-1848

TAYLOR, William to Mary Myers   7-13-1848

TED, William to Elizabeth Langly   lic. 8-17-1849

TELLMAN, Wilhelm to Mrs. Anna Broakride - widower and widow   5-2-1849

TILLING (TULLING), William to Catharine Schulta   9-13-1849

TIPPEE, Orin A. L. To Olive S. Orton   11-13-1849

TOMPSON, William to Sarah Carter   3-23-1848

TRAVIS, F. M. to Rebecca Brener   10-10-1849

URNSTED, Emanuel to Mary Jane Buckey   11-24-1848

VOGT, John Frederick to Helena Dahsonbrook   11-27-1849

WAGNER, Samuel to Caroline M. Katts   4-8-1848

WANER, Michael to Magdalena Bauer   3-7-1848

WATERS, Joseph to Agnus Jacobs   2-8-1849

WATT, John to Jane Fisher   6-19-1848

WEHRMANN, John Herr to Bernadina Winner   9-1-1848

WEIDERMANN, Frederick Arnold to Anna Mary Strow   12-4-1849

WELLS, Farries to Susanah Hines   12-28-1849

WESTBAY, Matthias to Mary Frances Webb   8-24-1849

*WHETSTONE, John to Catharine Randale   5-10-1849

*WHETSTONE, John to Catharine Rennels   8-8-1849

WHETSTONE, Samuel to Elizabeth Lockard   11-22-1849

WIERWILLE, Wilhelm to Christina Readvillens   7-28-1848

WILLIAMS, Abraham to Anna Maria O'Neal   9-29-1848

*May be same, if so, two dates.

WILLIAMS, Elias N. D. to Margret Bortz   7-21-1848
WILLIAMS, Thomas to Hannah Wagner   10-30-1849
WILSON (WILLIAMS), James to Margaret Hawthorn   7-19-1849
WITTE, Henrich to Anna Maria Knoben   5-28-1848
WITTE, William to Mary Olbers   11-9-1849
WOEDING, Bernhard Heinrick to Anna Mariah Schmissing   2-20-1849
WOLSEY, John T. to Sarah Ann Constant   6-18-1848

BELMONT COUNTY, OHIO - COMMON PLEAS COURT MINUTES 1805-1808

The following records were taken from Journal A. Pages were not numbered.

December Term 1805

John Bell and Margaret Price appointed adms. of estate of David Price, dec'd.
Security, Robert Bell and Alexander Gaston. -- John Henthorn appointed adms. of
the estate of James Henthorn, dec'd. -- William Holmes chose Archibald McElroy as
his guardian. -- Noah Zane adms. of Absalom Martin, dec'd made deed of conveyance
to Daniel Harris. -- John Workman appoirted adms. of estate of Samuel Hunter, dec'd.
-- Nancy Selby vs. James Cloyd. Bastardy. Female child born to Nancy on 18 August
1805 named Caroline. -- John Winter, native of England made application to be
admitted as citizen. -- Amos Sparks appointed adms. of the estate of Mark Sparks,
dec'd. Security, Jeremiah Burris and Joseph Linder.

April Term 1806

Will of William Outland produced and proven with letters granted to Margaret Outland,
James Edgerton and John Doudney. -- Margaret Hazlett, James Miller and John
Patterson appointed adms. of estate of Isaac Hazlett, dec'd. Security, William
Brown and Samuel Sullivan. -- Margaret Hazlett, James Miller and John Patterson
appointed guardians of Sarah, William, Mary, Cunningham, Isaac and James Hazlett,
children of Isaac Hazlett, dec'd.

August Term 1806

Will of William Thompson, dec'd produced and proven with letters granted to Sarah
Thomson and Samuel Stuart. -- Michael Ellis granted license to perform matrimony.

November Term 1806

John Simonson being next of kin was appointed adms. of estate of William P. Brooks,
dec'd. Widow, (not named) relinquished her right to administer estate. Security,
John Patterson and Andrew Moore. -- Will of John Fairhurst, dec'd produced and
proven with letters issued to William Woods, Jeremiah Fairhurst and Joseph Marshall.

December Term 1806

Alexander Caldwell, Jonathan Jennings and George Paull admitted to practice as
attorney at law.

April Term 1807

Jane Ward appointed administrator of Aaron Ward, dec'd. Security, Robert Forrens-
worth and Seth Ward. -- Zephemah Bell and Margaret Price appointed guardians of
Samuel Price aged 4 yrs. and 5 mos., John Price aged 2 yrs. and 7 nos. and Peter
Price aged 6 mos.; being ages of children at time of decease of David Price on
9th November 1805. -- John Patterson and Joseph Marshall appointed guardians of
Andrew Marshall, Samuel Marshall and John Marshall, minor children of John Marshall,
dec'd. -- Will of Thomas Plummer produced and proven with John Webster and Mahlon
Smith named as executors.

June Term 1807

James Lunday appointed adms. of the estate of James Lunday Sr., dec'd. Security, John Boyd and Matthew Patterson.

August Term 1807

William Giffen and Arch'd Giffen vs. John Johnston and James Johnston, heirs of William Johnston, dec'd and John Allen and Martha his wife. Robert Giffen guardian of John and James Johnston, minors. Partition of land described as E½ Section 8, Township 6, Range 3. -- Jacob Shuman appointed adms. of estate of Jonathan Kent, dec'd. Security, Thomas Lennon, Thomas Feeley and Samuel King.

September Term 1807

Easter Hotts will produced and proven with Samuel Connell and Hance Wiley named as executors.

October Term 1807

Grizzey Perrel appointed adms. of the estate of Alexander Perry. Security, Josiah Dillon and Thomas Gilham. -- Will of William Norris produced and proven, widow (not named) relinquished her right to dower. -- Hannah Carnes and Elias A. Deddle appointed adms. of the estate of Daniel Carnes, dec'd. Security, Sterling Johnston and John Thompson.

December Term 1807

Catherine Holtz chose William Hulse as her guardian, Ludwick, Mary, Peggy and George Holtz chose William McFarland and William Hulse as their guardian. Elizabeth Holtz chose William McFarland as her guardian. -- Elizabeth Edwards and William Bell appointed adms. of the estate of Thomas Edwards, dec'd. Walter Edwards aged 17 yrs. and John Edwards aged 15 yrs. chose William Bell as their guardian. -- Catherine Teters and John Brown appointed adms. of the estate of Francis Teters, dec'd. Security, Robert Gilkinson and Edward Bryson. -- Samuel Burns, Denny Burns by the said Samuel Burns his next friend, James Burns, David Burns, Agnes Burns and John Dickerson and Margery his wife late Margery Burns vs. John Clark. In Covenant.

January Term 1808

Susanna Davis, David Ruble and Edward Brison appointed adms. of the estate of John Davis, dec'd. Security, David Thomas and Matthias Noftsinger. -- Frederick Ault and Caty Ault chose Samuel Sullivan as their guardian for special purpose of recovering and receiving for their use a Legacy left them by Peter Law now in the hands of And'w Law. Court appointed Samuel Sullivan guardian of George Ault aged 14 yrs. for purpose aforesaid.

BELMONT COUNTY, OHIO - COMMON PLEAS COURT RECORDS 1828-1832

The following records were taken from Chancery Record 2, located in the Common Pleas Court (Clerk of Court's Office) at the court house in St. Clairsville.
Page on which the record may be found in the book is given in parenthesis.

Mar. 1828 - Martha SMITH vs. James E. NEWELL, etal. Petition for Dower. Filed 4-14-1827. John Smith, dec'd, died 1813. Widow, Martha Smith. John and Martha married 179_ (note: left blank). Land, Lots 57 & 58 St. Clairsville, which Smith purchased from Wm. Woods and Jane his wife; that James E. Newell claims right from Woods as do Hugh Cassady and Daniel Beighly. (1)

June 1828 - John CUNNINGHAM executor of will of Thomas ELDRIDGE, dec'd. Petition to make deed. Filed June 1828. Thomas Eldridge in his lifetime agreed to sell Isaac Workman and John Rose on 6-8-1825, land on McMahans Creek (no further description of land given). Heirs: Benjamin. Thomas, Elizabeth and Patty Eldridge, all minors. (7)

June 1828 - Margaret MEREDITH vs. Sarah MEREDITH, etal. Petition for Dower. Filed 4-10-1827. Land, two tracts--1st tract, 80 acres SW cor. NW¼ Section 19, Township 8 Range 4; 2nd tract, 10 acres Section 19, Township 4, Range 4, lines--George McWilliams and Samuel Patton. Children: Josiah Meredith and Israwl Meredith of Richland Co., Ohio, Albinah wife of James Morrison, Elizabeth Meredith, Mary Meredith, David Meredith, David Meredith, Benjamin H. Meredith, all of Belmont Co., Ohio, the last four named being minors. (8)

June 1828 - Mary WRIGHT and husband, Wm. WRIGHT vs. James GREEN, eta.. Petition for Dower. Filed 7-4-1827. Land, NE¼ Section 4, Township 7, Range 5 in Steubenville land district. Alexander Green, dec'd. Widow, Mary, now wife of Wm Wright; that Mary married Alexander Green in Ireland. Heirs: James Green being 21 yrs., Isaac Green and Sampson Green, both minors. That Alexander Green, dec'd was bequeathed above mentioned land by will. (13)

Sept. 1828 - Isaac STEVESON and Anna wife vs. Elizabeth WILSON, etal. Bill in Chancery. Filed 2-22-1827. Land, 73 acres Section 3, Township 9, Range 6. John Wilson, dec'd, died Oct. 1814 Belmont Co., Ohio. Widow, Sophia. Three children: Anna formerly Wilson wife of Isaac Steveson, Lewis Wilson resides in Tennessee and Daniel Wilson, dec'd, his children--Elizabeth and John Wilson. Will of John Wilson of Kirkwood twp., Belmont Co., Ohio; dated 9-24-1814; probated 12-5-1814 Ohio Co., Virginia; recorded 3-21-1815 Belmont Co., Ohio names: wife, Sophia; sons, Lewis and Daniel; daughter, Anna, Executors: brother, Joseph Wilson and William Groves. Signed: John Wilson. Witnesses: John McCullock, Henry Demest, and Lewis Willson. (32 & 89)

Sept. 1828 - Absalom KELLAR vs. Isaac KELLAR, etal. Petition for Partition. Filed 12-27-1827. Land, 100 acres Section 23, Township 7, Range 4, lines--Evan Philips, Joseph Irwin and Ned Mahan. George Kellar, dec'd. Widow, Comfort Kellar of Belmont Co. Heirs: Absalom Kellar of Belmont Co.; John Kellar of Monroe Co., Ohio; Ann wife of Lewis Wonsell of Morgan Co., Ohio; Levi Kellar of Guernsey Co., Ohio; Benjamin Kellar of Guernsey Co., Ohio; Isaac Kellar of Belmont Co.; and Thomas Kellar, who may not be living, if not then his family, of Morgan Co., Ohio. (84)

106

Mar. 1829 - In matter of David McCulloch gdn. of Isaac McCulloch, a minor. Petition to sell land. Filed Sept. 1828. Land, 104 acres Kirkwood twp. in NW corn. Section 4, Township 9, Range 6 being Lot 10 in survey of lands of John McCulloch, dec'd in partition among heirs. Isaac McCulloch aged 17 years on 26 Oct. 1827 is deaf and dumb and lives Ohio Co., Va. and is heir of John McCulloch. Guardian of said Isaac is his brother, David McCulloch. (91)

Mar. 1829- Letitia CRAIG admsrx. of Nathaniel CRAIG, dec'd vs. Robert CRAIG, etal. Petition to sell land. Filed June 1828. Land, 11 acres part Section 19, Township 7, Range 3 lines--Paul Preston, being in Steubenville land district. Nathaniel Craig, dec'd. Widow, Letitia Craig. Brothers: Robert Craig and James Craig of Ireland. Sister, Jane wife of Robert Wallace of Pennsylvania. (94)

Mar. 1829 - John FULKS executor of Joseph ARMSTRONG, dec'd vs. Priscilla ARMSTRONG and Maria ARMSTRONG. Petition to sell land. Filed June 1828. Land, 138 acres part Section 33, Township 6, Range 3, lines--Burris land. Widow, Priscilla Armstrong. Only child, Maria Armstrong. (97)

Mar. 1829 - John RICE vs. Thomas RICE, etal. Petition for Partition. Filed 12-26-1827. Land: 40 acres S end SE¼ Section 25, Township 8, Range 5; 60 acres being all balance of NE¼ Section 30, Township 7, Range 5 after deduction of 100 acres sold by Richard Rice to Samuel Rice from S end of quarter; 14 acres and 28 poles SE¼ Section 25, Township 8, Range 5 conveyed to Heirs of Richard Rice on 3-8-1822 by William Rice and Elizabeth his wife. Richard Rice, dec'd, died intestate in year 1817 or 1818. Children: John, Thomas, William, Elizabeth, Harriet and Nancy Rice, the last three named are not of age, all reside Belmont Co. except Thomas and William of parts unknown. (105)

Mar. 1829 - Luther PRYOR and Wm PHILIPS and wife Sarah vs. John PRYOR, etal. Petition for Partition. Filed June 1828. Land, 160 acres SW¼ Section 35, Township 6, Range 4. John Pryor Sr. of Belmont Co., dec'd, died fall 1828. Widow, Margaret Pryor of Belmont Co. Children: 1/12th part, Margaret wife of Francis Stephenson of Muskingum Co., Ohio; 1/12th part, Samuel Pryor of Monroe Co., Ohio; 1/12th part, Luther Pryor; 1/12th part, Sarah wife of Wm Philips; 1/12th part, Hannah wife of Elisha Lucas; 1/12th part jointly, Robert Pryor, dec'd, his children--Amos, Levi, Margaret, Thomas, John B. and Surete Pryor; 1/12th part, John Pryor; 1/12th part, Isaac Pryor; 1/12th part, William Pryor; 1/12th part, Joshua Pryor; 1/12th part, James Pryor; 1/12th part, Nathan Pryor; all reside Belmont Co. except first two named. (110)

Mar. 1829 - Joseph BAILEY and Susannah wife vs. Nicholas HEDGES, etal. Bill in Chancery. Filed Feb. 1826. Land, 60 acres (no further description) in Belmont Co. purchased from James Bell on 11-17-1813. Mary Hedges, dec'd, died October last (1825). Children: Susannah wife of Joseph Bailey, Nicholas Hedges, John Hedges, Joseph Hedges, Moses Hedges and Sarah wife of George Keller; Grandchild, Abigail Hedges. That Susannah and husband Joseph Bailey were living in Wheeling, Virginia in 1813 when her mother (Mary Hedges) came to western country and proposed that if they would move to farm and let her reside with them for the rest of her life, that she would purchase said farm for them. (121 & 192)

June 1829 - Launcelot BROWN adms. of William BROWN, dec'd vs. Barbara BROWN, etal.
Petition to sell land. Filed March 1829. Land, pt W½ Section 36, Township 3, Range
2, 121 acres, conveyed to Wm Brown, dec'd on 3-1-1627 by Noble Carothers. William
Brown, dec'd late of Belmont Co. Widow, Barbara Brown. Children: John Brown,
William Brown, Nancy Brown, James Brown, Jefferson Brown, Sally wife of Philip Ander-
son, David Brown, George Brown, Hiram Brown, Catharine Brown, Elizabeth Brown, Edward
Brown and Samuel Brown; the last seven named being minors. (155)

June 1829 - John CAMPBELL and John McNARY adms. of Alexander McNARY, dec'd vs.
Margaret McNARY, etal. Petition to sell real estate. Filed June 1828. Land,
205 acres Section 34, Township 9, Range 3, Jefferson Co., Ohio; part Section 19,
Township 8, Range 4, lines--Joseph Ralston and Carnes Fulton, being in Steubenville
land district, Belmont Co.; Lots 154-157, Cadiz, Harrison Co., Ohio. Alexander
McNary, dec'd. Widow, Margaret McNary. Children: John, Samuel, James, Eleanor,
Joseph, Alexander and William McNary, all of Belmont Co. (159)

June 1829 - Daniel BERRY vs. Thomas BERRY, etal. Petition for Partition. Filed
4-30-1829. Land, 41 acres pt. NE½ Section 35 and 61 acres pt SE½ Section 36,
Township 6, Range 3. John Berry, dec'd, died intestate Belmont Co. Heirs:
Daniel Berry of Belmont Co.; Thomas Berry of Coshocton Co., Ohio; Jacob Berry;
Isaac Berry; Enoch Berry; Delilah wife of N. Wells; Elizabeth wife of Jas. Welsh;
Rebecca wife of Thomas O'Heare; Mary wife of John Yost; and John Berry. (165)

June 1829 - David GRAY and Christiana his wife vs. Ruth EDGERTON, etal. Petition
for Partition. Filed 2-3-1829. Land: 160 acres SW½ Section 13, Township 8, Range
3; 160 acres SW½ and 159 acres NE½ Section 10, Township 7, Range 6, pt. SE½ Section
19, Township 8, Range 6. Richard Edgerton, dec'd. Widow Mary Edgerton of Belmont
Co. Six children: Christiana wife of David Gray. Ruth Edgerton, Ann. Edgerton,
Jesse Edgerton, Sarah(?) Edgerton and Thomas Edgerton; all of Belmont Co., the last
five named being minors. (168)

June 1829 - Ambrose DANFORD and Samuel DANFORD vs. Margaret DANFORD, etal. Petition
for Partition. Filed 7-1-1828. Land: NW½ Section 23, Township 5, Range 4, Belmont
Co.; SE½ Section 35, Township 7, Range 7, Monroe Co., Ohio; SE½ Section 25, Township
8, Range 7, Guernsey Co., Ohio. Peter Danford, dec'd, late of Belmont Co. Widow,
Margaret Danford. Children: William Danford, dec'd, his children--Hiram Michail,
Bathsheba Danford, Albraham Danford, Peter Danford and John Danford, all of Belmont
Co.; Rebecca widow of Nicholas Koontz, he being dec'd, of Maryland; Sarah wife of
Cornelius Bryan of Monroe Co., Ohio; Margaret wife of Samuel Thomas of Belmont Co.;
Nancy wife of James Groves of Belmont Co.; Ambrose Danford; Samuel Danford. (180)

Sept. 1829 - John PHILIPS vs. David PHILIPS, etal. Petition for Partition. Filed
5-2-1829. Land, 160 acres Section 23, Township 7, Range 4. Evan Philips, dec'd,
late of Belmont Co. Children: John Philips; Jane Knight; Matilda Philips; Nancy
wife of Peter Barnes of Belmont Co.; Evan Philips of Belmont Co.; David Philips
of Morgan or Guernsey Co.; William Philips of Morgan or Guernsey Co.; Enoch Philips,
dec'd, his children--Margaret wife of Ebenezer Demick, Jane wife of Peter Pickenpair
and George Philips a minor by John Westly Starr his guardian, all of Morgan or
Guernsey Co. (188)

Sept. 1829 - Daniel McVICKAR and Margaret his wife vs. Edward TOMPKINS, etal.
Petition for Partition. Filed 4-28-1829. Land, lot 12 in town of Belmont.
Benjamin Tompkins, dec'd, late of Belmont Co. Widow, Sarah Tompkins of Belmont
Co. Issue: Margaret wife of Daniel McVickar, Edward Tompkins, Lewis Tompkins,
Sarah Tompkins and Benjamin Tompkins, all of Belmont Co., the last four named
being minors by Wm Coffee their guardian. (203)

Sept. 1829 - Andrew BARNETT vs. Elizabeth GRANVILLE, etal. Petition for Partition
Filed 1-14-1829. Land, SE¼ Section 33, Township 5, Range 3. John Barnett, dec'd.
Children: Andrew Barnett, Elizabeth late Barnet wife of William Granville, Martha
late Barnet wife of Joseph David, Margaret Barnett, James Barnett, John Barnett
and David Barnett, all of Belmont Co., the last three named being minors. (290)

Mar. 1830- Jane FINCH guardian of John, William, Hannah and Nathaniel Finch.
Petition to sell land. Filed Sept. 1829. Land 172 acres NW cor. Section 18,
Township 6, Range 3, except 20 acres sold to Zephaniah Bell by Finch in his
lifetime. Jesse Finch, dec'd, late of Belmont Co., died in 1829. Jesse Finch
by last will and testament devised to his three children, Nathaniel Finch,
Hannah wife of John Bell and Ann wife of Peter Maring each one-fourth part of
said tract of land; he devised one-fourth part jointly to his grandchildren,
Jesse Finch Jr., Ann wife of Benjamin Brotherton, John Finch, William Finch,
Hannah Finch and Nathaniel Finch, the last four named being minors. (302)

Mar. 1830 - Wm COOK adms. of George LOVE, dec'd vs. Mary LOVE, etal. Petition
to sell real estate. Filed Sept. 1829. Land, SW¼ Section 15, Township 8, Range
4 and lots 37 and 38 in Shepherstown, Harrison Co., Ohio. George Love, dec'd,
late of Belmont Co. Widow, Mary Love. Children: Thomas, John and George Love;
all minors. Isabella Love, mother of said George Love, dec'd has dower rights
during her natural life in 20 acres of Section 15, Township 8, Range 4. (306)

Mar. 1830 - John NEFF vs. Peter NEFF, etal. Petition for Partition. Filed
7-17-1829. Land, 120 acres E½ Section 13, Township 7, Range 4, Richland twp.
Heirs: John Neff Jr.; Peter Neff; Henry Neff Jr.; Sarah late Neff wife of Isaiah
Frost; Elizabeth late Neff wife of Thomas Wright; Susannah late Neff wife of
William Wright; Anna late Neff wife of Elisha Combs; Hannah late Neff, dec'd,
late wife of Henry Coontz, her children--Jacob, Sarah, Peter and Catharine Coontz--
all minors except Jacob who is an idiot; Jacob Neff, dec'd, his children--John T.,
Sarah Ann and Mary Neff, all minors; all are of Allegheny Co., Maryland except
Henry Neff Jr. who resides in Belmont Co., Ohio. (312)

June 1830 - George BUCHANAN guardian of A. DOUGHERTY, etal. vs. Daniel VANMETER,
etal. Petition for Partition. Land, 69 acres pt. NW¼ Section 23, Township 8,
Range 6. Andrew Dougherty, dec'd, late of Belmont Co. Heirs: Margaret late
Dougherty wife of Daniel Vanmeter, Jane late Dougherty wife of Isaac Greer,
George Dougherty died without issue, Andrew Dougherty Jr., Alexander Dougherty,
John Dougherty, Rebecca Dougherty, and Young Dougherty; the last five named
being minors. By will of Andrew all were to have 1/8th part, but since death
of George each to have 1/7th part. (328)

Sept. 1830 - Jacob SMITH and Townsend EVANS adms. of Thomas EVANS, dec'd vs.
Widow and Heirs. Petition to sell land. Filed 2-22-1830. Land, NW¼ Section 17,
Township 5, Range 3. Widow, Catharine Evans. Heirs: Mahala wife of Jesse Hyatt,
Elias Evans, Sydney wife of John Reagon, Mevirel Evans, Burwell Evans, Thomas Evans,
Isaac Evans and Nancy Evans; the last five named being minors. (338)

Sept. 1830 - Henry FRESH Sr. and Henry FRESH Jr. adms. of George FRESH, dec'd vs.
Heirs. Petition to sell real estate. Filed 4-28-1830. Land, pt. SW¼ Section 21,
Township 8, Range 4, 11 acres of which was conveyed to dec'd on 4-1-1828 by Joseph
Gray and remainder conveyed by Margaret Henderson 4-2-1827; also 40 acres pt. Section
20, Township 8, Range 4 conveyed to dec'd 4-2-1827 by Wm Cook and Ruth his wife.
George Fresh, dec'd. Widow, Nackey Fresh. Children: Henry Fresh Jr., John Fresh,
Martha wife of James Hampson, George Fresh and Jacob Fresh, all of Belmont Co.,
the last two named being minors. (348)

Sept. 1830 - Thomas MILLER adms. of George MILLER, dec'd vs. Heirs. Petition to
sell real estate. Filed 6-8-1830. Land, 134.64 acres SE¼ Section 35, Township 9,
Range 6, Kirkwood twp., except four lots sold by dec'd in lifetime as follows:
Lot 1 cont. 3 and 3/10 acres to Susanna Sikes, Lot 2 containing 7.20 acres to
Elias Shoemaker, Lot 3 cont. 3.49 acres to Samuel Beall and Lot 4 cont. 1 acre
to Elias Hoemaker; also except 6 acres NE cor sold to Alexander McBrating.
Heirs: Rebecca wife of Wm Frizzle, Micha wife of Daniel Shipley, Rachael wife of
Zachariah Marsh, Elizabeth wife of Henry Gregory, Sarah Wife of Edward Marsh,
all of Belmont Co. (355)

Mar. 1831 - Robert A. ROBINSON and Hannah his wife vs Burgess McGRUDER, etal.
Petition for Partition. Filed 4-18-1830. Land, 320 acres E½ Section 20, Township
6 Range 3. Jacob Neff late of Cumberland, Allegheny Co., Maryland, dec'd, died
intestate leaving no widow. The following are entitled to 1/3rd part jointly
as children of dec'd: Hannah late Neff wife of Robert A. Robinson, Margaret late
Neff wife of Burgess McGruder, Mary late Neff wife of Emanuel Carter(?); all of
Allegheny Co., Maryland. (384)

Mar. 1831 - Nathan SHEPHERD vs. Noble TAYLOR, etal. Petition for Partition.
Filed 11-19-1830. Land, SE¼ Section 32, Township 8, Range 5. Nathan Shepherd Jr.
of Belmont Co. Partition: 1/9th of 2/11ths part, Mary wife of Aaron G. Tilton of
Richland Co., Ohio; 1/9th of 2/11th part, Sarah wife of Nemons Beebout of Washington
Co., Pa.; 1/9th of 2/11th part, Isabella wife of Joseph Rees of Washington Co.,
Pa.; 1/9th of 2/11th part, William Huston of Washington Co., Pa.; 1/9th of 2/11ths
part, Mordecia Huston of Philadelphia, Pa.; 1/9th of 2/11ths part, David Huston
of Washington Co., Pa.; 1/11th part, Noble Taylor of Belmont Co., Ohio. (392)

Mar. 1831 - Wilson SHANNON vs. James FAIRHURST, etal. Petition for Partition.
Filed 3-23-1830. Land, E½ lot 16 St. Clairsville. Jeremiah Fairhurst, dec'd,
late of Belmont Co. Children: John Fairhurst, Mariah wife of Perry Whitham,
James Fairhurst and David Fairhurst, all of Monroe Co., Ohio, the last two named
being minors. Wilson Shannon's interest by purchase from John and Mariah. (402)

110

Mar. 1831 - Robert WILLIS, etal. vs. Sarah WILLIS, etal. In Chcnaery. Filed
6-16-1830. Robert Willis, dec'd, late of Belmont Co. wrote will 2-10-1830, with suit
to decide if he was capable of willing his estate. Widow, Barah Willis. Children:
Robert Willis; John Willis; Isaac Willis; William Willis; Polly Willis; Catharine
wife of Elijah Copeland; Eleanor wife of Joseph Kincaid; Elizabeth wife of Jesse
Smith; James Willis; George Willis, dec'd his children--Catharine, Evan, Betsy,
James and Robert Willis; Margaret Jenkins, dec'd, her children--Hiram Jenkins, John
Jenkins, Catharine wife of Samuel Corbet, Jacob Jenkins and Robert Jenkins. Will of
Robert Willis Sr. Dated 2-10-1830. Wife, Sarah, plantation of 150 acres during
natural life and personal property. Sons: James Willis and William Willis.
Daughters: Elizabeth Smith and Polly Willis. Grandsons: George, Joseph and Robert
Willis sons of James Willis; Robert Willis son of son, George Willis, dec'd; Robert
Willis son of William Willis, Grand-daughter, Sarah Willis daughter of James Willis.
Land on which William Willis now living to be sold. Children not heretofore named
to have balance of estate. Executors: John Eaton and John Nichols. Signed;
Robert Willis. Witnesses: John Branson and John (mark) Arick(?). (411)

Mar. 1831 - John HART, etal. vs. Heirs of Wm CHAPLIN. Bill in Chancery. Filed
3-12-1830. Land, Leonard Hart, dec'd contracted to purchase part Section 20,
Township 8, Range 5. Leonard Hart, dec'd. Widow, Mary. Heirs: John Hart,
Elizabeth wife of Samuel Perkins, Margaret wife of Andrew Nixon, Catharine wife of
Amster B. Reed, and Leonard Hart Jr. Wm. Chaplin Heirs not named. (427)

June 1831 - Henry LONG vs Peter TALLMAN gdn. of minor BEATY Heirs. Petition for
Partition. Filed 3-23-1831. Land, 150 acres SW¼ Section 3, Township 10, Range 6.
John Beaty, dec'd. late of Belmont Co. Widow, Mary Beaty Sr. Heirs: Margaret
formerly Beaty wife of Absolum Kinsey, Nancy Smith formerly Beaty, Jane Beaty,
Sarah Beaty, and Mary Beaty Jr.; the last two named being minors with Peter Tallman
their guardian. (462)

June 1831 - Hetty GIFFIN and Robert her husband vs. Elizabeth SIMMONS, etal.
Petition for Partition. Filed 12-29-1830. Land: E½ Section 21, Township 7,
Range 4 called "Richland farm" near St. Clairsville, Belmont Co.; SE¼ Section
31, Township 8, Range 7, Guernsey Co., Ohio; NE¼ Section 36, Township 7, Range 7,
Monroe Co., Ohio. Note: name of deceased not given. Heirs: Hetty wife of
Robert Giffin of Knox Co., Ohio; Elizabeth Simmons of Ohio Co., Va.; Edy Hull
of Coshocton Co., Ohio; Rebecca wife of John Hannah of Guernsey Co., Ohio; Sally
wife of Jonathan Miller of Guernsey Co., Ohio; and Lovey wife of William Law of
Guernsey Co., Ohio. (466)

June 1831 - Peter TALLMAN adms. debonis non of Robert GRIFFITH, dec'd vs. Samuel
MEAD, guardian. Petition to sell land. Filed 3-24-1831. Land, 100 acres pt.
Section 31, Township 8, Range 5. Widow, Sarah Griffith. Only child, John Griffith,
dec'd, leaving Sarah Ann and Robert Griffith his only children, they being minors
by Samuel Mead their guardian. (470)

June 1831 - James REED, etal. vs. Samuel REED, etal. Petition for Partition.
Filed 7-8-1830. Land, SW¼ Sectio 1, Township 7, Range 4, except 40 acres in
SW corner deeded by Reed in lifetime to Adamigah and James Reed, balance containing
120 acres. David Reed, dec'd. Children: James Reed, Elizabeth wife of Richard
Elliott, Zeipheniah Reed, Samuel Reed, William Reed, Sarah Reed and Ann Reed;
the last four named being all of Belmont Co. and all minors. (474)

Sept. 1831 - Wm GROVES vs. Joseph GROVES, etal. Petition for Partition. Filed
3-25-1831. William Groves, Joseph Groves and Barnet Groves, now dec'd, he dying
12-1-1830 leaving widow Nancy and children--John, Rosanna, Lavina and Barnet
GROVES. Said William, Joseph and heirs of Barnet, dec'd all being tenants in
common in E½ Section 11, Township 9, Range 6 in Steubenville land district. (480)

Sept. 1831 - Samuel P. HUNT adms. of Joshua HUNT, dec'd vs. Rachel HUNT. Petition
to sell real estate. Filed 4-28-1830. Land 8 acres pt NW¼ Section 9, Township 6,
Range 8, conveyed to dec'd 1-29-1824 by Thomas Smith and Phebe his wife. Joshua
Hunt, dec'd. Widow, Rachel Hunt. Children; Mary wife of Jonathan Dye, Joshua
Hunt, Jonathan Hunt, John Hunt, Nathan Hunt, Charles Hunt and David Hunt; all of
Belmont Co., the last five named being minors. (491)

Sept. 1831 - John SINCLAIR adms. of William SINCLAIR, dec'd vs. Sarah SINCLAIR,
etal. Petition to sell land. Filed 3-7-1829. Land, SE¼ Section 8, Township
7, Range 4. Widow, Sarah Sinclair. Heirs: Alexander, Eleanor, John, Thomas,
Cecelia, Lydia, William and Western Sinclair, and Mary Ann Morrison; the last
six named being minors by Philip Ault their guardian. Alexander , Eleanor and John
are children of Wm., dec'd; relationship of others not stated. (497)

Sept. 1831 - Joseph EDGERTON and John EDGERTON executors of James EDGERTON, dec'd,
who was executor of James EDGERTON Sr., dec'd vs. Sarah MOTT, etal, Petition to
complete contract of Testator. Filed 7-27-1831. That James Edgerton Sr., dec'd in
his lifetime contracted to sell to his son, William Edgerton now dec'd 5 acres SW
corner SE¼ Section 36, Township 6, Range 5. William Edgerton, dec'd left issue
of his body--Jane, Bethsheba and Edgerton and left widow, Sarah; William by his
will bequeathed land to Bethsheba subject to interests of widow Sarah. James
Edgerton Sr., dec'd. Mentions widow but does not name. Heirs; William Edgerton,
dec'd, his children (named above); Joseph Edgerton; John Edgerton; Walter Edgerton
of Henry Co., Indiana; Sarah wife of Wm Mott of Monroe Co., Ohio; Christiana wife
of David Gray; Ruth wife of Asa Garretson; Anna Edgerton; Jesse Edgerton; Sarah
Edgerton; Thomas Edgerton (the last four named being minors); Rachel wife of
Tighman Patterson; Abigail Edgerton; David Edgerton; Rebecca Edgerton; Jane Edgerton;
Ann Edgerton; and Mary Edgerton; all residents of Belmont Co. except Walter Edgerton
and Sarah Mott. (503)

Mar. 1832 - Sarah COFFMAN vs. Daniel COFFMAN. Petition for Dower. Filed 9-3-1831.
John Coffman, dec'd. Widow, Sarah Coffman of Belmont Co. One child, Daniel
Coffman, not of age. (539)

Mar. 1832 - John BYRSON vs. Sarah McLAUGHLIN, etal. Petition for Partition. Filed
4-19-1831. Land, 640 acres Section 33, Township 4, Range 3 of lands sold at
Marietta, except tract conveyed by Hugh Bryson to his son Edward Bryson, now dec'd
on 11-28-1808 and also part of NW corner of same being 100 (or 125?) acres
being tract conveyed to John Bryson. Hugh Bryson, dec'd. Sons: John Bryson
and Edward Bryson, dec'd, his children--Sarah wife of Laughlin McLaughlin, Mary
wife of Henry Neff, Isaiah Bryson, Carcus Bryson, Jane Bryson, Elizabeth Ann Bryson
and Edward Bryson; all of Belmont Co., the last two named being minors. (544)

The following records are found in the Common Pleas Court and are the complete listing given in Chancery Record 1, with the exception of suits for debts which gave no genealogical information. Page on which record may be found is given in parenthesis.

June 1823 - Rhoda, Jesse J. and Martha WARD by Josiah DILLON their guardian vs. William POWELL, etal. About 1805, Aaron Ward and Timothy Ward of Belmont County purchased in partnership the NW¼ Section 10, Township 5, Range 4 in the Marietta land district; said quarter section being entered in the name of Aaron Ward with Aaron to have 100 acres off the north side and Timothy to have 60 acres off the south side. In 1807, Aaron Ward died intestate leaving Jane Ward his widow and children Rhoda, Jesse and Martha Ward, minors. In 1810, Jane Ward, widow, married William Powell of Belmont County and by him had five children; Reuben, Sally, James, John and Isaac Powell, all minors. (18)

May 1823 - Samuel SPRIGG, Esq. vs. David SMITH and Catharine his wife late Catharine SHAVER widow of John SHAVER, dec'd, Peter SHAVER, Elizabeth SHAVER, Alexander SHAVER and J. Calvin SHAVER heirs at law of John SHAVER, dec'd. Samuel Sprigg of Ohio County, Virginia on 8-31-1813 sold to John SHAVER of Washington Co., Pennsylvania since of Belmont County, now deceased; a tract of land on Ohio river in Belmont County. Land described as beginning at a small Sycamore on south bank of Wegee Creek opposite the mouth of Whites Run with lines Richard Rileys near top of River Hill, being 160 acres. (26)

June 1824 - Robert WOODS vs Zachariah JACOBS and Hetty WOODS, admrs. of Elijah WOODS, dec'd, Ebenezer Zane WOODS, Daniel WOODS, Elijah WOODS and John WOODS. Land, S½ Section 29, Township 2, Range 2. Land sold to Thomas Woods for $1535.00, with Hetty Wood contesting that she was highest bidder at $1900.00. Heirs of Elijah Wood, dec'd: Rebecca and Sarah Ann Woods. (36)

June 1824 - James R. BOGGS, etal. vs. Margaret BOGGS, etal. In Partition. Filed March 1824. Alexander Boggs, dec'd died intestate 3 January 1820. Widow, Hannah Boggs. Children: James R. Boggs of Belmont Co.; Ezekiel Boggs of Richland Co., Ohio; Reuben Boggs; Margaret Boggs; Jane Boggs; Elizabeth Boggs; Francis Boggs; Alice Boggs; Lucinda Boggs; William Boggs and Alexander Boggs; all of Belmont County, the last six not of age. Land, 254 acres part N½ Section 8, Township 7, Range 4 with lines: Thomas Tepton and Rice Boggs. (38)

May 1825 - John PATTERSON and Robert MORRISON executors of Will of George KERR, dec'd. In Chancery. Filed June 1823. Tract of land, lines: John Ryan on Wheeling Creek on Vances Run where it intersects with said creek, James Hannah, Patrick Nellon, George Paul; being 150 acres including a Grist Mill. Deceased left a widow (not named). (71)

Sept 1825 - David and Jane DEVER vs George DEVER, etal. In Chancery. Filed 8-30-1824. Land, 128 acres SE corner SE¼ Section 13, Township 9, Range 5. John Dever Sr., dec'd. Children: Jonathan Dever, dec'd, his children—David Dever of Jackson Co., Va. (Ohio?) and Jane Dever of Highland Co., Va. (Ohio?); George Dever of Jackson Co., Ohio; John Vanpelt and Mary his wife of Highland Co., Ohio; Robert Willis and Sarah his wife of Belmont Co.; Abraham Dever of Clinton Co., Ohio; James Dever of Bath Co., Va.; John Dever of Sciota Co., Ohio; William Dever, dec'd, his sons—William, George and Alexander Dever of Hampshire Co., Va. (82)

Feb. 1826 - Job BOGUE guardian of minor heirs of Jonathan BOGUE, dec'd. Petition to sell land. Filed May 1825. Land, two tracts, first tract being 60 acres in NW corner Section 11, Township 8, Range 6 of the Steubenville district, second tract being 10 acres SW corner adjoining Section 12, Township 8, Range 6, conveyed to said Jonathan in his lifetime by Samuel Embree and wife Hannah. Widow, Sarah Bogue of Harrison Co., Ohio. Children: Mary Ann, Ruth, Mark & John Bogue. (115)

Feb. 1826 - Jacob HOLLOWAY and Thomas CROZER adms. of James CROZIER, dec'd vs Levi PICKERING, guardian. Petition to sell land. Filed May 1825. Land, front lots 18 & 19 and back Lot 70 in Town of Flushing. Widow, Anne Crozer who has since married Curtis Grubb. Children: Samuel, Joshua and Sarah Crozer. (120)

Feb. 1826 - Benoni BRYANT and Jane his wife, late VERNON vs. Tamar VERNON, etal. In Chancery. Filed August 1817. Land, 100 acres SE¼ Section 14, Township 8, Range 6, lines: Moses Davis. Janes Vernon, dec'd. Widow, Tamar Vernon. Heirs: Benoni Bryant and Jane his wife late Vernon; Dola Vernon; William Vernon; Elizabeth Vernon; Amos Vernon; James Vernon; Asa Vernon; Jesse Vernon; and Eli Vernon; the last eight being minors of John Middleton their guardian. (125)

May 1826 - Samuel COPE and Sarah his wife vs. John COPE, etal. In Chancery. Filed 11-29-1824. James Steer, dec'd, died 17 December 1819. Children: Samuel Cope and Sarah his wife late Steer of Harrison Co., Ohio; Moses Biggott (also given as Piggott) and Hannah his wife late Steer of Belmont Co.; John Cope and Grace his wife late Steer of Harrison Co., Ohio; James Raley and Rachel his wife late Steer of Belmont Co.; Abigail Cope late Steer, widow of George Cope, dec'd of Belmont Co.; John Cowgill and Susannah his wife late Steer, residence unknown but not Ohio; James Steer of Belmont Co.; Joseph Steer, dec'd, died after his father, without issue but leaving widow, Emmy Steer of Jefferson Co., Ohio; Ruth Steer, dec'd, died after father, unmarried; Phebe Steer, dec'd, died after father unmarried. Will of James Steer. Dated 17th day, 12th month, 1819. Son, Joseph Steer, tract where he now lives, which was purchased from Bordon Staunton. Son, James Steer, all of tract purchased from Josiah Updegraff being place where testator lives except 14 acres off to Moses Piggot and 7 acres laid off for Meeting House lot. Daughter, Hannah Piggot, above mentioned 14 acres and $164.00. Daughters, Grace Cope, Rachel Raley and Abigail Cope each to have $300.00. Daughter, Abigail to have the old Meeting House lot except part laid off and made use of for a burying place which purpose executors are to make deed to Trustees for. Daughter, Sarah Cope wife of Samuel to have $1.00. Daughter, Susannah Cowgill wife of John to have $1.00. Mention land purchased from Isaac Pigeon in Madison Co., Ohio which is to be sold. Executor, friend, David Steer. Signed: James (his mark) Steer. Witnesses: Isaac Parker and Joshua Cope. (180)

May 1826 - Ruth LUCAS vs. Samuel LUCAS, etal. In Chancery and Petition for Dower. Filed 4-7-1826. Land, NW¼ Section 22, Township 6, Range 4 of lands sold at Steubenville. William Lucus, dec'd, died sometime in winter of 1824. Widow, Ruth Lucas. Heirs: Samuel, Elizabeth Ann, John Nelson, Sarah Anne, Mary Ellen, Temperance and William Lucas; William having been born since death of said William, dec'd; all of Belmont County. (191)

114

Sept. 1826 - David SMITH and Catharine his wife late SHAFER surviving adms. of
John SHAFER, dec'd vs. Susan SHAFER. In Chancery. Filed 4-25-1826. Land, John
Shafer, dec'd then of Washington Co., Pennsylvania made agreement with Samuel
Sprigg of Ohio Co., Virginia on 8-31-1813 to purchase for $1200.00 being 160
acres on Ohio River (previously described in suit of May 1823). Children of
John Shafer, dec'd: Susan, Elizabeth, Peter and Alexander Shafer. (235)

Feb. 1827 - John EATON adms. of Jacob DOVENBERGER, dec'd, late of Union Township.
Petition to make deed. Filed Feb. 1827. Land, Lot 77 in Morristown which on
11-2-1825, Jacob Dovenberger contracted to sell to Mary Tracy. Children: Mary,
John, Jacob and Margaret Dovenberger; all of Belmont County. (277)

Feb. 1827 - John McPHERSON adms. of John SHAY, dec'd. Petition to make deed.
Filed Feb. 1827. Land, Lot 77 in Morristown, which Shay in his lifetime on
9-3-1819 contracted to sell to Jacob Dovenberger. Widow, Barby Shay. Children:
Israel David Shay; John Shay; Abraham Shay; Catharine late Shay wife of Henry
Dougherty; Ann late Shay wife of Robert McFarland; Elizabeth late Shay wife of
Aaron Cain; Sarah late Shay wife of William Norris; Rebecca late Shay wife of
Joseph Hair; and Mary late Shay wife of James Wilson. (279 & 483)

Feb. 1827 - John KINNEY of Jefferson Co., Ohio, adms. of Abel TWEEZEY, dec'd,
late of Jefferson Co., Ohio. Petition to made deed. Filed Feb. 1827. On
4-24-1817 Abel Twezey then a resident of Belmont Co. agreed to sell to Benj.
Rickey of Jefferson Co., Ohio the West side of SE¼ Section 11, Township 6, Range
4, of lands sold at Steubenville. (280)

Feb. 1827 - Averhart PERKINS vs. Reuben PERKINS, etal. Petition for Partition.
Filed 3-15-1826. Land, NE¼ Section 28, Township 5, Range 4 of lands sold at
Marietta. Reuben Perkins, dec'd, died in 1816. Heirs: Averhart Perkins; Reubin
Perkins; Elias Perkins; Elijah Perkins; Crese Perkins; Ruth Perkins, a minor aged
11 yrs.; all of Belmont County; Rebecca wife of John King; Zopher Perkins aged
18 yrs.; Xerophen Perkins aged 15 yrs.; Calvin Perkins aged 13 yrs.; all of Mon-
roe County, Ohio; Rachel wife of George Christler of Beaver Co., Pennsylvania;
Elizabeth wife of Thomas Majilton of Greene Co., Pennsylvania. (293)

Feb. 1827 - Jonathan EDWARDS vs. Mordecai EDWARDS, etal. In Chancery. Filed
9-5-1825. Land, NE¼ Section 32, Township 6, Range 5 entered at Marietta land
office by Jonathan and his father, James now deceased, with certificate issued
in the name of James and letters of patent received July 19, 1824. James Edwards,
dec'd, died 20 December 1817. Children: Jonathan Edwards; Mordecai Edwards;
Phebe late Edwards wife of Alexander Moore of Indiana. Mordecai Edwards when last
heard of, his last known residence was in Georgia and at which time he removed from
Georgia, this being some twenty years ago; at that time he had some children, the
eldest of which was named John. Will of James Edwards late of Belmont County, Ohio.
Dated 20th day, 9th month, 1817. Daughter, Phebe to have $1.00. Son, Mordica to
have $1.00. Son, Jonathan, to have rest of estate during his lifetime, then to go
to children of testators son Mordica. Executor: Son, Jonathan. Signed:
James Edwards. Witnesses: Isaiah William, Elias Williams and Henry Williams.
(304)

Feb. 1827 - Jeremiah HARRIS vs. Henry BURKITT, etal. In Chancery. Filed March 1826. Land, 60 acres south side SE¼ Section 36, Township 7, Range 5 contracted on 9-3-1816 to be sold to Ason Settings. Jacob Burkitt, dec'd died without issue. Brother, Henry Burkitt of Frederick Co., Maryland. Nephews and Niece: Jacob, Joseph and Terracy Burkitt children of brother, Michael Burkitt, dec'd, of Berkley County, Virginia. (312)

Feb. 1827 - Joseph CANBY and Margaret his wife vs Thomas SMITH, etal. In Chancery. Filed 8-13-1824. Robert Haines of Frederick County, Virginia, dec'd, died in the year 1796 with his will having been recorded in that county on 2-3-1796. Widow, Margaret Haines. Children: Margaret late Haines wife of Joseph Canby of Warren Co., Ohio, married 1817, she arrived at age of 21 yrs in 1814; Mary Haines; Noah Haines of Warren Co., Ohio; John Haines; Amos Haines; Robert Haines; and Nathan Haines. (327)

Apr. 1827 - Edward NICHOLS adms. of John BOLTON, dec'd. Petition to make deed. Filed April 1827. On 3-22-1816 John Bolton contracted to sell to Samuel Sprigg out-lots 57, 58, 61, 62 and out-lot marked "C", being 27 acres in town of Pultney. (345)

Apr. 1827 - Anna REED admrx. of David REED, dec'd. Petition to make deed. Filed Apr. 1827. On 12-26-1815 said David, now deceased agreed to lease to Elizabeth Reed during her natural lifetime, part SW¼ Section 1, Township 7, Range 4: in the same instrument he agreed to deed land described above to Adonizah and James Reed; said Elizabeth Reed died in year 1822. Children of David Reed, dec'd: James Reed; Richard Reed; Elizabeth Reed now wife of Richard Elliott; Zachariah Reed, Samuel Reed; William Reed; Sarah Reed and Anna Reed; the last five being minors. (346)

Apr. 1827 - John TAYLOR and Robert McCONNEL, adms. of Jacob McELROY, dec'd. Petition to make deed. Filed Apr. 1827. On 4-23-1824 said Jacob agreed to sell to Bernard Elrick a lot west of town of St. Clairsville being described as adjoining lands of William Boggs, Sr. and being same lot lately owned by Thomas Rose. Jacob McElroy, dec'd, died 1 January 1825. Children: Mary Jane, James and John McElroy; all minors. (348)

Apr. 1827 - John NICHOLSON executor of Thomas ROBINSON, dec'd vs. William ROBINSON, etal. Petition to sell real estate. Filed Sept. 1826. Land, 46 acres Section 2, Township 7, Range 4; lines, Wm. Chambers. Heirs: Hannah wife of John Nicholson; William Robinson; all of Belmont County; Alban Robinson of Tyler Co., Virginia; Ira Robinson of Hamilton Co., Ohio; Lydia Yates formerly Robinson of Belmont County. (355)

Apr. 1827 - Matthew McCALL and Nancy his wife vs. George SHARP and Agness SHARP adms. of Joseph SHARP, dec'd, etal. In Chancery. Filed 6-29-1825. Joseph Sharp, dec'd died in March 1825. Widow, Agness Sharp. Children: Nancy wife of Matthew McCall; George Sharp and William Sharp. Mentions land owned by deceased in Muskingum and Belmont Counties. (378)

Aug. 1827 - David FULTON guardian minor heirs of John MAXWELL, dec'd. Petition to sell real estate. Filed Apr. 1827. Land, two tracts, first tract part Section 29, Township 6, Range 3; lines, George Beam, being 20 acres - 2nd tract, part NW¼ Section 28, Township 6, Range 3 being 88 acres. John Maxwell, dec'd died in fall season 1818. Widow, Nancy Maxwell. Children: James, dec'd, died since death of his father leaving infant son Thomas; Absalom Maxwell; John Maxwell; David Maxwell; Jane Maxwell; Senah Maxwell; Maria Maxwell; Lucinda Maxwell; Morgan Maxwell; Julia Maxwell; William Maxwell; Mary Maxwell; Eliza Maxwell; and Boswell Maxwell. John Turk has purchased interest of part of the heirs. (400)

Aug. 1827 - Joseph DAVID and Martha his wife vs. Andrew BARNET, etal. Petition for Partition. Filed Apr. 1827. Land, 184 acres SE¼ Section 33, Township 5, Range 3, John Barnet, dec'd died 1 May 1824. Children: Martha David; Andrew Barnet; Margaret Barnet; Elizabeth wife of William Granville; James Barnet; John Barnet and David Barnet; all of Belmont County. (405)

Aug. 1827 - Jemima HART vs. John HART, etal. In Chancery for Dower. Filed 3-22-1827. Land, East part Section 20, Township 8, Range 5 which was conveyed to Leonard Hart on 6-25-1808 by William Chaplin and Mary his wife. Leonard Hart, dec'd, died in winter of 1826 or 1827. Widow, Jemima Hart. Heirs: Leonard Hart; John Hart; Elizabeth wife of Samuel Perkins; George Hart, dec'd, his daughter— Catharine Hart aged 16 yrs.; all of Belmont County; Margaret wife of Andrew Nixon of State of Indiana. (410)

Aug. 1827 - Wm. BOOKER vs Heirs of George E. RICH, dec'd and David NEISWANGER. In Chancery. Filed 9-30-1826. George E. Rich, dec'd late of Hamborgh, South Carolina. Said Rich authorized David Neswanger to sell his land in Belmont County, which was contracted to Wm. Booker, described as lying near West end of town of St. Clairsville and being part of NE¼ Section 10, Township 7, Range 4. (419)

Aug. 1827 - Henry OWENS vs. Nancy IRWIN, etal. In Chancery. Filed Apr. 1827. Land, contracted on 1-27-1816 to be sold to Henry Owens, described as SE¼ Section 29, Township 5, Range 5 in Steubenville land district. John King, dec'd. Children: Nancy wife of William Irwin; William King; Sarah King; Andrew King; Samuel King; Catharine wife of Baptist Derbin; John King; James King; Alexander King; Robert King; Mary King; Rachel King and George W. King; all of Belmont Co. (425)

Aug. 1827 - John THOMPSON vs Townsend FRAZER and wife Elizabeth. In Chancery. Filed 6-12-1827. Henry Cassaday and Townsend Frazer were indebted to said Thompson for Lot #2 south side of Commons in Wm. Mathers addition to town of St. Clairsville. Henry Cassaday, dec'd, died 1 August 1826. Widow, Margaret Cassaday. Heirs: James, Jane and William Henry Cassaday. (438)

Mar. 1828 - William MERRITT adms. of Robert W. JONES, dec'd vs. Wilmeth JONES, etal. Petition to sell real estate. Filed Feb. 1827. Land, 22 acres part of Section 36, Township 2, Range 2. Heirs: Wilmeth Jones of Belmont County; Mary wife of Joseph Reynolds; Hannah wife of Samuel Bess; both of Washington Co., Pennsylvania; Nancy wife of John Irons; Sarah wife of Thomas Irons; both of Waynesburgh, Green Co., Pennsylvania; and William Jones of Pittsburgh, Pennsylvania. (477)

117

Mar. 1828 - James BROOMHALL vs. Sarah FIELDS, etal. Petition for Partition. Filed 7-4-1827. Land, 219 acres part NW¼ Section 13, Township 8, Range 5 in Steubenville district. Enos Broomhall, dec'd. Widow, Phoebe Broomhall. Children: James Broomhall; Sarah wife of John Fields; Susan wife of James Moore; Martha wife of Abraham Hoover; Barclay Broomhall; and three others (not named) who conveyed their interest in said land to petitioner. (489)

Mar. 1828 - Thomas H. GENIN vs. Jacob AULT. Petition for Partition. Filed 1-19-1828. Land, 69 acres part SE¼ Section 4, Township 7, Range 4; lines, Joseph Hulse, Joseph Foulke, George Paull, John McElroy and John Thompson. Valentine Ault, dec'd. Issue: Peter Ault; Andrew Ault; Susannah wife of John Rose; Catharine wife of Henry Rose; Michael Ault; Frederick Ault; George Ault; Jacob Ault. All except Jacob Ault signed their interest in land to said Genin who purchased land. (495)

Mar. 1828 - Daniel BERRY vs. Nancy KREMMER, etal. Petition for Partition. Filed 3-14-1827. Land, half quarter being in Section 29, Township 6, Range 3. Valentine Horn, dec'd. Children: Nancy Kremer of Knox Co., Ohio; Daniel Horn of Muskingum Co., Ohio; Hannah wife of Thomas Tipton of Belmont County; Susan wife of Daniel Bowman of Tennessee; Elizabeth wife of Adam Lessley of Maryland; Christiana, dec'd wife of Benjamin Croy of Indiana, her unknown heirs who also reside in Indiana; Catharine, dec'd, wife of John Berry, Sr., her children—Daniel Berry, Thomas Berry, John Berry Jr., Isaac Berry, Jacob Berry, Enoch Berry, Delilah wife of Nichols Wells, Elizabeth Carter, Rebecca McCarroll and Mary wife of John Yost, all of Belmont County. (500)

Mar. 1828 - Malcom STRINGER vs. William STRINGER, etal. In Chancery. Filed 2-8-1827. On Dec. 7, 1811 John Stringer and Jane his wife sold land being part E½ Section 21 & 27, Township 4, Range 2 in Steubenville land district to William Stringer Jr., being 150 acres with lines adjoining William Stringer Sr. William Stringer Jr., dec'd, died about last day of July 1826. Widow, Jenny Stringer. Children: Maria, William, Jane and George Marion Stringer. (518)

Mar. 1828 - Margaret HENERSON executor of Robert HENDERSON, dec'd. Petition to make deed. Filed Mar. 1828. Widow, Margaret Henderson. Children: James, John, Elizabeth, William Taggart, David and George L. Henderson. On 2-14-1823 said Robert now deceased verbally agreed to sell to Thomas White all of his interest in 180 acres in north part of Section 27, Township 8, Range 4 formerly the property of David Henderson being the same land bequeathed to said David Henderson by will of John Henderson, dec'd. (526)

BELMONT COUNTY, OHIO - PARTITION RECORDS 1832-1833

The following records were taken from Chancery Record 3, as found in the Common Pleas Court. Page number on which record may be found is given in parenthesis.

July 1832 - Elizabeth HARRIS adms. of William HARRIS, dec'd vs. Daniel HARRIS, etal. Petition to complete real contract. Filed 2-23-1832. On 9-18-1828 William Harris of Virginia with James Harris, dec'd entered into agreement with John Harris and George Harris of Ohio to divide all tracts of lands which their father had in his lifetime being lands in Virginia and in Belmont and Tuscarawas Counties, Ohio. William Harris, dec'd. Widow, Elizabeth Harris. Children: Daniel, Edie, George, Sarah Ann, Elizabeth, John and Savina Harris, all minors. (1)

July 1832 - Thomas MILLER adms. of George MILLER. Petition to make deed. Filed July 1832. Land, SE¼ Section 35, Township 9, Range 6 contracted to Christopher Shoemaker on 12-26-1825 for 1 acre and on 12-14-1826 for one acre. Brothers and Sisters of George Miller, dec'd; Thomas Miller, petitioner; Rebecca late Miller wife of William Frizel; Elizabeth late Miller wife of Henry Gregory; Rachel late Miller wife of Zachariah H. Marsh; Michel late Miller wife of Daniel Shipley; all of Belmont County; and Sarah wife of Edward Marsh of Guernsey Co., Ohio. (69)

Nov. 1832 - Thomas FOSTER and Nancy his wife vs. Hiram BROWN, etal. Petition in Chancery for Dower. Filed 12-15-1831. Land. from lot 25 and back lots 26,34,42, & 50 in town of St. Clairsville. William Brown, dec'd, died in year 1825. Widow, Nancy Brown now the wife of Thomas Foster. Heirs: Hiram Brown; William Brown; Jesse Brown; Samuel Brown; Ann Eliza Brown; all of Virginia; David Brown; Jacob Brown; and Therese Murphy; of Ohio. (83)

Nov. 1832 - John DOUDNEY and Anna PATTERSON executors of Exum PATTERSON, dec'd vs. Phebe PATTERSON, etal. Petition to complete real contract. Filed 9-24-1832. On 10-6-1825 40 acres NE corner NE¼ Section 19, Township 8, Range 6 was contracted to Joseph Edgerton. Children: Phebe, Elizabeth, Mary and Sarah Patterson, all minors of Belmont County. (88)

Nov. 1832 - Crawford Welsh executor of Obediah HARDESTY, dec'd. Petition to make deed. Filed 10-1-1832. On 3-5-1828 tract of four acres between said Obediah Hardesty and Jesse Campbell was contracted to Phillip Lanning; said Lanning on 11-26-1830 assigned his interest to John Ault son of Michael Ault. Children of Obediah Hardesty, dec'd; Urias Hardesty; Solomon Hardesty; Lewis (?) Hardesty; Rebecca wife of Ralph Hardesty; Elizabeth wife of John Hatcher; Mary wife of Thomas James; Sarah wife of Daniel Warren; and Catharine wife of Jesse Campbell. (90)

Nov. 1832 - John Kennon adms. of the Estate of Philip AUBERRY, dec'd vs. Rachel AUBERRY, etal. Petition to sell real estate. Filed 9-7-1831. Land, 49 acres SE¼ Section 35, Township 6, Range 6. Widow, Rachel Auberry. Children: William Auberry; Rebecca Auberry; Nancy wife of Norris Reed; Ruhamy Auberry; Leah Auberry; Elizabeth Auberry; John Auberry; Rachel Auberry; and Hannah Auberry; the last six being minors. (93)

119

Nov. 1832 - James EATON and George VANLAW adms. of Thomas VANLAW, dec'd vs. Joseph VANLAW, etal. Petition for sale of real estate. Filed 4-7-1832. Land, total of 56 acres part of Section 36, Township 6, Range 4. Thomas Vanlaw at time of his death left a widow (not named) who has since deceased. Children: Joseph, Rebecca and Elwood Vanlew; all minors. Joel Wilkinson and Jane his wife previously on 11-26-1827, deeded their interest. (97)

Nov. 1832 - John H. THORNBURGH adms. of Daniel THORNBURGH, dec'd vs. John STRAHL, etal. In Chancery. Filed 12-4-1830. John Strahl now of Monroe Co., Ohio on 12-4-1815 sold said Daniel Thornburgh the plantation on which he the said John then resided being 72 acres E½ SW¼ Section 34, Township 7, Range 5; Daniel died with equitable interest in said land. Heirs: William Thornburgh of Virginia; Elizabeth Martin of Harrison Co., Ohio; Mary Thornburgh; Jane wife of Noah Calhoon; Rebecca wife of Jacob Conrow; Hester Conrow; and John H. Thornburgh; all of Belmont County. (104)

Nov. 1832 - Jane SWAYNE adms. of estate of Joseph SWAYNE, dec'd vs. Thomas SWAYNE, etal. Petition for sale of land. Filed March 1832. Land, Lot 5 in town of Bridgeport. Widow, Jane Swayne. Heirs: Thomas, Mary, Evans, Eli, Barnett and Caleb Swayne; all minors. (118)

Mar. 1833 - John HOWALD adms. of John HOFF, dec'd vs. Heirs. Petition to sell real estate. Filed 2-24-1832. Land, one half of an undivided tract in E½ SE¼ Section 25, Township 4, Range 3 of Marietta district. John Hoff died without widow or heirs to administrators knowledge. (124)

Mar. 1833 - Sarah COFFMAN vs. Daniel COFFMAN. In Chancery for Dower. Filed 11-1-1832. Land, fractional Section 10, Township 4, Range 3, being 570 acres in all. John Coffman, dec'd. Widow, Sarah Coffman. Heir: Daniel Coffman. (132)

Mar. 1833 - John VANFOSSEN vs. Mary VANFOSSEN etal. In Chancery. Filed 6-13-1831. Land, part Section 19, Township 19, Range 6 in Steubenville land district. Benjamin Vanfossen, dec'd, died in 1831. Widow, Mary Vanfossen; Children: John Vanfossen; George Vanfossen; Jacob Vanfossen; Henry Vanfossen; William Vanfossen; Benjamin Vanfossen; Samuel Vanfossen; Margaret wife of Thomas Wright; and Mary wife of Allen Buckingham. (157)

May 1833 - Lavina MARRING adms. of John MARRING, dec'd vs. Moses MARRING, etal. Petition to sell land. Filed 11-11-1832. Land, part North side SW¼ Section 10, Township 7, Range 6 being 60 acres in Marietta land district. John Marring, dec'd died without issue. Widow, Lavina Marring. Brothers and sisters: Moses Marring; Jacob Marring; Peter Marring; Elizabeth Marring; Rhoda Marring; Rachel Marring; Margaret Marring; and Sarah wife of John McDaniel; all of Belmont County. (164)

May 1833 - Mary A. BALDWIN late CARSON surviving adms. of David CARSON, dec'd vs. Valentine L. CARSON etal. Petition to sell land. Filed 11-16-1832. Land, Lot 4 in town of York, Jefferson Co., Ohio. Widow, Mary A. Baldwin late Carson now wife of Eli Baldwin. Children: Valentine S., David G., Mary A., Wm. G., Jane A., Samuel G., Rebecca B., and Emelia M. Carson. (167)

The following records were taken from "Death Record 1". They include only records for persons 40 years and over. Residence is same as place of death unless stated. Abbreviations: d=died; a=age; m=married; w=widow or widower; s=single; pd=place of death; pb=place of birth; res=residence. Page on which record may be found is given in parenthesis.

SCOVILLE, Asabil - d 4-13-1867; a 82y 2m; w; pd Georgetown; pb Waterbury, Conn; father, Amasa Scoville; mother, Esther Scoville nee Muirell. (2)
CHANE, Adam - d 9-22-1867; a 42-5-5; s; pd Georgetown; pb Germany. (2)
McCOY, Rebecca - d 9-11-1867; a 59-9-26; s; pd Decatur, O.; pb Decatur, O. (2)
TWEED, Jane - d 7-10-1867; a 65-5-1; s; pd Ripley; pb Union twp. (2)
WATT, James - d 8-16-1867; a 63y; m; pd Sterling twp.; pb Kentucky. (2)
SOWERS, Joseph - d 7-19-1867; a 77y; s; pd Ripley; pb Germany. (2)
BOHRER, Catharine - d 9-24-1867; a about 72y; m; pd Jefferson twp.; pb Bavaria, Germany; res Straight Creek; parents, Jacob & Kezia Young. (2)
BROWN, Richard - d 9-5-1867; a 73y 6m; m; pd Huntington twp.; pb Faquier twp., Virginia; parents, Thomas and Margaret Brown. (2)
HAWKINS, Lewis - d 8-11-1867; a 51y; m; pd Ripley; pb Bracken Co., Ky. (2)
WHARTON, George Washington - d 7-13-1867; a 52-6-10; m; pd Ripley; pb Kentucky. (2)
YOUNG, Jesse - d 8-16-1867; a 70-3-12; m; pd Ripley; pb Kentucky. (2)
SNELL, Pleasant - d 8-10-1867; a ?; pd Edenton, Clermont Co., O.; pb-----. (2)
DIXON, William - d 9-25-1867; a 76-7-6; w; pd near Ripley, O.; pb Kentucky. (2)
DUNN, Henry - d 10-6-1867; a 44y pd Sardinia, O.; pb not known. (2)
PORTER, Mrs. John - d 10-19-1867; a 50y; m; pd near Sardinia; pb not known; res Highland Co. (2)
HARDING, Henry - d 8-20-1867; a 50-6-20; pd Huntington twp.; pb------. (2)
LEWIS, Edwin - d 12-8-1867; a 55y; m; pd Georgetown; pb not reported. (4)
OSBORN, Wilson S. - d 11-28-1867; a about 47y; m; pd Feesburgh; pb Brown Co.; father, Elij. Osborn. (4)
LARWELL, Mary Jane - d 11-28-1867; a 53-11-28½ pd Huntington twp.; pb same. (4)
VILNERS(?), To Derin - d 10-31-1867; a 55y; w; pd Perry twp.; pb Belgium (4)
BRAFFORD, Thomas - d 3-27-1868; a 76y 2m; m; pd Ripley; pb Old Virginia (4)
METHERS, Mrs. Sarah - d 2-24-1868; a 49y; m; pd Union twp.; pb Adams Co. (4)
MEFFORD, Rebecca - d Jan. 1868; a 82y; w; pd Ripley; pb Union twp. (4)
HANDMAN (or HARDMAN), Catherine - d 1-12-1868; a?; w; pd Ripley; pb Frourbach, Rhine. (6)
MOORE, James B. - d 5-11-1868; a 68-3-19; m; pd Byrd twp.; pb same. (6)
MATHEWS, Erefine - d 2-6-1868; a 61y; m; pd Lewis twp.; pb Clermont Co., Ohio. (6)
MINKLER, Mary Ann - d 6-30-1868; a 51y; m; pd Aberdeen; pb same; father, Andrew Griffin. (6)
HUEY, Catherine - d 2-25-1869; a 53-2-25; s; pd Hillsboro; pb------ (6)
LONG, Mary Ann - d 3-2-1869; a 68-11-17; w; pd Eagle Creek; pb Eppen Crame, Ger.(8)
FUHTER, Catharine - d 3-29-1869; a 69y; w; pd Ripley; pb Bavaria, Germany. (8)
WEAVER, David - d 2-19-1869; a 80-2-14; m; pd Brown Co.; pb Maryland. (8)
JOLER, Robert - d 3-4-1869; a 64y; pd Aberdeen; pb Lynchburg, Va.; father, Stephen Moler; mother, M. A. Joler. (8)
MADDOX, Elizabeth - d 9-27-1868; a 58y; m; pd Sprigg twp., Adams Co.; pb Fleming Co., Kentucky; parents, David W. and Elizabeth Early. (8)
SLADE, Ellen - d 10-25-1868; a 93-8-18; w; pd Georgetown, O.; pb------. (8)

121

BURCK, Ursula - d 11-15-1868; a 60y; m; pd Ripley; pb Europe. (8)
GREWER, Catharine - d 12-9-1868; a 74y; w; pd Russelville; pb Europe. (8)
BLY, Anna - d 9-9-1869; a 42y; m; pd Huntington twp.; pb-----. (8)
BOWER, Elizabeth - d 10-15-1868; a 70y 3m; w; pd Russelville; pb Armstrong Co.,
     Pa. (8)
WILEY, Calbreath - d 11-14-1868; a 67-11-21; m; pd Beechwoods Factory; pb Edgefield
     Dist., S. Carolina; res Byrd twp. (8)
MITCHELL, Thomas - d 12-14-1868; a 58-8-9; m; pd Russelville, O.; pb McLain Co.,
     Pa. (8)
FULTON, John - d 10-12-1868; about 62y; w; pd Ripley; pb-----. (8)
EWING, Thomas - d 12-6-1868; a about 62y; w; pd Ripley; pb-----. (8)
JONES, Mrs. Anna - d 2-2-1869; a 72y; w; pd Ripley; pb-------. (8)
MIDDLESWAITH, Jane - d 10-6-1868; a 80y 20d; m; pd Jackson twp.; pb Pennsylvania.(8)
PARKER, John - d 4-19-1869; a 72-5-19; w; pd near Georgetown; pb Washington, Ky. (10)
HAYWARD, Ezekiel - d 10-6-1868; a 86y 23d; m; pd Lewis twp.; pb Virginia. (10)
LEACH, Joseph - d 1-18-1869; a 60y 18d; m; pd Lewis twp.; pb Kentucky. (10)
RICHARDS, Wm - d 3-10-1869; a 60-2-9; m; pd Lewis twp.; pb West Virginia. (10)
GRAHAM, Miss Margrit - d 2-27-1869; a 60-1-58; s; pd Lewis twp.; pb Virginia. (10)
ABERS, Ann - d 4-26-1869; a 44y; m; pd Perry twp.; pb Salem twp., Highland Co.,
     Ohio. (10)
SELLERS, Catharine - d 7-4-1869; a 78y 2m; w; pd Franklin twp.; pb----; res
     Straight Creek. (10)
CRAWFORD, John - d 9-10-1869; a 73y; m; pd Union twp.; pb unknown. (10)
KNIGHT, Eliza P. - d 10-30-1869; a 68y; w; pd Ripley; pb Stonington, Ct. (10)
HELFINCH, Anna Othilia - d 9022-1869; a 79y 3m; m; pd Ripley; pb Germany. (10)
HELFINCH, Francis - d 11-19-1869; a 64y; w; pd Ripley; pb Germany. (10)
VOELKER, Rosa - d 11-26-1869; a 78y; m; pd Arnheim; pb France. (10)
HANZEL, Francis - d 12-13-1869; a 75y; m; pd Ripley; pb Austria. (10)
PRIEDLE, Thomas - d 11-21-1869; a 50y; m; pd Washington twp.; pb same. (10)
GILFILLEN, William - d 8-10-1869; a 50y 3m; m; pd Carlisle; pb near Londonderry,
     Ireland. (12)
SELLARS, Caroline - d 6-5-1869; a 77y 3m; pd Franklin twp.; pb Virginia. (12)
DAUNN, Earnest - d 4-8-1869; a 50y; s; pd Franklin twp.; pb Germany. (12)
VOLCHER, Rosa - d 9-26-1869; a 78-8-10; m; pd Franklin twp.; pb Germany. (12)
NEY, Frederick - d 9-29-1869; a 68y 7m; m; pd Franklin twp.; pb Germany. (12)
PURDON, Sarah - d 8-29-1869; a 81y; w; pd Scott twp.; pb-------. (12)
GREHUME, Samuel - d 8-21-1869; a 74-6-2; pd Scott twp.; pb New Jersey. (12)
GORDON, Minerva E. - d 12-20-1869; a 51-6-18; m; pd Pleasant twp.; pb Trumbull
     Co., Ohio. (14)
CRAWFORD, Elizabeth - d 9-15-1869; a 61y; m; pd Pleasant twp.; pb Virginia. (14)
LAYCOCK, Robert S. - d 11-3-1869; a 45-6-10; m; pd Pleasant twp.; pb Brown Co.,
     Ohio. (14)
PARKER, John - d 4-19-1869; a 73y; w; pd Pleasant twp.; pb Kentucky. (14)
FOORE, Joseph - d 7-27-1869; a 42-5-25; m; pd Pleasant twp.; pb same. (14)
LARYMAN, Margaret - d 8-28-1869; a 69y 8m; w; pd Pleasant twp.; pb Germany. (14)
VAN ANDER, Lawson - d 8-14-1869; a 63-2-14; m; pd Pleasant twp.; pb Maryland. (14)
HODGSON, James - d----1869; a old age; w; pd Green twp.; pb England. (14)
WILSON, Mary - d------1869; a old age; w; pd Green twp.; pb Virginia. (14)
HILLING, Mary A. - d 10-14-1869; a 40-4-27; m; pd Fincastle, Eagle twp; pb
     Pennsylvania; parents, William and Ann Calahan. (14)

122

SIMPKINS, Rebecca - d 4-20-1869; a 73-2-6- m; pd Sterling twp.; pb same; father,
------Pinkney. (16)
SIMPKINS, Sarah - d 5-7-1869; a 49-11-6; m; pd Sterling twp.; pb same; parents,
E. and Eliza Conover. (16)
ROSS, Misouri - d 9-24-1869; a 79y; n; pd Sterling twp.; pb Clermont Co., Ohio;
father, Baggess(?). (16)
PINDELL, Thomas - d 11-21-1869; a 54-10-9; m; pd Washington twp.; pb Brown Co. (16)
DUNN, Milley - d 11-11-1869; a 45y; w; pd Washington twp.; pb Brown Co. (16)
BELL, Joseph E. - d 11-17-1869; a 40-1-10; m; pd Washington twp.; pb Brown Co. (16)
CAMPBELL, William P. - d 8-28-1869; a 56y; m; pd Washington twp.; pb Penna. (16)
HUFF, Nancy - d 11-26-1869; a 82-4-3; w; pd Sardinia, Washington twp.; pb don't
know. (16)
KNIGHT, Eliza P. - d 10-29-1869; a 75y; w; pd Ripley; pb Ripley. (18)
DIXON, Cinderilla - d 12-22-1869; a 48-10-4; w; pd Union twp.; pb Union twp. (18)
GARDNER, Sarah - d 9-20-1869; a 75y 12d; m; pd Union twp.; pb unknown. (18)
HAMILTON, Alexander - d 1-18-1869; a 72y 3m; m; pd Union twp.; pb unknown. (18)
EVANS, Minerva - d 9-7-1869; a 45y; m; pd Union twp.; pb Union twp. (18)
FRERRIK(?), Sophia - d 11-6-1869; a 59y; s; pd Union twp.; pb Union twp. (18)
PETERS, R. C. - d 11-18-1869; a 41y 6m; m; pd Riple, O.; pb Ripley, O. (18)
TURNER, Jesse - d 10-29-1869; a 44y; m; pd Ripley, O.; pb Ripley, O. (18)
BERRY, Millie - d 4-29-1869; a 40y; m; pd Ripley, O.; pb-----. (18)
HOPKINS, Fanny - d 7-23-1869; a 75y; pd Union twp.; pb Union twp. (18)
EYLER, Henry - d 8-19-1869; a 69-4-6; m; pd Jackson twp.; pb Adams Co., O. (20)
GILFILLEN, William - d 8-11-1869; a 50-2-17; m; pd Jackson twp.; pb Ireland. (20)
RHOODS, Elizabeth - d 8-7-1869; a 52-7-18; m; pd Jackson twp.; pb Brown Co. (20)
WARDLOW, Samuel - d 7-29-1869; a 69-1-3; m; pd Pike twp.; pb Kentucky. (20)
APPLEGATE, Vincent - d 10-18-1869; a 74y; m; pd Pike twp.; pb Kentucky. (20)
THOMPSON, William - d 7-9-1869 a 69y; m; pd Clark twp.; pb Pennsylvania. (22)
HOLMAN, Michael - d 4-1-1869; a 77-7-18; m; pd Clark twp.; pb------. (22)
McGOHAN, John W. - d 4-29-1869; a 49y; m; pd Clark twp.; pb------. (22)
WRESLER, Henry - d 3-16-1869; a 77y; s; pd Clark twp.; pb Pennsylvania. (22)
LYONS, Catherine - d 10-1-1869; a 45y; w; pd Clark twp.; pb Clark twp. (22)
BRYAN, Mary A. - d 12-24-1869; a 68y; m; pd Aberdeen; pb Adams Co., O. (22)
ACKLIN, Martha - d 11-18-1869; a 74y; w; pd Aberdeen; pb Camil (Campbell) Co.,
Ky. (22)
CARTO, Franklin - d May 1869; a 48y; m; pd Aberdeen; pb Maysville, Ky. (22)
GLASCOCK, Wm H. - d 9-16-1869; a 46-1-12; pd Huntington twp.; pb same. (22)
STEWART, Elizabeth - d 7-22-1869; a 70y; m; pd Huntington twp.; pb Adams Co. O.(22)
GRIERSON, John - d 6-8-1869; a 68-3-21; m; pd Huntington twp.; pb Scotland. (22)
KING, Lydia - d 11-14-1869; a 52y; w; pd Huntington twp.; pb same. (22)

BROWN COUNTY, OHIO - DEATH RECORDS 1870-1872

The following records were taken from "Death Record 1". They include only records
for persons 40 years and over. Residence is same as place of death unless stated.
Abbreviations: d=died; a=age; m=married; w=widow or widower; s=single; pd=place of
death; pb=place of birth; res=residence. Page on which record may be found is given
in parenthesis.

BUTT, Samuel - d 4-15-1870 a 80y 16d; pd Franklin twp.; pb United States. (12)
GROW, Augusta - d 2-17-1870; a 70y; w; pd Franklin twp.; pb Germany. (12)
CAMPBELL, Abigal - d 2-25-1870; a 43-6-2; m; pd Scott twp.; pb Franklin twp. (12)
SARNS, Elizabeth - d 1-10-1870; a 70y; w; pd Scott twp.; pb Virginia. (12)
WILLS, Margaret - d 2-17-1870; a 80y; w; pd Pleasant twp.; pb New Jersey. (12)
WALKER, Hannah - d 3-6-1870; a 73y; w; pd Five Mile, Ohio; pb Virginia. (12)
MALOTT, David - d 3-14-1870; a 92y 7m; m; pd Sterling twp.; pb Ohio; parents,
   Joseph and Susan Malott. (16)
PATTON, Elizabeth - d 3-23-1870; a 57-4-11; m; pd Sterling twp.; pb Warren Co.,
   O.; parents, James and Margaret Patton. (16)
BALL, Daniel - d 1-7-1870; a 76y; m; pd Ripley; pb Ripley. (18)
COOPER, Margarett - d 3-17-1870; a ?; s; pd Union twp.; pb Union twp. (18)
CREEKBAUM, John - d 1-8-1870; a 60-11-22; m; pd Ripley, O.; pb-----. (18)
KUNTZ, George J. - d :-14-1870; a 73-5-15; m; pd Jackson twp.; pb Germany. (20)
ADAMS, Elizabeth - d 3-5-1870; a 50-4-19; m; pd Jackson twp.; pb Germany. (20)
HART, Daniel - d 2-18-1870; a 53-5-3; m; pd Jackson twp.; pb Brown Co. (20)
JOHNSON, William - d 3-22-1870; a 77y; m; pd Jackson twp.; pb England. (20)
BARR, Elnora - d 1-27-1870; a 53y 27d; m; pd Perry twp.; pb same. (20)
ROBBISON, Thomas - d 2-14-1870; a 56y; m; pd Pike twp.; pb Highland Co. O. (22)
HENDRIXSON, Elizabeth - d 1-9-1870; a 41y; m; pd Clark twp.; pb same. (22)
SHELTON, Thomas - d -----1870; a 94y; w; pd Aberdeen; pb Virginia. (22)
DAVIDSON, Mary - d 6-20-1870; a 79y 19d; w; pd Scott twp.; pb Maryland. (26)
LOVESSY, Susan - d 10-5-1870; a 48y; w; pd Scott twp.; pb Virginia. (26)
McCALL, Margaret - d 9-17-1870; a 86y; s; pd Scott twp.; pb Pennsylvania. (26)
PEDDICORD, Cunthia - d 3-7-1871; a 97y; w; pd Scott twp.; p! Pennsylvania. (26)
SCOTT, Thomas - d 3-17-1871; a 71y; m; pd Scott twp.; pb--------. (26)
FENTON, Benjamin - d 8-10-1870; a 59-11-20; pd Eagle twp; pb Winchester; parents,
   Jeremiah and Lorence Fenton. (26)
HEATON, Mary Ann - d 9-28-1870; a 70-1-6; w; pd Eagle twp.; pb Huntington twp.;
   parents, Abraham and Mary Ann Evans. (26)
SHAW, Geo. W. - d 11-11-1870; a 46-1-26; m; pd Eagle twp.; pb Eagle twp.; parents,
   Antony and Sarah Shaw. (26)
DRAKE, Hannay - d 3-15-1871; a 47-11-15; m; pd Jefferson twp.; pb Virginia. (26)
McILHENY, Alexander H. - d 7-12-1871; a 77y 4m; m; pd Jefferson twp.; pb Penna. (26)
WILLIAMS, John A. - d 1-17-1871; a 52-1-17; m; pd Jefferson twp.; pb Dover, Ky. (26)
FOY, Judith - d 1-21-1871; a 64-7-17; m; pd Pike twp.; pb Westmoreland, Va. (28)
WARDLOW, Rebecca - d 3-20-1871; a 77-3-7; w; pd Pike twp.; pb Kentucky. (28)
WISBY, Anna - d 8-29-1870; a 61-7-7; w; pd Pike twp.; pb North Carolina. (28)
FRY, Margaret - d 2-20-1871; a 83y; w; pd Pike twp.; pb-------. (28)
JOHNSON, Mary - d 12-12-1870; a 88y; w; pd Jackson twp.; pb unknown. (28)
WEST, Edward - d 5-26-1870; a 69y; m; pd Jackson twp.; pb unknown. (28)
WEST, Sarah - d 9-14-1870; a 72y; w; pd Jackson twp.; pb unknown. (28)
FRANCIS, Edward - d 11-7-1870; a 55y 9m; m; pd Jackson twp.; pb Ireland. (28)

STEVENSON, Sarah - d 1-15-1870; a 80y; w; pd Jackson twp.; pb Ireland. (28)
BRUNNER, Anna - d 1-29-1871; a 82-2-27; pd Franklin twp.; pb Virginia; father,
   Robinson Lucas; mother, Miss Prickett. (28)
SANDENBERGER, Catherine - d 8-31-1870; a 64-7-7; m; pd Arnheim; pb Oever Stienbach,
   Elsace, France; father, Henry Wagner; mother, Margaret Zimmerman. (28)
SHAUB, Conrad - d 11-14-1870; a 59-10-25; pd Franklin twp.; pb Germany; father,
   John Shaub. (28)
PICKERILL Thomas - d 4-19-1871; a 74-2-20; m; pd Byrd twp.; pb Byrd twp.;
   father, Samuel Pickerill. (30)
BURBAGE, Mary - d 3-2-1871; a 73y 15d; m; pd Byrd twp.; pb Byrd twp. (30)
CARSON, James - d 10-25-1870; a 68y; m; pd Byrd twp.; pb Byrd twp. (30)
CARSON, Mary D. - d 1-29-1871; a 66y; pd Byrd twp.; pb Byrd twp.; res Washington
   twp. (30)
BARE, David - d 12-31-1870; a 57y; m; pd Sardenia; pb Brown Co. (30)
BELL, Alice - d 2-17-1871; a 41y; w; pd Sardenia; pb Brown Co. (30)
DAVIS, Sarah - d 10-3-1870; a 73y; m; pd Sardenia; pb Ohio Co., Ky. (30)
DAVIS, Thomas - d 12-26-1870; a 74y; w; pd Sardenia; pb Virginia. (30)
KINCAID, Matthew - d 1-9-1871; a 77-5-11; m; pd Washington twp.; pb Allegheny
   Co., Pa. (30)
KINCAID, Robert - d 2-3-1871; a 74y 11m; pd Sardenia; pb Allegheny Co., Pa. (30)
SHUBERT, Rosa - d 4-5-1871; a 70y 4m; w; pd Washington twp.; pb Germany. (30)
CALVIN, Hugh - d 10-27-1870; a 56-9-27; m; pd Green twp.; pb Ohio. (30)
WALLACE, Ellen - d 3-27-1870; a 53-9-27; m; pd Green twp.; pb Green twp.;
   father, Isaac Wallace. (32)
COOK, Amanda M. - d 10-21-1870; a 84-4-13; w; pd Clark twp.; pb New Jersey. (32)
SLICK, David - d 9-13-1870; a 74y; m; pd Clark twp.; pb Clark twp. (32)
JONES, Sarah - d 2-12-1871; a 47y; m; pd Sterling twp.; pb New Jersey; parents,
   John and Hannah Hamilton. (32)
MOORE, Michael - d 2-22-1871; a 63y 2m; pd Sterling twp.; pb Virginia; parents,
   Levi and Mary Moore. (32)
MARSHALL, Eliza - d 1-22-1871; a 52y; m; pd Sterling twp.; pb Sterling twp.;
   parents, Philip and Catharine Fryman. (32)
BISHOT, Sarah - d 10-10-1870; a 95y 15d; w; pd Lewis twp.; pb France. (32)
SALISBURY, John - d 7-25-1870; a 70y; w; pd Lewis twp.; pb------. (32)
BARTON, Nancy - d Aug. (1870); a 70y; s; pd Lewis twp.; pb New York. (32)
WAGONER, Ruth - d Oct. 1870; a 84y; m; pd Lewis twp.; pb-----. (32)
WINTERS, John - d 8-15-1870; a 70y; m; pd Lewis twp.; pb-----. (32)
KOFLER, Anton - d 12-5-1870; a 42y 7m; m; pd Higginsport; pb Germany. (34)
HUTCHISON, John - d 8-3-1870; a 74y; m; pd Lewis twp.; pb Kentucky. (34)
COOPER, Charles - d 2-19-1871; a 70y; w; pd Huntington twp.; pb Ohio. (34)
HOLIDAY, Ann - d 2-11-1871; a 69y 1m; w; pd Aberdeen; pb Virginia. (34)
CALAGHAN, Hannah - d 8-4-1870; a 75y; pd Perry twp.; pb Ireland. (36)
HUBER, Anthony - d 10-15-1870; a 57y m; pd Perry twp.; pb Switzerland. (36)
THOMPSON, John - d 3-8-1870; a 75y 5m; m; pd Perry twp.; pb England. (36)
CAMPBELL, Robert - d 6-10-1870; a 65y; s; pd Perry twp.; pb Ireland; res Union
   twp. (36)
HARRISON, Adalaide M. - d 3-18-1871; a 48y; m; pd Ripley; pb------. (36)
BRUCE, Anna L. - d 11-26-1870; a 49-10-18; m; pd Ripley; pb--------. (36)
STANDER, Mary - d 3-18-1871; a 53-1-15; m; pd Ripley; pb--------. (36)

125

FRANCIS, Unis - d 8-3-1870; a 58y; m; pd Ripley; pb Kentucky. (36)
STIVERS, Jane - d 4-10-1870; a 80y; w; pd Ripley; pb------. (36)
NEWCOMB, James - d 11-22-1870; a 69-11-27; m; pd Ripley; pb---------. (36)
MATHERS, Richard - d 7-28-1870; a 50y; m; pd Ripley; pb Carlisle, Ky. (38)
SUMMERS, Lucinda - d 6-26-1870; a 46-2-8; pd Union twp.; pb Union twp. (38)
SIDWELL, Lydia - d 7-9-1870; a 53y; m; pd Union twp.; pb Kentucky. (38)
WILLOUGHBY, Miner - d 8-15-1870; a 87y; m; pd Union twp.; pb unknown. (38)
MEFFORD, Matilda - d 7-17-1870; a 73y 4d; m; pd Union twp.; pb unknown. (38)
CARR, Nancy - d 8-14-1870; a 51y; w; pd Union twp.; pb Kentucky. (38)
EDWARDS, George - d 10-28-1870; a 99y; s; pd Union twp.; pb unknown. (38)
NELSON, Nancy - d 3-31-1871; a 70y 7m; w; pd Ripley; pb Virginia. (38)
THEIS, Charlotte - d 10-12-1870; a 63-2-15; m; pd Georgetown; pb Germany. (38)
PURDUM, Sarah - d 3-13-1871; a 76y; w; pd Georgetown; pb Brown Co. (38)
STEWART, O. J. - d 5-22-1870; a 41y 7d; pd Vicksburg, Miss.; pb Brown Co.; res
   Brown Co. (38)
McLEMM, Annie - d 6-9-1870; a 56-7-9; m; pd Pleasant twp.; pb Ohio. (38)
LEIBERMAN, Elizabeth - d 12-19-1870; a 48y 1m; m; pd Georgetown; pb Germany. (40)
FRY, Margaret - d 2-13-1871; a 83y 3m; w; pd Pike twp.; pb Kentucky. (40)
ELLIS, Samuel - d 11-20-1870; a 76-8-5; m; pd Ohio River; pb Virginia; res
   Ohio Valley. (40)
STEPHEN, Henry J. - d 10-11-1870; a 48-7-2; m; pd Georgetown; pb Batavia. (40)
CAHAL, Thomas Sr. - d 1-28-1871; a 81y; m; pd Pleasant twp.; pb Maryland. (40)
CAHAL(?), Sarah - d 3-6-1871; a 83-9-6; w; pd Pleasant twp.; pb Virginia. (40)
KELLER, Catherine F. - d 1-2-1872; a 72-5-5; m; pd Franklin twp.; pb Alsace,
   France; father, Peter Haren. (42)
BOHL, M. Elizabeth - d 5-21-1871; a 80y; w; pd Franklin twp.; pb Bavaria;
   father, Adam Homings. (42)
LINDSEY, Jesse - d 6-22-1871; a 65-10-14; m; pd Franklin twp.; pb Franklin twp.;
   father, Philip Lindsey; mother, Drusilla Lucas. (42)
HARLOW, Francis - d 5-12-1871; a 86y; w; pd Franklin twp.; pb Virginia; father,
   Samuel Summers; mother, Lydia Moore. (42)
BEVERIDGE, John L. - d 8-24-1871; a 74y; m; pd Jackson twp.; pb------. (42)
EVANS, Dr. Jas. M. - d 1-30-1872; a 57y; m; pd Jackson twp.; pb-----; parents,
   Amos and Elizabeth Evans. (42)
KNOTT, John - d 3-26-1872; a 62y; m; pd Jackson twp.; pb Ireland. (42)
RISHFORTH, Joseph - d 10-16-1871; a 78y; m; pd Jackson twp.; pb England. (42)
HENRY, James - d 7-5-1871; a 51y 9m; s; pd Jefferson twp.; pb Ripley. (42)
HEUIZE, Eliza - d 12-9-1871; a 40y; m; pd Franklin twp.; pb Franklin twp. (42)
JOHNSON, Wm - d 4-8-1871; a 90y; m; pd Russelville; pb Ireland. (42)
JOHNSON, Sarah - d 10-24-1871; a 70y; m; pd Russelville; pb Ireland. (42)
PILSON, John L. - d 9-14-1871; a 66y; s; pd Jefferson twp.; pb Virginia. (42)
MOSS, Mary - d 8-28-1871; a 50-6-3; m; pd Washington twp.; pb Kentucky. (42)
KINNER, Katherine - d 11-28-1871; a 68-3-2; m; pd Pike twp.; pb Ohio. (44)
WORTHINGTON, Sarah - d 4-1-1871; a 63-9-5; m; pd Pike twp.; pb Clark twp. (44)
RAMSAY, Samuel - d 9-16-1871; a 40-2-21; m; pd Pike twp.; pb Scott twp. (44)
MONTJAR, Francis A. - d 12-30-1871; a 51-6-6; m; pd Pike twp.; pb Highland Co. (44)
BLAIR, Maria - d 12-5-1871; a 64y; w; pd Pike twp.; pb Lewis twp. (44)
RUSSELL, Peter - d 9-21-1871; a 61-4-24; m; pd Pike twp.; pb Lewis twp. (44)
LAUDERBACK, Peter - d 8-4-1871; a 71-1-24; m; pd Eagle twp.; pb Pennsylvania. (44)

126

CUMBERLAND, Moses - d 4-1-1871; a 51y; m; pd Eagle twp.; pb Ohio. (44)
BLAIR, William - d 7-30-1871; a 76y; m; pd Eagle twp.; pb Ireland. (44)
ANDREWS, Mary E. - d 7-16-1871; a 61y; w; pd Eagle twp.; pb Ohio. (44)
ELLIS, James - d 6-16-1871; a 71y; m; pd Eagle twp.; pb Virginia. (44)
HUDSON, John - d 1-9-1872; a 54y; w; pd Eagle twp.; pb Virginia. (44)
PENNY, Albert - d 1-5-1872; a 5-8-5; m; pd Clark twp.; pb Clark twp. (44)
DUNN, Mary - d 10-12-1871; a 73-6-2; m; pd Clark twp.; pb Kentucky. (44)
DUNN, James - d 10-26-1871; a 64-6-16; m; pd Clark twp.; pb Indiana. (44)
KELLUM, Jas. A. - d 10-17-1871; a 4-1-3; m; pd Clark twp.; pb Clermont Co. (44)
WILSON, Margaret A. - d 5-3-1871 a 50y 2m; m; pd Clark twp.; pb Adams Co., O.;
     parents Mathew (or Nathan?) and Mary P. Plummer. (44)
SPEES, George - d 7-26-1871; a 83-6-12; pd Clark twp.; pb Randolph Co., Pa. (44)
RICHARDS, Charles - d 6-6-1872; a 67-4-6; m; pd Clark twp.; pb Maryland. (44)
APPLEGATE, Adams - d 10-13-1871; a 71-3-21; w; pd Clark twp.; pb Trumbull Co.,
     Ohio. (44)
BLAIR, S.M. - d 6-30-1871; a 73-8-20; m; pd Clark twp.; pb Tennessee. (44)
FILO, Jacob - d 5-21-1871; a 51-6-2; m; pd Scott twp.; pb Kentucky. (46)
HILER, Jacob - d 1-28-1872; a 66y; m; pd Scott twp.; pb Pennsylvania. (46)
GATTS, John - d 4--8-1871; a 55y 2m; m; pd Scott twp.; pb Virginia. (46)
ANDERSON, Lucinthia - d 5-5-1871; a 73y; pd Scott twp.; pb Virginia. (46)
VISLSY, Mariah - d 9-5-1871; a 63y; s; pd Scott twp.; pb Virginia. (46)
BENJAMIN, Nancy - d 11-26-1871; a 49y 4m; m; pd Scott twp.; pb Brown Co. (46)
PATTON, Amanda M. - d 11-7-1871; a 40y; m; pd New Hope; pb Brown Co. (46)
DUM, Lydia Ann- d 9-6-1871; a 41-1-15; m; pd Green twp.; pb Washington twp.;
     father, J. I. Dum; mother, Lydia A. Vance. (46)
WAITS, Rachel - d 2-1-1871; a 78-3-15; w; pd Sterling twp.; pb Kentucky. (46)
WATT, Nancy - d 10-25-1871; a 63-9-20; w; pd Sterling twp.; pb Brown Co. (46)
CREMER, Jane C. - d 7-23-1871; a 57y; m; pd Sterling twp.; pb Brown Co. (46)
FOOTINBERRY, Hannah - d 3-27-1872; a 71y; s; pd Sterling twp.; pb Louisana. (46)

127

BUTLER COUNTY, OHIO - CHANCERY RECORDS 1827-1829

The following records were taken from "Chancery Record 3" located in the basement Archives of the court house at Hamilton. The page on which record may be found in the original book is given in parenthesis.

Sept. 1827 - Wm McCLELLAN adms. of John McCLELLAN vs. David CONNER and John SUTHERLAND. Petition for money due. Filed Oct. 1823. John McClelland and David Conner become partners in January 1814 in trading firm of McClelland and Conner. That John McClellan was killed by Indians 8-14-1814 while traveling from Greenville to Fort Recovery. (1)

Sept. 1827 - George SMITH and wife et al. vs. James McCREA and John McCREA. Filed 9-11-1826. That Catharine McDONALD late of Somerset Co., New Jersey made will on 6-10-1813 devising to her grandsons, James McCrea and John McCrea sons of Gilbert McCrea all land in Warrant #341 which at the time of the execution of the will was in possession of Gilbert McCrea the son of testatrix, said land warrant being in Section 2 of 1st twp., 2nd range being whole section 640, upon condition that Gilbert McCrea, her son, should have the undistributed possession of said land during his lifetime and that grandsons John and James McCrea upon one year after said Gilbert's death are to pay to daughters of Gilbert $150.00. Executors of Catharine McDonald's will being Richard McDonald's will being Richard McDonald and George McDonald. Gilbert McCrea, dec'd late of Butler Co., Ohio died June 1824. Children: Mary late McCrea wife of George Smith of Butler Co.; Catharine late McCrea wife of James Wilkerson of Hamilton Co., Ohio; James McCrea and John McCrea (note: petition mentions at time of Gilbert's death that there were three daughters living, but third daughter is not named, only two are named.) (15 & 57)

Sept. 1827 - Elizabeth RHEA et al. vs. SUTHERLAND and McCLELLAND. Henry Rhea, dec'd late of Butler Co., Ohio died in year 1813. Widow, Elizabeth Rhea. Children: Juliann wife of Joseph P. Wilson, Eliza wife of Samuel Dick Jr., Thomas Lyon Rhea and John Rhea, the last two being minors by Joseph P. Wilson their guardian. That Sutherland and McClelland were adms. of estate of Henry Rhea and that said Henry Rhea left large estate of $7000.00 and upwards from which money was collected by adms. from Pennsylvania. Petition asks that estate be settled and money distributed. (19&37)

Sept. 1827 - Daniel RUMPLE vs. George WHITE. Filed 2-26-1827. Petition to clear title to land being 60 acres part of Section 11, Township 3, Range 2. (42)

Sept. 1827 - John ROSS vs. James BARCALOW and Derick BARCALOW adms. of Tobias BARKELOW, dec'd late of Butler Co., Ohio. Filed Feb. 1827. Widow, Elizabeth Barcalow. Children: James Barcalow; William Barcalow; Rebecca late Barcalow wife of Polhamus Lane; Elizabeth late Barcalow, dec'd, late wife of Arthur Lefferson; John Barcalow; Eleanor Barcalow; Lydia Barcalow; Deborah Barcalow; Tobias Barcalow and Rachel Barcalow; the last six named being minors. That John Ross during life time of Tobias Barcalow contracted to purchase 100 acres in Wayne twp. in north end W½ Section 11, Township 3, Range 3 with Barcalow giving bond to make deed. (46)

128

Sept. 1827 - Nicholas JONES vs. James W. ROBINSON, et al. Filed 5-21-1827. Nicholas Jones had contracted to purchase land being 168½ acres S½ Section 2, Township 4, Range 1 from James W. Robinson now of Hamilton Co., Ohio. Said land being land laid off to Robinson as one of the heirs at law of Samuel Robinson, dec'd. (52)

Feb. 1828 - Elijah HUGHES vs. Daniel NELSON. Filed --------1828. Petition to obtain clear title to land. (63)

May 1828 - Isaac FALCONER vs. Maxwell PARKISON. Filed 10-17-1825. Petition to complete contract to purchase land including mill seat adjoining town of Rossville. (69)

May 1828 - William BROWN vs. Thomas WILSON and John W. WILSON. Filed 5-21-1827. Petition to obtain judgement. (95)

May 1828 - Nancy ENYART vs. Stephen CRANE, et al. Filed 5-21-1827. Land, 166 acres SE corner Section 20 Township 2 Range 2 in Symmes Purchase except 60 acres sold by John Enyart in his lifetime to his son, William Enyart; also 39 acres Section 14 Township 2, Range 2 joining above 166 acres on the east side. John Enyart late of Butler Co., Ohio, dec'd died about Dec. 1824. Widow, Nancy Enyart. Children of John and Nancy: Polly wife of Stephen Crane of Butler Co.; Sarah wife of David Slayback of Butler Co.; Catharine wife of William Butler (res. not stated); Ann wife of Joseph Camron of Hamilton Co., Ohio; Charlotte wife of Thomas Fleming of Butler Co.; William Enyart of Hamilton Co., Ohio; James Enyart of Butler Co.; and Thompson Enyart (res. not stated). (100)

May 1828 - KEYT and KEYT vs. KEYTS executors, et al. Filed 9-10-1827. Daniel Keyt, dec'd left will dated 5-25-1822 with executors of will being his wife Eleanor and James McBride. Widow, Eleanor now the wife of Robert Jones. Heirs: James Keyt and Ann Eliza Keyt of New Jersey children and heirs of David R. Keyt, dec'd, late of Butler Co., Ohio who died in year 1814. Benjamin Crane guardian of James and Ann Eliza. Mentions Joel Collins adms. of John R. Crane, dec'd late of Butler Co., Ohio. (77, 108 & 208)

May 1828 - Daniel SEWARD vs. Adam BLAIR and Wm BLAIR. Filed 2-25-1828. In April 1821 Adam Blair cam e to board with Seward and had with him a mulatto boy called Joe Hammond which he claimed was indentured to him for 8 yrs. 1 mo. & 19 ds. or until Joe Hammond arrived at 21 yrs. of age. Seward agreed to board Adam Blair for services of Hammond, now petitions to retain money due him from lack of services.(113)

May 1828 - Thomas FERGUSON et al. vs. Elizabeth Dennis. Filed 9-11-1826. Samuel Ferguson, dec'd., left will dated 2-8-1814, for which letters of adms. with will annexed were granted to widow, Elizabeth Ferguson. Widow, Elizabeth late Ferguson now wife of John Dennis. Children: Thomas Ferguson, Athel Ferguson, Nancy late Ferguson wife of Ebenezer Paddox, Letha late Ferguson wife of John Hall, Elizabeth late Ferguson wife of Joseph Chambers, Polly late Ferguson wife of Daniel Heaton, Sarah late Ferguson wife of Ebenezer Goble, Levinah late Ferguson wife of Archibald Reed, John Ferguson, James Ferguson, Melinda Ferguson, William Ferguson and Rosannah Ferguson; the last five named being minors by David Heaton their guardian. Will of Samuel Ferguson names children: Thomas, Athel, Nancy, Lethy, Elizabeth, Polly and Sarah, married at that time; also Levinah, Melinda, and Rosannah not married at that time. Will signed: Samuel (mark) Ferguson with witnesses: Thos. Ferguson, Thos. Pound and Elizabeth Goble. (116)

Sept. 1828 - Ezekiel McCONNEL vs. Jacob BURNETT, et al. Filed 9-7-1826. Ezekiel
McConnel files petition against Jacob Burnet, Martin Baum and William Corry executors
of Will of William McMillan, dec'd to complete contract on purchase of land. (121)

Sept. 1828 - John HILL Sr. vs. William JOHNSTON, et al. Filed Feb. 1828. Mentions
Thomas Hill, John Hill Jr. and Nancy Hill minors by John Hill Sr. their guardian,
Catharine wife of William Houk, Eliza wife of James Clark, all children of John
Hill Sr. the petitioner. John Hill Sr. in August 1824 having formed the intention
of traveling into Pennsylvania and having lost his wife by death and being concerned
for welfare of his family was compelled to leave family under care of his daughter,
Martha then unmarried but now the wife of William Johnson. That John Hill Sr.
gave Jacob Mong and said Martha control over the property of family, of which Martha
being easily swayed gave to said Mong. Petition now to recover said property. (127)

Sept. 1828 - George CASTO vs. William CASTO. Filed Feb. 1828. George Casto the
petitioner being a minor 7/21 years by Allen Mann his guardian. That William Casto
uncle of said petitioner, George Casto and George Casto, father of said Petitioner,
George Casto purchased a lot from a Mr. Davis in the Miami University lease tract and
now George Casto by guardian petitions to obtain title to said land. (134)

Sept. 1828 - James McCLUNG et al. vs. Ann MARTIN et al. Filed May 1828. That James
Martin now dec'd made will on 1-23-1826 devising to son, Joseph Martin farm where
testator lived, also devising to three daughters, Polly, Nancy and Betsey with Richard
Scott and George Kraner executors of will and witnesses to will being Matth. J. Richardson, Maria Richardson and Matt. Richardson. Petitioners maintain that at time of
making of will said James Martin was insane and could not remember who all his children were. Children of James Martin, dec'd late of Butler Co., Ohio: Mary late Martin wife of James McClung, Elizabeth Morris late Martin, Nancy late Martin wife of
John Herron and Joseph Martin a minor by Wm Douglass his guardian (note: names no
further children, petition pertains in body primarily to how property devised under
will). Widow of James Martin, dec'd, Ann Martin. (141)

Sept. 1828 - Heirs of James MOORE, dec'd vs. Adms. of James MOORE, dec'd. Filed
Feb. 1828. James Moore, dec'd, died in year 1820. Widow, Polly now wife of Joshua
Rowland. Children: George Moore, William White Moore and James Thompson Moore
all minors by John Beach and John Dunn their guardians. Court appointed James
Thompson, Jacob Piatt and Polly Moore now Rowland adms. of estate of James Moore,
dec'd. (144)

Mar. 1829 - Martha Jane CUMMINS vs. Michael AYERS and Jeremiah DAY executors of
will of Stephen CUMMINS. Filed 3-2-1829. Stephen Cummins dec'd died in year
1822 in Butler Co., Ohio. Child: Martha Jane Cummins a minor by David Bigham her
guardian. Will specified money from estate to be used to purchase congress land
for said Martha Jane and Petition requests that this be done. (144)

Mar. 1829 - Jacob MADEIRA et al. vs. Jacob WHITINGER and Jane WILSON. Filed
Mar. 1829. Land, Lots 245 & 246. Petition for partition with Jacob Maderia
maintaining that he has 1/3rd interest and that Joel Whitinger of Indiana has
2/3rds interest in said lots. (156)

Mar. 1829 - James BAIRD vs. widow and heirs of George HETFIELD, dec'd. Filed
Mar. 1829. Land, SW¼ Section 24, Township 3, Range 3. George Hetfield, dec'd.
Widow, Rachel late Hetfield now Rachel Broadberry, with Broadberry also now being
dec'd. Children: Mary late Hetfield wife of Samuel Culver; John Hetfield; Jacob
Hetfield; Abel Hetfield; Elizabeth Hetfield; Elihu Hetfield; Nancy Hetfield living
in Clark Co., Ohio; Sarah Hetfield; George Hetfield now living in Preble Co., Ohio;
the last five named being minors. Baird petitions that he purchased 3/9ths interest
in said land from John, Jacob and Abel Hetfield. (159)

May 1829 - John AYERS vs. Absalom CUMMINS, et al. Filed Feb. 1827. Petition to
collect debt. James Cummins father of said Absalom Cummins made will proven
2-27-1826 in which James having no son except Absalom devised away to his daughters
and nephews considerable personal and real property and petitioner claims that
nephew, James Cummins was devised S½ lots 41 and 42 in Middletown which were intended for use of testator's son, Absalom. (163)

May 1829 - James C. BECKET vs. Jonas GRAHAM, etal. Filed Feb. 1828. Bill in
equity for Judgment. (171)

May 1829 - James DELAPLANE vs. Samuel BENNETT. Filed May 1828. Petition for clear
title to land. (177)

May 1829 - Jane WILSON vs. Jacob WHITINGER. Filed May 1828. That James Wilson died
in Jan. 1828 leaving widow Jane Wilson who he married in Pennsylvania. That at time
of his death James Wilson owned 2/3rd interest in lots 245 & 246 in Hamilton which in
his lifetime he sold to Jacob Whitinger. Jane maintains that she did not release
dower and now claims dower in same. (181)

May 1829 - Margaret LINE vs. Jacob LINE and Dennis BALL executors of Solomon LINE
and Heirs of Solomon LINE, dec'd. Solomon Line, dec'd made will on 11-3-1817.
Widow, Margaret Line. Children: Jacob Line; Margaret late Line wife of Dennis Ball;
Martha late Line, dec'd late wife of Isaac Ball who is also dec'd, her children--
Solomon Ball, Topher Ball, Nancy late Ball wife of William Hunter, Margaret late Ball
wife of John Hunter, Sarah late Ball wife of Felix Hunter and Esther Ball; David Line;
Elihu Line; Jonathan Line; John Line; Nancy late Line wife of James Lyon. Copy of
will of Soloman Line of Fairfield twp., Butler Co., Ohio names: wife, Margaret.
Daughters: Nancy Lyon, Margaret Ball and Martha Ball, dec'd, her children. Sons:
David, Jonathan, Elihu and John have received their portions. Executors: son, Jacob
Line and son-in-law, Dennis Ball. Dated 11-3-1817. Signed: Solomon (mark) Line.
Witnesses: James Heaton and Rebecca Walker. (104 & 183)

May 1829 - John WILCOX and wife vs. Catharine McDONALD, et al. Filed Sept. 1828.
William McDonald late of Butler Co., Ohio, dec'd, died in the year 1812 intestate.
Widow, Catharine. Children: Harriet wife of John Wilcox, William McDonald, James
McDonald, Catharine Maria wife of Samuel Peirson, Margaret wife of John Winter,
Sarah wife of John Hart, Eliza wife of Ogden Harvey, and Jane Florence wife of
Ezekiel Beckwith. (195)

May 1829 - Thomas KENWORTHY vs. Benjamin BASY, et al. Petition in judgment for
money. (204)

May 1829 - Susan VANATER vs. Mark McMaken adms. of A. Vanater, dec'd. Filed March 1829. Andrew Vanater, dec'd, died in July 1828. Widow, Susan Vanater. Mentions Susan's children but does not name. (206)

Sept 1829 - Jesse WOODS and Joseph FOOTE vs. Patrick SHIELDS. Filed Feb. 1828. Jesse Woods purchased one half acre ground on 12-15-1825 from Patrick Shields in Township 2, Range 4 (no section given), said land adjoining canal at point in road from Hamilton to Middletown and Dayton crosses Miami Canal at Lock 3 on south side of Dicks Creek with lot including a storehouse. That Shields again sold said land in January 1827 to one James Dryer. (213)

Sept. 1829 - Heirs and adms. of Joseph ELY vs. MULFORD, BUTT, etal. In Chancery. Filed May 1828. On 12-2-1810 Jonathan Dayton executed a deed to David Mulford since deceased for tract of land in Section 36, Township 3, Range 3, that on 8-21-1815 the Heirs of David Mulford executed deed to said land to John P. Finkle and that on 4-19-1816 Finkle sold said tract to Joseph Ely. Petition to clear title to land. Joseph Ely, dec'd. Children and Heirs: William Ely, James Ely, Sarah late Ely wife of Thomas Anderson, Mary late Ely wife of John Marshall and John Ely, a minor. John N.C. Schenck and Joseph Tapscott were adms. of estate of Joseph Ely, dec'd. David Mulford, dec'd. Three children: Jane late Mulford wife of Edward Aldridge, John Mulford and Job Mulford, dec'd, his widow, Eupheme Mulford and his children--David, Harriet and Jane Mulford. (220)

Sept. 1829 - Joseph KIRKWOOD vs. S. DICK surviving executor of D. KIRKWOOD, dec'd. Filed Sept. 1828. That Joseph Kirkwood was the son and only heir of David Kirkwood who died in the year 1796 in Hamilton County, Ohio leaving a will therein. That David Kirkwood by his will appointed his brothers-in-law, George Gillespie Jr. and Samuel Dick executors of said will. Mentions 100 acres of land in Sycamore twp., Hamilton Co., Ohio. Mentions money to be collected in Pennsylvania. Also mentions money coming from Joseph Kirkwood's estate in Pennsylvania to daughters (Joseph's???) Martha and Mary. (232) (note: David Kirkwood's will probated in 1796 names sisters of testator as Martha and Mary--thus, it is not absolutely certain from the way the above chancery record record is worded whether the daughters Martha and Mary were daughters of Joseph Kirkwood the petitioner or of the Joseph Kirkwood who died in Penna.)

Although generally speaking, death records in Ohio do not begin until 1867, there are a few exceptions to the rule. The following record is found in the Butler County, Ohio, Probate Court and is entitled, DEATH RECORD ENDING ON 1st day MARCH, 1857. Death dates from March 1st through December 31st are for the year 1856; from January 1st through February 28th are for the year 1857. Children six (6) years and under have been omitted.

Name	Date of Death	Age	Marital Status	Place of Birth	Parents

OXFORD TOWNSHIP

Name	Date of Death	Age	Marital Status	Place of Birth	Parents
HUFFMAN, Margaret	5-26	60	wid.	Kentucky	(mulatto)
CROSBY, Juenia E.	6-18	32	mar.	Ohio	G. ELLIOTT
MAGIE, Mary A.	9-11	21	mar.	Ohio	W.R. & Elizabeth DEWITT
STRANDER, Fany	11-18	55	mar.	Virginia	(black)
BAIRD, William	9-1	72	wid.	Penna	Wm. & Jane BAIRD
STEBBENS, David	12-25	71	mar.	N. Jersey	E. & Rebecca STIBBENS
DAVIS, Ann	11-20	80	wid.	Penna.	- - - - -
HANNAH, James	1-26	56	mar.	Penna.	John & Sarah HANNAH
BECKETT, Wm. C.	1-24	23	sing.	Indiana	Wm. & Catharine
MOORE, Elizabeth	11-17	52	mar.	N. Jersey	Jos. & Permelia SELLERS
FREEMAN, Martha	2-4	41	mar.	Kentucky	Jos. & Catharine CROSS
CRULL, Michael	1-29-1857	67	mar.	Penna	Michael & Hettia CRULL
BONNEY, Margaret	11-16-1856	29	mar.	N. Carolina	David & Mary YOUNG (black)
COWAN, Elizabeth	6-13	13	sing.	Kentucky	Cyrus A. COWAN (black)
CLAY, Eliza	3-25	40	mar.	Kentucky	Mingo & S. HALL (black)
HOLLY, Mary	3-21	20	mar.	Ohio	Noble&Margaret CHURCHILL
PATTERSON, Wm. S.	4-17	30	sing.	Penna.	A.O. & M.S. PATTERSON
	(Note:- Died Nevada City, Calif. - Physician)				
HASELTIN, Nancy	8-18	58	mar.	Mass.	F.P. & Nancy HARDMAN
FEELY, Sue W.	5-25	25	mar.	Cincinnati	Oliver & Elizabeth WELLS

REILY TOWNSHIP

Name	Date of Death	Age	Marital Status	Place of Birth	Parents
BRIANT, Elizabeth	10-27	77	mar.	N. Jersey	David BAKER & Nancy SCUDDER
	(Note: d. N. Jersey - Residence: Darrtown)				
GOUDY, John	9-4	78	wid.	Scotland	. . . .
SMITH, James B.	11-22	33	mar.	Ohio	Charles & Phebe SMITH
YOUNG, John	2-11	21	sing.	Bavaria	. . . .
ROBESON, Sylvester	7-14	28	sing.	Carthage	J. & N. ROBESON
TUMBLY, Elizabeth	6-3	67	wid.	Penna	Jas. & Esther DENEEN
	(Note: Died at John BURGETT's)				
BURK, Elizabeth	10-20	81	mar.	Maryland	JONES
FUHRMAN, Phillip	Oct.	55	mar.	Germany	. . . .
KEEGAN, Peter	2-14	54	mar.	Ireland	Barney & Anna KEEGAN
HARRIS, Martha	4-2	27	mar.	Ohio	Thomas GRANT

Name	Date of Death	Age	Marital Status	Place of Birth	Parents

ROSS TOWNSHIP

Name	Date of Death	Age	Marital Status	Place of Birth	Parents
TIMBERMAN, Peter	10-25-1856	57	mar.	Tennessee	Jonathan & Barbara
ELLIOTT, Allen	Feb. 1856	—	sing.	Hamilton Co.	Samuel & Ruby
BURK, Mary	8-15-1856	40	mar.	Ireland	Lamy(?) WELSH

MORGAN TOWNSHIP

Name	Date of Death	Age	Marital Status	Place of Birth	Parents
BROWN, Robert	10-10	44	mar.	Ohio	John & Dorcas BROWN
HESLET, Samuel	5-2	53	mar.	Kentucky	. . . .
SNYDER, Rebecca	10-17	57	mar.	N. Jersey	Charles & Mary ENB
DAVIS, James L.	8-23	59	mar.	Penna.	Mesheck & Mary DAVIS
HALL, Eliza	1-4	19	sing.	Ohio	Jeremiah & Jane
SEPTON, Henry	8-15	44	—	——	Henry & Elizabeth SEPTON

HANOVER TOWNSHIP

Name	Date of Death	Age	Marital Status	Place of Birth	Parents
TIMBERMAN, Susan	1-10	22	sing.	Ohio	David & Sarah
HARNING, George	10-19	—	——	——	Lewis HARNING
DONLEY, Steven	12-23	—	——	——	Mich'l & Catharine DONLEY
GIFFEN, Elizabeth	4-24	—	mar.	Ohio	John & J. Smith

WAYNE TOWNSHIP

Name	Date of Death	Age	Marital Status	Place of Birth	Parents
ORR, Jane Ruth	——	28	mar.	Indiana	George & Nancy CURTS
CARTER, Margt L.	10-20	17	sing.	Preble Co.	A.B. & Margt. H. CARTER
MACY, George	10-25	41	mar.	Cincinnati	Reuben & Sarah MACEY
MACY, Jonathan	11-11	35	mar.	Cincinnati	Reuben & Sarah MACEY
KING, Sam'l W.	9-26	22	sing.	Germantown	Jacob & Maylin KING
THOMAS, Rodia Ann	11-2	33	mar.	Ohio	Wm. J. & Nancy HENRY
THOMAS, Sophia	12-5	9	sing.	Ohio	James H. & Rodia Ann
THOMAS, Catharine	9-8	27	mar.	Ohio	Andrew & Elizabeth
THOMAS, John H.	4-4	56	mar.	Penna.	. . . .

MADISON TOWNSHIP

Name	Date of Death	Age	Marital Status	Place of Birth	Parents
AUGSPERGER, Catharine	10-2-1856	17	sing.	Ohio	Jacob & Catharine
AUGSPERGER, Mary	4-17-1856	77	wid.	Europe	Not Known
DORR, Elizabeth	7-10-1856	40	mar.	France	Joseph & MagdalenaSCHERTZ
	(Note: Residence in Cincinnati)				
BUEHL, George	2-1-1856	26	mar.	Montgomery Co.	John C. & Willamine BUEHL
MILLER, Barbrea	3-1-1856	47	sing.	Penna.	David & Barbera MILLER
LONG, Nancy	5-15-1856	21	mar.	Illinois	John & Sarah GEPHART
GOUCHEY, Christian	7-3-1856	72	mar.	Germany	. . . .
GOUCHEY, Catherine	12-18-1856	67	wid.	Germany	. . . .
GEPHART, Lucinda	1-3-1856	11	sing.	Ohio	Henry & Nancy
HUFFMAN, Levi	5-5-1856		wid.	——	. . . .

(Note: States he died of old age, age not being known)

Name	Date of Death	Age	Marital Status	Place of Birth	Parents

MADISON TOWNSHIP (Continued)

Name	Date of Death	Age	Marital Status	Place of Birth	Parents
DEEM, Mary W.	2-8-1856	21	mar.	——	. . . .
KEMP, Daniel	8-29-1856	79	mar.	----	Daniel & Barbera KEMP

LEMON TOWNSHIP

Name	Date of Death	Age	Marital Status	Place of Birth	Parents
PARROT, Rachel	7-5-1856	24	sing.	Ohio	John & Matilda
FIELDING, Margaret	9-28-1856	27	mar.	Ohio	C. DENNIS
CUMMINS, Catharine	10-12-1856	36	mar.	Ohio	Absalom & Julia CUMMINS
VANHORN, James B.	12-31-1856	17	sing.	Ohio	Barnard & Eliza Jane
VANHORN, Mary M.	1-25-1857	14	sing.	Ohio	Bernard & Eliza Jane
CLANCEY, Margaret	9-28-1856	26	mar.	Ireland	Martin FLINN
DEARDOFF, Geo. W.	3-20-1856	24	sing.	Ohio	Jacob & Mary
ROBINSON, William	7-30-1856	40	sing.	Ohio	. . . .
DOTY, Joseph	4-24-1856	48	mar.	Ohio	Daniel & Betsy DOTY
WALDOE, Albert	10-8-1856	44	sing.	Ohio	Carlton & Rhoda WALDOE
CONKLIN, Frem	12-24-1856	72	sing.	N. Jersey	. . . .
HOLMES, Rachel	9-22-1856	22	sing.	Ohio	Geo. HOLMES
JEFFERSON, Ann	10-23-1856	66	sing.	N. Jersey	. . . .
GRIMES, Geo.	9-2-1856	68	mar.	Virginia	. . . .

LIBERTY TOWNSHIP

Name	Date of Death	Age	Marital Status	Place of Birth	Parents
WOODMANSEE, Lydia	9-1-1856	44	mar.	Butler Co.	Thomas & Miss BARKALOW
WILSON, Eliza Jane	7-20-1856	9	sing.	Maryland	Thomas & Jemima
PIERSON, Emma Irena	2-16-1857	5y7m	sing.	Butler Co.	Bethwell & Sophia
WILLIAMSON, Dav.B.	2-1-1857	39	mar.	Butler Co.	John & Christian
BUTLER, Malissa	4-3-1856	10	sing.	Warren Co.	Wm. & E. H. RUTLER
CLAWSON,Lydia Minerva	6-29-1856	18	mar.	Butler Co.	Jas. & Aseneth LEGGET
AYRES, Magdelana	2-4-1857	60	wid.	Holland	Roger & Cornelia FEUTINHOFT
WOODRUFF, Daniel	4-2-1857	77	wid.	N. Jersey	Stephen & Eliza
GARY, Cornelia	8-16-1856	87	mar.	Holland	Not Known
JOHNSON, Thomas Jr.	2-22-1857	76	wid.	Virginia	Thomas & Sarah JOHNSON

UNION TOWNSHIP

Name	Date of Death	Age	Marital Status	Place of Birth	Parents
AYDLOTT, Prudence	2-20-1857	40	mar.	Penna.	J. & P. COOVER
BARNARD, John	7-9-1856	30	mar.	N. Jersey	. . . .
CONOVER, Britton	4-9-1856	20	sing.	Union Two.	E. W. & C.
COY, Samuel	9-10-1856	40	mar.	Penna.	. . . .
FLINN, Milton	2-6-1857	19	sing.	Indiana	. . . .
	(Note: Residence - Indiana)				
NOBLE, Elizabeth	12-18-1856	73	wid.	Penna.	. . . .
QUINN, Thomas	2-20-1857	65	mar.	Ireland	. . . .
WILLIS, Rachel	4-14-1856	87	wid.	Virginia	. . . .
CUTTER, Jane	11-15-1856	29	mar.	Hamilton Co.	. . . .

Name	Date of Death	Age	Marital Status	Place of Birth	Parents

MILFORD TOWNSHIP

Name	Date of Death	Age	Marital Status	Place of Birth	Parents
SCOTT, Mary	11-4-1856	88	mar.	Ireland	Robert & Jane RICHEY
SCOTT, Rebecca Jane	4-14-1856	18	sing.	Ireland	John & Jane
SCOTT, John E.	7-20-1856	74	mar.	Penna.	John & Rebecca SCOTT
YERGEN, Margaret	4-24-1856	24	mar.	Butler Co.	John & Susan GRIMES
DAVIS, Nancy	9-10-1856	37	mar.	Butler Co.	Robert & Jane YOUNG

ST. CLAIR TOWNSHIP

Name	Date of Death	Age	Marital Status	Place of Birth	Parents
TROUTMAN, John	10-22-1857	37	mar.	St. Clair	Peter & Elizabeth
LEFLAR, Margaret	12-25-1856	47	wid.	Penna.	. . . .

FAIRFIELD TOWNSHIP

Name	Date of Death	Age	Marital Status	Place of Birth	Parents
DAUGHERTY, Mary	5-10	9	sing.	Ohio	Patrick & Margaret
BLACKBURN, Sarah	8-21	72	wid.	Fairfield	Robt. & Margt. LYTLE
BUTLER, Reuben T.	8-7	43	sing.	Ohio	William & Catharine E.
TYLER, Drusella	11-15	70	wid.	Fairfield	. . . .
McDONALD, James	6-13	74	sing.	Fairfield	. . . .
MAGEE, Richard	Sept.	—	wid.	- - - - -	. . . .
CARR, John	9-23-56	54	mar.	Lemon Twp.	John & Jane
HILLEBRECHT, Andy	8-24-56	76	mar.	Germany	. . . .
SHELEY, Regiah	1-3-57	65	mar.	Virginia	Wm. & Rachel CATTERLIN
JONES, Lucinda	11-5-56	40	mar.	- - - - -	. . . . (black)

CITY OF HAMILTON

Name	Date of Death	Age	Marital Status	Place of Birth	Parents
BEARDSLY, Laura	5-29-56	29	mar.	Hamilton	Jas. & Leah O'CONNOR
DAVIS, Susan	6-8-57	22	mar.	Hamilton	Jos. & Susan A. WATKINS
HUNTER, Wm.	1-29-57	59	mar.	Penna.	Thomas & Jane HUNTER
RUOFF, Daniel	12-8-56	15	sing.	Hamilton	Ludwig & Mary
HESS, John M.	9-6-56	13	sing.	Cincinnati	John & Elizabeth
SCHENCK, Aaron	3-9-56	53	mar.	N. Jersey	Obediah & Rhoda SCHENCK
TRICKLER, Henry	3-15-56	25	mar.	Germany	Henry & Elizabeth
BRANNAN, Margaret	7-4-56	73	wid.	N. Y. City	John SHAY
DOUGLASS, Jas. S.	10-7-56	41	mar.	Milford Twp.	Wm. & Ann DOUGLASS
WEHOTERING, Harmon	9-19-56	46	mar.	Germany	. . . .
MURRAY, James C.	11-10-56	24	sing.	Hamilton	Wm. & Mary MURRY
(Note: Residence - Richmond, Kentucky)					
SHUEY, Dr. Adam	9-29-56	27	---	Penna.	Christian & Magdalena
MELEY, Sarah	4-19-56	54	mar.	Penna.	Abner & Rebecca PATTERSON
DIXON, Delphi	7-15-56	16	sing.	Hamilton	. . . . (black)
WILDS, Mary Ann	3-15-56	34	mar.	England	WINGROVE
WEISER, George	7-19-56	73	mar.	Penna.	Jacob & Catharine
MAGNUS, Sam'l J.	10-11-56	14	sing.	Cincinnati	John & Julian
CRESS, John	12-11-56	42	sing.	Germany	Michael & Josephine
McELRY, Michael	10-1-56	7½	sing.	Ireland	Daniel & Mary
SHAFFER, Oscula	8-2-56	26	mar.	Germany	. . . .
ERWIN, Chas. R.	11-5-56	20	sing.	Camden, O.	J. W. & Ann E.

136

BUTLER COUNTY, OHIO - ORPHAN AND TESTAMENTARY RECORDS 1803-1810

From original records located in the Butler County, Ohio Archives located in the Court House Basement, Hamilton, Ohio; under the care of Mrs. Esther R. Benzing, Archivist. The following records are from Book 1803-1821, with page on which record is located, being given in parenthesis.

7-12-1803
WHITE, James, dec'd - Will proven - Tabitha White & Bladon Ashby, Executors. (1)

9-13-1803
GREGORY, David, dec'd - Margaret Gregory widow relict of David, adms. gave bond of $3000. with Mahlon Baker and William Long. (2)
GRAHAM, Patrick, dec'd - Isaac Swearingen, adms. gave bond of $600. with Joseph McMahon and Samuel Seward. (2)

10-21-1803
DILLON, Andrew, dec'd - Elizabeth Dillon and Thomas Dillon, adms. gave bond of $600. with William McClellan and Isaac Stanly. (3)
NOBLE, Robert, Dec'd - Agness Noble and William Noble, adms. gave bond of $1200. with Samuel Dillon and Darius Curtis. (3)

12-16-1803
LOY, Adam, dec'd - Will proven. (4)
MANSFIELD, Charles, dec'd - Rebeccah Mansfield and John Mansfield, adms. gave bond of $400. with Abraham Heath and Thomas Gray. (4)

5-15-1804
PARKISON, William, dec'd - Will proven. (5)
GORDON, John, dec'd - Request for adms. by Matthew Hueston and James Hamilton, request also filed by Phebe Griffin and Abner Enoch; Court decreed adms. to said Hueston and Hamilton, their having given bond of $4000. with John Buckhanon and David Beaty, surety. (5)
LOWRY, John, dec'd - Catharine Lowry widow relict of John, adms. gave bond of $400. with Thomas Davis and John Carson. (6)
EWING, Samuel, dec'd - Margaret Ewing widow relic of Samuel, adms. gave bond of $500. with David Beaty and John R. Beaty. (6)

STERRET, Alexander, a minor aged 13 years, son of Alexander Sterret late of Cumberland Co., Penna.; James Dunn, guardian gave bond of $3000. with John Torrence and Celadon Symms. (7)
MORROW, Lewis, a minor aged 13 years on 17th day Oct. next, one of sons of James Morrow late in Army of United States, dec'd; David Beaty, guardian gave bond of $500. with Celadon Symms and John Torrence. (7)

10-16-1804
GORDON, John, dec'd - Ordered that John Wingate, Joseph Hunter and Isaac Stanly are appointed commissioners to receive charges against estate. (8)
JONES, Edward, dec'd - Will proven. (8)
HAGAMAN, Michael, dec'd - Margaret Hagaman widow of Michael, adms. gave bond of $600. with Abraham Freeman and Garret Vannest. (9)

12-3-18-4
PERKINS, Jesse, dec'd - Nancy Perkins widow relict of Jesse, adms. gave bond of
$500. with William Spencer and Aaron Cherry; John Hamilton, Abraham Heath and
Capt. James Mills, appraisers. (10)

1-15-1805
KISER, John, dec'd - Elias Wallen, adms. gave bond of $200. with Charles Bruce
and Patrick Moore; John McCormack, William Brodrick and Robert Saunders, appraisers.)

4-29-1805
KING, John, late of Campbelle Co., Kentucky, dec'd - Phebe King widow of John, adms.
gave bond of $600, with Henry Thompson of Rossville, Benjamin Thompson and Archi-
bald Talbott; Samuel Ayers, William Curry and James White, appraisers. (12)

5-21-1805
KITCHEL, John, dec'd - Will proven. (13)
GOBLE, Isaac, dec'd - Will proven. (13)
HARRIS, Walter, dec'd, St. Clair Twp. - Elizabeth Harris widow relict of Walter,
adms. gave bond of $200. with Samuel Pottenger and Jacob Case. (14)
WALLEN, Elias, dec'd, St. Clair Twp. - Mary Wallen widow relict of Elias, adms.
gave bond of $800. with William McClellan and James Smith with Solomon Line and
John Wingate, sureties; Henry Taylor, James Mills and Samuel Davis, appraisers (14)
KISER, John, dec'd - Elias Wallen late adms. now dec'd; adms. granted to Mary Wallen
who gave bond of $200. with James Smith and William McClellan; Henry Taylor, James
Mills and Samuel Davis, appraisers. (14)
GILDERSLEVE, Isaac, dec'd, Liberty Twp. - Isaac Van Nuys, adms. gave bond of $1000.
with William Brodrick and John Vannice; Ralph W. Hunt, Joseph Stephens and Isaac
John, appraisers. (15)
RAIL, William, a minor aged 15 years on about the middle of Feb. last, son of
Eleanor Matheried; Samuel Ferguson of St. Clair Twp., guardian, gave bond of $200.
(15)

8-20-1805
DAVIS, Daniel, dec'd - Margaret Davis and Samuel Davis, adms. gave bond of $600.
with Matthew Hueston and John Scott; David Beaty, James Blackburn and Thomas
Alston, appraisers. (16)
GRAHAM, Aaron, a minor aged 14 years in Jan. last, one of sons and heirs of Patrick
Graham late of Liberty Twp.; Andrew Wilson, guardian gave bond of $100. (16)
GRAHAM, Sally, a minor aged 9 years in March last, one of daughters and heirs of
Patrick Graham late of Liberty Twp.; Andrew Wilson, guardian gave bond of $100.
with James Wilson and Isaac Wills. (17)

12-17-1805
REED, Mary, dec'd - Will proven. (18)
BAGGS, James, dec'd - Eleanor Baggs widow relict declines to adms. her husband's
estate; Adms. granted to James Brown, Jr., son-in-law of dec'd; Andrew Wilson,
William Mitchel and Samuel Dick, appraisers. (18)
VANCLEEF, Ann dec'd - Benjamin Vancleef and Joseph Baird, adms.; Tunis Vandavere,
William Bakalew and James Tapscott of Lemon Twp., appraisers. (19)
HARPER, William, dec'd, St. Clair Twp. - Ann Harper widow relict of William, adms.;
Samuel Pittinger, James McKean and James Withrow, appraisers. (19)
WALLIN, Elias, Estate - Charles Bruce, John Torrence and Henry Brown appointed
trustees. (19)

GORDON, John, Estate - Claims presented. (20)

4-15-1806
HAWKINS, Nathan, dec'd - Will proven. (22)
DEBOLT, Henry, dec'd, late of Lemon Twp. - Mary Debolt, adms.; Bladen Ashby,
Samuel Dickey of Elk Creek and John Barret, all of Lemon Twp., appraisers. (22)
STERRET, Alexander, a minor aged 14 years July last, only son and heir of Alex-
ander Sterret late of Cumberland Co., Penna., dec'd; James Dunn, guardian gave
bond of $1000. with Charles Bruce and Matthew Hueston. (23)
GRAHAM, Patrick, Estate - Settlement, claims balance cash on hand, thus, no dis-
bursement to heirs. (23)
EWING, Samuel, dec'd - Account presented. (24)

8-19-1806
WILKINSON, John, dec'd - Will Proven - Leah Wilkinson, widow now granted adms.
rights. (25)
MARKS, James, dec'd, Wayne Twp. - John Marks of same twp., adms. gave bond of $300.
with Moses Crume and James Harrell; John Withrow, Samuel Pottenger and Thomas
Pound, appraisers. (26)
BARTON, Martha, dec'd, late of Kentucky - Archibald Mahan of Ross Twp., adms. gave
bond of $600. with Joseph Walker and William Mahan; William Blackburn, James
Shields and Samuel Dick, appraisers. (26)
KISER, John, dec'd - Account filed. (27)
WALLIN, Elias, dec'd - Account filed. (27-29)

12-16-1806
STILES, Richard, dec'd - Will proven. (30)
LEMON, Jonathan, dec'd - Milford Twp. - Nancy Lemon widow relict, adms. gave
bond of $400. with Daniel Burch and Henry Oxly. (30)

2-13-1807
HOUGH, Thomas, dec'd, Hamilton, Fairfield Twp. - Benjamin Hough and Joseph Hough,
adms. gave bond with John Torrence and John Wingate, Sureties, $5000.; Henry
Brown, William Carry and William McClellan, appraisers. (31)

4-21-1807
SEWELL, Timothy, dec'd - Will proven. (32)
SCOTT, John, dec'd - Will proven. (32)
DELAPLANE, Joshua, Esq., dec'd, St. Clair Twp. - James Delaplane, adms. gave bond
of $400. with Solomon Line, John Torrence and Thomas McCullough; James Smith,
Matthew Winton and James Brown, appraisers. (33)
McNABB, John dec'd, St. Clair Twp. - William Patton, adms. gave bond with Benjamin
Line and Isaac Swearingen, $600.; James Smith, James Mills and William Brodrick,
appraisers. (33)
FISHER, James, a minor aged 10 years on 25th day Dec. last, one of sons and heirs
of James Fisher, dec'd; John Wingate of Hamilton, guardian gave bond of $250. with
John Sutherland. (34)
WEIGHT, Alexander, a minor aged 15 years on 23rd day March last, one of sons and
heirs of James Weight late of Berkly Co., Virginia, dec'd; George Harlan of
Hamilton, guardian gave bond of $300. with John Wingate. (34)

12-15-1807

FISHER, ,David, dec'd, Lemon Twp. - Andrew Waggoner of same twp., adms. gave bond
of $200. with Jonathan Garrison and Christopher Reed; Samuel Dickey of Elk Creek,
Isaac Reed and John Lingle, appraisers. (35)

WATTS, James, dec'd, Lemon Twp. - Resalinda Watts widow of James, adms. gave bond
of $500. with Amos Vallentine and Joseph Patterson; Ezekiel Ball, Esq., William
Trene and John Bridge, appraisers. (35)
HUNTER, Joseph, Esq., dec'd, Fairfield Twp. - Hannah Hunter and Anderson Spencer,
adms. gave bond of $400. with John Torrence and William Murray; Matthew Hueston,
John Mc Donald and James Watson, appraisers. (36)

1-13-1808

LOWRY, Elizabeth, dec'd - Will proven. (37)
CHAMBERLIN, John, dec'd, Lemon Twp. - Nancy Chamberlin widow of John declines adms.,
James Tapscott and John N. C. Schenck, adms. gave bond of $1500. with William Bark-
alow and John Cox; Moses Vail, Daniel Dubois and William Woodward, appraisers. (38)

2-8-1808

TORRENCE, John, dec'd, Hamilton, Fairfield Twp. - Emma Torrence, Robert Benham and
John Wingate, adm. gave bond of $2000. with Solomon Line and James Mills; William
Murray, William McClellan and James Smith, appraisers. (39)
PEEK, Thomas, dec'd, Liberty Twp. - Lucy Peek, adms. gave bond of $500. with
Peter Lintner and Brice Virgin; John Ayres, Ashbel Waller and William Legg,
appraisers. (39)

4-19-1808

BARKALOW, Eleanor, a minor aged 14 years in May last, one of daughters and heirs
of Derick Barkalow late of Menmouth Co., New Jersey, dec'd.; her brother Zebulon
Barkalow of Butler County, guardian gave bond of $2000. with James Tapscott and
Benjamin Barkalow. (40)
BALDWIN, Abraham, a minor aged 7 years on the 11th day Sept. last, son of Elias
Baldwin of Butler County, by his late wife, Elizabeth Piatt one of daughters and
heirs of Abraham Piatt late of Northumberland Co., Penna., dec'd.; Elias Baldwin
father of minor appointed guardian. (40)

5-25-1808

LOGAN, David, dec'd - Will proven. (42)

8-16-1808

COEN, James, dec'd, Ross Twp. - Will proven. (43)
McCLOSKY, Henry, dec'd, Ross Twp. - Will proven. (43)
OSBORNE, Cyrus, dec'd, Lemmon Twp. - Esther Osborne and Daniel Doty, adms. gave
bond of $500. with Moses Vail and Garret Vannest; Richard Watts, Aaron Vail, and
James Piper, appraisers. (44)
ARMSTRONG, Polly, a minor aged 14 years in Jan. last, one of daughters and heirs
of James Armstrong late of Hamilton Co., dec'd.; Joseph McMahan, guardian gave
bond of $300. with William Hayse and William Smith, sureties. (44)
DAVIS, Esther, a minor aged 13 years on 20th June last, one of daughters and heirs
of Daniel Davis, dec'd.; Matthew Hueston, guardian gave bond of $200. with Samuel
Davis and John Sutherland. (45)

8-16-1808

DAVIS, Samuel and James, minors, Samuel aged 7 years May last and James aged 5 years Oct. last, minor sons and heirs of Daniel Davis, dec'd on application of Margaret Davis, widow of said Daniel, guardian along with Matthew Hueston and William McClellan, giving bond of $400. with Samuel Davis and John Sutherland, security. (45)

KING, John, dec'd – Account filed by Phebe King and Henry Thomson, adms.; claims balance cash on hand, no disbursement to heirs. (46)

12-20-1808

VAIL, Stephen, dec'd – Will proven, Phebal Vail and Aaron Vail, executors. (47)
MARTIN, John, dec'd – Will proven, Margaret Martin and David Beaty, executors. (47)
THOMAS, James, dec'd – Lemon Twp. – Esther Thomas and Lewis Thomas, adms. gave bond of $2000. with Daniel Baker and John Freeman; John Carson, Robert Reed and Samuel Wilsen, appraisers. (48)
LOFFLAND, Branston, dec'd, Millford Twp. – William Loffland, adms. gave bond of $200. with William Symmes and Brice Virgin; James Martin, Matthew Richardson and Henry Taylor, appraisers. (48)
GARDNER, Henry, dec'd, Reily Twp. – Peter Sellman and Andrew Lewis, adms. gave bond of $4000. with Martin Rhinehart and John Richardson; William Mitchel, Benjamin Dungan and John Dungan, appraisers. (49)
SEWARD, James, dec'd, Fairfield Twp. – Caleb Seward and Daniel Seward, adms. gave bond of $300. with David Beaty and Patrick Cassidy; James Blackburn, John Cassidiy and John Maxwell, appraisers. (49)
OSBORNE, Daniel, a minor aged 17 years 23d day Dec. last, one of sons and heirs of Cyrus Osborne; Isaac Huff, guardian gave bond of $200. with Daniel Doty and Abraham Huff, sureties. (49)
OSBORNE, David, Oliver, Thomas and Polly, minors – On application of Esther Osborne widow relict of Cyrus Osborne, dec'd; guardian of David aged 11 years 23d May last, Oliver aged 9 years 30 day Nov. last, Thomas aged 8 years on 8th Oct. last and Polly aged 3 years on 8th July last, minors and heirs of said Cyrus, dec'd; with Isaac Huff and Shubal Vail also guardians gave bond of $800. with Daniel Doty and Abraham Huff, sureties. (50)
TORRENCE, John, dec'd – Adms. petition to sell real estate to pay debts. (51)

4-18-1809

HALL, Joseph, dec'd – Will proven, Sarah Hall and David Conger, executors. (52)
CRANE, Elias, dec'd – Will proven, Phebe Crane and Moses Crane, executors. (52)
TORRENCE, John, dec'd – Inventory of estate. (53)
SEWARD, Heirs of James, dec'd – On motion of Joseph Hahn one of the heirs at law of said James, dec'd, who requests bond be increased to $1000. (54)
SYMMES, William, dec'd – Rebeccah Symmes widow relict of William declines adms. of husband's estate; adms. granted to Celadon Symmes and Joseph To Randolph who gave bond of $500. with James Blackburn and Jacob Lewis; Thomas Fleming, Joseph Potter and Archibald Stark, appraisers. (54)
MOFFET, John, dec'd – William Riddle, adms. gave bond of $200. with John Sutherland and Hugh Wilson; William McClellan, William Murray and Isaac Stanly, appraisers. (55)
WATTS, John, Irene and Landson, minors – On application of Rosalinda Watts widow relict of James Watts, dec'd, guardianship of John K. aged 7 years March last, Irene aged 5 years Feb. last and Landson aged 2 years July last, heirs at law of said James, dec'd is granted to John Bigger, Esq. and Samuel Serring who gave bond of $300. with Amos Valentine and John Miller, sureties. (55)

141

8-15-1809
ORBISON, Robert, dec'd - Will proven, Matthew Orbison, executor. (56)
WHITE, Mary, dec'd - Thomas White, adms. gave bond of $300. with William McClellan and James Mills, sureties. (56)
MARKS, Nathaniel, a minor aged 16 years, a son and heir at law of John Marks, dec'd; Moses Crume, guardian gave bond of $200. with George Earhart and John Gray, sureties. (57)
GARDNER, Henry and John, minors; Henry aged 13 years and John aged 11 years, sons and heirs of Henry Gardner, dec'd; Samuel Dick, guardian gave bond of $1200. with William Smith and William Crooks; sureties. (57)
GARDNER, Samuel, a minor aged 9 years, one of sons and heirs at law of Henry Gardner, dec'd; John Richmond, Jr. guardian gave bond of $600. with William Murray and John Richmond, sureties. (58)
WATTS, John, dec'd - Account filed; $71.27½ to be disbursed to heirs of dec'd. (58)
FISHER, David, dec'd - Account filed, no disbursement to heirs. (59)

Sept. 1809
SLOAN, David, dec'd - His widow (not named) declines adms. of husband's estate; adms. granted to Stephen Crane and John K. Este who gave bond of $2000. with John Dickson and Uzal Edwards, Daniel Millikin, Matthew Hueston and John Dixon, appraisers. (60)

12-19-1809
GARDNER, William, a minor aged 15 years on 3rd Oct. last, one of sons and heirs of Henry Gardner, dec'd; William Murray, Esq., guardian. (61)
GARDNER, Henry, dec'd - Application of adms., Peter Sellman and Andrew Lewis to make payment to the United States for lands purchased by Henry Gardner in his lifetime. (61)

2-10-1810
CLARK, Stephen, Esq., dec'd - Will proven, Joannah Clark and Russel Potter, executors. (62)
WHITINGER, Francis Jr., dec'd - Deborah Whitinger and Jacob Whitinger, adms. gave bond of $1000. with Henry Whitinger and Joseph Spencer; William Smith, Knoles Shaw and Joseph Bolton, appraisers. (63)

4-17-1810
MURPHY, Peter, dec'd - Will proven, Eleanor Murphy, John M. Gary and Josiah Conklin, executors. (64)
SYMMES, William, dec'd - Adms. petition to sell real estate to pay debts. (65)

8-21-1810
SIMPSON, Abraham, dec'd - Will proven, Jane Simpson and Squire Littel, executors.(66)
HUFFMAN, Peter, dec'd - Will proven, George Huffman and Isaac Huffman, executors.(66)
SYMMES, William, dec'd - Valuation of real estate described as 288 acres Section 9, Township 2, Range 2; Lots 34,45,65,95,96 in Rossville and Lot 165 in Hamilton (67)
SINNARD, Abraham, a minor aged 19 years, one of sons and heirs of Thomas Sinnard; Joseph Potter, guardian gave bond of $200. with William Wallace. (68)
SINNARD, Thomas, a minor aged 17 years, one of the sons and heirs of Thomas Sinnard, dec'd; Joseph Potter, guardian gave bond of $200. with William Wallace.(68)
HAGEMAN, Abigail, a minor aged 15 years, one of daughters and heirs of Michael Hageman, dec'd; Margaret Hageman her mother, guardian gave bond of $2000. (69)

CHAMBERLIN, James aged 12 years and Mary aged 9 years on Nov. last, miners, son and daughter of John Chamberlin, dec'd; William P. Barkalow, gardian gave bond of $600. (69)

CHAMBERLIN, Lucy, a miner aged 4 years, one daughters and heirs of John Chamberlin, dec'd; Joseph Tapscott, guardian gave bond of $300. (70)

WHITINGER, Mary aged 7 years and Nicholas aged 5 years, miners, son and daughter and heirs at law of Francis Whitinger, dec'd; David Scott, guardian gave bond of $600. (70)

WHITINGER, James, a minor aged 2 years, one of sons and heirs of Francis Whitinger, dec'd; Nicholas Whitinger, guardian gave bond of $300. (71)

GILLESPIE, Thomas, dec'd - George Gillespie, Jr.; adms. gave bond of $600. with James McClellan and Patrick Moore; Michael Ayers, David Layman and Joseph Cox, appraisers. (71)

8-31-1810

FLENOR, Rudolph, dec'd - Magdalene Flenor widow relict of Rudolph relinquishes her right to adms. estate; George Flenor and Daniel Flener, adms. gave bond of $8000. with David Flener, Stephen Slipher and Jacob Slitsher; Paul Sanders, George Huffman and John Smalley, appraisers. (72)

10-4-1810

MARTIN, James, dec'd - Ann Martin widow and Matthew Richardson, Esq., adm. gave bond of $1400.; William Robison, James Scott and Robert Scott, appraisers. (73)

WOOD, Charles; dec'd - Dianah Wood, widow of Charles, adms. gave bond of $300.; Isaac Lindlay, John Clem and Thomas White, appraisers. (73)

GILLESPIE, Heirs of Thomas, dec'd - Jane Gillespie a minor aged 11 years Feb. last, George Gillespie a minor aged 9 years in Jan. last, Martha Gillespie a minor aged 8 years Sept. last and Margaret Gillespie a minor aged 5 years June last, son and daughters and heirs of Thomas, dec'd; Thomas Irwin and Joseph Williamson, guardians. (74)

12-18-1810

COAPSTICK, Samuel, dec'd - Will proven; Sarah and Thomas Coapstick, executors. (75)

143

The following records were taken from "Testamentary Record Book 1" located in the Butler County Archives, Court House, Hamilton, Ohio. Pages on which the record may be found in the original book are given in parenthesis.

1-3-1811
CUMMINS, David - Estate - Theodocia Cummins, widow, appointed admsrx. (76)

4-16-1811
COAPSTICK, Samuel - Estate - Appraisers appointed. (77)
SLOAN, David - Estate - petition to sell real estate to pay debts. (77)
McNABB, Dorothy aged 17yrs., daughter of John McNabb, dec'd. William Murray appointed guardian. (78)
McNABB, Mary aged 14 yrs., daughter of John McNabb, dec'd. Israel Woodruff appointed guardian. (78)

8-19-1811
PHELPS, John - Will presented. Peter Voorhees, executor. (79)
SLOAN, David - Inventory of real estate. Land in Section 28, Township 2, Range 2 valued at $9.00 per acre totaling $1170.00 and In-lots 12 & 39 Hamilton totaling $70.00. (79)
CRANE, Abigail aged 17 yrs., daughter of Elias Crane, dec'd. Stephen Crane, her brother appointed guardian. (80)
CRANE, William aged 11 yrs., son of Elias Crane, dec'd. John Dixon appointed guardian. (81)
HARLAN, Ishmael aged 18 yrs. George Harlan appointed guardian. (81)
PIERCE, James - Nuncupative Will presented. Wife, Elizabeth. Son, Joseph, not of age. Mentions "all my children", but does not name. Executors: wife, Elizabeth; William McClean; and Robert Irwin. (81)
WHITEHEAD, Stout - Estate - Gerusha Whitehead and Aaron Atherton appointed adms. (82)
HOUGH, Thomas - Accounting in Estate. $1576.66 balance to be paid to heirs (not named). (83)

11-29-1811
FULLENWIDER, John - Will presented. Jacob Fisher and Henry Cruse, Executors. (84)

12-16-1811
GILLESPIE, George aged 10 yrs., Martha aged 9 yrs., and Margaret aged 6 yrs., son and daughters of Thomas Gillespie, dec'd. Joseph Cox appointed guardian. (85)
GILLESPIE, Isabella aged 14 yrs. on 23 June last, daughter of Thomas Gillespie, dec'd. John Robeson appointed guardian. (85)
GILLESPIE, Jane aged 12 yrs. Feb last, daughter of Thomas Gillespie, dec'd. John Robeson appointed guardian. (86)
LYNN, Adam - Estate - John Lynn and Enoch Thompson appointed adms. (87)
CHAMBERLIN, John - Accounting in Estate - Balance to be distributed to heirs (not named) $301.31. (88)
MARTIN, James - Accounting in Estate - Balance to be distributed to heirs (not named) $456.85. (89)

2-21-1812
McCULLOUGH, Thomas - Estate - William Murray and James Heaton appointed adms. (90
TAYLOR, John - Estate - Esther Taylor and Robert Taylor appointed adms. (90)

2-21-1812
MARTIN, Robert aged 17 yrs on 1 Sept last, son of James Martin. William Murray,
    Esq. appointed guardian. (91)
MARTIN, Thomas aged 14 yrs on 6 June last, son of James Martin, dec'd. William
    Murray, Esq. appointed guardian. (91)
MARTIN, Betsey aged 10 yrs. in Jan. last daughter of James Martin, dec'd. William
    Murray, Esq. appointed guardian. (92)

3-21-1812
IRWIN, James late of Ross twp. - Will presented - Joseph Brown and James Elliott,
    executors. (93)

4-20-1812
STUART, Nancy aged 15 yrs., daughter of William Stuart, dec'd. Ezekiel Ball,
    Esq. appointed guardian. (94)
REED, David - Estate - Ruth Reed, widow appointed admsrx. (94)
McNABB, John - Accounting in Estate - $152.60 to be divided amongst heirs (not
    named). (95)
GILLESPIE, Thomas - Accounting in Estate - Distribution to Heirs: Isabella
    Gillespie $31.99; Jane Gillespie $40.61½; George Gillespie $31.51; Martha
    Gillespie $39.11½; Margaret Gillespie $22.69½. (96)
WHITINGER, Francis Jr. - Accounting in Estate - Deborah Whitinger, widow and
    adms.; $381.78 to be distributed to heirs (not named). (97)
WOOD, Charles - Accounting in Estate - $21.84 debt paid to Wm Wood; Dianah
    Wood, widow and admsrx.; $21.18½ to be distributed to heirs (not named). (98)

8-17-1812
GARDNER, Henry aged 15 yrs., son of Henry Gardner, dec'd. Samuel Dick appointed
    guardian. (99)
IRWIN, Robert James aged 8 months on 2 Aug instant, son of James Irwin late of
    Ross twp. James Shields appointed guardian. (99)
MONTGOMERY, David - Estate - John Wilson appointed adms. (100)

10-15-1812
CUMMINS, Jane - Will presented. Richard McKean, executor. (101)
ALEXANDER, Samuel - Estate - William Alexander, his son appointed adms. with
    widow, Elizabeth Alexander declining adms. (101)
RHEA, Henry - Estate - William Rhea, William McClellan and John Sutherland
    appointed adms. (102)

11-21-1812
SALLE, Israel - Estate - Abigail Salle and Daniel Salle appointed adms. (103)

12-21-1812

MORROW, Benjamin - Will presented. Mary Morrow, executrix. (104)

ROBY, Edward - Estate - Elias Roby, father of dec'd appointed adms. (104)

THOMAS, Lewis - Estate - Tabitha Thomas, widow appointed admsrx. (105)

DICKEY, Samuel - Estate - Adam Deem and Allen Simpson appointed adms. (105)

BROSIUS, Daniel - Estate - Sebastian Stonebreaker and John McClosky appointed adms. (105)

BROWN, Doctor Thomas - Estate - Ira Hunt appointed adms.; widow, Eliza B. Brown declining adms of estate. (106)

12-21-1812

DICKEY, James aged 19 yrs on 7 Feb last, son of Samuel Dickey, dec'd. George Kelly appointed guardian. (106)

DICKEY, George aged 18 yrs on 25 Oct last, son of Samuel Dickey. Isaac Hoff appointed guardian. (107)

DICKEY, Ebenezer aged 16 yrs on 8 Apr last, son of Samuel Dickey. Isaac Hoff appointed guardian. (107)

DICKEY, Sarah aged 14 yrs on 28 Feb. last, daughter of Samuel Dickey, Isaac Hoff appointed guardian. (107)

DICKEY, Isaac aged 11 yrs on 16 Mar last, son of Samuel Dickey. George Kelly appointed guardian. (108)

DICKEY, Mary aged 10 yrs. on 5 Nov last, daughter of Samuel Dickey. George Kelly appointed guardian. (108)

DICKEY, Samuel aged 8 yrs. on 1 Nov last, son of Samuel Dickey. George Kelly appointed guardian. (108)

DICKEY, Margaret aged 6 yrs. on 10 Dec. instant, daughter of Samuel Dickey. George Kelly appointed guardian. (109)

DICKEY, Nancy aged 3 yrs. on 6 August last, daughter of Samuel Dickey, George Kelly appointed guardian. (109)

McCLOSKY, Joseph aged 16 yrs on 11 Sept last, son of Henry McClosky. Samuel Dick appointed guardian. (110)

GREEN, Eli aged 14 yrs on Nov last, son of Henry Green, dec'd. Clinton Stack appointed guardian. (110)

PHELPS, John - Accounting in Estate - $131.74½ to be distributed to heirs (not named). (110)

FLENNOR, Rudolph - Accounting in Estate - Amount overpaid widow and heirs (not named) $337.62 3/4; Widow's third $995.75; two-thirds to be divided between heirs (not named) $1991.50. (111)

PIERCE, James - Accounting in Estate - Widow (not named) $146.00; son, Joseph $35.00; Widow $159.50½; to be divided between heirs of testator (not named) $159.50½. (112)

1-14-1813

COX, David - Will presented. John Cox and George Flennor, executors. (114)

2-12-1813

VANMATER, Abraham - Will presented, Sarah Vanmatre and Stephen Gard, exec. (115)

146

4-19-1813

GASTON, James - Will presented. Mary Gaston and Ezekiel McConnel, Executors. (116)
SIMPSON, Jonathan - Estate - widow, Elizabeth Simpson and Squire Little appointed
    adms. (116)
NICHOL, Joseph - Estate - Appraisers appointed. Father of deceased, Thomas
    Nichol, one of the adms. (117)

8-16-1813

POTTENGER, Thomas - Will presented. Elizabeth Pottenger and Samuel Pottenger,
    executors. (118)
QUICK, John - Will presented. Amy Quick and Samuel Bolton, executors. (118)
SACKET, Alexander - Will presented. Thomas Blair, executor. (119)
HOFF, Lewis - Estate - Abraham Tiesort appointed adms. Widow, Sally Hoff
    declining adms. of estate. (119)

8-16-1813

McDONALD, William - Estate - widow, Catharine McDonald appointed admsrx. (120)
COLEY, Samuel - Estate - Philip Drollinger appointed adms., widow, Hannah Colby
    declining adms. of estate. (120)
McKEAN, John - Estate - Robert McKean appointed adms. (121)
PIERSON, Elias aged 14 yrs. on Dec. last, son of Pioneer Pierson, dec'd. James
    Dunn appointed guardian. (121)
PIERSON, Joel aged 13 yrs. in Mar last, son of Pioneer Pierson. Robert Morehead
    appointed guardian. (121)
PIERSON, William aged 10 yrs., son of Pioneer Pierson. Robert Morehead appointed
    guardian. (122)
SALLE, Israel - Accounting in Estate - widow, Abigail Salle $132.21; $132.21 to
    be paid to heirs (not named). (122)
YOUNG, Benjamin - Accounting in Estate - widow, Elizabeth Young $74.80; $74.80 to
    be distributed to heirs (not named). (123)
THOMAS, James - Accounting in Estate - widow, Esther Thomas $35.69. $871.38
    to be distributed to heirs (not named). (124)

10-9-1813

BROSIUS, Peter - Estate - Michael Yeakle and Benjamin Saltman appointed adms.;
    widow, Elizabeth Brosius declining adms. of estate. (125)

10-20-1813

SQUIRE, David C. - Estate - Margaret Squire and Simeon Gard appointed adms. (126)

12-20-1813

HORNER, Edward - Estate - Elijah Horner appointed adms. (127)
VANSICKLE, Robert - Estate - Elizabeth Vansickle and Ephraim Carmack appointed
    adms.; security on bond by James Parkison and Evert Vansickle. (127)
ASHBY, Milton Estate - Bladen Ashby appointed adms. (127)
BROWN, Aaron - Estate - James Linn appointed adms. (127)
DICKEY, James - Estate - James Dickey appointed adms. (128)
HUFFMAN, Abraham - Estate - George Huffman appointed adms. (128)

147

SOUTHRELL, Edward - Estate - John Longfellow appointed adms. (128)
HARPER, James - Estate - John Harper appointed adms. (128)
CASSIDY, John - Estate - Obadiah Schenck and Thomas Blair appointed adms.; widow,
    Sally Cassidy declining adms. of estate. (129)
CRAIG, John - Estate - Eleanor Craig appointed admsrx. (129)
SUTTON, Edward - Estate - Matthew Richardson appointed adms. ; widow, Jane Sutton
    declining adms. of estate. (129)
KYLE, William - Estate - Ann Kyle appointed admsrx. (130)
WATTS, Henry - Estate - Catharine Watts and Robert Scott appointed adms. (130)
JOYCE, James - Estate - Joseph Hough and John Gilliland appointed adms. (130)
ANDREWS, John aged about 12 yrs. son of Moses Armstrong late of Hamilton County,
    Ohio. Henry Andrews appointed guardian. (131)
KING, Jacob aged 14 yrs. in Jan last, son of John King, dec'd, late of Kentucky.
    Henry Thompson appointed guardian. (131)
GRACEY, Polly aged 14 yrs. in June last, daughter of John Gracey late of Hamilton.
    Thomas Blair appointed guardian. (131)
BROSIUS, Rebecca aged 14 yrs. in July last, daughter of Daniel Brosius. Michael
    Yeakle appointed guardian. (132)
BROSIUS, Daniel aged 11 yrs. in Sept last, son of Daniel Brosius. John Rainey
    appointed guardian. (132)

12-20-1813
BROSIUS, Sarah aged 9 yrs in Mar last, daughter of Daniel Brosius. John Rainey
    appointed guardian. (132)
BROWN, Thomas - Accounting in Estate. Balance to be paid to heirs (not named)
    $4.70. (133)
HOFFMAN, Peter - Accounting in Estate - Delilah, daughter of dec'd, she not of
    age; other children (not named); amount to heirs under will $336.29½. (133)
STILES, Richard - Accounting in Estate - $289.00 paid for funeral expenses of
    Robert Glidel, testator's father-in-law; $270.00 for maintenance and schooling
    of testator's children; $250.00 paid for land purchased for Byrd Stiles and
    John Stiles under will; Widow, Elizabeth Stiles; $152.54 to be paid to heirs
    (not named). (134)
GARDNER, Henry - Accounting in Estate - $1153.73½ paid for support of family
    and schooling of children; $309.56 to be paid to heirs of dec'd (not named).
    (135)
TAYLOR, John - Accounting in Estate - Widow, Esther Taylor $206.55½ (note: no
    other heirs mentioned). (136)

1-1-1814
HOLLOWAY, Joseph - Estate - David Brant and Samuel Miller appointed adms.;
    widow, Catharine Holloway declining adms. of estate. (137)

1-15-1814
PAINE, Samuel - Nuncupative Will presented. Wife, Mary Paine; mentions "my
    several children" (not named); Executors--wife, Mary and two friends. William
    Phares and Joseph Hawkins. (138)
DOWTY, Reuben - Estate - Margaret Dowty and John Richmond appointed adms. (138)

1-25-1814
POTTER, Enos - Will presented. Noah Potter, executor. (139)
ROBY, Elias - Estate - George Roby appointed adms; widow, Mary Roby declining
   adms. of estate. (139)
STINE, Daniel - Estate - Martin Stine appointed adms. (140)
YOUNG, John - Estate - Samuel McCleary and Robert Young appointed adms. (140)
POTTS, Jacob - Estate - David Potts appointed adms. (140)
VANNEST, Garret - Estate - Jane Vannest and Joseph Walker appointed adms. (141)

3-14-1814
POTTER, Russel - Will presented. Samuel M. Potter and Levi Potter, executors. (142)
CRANE, Moses - Estate - Sarah Crane and Joshua Miller appointed adms. (142)
MASTERSON, Jeremiah - Estate - Mary Masterson appointed admsrx. (143)
DRIVER, William - Estate - Catharine Driver appointed admsrx. (143)
MULFORD, David - Estate - John Mulford appointed adms.; widow, Hannah Mulford
   declining adms. of estate. (143)
GIBSON, Isaac - Estate - James Mahan appointed adms. (143)

4-18-1814
CURRIER, William - Will presented. Sarah Currier, executrix. (144)
CLAP, John - Will presented. Joseph Gaston and Cornelius W. Hall, executors. (144)
YOUNG, John - Nuncupative will presented. Will given by John Young during his
   last sickness in January 1814 in presence of witnesses Samuel Young and James
   Ocheltree. John Young died at Samuel McClearys on Sabbath morning last, 16th
   January. Heirs named under will: Sally McCleary, Mary McCleary, Samuel
   McCleary and Andrew McCleary. (145)

4-18-1814
NELSON, Daniel - Will presented. Peter Voorhees, executor. (146)
WRAY, James - Will presented. William Martin and James Beaty, executors. (146)
JONES, Jonathan - Will presented. Washington Jones, Henry Jones and Jonas
   Jones, executors. (147)
HAND, Enoch - Will presented. Martha Hand, executrix. (147)
FERGUSON, Samuel - Will presented. Widow, Elizabeth Ferguson, executrix. (147)
MILLS, William L. - Will presented. Samuel Cunningham, executor. (148)
OGLE, Robert - Will presented. Alexander Ogle, William Ogle and Matthew
   Richardson, executors. (149)
DAVIS, Agnes - Estate - Jonathan Rardon and Samuel Davis Jr., appointed adms. (149)
WILSON, Thomas - Estate - Jane Wilson and Josiah Wilson appointed adms. (149)
DACKE, John H. - Estate - George Dacke appointed adms. (150)
BENZLY, William - Estate - John Benzly appointed adms. (150)
LEWMAN, William - Estate - William Reed appointed adms. (150)
SINKEY, John - Estate - William Harvey appointed adms.; widow, Mary Sinkey
   declining adms. of estate. (151)
DOTY, William - Estate - Margaret Doty appointed admsrx. (151)
CANFIELD, Nathan - Estate - Elizabeth Canfield and Jacob Widener appointed adms.
   (151)
MISNER, Richard - Estate - William Misner of Hamilton Co., Ohio appointed adms.
   (152)

149

SMITH, Robert - Estate - Mary Denny and Robert Denny appointed adms. (152)
RAY, John - Estate - Hannah Ray appointed admsrx. (152)
TEMPLE, Peter - Estate - Christian Coon appointed adms.; widow, Rachel Temple
    declining adms. of estate; security on bond by Michael Temple Jr. and Samuel
    McClure. (153)
COON, George - Estate - Christian Coon appointed adms. (153)
SLOAN, Rachel - Estate - Moses Crane and Uzal Edwards appointed adms. (153)
LONG, Noah - Estate - Isaac Hoff and John G. Long appointed adms. (154)
REED, John - Estate - William Hutchin and John Brelsford appointed adms. (154)
HAMILTON, George - Estate - William Hamilton appointed adms. (154)
QUICK, Aaron - Estate - Elizabeth Quick appointed admsrx. (155)
CASSIDY, Patrick - Estate - Sally Cassidy and James Heaton appointed adms. (155)
ANDREW, Doctor John - Estate - Elizabeth Andrew appointed admsrx. (155)
MILLER, John - Estate - Margaret Miller appointed admsrx; security on bond by
    Jacob Miller and Daniel Round. (156)
CURTZ, Michael - Estate - Zachariah Curtz appointed adms. (156)
REYNOLDS, John - Estate - Sarah Reynolds appointed admsrx. (156)
CUMMINS, Eleazer late of Washington Co., Georgia - Estate - John Cummins appointed
    adms.; security on bond by James Cummins and Richard McKean. (157)
MICHAEL, Paul - Estate - Samuel Hundman appointed adms.; Widow, Nancy Michael
    declining adms. of estate. (157)
BYRAM, John - Estate - Elizabeth Byram appointed admsrx. (157)
POTTER, Rhoda aged 16 yrs., daughter of Russel Potter. John Squire appointed
    guardian. (158)
GIBSON, Margaret aged 8 yrs in Mar. last, daughter of Isaac Gibson Jr. and
    Rebeccah his wife late of Butler Co., dec'd. David Beaty and Maxwell
    Parkison appointed guardians. (158)
GIBSON, Elizabeth aged 5 yrs., daughter of Isaac Gibson Jr. and Rebeccah his wife
    late Rebeccah McDonald, dec'd. David Beatty and Maxwell Parkison appointed
    guardians. (158)

4-18-1814
GIBSON, Esther aged 3 yrs., daughter of Isaac Gibson and Rebecca his wife late
    Rebecca McDonald, dec'd. William Mitchel and David Gibson appointed
    guardians. (159)
GIBSON, David aged 8 months, son of Isaac Gibson Jr. and Rebecca his wife late
    Rebecca McDonald, dec'd. William Mitchel and David Gibson appointed
    guardians. (159)
EWING, Joseph aged 16 yrs. on 11 June last, son of Samuel Ewing. John McDonald
    appointed guardian. (160)
GARDNER, John (age not given), son of Henry Gardner, dec'd. Emanuel Burget
    appointed guardian. (160)
REES, Elijah aged 15 yrs. on 8 Dec. last, son of John Rees late of Indiana Co.,
    Pennsylvania, dec'd. John Hutson appointed guardian. (160)
VANSKAIK, Tobias aged 19 yrs. on 9 Aug. last, son of David Vanskaik, dec'd.
    Ezekiel Ball, Esq. appointed guardian. (161)
VANSKAIK, Hannah aged 14 yrs. in Aug. last, daughter of David Vanskaik, dec'd.
    Ezekiel Ball, Esq. appointed guardian. (161)

ASHTON, Martha aged 9 yrs. on 1 May last, daughter of Joseph Ashton, dec'd. John
Brelsford appointed guardian. (161)

ASHTON, Catharine aged 8 yrs. on 21 Apr instant, daughter of Joseph Ashton, dec'd.
John Brelsford appointed guardian. (162)

ASHTON, Joseph aged 6 yrs. on 6 Sept. last, son of Joseph Ashton, dec'd. John
Brelsford appointed guardian. (162)

ASHTON, Sarah aged 3 yrs. on 31 March last, daughter of Joseph Ashton, dec'd.
John Brelsford appointed guardian. (162)

ASHTON, Mary aged 4 months, daughter of Joseph Ashton, dec'd. John Brelsford
appointed guardian. (163)

CLAP, William aged 11 yrs., son of John Clap, dec'd. David Beaty and John Dixon
appointed guardians. (163)

CLAP, Abigail aged 7 yrs. daughter of John Clap, dec'd. David Beaty and John
Dixon appointed guardians. (163)

CLAP, Catharine Ann aged 5 yrs. daughter of John Clap, dec'd. David Beaty and
John Dixon appointed guardians. (164)

MARTIN, Betsey aged 12 yrs. on 6 Jan. last, daughter of James Martin, dec'd.
Ann Martin, her mother appointed guardian. (164)

LOGUE, Samuel aged 16 yrs. on 4 Feb. last, son of Mary Logue, late of Kentucky,
dec'd. Benjamin Pursail appointed guardian. (164)

WHITEHEAD, Stout - Accounting in Estate - Widow, Gerusha Daubenshire late Gerusha
Whitehead; $91.12½ to be distributed to heirs (not named). (165)

IRWIN, James late of Ross twp. - Accounting in Estate - mentions widow and infant
son (does not name); brother, John Irwin. (165)

CUMMINS, David - Accounting in Estate - $121.73 to be divided between widow
and heirs (not named). (166)

BROSIUS, Daniel - Accounting in Estate - $406.87 to be distributed among heirs
(not named). (167)

The following records were taken from "Testamentary Record Book 1" located in the court house at Hamilton (basement archives). Page on which the record may be found is given in parenthesis.

8-15-1814

BEATY, Wilkins, a minor aged 14 yrs., son of Rebeccah Gibson late Rebeccah McDonald. On 8-28-1814 Wilkins Beaty age 15 yrs. on 15 July last, chose Jeremy Beaty as his guardian. (168)

JOYCE, James, dec'd, in lifetime purchased from United States NE¼ Section 8, Township 1, Range 2 and died prior to payment being made. Joseph Hough and John Gilleland, adms. are to sell land. (168)

HUNT, Thomas, will presented. Peter Voorhees and Arthur Orr, witnesses. (169)

FISHER, John, will presented. Thomas Irwin and Joseph McKnight, executors. (169)

DEWIT, Jacob, will presented. Nathan Horner and Zachariah P. Dewit, executors. (172)

MURPHY, Samuel - Estate - John Murphy appointed administor. (172)

CARRICK, Robert - Estate - Ruth Carrick and Thomas Coapstick appointed adms. (172)

SKILLMAN, Thomas - Estate - Nelly Skillman appointed adms. (173)

HART, Isaac - Estate - Sarah Hart and Thomas Hart appointed adms. (173)

BLACKBURN, Bryson - Estate - Esther Blackburne and Robert Blackburn appointed adms. (173)

LONG, Stephen - Estate - Lewis Moore appointed adms. (173)

DICKEY, Samuel of Lemon twp. - Estate - Mary Dickey and Henry Weaver appointed adms. (174)

JAMESON, John - Estate - Margaret Jameson and Thomas John appointed adms. (174)

RUSSELL, George - Estate - Mary Russell and Robert Ferris appointed adms. (174)

KYGER, John - Estate - Henry Miller appointed adms. (174)

ORWIG, Daniel - Aaron Bowen appointed adms. (175)

LONG, Thomas Jr. - Estate - Thomas Long appointed adms. Widow, Jemima Long relinquishes right to adms. (175)

THOMPSON, Andrew - Estate - Azarias Thorn, adms. (175)

BIRCH, Richard the Elder - Estate - Richard Birch the younger appointed adms. (175)

WOOD, Benjamin - Estate - Joseph Gaston and John Thornburg appointed adms. Widow, Jane Wood relinquishes right to adms. (176)

CUNNINGHAM, Samuel C. - Estate - Samuel Cunningham appointed adms. (176)

McCLELLAN, John late of St. Clair twp. - Estate - Wm McClellan appointed adms. (176)

MILLS, John - Estate - Julia Mills and Richard Jenkins appointed adms. (176)

8-18 1814

LOWRY, Elizabeth, a minor 15 yrs., daughter of John Lowry and Elizabeth his wife, dec'd. Samuel Hyndman appointed guardian. (177)

LOWRY, Martha, a minor age 14 yrs., daughter of John Lowry and Elizabeth his wife, dec'd. Samuel Hyndman appointed guardian. (177)

OGLE, Jane, a minor age 14 yrs. on 15 Dec. last, daughter of Robert Ogle, dec'd. Alexander Ogle appointed guardian. (177)

OGLE, Theresa, a minor aged 9 yrs. on 16 Jan. last, daughter of Robert Ogle, dec'd. Abraham F. Darr appointed guardian. (178)

152

OGLE, Franklin, a minor aged 6 yrs. on 30 Nov. last, son of Robert Ogle, dec'd.
Abraham F. Darr appointed guardian. (178)
OGLE, Nancy a minor aged 4 yrs. on 11 Jan. last, daughter of Robert Ogle, dec'd
Abraham F. Darr appointed guardian. (178)
OGLE, Eliza, a minor aged 2 yrs. on 11 Oct. last, daughter of Robert Ogle, dec'd
Abraham F. Darr appointed guardian. (179)
OGLE, Robert, a minor aged 18 days on 18 August instant, son of Robert Ogle, dec'd
Abraham F. Darr appointed guardian. (179)
YOUNG, David a minor aged 17 yrs. on 28 Sept. last, son of Andrew Young, dec'd.
Matthew Richardson appointed guardian. (179)
ISDELL, Thomas, a minor aged 14 yrs. on 25 Jan. last, son of Robert Isdell, dec'd.
John Kidd of Cincinnati appointed guardian. (180)
HOFFMAN, Delilah, a minor aged 13 yrs. in Jan. last, daughter of Peter Hoffman,
dec'd. Samuel Schenck appointed guardian. (180)
HOFFMAN, Campson, a minor aged 19 yrs. on 19 May last, son of Peter Hoffman,
dec'd. Samuel Schenck appointed guardian. (180)
TIMBERMAN, William, a minor aged 12 yrs. in Oct. last, son of Christopher Timber-
man, dec'd. Isaiah Wilson appointed guardian. (181)
TIMBERMAN, George, a minor aged 10 yrs. on 2 May last, son of Christopher Timberman, dec'd. Isaiah Wilson appointed guardian. (181)
TIMBERMAN, James, a minor aged 8 yrs. on 19 May last, son of Christopher Timberman, dec'd. Isaiah Wilson appointed guardian. (181)

8-22-1814
McKEAN, John - Estate - Account filed. (182)
MONTGOMERY, David - Estate - Account filed. (182)
SEWARD, James - Estate - Account filed by Caleb Seward and Daniel Seward, adms.(182)

10-5-1814
BONNEL, Moses, will presented. Hannah Bonnel and David Bonnel, executors. (184)
MOREHEAD, Robert, will presented. William Crooks, executor. (184)
BIGELOW, Aaron - Estate - Soloman Beach and James Cable appointed adms. Widow,
Hannah Bigelow relinquishes right to adms. (184)

12-19-1814
CORNELL, Richard, will presented. Sarah Cornell and Wm Cornell, executors. (185)
KIRKPATRICK, George, will presented. Alexander Kirkpatrick and Ninian Beaty,
executors. (185)
BIRCH, Richard - Estate - Account filed. (186)
VANVICKLE, Robert - Will - Property set off to widow (not named.) (186)
MOREHEAD, Robert - Estate - Account filed. (186)
CRAVEN, John - Estate - Thomas Craven appointed adms. Widow, Margaret Craven
relinquishes right to adms. (186)
NOBLE, James - Estate - Thomas McAdams appointed adms. (187)
FLEMING, Samuel - Estate - Abigail Fleming appointed adms. (187)
KEYT, Daniel - Estate - Daniel Keyt and John R. Crane appointed adms. (187)
DeKUYPER, Atto - Estate - Benjamin Cilley appointed adms. (187)
MONTGOMERY, Thomas - Estate - Elizabeth Montgomery appointed adms. (188)
MOORE, Solomon - Estate - Gerusha Moore appointed adms. (188)
MATTOX, William - Estate - David Mattox appointed adms. (188)
LOWRY, John - Estate - Fleming Lowry appointed adms. (188)

12-19-1814
McCLURE, Mary, a minor aged 16 yrs. in March last, daughter of Janet McClure,
dec'd, late Janet Officer late the wife of John McClure. William McClure
appointed guardian. (189)

12-19-1814
McCLURE, Jane, a minor aged 11 yrs. in May last, daughter of Janet McClure, dec'd,
late Janet Officer late the wife of John McClure. Wm McClure appointed
guardian. (189)
MILLER, Ellis, a minor aged 14 yrs. in August last, son of Jacob Miller, dec'd.
Samuel M. Potter appointed guardian. (189)
CRANE, Michael M., a minor aged 14 yrs. on 6 June last, son of Joseph Crane, dec'd.
David Crane appointed guardian. (190)
MILLER, Jacob P., a minor, son of Jacob Miller Jr., dec'd. Price Thompson of
Hamilton appointed guardian. (190)
LONG, Eli, a minor aged 15 yrs. in Nov. last, son of Noah Long, dec'd. Robert
Brown appointed guardian. (190)
FISHER, David, a minor aged 16 yrs. in August last, son of John Fisher, dec'd.
Robert Faris appointed guardian. (191)
PIERSON, Joel, a minor aged 14 yrs., son of Pioneer Pierson, dec'd. William
Morris appointed guardian. (191)
PIERSON, William, a minor aged 11 yrs., son of Pioneer Pierson, dec'd. Thomas
Moorehead appointed guardian. (191)
VANVICKLE, Robert, a minor age 1 yr. in April last, son of Robert Vanvickle, dec'd.
James Parkison appointed guardian. (192)
VANVICKLE, Ephrain, a minor aged 1 yr. in April last, son of Robert VanVickle,
dec'd. James Parkison appointed guardian. (192)
BROSIUS, Peter - Estate - Account filed by Michael Yeakle and Benjamin Sortman,
adms. (192)

4-17-1815
BARBEE, Benjamin, will presented. Mary Barbee, executrix. (194)
SWORDS, William, will presented. Widow, Mary Swords, executrix. (194)
SMALLEY, James, will presented. Joseph Worth, executor. John Smalley the other
executor renounces. (195)
BIRCH, Richard the Elder - Estate - real estate to be sold being 242.45 acres
in fractional Section 1, Township 1, Range 3. (195)
JOYCE, James - estate - Account filed. (196)
MULFORD, David - Estate - Account filed. (197)
ANDERSON, Samuel - Estate - John Anderson appointed adms. (197)
CRANE, Joseph - Estate - Margaret Crane appointed adms. (198)
LINE, Benjamin - Estate - John Line and Dennis Ball appointed adms. Widow,
Rebeccah Line relinquishes right to adms. (198)
DERROW, William - Estate - Sarah Derrow and Wm McClelland appointed adms. (198)
SHORT, Telghman - Estate - Ira Hunt appointed adms. (198)
BALL, Isaiah - Estate - Dennis Ball appointed adms. Widow, Phebe Ball relinquishes
right to adms. (199)
RITCHEY, John - Estate - Samuel Millikin appointed adms. (199)
WOOD, Rebecca, a minor aged 14 yrs. in June last, daughter of Benjamin Wood, dec'd
Isaac Sellers appointed guardian. (199)

154

4-17-1815

WOOD, Anthony S., a minor aged 11 yrs. in May last, son of Benjamin Wood, dec'd. David Powers appointed guardian. (199)

WOOD, Isabella, a minor aged 10 yrs., daughter of Benjamin Wood, dec'd. David Powers and Isaac Sellers appointed guardians. (200)

WOOD, Joseph, a minor aged 5 yrs. in March last, son of Benjamin Wood, dec'd. David Powers and Isaac Sellers appointed guardians. (200)

DICKEY, Isaac, a minor aged 14 yrs. on 16 March last, son of Samuel Dickey, dec'd, of Madison twp. George Kelly appointed guardian. (200)

BALL, Nancy, a minor aged 14 yrs. on 10 May last, daughter of Isaiah Ball, dec'd. Dennis Ball appointed guardian. (201)

BALL, Margaret, a minor aged 14 yrs. on 4 Sept last, daughter of Isaiah Ball, dec'd. Dennis Ball appointed guardian. (201)

BALL, Solomon aged 12 yrs. on 13 March last, son of Isaiah Ball, dec'd. James Cummins appointed guardian. (201)

BALL, Zepher aged 10 yrs. on 3 April instant, son of Isaiah Ball, dec'd. Dennis Ball appointed guardian. (202)

BALL, Esther, a minor aged 8 yrs. on 1st Jan. last, daughter of Isaiah Ball, dec'd. James Cummins appointed guardian. (202)

SUTTON, Matthew, a minor aged 14 yrs. on March last, son of Edward Sutton, dec'd. Jane Sutton appointed guardian. (202)

SUTTON, John Shaw, a minor aged 12 yrs. in Nov. last, son of Edward Sutton, dec'd. Jane Sutton appointed guardian. (203)

SUTTON, Thomas, a minor aged 6 yrs. on 22 Oct. last, son of Edward Sutton, dec'd. Jane Sutton appointed guardian. (203)

CRANE, Lucretia, a minor aged 15 yrs. on 22 March last, daughter of Moses Crane, dec'd. Samuel M. Potter appointed guardian. (203)

CRANE, Noah, a minor aged 12 yrs. on 8 March last, son of Moses Crane, dec'd. Samuel M. Potter appointed guardian. (204)

CRANE, Stephen Clark, a minor aged 5 yrs. on 12 Oct. last, son of Moses Crane, dec'd. Samuel M. Potter appointed guardian. (204)

NELSON, Betsey, a minor aged 15 yrs. in January last, daughter of Daniel Nelson, dec'd. David Beaty appointed guardian. (204)

NELSON, Nancy Ferguson, a minor aged 13 yrs. in March last, daughter of Daniel Nelson, dec'd. David Beaty appointed guardian. (205)

NELSON, Rebecca McDonald, a minor aged 8 yrs. in Oct. last, daughter of Daniel Nelson, dec'd. John Nelson appointed guardian. (205)

BROSIUS, Margaret, a minor aged 15 yrs. on 21 June last, daughter of Daniel Brosius, dec'd. Michael Yeakle appointed guardian. (205)

BROSIUS, John, a minor aged 10 yrs. on 1 Oct. last, son of Peter Brosius, dec'd. Peter Sellman and John Castator, guardians. (206)

BROSIUS, Eve, a minor aged 8 yrs. on 27 Sept. last, daughter of Peter Prosius, dec'd. Peter Sellman and John Castator appointed guardians. (206)

BROSIUS, Daniel, a minor aged 6 yrs. on 27 Sept. last, son of Peter Brosius, dec'd. Peter Sellman and John Castator appointed guardians. (206)

BROSIUS, Elizabeth aged 5 yrs. on 8 April instant, daughter of Peter Brosius, dec'd. Peter Sellman and John Castator appointed guardians. (207)

BROSIUS, Jonas, a minor aged 2 yrs. on 8 Jan. last, son of Peter Brosius, dec'd Peter Sellman and John Castator appointed guardians. (207)

POTTER, Amos, a minor aged 16 yrs. on 10 Oct. last, son of Moses Potter, dec'd. Joel Kennedy appointed guardian. (207)

4-17-1815
POTTER, Jonathan H., a minor aged 14 yrs. on 24 Dec. last, son of Moses Potter, dec'd. Stephen Paine appointed guardian. (208)
MARKLAND, Joshua, a minor aged 19 yrs. on 1st May last, son of Matthew Markland, dec'd. Ezekiel Ball appointed guardian. (208)
DAVIS, Rachell, a minor aged 10 yrs. in Feb. last, daughter of William Davis, dec'd. James Murray appointed guardian. (208)
DAVIS, Sally, a minor aged 8 yrs. in April instant, daughter of William Davis, dec'd. James Murray appointed guardian. (209)
DAVIS, Michael, a minor aged 4 yrs. in April instant, son of William Davis, dec'd. James Murray appointed guardian. (209)

4-17-1815
FULLENWIDER, Elizabeth, a minor aged 15 yrs., daughter of John Fullenwider, dec'd. John Dunn appointed guardian. (209)
SUTTON, Edward - Estate - Account filed. (210)
HOLLOWAY, Joseph - Estate - Account filed. (210)
CRANE, Moses - Estate - Account filed. (211)
LEMON, Jonathan - Estate - Account filed. (212)
CUMMINS, Eleazer - Estate - Account filed. (213)

5-22-1815
ROBINS, Benjamin late of Cincinnati, Hamilton Co., Ohio, will presented. Azarias Thorn, executor. (215)
MORRISON, James - Estate - Sarah Morrison and James Mathers appointed adms. (215)

8-21-1815
BIRCH, Richard the Elder - Estate; real estate sold to Samuel Morrison for $2620.50. (216)
JOYCE, James - Estate - petition to sell land of dec'd being 162 acres part of fractional Section 34 or 35, Township 3, Range 2. (216)
PECK, John H., will presented. Sarah Peck and William Enyart, executors. (217)
NICHOLS, William - Estate - Robert Irwin appointed adms. (218)
BOALS, Francis - Estate - James Matthews appointed adms. Widow, Mary Boals relinquishes right to adms. (218)
HAWKINS, Benjamin - Estate - Joseph Hawkins appointed adms. Widow, Olive Hawkins relinquishes right to adms. (218)
INLOES, William - Estate - Daniel Inloes appointed adms. (219)
BRYSON, Rachel - Estate - John Holmes appointed adms. (219)
HENRY, Joseph - Estate - Isaac S. Patton appointed adms. Widow, Catharine Henry relinquishes right to adms. (219)
HUFFMAN, George - Estate - Elizabeth Huffman and Isaac Huffman appointed adms. (219)
HORNADY, John - Estate - Hannah Hornady and Jonathan Hornady appointed adms. (220)
HALL, Joseph - Estate - Jacob Line appointed adms. (220)
FOREMAN, Jacob - Estate - William Murray appointed adms. (220)
CHASE, Valentine, will presented by Elizabeth Chase, widow. (220)

8-22-1815
CRANE, Joseph - Estate - Property set off to widow, Margaret Crane. (221)
REED, John, a minor aged 16 yrs. on 12 Feb. last, son of John Reed, dec'd. John Brelsford appointed guardian. (221)

8-22-1815

REED, Clementine, a minor aged 14 yrs. on 19 Sept. last, daughter of John Reed,
dec'd. Allen Simpson appointed guardian. (222)
REED, Washington, a minor aged 10 yrs. on 12 Feb. last, son of John Reed, dec'd.
Allen Simpson appointed guardian. (222)
REED, Samuel, a minor aged 6 yrs. on 21 Oct. last, son of John Reed, dec'd.
Allen Simpson appointed guardian. (223)
REED, Catharine, a minor aged 10 months on 22 August instant, daughter of John
Reed, dec'd. Allen Simpson appointed guardian. (223)
MARKLAND, Matthew, a minor aged 15 yrs., son of Matthew Markland, dec'd, Ezekiel
Ball, esq. appointed guardian. (223)
MARKLAND, Eleanor, a minor aged 12 yrs. on 24 July last, daughter of Matthew
Markland, dec'd. Ezekiel Ball, Ewq. appointed guardian. (224)

8-25-1815

SHORT, Peyton, a minor aged 18 yrs. on 11 March last, son of Teleghman Short,
dec'd. Ira Hunt appointed guardian. (224)
SHORT, Julia, aged 16 yrs. on 25 August instant, daughter of Telghaman Short,
dec'd. Ira Hunt appointed guardian. (224)
SHORT, Sally, a minor aged 12 yrs. on 26 March last, daughter of Telghman Short,
dec'd. Ira Hunt appointed guardian. (225)
SHORT, Amelia L., a minor aged 8 yrs., daughter of Telghman Short, dec'd. John
Strait appointed guardian. (225)
DYER, William, a minor aged 18 yrs. on 29 June last, son of Nathaniel Dyer late
of Virginia, dec'd. Robert Brown appointed guardian. (226)
VANMATRE, Joseph, a minor aged 12 yrs. on 25 August instant, son of Abraham
Vanmatre, dec'd. Jacob Bell appointed guardian. (226)
THOMPSON, James, a minor aged 15 yrs. on 22 Jan. last, son of Andrew Thompson,
dec'd. Azarias Thorn appointed guardian. (226)
LONG, Noah, a minor aged 3 yrs. on 24 Nov. last, son of Thomas Long Jr., dec'd.
Thomas Long Sr. appointed guardian. (227)
LOWRY, Elizabeth. Wm Goudy and John Bigger, executors. Account filed. (227)
HUFFMAN, Abraham - Estate - George Huffman, adms. filed account. (228)
VANMATRE, Abraham. Sarah Vanmatre and Stephen Gard, executors. Account filed. (228)
POTTER, Russel. Samuel M. Potter and Levi Potter, executors. Account filed. (228)
HART, James - Estate - Thomas Hart and Sarah Hart, adms. filed account. (230)
MILLS, William L. - Estate - Robert Scott, adms. filed account. (230)
LONG, Thomas Jr. - Estate - Thomas Long, adms. filed account. (231)
LEASON, James - Estate - Estate insolvent. (231)

9-25-1815

CHASE, Valentine, will presented. Jedediah Swift and L. Homedial Chase, executors.
Widow, Elizabeth Chase. (233)
BIGHAM, William, will presented. David Bigham, George R. Bigham and James
Bigham, executors. (233)
ROBY, Edward - Estate - Isaac Roby appointed adms. de bonis non in place of
Elias Roby previous adms. who is now dec'd. (234)
MICHAEL, William - Estate - Joseph H. McMaken appointed adms. (234)
FITZPATRICK, James, a minor aged 14 yrs. on 25 Oct. last, son of Benjamin
Fitzpatrick late of Kentucky, dec'd. Philip Schull appointed guardian. (234)
DAVIS, Samuel, a minor aged 15 yrs. on 20 May last, son of Daniel Davis, dec'd.
Matthew Hueston appointed guardian. (235)

157

10-16-1815

GARRIGUS, David, will presented. Jeptha Garrigus and James Heaton, executors. (236)
BAKE, John Jr. - Estate - Christopher Bake and Jacob Widener appointed adms.
   Widow, Hannah Bake relinquishes right to adms. (236)
SPENCER, Anderson - Estate - David Beaty and Joseph Hough appointed adms. Widow,
   Polly Spencer relinquishes right to adms. (236)
COURSON, George - Estate - Nancy Courson appointed adms. (237)
WILSON, William M., a minor aged 7 yrs. on 11 March last, son of Thomas Wilson,
   dec'd. Wm D. Jones and Robert Anderson appointed guardians. (237)
WILSON, Mary M., a minor aged 6 yrs. on 22 June last, daughter of Thomas Wilson,
   dec'd. WmD. Jones and Robert Anderson appointed guardians. (237)
WILSON, Hannah J., a minor aged 4 yrs. on 1st Feb. last, daughter of Thomas Wilson,
   dec'd. Wm D. Jones and Robert Anderson appointed guardians. (238)
WILSON, Thomas, a minor aged 2 yrs. on 27 Feb. last, son of Thomas Wilson, dec'd.
   Wm D. Jones and Robert Anderson appointed guardians. (238)

10-31-1815

ELLIOTT, William, will presented. Joshua Elliott and Arthur W. Elliott, executors.
   (239)
CAMPBELL, Archibald - Estate - Jacob Campbell appointed adms. Widow, Mary Campbell
   relinquishes her right to adms. (239)

12-18-1815

STAGGS, William, will presented. Thomas Pound and Isaiah Orr, executors. (240)
DENMAN, Moses, will presented. Elizabeth Denman and Wm Denman, executors. (240)
CLARK, Isaac - Estate - Sally Clark appointed adms. (241)
MILLER, Henry - Estate - John Ayers appointed adms. Widow, Eve Miller relinquishes
   right to adms. (241)
MONTGOMERY, William - Estate - John Hall of Rossville appointed adms. (241)
CHAPMAN, Nathaniel - Estate - Jacob Rozencrantz and John Freeman appointed adms.
   Widow, Peggy Chapman relinquishes right to adms. (242)
BOALS, Margery, a minor aged 10 months, daughter of Francis Boals, dec'd. William
   Jenkins appointed guardian. (242)
TIMMONS, George - Estate - Nathaniel Bell appointed adms. (242)
SYMMES, William, a minor aged 14 yrs. in May last, son of William Symmes, dec'd.
   John Ayers appointed guardian. (243)
GARDNER, Samuel, a minor aged 14 yrs., son of Henry Gardner, dec'd. John
   Richmond Jr. appointed guardian. (243)
GARRIGUS, Timothy L., a minor aged 17 yrs. on 24 April last, son of David Garrigus,
   dec'd. Daniel Millikin, Esq. appointed guardian. (243)
REED, Mary Ann, a minor aged 12 yrs. on 13 August last, daughter of John Reed,
   dec'd. William Hutchin appointed guardian. (244)
McDONALD, Nelson, a minor aged 16 yrs. on 10 May last, son of Levi McDonald, dec'd.
   Nancy Reddy appointed guardian. (244)
LEMON, Elizabeth, a minor aged 13 yrs., daughter of Jonathan Lemon, dec'd.
   Samuel Johnston appointed guardian. (244)
CASSIDY, Patrick - Estate - petition to sell land described as undivided one half
   of 71 acres part of Section 10, Township 1, Range 2. Land sold to Wm Hall
   for $49.37½. (245)
GIBSON, Isaac Jr. - Estate - Account filed. Account lists $151.69½ paid to heirs
   of Rebecca Gibson, dec'd widow and relict of said intestate and also $151.69½
   paid to children of intestate being heirs and representatives of Intestate
   (not named). (246)

OGLE, Robert - Estate - account filed. (247)
BIGELOW, Aaron - Estate - account filed. (248)
VAN VICKLE, Robert - Estate - account filed. (248)
KEYT, David R. - Estate - account filed. (249)

AYRES, Levi to Elizabeth Murphy	11-3-1803
AYRES, Michael to Abigail Williams	11-17-1803
BADGLEY, William to Polly Broadbury	8-23-1804
BALDWIN, William to Amy Crooks	8-1-1805
BALL, Abel to Mary Crooks	10-8-1805
BALL, Dennis to Margaret Linê	9-12-1805
BALL, Joshua to Sarah Drybread	7-4-1805
BALL, Zopher to Elizabeth Hunter	4-24-1806
BOWMAN, Jonas to Susanna Campbell	9-26-1805
BOYD, Daniel to Anne Wilson'	9-20-1804
BOYD, Nicholas to Catharine Boyd	6-21-1804
BRADY, John to Jane Bell	6-28-1804
BRANIN, James to Polly Hardesty	11-20-1803
BROWN, John to Hannah Bell	9-10-1805
BUOSSO, Henry to Mary Long	9-4-1806
CAMPBLE, Cornelius to Diana Round	1-13-1805
CARSON, William to Mary McGuire	6-30-1806
CARTER, Nichlas to Anne Hanond	9-8-1800
CASTOR, Solomon to Hannah Goodwin	6-25-1805
CATIO, Peter to Christianna Loy	1-1-1805
CATTERLIN, Ephraim to Sally McKinstry	10-13-1805
CAVENAUGH, Laurence to Anne Martin	1-23-1806
CLARK, James to Margaret Watson	7-3-1804
COMPTON, Richard to Mary Line	12-13-1804
COREY, David to Johannah Easton	1-11-1804
CRAIG, John to Mary Valentine	2-8-1804
CRANE, Noah, Jr. to Eliza Pearce	1-9-1800
Noah of Hamilton Co., Ohio	
CUMMINGS, David to Hogpy(?) Halloway	6-26-1804
DOTY, Reuben to Margaret Richmond	3-25-1806
DRAKE, William to Sarah Liston	1-31-1804
DUNN, John to Lettice McClosky	3-14-1805
EMERSON, John Prat to Sophia Perry	10-6-1803
EVANS, Moses to Sarah Castor	3-27-1806
GARD, William to Sarah Campbell	9-18-1800
GIBSON, Isaac, Jr. to Rebecca McDonald	3-19-1805
GOBLE, Isaac, Jr. to Elizabeth Ayres'	2-9-1804
GRAY, Abraham to Jane Paugh	6-25-1806
GRIFFIN, David to Betsey Rush	8-26-1806
HAMILTON, John, Jr. to Anne Wilson	9-18-1800
HARPER, John to Polly Decker	2-4-1806
HEATON, Daniel to Mary Ferguson	6-12-1806
Daniel of Warren Co., Ohio	
HUDGEL, Joseph to Phebe Pue	3-6-1804
HUFF, Lewis to Sarah Parker	10-9-1806
HUNT, Abraham to Elizabeth Gee	9-13-1804
HUNT, Ira to Elizabeth Vanduyn	3-12-1806
JOHNSTON, John to Elizabeth Rnearson	1-1-1806
JONES, Abraham to Agness Clark	2-17-1804
KELLER, Jacob to Anna Redingbough	11-10-1805
KELLY, Alexander to Rachel Haines	10-8-1806
KENNEDY, James to Rebecca Skyles	10-9-1806
KERCHAVEL, Benjamin to Nancy Pound	2-2-1804

KERCHEVAL, Reuben to Mary Crume   1-15-1806
LEAMONS, John to Peggy Huffman   3-11-1806
LEE, John to Massey Lucas   9-26-1804
LINE, Jacob to Ruth Hall   9-21-1806
LINE, Jonathan to Johannah Bonnell   8-11-1804
LODER, John to Isabella Ringland   9-25-1806
LONG, Robert to Jane Cartwell   1-10-1805
LYON, Jonham to Elizabeth Sellers   12-21-1806
McADAMS, Thomas to Elizabeth Noble   10-18-1804
McCARREN, Barnabas to Polly Hunter   6-27-1805
McCLURE, Samuel to Margaret Hannah   3-13-1806
MANSFIELD, John to Jane Ray   10-11-1804
MARTIN, William to Catharine Harden   7-31-1804
MASSACK, James to Mary Crume   9-30-1806
MEIDETH, Caleb to Nancy Harper   6-5-1806
MENAN, Michael to Jane Simpson   4-5-1805
MILLHOLLAND, Thomas to Margaret Drybread   7-4-1805
MILLS, John to Sarah Hardesty   5-12-1805
MOORE, Jesse W. to Lucy Milner   1-31-1804
MOORE, Lewis to Susannah Enyart   8-2-1804
MORTON, James T. to Abigail Bonnell   11-5-1806
OGLE, William to Elizabeth Irwin   4-3-1804
ORBISON, John to Louisa Randall   6-20-1805
OXLEY, Henry to Betsey Burch   7-14-1806
PAINE, Elijah to Rebecca Paddix   9-7-1806
PARK, Arthur to Elizabeth McCloskey   5-12-1806
PARKER, Jacob to Mary Loy   11-20-1803
PATTON, Isaac to Elizabeth Sheafer   2-2-1806
PERKINS, Andrew to Allice McKee   12-3-1804
PERKINS, John to Nancy Reed   3-1-1804
POWERS, Daniel to Abigail Skyhawk   5-12-1806
PRICE, David to Elizabeth Cump   7-5-1804
PRUDDY, John to Nancy Fleming   7-16-1806
REED, Isaac to Latitia Clark   3-25-1804
RICHMOND, Jonathan to Barbara Burget   1-17-1805
ROSS, Austin to Catharine Kitterow   12-19-1806
     Austin of Warren Co., Ohio
ROUND, Martin to Susanna Boyers   8-15-1805
ROWLAND, Joshua to Margaret Andrew   9-19-1805
SAMPLE, Jacob to Jane Hueston   9-3-1803
SAMPSON, David to Jane Carrick   4-28-1804
SARGENT, Sampson to Rebecca Martin   1-3-1805
SCHENCK, John N. C. to Sarah Tapscott   9-2-1804
SCHENCK, Obadiah to Abigail Freeman   6-22-1806
SHIELDS, James to Christianna Cook   9-1-1803
SIMPSON, Isaac to Betser Richardson   3-8-1804
SIMPSON, Jonathan to Elizabeth Berry   12-25-1806
SLOAN, David to Rachel Crane   1-22-1806
SMITH, Amos to Elizabeth Ashby   8-12-1805
SMITH, Andrew to Margaret Fleming   2-22-1804
SNUFF, Jacob to Rachel Cook   2-9-1806
SPENCER, Joseph to Eleanor Johnston   4-5-1804
SPINNING, William to Hannah Oseborne   2-7-1805

```
SQUIRE, David to Sally Gard                        11-30-1805
        David of Montgomery Co., Ohio
STALEY, Jacob to Charlotte Catterlin               12-19-1805
STEPHENS, James to Leah Banta                      10-3-1805
STILL, Alexander to Mary Broadbury                 12-19-1805
STOUGHTON, William to Cathárine Vanderpool         8-21-1805
SUTTON, Elisha to James Copestick                  8-12-1806
TEAGARD, Abraham to Abigail Enoch                  11-21-1805
THOMPSON, Smith to Badgley                         10.-3-1805
TIETSORT, Peter to Elizabeth Auspaw                12-21-1806
TOLES, John to Elizabeth Wilson                    6-3-1805
TORRENCE, John to Phebe Cotton                     10-2-1804
TURNER, Matthias to Susannah Neighbors             5-14-1804
VAIL, Henry to Pamelia Bridge                      6-19-1806
VANNEST, John to Polly Taylor                      4-10-1806
WAGGONER, Martin to Sarah Hahn                     12-11-1803
WALDRON, Garret to Catharine Huff                  6-8-1806
WATSON, Eber to Phebe Thompson                     12-31-1805
WATSON, Isaac to Polly Round                       1-8-1805
WATTS, Joseph to Jemima Harden                     1-3-1805
WELCH, William to Rebecca Castor                   4-10-1806
WHITMORE, Miles to Clarissa Kelley                 5-4-1806
WILCOCKS, John to Harriot McDonald                 6-12-1806
WILLIS, John to Mary Fisher                        10-24-1803
WILSON, James to Rebecca Dailey                    11-13-1804
WILSON, John to Nancy Harvey                       10-21-1806
WINTON, Robert to Ann Richardson                   11-22-1804
WOOLVERTON, Thomas to Mary Bozworth                12-18-1806
YOUNGBLOOD, Thomas to Martha Demoss                2-7-1805
```

ALEXANDER, William to Pamelia Givirup	8-27-1807
ALSTON, Wallace to Martha Buckley	4-27-1809
ARMSTRONG, James to Rebecca STILES	9-29-1808
AYRES, James to Julia Cummins	9-7-1809
BAIRD, Alexander to Kezia Jones	3-25-1809
BAIRD, John to Nancy Troxell	3-10-1808
BALL, Abner to Rhoda Martin	6-30-1808
BALL, Isaiah to Phebe Breese	9-1-1808
BALL, Stephen to Rebecca Treene	1-1-1807
BAXTER, Thomas to Lydia Murphy	2-15-1809
BEATY, Nenian to Jane McKinsey	4-13-1809
BEELER, James to Betsey Kyger	8-21-1808
BEELER, Thomas to Hannah Drybread	9-14-1809
BELL, Henry to Polly Bell	1-15-1809
BISHOP, John to Anne Hankins	4-7-1808
BLAIR, Thomas to Margaret Lytle	3-28-1809
BOWLES, William to Anne Martin	6-22-1809
BOWLS, James to Mary Debolt	10-20-1808
BREES, John to Eleanor Smith	6-2-1809
BRIDGE, William to Rebecca Grimes	11-3-1808
BRODBURY, James to Elizabeth Crane	2-26-1807
BROWN, Samuel to Jane Bell	3-12-1807
BRUGET (BENGET), Emanuel to Catharine Gardner	12-21-1808
BRYANT, Cornelius to Sarah Moore	9-30-1809
CALAHAN, Samuel to Polly Iseminger	2-20-1809
CAMPBELL, Albert to Rebecca Bake	4-13-1809
CARLISLE, James to Harriot Greer	7-12-1808
CARROL, Thomas to Rachel Simpson	10-29-1807
CASE, David to Sally Staggs	4-5-1808
CASE, William to Mary Paine	4-4-1807
CHAMBERS, David to Mary Sexton	10-29-1807
CHAMBERS, Joseph to Elizabeth Ferguson	12-21-1809
CHAMBERS, Samuel to Rebecca Thomas	10-30-1808
CLARK, Charles to Elizabeth Barclay	4-2-1809
CLARK, Daniel to Eunice Garrigus	3-26-1807
CLARK, Isaac to Sarah Davis	10-23-1809
CLARK, John to Clarissa Legg	3-22-1808
CLEM, George to Mary Curry	1-14-1808
COLBY, Joseph to Parmlia Boothe	2-10-1807
CONKLIN, Freeman to Sarah Noble	8-24-1807
CONNER, John to Eleanor Carmichael	10-21-1809
CONNER, Moses to Mary Wolf	8-20-1809
CORNELISON, Marsh to Elizabeth Crooks	6-15-1809
COX, Gilbert to Anne Craig	2-5-1807
CRANE, Robert to Rebecca Gard	3-29-1808
CRANE, Stephen to Polly Enyart	5-25-1809
CREEKMORE, Horatio to Diana Townsend	8-3-1809

```
CRESSEY, William T. to Margaret Templeton          12-22-1808
DANFORD, Cilly to Nancy Knight                      4-13-1808
DAVIS, Eli to Ruth Long                             1-10-1808
DAVIS, John to Polly Reno                           5-13-1808
DAVIS, John to Jane Moore                           2-2-1809
DAVIS, Samuel to Margaret Ogle                     10-26-1809
DAVIS, Vincent to Anne Smalley                      1-17-1807
DENEEN, John to Mary Burgett                        8-27-1809
DRYBREAD, Joseph to Catharine Iseminger             6-9-1808
DUFFEE, James to Ann Eddes                          8-11-1808
DUNGAN, Benjamin to Margaret Mitchel                2-9-1808
DUNN, James to Mary McLaskey                        7-7-1807
EARHART, Jacob to Sally Seybold                    11-19-1807
ELWELL, John to Ann Deneen                          9-29-1807
EMMERSON, James to Eve Allrid                       6-2-1807
ENYART, James to Mary Hahn                          9-1-1808
EVANS, William to Jane Rollands                     6-3-1808
FISHER, John of Indiana Territory to Isabel Richardson 7-6-1807
FLENNOR, George to Polly Andrew                     9-29-1808
FOWLER, James to Elizabeth Devore                   7-21-1808
FRAZEE, Samuel to Rhoda Emmerson                    7-10-1807
FREEMAN, Henry to Mary Campbell                    12-17-1807
FREEMAN, Thomas to Ruth Campbell                    3-24-1807
FREEMAN, York to Judy Holen                         9-27-1808
FRUIT, Geryi (?) to Catharine Stonebreaker         10-29-1808
FRUITS, John to Anny Beaty                          3-2-1809
FULLER, James to Polly Johnson                      8-24-1808
GARD, Daniel to Elizabeth Sutton                   12-25-1809
GARVER, Leonard to Catharine Fisher                 3-17-1809
GARVER, Samuel Jr. to Catharine Lingle              3-20-1808
GEE, William to Elizabeth Flowers                   2-22-1807
GERRARD, Reece to Margaret Syres                    8-15-1809
GOBLE, Jacob to Mary Case                          12-27-1808
GOBLE. Robert to Rebecca Mansfield                  7-28-1807
GOBLE, William to Elizabeth Clark                  11-1-1809
GRAY, Thomas to Sarah White                         3-30-1809
GREEN, Henry to Catharine Rose                     11-19-1807
GRIFFITH, John to Ruby Willey                       4-14-1807
GRIMES, John to Rebecca Paine                       9-18-(1808)
GWILLY, Morgan to Elizabeth Evans                   4-18-1808
HARDEN, Peter to Jane Decker                        3-30-1809
HARPER, Thomas to Jemima Reed                       9-24-1807
HARPER, William to Mary Swift                       6-17-1808
HART, John to Sally McDonalds                       1-8-1809
HART, William to Anne Piatt                         3-24-1808
HARVEY, William to Elizabeth Ringland              12-31-1807
HEADY, Stilwell to Susanna Stonebreaker             7-10-1808
HITTLE, Solomon to Elizabeth Patterson              7-16-1807
HOLLAND, Joshua to Nancy Jones                      7-17-1808
HOUGHMAN, Aaron to Elizabeth Harris                 6-26-1808
```

164

```
HOWARD, George to Nancy Irvin                                    1-1-1809
HUFFMAN, Jacob to Elizabeth Marks                                2-5-1807
HUNT, Isaac to Mary Woodruff                                    10-13-1808
HUSLER, George to Catharine McCaskey                            2-19-1807
JENKINSON, Joseph to Sally Vail                                 9-13-1807
JOHNSTON, Gideon to Polly Smith                                  6-5-1808
JOHNSTON, Samuel to Nancy Lemon                                  8-2-1807
JONES, Jonas to Nancy Hancock                                   7-20-1809
JONES, Ned to Lettice Harris                                     9-7-1808
KENNARD, John to Sarah Richardson                              5-23-1809
KNEESE, Peter to Peggy Waggoner                                8-13-1807
LARUE, William to Lydia Lee                                     6-15-1809
LEESE (LUSE), Robert to Mary Jones                              6-9-1808
LEGG, Owen to Lucy Davis                                      12-17-1807
LENNIN, Samuel to Elizabeth Beaver                              1-1-1808
LIMPUS, Enoch to Sarah Sacket                                   7-6-1809
LIMPUS, Levi to Betsy Erskin                                   8-30-(1808)
LINE, Henry to Sarah Ball                                      3-20-1807
LINE, John to Sarah Hall                                        3-5-1809
LINTNER, Andrew to Rachel Lytle                                3-28-1809
LISTER, Eliphas to Margaret Lennin                            12-29-1808
LISTON, Charles of Hamilton Co. Ohio to Eleanor Boyer          1-15-1807
LONG, William to Catharine Freeman                            12-12-1809
McCLURE, William to Esther Gregory                             6-2-1808
McCOWEN, James to Margaret Mansfield                          11-15-1809
McDONALD, Jupiter, a negro man to Lydia Moore, a negro woman
                                                              3-19-1808
McDONALD, Daniel to Catharine Logan                            6-4-1807
McKLEAN, Robert to Jane Lytle                                 12-22-1807
McKLEAN, Samuel to Mary Francis                               3-17-1807
McMANUS, Robert to Margaret Nelson                           12-28-1809
McMANUS, William to Rebecca Shields                           3-28-1809
MADDOX, Jacob to Catharine Paddox                            10-18-1807
MAHAN, William to Nancy Burns                                 2-16-1808
MARTIN, James to Polly Durden                                  8-7-1808
MASTERS, John to Hannah Goodwin                               3-12-1807
MAXWELL, James to Elizabeth Davis                             8-11-1808
MAXWELL, Thompson to Mary Little                              6-25-1807
MEDCALF, Isaac to Mary Spencer                                2-24-1808
MEEK, Jeremiah L. to Rebecca Grimes                           6-18-1807
MILLS, Joseph to Nancy Taylor                                12-24-1807
MISNER, Charles to Catharine Vanleerer                        8-24-1809
MITCHELL, Fergus to Mary Gregory                              3-10-1808
MITCHELL, Park to Elizabeth Armstrong                         4-30-1808
MOORE, Alexander to Mary Orbison                             12-24-1807
MOORE, Reuben to Betsey Liston                               10-27-1808
MOOREHEAD, Thomas to Hetty Shields                            7-28-1807
MURPHY, Samuel to Lavina Mack                                12-15-1807
MURRAY, Abraham to Hannah Brodrick                           12-31-1809
MURRAY, James to Parmelia Woodruff                            1-18-1807
```

165

MURRAY, William to Johanna Shaik   12-14-1809
MYERS, David to Hannah Waller   3-23-1809
NEWTON, Thomas to Ann Newton   9-22-1807
NICHOLAS, Matthew to Abigail Ball   11-8-1807
NICHOLS, Humphry to Isabella Murphy   1-19-1808
ORR, Isaiah to Nancy Staggs   3-5-1807
ORSON, Joseph to Leah McDonald   5-5-1808
OWENS, Silas to Polly Reed   1-24-1808
PARCELL, John to Isabella Gray   12-21-1809
PARKER, George to Sarah Allen   7-28-1808
PARKISON, Maxwell to Mahela Johnston   6-23-1807
PARTELOW, Amos to Sarah Bailey (Sarah's name also given as "Beaty"
                         marriage recorded twice)   5-25-1809
PARTILOW, William to Susanna Price   6-4-1809
PHILIPS, Richard to Esther Harding   8-18-1807
PIATT, Abraham to Jane Hageman   6-25-1807
PIERSON, Ludlow to Eleanor Davis   4-5-1807
PRICE, William to Esther Vanzant   12-26-1809
POWERS, Aaron to Martha Colby   2-9-1807
RAINS, Isaac to Rachel Hammer   1-27-1808
RANDOLPH, Drake to Sarah Woodruff   12-3-1809
RAYNOLDS, John to Sarah Bills   10-22-1807
REED, John Jr. to Nancy Buck   6-16-1808
REILY, John to Nancy Hunter   2-23-1809
RICHMOND, John Jr. to Polly Gardner   3-9-1809
ROBBINS, Samuel to Jane Marks   2-4-1808
ROBISON, Charles to Sarah Partilow   3-5-1809
ROSS, Jacob to Margaret Montgomery   8-13-1807
RUSSELL, Thomas to Polly Kemp   2-16-1809
SACKET, Thomas to Catharine Chambers   11-23-1808
SALLE, Israel to Abigail Martin   3-23-1809
SALLEE, Daniel to Sarah Gray   1-15-1807
SANDERSON, James to Peggy McKean   12-28-1809
SCROUFE, George to Sally Flowers   9-24-1807
SELVEY, Leonard to Elizabeth Morningstart   12-28-1809
SEWELL, Amos T. to Sarah Russell   5-24-1808
SEWELL, David to Esther Browder   3-12-1807
SEXTON, Zadock to Nancy Enoch   9-17-1807
SHAPPELL, George to Sindy Shaw   9-28-1809
SHEPHARD, William to Nancy Griffith   7-20-1807
SHEPHERD, Frederick to Mary Onspough   9-14-1809
SKYHAWK, John to Elizabeth Freeman   1-22-1807
SLIFER, Jacob to Susanna Flenor   10-22-1809
SMALLEY, Jonathan to Phebe Moore   9-10-1807
SMILEY, John to Polly Harper   7-23-1807
SMITH, Benjamin to Tamer Hawkins   8-4-1808
SMITH, David to Margaret Crooks   7-13-1809
SMITH, James, Esquire to Catharine Beverly   5-18-1809
SMITH, John H. to Joicey Watson   3-10-1807
SMITH, William to Lydia Bell   5-21-1809
SQUIRE, John to Mary Potter   10-12-1809

STACKHOUSE, Clinton to Cintha Green	1-15-1807
STINE, John to Polly Wilcox	9-14-1809
STONEBREAKER, John to Jane Williams	7-2-1807
STOUT, Charles to Polly Duvall	9-14-1809
TALBOTT, John to Rhoda Page	2-23-1809
TAYLOR, John to Esther Beauch	4-2-1807
TROXELL, Frederick to Jane McGarey	10-15-1807
VAIL, Randolph to Mary Vansickle	5-7-1807
VANDUYNE, Matthias to Fanny Misner	8-10-1809
VANSYCKLE, John to Rachel Sheafer	3-10-1808
WADE, Aaron M. to Julia Ward	3-31-1807
WAGGONER, Christopher to Betsey Denman	11-12-1807
WALTON, John to Lydia Marsh	6-9-1808
WARD, Samuel to Nancy Ward	8-13-1807
WATSON, Isaac to Deborah King	4-2-1809
WATTS, Israel to Mary Deweese	11-15-1809
WATTS, Richard to Parmilia Ward	4-20-1807
WEBSTER, Thomas to Rachel Robbins	6-1-1809
WEST, Henry to Elizabeth Barber	3-4-1807
WHITINGER, Francis to Deborah Brown	1-19-1807
WILKINS, Daniel to Betsey Vantrees	5-23-1809
WILKINS, Michael to Martha Shirk	8-11-1808
WILKINS, Michael to Elizabeth Vantrees	6-6-1809
WILKINSON, Gideon to Abigail Vannest	5-21-1807
WILKINSON, John to Polly Kerr	4-27-1809
WILLIAM, Thomas to Sarah Ball	5-8-1808
WILLIAMS, Samuel to Nancy Bunch	1-28-1808
WILSON, Brown to Mary Burns	2-9-1808
WILSON, Thomas to Eleanor Gaterel	2-17-1807
WINGATE, John, Esquire to Emma Torrence	5-16-1809
WOOD, Israel to Sarah McNabb	8-11-1807
WORTH, Joseph to Elizabeth Gard	9-6-1807
YOUNG, Alexander to Kitty Warnock	3-31-1808
YOUNGS, Abijah to Charity Rynearson	10-29-1807

ABERCROMBIE, James to Jane Cox	5-31-1810
ALBERTSON, William to Mary White	8-15-1811
ALDRIDGE, Edward to Jane Mulford	10-4-1810
ALEXANDER, Samuel to Elizabeth Dillon	4-12-1810
ALGER, William to Nancy Carnes	1-19-1812
ALLEN, James to Elizabeth Busby	4-16-1812
ANDERSON, James to Mary Blackburn	5-24-1810
ARCHER, Simon to Mary Gosset	7-25-1811
ASBEL (or ASHEL), John to Massy Worth	4-30-1812
BAIL, John to Delilah Tait	3-25-1812
BAIRD, James to Mary Robbins	8-1-1812
BAKE, Christopher to Elizabeth Stoat (Stout)	10-1-1812
BALDWIN, Thomas to Susan Steele	9-12-1810
BALL, Doctor to Rachel Denman	11-21-1811
BARBER, Henry to Catharine Roby	1-12-1811
BARKALOW, Zebulon to Emma Vail	11-17-1811
BAYLESS, Platt to Fanny McGarey	4-1-1812
BALENGER, Mizel to Elizabeth Partilow	8-14-1812
BAUM, Jacob to Anne Coleman	1-5-1812
BEATY, David Jr. to Margaret Johnston	3-8-1810
BOYER, John to Anne Vankeuren	10-27-1812
BRANNON, Henry to Polly Adams	11-17-1811
BRINEY, Mark to Sarah Stephenson	8-16-1810
BROADBURY, Hezekiah Jr. to Lucy Wright	11-12-1812
BRODRICK, Soloman to Mary Doan Wilson	5-2-1811
BROWN, Andrew to Phebe Goble	3-31-1810
BROWN, William to Isabella Cornthwaite	2-28-1811
BURGET, John to Betsey Deneen	1-24-1811
BURGETT, Daniel to Betsey Ettles	9-6-1810
BURK, John to Eleanor Duvall	7-4-1811
BUTLER, George to Polly Powers	12-19-1811
CAHILL, Abraham to Elsey Watson	4-22-1810
CAMPBELL, James to Margaret Shellhouse	3-22-1810
CARMICHAEL, John to Betsy Pinkley	10-17-1812
CARSON, Samuel to Leah Loury	2-26-1811
CLAP, James to Catharine McCrea	10-5-1811
CLARK, Isaac to Polly Enyart	3-12-1812
CLARK, Johnston to Elizabeth Harris	1-12-1811
CLARK, William to Elizabeth Jenkins	3-15-1812
CLEM, John Jr. to Nancy Wood	2-8-1810
CLENN, Henry to Isabell Hancock	4-2-1812
COAPSTICK, Thomas to Elizabeth Fisher	11-1-1810
COOK, Andrew to Susanna Rowen	8-8-1811
COOPER, Jacob to Elizabeth Walls	4-24-1810
COOPER, Ralph to Mary Guest	6-12-1810
CORRY, William, Esquire to Eleanor Fleming	1-3-1810
COX, John to Elizabeth Patterson	1-3-1811
COX, John Jr. to Nancy Chambers	7-25-1811

CORNELISON, John to Anne Shenard	8-13-1812
COZAD, Benjamin to Patty Shaw	7-23-1810
CRAIG, David to Jemima Masterson	11-5-1812
CRAIG, John to Eleanor Hurley	8-26-1811
CRAIG, Samuel to Hannah Wilson	10-22-1812
CRANE, David to Elizabeth Hoff	10-25-1812
CRANE, Ichabod G. to Esther Gutherie	3-24-1812
CROCKET, James to Sarah Woodruff	6-26-1810
CULLEY, Samuel to Hannah Drollinger	4-24-1810
DANIEL, James to Hannah Hunt	2-26-1811
DAVIDSON, James to Mary Doty	8-13-1812
DAVIS, Benjamin to Jane McKinstry	3-1-1812
DAVIS, Daniel to Eleanor Beasley	3-28-1811
DECKEE, George to Sarah Line	1-3-1811
DELAHAND, Robert to Sally Beeler	4-30-1812
DRAKE, Joel to Elizabeth Grimes	12-24-1812
DUNWOODY, William to Mary Burns	2-13-1810
DUTY, Zina to Sarah Moore	12-2-1810
EARHART, Andrew to Nancy Overpeck	4-23-1812
EATON, Ebenezer to Phebe Ferguson	9-17-1811
EDDENFIELD, John to Hannah Thompson	6-14-1810
ELLIOTT, Micajah to Polly Murphy	10-17-1811
EMANS, James to Elizabeth Brusenbark	12-17-1812
ENYART, Lewis to Lydia Moore	8-1-1811
EVANS, William to Sarah Ross	9-20-1810
FERRIS, John to Nancy Lee	10-8-1810
FISHER, Thomas to Martha Reed	1-23-1810
FLENNOR, Daniel to Hannah Andrew	2-14-1811
FORBES, John G. to Jane Boley	4-2-1811
FREAM, Thomas to Mary ___len(?)	4-10-1812
FREEMAN, Abraham Fitz. to Catharine Buchanan	5-13-1812
FRENCH, Samuel to Elizabeth Decker	6-21-1810
FRUITS, David to Mary Whitinger	1-30-1812
FRUITS, Jonathan to Polly Noble	2-26-1812
GARD, Ezekiel to Elizabeth Gill	1-1-1811
GARDNER, Richard to Ann Bishop	9-2-1812
GARDNER, William to Rebecca Stuart	12-19-1811
GASKILL, Thomas to Nancy Sewell	1-8-1810
GEE, Henry to Eve Ferguson	12-12-1811
GROVE, Daniel to Betsey Smith	8-6-1810
GUSTON, Samuel to Margery Anderson	7-23-1812
HALL, Abraham to Polly Tietsort	9-10-1812
HAND, Joseph to Elizabeth Eller	12-20-1812
HANEL (or HAVEL), Jesse to Hannah Frakes	10-15-1812
HARDEN, John to Jane Ashcraft	9-10-1811
HARELL, Philip to Catharine Reading	11-26-1812
HARLAN, Edward to Sarah Hickman	4-29-1810
HARRIS, Joseph to Rachel Horniday	7-5-1812

169

HARRISON, Robert to Polly Hammer	4-25-1811
HARTSELL, Frederick to Sarah Houghman	11-10-1810
HAWKINS, James to Susan Jones	11-12-1812
HAYS, William Esquire to Sarah Fleming	3-27-1810
HAYSE, James to Sarah Cushman	8-30-1810
HENDERSON, Adam to Mary Armstrong	8-29-1811
HENDERSON, William L. to Ann Wilson	10-18-1810
HENDRICKSON, Eli to Polly Paugh	4-18-1811
HOFFMAN, Robert to Mary Waggoner	2-14-1811
HORNER, John to Mary Horner	4-16-1812
HOSTILLER, John to Mary Wood	1-24-1810
HOUGH, Joseph to Jane Hunter	12-27-1810
HOUGHAM, David to Sarah Morris	7-30-1812
HOWARD, James to Alice Gunyon	3-13-1812
HOWEY, Samuel to Maria Roseboom	7-17-1811
HUBBARD, William to Eunice Van Blair	11-5-1812
HUESTON, John to Ruth Reece	5-7-1812
HUTCHIN, Thomas to Sally Brelsford	6-20-1811
IRWIN, Morton to Anne Crawford	11-28-1811
JAQUES, Richard to Sarah Hamilton	3-29-1812
JEWELL, Elihu to Christiana Dale	2-27-1812
JOHNSTON, David to Mary Caldwell	7-28-1811
JOHNSTON, Thomas to Elizabeth Moore	10-11-1810
JONES, Alexander to Sarah Lane	4-26-1812
JONES, John to Polly McClellan	5-10-1810
KELLEN (or KELLER), Nathaniel to Priscilla Green	11-12-1812
KERR, Alexander to Rachel Potter	3-19-1811
KERR, Jacob to Hannah Wikert	9-5-1811
KIRKPATRICK, William to Betsy Huffman	7-21-1810
LANDPHER, Thomas to Polly Mehaffy	8-6-1812
LANE, George to Elizabeth Phillis	3-22-1812
LANE, John to Polly Baird	2-21-1811
LANGDON, John to Elilah Cullum	5-7-1812
LEDWELL, John to Martha Moore	6-9-1810
LEE, John to Massey LONGBURY	5-28-1812
LEFFERTON, Arthur to Elizabeth Barkalow	9-24-1812
LIMPREST, Elijah to Lydia Young	2-4-1810
LINE, Elihu to Nancy Bell	5-6-1810
LISTON (or LISTOR), William to Nancy Patton	7-4-1811
LITTLE, John to Susanna Gunyon	7-9-1810
LOGAN, Alexander to Ann McClure	2-20-1812
LOGAN, Charles to Elizabeth Johnston	9-6-1810
LONG, James to Margaret Martin	1-11-1811
LONG, John to Phebe Bailey	5-3-1810
LONG, Thomas Jr. to Jemima Pine	2-20-1810
LOWES, James A. to Mary Andrew	1-30-1812
McCLOSKEY, John to Elizabeth Brocius	12-13-1810
McCORMACK, John Jr. to Bethea Case	8-9-1810

McCRAY, Samuel to Elizabeth Lucus   1-4-1810
McGREGOR, John to Elizabeth Malone   12-24-1812
McGUIRE, John to Betsey Street   7-10-1811
McKENZIE, Andrew to Mary Ann Thompson   2-21-1811
McKINSTRY, James to Margaret Craine   7-28-1811
McKINSTRY, John to Charity Good   9-27-1810
McMANUS, Charles to Christiana Smiley   2-27-1812
MARSH, Eliakim to Hannah Sutton   2-12-1812
MARTIN, Isaac to Mary Hand   4-30-1809
MARTIN, John to Margaret Ward   8-15-1811
MARTIN, John to Betsey McGarey   1-30-1812
MASEY, Reuben to Lettitia Smith   3-31-1811
MEGART, Matthias to Catharine Kyger   3-26-1812
MILLIKIN, William to Phebe Richards   11-5-1811
MISENER, Zebulon to Elizabeth Mench   3-18-1810
MONTGOMERY, Henry to Polly Howard   4-11-1811
MOORE, James to Sarah Stackhouse   7-2-1812
MORGAN, Stafford to Delilah Harris   3-26-1812
MULFORD, John to Polly Clark   1-1-1812
MURPHY, Cornelius to Sarah Elliott   7-2-1812
MURPHY, John to Susanna Conklin   8-23-1810
NOBLE, Daniel to Barbara Fruit   1-20-1811
OLLIFANT, William to Susanna McCain   2-6-1811
ORNDORF, Perry to Jane Watson   5-29-1810
OSBORNE, Joseph to Lydia Pardesty   7-7-1811
PAINE, Stephen to Sally Potter   12-5-1810
PAITELOW, Joseph to N;ancy Seward   4-2-1811
PARKER, James Jr. to Susanna Randle   10-22-1811
PARTLOW, Isaac to Rachel Seward   6-11-1811
PARTLOW, Stephen to Anne Partlow   1-4-1810
PAUGH, Michael to Susanna Seward   5-23-1811
PERINE, James to Hannah Hutchins   7-2-1811
PEYTON, John to Rebecca Perry   7-12-1810
PHARES, Joseph H. to Eleanor Witherow   10-9-1812
PIERSON, Jonathan to Matilda Davis   3-1-1810
POGUE, John to Catharine Emery   9-13-1810
POPEJOY, Nathan to Mary Gregory   5-2-1811
POTTER, John to Susanna Vanlear   10-12-1810
PREDDY, Thomas to Elizabeth Orbison   12-31-1811
PRICE, Thomas to Selah Harper   3-10-1810
PRICE, William to Martha Shields   3-19-1812
PRIDDY, Daniel to Elizabeth Goble   10-30-1810
PRIDDY, Thomas to Elizabeth Wilson   7-30-1812
PUGH, Hulet to Abigail Miller   9-15-1812
RAIL, William to Mary Urmston   8-2-1810
REA, William to Sarah Miller   9-12-1810
REED, Benjamin to Betsheba Lindley   4-18-1811
REED, William to Rebecca Looman   1-30-1810
REEVES, Augustus to Lucy McSherry   12-4-1811

171

```
RHODE, Jonathan to Harriet Anderson               10-17-1811
RHINEHART, Jacob to Esther Burgett                10-4-1810
RICHARDSON, John to Polly Bridget                 8-13-1812
RIKER, Jacob to Delilah Crooks                    11-5-1811
RINGLAND, Joseph to Polly Edminston               1-30-1812
ROGERS, Joseph to Nancy Holloway                  2-28-1811
ROSEBOOM, Gilbert to Elizabeth Pierson            1-29-1812
ROUND, Jacob Jr. to Nancy Miller                  4-9-1811
ROWE, Abraham to Elizabeth Hand                   12-6-1812
RUSH, Jacob to Jemima House                       12-11-1810
RYCRAFT, Joseph to Mary Huffman                   6-12-1810
RYON, Reubon to Ann Baldwin                       5-17-1810
SALMON, Jacob to Elizabeth Montgomery             11-14-1811
SCHENCK, Samuel to Polly Hougham                  11-28-1811
SCUDDER, Stephen to Elizabeth Thomas              2-8-1810
SEWARD, Samuel to Anne Van Blear                  6-18-1812
SHAFER, Daniel to Evy Burgett                     8-28-1810
SHAFER, William to Jane Ryerson                   7-18-1811
SHARP, Horatio to Polly Jewell                    8-18-1811
SHAW, Reverand Hezekiah to Rebecca Halstead       9-30-1811
SHERWOOD, James to Nancy Cornelison               1-26-1812
SHOOKMAN, John to Mary Wquire                     4-16-1811
SILLINGER, James L. to Elizabeth Craig            8-17-1812
SIMCOCK, James to Mary Wright                     3-15-1812
SIMMONS, Solomon to Rebecca Schenck               6-28-1810
SLAYBACK, Levi to Dorcas Andrews                  1-4-1810
SMITH, John to Eleanor Long                       11-21-1811
SOWARD, Biram to Phebe Thomas                     2-2-1811
SQUIRE, William to Precise Osborne                1-20-1810
STAGGS, Jonathan to Polly Smith                   3-3-1811
STARR, James Jr. to Eleanor Thornhill             12-17-1812
STEEL, Alexander to Maria Reed                    9-5-1811
STILWELL, James to Rachel Stilwell                1-23-1811
STILWELL, John to Betsey Martin                   1-19-1810
STOCKMAN, John H. to Margaret Stuart              2-13-1812
STONE, Thomas to Elizabeth Martin                 8-25-1812
STRANGE, John to Ruth Waller                      8-29-1812
SULLIVAN, William to Catharine Rhinehart          3-24-1812
SUNDERLAND, Cornelius to Nancy Page               12-24-1812
SWAFFORD, Isaac to Sarah Armstrong                3-21-1810
SWALLOW, Garret to Polly Richey                   9-15-1811
TANNER, William to Betsey Blue                    12-29-1811
TAYLOR, Joseph to Rhoda Pearce                    9-17-1812
TAYLOR, Robert to Mary Bigham                     4-2-1811
TEGARDEN, George Jacob to Nancy Price             10-17-1811
TEMPLER, James to Lucy Dailey                     10-11-1810
THOMAS, Lewis to Tabitha Roby                     3-22-1810
THOMPSON, Enoch to Polly Linn                     5-10-1810
THOMPSON, Isaac to Elizabeth Tietsort             8-9-1812
```

172

```
THORN, Azarias to Nancy Thompson                        8-30-1810
TURNER, Charles to Sally Downing                        12-25-1810
UNDERWOOD, Stephen to Jane Shannon                      4-11-1811
URMSTON, Samuel to Kiziah Hale (or Hall)                11-2-1811
VAIL, Thomas to Nancy Bridge                            3-22-1811
VAIL, William to Eleanor Barkalow                       1-2-1812
VANBLEER, Daniel to Belinda Bean                        5-1-1811
VANSICKLE, Robert to Elizabeth Parkison                 8-11-1812
VANSICKLE, Robert to Elizabeth Parkison                 8-11-1812
VINNEDGE, David to Elizabeth McKean                     5-21-1812
WALDO, Carlton to Mary Magdalene Flennor                11-4-1811
WARD, Henry to Polly Timberland                         8-27-1812
WEAR, James to Mary Lister                              10-12-1811
WELCH, William to Mary Burgett                          11-20-1811
WHITAKER, Jonathan of Hamilton Co., Ohio to
                 Jane Irwin of Butler Co.               8-23-1810
WHITE, John to Hannah McDonald                          4-9-1810
WHITSON, John to Cinthia Tacket                         8-6-1812
WIDENER, Jacob Jr. to Mary Hannah                       4-23-1812
WILLEY, George to Patty Bolton                          9-8-1811
WILLSON, William to Margaret Brodrick                   5-30-1811
WILSON, James to Anne Gilmore                           3-26-1812
WILSON, Joseph to Betsey Dick                           1-9-1812
WILSON, William to Mary Gaston                          2-14-1811
WOOD, James to Sarah McCray                             11-7-1811
WOOD, William to Barbara Clem                           3-1-1810
WOODRUFF, Jesse to Rachel Davis                         3-19-1812
_____, John to ____ _____(note: page torn away)      1-9-1812
```

BUTLER COUNTY, OHIO - WILLS 1803-1810

Abstracted from Old Will Book I, Butler County Probate Court Records.

WHITE, James of Hamilton County, Ohio - page 1 - dated 7-12-1802; recorded July 1803 - Wife: Tabithey - Children: mentioned, but not named - Executors: wife, Tabithey White and Bladen Ashby - Signed: James White - Witnesses: Wm. Milner, John Drake and Mary Drake.

LOY, Adam of Lemon Twp. - page 3 - dated 11-11-1803; recorded 12-16-1803 - Wife: mentioned, but not named - Children: mentions children and designates 3 oldest sons, but does not name - Executors: John Lucas and Peter Cossel - Signed: Adam Loy - Witnesses: Joseph Ely, Jacob (mark) Parker and Rachel (mark) Higgins.

PARKISON, William of St. Clair Twp. - page 4 - dated 5-5-1802; recorded May 1804 -
Sons: John, James, Maxwell and Richard - Daughters: Nancy, Elizabeth and Mary -
Mentions: William and Jane, son and daughter of son Richard - Mentions: 279 acres
land in Nottingham Twp., Washington Co., Penna. - Executors: sons, John and Maxwell - Signed: Will Parkison - Witnesses: Emanuel Vantrees(?) and John Scott.

JONES, Edward - page 6 - dated 10-26-1803; recorded Oct. 1804 - Wife: Jane -
Sons: Daniel, Abraham and Justus - Daughters: Esther and Nancy - Son-in-law:
Daniel Baker - Mentions money in Monongalia Co., Virginia - Executors: son-in-law,
Daniel Baker and son, Justus Jones - Signed: Edward Jones - Witnesses: Jacob
Minturn and John Clark.

KITCHEL, John - page 8 - dated 12-29-1804; recorded 5-21-1805 - Wife: Abigail -
Sons: Ashbell and Mildan - Daughters: Rosalindah, Polly, Alurah, Johannah,
Matildah, and Abigail - Executors; wife, Abigail, William McClure and Daniel Doty
- Signed: John Kitchel - Witnesses: Squire Little, Isaac (mark) Vail and James
Barnet.

GOBLE, Isaac - page 10 - dated 4-7-1805; recorded 5-24-1805 - Wife: Elizabeth -
Mentions: one child, does not name - Signed: Isaac (mark) Goble - Witnesses:
Robert Goble and Thomas Baldwin - Codicil mentions brother, Robert Goble.

REED, Mary - page 11 - dated 4-5-1805; recorded 12-18-1805 - Sons: oldest son,
David Reed and his wife Ruth; Robert and his daughter Jenny; William Reed -
Daughters: Christian, Margaret and Martha, all unmarried - Mentions: that one
case of drawers is at Mr. James Duncan's in Kentucky - Executors: sons, Robert
and William Reed - Signed: Mary (mark) Reed - Witnesses: Joseph Henry, Platt B.
Dickson and W. McClure.

HAWKINS, Nathan - page 13 - dated 1st day, 12th month, 1805; recorded April 1806 -
Sons: John, James, Henry, Nathen and Amos - Daughters: Rebecca Compton, Anne and
Mary Hawkins - Executors: sons, Amos and Nathen and brother, Benjamin - Mentions:
land in South Carolina - Signed: Nathan Hawkins - Witnesses: Amos Hawkins, Levi
Hawkins and Joseph Conner.

WILKINSON, John of Fairfield Twp., Hamilton Co., Ohio - page 15 - dated (da. & mo.
not given) 1800; recorded August 1806 - Wife Leah - Children: Samuel, John, Elijah,
Mary and Margaret - Children of first wife Elizabeth, deceased: John, Jehu, Abner,
Elizabeth, Jean and James - Executor: Moses Miller of Springfield Twp., Hamilton
Co., Ohio - Mentions; Money due from John Kain, Esq. of Winchester, Virginia -
Signed: John Wilkinson - Witnesses: Robt. McClure, Ferdinand Brokaw, Joseph Powers.

STILES, Richard - page 18 - dated 9-1-1806; recorded December 1806 - Wife: Elizabeth
- Sons: Byrd and John (note: possibly more children) - Executors: Abraham Lee
and Samuel Lee - Signed: Richard (mark) Stiles - Witnesses: Abraham Lee, Samuel
Lee and David McCance.

SCOTT, John - page 19 - dated 3-28-1806; recorded April 1807 - Wife: Rebecca - Sons:
James, David, Robert, John and Richard, Richard not of age - Daughter: Jennet
Young - Mentions Tanyard included in land willed to son Robert - Executors: sons,
David and Robert - Signed: John Scott - Witnesses: Mathew Richardson, R. Lytle
and Wm. Robeson.

SEWELL, Timothy - page 22 - dated 9-9-1806; recorded April 1807 - Wife: Sarah - Sons: John R. and Amos, who have been absent for some time; Peter and David - Daughters: Jane Russel, Mary Cowen, Hester Shaw and Nancy Sewell - Grand-daughters: Sarah Sewell and Susannah Sewell, not of age - Executors; sons, Peter and David - Signed: Timothy Sewell - Witnesses: Ezekiel Ball, Nathaniel Bone and James Marshall.

LOWERY, Elizabeth wife of John Lowery, deceased - page 26 - dated 10-24-1807; recorded 1-13-1808 - Sons: Abraham and Fleming, both not of age - Daughters: Sarah, Eliza and Martha, not of age - Sisters: Martha Wilson, Mary Hundman, Isabella Goudy and Margaret Robison - Mentions: Samuel Wilson to serve as guardian of Fleming and Martha; Samuel Hundman to serve as guardian of Sarah and Eliza; Abraham may choose own guardian - Executors: William Goudy and John Bigger, Jr. - Signed: Elizabeth Lowery - Witnesses: Sam'l Wilson, Sam'l Hyndman and John Wilson.

LOGAN, David - page 29 - dated 4-23-1808; recorded 5-25-1808 - Brother: John Logan - Nephews: John McKnight, Joseph McKnight, David Curry, John Laurimer, James Cunningham, John Mathew and Thomas Irwin - Niece: Jean Mathers wife of John Mathers - Executors: John Mathers and Joseph McKnight - Signed: David Logan - Witnesses: Sampson McCullock and James Leason.

McCASKEY (McCLASKEY-McLASKY), Henry of Ross Twp. - page 31 - dated 6-6-1806; recorded August 1808 - Wife: Isabella - Sons: James, John and Joseph - Daughters: Elizabeth, Letty and Polly - Executors: sons, John and Joseph - Signed: Henry McCaskey - Witnesses: Wm. Murray, David Smith and John Reily.

COEN, James - page 33 - dated 5-27-1808; recorded August 1808 - Wife: Margaret, also to serve as executrix - Children: Jane and Edward Jr., both not of age - Signed: James Coen - Witnesses: Maxwell Parkison and James Shields.

VAIL, Stephen of Lemon Twp. - page 36 - dated 4-18-1808; recorded December 1808 - Wife: Mary - Sons: Samuel, Moses, Shobal, Hugh, Aaron and Randal - Daughters: Sarah Burge, Mary Russell and Catharine Smith - Grand-children: Rachel Burnett, Mary Burnett and Catharine Jeffers, not of age - Mentions money due from William Jeffers of Penna. - Executors: sons, Shobal and Aaron - Signed: Stephen Vail - Witnesses: Jonas Smalley, Abrm, Van Sickle and Henry Weaver.

MARTIN, John of Fairfield Twp. - page 38 - dated 11-8-1808; recorded December 1808 - Wife: Margaret - Mentions: four sons and four daughters, but names only son John - Executors: David Beaty; wife, Margaret Martin - Signed: John (mark) Martin - Witnesses: Anderson Spencer, David Sloan and George (mark) Bonsbarger.

CRANE, Elias of Fairfield Twp. - page 41 - dated 6-27-1807; recorded April 1809 - Wife: Phebe - Children: Polly Edwards, Rachel Sloan, Moses, William, Jabez, Cyrus, Stephen, David and Abigail Crane, some are not of age - Executors: wife, Phebe and son, Moses - Mentions: "Stephen and David enjoy the future advantages of their grandfather's favour." - Signed: Elias Crane - Witnesses: David Powers, Godfrey Wagner and John Dixon.

HALL, Joseph of Liberty Twp. - page 43 - dated 1808; recorded April 1809 - Wife: Sarah - Sons: Stephen, Thomas, Jacob and Joseph, last two not of age - Daughters: Jane, Elizabeth, Kiziah and Sarah - Executors: wife and David Conger - Signed: Joseph (mark) Hall - Witnesses: John Ayers and David Urnestand.

ORBISON, Robert of Wayne Twp. - page 45 - dated 7-22-1809; recorded Aug. 1809 - Wife: Elizabeth - Sons: Matthew, John and Robert - Daughters: Ellanor Smith, Margaret Smith, Mary Moor, Catharine and Elizabeth Orbison - Executor: son, Matthew - Signed: Robert Orbison - Witnesses: R. Lytle, Wm. McClelland and James Brown.

CLARK, Stephen - page 47 - dated 12-16-1809; recorded 2-12-1810 - Wife: Joannah - Sons: Jonas and David - Daughter: Jane, not of age - Father-in-law: Jacob Miller - Executors: wife, Joanah and Russel Potter - Signed: Stephen Clark - Witnesses: Jacob Miller, Joshua M. Miller and Elias Miller.

MURPHY, Peter of Liberty Twp. - page 50 - dated 2-10-1810; recorded April 1810 - Wife: Elanor - Sons: James, Cornelius and Peter - Daughters: Ezbal, Mary and Ellanor - Executors: wife, John Megary and Josiah Conklin - Signed: Peter (mark) Murphy - Witnesses: R. Brown, Jacob S. Conkling and Rezin Virgin.

SIMPSON, Abraham - page 52 - dated 6-16-1810; recorded 9-22-1810 - Wife: Jane - Sons: Jonathan, Samuel and Jerry - Executors: Jane Simpson and Squire Little - Signed: Abraham Simpson - Witnesses: Squire Little and Abner Ball.

HUFFMAN, Peter - page 54 - dated 4-19-1810; recorded Aug. 1810- Wife: Anna - Sons: Sampson and Isaac, not of age - Daughters: Polly, Sally and Lily, the last not of age - Executors: father, George Huffman and brother, Isaac Huffman - Signed: Peter (mark) Huffman - Witnesses: John Cox and Edward Leston.

COAPSTICK, Samuel - page 55 - dated 10-1-1810; recorded Dec. 1810 - Wife: Sarrah - Sons: John and Thomas - Daughters: Elizabeth, Ruth and Jean - Executors: wife, Sarah and son, Thomas - Signed: Samuel Coapstick - Witnesses: James Clark and John Robison.

PRINCE CEMETERY
Champaign County

Located in the northwest quarter of Section 28, Mad River Township. The cemetery is situated on Nettle Creek Road, one-eighth mile west of its intersection with Vance Road. The cemetery is fenced, but is overgrown. The following is a complete listing of all stones that could be found:-

LOUDENBACK, Adam died Sept. 14, 1876 aged 57 yrs. 2 mo. 28 d.
GRABILL, Infant son of E. & S. died Feb. 1, 1869
BURROKER, Molly wife of M. Burroker died Sept. 25, 1848 aged 68 years
        Martin died Nov. 1, 1855 aged 75 yrs. (note: broken)
VANCE, Sarah daughter of D. & N. died June 1, 1834 aged 1 yr. & 2 ds.
        William son of D. & N. died Dec. 13, 1850 aged 1y 11m 22d
HOWER, John died June 1866 in his 76th year (note: no death day given)
        Sarah wife of John Hower died Nov. 12, 1854 aged 62 yr. 11 mo. 14 ds.
        Henry died Jan. 21, 1854 aged 26y 3m & 26d
BUROKER, Adam died Sept. 18, 1851 aged 65y 5m
        Elizabeth wife of A. Buroker died Feb. 29, 1868 aged 74 ys. 4 ms. 24 d.
. . . . (note: base for large stone, stone gone)
LOUDENBACK, Washington died Oct. 21, 1863 aged 30y & 16d (broken)
        Salina daughter of Jacob & Sarah died Dec. 22, 1861 aged 8 yrs. 2 m.
                                              12 ds.

        Joseph died Dec. 11, 1858 aged 62 yrs. 5 m. & 17 d.
        Noah died April 17, 1854 aged 32 yrs. 9 mo. & 9 d.
        Benjamin died April 12, 1854 aged 12 yrs. 10 mo. & 18 ds.
= = = = = = =

MILLER CEMETERY
Champaign County

Located in the northwest quarter of Section 32, Concord Township. The cemetery is on the north side of the Miller-Eris Road, one-half mile east of Millersport. It is fenced, but is overgrown. The following is a complete listing of all stones that could be found:-

MILLER, John T. died Sept. 21, 1870 aged 82 ys. 3 ms. 26 ds.
        Barbara wife of John Miller died July 2, 1871 aged 80 yrs. 11 mo. 14 ds.
COMER, Elizabeth dau. of B. & B. A. died Oct. 17, 1843 aged 14 d.
= = = = = = =

BODEY CEMETERY
Champaign County

Located in the southeast quarter of Section 10, Adams Township. The cemetery is on the north side of the Woodville Pike Road just west of its intersection with Cemetery Road. The cemetery is fenced but overgrown. The following is a complete listing of all stones that could be found:-

BODEY, Lewis died Sep. 1, 1839 aged 56y 6m 27d
        Margaret wife of Lewis Bodey died Feb. 10, 1891 aged 88y 10m 12d (ss as Lewis)
MERICA, Daniel son of H. & D. died Dec. 29, 1846 aged 1 yr. 9 mo. 21 ds.
PRESSLER, Inf. son of D. & E. born Nov. 1863; Daniel son of D. & Elizabeth died
                Jan. 15, 1861 aged 6y 7m 5d
. . . . .died May (or Mar.)__, 1886 aged 55y 1(or 4)m & 21d

MUDDY RUN CEMETERY - CHAMPAIGN and LOGAN COUNTIES, OHIO

Cemetery is located in Champaign County, Section 32, Salem Township immediately south of the Logan County line. Access is from Logan County, State Route 245 to Liberty Twp. road #195 about one-quarter mile from Route 245. Cemetery is completely overgrown with the majority of tombstones no longer in an upright position. It has been a fair-sized cemetery at one time and there most likely were more stones (monuments) than were found; however, inscriptions were transcribed from all legible tombstones. Inscriptions taken spring 1969.

BAIRD, Catharine died Aug. 25th 1842 aged 45 years 10 mo. & 3 days.
    Robert died Oct. 8, 1841 aged 35 Y. 1 M. & 8 D.
McCONNEL, Catharine died June 3, 1852 aged 74 y'rs. 6 mo. & 6 d's
ENGLAND, Mary Ann wife of Isaac England died 27. of Feb. 1837 in her 26 year.
CLAYTON, S. B. died March 14, 1843 aged 23 yrs. & 6 ds.
WALL, Susannah E. wife of Daniel Wall died Aug. 11, 1837 aged 20 years & 9 days
CLAYTON, Ruhama wife of J. Clayton died May 13, 1841 aged 62 yrs. 3 mo. & 7 ds.
    In memory of John Clayton who was born near Harpers Ferry, Va., Oct. 10,
        1778 & died Jan. 9, 1835 aged 56 years 2mo. & 30 days.
CLAYTON,_____(?) son of J. & E. died Sep. 8, 1851 aged 1 m. 10 ds. (note; effaced)
CLARK, Robert M. died Oct. 11, 1851 aged 31y 2m 19d
BAIRD, In memory of Thomas Baird Sr. who died March 14th, 1844 in the 80th year
        of his age
CLARK, Catharine wife of Robert Clark died Sept. 11, 1849 aged 62 Y. 11 M.
BAIRD, John R. died July 4, 1846 aged 57 Yr. 9 M. 2 D.
CLARK, Richard died August 12, 1814 in the 33d year of his age (note: date of
        1814 is very plain)
(Note: Next stone is effaced but is same style and design stone as that of
        Richard Clark)
SHIELDS, D., died July 1, 1826 aged 45 Y.
(Note: Large yellow slate stone, completely effaced)
McBETH, Sacred to the memory of Wm. McBeth who died March 25, 1844 aged 59 yrs.
        7 mo. & 9 days.
OWENS, William_____(Note: Rest of inscription completely effaced)
KAVANGH, Rachel wife of James Kavangh died May 15, 1839 aged 36 yea 2 mo. 18 days.
(Note: Next stone is large stone, completely effaced—footstone has initial J.K.)
HANGER, Elizabeth wife of D. G. Hanger died Apr. 3, 1848 aged 28yrs. 9M & 1 day
Mc_ain, R. died March 22, 1849 aged 52 yrs. 10 mo. & 8 d. (Note: Partly effaced)
(Note: Large stone of yellow slate, completely effaced)
KIRKWOOD, Thomas H. son of Wm. & S. Kirkwood, a member of Co. G. 66th Reg., died
        Feb. 11, 1863 aged 27y & 16d
KIRKWOOD, Wm. died May 26, 1849 aged 67 Y.
KIRKWOOD, Mary & Wm. H. & Mariah E., children of Wm. & Sarah died Feb. 17, 1831,
        June 19, 1836, Oct. 3, 1844 from____ to 5 years (Note: Partly
        effaced.)
(KIRK)WOOD, ____ died Sept. 3, 1855 aged 34 yrs. & 8 days (Note; Broken)
KIRKWOOD, Margaret & Elizabeth daughters of Wm. & Sarah _____(broken)
(Note: Large yellow effaced stone)
(Note: Stone with top gone) died June, 1849 aged 37 years.
McBETH, John died Sept. 2 A. D. 1830 aged nearly 100 years (Note: Inscrip. plain)
NILES, W. H. died Dec. 8, 1825 aged 46 Y 1 M. & 2 D.
KIRKWOOD, David son of J. & N. died Jan. 11, 1833 aged 1 yr. 8 mo. & 20 ds.
    Martha J. dau. of J. & N. died Sept. 29, 1823 aged 9 mo. & 2 ds. (Note:
        David and Martha J. on same stone)

MYRTLE TREE BAPTIST CHURCH CEMETERY
Concord Twp. - Champaign Co., Ohio

This cemetery is located on State Route 36 just east of Neal Road, between the villages of St. Paris and Westville. The following inscriptions were taken from a small grouping of older stones located by themselves in the southeast corner of the cemetery.

MILLER, Malchel son of J. & M. d. 6-20-1849; ae 6y 4m 27d
  Marcahet R. dau. of J. & M. d. 5-3-1839; ae 3y 1m 7d
MILLER, John Miles son of S. & R. d. 10-5-1848; ae 4y 1m 28d
  Valentine son of John & Mary d. 2-24-1840; ae 1y 3m 9d
MILLER, John b. 12-11-1794; d. 3-6-1847 (same stone as Polly)
  Polly b. 12-14-1800; d. 2-1-1885
PACKER, Joseph V. son of Stephen J. & Mary E. d. . . 1859 (stone cemented in base)
WELLER, Sarah J. d. 1-29-1864; ae 37y 1m 18d.
MILLER, Samuel W. son of S. & R. d. 7-12-1851; ae 1m 20d.
SHRIVER, James C. son of John & Ann d. 8-18-1831
RUSSELL, . . .h d. 1-13-1832; ae (?) y. 10m 30d. (stone effaced)
MILLER, Jas. Mar_n son of S. & M. d. 7-6-1839 ae 10m 22d (stone effaced)
RUSSELL, sarah dau. of Joseph & Ann d. 1-22-1831; ae 1y 2m 14d
MILLER, Jos. Hill son of S. & R. d. 3-30-1836; ae 1y 2m 29d
NILES, Rebecca J. dau of E. & L. d. 3-31-1851
  Amanda M. dau of E. & L. d. 12-9-1835; ae 2y
  Thomas J. son of E. & L. d. 2-9-1839
ROBERTS, "In memory of Sarah who died March 10, 18__, aged 72 years and 6 mos."
               (stone effaced)
NEER, Martha dau. of Conard & Ann d. 9-20-1845; ae 43y 6m & 16d
MILLER, "In memory of Valentine, died Nov. 29, 1843, aged 80 years 11 mo. & 2 das."
TAYLOR, Infant son of R. S. & S. d. 1-2-1832
. . . . (Footstone - S. M.)

ZEEGLER-ZIEGLER CEMETERY
CHAMPAIGN COUNTY, OHIO

Located in Section 1, Harrison Township; on west side of Sullivan Road, one and one-half miles south of State Route 245 or one mile east and north from Yearin Road. Fenced but overgrown. Only four stones in cemetery, Inscriptions transcribed in 1969.

ZIEGLER, In memory of John son of J. & B. Ziegler who died Aug, 1840 aged 9
    years 10 mo. & 21 days.
ZEEGLER, Martha daughter of Jacob & Barbara Zeegler died Apr. 26, 1849 aged
    2 yrs. 3 m 25 ds.
  Mariah wife of David M. Zeegler died Aug. 8, 1853 aged 23 yrs.
    10 m. & 28 days
  Mariah daughter of David & Mariah died Sept. 10, 1853 aged 1 mo. 14 ds.

WILSON (aka. RUSSELL) CEMETERY
CHAMPAIGN COUNTY, OHIO

Located in the northwest quarter of Section 6, Adams Township; on Cemetery Road
about one-fourth mile north of State Route 29. Cemetery is overgrown but it is
fenced. Only three stones in cemetery, Inscriptions transcribed 1969.

WILSON, William born June 12, 1821 died Oct. 3, 1891
Sylvester son of Wm. & P. died Feb. 1851 aged 6 mo. & 21 ds.
Jas. P. Willson died Jan. 24, 1881 aged 35y 4m 9d (Note: Same stone
as Rosanna)
Rosanna wife of Jas. P. Wilson died Jan 2, 1879 aged 29y 1m 13d,
also infant son died May 9, 1871

CHAMPAIGN COUNTY, OHIO
Will Abstracts 1806-1819

The following is a complete listing for all wills appearing in Will Book "A":-

REYNOLDS, Joseph - page 1 - dated 7-5-1808; recorded (not given) - Wife: Sarah - Sons: John, Isaac, Joseph Smith, Jas., Thos., Robt., Martin and Samuel - Daughters: Elizabeth Bonner wife of David G. Bonner, to have land in Greene Co., Ohio where David Bonner now lives; Mary and Sarah Reynolds - Executors: Wife, Sarah, and sons, John and Joseph S. Reynolds - Signed: Joseph Reynolds - Witnesses: Thomas L. Lamdal, John Kain and Thomas Parish.

RUSSEL, Caleb - page 3 - dated 3-6-1810; recorded (not given) - Wife: Lydia - Sons: William and Caleb - Daughters: Martha Hester, Rebecca and Lydia - Executors: Wife, Lydia; and brother, Robert Russel - Signed: Caleb Russel - Witnesses: Edward H. Pearce and James Devore.

MORRISON, Ephraim - Springfield Twp. - page 4 - dated 1-13-1806; recorded 5-20-1806 - Wife: Lettice - Son: Ephraim - Daughter: Nancy - Mentions Nancy Gibson, may be same as daughter, Nancy - There may be more children not named - Executors: Wife, Letty and Joseph Leyton - Signed: Ephraim Morrison - Witnesses: Ira Smith and Hugh M. Wallace.

McDONALD, William - page 5 - dated 8-23-1807; recorded 9-22-1817 - Wife: Jennet - Sons: Andrew, James, William, John, Samuel, Ebenezer and Rober; last three are minors - Daughters: Jane Yearnal and Polly - Executors: Sons, William and John - Signed: William McDonald - Witnesses: Thomas Moore and Alex'r McBeth.

MITCHEL, Samuel - Concord Twp. - page 7 - dated 4-6-1811; recorded 1-31-1812 - Wife: Margret - Sons: Howard, James, John and Sam'l - Daughters: Mary, Martha, Sarah Enos - Brother: Edward, deceased - Executors: Sons, James and John Mitchel; William Streaet - Signed: Samuel (mark) Mitchel - Witnesses: Henry (mark) Smith, Phelix Rock and Wm. Street.

KAIN, Maurice - page 9 - dated 10-8-1809; recorded 9-25-1812 - Bequeath to John and William Kain, sons of Hugh Kain - Mentions John Kain's two daughters, Elizabeth and Mary; and William Kain's daughter, Julian Kain; and son, John Maurice Kain - Mentions land in Kentucky and gives various land descriptions for Ohio land - Executors: Nephew, John Kain and John Lafferty - Signed: Maurice Kain - Witnesses: William Stevens and Zephimieh Luce.

EVANS, Isaac Sr. - page 12 - dated 7-29-1812; recorded 9-28-1812 - Wife: Mary - Children: Margaret Harland (or Hainlan), Jeremiah, Isaac, Edward, George, Ailsey, James and Nancy - Executors: Wife, Mary Evans and Joseph Hedges - Signed: Isaac Evans - Witnesses: Joseph Hedges, Christopher Kenaga (or Renaga) and William Glenn - Codicil dated 8-8-1812 - no further information.

BEEZLEY, John - page 16 - dated 8-9-1812; recorded 1-18-1813 - Step-sons: John, Nicholas and Isaac Pricket - Bequests to: Gitta Davis; William, Joseph, Thomas, and Isaac Beezley; Sarah, Jane and Rachel - Executors: Nicholas Pricket and William Beezley - Signed: John Beezley - Witnesses: John Warren, Robert Crossley and Wm. Christy.

HAMILTON, John – page 18 – dated 8-13-1813; recorded 10-21-1813 – Wife: Sarah – Mentions his children but only names oldest daughter, Eliza – Executors: John Humphreys and John Perrin – Signed: John Hamilton – Witnesses: Robert Remck, John Nelson and Peter (mark) Shaffer.

GOODE, John – page 20 – dated 4-22-1813; recorded 10-28-1813 – Wife: Mary – Children: Robert, Samuel, Gardenar, Thomas, Joseph, James, Francis and Sail – Executors: James Spain, Thomas Goode and Joshua Spain – Signed: John Goode – Witnesses: Thomas Spain and Daniel Spain.

WALLACE, Thomas – page 21 – dated 3-13-1813; recorded 10-28-1813 – Wife: Elaner – Sons: John, Ross, William, Moses, Joseph and James – Daughters: Nancy, Deborah and Rachel Wallace – Grandson: Thomas Wallace son of Ross Wallace – Executors: Wife, Eloner and John Warwick – Signed: Thomas Wallace – Witnesses: Richard Peeirson, Jonathan Johnson and John Paul.

LAYTON, William – page 23 – dated 12-15-1813; recorded 1-24-1814 – Sons: John, Elisha, Joseph, Arthur and William – Daughter: Hetty – Step-daughter: Dinah Williams, mentions Dinah's son Bill – Mentions that balance of estate is to be divided amongst children by my first wife including Robert Layton's heirs and Thomas Williams Children by my daughter, Sarah – Executors: Sons, Joseph and Arthur – Signed: William (mark) Layton – Witnesses: Samuel McKenney and Sarah (mark) McKenney.

HUGHS, Abraham – page 24 – dated 10-6-1813; recorded 1-25-1814 – Wife: Sarah – Sons: Isaac and Wesley – Daughters: Ruth, Rebeckah Duvall, Margaret Lee, Mary Hughes, Lydia Hughes and Hannah Hughes – Mentions land sold to Benjamin Lee – Mentions that one acre of his land is to be used for a burying ground – Executors: Wife, Sarah and Isaac Hughes – Signed: Abraham Hughes – Witnesses: Reuben Paxson and Jeremiah Baldwin.

ROGERS, John – page 27 – dated 10-19-1813; recorded 1-25-1814 – Wife: Mary – Son: Hamilton – Daughters: Mary, Rebeckah and Ann Rogers – Administrators: Mary and Hamilton Rogers – Signed: John(mark) Rogers – Witnesses: John Collins and James (mark) Merrifield.

BALLINGER, Joshua – page 28 – dated 23rd day, 12th month, 1812; recorded 1-25-1814 – Wife: Sarah – Sons: Henry, Caleb and Thomas; Thomas not of age – Daughters: Hope Winder, Elizabeth Sherb(?), Rachel and Sarah – Brother: Samuel Ballinger – Executors: Wife, Sarah and John Garwood, Sr. – Signed: John Ballinger – Witnesses: John Garwood, Henry Jones and Samuel Curl.

GARBER, John – page 31 – dated 12-11-1813; recorded 6-3-1814 – Children: Jacob, Elizabeth, Nancy, Mary, Abraham, Barbara, Magdalene wife of Peter Minnich Sr., Joseph and Samuel – Mentions land in Hamilton Co., Ohio – Executors: Peter Minik, Sr. and son, Jacob Garber – Signed: Johannis Garber – Witnesses: George Keefer and Peter Minnich, Jr.

FOOS, Benjamin - page 35 - dated 3-23-1814; recorded 6-18-1814 - Wife: Sarah, also to serve as Executrix - Mentions family, not of age, but does not name - Verbal Will - Witnesses: William Holl and Griffith Foos.

DARNALL, William - Mad River Twp. - page 36 - dated 2-3-1814; recorded 12-22-1814 - Wife: Mentioned but not named, she is also to serve as Executrix - Children: Mentioned but not named - Signed: William Darnall - Witnesses: David Boyle, Nathen Hill and David Beely.

REED, Hugh - Verbal Will - page 37 - dated 4-5-1814; recorded 8-22-1814 - Requests that Daniel and Thomas Goble assist Hannah Reed, wife, in managing affairs of estate - Children mentioned but not named - Witnesses: Daniel Goble and George Benson.

STEVENSON, David - Verbal Will - page 38 - Will given 2-21-1814; deposition named 5-19-1814; recorded 8-22-1814 - Wife: Martha - Children: Arthur, Martha, Anna, David, Charles, John and Jane - Mentions money due from Virginia - Witnesses: James Dunlap and Thomas Watt.

WARWICK, John - Bethel Twp. - page 39 - dated 2-21-1814; recorded 8-22-1814 - Wife: Mary - Sister: Anne Ingrun - Mentions: "all my children", but does not name - Executors: William Page, Sr., Rueben Wallace, John Lamme and William Lamme - Signed: John Warwick - Witnesses: James Henderson and James Lamme.

WARD, Joseph - page 40 - dated 7-4-1814; recorded 9-29-1814 - Wife: Sarah - Son: Richard - Grandsons: John and Joseph Ward - Grand-daughter: Mary Crosly - Executors: Wife, Sarah and son, Richard - Signed: Joseph (mark) Ward - Witnesses: Henry Vanmeter and Edward Johnston.

THARP, Nathan - Verbal Will - page 43 - dated 8-29-1814; recorded 9-29-1814 - Wife: Mentioned, but not named - Witnesses: Abner Tharp and Hannah Tharp.

EVANS, Mary - page 44 - dated 8-5-1814; recorded 9-29-1814 - Sons: George, James, Isaac and Edward - Daughters: Margaret Harlin of Virginia and Nancy - Executor: Nathan Pruckard - Signed: Mary Evans - Witnesses: Nathaniel Prickard, Isaac and George Evans.

LEE, Benjamin - page 45 - dated 8-31-1814; recorded (not given) - Wife: Peggy - Children: Mentioned but not named - Executors: Jeremiah Baldwin and Aaron L. Hunt - Signed: Benjamin Lee - Witnesses: Aaron L. Hunt, David Norton and Jacob Paxton.

GLOVER, Samuel - page 46 - dated 10-5-1813; recorded (not given) - Sons: Joshua and Samuel, also to serve as administrators - Daughters: Sally Thornton, Elizabeth, Anne and Marget Glover - Signed: Samuel (mark) Glover - Witnesses: John Caraway and Elisha Taber.

RICE, Ezekiel - page 47 - dated 11-29-1814; recorded January 1815 - Memorandum of Ezekiel Rice of Springfield and his wife in regard to a conversation that took place between them and William Moody, Sampson Hubble, Nathan Adamson and Samuel Smith in relation to the disposal of his property - Property to be divided among children should wife not recover from present illness - Son: Ezekiel - Daughter: Susannah Dean - Mentions: Jeny Spencer, Abraham Spencer and his daughter Ann - Sons: Reuben and Russel - Witnesses: Samuel Smith, William Moody and Joseph Adamson.

RICE, Sophia - page 48 - dated 1-13-1815; recorded 2-4-1815 - Sons: William Daugherty and Thomas Doyle - Daughters: Sophia Doyal and Harriet McCulloch - Mentions that children Harriet, Thomas and Sophia are heirs of their uncle, Thomas Doyle - Mentions that John Dougherty is father of William and that William is to be bound to John McCulloch until of age - Signed: Sophia Rice - Witnesses: John Hall, Jacob Lingle and Samuel Smith - Codicil dated 1-13-1815, same witnesses - requests that son-in-law, John McCulloch serve as executor and guardian of children.

PENCE, Samuel- page 51 - dated 2-20-1815; recorded 6-13-1815 - Wife: Elizabeth - Children: Tabitha, David and John; not of age - Executors: Wife, Elizabeth and brother, Joseph Pence - Signed: Samuel (mark) Pence - Witnesses: John Nowman, Henry Pentz, Abraham Pentz and Isaac Myers.

CAMRON, Hugh - page 53 - dated 4-12-1815; recorded 6-14-1815 - Niece and Nephew: Hugh and Jane Camren children of brother James Camron - Mentions: George Richarson and Levena (or Laura) Richison - Executor: David Lowery - Signed: Hugh (mark) Camran - Witnesses: Jane Lowry and Reuben William.

DICKSON, Robert - page 55 - dated 2-3-1815; recorded (not given) - Wife: Betsy, also to serve as executrix - Children: William, Thompson, John, Jane, Betsey and Polly Dickson; not of age - Signed: Robert Dickson - Witnesses: Eleazer Piper, William Dougless, Zepamize Cumer, James Moore and James Stewart.

LAMME, James - Bethel Twp. - page 57 - dated 9-25-1815; recorded (not given) - Sons: John and James, also to serve as Executors - Daughter: Nancy G. Lamme - Sons-in-law: John Wallace, Reubin Wallace, Abraham McNeale, John L. Boswell - Grandsons: James H. Boswell and James W. Lamme - Signed: James Lamme - Witnesses: William Lewerie and Samuel McKinny.

DAVISON, James - page 59 - dated 9-12-1815; recorded (not given) - Wife: Mary - Father: Isaac Davison - Brothers and Sisters: Not named except for Isaac Davison - Nephew: Thomas Davison - Executors: Wife, Mary; friend, John Reynolds and brother, Isaac Davison - Signed: James Davison - Witnesses: Jno. Rhodes and Jno. C. Pearson.

NEAL, St. Leger - Salem Twp. - page 63 - dated 7-13-1816; recorded (not given) - Wife: Rachel - Son: Henry - Grandsons: St. Leger and Henry Neal - Mentions: John Stewart - Executors: Wife, Rachel and John Stewart - Signed: St. Leger Neal - Witnesses: J. J. Eckasen, John Martin and Thomas (mark) Burten.

MILLER, William - Montgomery Co., Ohio - page 60 - dated 10-5-1810; recorded (not given) - Being about to make a journey to Europe bequeaths to Prudence Giddies daughter of Prudence Tarince who is a daughter of James Torence of Fayett Co., Penna. - Prudence Giddies was born sometime in the fall or autumn of 1797 - Mentions land in Miami Co., Ohio - Bequeath to friends, Thomas Simpson of Greene Co., Ohio and Benjamin Van Cleave, Esq. of Montgomery Co., Ohio who are also to serve as executors - Signed: William Miller - Witnesses: Lilly Simpson and Margret (mark) Rough.

HUFFMAN, Lewis - German Twp. - page 65 - dated 12-26-1815; recorded (not given) - Wife: Barbary - Children: Abraham, Mary, Elizabeth, Moses, Mathias, Sarah, Ann, Christana and William - Signed: Lewis Huffman - Witnesses: David Jones, John Kamy and Henry Baker.

REESE, Jacob - page 66 - dated 6-27-1816; recorded (not given) - Wife: Elsa - Children: Mentioned but not named - Executor: John Price - Signed: Jacob Reese - Witnesses: Peter Sewell and Nathan Rees.

WARD, Abijah - Union Twp. - page 68 - dated 10-14-1813; recorded 8-8-1816 - Wife: Esther - Children: Mentioned but not named - Executors: Friends, James Dunlap and John Thomas - Signed: Abijah Ward - Witnesses: Zephaniah Luse and William Dunlap.

POWELL, Abraham Sr. - Urbana Twp. - page 69 - dated 10-4-1816; recorded Feb. 1817 - Wife: Ann - Sons: Elijah, Abraham, Joseph, Benjamin, Timothy and Enoch - Daughters: Leah, Rachel, Rhode, Mary and Ann - Executors: Sons, Elijah and Timothy - Signed: Abraham Powell - Witnesses: Samuel Powell, James Smith and Abraham Powell.

SMITH, Peter - Bethel Twp. - page 72 - dated 6-1-1816; recorded 6-26-1818 - Wife: Catharine - Heirs: Ira, Samuel, Sarah, Hezekiah, heirs of Elizabeth Faris, Abraham, heirs of Nancy John, Polly and Rhoda - Executors: Wife, Catharine and son, Samuel. - Signed: Peter Smith - Witnesses: Reuben Wallace and George Keifer.

HALL, John - Springfield - page 74 - dated 1-20-1817; recorded 6-26-1818 - Requests to be buried on ground where he now lives - Brother: Hezekiah Hall of New Lebanon, New York - Father: John Hall of Windsor, Berkshire Co., Mass. - Executor: Joseph Perrin - Signed: John Hall - Witnesses: J. B. Coleman and Joseph O. Lemon.

YARNALL, Amos J. - page 77 - dated 8-22-1817; recorded 6-26-1818 - Wife and Children mentioned but not named - Executors: Wife (not named) and friend, Sam'l McCord - Signed: Amos J. Yarnall - Witnesses: Sam. McCord and W. Ward, Jr.

SPAFFORD, Amos - Waynesfield Twp. - page 78 - dated 4-29-1817; recorded 6-26-1818 - Wife: Oliver - Children: Samuel and Ausora Spafford; Chloe Hecox - Grandchildren: John Craw and Richard Craw - Executers: Sons, Ausora and Seneca Allin - Signed: Amos Spafford - Witnesses: David Hull, Jacob Wilkison and Wm. Baldwin.

STRETCH, William - Concord Twp. - page 79 - dated 2-17-1817; recorded 6-26-1818 - Wife: Jemima - Son: Thomas - Grandson: Andrew - Executors: Wife, Jemima and son, Thomas - Signed: William Stretch - Witnesses: John Luse, Robert McFarland and Joseph (mark) Longfellow.

ALLEN, James - page 81 - dated 1-10-1818; recorded 6-27-1818 - Children: Samuel, Elijah and Belinda - Bequeath to friend, Vacheal Blaleck all bounty for service in last war and Warrant #173 - Executor: Vacheal Blaleck - Signed: James (mark) Allen - Witnesses: John Thomas, Randal Largent and James Gillaspie.

BALLINGER, Sarah - page 83 - dated 17 of 11 mo. 1817; recorded 6-27-1818 - Mentions: Sarah Winder; Elizabeth; Phebe Sharp; Rachel; Sarah; Patience; Ann Ballinger; Achsah M'Waid; Caleb; Thomas; does not give relationship except mention fact that she has at least four daughters - Executors: Caleb Ballinger and Allen Haines - Signed: Sarah Ballinger - Witnesses: Job Sharp and Samuel Ballinger.

MALIN, William - page 85 - dated 8-7-1818; recorded 9-14-1818 - Wife: Vashti - Children: Joseph, Mahlon, Jacob and Mary - Mentions that Mahlon is now absent - Bequeath to Nancy Rymond - Executor: John McAdams - Signed: Wm. Malin - Witnesses: E. L. Morgan, Thomas Stewart and John (mark) Foster.

BAYLES, John - page 87 - dated 1-1-1819; recorded March 1819 - Son: David; Mentions his sons Joseph and Jefferson and daughter Peggy - Mentions father and mother (does not name) whose welfare to be in care of Nathan Darnal and John West - Mentions brothers, but does not name - Executors: Father (not named) and Ninian Taunahill - Signed: Jno. Bayless - Witnesses: J. R. Hughs and Asael Sweet.

HAGGARD, Rice - page 89 - dated 5-1-1819; recorded (not given) - Wife: Nancy - Children: Nancy, James, Okelly, Elizabeth and David Rice Haggard - Executors: Brother, Levy Haggard of Cumberland Co., Ky.; Reuben Paxson of Champaign Co.; and wife, Nancy - Signed: Rice Haggard - Witnesses: Peter Black and Joshua Richardson.

SPAIN, William - page 90 - dated 10-27-1819; recorded Dec. 1819 - Father: Mentioned but not named; states that he lives with his father - Brothers and Sisters: Abraham, John Peterson, Daniel, Sarah Eppes, Mary Leads (?), Elizabeth Spain - Executors: Brother, John Peterson Spain - Signed: William (mark) Spain - Witnesses: James Spain, William Auders and William Eppes.

CHAMPAIGN COUNTY, OHIO - WILL ABSTRACTS 1818-1826

The following records were taken from Will Book B, located in the Probate Court at the court house in Urbana. Pages on which the record may be found in the original record are given in parenthesis.

SPAFFORD, Amos of Waynesfield twp. - dated 4-29-1817; recorded 6-26-1818. Wife, Olive. Children: Samuel Spafford, Cloe Hecox and youngest son, Aurora Spafford. Grandchildren: John Craw and Richard Craw. Executors: Aurora Spafford and Seneca Allen. Signed; Amos Spafford. Witnesses: David Hull, Jacob Wilkins, William Baldwin. (1)

STRETCH, William of Concord twp. - dated 2-17-1817; recorded 6-26-1818. Wife, Jemima, also to serve as executrix. Son, Thomas, to have 100 acres Congress land. Grandson, Andrew, who lives with testator, not of age. Mentions "rest of my children" but does not name. Signed: William Streach. Witnesses: John Lyle, Robert McFarland and Joseph (his mark) Longfellow. (3)

JOHNSTON, William - dated 4-30-1815; recorded 8-27-1820. Wife, Ellen. Sons: Barnet Johnston, dec'd; Otho Johnston; and Jacob Johnston. Daughters: Ann, Hannah, Jean, Ellen and Lidia. Four grandsons: William, John, Barnet and Joseph Johnston, sons of Barnet Johnston, dec'd. Mentions Elizabeth Johnston, widow of Barnet and mother of four grandsons. Executor, Otho Johnston. Signed: William Johnson. Witnesses: Jacob Strattan, Isaac Everitt, and John Thomas. (5)

OWENS, William - dated 10-16-1821; recorded 11-27-1821. Wife, Jane, also to serve as executrix. Sons: Alfred and Asahel. Possibly more children not named. Signed; William (mark) Owens. Witnesses: J. D. Carter, J. Cooley and Benj'n L. Holler. (7)

ROWIN, Peter - Yeoman - dated 9-17-1820; recorded 11-28-1821. Wife, Katharine, also to serve as executrix. Grandson, Peter Shay. Signed: Peter (mark) Rowin. Witnesses: William Bridge, Edward Quinn and Benjamin Ward. (9)

COLBERT, Joshua - Verbal Will - Deposition made by John B. Culbersson with will taken 8-15-1820 shortly before death of Joshua Colbert, Salem township; recorded 8-25-1821. Son-in-law, James Mathers. Daughter, Mary. Youngest daughters, Catharine and Anny. Son, Thomas. Witnesses: John B. Culbertson and Susana (mark) Colbert. (10)

MACLAY, Charles of Salem twp. - dated 12-26-1814; recorded Apr. 1821. Wife, Susana. Six children: William, Charles, John, Elijah. Jane and James Linn Dixon; not all of age and three youngest children to have schooling. Executors: son, William; brothers-in-law, Abraham Smith and James Smith. Signed: Charles Maclay. Witnesses: George Petty, Jas. Smith, Thomas Thomas. (11)

COMER, Peter of Urbana - dated 2-15-1822; recorded 6-14-1822. Wife, Mildred. Son, Peter Comer, a minor. Executors: John Glenn and William Runkle. Signed: Peter Comer. Witnesses: J. Cooley and M. Malgrew. (13)

CROW, Sarah - dated 2-19-1821; recorded Apr. 1821. Brother, Joseph Crow to have half of 140 acres in Pique County (Pickaway County). Sisters: Susanah Fielder and Mary R. Fielder. Executor; brother, Joseph Crow. Signed: Sarah (her mark) Crow. Witnesses: James (mark) Thomas, Elizabeth Thomas. (14)

LAFFERTY, John - dated 3-13-1819; recorded 6-17-1822. Wife, Sally. Children: Jane, Thomas, William, Molly, John, David, Wesley, Catharine and also child wife is now pregnant with. Daughter, Jane to have testator's Bible and wife, Sally to have Big Bible. Mentions money coming to testator from Virginia. Executor; friend, Theodorick Spain. Signed: John Lafferty. Witnesses: William Bay, Sally Dockam and Richard Tennyon(?). Codicil dated 1-19-1822 names children unborn at writing of will; daughter, Sarah and youngest child, daughter, Hester Ann. (15)

ROBINSON, John - dated 19th, 6th month 1822; recorded 11-4-1822. Wife, Hannah. Sons: Nicholas, John, James, Joshua and Jehu. Daughters: Mary, Lydia and Rachel. Executors: sons, Nicholas and John Roberson. Signed: John Robinson. Witnesses: John Williams, Silas Williams and Nicholas Williams. (17)

BEAL, Obadiah - (not dated); recorded 11-5-1822. Wife, Rebecca. Son, Daniel M. Beal. Daughter, Corry Beal. Signed: Obadiah Beal. Witnesses: Jesse Bates, Ebenezer Culver and James Douglass. (18)

COWAN, John - dated 11-2-1820; recorded 11-5-1822. Sons: William, John, David, James, Thomas, Samuel, Alexander and Wilson Cowan. Daughters: Mary Kerkley, Margaret Frankelberger and Caroline Cowan. Mentions 10 acre plantation where testator now lives which includes tanyard. Sons, John and David are not of age. Executors: son, William Cowan and Benjamin Chenny. Signed: John Cowan. Witnesses: Benjamin Chenny, John Hoover, Jonathan Harbert and Cashore (mark) Karkley. (18)

SMITH, Abraham of Salem township - Nuncupative Will - will given 10-21-1822; recorded 11-14-1822. Lands in Salem township to be divided equally and to go to the use of the family of James Smith and the family of Widow McClay. Mentions lands in Missouri. Executors: brother, James Smith and nephew Charles McClay. Witnesses: James Turner, John B. Culbertson and Archibald Stewart. (19)

WARD, William - dated 12-21-1822; recorded (not given). Wife, Peggy; mentions "her children born by me". Sons: John A., William Jr., Syras (Cyrus) F., James and Marshall. Daughters: Phebe Barr, Peggy, Betsy, Frances and Rebecca. Executors: John A. Ward, William Ward Jrl, Cyrus F. Ward, Robert Barr and brother, James Ward of Kentucky. Signed: Wm. Ward. Witnesses: W. H. Fyffe and George Hite. (20)

CARSON, Robert of Jackson township - dated 6-2-1818; recorded 12-2-1823. Wife, mentioned but not named. Sons: James, Robert and Ambrose Carson. Daughters: Peggy Huston, Betsey, Jinny, Nancy Carson, and Polly Carson. Executors: sons, James and Ambrose. Signed: Robert Carson. Witnesses: George Fithian, Nathan Hill and William Fithian. (24)

POWELL, Samuel of Urbana township - dated 7-3-1823; recorded 12-2-1823. Wife, Catharine. Sons: Abraham, Alfred, Joseph, Abel, Samuel, Henry, George and James Powell; James is youngest son and not of age. Daughters: Sarah, Mary, Nancy, Christina, Roxvina and Matilda. Executor: son, Abraham Powell. Signed: Samuel (his S mark) Powell. Witnesses: Elijah Powell, Timothy Powell and James Smith.(25)

CARY, Calvin Sr. - dated 6-28-1823; recorded 12-2-1823. Wife, Jane. Sons: Ezra and Samuel Cary. Daughters: Margaret, Liddy and Mary Cary. Executors: wife, Jane and son, Ezra. Signed: Calvin Cary Sr. Witnesses: Lewis Sroufe and George Sroufe. (26)

WILLSON, Francis - dated 4-19-1823; recorded 12-3-1823. Wife, Prissilla. Two youngest sons, Francis and George. Son, Alexander. Daughters: Jane and Eliza Willson. Mentions money coming from Pennsylvania. Owns lot #40 in Sidney, Ohio. Bequeaths money to William Bothell for use of Anna Bothwell and his youngest son; also money to Margery Durgman and her daughter Anny. Son, Thomas Willson and his son, Francis. Executors: Thomas Willson and William Bothell. Signed: Francis Willson. Witnesses: William Bothel and Francis Willson. (27)

BROWN, Benjamin of Salem township - dated 6-23-1822; recorded 12-3-1823. Sons: Ira and Elisha. Daughter. Rhoda. At death of Eliza Brown, property to be divided equally between William Brown and Eunice Brown, Executor: Ebenezer Culver. Signed: Benjamin Brown. Witnesses: Ebenezer Culver. Obadiah Beal and Roswell Culver. (29)

JOHNSTON, Mary - dated 3-21-1823; recorded 12-3-1823. Son, Edward Johnston, dec'd, his children--Martha, Noel, Delila, William, Nancy, Alfred and Mary to have a bond made 6-24-1812 by Edward Johnston Jr. to Edward Johnston Sr. and Mary his wife for $1000.00, said bond made for a dwelling house now occupied by Gerrard McKennie and his wife and children of the said dec'd Edward Johnston (Jr.). Son. Alexander Johnston, dec'd, his children (not named). Children: Mary Osborn, Nancy wife of Levi Osborn, James Johnston, Jesse Johnston, Elizabeth Henry, Milly Dunlap and Patsey Osborn. Requests to be buried near the place where her deceased husband is buried. Executor, Douglass I. Winn. Signed: Mary (mark) Johnston. Witnesses: John G. Colwell, Aquilla Bishop and Charles Winn. (30)

OSBORN, Levi - dated 11-14-1823; recorded 12-20-1823. Bequeaths to: Joseph Osborn land S½ NW¼ Section 1, Township 5, Range 11 provided he pays $350.00 to Jeremiah Osborn two years after testator's death; to Heirs of James Osborn (not named) living with their mother; to Heirs of Alexander Johnston; to Heirs of Jesse Johnston; to Heirs of David Osborn; to Heirs of Samuel Kincade. Executor, William Glenn. Signed: Levi Osborn. Witnesses: John Willey and John Ashing. (31)

HORNBACK, John of Harrison township - (not dated); recorded 2-6-1824. Wife, Jane. Children: Elizabeth Hopkins, Doly Core, John Hornback, James Hornback and Abraham Hornback. Son, John to have "house bible". William and James Campbell to have note on Samuel Hopkins. Adms.: Daniel Deerduff and James Carmy. Signed: John Hornback. Witnesses: Thomas Daniel and John Kirkwood. (32)

STEWART, Charles - dated 2-1-1824; recorded 2-13-1824. Wife, Rachel. Sons: Thomas Stewart and his heirs; Abram S. Stewart and his heirs; and James Stewart. Grandchild, Charles Stewart, son of Abram S. Stewart. Mentions one acre of land on which the graveyard now is to be set apart for the express purpose of a burying ground. Other children: John Stewart, Elizabeth Pearce, Rachel Williams, Mary Foodery and Ann W. Prater, Ann now being dec'd. Executors: wife, Rachel and son, James, Signed: Charles (mark) Stewart. Witnesses: William Patrick, John Voorheess and David Voorheess. (33)

CHENEY, Edward - dated 3-16-1824; recorded 4-8-1824. Son, Samuel Cheney, also to serve as executor. Signed: Edward (mark) Cheney. Witnesses: John Myers, Benjamin Cheney and Jesse Pearce. (35)

MILLER, John - dated 5-5-1824; recorded 6-17-1824. Wife. Christena. Son, Isaac Miller, not of age. Daughter, Delilah Miller, not of age. Executors: brother, Martin Miller and John Yutsler. Signed: John (mark) Miller. Witnesses: Christopher Scrouffe, Jeremiah Huffman and Thomas D. Scroufe. (36)

GUKIDGE (GUTRIDGE), John Sr. - dated 6-22-1822; recorded 7-19-1824. Wife, Elizabeth. Children: John Gutridge. William Gutridge, Sarah Rhodes, Jane Hathaway, Catharine Loury, Jesse Gutridge, Moses Gutridge, Aaron Gutridge, Richard Gutridge, and James Gutridge. Executors: James Daniels and Solomon Vauss. Signed:John Gutridge. Witnesses: Absalom Fox, John Thomas and Henry Sibert. (37)

DILTZ, Joseph - dated 3-23-1824; recorded 7-19-1824. Wife, Mary, to have large Bible. Sons: John, Samuel, Wesley, Jarrett and Wilkinson. Daughters: Susanna Crone, Sarah, Rebecca, Elizabeth and Cynthea. Executors: wife, Mary and Abner Barrett. Signed: Joseph (mark) Dilts. Witnesses: James Daniels and Susanna Dilts. (39)

VINYARD, Stephen of Urbana township - dated 11-10-1822; recorded 9-18-1824. Wife, Elizabeth. Sons: eldest son, William; youngest son, Stephen. Daughters: Rebecca wife of James Baer, Elizabeth, Jane and Nancy. Signed: Stephen Vineyard. Witnesses: Joseph Twaddle and William Boyd (41)

COWAN, Rachel - dated 9-29-1824; recorded 12-15-1824. Sons: Miles, James, William, Thomas, John S. and David M. Cowan; William to have large Bible. Daughters: Caroline Cowan, Polly Kirkley and Margaret Frankerberger. Deborah Smith to be well paid for nursing extatrix. Executor, William Cowan. Signed: Rachel (mark) Cowan. Witnesses: John Peper, William Marrs and David Porter. (42)

PENCE, Henry - dated 4-10-1820; recorded 12-1-1824. Son-in-law, John Norman. Children: Jacob Pence; Benjamin Pence; Samuel Pence, dec'd, his heirs (not named); Henry Pence; Abraham Pence; John Pence; David Pence; Joseph Pence; Isaac Pence; Rubin Pence; Susanah Inkens; Anna Norman; Elizabeth Stoneberger; Mary Runkle; and Barbary Stewart, dec'd, her two sons--Joseph Rosenbarger and Henry Stewart. Executors: John Norman and William Runcle. Signed: Henry Pence. Witnesses: John Taylor, Peter Runcle, Adam (mark) Kite and Martin Frank. (47)

LOWRY, James - dated 11-23-1824; recorded 12-15-1824. Children: John Lowry, Sara Bowen, Nancy, James, Joseph, Elizabeth, Justice, Lucinda, Mary Ann and Catharine. Executors: son, John Lowery and Elisha D. Berry. Signed: James (mark) Lowery. Witnesses: James Daniels, James Gutridge and James Coile. (44)

ASBERRY, Rachel of Urbana - dated 1-31-1825; recorded 4-19-1825. Husband, Thomas Asberry to have all of estate. Land in town of Cohossitt, Plymouth Co., Mass. which came to testatorix from her father, Spencer Benney; lines--north by Atlantic Ocean, east by Elisha Doan and land set off to Rebecca Benny; south by widow of Theophilas Cushing and west by Widow of Lot Nichols; Land on west head of Pedon Island, Plymouth Co., Mass. being undivided with heirs of Ann Benny, dec'd and heirs of Spencer Benny. Also land called Pointattan lying in town of Hull at head of Boston Bay, Plymouth Co., Mass. with other half owned by Ann Benny. Signed: Rachel Asberry. Witnesses: Margaret Corwine and Electa Colwell. (49)

DONAVAN, Robert of Franklin County, Pennsylvania - dated 7-2-1822; recorded Franklin Co., Pa. 12-8-1823; recorded Champaign Co. 11-2-1824. Sons: John, Robert, Joseph, William and James. Daughters: Jane (Jean) wife of Robert Wilson; Martha. Owned land Champaign and Fairfield Cos., Ohio; Franklin Co., Pa.; Shippensburg and McKeesport, Pa. Executors: Thomas McClelend, James Turner Sr., William M. Turner and James E. Turner. (51)

HUDDLESTUN, William - dated 8-14-1824; recorded 3-21-1825. Wife, Rachel. Sons: Henry, William and John. Daughters: Elizabeth, Patcey, Sally, Lithe. Son-in-law, Joseph Sterris (Sterns?). Grandchild, Lysander Francis Sterns. Executors: wife, Rachel and William Huddlestun Jr. Signed: William Huddlestun. Witnesses: Jonathan Pruity and Archibald Dowden. (54)

HEYLIN, Marcus - dated 8-25-1824; recorded 5-4-1825. Wife, Jane. Son, Isaah. Executors: wife Jane and son Isaah. Other children not named. Signed: Marcus (mark) Heylin. Witnesses: Sam'l McCord, I. Slicer. (56)

GWYNNE, Thomas - dated 7-4-1825; recorded 7-15-1825. Wife, Jane. Children, mentioned but not named. Executors: wife, Jane; Eli W. Gwynne and Robert Murdock. Signed: Thomas Gwynne. Witnesses: Philip Grandin, John Armstrong and John Moorhead. (57)

TAYLOR, John - dated 8-19-1825; recorded 10-31-1825. Sons: William, Levi and Thomas; also to serve as executors. Daughters: Ruhanna, Blanch and Elizabeth; unmarried. Signed: John Taylor. Witnesses: Thomas Stewart and Cornelius M. Canegies(?). (59)

JOHNSTON, James - (not dated); recorded 10-31-1825. Wife, Caroline. Children: Nancy, Elizabeth, William, Peggy, Luisy and child wife is now pregnant with. Executor, John McAdams. Signed: James Johnston. Witnesses: Aaron L. Hunt and John McAdams. (61)

192

COMER, Philip - dated 5-15-1823; recorded 2-20-1826. Sons: David, Martin and Reuben. Daughters: Catharine, Elizabeth, Barbara and Susan. Grandson, Peter Comer. Executors: Joseph Comer and William Runkle. Signed: Peter Comer. (63)

McCUMSEY, Alexander of Urbana - dated 2-1-1826; recorded 3-20-1826. Wife, Barbara. Sons: Thomas, Matthias, Joseph, Carter, Henry and Davison McCumsey. Daughters: Mary McCumsey alias Updike and Josina White Mc Cumsey. Executors: sons, Matthias and Joseph. Signed: Alexander McCumsy. Witnesses: R. G. Swann and John Owin. (64)

CRONKLETON, Joseph of Delaware Co., Ohio - dated 11-30-1822; recorded Delaware Co. 11-22-1824; recorded Champaign Co. 6-19-1826. Wife, Mary. Sons: William, dec'd, his widow and 2 daughters (not named); Samuel; John; Joseph; and Robert; Robert is not of age. Daughters: Elizabeth Taylor, Ann and Margarette Cronkleton. Reserve for family 2 perches square on land where son, William's widow lives and where William is buried for a burying ground. Executors: son, Joseph and James Gillis. Signed: Joseph Cronkleton. Witnesses: Robert McCoy, Joseph Cunningham and Joseph Eaton. (67)

BROWN, Alexander - dated 3-20-1826; recorded 10-23-1826. Brothers: Samuel Brown, John Brown and David Brown. Five nephews: John, Andrew, Jacob, Nathan and Joseph Brown. Executor, William Darnall. Signed: Alexander (mark) Brown. Witnesses: John West, Andrew Davis and Henry Oiler. (71)

CHAMPAIGN COUNTY, OHIO - WILL ABSTRACTS 1827-1836

The following abstracts were taken from 'Will Book D" located in the Probate Court of the court house at Urbana. The page on which the record begins in the original book is given in parenthesis.

LONG, Jonathan - dated 3-10-1825; recorded 3-27-1827. Sons: James and William, also to serve as executors. Daughters: Sarah, Mary and Jane. Signed: Jonathan Long. Witnesses: Amos Parker, Edward S. Morgan. (73)

SPAIN, Hezekiah - dated 1-22-1827; recorded 8-13-1827. Wife, Martha. Sons: Thomas Spain land where he now lives containing 200 acres and the land his mill pond covers; Willis Spain tract of 144 acres where he now lives including the creek and head of the millpond. Daughters: Mary M. Spain, land where she and her husband now reside containing 106 acres; Martha Spain. Executors: sons, Thomas and Willis Spain; and friend, William Sharp son of John Sharp. Signed: Hezekiah Spain. Witnesses: Joshua Spain, Edward Spain and Daniel Spain. (75)

DOUGLASS, Elihu - dated 4-2-1828; recorded 8-18-1828. Wife, Mary, real and personal property to raise the children. Son, Preston Doughlas. Three daughters: Elizabeth, Catharine and Sarah. Mentions, David son of wife, Mary, he not being of age. Signed: Elihu (his mark) Douglass. Witnesses: Wm Sutton, Samuel Rector. (77)

COOLEY, James of Urbana - dated 7-21-1826; recorded 8-18-1828. Wife, Jennett. Father-in-law, Abraham J. Chittenden to have lands in Oxford, Butler County in trust for use of the children of said Chittenden. Sister, Eunice. Executors: friends, Sampson Mason of Clark County, John Wallace and John C. Pearson of Champaign County. Signed: James Cooley. Witnesses: Obed Hor, James Campbell, Wm Bayless. (79)

CARTER, Caleb of Goshen twp. - dated 6-17-1828; recorded 11-17-1828. Wife, Mary, also to serve as executrix. Son, Levi Carter to have large Bible. Signed: Caleb (his mark) Carter. Witnesses: Joseph Mitchel Jr., Irene Mitchell, and Eliphaz Bigelow. (81)

MEREDITH, John of Urbana - dated 12-15-1823; recorded 11-17-1828. Sister Anne Cawley. Wife, Elizabeth to have lot 104 in Urbana where now living, also to serve as executrix. Sister's daughter Hannah Sabin. Signed: John Merredeth. Witnesses: James Cooley, Jona E. Chaplin, George Hunter. (82)

JUDY, Jacob - dated 2-1-1829; recorded 4-6-1829. Wife, Dolly Judy. Two sons: Joseph Judy and David Judy. Two grandchildren, Linay and Susanna Smith. (note: no executor named). Signed: Jacob (his mark) Judy. Witnesses: Achory Berry, John Long, Elijah Berry. (84)

DAVIS, Andrew - dated 3-3-1824; recorded 8-14-1829. Sons: Andrew, John, Samuel, and William. Daughter, Ruana Davis. Each of the afore-mentioned to have a coverlet. Daughters: Peggy Brown, Betsey Brown and Rebecca Kelly. Grandson, Aaron Pence. Niece, Ruth Pence, daughter of Rebecca Kelly. Executor, William Runkel. Signed: ' Andrew (his mark) Davis. Wit: Joel Frankelberger, John Paisley. (85)

COCHRAN, Hugh - dated 7-29-1829; recorded 9-22-1829. Wife, Rebecca. Three sons; George Washington, William Harrison and Jackson Cochran. Executors: wife, Rebecca and James McClain. Signed: Hugh Cochran. Witnesses: Benj'n Cheney, Thomas Pearce, George Grubb and Asa Cooney. (89)

PAXTON, James of Marion County, Indiana; dated 4-3-1829; recorded Marion Co., Ind. 5-21-1829; recorded Champaign Co. 10-19-1829. Wife, Elizabeth Paxton to have lot in Indiana. Testator owned store, building and lot in Indianapolis at the corner of Conner and Harrison; bequeathed money to the Methodist church at Indianapolis; also owned other land in Indianapolis and Marion County. To James Paxton Lease son of F. T. Lease and to his younger brother (not named) both not of age, each to have two lots on Washington St. in Indianapolis. To Joseph Smith, not of age, 100 acres of land when he comes of age. Requests money to be set aside for tombstones on his and his wife's graves. Executors: wife, Elizabeth and friend, Calvin Fletcher. Signed: James Paxton. Witnesses: Israel P. Griffith and Chas. McDougal. (89)

DONNALLAN, Thomas - dated 4-26-1824; recorded 3-29-1830. Wife, Hester. Children: Elizabeth wife of Ambrose Blount, Ann Mariah, Thomas, Nelson, Edward, John, William, Mary and Benjamin. Executors: friends, Samuel McCord and Edmund B. Cavalier. Signed: Thomas Donnallan. Witnesses: J. Cooley and James McNutt. Codicil dated 4-26-1824 mentions money coming to other children--all except four youngest--from their grandfather (not named); same witnesses. Codicil dated 3-10-1829 mentions youngest son, Edmund born after original will and first codicil were made. Witnesses: William Glenn and Amos Andrews. (93)

LEWIS, George of King George County, Virginia - dated 3-19-1819; recorded King George Co., Va. 4-28-1827; recorded Champaign Co., Ohio 3-29-1830. Wife, Catharine. Sons: Dangerfield and Samuel. Daughter, Mary W. Willis. Mantions "western country land" and that son Dangerfield is to reside with his mother. Executors: sons, Samuel and Dangerfield. Signed: George Lewis. Witnesses: (not given). (97)

REED, Robert - dated 7-21-1829; recorded 8-30-1830. Wife, Sarah Reed. Son, Joel Reed. Daughters: Elizabeth Reed, Mary Reed, Rebecca Reed, Sarah wife of French Rambo, Rachel wife of William Werden and Achsa wife of Thomas Walker. Executors: Jacob Ware and testators two daughters, Elizabeth Reed and Mary Reed. Signed: Robert Reed. Witnesses: John Thomas and Thomas Cowgill. (98)

CROWDER, Harbert - dated 1-8-1831; recorded 4-11-1831. Wife, Martha Crowder to have plantation where now live containing 75 acres. Eight children: Mark, John, William, Mary, Elizabeth, Nathaniel, Martha and Nancy. Executors: son, William and son-in-law, Edwin Spain. Signed: Harbert Crowder. Witnesses: Thomas Spain and Jesse R. Reams. (100)

MARTIN, Job - will made Sept. 1826 and established in Chancery Court August Term 1828 in case of William Scott and Arthur Scritchfield vs. widow and Heirs of Job Martin, dec'd; recorded 4-21-1832. One third of all property to wife, Ann Martin who survived him until eldest of five children by said Ann, to-wit:--Polly Martin, Sarah Martin, Nahala Martin, Charity Martin and Eli P. Martin. Mentions that daughter, Polly is now of full age. Testator's sons by a former marriage: George Martin and John Martin. Grandson, Ezekiel Martin. Executors: William Scott and Arthur Scritchfield. Witnesses: Edward Bates and Daniel Downs. Deposition given 3-29-1828 by Edward Bates states that Polly is eleven years and that daughter Nancy was born three months after death of testator. (101)

STUBBLEFIELD, George of Frederick County, Virginia; dated 2-9-1801; recorded Frederick Co., Va. 10-7-1801; recorded Champaign County, Ohio 4-20-1832. Wife, Sally. Three children; John Jourg Stubblefield, William Tabb Stubblefield and Patsy wife of Bushrod Raylor received shares at time of testator's marriage to wife Sally. Mentions son-in-law, Thomas Hernden (or Hemden). Children: son, Beverly Wislow Stubblefield; son, Henry Stubblefield; daughter, Susannah Beverly Hernden (or Hemden). Mentions also Robert Beverly Stubblefield and Peter Stubblefield may be children, but if so testator is not specific. Daughter, Susannah Beverly Hernden (or Hemden) to have all the "plate" testator possessed as he did not get by his present wife Sally. Executors: brother, Veverly Stubblefield and friend, Richard Baylor. Signed: George Stubblefield. Witnesses: W. M. Peck, Geo. Barnett, and Tarlton T. Webb. (104)

HALL, Maryland of Salem twp. - dated 2-19-1833; recorded 4-15-1833. Wife, Elizabeth, to have farm where now reside for rest of her natural life, also to serve as sole executrix. On death of wife, Elizabeth to be divided: one-third to William Shepard and Albert Shepard; one-third, son, Henry Hall; one-third, Emma Cooksey and her heirs. Signed: Maryland Hall. Witnesses: Archibald Stewart and Charles Lewis. (107)

HILL, Nathan - dated 4-8-1833; recorded 7-22-1833. Wife, Druzilla. Son, Joseph Henry. Three daughters: Rebeckah, Adnne(?), and Mary. Executor: Joseph Henry Hill. Signed: Nathan Hill. Witnesses: Robert Kelley and William Darnal. (109)

NICHOLS, Daniel - dated 4-25-1833; recorded 7-26-1833. Wife, Elizabeth. Six children (not named). Signed: Daniel (his mark) Nichols. Witnesses: Achory Berry and John Miller. (110)

WATSON, Eunice - dated 5-20-1833; recorded 7-22-1833. Sister, Irena Martin. Daughter, Eliza Watson, not of age. Niece, Eunice Martin. Executor: Thomas Cowgell. Signed: Eunice Watson. Wit: Lymor North and Lucy North. (111)

AYRES, John - dated 3-15-1833; record3d 7-25-1833. To St Ledger Neal the farm now in his occupancy containing 52 acres. Daughters: Veturah and Clarissa. Executors: St. Ledger Neal and Richard D. George. Signed: John (his mark) Ayres. Witnesses: Richard D. George, William (his mark) Copes and Caleb Hitt. (112)

HANDBACK, Barbara wife of Lewis Handback, dec'd, of Johnston twp. - dated 9-19-1833; recorded 10-18-1833. One third to daughter, Hannah Handback. Two-thirds to son, David Handback. Signed: Barbara (her mark) Handback. Witnesses: David Berry, Lyman Graves. (114)

THOMAS, Edward - dated 12-3-1833; recorded 1-18-1834. Five children: Margaret Thomas, William R. Thomas, Osborn Thomas, Carahniis Davison and Emily Thomas. Son-in-law, Jacob C. Davison, Nephew, Orlando Williams. Mentions court suit in Augusta Co., Virginia. Executors: John Wesley Hitt, Samuel Davison and Jacob C. Davison. Signed: Edward Thomas. Witnesses: John B. Magruder, John Ordway. (115)

CRICHFIELD, Arthur - dated (not given); recorded 1-18-1834. Sons: Isaac and John. Children of son, Isaac--Arthur and John. To Rosannah Scrichfield daughter of Phebe Davis, now living with her mother, not of age. To Westley Scrichfield son of Mahala Martin now the wife of one Falkner, not of age. Specifies that land is to be purchased in the names of the three sons of his sister, Charity Davison. Executors: Georgt Pettey and William Black. Signed: Arthur Chrichfield. Witnesses: Jonah Baldwin, John Scott and Israel Hamilton. (116)

McADAMS, Samuel - dated 2-17-1832; recorded 4-9-1832. Land near Taylor's Mill to sister, Ellen Dellen. Personal Property to father, John McAdams who is to serve as sole executor. Signed: Samuel McAdams. Witnesses: Neil McNaighton, A. S. Todd, Samuel Merchant and Michael McCaily. Depositions taken in Ohio County, Virginia.(118)

BERRY, Achory - dated 12-25-1833; recorded 3-27-1834. Sons: David, Elijah and Joseph Berry. Daughters: Elizabeth Mars and Anna Smith. Signed: Achory Berry. Witnesses: Robert Jones and Abraham Huffman. (121)

HAYNES, Jonathan - dated 3-30-1833; recorded 3-27-1834. Wife, mentioned but not named. Sons: Joseph, Allen, Job and Jonathan; the last two named being two youngest sons. Daughter, Elizabeth Black. Signed: Jonathan (his mark) Haynes. Witnesses: Samuel Haynes, Peter Black Jr. (122)

EBERT, John of Jackson twp. - dated 1-16-1834; recorded 4-3-1834. Wife, Sarah. Sons: eldest son, John Ebert; Andrew Ebert; William H. Ebert; Enoch Ebert. Daughters: oldest daughter, Sarah Ebert (mentions her husband but doesn't name); second daughter, Mary Ann Ebert; youngest daughter, Elizabeth Ebert. Mentions that three youngest children are Wm H., Mary Ann and Elizabeth. Executors: sons, John Ebert and William H. Ebert. Signed; John Ebert. Witnesses: Daniel Snap and Abraham Stuck. (124)

SPAIN, Thomas - dated 6-13-1834; recorded 6-27-1834. Present wife, Sally Spain to have all farm where testator now lives on waters of Darby Creek containing 150 acres with Sawmill. Mentions all his children, some not of age, but does not name. Executors: son, Robert Spain; John Cantrill and John D. Elbert Jr. Signed: Thomas Spain. Witnesses: Joseph Everett Jr., Allen Haines and John Bishop. (126)

McLAIN, Joseph - dated 4-15-1834; recorded 8-9-1834. Wife, Betsy McLain. Children: John R., Stephen, James A., William, Sarah and Jane Polly McLain. Executors: sons, John R. and James A. McLain. Signed: Joseph McLain. Witnesses: James McLain and Richard Runyon. (128)

CLEVINGER, Joseph - dated 9-28-1834; recorded 11-24-1834. Requests to be buried beside deceased wife. Son, William Clevinger, 80 acres in Allen Co., Ohio. Daughters Anna Mariah Cashad, four youngest daughters--Kizziah, Nancy, Jane and Margaret. Executor: brother-in-law, Charles Rector. Signed: Joseph (his mark) Clevinger. Witnesses: Hugh McDonald and Sam'l Goldamith. (130)

WOOD, William of Goshen twp. - dated 11-28-1832; recorded 1-1-1835. Wife, Mary Wood. Sons: Aaron Wood, Jesse Wood, Enoch Wood, Moses Wood. Daughters: Lydia Lafferty, Maryon Underwood and Rachel Wood. Executors: James Underwood and Charles Joiner. Signed: Wm. Wood. Witnesses: William N. Ross, Joh Owen, J. H. Spain. (131)

ANDERSON, Thomas R. - dated 11-6-1834; recorded 4-14--1835. Wife, Nancy. Sons: Bartolomew Anderson, Elias Anderson and James Anderson. Two daughters: Miriam and Nancy. Executor: Samuel McCord of Urbana. Signed: Thomas R. (his mark) Anderson. Witnesses: Israel Aikins and Joseph H. Woods. (133)

WILEY, John of Springfield, Clark County, Ohio dated 1-6-1835; recorded 1-13-1835. Wife, Lucy Ann Wiley. Son, John Morison Wiley. Owned late on Connelsville, Fayette Co., Pa. Executors: brother-in-law, Albert Morison. Signed: John (his mark) Wiley. Witnesses: James S. Halsey, John Osborn. (135)

CLAYTON, John of Logan County, Ohio - dated Sept. (no day given) 1834; recorded Champaign Co. 3-23-1835. Wife, Ruhanna. Sons: George Washington, Samuel, Jonathan and Joseph. Daughter, Susannah Elizabeth. Executors: wife, Ruhanna and son, Jonathan, Signed: John Clayton. Witnesses: Shepherd Green and Joseph Earl.(136)

BALEY, Thomas M. of Accomack Co., Virginia - dated 3-9-1838; recorded Accomack Co., Va. 1-27-1834; recorded Champaign Co., Ohio 5-28-1835. Wife, Jane O. Baley, land including "Mount Custis" where now live. Children: Thomas H. Bayley, Anna Bayley, Sally Bayley, Elizabeth W. Bayley, Margaret P. Bayley and Jane O. O. Bayley. Owned 10,000 acres of land in Ohio, owned land in Illinois, also owned lots and houses in Chillicothe. Mentions "the Boy, William P. Bayley", not of age who is to be bound by son, Thomas to Mechanical or manufacturing trade in Massachusetts. Wife, Jane O. to serve as guardian of son, Thomas and five daughters. Executors: wife, Jane O. Baley and son, Thomas H. Bayley. Signed: Thomas M. Bayley. Witnesses: (not given). (138)

CRAIN, Lewis F. of Tazwell County, Illinois - dated 9-3-1834; recorded Tazwell Co., Ill. 9-27-1834; recorded Champaign Co., Ohio 6-8-1835. Wife, Clara. Children: Lucinda Jane, James Addison and Louisa Caroline Crain. Executors: William M. Roberts of Champaign Co., Ohio, William Foreman of Clark Co., Ohio, James W. Crain andAddison Shanklin of Tazwell Co. Ill. Signed: Lewis F. Crain. Witnesses: Josiah B. Smith, Charles Winn and Dan Stone. (142)

WEAVER, Christopher - dated 9-5-1835; recorded 10-7-1835. Sons: William and Henry. To children of my daughter, Polly wife of Samuel Rector. Executor; son, Henry Weaver. Wife mentioned but not named. Signed: Christopher (his mark) Weaver. Witnesses: Samuel Furman, Halron Rowlison and David Jones. (144)

PENCE, Frederick - dated 3-8-1832; recorded 1-1-1836. Wife, mentioned but not named. Son, Martin. Mentions other sons and sons-in-law, butdoes not name. Executor: son-in-law, Westley Arrowsmith. Signed: Frederick Pence. Witnesses: David Berry, Wm Fuson. (145)

SEWARD, Canfield of Surry County, Virginia - dated 5-28-1810; recorded Surry Co., Va. 2-22-1819; recorded Champaign Co., Ohio 4-18-1836. Wife, Hannah Seward, also to serve as executrix. Signed: Canfield Seward. Witness: Daniel Marks. (147)

WEAVER, Rebecca - dated 12-15-1835; recirded 4-18-1836. To John Wiley, 1/4th part of estate; to James Rouse, 1/4th part of estate; to George Becker, 1/4th part of estate; to James Montgomery, dec'd, his heirs, 1/4th part of estate. Executor, John Wiley. Signed: Rebecca (her mark) Weaver. Witnesses: Emanuel Hupp and Robert Calvin. (148)

TUCKER, Isaac - dated 6-27-1835; recorded 4-18-1836. Wife, Elizabeth Tucker. Son, John Tucker, also to serve as sole executor. Mentions "all my other children having heretofore received from me all that I could conveniently give them." Signed: Isaac (his mark) Tucker. Witnesses: (his mark) Groves and John Owen. (149)

HEWLINGS, Joseph of Harrison twp. - Verbal Will - will made 3-27-1836 two days previous to testator's death; deposition given 4-4-1836; recorded 4-18-1836. Sons: Joseph Hewlings and Abel Hewlings. Witnesses: James Fuson and John W. Brooks. (150)

Abbreviations used:- MS=Military Service; MW=Military Warrant; a/o=
assignee(s) of; S=Section; T=Township; R=Range.

BARETH, John - 10-17-1807 - 150 acres MW #506 - MS, soldier in the Va. Contl.
Line - Volume A, page 59.

GALLOWAY, James Jr. - 6-5-1813 - 50 acres MW #205 - Galloway received by de-
cree of the Franklin Co., Ohio Chancery Court as a/o David Mitchell, John
Taylor and William Gabriel, a/o Alexander Kerr, a/o David Reed, a/o Byrd Previtt, a/o Thomas Thweatt for his MS as Capt. for 3 yrs. in Va. Contl Line -
Volume C, page 34.

GOODFELLOW, Moore a/o Thomas Herd - 3-1-1815 - NE¼ S22, T6, R9 -
Volume C, page 193.

WATTS, John a/o Hezekiah Morton - 6-10-1810 - 293 acres part of MW #660 - MS
of Morton as Capt. from 8-30-1777 to 12-28-1782 in Va. Contl Line -
Volume C, page 246.

HULTZ, Joseph a/o Lewis Davis - 2-6-1813 - fractional S5&6, T6, R9 -
Volume C, page 261.

MOORE, Patrick - 6-26-1816 - NE¼ S31, T4, R14 - Volume C, page 266.

ZANE, Isaac - 8-28-1806 - S14&15, T4, R12 and S2, T4, R12 - Volume C, page 296.

MALIN, Jacob a/o Coates Thorton - 6-11-1816 - SE¼ S17, T3, R11 -
Volume C, page 450.

AERL, Isaac of Adams Co. (Ohio) - 7-30-1814 - fractional S12, T1, R8 -
Volume C, page 474.

MALLERY, Wm. a/o James Hendrick - 2-22-1811 - E½ S10, T5, R12 -
Volume D, page 64.

KESLER, Henry - 10-7-1816 - NE¼ S21, T4, R10 - Volume D, page 133.

KESLER, Barbara a/o Lewis Huffman - 10-7-1816 - NW¼ S21, T4, R10 -
Volume D, page 133.

NEWCOMB, Daniel - 8-24-1813 - SE¼ S 34, T5, R12 - Volume D, page 233.

HUFFMAN, Ambrose of Hamilton Co. (Ohio) - 5-5-1818 - NE¼ S18, T3, R11 -
Volume D, page 397.

HUFFMAN, Ambrose of Hamilton Co. (Ohio) - 2-8-1817 - NW¼ S12, T3, R11 -
Volume D, page 397.

DUNLAP, Alexander - 2-18-1817 - SW¼ S8, T4, R12 - Volume E, page 16.

HEWLINGS, Joseph of Warren Co. (Ohio) - 6-1-1807 - SW¼ S7, T4, R13 - Volume E, page 37.

CRAIG, Abraham a/o Charles Sinks - 10-1-1814 - NE¼ S4, T5, R10 - Volume E, page 73.

DAWSON, George - 7-13-1812 - 750 acres, 500 acres MW #5807, 250 acres MW #5808 - Dawson a/o Thomas McKinley only son and heir of John McKinley for John's MS as Lieut. for 3 yrs. in Va. Contl. Line - Volume E, page 258.

HARBOUR, Noah of Virginia - 12-22-1808 - NE¼ S19, T4, R12 - Volume e, page 291.

VANCE, John Wm. - 6-27-1817 - NW¼ S25, T5, R12 - Volume E, page 323.

McGREW, Archibald a/o James Lowery - 4-29-1814 - NW¼ S11, T4, R11 - Volume F, page 240.

McGREW, Archibald Sr. a/o Mathew McGrew - 7-13-1814 - NE¼ S11, T4, R11 - Volume F, page 241.

DUNLAP, Alexander - 7-27-1819 - NE¼ S8, T4, R12 - Volume F, page 493.

DOWNS, Joseph - 12-6-1823 - 100 acres MW #4619 - Downs a/o Alexander Dunlap a/o Henry Wilson for Wilson's MS as soldier 3 yrs. in Va. Contl Line - Volume F, page 496.

GOODE, John - 370 acres MW #5051 - Goode a/o John Verell, a/o Erasmas Gill a/o Peter Minor for Minor's MS as Capt. for 3 yrs. in Va. Contl. Line. Volume F, page 554.

LONG, Samuel of Penna. - 7-1-1818 - SE¼ S11, T5, R11 - Volume G, page 136.

SNIP (SCHNEPP), Solomon of Montgomery Co. (Ohio) - 6-10-1826 - E½ NE¼ S11, T3, R11 - Volume G, page 414.

SNIP (SCHNEPP), Daniel of Montgomery Co. (Ohio) - 6-10-1826 - 80 acres, W½ NE¼ S11, T3, R11 - Volume G, page 415.

SNIP (SCHNEPP), John Jr. of Montgomery Co. (Ohio) - 6-10-1826 - 80 acres W½ SW¼ S11, T3, R11 - Volume G, page 416.

SNIP (SCHNEPP), John Jr. of Montgomery Co. (Ohio) - 6-10-1826 - 80 acres E½ SW¼ S11, T3, R11 - Volume G, page 417

VANCE, David - 12-9-1822 - 160 acres NW¼ S35, T6, R10 - Volume G, page 46.

KING, David a/o Samuel McCord - 7-19-1834 - 80 acres W½ NW¼ S18, T3, R11 - Volume H, page 78.

KING, David a/o Samuel McCord - 7-19-1824 - 75 acres pt. NW¼ S32, T3, R12 - Volume H, page 79.

MAUZY, Joseph a/o John Long - 3-10-1820 - 160 acres NE¼ S21, T3, R12, - Volume H, page 141.

ADAMSON, Heirs of Elisha, dec'd - 3-18-1814 - SE¼ S32, T5, R11 - Volume H, page 399.

BOYLE, Hugh - 4-19-1825 - tract of 675 acrew on MW #997, 1481, 2941, 3228, 2974 and part of #3997 - Boyle a/o Robert Howard, Shadrack Pinkstone, John Evans, Lodowick Miller and George Ryan each a soldier for 3 yrs. and David Pew a soldier for the war in Va. Contl Line - Volume H, page 495.

MILLER, Jacob of Montgomery Co. (Ohio) - 6-10-1826 - 78 acres E½ SW¼ S12, T3, R11 - Volume I, page 567.

MILLER, Jacob of Montgomery Co. (Ohio) - 6-30-1826 -78 acres W½ SE¼ S12, T3, R11 - Volume I, page 568.

WARD, Abijah a/o John Smith - 7-20-1812 - SW¼ S31, T6, R11 - Volume J, page 2.

WARD, Abijah a/o John Smith - 7-20-1812 - SE¼ S31, T6, R11 - Volume J, page 3.

HAMILTON, John of Scioto Co. (Ohio) - 2-24-1820 - 160 acres SW¼ S19, T4, R11 - Volume J, page 217.

WALLACE, Cadwallader - 10-13-1819 - 150 acres MW 111 - Wallace a/o Cicely A. Waller wife of Absalom Waller formerly Cicely A. Shelton, William A. Shelton, Nelson F. Shelton, Mary C. Anderson wife of Robert Anderson formerly Maria C. Shelton children and heirs of Clough Shelton, dec'd, for Shelton's MS. as Capt. for 3 yrs. in Va. Contl Line - Volume J, page 226.

HUFFMAN, David - 2-21-1821 - SW¼ S18, T3, R11 - Volume J, page 238.

HUFFMAN, David - 8-5-1817 - SW¼ S18, T3, R11 - Volume J, page 238.

HUFFMAN, David - 4-1-1825 - 154 acres NW¼ S24, T3, R11 - Volume J, page 238.

JENKINS, Jesse - 11-1-1830 - 79 acres E½ NE¼ S4, T3, R11 - Volume J, page 299.

PENCE, William - 11-1-1830 - 80 acres E½ NW¼ S32, T4, R12 - Volume J,page 344

WEEKS, John of Warren Co. (Ohio) - 9-2-1830 - 81 acres E½ NE¼ S19, T(not given), R11 - Volume J, page 265.

CAMPBELL, John – 3-12-1837 – NE$\frac{1}{4}$ S17, T3, R11, 81 acres – Volume J, page 271.

DUNN, Walter – 3-15-1819 – 120 acres MW #708 – Dunn a/o Anthony Walke a/o James Gammell, Anne Bully and Nathan Gammell only heirs of Nathan Gammell, dec'd for his MS as Sgt. for 3 yrs. in Va. Contl Line – Volume K, page 85.

STEPHENSON, Hamilton a/o John Harbert – 8-7-1817 – SE$\frac{1}{4}$ S3, T5, R11 – Volume K, page 379.

SCHNEPP, Daniel – 8-9-1831 – 81 acres W$\frac{1}{2}$ NW$\frac{1}{4}$ S5, T3, R11 – Volume K, page 396.

DUER, Joh of Miami Co. (Ohio) – 7-2-1831 – E$\frac{1}{2}$ SW$\frac{1}{4}$ S28, T3, R12 – Volume k, page 454.

TAYLOR, John a/o Philip Miller – 12-2-1830 – NE$\frac{1}{4}$ S19, T4, R13 – Volume K, page 477.

DONAVAN, Robert of Penna. – 9-23-1812 – SE$\frac{1}{4}$ S29, T4, R11 – Volume K, page 584.

PINE, Jacob – 7-10-1832 – E$\frac{1}{2}$ SW$\frac{1}{4}$ S21, T4, R13 – Volume L, page 19.

WARD, Richard – 5-5-1818 – NW$\frac{1}{4}$ S32, T6, R11 – Volume L, page 576.

PRINCE, Martin – 12-1-1831 – 157 acres SW$\frac{1}{4}$ S27, T3, R12 – Volume L, page 605.

DENNY, James – 12-16-1813 – 180 acres; 80 acres part MW #732, 50 acres part of MW #660 – Denny a/o Thomas Hewett and Thomas Parker, for their MS as Capts. for 3 yrs. and Hezekiah Morton for MS as Capt. from 30 Aug. 1777 to 28 Dec. 1782 in Va. Contl Line – Volume L, page 615.

HALL, Daniel S. – 7-1-1833 – Survey 568, 100 acres MW #5008 – Hall a/o Edward Stokes for his MS as soldier 3 yrs. in Va. Contl Line – Volume M, page 21.

"Minute Book 1-3-4-5-" is found in the Common Pleas Court (Clerk of Court's Office) at the court house in Urbana. This book contains four separate volumes, each numbered individually, which have been bound into one book. When they were bound they were not all numbered in the correct chronological order. They are as follows: Minute Book 1 covers Sept. 1805 to 1809. Minute Book 3 covers Jan. 1816 to Feb. 1817. Minute Book 4 covers Apr. 1817 to Sept. 1817. Minute Book 5 covers Sept. 1814 to Nov. 1815. However, for the purpose of this record we will give them in the correct chronological order and will at the beginning of each book, give its number. Page on which record may be found in the original book is given in parenthesis. It should be mentioned that while Minute Book 2 was not found in this book it does exist as a separate individual book.

MINITE BOOK 1

Sept. 1805 - James McPHERSON granted license to vend merchandise. (5)

Jan. 1806 - Fabien EAGLE granted license to vend mercha dize. (6)

Jan. 1806 - Elizabeth Lowry and Joseph Tatman appointed adms. of the estate of Thomas LOWRY, dec'd. (6)

May 1806 - This term of court held at Springfield. (9)

May 1806 - Benjamin SIMONTON granted permit to keep house of entertainment. (15)

May 1806 - Griffith FOOS granted permit to keep house of entertainment. (15)

9-2-1806 - This term of court held at Urbana. (15)

9-2-1807 - John THOMSON, Esq. admitted to practice as an attorney at law in said county. (15)

9-2-1807 - Samuel SIMONTON granted license to vend merchandize and also a license to keep a house of entertainment. (15)

1-6-1807 - George FITHIAN granted license to keep tavern. (22)

1-6-1807 - Francis LAYCROX granted license to vend merchandize as a traveling merchant. (22)

1-6-1807 - John Jackson appointed adms. of the estate of Peter McCANNY, dec'd. (28)

9-8-1807 - Samuel SIMONTON granted license to keep store and tavern. (36)

9-8-1807 - Robert Renick and Daniel McKinnon, Esq. appointed adms. of the estate of Archibald LOWRY, dec'd, the executor of said Lowry now being dec'd. (36)

9-8-1807 - D. Lowry and Benjamin Simonton appointed adms. of the estate of Elizabeth LOWRY, dec'd. (36)

9-8-1807 - Mary LEMMON aged 16yrs. chose John Reynolds as her guardian. (36)

9-8-1807 - Robert Renick appointed adms. of the estate of Andrew HODGE, dec'd. (37)

9-8-1807 - Elijah Standerford appointed adms. of the estate of Wilden ROWZE, dec'd. (37)

9-8-1807 - Abigail ROUZE (note: no age given) chose Rebeckah Rouze as her guardian. (37)

9-8-1807 - Wm McDannel, Ezekiel Thomas, Thomas M. Pendelton and Thomas Moore appointed appraisors of the estate of William McDONNEL, dec'd. (37)

1-5-1808 - Mary OWENS appointed adms. of the estate of John OWENS, dec'd. (44)

1-5-1808 - John PERRIN granted license to keep store. (44)

5-10-1808 - Thomas DONAVEN granted license to keep public house in Urbana. (58)

5-5-1807 - Richard STANUP and Gracy STANUP wife of said Richard, persons of colour have made application as directed by law for their names being recorded in the clerk's office, dated at Urbana. (un-numbered page following page 67)

Jan. 1809 - John REYNOLDS granted license to vend merchandize. (un-numbered page following page 67)

9-19-1814 - Andrew BLACK appointed adms. of the estate of Samuel BLACK, dec'd. (1)

9-19-1814 - Caleb BALLINGER aged 19 yrs., Thomas BALLINGER aged 16 yrs. and Sarah BALLINGER aged 15 yrs. chose Sarah Ballinger as their guardian. (2)

9-19-1814 - Richard D. George appointed adms. of the estate of William GEORGE, dec'd. (2)

9-19-1814 - George Kitt and William Moody appointed adms. of the estate of Peter KITT, dec'd. (3)

9-19-1814 - Joseph Butcher appointed adms. of the estate of David BUTCHER, dec'd.(3)

9-19-1814 - Isaac Evans appointed adms. of the estate of Alice EVANS, dec'd. (4)

9-20-1814 - James Elliot appointed adms. of the estate of James STEELE, dec'd. (7)

9-20-1814 - Joseph MITCHEL a minister of the Methodist Episcopal church granted license to solemnize marriages. (7)

9-20-1814 - Jeremiah Symmes appointed adms. of the estate of Zebulan BARD, dec'd. (8)

9-20-1814 - John Pence appointed adms. of the estate of Henry VENUS, dec'd. (8)

9-20-1814 - Unis Rees and Thadius Tuttle appointed adms. of the estate of Moses REES, dec'd. (8)

9-20-1814 - Job Sheck appointed adms. of the estate of Arthur McWADE, dec'd. Widow (not named) relinquishes right to adms. (9)

9-20-1814 - Notice is given to Jerusha GILMORE that if she does not take out letters of adms. on the estate of her dec'd husband at the next court, court will appoint an adms. (9)

9-21-1814 - John Reynolds appointed guardian of James EVANS aged 10 yrs. and Nancy EVANS aged 7 yrs. (14)

9-21-1814 - James BIRDWHISTLE granted license to keep tavern in Urbana. (15)

9-21-1814 - Elijah BEARDSLEY granted license to keep tavern in Urbana. (18)

9-29-1814 - George Fithian appointed adms. of the estate of Alexander WOODS, dec'd. Widow (not named) relinquishes right to adms. (22)

9-29-1814 - Court appointed John McAdams and Matthew Stewart to collect and secure estate of Jane PHILLIPS late Jane RIDDLE, dec'd until letters of adms. can be granted. (23)

11-11-1814 - Barbary Arbagast and George Arbagast appointed adms. of the estate of Michael ARBACAST, dec'd. (24)

11-11-1814 - Sarah Valentine and John Lafferty appointed adms. of the estate of David VALENTINE, dec'd. (24)

11-11-1814 - John Wiley appointed adms. of the estate of Samuel LOGAN, dec'd. Widow (not named) relinquishes right to adms. (25)

12-5-1814 - Joseph Hedges and William Miller appointed adms. of the estate of Samuel McCULLOCH, dec'd. (26)

12-5-1814 - Elisha Harbour appointed adms. of the estate of Joel HARBOUR, dec'd.(26)

12-15-1814 - Abel Crawford appointed adms. of the estate of Adin HOWELL, dec'd. Widow (not named) relinquishes right to adms. (27)

1-16-1815 - Acashe McWade appointed guardian of Joshua McWADE aged 7 yrs., Job McWADE aged 5 yrs. and Samuel McWADE aged 3 yrs. (29)

1-16-1815 - Hezekiah Wilcox appointed adms. of the estate of William GILMORE, dec'd. (31)

1-16-1815 - Otho Johnston and Adam (or Abram) L. Hunt appointed adms. of the estate of Barney JOHNSTON, dec'd. (31)

1-16-1815 - Benjamin Chaney appointed adms. of the estate of William MARTIN, dec'd. (31)

1-16-1815 - Ann N. Bell appointed guardian of John F. BELL (no age given) a minor. (31)

1-16-1815 - Ann Paul and Daniel Baker appointed adms. of the estate of William PAUL, dec'd. (31)

1-16-1815 - John Hall appointed guardian of German HALL aged 6 yrs. (31)

1-16-1815 - George Lowman appointed adms. of estate of Joseph LOWMAN, dec'd. (32)

1-16-1815 - William M. Reyburn appointed adms. of estate of James REYBURN dec'd. (32)

1-17-1815 - John REYNOLDS granted store license to vend merchandize in Urbana. (33)

1-17-1815 - James Gates appointed adms. of the estate of Henry HAINES, dec'd. (33)

1-17-1815 - Sarah Johnston appointed admsx. of the estate of Alexander JOHNSTON, dec'd. (35)

1-17-1815 - Pierson SPINING granted store license to vend merchandize in Springfield. (37)

1-17-1815 - Ann Herd appointed admsx. of the estate of Stephen HERD, dec'd. (37)

1-17-1815 - James HUGHS a minister of the Presbyterian church granted license to solemnize marriages. (37)

1-18-1815 - William McKinnon appointed adms. of the estate of Thomas PLUMMER, dec'd. (38)

1-19-1815 - Richard Bacon appointed guardian of Howard HOPKINS aged 16 yrs. (46)

1-19-1815 - Samuel Hitt appointed guardian of Benjamin J. BALL aged 17 yrs. (46)

1-19-1815 - Alexander Dake appointed guardian of John LAW (LAER or LAEO?) aged 16 yrs. (46)

1-19-1815 - Ezekiel Rice appointed adms. of the estate of Ezekiel RICE, dec'd with the will annexed.

1-20-1815 - John THOMAS granted license to vend merchandize in Urbana. (48)

1-20-1815 - Nathaniel -?- (note: surname not given) appointed adms. of the estate of Elizabeth LAYBURN, dec'd. (58)

2-4-1815 - Thomas DOYLE aged 16 yrs. chose John McCul as his guardian. (60)

2-4-1815 - Thomas MOORE aged 19 yrs. chose Robert Moore as his guardian. William MOORE aged 17 yrs. chose David Askew as his guardian. (60)

2-4-1815 - Robert Moore and John Moore appointed adms. of the estate of William MOORE, dec'd. Widow (not named) relinquished right to adms. (60)

2-4-1815 - Mary Lemon and Joseph Lemon appointed adms. of the estate of William LEMON, dec'd. (61)

2-4-1815 - John McCullock appointed guardian of Sophia BAYEE aged 11 yrs. (61)

5-11-1815 - Polley BRAYDEN aged 15 yrs. chose William McBeth as her guardian. (66)

5-15-1815 - James PAUL aged 17 yrs. chose John Lafferty as his guardian. (69)

5-15-1815 - Anne PAUL aged 13 yrs. and Sarah PAUL aged 18 yrs. chose Joseph McLean as their guardian. (72)

5-15-1815 - Thomas Newell and Benjamin Schooler appointed adms. of the estate of William NEWELL, dec'd. (72)

5-15-1815 - Dan'l Kiblinger appointed adms. of the estate of Jacob KIBLINGER, dec'd. (72)

5-15-1815 - James McIlroy appointed adms. of the estate of Thomas MURPHEY, dec'd. (72)

5-15-1815 - Sidney Hedges appointed adms. of the estate of Robert HEDGES, dec'd. Widow (not named relinquishes right to adms.) (73)

5-16-1815 - William M. REYBURN granted license to vend merchandize in Bethel twp.(76)

5-16-1815 - Samuel POAGE granted license to vend merchandize in Jefferson twp. (78)
5-16-1815 - Benjamin DOOLITTLE granted store license in Urbana. (80)
5-16-1815 - James TAMPLIN granted tavern license in Springfield. (80)
5-16-1815 - Joseph VANCE granted store license in Urbana. (80)
5-16-1815 - Calvin H. CAVIN granted store license in Urbana. (80)
5-16-1815 - Hezekiah STOUT granted tavern license in Boston. (80)
5-17-1815 - Lewis Rigdon appointed adms. of the estate of John RIGDON, dec'd. (85)
5-17-1815 - Henry Pence appointed guardian of Lucy MAGERT aged 11 yrs. and Benjamin
    MAGERT aged 11 yrs. (86)
5-17-1815 - William Malin appointed adms. of the estate of Joshua MALEN, dec'd. (86)
5-17-1815 - Jonathan Milhollin and John Ambler appointed guardians of Eliza Cather-
    ine HAMILTON aged 6 yrs. on 12th this inst., Ruthy Eleanor HAMILTON aged 5 yrs.
    on 1st Dec. next, Amanda Jane HAMILTON aged 3 yrs. on 5th Oct. next, and Sarah
    Ann HAMILTON aged 2 yrs. on 20th Oct. next. (75)
5-18-1815 - Alexander DAKE granted tavern license in Urbana. (88)
5-18-1815 - Maddox FISHER granted tavern license in Springfield. (88)
5-18-1815 - Samuel Gibbs appointed guardian of Thomas FITCH aged 12 yrs. (89)
5-18-1815 - James RIDDLE aged 14 yrs. chose John McAdam as his guardian. (89)
5-19-1815 - Polly MAGERT aged 14 yrs. chose Henry Pence as her guardian. (92)
5-19-1815 - Walter MUNSAN granted store license in Springfield. (92)
5-30-1815 - Elizabeth Rigdon appointed admx. of the estate of John RIGDON, dec'd.(110)
5-31-1815 - William WILLIAMS aged 17 yrs. chose Robert Smith as his guardian. (111)
5-31-1815 - Samuel PAGE (POAGE?) granted store license in Urbana. (111)
9-18-1815 - Andrew G. DUGBEE granted store license in his tavern at Springfield.(115)
9-18-1815 - Abraham R. CALDWELL granted license to vend merchandize. (117)
9-18-1815 - E. & E. W. GUYNNE granted license to vend merchandize in Urbana. (117)
9-18-1815 - John Reed and Edward Armstrong appointed guardians of George Chambers
    LAMME and Betsey Chambers LAMME, minors (note: no age given). (118)
9-18-1815 - Eliza GULLENLIN aged 15 yrs. chose Robert Rendick as her guardian. (118)
9-19-1815 - Catharine Taylor appointed admsx. of the estate of Peter TAYLOR, dec'd.
    (120)
9-19-1815 - Thomas MOORE aged 20 yrs. and Sam'l MOORE aged 18 yrs. chose William
    Moore as their guardian. (121)
9-19-1815 - Rachel Kirkpatrick and Benjamin Kirkpatrick appointed adms. of the
    estate of Hugh KIRKPATRICK, dec'd. (122)
9-19-1815 - Othia Johnston appointed adms. of the estate of Elizabeth JOHNSTON,
    dec'd. (122)
9-19-1815 - Ruth Campbell and Alexander McBeth appointed adms. of the estate of
    John CAMPBELL, dec'd. (123)
9-19-1815 - James JOHNSTON an alien took oath agreeable to law of his intention
    to become citizen of the United States. (127)
9-20-1815 - James McILREY granted tavern license in Springfield. (131)
9-20-1815 - Sarah MOORE aged 15 yrs. chose William Moore as her guardian. (132)
9-20-1815 - John W. VANCE aged 17 yrs. chose James Johnston as his guardian. (132)
9-20-1815 - Elijah BEARDSLEY granted tavern license in Urbana. (132)
9-20-1815 - James JOHNSTON a minister of the Baptist church granted license to
    solemnize marriages. (132)
9-20-1815 - Reuben Wallace appointed guardian of Elizabeth DANIELS, Rachel DANIELS,
    John DANIELS, Lucinda DANIELS and Jonathan DANIELS, all minors (note: no ages
    given. (134,135)

9-20-1815 - James MONTGOMERY a minister of the Methodist Episcopal church granted license to solemnize marriages. (135)

9-20-1815 - John FITCH granted tavern license in Urbana. (135)

9-21-1815 - Andrew Richard appointed adms. of the estate of Jonathan ROSS, dec'd.(141)

9-21-1815 - John GILSON aged 18 yrs. chose John Lamme as his guardian. Betsey GILSON aged 15 yrs. also chose John Lamme as her guardian. (142)

9-22-1815 - Edwin MATTHEWS granted store license in Urbana. (156)

9-22-1815 - Daniel DAVIDSON a minister of the Methodist Episcopal church granted license to solemnize marriages. (162)

9-22-1815 - Joseph Layton appointed guardian of Arthur LAYTON, Carmen LAYTON, Joseph LAYTON and Lavina LAYTON, all minors (note: no ages given). (162,163)

11-1-1815 - James Rhea and Joseph Reed appointed adms. of the estate of Joseph LAMME, dec'd. (166)

11-11-1815 - Abraham Shepherd and William Bay appointed adms. of the estate of Henry BLUE, dec'd. (167)

11-11-1815 - James Hual appointed adms. of the estate of Elizabeth DAVISSON, dec'd. (167)

11-11-1815 - David Hanah appointed adms. of the estate of Elizabeth VANCE, dec'd. (167)

11-11-1815 - Olive Munsan and Thado Norton appointed adms. of the estate of Walter MUNSAN, dec'd. (168)

11-11-1815 - Samuel Wright appointed guardian of James DAVIDSON aged 5 yrs. and Hugh DAVIDSON aged 3 yrs. (168)

MINUTE BOOK 3

1-15-1816 - Alexander BEATY aged 17 yrs. chose Mary Beety as his guardian. (1)

1-15-1816 - John CANTRALL aged 15 yrs. chose Richard D. George as his guardian. (2)

1-15-1816 - A. & O. SIMPSON granted license to vend merchandize in town of Springfield. (2)

1-15-1816 - John REYNOLDS granted license to vend merchandize in Urbana. (2)

1-15-1816 - James McOLRAY appointed adms. of the estate of Joseph MURPHEY, dec'd.(2)

1-15-1816 - Reuben RICE aged 16 yrs. chose David Hanna as his guardian. Russel RICE aged 14 yrs. also chose David Hanna as his guardian. (3)

1-15-1816 - Henry Smith appointed adms. of the estate of James SMITH, dec'd. Widow (not named) relinquishes right to adms. (3)

1-15-1816 - Reuben Wallace appointed adms. of the estate of John JOHN, dec'd. Widow (not named) relinquishes right to adms. (3)

1-15-1816 - Will of James LAWRENCE produced and proven in court. (3)

1-16-1816 - Hannah SWING aged 19 yrs. chose Alexander Dake as her guardian. (5)

1-16-1816 - Elijah BEADRLEY granted tavern license in Springfield. (7)

1-16-1816 - Joseph CARTMILL granted tavern license in Urbana. (7)

1-16-1816 - Pierson SPINING granted store license in Springfield. (7)

1-16-1816 - COREGTIE(?) & Co. granted store license in Springfield. (7)

1-17-1816 - WORKMAN and NEWELL granted store license in Jefferson twp. (8)

1-17-1816 - James ROBINSON granted tavern license in Urbana. (8)

1-17-1816 - William WILSON aged 16 yrs. chose George Petty as his guardian. (8)

1-18-1816 - Mary Brothers appointed admsx of the estate of Francis BRETHERS, dec'd. (15)

1-18-1816 - Hugh GIBBET granted store license in Urbana. (26)

1-18-1816 - PERRIN and GIBBS granted store license in Springfield. (26)

1-18-1816 - Enos THONS granted store license in Urbana. (26)

1-19-1816 - Thado Norton and Olive Munsan appointed adms. of the estate of Walter MUNSAN, dec'd. (30)

1-19-1816 - On application of Josiah Baldwin guardian of John Clinton BOARDMAN one of the heirs of John BOARDMAN, dec'd that Elijah Hornet and Rachel Boardman the adms. are to show cause why estate has not been settled. (30)

1-19-1816 - Warret OWEN granted store license in Mechanicsburg. (32)

1-20-1816 - On application of Reuben Wallace guardian of Palina HODGE and Andrew HODGE heirs of Andrew HODGE, dec'd, that Robert Renick and John Snodgrass the adms. show cause why estate has not been settled. (43)

3-6-1816 - Deposition to be taken from Margaret JOHNSTON wife of Gavin JOHNSTON late Margaret RAUGH one of the witnesses to a will, said deposition to be taken in Ross County. (52)

3-6-1816 - Zephemiah Plat and Jesse Demint appointed adms. of the estate of James DEMINT, dec'd. (52)

4-9-1816 - John HUNT granted license to keep tavern in Springfield. (62)

4-9-1816 - James MORTEN granted license to keep tavern in Springfield. (66)

4-9-1816 - Mary Bennet and Israel Carter appointed adms. of the estate of Reynolds BENNET, dec'd. (66)

4-12-1816 - Sarah Cumings appointed guardian of Elmira CUMMINGS and Thomas CUMINGS, both minors under 12 yrs., heirs of Joseph CUMINGS, dec'd. (84)

4-12-1816 - Thomas Pearce appointed guardian of William Francis GEORGE aged 1 yr., heir of William GEORGE, dec'd. (84)

4-12-1816 - Ira Smith appointed guardian of Ira S. JOHN, James JOHN and Catharine JOHN, minors under 12 yrs., heirs of John JOHN, dec'd. (84)

4-13-1816 - Hezekiah STOUT granted license to keep tavern in New Boston. (87)

4-13-1816 - John HARRISON a minor (no age given) chose Charles Harrison as his guardian. (88)

4-13-1816 - James WILLIAMS aged 18 yrs. chose William Millan as his guardian. (88)

4-15-1816 - Andrew PORTER aged 18 yrs. chose Richard S. Collins as his guardian. (89)

4-15-1816 - William WILSON aged 17 yrs. chose Richard S. Collins as his guardian. (89)

4-16-1816 - Enos THOMAS granted license to vend merchandize in Harmony twp. (91)

4-16-1816 - VANCE and NEEL granted license to vend merchandize in Urbana. (91)

4-17-1816 - John Pence appointed guardian of Debitha PENCE aged 6 yrs., David PENCE aged 5 yrs. and John PENCE aged 2 yrs., heirs of Samuel PENCE, dec'd. (92)

4-17-1816 - Deposition of Lewis Rigdon adms. of the estate of John RIGDON states that John RIGDON in his lifetime ebtered SW¼ Section 19, Township 5, Range 11 in Champaign County and paid only first installment and now no funds are available in the estate to complete payment. (92)

4-17-1816 - Settlement of the estate of William PARKISON, dec'd by Samuel Wilcox, adms. (92)

4-17-1816 - Lewis a man of colour produced in court a certificate of his emancipation which was ordered recorded as follows: Shelby County, Kentucky. To whom it may concern that at the court held in said county March 15, 1813 John Hite and William Adams emancipated and set free certain slaves including Lewis, dated the 15th day of March, 1813. (102)

4-17-1816 - Robert MILLER a minister of the Methodist Episcopal church granted license to solemize marriages. (102)

5-29-1816 - Mahala Lewis and George McPheoin appointed adms. of the estate of Benjamin LEWIS, dec'd. (106)

5-29-1816 - Raxlani Gifford appointed admsx. of the estate of Richard GIFFORD, dec'd. (109)

8-5-1816 - John NEWELL and Co. granted store license. (112)

8-5-1816 - Rebecca Hill appointed admsx. of the estate of William R. HILL, dec'd. (112)

8-5-1816 - Edmund Marmon appointed adms. of the estate of John TAYLOR, dec'd. (112)

8-5-1816 - Mary Moore and Samuel Moore appointed adms. of the estate of Robert MOORE, dec'd. (114)

8-5-1816 - Abner Cox Sr. appointed adms. of the estate of Abner COX, dec'd. (114)

8-6-1816 - Marcus HEYLIN and Co. granted store license to vend merchandize in Urbana. (118)

8-6-1816 - Sally Plummer appointed guardian of Mason PLUMMER, Hiram PLUMMER, Lucinda PLUMMER, Tilman PLUMMER, Thomas PLUMMER and James PLUMMER, all minors (no ages given). (119)

8-6-1816 - James McILROY granted license to keep tavern in Springfield. (119)

8-6-1816 - John R. Lemon appointed guardian of Orrange Vandiver LEMON, Simon Kenton LEMON and Jane LEMON, all minors (no ages given). (120)

8-6-1816 - Obadiah Beal appointed guardian of Elmira CUMMINS and Unis CUMMINS both minors. Samuel Porter appointed guardian of James CUMMINS, a minor. (note: no ages given). (120)

8-6-1816 - Michael TUCKER aged 15 yrs. chose James Davis as his guardian. (120)

8-7-1816 - William M. REYBURN granted store license to vend merchandize in Bethel twp. (136)

8-8-1816 - George McPherrin appointed guardian of Betsey LEWIS, John LEWIS and Samuel LEWIS minors all under 12 yrs., heirs of Benjamin LEWIS, dec'd. Mahala Lewis appointed guardian of Phebe LEWIS a minor (no age given), heir of said Benjamin LEWIS, dec'd. (141)

8-14-1816 - John KELLY granted store license to vend merchandize in Mechanicsburg. (159)

8-14-1816 - James TAMPLIN granted tavern license in Springfield. (161)

8-14-1816 - Lettice BUTCHER late Lettice MORRISON surviving adms. of the estate of Peter GILSON, dec'd filed settlement. (161)

9-25-1816 - Ann Walter and Eleazor Hunt appointed adms. of the estate of William WALTER, dec'd. (177)

12-9-1816 - Robert RUSSEL license to vend merchandize in Springfield. (189)

12-9-1816 - ROSS and COLEMAN license to vend merchandize in Springfield. (189)

12-10-1816 - Henry McPHERSON and Daniel WORKMAN license to vend merchandize at the house of James McPHERSON. (191)

12-10-1816 - W. & E. W. GUYNNE and Co. license to vend merchandize in Urbana. (191)

12-10-1816 - CAMPBELL, RHODS and Co. license to vend merchandize in Urbana. (191)

12-10-1816 - Robert RENICK license to vend merchandize in Springfield. (191)

12-10-1816 - Joseph ROSENBERGER a minor (no age given chose John Pence as his guardian. (192)

12-10-1816 - Zepheniah B. TENNERY a minor (no age given) chose Henry Bacon as his guardian. (193)

12-10-1816 - David Jones appointed adms. of the estate of Peter BRUNER, dec'd.(194)

12-10-1816 - John McCalley appointed adms. of the estate of Adam ASH, dec'd. (194)

12-12-1816 - David Andrews appointed guardian of Joseph, Abner, Moses, John, George, Adelene, Sarah and David LAMB, minors (no ages given), heirs of Joseph LAMB, late of this county, dec'd. (208)

12-13-1816 - Joseph C. Neel appointed guardian of William BALDWIN Jr. a minor (no age given), heir of William BALDWIN, dec'd late of this county. (220)

12-13-1816 - Samuel Cary appointed adms. of the estate of Abraham CARY, dec'd.(225)

12-14-1816 - John FITCH granted tavern license in Urbana. (237)

12-14-1816 - James ROBENSON granted tavern license in Urbana. (237)

12-17-1816 - John Garwood adms. of the estate of Joshua BALLINGER, dec'd filed settlement. (241)

12-18-1816 - John Hollow adms. of the estate of Squire Herringdon, dec'd filed settlement. (242)

12-18-1816 - John REYNOLDS and Co. granted license to vend merchandize in Urbana.(244)

12-18-1816 - Rosswell Miner and Maryan Miner appointed adms. of the estate of John LOWE, dec'd. (247)

12-18-1816 - Moses Miller and Jonathan D. Miller adms. of the estate of Caleb BOYLSTON, dec'd filed settlement. (248)

12-19-1816 - Sampson Tolbert and Joseph Hill adms. of the estate of Nathan FITCH, dec'd filed settlement. (249)

2-25-1817 - Barton Minturn and George Minturn appointed adms. of the estate of Jacob MINTURN, dec'd. (262)

MINUTE BOOK 4

4-7-1817 - Phebe BOYLSTON aged 16 yrs. on June last, heir of Caleb BOYLSTON, dec'd chose Daniel Miller as her guardian. Susan BOYLSTON aged 11 yrs. on May last, daughter of Caleb BOYLSTON, dec'd chose Daniel Miller as her guardian. (3)

4-8-1817 - Rosetta JONES aged 3 yrs., daughter of Edward JONES, dec'd with court appointing Esther Jones as her guardian. (9)

4-8-1817 - John Heaton appointed adms. of the estate of Jesse GILLAND, dec'd. Widow (not named) relinquishes right to adms. estate. (15)

4-9-1817 - Benjamin Downs appointed adms. of the estate of Benjamin DOWNS, dec'd. Widow (not named) relinquishes right to adms. (16)

4-9-1817 - Daniel HOPKINS aged 16 yrs. chose Thomas Thompson as his guardian. (16)

4-9-1817 - William Lamme appointed adms. of the estate of Andrew HODGE, dec'd. (17)

4-11-1817 - Thomas Thompson appointed adms. of the estate of Simeon BLACKMAN. dec'd. (38)

4-15-1817 - Thomas FITCH aged 13 yrs., heir of Nathan FITCH, dec'd chose Sampson Tolbert as his guardian. (55)

4-16-1817 - Mary MOORE widow of Curtis MOORE, dec'd petition to have dower set off. (60)

4-17-1817 - Christopher FRANCE a minister of the Baptist church granted license to solemnize marriages. (67)

4-17-1817 - Jacob Baker appointed adms. of the estate of Valentine HUMFILL, dec'd.(67)

7-28-1817 - Daniel Garwood appointed guardian of Joseph GREEN aged 11 yrs. and 9 mos. and Abigail GREEN aged 8 yrs. and 6 mos., children of John GREEN a lunatic, agreeable to the overseers of the poor of Zane twp. (71)

7-28-1817 - Isreal Howel appointed guardian of George WILKISON aged 15 yrs. and Nancy WILKISON aged 12 yrs. Christopher Pipher and wife appointed guardian of John WILKISON aged 6 yrs. and Ibby WILKISON aged 4 yrs. All being minor heirs of Thomas WILKISON, dec'd. (72)

7-29-1817 - David Hanna appointed adms. of the estate of Abednego DAVISON, dec'd. Widow (not named) relinquishes right to adms. (78)

7-29-1817 - Christopher SHROFE and Sebastrian SHROPE granted license to retail merchandize. (78)

8-8-1817 - Daniel McKinnon adms. of the estate of Archibald Lowry, dec'd filed settlement. (124)

8-8-1817 - Sara CUMMINS widow of Joseph CUMMINS, dec'd petitions for dower. (124)

8-8-1817 - George Caraway adms. of the estate of John VINEY, dec'd filed settlement. (125)

9-30-1817 - Elizabeth Lewis and Edward L. Morgan appointed adms. of the estate of William LEWIS, dec'd. (142)

CLARK COUNTY, OHIO - Will Abstracts 1819-1824

The following abstracts were taken from Will Book A-1. Pages are given in parenthesis following each will. Wills do not begin until numbered page 15.

MARK, William of Madison Co., Ohio - dated 10-16-1815; recorded 1-19-1819 - Wife:- Sarah - Three youngest sons:- Joseph, Elijah and David - Youngest daughter:- Polly, wife of John Moler - Esecutor:- Son, James Mark - Signed:- William (mark) Mark - Witnesses:- R. Powers and Levi Shinn. (15)
KIZER, Philip of Champaign Co., Ohio - dated 3-2-1818; recorded 1-19-1819 - Wife:- Mentioned but not named in will, in recording of will named as Elizabeth Kizer - Sons:- Michael, William, George and John - Daughters:- Sarah, Elizabeth, Caty, Anna, Mary and Peggy - Mentions that negro boy, Tom, is to nave 80 acres in Section 30, Township 4, Range 10 on condition that he stay with widow and family until he is 26 years old. - Executors:- Wife (not nmed) and Daniel Kiblinger - Signed:- Philip Kizer - Witnesses:- David Kizer, William Reetor and Charles (mark) Reetor. (17)

BOWMAN, Jacob - dated 7-8-1818; recorded Jan. 1819 - Wife:- Rebecca - Two children:- Joseph and Sarah Bowman - Executor:- Jeptha Johnson - Siged:- Jacob Bowman - Witnesses:- John Wade, Harmon B. Robinson and Thos Strawbridge. (20)

McCLURE, William - dated 3-25-1818; recorded 1-20-1819 - Wife:- Margaret - Sons:- Samuel, Matthew, Robert and William - Daughters:- Rebecca, Elizabeth, Margaret, Nancy, Jane and Mary - Mentions:- Wife's youngest son, James Michel - Execitors:- Wife, Margaret; John Forgy and John Black - Signed:- William McClure - Witnesses:- Adam Verdier and Joseph Chesnut. (21)

REID, Joseph - dated 10-23-1818; recorded 1-20-1819 - Wife:- Elizabeth - Six children:- Thomas, James, Daniel, Eleanor, William and Sally Reid; none are of age - Executors:- Wife, Elizabeth and brother, John Reid - Signed:- Joseph Reid - Witnesses:- Mathew Woods and James Rea. (24)

DAVIS, Owen of Miami Twp., Greene Co., Ohio - dated 8-24-1811; recorded 1-20-1819 - Wife:- Lettia - Son:- Lewis Davis - Daughter:- Catharine Whiteman - Executors:- James Popence and John T. Stewart - Signed:- Owen Davis - Witnesses:- Sam'l Stewart and Elizabeth Stewart. (25)

STEWART, James of Pile Twp., Champaign Co., Ohio - dated 1-12-1818; recorded 4-27-1819 - Brothers:- Joseph and Stephen - Sisters:- Mary Stout and Mercy Davis - Executor:- Henry Pence (or Pierce) - Signed:- James Stewart - Witnesses:- John Thomas and Daniel (mark) Baker. (28)

WEST, Thomas - dated 1-1-1819; recorded 4-27-1819 - Grandsons:- Abner West; Benjamin; Thomas son of Thomas; Julian West - Grand-daughters:- Eliza daughter of son Thomas; Deborah; Catherine - Daughter-in-law:- Polly, wife of my son Thomas - Bequeath to John Patterson, relationship if any, not given - Executors:- Son, Thomas West and Griffith Foos - Signed:- Thomas West - Witnesses:- John Patterson, William (mark) Irwin and Sam'l Henkle. (29)

213

TAYLOR, Thomas - dated 4-26-1819; recorded 9-11-1819 - Wife:- Rosanna - Executors:- Wife, Rosanna and Samuel Lafferty - Signed:- Thomas Taylor - Witnesses:- Arch'd M. Maronkey and Israel Marsh. (32)

HUNTER, Ann - widow of the late Jonathan Hunter, dec'd - dated 2-8-1819; recorded 9-13-1819 - Sons:- John, William, George, Jonathan, Jeremiah and James Hunter - Daughters:- Rachel wife of Richard Bull, Nancy Reed, Mary Ward widow of the late James Ward and Sarah Hunter - Grandson:- Aaron Reed, son of Nancy Reed - Grand-daughters:- Mary Ann Reed and Juliet Ann Violet - Executor:- Son, James Hunter - Signed:- Ann (mark) Hunter - Witnesses:- Sam'l Lafferty and William Hend. (33)

S'EDIKER, Christian - dated 10-10-1818; recorded 9-13-1819 - Wife:- Rebecca - Sons:- Gabrial, John and Isaac - Oldest daughter:- Anna, now Anna Wickoff - Executors:- Wife, Rebecca and John Lingle - Signed:- Christian Snedeker - Witnesses:- Sam'l Henkle and Jeremiah A. Minter. (35)

BENDURE, William - dated 5-9-1818; recorded 9-14-1819 - Wife:- Elizabeth - Children:- Mentioned but not named - Executor:- Brazil Harrison - Signed:- William Bendure - Witnesses:- Timothy Beach and Thomas Rathbun. (37)

WEED, John of Springfield Twp. - dated 2-6-1819; recorded 9-14-1819 - Wife:- Elizabeth - Children:- Mentioned but not named - Executor:- John Lingle - Signed:- Johannis Weed (German signature) - Witnesses:- Sam'l Henkle and Mary Lingle. (38)

BEESON, Amaziah - dated 10th day, 12th month, 1819; recorded March 1820 - Wife:- Isabel - Sons:- Igal (Isaac?) and Darius - Daughters:- Rachel and Rosana - Bequeaths to Friends, the lot where Meeting House now stands, known by the name of Green Plains - Executors:- Wife, Isabel and Elijah Anderson - Signed:- Ammasia (mark) Beson - Witnesses:- Samuel Sleeper, Wm. Willis and Matthew Crispen. (40)

ALBIN, John of Green Twp. - dated 4-4-1820; recorded Aug. 1820 - Wife:- Ann - Sons:- Gabriel and Samuel - Daughter:- Mary - Son-in-law:- Amos Lambert - Executors:- Son, William and Joseph - Signed:- John Albin - Witnesses:- Jacob Morgan, Samuel Martin and Tunis Miller. (42)

SIMPSON, Alex - Verbal Will - Will made 5-19-1820; deposition 5-25-1820; recorded Aug. 1820 - Wife:- Mentioned but not named, named in recording as Abigail - Children:- Mentioned but only sons, Abraham and Stephen are named - Executors:- Wife and son, Abraham - Witnesses:- Trustram Hull, Louisa Hull and Samuel Patrick. (45)

BABCOCK, Thomas of Bath Twp., Greene Co., Ohio - dated 3-22-1815; recorded Nov. 1820 - wife:- Martha - Five sons:- William and Simmeon are only two named - Daughters:- Martha, Anna and Judith - Executors:- Wife, Martha and son, Simmeon - Signed:- Thomas Babcock - Witnesses:- Anna Davis, Jacob Babcock and William Lambert. (47)

LINGLE, John - dated 9-18-1820; recorded Nov. 1820 - Wife:- Mary - Children:- Mentioned but not named - Mentions land one mile from Springfield on the Springfield and Xenia pike now occupied by Mrs. Weed - Executors:- Wife, Mary, and Jacob Lingle - Signed:- John Lingle - Witnesses:- Ambrose Blount, John Boyce and Sampson Hubbell. (49)

BEST, Francis of Springfield Twp. - dated 10-9-1820; recorded Nov. 1820 - Wife:- Rosanna - Sons:- John, Francis, William, Thomas, Joseph and David - Daughters:- Jane, Isabella, Plly and Elizabeth - Executors:- John Perrin and John Best - Signed:- Francis Best - Witnesses:- Sam'l Henkle and Cooper Ludlow. (51)

HALL, William - dated 1-12-1821; filed 3-27-1821; recorded 4-18-1821 - Wife:- Nancy - Seven Children:- Son, Philip Hall; Daughter, Nancy Hunt and her six children, to-wit:- Ellinor, William, Nancy, Griffith, Joseph and Benjamin Foose; Daughter, Christiany Whiteley; Son, John Hall; Daughter, Freelove Vanhook; Daughter, Polly Dugan; and Daughter, Nancy Dalrymple - Executors:- Son, John Hall and son-in-law, John Whiteley - Signed:- William Hall - Witnesses:- Benjamin D. Sweet and Alex Elliot. (55)

LORTON, James - dated 7-29-1818; recorded 8-14-1821 - Wife:- Mentioned but not named; named Sarah in recording of will - Sons:- Jonathan, James William and John - Daughters:- Nancy, Polly, Salley and Rachel - Signed:- James Lorton - Witnesses:- Revel Rouch, Henry Baker and Henry (mark) Baker. (57)

BAKER, Jacob Sr. of German Twp. - dated 9-17-1821; filed and recorded 10-1-1821 - Wife:- Mentioned but not named; named in recording as Magdalane - Sons:- Henry, Jacob, Martin, John and Samuel - Mentions three daughters but only names one, Magdalane - Executors:- Wife and son, Jacob - Signed:- Jacob Baker - Witnesses:- William Miller, Lewis Pentz and John Beamer. (59)

GILBERT, Allen - Verbal Will - Will made 10-19-1821; deposition 10-23-1821; recorded 1-22-1822 - Mentions wife and family but does not name - Witnesses:- Abram Sprague and Nathan Hammen, Jr. (62)

MILLER, Frederick - dated 9-1-1822; recorded 12-17-1822 - Wife:- Elizabeth - Sons:- Henry, Daniel, John and David: David not of age - Daughters:- Mary wife of Anthony Leffel, Elizabeth wife of James Leffel and Delilah - Executors: Henry and John Miller - Signed:- Frederic (mark) Miller - Witnesses:- Benjamin P. Gains, Jacob Ebersole and Hugh M. Wallace. (63)

REEDER, Jacob - dated 9-1-1821; recorded 1-7-1823 - Wife:- Elizabeth - Sons:- Elan and Jacob - Daughters:- Marianne, Rachel and Susan - (note:- Possibly more children not named) - Step-son:- William Faris - Step-daughters:- Nancy, Polly and Priscilla Faris - Executors:- John Crain and John Layton - Signed:- Jacob Reeder - Witnesses:- Samuel Martin, Isaac Martin and Jacob G. Reeder. (65)

215

FARNHAM, John S. - dated 1-13-1822; recorded 1-10-1823 - Wife:- Minda, also to serve as executrix - Sons:- Stephen, John, James, Timothy and George - Daughters:- Elizabeth Town, Sarah Sawyer, Fanny Farnham and Permelia Barret - Signed:- John S. Farnham - Witnesses:- Amos Atkins and William Holloway. (68)

WOODS, John - dated 9-15-1822; recorded 1-10-1823 - Son:- Thomas and his wife Catherine - Daughters:- Mary wife of Joel Jinkings, her heirs and Elizabeth, deceased, her daughter Anna who is grand-daughter of testator - Executors:- Reuben Wallis - Signed:- John (mark) Woods - Witnesses:- Benjamin P. Gains, Philip Minnick and Caleb (mark) Key. (70)

GOBLE, Daniel - dated 4-18-1822; recorded 6-10-1822 - Wife:- Elizabeth, also to serve as executrix - Signed:- Daniel Goble - Witnesses:- John Snodgradd, Daniel (mark) Kimbell and George Buffinburger. (72)

GARLOUGH, John Sr. of Green Twp. - dated 6-5-1823; recorded 10-20-1823 - Wife:- Margaret Ann - Sons:- John, Jacob and Henry - Daughters:- Eve Hattfield, Margaret, Magdelene Hatfield, Saloma, Elizabeth Todd, Anna, and Kathrina Neve - Executors:- Jacob Garlough and James Todd - Signed:- John (mark) Garlough - Witnesses:- Thomas Pattan and Samuel Stewart. (74)

ROSS, John of Green Twp. - dated 9-17-1823; recorded 10-20-1823 - Wife:- Mary - Son:- William - Mentions that farm is to go to William Miller in trust for my son William - Executors:- Wife, Mary and William Miller - Signed:- John Ross - Witnesses:- Timothy Straton, Thomas Mills and Stephen Straton - Codicil dated 9-17-1823 - Grandson:- Jonathan Miller - Mentions his other children, but does not name - same witnesses. (77)

STEELE, James - dated 9-4-1823; recorded 10-20-1823 - Wife:- Ann - Son:- James - Daughters:- Jane Cowan, Sarah Kirkpatrick, Mary Stephenson and Elizabeth Steele - Executors:- Wife, Ann and son-in-law, David Cowan - Signed:- James Steele - Witnesses:- Thomas Patton, Wm. Wilson and Wm. Gowdy. (79)

ROUZER, Daniel - dated 3-22-1823; recorded 10-20-1823 - Wife:- Margaret, also to serve as executrix - Mentions children (does not name) of brother John Rouzer - Signed:- Daniel Rouzer - Witnesses:- Joseph Perrin and Thomas H ays. (81)

ELDER, Charles F. - dated 10-11-1823; recorded 12-3-1823 - Wife:- Susannah - Children:- Mentions but does not name, they are not of age - Executor:- John Black - Signed:- Charles F. Elder - Witnesses:- James Stafford and James Stafford, Jr. (83)

AKIN, James - dated 9-3-1823; recorded 12-3-1823 - Mother:- Anna Akin - Brothers and Sisters:- John Akin, Polly Curtis, Anna Mills, Betsy Haniman and Martha Cummins - Executors:- Asaph Butler, Henry Oxtoby and John Whiteley - Signed:- James Akin - Witnesses:- Robert Tharpe, Zimri F. Butler and John Craig. (85)

216

REPLOGEL, Adam - dated 10-2-1823; filed 10-20-1823 - Two oldest sons:-
David and Adam - Daughters:- Catharine - Executors:- George Keefer and
Peter Minnich - Signed:- Adam (mark) Replogel - Witnesses:- ____(?) Ohmart,
Adam Ohmert and Elizabeth (mark) Kizer. (87)

MILLER, Christley - dated 7-23-1823; filed 10-20-1823 - Wife:- Liddy - Sons:-
Eldest, John and second son Aaron - Daughters:- Eldest, Sarah; second, Sarah
and youngest, Mary - Executor:- Timothy Searl of Greene Co., Ohio - Signed:-
Christley (mark) Millar - Witnesses:- William Lambert, Jonathan Davis and
Timothy Searl. (89)

CARTMILL, Ann - dated 8-30-1821; filed 5-26-1823 - Sons:- James P., Nathaniel, Joseph, John and Thomas - Daughters:- Rachel wife of James Null, Ellen
wife of James Hunter, Sarah Morris and Elizabeth wife of John Supton - Executor:- Son, Jacob P. - Signed:- Ann (mark) Cartmill - Witnesses:- Jacob P.
Cartmill, Roecha Cartmill and John Cartmill. (92)

SIMS, Jeremiah - dated 1-8-1824; filed 1-28-1824 - Wife:- Sarah - Sons:-
William, James, Jeremiah and Thomas - Daughters:- Phebe - Executors:- John
Beamer and son, Thomas Sims - Signed:- Jeremiah Sims - Witnesses:- Samuel
Henkle, John Calleson and James Callison - Codicil:- Names two colored boys,
Charles and John - same witnesses. (94)

FOX, John - dated 12-9-1823; filed 3-22-1824; recorded 5-18-1824 - Wife:-
Catherine - Children:- Sarah, Daniel, Heirs of John Fox Jr., Nancy, Catherine, Mary, David, Joseph, Samuel, Asher and Aaron - Executors:- Sons, Aaron
and Asher - Signed:- John Fox - Witnesses:- John R. Lemon and John Skinner.
(97)

BLOXSOM, Richard - dated 1st day, 9th month, 1820; filed 3-22-1824 - Sons:-
Williar, Richard, Gregory, Gedion and Charles - Daughters:- Sarah Johnson,
dec'd; Mary Worriner; Ann Bloxsom and Elizabeth Gil - Mentions children of
daughter Sarah Johnson; Obadiah Johnson and Richard Johnson, with Richard's
part to go for benefit of his son, John Johnson - Mentions Mary and Ann,
two children of daughter Mary Worriner - Executors:- Gedion Bloxsom and
Jeptha Johnson - Signed:- Rich'd Bloxsom - Witnesses:- Charles Bloxsom,
Anne Bloxsom and Obadiah Johnson. (98)

MEFFORD, Casper - dated 2-9-1824; filed 3-22-1824 - Wife:- Cathrine - Sons:-
Don Doverd, George Ciles and Andrew Hodge Mefford - Daughter:- Jane Gibins
Mefford - Executors:- Thomas Thompson and John D. Mefford - Signed:- Gasper
(mark) Mefford - Witnesses:- James Donnell, James McQuaddy and John Bishop.
(101)

DOUGHERTY, Patrick - dated 10-8-1823; filed 3-22-1824 - Wife:- Nancy, also
to serve as executrix - Sons:- Daniel, Michael, Barnard, William, James and
John - Daughters:- Mary, Catherine, Nancy, Jane and Elizabeth - Signed:-
Patrick Dougherty - Witnesses:- Laughlin Kenny and Michal (mark) Kenny. (103)

ADAMSON, Lloyd B. - dated 3-2-1824; filed and recorded 6-28-1824 - Mother:-
Nancy Adamson - Sister:- Anna Adamson - Brothers:- John, Nathan and Elisha -
Mentions land in Champaign Co., Ohio - Executor:- Brother, John Adamson -
Signed:- Lloyd B. Adamson - Witnesses:- James C. Beall, Joseph N. Husted
and Isaac Elwell. (106)

REA, James - dated 3-6-1824; filed 6-28-1824; recorded 7-3-1824 - Wife:-
Agnes - Sons:- John, James William and Andrew - Daughters:- Betsy and
Luesy Rea - Executors:- Wife, Agnes and John Snodgradd - Mentions land in
Franklin Co., Penna. - Signed:- James Rea - Witnesses:- Andrew Edgar and
James Reed. (108)

VICKER, Joseph - dated 2nd day, 7th month, 1824; filed and recorded 12-7-1824
- Mother:- Celia Vicker - Three youngest sisters:- Mary Ann, Ruth and Emily
Vickers - Signed:- Joseph Vicker - Witnesses:- Elijah Anderson, Margaret
Wildman and Alex'r Morton. (112)

Heirs of TUNIS MILLER to Matthew ANDERSON - 4-8-1847; $1800; part north part SW¼ Section 20, Township 5, Range 10 - James B. McKinnon and Elizabeth his wife late Elizabeth Miller of Logan Co., Ohio; Abraham Trout and Catharine L. his wife late Catharine Miller; and Amanda Miller all of Clark Co.; heirs of Tunis Miller dec'd who died intestate - Volume X, page 69

Reuben SHELLABARGER, et al to John BEARD - 4-17-1847; 40 acres part SE¼ Section 11, Township 3, Range 8; part of Section 6, Township 3, Township 3, Range 8 and W½ SW¼ Section 36, Township 4, Range 3; $2400. - Reuben Shella- barger and Elizabeth, his wife, Thomas Johnston and Elizabeth, his wife, Martin Shellabarger and Elizabeth, his wife, all of Clark Co.; land belong- ing to the estate of Ephraim Shellabarger, dec'd. - Volume X, page 75

David COWAN and others to Nicholas MOORE - 9-14-1847; lots #202 and #203 in Mill Run - David Cowan and Jane, his wife, late Steel; John Gowdy and Ann, his wife, late Steel; Robert Gowdy and Elizabeth, his wife, late Steel; all of Clark Co.; Thomas Stevenson and Mary, his wife, late Steel, Thomas Gowdy and Nancy, his wife, late Kirkpatrick; Edward Reid and Margaret, his wife, late Kirkpatrick; Jane Kirk- patrick; all of Greene Co., Ohio; being heirs of William KIRKPATRICK and Sarah, his wife, late Sarah STEEL who died intestate being heirs of James STEEL, dec'd, who died in Clark Co. leaving a will by which he devised to his five heirs, to- wit:- Jane, Elizabeth, Ann, Mary and Sarah. - Volume X, page 372

David J. CORY and others to Jacklen BARRINGER - 5-20-1845; Lot 51 in Enon - David J. Cory and Martha, his wife of Henry Co., Ohio; David J. Smith and Sally, his wife; David Cross and Rhoda W., his wife; Samuel E. Stafford and Malissa, his wife; Jane Cory; Joseph V. Cory and Martha, his wife; all of Clark Co. - Volume X, page 192

Nathan NEER, et al. to Andrew B. RUNYON - 2-25-1846; $500.; E½ SE¼ Section 21, Township 6, Range 10 - Nathan Neer and Mary Ann his wife; Enos Neer, Sr. guardian of Joseph Hill Neer and Hannah Neer minor heirs of Amos Neer, dec'd; Mary Neer widow and heir of Jonathan Neer, dec'd; all of Clark Co. and Michael Couchman and Elizabeth, his wife, of Champaign Co., Ohio; all heirs of Amos Neer, dec'd. - Volume X, page 100

John LAMAN and Rachel, his wife, formerly SIPE of Tippecanoe Co., Indiana; Power of Attorney to Joseph SIPE of Clark Co. - 1-27-1846; all their inter- est in lands of Francis SIPE, dec'd, father of said Rachel. - Volume X, page 110

Nancy NEER to Nathan NEER - 3-17-1847; release of dower interest. - Volume X, page 115

Heirs of Samuel McINTIRE to Joseph McINTIRE - 9-27-1846; N½ Lot 91 in Springfield - Reuben Merriweather and Rachel, his wife, of Clinton Co., Ohio; William T. McIntire and Mary, his wife; John S. McIntire and Esther, his wife; James Fleming and Sarah, his wife; James W. McIntire; Amariah McIntire; and Margaret McIntire; widow and heirs of Samuel McIntire, dec'd. - Volume X, page 163. - Joseph McINTIRE and Maria, his wife to John McINTIRE; 7-8-1847, W½ of N½ Lot 91 in Springfield. - Volume X, page 163

Abraham RUNYON in his own right and as assignee of Andrew BUMGARDNER from President United States - 5-4-1815; S W¼ Section 20, Township 6, Range 10 - Volume X, page 551. Thomas STIMPES and wife to Hiram L. RUNYAN - 3-3-1848; all interest as heirs of Abraham RUNYAN in S½ SW¼ Section 20, Township 6, Range 10; Volume X, page 552. Nathaniel BUNNELL Jr. and Susannah his wife of White Co., Indiana to Hiram RUNYAN - 12-10-1847; undivided 1/9th of all real estate of Abraham RUNYAN, dec'd; Volume X, page 553 —— Peter L. RUNYAN and Mary his wife of Clark Co. to Hiram L. Runyan - 9-25-1844; undivided 1/9th part of estate of Abraham RUNYAN, dec'd; Volume X, page 554 —— John W. RUNYAN, et al to Hiram L. RUNYAN - 1-29-1848; John W. Runyan and Rachel his wife of Champaign Co., Ohio; Sophia Runyan; Henry Runyan and Rachel his wife; Samuel Wright and Esther his wife; Andrew B. Runyan and Matilda his wife; Archibald McKonkey and Lydia his wife; James McMillice and Ann Sophia his wife; all of Clark Co.; our undivided interest in estate of Abraham RUNYAN, late of Clark Co., dec'd; Volume X, page 554

Heirs of Susan KIRKPATRICK to George McCULLAH - 12-13-1847; John Kirkpatrick, Susan Kirkpatrick, James Kirkpatrick and Malina his wife, Stephen R. Martin and Nancy his wife, John Kirkpatrick Jr. and Mary Ann his wife, and Daniel Pittenger, all of Delaware Co., Indiana; John H. Ellis and Phebe his wife, Robert Kirkpatrick and Susan his wife; heirs of Susan Kirkpatrick; all right, title and interest to estate of Robert LAYNE of Clark Co., which said Layne in his last will devised to Susan Kirkpatrick and her heirs being 1/6th part - Volume Y, page 248

Heirs of Richard BLOXSOM by Sheriff to Samuel HOWELL - 4-8-1847; Mary Warner of Clark Co. filed her petition in the Common Pleas Court against Gideon Bloxon, James Bloxon, Ann S. Morgan wife of Jonathan Morgan, Elizabeth King wife of John King, Maria Wastfall wife of Albert Wastfall, Sarah Scott wife of Charles Scott, Eliza Bloxon, Mary Bloxon, Nancy Bloxon, Ann Man wife of John Man, Mary Van Brunt wife of Thomas Van Brunt, George Bloxon, Elizabeth Montgomery wife of Samuel Montgomery, Richard Bloxon, Catharine Bloxon, Christian Bloxon, William Gill, James Gill, Lavina Baker wife of Miller Baker, Unity Johnston wife of Richard Johnston, John Johnston, Gideon Johnston, Harriet Seller wife of Albert Seller, Maria Johnston, Nancy Johnston, Arabella James, Parmela and William H. Johnston; demanding partition of real estate; land described as border on north by Ann Bloxon's land, on east by Mary B. Warner's land, on south by Xenia and Columbus pike and on west by Chillicothe and Dayton road being 75 acres - Volume Y, page 297

REEDER Heirs to Enos REEDER - 9-13-1848; part of tract #3957 sold by Charles THOMPSON to Jacob REEDER, dec'd; John Reeder and Mary his wife of Clark Co., Henry Harrington and Hannah his wife of Greene Co., Ohio; Isaiah Jones and Mary his wife of Madison Co., Ohio; James M. Reeder and Sarah his wife of Clark Co.; George W. Lohr and Sarah F. his wife of Madison Co., Ohio; Ann Reeder, Trusdale Reeder, Russel B. Reeder and Amanda Reeder of Clark Co. - Volume Y, page 400

Heirs of Henry SEITZ, Sr. to Isaac Miller - 4-15-1848; $2800.; part SE¼ Section 6, Township 4, Range 9, 100 acres; Isaac Seitz and Elizabeth his wife of Illinois, Andrew Seitz and Mary his wife, Jacob Seitz and Mary his wife, Jacob Beard and Catharine his wife, Mary Seitz widow of Henry Seitz Sr., dec'd - Volume Y, page 38

Benjamin CARMAN's Heirs to William DEATON and James LEFFEL - (not dated); recorded 9-3-1847; part NE¼ Section 35, Township 3, Range 10 - Samuel Carmin and Anna his wife; William Car--- ~~~ Rhoda his wife, ~~ Delaware Co., Indiana; Elijah Carmin and ----- his wife; Lewis Carmin and Jane his wife; John Carmin ---- ------ his wife, Thomas Buckles and Mary his wife late Carmin, Henry Long and Elizabeth his wife late Carmin, William Richeson and Eliza his wife late Carmin, Samuel Deaton and Nancy his wife late Carmin, Sarah Priest widow of Jeremiah Priest, dec'd, late Carmin, and Sootha Carmin; heirs of Benjamin Carmin, dec'd, late of Clark Co. - Volume X, page 229

Ruth TOWN's Heirs to James S. HALLEY - Power of Attorney - 1847; E½ W½ SE¼ Section 16, Township 5, Range 8 - Nathan Town, Joseph Galloway and Fanny his wife, Ephraim Scarlett and Lucinda his wife, all of Noble Co., Indiana; Reuben B. Perry and Sally his wife, Emanuel Wineland and Delecta his wife and James Town; said Sally Perry, Delecta Wineland, Lucinda Scarlett and James Town being only children and heirs of Ruth Town, late of Clark Co., dec'd. - Volume X, page 272

James M. SLOAN, guardian to James TURNBELL - 11-11-1847; Lots 22 and 23 in town of Harmony - James M. Sloan guardian of James Sloan, Jr. heir of Alexander Sloan, dec'd. - Volume X, page 406

Thomas NAUMAN, et al. to Samuel HARSHBARGER - 11-13-1847; SE¼ Section 27, Township 4, Range 10 - Thomas Nauman and Catharine his wife, Samuel Baker and Mary his wife; John Baker and Christena his wife, Henry Baker and Varonica his wife, David Baker and Elizabeth his wife, Jacob Rust and Elizabeth his wife, John Roler and Rebecca his wife, all of Clark Co. - Volume X, page 410

Heirs of Israel MARSH to Joseph LAYBOUR - 9-1-1847; in-lots 18,19 & 20 Pleasant township in Israel Marsh's plat of town of Catawba - Andrew Ward and Sarah his wife, Noah Marsh and Eliza his wife, of Madison Co., Ohio; Lemuel Hunter and Nancy his wife, Susannah Marsh and Samuel Marsh of Clark Co. - Volume X, page 442

Heirs of Henry COSLER to John DERREN - 12-1-1847; part SE¼ Section 29, Township 4, Range 8 - Mary Cosler widow of Henry Cosler, Clarke Co.; Martin Cosler and Lewis Cosler of LaSalle Co., Illinois; Michael Leffel and Elizabeth his wife of Miami Co., Ohio; Jacob Drake and Catharine his wife, John M. Cosler and Elizabeth his wife, James M. Cosler and Lavenia his wife; heirs of Henry Cosler, dec'd. - Volume X, page 514

Jer. WARDER and Children to William M. COOPER - 1848; part NW¼ Section 29, Township 5, Range 9, Springfield Twp. - Jeremiah Warder and Ann A. his wife and the following persons, children of said Jeremiah and Ann; John A. Warder and Elizabeth B. his wife of Hamilton Co. Ohio, Edward H. Cumming and Sarah his wife late Warder of Knox Co. Ohio, Charles S. Rannelle and Mary his wife late Warder of St. Louis, Missouri; George A., William, James T., Benjamin H. and Elizabeth A. Warder. - Volume X, page 555

The following marriage records were transcribed from Book 1-B

ADAIR, John to Elizabeth Vickers		11-11-1823
ADAMS, Robert to Elizabeth McIntire = his father John Adams		7-5-1821
ALEXANDER, Richard to Susanna Hembleman	lic.	9-16-1823
ALLEN, Joseph to Mary Johnson		6-27-1822
ALLEN, Samuel to Nancy Morris		4-4-1822
ARBOGART, Enos to Catherine Fleming		6-1-1823
ARBOGART, Otho to Dorothy Curl (Carl)		12-18-1823
ARMSTRONG, Thomas to Nancy Ray		10-25-1821
ARNETT, James to Ruth DeWitt		12-9-1823
ARNETT, William to Mary Furrow		11-15-1821
BABCOCK, Hiram to Lydia Hutcheson		10-10-1822
BAILEY, James to Fanny Wyeth		7-17-1822
BAKER, Melyn D. to Margaret McClure		9-5-1822
BALDWIN, Enoch to Catharine Scott		7-19-1821
BALDWIN, Jonah to Mrs. Amelia Vanpelt		2-27-1823
BANCROFT, Richard to Mary Graham		2-18-1822
BANES, Gabrie to Sally McKinnon		12-26-1822
BARDWELL, Seth to Nancy Jones		11-8-1821
BASINGER, Peter to Rebecca Miller		5-31-1821
BEALL, Walter to Sarah Akins		2-13-1823
BARRETT, Dickison to Fanny Farnham		12-26-1822
BEASLE (BEEZLEY), Paul to Mary Plum		8-1-1822
BELL, George of Urbana to Elizabeth Kizer		5-2-1822
BERRY, James D. to Julia Ann Hibbard		6-21-1821
BISHOP, Edward to Bethiah Winchester		1-16-1823
BLACK, James R. to Margaret Winget		3-6-1822
BLUE, Andrew to Nancy Pentz		4-18-1822
BOND, Edward to Rachel Woolman		3-20-1823
BRACKNEY, Samuel to Jane Willis		4-25-1822
BRANSON, John to Miriam Thomas (no day given)		Sept. 1822
BRANSTELLER, Daniel to Elizabeth Baker		8-21-1823
BREVARD, Zebulon to Sarah Fleming		7-25-1823
BRIGGS, Samuel to Elizabeth Hempleman-father, Geo. Hambleman		5-10-1821
BRUBACKER, Benjamin to Eliza Rosigrant		12-12-1822
BURNHAM, William A. to Cinthia Marshall		3-20-1823
BUTLER, William to Byanca Butler - Wit: Joel Butler		9-5-1821
CALLISON, James to Elizabeth Franklin		9-12-1822
CAMPBELL, William C. to Rebecca Roach		6-28-1821
CARTER, Thomas to Martha Martin	lic.	2-15-1823
CARLETON, Amos P. to Charlotte Hale		3-7-1823
CENTER, Roderick to Barbara Smith		10-1-1822
CHANCELLER, Jesse to Mary C. Warrick		12-26-1822
CHARD, James to Sarah Burnett		10-31-1822
COCHRAN, Thos. to Emelia Peterson	lic.	10-20-1821
COFFY, Joseph Jr. to Susana Hunter		2-13-1823
COLEMAN, Dr. Asa to Polly Keifer		10-25-1822
COLLINS, Daniel to Rebecca Fisher		1-2-1823
CONFER, Michael to Sally Winget		9-11-1823

CONKLIN, Joseph to Clarissa Baird   8-29-1821
COOK, James to Jane Richardson   3-12-1822
COWGILL, Benjamin to Rebecca Sparrow   2-28-1822
COX, John to Polly Laferty   2-7-1822
CRAIG, James to Eliza Enoch   12-25-1823
CRAIG, Robert to Fanny Joiner   1-5-1823
CRAWFORD, Abel to Caty Pierce - widower and widow   12-25-1823
DALLINGER, Thomas to Polly Courtney   5-29-1823
DEBOY, John to Rachel Franch   8-4-1822
DENHAM, James to Ruth Baxter   5-26-1822
DICKENSON, Elisha to Susanna Miranda   10-3-1822
DODSON, William to Martha Kinnan   8-15-1821
DOUGHERTY, Dan'l to Elizabeth Long   8-9-1823
DREW, Abner to Edith M. Harris   2-14-1822
DRISCOL, John to Nancy Faris   5-15-1823
DUNHAM, Amos to Elizabeth Heaton   6-12-1823
ELDER, Thomas to Mary Anderson   10-2-1823
ELLIOTT, Alexander to Sarah Moore   12-6-1821
ENOCH, Henry to Mary Jones   8-28-1822
FARNHAM, John to Mercy Hawley   3-13-1823
FENTON, John to Margaret Fenton   5-29-1823
FENTON, Samuel to Nancy Fenton   12-24-1822
FENTON, Wm. Jr. to Jane Fenton   6-20-1821
FIELDS, Walter to Sarah Syre   12-27-1821
FISHER, John to Elizabeth N. Crockett   7-17-1823
FLEMING, Benjamin to Elizabeth Bunnell   8-8-1822
FLEMING, Norris to Mrs. Lucinda Boyce   3-27-1823
FOLEY, Thomas to Sarah Bear - Wit. James Foley   4-19-1821
FOSTER, Nelson to Cassa Priest   11-22-1821
FRANTZ, Daniel to Madelina Minnick   8-21-1821
FRANTZ, David to Catharine McGinty   10-9-1823
FRANTZ, John to Anna Omit   9-20-1821
FRANTZ, Michael to Susanna Neher   10-16-1823
FUNSTON, William to Anna Barr   6-12-1822
FURROW, William to Elizabeth Maxson-her father, Jesse Maxson   4-18-1821
GAFFIELD, Benjamin to Luana Smith   3-11-1823
GAINES, Alexander to Mary Crispin   12-26-1822
GARLOUGH, John to Ann Patten   6-5-1821
GAY, Benjamin to Elizabeth Blanchard   10-26-1823
GEARHEART, John to Blanor Beaty   11-7-1822
GOODRICH, Price to Livina Park - Wit. Jno. Park   7-23-1821
GOWDY, Andrew to Elizabeth McBeth   2-18-1823
GRIFFITH, Azel to Mary Magee   5-1-1822
HAIN, Joseph to Jane Holmes   10-30-1823
HALE, Calvin to Sarah Smith   1-5-1822
HAMMOND, Nathan to Submit Monson   7-4-1822
HAMPTON, Ephraim to Polly Monger   6-7-1821
HANDLEY, Obadiah E. to Catherine Walburn - widow   6-15-1823
HANEBY, John to Mrs. Mary Miller   12-11-1823
HANELINE, George to Polly Husted - Wit: Solomon Husted   6-21-1821

223

HARBERT, Robert to Huldy Barnes   6-19-1823
HARDESTY, Benjamin to Leah Cannon-colored widower and widow   2-2-1822
HARRIS, Reuben to Ruth Van Meter   5-3-1821
HARRISON, Caleb to Cinthia Hamilton   2-22-1823
HARRISON, Hoses to Elizabeth Compton   12-28-1823
HARRISON, Nathan to Anna Bodkin   6-7-1821
HARVEY, Andrew to Caty Hill   2-27-1823
HAWKINS, John to Jane Diner   9-8-1822
HAYMAKER, John to Elizabeth Madden   4-10-1823
HAYS, James to Rebecca Clark - Wit: Jas. Clark   11-1-1821
HODGE, William to Mary Wolfe   2-27-1823
HOFF, James to Margaret Hampton   7-4-1821
HOLLOWAY, George to Mary Woolman   2-6-1823
HOUSTON, Robert to Eliza Pierce   12-10-1822
HUFFMAN, Mathias to Christina Freiermood   5-19-1821
HUFFMAN, Moses to Rhoda Winn   12-28-1823
HULET, Lewis to Martha Hulett   10-29-1822
HUNT, James to Nancy Jones - Wit: John Jones   11-9-1821
HUNT, John of Dayton to Elizabeth Brooks   4-10-1823
HURD, William to Mary Reynolds   4-10-1821
HURD, William to Corella Brook   2-26-1822
HUSTED, John to Elizabeth Reeder   9-18-1823
JACKSON, Hiram to Abigail Cooley   5-14-1821
JAMES, Isaac to Elizabeth Bates   1-3-1822
JAMISON, Andrew C. to Mary Durlin   6-20-1822
JESSUP, Thomas to Rosanna Beason - Wit: Amaziah Beeson   4-18-1821
JONES, David to Polly Owens   6-18-1823
JUDY, John to Lydia Hull   12-10-1822
KAIN, John to Jane Petticrew - Wit: James Petticrew   9-19-1822
KELSO, Robert to Jane Music   8-4-1823
KIBLINGER, Peter to Rebecca Peacock   8-9-1821
KING, John to Elizabeth Cavenger   8-6-1822
LAYTON, John to Mary Russell - Wit: Jno Russell   1-24-1822
LAYTON, William to Deziah Botkin   6-8-1822
LAYTON, William to Elizabeth Marquart   11-13-1823
LAZURE, William to Margaret Bayles   7-8-1823
LEFFEL, James to Elisabeth Miller   1-1-1822
LEHMAN, Jonathan to Mary Canan   11-30-1823
LEONARD, Jos. to Nancy Thomas   lic. 9-22-1823
LESH, John to Anna Frantz   1-9-1823
LITTLE, Jacob to Nancy Demint   7-12-1821
LOGAN, John to Polly Robinson   11-15-1821
LORTON, Jonathan to Elenor Johnston   12-12-1822
LOWRY, James to Eliza Smeed   3-18-1821
LYNES, Absalom to Sally Smith - colored   lic.10-19-1821
McKINNON, Theophilus to Priscilla Houston   1-2-1823
McMILLER, William to Polly Rathburn - Wit: Thos. Rathburn   10-18-1321
McPHERSON, Joseph to Sarah Peticrew   9-12-1821
MACBEATH, William to Amelia Gowdy   12-11-1823

```
MACKEY, James to Anna Bennet - Wit:  John Bennett          8-8-1821
MADDEN, John B. to Permelia Ingave                         6-4-1822
MARQUART, David to Eliza Ann Wright                         10-30-1823
MARSHALL, James to Hannah Bond                             12-19-1822
MARTS, George L. to Margaret Kizer                         1-2-1823
MASON, Samson to Minerva Needham                           11-24-1823
MASON, Thomas to Mary Tonkinson                            10-10-1822
MAXON, Ephraim to Mary Smith                               5-22-1823
MERENESS, Abraham D. to Jane Coen                          1-6-1822
METSKER, John to Mary Orpurd                               7-6-1823
MICHAEL, Adam to Mary Wone                                 12-18-1823
MILLER, Daniel to Elizabeth Neff                           5-2-1822
MILLER, John P. to Eliza Cory                              10-10-1822
MILLER, William to Ellen Drake                             6-17-1821
MINNICH, Peter to Elizabeth Croft                          11-27-1823
MITCHEL, Howard to Nancy Stafford                          11-6-1823
MONOHAN, Gershom to Elizabeth Rakestraw                    1-2-1823
MOREHOUSE, Thomas to Polly Oliver                          5-10-1823
MORRIS, William to Elizabeth Beaty                         12-12-1822
MORRISON, Samuel F. to Elizabeth Stephenson                4-30-1823
NAGLE, Frederick to Charlotte Carys                        4-17-1822
NEWCOM, John to Jane Coulter                               12-11-1823
OSBURN, Elijah to Mary (Polly) Write - Wit: L. D. Osborn   9-14-1821
PAGE, Lindsey A. to Achsah Harris - Wit: Evan Page & Isaac Harris 1-24-1822
PATTON, John to Rachel Clawson                             1-8-1823
PEARSON, James P. to Elizabeth Wilson                      4-17-1823
PEFFLER, John to Nancy Reed - widower and widow            10-16-1823
PENCE, Sam'l to Phebe Glass                                9-11-1823
PERRIN, Urias to Anna Huffman                       lic.   6-5-1822
PETTICREW, John to Elizabeth Hamilton, a widow             6-26-1823
PLUMMER, Washington to Rebecca Smith                       5-22-1823
POPENOE, James to Sarah Parkham                            11-13-1821
PRICKETT, John to Rachel Plum                              4-17-1823
PRIEST, Jeremiah to Sally Carmin                           6-21-1821
PRIEST, Wm. to Nancy Myers - Wit: Jos Myers         lic.   8-14-1821
RAKESTRAW, Charles to Polly Wise                           5-27-1821
RAKESTRAW, Joseph to Priscilla Bates                       10-21-1823
RAKESTRAW, William to Jennetty Vandevanter                 8-15-1822
RANDOLPH, James B. F. to Rachel Stanley                    5-18-1823
RENDESIL, Jacob to Eleanor Vance                           4-11-1822
RICHARDS, Elias to Mrs. Elizabeth Hulse - Wit: her brother 7-12-1821
                           Michael Rudicilly
RICHARDS, Joseph to Rachel Davidson                        5-2-1822
RICHARDS, Silas to Ellen Richards-her father, Arnold Richards 6-24-1821
RICHARDSON, John to Elizabeth Corey                 lic.12-4-1821
ROACH, John to Mary Ann Parent                             8-21-1823
ROBINSON, Nathan to Mary Kitts                             3-13-1823
ROBISON, William to Nancy Patrick                          2-15-1823
SANDERS, John to Magdalena Baker                           10-2-1823
```

```
SCARLET, Barney to Lois Pool                                      11-27-1821
SCOTT, Israel T. to Deborah Roll                                  6-27-1822
SELLERS, Henry to Barbary Ohmert                                  5-30-1822
SERFIS, John to Elizabeth Weaver                                  6-10-1821
SHAFER, David to Polly Shannon                                    4-19-1821
SHALLINGHEEPER, Isaac to Polly Clark                              10-26-1821
SILS, Michael to Peggy Myers                                      12-25-1823
SIMS, Thomas to Sarah Donovan                                     4-4-1822
SLEETH, William to Sarah Drummond                                 8-2-1821
SMALLEY, John to Martha Babcock                                   11-1-1822
SMITH, Jacob to Priscilla Arbogast                                4-22-1821
SMITH, Samuel to Anna Hedreck                                     12-20-1821
SMITH, Solomon to Catherine Swan                                  6-27-1822
SNODGRASS, Joseph to Margaret Bird                                3-20-1823
SPELMAN, Thomas to Elizabeth Swisher                              6-5-1823
STEELE, James W. to Nancy Worthington                     lic. 5-5-1823
STEELE, Joseph Smith to Elizabeth Deny                            1-30-1823
STEPHENSON, David to Ann Kizer - Wit: Dan'l Kizer                 6-12-1821
STEWART, Asa to Melinda Franklin                                  12-4-1823
STOKES, Stephen to Martha Wright                                  9-25-1822
STRATTON, Stephen to Harriett Holcomb                             3-6-1823
STRAUSS, Daniel to Nancy Enoch                            lic.  4-9-1823
SWANN, Richard to Verlinda Dawson                                10-10-1822
TAMPLIN, John to Sarah Lyon                                       9-18-1823
TELLER, Isaac to Mrs. Susanna Rogers - widower and widow lic.    10-26-1822
                    note - no date given                  ret.  1-28-1823
THRASHER, Solomon to Mary Cooper                                 8-8-1822
TURNER, Aquila to Frances Judy - Wit: Rich'd Judy               11-29-1821
TURNER, Samuel to Leah Jones                                      3-14-1822
TURNER, William to Polly Catterlin                                1-23-1823
TUTTLE, Caleb to Mary Pricket                                     3-21-1822
TUTTLE, David to Rebecha Buckles -(no date given)         lic. 10-22-1821
                                                          ret. 3-6-1822
VALENTINE, Jonathan to Elizabeth Kress,Wit: Jacob Kress          4-25-1822
VANCE, George B. to Margaret Beach                                7-17-1823
VANCE, John to Abigail Simpson                                    1-24-1823
WAGGONER, Jacob to Nancy Harshman, Wit: Charles Harshman          4-26-1821
WARD, Andrew to Sarah Marsh                                      11-21-1822
WARNER, Lewis, a widower, to Mrs. Mary Olinger                   12-2-1823
WEEKS, John to Barbara Waggoner                                   5-15-1823
WEST, Joseph to Sarah Jones                                       6-12-1823
WILLET, John to Harriet Peterson                                  9-5-1822
WILSON, Daniel to Nancy Davis                                     3-4-1822
WILSON, Isaac G. to Mary Ann Patterson                          12-28-1822
WILSON, James C. to Sarah Daniels                                 9-6-1821
WINGET, John to Mary Boyce                                        6-13-1822
WINN, John to Margaret Turman                                     5-26-1823
WINN, Richard to Rhoda Turman                                     7-15-1823
WOLF, Amos to Rebecca Gowdy                                       2-24-1822
```

WOLF, Henry to Barbara Jentis   lic.6-22-1822
WOOD, Andrew to Elizabeth Beezley (No date given)   lic.2-16-1822
                                                                      ret.3-4-1822
WOOD, Isaac to Sarah Wood — Wit: Widow Wood   lic.9-19-1821
                                  (No date given)   ret.3-6-1822
WREN, Thomas to Elizabeth Gordon   lic.3-11-1823
WRIGHT, John to Jane Eddy   7-6-1823
WYLAND, Jonathan to Catherine Plumb   12-8-1823
YOUNG, Patrick to Jennet Arthur   lic.11-9-1822
YOUNG, Samuel to Mary McManorey   4-24-1823

CLARK COUNTY, OHIO - COLUMBIA STREET CEMETERY, SPRINGFIELD

Contributed by Julie Overton, 405 N. Winter St., Yellow Springs, Ohio 45387

Mrs. Overton states that this cemetery was copied in 1924 by George S. Dial, Trustee, Clarke County Historical Society with a copy being placed in the Warder Public Library. Mrs. Overton further states that she passed the cemetery about two years ago and only 4 tombstones could be seen. According to Beers "History of Clark County, Ohio", p 597 the cemetery extends back to when the city was laid out and its use was abandoned with the growth of the city.

ANTHONY, Mrs. Elizabeth E. wife of Charles Anthony, Daughter of Joseph and
    Rachel Evans d Apr. 20th, 1839 age 37 yrs 10 mo. 6 days.
EVANS, Mrs. Rachel, widow of Joseph Evans d Sept. 7th 1839 aged 64 yrs 9 mo 11 da
ANTHONY, Rebecca Sarah, age 5mo. 18 days; Oliver Benton aged 37 days
    Charles McDonald, age 2 yrs 2 mo 23 days
    (note: the above inscriptions are all on the same stone, which
    includes the inscription) "Erected Sept. 1839 by Family of C. Anthony"
ANTHONY, Joseph b Jan. 26, 1824 d Sept 18, 1847
GARDNER, Elizabeth Jane Gardner, niece of Jacob & Jane Hardey and daughter of
    Archibold and Sarah Gardner d Oct 31st 1830 aged 9 yrs & 6 days
HILL, Miss Elmina A. d Jane. 24, 1832 age 16 yrs 3 mo 24 days
HEISKELL. Erected in memory of family of J. & E. Heiskell.
    Margaret Caroline daughter of John & Elizabeth Heiskel, wife of
    E. LAWRENCE, who died May 9th 1830 aged 21 yrs. 2 mo. 7 days
    Margaret Elizabeth dau. of E. & M. C. Heiskell d Jan 17, 1841 aged 14 yrs.
    Adam, son of J.&E. Heiskell d Sept. 2nd 1835 age 12 yrs 3 mo 22 ds
    (note; above inscriptions for Heiskells all on same stone)
(note: next tombstone illegible)
McENTIRE, Daughter of W. & B. McEntire, July 20, 1815
MERENESS, Margaret, wife of A. D. Mereness d Oct 2nd 1821 age 30 yrs 9 mo.
(note: next stone) S.W.C.
FREEZE, Mary wife of Jefferson Freeze d Apr. 19, 1840 aged 25 yrs 2 mo 26 days
HUNT, Sarah Matilda, daughter of Doc. B. W. & Frances Hunt d June 3, 1839, aged
    6 yrs. 6 mo. 11 days
    Sarah_____of John Hunt_____
(nest stone)   MCH. U.B.H.
HUNT, Mary C. dau of Doc. Hunt; Hen__son of Doc. Hunt (note: no dates)
HUBBELL, Elizabeth A.W. wife of R.H. Hubbell and dau. of Isaac Cowgill, Esq.
    b Nov 28, 1812 in Culpepper Co. Va.
CULLEN, Patrick of April 10th 1835 age 31 yrs.
    John son of Patrick & Catharine Cullen d Oct 2, 1831 age 24 yrs & 5 mo.
SHIPMAN, Anna d Nov 14, 1837 age 18 yrs 5 days
STEELE, Elizabeth d Nov 9, 1842 age 63 yrs 5 days
    Jo____d June 2, 1836
JOHNSTON, Paul F. son of Andrew & Elizabeth b Jan. 15, 1825 d July 10, 1825
_____, Elizabeth Ann, wife of _____
WEATHERSHINE, Jacob son of George & Jane, d Jan. 27, 1845 age 2 yrs.
(note: next stone illegible)
FISHER, John Reynolds son of W. L. & Sarah Fisher died in infancy.
(note: next stone illegible)
KENNEY, Martha d Mch. 10, 1838 aged _____
FOOS, Elizabeth consort of Griffith Foos d Oct 10, 1833 aged 56 yrs.
HUGHES, David infant son of David & Emily d Aug 26, 1836 age _____

228

KAUFMAN, J.E. son of Michael & Catharine Kaufman.
BELL, Ann Elizabeth Bell, consort of_____ d Oct 27_____
WOST, Florence May dau. of J.M. & G. S. Wost d July 3, 1848 age 13 mo 3 days.
(note: next stone illegible)
THOMPSON, James Sr. d Oct 25, 1846 age 76 yrs.
RENSHAW, Thomas S._____
RENSHAW, Thomas son of T.S. & E.C. Renshaw d Oct 3 1839
(note: next inscription reads as follows, evidently grave of John Bancroft)
    "John B., d Sept. 1837 age____. Revolutionary war."
SHIPLEY, Vachel Henry son of Richard & Mary Shipley d Oct 31, 1838 age 9 mo 12 ds
(note: next stone) M.L.
CONWAY, Sarah dau. of Patrick & Margaret d Mch 24, 1840 age 17 mo.
    John son of P. & S. Conway d Aug 12 1834
STRAIN, Robert d Dec 20, 1840 (note: date in 1840 as transcribed by Mr. Dial,
    it has been changed to 1841), age 40 yrs 4 mo. (note: "see Weekly
    Republican, Vol 10 Dec 20, 1841 has been written in)
    Robert Montgomery, son of Robt and Mary Strain d Jan 24, 1842 age 8 mo
    18 days (note: it has been added that Mary was second Wife)
    Elizabeth consort of Robert Strain d Dec 20, 1835 age 30 years, born
    Faunettsburg, Pa. (note: added is the information that Elizabeth's
    maiden name was Geddes, also to see "Springfield Pioneer, Vol 7,
    Dec. 25th, 1835. Also states that tombstones were in good condition
    in Dec. 1921--that son Isaac not bu. in this cemetery and for
    Lieut Isaac Strain, see Vol 22, Weekly Republic)
STARRETT, Ellen C. consort of J. A. Starrett d March 12, 1844 age 52
HOWELL, Lemira Lee
SPENSER, Lemira wife of Josiah Spenser d Mar 2, 1860 age 23 yr.
SPENCER, Mary Ann wife of Josiah Spencer d June 4, 1841 age 57 yr.
MARSHALL, Sarah Ann dau. of Michael & Louisa b Nov 24, 1852 d Oct 18, 1857
    Charles Albert son of Michael & Louisa b Feb 7, 1835 d April 17, 1840
    Laura Louisa dau of Michael & Louisa b Jan 24, 1838 d Apr 12, 1840
WERTZ, George d Jan 17, 1833 age 20 yrs.
HENDERSHOTT, Charity d March 12, 1832
KNEPELY, Lawrence d Nov 27, 1839 age 36 yrs.
    Thomas Jefferson son of Lawrence & Ann d July 4, 1837 age 5 mo 16 ds
FLOWER, Ann Mary daughter of A.&P. d July 21, 1840 age 6 2ks.
    Josephine daughter of A. & Phebe d Aug. 30, 1839 aged 2 yr 9 mo 6 ds
FLOWER, D. L. Fletcher, d Aug 21, 1839, son of A. & P. Flower
(note: next stone illegible)
MOTT, Samuel d Oct 23, 1841 aged 60 yrs.
WILSON, James d April 11, 1843 aged 26 yrs.
(note: next stone illegible)
STEWART, Robert Peeble, son of Adam & Mary d Sept. 28, 1833 aged 9 mo. 3 wks 4 ds.
MAHR, Nicolaus b Jan 16, 1801 d Sept 3, 1849
    Elizabeth dau of N. & Tordy Mahr d Aug 25, 1848 aged 16 mo.
WELDON, George Henry son of Joseph & Elizabeth d March 3, 1837 aged 3 mo.
CONWAY, Sarah dau of Patrick & Margaret d March 24, 1840 aged 17 mo.
    John son of Patrick & Margaret d Aug 12, 1834
BELL, Charles d Jan 10, 1839 aged 29 yrs.
BALDRIDGE, Mary J. wife of A. P. Baldridge d Aug 10, 1850 age 35 yrs 1 mo 3 ds
    Flora D, d 1846; Sam A., d 1846; James S., d 1850, children of A. P.
    Baldridge

BALDRIDGE, Adeline wife of A.P. Baldridge d July 24, 1838 age 27 yrs.
          (note: all Baldridges on same stone)
PHILLIPS, Frances M. dau. of Jason & Athalinda d July 20, 1835 aged 1 yr. 6 ds.
(note: next stone is illegible)
CLINTON, Thomas b in Wales, Sept. 10, 1821(?) d Sept. 13, 1838 aged 27 yrs.
DOUGLAS, Charles d Feb. 12, 1839 aged 39 yrs. Native of Scotland.
WINN, John d Sept. 11, 1838 aged _____
(note: next stone) M.H.M.
ANDERSON, Archibald P. son of Robert & Agnes d Aug 24, 1839 aged 5 yrs._____
          Esamiah dau. of Robert & Agnes d May 4, 1858 aged 19 yrs. 11 mo.
(note: next stone) E.V.
TRIMMER, Mary Ann wife of Matthias Trimmer, daughter of Abraham and Elizabeth
          Mones(?), d Nov 22, 1812 aged 21 yrs. 7 mo.
          David B son of Matthias & Mary Ann d July 19, 1812 aged 1 mo 28 ds.
SMYTH, William, June 18, 1838, aged 2 yrs 5 mo
(note: the following inscriptions are from center west of path)
LOHNES, Catharine wife of Peter Lohnes d Nov 23, 1852
SHORT, Nancy daughter of A. & M.F. Short d Jan 3, 1852 aged 3 yrs 9 mo.
SNIVELY(?), Sacred to memory of David (Snively?)
SNIVELY William H. son of David and Hannah Snively.
          Ann Elizabeth daughter of David and Hannah E. Snively.
BOGGS, Andrew 1779-1845; Sarah Biddle Boggs 1793-1845
MILES, Theodore aged 16 yrs.; Hilda aged 2 yrs.
BIDDLE, Sophia 1753-1837 (note: Boggs, Miles and Sophia Biddle all on same stone)
BOGGS, John Johnston d May 3, 1840 aged 23 yrs. 9 mo.
          Miss Rebecca d Dec. 10, 1839 aged 24 yrs. 8 mos.
WALLACE, Elizabeth S. wife of James Wallace, daughter of William and Sareph
          Mc_____ d Nov 20, 185_ aged 55 yrs.
          Mary E. R. daughter of James & E.S. d March 6, 1832 aged 4 yrs.
          Wm. McMahon, only son of James & E.S. d Sept. 24, 1832 aged 3 yrs.
SCOTT, Solomon d Sept. 19, 1837 aged 70 yrs.
_____, Frances Penelope, daughter of_____1838.
BERRY, Alice b Nov 12, 1803 d May 16 1863
(note: next stone illegible)
EBERLE, Elizabeth L. wife of William Everle, daughter of Samuel and Hannah Beers
          d March 1, 1842 aged 19 yrs. 5 mo. 14 ds.
PITTENGER, Elizabeth Jane dau. of John & Mary Ann d March 24, 1840 aged 1 yr 6 m.
          William son of John & Mary A. d April 12, 1842 aged 2 yrs.
          Mary Elizabeth dau of John & Mary A. d Dec 12 1836 aged 2 yrs.
HARRISON, Sylvania Elizabeth, dau. of Peter and S. E. Harrison.
(note: the following inscriptions are from east of center walk)
WOODS, William b Nov.__, 1802, d _____
KELLEY, James, April 30, 1837 aged 85 yrs. (Rev. Sol.)
          Catharine wife of James Kelley, deceased.
          James d Sept. 5, 1849.
ROCK, Leah d July 17, 1847 in the 11th yr. of her age.
KELLEY, Frances, June 9, 1840 in the 38th(?) yr. of his_____.
McCORD, Elizabeth dau. of John & Celia d Nov. 9, 1839 aged 10 yrs. 7 mo.
          Celia W. dau. of John & Celia d May 4, 1840 aged 11 yrs.
          Nancy infant dau. of John & Celia d June 19, 1835.
INLOW, James b Feb 4, 1809 d Jan 17, 1845 aged 36 yrs 11 mo 13 days

CRAIG, Samuel d May 28, 1839 aged 41 yrs 2 mo 12 da.

MOFFETT, Frances C. dau. of William & Sarah d Sept. 20, 1837 aged 1 yr 10 mo 18 ds.

FOGLESOII, John S. son of John S. & Ann Elizabeth d July 11, 1844 aged 1 mo 7ds.

VANCE, John d Nov 16, 1852 in his 55th yr.

    Lydia wife of J. Vance d March 6, 1825 aged 34 yrs. (same stone as John)

(note: next stone illegible)

(note: the following inscriptions are from east side)

IRDOUR, Keturah Ann wife of Drydent Irdour, daughter of Daniel and Anna Bachout,
      d Sept. 9,_____

____. Infant son of _____

HELLER, Sarah Ann wife of William Heller d May ..., 184_ in the __yr. of her age.

HOWD, George W. b Dec 19 1800 d Feb 9, 1830

    Rerec I. (?) (note: on same stone with George W.)

_____, John son of _____

(note: next two stones are illegible)

BORMAT, John son of Terrance and Elizabeth Bormat d 1815

    Elizabeth daughter of____ and Elizabeth Bormat, 1842

WATSON, John son of John & Elizabeth d Oct 25, 1845 aged 9 yrs 2 mo.

    William son of John & Elizabeth d June 17, 1818 aged 17 yrs 10 mo 8 ds.

HUNTER, Daniel d Feb. 2, 1846 aged 69 yrs.

    Rebecca wife of Daniel Hunter d March 12, 1818 aged 63 yrs. of age.

CONKLIN, William son of John and Mary, died_____

LEE, Mary d Dec. 14, 1813 about____yrs of age.

EASTMAN, Moses(?) late resident of Newhamshire, Grafton County, son of James
    and Polly Eastman d Feb. 20, 1818 aged 22 yrs.

JEWETT, Mrs. Sophia d Oct 20, 1826 aged 36 yrs.

REHLY, Jane_____of John Renly d Sept. 2, 1839 aged 19 yrs 2 mo. 29 ds.

REID, John d Aug 18, 1849 aged 60 yrs 3 mo 18 ds

KENNEY, John husband of Katharine Kenney(?)

HALL, Tobitha Jane wife of George Hall d Oct 1, 1840 aged 23 yrs.

_____./_____raha wife of Isaac_____ died M. April 21, 1853 aged 41 yrs 2 mo.__ds.

ROSS, Cyrus Presty, son of William & Ann b May 18, 1823 d April 9, 1824.

KIRKPATRICK, John Jr. d Sept 13, 1826 aged 32 yrs. 6 mo.

BEST, T.

    Jane

ADAMSON, John d Oct 8, 1841 aged 40 yrs.

SHAW, William d May 26, 1844 aged 47 yrs., a native of Chesterfield____Maryland.

    Louisa dau. of William & Sarah d Sept. 28, 1842 aged 10 mo. 11 ds.

    A____ _____(?) dau. of William & Sarah d July 7, 1849 aged 2 yrs 2 mo.

    Mary dau. of William & Mary d May __, _____; _____

PAGE, William W. son of Ha. and Sarah Page d March 4, 1831 aged 12 yrs 6 mo. 16 ds.

(note: next two stones have nothing on)

REED, Robert d Aug 21, 1830 aged 89 yrs.

    Sarah wife of Robert Reed d July 3, 1845 aged 86 yrs.

(note: next stone illegible)

(The following records were abstracted only as a finding aid for .the genealogist, complete land descriptions were not included. Pages on which original record may be found are given in parenthesis. William Lytle and Philip Buckner, among others, purchased large tracts of land that had originally been granted for military service in the Virginia Military District, they then divided these tracts into smaller tracts which they then sold.)

8-15-1800	Wm. LYTLE & Eliza N. wife of Fayette Co., Ky. to Elizabeth KELLY of Fayette Co., Ky. (1)
8-15-1800	Wm. LYTLE & Eliza N. wife of Fayette Co., Ky. to Nancy KELLY of same.(2)
3-20-1801	Wm. LYTLE & Eliza N. wife of Clermont Co. to James CAROTHERS. (3)
1-28-1801	Reubin TAYLOR of Jefferson Co., Ky. to Nathan MANNING of Clermont Co.(4)
1-28-1801	Reubin TAYLOR of Jefferson Co., Ky. to Elishua MANNING of NW Terr. (5)
-----1801	Joseph TATMAN Sr. to Nathan TATMAN. Bill of Sale. (6)
4-7-1800	Archibald BEARD & Elizabeth wife of Franklin Co. Pa. to William LYTLE of Fayette Co. Ky. (7)
4-7-1800	Archibald BARD & Eliza wife of Franklin Co. Pa. to William LYTLE of Fayette Co. Ky. (8)
7-28-1800	Wm. LYTLE & Eliza N. wife of Fayette Co. Ky. to Wm. HANSON of same. (9)
8-14-1800	Wm. LYTLE & Eliza N. wife of Hamilton Co. O to Wm. CAMPBELL of same.(10)
8-14-1800	Wm. LYTLE & Eliza N. wife of Fayette Co. Ky. to Daniel KAIN of Hamilton Co., Ohio. (11)
8-15-1800	Wm. LYTLE & Eliza N. wife of Hamilton Co. to James KAIN of same. (13)
7-28-1800	Wm. LYTLE & Eliza N. wife of Fayette Co, Ky. to William READ. (14)
8-16-1800	Wm. LYTLE & Eliza N. wife of Hamilton Co. to Sampson MURFEY of same (15)
8-15-1800	Wm. LYTLE & Eliza N. wife of Fayette Co. Ky. to David GIBSON of same.(16)
8-16-1800	Wm. LYTLE & Eliza N. wife of Hamilton Co. to Ann McADAMS of same. (17)
8-15-1800	Wm. LYTLE & Eliza N. wife of Hamilton Co. to Ephraim McADAMS of same.(18)
8-15-1800	Wm. LYTLE & Eliza N. wife of Hamilton Co. to Amos SMITH of same. (20)
8-14-1800	Wm. LYTLE & Eliza N. wife of Fayette Co. Ky. to Isaac MILLAR of Hamilton Co., Ohio, (21)
8-28-1800	Wm. LYTLE & Eliza N. wife of Fayette Co. Ky. to Polly KAIN of Hamilton Co., Ohio. (22)
8-16-1800	Wm. LYTLE & Eliza N. wife of Hamilton Co. to Thomas KAIN of same. (23)
8-16-1800	Wm. LYTLE & Eliza N. wife of Hamilton Co. to Mary BUNTING of same. (24)
3-28-1799	John Adams, Pres. United States to Daniel De BENNEVILLE, Surgeon for the War in consideration of Military Service of the U. S. in the Virginia line on the Continental Establishment. (25)
6-30-1800	Daniel De BENNEVILLE & Elizabeth wife of Phila. Pa. to William LYTLE of Lexington, Fayette Co. Ky. (26)
6-18-1798	John Adams, Pres. United States to Daniel DeBENNEVILLE, Surgeon for the War in consideration of Military Service in the Virginia line on the Continental Establishment. (28)
6-30-1800	Daniel De BENNEVILLE to William LYTLE. Assignment. (29)
6-30-1800	Daniel De BENNEVILLE & Elizabeth wife of Phila. Pa. to William LYTLE of Fayette Co. Ky. (30)
8-16-1800	Wm. LYTLE & Eliza N. wife of Hamilton Co., O. to John CORBLEY. (32)
5-25-1801	Wm. LYTLE & Eliza N. wife of Clermont Co. to Archibald McILVAIN of Fayette Co., Ky. (33)

5-11-1801   Wm. LYTLE & Eliza N. wife to Nicholas SINKS. (34)
5-11-1801   Wm. LYTLE & Eliza N. wife to Thomas BROWN of Hamilton Co. Ohio. (36)
5-11-1801   Wm. LYTLE & Eliza N. wife to Thomas BROWN and Nicholas SINKS. (37)
12-16-1800 Wm. LYTLE & Eliza N. wife to Ephraim McADAMS of Hamilton Co. O. (38)
8-15-1800   Wm. LYTLE & Eliza N. wife to Hamilton Co. to Wm. DODDS of same. (40)
9-29-1800   Wm. LYTLE & Eliza N. wife of Fayette Co. Ky. to David DODGE of same. (41)
8-15-1800   Wm. LYTLE & Eliza N. wife of Fayette Co. Ky. to John KAIN of Hamilton
            Co., Ohio. (42)
3-18-1801   Wm. LYTLE & Eliza N. wife of Clermont Co. to Jacob TEAL. (43)
7-30-1800   Wm. LYTLE & Eliza N. wife of Fayette Co. Ky. to John L. MARTIN of
            same. (44)
7-28-1800   Wm. LYTLE & Eliza N. wife of Fayette Co. Ky. to John McCORD of same. (45)
7-28-1800   Wm. LYTLE & Eliza N. wife of Fayette Co. Ky. to Isabella McCORD of
            same. (47)
7-21-1800   Wm. LYTLE & Eliza N. wife of Fayette Co. Ky. to Leven YOUNG of same. (48)
5-25-1801   Wm. LYTLE & Eliza N. wife of Clermont Co. to Wm. HANSON of Fayette
            Co. Ky. (49)
3-25-1801   Wm. LYTLE & Eliza N. wife to John MEHARD of Hamilton Co. O. (50)
5-9-1801   Wm. LYTLE & Eliza N. wife to Daniel MILLER Sr. (51)
5-9-1801   Wm. LYTLE & Eliza N. wife to David MILLER Sr. (53)
5-7-1801   Wm. LYTLE & Eliza N. wife to Charles REDMAN. (54)
5-8-1801   Wm. LYTLE & Eliza N. wife to William TERRY. (55)
3-2-1801   Robert TYLER & Margaret wife of Shelby Co. Ky. to Daniel TEAGARDEN
            of Clermont Co. (56)
6-19-1801   Wm. LYTLE & Eliza N. wife to Jacob BROADWELL assignee of Bambo HARIS
            assignee of Mr. NELSON of Hamilton Co., Ohio. (57)
10-18-1800 Wm. LYTLE & Eliza N. wife of Hamilton Co. to Nath'l DONHAM of same. (59)
6-15-1801   Robert TYLER of Shelby Co. Ky. to Jacob ULRY of Clermont Co. (60)
10-8-1800   Nathaniel MASSIE & Susan Everrard wife of Adams Co. Ohio to William
            JONES of Hamilton Co., Ohio. (61)
8-1-1800   Philemon THOMAS & Fanny wife of Mason Co. Ky. to Alexander MARTIN of
            Hamilton Co. Ohio. (62)
8-1-1800   Philemon THOMAS & Fanny wife of Mason Co. Ky. to William ELLIS of
            Hamilton Co. Ohio. (64)
8-1-1800   Philemon THOMAS & Fanny wife of Mason Co. Ky. to Heirs of William
            MOORE, dec'd of Hamilton Co., Ohio. (65)
7-30-1800   Philemon THOMAS & Fanny wife of Mason Co. Ky. to James HENRY of
            Hamilton Co., Ohio. (67)
8-1-1800   Philemon THOMAS & Fanny wife of Mason Co. Ky. to Wm. LACOCK of
            Hamilton Co., Ohio. (69)
8-1-1800   Philemon THOMAS & Fanny wife of Mason Co. Ky. to Valentine McDANIEL
            of Hamilton Co. Ohio. (70)
8-1-1800   Philemon THOMAS & Fanny wife of Mason Co. Ky. to Thomas McCONNELL
            of Hamilton Co. Ohio. (72)
7-22-1800   Wm. LYTLE & Eliza N. wife of Fayette Co. Ky. to Lawson McCULLOUGH of
            same. (73)
8-16-1800   Wm. LYTLE & Eliza N. wife of Hamilton Co. O. to Benjamin HOOD of same. (75)
4-28-1801   Wm. LYTLE & Eliza N. wife of Clermont Co. to John COTTERAL. (76)
8-15-1800   Wm. LYTLE & Eliza N. wife of Fayette Co. Ky. to Robert BOYD of
            Franklin Co. Pa. (77)

6-20-1801 Wm LYTLE & Eliza N. wife of Clermont Co. to Thomas McKEE of Franklin
Co. Pa. (78)
9-30-1800 Wm. LYTLE & Eliza N. wife of Fayette Co. Ky. to Peter JANUARY Jr.
of same. (80)
8-24-1801 Wm. LYTLE & Eliza N. wife of Clermont Co. to Luther STEPHENS of
Fayette Co. Ky. (81)
8-24-1801 Wm. LYTLE & Eliza N. wife of Hallet M. WINSLOW of Fayette Co. Ky. (82)
8-24-1801 Wm. LYTLE & Eliza N, wife to David DODGE of Fayette Co. Ky. (83)
1-9-1801 Charles PATTERSON & Elizabeth wife of Franklin Co. Ky. by Peter
PATTERSON to Morris WITHAM of Hamilton Co. Ohio. (85)
11--8-1801 Wm. LYTLE & Eliza N. wife to Ignatius WOLF of Hamilton Co. Ohio. (87)
8-3-1800 Wm. LYTLE & Eliza N. wife to Capt. Isnatius ROSS. (88)
4-22-1801 Charles PATTERS & Elizabeth wife of Franklin Co. Ky. by Peter
PATTERSON to Ignatius ROSS of Hamilton Co. Ohio. (89)
7-25-1801 Wm. LYTLE & Eliza N. wife to Hugh McLANE. (91)
8-16-1800 Wm. LYTLE & Eliza N. wife to John EARHEART of Hamilton Co. O. (92)
8-16-1800 Wm. LYTLE & Eliza N. wife of Hamilton Co. to George EARHEART Jr. of
same. (94)
11-28-1801 Wm. LYTLE & Eliza N. wife of Clermont Co. to Moses LEONARD. (95)
7-25-1801 Wm. LYTLE & Eliza N. wife to George EARHEART of Clermont Co. (96)
11-28-1801 Wm. LYTLE & Eliza N. wife to John ANDERSON. (97)
6-28-1801 James TATMAN & Elizabeth wife to Stephen POLANDER. (98)
2-3-1801 James TAYLOR of Jefferson Co. Ky. to James TATMAN of Clermont Co. (99)
2-10-1801 Philip BUCKNER & Tabbie wife of Bracken Co. Ky. to Gabriel AKINS of
Clermont Co. (100)
6-28-1801 Philip BUCKNER & Tabbie wife of Bracken Co. Ky. to James TATMAN of
Clermont Co. (101)
2-12-1801 Thomas PAXTON & Martha wife to Silas HUTCHINSON. (102)
2-10-1801 Philip BUCKNER & Tabie wife of Bracken Co. Ky. to Charles McCLAIN
of same. (104)
1-31-1801 Philip BUCKNER & Taby wife of Bracken Co. Ky. to James BUCHANNON of
Clermont Co. (105)
1-31-1801 Philip BUCKNER & Taby wife of Bracken Co. Ky. to Alexander BUCHANNON
Sr. of Clermont Co. (106)
1-31-1801 Philip BUCKNER & Taby wife of Bracken Co. Ky. to Alexander B. SHANNON
Jr. of Clermont Co. (107)
6-26-1801 Philip BUCKNER & Tabie wife of Bracken Co. Ky. to Mordaccai FORD of
Clermont Co. (109)
2-2-1801 James TAYLOR Jr. of Jefferson Co. Ky. to Nathan TATMAN of Clermont
Co. (110)
3-19-1801 Jacob FRAZEE & Elizabeth wife of Hamilton Co. to James GERARD. (111)
8-12-1801 Jacob FRAZEE & Elizabeth wife of Hamilton Co to Wm. SMALLY of same.(112)
3-26-1801 George KERR (KARR) & Martha wife of Hamilton Co. to Jacob VORIS of
same. (114)
6-19-1801 Wm. LYTLE & Eliza N. wife to James KNIGHT assignee of Jacob BROADWELL.(115)
6-19-1801 Wm. LYTLE & Eliza N. wife to James ARTHUR assignee of Jacob BROADWELL.(116)
6-24-1801 Philip BUCKNER & Tabitha wife of Bracken Co. Ky. to David WOOD of
Clermont Co. (118)
2-10-1801 Philip BUCKNER & Tabie wife of Bracken Co. Ky. to Joseph CLARK. (119)

234

2-10-1801 Philip BUCKNER & Tabie wife of Bracken Co. Ky. to David WATSON of
           Northumber land Co. Pa. (120)
2-10-1801 Philip BUCKNER & Tabie wife of Bracken Co. Ky. 'to Wm. CAROTHERS. (121)
8-5-1801   Philip BUCKNER & Tabie wife of Bracken Co. Ky. to Sanford MITCHELL
           of Mason Co. Ky. (122)
7-8-1801   Jas. TAYLOR of Jefferson Co. Ky. to Philip BUCKNER of Bracken Co.Ky.(123)
9-9-1801   Wm. LYTLE & Eliza N. wife to Heirs of William REGGS, dec'd, of
           Hamilton Co. Ohio. (124)
9-7-1801   Wm. LYTLE & Eliza N. wife to Charles WAITE of Ky. (126)
7-1-1801   Wm. LYTLE & Eliza N. wife to John REILY of Hamilton Co. Ohio. (127)
8-20-1801 Wm. LYTLE & Eliza N. wife to Roger Walton WARING. (128)
4-20-1802 Wm. LYTLE & Eliza N. wife to Daniel ROUDEBUSH. (129)
9-22-1800 John BLANCHARD & Elizabeth wife of Bracken Co. Ky. to Isabell
           McCONNELL of Hamilton Co. Ohio. (130)
9-17-1801 Wm. RADFORD of Va. to Wm. LYTLE of Clermont Co. (132)
5-16-1800 Stephen THOMPSON & Mary wife of Loudon Co. Va. to John BROWN of
           Frankford, Ky. (133)
10-4-1801 Bennet TOMPKINS by his atty. Wm. CLARK of Caroline Co. Va. to Wm.
           LYTLE of Fayette Co. Ky. (134)
10-27-1801 Wm. LYTLE & Eliza N. wife of Clermont Co. to Benajah BOSWORTH of
           Fayette Co. Ky. (135)
7-14-1801 Isnatius ROSS & Mary wife of Hamilton Co. to Zadock WATSON. (137)
7-14-1801 Isnatius ROSS & Mary wife of Hamilton Co. to John McGRAW. (138)
9-1-1801   Wm. LYTLE & Eliza N. wife of Jacob BURNET of Hamilton Co. Ohio. (140)
9-1-1801   Wm. LYTLE & Eliza N. wife of Jacob BURNET of Hamilton Co. Ohio. (141)
1-31-1801 Philip BUCKNER & Taby wife of Bracken Co. Ky. to Adam FISHER. (142)
1-31-1801 Philip BUCKNER & Taby wife of Bracken Co. Ky. to John CARMERAR. (143)
7-24-1801 Jacob FRAZER & Elizabeth wife of Hamilton Co. to Oliver POLLOCK.
           of same. (145)
7-24-1801 Jacob FRAZIER & Elizabeth wife of Hamilton Co. to John POLLOCK Jr.
           of same. (146)
8-28-1801 Wm. LYTLE & Eliza N. wife to William PERRY. (147)
8-3-1801   Wm. LYTLE & Eliza N. wife to Christopher HARTMAN of Jessamine Co. Ky.(148)
12-25-1801 Wm. LYTLE & Eliza N. wife to Thomas Steel CAVENDER. (150)
12-21-1801 Wm. PERRY & Nancy wife to Thomas BROWN of Hamilton Co. Ohio. (151)
8-26-1801 Wm. LYTLE & Eliza N. wife to Robert TOWNSLEY of Hamilton Co. (152)
12-22-1801 Wm. LYTLE & Eliza N. wife to Joseph GEST. (154)
9-15-1801 Wm. LYTLE & Eliza N. wife to Lewis FRYBERGER of Hamilton Co. (155)
1-8-1802   Wm. LYTLE & Eliza N. wife to Hannah SMITH, John PARKER and Levi
           TODD, Executors of the will of Elijah SMITH, dec'd. (157)
1-19-1802 Wm. LYTLE & Eliza N. wife to Amos SMITH. (159)
1-20-1802 Wm. LYTLE & Eliza N. wife to James WINTERS. (160)
1-26-1802 Wm. LYTLE & Eliza N. wife to Wilson HUNT of Fayette Co. Ky. (161)
1-26-1802 Wm. LYTLE & Eliza N. wife to Jonathan HUNT of Clermont Co. (162)
1-26-1802 Wm. LYTLE & Eliza N. wife to James HUNT of Clermont Co. (164)
1-26-1802 Wm. LYTLE & Eliza N. wife to Daniel BRYAN of Fayette Co. Ky. (165)
1-26-1802 Wm. LYTLE & Eliza N. wife to Jasper SHOTWELL, Esq. (166)
1-26-1802 Wm. LYTLE & Eliza N. wife to John SHOTWELL. (167)

235

11-27-1801 John BROWN & Margaretta wife of Franklin Co. Ky. to Benjamin PARISH OF Fayette Co. Ky. (169)

8-20-1801 Wm. LYTLE & Eliza N. wife to Ebenezer OSBURN. (170)

3-1-1802 Nathaniel MASSIE & Susan wife of Ross Co. O. to Joseph DUGGIN. (171)

3-18-1802 James CURRY & Mary wife of Ross Co. O. to Representatives of Robert CURRY, dec'd, of Clermont Co. (172)

2-20-1802 Richard TAYLOR of Jefferson Co. Ky. to Stephen BOLANDER of Clermont Co. (174)

8-17-1801 Edward MILLER & Elizabeth wife to Jacob TEAL. (175)

2-23-1802 Wm. LYTLE & Eliza N. wife to Robt. DICKEY. (176)

8-28-1801 Wm. LYTLE & Eliza N. wife to Abel DONHAM. (177)

8-28-1801 Wm. LYTLE & Eliza N. wife to Robert DONHAM. (180)

8-20-1801 Wm. LYTLE & Eliza N. wife to John DONHAM. (181)

12-16-1801 Wm. LYTLE & Eliza N. wife to John McADAMS of Hamilton Co. (182)

3-29-1802 Wm. LYTLE & Eliza N. wife to Ignatius ROSS of Hamilton Co. (184)

3-15-1802 Wm. LYTLE & Eliza N. wife to Wm. CAMPBELL. (185)

10-26-1801 Hezekiah CONN of Clermont Co. to William BLIETH, Merchant of Hamilton Co. Ohio. Said land granted to Hezekiah Conn by indenture executed and recorded Bourbon Co., Ky. 5-23-1800 between Thomas Conn and said Hezekiah for love and affection of Thomas for his son the said Hezekiah. (186)

2-12-1801 Joseph CLARK & Sarah wife to Alexander KENNEDY. (189)

2-13-1802 Nathan TATMAN of Clermont Co. to John DAY of Bracken Co. Ky. (190)

4-4-1802 Philip BUCKNER & Tabie wife of Bracken Co. Ky. to John MILLAR. (191)

10-5-1801 James TATMAN & Elizabeth wife to Jacob JONES. (192)

4-20-1802 Wm. LYTLE & Eliza N. wife to Owen TODD. (193)

5-25-1802 Hezekiah CONN to Rodham MOURNING. (194)

5-22-1802 Wm. LACOCK & Silruce wife to Heirs of Joseph LACOCK, dec'd. (195)

7-8-1801 Pugh PRICE of Fayette Co. Ky. to Wm. LYTLE of Clermong Co. Power of Attorney. (196)

5-6-1801 George Rogers CLARK of Jefferson Co. Ky. to William CROGHAN of same. Mortgage. (197)

5-4-1802 Wm. LYTLE & Eliza N. wife to Heirs of Richard BARD, dec'd of Franklin Co. Pa. (199)

5-4-1802 Wm. LYTLE & Eliza N. wife to Heirs of Richard BEARD, dec'd of Franklin Co. Pa. (200)

----1802 Alexander McLAUGHLIN, Collector of Territorial Taxes to Nathan ELLIS of Adams Co. Ohio. (202)

7-10-1801 Nathaniel MASSIE & Susan wife of Adams Co. Ohio to Wm. LYTLE of Clermont Co. (203)

6-12-1802 Wm. LYTLE & Eliza N. wife to John COLTHER Sr. (204)

6-12-1802 Wm. LYTLE & Eliza N. wife to John COLTHER Jr. (205)

8-12-1802 Wm. LYTLE & Eliza N. wife to John FAGIN. (207)

CLERMONT COUNTY, OHIO - DEED BOOK D-3 - 1799-1806

By Anita Short, C.G., Editor, GATEWAY TO THE WEST

(The following records were abstracted as a finding aid for the genealogical researcher, complete land descriptions have not been included. Pages on which original record may be found are given in parenthesis.)

2-7-1799 Matthew WINTON, carpenter of Hamilton Co. O. to Thomas GOUDY of same. (1)
9-4-1804 Wm. C. SCHENCK, Esq. of Hamilton Co. to James SMITH & James FINDLAY, (2)
9-6-1805 John SAVORY of Bourbon Co. Ky. to Thomas PAGE.   (5)
6-14-1804 Robert Clark JACOB of Northampton Co. Va. to James JOHNSON. Power of
          Attorney.   (7)
6-15-1805 Jas. JOHNSON by Power of Atty. of Robert Clark JACOB to Christian SHINKLE
          of Clermont Co.   (8)
6-16-1804 Robert Clk. JACOB of Northampton Co. Va. assignee of Henry WILLIS a Capt.
          of U. S. in Virginia Continental Establishment to James JOHNSON.
          Power of Attorney.   (10)
12-7-1805 Jas. JOHNSON by Power of Atty. of Robert Clark JACOB to Green CLAY of
          Madison Co. Ky.   (11)
1-8-1806 Will of Lewis JOYNES (note: surname spelled interchangeably as Joynes
          and Jones). Wife, Ann, also to serve as executrix. Sons: John,
          Lewis and Thomas Robinson Joynes. Daughters: Susannah, Ann Smith
          and Sarah Joynes. Dated 12-15-1793. Signed, Lewis Joynes. Codi-
          cil, gives no additional information. Recorded 10-27-1794 Accomack
          Co. Va. Recorded 1-8-1806 Clermont Co. Ohio.   (13)
6-25-1806 John SMITH adms. of Lewis JOYNES of Accomack Co. Va. to James JOHNSON
          of Northampton Co. Va. Power of Attorney.   (17)
7-15-1805 John LIGGERT of Clermont Co. by Power of Atty. of Jane BRECKENRIDGE
          Executrix & Devisee of Alexander BRECKENRIDGE, dec'd to Robert POGUE.(19)
7-15-1805 John LIGGERT by Power of Atty. of Jane BRECKENRIDGE to Henry CHAPMAN.(20)
7-15-1805 John LIGGERT by Power of Atty. of Jane BRECKENRIDGE to Wm. CHAPMAN. (21)
7-15-1805 John LIGGERT by Power of Atty. of Jane BRECKENRIDGE to William FORSYTHE
          and John McCONAUGHTY.   (22)
7-27-1805 Philip BUCKNER & Tabie wife of Bracken Co. Ky. to Thomas CORNICH. (23)
7-5-1805 Philip BUCKNER & Tabie wife of Bracken Co. Ky. to Abram SILLS. (24)
7-5-1805 Philip BUCKNER & Tabie wife of Bracken Co. Ky. to Joshua JORDON. (25)
7-5-1805 Philip BUCKNER & Tabie wife of Bracken Co. Ky. to Jeremiah WASHBURN. (26)
7-5-1805 Philip BUCKNER & Tabie wife of Bracken Co. Ky. to John MORECRAFT. (27)
7-5-1805 Philip BUCKNER & Tabie wife of Bracken Co. Ky. to John LEAGERT. (28)
3-10-1804 Thomas HARELL of Hanover Co. Va. to William MARSHALL of Richmond, Va.(29)
6-7-1804 Thomas CARMEAL of Kentucky to William MARSHALL of Virginia. (30)
11-3-1804 John FINLEY of Fleming Co. Ky. to John Whetstone. (31)
9-17-1805 Mathew COULTER to John BROOKS, both of Clermont Co.   (33)
9-6-1805 John SAVORY of Bourbon Co. Ky. to George SEVING of Clermont Co. (34)
6-6-1805 Thos. PAXTON & Martha wife to William LYTLE, both of Clermont Co. (37)
7-28-1803 Wm. LYTLE & Eliza N. wife to John LYTLE. (38)
7-2-1805 Robert MEANS of Richmond, Va. by Power of Atty. to James TAYLOR of Norfolk
          Co. Va. executor of will of James HERON of Richmond, Va., dec'd to
          William LYTLE. Power of Atty. recorded 3-1-1805 Ross Co. Ohio (39)
----1805 Wm. LYTLE & Eliza N. wife to Absolam BROOKS.   (42)

11-4-1804 John FINLEY of Fleming Co. Ky. to Richard ALLISON. (43)
8-24-1805 Wm. Lytle & Eliza N. wife to Benjamin WOOD of Adams Co. Ohio. (44)
--1805 William ROSE of Mason Co. Ky. to Alexander ROBB of Clermont Co. (47)
9-7-1804 Wm. PERRY & Nancy wife to James McGARWICK of Kentucky. (48)
6-7-1805 Philip BUCKNER & Tabie wife of Bracken Co. Ky. to John Phlip SHINGLE. (49)
9-5-1805 Wm. LYTLE & Eliza wife to Jacob STROUP, both of Clermont Co. (50)
2-9-1805 Thomas PAXTON & Martha wife to James DAVISON, both of Clermont Co. (51)
--1805 John COLLINS & Sarah wife to David WHITE, both of Clermont Co. (52)
-(1805?) John COLLINS & Sarah wife to Robert LEIDS, Thomas PAGE, Daniel TEAGARDEN,
        William SIMONS, Benjamin CLARK and David WHITE. (53)
4-4-1805 Edward S. HACKLEY of Fredericks, Va. & Ann wife to Robert PATTON and
        Robert WALKER of same. (56)
10-12-1805 John MILLER & Catherine wife to Peter DEWITT, both of Clermont Co. (57)
12-5-1805 Wm. LYTLE & Eliza wife to Benjamin SNIDER, both of Clermont Co. (59)
12-10-1805 Levi ROGERS, Doctor of Medicine & Anna wife to John CHARLES. (60)
8-4-1805 John COLLINS to Robert DAUGHTY, both of Clermont Co. (61)
8-2-1805 John WHITSTONE of Hamilton Co. to George BOLTS of Clermont Co. (62)
12-10-1805 Wm. LYTLE & Eliza wife to John Metcalf. (63)
12-17-1805 Wm. LYTLE & Eliza wife to Richard HALL. (64)
----1805 Abel DONHAM of Clermont Co. by Power of Atty. of Nathaniel LUCAS of
        Montgomery Co. Va. to John FRANTS. (65)
12-28-1805 Francis GRAHAM of Franklin Co. Ky. to Wm. LYTLE of Clermont Co. (65)
8-13-1805 Wm. LYTLE & Eliza wife to John CHARLES, both of Hamilton Co. O. (67)
10-30-1805 Charles REDIMON & Mary wife of Harrison Co. Ky. to Joseph MOOR(E) (68)
1-7-1806 Obed DENHAM & Mary wife to William SOUTH, both of Clermont Co. (69)
1-27-1806 Obed DENHAM & Mary wife to James SOUTH, both of Clermont Co. (71)
2-7-1806 Green CLAY of Madison Co. Ky. to Robert C. JACOB of Northampton Co. Va.(72)
10-10-1805 John CHARLES to Samuel MILLER. Agreement. (74)
11-5-1805 Thomas WATTS & Elenor wife to John REDDEBOUGH, both of Clermont Co.(75)
4-25-1805 Wm. LYTLE & Eliza wife to Levi ROGERS, both of Clermont Co. (76)
11-14-1805 Joseph MOORE & Nancy wife to Thomas COOK, both of Clermont Co. (78)
9-10-1805 John TRASEY & Esther wife to Mathew COLTER, both of Clermont Co. (79)
1-20-1805 Thomas GOUDY & Sarah wife to William HUGHES, both of Clermont Co. (80)
10-18-1805 William DENHAM of Pulaski Co. Ky. to Samuel BECK of Clermont Co. (81)
10-18-1805 William DENHAM of Pulaski Co. Ky. to Kilby BURK of Clermont Co. '83)
2-4-1806 Thomas GOUDY of Warren Co. O. to Heirs of Robert TODD, dec'd. of Ky.(84)
1-3-1805 William HUGHES to Thomas GOUDY, Esq., both of Clermont Co. (85)
2-13-1805 Archibald SMITH to Philip TURPIN, both of Anderson twp., Hamilton Co.(86)
2-18-1806 Wm. LYTLE & Eliza wife to J. William JEDD, both of Clermont Co. (87)
2-18-1806 Wm. LYTLE & Eliza wife to Joshua DAVIS. (88)
2-6-1806 Wm. LYTLE & Eliza wife to Isaac EDWARDS, both of Clermont Co. (90)
12-8-1804 John KAIN & Elizabeth wife to David KIDD. (92)
3-3-1806 Adam SNIDER to Ramoth BUNTING. (94)
3-8-1806 David KIDD & Nancy wife to James KAIN, both of Clermont Co. (95)
6-13-1805 Richard GERNON of Phila. Pa. to John SAVARY of Millsburgh, Ky. (96)
1-18-1806 Abel DUNHAM to John FRANCE, both of Clermont Co. (99)
2-20-1810 Sylvester HUTCHINSON to Ezekiel HUTCHINSON, both of Middlesex, N.J.(101)
3-1-1806 Sylvester HUTCHINSON of Middlesex, N.J. to Joseph JAMES of Warren Co.
        Ohio. (102)

238

3-24-1806 Obed DENHAM of Clermont Co. to James DENHAM of Harrisfield twp., Pa.(103)
2-15-1806 James HILL & Amelia wife to Rose RONEY, both of Clermont Co. (106)
10-17-1805 Morgan BRYAN & Maxsymealy wife of Henry Co. Ky. to Thomas FER of Clermont
               Co. (108)
3-25-1806 Andrew APPLE Sr. & Catherine wife to Henry APPLE, both of Clermont Co.(109)
1-29-1806 Wm. LYTLE & Eliza wife to John DUNHAM, both of Clermont Co. (110)
4-15-1806 Wm. LYTLE & Eliza wife to Joseph GEST, both of Clermont Co. (112)
4-15-1806 Wm. LYTLE & Eliza wife to Ezekiel DUNWITT(?), both of Clermont Co. (113)
Sept.1805 Col. Wm. LYTLE & Eliza wife to Dr. Levi ROGERS, both of Clermont Co.(115)
9-8-1805   Col. Wm. LYTLE & Eliza wife to Dr. Levi ROGERS. (116)
2-14-1806 Col. Wm. LYTLE & Eliza wife to Dr. Levi ROGERS. (117)
2-14-1804 Col. Wm. LYTLE & Eliza wife to Dr. Levi ROGERS. (118)
3-15-1806 Col. Wm. LYTLE & Eliza wife to Adam BRICKER, both of Clermont Co. (119)
2-14-1806 Levi ROGERS & Anna wife to William LYTLE, Esq. (121)
3-1-1806   Matthew COLTER to John COLTER, both of Clermont Co. (123)
12-11-1805 Wm. LYTLE & Eliza wife to Samuel WALKER of Warren Co., Ohio. (125)
3-12-1806 Joseph KERR & Nancy wife of Ross Co. O. to Jenathan LINING. (126)
4-7-1806   James SCHANTLING & Nancy wife to Benjamin PARISH, both of Fayette Co.
               Ky. (127)
3-20-1806 Joseph KERR & Nancy wife of Ross Co. O. to Thomas LINING. (129)
4-14-1806 Wm. LYTLE & Eliza wife to John CHARLES, both of Clermont Co. (131)
4-14-1806 Wm. LYTLE & Eliza wife to John EARHART. (132)
4-15-1806 Wm. LYTLE & Eliza wife to John IRVINE. (135)
10-1-1805 Isaac HIGBY & Sophia wife to Cornelius McCALLUM. (137)
10-1-1805 Cornelius McCALLUM to Isaac HIGBY, both of Clermont Co. (138)
4-29-1806 Samuel BOYD to Abigail Roorland BOYD. (140)
6-16-1800 Thomas BAXTON of Hamilton Co. O. to Redman McDOUGH. (141)
3-20-1806 Rancoth BUNTING & Sarah wife to Nicholas SINKS, both of Clermont Co.(142)
12-20-1805 Nathaniel MASSIE & Susan wife of Ross Co. O. to Samuel SALISBURY. (143)
——1806   Thomas SCOTT, Tax Collector to John CARLISLE. (145)
3-26-1806 Thomas Jefferson, Pres. United States to Philip EASTON, a Lt. in consid-
               eration of Military Service for 7 yrs. in Virginia Line on the Contin-
               ental Establishment. (146)
4-11-1806 Morris WITHAM to John BENNETT, both of Clermont Co. (148)
4-12-1806 Morris WHITHAM to James BENNETT, both of Clermont Co. (150)
4-11-1806 Morris WHITHAM & Hannah wife to John WARREN. (152)
4-12-1806 Morris WHITHAM & Hannah wife to Abraham REDDIN(?). (153)
4-12-1806 Morris WHITHAM & Hannah wife to Isaiah PRICKET. (155)
4-12-1806 Morris WHITHAM & Hannah wife to Nicholas PRICKET. (156)
4-19-1806 William LINDSEY & Nancy wife to James FITZPATRICK. (158)
10-3-1805 George BOTTS & Sarah wife to Matthew BONER. (160)
3-28-1806 John O. SANNON(?) of Woodford Co. Ky. to Philip MAINS. (161)
2-22-1806 John RAY & Mary wife to Nathan MORGAN. (162)
10-11-1805 James ROLSTON & Matthew ROLSTON executor of John McDAGAL, dec'd of Mason(?)
               Co. Va. to John DEMOS. (163)
5-20-1806 Wiley CAMPBELL by Power of Atty. of Beverly RAY of King & Queen Co. Va.
               to Philip BUCKNER of Bracken Co. Ky. (164)
5-22-1806 Philip BUCKNER & Tabie wife of Bracken Co. Ky. to George HUMLONG(?).(165)
6-24-1805 James ALLEN Sr. & Margaret wife of Augusta Co. Va. to John BELL of
               Fayette Co. Ky. (167)

3-12-1806 John POLLOCK & Anna wife to John Pollock HARE, both of Clermont Co.(168
4-11-1806 James POLLOCK & Rachael wife of Hamilton Co. O. to Thomas HAIR. (169)
4-9-1806 Thomas SCOTT, Tax collector to James BUCHANUN. (170)
4-11-1806 Thomas SCOTT, Tax collector to John CARLISIE. (171)
4-12-1806 Morris WHITAM to Gibbons BRADBERRY, both of Clermont Co. (173)
5-29-1806 Deposition of Francis DUNLAVY, Esq. taken 5-29-1806 concerning survey lines of a tract surveyed in name of John BRECKENRIDGE. (174)
2-14-1806 John McGILMORE of Lancaster Co. Va. to Samuel DAVID of Jefferson Co., Ky. (176)
4-2-1806 John PRUTON(?) and Wm. MUNFORD executors of will of William RADFORD of Richmond, Va. to John RADFORD, their brother-in-law. Power of Atty. (178)

CLERMONT COUNTY, OHIO - DEED RECORDS

H. PACKARD HEIRS by Sheriff to Peter PACKARD - 3-11-18__ On 9-5-1853 Peter and Benjamin Packard of Clermont Co. filed their petition in the Court of Common Pleas for said county against Richard Frazee, Mary Frazee, Harmon Osburn, Eliza Osburn, Hannah Williams, Moses Williams, Stephen Golden, Ann Golden, Charles Pasquer, Martha Pasquer, Frazee Packard, Henry Packard, Phebe Packard, Rebecca Packard, James Packard, Harriet Packard, John Packard and Rachel Packard heirs of Henry Packard, dec'd, demanding partition of real estate. Said real estate was sold at public auction to Peter Packard for $33.50 per acre and consisted of 131½ acres; lines—Samuel Potts, County Road, Thomas Paxton. Deed Book W-3 (or 36), pages 357-359.

Benjamin CRAMER and Chalista his wife, Samuel CRAMER and Esther his wife, William BROWN and Sarah his wife, Joel CURLESS and Rachel his wife, Joseph CURLESS and Mary his wife, Thomas ASHTON and Elizabeth his wife of Brown and Clermont Cos. to Richard CRAMER of Clermont Co. - 12-21-1827 - $300. - on waters of Grassy run in Survey entered by William Johnston #1209, lines-three dogwoods, Grassy Run, etc. Deed Book M-2 (or 36), page 82.

Robert FEE, John HALL, John BARKLEY and Margaret his wife, John G. BUCHANAN and Catherine his wife, William P. DAUGHTERS and Hannah his wife, Alexander BUCHANA and Lamira I. his wife, Dickson BUCHANAN and Robert BUCHANAN heirs of Robert BUCHANAN, dec'd, all of Clermont Co. to Azariah JARMAN of Clermont Co. - 6-5-1836 - $400. - 76 acres and 80 poles being on Bear Creek part of tract known as Buchanan saw mill tract being part of Daniel Morgan's survey #659 and part in Daniel Flowers survey #1318 and part in John Nevills survey #388; lines-bank of creek, Squire Frazee, Elisha Manning, Philip Main and Neville Road. Deed Book M-2 (or 36), page 130.

Henry FISHER of Shelby Co., Indiana, John and Daniel FISHER of Clermont County to David FISHER of Clermont County - 10-28-1836 - $150. - farm formerly owned by Acrn Fisher, dec'd being part of Beverly Roys survey #1064; lines—Andrew Buchanan, John Cramer, Thomas Fee, Samuel Wilson, John McWilliams, Samuel Buchanan, nd Anthony Jones; being 140 acres. Deed Book Z-2 (or 44) page 389.

John NEEDHAM and Rozannah his wife, Joseph NEEDHAM and Rebeckah his wife, Joseph KIDD and Sarah his wife, George NEEDHAM, James NEEDHAM and Agnes his wife all of Clermont Co. to William NEEDHAM of Clermont Co. - 1-14-1834 - in consideration of certain lots of land willed to John, Joseph, George, and James Needham and Joseph Kidd by John Needham, Sr., being land on waters of Stonelick part of a patent granted to James Taylor of Newport, Ky.; lines—George Needham, James Needham, Joseph Brunk; being 92 acres. Deed Book G-2 (or 31), pages 79-80.

Jane FLANEGAN widow of John FLANEGAN, dec'd, Joseph DURHAM and Jane his wife, John GARRETT and Elizabeth his wife, Robert SWEET and Rebecah his wife, William CONKLIN and Sarah his wife, all late of Clermont Co. to James Flanegan of Clermont Co. - 10-28-1833 - $280. - 70 acres near margin of Ohio River in Monroe township; lines—bank of river and James Cooper; survey formerly belonging to John Flanegan originally part of a tract of 1300 acres, Warrant #1892 patented to Alexander Parker on Feb. 20, 1793. Deed Book G-2 (or 31), page 199.

Hannah BRYAN widow of Melancthon A. BRYAN, dec'd, David C. BRYAN and Thomas L. BRYAN to John M. BROWN at Clermont Co. - 2-25-1834 - Quit Claim of Lot #8 in Batavia - Deed Book G-2 (or 31), page 130.

David C. BRYAN and Mary Malvina his wife, Thomas BRYAN and Katharine his wife, Nancy EVERHEART late BRYAN and Titus EVERHEART her husband heirs of David C. BRYAN late of Clermont Co., dec'd and Ruth BRYAN widow of said David C. BRYAN, dec'd, Mary BRYAN widow of George S. BRYAN, dec'd and Hannah BRYAN widow of Malacthon BRYAN, dec'd, all of Clermont Co. to Wm. MOUNT of Clermont Co. - 12-5-1836 - $5.00 - SW½ of in-lot #114 in Batavia. Deed Book M-2 (or 36), page 322.

Rhoda WHETSTONE widow of Jacob WHETSTONE, dec'd, Jasper WHETSTONE, Elnathan WHETSTONE and Nancy his wife, John WHETSTONE, Abijah WHETSTONE and Lucinda his wife, McCalla STOUT and Cynthia his wife late Cynthia WHETSTONE and Frances WHETSTONE heirs of Jacob WHETSTONE, dec'd to William CURRY of Clermont Co. - 5-30-1833 - $3324. - 443 acres except 49 acres conveyed by Elnathan Whetstone and wife to Wm. Curry by deed of 11-1-1832, being on East fork of Little Miami part of James Winlocks survey #1771; lines—creek. Deed Book G-2 (or 31), page 346.

David R. CARRALL and Elizabeth his wife, John W. CARRALL and Amalthe his wife, William HETH and Mary Ann his wife, John GERGUSON and Sarah his wife, John B. D. VEIRS all of Harrison Co., Indiana to Enos J. SEARL of Clermont Co. - 5-8-1834 - $30. - N½ lot #2 in New Richmond. Deed Book G-2 (or 31), page 365.

Ama FLETCHER and Caroline FLETCHER heirs of John FLETCHER, dec'd late of Clermont Co., Thomas BRACKEN, John STEWART and Mary his wife late BRACKEN, Isaac BREWER and Ann his wife late BRACKEN, John BRACKEN and James BRACKEN heirs of William FLETCHER, dec'd, late of Clermont Co. to Robert GALBREATH of Clermont Co - 8-7-1836 - $800. - 52 acres and 140 poles on Ohio River, lines—Robert Galbreath, Heirs of Thomas Fletcher, dec'd, Azariah Jarman; being part of Daniel Morgan's survey #659 - Deed Book M-2 (or 36), page 208.

Elizabeth RANKINS, John LIGHT and Mary his wife, David LIGHT and Harriet his wife, Daniel LIGHT and Cynthia his wife, Jacob LIGHT and Elizabeth his wife, Peter LIGHT and Hesibeth his wife, Benjamin LIGHT and Elmira his wife all of Clermont Co., William DORREL and Mary his wife late Mary LIGHT, Timothy CONNER and Susannah his wife late Susannah LIGHT all of Dearborn Co., Indiana, Samuel REARDEN and Catharine his wife late Catharine LIGHT of Campbell Co., Kentucky, children and heirs of Jacob LIGHT, dec'd late of Clermont Co. to Hugh FERGUSON - 5-19-1836 - $100. - Lots #114 and 115 in New Richmond. Deed Book M-2 (or 36), page 252.

Joseph LEEVER and Margaret his wife, Lewis LEEVER and Mary his wife, Benjamin LEEVER and Margaret his wife, Peter LEEVER and Sally his wife, Samuel LEEVER and Nancy his wife, George LEEVER and Elizabeth his wife, Elizabeth ANSHUTZE, Adam LEEVER and Elizabeth his wife all of Clermont Co. to Ludwell G. GAINS of Clermont Co. - 5-9-1835 - $81. - 6 and 3/4ths acres and 13 poles; lines-- Peter Fryberger, David Roudebush and David Shederly. Deed Book M-2 (or 36), page 261.

Joseph FAGIN and Rachel, his wife, Andrew GRAY and Lucy, his wife, Jeremiah GRAY and Susan, his wife, Henry GRAY and Rachel, his wife, James H. GRAY and Lucy, his wife, Aaron GRAY and Nancy, his wife, John G. SCOTT and Mary, his wife, Nancy WINNANS late GRAY, Aaron PARKER husband of Elizabeth PARKER, dec'd, late Elizabeth GRAY all of Clermont Co. to Hiram GRAY of Clermont Co. - 12-10-1836 - $450. - 125 acres, lines--Ohio River, Isaac Ferguson; as survey- ed in name of Robert Joull(?) and part to Nathaniel Massie and conveyed by Massie to Archibald GRAY. Deed Book M-2 (or 36), page 315.

WHITE PILLARS-PAXTON CEMETERY - CLERMONT COUNTY, OHIO

Located near Loveland, Ohio on State Route 48
RAMSEY, James b 12-28-1827 d 10-31-1909 (same stone as Minerva)
 Minerva Arbuckle, his wife b 1-21-1831 d-------(not engraved)
PAXTON, Thomas Paxton, a soldier_____Revolution. Colonel Thomas Paxton was born
   In Lancaster Co., Pa._____in_____he was_____Lt.
   Col of_____Battalion of Pa._____Bedford Co. in 17__
   until the close of the_____. He participated _____West campaign
   against the Indians under Gen. Anthony Wayne and was present at the
   battle of Fallen Timbers. Died____(note: much of stone unreadable)
_____, Augustus M., son of _____ d 12-8-1887
RAMSEY, Catherine d 1-20-1879 a 76y 8m 23d
  John d 10-8-1872 a 76y 8m 3d
  Isabella wife of John Ramsey d_____1837

     PAXTON CEMETERY - CLERMONT COUNTY, OHIO

Located on Guinea Pike, near Branch Hill, Ohio
ORR, Sanders son of William and Sarah b 6-9-1846 d 6-22-1872 a 26y 13d (note:
     Sarah Orr was daughter of Thomas Paxton)
  William d 7-6-1863 a 63y
PRICE, In memory of Catherine wife of John S. Price who died 8-2-1846 a 22y 10m 15d
LEEVER, Lizzie A. wife of A. A. Leever d 9-15-1857 a 28y 1m
MOTSINGER, Mary wife of Felix Motsinger b 1-11-1792 d 3-18-1866
HUTCHINSON, Joseph d 6-28-1853 a 71y 7m 14d
  William H. d 1-29-1855 a 30y 3m 12d
other names in cemetery for which most of stones are readable: SANDERS. REDDING,
YOUNG, CREAGER, FITZWATER, NEWLOVE, HAWLEY, NELSON, CROOKS, HOMER, POTTS,
BUCHANAN, RIGGS AND COOK.

Copied and contributed by Mr. and Mrs. Clyde Shilt, Rt. 3, Westbrook Rd., Brookville, Ohio 45309. Cemetery is located south of Port William one-half mile on Route 134 to Horseshoe Rd., three-fourths mile on north side back in field.

JOSEPH H. DANIEL died Oct. 26, 1866 aged 55 yrs.
ROBERT W. son of J.H.(?) & M.C. DANIEL died Mar. 8, 1865. Aged 14y 10m 12d
MARGARET wife & infant son of JOSEPH WILLIAMS who died Aug. 4, 1843
aged 43 yrs. 9 ms.
SUSAN wife of J. WILLIAMS died Aug. 5, 1902 aged 91 yrs. 3 m. 21 ds. Mother
JOSEPH WILLIAMS died June 17, 1874 aged 80 yrs 3 mo 5 ds. Father (ss Susan)
MARY - Consort of JOSEPH WILLIAMS Senior died Nov. 4, 1843 aged 92yrs 5 ms.
ANDREW MARION son of JOHN C. & DELILA EARLEY died June 1, 1866
aged 11 yrs. 10 ms. 10 ds.
SILAS EARLEY son of J.C. & D. EARLEY died Aug. 4, 1855 aged 1y 6m 18d.
SARAH daug. of A. & E. JOHNSON died Nov. 1833 6 yrs.
JOHN M. CASELDINE died Aug. 9, 1846 in the 37th yr. of his life.
LUELLA JANE daug. of DANIEL & LOUISE EARLEY died Mar. 9, 1868 aged 1 mo 14 ds.
HENRY E. son of D.S. & DEBORAH SHIELDS died Dec. 21, 1860 aged 11 yrs. 12 ds.
MARY E. daug. of D.S. & DEBORAH SHIELDS died Sept. 4, 1852 aged 1 yr 6m 2ds.
JOHN A. son of D.S. & D. SHIELDS died Aug. 16, 1849 aged 9m 23ds.
DAVID SHIELDS died July 21, 1841 aged 88 yrs. (Revolutionary War)
ELIZABETH_____(?) of Daniel & _____(?) died July 11, 1838 aged (8)4 yrs.
(Note:- Stone effaced)
JAMES SHIELDS died May 25, 1856 aged 72 yr. 9m 8d
(Note:- Marker Stones) J.S., J.A.S., J.L.S., B.S., D.S.S.
ISABEL A BEAL 1826-1827; KATHARINE A. BEAL 1834   (Note: ss)
GEORGE BEAL 1825-1846
JACOB BEAL 1835-1837
WM. BEAL Jan. 4, 1837 - Dec. 31, 1837
JACOB BEAL 1779-1850
MARGARET BEAL 1801-1892
PETER H. STEPHENS died Mar. 16, 1876
MARY A. wife of P.H.STEPHENS died Feb. 1, 1883 aged 74 yrs. 1 mo. 6 ds.
SARAH A. wife of CHRISTOPHER ELLIS and daug. of D.C. STEPHENS died June 29,
1855   18yrs 9mo 3ds
BIRDY son of J.H. & I.A. STEPHENS died Feb. 11, 1873 aged 3 days
DAVID M. STEPHENS died Aug. 25, 1878 aged 48 yrs 7 ms 21 ds
W. S. STEPHENS died June 3, 1863   30 yrs 10 mo 23 ds
(Marker Stone) J.W.
CHARITY daughter of JOSEPH N. LARGE died Aug 3, 1842 aged 1 yr 2m 14 days
CALVIN LOUIS son of DANIEL & LOUISA EARLEY died Aug. 24, 1853 aged 1y 10m 21d.
MAUD infant daug. of J.C. & M.E. EARLEY died Mar. 25, 1877
W.M.T. son of D.R. EARLEY died Feb. 23, 1838 aged 18yr 9m 25 days
CHARLES L. died Feb. 4, 1861 aged 1 year
CHARLES L. son of J.T. & I. EARLEY died Feb. 4, 1861 aged 1 year (2 stones)
(Stone Markers) EE, J.H.J, A.E., I.E., L.J.E., W.T.E., C.L.E., R.S.E.
AARON H. son of A. & E. ELLIS died Mar. 4, 1849 aged 7mo 4ds
(Stone Markers) M.H., S.B.
ELIZABETH - consort of A.W. HOBLIT died March 22, 1847 aged 25 yrs 1m 1d

MARY wife of PETER STEPHENS died May 1836 aged 72 yrs.
PETER STEPHENS died Mar. 10, 1838 aged 78 yrs.
Infant dau. of J.A. & P.C.B. FIELDS born and died Sept. 9, 1855
ANDREW CALDWELL died Sept. 21, 1869 aged 65 yr 5m 13ds
LIEULLA J. dau of T.J. & S.I. HAWS died Aug 23, 1812 aged 1m 3ds (1842?)
JOHN WILLIAM son of ISAAC & SARAH WILSON died Aug. 9, 1845 aged 3 yrs 5m
MARGARET M.H. SABIN died Sept. 8, 1838 aged 7 yr 8 m
SARAH daug. of A.&E. WILSON died Nov. 1833 aged 6 yrs.
Infant son of T.W. & M.J. DORAN died Mar. 25, 1854 aged 10 ds.
LEUIRA dau of T.W. & M.J. DORAN died Mar. 18, 1862 aged 1 mo 18 ds.
DANIEL EARLEY died Oct. 20, 1876 aged 77 yrs. 9 m. 10 ds.
RACHEL wife of D. EARLEY born July 15, 1807 died Jan. 28, 1881
JOHN LOUIS son of P.H. & M.A. STEPHENS died Aug. 3, 1860 aged 21 yrs 1m 14ds
ISABEL A. wife of J.M. STEPHENS died Feb. 27, 1873 aged 26yrs 8mo 5ds
MARY F. daug. of JOHN & LEAH OWENS died Sept 16, 1858 aged 10mo 3ds
(Stone markers) I.A.S., M.O., M.F.O.
ELIZABETH J. wife of Wm. M. ADAIR died May 29, 1856 aged 23 yr 8m 6d
HUGH ADAIR died Mar. 16, 1859 aged 11yr 1m 18ds
ISAAC M. STEPHENS died Nov. 22, 1864 aged 34 yrs
CHARLES W. son of I.H. & A.J. STEPHENS died Nov. 28, 1861 aged 5y 11m 4ds
CHRISTINA STEPHENS died June 7, 1860 aged 79 yrs
SARAH wife of CHRISTIAN STEPHENS died Mar. 22, 1866 aged 81 yrs
ALLETTA STEPHENS died Mar. 20, 1871 33 yrs.
(Stone markers) C.W.S., I.M.S., S.S., C.S.
DAVID CALDWELL died Aug. 19, 1872 aged 32y 9m 9d
MARY E. wife of JOSEPH WILLIAMS died Sept. 19, 1869 in the 22nd year of
                                                              her age.
JOSEPH WILLIAMS died Aug. 10, 1874 aged 42 yr. 10m 23 days.
ELIZABETH wife of ASHLEY JOHNSON died Dec. 13, 1883 aged 92yr 10m 21ds
ASHLEY JOHNSON died Sept. 4, 1870   79 yr 2m 15d
(Stone Markers) D.C., J.W., A.J.
REV. CHARLES HUMMEL died July 27, 1872 aged 56 yrs. 4 ms. 23 ds.
LUCY ANN wife of C. HUMMEL died May 25, 1885 aged 77 yrs 7 ms 26 ds
(Stone Markers) C.H., W.H., L.A.H.
MARY W. HOBLITT born Nov. 4, 1814 died Apr. 17, 1894
DEACON WILLIAM HOBLIT died Dec. 20, 1870 aged 87yr 1m 1d
MARGARET wife of WILLIAM HOBLIT died March 18, 1867 aged 80y 1m 27d

Contributed by:- Carrie Purtell, Box 85, Leesburg, Ohio 45135
Located on Luttrell Rd. close to the Memphis Church. Copied by Kathryn Murphy
and Carrie Purtell in Sept. 1972.
LEE, Henry 1857-1917   Laura 1863-1936
    Grethel 1892-1898
    Alfred 1884-1958 Bessie 1889-1972 (News item, Sabina, died July 8, 1972,
                        83 yrs., wife of Alfred Lee)
MAY, Allena 1884-1900
ROCKHOLD, Martha wife of James Rockhold died Jan. 24, 1883 aged 42y 3m 73
STEWART, John died April 17, 1859
NANCE, Herbert M., Ohio Wagoner U. S. Army, World War I, May 2, 1893, May 29, 1969
FOWLIS, Millie J. dau. of A. & S. Fowlis, d. Oct. 1855 in the 8th year of her age.
       _____? died Jan. 19, 1861, age 7y 1m 21d
       (note: above stones stacked around tree.)
MASON, J. W. d. Sept. 9, 18__?, age 1y 5m 23d
WILLSON, Sarah wife of William B. Willson, died Aug. 20, 1867 aged 19y 4m 20d
       Rebecca wife of Henry Willson, died Feb. 14, 1868, aged 40y 4m 23d
NANCE, Elbertha 1877-1924
NANCE, Maggie 1883
      William Lewis (no dates) Alena May (no dates Polly Ann (no dates)
ALFRED, Isabell wife of George Alfred born Sullivan Co., Tenn., Sept. 27, 1856,
             died Clinton County, Ohio, Aug. 29, 1900
NANCE, William 1844-1918   Alice, his wife 1854-19_
NANCE, Harry W., Ohio Pvt., 813 Pioneer Inf. Sept. 28, 1918
FOWLIS, Jane wife of Paul Fowlis, died Jan. 28, 1867, age 44 yrs. & 24 days

---

Contributed by: Carrie Purtell, Bos 85, Leesburg, Ohio 45235
Copied Apr. 1972 by Kathry Murphy of Sabina and Carrie Purtell.
Cemetery located on Route 72.
SEXTON, Infant son of D.&L.M. Sexton, d. March 25, 1866, aged 1 day
    Lavina M. wife of Dempsey Sexton, departed this life Dec. 28, 1876,
          aged 29 years and 3 months.
DAILY, Elmira, dau. of T. & H. Daily, d. June 12, 1857
DALEY, Martha J., dau. of T. & H. Daley, d. Dec. 15, 1854, age 2 m.
    Thomas died March 29, 1858
    Frances W. died Oct. 1838, aged 43 yrs. & 4 mon. (note: listed in county
        history also)
    Mary A., dau. of T. & F. Daley, d. May 12, 1838, aged 23 yrs. 21 days.
(note: Two different spellings of Daley. Dr. Fred Wollard, Washington C.H.
and his brother Robert Woolard, Samantha, Ohio told Mrs. Purtell that their
Grandparent Wollards are buried in this cemetery. The cemetery was surrounded
by an oval shape fence made of very large stones, but many have fallen inside
and outside. Probably more stones here but could not locate; hogs were rooting.)

CLINTON COUNTY, OHIO - TERRELL PASTURE CEMETERY - WAYNE TOWNSHIP

Contributed by:- Carrie Purtell, Box 85, Leesburg, Ohio 45135
Located on Terrell Road in a pasture field. Stones are no longer on graves but are
stacked around two stumps. Copied by Mary Lane, Kathryn Murphy and Carrie Purtell in
September, 1972.
ALMOND, John Thomas son of Kelly & Catherine Almond, d. July ___. 1849, age 11y 3m
                                                                    20d

CURTIS, Thomas son of E. & E. Curtis died February 27, 183_?
EDWARDS, Emily wife of Elisha, E. & S., Sept. 14, 1843, aged 196 1m 15d
GRICE, John Abraham son of William R. Grice, _____(?)
GRICE, Ruth wife of Joseph Grice, who died Oct. 4, 1846, 80 years.
        Joseph Grice who died April 9, 1852, in the 85th year of his age.
GRICE, Mary wife of John Grice, Sr., died 1850, Nov. 19, 58y 6m
        John Sr. died Nov. 14, 1859, 87 years
_____, _____1853, aged 36 years (note: stone broken in too
                              many pieces to read)
YOUNG, John C. died Feb. 3, 1850, aged 81 yrs. 11m 25 dys.
_____, Pannety _____(note: top of head stone, rest of stone broken) **
    (note: small broken pieces of stones are as follows)
_____, aged 1 year 3 mon 20 days
_____, Jose _____?
_____. Amos _____(note: could be Paris??)
_____, _____1852
_____, _____ 6 yrs (?) 10 ds
_____, _____(?) & 7 day
_____, _____58y 6m 17days
** a marriage record at courthouse gives Joseph Grice & Phynetty Clifton
                Oct. 5, 1833.

CLINTON COUNTY, OHIO - GEORGE CEMETERY - RICHLAND TOWNSHIP

Contributed by:- Carrie Purtell, Box 85, Leesburg, Ohio 45135
Located on Texas Road at Cherry Bend. Copied in July 1972 by Mary Lane of Xenia and
Carrie Purtell.
CLEMENT, Jane, dau. of Louis & Lizzie Clement, d. Sept. 21, 1901, age 28d
BIGONVILLE, John P. d. Nov. 23, 1888, aged 71y 3m 22d
MATSON, Mary J., wife of James Matson, d. Sept. 26, 1878, aged 27y
        Infant son of James & Mary Matson
CLEMENT, James, son of Mary & _____(?) Clement, d. Sept. 8, 1874, aged 1y 6d
        Victoria, wife of Hubert Clement, d. Sept. 14, 1871, aged 52y 7m 25d
        Hubert d. Mar. 10, 1886, aged 81y 2m 24d
QUINN, Infant son (?) of Charles &_____(?) Quinn, d. June (?) 10, 1898 (or 1878?)
DABE, Hannah E., wife of James Dabe, d. Jan. 31, 1872, aged 30y 3m 1d
ROGERS, Eliza, wife of John Rogers, d. June 21, 1870, in the 64th year of her age.

247

CLINTON COUNTY, OHIO - ZURFACE CEMETERY - WAYNE TOWNSHIP
Contributed by: Carrie Purtell, Box 85, Leesburg, Ohio 45135
Copied by Mary Lane, Kathryn Murphy and Carrie Purtell.
COCHRAN, Daniel d. Sept. 12, 1849, aged 61y 2m 22d
        James, son of J. & S. Cochran, d. Dec. 23, 1846, aged 20 ds.
        John d. Sept. 11, 1818, aged 23y 11d
DRAGOO, Polly, wife of Andrew Dragoo, d. Dec. (8):, 1832, aged about 11y (41?)
HARDESTY, Joshua d. May 20, 1858, aged 102 years 7 mo.
            (Stone)-----wife-------(not legible)
        Joshua d. Feb. 16, 1848, aged 83y 11m 21d
LINDSEY, Louisa, wife of Isaiah Lindsey, d. Apr. 27, 1873, aged 27y 8m
            (note: small stone, either head or foot - no name)
MIERS, Sarah G., dau. of J.&E.M. Miers, d. Aug. 28, 1856, aged 5y 11m 2d
MYERS, Alice J., dau of J.&A.E. Myers, d. Oct. 31, 1860, aged 1m 10d
NELSON, Samuel J., son of I.&A.S. Nelson, d. Feb. 18, 1844, aged 1y 4m 25d
REED, Arabella, wife of Samuel Reed, who d. Dec. 21, 1845, age 60y 9m
        James Madison, son of Samuel & Arabella Reed, b. Oct. 21 (or 27), ____(?)
WILSON, George W. d. Feb. 20, 1850, aged 53y 8m 11d
ZURFAS, Martha, wife of Samuel Zurfas, d. June 9, 1872 (or 1873), aged 62y
        Margaret E., dau. of S.&M. Zerfas, d. Oct. 22, 1850, aged 1y 15d
Cemetery located about 1 mile from Rt. 72 and Memphis Church on the old Samuel
Zurface farm on Larrick Road. This cemetery is in a woods close to the highway
and was clean and well kept. Most of the stones are stacked against a large
tree, a few broken. Probably some are gone.

CLINTON COUNTY, OHIO - WADE CEMETERY - RICHLAND TOWNSHIP
Contributed by: Carrie Purtell, Box 85 Leesburg, Ohio 45135
Copied June 18, 1972 by Mary Lane of Xenia and Carrie Purtell.
FORD, William d. January 10, 1892, age 45y & 2m
WADE, Andrew J. d. July 11, 1865, 28y 10m 19d
        George d. Aug. 4, 1884, 60y 3m 29d
        Mary Jane d. Dec. 5, 1884, 88y 5m 14d
WADE, George d. Feb. 17, 1891, 89y 1m 22d
WADE, Nellie M. dau. of William C. & Rosanie Wade, d. May 10, 1881, 2m & 14d
WADE, Polly Ann d. May 18, 1850, 20y 11m 29d
WADE, Alexander H. d. Jan. 1, 1864, 23y 6m 11d
WADE, Plesant d. Sept. 12, 1846, aged 86y
        Dorcas, wife of Plesant Wade, d. Sept. 12, 1845, aged 73y
HOLLY, Elizabeth W. wife of David Holly, d. Feb. 23, 1861, 37y & 4d
        David, 72 years (?)
        John Holley Jr., d. Aug. 18, 1866, aged 45y 7m 23d (note: surname HOLLEY)
        John Holly Jr., d. Mar. 18, 1880, aged 20y 2m 5d
HOLLY, William, son of John & Mary Holly, d. May 25, 1883, aged 20y 4m 27d
WADE, James d. Mar. 17, 1881, aged 81 year.
TAYLOR, Martha, dau. of J. & M. Taylor, d. Dec. 1835, aged 14 yr
        Martha, wife of James Taylor, d. Jan. 9, 1855, aged 37y
_BISLEY, __nidas, son of ____(?) & Susan _bisley(?) (note: tree grown into
        stone covering half of marker; fot stones LWH & TER)
Cemetery is located on Rt. 22, about 1/2 mile from Melvin Crossroad, south on right
side of highway. Can be seen from road.

Contributed by: Carrie Purtell, Box 85, Leesburg, Ohio 45135
Located in the Snow Hill Road. Cemetery is in very bad condition, stones buried,
some broken in several places, ground hog holes all over and trees and shrubbery
growing into stones. Copied June 1972 by Mary Lane of Xenia and Carrie Purtell.
CUNNINGHAM, Cora, dau. of J. & G. Cunningham d Oct. 23, 1876 aged 3y 4m 11d
      Emily C., dau of J. & G. Cunningham d Aug. 14, 1872, aged 1y 8m 27d
ANDERS, Mar___iet(?) J., dau. of _____ Anders, d _____1831, aged 19 y 9m 1d
      Sarah, wife of Adam Anders, d. Dec. 27, 1864, aged 75y 3m 9d
      Adam, died Oct. 9, 1855 in his 70th year.
      Jacob Mar. 11, 1840, Apr. 6, 1904
      Elizabeth, wife of Jacob Anders, d. Sept. 5, 1880, age 36y 11m 18d
NIELAND, Mary A., wife of Andrew Neiland, d. Aug. 17, 1877, age 49y
      Allen A. son of A. & M. A. Neiland, died Sept. 20, 1868, age 14d
SHERIDAN, James M. died Feb. 12___1 (?)
      Mary E. dau. of Patrick & Margaret, d. July 28, 1889, age 19y 4m 14d
      Patrick died Mar. 25, 1888, age 16 yrs.
      Margaret, wife of Patrick Sheridan, d. Jan. 17, 1872 age 37y 2m 25d
(note: stone with top gone)
McCANN, George son of J. J. &___ McCann, d Sept. 16, 18(52?), age __y 11m 8d
      (note: above stone is broken)
EVANS, Mary B., born Mar. 6, 1856, died Nov. 21, 1919
      Sarah A., dau. of A. & S., d. Mar. 13, 1887 24y 12d
      Allan died Feb 13, 1885, aged 53y 10m 10d
      David d Mar. 6, 1840, aged 70y 9m 1d
      Sarah died Oct 2, 1900, age 67y 4m 20d
      David died Dec. 30, 1860, aged 83y 10m 18d
      "Evans Sisters" Martha 1833-1912 Sarah 1836-1907 Margaret 1841-1927
      Clark born July 21, 1898, 38y (?)m
      Emily dau of Stephen and Mary, died Mar. 17, 18__(?), aged 60y & 11d
      Stephen died May 11, 1879, age 76y 1m 18d
      Mary, wife of Stephen, died Sept. 1, 1876, age 72y 9m 8d
      Harvey, a member of Co. D, 114 Regt. OVI, Died at Vicksburg, Miss.,
          July 29, 1863 aged 26y 7m 4d, son of Stephen and Mary Evans
ALLEN, C.G.A._____dau. of P. C. Allen died June 3, 18__(?) aged____ (note:
      broken in several pieces.
      William June 26, 1872, May 18, 1891
      J. W. infant son (?), Sept. 28, ____(?), Aug. 185_(?)
      Earl son of C. & S. J. Allen, born July 12, 1891, died Feb. 4, 1899
      (note: footstone) S E A
ALLEN, Jacob died May 9, 1898, aged 65y 3m 2d
      Sarah, wife of Benjamin Allen, died Jan. 7, 1887, aged 84 yrs.
      Samuel died Feb. 2, 1881, age 85y 9m 8d
      Benjamin F. died Sept. 9, 1871, age 40y & 13d
      Albert 1870-1927 Rebecca 1866-1933
      Margaret, wife of B. F. Allen 1836-1921
      Samuel R., son of Clement Allen, died Feb. 21, 1878, age 1y 22d
      Sarah C. dau. of Clement & Sarepta J. Allen, died Oct. 17, 1879 aged
          4y 8m 4d (note: this stone was dug upP
HAGGARD, Sarah Jane, wife of John Haggard, died Mar. 7, 1870, age 32y 4m 21d
      Samuel son of J. & S. Haggard, died Apr. 21, 1870, age 1m 2d

DRAPER, Rebecca A., dau. of J. & M. Draper, died Oct. 5, 1870, age ly 17d
LIVERY, Sarah, wife of Joseph Livery, Oct. 4 (or 5), 1852, Sept. 18, 1904 (note:
               against fence in rear of cemetery)
SPURLOCK, George W. died Jan. 1, 1870, age 17y 6m 30d
        Levi died May 20, 1862 age 12y 1d
        Mandie dau. of Riley & Hattie Spurlock, died Dec. 5, 1903 age 3y 3m 19d
           (note: stone in trees in the rear of cemetery)
        Emily A. dau of L. & E. Spurlock, died Apr. 8, 1861, age 7y 5m
WEBB, Benjamin died Nov. 10, 1876, age 43y 4m 2d
        Byrd b. Dec. 7, 1802, d. Jan. 9, 1889, age 86y 10m 26d
        Francis J. died Sept. 17, 1874, age 28y 10m 11d
        Armilda dau. of J. W. & M. E. Webb, died Jan. 19, 1868, age ly 1m 6d (note:
           court house has date Jan. 18, 1867)
        Infant dau. of J. W. & M. F. Webb, died Dec. 17, 1871, age 10m
        Martin, N. G. (or O.N.E.) died Aug. 6, 1866, aged 24y 3m 12d (Civil War)
BONECUTTER, Ferdinand died Nov. 8, 1865, age 28y 7m 21d
        Charlotte, wife of Christopher Bonecutter, died Jan. 14, 1890; 74y 19d
        John born Aug. 22, 1818, died Aug. 22, 1892, age 76yrs.
        Sophia, wife of John Bonecutter, died Sept. 25, 1896, age 75 yrs.
        Christopher died Jan. 17, 1884, age 79 yrs.
        John H. died June 21, 1898, age 48y 4m 13d
(note: broken pieces of another stone; could not read any part.)
BONECUTTER, Job, son of J. & F. Bonecutter, died Mar. 22, 1864, age 8y 7m 26d
MARTIN, _____ J. & M. J. Martin died Feb. 10, 1869, aged ly 9m 26d (broken)
CLINE, Infant dau. of W. H. & Ollie Cline died July 12, 1900, age 9d
        Harrison born Aug. 14, 1338, died Jan. 27, 1901
        Annie, wife of Harison born June 9, 1831, died Oct. 13, 1906
        John H., son of H. & A. Cline, died Jan. 30, 1890, aged 30y 7m 23d
        Mary E. dau. of Harrison & Anna Cline, died June 12, 1877, age 4m
CLINE, Philip born May 27, 1816, died Aug. 18, 1903
        Delila born Oct. 3, 1820, died Dec. 8, 1875
        Infant son of P. & D. Cline "Born to Die" Aug. 4, 1837
        Laura E. dau. of P. & D. Cline born Mar. 18, 1858, died Mar. 18, 1859
CLINE, Armilda dau. of Eli & Lillie Cline, d Feb. 26, 1908, aged 8d
        Eve dau. of Eli & Lillie Cline 1898-1910
        Ona Apr. 7, 1913, March 22, 1917
CLINE, Lillie M. 1873-19__(not engraved) Eli W. 1868-1935
        David 1857 (not engraved) Alice, his wife, 1861-1906
CLINE, John M. son of C. & S. Cline d. June 27, 1870 aged 4y 10m 27d
        Philip died Jan. 21, 1865, age 84y 10m 5d
        Doris Marie dau. of H. & H. Cline, July 10, 1904
CLINE, Arminta R. dau. of Alfred & Louisa Cline, d Apr. 1876, age 5y 8m 29d
CLINE, John J. died Oct. 22, 1890 age 84y 7m 12d (headstone: Mother-Father)
        Ida died Apr. 29, 1890, aged 83y 8m 19d
GOODSON, Thomas E. son of W. & E. W. Goodson, d Nov. 19, 1861, age 21y 2m 4d
        Richard H. son of O. & E. Goodson d Mar. 28, 1853, aged 15y 6m 1d
PIERCE, Joel E. son of Stephen & Maria Pierce d Jan. 17, 1851, aged 4y 1m 19d
SHARP, Mary E. dau. of Rachel Sharp, d. Sept. 1, 1873, age 22y 5m 7d
        David Henry son of J. & K. Sharp, d. Sept. 15, 1876, age 23y 8m 22d
        Lewis R. son of R. R. & M. J. Sharp (note: from broken pieces at foot of
                                                     Monument)

SHARP, Kizzirh, dau. of James & K. Sharp, d. Feb. 22, 1840, aged 1y 11m 11d
        Infant son of James & K. Sharp, d. Mar. 11, 1842, age 1 day
        Lucinda dau of J. & K. Sharp, d. Nov. 28, 1845 aged 1m 3d
BINEGA., Moses, Co. J., 1st Legt. OVI, d. Feb. 28, 1863, age 23y 11m 21d
SHARP, Burt(?) son of .. B. & M. Sharp d. Feb 17, 18__aged 5y & 27d
HENKLE(?), Nelson M._____died Nov. 6, 1836, aged 31 yrs. 11 mo. 21 ds.
(note: broken pieces of stone in thick brush along fence on right side) C.H.(??)
PLUMMER, Eli 1797-1871
LINCH, Edwards d Mar. 1, 1867, aged 32y 14d
MORRIS, Elwood 1866-1885
        Lorenzo 1834-1906   Deborah, wife of Lorenzo Morris 1836-1884
(note: MORRIS stone in small pieces could not be put together)
LYNCH, George H. son of F. & A. M. Lynch b July 16, 1859, d. Apr. 25, 1882
LYNCH, Sarah C., wife of W. H. Lynch. 1860-1893
        Elizabeth, wife of Joseph Lynch, d Sept. 21, 1866, aged 78y 7m 16d
ANDERS, Ollie, dau of G.W. & Ellen Anders, d. Jan. 2, 1892, age 17y 7m 26d
        Ellen, wife of George W. Anders, 1823-1905 "At Lest"
        George W. d Aug. 6, 1886, aged 60y 11m 3d
        Rebecca 1850-1886
DRISCOLL, Children of J. B. & E. Driscoll
          Joseph William died Aug. 23, 1869, aged 2m 20d
          Clara Belle died Aug. 5, 1868, aged 3m 21d
        Eliza Ann, wife of John Driscoll, d. Jan. 3, 1879, aged 35y 5m 9d
ANTRIM, Adin died Mar. 7, 1833, aged 48y 1m 21d
ANTRIM, Alonza son of T. & H. Antrim d. Apr. 19, 1855, aged 5m 27d
REED, Gilyann 1829-1908
        gracia dau of R. M. & T. J. Reed, d. Apr. 23, 1891, age 1m
        Phila, wife of R. M. Reed, d. Aug. 4, 1893, age 24y 1m 4d
DITMOUSE, _____(?) city (?) Ditmouse & Catherine Ditmouse
ANTRIM, Mary, wife of Adin Antrim, died July 27, 1835, aged 1ly 6m 2d (41?)
ELLIOTT, Martin died Aug. 28, 1867, in the 66th yr. of his age.
        Patience, wife of Martin Elliott, died May 20, 1872, age 66y 10m 12d
        Benjamin, son, died June 5, 1863, aged 25y 4m 7d, Died at Camp, Vetern marker
        Mary d June 19, 1861, age 48y 9m
HEFLEY, Ferdinand born Jan 22, 1818, died May 29, 1895.
BONECUTTER, Lizzie M. dau. of (AT ?) & Sarah Bonecutter, died June 22, 1882,
        age 2y 11m 17d
REED, Henry B. son of J. W. & L. A. Reed, d Oct. 17, 1868, age 1m 17d
        Joseph P. June 2, 1878, Oct. 17, 1868, aged 65y 6m 21d
REED, Jane, wife of J. P. Reed, d. July 3, 1867, age 48y 4m 15d
ROGERS, Jemina, wife of Joel Rogers, died May 4, 1865, age 61y 11m 10d
MORITZ, Son of S. M. Moritz, died July 18, 1889, aged 8y 10m 8d
ROBERTS, Jehu died Sept. 19, 1952 age 22y 5m 15d
        Almira, dau of J.&(?) Roberts, died Sept. 15, 1852, aged 7m 23d
MARTIN, Eli 1823-1866   Rachel 1830-1904
MARTIN, Martha, wife of Stephen Martin, died July 19, 1888, age 86y 10m 24d
        Frank son of John & Annie Martin, died Oct. 15, 1879, age 1m 22d
        Anna, wife of John Martin, died Nov. 8, 1883, aged 36y 11m -?
        Elijzh son of John & Anna Martin died Mar. 24, 1885, age 9y 7m
WADDLE. Francis d. June 21, 1865, age (83 yrs.?)
        Anna, wife of F. Waddle, died May 10, 1868, aged 856
BEVERLY, Malinda Jan. 10, 1824, Feb. 14, 1914
WILSON, Delbert son of J. & M. Wilson, died Mar. 13, 1865, age 19y 21d

Contributed by: Carrie Purtell, Box 85, Leesburg, Ohio 45135
Located on Rt. 72 near the Memphis area. Copied by Mary Lane of Xenia and
Carrie Purtell.

GEFFS, William, d. Apr. 23, 1841, 8y 11m
   William d. Apr. 23, 1882, aged 80y 5m 13d
   Harrison, son of Thomas & Mary Geff, d. Jan. 29, 1864, age 16y 4m 22d
   Harrison, b Feb. 11, 1814, d. Nov. 25, 1844, 30y 9 m 14d
   Thomas, 1820 or 1826-1908   Mary, his wife, 1821-1912
   John d May 23, 1840 aged 50y 6m
   Tamer, his wife, d. Mar 25, 1881, aged 91 (or 92)y 6m 2d
   Robert D. d. May 23, 1879, aged 30y & 29d (fenced)
   Jane, dau. of Thomas & Mary, d. May 20, 1854, age 9y
   Elizabeth Geffs, who departed this life Aug. 23, 1832 (or 1839?) aged
      80 (or 86?)y 5m 13d
   Lydia, d. May 8, 1856, age 32y 8m 8d
GROVE, Henry d Oct. 18 (or 19?), 1849, aged 30y 5m
   Margaret Ann, his wife, d August 29, 1875, age 53y 5m 3d
   Irvine, son of Henry & Ann Grove, d. Sept. 16, 1844, age 2y 4m 21d
McKAY, Jessie R., 1861(?), son of J. & A. M. McKay, d May 8, age 2y 3m 25d
   David M. d. July 16, 1870, aged 26y 7m 2d
   Jesse d Nov. 5, 1864, 83y 3m 25d
   Jesse d Jan. 9, 1883, age 52y
   Mary, wife of Jessie McKay, d. July 2, 1871, aged 28 (or 78) ys.
   Robert, d Nov. 13, 1852, age 70y
ADAMS, Ann d Nov. 1, 1864, age 44y
   Edward d Feb. 2, 1845, 49 Years of his age
   Henry S. b. Apr. 17, 1831, d. Apr. 26, 1806 (1906?)
   Susan A. Oct. 15, 1833, July 9, 1913
   John Q. d Sept. 10, 1876, age 93y - Veteran Marker 1812 (note: Bible
     record in Beers History aives. Birth June 4, 1783)
   Thomas d. July 12, 1875, aged 104 yrs., Veteran 1812
   Patience, wife of Thomas d. July 17, 1851, aged about 60y
   Peter d Dec. 4, 1858 (or 1856), in the 72nd life of his age.
   Polly, wife of Peter Adams, 1869, May 30, age 77y 1m 20d
   Thomas d. July 24, 1851, age 55y
BENNETT, Jane wife of Jesse K. Bennett, d. Oct. 18, 1846, aged 46y 4m 9d
   Jesse, aged 46y 4m 9d 1846
   Joseph, d 20th, 10th mon, 1865, aged 84y 2m 15d
   Ann, wife of Joseph, d 2nd mo. 17th, 1857, age 87y 5m 5d
DOGGETT, Benjamin B. d June 7, 1860, about 29y
   Martha J., 1842.
   George R. d Nov. 8, 1865, age 70y 7m
   Elizabeth, wife of G.R. Doggett, d July 4, 1868, age 79y 10m 14d
   Sarah M. R. d Mar. 24, 1867, age 39y 8m 1d
   Mary R. d Nov. 18, 1865, age 80y 7m 7d
COX, Valentine d. Oct. 31, 1874, age 64y 6m 28d
HUBBARD, Levin d June 19, 1849 in 80th year.
SEVERS, Charity A., wife of James, d Dec. 18, 1857, age 38y (footstone C.A.S.)
HILL, Eliza M., dau. of D. & E. Hill, d. July 18, 1840, age 9m 5d
MORRIS, Osco, son of Isaiah & Tamer Morris, d. Feb. 25, 1875, age 7y 8m 23d
   Willie, son of M.C.&L. Morris, d. Apr. 21st, 1861, age 5m 3d

CAMPBELL, James d June 9, 1864, age 27y 3m 6d
NOBLE, Susan, wife of William Noble, d. Nov. 19, 1850, aged 40y 6m
WILKENSON, Susan M., wife of William S., d Oct. 15, 1874, age 35y 11m 7d
SNOW, Robert b Patrick Co., Va., Mar. 15, 1815 d Jan. 23, 1892, age 76y 10m18d
     Frances Ellen, wife, b Culpepper Co., Va., Feb. 21, 1818, d Oct. 1867,
       age 56y 7m 15d
    Children of Robert & Frances E.
      Martha J. d Sept. 23, 1842, aged 0y 10m 13d
      Sarah M. R., d Oct. 25, 1873 age 17y 8m 11d
GRIFFITH, Wrightsle, d Jan. 21, 184_(?), aged 38y
    Henry d Nov. 27, 1835, age 2y 10m 13d
    Standsbery, son of W. & E., d. Oct. 1845, age 19y 1m 26d
    Elizabeth W. d. May 3, 1854, age 48y
WOOLARD, Walter A., son of Joseph M. & Elizabeth, d. Feb. 20, 1881, age 2y 1m

CLINTON COUNTY, OHIO - LUTTRELL CEMETERY - WAYNE TOWNSHIP

Contributed by: Carrie Purtell, Box 85, Leesburg, Ohio 45135
Located on Luttrell Road about 1/4th mile from Rt. 72 on hill just back of the Geff
Cemetery. Cemetery is in bad shape. Ground hogs have undermined the stones.
Twenty-two stones were dug up and the transcribers feel sure that there are more
there that were not found. Copied in Oct. and Mar. 1972 by Kathryn Murphy, Mary
Lane and Carrie Purtell.
HAYNES, Milly, wife of P. Haynes died Sept. 1918, aged --y --m 11 days
    Sarah, wife of P. Haynes d June 11, 1846, aged 42y 9m 24d
    Nancy Haynes departed this life Aug._____ age 42 yrs.
    Jefferson died May 21, 1849, aged 34 yrs.
LUTTRELL, Polly, wife of Richard Luttrell died Nov. 18, 1810 aged 36y 8m 12d
    Richard, died 1848 (Dates from County History died Mar. 23, 1848,
       age 50y 7m 8d)
    Ruth, wife of Richard Luttrell died July 20, 1889, aged 86y 4m 24d
    Barbara J., dau. of Robert & Fanny(?) Luttrell, died Oct. 25, 1863
       aged 48 yrs. 4 mo.
    Mary, wife of Robert Luttrell d. Dec. 5, 1857, aged 56y & 23d
(note: these dates from County History - other graves in the area could
     not be identified as stones broken and scattered)
GROVE, Elizabeth, wife of Albra. died Oct. 17, 1847, aged 42y 6m 20d
    Nancy, wife of John Grove, died July 10, 1840, aged 44y 11m 15d
    Jacob d. Nov. 15, 1860, aged 86y 8d
    Catherine, wife of Jacob Grove died Dec. 2, 1862, aged 91y 29d
    Martha, wife of George Grove, Mar. 26, 1815, April 21, 1909
(note: on Grove Lot is broken stone in several pieces with only____16.
     This could be David Grove, Apr. 16, 1863, aged 55y 11m 18d--taken from
     Doun5y History--with the date being 16 in both places.)
GROVE, Susan M. dau. of J. & M. Grove d Mar. 20, 1845, age 15y 2m 29d
    Louisa, dau. of David & Mary Grove, died Aug. 11, 1800(?) aged 5y
CANNEY, Mary dau. of E.W.&H.J. Canney, died Oct. 13, 186_(?), aged 2y 2m 3d
LARRICK, Sarah J., wife of Hiram, died Sept. 12, 1875, aged 33y 11m 23d
_____, Lenora, dau. of M. & R._____(note: could not read)
HUBBARD, Levin died June 19, 1849 in the 80th yr. of his life (note: this is from
       the record of George Robinson of Washington C.H., taken several years ago.)

McVEY, Sarah, wife of Edmund McVey, d Feb. 3, 1850 aged 36y 2m 26d
CANTER, Mary died Feb. 7, 1873, aged 86 yrs. 6 mo. 6 days
        John, died July ____(?), 1867, aged 93y 29d
        Joseph, died Aug. 24, 1877, aged 69y
        Mary, wife of Joseph Canter died June 16, 1869, aged 48y 3m 7d
        Catherine, wife of J. C. Canter died May 1, 1848, aged 38y 8m 5d
REED, Levi, died Dec. 9, 1840, aged 17y 10m 18d
ICE & SNOW, Ice & Snow died Apr. 29, 1860, aged 79y 2m 16d
        Mary, wife of Ice & Snow died July 8, 1864, aged 73 yrs. 4mo. 4ds.
SNOW, D. G., died Oct. 19, 1871, aged 26y 7m 14d, son of Thomas & Mary Snow
                (footstone D.G.S.)
        Arminta, dau. of Thomas & Mary Snow, died Nov. 18, 1857, aged 1y & 21d
        Thomas J., son of F. L. & E. Snow, died Oct. 12, 1871, aged 21y 10m 13d
        Mary C., dau. of F. & E. Show, died May 13, 1853, aged 1y 5m 4d
WOOLARD, Catherine, wife of Isaac Woolard, died Apr. 19, 1859, aged 25y 11m 21d
LEWIS, Fielding, died Dec. 25, 1861, in the 82nd year of his life
        Elizabeth, wofe of Fielding Lewis, died Dec. 4, 1874 aged 81y 5m 7d
RUNNELLS, (top of stone broken in small pieces) "our Infant", dau of
                I. & R. Runnells, Aug. 6, 1865
MARTIN, Mahalla, wife of Eli Martin b Nov. 27, 1823, d Aug. 1st, 1846,
                aged 22y 8m 3d
MILBURN, Susanna, wife of John W. Milburn, died May 10, 1860, aged 10(?) y
                1m 11d (1840?)
        Hanson L., son of J. W. & S. Milburn, died Oct. 27, 1860, age 1y 8m 30d
                J. W. & C____? Sept.____? age 1 yr &____?
EASTLACK, a son of J. & A. Eastlack
ROGERS, Joshua son of Robert & Cynthia (Moore) Rogers, d. 19 yrs.
        Mattie dau. of Robert & Cynthia (Moore) Rogers, d. infancy
        Eva dau. of Robert & Cynthia (Moore) Rogers, d. infancy
        (note: the above children were brother and sisters of Mrs. Purtell's
                mother-in-law, Millie Rogers Purtell and had no grave stones.
                Graves are located in upper left corner of cemetery)

Contributed by:- Carrie Purtell, Box 85, Leesburg, Ohio 45135
Cemetery is located on Van Pelt Road, just off Rt. 72, in grove, in pasture close
to road. Many of the large trees have fallen on monuments. Transcribers dug out
and pieced together stones to get inscriptions. Cemetery could easily be cleaned.
Legend says it was an Indian Cemetery. Copied by Mary Lane of Xenia, Kathryn
Murphy of Sabina and Carrie Purtell in April 1972.
ELLIOTT, Sarah E. dau. of Benjamin & Louise Elliott d. Aug. 7, 1871, aged 5m 19d
    Son of Benjamin & Louise Elliott, d. Dec. 6, 1856 aged 2m 7d
    Mary A. dau. of Benjamin & Louise Elliott, d. Jan. 30, 1871, aged 13y 3m 11d
    Louise, wife of Benjamin Elliott d. Oct. 18, 1873 aged 40y dm 15d
    Catharine, wife of Benjamin Elliott, d. Dec. 13, 1816, aged 32y 9m 8d (1846?)
    Children of Benjamin & Catherine Elliott
        James_____ Mar. _____ 1846
        Catherine d. July 13, 1847
McVEY, Kesiah, wife of James McVey, died June 23, 1860, aged 73y 1m 26d
    James died Apr. 2, 1859, aged 72 yrs. (?)
ADAMS, Mary F. dau. of D. & R. Adams, d. Apr. 23, 1845, aged 11m
MARTIN, David E. son of D.(?) & E. Martin, d. Jan. 27, 1842, aged 2y 6m 25d
MARTIN, Stephen Sr. died Apr. 28, 1814, age about 45 yrs.
MARTIN, Elizabeth, wife of Charles Martin, b. June 20, 1797, d. Nov. 16, 1849
                  aged_____(?) (E.M.)
(note: foot stones) M.C.F. ___ & ___ P.F.
MORRIS, Jane, wife of Isaac Morris, died Apr. 17, 1848, aged 26y 4m 6a
FRY, Peter A. _____pf Pvt. Comp. 2, 48 Regt. OVI USI died Apr. 27, 1862
                age 20 yrs. 10 ms. 1 day.
FRY, Susan, dau. of John & Christiana Fry. d. May 27, 1863 age 18y
    Peter A. son of John & Christiana Fry d. May 17, 1863, age 2y 3m 17d
FRY, Michael C. d. April 13, 1866, aged 71y 6m 7d
    Martha Fry, departed this life June 13, 1857 in the 31st year of her life.
    Hazell son of M. & M. Froy, died Oct. 1, 1858 in the 5th year of his age.
(note: many field stones with initials scratched on them--some plain. All
    stones are the same shape. Some have the "S" backward. Some may be Indian?)
    M.C.F.   P.F.   J.S.   _.(L)?   E.M.   W.E.   S.B.   S.D.   J.S.
        C.P. (note: another that could not be made out).

CLINTON COUNTY, OHIO - COMMON PLEAS JOURNAL 1830-1834

The following records were taken from "Common Pleas Journal 1830-1834" as found located in the Common Pleas Court (Clerk of Courts Office) in the court house at Wilmington. Page on which record may be found in original book is given in parenthesis. A note on inside of cover on first blank page states "1907 Aug. 27 This volume delivered to me, this day having been taken from the corner stone about one year ago while workmen were execavating to make room for the Court House Barber Shop. (Signed) W. Lawhead, Clerk"

3-29-1830 - Wiatt C. HUNDLY and John WRIGHT license to keep grocer and tavern in Martinsville. James DALBY license to keep tavern at residence. Samuel HARBIN license to keep tavern at residence. Jehu REED license to keep tavern on Wash. Road. (6)

3-29-1830 - Samuel H. HALElicense to keep tavern in Wilmington. Charles CLINE license to keep tavern renewed. Warren SABIN license to keep tavern renewed. Daniel PARIS license to keep tavern renewed. (7)

3-29-1830 - Will of Joshua STACKHOUSE presented. Will of Ruth THATCHER presented.(8)

3-29-1830 - Absalom Douglass appointed adms. of Estate of Samuel McGILL, dec'd. Fenton McGILL aged 16 yrs. chose Jas. S. Taylor as his guardian with Taylor to also serve as guardian of Jackson McGill aged about 13 yrs. and Jane McGill aged about 9 or 10 yrs., all minors of Fenton McGill, dec'd. (9)

3-30-1830 - Will of John FALLIS presented. (17)

3-30-1830 - Robert HOOTEN aged 17 yrs. chose Gideon Fuller as his guardian with Fuller to also serve as guardian of Rebecca Hooten aged 6 yrs. and upwards and Jemima Hooten aged about 5 yrs., all orphan minors of James Hooten, dec'd. (18)

3-31-1830 - Catharine HOOTEN aged 15 yrs., orphan of James Hooten, dec'd, chose Gideon Fuller as her guardian. (20)

3-31-1830 - John McINTIRE granted renewal of his tavern license. (20)

3-31-1830 - David Reed adms. of Estate of Stephen SAVAGE, dec'd, granted further time to settle estate. (20)

4-1-1830- Samuel Miller adms. of Estate of Henry WELCH, dec'd filed account for settlement of estate. Joshua Betterton adms. of Estate of Owen WEST, dec'd granted more time. (23)

4-2-1830 - Joshua Noble and Mary Noble adms. of Estate of Benjamin NOBLE, dec'd filed account. Will of Jacob BEALS settled. (27)

4-3-1830 - Will of Philip CRIHFIELD presented. Estate of William DILLON, dec'd with Malon Haworth adms. settled. Alexander Jay guardian of Elizabeth REAGON now Elizabeth LENTEN filed settlement. Michael Bennet and Catharine Jacks late Catharine Doan, adms. filed account in Estate of Joseph DOAN, dec'd. (28)

4-6-1830 - Will of Mordecai WALKER presented. (31). Will of William COCHRAN presented. (32)

4-7-1830 - Sarah Mills and Ambrose Jones adms. of Estate of Joseph MILLS, dec'd filed account. (33)

4-8-1830 - Martin H. Venard appointed guardian of Harriet Amanda LEE aged 4 yrs. and upwards daughter of Sarah Venard wife of said Martin Venard. (34)

4-26-1830 - William Hibben appointed adms. of Estate of Peter BORDEN, dec. (49)

7-26-1830 - Will of Andrew BROWN presented. Cephas Atkinson appointed adms. of Estate of Joseph ATKINSON, dec'd. (57)

256

7-26-1830 - Benjamin BENTLEY granted license to sell merchandise. Joseph WISONG
    license to keep tavern. David CARTER license to keep tavern. Rev. Elisha
    KNOX a minister of M.E. Church granted license to solemnize marriages. (58)
7-26-1830 - Will of Hezekiah STARBUCK presented. (59)
7-27-1830 - James Rees adms. of Estate of John ELMORE filed account--estate
    originally filed pre-1823. (64)
7-27-1830 - Request that guardian be appointed for Jehu SHIELDS 9 no age given)
    and Eliza Shields aged 12 yrs., children of William Shields. (66)
7-29-1830 - Hannah TAYLOR aged 14 yrs. chose her mother, Mary Taylor as her
    guardian with Mary to also serve as guardian of Maria Taylor aged 13 yrs.,
    Sarah Taylor aged 11 yrs. and Susannah Taylor aged 8 yrs., all orphans of
    Israel Taylor, dec'd. (69)
7-31-1830 - Account filed in Will of Joseph HOWARD. Account filed in Will of
    Jane B. OXLEY. (78)
8-2-1830 - William Rhonemus adms. of Estate of Andrew RHONEMUS filed account
    for settlement. Account filed in Will of Josiah BAILEY. (79)
8-2-1830 - Barnet Basehore adms. filed account for settlement in Estate of Caleb
    RULON. Account filed in Will of Isaac PERKINS. (80)
8-7-1830 - Robert Rees and Elizabeth Linton adms. of Estate of William B. LINTON,
    dec'd granted more time. John McElwain and Benj. McElwain adms. of Estate of
    David McELWAIN, dec'd, granted more time. (97)
8-27-1830 - James Morrow appointed adms. of Estate or Robert MORROW. (99)
10-20-1830 - Stratton GORHAN renewal of tavern license. SHIPLEY and GRAY
    merchants granted license to sell merchandise. MORGAN and SABIN granted
    license to keep grocery in Chester twp. (102)
10-20-1830 - Will of John BASEHORE presented. (103)
10-21-1830 - Nathan HOCKET granted license to vend merchandise in Green twp.
    Robert Stoops adms. filed account for settlement in Estate of Margery
    McGREW. Nancy FLOYD a resident of Richland twp. an unmarried woman vs.
    Samuel SPURGEN for bastardy. (107)
10-21-1830 - Jane WAKEMAN of Chester twp., an unmarried woman vs. David HILSAMER
    for bastardy with Hilsamer being declared father of said child. (109)
10-22-1830 - Leah GALLAHER an unmarried woman of Richland twp. vs. Charles HALLEN
    and William HALLEN for bastardy. (110)
10-25-1830 - David Bailey guardian of Mary HUNNICUTT filed account for settlement.
    (117)
10-27-1830 - James MORROW granted renewal of his tavern license. Benjamin
    HAIKSON adms. of Estate of Reuben ADAMS, dec'd, granted more time. (124)
10-27-1830 - Rebecca Rulon appointed guardian of her children, Samuel H. RULON
    aged 3 yrs. and upwards and Joseph RULON aged 2 yrs. and upwards, orphans
    of Caleb Rulon, dec'd. (124)
10-28-1830 - Daniel Redington guardian of Josiah, Jane and Nancy JEWETT, minor
    orphans of Josiah Jewett, dec'd, filed account. (127)
10-29-1830 - John W. Jones appointed guardian of Eliza SHIELDS aged 12 yrs. and
    upwards and Jehu Shields aged 2 yrs. and upwards, minor son and daughter of
    William Shields. (129)
12-31-1830 - Will of Caleb Harvey presented. (138)
2-25-1831 - Will of Joseph STRATTON presented. (139)

3-30-1831 - Will of Mary BAXTER presented. (140)
(note: at this point there is an error in page numbering and numbers jump from
140 to 241 and are numbered from 241 on through the rest of the book.)
4-18-1831 - Charles HARRIS license to keep tavern at his residence. Samuel HARBIN
license to keep tavern in Martinsville. (251)
4-18-1831 - Ephran SMITH license to keep tavern at residence. James DALBY license
to keep tavern at residence. John ANTRAN license to keep tavern in Wilmington.
John McINTIRE license to keep tavern at residence. Daniel PARIS license to
keep tavern at residence. John WRIGHT and Wiatt E. HUNDLEY license to keep
tavern at Martinsville. (252)
4-18-1831 - Jehu REED license to keep tavern at residence. Jesse Harvey and
Isaac Harvey appointed adms. of Estate of Joshua HARVEY, dec'd. James Shalds
and William Hoblett appointed adms. of Estate of John KING, dec'd. Will of
James DAVIS presented. (253)
4-18-1831 - Will of William H. HAYNES presented. (254)
4-18-1831 - Mary Owen appointed guardian of her children, Harriet OWEN aged
6 yrs., Benjamin Owen aged 3 yrs. and Ruth Ann Owen aged 2 yrs., minor
orphans of George Owen, dec'd. (254)
4-18-1831 - Isaac Collett appointed adms. of Estate of Mary Baxter with will
annexed. (254)
4-18-1831 - Widow, Rebecca STRATTON relinquished right to dower in Estate of
Joseph STRATTON. (255)
4-19-1831 - Elizabeth HARVEY aged 15 yrs. chose Joshua Harvey as her guardian
with said Joshua to also serve as guardian of Rebecca Harvey aged 17 yrs. (259)
4-20-1831 - Warren SABIN license to keep tavern in Wilmington. (264)
4-21-1831 - Will of Richard THORNBURG presented. (270)
4-21-1831 - Jane PHILIPS aged 16 yrs., orphan of Joshua H. Philips, dec'd, chose
her mother, Lucinda H. Philips as her guardian. (270)
4-21-1831 - Autenticated copy of Will of John WATTS presented and received from
Bedford Co., Virginia. (271)
4-23-1831 - Account filed in Estate of William McMILLAN, dec'd. (275)
4-23-1831 - Account filed in Estate of Jesse HINES, dec'd. Jonathan Fallis adms.
of Estate of Amos FALLIS, dec'd filed account for settlement. (276)
4-27-1831 - Aaron Sewell guardian of Aaron and Mirian SEWELL filed account. (280)
4-30-1831 - Adms. of Estate of William WHITAKER, dec'd granted further time. (290)
5-7-1831 - Will of Joseph CAMP presented. Asahel Tribbey and Lemuel Garrison
adms. of Estate of Parsons GARRISON, dec'd, filed account. (306)
6-11-1831 - Will of Ezekiel CAST presented. (308)
8-22-1831 - David Ashly and John Gaddis appointed adms. of Estate of Thomas
GADDIS, dec'd; widow, Margaret Gaddis relinquishes right to adms. estate. (318)
8-22-1831 - Huldah Giddings appointed guardian of her son, John H. H. T. GIDDINGS
aged 10 yrs., orphan of Zebalon Giddings, dec'd. (319)
8-22-1831 - Sarah HARVEY aged 16 yrs. chose her mother, Rebecca Stratton as
her guardian with Rebecca to also serve as guardian of her children,
Rebecca Stratton ag d 2 yrs. and Edward Stratton aged 4 mos., orphans
and minors of Joseph STRATTON. (319)
8-22-1831 - Nancy Biggs appointed guardian of her daughter, Charlotte BIGGS
aged 8 yrs. (319)
8-22-1831 - Sarah FLETCHER aged 17 yrs. and John FLETCHER aged 16 yrs. chose
their father, Henry Fletcher as their guardian. (320)

8-22-1831 - David CARTER granted renewal of tavern license. Andrew LOVE granted license to keep tavern. (320)

8-23-1831 - Joseph WYSONG granted license to keep tavern. (327)

8-27-1831 - William Milikin adms. of Estate of Palmer ADSIT, dec'd filed account. David F. Eachus adms. of Estate of Robert EACHUS, dec'd, filed account. (343)

8-27-1831 - Huldah Giddings adms. of Estate of Zebulon GIDDINGS, dec'd filed account. (344)

9-2-1831 - Julia A. COLLINS an unmarried woman vs. George M. SABIN for bastardy.(362)

10-13-1831 - William Hadley and Nathan Linton appointed adms. of Estate of Josiah TOWNSEND, dec'd; widow, Abigail Townsend relinquishes right to adms. estate.(367)

10-13-1831 - Will of Thomas PENNINGTON presented. (367) Will of Aquila CAST presented. (368)

11-7-1831 - Edward ROBERTS, application for a pension. On this day Edward Roberts an applicant for a pension personally appeared in open court and made his declaration in order to obtain a pension in due form of law and exhibited to Court his schedule of his whole estate &c. Subscribed by him by which it appears that the whole of applicants estate amounts to the sum of one hundred and thirty-six dollars and twenty-five cents. And the said Edward Roberts took and subscribed the oath aquired by the law of Congress. (371)

11-7-1831 - James Morran license to keep tavern renewed. Thornton NICHOLS granted license to keep tavern in Clarksville. (371)

11-7-1831 - Will of Thomas GOE presented. (372)

11-8-1831 - Will of William CAST presented. (373)

11-9-1831 - Stratton GORHAN license to keep tavern. (379)

11-12-1831 - Jonathan Fallis appointed adms. de bonis non of Estate of Ellis PUGH, dec'd. (393)

11-14-1831 - John Lewis guardian of Esther, Perry, Heprpha(?), Ursula and Polly NOGGLE, minor heirs of George Noggle, dec'd, filed account. (394)

11-14-1831 - More time granted in Will of William BIGGS. (395)

11-16-1831 - James NEAL aged 16 yrs. and upwards chose George D. Haworth as his guardian. (405)

1-12-1832 - Sampson Wright one of the sons of dec'd appointed adms. of Estate of John WRIGHT, dec'd; widow, Elizabeth Mary Wright relinquishes right to adms. estate. (412)

2-20-1832 - Jonanna AYARS aged 15 yrs. and upwards and Annas AYARS aged 18 yrs. and upwards chose Peter T. Shaw as their guardian with Shaw also to serve as guardian of John Ayars aged 13 yrs. and upwards. (413)

3-6-1832 - Will of Jesse ARNOLD presented. (414)

4-9-1832 - Warren SABIN tavern license renewed. John MITCHELL granted license to keep tavern. Samuel HARBIN tavern license renewed. Charles HARRIS tavern license renewed. Samuel A. HALE granted license to keep tavern. (420)

4-9-1832 - Daniel R. FURGUSON granted license to keep tavern. (421)

4-9-1832 - John Lewis appointed guardian of Perry NOGGLE aged 11 yrs. and upwards, minor orphan of George Noggle, dec'd. (421)

4-9-1832 - John Arnold appointed adms. of Estate of Ralph MYERS, dec'd. Susanna Hollcraft appointed adms. of Estate of Robert HOLLCRAFT, dec'd. (421)

4-9-1832 - Will of Charlton BARNES presented. Will of Oliver WHITAKER presented.(422)

4-11-1832 - John Stout guardian of James Arthur WHINNERY, orphan of John Whinnery, dec'd, filed account. (437)

4-14-1832 - Joseph Vanmater adms. of Estate of William COMPTON, dec'd, filed account, Robert Rees and Elizabeth Linton, adms. resigned and Nathan Linton appointed adms. of Estate of William LINTON, dec'd. Benjamin Howland and Stratton Gorhan appointed adms. of Estate of Joseph P. GORHAN, dec'd; widow, Abigail Gorham relinquishes right to adms. estate. (445)

4-11-1832 - Milo BRAY aged 17 yrs. and upwards, Mary BRAY aged 16 yrs. and
upwards and Peter BRAY aged 15 yrs. and upwards chose Obed A. Bonem as
their guardian with Bonum and William Hadley to serve as guardians of
Charles Bray aged 12 yrs. and upwards, Alice Bray aged 9 yrs. and upwards,
Dinah Bray aged 8 yrs. and upwards, Matilda Bray aged 4 yrs. and upwards,
Venus Bray aged 11 yrs., Jenny Bray aged 10 yrs. and Joseph Bray aged 9 yrs.,
all minor persons of colour. (435)
4-18-1832 - Ebenezer GORHAM aged 15 yrs. and upwards, orphan of Joseph P. Gorhan,
dec'd, chose Perry Dakin as his guardian. Azariah Wall appointed guardian
of John Gorhan aged 13 yrs., orphan of Joseph P. Gorhab, dec'd. (453)
4-19-1832 - Ephraim SMITH granted license to keep tavern. Daniel PARIS granted
license to keep tavern. (455)
4-20-1832 - Rev. William RUBLE a minister of the Church of Christ granted license
to solemnize marriages. (462)
5-3-1832 - Will of Solomon STANBROUGH presented. (465)
8-28-1832 - George R. HAYS granted license to keep tavern in Martinsville. (470)
8-28-1832 - Ann King appointed guardian of her children, David KING aged 10 yrs.
and upwards, Sarah King aged 9 yrs. and upwards, Elizabeth King aged 7 yrs.
and upwards, Mary King aged 5 yrs. and upwards, Margaret King aged 4 yrs. and
upwards, orphan minors of John King, dec'd. (470)
8-28-1832 - Will of John NEWLIN presented. (470)
8-27-1832 - Harry BRAY a person of colour aged 20 yrs. chose Obed A. Borum as
his guardian. (471)
8-27-1832 - Charles HARRIS made application for the vacation of the town of
Snowhill. (471)
8-28-1832 - John REED granted renewal of tavern license. (474)
8-31-1832 - Obed A. BORUM released as guardian of BRAY children in favor of
William Hadley who was appointed guardian. (488)
9-3-1832 - Widow, Christiana Roberts and son, Henry Roberts appointed adms. of
Estate of Edward ROBERTS, dec'd. (492)
9-4-1832 - James Lundy and Charlotte Lundy adms. of Estate of Enoch LUNDY filed
account. (494)
9-5-1832 - Lydia Smith and William Smith appointed adms. of Estate of Joseph
SMITH, dec'd. (496)
9-5-1832 - Daniel Paris appointed guardian of Rosella Jane RAMSEY aged 11 yrs.
and upwards, daughter of Margaret Ramsey, dec'd. (496)
9-6-1837 - James SPENSER, Application for a pension. The said James Spencer having
exhibited to the court his declaration in order to obtain pension it is the
opinion of the Court after the investigation of the matter, that the above
named applicant was a revolutionary soldier and served as he states, and it
further appears to the Court that John Allen and John Roberts, who signed the
certificate attached to the declaration aforesaid are credible persons, and
that their statement is entitled to credit. (500)
9-6-1837 - Thomas HARDIN, Application for a pension. The said Thomas Hardin having
exhibited his declaration in order to obtain a pension, it is the opinion of
the Court, after investigation of the matter, that the said applicant was a
revolutionary soldier, and served as he states, and the Court and further of
the opinion, that Ashahel Tribbey and William Austin, who signed the certificate attached to said declaration, are clergymen, residents of Vernon Township,
in said county of Clinton, and are creditable persons and that their statement
is entitled to credit. (500)

9-6-1837 - John ALLEN, Application for a pension. The said John Allen having
exhibited his declaration in order to obtain a pension it is the opinion of
the court after the investigation of the matter, that he the said applicant was
a revolutionary soldier, and served as he states, and it is the opinion of
the court that Jesse Rhonemus and David Carter, who signed the certificate
attached to the said declaration, are residents of Richland township in said
County and that their statement is entitled to credit. (500)

9-6-1832 - Elijah SABIN, Application for a pension. The said Elijah Sabin having
exhibited his declaration in order to obtain a pension, it is the opinion of
the Court, after the investigation of the matter, that the said applicant was
a revolutionary soldier, and served as he states, and it is also the opinion
of the Court that Jesse Thatcher and Benjamin Hinkson who signed the certificate attached to said declaration are residents of Clinton County and credible
persons and that their statement is entitled to credit. (501)

9-6-1832 - David SHIELDS, Application for a pension. The said David Shields having
exhibited his declaration in order to obtain a pension, it is the opinion of
the Court, after the investigation of the matter that the said applicant was
a revolutionary soldier and served as he states, it is also the opinion of the
Court that William Hoblett and Ashley Johnson are residents of Richland township in said County, and are persons of credibility, and that their statement
is entitled to credit. (501)

9-6-1832 - William FLOYD, Application for a pension. The said William Floyd having
exhibited his declaration in order to obtain a pension, it is the opinion of
the Court after the investigation of the matter that the said applicant was a
revolutionary soldier and served as he states. (501)

9-6-1832 - John WOOLARD, Application for a pension. The said applicant having
exhibited his declaration in order to obtain a pension, it is the opinion of
the Court, after the investigation of the matter, that said applicant was a
revolutionary soldier, and served as he states, it is also the opinion of the
court that John Allen and William St. Clair who signed the certificate attached
to said declaration are residents of Richland township in said county and are
persons of credibility and that their statement is entitled to credit. (501)

9-7-1832 - Joshua Harvey appointed adms. of the Estate of Cynthia HARVEY, dec'd.(505)

9-7-1832 - Authenticated copy of will and codicil of General Peter MUHLENBERG,
dec'd presented and received from Philadelphia, Pa. where will was proved
on 10-5-1807. (506)

9-8-1832 - William ROBISON, Application for a pension. The said William Robison
exhibited his declaration in order to obtain a pension, it is the opinion of
the court, after the investigation of the matter that the said William Robison
was a soldier of the Revolution and served as he states, it is also the
opinion of the court that John Hamrich and Joshua Bettester(?) who signed the
certificate attached to said declaration are residents of Clark township in
said county and credible person, and that their statement is entitled to
credit. (508)

9-8-1832 - Isaac GRANT, Application for a pension. The said Isaac Grant having
exhibited to the court his declaration in order to obtain a pension, it is
the opinion of the Court, after the investigation of the matter that said
Isaac Grant was a soldier of the revolution and served as he states, it is
also the opinion of the Court that Joshua Betterton and John Hanbrich who signed
the certificate attached to said declaration are residents of Clark township in
the county aforesaid and that their statement is entitled to credit. (508)

9-8-1832 - John HALL, Application for a pension. The said John Hall having exhibited
to the court his declaration in order to obtain a pension, it is the opinion
of the Court, after the investigation of the matter that said John Hall was
a soldier in the revolution and served as he states, it is also the opinion of
the Court that Charles Cline and William Shepherd who signed the certificate
attached to said declaration are residents of Clark township in said county
and credible persons and that their statement is entitled to credit. (508)
9-8-1832 - Samuel Buch appointed adms. of Estate of John McGREW, dec'd. Will of
Ritesman WILL presented. (512)
9-8-1832 - Widow, Elizabeth Whitaker relinquishes dower in Estate of Oliver
Whitaker, dec'd. (513)
9-8-1832 - John CLELAND, application for Naturalization. Declaration of Intention
made at Oct Term 1827 court at which time John Cleland was 30 years, born in
County Antrim, Ireland. Affidavits by James Christy and William S. Wilson.(513)
11-6-1832 - William C. EVANS aged 14 yrs. and upwards chose Alexander Wilson as
his guardian. (519)
11-6-1832 - Robert B. HUNNICUTT aged 18 yrs. and Abel Hunnicutt aged 16 yrs.
chose William P. Hunnicutt as their guardian with William also to serve as
guardian of Susannah Hunnicutt aged 13 yrs. and Joseph Hunnicutt aged 6 yrs.(519)
11-6-1832 - David CARTER granted license to keep tavern. (520)
11-6-1831 - David HAMRICH, Application for a pension. The said David Hamrich
having exhibited to the Court his declaration in order to obtain a pension,
it is the opinion of the Court after the investigation of the matter, that
the said David Hamrich was a soldier of the revolution and served as he states.
(523)
11-9-1832 - Will of David COUCKLIN (CONCKLIN?) presented. (533)
11-9-1832 - Abraham ELLIS, Application for a Pension. The said Abraham Ellis having
exhibited to the Court his declaration in order to obtain pension, it is the
opinion of the Court after the investigation of the matter, that said applicant
was a Soldier of the revolution and served as he states. It is also the
opinion of the Court, that Samuel Miller and William M. Irvin who signed the
certificate attached to said declaration are residents and citizens of Clinton
County and credible persons and that their statement is entitled to credit.(533)
11-9-1832 - William BOATMAN, Application for a Pension. The said William Boatman
having exhibited to the Court his declaration in order to obtain a pension,
it is the opinion of the Court, after the investigation of the matter, that
said applicant was a soldier of the revolution and served as he states, it is
also the opinion of the Court that George W. Barrier who signed the certificate
attached to said declaration is a citizen of Highland County, Ohio, that he is
a credible person and that his statement is entitled to credit. (533)
11-11-1832 - Emeline MAPEN aged 13 yrs. and upwards chose George B. Moon (or Moore?)
as her guardian. (536)
11-11-1832 - Samuel Southwich appointed adms. of Estate of Melzer STEARNS; widow,
Achsah Stearns relinquishes her right to adms. estate. (536)
12-4-1832 - Will of James MILLS presented. (550)
4-15-1833 - Charles HARRIS license to keep tavern at his residence. Samuel HIATT
license to keep tavern at Martinsville. Ephrain SMITH license to keep tavern
renewed. Joshua WRIGHT license to keep tavern at Martinsville. (553)
4-15-1833 - Harrison STEA NS aged 18 yrs. and upwards and Sally STEARNS aged 16
yrs. and upwards chose Edward Crossen as their guardian. (555)

4-15-1833 - Moses HALL aged 14 yrs. and upwards chose George McManis as his guardian. (555)

4-16-1833 - Authenticated copy of Will of John HENRY presented and received from Richmond, Va. where it was originally recorded on 9-8-1807. (559)

4-16-1833 - John JONES, Application for a pension. The said John Jones having exhibited his declaration in order 6o obtain a pension, it is the opinion of the Court, after the investigation of the matter, that the said applicant was a revolutionary soldier and served as he states. It is also the opinion of the Court that Thomas Cloud Jr., John Terrell and David Hays who signed the certificate attached to said declaration are residents of Clark township in said county, are persons of credibility and that their statement is entitled to credit. (560)

4-17-1833 - Widow, Mary ANTRAN appointed adms. of the Estate of Aden ANTRAN, dec'd. (562)

4-17-1833 - David S. Miller appointed guardian of his children, Adam MILLER aged 11 yrs. and John Miller aged 5 yrs. (562)

4-17-1833 - John McINTIRE license to keep tavern at his residence. (563)

4-18-1833 - John MITCHELL granted license to keep tavern. (568)

4-20-1833 - Account filed in Will of Alice GREEN. Legatees are: Joab Hunt, Lydia Hunt, Ruth Green, John Cary, Margaret Carey, Mary Green, Isaac Green, John Green, Jesse Green, Robert Green, Jesse Lundy, Abigail Lundy, Alice Green and Charlotte Lundy. (575)

4-22-1833 - Abraham ELLIS, Application for a Pension. The said Abraham Ellis having exhibited his amended declaration in order to obtain pension it is the opinion of the Court after the investigation of the matter, that said applicant was a revolutionary soldier and officer and served as he states. It further appears to the court that William M. Irvin, who has signed the necessary certificate to the original declaration of said Ellis produced at the last term of Court was then and still is a clergyman resident of said County of Clinton and that the statement made by him and Samuel Miller from the good standing and character of said William M. and Samuel is entitled to credit. (577)

4-23-1833 - License granted to Rev. Jacob DOUP (or DOUSS) a minister of the M. E. Church to solemnize marriages. (579)

4-25-1833 - James SPENCER, Application for a pension. The said James Spencer having exhibited his amended declaration in order to obtain a pension, it is the opinion of the court after the investigation of the matter, that George McManis who signed the certificate attached to said amended declaration, is a Clergyman, resident of Clinton County and a credible person. (589)

5-20-1833 - Thomas Hibben and John Hibben appointed adms. of Estate of Thomas HIBBEN, dec'd; widow, Mary Hibben relinquishes her right to adms. estate. (590)

7-22-1833 - Eza S. Quinby license to keep tavern in Wilmington. (595)

7-22-1833 - Charles L. Kelly and Thomas Anderson appointed adms. of Estate of John KELLY, dec'd. (595)

7-22-1833 - Will of Melzor STEARNS presented. (596)

7-24-1833 - Daniel PARIS license to keep tavern granted. (608)

7-27-1833 - Lydia FALLIS guardian of Turner Fallis, John Fallis, Isaac Fallis and Susan Fallis, minor heirs of Amos Fallis, dec'd filed account. (615)

7-30-1833 - George NIXON, Application for a pension. The said George (Nixon) having presented his petition in order to obtain a pension, the court here declares their opinion, after the investigation of the matter, that the above named applicant was a revolutionary officer and served as he states. And the Court is also of the opinion that James Brown and Asa Brown, who also

signed certificate are residents of Clark township in the vicinity of the
applicant and are credible persons and that their statement is entitled to
credit. And the (court) is satisfied that the said applicant could not
produce a clergyman in court as one of the said persons without to much
in convenience to him the said applicant. (621)

11-4-1833 - Thomas Austin appointed adms. of the Estate of Noah BURGE, dec'd;
widow, Rachel Burge relinquishes her right to adms. estate. (632)

11-4-1833 - Daniel H. Collett appointed guardian of Mary McKAY aged 11 yrs. and
upwards, orphan of Moses McKay, dec'd. (633)

11-4-1833 - Eliza DAKIN aged 14 yrs. and upwards, orphan of Henry DAKIN, dec'd,
chose James Pilcher as her guardian. (633)

11-4-1833 - Edward Adams and John C. Spencer resigned as adms. of Estate of
Thomas HALLAM, dec'd; widow, Sarah Hallam relinquishes her right to adms.
estate and Elisha Doan is appointed adms. de bonis non. (633)

11-4-1833 - Joseph WYSONG license to keep tavern in Clarksville. Thornton NICHOLS
license to keep tavern in Clarksville. Robert LONG license to keep tavern
at his residence. Jonathan BALDWIN license to keep tavern at residence.(634)

11-5-1833 - Will of Joseph ANTHONY presented. (639)

11-5-1833 - Samuel Williams appointed adms. of Estate of Elijah JESSUP, dec'd;
widow, Emily Jessup relinquishes right to adms. estate. (640)

11-5-1833 - Will of Ezekiel FRAZER presented. Richard PIERCE license to keep
tavern in Wilmington. (640)

11-5-1833 - Thomas WAY license to keep tavern at his residence. Jehu REED license
to keep tavern at Claysville. (641)

11-9-1833 - James Standford appointed guardian of Henry WELCH aged 13 yrs. and
upwards, Lorenzo C(?). Welch aged 11 yrs. and upwards, Daniel Welch aged 8
yrs. and upwards, and Catharine Welch aged 7 yrs. and upwards, orphans of
henry Welch, dec'd. (658)

11-9-1833 - John Kester appointed adms. of the estate of Abigail WILSON, dec'd.(658)

11-11-1833 - Widow, Susanna Parsel appointed adms. of Estate of Bergoon PARSEL,
dec'd. (661)

11-12-1833 - Will of Timothy BENNET with Elizabeth Jennings late Elizabeth Bennet
as executrix, account filed. (663)

1-3-1834 - Widow, Priscilla Titus and William Titus Sr. appointed adms. of Estate
of Philip TITUS. (677)

4-7-1834 - Will of Francis JACKSON presented. (682)

4-7-1834 - William HOGUE license to keep tavern in Cuba. (683)

4-8-1834 - Will of Martin RYAN presented. (687)

4-8-1834 - Benjamin EVANS aged 14 yrs. and upwards Joseph Josephus Reed as his
guardian. (687)

4-8-1834 - Samuel HIATT license to keep tavern in Martinsville. John McINTIRE
license to keep tavern at his residence. (687)

4-14-1834 - Levi Smith appointed guardian of Thomas HAWS aged 11 yrs. and upwards,
Lavina Jane Haws aged 8 yrs. and upwards and James Haws aged 7 yrs. and upwards,
orphans of John Haws, dec'd. (706)

Mary HARVEY, etal. to William HARVEY - 10-4-1829 - $1.00 - Parcel of land lying on Toddy Fork of the Little Miami, part of survey #2372 patented to Robert POLLARD - Mary HARVEY of Clinton County, Ohio; Simon MOON and Lydia MOON, wife; William HADLEY and Ann HADLEY of Morgan County, Indiana; Isaac CHEW and Martha CHEW, wife; Elizabeth HARVEY, Aikin DAKIN and Mary DAKIN, wife, and Cynthia HARVEY of Clinton County, Ohio, who are special legatees of the estate of Eli HARVEY, deceased, late of Clinton County; parties of the first part to William HARVEY, son of Eli Harvey, dec'd, of Clinton County, Ohio, party of the second part - Volume F, Pages 482-483

Elizabeth NORDYKE, etal. to Morgan E. NORDYKE - 4-2-1829 - Part of William TALLEFARO's survey number of entry 1192 on East fork of Little Miami River - 69 acres - Elizabeth (mark) NORDYKE, Benajah NORDYKE and Ann NORDYKE, wife; Hesekiah NORDYKE, Abraham NORDYKE and Henrietta P. NORDYKE, wife; William LUPTON and Anna LUPTON, wife, heirs of Israel NORDYKE, deceased, late of Clinton County, Ohio, of the first part and Morgan E. NORDYKE, as quit claim for his portion of estate of Israel NORDYKE, deceased, of the second part - Witnesses: Joshua NOBLE and Hiram NORDYKE - Volume F, pages 184-185

Henry LEEKA, etal to John LEEKA - 8-21-1830 - Henry LEEKA and Jane (mark) LEEKA, wife; Philip LEEKA and Elizabeth LEEKA, wife; George LEEKA and Lydia (mark) LEEKA, wife; Robert ANTRIM and Justena (mark) ANTRIM, wife, late Justena LEEKA; William SHARP and Elizabeth (mark) SHARP, wife, late Elizabeth LEEKA heirs and representatives of Christain LEEKA, late Clinton County, Ohio, deceased and Elizabeth (mark) LEEKA, widow of said LEEKA, deceased; all their right to interest in estate of deceased for $100. each; parties of the first part - John LEEKA, legal representative of said LEEKA, deceased, party of the second part - Volume F, page 478

Thomas P. McCOOL, etal. to Amarilla DINSMORE - 11-20-1830 - $1.00 In-Lot #20 in Faulkners addition of the town of Wilmington - Thomas P. McCOOL and Hannah McCOOK, wife; Daniel Anderson and Jane Anderson, wife; John DINSMORE and Elizabeth DINSMORE, wife; James DINSMORE and wife; of Green County, Ohio; brothers and sisters, brothers-in-law and sisters-in-law of Amos DINSMORE, deceased, late of Clinton County, Ohio; parties of the first part - Amarilla DINSMORE, widow of said Amos DINSMORE, deceased; party of the second part - Witnesses: John OZBURN and Jacob WEAVER - Volume G, pages 259-260

John R. DUNLAP, etal. to George DUNN - 10-21-1854 - $15.16 - Lots 25, 26, 22 and south side of 24 in the town of Clarksville - Signed: John R. DUNLAP and Emely DUNLAP, wife; William BOYCE; Levi PREWETH and Peggy PREWETH, wife; Bayll PREWETH and wife by John R. DUNLAP, their attorney in fact; Isear P. FISHER and Virginia A. FISHER, wife; Benjamin F. McKENNY; George ARMSTRONG and Elizabeth C. ARMSTRONG, wife, by Isear P. FISHER, their attorney in fact; all of Fayette County, Kentucky - Volume 1, page 1

Abigail CHEW, etal. to George MADEN - 13th day, 4th month, 1828
Power of Attorney - Abigail (mark) CHEW widow of Samuel CHEW late of
Clinton County, Ohio, deceased; Joshua HARVEY and Alice (mark) HARVEY,
wife; Reuben CHEW and Rebecca CHEW, wife; Harlan HARVEY and Ruth
HARVEY, wife, of Clinton County, Ohio, appoint George MADEN, their
lawful attorney, to collect monies owing estate of Samuel CHEW, de-
ceased - Witnesses: John TENEL, John PUCKETT, Jesse MOORE, John
HAZARD and Absalom GIBSON - Volume F, page 81

David WILLIAMS, etal. to Mary DAVIDSON - 8-9-1827 - David WILLIAMS
and Rachel WILLIAMS, wife; Abel WILLIAMS, Jr. and Enoch WILLIAMS of
Warren County, Ohio; William WILLIAMS and Nancy WILLIAMS, wife and
Ann DAVISON of Preble County, Ohio; Abel WILLIAMS and Rebecca WILLIAMS,
wife, of Fairfield County, Ohio; Joel AUSTIN and Hannah AUSTIN, wife
of Clinton County, Ohio; Jane WILLIAMS and Hannah WILLIAMS of Warren
County, Ohio; on the first part - Mary DAVIDSON of Preble County, Ohio
on the second part - Lot #118 in the original plat of Wilmington -
Volume F, pages 98-99

Benjamin McDUFFE, etal. to Charles P. GALLAHER - 8-14-1830 - part of
Survey #729 entered by John FRENCH - Benjamin McDUFFE and Elizabeth
McDUFFE, wife, late Elizabeth GALLAHER; Rachel GALLAHER; Leah GALL-
AHER; Alfred SABIN and Catharine SABIN, wife, late Catharine GALLA-
HER of Clinton County, Ohio, legal heirs of James GALLAHER, deceased;
parties of the first part - Charles P. GALLAHER, son and one of heirs
of said James GALLAHER, deceased; party of the second part -
Witnesses: Absalom REED and Andrew LOVE - Volume G, page 29

Reference:- See July, 1969 issue (VOL. II, No. III) of GATEWAY for marriages for this period. After the marriages mentioned above were published, it came to the editor's attention that there was a separate book containing, "Consents for Marriages" occuring during this period. Feeling that this information should not be omitted, we are now publishing it although it will be necessary to use the previously published record in connection with the use of this record.

ALEXANDER, John
  his father, Robert Alexander
THORNHILL, Rhoda
  her father, John Thornhill
LUKUS, Sarah
  her father, Caleb Lucas
FAIRFIELD, Lydia
  her father, David Fairfield
HUGHES, Polly
  her brother, John Hughes
LEWIS, Ruth
  her father, John Lewis
MILLS, Lydia
  her mother, Mary Mills
BARKLEY, Moses
  his father, John Barkley
OXLEY, Frances
  her mother, Jane Oxley
BARRETT, Jacob
  his father, William Barret
JONES, Sarah
  her father, John Jones
HARVEY, Mary
  her father, Samuel Harvey, Esq.
FORMAN, Margot
  her father, Thomas Foreman
JESSAP, Catharine
  a widow, former husband dec'd
BURROWS, Elizabeth
  her father, Isaac Burrows
BIGGS, William B.
  his father, Wm. Biggs. Esq.
BURGE, Noah
  his father, Henry Burge
WILKINSON, Rachel
  her father, Wm. Wilkison
CAR, Jane
  her uncle, George Green
GARRISON, Mary
  her brother, Jeremy Garrison
MOUNT, Jane
  her father, Wm. Mount

LAYMAN, Anne
  her father, Jacob Layman
PRATER, Mary - aged 22 yrs.
CART, Sabrath
  her father, Ezekiel Cast
SMITH, Elizabeth
  her father, John Smith
WILSON, Lettitia
  her father, Amos Wilson
DAKIN, Hiram
  his father, William Dakin
CRAW, Hannahretty
  her father, John Craw
HAINES, Rachel
  her father, Isaac Haines
HOSKINS, Hannah
  her father, Moses Hoskins
SEWELL, Sarah
  her father, John Sewell
OBLEBEE, Eliza
  her brother, Jacob Oglesbee
CAMP, Mary
  her father, Ezekiel Camp
FISHER, Daniel
  his father, Moleston Fisher
FISHER, Isaac
  his father, Moleston Fisher
BENNETT, Margaret
  her father, Timothy Bennet
BENNET, Amy
  her father, Timothy Bennet
RICHARDS, Betsey
  her father, Geo. Richards
CAMB, Jane
  her father, Ezekiel Camp
HARDIN, Thompson
  his father, Thomas Hardin
SEWELL, Elizabeth
  her father, Jno. Sewell
SMITH, Avalina
  her brother, Reuben Smith
VANDERVOURT, Mary
  her father, Jonah Vendervort

CLEVER, James
    his father, David Clever
POWERS, Mary
    her father, Stephen Powers
KIMBROUGH, Elizabeth
    her father, Jeremiah Kimbrough
GOODALL, Sally
    her step-father, John Bowermaster
BARRETT, Elizabeth
    her father, William Barrett
MORROW, Almira
    her father, James Morrow
HENDRICKSON, Rhoda
    her father, Cornelius Hendrickson
LARUE, Jacob
    his mother, Deborah Larue
LEE, William
    his step-father Richard Cast
SEWELL, Rebecca
    her father, John Sewell
NOBLE, Priscilla
    her father, William Noble
McKINNY, Joel
    his father, Stephen McKinny
McKINNY, Lewis
    his father, Stephen McKinney
CURTIS, Martha
    her brother, Edward Curtis
CROUSER, Margaret
    her father, John Crouser
McGEE, Polly
    her mother, Elizabeth McGee
CLARK, Sally
    her brother, Benjamin Clark
WHITE, Jemima
    her father, Joshua White
PARKER, Abraham
    his mother, Elizabeth Parker
GARNER, Elizabeth
    her father, James Gardner

THATCHER, Mary
    her father, Thomas Thatcher, Esq.
HOGE, Alivia - consent by John
        McWhorter who she lived with
        since a child
SEWELL, Hannah
    her father, John Sewell
DRAPER, Hannah
    her father, Thomas Draper
MORRISON, Nancy
    her father, Gaven Morrison
SEWELL, Mary
    her father, John Sewell
SMITH, John
    his father, Wm. Smith
BREWER, Siner
    her brother, Jemermiah Brewer
McCUGH, Jane (McHUGH on consent)
    her step-father, Elisha Whitaker
McINTIRE, Polly
    her father, John McIntire
RIDINGER, Celia
    her father, Andrew Redinger
LEGGETT, Betsey
    her father, Wm. Ligget
WILKASON, Elisha
    his father, Wm. Wilkason
RUBLE, Rachel
    her brother, Walter Ruble
MITCHEL, James H.
    his father, John Mitchel
MOORE, James (MOON on consent)
    his father, William Moon
McGEE, Rebecca
    her mother, Rebecca McGee
WALTERS, Sally
    her grandfather, William Spencer Sr.
McVEY, Charity
    her mother, Mary McVay

The following records were taken from Marriage Return Book 1, Marriage License Book 1 and Marriage Book 2; marriages from Aug. 21, and after are from Book 2 with licenses for same being from Book 1. Abbreviations: c=consent; o=oath.

ABRAMS, Israel to Sarah Biggs	9-22-1815
ADAMSON, James to Lydia Roberts - c. his father John Adamson	8-21-1817
her father Joseph Roberts	
ADAMSON, John to Sarah Roberts	11-28-1816
AIRY (AERY), John to Margaret Turner - c. her father Walter Turner	8-14-1817
AKIN, Harman L. to Harriatt Haynes - c. his father David Akin	6-4-1817
her father Wm. Haynes	
ALLEN, John Jr. to Kesiah Jackson	3-12-1811
ANTRIM, Adan to Mary Sharp - o. William Antrim	11-8-1810
ANTRIM, William to Sarah Sharp	11-4-1810
ARNOLD, William to Elizabeth Townsend - o. Isaac Jay	7-4-1815
BABB, Thomas to Mary Babb	8-15-1815
BAILES, Solomon to Elizabeth John	12-21-1815
BAILISS (BALIFF), Joshua to Ann Haines	2-13-1817
BARKLEY, John to Elizabeth Cast	9-12-1816
BARRET, William to Kesiah Sharp	4-12-1812
BARRETT, David to Nancy Criswell	10-16-1814
BATY, William Beall to Elizabeth Haines	6-9-1814
BEALS (BAILES), John to Elizabeth Puckett	4-20-1815
BETTERTON, William to Margaret McKebbin	2-27-1817
BLOOMER, Gilbert to Susanna Thompson	9-24-1816
BOTKIN, Charles to Sarah Griffin - both have been married	10-11-1812
BOWERMASTER, John to Mary Haws (Hanes)	5-25-1813
CARMON, James to Rosanna Ellis	2-1-1816
CHAMBERS, Nathan to Emily Denny	1-23-1817
CHENOWETH, Isaac to Isabella McElwain - c.her father David McElwaine	6-12-1817
CHEW, Isaac to Martha Harvey	5-7-1816
CHRISTY, James to Anna McDonald	11-1-1815
COATS, Aquila to Hannah Cogle	1-25-1816
COATS, William to Charlotte Wright	10-30-1817
COMER, Nathan to Susannah Stount	9-23-1813
COPELAND, Abner to Peggy Morgan - c. her grandfather Thomas Morgan,	4-10-1817
as her parents do not reside in this state	
COPUS, John to Charity Little	6-6-1811
CORAH, John to Mary Osborn	2-15-1816
COX, John Jr. to Pamelia Quick	8-9-1810
COX, Samuel Esq. to Anna Reed	9-2-1811
CREE, Robert to Elenor Barkley	11-20-1811
CROSSON, Edward Jr. to Hannah Burroughs	10-4-1817
CROUSE, John to Rhoda Matson - c. her father John Matson	5-8-1817
CURTIS, John to Ann Sinclear	7-25-1815
DAKIN, Elias to Phebe Hazard	3-16-1815
DAKIN, John to Phebe Clever - c. his father William Dakin	12-25-1817
DANIELS, Benjamin to Margaret Burge	2-13-1817
DANIELS, Samuel to Elizabeth Corry	6-25-1816
DARROW, Jason to Mary Nordyke	6-4-1817

DAUGHERTY, John to Rebecca Larue   12-5-1816
DAUGHERTY, William to Tamar Thornburgh   1-17-1815
DOAN, Joseph Jr. to Caty Bennett   9-23-1813
DRAPER, Thomas to Elizabeth Dunkreeg   11-20-1810
DUCKWALL, Frederick to Catherine Ellis - return not dated-1814-lic.   11-3-1813
ELLIS, Isaac of Green Co. to Rebecca Copeland - o. brother   6-8-1815
                                      Joseph Copeland
ELLIOTT, James to Cynthia Sterns - c. his father Edmund Elliott   4-17-1817
                          her father David Sterns

ELLISON, Andrew to Welmet Thornburg   5-4-1815
ENSMINGER, Andrew W. to Jane Buckner   5-29-1817
FAGANS (HIGGINS on lic.), Willis to Elizabeth Jones   2-3-1816
FISHER, David to Hannah Clevenger   12-24-1812
FISHER, Thomas to Susanna Hodgson   11-29-1810
FROST, Barnard to Phebe Cook   11-15-1810
GARNER, Henry to Unice Cavit   5-17-1814
GARNER, Jobe to Rebeccah Jones   9-26-1815
GARNER, William to Anne Hockett - o. Seth Hockett   4-24-1817
GARRISON, Benjamin to Rebecka Garrison - o. brother David Garritson 12-24-1810
GARRISON, John to Jane Foreman   12-10-1811
GARRISON, Reed to Jane McGee   1-16-1812
GARRITSON, David to Nancy Elsey   9-23-1813
GARWOOD, Joseph to Margaret Ann Borden   11-28-1816
GARWOOD, Joshua to Polly Stephens   6-10-1813
GRAGOREE(?), Levi to Catherine Walker   10-18-1814
GREEN, Jesse to Sarah Davis   9-21-1815
GRICE, Henry to Frankey Curtis   5-20-1812
GRICE, John to Mary Curtis - c. her father Edward Curtis   7-9-1812
GRIFFIN, James to Susanna Hester   5-10-1810
HAIE, Em. to Maria Sabin   1-16-1817
HALL, Hutson to Nancy Alley   4-24-1817
HALLEWAY, John to Levisa Hodgson   2-19-1817
HANES, Joab to Elizabeth Doan   9-3-1812
HARDEN, Samuel to Hannah Burr   10-22-1814
HARDWICK, William to Sarah Stewart   1-22-1811
HARDY, James to Susannah Shockley - c. her father Eli Shockley   8-28-1817
HARPER, John to Delilah Hughes   4-15-1813
HAWKINS, Jehu to Susanna Brock   5-4-1817
HAYNES, Joseph to Sarah Fisher   12-28-1815
HAYNES, Samuel to Elizabeth McCloud   8-25-1811
HAYS, Jacob to Elizabeth Baser (Baysore)   1-21-1816
HAYS, John to Ann Cowgill   2-19-1815
HAZARD, John to Rebecca Conger   1-6-1817
HESTER, Henry to Nancy Painter   12-25-1817
HESTER, Martin to Eve Hushaw   7-12-1814
HIATT, Reuben to Mary Stout   9-13-1817
HOBSON, Cornelius to Mary Hobson   3-11-1813
HODGSON, Joel to Elizabeth Caster - c. her father Thomas Caster   11-12-1812
HOLESTER, John to Hannah Haynes   5-29-1815
HOSKINGS, George to Mary Hodgson - o. John Hoskins   3-13-1817

270

```
HOSKINS, Jonathan to Lydia Hodson                                      9-30-1813
HOW, James to Katherine Totherow                                       5-17-1810
HOWELL, Charles to Mary Stout                                          2-4-1813
HUMPHREY, Robert to Hephzibah Perkins                                  10-22-1813
HUNT, Ira to Mary Grayham                                              11-13-1814
JACKSON, Amur to Ancenth St. Clair                                     12-19-1816
JACKSON, Elemiel to Sarah Barrett                                      5-7-1813
JACKSON, Henry to Elizabeth Jones                                      1-23-1817
JOHN, Samuel to Elizabeth Bails (Bailes)                               4-6-1815
JOHNSON, Ashla to Sarah Malon                                          12-28-1816
JOHNSTON, Ashly to Elizabeth Shields - c. brother William Shields      11-18-1813
JONES, Daniel to Elizabeth Star                                        4-13-1817
JONES, Elisha to Elizabeth Brown                                       3-13-1817
JONES, Thomas to Nancy Star                                            2-11-1814
KEENAN, Peter to Nancy Mitchell                                        9-26-1816
KELLEY, Nathan of Warren Co. to Mary Vanmater                          12-25-1816
KELSEY, William to Betsy Keenon                                        12-12-1816
KERSEY (KELSEY), David to Lydia Keenan                                 12-22-1814
KERSEY, John to Anna Stedhan                                           2-13-1813
LINSY, John to Bula Head                                               5-7-1816
LORANCE, Elijah to Snythia Wright                                      6-24-1813
LOW, James to Ann Grewness (Grimary)                                   8-27-1816
LUKA, Henry to Jane Fry                                                3-7-1816
LUPTON, Jonathan to Catherine Stephens                                2-1-1814
LYONS, John to Betsy Brown - c. her father John Brown                 5-1-1817
LYTLE, John to Scina Mounts                                            11-5-1816
McDANIEL, John to Jane Christy                                         1-19-1815
McGrager, John to Elizabeth Harris                         lic. 7-2-1811
McGRIFF, Richard to Henry Janny - o. Allen Reed                        4-3-1817
McKIBBINS, Gideon to Jane Stewart                                      8-23-1810
McVAY, James to Susannah Jones                                         1-9-1817
MALONE, Jesse to Jane Jones - o. Thomas Jones                         1-1-1814
MANN, David to Rachel Jones Ervin (Irvin) - c. her grandfather         3-10-1811
                                  John Jones
MARKER, Jacob to Mirriam Jones                                         7-29-1815
MARKER, Jonathan to Polly Brockney                                     12-12-1816
MARRET, Isaac to Elizabeth Crawford                                    4-4-1815
MASON, Richard to Sarah Jackson                                        2-2-1812
MATHEWS, Peter to Catharine Noble - c. her father Wm. Noble            5-29-1817
MEDSCAR, Isaac to Rebecka Richards                                     9-24-1816
MILLS, Alexander to Sally Gilpin                                       4-2-1813
MILLS, Hezekiah to Darcus Bently                                       9-7-1815
MILLS, William to Mary Elsey                                           7-1-1813
MILS, Daniel to Mary Bennit - return not dated-1815        lic. 2-7-1815
MIRANDAY, Jonathan to Sarah Stewart                                    5-20-1812
MOON, Henry to Sarah Mills                                             9-29-1814
MOON, James to Anna Hockett                                            5-23-1816
MOON (MOORE), Thomas to Elizabeth Hockett - c. his father Jos. Moore   12-25-1817
                                  her father Jos. Hockett
MORRIS, Owin to Abigail Wilson                                         10-13-1813
```

```
NICASON (NICKERSON), David to Catharine Spencer                              11-28-1816
NICKERSON, Arteunas to Elizabeth Reed                                        4-10-1817
NOBLE, Benjamin to Betsy Matthews                                           9-21-1815
NOBLE, Joshua to Susannah Matthews                                          2-13-1817
OREN, Joseph to Sarah Hayworth                                              11-19-1812
OSBORN, Thomas to Margaret Rinard                                           12-18-1817
OVEN, James to Margaret Atkinson                                            12-22-1814
OXLEY, Aaron to Elizabeth Sewell - c. her father Aaron Sewell              10-30-1817
PAINTER, Edward to Nancy Fairfield - c. her father David Fairfield         11-26-1810
PARCELS, Burgoon to Susanna Jones                                          12-10-1812
PARKER, William to Nancy Stanley                                            1-19-1815
PATERSON, David to Tempe Taylor - c. brother Drury Taylor                   1-17-1811
PATTERSON, Thomas to Abigail Hester                                         8-21-1816
PETTIT, James to Jane Conner                                               12-23-1817
POFF, Samuel to Frankey Jones                                               5-1-1817
PORTER, Nicholas to Mahala Garrison                                         6-20-1811
RATLIFF, Edam to Hannah Smith                                              12-9-1814
REED, David to Hannah Dougherty                                            3-2-1815
REEDE, John to Susanna Lefler                                              3-29-1814
REEDER, John to Elizabeth Thompson                                         1-7-1813
REEL, John to Mary Smith                                                   2-23-1815
RHONEMOUS, Jacob to Sophia Cluster                                         5-26-1814
RICH, Thomas to Ann Ballard                                               1-31-1811
RIGEL, Abraham to Elizabeth How - Abraham married before, wife            11-20-1817
                                 believed to be deceased
RIGGS, Isaac to Sarah Ridinger                                            10-12-1817
RINARD, Jeremiah to Sarah Howell                                          4-27-1815
RINARD, Solomon to Rachel Green - c. her father Jesse Green               8-28-1817
RUBLE, Samuel to Mary Jothers (or Lothers)                                7-2-1814
RUBLE, Walter to Hannah Hayworth                                          11-19-1811
RUBLE, Walter to Sarah Wright                                             5-26-1814
RYUN, Mashack to Elizabeth Arner - c. her brother Vinsum Garner           12-12-1817
SABIN, Warren to Margaret McManis - o. James McManis                      4-4-1811
SANDERS, Hezekiah to Massey Sanders                                       1-10-1811
SEAMAL, Ebenezer F. to Lillus Mitchell                                    10-21-1813
SHARP, Solomon to Rebecca Stokesbury                                      7-22-1813
SHARP, William to Elizabeth Leaky                                         2-21-1817
SHEPHERD, Moses to Rebecca Lee                                            2-16-1815
SHIELDS, George to Nancy McDanald                                         10-10-1811
SHIELDS, William to Isabella McDaniel                                     9-24-1816
SHORT, Henry to Lydia Williams - o. Obadiah Williams                      11-12-1810
SIMERMAN, George to Elizabeth Martin                                      2-24-1816
SMALLY, John to Salome Swallow - his father Wm. Smalley says              7-19-1812
                                 Salome is 21 years
SMETHERS (SNETHEN), George W. to Elizabeth Thornburgh                     10-10-1816
SMITH, Elisha to Lydia Mills - c. her brother Wm. Mills                   7-31-1817
SMITH, Henry to Ann Reddecks                                             11-17-1812
SMITH, Peter to Nancy Rinard                                             11-29-1817
SMITH, William to Elizabeth Atha                                         2-3-1814
SMITH, Wm. to Nancy Wrightsman                                           5-23-1816
```

```
SPENCER, John to Mary (Polly Lually) Hinkston                          1-25-1816
SPRAY, Samuel to Elizabeth Hayworth - c. her father Absalom Hayworth 8-5-1816
STANBERRY, James to Mary Hodgson                                       2-11-1814
STANBERRY, Nehemiah to Elizabeth Hester                               7-19-1810
STEEL, Jesse W. to Elizabeth McGragor                                 9-16-1815
STEPHENS, James to Exsha (Axsha) Engle                                5-15-1814
STAR, William to Lydia Jackson                                       10-14-1815
STEWARD, John to Ann Lee                                              3-10-1814
STEWART, Samuel to Mary McKibban                                     10-2-1815
STOUT, Ephraim to Ruth Howell                                        4-2-1815
TEAGUE, Elijah to Rebecca Atha                                       12-26-1817
TENARY, Thomas to Susannah Acre - c. her father John Acre            12-11-1817
THORNBERRY, Abel to Rhoda Johnson                                    9-20-1817
THORNBURGH, Joseph to Rachel Burris - c. his father Richard Thornburg 12-4-1817
                                       her father William Burris
THORNHILL, Barrett to Ruth Jones                                     12-23-1813
TOWELL, Henry to Ruth Harvey                                         8-1-1815
TURNER, John to Mary Lucas                                           2-23-1815
TRENARY, Thomas to Fanny Dawson - c. her father Nathaniel Dawson     12-29-1817
VANMETER, Solomon to Mary Ann Babb                                   1-19-1813
VENARD, James to Delilah Linn                                        12-10-1812
VESTAL, Nathan to Mary Poe - both of Chester twp.                    12-26-1811
VESTALL, William to Anna Hobson                                      10-13-1817
VILLARS, John to Elizabeth Magee                                     9-15-1816
WALTER, Robert to Mary Ward                                          3-13-1817
WALTERS, Conrad to Sarah Ann Heaton                                  11-20-1817
WASSON, Samuel to Sally Harris          (note:  no day given)        Feb. 1816
WHINERY, Joseph to Lydia Pirkins                                     8-10-1815
WILES, William to Dinah Stout                                        5-23-1811
WILKERSON, John to Elizabeth Faris                                   12-5-1811
WILLIAMS, Benazah to Jane Whinnery - o. Joseph Whinery               5-29-1817
WILSON, Joseph to Mary Cochrin                                       4-25-1815
WIRE, William to Abigail Vandervort - c. her father Jonah Vandervort 12-4-1817
WRIGHT, Abraham to Elizabeth Tomlin - c. by himself as his father    3-27-1817
             is in Indiana to plant corn and clear land
WRIGHT, Amos to Mary Lieurance - c. Peter Lieurance  = = = = = = = = 2-20-1817 = = =
```

273

ABERNATHY, Samuel to Sarah Lee	6-29-1820
ACRE, John, Jr. to Sally Jones	3-11-1819
ADAMS, Allen to Arksie Hobson	10-8-1820
ADSET, Palmer to Isabella Reynolds	12-23-1819
ALEXANDER, John to Rhoda Thornhill	12-28-1820
ARNOLD, Luke to Sarah Lukus	3-13-1818
ATKINSON, Robert to Lydia Fairfield	7-30-1818
BABB, Jasper to Polly Hughes	1-15-1818
BABB, Peter to Ruth Lewis	6-24-1819
BAILY, William A. to Lydia Mills	8-20-1820
BARKLEY, Moses to Frances Oxley	4-9-1818
BARRETT, Jacob to Sarah Jones	8-5-1818
BASHORE, Barnet to Mary Harvey	8-15-1820
BEGGS, William to Margot Forman	1-1-1818
BENTLEY, Benjamin to Catharine Jessap	2-6-1818
BIGGS, Daniel to Elizabeth Burrows	12-8-1818
BIGGS, William B. to Rhoda Whittaker	12-10-1818
BOTTS, Williamson J. to Sarah Moon	4-8-1819
BOUTON, Josiah to Hannah Fairfield	9-21-1820
BURGE, Noah to Rachel Wilkinson	9-10-1818
BURLEY, James to Jane Car	1-11-1820
CAMP, Joseph to Mary Garrison	8-11-1819
CAMP, Zephianiah to Prudence Garrison	3-24-1818
CARSON, James to Prudence Cloud	1-25-1820
CAST, Horatio to Jane Mount	9-3-1818
CLARKE, John to Rebecca Matthews	12-31-1818
CLEVER, James to Mary Powers	11-9-1820
CLOUD, Henry to Anne Layman	12-14-1820
COCHRAN, William S. to Ruth Manker	10-21-1818
COCK, George to Mary Prater	10-26-1820
CONKLIN, Jacob to Sabrath Cart	3-9-1820
COX, Isaac to Mary Spray	1-18-1818
CREE, John to Elizabeth Smith	11-19-1818
CRISWELL, Samuel to Lettitia Wilson	11-23-1820
CUNNINGHAM, Moses to Betsy Marts	5-6-1819
CURTIS, Edward to Elizabeth Lyons	6-27-1820
DAKIN, Henry to Merandy Barnes	3-2-1820
DAKIN, Hiram to Hannahretty Craw	4-20-1820
DAVIS, Anthony to Rachel Haines	10-7-1819
DENNIS, Richmond to Hannah Tomlin	10-29-1818
DILLON, William to Hannah Hoskins	3-5-1818
DOLBY, James to Sarah Sewell	4-13-1820
ELLIS, Isaac to Eliza Oglebee	11-18-1819
ELWAINE, John M. to Peggy McGregor	8-27-1818
ELZEY, James to Mary Camp	10-12-1820
ENSLY, Aaron to Rachel Wollard	10-15-1818
FIFE, James to Jane Dillon	11-29-1819
FISHER, Daniel to Margaret Davis	2-12-1818
FISHER, Isaac to Margaret Bennett	10-12-1820
FISHER, James to Amy Bennet	5-3-1818

FREY, Michael to Jane Trenary	12-31-1820
FULLER, William to Betsey Richards	6-18-1818
GARRISON, Lemuel to Martha Garrison	10-12-1820
GARRISON, Parsons to Elizabeth Mart	4-14-1819
GARRISON, William to Jane Camb	2-5-1818
HAMPTON, Abraham to Rebecca Harlin	12-24-1818
HARDIN, Thompson to Elizabeth Turner	1-28-1819
HARDIN, William to Elizabeth Sewell	10-26-1820
HARNDEN, Jeduthan to Avalina Smith	2-25-1818
HAWORTH, James to Amillia West	3-18-1819
HAY, William to Nancy Evans	1-7-1818
HAYNES, William to Rhoda Shepherd	10-8-1818
HESTER, David to Mary Vandervourt	2-18-1820
HIATT, Gideon to Mary Thatcher	8-5-1819
HIBBIN, Thomas to Nancy McFadden	6-27-1819
HOW, John to Alivia H oge	1-28-1819
HOWELL, Benjamin to Elizabeth Kimbrough	1-6-1820
IVINS, Samuel to Sally Goodall	1-1-1818
JACKSON, Thomas to Polly Brooks	2-8-1820
JEWETT, Josiah to Sarah Redington	12-31-1820
JOHNSON, Achillis C. to Susannah Wright	8-22-1820
JONES, Solomon to Elizabeth Barrett	1-13-1820
JONES, William to Esther Johnson	4-25-1820
KIRK, Elisha to Almira Morrow	12-28-1820
KISER, Philip to Rhoda Hendrickson	2-24-1820
LARUE, Jacob to Mary Reeder	1-7-1819
LEE, William to Rebecca Sewell	2-5-1818
LEONARD, Thomas to Hannah Starbuck	6-22-1820
LIEURANCE, George to Priscilla Noble	2-12-1818
LONGSTRETH, Jacob to Peggy Ditto	1-1-1818
McKINNY, Joel to Polly Black	3-9-1820
McKINNY, Lewis to Sarah Dowas	3-10-1818
McVAY, Peter to Hannah Martin	2-7-1819
MAGEE, James W. to Elizabeth McManis	1-11-1818
MARSHALL, James to Sarah Burr	10-8-1818
MARTIN, Charles to Clarinda Howland	12-31-1820
MARTIN, Levi to Anne Mills	8-12-1819
MARTIN, Stephen to Martha Curtis	11-16-1820
MICHAEL, John to Margaret Crouser	6-18-1820
MILES, Burwell B. to Lydia Wilson	8-2-1818
MILLS, William to Elizabeth Taylor	4-11-1820
MITCHEL, James H. to Polly McGee	12-3-1818
MOON, Joseph to Rachel Hocket	8-6-1818
MOON, William to Hannah Hocket	11-21-1818
MOORE, James to Rody Vanmatre	5-20-1818
MOORE, James to Sally Clark	12-23-1819
MOORE, Micajah H. to Rebecca McGee	8-19-1819
MORROW, William to Susanah Nickerson	6-17-1819
MOUNT, William to Catherine Baker	10-26-1820
MURFY, John to Jemima White	1-21-1819
MYERS, David to Sally Stout	5-23-1819

```
ORNEY, Athony to Sally Walters                                    5-30-1818
PARKER, Abraham to Charity McVey                                  11-5-1820
PENINGTON, Thomas to Isabella Rogers                             3-9-1820
PORTER, John to Rachel Elzey                                     2-10-1820
POWERS, Samuel to Rhoda Lucas                                    9-13-1819
PUCKET, James, Jr. to Mary Grant                                3-12-1818
PYLE, Jehu to Esther Stratton                                    2-24-1820
RADCLIFF, Daniel to Rachael McManis                             8-28-1819
RATLIFF (RATCLIFF), John to Elizabeth Garner                    7-8-1819
REEDER, Jacob to Elizabeth Faris                                3-13-1818
REES, Moses to Lydia Rockhill                                    3-5-1820
RICHEY, JOHN to Phebe Smith                                      12-28-1820
RYAN, Martin to Margaret Harlan                                 5-14-1818
SAILOR, William to Hannah Sewell                                11-10-1818
SHEPHERD, Moses to Hannah Draper                                10-29-1819
SHIELDS, John to Jemima St. Clair                               2-11-1819
SIDLES, Israel to Nancy Morrison                                12-17-1818
SMITH, James to Mary Sewell                                      3-5-1818
SMITH, Joshua to Lydia Babb                                      8-19-1820
SMITH, John to Elizabeth Crowser                                6-3-1819
SMITH, William to Sarah Jones                                    5-4-1820
SMITHSON, Drummond D. to Siner Brewer                           3-30-1820
SPURGEN, William to Hannah Davis                                10-26-1820
STANSBERRY, Recompence to Jane McCugh                           12-25-1820
STAR, Richard to Sarah Jackson                                   6-15-1820
STEWART, Timothy to Catharine Creswell                         12-31-1818
STRAUGHN, Merriman to Hannah Vickery                            8-2-1818
TALLY, Oliver H. to Abigail Brackney                            1-1-1818
THOMPSON, James to Pelly McIntire                               9-24-1818
THORNHILL, Thomas to Nancy Starr - lic. granted Clark Co. 2-5-1818
TIBBETT, Henry to Jane Bradshaw                                 5-1-1818
TRADER, Arthur to Celia Ridinger                                1-29-1818
TROTTER, William R. to Hannah Hughes                            4-27-1820
UNDERWOOD, William to Mary Thomas                               1-21-1819
VANDEVORT, John to Martha Reed                                  1-10-1819
VAN MATRE, Joseph to Catherine Matthews                        9-17-1818
VESTALL, Lemuel to Nancy Howell                                 9-3-1819
WALKER, Robert, Jr. to Elizabeth Rulon (Rubon?)                10-7-1819
WELCH, , Turner to Esther Fallis                                8-22-1819
WEST, James to Betsey Leggett                                   6-8-1820
WEST, William to Sary Hardon                                    1-26-1819
WILKASON, Elisha to Mary Jones                                  9-7-1820
WILKENSON, James to Jane McDaniel                               6-25-1818
WILKISON, William to Nancy Atha                                 11-12-1818
WILSON, Alexander to Sarah Ireland                             12-23-1819
WILSON, Amos to Mary Coulter                                     7-12-1818
WILSON, James to Elenor Ireland                                 8-17-1820
WOOD, Solomon to Phebe Lucas                                     6-10-1819
WRIGHT, Emson to Rachel Ruble                                   3-23-1820
WRIGHT, Isaac to Esther Thatcher                                3-25-1819
YOUNG, James to Mary Cluster                                    11-24-1819
```

Estate of John ACRE, Sr. - Feb. Term 1814 - Bond of $200. by John Acre, Jr. adms. with Amos Hankins and William Clevenger as sureties

Estate of Peter BURR - 9-28-1816 - Bond by Hannah Burr, adms. with Samuel Cox and Joel Woodruff as sureties

Estate of James CRAWFORD - 11-20-1818 - Bond by Mary Crawford, widow and Thomas Thatcher, adms. with Thomas Thatcher, Jr. and John Adamson as sureties

Estate of John CRAWFORD - 3-1-1814 - Bond of $500. by Elizabeth Crawford and Thomas Thatcher, adms. with John Balanger as surety

Estate of George CRISWELL - 12-1-1812 - Bond by Elizabeth Criswell and Martin Hester, adms.

Estate of William COULTER - 3-19-1814 - Bond of $400 by Mary Coulter, adms. with John Coulter as surety

Estate of Joseph CU - 4-18-1814 - Bond by William Cu, adms. with John Hays as surety

Estate of Robert GRIFFIN - 12-14-1811 - Bond by Sarah Griffin, adms. with James Griffin as surety

Estate of Archibald HENDERSON - 10-6-1810 - Bond by John Barkley, adms. with Benjamin Smally, Sr. and John Cox as sureties

Estate of Thomas JOHNSTON - June 1814 - Bond of $200. by John Johnston, adms. with John Schooly and Isaac Harvey as sureties - Mother of Thomas Johnston (not named) relinquishes right to administer estate

Estate of John LOSA - June Term 1814 - Bond by Sarah Losa, adms. with John Allen and Joseph Gric as sureties

Estate of John McGREGOR - 9-18-1813 - Bond $800. by James Harris and Elizabeth McGregor, widow, executors with Elisha Last(?) and James M. Manes as sureties

Estate of Joseph MIRES - 11-9-1814 - Bond of $500. by William Jackson, adms. with James Jackson and Thomas Stilt as sureties

Estate of James MOON - Clark Twp. - 1-26-1818 - Bond of $300 by Seth Hocket and Joseph Moon, adms. with Daniel Moon and Jesse Moon as sureties

Estate of Michael Tethero - 9-28-1816 - Bond of $1000. by Rachel Tethero, Samuel Ruble, Jr. and Thomas Thatcher, adms. with Peter Tomlin, Robert Stoap and Samuel Ruble, Sr. as sureties

Estate of William Ward - 6-15-1817 - Bond $1000. by Elizabeth Ward and Thomas Thatcher, adms. with Edward Powers, Abel Wright and Matthew Calloway as sureties

Estate of Jacob WRIGHTSMAN - 4-18-1814 - Bond of $200. by Nancy Wrightsman, adms. with Jeremiah Rinard as surety

*Refers to only those estates which were included in Will Volume A-B. In addition, the Clinton County Common Pleas Docket, p. 302 refers to an estate of one Thomas Wright, July 1818, as follows: Widow—Ann Wright, David Wright and Walter Rubel—applicants for letters of administration. GATEWAY TO THE WEST, Vol. 1: No. 3 (July-Sept. 1968).

Editors' Note:- From Volume A-B
Volume A & Volume B are two individual books, but have been
bound as one book known by cover as Volume <u>A-B</u>.

BABB, Henry - Union Twp. - Volume A, page 37 - Dated 10-18-1821
Recorded 1-30-1811 - Wife: Elizabeth - Sons: Azel, Sampson, Peter,
Thomas and Henry, last two not of age - Daughters; Rachel, Lydia, Mary,
Rebecca, Margaret, Elizabeth and Hannah. Executors: wife, Elizabeth
and son, Peter - Signed: Henry (mark) Babb - Witnesses: Azel WALKER,
Thomas Babb, 2nd, and Robert EACHUS

BAILEY, Josiah - Volume A, page 21 - Dated 12th day, 6th month, 1816 - Recorded
(not given) - Wife: Susanna - children: Almeida, Robert B., Judith,
Daniel, James E. and Mary B. Bailey - Mentions Lot #2 Jefferson Square,
Town of Waynesville, Warren Co., Ohio - Signed: Josiah Bailey -
Witnesses: Hezekiah HIATT and Eleasor HIATT

BALLARD, John - Volume A, page 11 - Dated 20th day, 3rd month, 1814 - Recorded
6-16-1814 - Wife: Dinah - Children: mentioned, but not named, not all
of age - Executors: Reuben GREEN and William BUTLER - Signed: John
Ballard- Witnesses: Joseph Ballard, Nathan LUNDY and Wm. Ballard

DAVIS, William - Volume A, page 29 - Dated 2-14-1818 - Recorded 1-4-1821 - Wife:
Sarah - Sons: James, John, Samuel, William and Henry - Daughters:
Polly DOWNING and Elizabeth FLOREA - Executors: wife, Sarah and neigh-
bor, John LYTLE - Signed: William (mark) Davis - Witnesses: Benjamin
HUNTER, John LYTLE and John SHIELDS

DILLON, John - Volume A, page 10 - Dated 10-2-1813 - Recorded 6-16-1816 Sons:
James, eldest son; William - Daughters: Mary EDWARDS eldest daughter;
Phebe FOLLACE; Lydia BABB and Hannah FOLLACE - Grandson: Malon DILLON -
Mentions land in Highland Co., Ohio - Executors: Richard Follace of
Union Co., Pa. and Daniel DILLON of Clinton Co., Ohio - Signed: John
Dillon - Witnesses: William DILLON, Hn.(?) DILLON and Absalom DILLON

GALLASPY, Thomas Sr. - Green Twp. - Volume A, page 19 - Dated 4-6-1816 - Recorded
(not given) - Specified as being codicil to a former will, however no
former will was found in the Clinton Co. records - Grandchildren:
Virginny TRIMBLE, Hugh THOMAS, James THOMAS, Thomas THOMAS, Elixander
THOMAS and Jonathan TRIMBLE - Signed: Thomas Gallaspy - Witnesses:-
Joseph HATHAWAY and Justice COOPER

GREEN, Alice - Volume A, page 25 - Dated 25th day, 4th month, 1818 - Recorded
10-14-1818 - Mentions: brothers and sisters, but does not name except
for John Green and Reuben Green - Mentions: children of brothers and
sisters, but does not name - Executors: brothers, John Green and Reuben
Green - Signed: Alice (mark) Green - Witnesses: Owen WEST, Jr., William
WEST, Mary (mark) McLIN

GARRISON, Lemuel Sr. - Volume A, page 24 - Dated 12-1-1817 - Recorded 7-17-1818 -
Wife: mentioned, but not named - Sons: Benjamin and Arwine - Daughter
- Mehaley BIGGS - Grandson: Elias PORTER - Mentions: four other sons,

(GARRISON)BUT does not name - Executors: wife, not named and son, Benjamin Garrison - Signed: Lemuel (mark) Garrison, Sr. - Witnesses: Elijah BURGE and Ebenezer H. HENNER

HAWS, Conrad - Volume A, page 30 - Dated 1-25-1831 - Recorded 6-7-1821 - Wife: Fanne - Sons: John, Abraham, Conrad, David and Jacob - Mentions: John BOWERMASTER and wife Polly, late Polly HAWS - Executors: John Haws and Jacob Haws - Signed: Conrad (mark) Haws - Witnesses: Thomas McCOY, Robert DWIGGINS and William RUNNELS

HAYNES, William - Volume A, page 34 - Dated 9-8-1821 - Recorded 10-18-1821 - Wife: mentioned, but not named - Sons: William Henry Hains, Lewis Harmon Haynes and Archibald Haynes- Daughters: Emaline AKIN, eldest daughter Jane Lina Haynes, youngest daughter - Son-in-law; Harmon L. AKIN - Executors: John LEWIS and Jonathan COLLETT - Signed: William Haynes - Witnesses: James DAKIN, John CRAW and Gideon WAKEMAN

HOBSON, William - Wilmington - Volume A, page 12 - Dated 15th day 11th month 1813 - Recorded 6-17-1814 - Wife: Sarah - Sons: William, John, Joseph, Samuel and George - Daughter(?): Deborah - Executors: Joseph DOAN and William BUTLER - Signed: William Hobson - Witnesses: Samuel H. HALE, Isaac GARRETSON, Alice GARRETSON and William BUTLER

HODGSON, Jonathan - Volume A, page 5 - Dated 6th day 11th month, 1811 - Recorded (not given) - Brothers: Joseph, John, George Hur and Solomon - Sisters: Sarah LOVET; Ruth HAUSKINS and Mary HESTER - Nephews: Amos and Joel Hodgson; Daniel Hodgson - Executors: Nephews, Amos and Daniel Hodgson - Signed: Jonathan Hodgson - Witnesses: Daniel DILLON, Evean STANBROUGH and Elizabeth STANBROUGH

HODGSON, Jonathan - Volume A, page 28 - Dated 4-21-1820 - Recorded 1-3-1821 - Wife: Mary - Sons: Jonathan, John, Matthew and Enos - Daughters: Elizabeth, Sarah and Mary Hodgson - Executors: wife, Mary and Solomon HODGSON of Highland Co., Ohio - Signed: Jonathan Hodgson - Witnesses: Matthew Hodgson and George Hodgson

JACKSON, John - Volume A, page 1 - Dated 2nd day 8th month, 1810 - Recorded 11-1-1810 - Wife, Phebe Jackson - Sons: Uriah, William, Ames and Jesse Daughters: Keziah and Mary, two youngest; Hannah BRANSON; Sarah CHAINY; Charity FOSTER; and Elizabeth ROOKS - Executors: wife, Phebe Jackson and nephew, Curtis (?) BAILES - Signed: John (mark) Jackson - Witnesses: Jacob Jackson and Ennion WILLIAMS

JONES, John - Volume A, page 8 - Dated 9th day, 11th month, 1813 - Recorded 2-17-1814 - Wife: Sarah Jones - Children: mentioned, but not named - Executors; Wife, Sarah; Jesse HOLE - Signed: John Jones - Witnesses: Thomas Kersay and George MADDAN

KIRBY(KERBY), Benjamin - Verbal Will - Volume A, page 23 - Will given 7-11-1817 - Deposition 7-17-1817 - Recorded 10-29-1817 - Wife: Mary - Witnesses: Robert EACHUS and John HOBSON

279

LEONARD, John Sr. - Volume A, page 7 - Dated 6-14-1812 - Recorded 10-23-1812
Wife: Abigail - Sons: John, Ezekiel, Joseph and George - Daughters:
Feniah, Silinah, Lidah, Mary, Ellenor, Abigail and Sarah - Executors:
Wife, Abigail and son, Ezekiel - Signed: John Leonard - Witnesses:
John GRIFFITH, John (mark) HOBSON and Robert EACHUS

McKIBBIAN, John - Highland Co., Ohie - Volume A, page 14 - Dated 6-3-1812 - Recorded 10-27-1814 - Wife: Margaret - Sons: James and Gideon - Daughters:
Martha and Polly - Mentions: Isaac MILLER, Joseph McKIBBON and John
McKIBBON, relationship not stated - Executors: friends, Morgan VANMETER
and Isaac MILLER - Signed: John McKibbian - Witnesses: Absalom VANMETER
and Charles HARRIS

McMILLAN, Thomas - Chester Twp. - Volume A, page 36 - Dated 27th day 10th month,
1821 - Recorded 1-29-1822 - Wife: Jane - Daughters: Edith and Deborah
McMillan - Executors: wife, Jane McMillan and Samuel COX - Signed:
Thomas McMillan - Witnesses: David McMillan and Thomas COX

MASTERS, William - Volume A, page 15 - Dated 10-4-1814 - Recorded 10-20-1814 -
Wife: Sarah - Daughters: Rachel SHARP, her children and Anne WOLVY
(WOLLIVUS?), her children - Wife's daughter: Nancy STEWART - Mentions:
Solomon SHARP - Executors: Amos WILSON and James MILLS - Signed;
William Masters - Witnesses: John MATHEYS and David STOKSBURY

MILHOUS, Henry - Volume A, page 32 - Dated 9th day, 12th month, 1819 - Recorded
10-17-1821 - Wife: Anna - Son: Robert - Daughters: Ann HAWKINS, Mary,
Rebekah, Sarah and Dinah - Executors: wife, Anna and son, Robert -
Mentions: land on Caesars Creek - Signed: Henry Milhous - Witnesses:
Daniel NICHOLSON, Elizabeth NICHOLSON and Caleb EASTERLING

MILLS, John - Volume A, page 16 - Dated 3rd day, 7th month, 1813 - Recorded
10-20-1814 - Wife: Mary - Sons: Enoch and Elijah - Signed: John (mark)
Mills - Witnesses: William CASY, John Mills, Jr. and Charles Mills

MYERS, Ralph - Volume A, page 27 - Dated 24th day, 4th month, 1820 - Recorded
10-13-1820 - Step-daughter: Mahala ELMORE, also to serve as guardian
of children - Children: William ELMORE, Nathan, Samuel, Mary and Ralph
Myers, not of age - Mentions: Caesars Creek Monthly Meeting - Executor:
Jesse ARNOLD - Signed: Ralph Mires - Witnesses: Josiah FARQUHAR, William
EDWARDS, and Samil WHITSON

PENDERY, Richard - Volume A, page 13 - Dated 8-24-1814 - Recorded 10-27-1814 -
Sons: Robert, James, Thomas, Richard and William - Daughters: Martha
RYNERAND and Elizabeth KINDER - Mentions: land in town of Hardinburgh,
Breckinridge Co., Ky. - Executors: son, Robert and son-in-law, Jacob
KINDER - Signed: Richard Pendery - Witnesses: David SEWELL, Isaac
JOHNSON and Robert LOMAN

REED, James - Volume A, page 26 - Dated 1-8-1819 - Recorded 6-15-1819 - Wife:
Jane - Son; James Reed - Mentions children, but does not name except for
Thos. McAFARTY and Jacob DANNER (called children) who were each willed
one dollar - Executors: son, James Reed and wife, Jane Reed - Signed:
James (mark) Reed - Witnesses: David STOOKSBURY and John ALLEN

RUS,* Robert Sr. - Volume A, page 16 - Dated 9-14-1841 - Recorded 3-27-1815 - Wife: Rachel - Sons: David, Thomas, Lewis and Robert - Daughters: Elizabeth WRIGHT, eldest dau.; Mary PUGH; Margaret PUGH and Sidney GOLDENBURGH - Mentions money due from Va. - Executors: John LEWIS, Sr. and Daniel DILLON - Signed: Robert Rus - Witnesses: Jacob MARKER, Marmeduke BRACHNEY and Mary (mark) BRACKNEY

SANDERS, John - Volume A, page 6 - Dated 25th day, 11th month, 1811 - Recorded (not given) - Son: Benjamin - Daughters: Miriam, Sarah and Susanna - Sons-in-law: William FARMER and Hezekiah SANDERS - Grand-daughter: Massey KENNADY - Executor: son-in-law, William FARMER - Signed: John (mark) Sanders - Witnesses: Samuel SPRAY, John MILLS and Samuel WHITSON

SEWEL, David - Volume A, page 20 - Dated 7-20-1816 - Recorded (not given) - Wife: Mary, also to serve as Executrix - Signed: David Sewel - Witnesses: Ezekiel CART and Aaron OSBY

WHINERY, John - Volume A, page 18 - Dated 7-12-1815 - Recorded (not given) - Wife: Patsey - Children: mentioned, but not named, not all of age - Mentions: Solomon (no surname given, possibly a son) - Executors: friends, David STOUT and Gideon FULLER - Signed: John Whinery - Witnesses: Charles STOUT, John SKOOLY and William STUBS

WRIGHT, James - Volume A, page 9 - Dated 12th day, 9th month, 1812 - Recorded 2-10-1816 - Wife: Sarah -Sons: John, James, William and Isaac - Daughters: Sarah ELLIS, Rachel HAYWORTH, Betty DILLON, Ruth HAWORTH, Charity WRIGHT, Phebe HAYWORTH and Susanna - Executors: son, John WRIGHT and son-in-law, James HAWORTH - Signed: James Wright - Witnesses: George HAWORTH, Daniel DILLON and William DILLON

*For *Rus, Robert Sr.* read *Rees, Robert Sr.* GATEWAY TO THE WEST, Vol. 1: No. 3 (July-Sept. 1968).

The following records were taken from Will Book A-B, which is a combination of will books "A" and "B" being bound in one cover. Pages on which record may be found are given in parenthesis; Will Book B begins with will of Stephen Mendenhall.

BURK, John - dated 9-7-1815; recorded 1-30-1822. Wife, Elizabeth, also to serve as Executrix. Children: Martha Meloy of Warren Co., Ohio; Margaret; Elizabeth; Mary; Sarah and Matthew; the last five not of age. Signed: John (his mark) Burk. Witnesses: Abel Wright and Thomas Thatcher Sr. Codicil dated 12-31-1820 mentions wife as present wife. Witnesses: Thomas Thatcher and Edward Powers.   (40)

RAINS, McKegah - dated 12-11-1821; recorded 10-24-1822. Wife, Elizabeth, also to serve as executrix. Signed: McKegah (his mark) Rains. Witnesses: Obed Waln(?) and Samuel Miller.   (42)

COWGILL, John Sr. - dated 3-12-1822; recorded 10-31-1822. Wife, Catharine. Sons: Henry, John, William, Elisha, Asa and Amos. Daughters: Lidy Patterson and William Patterson, Hannah Coates and Ann Hays. Grand-daughter, Catharine Patterson, not of age. Executors: wife, Catharine and sons, Asa and Amos. Signed: John Cowgill. Witnesses: Jonas Crawford, Henry Patterson and James Johnson.   (43)

THATCHER, Thomas - dated 7-24-1822; recorded 1-31-1823. Wife, Susannah. Children, mentioned but not named, not of age. Executors: Joseph Stratton and Joseph Thatcher. Signed: Thomas (his mark) Thatcher. Witnesses: James W. Magee, William Butler and James Curl.   (45)

HARVEY, Eli - dated 3rd day, 1st month, 1819; recorded 2-8-1823. Wife, Mary. Son, William Harvey. Daughters: Lydia, Marth, Elizabeth, Ann, Mary and Cynthee. Executors: brothers, William Harvey and Caleb Harvey. Signed: Eli Harvey. Witnesses: John Hadley, Melzar Stearns and Ezekiel Hornaday.   (47)

SMART, David of Wilmington, presently in City of Baltimore, Maryland - dated 8-9-1822; recorded 2-26-1823. Wife, Deborah Tresse Smart. Mentions unborn child. Brothers: James, William, John and Hugh Smart. Sisters: Jane Smart, Martha wife of Jonathan Schaeffer and Elizabeth Thomas. Mentions land in Wilmington owned with Elie Gaskill. Executors: friends, Elie Gaskill and William Hubben. Signed: David Smart. Witnesses: John Barr, Asahel Hulsey and Fielder Israel.   (50)

HUNTER, Benjamin - dated 12-11-1820; recorded 5-30-1823. Wife, Marget, also to serve as executrix. Three children: Nathaniel, Eleanor and James Hunter. Signed: Benjamin Hunter. Witnesses: Isaac Florea, John W. Jones and Joel Walmsley.   (53)

BALLARD, David of Union township - dated 9th day, 6th month, 1820; recorded 5-30-1823. Wife, Martha, mentions property she claims at her father's, David Marmon at Mad River. Children: Joseph, Rhoda, Lydia, Nathan, Mary, Anna, Edith, William, Asa and John. Mentions that son John's portion is to be divided between his children. Executors: friends, Nathaniel Carter and Reuben Green. Signed: David Ballard. Witnesses: George Carter, David Stratton and John Miler.   (55)

DALE, John - dated 8-20-1821; recorded (not given-1823). Wife, Eleanor. Children: Elizabeth, Margaret, James, Daniel, Nancy, Ebenezer, Anna and John; last four not of age and mentions that son Daniel is now away from home. Mentions money in Redstone Country on waters of the Monogahela in Fayette Co., Pennsylvania. Mentions lot in town of Paris, Clinton Co. Executors: wife, Eleanor and son, James. Signed: John (his mark) Dale. Witnesses: Thomas Thatcher and William Thatcher. (56)

MENDENHALL, Stephen - dated 18th day, 12th month, 1822; recorded 7-31-1823. Wife, Elizabeth. Sons: John, Nathan, Isaac, Stephen, Eli, Thomas, James and Mordecai. Mentions son Mordecai's heirs who are not of age. Daughters: Sarah Kimbrough; Rachel Gibson, her heirs; Hannah Moreman, her heirs; and Elizabeth Gibson. Grandchildren: Thomas, David and Rachel Harris; Stephen and Samuel Mendenhall sons of Isaac Mendenhall. Mentions land in Wayne County, Indiana near New Garden Meeting House. Executors: wife, Elizabeth and sons, Nathan and James. Signed: Stephen Mendenhall. Witnesses: Jeremiah Kimbrough and George Carter. (1)

FITZHUGH, Nicholas - dated 8-12-1813; recorded Orphans Court, Alexandria County, District of Columbia 1-14-1817; recorded 8-1-1823 Clinton County, Ohio. Wife, Sarah. Sons: Augustine, Edmund, Burdett, Henry William, Charles and Lawrence. Daughters: Henrietta Sarah, Lucy Battaile, Anne Elizabeth, Sophia and Sarah Nicholas Fitzhugh. Brothers: Giles and Mordecai Fitzhugh. Mentions "tract of land which on a division of the estate of the late General George Washington, deceased, was allotted to the heirs of the late Anne Ashton, deceased, one third part whereof belonging to my wife, being one of the children of said Anne Ashton, conveyed by her and myself to Noblett Herbert and by him reconveyed to me, the remaining two thirds part thereof I bought from Burdett Ashton Jr. the son of Burdett Ashton the late husband of the said Anne Ashton. This tract lies in Mason County in the State of Virginia and contains by survey fourteen hundred and twenty five acres". Mentions 6000 acres of land lying between the Little Miami and Scioto Rivers in Ohio purchased from Alexander Spottswood; 620 acres of land purchased from brother, Giles Fitzhugh adjoining Nicholas's land Revenworth in Fairfax Co., Virginia; 196 acres bought from brother, Mordecai Fitzhugh, commonly called the upper tract; three lots of land in town of Alexandria, District of Columbia; and other land descriptions. Executors: wife, Sarah; John Thompson Mason and Walter Jones. Signed: N. Fitzhugh. (2)

CASSADA (CASSADY), John - verbal will - will given 8-31-1823; deposition 9-2-1823; recorded 11-18-1823. Mentions James R. Smith. Witnesses: James D. Massey, Geo. Bruce, Abraham Jefferies, James Fife and Jeremiah Reynolds. (6)

DILLON, Jesse - dated 7th day, 2nd month, 1818; recorded 11-18-1823. Wife, Hannah. Children: Achsah Hodgson, Susannah Starbuck, Jonathan Dillon, Sarah Dwiggins, Martha Fisher, Luke Dillon, Hannah Wright and Abigail Wright. Signed: Jesse Dillon. Witnesses: Malon Haworth, George D. Haworth and Ezekiel Haworth. (7)

VILLARS, James - dated 8-21-1823; recorded 11-19-1823. Wife, Rebeckah. Mother-in-law, Rachel Davidson. Five sons: John, George, Hiram, James and William; last two not of age. Three daughters: Rachel, Rebeckah, and one not named. Mentions one-fourth acre of land adjoining the lot of land which he gave to Mount Pleasant Meeting House and he reserves this one-fourth acre as a burying ground for use of his family. Mentions land in Warren County, Ohio. Executors: sons, John and James. Signed: James Villars. Witnesses: Wm. Austin, Asahel Tribbey and Samuel B. Austin. (8)

MADDEN, George - dated 25th day, 9th month, 1823; recorded 11-19-1823. Wife, Elizabeth. Sons: Hiram, Eli, George and Solomon. Daughters: Martha Towell, dec'd; Elizabeth Reeves; Ann Harvey and her husband H. Harvey; five unmarried daughters, Edith, Rebecca, Mary, Ruth and Deborah. Mentions heirs of daughter Martha Towell, dec'd, but does not name. Mentions land in Wayne County, Indiana. Executors: son, Hiram; George Carter. Signed: George Madden. Witnesses: William Millikan and Thomas Kersey. (10)

HESTON, William Sr. - dated 2nd day, 1st month, 1824; recorded 5-21-1824. Sons: Amos, William and Phineas. Daughter, Mercy Garwood. Executor: son, Phineas. Signed: William Heaston. Witnesses: Caleb Easterling and Lot Bowen. (12)

MOUNT, William - dated 6-24-1823; recorded 6-4-1824. Sons: John, William and Thomas. Mentions six daughters, names Elizabeth Moon, but does not name the other five; states that two live with estator. Executors: John Lytle, Horatio Cast and John Mount. Signed: William (his mark) Mount. Witnesses: Horatio Cast, John Mount, John Lytle, Isaac Florea and Henry Davis. (13)

HOWARD, Joseph - dated 12-18-1822; recorded 6-17-1824. Wife, Mary Hannah. Mentions father but does not name. Mentions children but does not name except for son, Burr Howard. Mentions tracts of land in Indiana and Illinois. Executor: John Villars. Signed: Joseph Howard. Witnesses: Wm. Austin, Benjamin Dannels and William Hollaman. (14)

COLE, Solomon - dated 9-4-1823; recorded 9-16-1824. Sons, Samuel and William R. Executor, son, William R. Signed: Solomon Cole. Witnesses: Daniel Radcliff, Rich'd Peirce and Israel Johns. (16)

GREEN, George - dated 4-30-1824; recorded 9-25-1824. Wife, Charlotte. Mentions children but does not name, possibly not all are of age. Executors: wife, Charlott and Thomas Babb Jr. son of Thomas Babb Sr. Signed: George Green. Witnesses: Nathan Linton, George Hartman, Ganer (his mark) Hartman and James (his mark) Hartman. (17)

CARRINGTON, Paul of Charlotte County, Virginia - dated 11-21-1817; recorded 7-6-1818 Charlotte County, Va.; recorded 11-19-1824 Clinton County. Sons: Henry and Robert. Daughter, Lettice Carrington. Grandchildren: Lettice and Robert, children of son, Henry. Brother: Edward Carrington, dec'd; his widow Eliza J. Carrington. Appoints son-in-law, S. W. Venable guardian of son Robert Carrington and Edward C. Carrington guardian of daughter Lettice Carrington. Mentions Ohio land company grant which descended to testator by death of his brother, Edward Carrington. Mentions various Virginia land descriptions. Executor, son Henry Carrington. Signed: P. Carrington. (18)

LOGAN, Benjamin - dated 6-25-1824; recorded 11-20-1824. Friend, John Grice. Mentions: Jacob Fry Sr.; Jacob Fry Jr.; Michael Fry and Jane Keeky, each to have $1.00 and a Bible; no relationship given. Signed: Benjamin (his mark) Logan. Witnesses: Samuel Reed and Henry Grice. (20)

284

GREEN, John of Union township - dated 23rd day, 5th month, 1824; recorded 5-8-1824. Wife, Ruth. Sons: Jesse, Robert, Isaac and John. Mentions five daughters but only names four single daughters: Mary, Abigail, Alice and Charlotte Green. Executors: sons, Isaac and Jesse Signed: John Green. Witnesses: Enoch Wickersham, Job Hains, James Lundy and Margaret Wickersham. (22)

RITSMAN, Peter - dated 12-20-1823; recorded 5-29-1825. Wife, Abigail. Sons: James Eli and John. Daughters: Lucretia, Phenia, Mary, Lydia L. V., Sarah and Rebecca. Executors: wife, Abigail and friend, Jacob Hains. Signed: Peter Ritsman. Witnesses: Isaac Perkins, Thomas Perkins and Rob't Eachus. (23)

GILLESPEY, James - dated 7-17-1825; recorded 3-14-1826. Wife, Catharine. Mentions children and unborn child, but does not name. Executor: brother-in-law, William Peck. Signed: James Gallespey. Witnesses: Rameth Hankins, Samuel Love, Charles P. Gallaher and James Gallar. (27)

LINN, Samuel - dated 5-20-1825; recorded 3-14-1826. Wife, Jane, also to serve as executrix. Signed: Samuel Linn. Witnesses: Samuel Harvey and William Ruble. (28)

NORDYKE, Abraham - dated 3rd day, 3rd month, 1824; recorded 3-14-1826. Sons: Hiram, Aden, Israel, Benajah, Micajah and Daniel Nordyke. Daughters: Bulah wife of Elijah Foley and Phebe wife of Jehu Ellis. Executors: friend, James Hadley and son-in-law, Jehue Ellis. Signed: Abraham Nordyke. Witnesses: Benj. Puckett, Robert Ellis and Joseph R. Moon. (29)

SMITH, Barnabas - dated 10-10-1825; recorded 3-15-1826. Wife, Phebe. Children: William Smith, Anna Oliver late Smith, Levi Smith, Elizabeth Shaw late Smith, Thomas Smith, Barnabas Smith, John Smith, Sanford Smith, Silas Smith, Sidney Smith, Nancy Smith and David Smith. Executor: friend, James Harris. Signed: Barnabas (his mark) Smith. Witnesses: Richard Cast, David Stearns and John Cree. (30)

GALLAHER, James - dated 7-28-1822; recorded 3-16-1826. Wife, Leah. Children: son, Charles P.; mentions other children but does not name. Executor; son, Charles P. Signed: James Gallaher. Witnesses: James Gillespey, John C. Spencer and Thomas Spencer. (32)

FRAIZER, Alexander - dated 16th day, 4th month, 1824; recorded 3-16-1826. Wife, Mary. Mentions children but does not name, not all of age. Executors: wife, Mary and Jonah Fraizer. Signed Alexander Fraizer. Witnesses: Ashley Johnson, Moses Fraizer and John Atkinson. (33)

EVANS, Samuel of Union township - dated 2-20-1826; recorded 6-12-1828. Children: William Clarke, Benjamin, Mary, Susannah and Samuel Goodall Evans. Mentions tract of land in Brown County, Ohio on Indian Crick adjoining Nancy McPherson, Charlotte Redman and Elijah Hopkins. Executor, Robert Dwiggins of Union township. Signed: Samuel Evans. Witnesses: Isaac Johnson, Alexander Wilson and Peter Hester. (34

ADAMS, Absalom of Richland township - dated 1-3-1826; recorded 6-15-1826. Wife, Mary. Sons: eldest son, William; 3rd son, John; and son, Edward. Daughter, Polly Adams wife of Peter Adams. Executor: son, John Adams. Signed: Abslom (his mark) Adams. Witnesses: Isaac Pavey and Thomas (his mark) Draper. (35)

BIRDSALL, Priscilla - dated 1-8-1826; recorded 9-26-1826. Sons: James, Daniel, Maurice and Matthias Birdsall. Two daughters, Olive Mary and Sarah Hendrake. Executor: son James Birdsall. Signed; Priscilla Birdsall. Witnesses: William Vantress and Richard Vantress. (37)

SCOTT, William - dated 27th day, 8th month, 1826; recorded 10-24-1826. Wife, Sarah. Children: John, Isom, Eli and James Scott. Executor, William Sanders. Signed: William Scott. Witnesses: John Whitson and Enoch Mills. (38)

O"LAUGHLIN, Dennis - dated 3-2-1826; recorded 10-25-1826. Wife, Martha Matilda. Executor: James Brown. Signed: Dennis (his mark) O'Laughlin. Witnessese: James Dakin, John Craw and Abraham Campbell. (39)

BENNETT, Timothy - dated 11-24-1823; recorded 4-12-1827. Wife, Elizabeth. Sons: Michael, Nathaniel and Timothy; Timothy not of age. Daughters: Phebe Done, Mary Mills, Caty Doan, Sarah Roberts, Amy Fisher, Peggy Fisher, Kizih Bennett, Betsy Bennett, Unice Bennett and Milly Bennett. Executors: wife, Elizabeth and sons, Michael and Nathaniel. Signed: Timoth (his mark) Bennett. Witnesses: Gideon Edwards, James Edwards and Wm. Newcomb. (40)

McCONNELL, Sarah - dated 8-31-1826; recorded 4-12-1827. Sons: John D., Thomas, Joseph M. and Reason. Daughters: Harriet McConnel, Elizabeth Wilson, Mary Barnerd and Dorcehus McConnell. Mentions lots in Ripley, Brown County, Ohio. Executor: eldest son, John D. McConnell. Signed: Sarah McConnell. Witnesses: Wm. Newcomb and John (his mark) Young. Codicil dated 10-31-1826 mentions money coming from her father's estate. Witnesses: Ruben Hodson and Wm. Newcomb. (42)

STEVENS, General Edward of Culpeper County, Virginia - dated 6-1-1820; recorded 11-11-1823 Culpeper Co., Virginia; recorded 1-26-1827 Clinton County. Wife, Gelly. Daughter-in-law, Polly Stevens. Owns 750 acres adjoing town of Wilmington, Ohio which is to be sold and proceeds divided between children of his sister, Polly Edmondson: James Scanland of Kentucky; John Edmondson; Robert chandler, dec'd, his portion to his children; Joseph Edmondson, dec'd, his children; Edward Evans; Nancy wife of_____(left blank) Blane; James Edmondson; Betsy Emery late Edmondson; and Robert Edmondson, believed to possibly be deceased. Also mentions William Edmondson and Richard Chandler. Mentions 1000 acres patented in Dismal Swamp, Norfolk County to George Pollard son of friend, Robert Pollard of the City of Richmond. Mentions land to Protestant Episcopal Church to build church on and also an acre to Presbyterian church adjoining town of Fairfax. Mentions 1 acre to Freemasons Lodge of town of Fairfax adjoining his family burial ground. Executors: wife, Gelly; daughter-in-law, Polly Stevens; nephew, Robert Pollard; friends, John McNeal, Richard Johnson Test, Philip Lightfoot and Thomas Hall. Signed: Edward Stevens. (45)

SIMCOCK, John - dated 14th day, 4th month, 1825; recorded 8-16-1827. Wife, Mary. Six children that are married: John, Aaron, James, Ann Johnson, Jane Johnson and Mary Lundy. Grandson, Job Simcock. Executors: wife, Mary and friends, Nathan Statker and Samuel Andrews. Signed: John Simcock. Witnesses: Isaac Stout and George Carter. (44)

FARQUHAR, Benjamin - dated 24th day, 2nd month, 1827; recorded 1-28-1828. Wife, mentioned but not named. Children: Josiah, Susanna, Rebecca, Rachel, Uriah, Cyrus and Allen. Executors: son, Josiah Farquhar and friend, George Carter. Signed; Benj'm Farquhar. Witnesses: Isaac Carpenter and Jonathan Fallis. (50)

JOHN, Ebenezer - dated 9th day, 3rd month, 1828; recorded 4-16-1828. Wife, Sarah. Youngest son, Ebenezer, not of age. Mentions five daughters but does not name. Executors: son, Elisha John and Micajah H. Moore. Signed; Ebenezer John. Witnesses: Micajah H. Moore, Samuel John and Elisha John. (52)

BIGGS, William - dated 5-4-1828; recorded July 1828. Wife, Nancy. Sons: William, Robert, Daniel and Alfred. Daughters: Nancy, Rebeccah and Charlotte. Sons-in-law: James Faris, Israel Abrams and Jacob Runamus. Mentions Rachel Runamus, dec'd, her son, William Runamus who is not of age; no relationship stated. Brother, Daniel Biggs. Executors: son, William Biggs and Thomas Woodmansee. Signed: William Biggs. Witnesses: Samuel H. Woodmansee, Oliver Whitaker and William Darby. (53)

BEALS, Jacob of Vernon township - dated 21st day, 4th month, 1826; recorded July 1828. Wife, Elizabeth. Sons: Jacob, Daniel, John and Solomon. Daughters: Hannah Ellis and Elizabeth John. Executor: son, Jacob Beals. Signed: Jacob Beals. Witnesses: Isaac Flores and William Thompson. (56)

COCHRAN, William - dated 5-29-1828; recorded July 1828. Daughters Mary Wilson and Fanny Cochran. Mentions William Cockran, Robert Cockran and Elizabeth Winter; relationship not clearly stated, may be children. Executor: Jacob Strickle. Signed: William Cochran. Witnesses: T. Welch, Jacob Strickle and Wm. R. Cole.(58)

PERKINS, Isaac - dated 12th month, 13th day, 1827; recorded October 1828. Wife, Pheniah. Daughters: Salina Perkins and Abigail Paist. Mentions other children but does not name. Executor: brother-in-law, William Adams. Signed: Isaac Perkins. Witnesses: James Moon, Charles Potts and Timothy Scott. (59)

Contributed by: Carol Willsey Bell, C.G., 4649 Yarmouth Lane,
Youngstown, Ohio 44512

ACKLEY, Aaron to Sooy, Mary	1-6-1814
ADAMS, John to Prouse (Crouse) Leah	2-21-1811
ADAMSON, Thomas to Woods, Elizabeth	11-21-1816
ALDOFFER, George to Altman, Mary	9-16-1810
ALEXANDER, John to Rudisill, Lena	9-25-1817
ALLEN, William to Summerville, Mary	11-6-1817
ALLIN, James to Shiveley, Sarah	9-12-1815
ALLMON, Ebenezer to OLIPHANT, Rebeccah	11-16-1809
ALLMON, William to Walker, Lydia	10-18-1809
ALTMAN, Ludwick to Bair, Catharine	4-13-1813
ALTON, Reason to Rogers, Anna	1-6-1814
AMON, James to Merrel, Ann	3-23-1814
ANDERSON, John to Andrews, Jane	2- -1808
ANDREWS, James to Helfrick, Christiana	5-25-1814
ANDREWS, William to McClarren, Polly	7-13-1809
ARMSTRONG, Andrew to King, Rachel	6-30-1809
ARMSTRONG, Bennet to Craig, Elizabeth	4-14-1814
ARMSTRONG, James to Craig, Deborah	10-23-1812
ARMSTRONG, James to Heald, Mary	1-3-1811
ARMSTRONG, John to McKaig, Isabella	4-2-1816
ARTHUR, Michael to Richardson, Lydia	12-12-1816
ASHFORD, George to Whitacre, Patience	8-28-1817
ATTERHOLT, Peter to Koontz, Mary	11-8-1811
AUGUSTEEN, Abraham to Forney, Elizabeth	3-26-1815
AUGUSTINE, George to Shitz (Shultz), Barbara	4-21-1807
AUGUSTINE, Henry to Shnok, Caty	1-15-1811
AYRES, John to Wollihan, Sarah	9-23-1806
BAKER, Philip to Gooden, Jane	12-9-1817
BALIS, Nathin to Booth, Elizabeth	9-19-1816
BALSURE, David to Hoy, Sarah	12-16-1806
BARBER, Abraham to Gaus, Drusilla	2-21-1810
BARBER, Robert to McIntosh, _____	7-10-1815
BARKDULL, John to Slater, Nancy	10-12-1810
BARKDULL, John to Dicks, Sarah	11-12-1816
BASSET, Amos to Rogers, Elizabeth	4-21-1814
BATES, David to Emmens, Margaret	9-3-1812
BATES, Frederick to Freed, Magdalena	12-30-1818
BATTERSHELL, William to Stauffer, Nancy	3-28-1809
BATTIN, Eli to Pennock, Phebe	3-21-1816
BATTIN, Jonathan to Reeder, Priscilla	10-25-1809
BEANS, John to Burns, Mary	9-25-1815
BEANS, Mathew to Whitacre, Elizabeth	12-4-1817
BEARD, George to Mouen, Elizabeth	6-23-1813
BEATY, Wibrents (?) to Filson, Polly	8-2-1810
BECHT, Jacob to Mosser, Susanna	9-2-1811
BECK, Christian to Houston, Polly	10-17-1815
BECK, Paul to Dickinson, Mary	11-29-1809

```
BEESON, John to Schooley, Sarah                     3-18-1804
BEESON, Richard to Oliphant, Ann                    9-13-1804
HEIGHT, John to Roads, Julian                       4-9-1818
BELL, William to Altman, Barbara                    11-8-1810
BENNET, Peter to Rakestraw, Mary                    5-9-1816
BERBICK, Arthur to Hamilton, Sarah                  10-22-1816
HERSON, Jesse to Themsten, Elisa (?)                7-11-1814
BETZ, George to Summers, Susannah                   4-9-1812
BEVINGTON, Henry (jr) to Randolph, Rachel           2-15-1816
BISHOP, Joseph to Young, Elizabeth                  10-9-1814
BISHOP, Thomas to Silvers, Mary                     1-13-1814
BLACK, Mathew to Bough, Elizabeth                   3-16-1815
BLACKBURN, Johns to Kerr, Eleanor                   8-28-1810
BLACKBURN, Josiah to Blackburn, Nancy S.            6-2-1816
BLACKBURN, William to Armstrong, Janie              9-29-1814
BLACKFORD, Joseph to Walker, Amelia                 1-1-1818
BLACKLEDGE, Joseph to Grissel, Rachel               3-17-1808
BLACKLEDGE, Robert to Sooy, Elizabeth               10-28-1806
BLECHER, John to Stock, Elizabeth                   1-29-1807
BLORE, Joseph to Dunlap, Rachael                    1-2-1817
BOLAND, James to Pearce, Sophia                     4-16-1813
BOLLMAN, Charles to Gash, Julianna (?)              5-10-1807
BONER, John to Willington, Harriett                 7-8-1806
BONSALL, Edward to Warrington, Rachel               5-11-1807
BOREMAN, Henry to Loop, Catherine                   7-13-1815
BOST, Jacob to Williams, Tasey                      12-8-1814
BOULTON, Levi to Heald, Anna                        11-15-1815
BOWER, Alexander to Stevenson, Margaret             1-24-1814
BOWER, David to Smith, Barbara                      3-2-1809
BOWLER, William to Brady, Rachel                    2-17-1818
BOWMAN, David to Eyster, Anna                       8-9-1814
BOYCE, Richard to Moore, Ruth                       11-7-1815
BOYD, Frederick to Roberts, Jamima                  9-28-1813
BOYER, Amraham to Hively, Mottlena                  9-10-1812
BRADFIELD, Benjamin to Feasill, Nancy               8-12-1807
BRADFORD, Thomas to Thompson, Hannah                5-20-1807
BRADY, John to Mercer, Jane                         10-8-1816
BRAKESTRAW, Jonathan to Molonsbury, Elizabeth       12-31-1812
BRANDEBERRY, Abraham to Culbertson, Sarah           5-28-1817
BRANDEBERRY, Conrad to Cameron, Susannah            5-28-1805
BRANDEBERRY, Isaac to McConesshey, Mary             3-20-1817
BRANDEBERY, Rudolph to Deverbaugh, Susannah         nd -1808
BRANDSBERRY, Phillip to Zimmerman, Catherine        12-9-1808
BRICKER, John to Brinker, Mary                      4-6-1817
BRICKER, John to Sampsell, Hannah                   11-9-1817
BRIGGS, Francis to Craig, Isabella                  9-12-1805
BRIGGS, Israel to Strahl, Mary                      6-30-1813
BRIEN, John to Kuntz, Sophia                        8-20-1811
BRINKER, Peter to Hart, Rebeccah                    6-29-1817
```

BRITIN, Archibold to Hipner, Caty	1-3-1815
BROLEN, Benjamin to Marshall, Mary	4-6-1814
BROOKS, James to Cameron, Jane	3-5-1811
BROWN, Benjamin to Patterson, Abigail	7-9-1814
BROWN, Nathan to Stratton, Amy	12-18-1806
BROWN, Samuel to Lesley, Mary	11-26-1805
BROWN, William Rhodes, Anna Maria	12-24-1812
BROWN, William to Young, Mary Magdalena	11-25-1813
BRUCE, John to Downand, Latrenna	11-13-1813
BUCK, George to Irey, Martha	8-14-1817
BURDEN, Levi to Holloway, Rhody	1-1-1812
BURGER, Jacob to Risher, Catharine	3-27-1810
BURNS, George to Gaunt, Elizabeth	10-28-1817
BURSON, David to Whinnery, Jane	11-23-1809
BURSON, James to Myers, Elizabeth	3-11-1807
BURSON, Laben to McFarling, Sarah	10-19-1809
BUSHMAN, George to McIntire, Mary	3-31-1807
BUSHONG, Augusteen to Keller, Barbara	8-11-1807
BUSHONG, George to Keller, Fanny	6-14-1818
BUSK, James to Grafton, Casandrew	6-11-1812
BUTLER, George W. to Keller, Elizabeth	2-24-1818
BUTLER, John to Alexander, Amelia	4-14-1811
BUTTS, William to Eyster, Barbary	10-26-1813
BYXBY, Willis to Cross, Catherine	10-12-1815
CALDWELL, James Ewen to Tucker, Sarah	7-17-1804
CALDWELL, Thomas to Kinneman, Margaret	10-29-1811
CALDWELL, William to Crawford, Elizabeth	12-19-1811
CALHOUN, Robert to Young, Mary	3-12-1818
CALLIHAN, Elias to Bayler, Catherine	12-17-1817
CALLIHAN, Thomas to Zimmerman, Catherine	1-5-1817
CAMERON, John to Zimmerman, Barbara	9-11-1817
CAMERON, Simeon to McDonald, Margaretta	9-19-1814
CAMPBELL, Obadiah to Beans, Rachel	8-14-1815
CANON, John to Cross, Eleanor	1-11-1807
CARL, Charles to Blackburn, Elizabeth	9-15-1808
CARLE, Richard to Firestone, Mary	12-17-1807
CARR, Samuel to Thomas, Patience	2-17-1815
CARROLL, Joseph to Ellis, Elizabeth	12-24-1817
CARSON, John to Yates, Jamima	4-5-1810
CASTY (?), Amos W. to Parmer, Terison (?)	8-12-1807
CATT, George to Smith, Mary	4-17-1810
CATT, John Jr. to Rupert, Leah	8-15-1809
CHAMBERLAIN, Isaac to Coburn, Elizabeth	7-1-1817
CHAMBERLAIN, John to McCoy, Rachel	4-9-1807
CHAMBERLAND, Samuel to Ashford, Susannah	1-9-1817
CHANCE, Peter to Cannon, Sarah	3-9-1809
CHANEY, John to Glenn, Anne	12-25-1815
CHANEY, Jonston to Brooks, Mary	12-10-1815
CHASESSON, Alexander to McPherson, Jane	3-12-1812
CHRIST, Abraham to Eyster, Mary	1-5-1808

CHRIST, Andrew to Firestone, Catharine	6-5-1800
CHRIST, Christian to Slosher, Sussannah	12-23-1806
CHRIST, Henry to Firestone, Mary	6-13-1811
CHUB (?), John to Little, Catharine	11-30-1813
CLAPSADDLE, Jacob to Bleecher, Magdalina	10-2-1810
CLAPSADDLE, John to Keefer, Elizabeth	2-15-1817
CLAPSADDLE, William to Prans, ____(?)	1-6-1816
CLARK, Abel to Burton, Mary	9-21-1815
CLARKE, Hugh to Kerr, Letticia	1-11-1815
CLAY, Isaac to Penick, Mary	12-29-1808
CLETS, Frederick to Deterecht, Anna Margaret	5-15-1807
CLINKER, John to Coy, Hannah	8-1-1817
COBURN, David to Kinder, Nancy	11-25-1817
COBURN, James to Bowland, Elizabeth	11-27-1810
COBURN, Samuel to Crawford, Mary	4-11-1805
Cohey (coy), James to Young, Elizabeth	5-24-1808
COMBS, John to Milner, Ann	4-11-1816
COMSTOCK, Calvin to Kinney, Mary	1-20-1814
CONON, Linsy to Fife, Elizabeth	5-2-1809
CONOVER, John to Hoover, Sarah	7-4-1818
COPE, Caleb Jr. to Strattan, Rebecca	11-13-1817
COPE, Israel to Dixon, Elizabeth	12-16-1806
COPE, John to Stratton, Ann	12-14-1814
COPE, Joshua to Earle, Mary	8-27-1816
COPELAN D, George to Dixon, Ruth	3-6-1814
COPPOCK, Jehu to Stanley, Judith	1-20-1814
COPPOCK, John to Stanley, Judith (rec twice)	1-20-1814
COPPOCK, Samuel to Cobbs, Rebecca	10-21-1813
COPUS, Aaron to George, Phebe	8-11-1814
COOK, Jacob to Parshell, Elizabeth	1-31-1809
COOK, Job to Moreland, Mary	5-1-1809
COOPER, Joshua to Fletcher, June	2-20-1817
COULSON, Uriah to Winder, Ann	10-23-1816
COUNTRIMAN, David to Mall, Anna	10-28-1813
COURTNEY, Jacob to Moore, Esther	5-7-1818
COUSINS, William to Jones, Martha	4-22-1808
COWGILE, Caleb to Oliphant, Rachel	2-20-1806
COX (EN), Michael to Fox, Catharine	12-9-1806
COX, Thomas to Beal, Kesiah	4-29-1813
COY, Henry to Windal, Elizabeth	9-18-1815
COY, Samuel to Boyer, Nancy	1-9-1817
CRABLE, David to Erwin, Rebeckiah	6-22-1815
CRAIG, Absalom to Keith, Sarah	4-17-1817
CRAIG, Hugh to Martin, Martha	4-10-1811
CRAIG, Isaac to Davis, Elizabeth	4-7-1808
CRAIG, Robert to Stevenson, Sarah	2-27-1816
CRAIG, William to Guthery, Margaret	12-17-1812
CRAM, John to Pritchard, Tabitha	1-3-1815
CRAMRIN, John to Rinehard, Catharine	5-5-1808

CRANE, William to Beer, Ann   11-15-1810
CRAWFORD, Daniel to Robinson, Margaret   4-30-1811
CRAWFORD, Edward to McLaughlin, Elizabeth   6-10-1806
CRAWFORD, James to Crawford, Nancy   3-8-1814
CREW, Joshua to Stanley, Milley   10-15-1812
CROFT, Henry to Davis, Margaret   6-8-1807
CROSS, John to Fitzpatrick, Mary   6-8-1818
CROSS, Thomas to Eades, Nancy   2-15-1810
CROSSER, Adam to Roach, Margaret   7-25-1817
CROSSER, James to Moon, Margaret   1-13-1814
CROW, Abraham to Thomson, Sariah   11-14-1811
CROW, James to Morelan, Elizabeth   10-3-1811
CROWL, George to Barger, Susanna   1-31-1809
CROWL, Jacob to Roach, Ann M.   3-23-1815
CRUMBACKER, Daniel to Overholtser, Esther   12-21-1811
CRUMBACKER, John to Myers, Lydia   6-25-1818
CULBERTSON, James to Airhart, Catharine   4-3-1817
CULBERTSON, Thomas to Gonter, Betsy   4-14-1814
CULP, Anthony to Shellinberger, Nancy   5-1-1817
CULP, Balser to Hoveler, Catharine   4-7-1808
CUMMINGS, Barney to Pearce, Sarah   4-11-1815
CUNNING, Robert to Cunning, Margaret   2-14-1810
CURLE, Samuel to Pointer (Painter) Susannah   7-26-1809
CURRY, Mosses to Gilson, Anney   1-?-1815
DANHOUDON, Cornelius to Brouse, Mary   12-31-1809
Daniels, William to Daniels, Ruth   7-14-1818
DAUGHERTY, Samuel to Sheehan, Isabel   8-18-1803
DAVIDSON, James to Johnson, Mary   5-3-1807
DAVIDSON, William to Moore, Ann   10-30-1817
DAVIS, Eli to Huston, Hannah   4-22-1806
DAVIS, Jehu to Bushaw, Edith   8-11-1814
DAVIS, John to Gilbert, Lydia   9-5-1811
DAVIS, John to Hamilton, Mary   12-26-1816
DAVIS, Joseph to Smith, Lenor   10-3-1816
DAVIS, Nathan to Koffel, Sarah   9-25-1817
DAVIS, Robert to Riley, Margaret   7-23-1805
DAVIS, William to Ramsey, Mary   2-21-1811
DAVIS, William to Fawcett, Ann   11-24-1813
DAVIS, William to Whitacre, Phebe   8-25-1818
DAVIS, William to Warrington, Hannah   12-16-1815
DEAN, John to Duck, Elizabeth   9-23-1806
DeHOFF, George to Whitacre, Catharine   9-26-1813
DeHOFF, John to Mountz, Mari   3-12-1816
DeLONG, John to Cross, Sarah   9-4-1807
DIEBL, Charles to Sheets, Elizabeth   6-16-1818
DILLIHAN, John to McCaskey, Jane   9-4-1806
DILLON, James to Underwood, Elizabeth   11-21-1816
DINGER, John to Walton, Bersheba   1-20-1809
DIRKE, Henry to Guy, Elizabeth   8-21-1815
DIXON, John to Beal, Hannah   12-18-1806
DIXON, Nathan to Pettit, Lucretia   3-13-1814
DIXON, Simon to James, Elizabeth   12-18-1806

DRISKELL, William to Brody, Mary	2-23-1804
DRISKILL, Denis to Taylor, Hannah	7-21-1809
DOWNARD, John to Kerr, Mary	12-25-1817
DUCKS, George to Ritchie, Mary	6-8-1807
DUFFY, James to Butts, Susannah	11-13-1817
DUGALLES, John to Coburn, Margaret	11-13-1810
DUTCHOS (?), Oswald to Tritt, Rachel	9-20-1817
EADES, James to Whitacre, Phebe	2-20-1812
EARL, Joseph to Gibson, Margaret	8-20-1810
EARLY, David to Cott, Maryan	7-18-1810
EDWARDS, John to Whitacre, Hannah	11-7-1806
EIK, John to Grogg, Sarah	4-20-1813
ELDER, Mathew to Frederick, Polly	9-11-1815
ELIANDER, John to Robinson, Elizabeth	2-11-1817
ELLIS, Gainer to Jackson, Mercy	4-25-1816
ELLISON, Isaac to Cattell, Elizabeth	5-25-1815
EMERICK, Christian to Weem, Catharine	9-21-1818
EMERICK, Peter to Taylor, Mariah	6-29-1808
ERWIN, Joseph to Young, Oliviah	4-7-1814
ESPY, George to Turnipseed, Susannah	9-25-1811
ESTEP, George to Wolf, Catharine	5-3-1808
ESTEP, Henry to Anderson, Abigel	10-26-1815
Estep, William to Campbell, Martha	10-7-1806
ESTERLY, George to Hafily, Christiana	2-16-1815
ESTERLY, Jacob to Murcessusn, Barbarah	9-4-1817
EVERHART, Jacob to Smith, Betsy	1-24-1815
EWING, James to Hephner, Dolly	(?)-(?)-1808
EWING, Samuel to Franks, Ann	7-21-1818
EYSTER, William to Keller, Fanny	6-21-1817
FARR, Jesse to Robinson, Eliza	3-31-1816
FARSON, John W. to Rose, Marjory	3-17-1808
FAUSNAUGHT, Jacob to Moran, Magdalena	9-10-1815
FAWCETT, David to Ball, Hannah	5-24-1815
FEASEL, Jeremiah to Murphey, Hannah	7-18-1811
FEGGINS, Samuel to Merrison, Ester	5-24-1816
FENIMORE, Caleb to Snyder, Laruw	12-31-1816
FEREL, William to Beck, Rachel	8-11-1812
FERGUSON, Samuel to Reed, Rosannah	1-7-1812
FERRIL, John to Zeupurnich, Elizabeth	2-1-1816
FESSEL, James to Rogers, Jane	2-28-1809
FIELD, John to Pine, Elizabeth	10-3-1812
FIFE, James to Hamilton, Susanah	8-13-1810
FIFE, John to Heey, Mary	1-29-1807
FIFE, Joseph to Hamilton, Catharine	4-19-1814
FIFE, Samuel to Robinson, Elizabeth	2-18-1817
FIFE, William to Robinson, Jane	1-5-1807
FIGLEY, Abraham to Hughs, Elizabeth	3-21-1809
FIRESTONE, John to Rowler, Rachel	2-18-1806

FIRESTONE, Peter to Brinker, Elisabeth	2-15-1818
FISHELL, John to Knapp, Amelia	6-2-1808
_____, Jacob to Fisher, Catherine	2-18-1806
FISHER, Frederick to Clark, Elenor	6-20-1815
FISHER, Henry to Fulk, Nancy	3-29-1809
FISHER, Peter to Sheppler, Catharine	3-28-1811
FLECKINGER, John to Bernhart, Elizabeth	9-10-1816
FLOWERS, Samuel to Pickrel, Mary	12-2-1817
FORBES, William to Lindsey, Fanny	1-14-1818
FORNEY, Adam to May, Sarah	1-31-1811
FORNEY, Nicholas to Sponsailer, Elizabeth	4-28-1807
FORNEY, William to Lipley, Christian	5-18-1815
FOULKS, Charles to McKinley, Sarah	9-19-1815
FOULKS, William to Reems, Sarah	1-11-1816
FOUST, Philip to Binomen(?), Catharine	7-6-1813
FOUTS, Philip to Preil, Mary	1-20-1816
FOWLER, Thomas to Clark, Esther	8-7-1805
FOX, Abraham to Pontious, Polly	1-11-1810
FOX, Henry to Rubert (Rupert), Rachel	5-5-1812
FOX, Jacob to Wilyard, Elizabeth	1-11-1816
FOX, John to Roller, Agnes (mary)	1-2-1817
FOX, John to Roller, Mary	12-24-1805
FOX, John to Fox, Mary	2-8-1810
FOX, Philip to Hoffman, Susannah	8-19-1806
FOX, Philip to Roller, Sarah	9-3-1812
FRANKS, Henry to Routson, Susannah	8-22-1815
FRANKS, Michael to Thompson, Martha	1-14-1813
FRASER, Daniel to Obilvie, Uphemia	5-27-1817
FRASER, William to Kennedy, Jannet	1-18-1809
FREDERICK, John to Gloss, Sophia	4-7-1808
FREDERICK, Samuel to Caldwell, Elizabeth	5-27-1813
FREED, Peter to Caldwell, Rebecca	9-28-1812
FREEMAN, Jacob to McLillery, Margaret	8-20-1807
FREEMAN, Jeptha to Wilson, Lydia	3-21-1816
FRENCH, Barzilla to Yatts (Yeates), Mary	11-1-1810
FRENCH, Elijah to Curle, Susannah	3-4-1807
FRENCH, Robert to Street, Anna	2-25-1807
FRENCH, Samuel to McLaughlin, Catharine	7-26-1804
FREW, Henry to Crowl, Peggy	11-8-1815
FRINK(?), Peter to Boyer, Barbara	4-5-1814
FULKS, Daniel to McCoy, Elizabeth	10-15-1816
FULLER, Luther to Beymer, Anna	2-9-1816
GALBREATH, Thomas to Star, Olovia	12-19-1811
GALLOWAY, William to Gilson, Agness	3-16-1813
GARDNER, William to Muma, Lena	12-16-1815
GARWOOD, Daniel to Holloway, Mary	3-19-1807

294

GARWOOD, Thomas to Stratton, Mary	3-16-1809
GASKILL, Israel to Reed, Rebecca	4-19-1817
GASKILL, Thomas to Welch, Jane	5-28-1818
GAUNT, John to Burns, Susanna	4-23-1817
GAUS, Henry to Root, Elizabeth	12-11-1817
GAUSE, Isaac to Shores, Rebecca	7-15-1810
GAUSE, Robert to Bowman, Charlotte	2-22-1814
GEDDES, James to Conkel, Elizabeth	7-15-1817
GEISSINGER, Joseph to Fox, Rebecca	9-12-1811
GEORGE, Thomas to Gonsallus, Sarah	2-14-1810
GIBBONS, William to Hooten, Fanny	12-6-1808
GIBBONS, Windsor to Houton, Hannah	2-7-1807
GIBBS, Isaac to Norris, Polly	3-14-1815
GIBSON, Andrew to Pine, Mary	7-5-1814
GILBERT, Barnace to Fox, Mary	12-3-1810
GILBERT, Henry to Gongower, Susanna	12-30-1813
GILBERT, Thomas to Sinclair, Mary	2-2-1809
GILMORE, William to Fisher, Susannah	9-16-1810
GILSON, William to Clarrin, Margaret M.	9-2-1806
GIMBLE, John to Marietta, Hannah	8-7-1817
GISER, John to Eyster, Esther	9-15-1814
GLASS, David to Worrel, Mary	11-25-1816
GLOSS, David to Driskill, Elizabeth	10-2-1809
GOBLE, Silas to Burger, Mary	10-22-1812
GODDIS (GEDDES), Wm. to Beens, Pleasant	3-3-1812
GONEN, Joseph to Gilbert, Sarah	12-26-1811
GORMAN, Daniel to Pain, Nancy	5-9-1815
GRACE, Henry to Boots, Mary	11-27-1810
GRAHAM, Thomas to Ketchum, Susan	7-8-1817
GRAYHAM, David to Binshop, Sarah	4-15-1817
GREEN, Elisha to Madams, Margaret	4-30-1818
GREEN, Joseph to Balin, Nancy	8-26-1817
GREEN, William to Frederick, Margaret	1-25-1811
GREENEMY, Daniel to Heck, Elizabeth	5-15-1810
GRIM, George to Bushong, Elizabeth	5-9-1807
GRIMES, George to Brown, Hannah	11-29-1813
GRIMES, James to Downs, Nancy	6-13-1817
GRIMES, John to Allender, Catharine	3-28-1816
GRIMES, John to Dillen, Elizabeth	1-19-1815
GRIMES, Samuel to Alexander, Nancy	3-11-1817
GRIMM, John to Miller, Charlotte	5-7-1811
GRIMM, Nicholas to Miller, Mary	9-23-1806
GRISOL, Samuel to Whitacre, Nancy	7-4-1813
GRISSELL, Joseph to Whitacre, Leticia	8-20-1810
GUANT, Isaac to Mall, Calse	3-25-1817
GUTCHER, Gottleeb to Bair, Catharine	1-16-1816
GUTHERIE, Richard to Vanfosson, Mary	2-11-1812
GUTTERY, Samuel to Pollock, Mary	2-20-1812
GUY, Jesse to Shirts, Jane	9-5-1816
GUY, William to Shirts, Ally	4-4-1816

```
HACKATHORN, John to Altman, Susana              2-16-1816
HACKHART (ECKHART?), Mich. to Hook, Margaret     6-28-1808
HAHN, Adam to Weisleder, Magdalena               4-19-1808
HAHN, Israel to Menser, Elizabeth                5-22-1817
HAHN, Jacob to Wickart, Mary                     6-16-1812
HAHN, Peter to Stump, Maria                      3-17-1812
HAINES, Levi Jr. to Hatcher, Sarah               10-24-1811
HAINES, Mahlon to Hatcher, Rachel                5-13-1806
HAMBLE, James to Fisher, Elizabeth               9-22-1814
HAMBLETON, Benjamin to Hanna, Anna               12-14-1815
HAMILTON, Henry to Woods, Sarah                  1-1-1807
HAMILTON, Joseph to Spence, Hannah               5-28-1812
HAMILTON, William to Davis, Elizabeth            4-4-1816
HAMLIN, William to Holloway, Hannah              9-19-1816
HANNA, Benjamin to Dixon, Rachel                 12-15-1803
HANNA, Benjamin to Fisher, Anna                  7-14-1808
HANNA, David to Gilson, Margaret                 4-28-1814
HARMAN, Frederick to Shennabarger, Elizabeth     10-2/-1806
HARMAN, Jonas to Rhoads, Frances                 11-16-1813
HARMAN, William to Roads, Elizabeth              1-22-1818
HARPER, James to Shaw(ke), Rachel                3-30-1815
HARRISON, Benjamin to Smith, Lena                11-16-1815
HARRISON, Latham to James, Mary                  4-12-1809
HARRISON, William to Dixson, Mary                3-15-1810
HARTER, Charles to Shirts, Mary                  3-5-1816
HARTSILL, Abraham to Smith, Sally                9-18-1812
HATCHER, John to Adamson, Rebecca                1-18-1816
HATCHER, Thomas to Adamson, Ruth                 9-15-1814
HAWLEY, David to Beal, Rachel                    8-17-1809
HAYCOCK, Jacob to Underwood, Susannah            10-22-1807
HAYES, Jehu to Altman, Polly                     10-24-1814
HAYES, Mordecai to Hogue, Esther                 10-20-1813
HAYS, Adam to Stevens, Sisson                    10-6-1803
HAYS, David to Early, Sally                      12-18-1810
HEACOCK, Jonathan to Underwood, Sarah            4-5-1808
HEADLY, John to Bricker, Susanna                 3-12-1818
HEALD, James to Wilson, Mary                     1-14-1808
HEALD, Joseph to Hole, Ury Betsy                 11-14-1816
HELMAN, Jacob to Welch, Mary                     4-18-1816
HELMAN, William to Dutro, Mary                   1-3-1813
HELMICK, John to Manning, Sophia                 2-16-1813
HENDERSON, James to McClure, Jane                6-1-1817
HENDERSON, William to Welch, Catharine           9-1-1817
HENNUH (HANNA?), Jacob to Haun, Elizabeth        7-5-1`3
HENRY, James to Young, Elizabeth                 5-11-1815
HENRY, William to Hurst, Abigail                 9-14-1804
HEPNER, John to Earhart, Barbara                 9-5-1814
HERMAN, Christian to Bowker, Nancy               6-27-1815
HERMAN, Henry to Neidick, Ann                    10-27-1811
```

```
HERROLD, David to Bair, Rebecca                      3-21-1812
HESTON, Martin to Stough, Mary                       11-30-1809
HESTER, John to Mueller, Hana                        8-13-1818
HIBBIT, James to Bidinger, Susanna                   9-23-1814
HICKMAN, Jeremiah to (?? no name given)              10-17-1815
HICKMAN, John to Reed, Deborah                       3-31-1814
HIGINS, Samuel to Franks, Elizabeth                  11-20-1810
HILES, Nicholas to Reeder, Mary                      8-19-1812
HILLIS, William to Hayes, Mary                       8-14-1817
HIN, Joshua to Martin, Catharine                     6-9-1814
HIPNER, Henry to Benner, Nancy                       10-15-1815
HIVELY, Christopher to McGregor, Mary                7-27-1809
HIVELY, Michael to Bushong, Catherine                3-19-1812
HOCK, George to Young, Elisabeth                     7-16-1818
HOFFMAN, Jacob to Meece, Polly                       5-2-1815
HOGE, James to Murren, Sarah                         3-21-1810
HOGUE, James to Buck, Mary                           10-1-1812
HOLE, Charles to Hanna, Esther                       5-15-1811
HOLLOWAY, Aaron to Mercer, Olive                     10-14-1812
HOLLOWAY, Aaron to Garwood, Sara                     9-15-1816
HOLLOWAY, Isaac to Garwood, Hope                     9-17-1815
HOLLOWAY, Joel to Alfred, Mary                       12-7-1815
HOOFMAN, John to Shnok, Elizabeth                    5-26-1808
HOOK, George to Mellinger, Catharine                 1-11-1805
HOOVER, Jacob to Shelenberger, Elizabeth             1-27-1814
HOSTETTER, David to Wiley, Nancy                     11-4-1813
HOUGH, Gustavus to George, Margaret                  7-13-1818
HOUTS, Philip to Ritz, Polly                         3-17-1814
HOUTY, William to Crowl, Rosana                      2-28-1811
HUBBARD, Ephraim B. to McGowen, Polly                7-1-1817
HUCKMAN, Nicholas to Martain, Eloner                 6-2-1814
HULL, Aaron to Wiseman, Easter                       4-7-1812
HULL, Henry to Pool, Elizabeth                       11-7-1811
HULL, Jesse to Beard, Mary                           2-7-1804
HULL, John to Sheehan, Nelly                         11-9-1813
HULL, Samuel to Norris, Ann                          (?)-30-1817
HUNT, Nathan to Warrington, Ann                      6-25-1808
HUNT, Samuel to Black, Mary                          3-25-1812
HUNT, Stacy to Mercer, Rebecca                       5-23-1816
HUNT, William to Webb, Elizabeth                     5-26-1808
HUNTER, Samuel to Paul, Jane                         5-17-1813
HUSTEN, Samuel to Molten. Esibela                    10-29-1811
HUSTING, Robert to Bowman, Elizabeth                 12-5-1811
HUSTON, Benjamin to Booth, Hannah                    10-16-1817
HUSTON, John to Coburn, Rachel                       3-18-1806
HUSTON, Samuel to George, Elinor                     11-18-1808
HUSTON, Samuel to George, Elinor (2nd entry)         11-18-1809
HUSTON, William to Perry, Margaret                   1-22-1817
HUTTON, William to Burden, Hannah                    4-24-1813
HYELS, Joseph to Murrel, Mary                        2-19-1811
HYETH, David to Gonsalus, Elizabeth                  5-1-1817
HYLES, Levi to Estep, Catharine                      11-21-1811
```

IDDINGS, Joseph to Grafton, Hannah	9-5-1815
IRAY, John to New, Elizabeth	10-3-1811
IREY, Isaac to Irey, Margaret	9-30-1813
IREY, Phineas to Whitacre, Martha	10-20-1815
JACKSON, Benjamin to Stackhouse, Alice	2-4-1813
JAMES, John to Richards, Esther	6-14-1809
JAMES, Joseph to Harrison, Ann	9-16-1812
JENINGS, Levi to Myers, Mary	6-27-1816
JENNINGS, Simion to Watkins, Nancy	3-19-1812
JEWEL, Hopewell to Smith, Delilah	5-13-1811
JOHN, Abner to Reeder, Hannah	10-25-1815
JOHN, Benjamin to Winder, Hanah	10-22-1817
JOHNSON, John to Murrell, Nancy	3-25-1817
JOHNSON, John H. to Penok (Pennock) Hannah	1-25-1809
JOHNSTON, William to Middleton, Sarah	11-14-181?
JOLLY, Samuel to Strough, Mary	9-7-1809
JONES, John to Crawford, Harriet	7-2-1818
JONES, Jurdan to Feral, Nancy	9-27-1810
JONES, Lawrence to Littil, Sarah	10-14-1817
JONES, Samuel to Roller, Elizabeth	12-21-1811
JONSTON, Robert to Tradfield, Susannah	11-1-1808
KAILER, Abraham to Matz, Mary (Matilda)	8-6-1805
KAYLE, Philip to Rudisill, Mary	5-20-1810
KECK, Daniel to Given, Catherine	5-7-1815
KEHL, Martin to Gindner, Catharine	7-12-1812
KELLER, Jacob to Benner, Catharine	4-9-1816
KELLER, John to Kindeheut, Catharine	5-14-1817
KELLEY, Alexander to McCarty, Rebecca	3-14-1807
KELLEY, David to Rish, Hannah	9-8-1808
KELLEY, Isaac to Miller, Leanor	4-24-1816
KELLEY, William to Bower, Barbara	9-22-1807
KENT, Asfor(d) to Thompson, Nancy	1-1-1818
KERN, George to Boulin, Margaret	1-16-1816
KERR, William to Beard, Mary	4-25-1811
KERSCHER, John to Musser, Eve	7-11-1816
KHAN(?), Arthur to Roach, Elizabeth	9-26-1815
KIM, Peter to May, Elizabeth	11-15-1814
KIMBLE, William to Greet(?), Elizabeth	9-23-1813
KING, Robert to Bishop, Naomi	11-7-1816
KING, Thomas C. to Copeland, Abigail	5-19-1818
KIRK, Caleb to McBride, Hannah	12-25-1816
KLINKER, Isaac to Shafer, Elizabeth	4-9-1816
KNIPPER, Godfrey to Stnier, Magdalena	7-9-1818
KOFFIE, Adam to Poe, Sarah	6-18-1811
KOONTS, Michael to Catt, Elizabeth	1-23-1817
KRUMM, Christian to Billger, Catareena	5-19-1807
KUNS, William to Roller, Margaret	9-1-1814
KUNTZ, John to Airhart, Margaret	9-5-1816
KUSEY, Henry to Cook, Catharine	12-15-1817

```
LAUGHTEN, Robert to Brown, Moriah              4-24-1817
LESLIE, Elisha to Fitzpatrick, Elizabeth       8-22-1811
LESLIE, Joseph to Gallaway, Nancy              5-4-1809
LEWIS, Francis to Ralphenider, Magdalena       5-31-1812
LEWIS, Jason to Ashfow, Nancy                  4-7-1813
LEWIS, John to Stinger, Mary                   12-17-1816
LINDESMITH, Peter to Earhart, Susannah         1-10-1808
LOORY, Benjamin to Sheets, Elizabeth           11-24-1814
LOSINE(?), Henry to Shook, Elizabeth           8-27-1805
LOSLEY, Elijah to Galloway, Maryann            3-31-1814
LOWE(R), John to Alouhsser, Sarah              9-12-1817
LYON, Abraham to Shaw, Margaret                10-11-1804
LYON, Jonathan to Davis, Elizabeth             2-18-1807
MACKELROY, Hugh to Brooks, Susannah            11-21-1816
MALER, Jacob to Bradfield, Ann                 4-28-1813
MALONE, Daniel to Wiseman, Margaret            1-15-1811
MANKIN, Isaac to Monlen (Morlen), Judy         12-8-1814
MANKINS, George to Wright, Charity             12-20-1817
MANKINS, Thomas to Morlan, Elizabeth           10-26-1816
MANN, Phillip Jr. to Wollman, Susanna          5-23-1809
MARSH, Elias to Townsend, Edith                6-8-1810
MARSH, Jonathan to Armstrong, Phebe            12-22-1808
MARSH, Joseph to Rigbey, Hannah                1-25-1816
MARSHALL, Benjamin to Cattell, Ann             4-22-1813
MARSHALL, David to Maple, Elizabeth            4-20+1814
MARSHALL, Joseph to Wilman, Mary               12-3-1812
MARTIN, Andrew to Amons, Elizabeth             4-25-1805
MARTIN, Nathaniel to Hickman, Mary             4-3-1814
MARTIN, Robert to Amons, Mary                  4-23-1811
MARTIN, Samuel to Watson, Mariah               7-26-1808
MARTIN, Simeon to Dye, Achsa                   8-31-1815
MASIMORE, Joseph to Frew, Barbara              11-8-1815
MATHEWS, Isaac to Hamilton, Nancy              10-9-1806
MAY, John to Miller, Catharine                 5-13-1811
MAY, William to Miller, Polly                  6-10-1817
McADAMS, Patrick to Clomens, Margaret          5-5-1814
McBRIDE, Stephen Jr. to Sandres, Charity       1-21-1808
McCALLISTER, Heiter(?) to Brannan, Mary        6-25-1816
McCALLISTER, Walter to Robsh, Caty             3-22-1815
McCALNY, George to McGinnis, Mary              9-13-1809
McCARRON, John to Earl, Rachel                 9-23-1809
McCLARAN, Richard to Gilson, Nancy             4-14-1808
McCLARAN, Robert to Cook, Grace                6-18-1812
McCOLLESTER, John to Green, Margaret           3-7-1811
McCONNAL, Jesse to Byrns, Rachel               5-17-1810
McCONNEL, Edward to Townsend, Lydia            6-17-1812
McCONNEL, Levi to Townsend, Ruth               3-18-1813
McCONNER, Samuel to Wright, Clarissa           1-5-1815
McCOOK, Daniel to Lattimore, Martha            8-28-1817
McCOY, Alexander to Singer, Nancy              5-5-1804
```

McCOY, John to Dimpsey, Elizabeth	3-25-1813
McCRAKEN, Thomas to Moore, Susannah	12-15-1808
McCREADY, Daniel to Douglass, Margaret	11-1-1816
McCUTCHEON, Samuel to Speer, Elizabeth	10-2-1817
McELROY, John to Hepner, Sarah	9-19-1815
McFAIL, Daniel to McPherson, Nancy	6-18-1812
McGREGORY, George to McKnight, Lydia	4-23-1810
McINTOSH, William to Graser, Isabell	2-22-1809
McKABY, Thomas to Siben, Lydia	3-19-1808
McKAN, John to Ritchie, Margaret	1-26-1809
McKEAN, Alexander to Boland, Clara	4-4-1809
McKECHIN, Brice to Kinney, Mary	2-14-1817
McKEE, Daniel to Willington, Rachel	4-29- 1813
McKEE, Robert to Kirkendall, Rebecca	7-13-1813
McKINLEY, David to McLane, Eleanor	9-1-1815
McKINNON, Joseph to Babbs, Hannah	8-14-1817
McKNIGHT, John to Willington, Pryphena	n.d. 1807
McLane, John to Spence, Sarah	4-11-1816
McLAUGHLIN, James to Tucker, Anna	4-16-1809
McLAUGHLIN, Joseph to Fisher, Sarah	6-28-1808
McLAUGHLIN, Thomas to Jolly, Maria	7-10-1817
McLISH, Jacob to Thatcher, Esther	11-4-1809
McLISH, Robert to Hatcher, Lydia	6-24-1806
McMILLAN, John to Adams, Sarah	1-31-1811
McNeelance, George to Craine, Ann	11-26-1816
McPHEATERS, Moses to Reaich, Elvira	11-28-1816
McQUITTON, John to Laughlin, Nancy	5-12-1818
MECREL, Abel to Lastly, Elizabeth	6-15-1809
MEEK, John to Turner, Mary	9-26-1805
MEGILTON, John to Whitacre, Elizabeth	12-29-1806
MELINGER, Melchoir to Color, Mary	11 -26-1809
MELLINGER, Jacob to Draher, Catharine	4-16-1811
MENDENHALL, Aaron to Richardson, Lydia	11-21-1805
Mercer, Daniel to Hole, Jacy (?)	9-19-1816
Mercer, Thomas to Richardson, Hannah	3-17-1808
MERE, Philip to Emerick, Elizabeth	1-2-1816
MIDDLETON, Nathaniel to Sharp, Dorrity	6-11-1816
MIGHT, John to SMITH, Susanah	3-20-1816
MILBOURN, Jonathan to Stackhouse, Margery	3-25-1811
MILBOURN, Samuel to Craig, Jane	10-23-1811
MILLEN, John M. to Pool, Catharine	3-21-1815
MILLER, Abraham to Blackburn, Nancy	4-4-1811
MILLER, Edward to Rhodes, Rebecca	9-21-1809
MILLER, Eli to Sinclair, Rhoda	12-22-1814
MILLER, Henry to Seitner, Elizabeth	5-12-1811
MILLER, John to Frederick, Elizabet	7-16-1818

```
Miller, John to McCalmont, Mary                    9-11-1817
MILLER, Peter to Stewart, Mary                     12-28-1813
MILLNOR, Charles to Norris, Roseannah              2-13-1817
MILNER, Isaac to Gilbert, Priscilla                12-24-1807
MILNER, Jesse to Craig, Mary                       12-24-1807
MILNER, Joseph to Ware, Jane                       1-15-1818
MITS, David to Moneysmith, Susanna                 7-1+1816
MITS, George to Chibns, Polly (?)                  12-15-1814
MOORE, Henry to Morfoot, Onuro Elinor              7-16-1817
MOORE, Joseph to House, Elizabeth                  9-12-1811
MOORE, Kinder to Cook, Sarah                       8-5-1814
MOORE, Samuel to Willibey, Mary                    4-1-1811
MOORE, William to Cogan, Rachel                    3-20-1806
MORELAND, Jonah to Armstrong, Amelia               1-28-1807
MORGAN, Thomas C. to Lodge, Susanna                5-29-1817
MORLAN, Isaac to Wright, Martha          1 or 19-Jan 1814
MORLAN, Jonah to Howell, Martha                    3-21-1817
MORLAND, Stephen to Ashford, Elizabeth             9-4-1806
MORLEDGE, John to Westfall, Hannah                 12-11-1817
MORRIS, James to Wallom, Mary                      2-20-1816
MORRIS, Joseph to Blecher, Mary                    10-10-1816
MORRIS, Joshua to Coppock, Rachel                  6-20-'1814
MORRIS, Joshua to Coppock, Rachel (2nd entry)6-3-1814
MORRISON, John to Custard, Catherine               2-24-1818
MORRISON, Joseph to Todd, Catherine                3-24-1814
MORTON, George to Estes, Mary                      1-8-1818
MORTON, Israel to Conn, Hannah                     1-5-1813
MORTON, Samuel to Baker, Catharine                 12-25-1817
MOWEN, Jacob to Nagle, Catarina                    2-10-1815
MOWEN, Peter to Fasennaugh, Elizabeth              4-28-1811
MUFIT, John to Skelton, Nancy                      11-4-1813
MURRAY, William to McMullen, Barbara               9-24-1807
MURREL, Joseph to Owen, Lidia                      4-21-1809
MURRELL, Samuel to Sheets, Ann                     7-21-1814
MUSSER, John to Shafer, Hetty                      12-5-1816
MYERS, David to Turnipseed, Cathareine             10-27-1807
MYERS, David to Enrig, Mary (?)                    10-14-1815
MYERS, Frederick to Relker, Catharina              9-6-1814
MYERS, Jonathan to Snyder, Sarah                   3-13-1810
MYERS, Silas to Miller, Elizabeth                  6-3-1806
NANSISTIN (?), Arnold to Gilmore, Amy              1-29-1807
NICEWONGER, John to Thomas, Mary                   1-3-1806
NIXON, Francis to Kennedy, Ann                     8-27-1817
NIXON, William to Bell, Mary (alias Fulcorson)4-28-1804
NORMAN, Joshua to Carrick, Ilana                   11-31-1814
NOWLING, William to Thompson, Rebecca              1-5-1 815
OAGLE, Hercules to Gibbens, Frances                6-9-1816
OGLESBEE, David to Stratton, Margaret              7-3-1810
OKLEY, Abraham to Tayler, Elizabeth                2-21 -1811
OLIPHANT, Ephraim to Heald, Elizabeth              1-18-1816
```

```
OLIPHANT, Samuel to Heald, Rachel              11-17-1814
OMERMAN, _____ to Hill, Mary               4-18-1805
ORR, John to Bowman, Sarah                     5-19-1814
Overhattser, Jonathan to Stauffer, Elizabeth   4-22-1817
OVERHOLTZER, Jacob to Mellinger, Elizabeth     7-19-1807
PAINTER, David to Web, Ann                     10-27-1813
PAINTER, Samuel to Hendrix, Mary               2-21-1816
PALMER, Jesse to Pugh, Charity                 7-12-1814
PANCAKE, William to Crawford, Mary             6-11-1816
PATRIDGE, John to Graham, Mary                 2-8-1816
PAUL, Henry to Hunter, Sarah                   1-6-1818
PAXON, Benjamin to Walker, Mary                9-18-1811
PEARCE, Aaron to Cummings, Hannah              1-13-1814
PEARCE. Lewis to Clark, Polly                  n.d. 1808
PEARSEL, Barnard to Welker, Sariah             5-9-1805
PEDDRICK, Philip to Townsend, Judith           5-21-1806
PENNOCK, John to Walker, Sarah                 1-16-1811
PENNOCK, William to Welch, Abigail             7-21-1818
PETIT, Fenias to Davis, Hannah                 2-1-1813
PETTIT, Phineas to Middleton, Margaret         12-11-1817
PHILIP, Smith to _____, Janet              1-24-1811
PHILIPS, Derias to Smith, Elizabeth            6-6-1816
PHILIPS, George to Earles, Eleanor             12-4-1817
PHILIPS, Reuben to Philips, Polly              9-12-1816
PHILIPS, Samuel to Smith, Elizabeth            12-10-1816
PHILIPS, William to Boyce, Susanna             3-7-1811
PHILSON, William to Comssi (?), Nancy          1-5-1814
PICKERING, Levi (Bel Co) to Groser, Susannah   6-13-1808
PIERCE, James to Gibson, Jane                  4-5-1814
POE, Andrew to Hoy, Ann                        9-8-1803
POE, Isaac to TOTTEN, Jane                     11w-25-1806
POE, John to Amens, Betsey                     6-22-1815
POE, Thomas to Hephner, Elizabeth              10-22-1807
POLLOCK, Thomas to Graham, Betsy               2-2-1814
POLLOCK, William to Starr, Mary                3-26-1818
POOL, Thomas to Burger, Sarah                  9u-21-1815
POWELL, Joseph to Powell, Sarah                3-16-1815
POWELL, William to Brandeberry, Sarah          10-30-1816
POWNELL, John to Quin, Mary                    2-13-1811
PRESTON, Amos to Reeves, Drusila               3-28-1811
PRITCHARD, Benjamin to Arter, Mary             11-14-1816
QUAINTANCE, Fisher to Irey, Sarah              1-25-1816
QUILLEN, Alexander to McKinly, Esther          11 -5-1816
RALPHSNIDER, John to Goodnel, Polly            6-16-1814
RAMBLER, John to Augustine, Catharine          10-12-1813
RAMSEY, David to Kinney, Elizabeth             2-2-1814
RAMSEY, James to Fout, Rachel                  4-5-1810
RAMSEY, John to Coulter, Mary                  1-13-1812
RANDOLPH, Jonas to Bevenington, Mary           3-6-1817
RANDOLPH, William to Johnston, Rachel          1-29-1818
```

```
RANNELLS, Joseph to Aldoffer, Elizabeth        12-1-1811
RAUZEN, John to Frank, Sara                    2-29-1816
REAM, Philip to Hartman, Maryann               2-12-1811
REDECK, William W. to Kenedy, Jane             4-23-1816
REED, Ruel to Wray, Rebecca                    7-18-1815
REEDER, Jacob to Byers, Elizabeth              6-24-1813
REEDER, Joseph to Haines, Hannah               1-17-1805
REEN, Aaron to Gorden, Elizabeth               5-13-1813
REESE, John to Clapsaddle, Mary                12-27-1808
RENKENBERGER, George to Esterly, Catharine     12-23-1813
RHODES, Frederick to May, Anna                 4-22-1817
RHODES, Moses to Hewit, Susannah               11-22-1815
RHODES, Sandford to Moore, Margery             10-8-1812
RHODES, William to Amen, Susanna               1-6-1817
RIBSÁMAN, Adam to Ruff, Sarah                  9-27-1814
RICHARDSON, Joseph to Myers, Lydia             6-11-1812
RICHEY, Abraham to Glass, Catherine            2-26-1815
RICHEY, David to McLaughlin, Jane              6-14-1805
RIGBY, Aaron to Irey, Hannah                   2-15-1816
RIGBY, James to Townsend, Elizabeth            10-31-1816
RITCHEY, Jacob to Glass, Sofen (?)             5-27-1817
RITTER, Benjamin to McCoy, Sarah               5-18-1813
ROAR, Peter to Shoemaker, Elizabeth            5-9-1816
ROADS, William Jr. to Brown, Mary              5-18-1815
ROBERSON, Jona to Morrison, Sarah              9-8-1814
ROBERTS, George to Cross, Mary                 10-6-1807
ROBINSON, Aaron to Smith, Sarah                6-3-1811
ROBINSON, Janonah to Lewis, Catharine          5-4-1813
ROBINSON, John to Hustin, Eliner               11-21-1811
ROGERS, Eli to Chance, Elizabeth               9-24-1814
ROGERS, James to Zimmerman, Margaret           12-26-1809
ROLLER, Jacob to Betz, Joredia (?)             11-24-1808
ROLLER, Jacob to Roller, Susanna               3-30-1809
ROLLER, Jacob to Gilbert, Elizabeth            12-121-1814
ROLLER, William to Teeters, Agnes              12-20-1810
ROOSE, Abraham to Shineberger, Catharine       1-7-1808
ROOSE, Frederick to Culp, Barbara              11-13-1817
ROSE, John to McClane, Margery                 3-9-1810
Rossell, Caleb to Holloway, Hannah             11-7-1805
ROUGH, John to Zimmerman, Susannah             7-13-1809
RUDISILL, Daniel to Painter, Elizabeth         9-7--1817
RUFF, Christopher, to Dehoff, Magdalena        10-8-1812
_____, Michael to Ruff, Isabella             10-10-1815
RUMEL, Henry to Shields, Margaret              3--19-1816
RUMMELL, Jacob to Altman, Susana               5-12-1818
RUPERT, Christian to Steller, Mary             9-1-1818
RUPERT, John to Bair, Sarah                    12-16-1806
RUPPERT, Jaclb to Shook, Sarah                 10-10-1816
RUSSELL, Henry to Hulpruner, Susannah          11-9-1815
RYRHGER, (?) Peter to Shanuon, Barbery         10-15-1814
SAINT, John to Lesdsly, Deborah                12-20-1810
```

303

```
SAINT, Thomas to Smith, Sarah                        5-27-1813
SAMPSEL, Nicholas to Bricker, Catharine             12-19-1810
SAMPSELL, Paul to Bricker, Rachel                    4-3-1817
SANDERS, Abishai to McIntire, Rachel                 1-7-1812
SANDERS, Benjamin to Wilkins, Sarag                  9-5-1810
SANER, George to Ream, Mary                          4-9-1818
SANOR, Jacob, Esq. to Yengling, Elizabeth            2-6-1816
SANTFORD, James to Bair, Elizabeth                   5-11-1818
SAWER, John to Lawferbark, Catherine                 7-28-1814
SCATTERGOOD, David to Carlile, Nancy                 5-2-1816
SCHOOLEY, John to Beeson, Phebe                      5-14-1807
SCHOOLEY, William to Reeve, Hannah                  10-23-1816
SCOTT, David to Rudisell, Elizabeth                  6-27-1805
SCOTT, Israel to Holloway, Sarah                    10-13-1808
SCOTT, John Sr. to Smith, Jane                       9-12-1815
SCOTT, Joseph to Marsh, Jane                         9-25-1817
SEBRELL, Joseph to Shinn, Mary                       2-19-1817
SEIDNER, Christian to Altman, Sarah                  6-23-1814
SEIDNER, John to Harmon, Margaret                   10-31-1808
SEYDEL, Michael to Buck, Elizabeth                  12-4-1817
SHAFER, Michael to Frankforter, Caty                11-28-1816
SGAFFERM Henry to Gilbert, Elizabeth                 3-8-1808
SHAHAN, John to Hood, Carrie                        10-18-1804
SHARER, James to Towel, Frances                      1-20-1815
SHAW, John to Hough, Sarah                           7-8-1813
SHAW, Jonathan to Wollum, Sally                     10-13-1807
SHAW, Philip to Bashong, Mary (Bushong)              9-5-1811
SHAW, Samuel to Samms, Sarah                        11-17-1803
SHAW, Thomas to Heald, Rachel                        9-20-1810
SHAWK, Henry to Rice, Sarah                          4-16-1812
SHAWKE, Jacob to Lewis, Elizabeth                   11-9-1816
SHEAKLER, J. TO Houselman, Crestina                  7-(?)-1817
SHEARER, William to McLaughlin, Rebecca              4-27-1809
SHEEHAN, Cornelius to Allison, Elizabeth             2-28-1804
SHEETS, Jacob to Wolf, Mary                          7-9-1811
SHEETS, John to Rubert (Rupert), Catherine           9-5-1809
SHELL, John to Estep, Sarah                          9-24-1818
SHIELDS, Samuel to Piper, Rachel                    12-26-1816
SHINN, Thomas to Sebrell, Sarah                     12-25-1816
SHINN, Thomas to Daniel, Rebecca                     6-12-1805
SHIPPY, William to Walters, Nancy                    9-30-1817
SHOEMAKER, John to Shafer, Susannah                  5-18-1817
SHOOK, John to Grogg, Mary                           3-5-1808
SHORE, John to Smith, Sarah                          4-22-1818
SHOUNKE, Jacob to Brady, Elizabeth                   1-13-1815
SIDDALL, Tisenis to Makins, Elizabeth                9-3-1818
SINCLAIR, Abner to Wilkins, Elizabeth                6-13-1813
SINCLAIR, William to Gilbert, Mary                   8-10-1808
SKELTON, John to See, Hanna                          4-4-1811
SLATER, Isaac to Gutherie, Hannah                    4-6-1812
SLOSHER, Peter to Augusteen, Susan                  11-1-1807
```

```
SMACHTEBARI, Adolph to Rubert, Margaretta          7-2-1815
SMALLY, John to Bradfield, Elizabeth               12-1-1808
SMARTE, Henry to House, Mercy                      4-11-1809
SMITH, Jacob to Lee, Sarah                         8--28-1817
SMITH, Jesse to Shaw, Susannah (1st in Co.)        5-17-1805
SMITH, John to Bear, Susannah                      12-11-1817
SMITH, John widower to Apple, Mary widow           8-18-1815
SMITH, John to Pearce, Hannah                      12-13-1809
SMITH, John to Middlebrook, Ann                    1-24-1811
SMITH, John to Fisher, Mary                        5-20-1806
SMITH, Joseph to Whitacre, Ann                     9-15-1807
SMITH, Peter to Robinson, Lainey                   10-14-1804
SMITH, Peter to Keel, Sofia                        1-21-1810
SMITH, Philip to McIntosh, Issabella               1-13-1815
SMITH, Samuel to Harvey, Catherine                 10-13-1806
SMITH, Vallantine to Crawford, Rebecca             6-9-1809
SMITH, Ward to Wood, Mary                          11-6-1805
SMITH, William to Kettenack, Issabella             12-22-1814
SNIDER, Henry to Minor, Elizabeth                  12-5-1816
SNIDER, Henry to Kendles, Catharine                2-17-1817
SNIDER, Martin to Rish, Mary                       5-7-1816
SNIDER, William to Gault, Charlotte                6-13-1816
SNYDER, Abraham to Fox, Polly                      4-30-1812
SNYDER, George to Derr, Mary                       12-26-1811
SNYDER, Henry to Ferrall, Elizabeth                11-13-1811
SOMER, David to Keck, Magdalena                    10-30-1808
SONG, George to Coulter, Rebecca                   11-24-1812
SPIKER, Peter to Tritt, Harriett                   3-24-1812
SPONSLER, Michael to Miller, Elizabeth             9-12-1808
SPRINGER, Joseph to Shafer, Mary                   3-10-1810
SPRINGER, Mathias to Miller, Susanna               7-11-1817
STACKHOUSE, Evan to Daniels, Hannah                7-8-1816
STACKHOUSE, Owen to Heston, Tacy                   10-2-1817
STACY, John to Amens, Sarah                        11-2-1815
STAINBROOK, Henry to Livermore, Polly              6-6-1815
STANDLY, Joseph to Cobbs, Abigail                  7-18-1812
STANLEY, Abraham to Blackbourn, Sarah              10-14-1812
STANLEY, Benjamin to Cobbs, Elizabeth              6-30-1813
STANLEY, Garland to Burden, Sarah                  7-24-1811
STANLEY, James Jr. to Cowgill, Rachel              1-8-1815
STANLEY, James to Cobbs, Rhody                     12-26-1811
STANLEY, John to Wollman, Mary Ann                 10-28-1809
STANLEY, Joshua to Reeves, Milisent                5-22-1816
STANLEY, Moses to Holloway, Susanna                6-17-1807
STANLEY, Nathaniel J. to Hinchsman, Hannah         8-28-1816
STANTON, Benjamin to Townsend, Martha              7-1-1816
STANTON, Benjamin to Townsend, Martha (2nd entry)9-21-1816
STARR, Richard to Young, Mary                      6-13-1816
STAUFFER, David to Coy, Margaret                   12-9-1816
STAUFFER, Jacob to Minor, Amelia                   11-28-1806
STAUFFER, John to Fry, Elizabeth                   10-25-1816
STEEL, William A. to Williams, Mary                2-22-1811
```

```
STEAPLETON, Samuel to Booth, Sarah              12-1-1814
STEVENS, Benjamin to Mite, Mary                 3-31-1807
STEWART, James to Robinson, Sally               4-22-1811
STEWART, Joseph to Long,Catharine               5-5-1818
STEWART, Samuel to Long, Elizabeth              10-16-1817
STEWARD, Mahlan to Parks, Elizabeth             12-7-1809
STIBBS, Joseph to Bealle, Elizabeth Johnson     9-21-1809
STININGER, George to Boadman, Ann               11-26-1816
STOFFER, Abraham to Coombacher, Susana          3-28-1809
STOMB, Jacob to Hibel, Catherine                6-22-1813
STRATTON, David to Garwood, Mary                3-26-1807
STRATTON, Joseph to Test, Sarah                 5-25-1814
STRATTON, Josiah to Schooley, Deborah           9-30-1812
STRAUGHN, Isaiah to Gaskill, Elizabeth          4-14-1808
STRAUGHN, Jacob to Barber, Rebecca              4-19-1808
STREET, Jesse to Hambleton, Sussan              8-18-1806
STRIEBY, Christopher H. to Pontious, Elizabeth 8-15-1815
STRONG, George to Lewis, Elizabeth              6-10-1813
SUMMER, Peter to Widericht, Elizabeth           3-24-1807
SWEARINGEN, Henry to Swearingen, Mary           7-16-1807
SWIM, Rinear to Gaskell, Sarah                  4-16-1818
SWINEHART, Adam to Grim, Elizabeth              8-21-1804
SWITSER, George to Macherman, Catharine         7-14-1811
SWITSER, Jacob to Brinker, Caty                 2-26-1811
SWITSER, John to Wisbaum, Elizabeth             5-7-1818
SWITSER, Jacob to Shelton, Polly                1-17-1816
TAGGART, Simeen to _____, Mary             1-16-1816
TAILOR, Adam to Landstreet, Elizabeth           7-4-1811
TAYLOR, Persifo (?) to HOOPES, Esther           8-9-1810
TAYLOR, Pinem to Whitacre, Kesiah               2-20-1818
TEETERS, Elisha to Raynolds, Elizabeth          10-15-1812
TEETERS, John to Cook, Mary                     5-30-1805
TEETERS, William to Webb, Martha                12-19-1810
TEMPLE, William to Williams, Martha             2-7-1818
TEST, Benjamin to Schooley, Mary                6-12-1805
TEST, Isaac to Straughan, Margaret              5-23-1810
TEST, Samuel to Barber, Maryann                 9-30-1815
THIBS, John to Bricker, Magdalena               8-9-1814
THOMAS, Ethan to Edes, Nancy                    12-11-1806
THOMAS, Evin to Henderson, Elizabeth            12-20-1816
THOMAS, Henry to Smith, Elizabeth               8-7-1805
THOMAS, Peter to Giselman, Elizabeth            10-1-1810
THOMAS, Robert to Sackett, Lucinda              3-25-1807
THOMAS, William to Saltscaver, Eva              12-4-1810
THOMPSON, Farling to Reeder, Pleasy             10-4-1810
THOMPSON, Isaac to Underwood, Nancy             10-16-1813
THOMPSON, Joseph to Underwood, Ruth             1-13-1814
```

THOMPSON, Samuel to Underwood, Hannah   .6-13-1816
THOMPSON, Thomas to Shinn, Mary   4-8-1816
TILLIS, Richard to Bassot, Rachel   8-14-1817
TIPTON, William to Mathews, Rebecca   6-7-1808
TOD, Samuel to Ralphsnider, Sarah   8-30-1812
TODD, Lot to Ralphsnyder, Hannah   6-2-1812
TODD, Lot to Witharow, Hannah   12-23-1817
TOWNSEND, Isaac to Dixson, Elizabeth   12-15-1808
TOWNSEND, Lewis to David, Rachel   2-20-1818
TOWNSEND, Talbot to Ware, Edit   9-20-1815
TRIPPY, George to Shively, Mary   3-14-1814
TUKLE, Mathus to Fouts, Mary   4-4-1816
TURNER, John to Fessel, Sarah   8-20-1812
TURY, Lewis to Welker, Cahriot   2-5-1818
UMPHRIES, Joseph to Lodge, Mary   9-13-1810
UNDERWOOD, John to Vie, Nancy   3-2-1809
UNKEFER, John to Thomas, Mary   10-9-1817
VanFOSSEN, Amos to Flowers, Rebecca   11-6-1817
VanFOSSON, Jacob to Flowers, Anne   7-4-1815
VANKIRKENDALL, _____ to Milburn, Kisiah   6-23-1812
Van METER, Isaac to Downing, Susannah   11-19-1803
VAUGH, Mathew to Pennock, Phebe   12-3-1812
VORE, Benjamin to Shaw, Margaret   7-19-1815
VOTAW, Thomas to Brown, Elizabeth   6-8-1807
WALKER, Benjain to Dillon, Susannah   2-21-1811
WALKER, George to James, Sarah   9-7-1815
WALKER, George to Randolph, Elizabeth   4-23-1815
WALKER, John to Rogers, Sarah   12-29-1814
WALLIHAN, John to Lodge, Catherine   2-27-1817
WALTER, Daniel to Moyer, Mary   4-11-1816
WALTER, Henry to Bowman, Salome   5-7-1816
WARNER, Paul to Johnsθn, Margaret   7-12-1818
WARRINGTON, Abraham Jr. to Wollman, Kesiah   12-25-1806
WASLIT, John to Hines, Sarah   10-11-1814
WATKINS, John to Benit, Macy   10-22-1807
WATSON, Jacob to Hoyle, Elizabeth   3-16-1812
WATSON, John to Helman, Magdalena   6-4-1816
WATT, David to Wells, Mary   1-3-1811
WAY, Caleb to Candles, Sarah   12-18-1810
WEB, James to Bowman, Casia   2-17-1807
WEBB, John Sr. to Morris, Leah   2-3-1817
WEBB, Richard to Dillon, Susanna   7-31-1817
WEBB, Thomas to Smith, Naomi   5-17-1804
WEBBER, Joseph to Reeder, Harriett   4-9-1816
WELCH, Jacob to Van Fustion, Mary   1-31-1809
WELCH, Lewis to Henderson, Mary   4-24-1816
WELKER, John to Randolph, Ruth   3-25-1818
WELKER, William to Mitetry, Elizabeth   10-18-1814
WELLS, Isaacℓ. to Allison, Leanor   12-11-1815
WERMAN, Henry to Brinker, Margaret   3-19-1814

```
WESTFALL, Levi to Maxwell, Nancy              4-9-1818
WHAN, William to Montgomery, Aeloner          4-28-1814
WHEALIN, Frederick to Burger, Jane            12-25-1810
WHINERY, Zinni to Wright, Judith              4-28-1818
WHINERY, William to Canoll (Carroll?),Margery 5-2-1811
WHINNERY, James to Carroll, Sally             5-22-1810
WHINNERY, John to McBride, Mary               12-20-1809
WHITACRE, Aaron to Stacy, Sarah               3-17-1808
WHITACRE, Asa to Irey, Susan                  9-30-1813
WHITACRE, Cornelius to Ades, Lenna            12-20-1811
WHITACRE, Daniel to Paxton, Elizabeth         3-28-1816
WHITACRE, Isaac to Richard, Phebe             12-11-1817
WHITACRE, John to Bye, Lydia                  11-2-1815
WHITACRE, Stephen to Vole, Margaret           8-20-1818
Whiteleather, Christian to Sanor, Susannah    11-9-1810
WHITELEATHER, John to Harrison, Elizabeth     5-7-1816
WHITROW, William to Norris, Mary              9-2-1817
WICKERSHAM, Ellis to Morgan, Elisa            12-19-1816
WICKERSHAM, George to Reeves, Elizabeth       5-18-1815
WICKERSHAM, Thomas to Samus, Ann              9-16-1813
WIGAST, John to Sheets, Mariah                6-21-1807
WILKINS, Daniel to Davis, Pheby               11-29-1810
WILLIAMS, Abraham to Bost, Elizabeth          8-17-1815
WILLIAMS, Benjamin to Battin, Catharine       2-19-1807
WILLIAMS, Jesse to Vanfussin, Elizabeth       11-20-1806
WILLIAMSON, Isaai to Dillon, Elizabeth        12-28-1813
WILLIBY, Andrew to Ralphsnider, Mary          3-13-1810
WILLINGTON, Mergan to Garrison, Elizabeth     2-11-1816
WILLINGTON, Thomas to Sanebary, Elizabeth     10-9-1810
WILLINGTON, William to Sheehan, Elizabeth     11-21-1811
WILLIS, William A. to Tucker, Clementy        9-19- 1815
WILSON, Benjamin to Ralphsnider, Anna         11-25-1817
WILSON, Jacob to Grissell, Ann                6-6-1814
WILSON, James to TAGGART, Sarah               11-20-1817
WILSON, Uriah to Howell, Deborah              9-6-1816
WINDLE, John to Bushong, Elizabeth            6-16-1807
WIRTS, Michael to Borman, Christena           8-15-1815
WISELEATHER, Andrew to Moyer, Mari Magdalena  5-1-1817
WISEMAN, George to George, Mary               3-11-1817
WITERECHT, Peter to Shoemaker, Elizabeth      4-2-1809
WOLF, Adam to Mountz, Catharine               2-3-1807
WOLF, Jacob to Kelley, Sarah                  1-6-1812
WOLF, Jacob to Shad, Elizabeth                7-7-1818
WOLF, Philip to Whiteleather, Mary            3-9-1810
WOLF, Philip to Hannah, Mary                  10-19-1815
WOODBURN, John to Strain (Strawn), Sarah      3-18-1806
WOODS, Enos to Hughes, Elizabeth              8-13-1807
WOODS, Frederick to Burk, Mary                1-2-1812
WOODS, Joshua to Bishop, Elizabeth            11-24-1809
WOODSIDE, Robert to King, Ann                 11-11-1817
```

```
WOODWARD, John to Harland, Mary                        6-9-1818
WOOLF, John to Sanor, Elizabeth                        8-9-1814
WORLL, Richard to Tenner, Catarina                     8-23-1809
WRAY, Samuel to Moore, Penelope                        5-3-1814
WRIGHT, Benjamin to Atkinson, Mary                     12-31-1812
WRIGHT, Gilbert to Murray, Mary                        10-9-1810
WRIGHT, John to Gilbert, Hannah                        10-26-1809
WRIGHT, Ruel to McCracken, Jane                        3-6-1817
WYLEY, David to Stanley, Elizabeth                     9-20-1815
YARIAN, Conrad to Rupert, Eva                          7-2-1805
YARNALL, Abraham to Whitacre, Sarah                    1-16-1816
YARRIAN, Matthias to Bair, Christiana                  12-16-1806
YATES, Benjamin to Blackledge, Margaret                4-21-1814
YATES, Benjamin to Palmer, Jane                        7-9-1818
YOUNG, Jacob to Todd, Sarah                            5-10-1818
YOUNG, Silas to Armstrong, Jane                        12-30-1806
ZEPPERNICK, Daniel to Rinehart, Betsy                  8-17-1810
ZIMMERMAN, John to Fox, Catharine                      2-21-1809
ZIMMERMAN, Joseph to Whiteleather, Elizabeth           11-7-1810
```

COLUMBIANA COUNTY, OHIO MARRIAGE BOOK I - 1803-1818

A word of explanation:- Prior to this time, Book I of marriages has been kept locked in the safe, due to its valuable and delicate condition. The only way to consult it, has been to use the TYPEWRITTEN copy prepared by someone several years ago. Recently, this compiler was allowed access to the original, and made a careful comparison between the original and the copy. A number of errors were discovered, and are included here. The corrected part is underlined in each case, and those marriages shown with * are new additions which did not occur in the typewritten copy. -----Carol Willsey Bell, 4649 Yarmouth Lane, Youngstown, Ohio 44512 Compiler

```
 BARBER, Robert to McIntosh, Nancy                     7-10-1815
*BLAZURE, David to Hoy, Sarah                          12-16-1806
 BRADFIELD, Thomas to Thompson, Hannah                 3-6-1807
 BRAKESTRAW, Jonathan to Malmsbury, Elizabeth          12-31-1812
 BRANDEBERRY, Isaac to McConeighy, Mary                3-20-1817
 BROWN, Nathan to Stratton, Anny                       12-18-1806
 BUTZ, William to Eyster, Barbary                      10-26-1813
*CARICK, George to Makerman, Easter                    11-31-1814
 CLAPSADDLE, William to Pearce, Mary                   1-6-1816
 CLETS, Frederick to Weterect, Anna Margaret           5-15-1807
 COOK, Job to More, Mary                               5-1-1809
 CRAIGE, James to Moore, Margaret                      1-13-1814
 CRAIN, John to Pritchard, Tabitha                     1-3-1815
 CULBERTSON, Thomas to Porter, Betsy                   4-14-1814
 CUNNING, Barney to Pearce, Sarah                      4-11-1815
 CURL, Charles to Blackburn, Elizabeth                 9-15-1808
*DAVIS, Isaac to Richards, Edith                       8-11-1814
 DELONG, John to Croy, Sarah                           9-4-1807
 DINGEE, John to Walton, Bersheba                      1-20-1809
```

```
FEASEL, Barnard to Welker, Sariah            5-9-1805
FEZEL, James to Rogers, Jane                 2-28-1809
*FIFE, David to Murren, Sarah                3-22-1810
 FREEMAN, Jacob to McLilley, Margaret        8-20-1807
*FULKS, Charles to McKindley, Sarah          9-19-1815
 GIGER, John to Eyster, Elizabeth            9-15-1814
 GIKSON, William to McClarrin, Margaret      9-2-1806
 GRIM, George to Bushong, Elizabeth          5-9-1813
 GRIMES, Samuel to Allender, Nancy           3-11-1817
*GUANT, John to Burns, Susanna               4-23-1817
*HEPNER, Henry to Benner, Nancy              10-15-1815
 HEPNER, John to Eirhart, Barbary            9-5-1814
*HICKMAN, Jeremiah to Martin, Mary           10-17-1815
 HOGE, James to Gilmore, Jane                3-13-1810
 HOGUE, James to Buck, Nancy                 10-1-1812
*HULL, Samuel to Armstrong, Mary             3-14-1804
*KECK, Christian to Routson, Polly           10-17-1815
 KECK, Daniel to Gilbert, Catharine          5-7-1815
 KELLY, William to Bowers, Barbara           9-22-1807
 KERNS, William to Roller, Margarette        9-1-1814
 KERR, William to Baird, Mary                4-25-1811
 KIMBLE, William to Freet, Elizabeth         9-23-1813
 KINE, Peter to May, Elizabeth               11-15-1814
 LONG, George to Coulter, Rebecca            11-24-1812
*LUM, Jonas to Tillis, Jane                  10-10-1817
*MAIER, John to Fasenicht, Elizabeth         3-24-1807
*MARTIN, Simeon to Taggart, Mary             1-16-1816
*MATZ, John to Miller, Elizabeth             6-3-1806
 MERREL, Abel to Lastly, Elizabeth           6-15-1809
 MILBURN, Jonathan to Stackhouse, Margery    2-30-1811
 MITE, George to Chiene, Polly               12-15-1815
*MORRISON, James to Wallon, Mary             2-20-1816
 MURRELL, Samuel to Shirts, Anne             7-21-1814
 MURRY, William to McMullen, Barbara         9-24-1807
 McCARTY, Amos to Parmer, Terrison           8-12-1807
 McCOLLISTER, Hector to Brannon, Mary        6-25-1816
 McCOLLISTER, Walter to Roach, Caty          3-22-1815
 McFARSON, John to Rose, Marjory             3-17-1808
*McKENTIFFER, Jacob to Fisher, Catharine     2-18-1806
 McPHEATERS, Moses to Redick, Elvira         11-28-1816
*ORWICK, Samuel to Penner, Sarah             11-11-1817
 PICKERING, Levi to Crozer, Susannah         6-13-1808
 POWEL, Joseph to Paul, Sarah                3-16-1815
 REESE, Aaron to Gorden, Elizabeth           5-13-1813
 ROBERTS, Gworge to Croy, Mary               10-6-1807
 ROBISON, John to Hustin, Eliner             11-21-1811
 ROCK, George to Young, Elizabeth            7-16-1818
 RUPERD, John to Bair, Sarah                 12-11-1806
 RUPPERT, Jacob to Snook, Rebecca            10-10-1816
 SAWER, John to Lawderbush, Catherine        7-28-1814
```

```
SHAW, Jonathan to Wolum, Sally              10-13-1807
*SHAWKE, Jacob to Brady, Elizabeth           1-13-1815
*SHORES, James to Powel, Frances             1-20-1815
 SKELTON, John to Lee, Hanna                 4-4-1811
*SMITH, Philip to _____, Jannet          1-24-1811
 SMITH, Waide to Wood, Mary                 11-6-1805
 STANLEY, John to Woolman, Mary Ann          9-21-1809
*STANLEY, Solomon to Cobbs, Mary             6-24-1813
 STEPHENS, Benjamin to Mite, Mary            3-31-1807
*TAYLOR, Christopher to Emerick, Elisabeth   1-2-1816
 TURNER, John to Fezel, Sarah                8-20-1812
*VAN FUSTIN, Arnold to Gilmore, Anny         1-29-1807
 WELKER, William to Mite, Mrs. Elizabeth    10-18-1814
 WHAN, Arthur to Roach, Elizabeth            9-26-1815
 WHITACRE, Aaron to Stacy, Mariah            3-17-1808
 WHITACRE, Cornelius to Ades, Luisa         12-20-1811
 WIGURT, John to Sheetz, Mariah              6-21-1807
*WILLIAMS, William to Higgins, Sarah         1-5-1815
 WILLIAMSON, Isaac to Dillon, Elizabeth     11-25-1813
 WILLINGTON, Thomas to Sensbary, Elizabeth  10-9-1810
*WITHROW, William to Norris, Mary            9-2-1817
*WORMAN, Joshua to Carick, Hana             10-17-1814
*ZEENER, Michael to Ruff, Issabella         10-10-1815
```

HUM FAMILY CEMETERY - COLUMBIANA COUNTY, OHIO - FAIRFIELD TOWNSHIP

Contributed by: Carol W. Bell, C.G., 4649 Yarmouth Lane, Youngstown, Ohio 44512

Cemetery is located in Section 14, off Rte 7, turn west on Metz Rd., located on a hill on south side of road. Established 1812 on land donated by Adam Hum. Completely copied except for one stone face down and two illegible stones.

CALDWELL, Cora M. 1867-1882
HARDMAN, Leah died Nov. 12, 1856 aged 29 y 10m 9d
         Simeon died Oct. 22, 1867 aged 44y 11m 22d
HOULETTE, Nicholas B. 1828-1899 "Father"; Susan nee REIMER 1826-1912 "Mother"
         Nicholas B. Jr. (note: no dates)
         Lizzie S. dau. of N. B. & S. died Sept. 27, 1877 aged 11y 8m 2d
HUM, Jacob 1827-1884   Lucinda 1827-1904 (note: same stone)
         Elizabeth wife of Jacob Hum died Oct. 25, 1846 aged 67 yrs.
         David died July 26, 1876 aged 72y 5m 11d Mary died 1841 (note: no age
             given, same stone as David)
         Ulysses C. son of J.W. & M.M. died Oct 2, 1865 aged 2y 6m
         Adam C. son of J. W. & M.M. died Oct. 2, 1865 aged 10m(same stone as Ulysses)
         Margaret dau of J. & E. died Jan. 31, 1875 in her 67th year

HUM, Adam 1810-1895 Elizabeth 1815-1896 (note: same stone)
    John died July 26, 1876 aged 81y 3m 21d
    Martha wife of John Hum died Dec. 16, 1877 aged 74y 5m 4d
LOWER, Elizabeth wife of George Lower died Feb. 4, 1877 aged 71y 20d
    Henry died Jan. 16, 1869 aged 31y 23d "Our Brother"
    Cora A. dau. of E. & A.J. died Jan 2, 1878 aged 3y (8?)m 6d
    Samuel Jr. son of S. & R. died May 5, 1869 aged 2y 6m 16d
    Sarah Ann dau of S. & R. died July 14, 1862 aged 1 y 14m 6d
    George son of S. & R. died Oct. 7, 1861 aged 3y 5m 10d
    Jacob son of S. & R. died Apr. 15, 1869 aged 4y 11m
    Ella Louada dau. of F. P. & M. died Nov. 21, 1875 aged 3d
MILLER, George died Feb. 13, 1869 aged 87y 6m
RAY, Homer B. 1885-1965 "Father" Hester L. 1884-1959 "Mother"
REIMERS, William born July 1, 1793 died Oct. 9, 1869
    William born Mar. 6, 1798 died Oct. 19, 1867 (note: this and abo ve stone
        are side by side)
ROTHWELL, Jared B. 1826-1892 "Father" Hester A. 1837-1921 "Mother"
    Dr. Joseph O. 1858-1938
RYMER, William died May 21, 1891 aged 23y
SCARLOTT, Fletcher 1845-1926 Elizabeth 1855-1936 (note: same stone)
SEACHRIST, Elizabeth wife of Jacob Seachrist died Jan. 22, 1862 aged 22y 4m 18d
    William son of_____ died Dec. 27, 1860 aged 1 d
SEEDERLY, Fredie M. 1889-1894 Ruby M. 1886-1887 Johnie W. 1891-1892 (same stone)
SHULTZ, Christian, Co. D, 175th Ohio Inf. (note: no dates)
WOODS, Joseph died Apr. 1, 1854 aged 82 yrs.
    Sarah wife of Joseph Woods died May 23, 1842 aged 68y 10m 23d
    James P. died Apr. 7, 1876 aged 67y 4m 8d (same stone Hannah, Caroline,
        Mary A., Arvine and James)
    Hannah died Oct. 11, 1902 aged 90y 9m 12d
    Caroline dau. of J. P. & H. died Sept. 21, 1836 aged 1m 23d
    Mary A. dau. of J. P. & H. died Dec. 18, 1841 aged 1y 19d
    Arvine W. ch. of J. P. & H. died Aug. 1, 1847 aged 1y 3m 2d
    James H. son of J. P. & H. died Oct. 6, 1863 aged 13y 9m 29d
    Sgt. J. F., Co. f 143rd Ohio Inf. (note: no dates)
    Albirda wife of W. R. Woods died May 20, 1897 aged 33y 6m 6d
WORMAN, Noah died June 30, 1875 aged 57y 6m 25d
    Henry died Dec. 6, 1893 aged 75y 1d
    David died Feb. 12, 1892 aged 70y 20d

COSHOCTON COUNTY, OHIO – COMMON PLEAS JOURNAL, 1829-1832.

The following records are from "Journal 4" found in the Clerk of Court's office at the court house at Coshocton. Page on which record may be found in the original book is given in parenthesis.

11-17-1829 - James CRAWFORD a native of Ireland. Naturalization. Declaration of intention made at November term 1827 court. Oath by John Mitchell and Henry Grim. (1)

11-17-1829 - Account filed in estate of John SCOTT, dec'd. (1)

11-17-1829 - John ALEXANDER, native of Ireland. Naturalization. Declaration of intention filed at Nov. term 1827 court. Oath by John Mitchell and Henry Grim. (2)

11-17-1829 - Robert CRAWFORD a native of Ireland. Naturalization. Declaration of intention filed at Nov. term 1827 court. Oath by John Mitchell and Henry Grim. (2)

11-17-1829 - Washington JOHNSTON appointed adms. de bonis non of the estate of James CRAIG, dec'd. (3)

11-17-1829 - Joshua Cochrane appointed adms. of the estate of Joshua COCKRANE, dec'd. (4)

11-17-1829 - Jane Montgomery appointed guardian of John MONTGOMERY aged 8 yrs., James Montgomery aged 4 yrs. and Nancy Montgomery aged 2 yrs., minor heirs of James Montgomery, dec'd. (4)

11-17-1829 - Will of Samuel THOMPSON proven in court. (4)

11-17-1829 - Account filed in estate of Josiah SIMPSON, dec'd. (9)

11-17-1829 - Account filed in estate of Jacob COURTRIGHT, dec'd. (9)

11-17-1829 - Account filed in estate of Benjamin KILBOURN, dec'd. (9)

11-17-1829 - Account filed in estate of Wm JOHNSON, dec'd. (9)

11-17-1829 - Account filed in estate of George MILLER, dec'd. (10)

11-17-1829 - Phebe Smith, widow and Sianey Smith appointed adms. of the estate of Amos SMITH, dec'd. (12)

11-17-1829 - John Frew appointed guardian of Calvin REASONER aged 7 yrs., minor heir of Peter D. Reasoner, dec'd. (18)

12-25-1829 - Rebecca Johnston and Joseph W. Rue appointed adms. of the estate of James JOHNSTON, dec'd. (21)

3-29-1830 - Jacob Stauffer appointed adms. of the estate of Joshua RUSSELL, dec'd. (25)

3-29-1830 - Wm McCASKEY and Elizabeth McCaskey appointed adms. of the estate of David ANDREWS, dec'd. (25)

3-29-1830 - Wm McCaskey appointed adms. of the estate of Hugh McCASKEY, dec'd. (26)

3-29-1830 - William Lynch appointed guardian of Mary WOLF aged 14 yrs. (26)

3-29-1830 - Catherine Miller appointed admsrx. of the estate of Jacob MILLER, dec'd. (26)

3-29-1830 - Charles WILLIAMS granted license to keep a ferry over the Muskingum, Tuscarawas and Whitewoman Rivers opposite the town of Coshocton for one year. (26)

3-29-1830 - James OSBURN granted license to keep tavern in town of Caldersburg. (26)

3-29-1830 - John Rodgers and Tamson Brownfield appointed adms. of the estate of Robert BROWNFIELD, dec'd. (28)

3-29-1830 - Nathan Wright appointed guardian of Sally Ann McCURDY aged 8 yrs., Mary Jane McCURDY aged 7 yrs., John McCURDY aged 5 yrs. and Malinda McCURDY aged 4 yrs. (28)

3-29-1830 - Account filed in estate of Andrew SCOTT, who left will. (28)

313

3-29-1830 - Will of John CRAWFORD proven in court with George Crawford as executor; widow, Ann Crawford having refused to be executor. (28)

3-29-1830 - Will of John GRAVES proven in court; Westley Graves and Joseph McMorris, executors; widow, Mary Graves elected to retain dower. (29)

3-29-1830 - Samuel Lee appointed guardian of Charles SCOTT aged 18 yrs. and Joseph SCOTT aged 15 yrs. (29)

3-29-1830 - Stephen Morris appointed guardian of James RUSEL (RUPEL) aged 5 yrs., minor heirs of Joshua RUSEL (RUPEL). (note: surname is spelled as Rusel but given as Rupel in parenthesis in the original record.) (30)

3-29-1830 - William HENDERSON granted license to keep tavern in West Carlisle. (30)

3-29-1830 - Account filed in estate of William DAVIDSON, dec'd. (32)

3-29-1830 - Account filed in estate of John SCOTT, dec'd. (32)

3-29-1830 - Theopholies PHILLIPS granted license to keep tavern in Caldersburgh.(38)

3-29-1830 - Styker MORGAN granted license to keep tavern in town of Tuscarawas. (39)

3-29-1830 - Oliver B. Randles appointed guardian of Mary Margarett SOVERNS and Daniel SOVERNS (note: no ages given). (39)

3-29-1830 - Account filed in estate of James ROBINSON, dec'd. (41)

3-30-1830 - Adam FLETCHER granted ferry license over the Tuscarawas River in Oxford twp. from Coshocton to New Philadelphia. (41)

3-30-1830 - Account filed in estate of Elijah SHAW, dec'd. (41)

3-30-1830 - William RAVENSCRAFT, a Rev. soldier. On this 30 March 1830 personally appeared in open court William Ravencraft a resident of said county aged between 65 and 70 years who being duly sworn...makes the following declaration in order to obtain the provisions made by the act of Congress of March 1818 and the 1st May 1820...enlisted for the term of 3 yrs. in the company of Capt. Benjamin Oates of Col. Ruford's Regt and Gen. Scotts Brigade in 1778 in the Virginia line upon the continental establishment, that he was enlisted in the county of Beckly, Virginia and that he continued to serve in the said corps until Oct. 1780 when he and regiment was discharged from the service in Nilesborough, North Carolina...that his name is not on the pension roll of any state...further states that in May 1818 he made application for a pension but was not able to procure the necessary evidence of his service and that he has made attempts since to obtain such pension but failed...and in pursuance of the act of 1 May 1820 swears that he was a resident citizen of the United States on 18 Mar. 1818...Schedule of my property of every kind which I was the owner of this 18 Mar 1818 except necessary beds and bedding and wearing apparel. Two horses worth $120., 2 cows worth $18., 18 head of young cattle worth $5. each, 12 sheep worth $1. each, 2 horses same as above stated worth $70., 20 head of hogs worth 50 cents each, 3 cows worth $7. each. I have no real estate of any kind whatever, am a farmer but able to labour very little. I have a wife named Rebecca and no other person who renders me any assistance or contributes to my support. Signed: Wm. Ravenscraft. (44)

3-31-1830 - Benjamin CHANCE granted license to keep tavern in Caldersburg. (55)

3-31-1830 - Jeremiah Collens SMITH aged 19 yrs., Laura SMITH aged 16 yrs. and Amy Maria SMITH aged 14 yrs. chose Asahel Platt as their guardian and said Platt also appointed to serve as guardian of Mary Abigail SMITH aged 11 yrs., Isaac SMITH aged 9 yrs., Amos SMITH aged 6 yrs. and Clarissa SMITH aged 1 yr. in place of John Williams who was former guardian. (56)

3-31-1830 - Robert WHITTEN aged 16 yrs. and Nanlua WHITTEN aged 14 yrs. chose Joseph
Burns as their guardian and Burns also appointed to serve as guardian of
Joanna WHITTEN aged 10 yrs., Eliza WHITTEN aged 4 yrs. and William WHITTEN
aged 7 yrs. (56)
3-31-1830 - James Robinson appointed guardian of Amanda JOHNSTON a deaf and dumb
woman. (56)
7-27-1830 - Phillip RUREH granted license to keep tavern in New Bedford. (58)
7-27-1830 - Richard FOWLER granted license to keep tavern where he now lives on state
road between Coshocton and Plainfield. (58)
7-27-1830 - Henry RAMSEY granted license to keep tavern in Keene. (58)
7-27-1830 - Christena Billman appointed admsrx. of the estate of Andrew BILLMAN,
dec'd. (59)
7-27-1830 - George Saucerman and Elizabeth Macoray appointed adms. of the estate
of John MACORAY, dec'd. (59)
7-27-1830 - Aaron HEATON granted license to keep tavern in West Bedford. (61)
7-27-1830 - Henry Bice appointed adms. of estate of Samuel BICE. (63)
7-28-1830 - Rebecca JOHNSTON granted license to keep tavern in Coshocton. (68)
7-28-1830 - Thomas C. RICKETT granted license to keep tavern in Coshocton. (68)
7-28-1830 - John Pingery appointed adms. of the estate of John PINGERY, dec'd. (69)
7-29-1830 - Thomas PLATT aged 17 yrs. chose Thomas Johnston as his guardian. (79)
7-29-1830 - Thomas PICKETT appointed adms. of the estate of Joseph HENDERSON, dec'd.
(79)
7-29-1830 - Samuel LOVE native of Ireland. Naturalization. Declaration of intention
made at Aug. term 1827 of court. Oaths by Mordicai Chalfant and John Frew.(80)
7-29-1830 - John RODERICK granted license to keep tavern in Plainfield. (81)
11-15-1830 - Charles WILLIAMS granted ferry license over Muskingham, Tuscarawas and
Whitewoman River opposite town of Coshocton. (84)
11--15-1830 - Conrad Powelson appointed adms. of the estate of Peter RAMBO, dec'd.(85)
11-15-1830 - Simon WOLF (no aged stated) chose Kitty Wolf as his guardian. (85)
11-15-1830 - William LYNCH granted license to keep tavern in Perry twp. where he
now lives. (85)
11-15-1830 - Peter Rigle appointed guardian of George MILLER. aged 10 yrs. & 10 mos.,
Rebecca MILLER aged 2 yrs. & 10 mos. and Mary MILLER aged 4 yrs. & 10 mos.,
minor heirs of Jacob MILLER, dec'd. John MILLER aged 14 yrs & 10 mos. and
Anne MILLER aged 12 yrs. chose Peter Rigle as their guardian. (86)
11-15-1830 - George McCASKEY a native of Ireland. Naturalization. Declaration of
intention filed at Nov. term 1827 court. Oath of Henry Grim and John Mitchell.
(86)
11-15-1830 - Will of John DUNLAP proven in court. (87)
11-15-1830 - William Henderson appointed guardian of Andrew McLANAHAN aged 10 yrs.,
Elizabeth McLANAHAN aged 9 yrs., Mary McLANAHAN aged 7 yrs., Susannah
McLANAHAN aged 6 yrs., Jane McLANAHAN aged 4 yrs. and John L. McLANAHAN
aged 2 yrs., minor heirs of John McLanahan, dec'd. (88)
11-15-1830 - Joseph Wright appointed guardian of Emily GRAVES aged 11 yrs., minor
heir of John Graves, dec'd. (88)
11-15-1830 - Daniel BOYD a native of Ireland. Naturalization. Declaration of intention made at July term 1828 court. Oaths by John Crowley and Ephraim
Thayer. (89)
11-15-1830 - John Clark and John Horn appointed adms. of the estate of John Denlap,
dec'd. (89)

11-15-1830 - John Carnahan and Adam Carnahan appointed adms. of the estate of James
        CARNAHAN, dec'd.   (95)
11-15-1830 - Andrew NULL a native of Scotland made his declaration of intention to
        become citizen.   (95)
11-15-1830 - Eliza McMillen appointed admsrx. of the estate of John McMILLEN, dec'd.
        (95)
11-15-1830 - John Smith appointed guardian of Mary JEFFERIES a girl incapable of
        handling her affairs.   (96)
11-15-1830 - John TRIMBLE a native of Ireland. Naturalization, Oath by Wm. Hender-
        son. Trimble arrived in United States before 1812.   (97)
11-15-1830 - Will of John JONES proven in court.   (97)
11-16-1830 - Will of Abraham THOMPSON, swc'd proven in court.   (103)
11-17-1830 - Francis A. STAFFORD granted license to keep tavern at his home in
        Washington twp.   (105)
11-19-1830 - John CROWLEY appointed inspector of pork, beef, lard and butter.   (119)
3-21-1831 - John McCULLON granted license to keep tavern in Coshocton.   (123)
3-21-1831 - Will of Richard WILLIAMS, dec'd proven in court.   (124)
3-21-1831 - Francis Miller appointed adms. of the estate of George MILLER, dec'd.(124)
3-21-1831 - Evelina GRAVES (no age given) chose Joseph Wright as her guardian.   (124)
3-21-1831 - Frederick Bentley appointed as guardian of heirs of Joshua RUSSEL (RUPEL)
        to replace Jacob Bice.   (127)
3-21-1831 - Nathan Dean appointed adms. of the estate of James WILLIAMS, dec'd. (127)
3-21-1831 - Thomas B. LEWIS granted licenseto keep tavern in Newport.   (127)
3-21-1831 - George ECKMAN granted license to keep tavern at home in Jefferson twp.
        (127)
3-21-1831 - Elias JAMES granted license to keep tavern at Claysville.   (127)
3-21-1831 - James CARSON a native of Ireland made his declaration of intention to
        become citizen.   (127)
3-21-1831 - Robert SHANKLIN a native of Ireland made his declaration of intention to
        become citizen.   (128)
3-21-1831 - Will of Thomas HESLIP proven in court.   (128)
3-21-1831 - Will of William WILLIS proven in court.   (129)
3-21-1831 - Theopolus PHILIPS granted license to keep tavern in Roscoe.   (130)
3-21-1831 - Wilson CARP (no age given) chose James Lisk as his guardian, said Wilson
        being a minor heir of Adam CARP, dec'd.   (130)
3-21-1831 - John Smith appointed guardian of Emily JEFFERS aged 11 yrs. and Robert
        JEFFERS aged 2 yrs., minor children of Mary Jeffers.   (132)
3-22-1831 - Windell Miller appointed adms. of the estate of Isaac MILLER, dec'd.(133)
3-22-1831 - Henry EVANS aged 20 yrs. and George W. EVANS aged 16 yrs. chose James
        Jones as their guardian, they being minor heirs of Isaac Evans, dec'd.   (134)
3-22-1831 - William RANKLIN aged 17 yrs., minor heir of David RANKLIN, chose James
        Renfrew as his guardian.   (137)
3-22-1831 - Joseph KILLY aged 18 yrs., minor heir of Eli KILLEY chose Joseph Burres
        as his guardian.   (137)
3-23-1831 - Moses L. NEEL granted license to keep tavern in Coshocton.   (146)
3-23-1831 - Benjamin CHANCE granted license to keep tavern in Jackson twp.   (146)
6-13-1831 - Robert HOPPER aged 14 yrs. and Arabelle HOPPER aged 12 yrs. chose William
        Brown as their guardian with Brown also appointed to serve as guardian of Jane
        HOPPER aged 10 yrs. and Elenor HOPPER aged 8 yrs., all minor heirs of Samuel
        HOPPER, dec'd.   (151)

6-13-1831 - John Frew appointed adms. de bonis of estate of James CRAIG in stead
   of Washington B. Johnston adms. de bonis who has since dec'd.   (153)
6-13-1831 - John Frew appointed adms. de bonis of estate of Esther CRAIG, dec'd
   in stead of Washington B. Johnston adms. de bonis who has since dec'd.(153)
6-13-1831 - John G. Pigman granted ferry license over Wills Creek at Taylors. (154)
6-13-1831 - Calvin HILL granted license to keep tavern at home in East Union. (154)
6-14-1831 - Joseph Burns appointed guardian of Emiline JONES under age of 14 yrs.,
   minor heir of Thomas Jones, dec'd.   (171)
6-14-1831 - Andrew Weather appointed adms. of estate of William SPEAKS, dec'd.(171)
10-6-1831 - David Moor appointed adms. of the estate of Margaret THOMPSON, dec'd.
   (183)
10-6-1831 - Samuel Elliott and Daniel Boyd appointed adms. of estate of Moses
   ELLIOTT, dec'd.   (183)
10-6-1831 - Isabel Platt appointed adms. of estate of Joseph RUSSELL, dec'd. (183)
10-6-1831 - Isabel Platt appointed guardian of Asahel RUSSELL aged 2 yrs. in Aug.
   last and Laura RUSSEL aged 4 yrs. & 8 mos., minor heirs of Joseph Russel.
   (183)
10-6-1831 - Will of George AMORY proven in court.   (184)
10-6-1831 - Joseph Burns and Mary Cartright appointed adms. of the estate of Abraham
   CARTRIGHT, dec'd.   (185)
11-21-1831 - Joseph Welch of Roscoe appointed adms. of the estate of Joseph SHOE-
   MAKER, dec'd.   (188)
3-12-1832 - Samuel THOMAS aged 14 yrs. & 8 mos. chose Moris Morgan as his guardian.
   (189)
3-12-1832 - David WYLIE aged 15 yrs., minor heir of Samuel Wylie chose Abraham
   Gardner as his guardian.   (190)
3-12-1832 - Will of Elisha BURRIS, dec'd proven in court.   (190)
3-12-1832 - John MONROE a native of Scotland makes his declaration of intention to
   become citizen.   (191)
3-12-1832 - John QUIGLEY granted license to keep tavern in West Bedford.   (194)
3-12-1832 - William LITTLE granted license to keep tavern in West Bedford.   (194)
3-12-1832 - Jacob LASH aged 15 yrs. chose Catherine Lash as his guardian.   (194)
3-13-1832 - Phillip RHINEHARTT granted license to keep tavern in New Bedford. (196)
3-13-1832 - Rebecca JOHNSTON granted license to keep tavern at home in Roscoe.(197)
3-13-1832 - Thomas L. Rue appointed adms. de bonis non of the estate of William
   DAYTON, dec'd.   (197)
3-13-1832 - Rev. James PEREGIN a minister of the Presbyterian Church granted license
   to solemnize marriages.   (197)
3-13-1932 - William Henderson appointed guardian of Manuel THOMPSON aged 12 yrs.,
   William THOMPSON aged 10 yrs., Rhode THOMPSON aged 8 yrs. and Hanah THOMP-
   SON aged 6 yrs.   (198)
3-13-1832 - Charles ADAMS a native of Ireland files his declaration of intention
   to become citizen.   (198)
3-13-1832 - Moses ADAMS a native of Ireland files his declaration of intention to
   become citizen.   (198)
3-13-1832 - Will of Clauna BACKUS certified in Ross Co., Ohio by David W. Matthews
   a legatee with copy forwarded to this county.   (199)
3-13-1832 - Will of James HAMILTON certified in Cumberland Co., Penna. with copy
   forwarded to this county.   (199)
3-13-1832 - Moses MORGAN granted license to keep tavern at his home in Oxford Twp.
   (199)

3-13-1832 - Richard FOWLER granted license to keep tavern at his home in Linton
       twp, (199)
3-13-1832 - Theopholis PHILLIPS granted license to keep tavern in Roscoe. (200)
3-13-1832 - Stryker MORGAN granted license to keep tavern in Tuscarawas twp. (200)
3-13-1832 - Isaac EVANS granted ferry license across the Tuscarawas River near
       Evansburg. (200)
3-13-1832 - John BOYD a native of Ireland files his declaration of intention to
       become citizen. (205)
3-13-1832 - John ROSS a native of Ireland files his declaration of intention to
       become citizen. (206)
3-13-1832 - Samuel Lee guardian of Joseph SCOTT a minor by indenture dated 7-5-1831
       bound said minor as an apprentice to William ROBINSON of said county until
       minor is 21 years of age. (214)
3-14-1832 - Charles WILLIAMS granted ferry license across the Muskingum and
       Tuscarawas River near Coshocton. (217)
3-14-1832 - Joseph DAVIS aged 15 yrs. chose Thomas Powell as his guardian. (217)
3-14-1832 - John Wagner appointed adms. of the estate of George LOCE, Jr. (217)
3-14-1832 - Samuel SPENCER aged 19 yrs., Joshua Osburn SPENCER aged 18 yrs.,
       Elisa SPENCER aged 17 yrs. and Sarah SPENCER aged 15 yrs. chose Nathan
       Spencer as their guardian and Nathan also appointed to serve as guardian
       of William SPENCER aged 9 yrs., Edmund SPENCER aged 7 yrs. and Nathan
       SPENCER aged 6 yrs. Sarah SPENCER aged 14 yrs. and Nancy SPENCER aged
       12 yrs. chose Joseph Welsh as their guardian with Welsh also appointed to
       serve as guardian of Catharine SPENCER aged 10 yrs., Margarite SPENCER
       aged 8 yrs. and Elisa SPENCER aged 2 yrs. (218)
3-14-1832 - Lucinda SPEAKES aged 18 yrs. and Elisa SPEAKES aged 14 yrs. chose
       Michael Nogle as their guardian. (218)
3-14-1832 - Michael Nogle appointed to serve as guardian of Namott SPEAKES aged
       11 yrs. and John SPEAKES aged 18 yrs. (219)
3-15-1832 - Jeremiah C. Smith appointed guardian of Jane SMITH aged 18 mos. (226)
3-15-1832 - Thomas Powell guardian of Joseph DAVIS a minor by indenture dated
       3-4-1832 bound said minor as apprentice to Wm. H. Johnson until he is
       21 years of age. (226)

COSHOCTON COUNTY, OHIO - COMMON PLEAS RECORDS 1832-1835

The following records were abstracted from Record Book D. Pages on which original record may be found are given in parenthesis.

Mar. 1832 - Wm. HENDERSON guardian of minor Heirs of John McLENNAHAN, dec'd. Petition to sell land. Filed 3-17-1830. Land, NW¼ Section 6, Township 4, Range 8. Children: Andrew, Elizabeth Susannah, Mary Jane and John L. McLennahan, aged 2 to 11 yrs. (9)

3-12-1832 - John MONROE, native of Scotland makes Declaration of Intention to become citizen. (50)

3-13-1832 - Charles ADAMS, native of Ireland, makes Declaration of Intention to become citizen. (51) Moses ADAMS, native of Ireland, makes Declaration of Intention to become citizen. (52) John BOYD, native of Ireland, makes Declaration of Intention to become citizen. (53) John ROSS, native of Ireland makes Declaration of Intention to become citizen. (54)

Mar. 1832 - Nancy EDINGTON, unmarried, of Pike twp. vs. Samuel CHANEY. Bastardy. (55)

Mar. 1832 - Joseph EVANS vs. George EVANS, et al. In Partition. Filed 3-22-1831. Isaac Evans, dec'd. Land; 414 acres pt. 2nd ¼, Township 5, Range 4 conveyed by deed recorded 2-7-1805 Muskingum Co., Ohio, also pt. 2nd ¼ and 1st ¼, Township 5, Range 4, Military tract and other land descriptions, mentions land in Tuscarawas County, Ohio. Children: Mary wife of George Harris, Isaac Evans, Elizabeth Evans, Martha Evans. Henry Evans and George W. Evans; the last two being minors. (59)

Mar. 1832 - Rev. James PEREGIN, Presbyterian, granted license to perform marriages. (70)

May 1832 - John WAGONER and Mary his wife vs. James GRAVES, et al. Petition for Dower. Filed 11-13-1830. Land; 73 acres E pt. SW¼, 77 acres W pt. SW¼ and 160 acres SE¼ Section 16, Township 4, Range 7. John GRAVES Sr., dec'd. Widow, Mary now the wife of Joseph Wagner; she married Graves in Ohio, married 10-21-1830 to Wagoner. Children: James Graves, Bailess Graves, Westley Graves, Henderson Graves, John Graves, Nancy late Graves wife of Phillip Williams, Betsey late Graves wife of Zachariah Ogle, Emily Graves and Enilina Graves. (75)

May 1832 - Mary Magdalene MOORE vs. William BARKLESS. Bastardy. (91)

May 1832 - Matthew DUNCAN vs. Elizabeth DUNCAN, et al. Land, NW¼ Section 5, Township 5, Range 8, Matthew Duncan exchanged said land with Samuel Duncan in his lifetime for tract of land in Fayette Co., Pa. Samuel DUNCAN, dec'd. Widow, Elizabeth Duncan. Heirs: Isabella and Mary Jane Duncan. (110)

5-28-1832 - Henry RAMSEY, native of Ireland, makes Declaration of Intention to become citizen. (149) Gilbert McKEE, native of Ireland, makes Declaration of Intention to become citizen. (151)

319

5-30-1832 - James McCOY, native of Ireland, makes Declaration of Intention to become citizen.   (151)

Oct. 1832 - Sarah GIBSON vs. Bradford BORDEN. Bastardy.   (166)

Oct. 1832 - Richard MOOD vs. Sarah CAIN et al. Petition to make deed. Filed 5-30-1832. Land, 200 acres whereon the town of West Bedford lays. Frederick CROW, dec'd. Widow, Sarah late Crow now the wife of Aaron Cain. Heirs: Elizabeth and Daniel Crow.   (179)

Oct. 1832 - Alexander McCOWAN adms. of James CALDER, dec'd vs. Sophronia CALDER. Petition to make deed. Filed 5-30-1832. Land, Lot #16 in Caldersburg (now called Roscoe) contracted to John Darnes by Calder. Widow, (not named) now the wife of Benjamin Chance. Heirs: Sophronia, Emily and James Calder; minors, Alexander McGowan, guardian.   (181)

Oct. 1832 - Joseph WELCH adms. of Joseph Shoemaker, dec'd vs. Lena SHOEMAKER, et al. Petition to make deed. Filed 5-30-1832. Land, 80 acres W pt. SE¼ Section 11, Township 5, Range 4, also 80 acres E½ SW¼ Section 11, Township 5, Range 7, contracted to Anthony Ricketts and Sarah Compton. Widow, Lena Shoemaker. Heirs: George and Anna Shoemaker, minors.   (183)

10-15-1832 - Thomas CRAWFORD, native of Ireland. Naturalization. Crawford arrived in United States prior to 1812.   (198)

10-16-1832 - Benjamin FORD, native of England, makes Declaration of Intention to become citizen. (198) Mathew TRIMBLE, native of Ireland. Naturalization. Trimble arrived in United States before 1812. (199) Alexander HAY, native of Ireland. Naturalization. (199)

10-17-1832 - Andrew HUTCHINSON, native of Ireland. Naturalization. Made his Declaration of Intention Nov. 1829. (200) William BACH, native of England, makes his Declaration of Intention to become citizen. (200) John LOVE, native of Ireland. Naturalization. Made his Declaration of Intention August 1827.(201)

4-8-1833 - Conyngham ROSS, native of Ireland. Naturalization. (241) Francis CUNNINGHAM, native of Ireland. Naturalization. (241)

4-9-1833 - John ELLIOTT, native of Great Britian. Naturalization. (242)

4-10-1833 - Patrick McKEE, native of Ireland. Naturalization. Has been in United States 14 yrs. (242) William NEILL, native of Scotland. Naturalization. (243) John ROLES, native of England. Naturalization. (243)

4-7-1833 - William STUBBS, native of England, makes his Declaration of Intention to become citizen.   (244)

10-29-1833 - Jacob BOWEN, native of England, makes Declaration of Intention to become citizen.   (351)

10-30-1833 - James JENNINGS, native of England, makes Declaration of Intention to become citizen. (351)

11-1-1833 - Francis JOHNSON, native of Ireland makes Declaration of Intention to become citizen. (352) Isaac LIGHTBODY, native of Ireland, makes Declaration of Intention to become citizen. (352) Isaac HINGOOD(?), native of England makes Declaration of Intention to become citizen. (353) William K. Johnson, native of Ireland. Naturalization. Made Declaration of Intention Sept. 1825.(354) Robert BARTON, native of Ireland, makes Declaration of Intention to become citizen. (354)

10-31-1833 - William LOVE, native of Ireland. Naturalization. Love arrived in United States before 1812. (355) James TAYLOR, native of England, makes Declaration of Intention to become citizen. (355)

10-28-1833 - Rev. Hiram WRIGHT, Church of Christ, license to perform marriages. (356) Rev. Seth WICKHAM, Baptist Church, license to perform marriages. (356)

10-29-1833 - Edward Laughead, native of Ireland, makes Declaration of Intention to become citizen. (356)

Oct. 1833 - John ROBINSON and Martha his wife vs. Henry C. COOPER. Petition for Partition. Filed 10-28-1833. Land NE¼ Section 22, Township 4, Range 8. Noah COOPER, dec'd. Widow, Martha late Cooper now wife of John Robinson. Five children: Mary M. wife of James Robinson; Henry C. Cooper, a minor of Crawford Co., Ohio; two children deceased without heirs; fifth child not mentioned or named. (357)

4-22-1834 - Richard D. WALLES, native of England, makes Declaration of Intention to become citizen. (418) Alexander McCULLOH, native of Ireland. Naturalization. (418) John COLES, native of England, makes Declaration of Intention to become citizen. (419)

4-24-1834 - William GORAM, native of England. Naturalization. (419)

4-21-1834 - Sedwick RICE, Baptist Church, license to perform marriages. (420)

June 1834 - Joseph WILLIAMS, adms. de Bonis non of Samuel BICE, dec'd vs. Heirs of Samuel BICE, dec'd. Petition to sell land. Filed 4-9-1833. Henry Bice former adms. moved from county. Land, W½ lot 12, 3rd Section, 7th Township, 6th Range. Heirs: Catharine Smith formerly Bice wife of Jeremiah C. Smith, her daughter—Mary Jane Smith; Henry Bice; John Bice; William Bice; Joseph Bice; Jacob Winner and Mary his wife; and Samuel Bice. (434)

6-30-1834 - Rev. James HAYS, Central Christian Church, license to perform marriages. (503)

7-2-1834 - John LOCKART, native of Ireland. Naturalization. Made Declaration of Intention Nov. 1830 in Jefferson Co., Ohio. (504) Thomas LOVE, native of Ireland. Naturalization. (504) Andrew McKEE, native of Ireland makes Declaration of Intention to become citizen. (504)

June 1834 – Moses MORGAN adms. of Benjamin NORMAN Sr., dec'd vs. Heirs of Benjamin NORMAN Jr., dec'd. Petition to sell land. Filed 7-30-1831. Land, 266 acres 2nd quarter, 5th Township 4th Range, Military tract. Benjamin Norman, Sr., dec'd. Widow, Elizabeth now the wife of Thomas Norris. Heirs: John Norman, dec'd, his widow Mary now Mary Ponday; Daniel Norman; Jabez Norman; Isaac.Norman; Abraham Norman; Benjamin Norman; Samuel Norman; James Norman; George Norman; William Norman; Rosannah Norman; Andrew Norman; Thomas Norman; Jonathan Johnston Norman; John Norman, Elizabeth Norman; Nancy Norman; Mary Norman; Andrew Norman; and Margaret Norman; the last eleven named are minors. (494)

Oct. 1834 – John RODGERS and Tamson BROWNFIELD adms. of Robert BROWNFIELD Sr., dec'd vs. Robert BROWNFIELD Jr., et al. Petition to sell land. Filed 7-13-1833. Land, lot 29 in Plainfield. Widow, Tamson Brownfield. Only son, Robert Brownfield Jr. (520)

Oct. 1834 – John FREU guardian of Minor Heirs of Adam JOHNSTON, dec'd. Petition to sell real estate. Filed 4-24-1834. Heirs: Susan, Charles H., George W., Mathew, William and Hannah Johnston. (557)

Oct. 1834 – David MEREDITH executor of John WELDON, dec'd vs. George WELDON, et al. Petition to execute deed. Heirs: George Weldon, Jacob Weldon, Michael Weldon, Christopher Weldon, Henry Fry and Catharine his wife and Frederick Weldon. (561)

10-27-1834 – John DANIS (or DAVIS), native of England, makes his Declaration of Intention to become citizen. (604) John Ockendon, native of England. Naturalization. Made Declaration of Intention Oct. 1829 in Muskingum Co., Ohio. (604)

10-28-1834 – John ARNOLD, native of England. Naturalization. Made Declaration of Intention Aug. 1829 in Muskingum Co., Ohio. (605) Rev. Thomas DUNN, M. E. Church, license to perform marriages. (605)

10-29-1834 – Fracis FRITSCHY, native of Germany. Naturalization. Made Declaration of Intention 9-24-1832. (606)

Apr. 1835 – Shadrack CASTEEL and Mary CESSNA adms. of John CESSNA, dec'd vs. Stephen CESSNA, et al. Petition to sell land. Filed 10-29-1833. Land, 68 acres E½ SW¼ Section 4, Township 4, Range 9. Widow, Mary Cessna. Heirs: Stephen Cessna, Jonathan Cessna, Charles Cessna, John Cessna Jr., William Cessna, Oliver Cessna, Rachel late Cessna wife of John Shrake, Nancy late Cessna wife of William Lement, Rebecca late Cessna wife of Lyod Lement, Elizabeth Cessna, Mary Cessna and Hannah Cessna. (609)

Apr. 1835 – James RAVENSCRAFT vs. James PERCIVAL, et al. In Partition. Filed 11-21-1833. Land, 450 acres Lot 1 NW corner 2nd quarter, 6th township, 4th range, military tract. James PERCIVAL, dec'd. Four children: Milton Percival, James Percival, Dolly wife of Moses Cook and Charlotte wife of Albert Odell.(614)

Apr. 1835 – William BROWN guardian of the HEIRS of Samuel HOPPER, dec'd. Petition to sell land. Filed 7-1-1834. Land, being with log house in West Carlisle. Heirs: Jane, Elenor, Anabella and Robert Hopper. (630)

Apr. 1835 - Aaron SPEAKES vs Francis SPEAKES, et al. Petition for Partition. Land, N½ part 2nd Section 6th township, 7th range, military tract. William SPEAKES, dec'd. No widow. Nine children: Aaron Speakes; Francis Speakes; Delia wife of John Holt; Elizabeth wife of Silas Bain; Margaret wife of Elias D. Albert; Catharine, dec'd wife of Nathan Spencer, her seven children—Osburn, Alice, Sarah, William, Mary, Edmund and Nathan Spencer; Mary, dec'd, wife of Phineas Spencer, her five children—Sarah, Eliza, Nancy, Catherine and Margaret Spencer; John Speakes, dec'd, his five children—Lucinda, Charles, Elizabeth, Harriett and John Speakes; Maria wife of Nathan Spencer. (616)

4-13-1835 - John LOCKARD, native of Ireland, makes Declaration of Intention to become citizen. (661) William WALKER, native of Ireland, makes Declaration of Intention to become citizen. (661) Hugh CASSIDY, native of Ireland makes Declaration of Intention to become citizen. (662) Alexander LAUGHEAD, native of Ireland, makes Declaration of Intention to become citizen. (662) Robert ADAMS, native of Ireland, Naturalization. (663) John ADAMS, native of Ireland. Naturalization. (663) Alexander SCOTT, native of Ireland. Naturalization. (664) George McCULLOUGH, native of Ireland. Naturalization. (664)

4-14-1835 - Benjamin FORD, native of England. Naturalization. (665)

July 1835 - Andrew McCLENNAHAM, et al vs. Elizabeth and Stephen Cessna. In Partition. Filed 6-14-1834. Land, NW¼ Section 6 and SE¼ Section 5, Township 4, Range 8. John McCLENNAHAM, dec'd. Widow, Elizabeth late McClennaham now wife of Stephen Cessna of Hardin Co., Ohio. Heirs: Andrew, Elizabeth, Mary, Susannah, James and John McClennaham; all minors by Charles Wright their guardian. (676)

July 1835 - David MYERS vs. Isabella MYERS, et al. Petition for Partition. Filed 2-11-1835. Land, S¼ Section 6, Township 5, Range 9 Coshocton Co. and pt. NE¼ Section 10, Township 5, Range 10 Knox County, Ohio. Henry MYERS Sr., dec'd. Widow, Isabella Myers. Children: James Myers, John Myers, dec'd, leaving no heirs, Nancy Myers, Margaret Myers, Mary late Myers wife of Van Farmer of Licking Co., Ohio, Eliza late Myers wife of Samuel Hains (or Harris) of parts unknown, David Myers, Rebecca Myers and Henry Myers Jr.; the last two being minors. (701)

The following records were taken from Book E. Pages on which record may be found in original records are given in parenthesis.

July 1835 - Samuel GREGG, native of Ireland makes his declaration of intention to become citizen - 7-20-1835. (2)

July 1835 - Thomas DAVIS, native of England makes his declaration of intention to become citizen. John McCOY, native of England makes his declaration of intention to become citizen. 7-20-1835. (3)

July 1835 - John ELDER, native of Ireland; Naturalization; declaration of intention made July 1829 at Coshocton. Benjamin GRAHAM, native of Ireland makes his declaration of intention to become citizen. 7-21-1835. (4)

July 1835 - Condy BOYLE, native of Ireland makes his declaration of intention to become citizen. 7-21-1835. (5)

July 1835 - John LOOZE, etal. vs. Polly KNISELY widow of George LOOZE Jr. and Margaret Looze heir of George Looze Jr. - Petition for Partition. Filed 6-13-1829. George Looze Sr., dec'd. Widow, Barbara Looze. Land: 151 acres SE¼ Section 1, Township 4, Range 5; 81½ acres pt. SW¼ Section 5, Township 4, Range 4; 5 acres pt. 2nd quarter Township 5, Range 4 Military Donation lands; Lots 240 & 319 Coshocton; and Lot 18 Plainfield. Children: John; Jacob; Christian; David; Philip; Adam; Daniel; George Looze Jr., his widow Polly, his children-- Catherine Looze and Margaret Looze of Muskingum Co., Ohio. (6)

Oct. 1835 - John BURTNOTT, etal. vs. John DILLON, etal. Petition for Partition. Filed 7-16-1835. Land, SW¼ Section 8, Township 5, Range 9. Peter Dillon, dec'd; his will dated 6-30-1823, probated August 1823. Widow, Mary Dillon now Mary Burtnett. Children: Anna Dillon wife of Daniel Berry, aged 22 years; John Dillon aged 19 yrs.; Simon Dillon aged 17 yrs.; and Thomas Dillon aged 14 yrs. (58)

Apr. 1836 - Nathaniel KERAN, etal. vs. Elizabeth LYNCH, etal. Petition for Partition. Filed 2-18-1834. Cornelius Lynch, dec'd, died fall of 1828. Land, 80 acres W½ NW¼ Section 11, Township 5, Range 9, Widow, Elizabeth Lynch. Children: Eliza Lynch now wife of Nathaniel Keran, Cynthia Lynch, Nancy Lynch, Letty Lynch, Mathus Lynch and Aaron Lynch. (114)

Apr. 1836 - Jehu WRIGHT adms. of estate of John FOGLE, dec'd vs. Charles NORRIS, etal. Petition to sell real estate. Filed 6-15-1834. Land, Lot 28 in Town of West Bedford. John Fogle, dec'd. Widow, Susannah Fogle now the wife of Charles Norris. Children: Julyan Fogle and Mary Fogle. (119)

Apr. 1836 - Abner NORRIS adms. of estate of Samuel COOKSEY, dec'd vs. Elizabeth COOKSEY, etal. Petition to sell real estate. Filed 1-23-1835. Land, E½ NE¼ Section 17, Township 4, Range 7, Military District. Widow, Elizabeth Cooksey. Children: Abner Cooksey aged 3 yrs. and James W. Cooksey aged 18 months. (123)

Apr. 1836 - William KING, native of Germany makes his declaration of intention to become citizen. Jacob METZ, native of Germany makes his declaration of intention to become citizen. Godlip STINE, native of Germany makes his declaration of intention to become citizen. 4-25-1836. (176)

Apr. 1836 - John CROFT, native of Germany; has resided in United States 3 yrs. next; was 21 yrs. when arrived; Naturalization. William CRABTREE, native of England; has been in United States 5 yrs.; in Ohio 1 year; made his declaration of intention in November 1831 in Muskingum Co., Ohio. 4-25-1836. (177)

Apr. 1836 - Francis JOHNSON, native of Ireland; Naturalization; made declaration of intention Oct. 1833. James TAYLOR, native of England; Naturalization; made declaration of intention Oct. 1833. 4-27-1836. (178)

Apr. 1836 - Francis ELLIS, native of Ireland makes his declaration of intention to become citizen. 4-26-1836. (179)

Apr. 1836 - Rev. Linos GILBERT, minister of the Baptist Church granted license to perform matrimony. 4-25-1836. (179)

Aug. 1836 - James LISK adms. of estate of Joseph LAKE, dec'd vs. Eveline WARDEN, etal. Petition to sell land. Filed 4-14-1835. Land, 100 acres pt. 1st quarter, Township 5, Range 4, U.S. Military District. Joseph Lake, dec'd. Widow, Eveline Lake now the wife of Maleon W. Warden. Children: Cornelius Lake aged 5 yrs. and Florentine Lake aged 4 yrs. (211)

Aug. 1836 - Joseph MARSHAL adms. of estate of George MARSHALL, dec"d vs. Elinor MARSHALL, etal. Petition to convey land. Filed 4-26-1836. Land, being 170 acres part of Tract 3, Section 4, Township 6 which deceased contracted to sell half to George Beaver; deceased purchased said land from estate of the Honorable James Hamilton, Esq., father of Susan Thorn and partitioned at his death to said Susan Thorn, James Hamilton, Sarah Hamilton and Mary Hamilton. George Marshall, dec'd. Widow, Elenor Marshall. Heirs: Isabella Marshall aged 10 yrs., Wm. Marshall aged 7 yrs., Jane Marsahll aged 6 yrs., Catharine Marshall aged 4 yrs. and George Marshall aged 1 year. (249)

Aug. 1836 - Andrew McKEE, native of Ireland; Naturalization; declaration of intention made July Term 1834. David LITTLE, native of Ireland; Naturalization; declaration of intention made June Term 1834. 8-1-1836. (277)

Aug. 1836 - Edward LAUGHEAD, native of Ireland; Naturalization; declaration of intention made April 2, 1835; 8-8-1836. Isaac LOGHTBODY, native of Ireland; Naturalization; 8-10-1836. (278)

Aug. 1836 - William BACK, native of England; Naturalization; declaration of intention made Oct. 1832. 8-11-1836. (279)

Oct. 1836 - Peter BARGER vs. Catharine DUNLAP, etal. Petition to sell land. Filed 3-21-1835. Land, 100 acres pt. 3rd quarter, Township 6, Range 9, U.S. Military District. John Dunlap, dec'd. Children: Catharine, Sarah Ann, William, Lewis and Henry Dunlap by Peter Barger their guardian, of Harrison County, Ohio. (286)

Oct. 1836 - Henry RICHARDS and Mahala his wife vs. Rufus INGLES and Martha his wife.
Petition for Partition. Filed 4-22-1836. Land, 80 acres NE½ SE½ Section 19, Township 6, Range 9. Martin SMITH, dec'd. Widow, Martha now the wife of Rufus Ingles.
(352)

Oct. 1836 - James McKEE, native of Ireland makes declaration of intention to become
citizen; 10-25-1836. (359) William TRIMBLE, native of Ireland; Naturalization;
10-25-1836. (360) Walter TURNER, native of England; Naturalization; declaration of
intention made New York City 9-27-1831; 10-24-1836. (361) John DAVIS, native of
England; Naturalization; declaration of intention made Oct. 1834; 10-24-1836. Alexander GIBSON, native of Ireland; Naturalization; 10-24-1836. (362)

Oct. 1836 - John JACK, native of Ireland makes declaration of intention to become
citizen; 10-25-1836. Richard HUNTER, native of Ireland makes declaration of intention to become citizen; 10-25-1836. (363) Richard PARKER, native of Ireland
makes declaration of intention to become citizen; 10-27-1836. William STUBBS,
native of Ireland; Naturalization; declaration of intention made April 1833,
10-27-1836. (364)

Feb. 1837 - David WAGGONER adms. of estate of John KNOFF, dec'd vs. Lydia KNOFF,
etal. Petition to sell land. Filed 10-20-1835. Land, 50 acres SE corner lot 16,
Section 1 Township 5, Range 6 U.S. Military land. Heirs: Lydia Knoff, widow; Heirs
of Susan Rundel--Mary Ann, Margaret and Lydia Rundel; Wm. G. Williams and Margaret
his wife; John McCulloch minor heir of Elizabeth Daniels(?), dec'd; Sanford F. Madden
and Mary his wife; John Knoff; and John Tish and Sarah his wife. (394)

Feb. 1837 - Thomas GILLUM, etal. vs. Jacob BLACK, etal. Petition to sell land.
Filed 10-29-1834. Land, pt. Lot 21, 1st section, Township 5, Range 8 conveyed
to Jared Black, dec'd by Samuel Gillum and Jemima his wife on 2-4-1828. Jared
Black, dec'd. Widow, Sarah Black now the wife of Thomas Gillum. Children: Jacob
Black aged 13 yrs., Shepherd Black aged 12 yrs., Margaret Black aged 10 yrs.,
Charles A. Black aged 8 yrs., and Thomas Black aged 6 yrs. (403)

Feb. 1837 - John POLLOCK, native of Ireland; Naturalization; declaration of intention made Nov. 1827; 2-13-1837. (407) Thomas BROSNAHAN, native of Ireland makes
his declaration of intention to become citizen; 2-15-1837. Edward STEVENSON, native
of Great Britian makes his declaration of intention to become citizen; 2-15-1837.(408)

May 1837 - Leonard REICHARD adms. of estate of Abraham LENT, dec'd vs. Enos BARTO,
etal. Petition to sell land. Filed 4-21-1836. Land, pt. 2nd quarter, Township 5,
Range 4 Military lands. Widow, Rebecca (also known as Margaret) now wife of Enos
Barto. Heirs: Lewis Lent and Susuanna Lent; both minors. (446)

May 1837 - Henry McGLAUGHLIN and Susan his wife vs. Casper SEVERS, etal. Petition for
Partition. Filed 5-9-1836. Land, 160 acres SW½ Section 12, Township 5, Range 9, of
unappropiated military land, Perry twp. John MOWREY, dec'd. Widow, Elizabeth Mowrey
now the wife of Casper Severs. Heirs and Partition: 1/10th part, Susan late Mowrey
wife of Henry McGlaughlin; 1/10th part, Martin Mowrey; 1/10th part, Catharine Mowrey;
1/10th part, Polly Mowrey; 1/10th part, Henry Mowrey; 1/10th part, John Mowrey; 1/10
th part, Betsey Mowrey; 1/10th part, Andrew Mowrey; 1/10th part, Alexander Mowrey;
1/10th part, Conrad Mowrey; the last six named being minors. (453)

May 1837 - Moses MUSGROVE adms. of estate of James THOMAS, dec'd vs. Elizabeth
THOMAS, etal. Petition to sell land. Filed 8-9-1836. Land E½ NW¼ Section 9,
Township 4, Range 8 of unappropriated military lands. Widow, Elizabeth Thomas.
Children: Elijah, Allice Ann, Moses, George and Silas Dexter Thomas. (465)

May 1837 - Christian GAMMITSFELDER, native of Wertenburg makes declaration of
intention to become citizen; 5-15-1837. (512) William DAVIS, native of England
makes declaration of intention to become citizen. Robert BOYD, native of Ireland
makes declaration of intention to become citizen. John POWELL Sr. native of
England makes declaration of intention to become citizen. 5-15-1837. (513)
John POWELL Jr. and William POWELL, natives of Ireland make their declaration
of intention to become citizens; 5-15-1837. William MOORE, native of Ireland
makes his declaration of intention to become citizen; 5-16-1837. (514)

May 1837 - James LYNCH, native of Ireland makes his declaration of intention to
become citizen; 5-16-1837. Andrew CARROL, native of Ireland makes his declaration
of intention to become citizen; 5-17-1837. James BENNING, native of Ireland;
Naturalization; declaration of intention made 7-28-1828; 5-17-1837. (515)

Aug. 1837 - Andrew McFARLAND vs Almon CHEADLE, etal. Petition for Partition.
Filed 8-12-1836. Land, 200 acres pt. 1st quarter, Township 5 Range 4 U.S. Military
Lands; conveyed to Ezekiel McFarland by James Lesk adms. of Andrew McFarland, dec'd
by deed of 4-14-1823 and by Sheriff's deed dated 4-12-1826. Ezekiel McFarland,
dec'd. Children: Andrew McFarland; Margaret wife of Almon Cheadle, Hannah McFarland;
George McFarland, dec'd, his widow, Clarissa, and his khildren--Louiza, Hannah and
John McFarland, minors; David McFarland, a minor; Robert McFarland, a minor. (534)

Aug. 1837 - Joseph BURNS adms. of Adam JOHNSTON, DEC"D VS. Sarah JOHNSTON, etal.
Petition to sell land. Filed 8-3-1836. Land; Lots 13,17,19,28,31,37 and many more
in Millersburgh Holmes Co., Ohio; 93 acres SE¼ Section 12, Township 9, Range 7.
Widow, Sarah Johnston. Heirs: Susan and Joseph F. Oliver; Charles H. Johnston;
George W. Johnston; Matthew W. Johnston; William Johnston; and Hannah Johnston. (539)

Aug. 1837 - Richard TAYLOR; Naturalization. Daniel McCULLOCK, native of Ireland
makes his declaration of intention to become citizen. 8-14-1837. (564) Robert
McCULLOCK, native of Ireland, being 21 yrs. of age when he arrived in United States;
Naturalization; 8-14-1837. John HALSEY, native of Ireland makes his declaration of
intention to become citizen. Thomas DAVIS, native of Great Britain; Naturalization;
declaration of intention made July 1835. 8-14-1837. (565)

Aug. 1837 - James SCOTT, native of Ireland makes his declaration of intention to
become citizen. Samuel Henry SCOTT, native of Ireland makes his declaration of
intention to become citizen. 8-16-1837. Michael NORTON, native of Ireland makes
his declaration of intention to become citizen; 8-18-1837. (566) Charles MURPHY,
native of Ireland makes his declaration of intention to become citizen; 8-18-1837.
(567)

327

The following records were taken from "Common Pleas Record F" located in the Clerk of Court's Office at the court house at Coshocton. Page on which record may be found is given in parenthesis.

Apr. 1838 - Gideon FITCH and Mary FITCH executors of will of Wm. FITCH, dec'd vs. Gideon FITCH, et al. Petition to complete contract. Filed 4-9-1838. William Fitch, dec'd late of Perry twp. in his lifetime entered contract to sell land he was then seized of to William Crow being 40 acres off East end NW¼ Section 9, Township 5, Range 9. Widow(?), Mary Fitch. Heirs: Gideon Fitch, Margaret wife of Thomas Almach, Catharine wife of Wm Vincent, Peter N. Fitch, Elizabeth Jane Fitch, John R. Fitch, Eliza Ann Fitch and Mary Martha Fitch, the last five named being minors. (1)

Apr. 1838 - Mary WRIGHT vs. Lewis WRIGHT et al. Petition for Dower. Filed 3-7-1837. William Wright, dec'd died seized of an estate of inheritance in 62½ acres part E½ Section 19, Township 4, Range 9. Widow, Mary Wright. Heirs: Lewis Wright; Albert Wright; Mary Smith, dec'd, her children--Theodore Smith, Garrison Smith, Mary Smith and Alexander Smith, all minors; Charles Wright; William Wright; Patsy Wright; Elwood Wright; Edward Wright; Martin Wright; and Daniel Wright. (17)

Apr. 1838 - Lucinda BRICKER an unmarried woman vs. Daniel M. CROUCH. Bastardy. Filed 7-19-1837. Child conceived about October. Bond by Daniel M. Crouch and Robert Crouch. Crouch found to be the father and to pay support of child. (25) (note: on page 35 this record at same term of court Lewis Bricker sued Daniel M. Crouch, this record states that Lewis Bricker was father of Lucinda.)

Apr. 1838 - Wm G. WILLIAMS and Jabius NORMAN adms. of estate of Wm DAVIDSON, dec'd vs. James DAVIDSON et al. Filed 4-29-1836. Wm. Davidson, dec'd, died seized of 60 acfes off lot 12 Section 1, and 50 acres off NE corner Section, all in Township 7, Range 7. Deceased left no widow. Heirs: James Davidson of Coshocton Co.; William Davidson of Coshocton Co.; Susana wife of Jabes Norman of Coshocton Co.; Polly Davidson of Hancock Co., Ohio; Betsey Davidson of Holmes Co., Ohio; Reason Davidson of Coshocton Co. (37)

Apr. 1838 - Rev. Amour McFARLAND a minister of the Reformed Prewbyterian Church granted license to solemnize marriages. (58)

Apr. 1838 - Rev. Seely BLOOMER a minister of the Methodist Church granted license to solemnize marriages. (58)

Apr. 1838 - Rev. Joel TUTTLE a minister of the Methodist Episcopal Church granted license to solemnize marriages. (58)

Apr. 1838 - Jacob BENSE late of Switzerland under Austria filed his declaration of intention to become citizen. (58)

Apr. 1838 - Anastasias YOST late of Darnstadt filed his declaration of intention to become citizen. (59)

Apr. 1838 - John SWIGERT late of Wertemburg filed his declaration of intention to become citizen. (59)

Apr. 1838 - Frederick SMALTZ late of Wirtemburgh filed his declaration of intention to become citizen. (60)

Apr. 1838 - Samuel BYERLY late of Wertemburg filed his declaration of intention to become citizen. (60)

Apr. 1838 - John Frederick SHNIDE late of Germany filed his declaration of intention to become citizen. (60)

Apr. 1838 - James HOLBROOK late of Great Britain filed his declaration of intention to become citizen. (61)

Apr. 1838 - Samuel McBRATTNEY late of Ireland filed his declaration of intention to become citizen. (61)

Apr. 1838 - James CREGHORN late of Scotland filed his declaration of intention to become citizen. (61)

Apr. 1838 - Anthony MASSA late of England filed his declaration of intention to become citizen. (62)

Apr. 1838 - David MAKLE late of Switzerland filed his declaration of intention to become citizen. (62)

Apr. 1838 - Rodolph BONGARNER late of Switzerland filed his declaration of intention to become citizen. (62)

Apr. 1838 - Robert HUTCHINSON late of Ireland filed his declaration of intention to become citizen. (63)

Apr. 1838 - James BURGESS late of England filed his declaration of intention to become citizen. (63)

Apr. 1838 - John TROTT late of England filed his declaration of intention to become citizen. (63)

Apr. 1838 - Thomas McFARLAND late of Ireland files his declaration of intention to become citizen. (64)

Apr. 1838 Patrick EAGEN, native of Ireland. Naturalization. Declaration of intention filed 4-14-1835. Oath as to character by John R. Gamble. (64)

Apr. 1838 - William KING late a native of Germany. Naturalization. Declaration of intention filed April term 1836. Oath by George Croft and Henry Gonsar. (64)

Apr. 1838 - Jacob METZ late a native of Germany, Naturalization. Declaration of intention filed April term 1836. Oath by George Croft and George Shultz. (65)

Apr. 1838 - Isaac THURGOOD late a native of England. Naturalization. Declaration of intention filed 11-1-1833. Oath by Francis Johnson and Wilson McGowan. (65)

July 1838 - Jane ADAMS an unmarried woman vs Humphrey SCOTT. Bastardy. Filed 3-16-1838. Jane has been a resident of Coshocton County for more than 12 years. Child born Dec. 29, 1838 (1837) with conception 4-1-1837. Scott gave bond in New Castle twp. (84)

July 1838 - John BLEASDALE late a native of Great Britain and Ireland. Declaration of intention filed 4-25-1835. (111)

July 1838 - Abraham COURTWRIGHT and Wm KAY adms. of estate of Isaac GOOD vs. Elisha MUSGROVE et al. Petition to sell land. Filed 5-27-1837. Land, lot 12 in Section 3 (known as Rathbone section by title bond from John Rathbone Jr. of New York City), Township 6, Range 7. Widow, Martha Good now the wife of Elisha Musgrove. Heirs: Abraham Good and Mary Jane Good, Both minors. (129)

July 1838 - Timothy EMERSON Sr. adms. of estate of Hiram K. FARMER, dec'd vs. Elizabeth FARMER, et al. Filed 8-2-1838. Petition to complete real estate contract. Hiram K. Farmer in lifetime contracted to sell lot 15 in Ransom and Swayne addition to town of Roscoe formerly town of Caldersburgh. Widow, Elizabeth W. Farmer. Heirs: Francis H. Farmer aged 5 yrs., Elizabeth E. Farmer aged 3 yrs., and Polly Farmer aged 1 yrs. (150)

July 1838 - John LYONS and Arbuthnott H. LYONS executors of Will of Hugh LYONS, dec'd vs. William BROWN, et al. Petition to sell land. Filed 7-21-1837. Hugh Lyons, dec'd died about 11-1-1836 leaving a will which reads as follows: Will of Hugh LYONS; dated 7-23-1835; proved 11-15-1836. Wife, Jane, interest from one third of all property during her natural life. Son, Thomas $1.00. To heirs of said son Thomas $50.00. Grandson, Hugh Robert Lyons $250.00. Son, John $250.00. Son, Arbuthnot $200.00. Daughter, Mary (Deceased) or her heirs $200.00. Daughter, Arabella or her heirs $200.00. Rest of estate to be divided between sons: Thomas, John, Arbuthnot and Hugh Robert. Executors: sons, John and Arbuthnot Lyons. (end of will). Land, 160 acres NE¼ Section 9, Township 4, Range 9. Hugh Lyons, dec'd. Widow, Jane Lyons. Children: daughter, Mary (dec'd since will and her husband also dec'd, her children--Robert Hopper aged 20 yrs., Arabella Hopper aged 19 yrs. , Jane Hopper aged 17 yrs. and Eleanor Hopper aged 15 yrs. all of Cochocton Co.; son, Thomas Lyons, dec'd (dec'd since will was made), his children--Hugh Lyons aged 25 yrs., Robert Lyons aged 23 yrs., John Lyons aged 21 yrs., Arabella Lyons aged 19 yrs., William Lyons aged 17 yrs. and Arbuthnot Lyons aged 11 yrs., all of Muskingum Co., Ohio; daughter Arabella (dec'd) since will was made) late wife of William Henderson of Coshocton Co., her children--Nancy McKee formerly Henderson wife of Daniel McKee, Eleanor formerly Henderson wife of William McGruder, Maria Henderson aged 14 yrs., Arabella Henderson aged 10 yrs., Mary Jane Henderson aged 8 yrs., Sarah Ann Henderson aged 6 yrs., Eliza Jane Henderson aged 4 yrs. andAdeline Henderson aged 2 yrs., all of Coshocton Co.; (daughter?), Eleanor formerly Lyons wife of William Brown of Coshocton Co. (note: states that Eleanor is mentioned in will, but she is not found mentioned in copy given above); Grandson of testator--Hugh Robert Lyons aged 13 yrs., whose father was Hugh Lyons, dec'd, who left widow, Jane Lyons. (158)

Oct. 1838 - Robert HAY vs. Levi JOHNSON et al. Petition to sell land. Filed
10-28-1836. Land, 134 acres NW¼ Section 15, Township 4, Range 4 in U.S. Military
land. William Johnson Jr., dec'd. Widow, Eleanor Johnson now the wife of William
Renfrow of Coshocton Co. Two sons: Levi Johnson aged 12 yrs and Richard Johnson
aged 10 yrs., both of Coshocton Co. Hay appointed guardian of minor children. (170)

Oct. 1838 - Eliza METHAM vs. Henry YONKER, et al. Petition for Dower. Filed
4-23-1838. Pren Metham at his death was seized of estate of inheritance in 3rd
quarter, Township 6, Range 8 near White Woman Run--96 acres NW corner ofDarbys tract,
76 acres in lot 8, 163 acres in lot 9, 118 acres in lot 10, also Island set in
meddle of White Woman River at No 9 & 1, deeded to Pren Metham by deed dated 3-15-
1821 and recorded in Book 3, pages 36 & 362 by Wm Bell and Hannah. That Pren Metham
left will probated 9-30-1836. Pren Metham, dec'd died 11-12-1826. Widow, Eliza
Metham. Heirs: Emily formerly Metham wife of Henry Yonker, Mary Metham aged 24 yrs.,
Margaret Metham aged 22 yrs., Henry Metham aged 16 yrs., Eliza Ann Metham aged 14 yrs.,
William Metham aged 12 yrs., Charlotte Louisa Metham who died in fall of 1837 intest-
ate as a minor, Pren Metham aged 8 yrs., Caroline Metham aged 7 yrs., and Josephine
Metham aged 3 yrs. (206)

Oct. 1838 - Joseph SMITH and Selina SMITH adms. of estate of Aaron SMITH, dec'd vs.
James SMITH, et al. Petition to sell land. Filed 5-3-1837. Land, 73.94 acres E½
NE¼ Section 1, Township 8, Range 11 unappropriated military lands sold at Chillicothe,
said land being in Knox Co., Ohio. Widow, Selina Smith of Coshocton Co. Children:
James Smith aged 11 yrs., Nancy Smith aged 9 yrs., Frances Smith aged 7 yrs. and
Sarah Smith aged 2 yrs., all of Coshocton Co. except Nancy who is of Knox Co. (212)

Oct. 1838 - Thomas CASSINGHAM and James AUSTEN vs Joseph F. MONROE and Calvin
RESONER. Petition for Partition. Filed 2-9-1837. Petitioners both of Coshocton
Co. and joint tenants with Joseph Munroe in SE¼ Section 24, Township 4, Range 7 in
U. S. Military district patented by U. S. to Peter D. Reasoner and Joseph F. Munro.
Petitioners represent that Peter D. Reasoner'd interest descended to his children--
Harriet wife of George Wheelan, Harmon Reasoner, Levina wife of James G. Honnold,
Lucinda wife of Joseph Adams, Greenwell Reasoner, Maria Reasoner and Calvin Reasoner.
That Wheelans, Harmon Reasoner, Adams, Honnolds, Greenwell Reasoner and Maria
Reasoner by deed of 6-17-1836 conveyed interest to 6/14th parts to petitioners and
that Joseph F. Munroe of Muskingum Co., Ohio and Calvin Reasoner a minor under 21
yrs. of Coshocton Co. retain remaining parts. (257)

Oct. 1838 - Elizabeth Ann CREPPLEIVER vs. William ALEXANDER. Bastardy. Filed
10-24-1838. Elizabeth Ann an unmarried woman had child on 1-30-1837. Alexander of
Whites Eyes twp. gave bond with John Alexander. (242)

Oct. 1838 - John COROTHERS and James COROTHERS vs. Joseph COROTHERS, et al.
Petition for Partition. Filed 6-11-1838. Land, 160 acres NW¼ Section 9 and 160
acres NE¼ Section 10, both in Township 4, Range 9; also lots 68,36,35&31 in
West Carlisle. Christopher Corothers, dec'd late of Coshocton Co. died about
July 1837. Widow, Mary Corothers entitled to dower. Children: James Corothers;
John Corothers; Batey Corothers; Joseph Corothers, all of Coshocton Co.; Ann
Thompson (late Corothers and daughter of Christopher), dec'd, who died about 1834,
her children--Elizabeth, William, James, Ruth Ann and John Thompson all of Knox
Co., Ohio. (244)

331

Oct. 1838 - Samuel (as given in title--name given as James in body of document) McKEE, native of Ireland. Naturalization. Declaration of intention filed 10-24-1836. Oaths by Wm Henderson and William Noland. (253)

May 1839 - Polly Shepherd vs. Jeremiah WILLIAMS. Bastardy. Filed 1-5-1839. Case dismissed. (327)

May 1839 - James MATHEWS and Elizabeth RODGERS adms. of estate of David RODGERS, dec'd vs. Elizabeth RODGERS, et al. Petition to sell real estate. Filed 4-30-1838. Land, 255.77 acres lot 10, Section 4, Township 5, Range 6 of U. S. Military lands. Widow, Elizabeth Rodgers. Heirs: Madison Rodgers, Washington Rodgers, Eliza Rodgers, Solomon Rodgers, Freelove Jane Rodgers and Jacob Rodgers, all of Coshocton County. (338)

May 1839 - David FREW vs. James Taylor CALDER and Emily CALDER. In Partition. Filed 9-12-1838. Land, part 2nd quarter, Township 5, Range 6 in U. S. Military lands being lot 7, also in-lots 36 & 37 in town of Rosco (formerly Caldersburgh) and land north of Rosco except 44 acres conveyed by James Taylor and Frances his wife to Samuel Brown leaving 21 acres. Partition: 1/3 part, David Frew; 1/3 part, James Taylor Calder aged 14 yrs of Columbiana Co., Ohio; 1/3rd part, Emily Calder aged 16 yrs. of Coshocton Co. (342)

May 1839 - Benjamin Ricketts and Joseph W. RUE vs. Joseph F. OLIVER, et al. In Partition. Filed 9-12-1838. Land, 71.54 acres part of 3rd quarter, Township 5, Range 6 of U. S. Military land known as Samuel Fulton tract. 1/9th part, Benjamin Ricketts; 2/9th parts, Joseph W. Rue; Adams Johnson, dec'd died seized of 6/9ths part, his children--Susan formerly Johnson wife of Joseph F. Oliver of Coshocton Co.; Charles H. Johnson aged 23 yrs. of Hamilton Co., Ohio; George W. Johnson; Matthew Johnson; William Johnson; Hannah Johnson; all of Coshocton Co. (363)

Aug. 1838 - Joseph BURNS guardian of minor heirs of James JOHNSON, dec'd vs. Mille A. JOHNSON, et al. Petition to sell real estate. Filed 5-2-1838. Land, Lot 39 in 1st quarter, Township 5, Range 2 of Military land located in Tuscarawas Co., Ohio. James Johnson, dec'd, died intestate eight years ago. Widow, Rebecca Butler late Johnson now the wife of Thomas Butler. Children: Mary late Johnson wife of Alexander Hay, Mille A. Johnson, Anderson Johnson and James Johnson, the last three named being minors by Joseph Burns their guardian. (433)

May 1840 - Thomas JOHNSON and Garner HUNT vs. Zechariah BAKER, et al. In Parrition Filed 8-27-1839. Land, 160 acres SE¼ Section 10, Township 4, Range 5. 1/4th part, Thomas Johnson of Coshocton Co. 1/4th part, Garner Hunt of Coshocton Co. Remaining part belongs to Bazil BAKER dec'd and his heirs; widow, Mary entitled to dower. Children: Aaron Baker, dec'd, his widow Mary Ann Baker entitled to dower and his only child--Nancy Catharine Baker; Zechariah Baker; Cassia Baker; the last two named are of age and also children of Bazil Baker along with Aaron, dec'd. All Baker heirs are of Coshocton Co. (607)

Marriages listed below were copied from Marriage Record Book 1 as found in the Probate Court.

ALBRIGHT, Daniel to Judith Lashley		10-21-1832
ANDREWS, Thomas S. to Eliza Ritchey		9-3-1832
ARMSTRONG, Silas to Sarah Preston		10-9-1832
BLAIR, Daniel to Sarah Jewell		9-25-1831
BALL, Daniel to Catharine Ziegler		8-30-1832
BECK, Jacob to Mary Berlene		12-6-1832
BEVINGTON, William to Sarah Jane Woolsey		12-19-1832
BLOWERS, Refus L. to Susan Smith		6-12-1831
BRUNDAGE, Samuel O. to Angeline Fish (Lish)		2-12-1832
BUSH (BUSK), Joseph to Phebe Casto		7-12-1832
CHILCOAT, Joshua to Mary Mix		5-3-1832
CLEMENS, Benjamin to Susan Stuckman		3-1-1832
CLIN, John to Rachel Casto		10-21-1831
CONLEY, Thomas to Sarah Swartz		10-11-1832
CRANDALL, John S. to Elizabeth Bibler		11-22-1832
DAVIS, William to Lucy Brayton		9-25-1832
DOUGHMAN (DUKEMAN), Stephen to Margaret Deeds		11-6-1832
DUCKER, Samuel to Catharin Duddleston		4-24-1832
DUNCAN, John to Mary McMichael, Jun.		12-9-1832
EBY, Peter to Rebecca Guisinger		10-9-1831
EVET (ERRET), John to Nancy Berlene		2-14-1832
FISHEL, Michael to Anna Humond		9-7-1832
FLEMING, Jacob to Kittury Hesser		3-15-1832
FLORA, Archibald to Sarah Kroft		10-30-1832
FOY, Jacob Jr. to Mercy Lupton		1-26-1832
GIBSON, David to Harriet White		11-8-1831
GIBSON, James to Emilim Dunn	lic.	6-6-1832
GORTON, Amos to Nancy Bibler		7-26-1832
GREEN, Frederick to Rakina Moyer		11-25-1832
HEMRY, William to Jane Morgan		2-28-1832
HILL, Joseph M. to Fanny Chatfield		12-1-1831
HITCHCOCK, Thomas to Naomy Corey		3-1-1832
JOHNSTON, Alexander to Polly Adams		12-15-1831
KING, David B. to Sarah B. Sweet		3-9-1832
LANGDON, Gabriel to Elisa Booes (Boves)		11-18-1832
LEY, Sebastian to Magdalene Bertoon	lic.	8-6-1832
LONG, Hugh to Sarah Hinkle	lic.	12-4-1832
McCRACKEN, James to Ruth Marquis		12-4-1832
MAGERS, William to Mary Andrews		10-23-1832
METCALF, Daniel to Lene Staffer		12-25-1832
MILLER, Thomas to Betsey Maria Miner		11-8-1832
NOACRE, John to Sarah Yawky		12-8-1831
PERKA, John to Elizabeth Whetstone		1-27-1832
PETERMAN, Michael to Sarah Ridgley		4-12-1832
PORTER, Edward to Rachel Shupp	lic.	Aug. 1832
RAGON, John to Sarah Curtis	lic.	11-19-1831

READ, George to Catharine Bash	9-6-1832
REID, George to Mary Ann Foster	10-18-1831
ROCKWELL, Joseph to Rachel Gurnes	10-7-1832
SHAFFNER, Martin to Susan Aurandt	6-14-1832
SHAFFNER, Samuel to Frances Shultz	5-8-1832
SHAY, David to Sarah McWarden	11-14-1831
SHOEMAKER, Adam to Catharine Staffer	9-30-1832
SPROAT, William to Elizabeth Cooper	5-10-1832
SHULTZ, John to Mary McMichael	12-9-1832
SINCLAIR, William to Laura Barney	11-21-1832
SMALLY, Chester to Esther Scott	11-16-1831
SMALLY, Horan to Hannah Chandler	1-5-1832
SNYDER, John to Mary Albertson	10-4-1832
SOCKRIDER, David to Sarah Hodge	lic. 11-19-1831
STUCKMAN, John to Betsey Slichg	11-3-1831
THOMAS, David to Jane Farmer	10-13-1832
VAN VLEET, Benjamin to Sarah Ann Champion	12-20-1832
VANVOORHIS, Charles Edward to Susan Jones	7-9-1832
WALLAN, William to Ellen Davis	4-5-1832
WALTERS, Anthony to Elizabeth Henry	9-18-1832
WHETSTONE, Peter to Mary Stine	3-6-1832
WHETSTONE, Samuel to Elisabeth Patterson	11-3-1831
WIGHT, Daniel to Eliza Gibson	3-19-1832
WILLIAMS, Daniel to Jerusha Switzer	10-18-1832
WRIGHT, Daniel to Elizabeth Woolsey	11-15-1832
YOST, Jacob to Julia Crosby	7-28-1832

MINISTERS' LICENSES

SEITZ, Rev. Lewis - Baptist; date issued 6-4-1831; place issued, Seneca County; date recorded Crawford County 12-24-1832

SIMS, Thomas - (denomination not given); date issued 10-6-1830; place issued, Clark County; date recorded Crawford County 1-18-1833

HAIRNS, John C. - (denomination not given); date issued 10-17-1827; place issued, Fairfield County; date recorded Crawford County 3-2-1832

SECREST, John - "Church of God"; date issued 5-8-1827; place issued, Belmont County; date recorded Crawford County 7-10-1832

STOUGH, Rev. John - (denomination not given); date issued 11-18-1806; place issued, Columbiana County; date recorded Crawford County 10-3-1832.

Located Whetstone Township, Range 17, Section 6, behind old gas station R.30 east of
Bucyrus. Inscriptions by: Vicki Layman, Mary Axel, Ellen Lash. Contributed by
Vicki Layman, 1202 Kinamoor Ave., Fort Wayne, Indiana 46807

SHROLL, Eli died Feb. 15, 1851 aged 18y 6m 15d
SHROLL, John died June 17, 1835 aged 55y 8m 8d
LAYMAN, Mathias died April 25, 1845 aged 29y 6m 1d
SHROLL, George died June 11, 1835 aged.45y 11m
ALBRIGHT, John H. s/o T.(?) and E., died Mar. 28, 1830(?) aged 5m (5y?)
STERNER, Dianna d/o Daniel and Rosina, d Aug. 8, 1849 aged 1y 9m 21d
STERNER, Francis s/o Daniel and Rosina, d Aug. 22, 1849 aged 1y 10m 5d
MANN, Mary died Mar. 30(?) 1855 aged 66y 9m 19d
SNYDER, Sally wife of Samuel, died Jan. 1, 1840 aged 35 years
STEM, Rebecca d/o C. and M., died July 9, 1848 aged 6y 9m 16d
STEM,_____(note: stone beside above, same info. par. "C. and A.")
STERNER, Caroline - 1846
LUDWIG, Charles s/o Wm. and Hannah P., died Jan. 29, 1846 aged 1y 3m 19d
LUDWIG, Hannah died Mar. 13, 1833 aged 16y 10m 6d
LUDWIG, Catherine w/o Isaac, died Dec. 28, 1833 aged 25y 11m 4d
SHROLL, Abraham - 1800-1883
SHROLL, Nancy w/o A. - 1808-1829 (on 2nd stone d. April 28, 1829)
SHROLL, Sophia w/o A. - 1805-1881
DECKER, Mary w/o Aron, died March 31, 1840 aged 48 years
ALBRIGHT, Daniel born April 22, 1766 - died Nov. 17, 1856
BANKS, Anna died Nov. 15, 1867 aged 76y 1m 3d
SHECKLER, John w. s/o D.J. and S.A., died Jan. 8, 1852 aged 1m 18d
ZIEGLER, Jacob H. born Dec. 10, 1786 died Dec. 1, 1830 aged 44y
ZIGLER, Catherine w/o Jacob died Mar. 21, 1843 aged 44y 10m 11d
BRESLAR, Rebecca - 1837-1889

CRAWFORD COUNTY, OHIO - BIRTH AND BAPTISMAL RECORDS 1850-1855
ST. MARK METHODIST CHURCH, FORMERLY GERMAN METHODIST, GALION, OHIO

Contributed by: Mrs. Ira R. (Mary Louise) Rizor, 410 Cherry St., Galion, Ohio 44833

CHILD	BIRTH AND PAPTISM	PARENTS
GIVINER, Susanna	b. 7-10-1843 bapt. 1-21-1850	John Giviner and wife Christina
NUHFER, Helena Katharina	b. 3-5-1850 bapt. 3-14-1850	Nikolaus Nuhfer and wife Elizabeth
RUKART, Peter	b. 1-20-1850 bapt. 3-14-1850	Georg Rukart and wf. Anna Katharina
SEIF, Aron	b. 10-11-1849 bapt. 6-2-1850	Jacob Seif and wife Sophia
KANZLEITER, Katharina Barbara	b. 5-17-1850 bapt. 6-30-1850	Johanas Kanzleiter & wf. AUrsula Katharina
STAEGER, Rosina	b. 9-17-1849 bapt. 6-30-1850	Abraham Staeger and wife Rosina Barbara
LEITPF, Georg	b. 4-15-1850 bapt. 7-7-1850	Greorg Leitpf and wife Katharina
HABER, Adam	b. 12-6-1849 bapt. 8-18-1850	Rudolf Haber and wife Margaratha
HABER, Maria Ava	b. 4-24-1848 Lapt. 8-18-1850	Rudolph Haber and wife Margaratha
LANGADORFOR, Susanna	b. 12-10-1850 bapt. 8-18-1850(?)	Georg Landadorfor and wf. Katharina
SCHAFER, Johannas	b. 7-17-1846 bapt. 8-24-1850	Konrad Schafer and wife Katharina
SCHAFER, Luisa Wilhelmina	b. 9-26-1840 bapt. 8-24-1850	Konrad Schafer and wife Katharina
SCHAFER, Magdalena	b. 4-10-1842 bapt. 8-24-1850	Konrad Schafer and wife Katharina
KRAMER, Adam	b. 1-1-1850 bapt. 9-9-1850	John Adam Kramer and wf. Katharina
KRAMER, Rebecca Karolina	b. 9-5-1850 bapt. 12-15-1850	Christofer Kramer & wf. Elizabetha (Munshun)
HIRSCHBERGER, Eva	b. 11-28-1830 bapt. 1-12-1851	Jacob Hirschberger and wife_____
HIRSCHBERGER, Susanna	b. 10-16-1822 bapt. 1-12-1851	Jacob Hirschberger and wife_____
SEITZ, Rebecka	b. 12-18-1834 bapt. 1-12-1851	Philipp Seitz and wife Elizabetha
HERMAN, Elizabeth Ana	b. 1-28-1850 bapt. 2-8-1851	Johann Herman and wife Elizabeth
HIRSCHBERGER, Lidia	b. 3-13-1850 bapt. 2-8-1851	Jacob Hirschberger and wife_____
SCHIEBER, Jacob	b. 12-13-1849 bapt. 2-8-1851	Lidia Schieber
ULMER, Wilhelm	b. 1-22-1851 bapt. 2-9-1851	Adam Ulmer and wife Katharina
ULMER, Wilhelmia	b. 1-22-1851 bapt. 2-9-1851	Adam Ulmer and wife Katharina

CHILD	BIRTH AND BAPTISM	PARENTS
LINGEN, Elizabeth Barbara	b. 11-6-1850 bapt. 2-19-1851	Daniel Lingen and wife Elizabeth
SCHNEIDER, Johanes Wilhelm	b. 12-4-1850 bapt. 2-26-1851	Wilhelm Schneider and wife Sofia
PERLE, Maria	b. 3-20-1851 bapt. 3-30-1851	Johanes Perle and wife Ana
GERBERISH, Ana Katharina	b. 6-21-1850 bapt. 5-4-1851	Samuel Gerberich and wife Margaretha
EKERT, Heinrich	b. 2-25-1851 bapt. 6-8-1851	Burghart Ekert and wife Barbara
PLETCHER, Johannas	b. 8-6-1849 bapt. 6-15-1851	Israel Pletcher and wife Helena
PLETCHER, Johan Wesley	b. 11-7-1850 bapt. 6-15-1851	Christian Pletcher and wife Maria
ZIMMERMAN, Maria Sophia	b. 2-12-1851 bapt. 6-15-1851	Daniel Zimmerman and wife Scharlotta
KANZLEITER, Elisa	b. 10-30-1851 bapt. 11-16-1851	Johannes Kanzleiter and wife Ursula Katharine (Rabach)
HAUS, Johann Georg	b. 12-5-1851 bapt. 1-28-1852	Peter Haus wife Anna Margaretha
ZITZLER, Johann	b. 11-27-1838 bapt. 4-26-1852	Johannes Zitzler wife Elizabetha
ZITZLER, Lidia	b. 12-3-1840 bapt. 4-26-1852	Johannes Zitzler wife Elizabetha
BARTSCH, Margaretha Magdalena	b. 3-2-1852 bapt. 4-30-1852	Christoph Bartsch wife Magdalena
HORLE, Johann Wilhelm	b. 4-20-1852 bapt. 4-30-1852	Johannes Horle wife Anna
BAUSCHLICHER, Jacob Heindrich	b. 12-7-1851 bapt. 5-2-1852	Daniel Bauschlicher wife Magdalena
SCHAUB, Georg	b. 6-24-1849 bapt. 5-23-1852	Peter Schaub wife Katharina
SCHAUB, Margaretha	b. 10-16-1850 bapt. 5-23-1852	Peter Schaub wife Katharina
KELLER, Gristian	b. 9-4-1851 bapt. 5-30-1852	Georg Keller wife Margaretha Barbara
EKERT, Katharina	b. 4-30-1852 bapt. 6-6-1852	Burkhardt Ekert wife Barbara
SEIF, Johann	b. 10-14-1851 bapt. 6-6-1852	Michael Seif wife Katharina
SEIF, Sophia	b. 3-11-1852 bapt. 6-6-1852	Jacob Seif wife Sophia
RUCKERT, Maria Elizabeth	b. 5-22-1852 bapt. 8-13-1852	George Ruckert wife Anna Katharina
KNAPPENBERGER, Katharina	b. 10-2-1852 bapt. 10-18-1852	Johann Georg Knappenberger wife Rosina
HERRMANN, Christina	b. 10-22-1852 bapt. 11-29-1852	John Hermann wife Elizabeth

CHILD	BIRTH AND BAPTISM	PARENTS
HIRSCHBERGER, Anna	b. 7-1-1838 bapt. 12-7-1852	Jacob Hirschberger wife_____
SOMMER, Gottlieb Friedrich	b. 1-16-1852 bapt. 12-7-1852	Daniel Sommer wife Rosina
FENHAL, Adam Friedrich	b. 11-5-1852 bapt. 1-24-1853	Johann Adam wife Christina
KRAMER, David	b. 12-7-1852 bapt. 3-4-1853	Christoph Cramer (K,C?) wife Anna Elizabetha
SCHILLINGER, Jacob Freadrick	b. 3-1-1853 bapt. 3-7-1853	Jacob Schillinger wife Magdalena
HORLE, Alexander Alias	b. 3-16-1853 bapt. 4-3-1853	Johann Horle wife Anna
EICHORN, Anna Maria	b. 10-20-1852 bapt. 4-8-1853	Friedrich Eichorn wife Christina
EICHORN, David	b. 9-14-1852 bapt. 4-14-1853	Phillipp Eichorn wife Margaretha
BUSCH, Wilhelmina	b. 5-15-1847 bapt. 4-15-1853	Wilhelm Busch wife Sophia
BUSCH, Margaretha	b. 7-29-1850 bapt. 4-15-1853	Wilhelm Busch wife Sophia
BUSCH, Charlotte	b. 1-11-1853 bapt. 4-15-1853	Wilhelm Busch wife Sophia
BECKER, Wilhelm	b. 4-8-1842 bapt. 4-15-1853	Jacob Becker wife Charlotte
BECKER, Maria	b. 4-16-1848 bapt. 4-15-1853	Jacob Becker wife Charlotte
BECKER, Johannes	b. 11-4-1840 bapt. 4-15-1853	Jacob Becker wife Charlotte
BECKER, Jacob	b. 6-16-1850 bapt. 4-15-1853	Jacob Becker wife Charlotte
BECKER, Emilia	b. 8-19-1846 bapt. 4-15-1853	Jacob Becker wife Charlotte
BECKER, Cornelius	b. 11-28-1843 bapt. 4-15-1853	Jacob Becker wife Charlotte
FUHRER, Anna Maria	b. 10-5-1852 Bapt. 4-24-1853	August Fuhrer wife Elizabethe
ULMER, Israel	b. 3-18-1853 bapt. 4-30-1853	Adam Ulmer wife Katharina
HEINLE, Andreas Jeferson	b. 8-29-1852 bapt., 5-15-1853	Johannes Heinle wife Elizabetha
SCHUPP, Johann Levi	b. 1-9-1852 bapt. 6-25-1853	Samuel Schupp wife Elizabetha Rosina
SCHUPP, Mariana	b. 2-3-1853 bapt. 6-25-1853	Samuel Schupp wife Elizabetha Rosina
SCHAUB, Jacob	b. 10-30-1852 bapt. 7-3-1853	Peter Schaub wife Katharina
LEITPF, Johannes Ludwig	b. 7-2-1853 bapt. 7-29-1853	Georg Heinrich Leitpf wife Anna Christina

CHILD	BIRTH AND BAPTISM	PARENTS
HIRN, Adam	b. 10-9-1852 bapt. 7-31-1853	Christoph Hirn wife Veronica
GEIGER, Magdalena Luise	b. 2-19-1853 bapt. 7-31-1853	Daniel Geiger wife Elizabethe
SCHNEIDER, Helena Alisa	b. 10-5-1852 bapt. 8-12-1853	Johannes Schneider wife Carolina
SCHNEIDER, Katharina	b. 10-26-1838 bapt. 8-12-1853	Johannes Schneider wife Carolina
SCHNEIDER, Maria Luisa	b. 6-6-1842 bapt. 8-12-1853	Johannes Schneider wife Carolina
SCHNEIDER, Jacob	b. 10-16-1847 bapt. 8-12-1853	Johannes Schneider wife Carolina
SCHNEIDER, Johannes Wesley	b. 11-12-1850 bapt. 8-12-1853	Johannes Schneider wife Carolina
SCHAAL, Johannes	b. 7-19-1853 bapt. 8-27-1853	Gottlieb Schaal wife Dianna
PLETCHER, Anna Elizabetha	b. 7-2-1853 bapt. 9-3-1853	Christian Pletcher wife Maria
GWANDT, Friedrich Jacob	b. 7-24-1853 bapt. 9 14-1853	Ludwig Gwandt wife Maria
SCHNEIDER, Peter	b. 6-16-1853 bapt. 10-9-1853	Wilhelm Schneider wife Sophia
BACKER, Daniel	b. 4-16-1853 bapt. 12-15-1853	Jacob Backer wife Scharlott
NIERLE, Elizabetha	b. 10-20-1853 bapt. 1-4-1854	Gottlieb Nierle wife Elizabeth
EHRIE, Gottlieb	b. 11-20-1853 bapt. 1-18-1854	Gottlieb Ehrle wife Maria
PALM, Ludwig	b. 9-27-1852 bapt. 1-20-1854	J. Gottlieb Palm (R?) wife Maria
HERGER, Luisa Matilda	b. 12-25-1853 bapt. 3-12-1854	Gottlieb Herger wife Christena
HERGER, Karoliene	b. 12-26-1853 bapt. 3-13-1854	Gottlieb Herger wife Karolina
BAUSCHLUHER, Margaretha	b. 8-7-1853 bapt. 3-13-1854	Daniel Bauschluher wife Magdalena
KNAPPENBERGER, Elizabeth	b. 2-24-1854 bapt. 5-21-1854	Georg Knappenberger wife Rosina
SCHAAL, Edward David	b. 4-18-1854 bapt. 5-21-1854	David Schall wife Maria
SEIBOLD, Anna Maria	b. 4-22-1854 bapt. 5-21-1854	Friedrich Seibold wife Christena Katharina
LEITPF, Georg Friedrich	b. 5-3-1854 bapt. 5-25-1854	Friedrich Lietpf wife Elizabetha
STEINHELFER, Johannes	b. 1-1-1854 bapt. 6-2-1854	Christof Steinhelfer wife Lidia
STEINHELFER, Samuel	b. 5-19-1851 bapt. 6-2-1854	Christof Steinhelfer wife Lidia

CHILD	BIRTH AND BAPTISM	PARENTS
STEINHELFER, Tobias	b. 8-17-1847 bapt. 6-2-1854	Christof Steinhelfer wife Lidia
STEINHELFER, Wilhelm	b. 3-26-1854 bapt. 6-2-1854	Christof Steinhelfer wife Lidia
NACHE, Georg	b. 5-20-1854 bapt. 6-11-1854	Wilhelm Nache wife Elizabetha
ECKHARDT, Lidia	b. 12-20-1853 bapt. 7-9-1854	Burkhard Eckhardt wife Barbara
KINSI, Jacob	b. 12-7-1853 bapt. 7-9-1854	Christian Kinsi wife Maria
SEIF, David	b. 3-13-1854 bapt. 7-9-1854	Jacob Seif wife Sophia
NEFF, Johannes	6-23-1851 bapt. 7--29-1854	Gottlieb Neff wife Rosina
NEFF, Jacob	b. 1-8-1847 bapt. 7-29-1854	Gottlieb Neff wife Rosina
NEFF, Elizabeth	b. 12-8-1853 bapt. 7-29-1854	Gottlief Neff wife Rosina
NEFF, Anna Maria	b. 12-20-1848 bapt. 7-29-1854	Tottlieb Neff wife Rosina
SEITZ, Wilhelm	b. 1-1-1835 bapt. 8-14-1854	Philippa Seitz wife Elizabetha
BURKHARDT, Elizabetha	b. (no date) bapt. 9-3-1854	Gottlieb Burkhardt wife Margaretha
DIETHER, Karl Franz	b. 7-4-1854 bapt. 9-3-1854	Barnhardt Diether wife Christina
HANGER, Johannes	b. (no date) bapt. 9-3-1854	Georg Hanger wife Katharina
BAUMARDT, Simion (Simon?)	b. 10-1-1852 bapt. 9-8-1854	Adam Baumardt wife Sarah
BURKHART, Johannes	b. 2-23-1843 bapt. 9-8-1854	Michael Burkhart wife Rosina
BURKHART, Maria	b. 1-1-1847 bapt. 9-8-1854	Michael Burkhart wife Rosina
WANER, Jacobus	b. 6-22-1854 bapt. 9-8-1854	Wilhelm Waner wife Margareth
HALLER, Karl Gottlieb	b. 6-14-1854 bapt. 9-24-1854	Ernst Haller wife Elizabetha
SCHAUB(P), Katharina	b. 6-5-1854 bapt. 9-24-1854	Peter Schaub(p?) wife Katharina
HIERZ, Elizabetha Maria	b. 8-30-1854 bapt. 10-29-1854	John Georg Hierz wife Eva
HENNACK, Herman	b. 11-1-1854 bapt. 11-30-1854	Friederich Hennack (Heneck?) wife Rosina
DORR, Ruban Homart	b. 8-14-1854 bapt. 12-4-1854	Jacob Dorr wife Elizabetha
HAUS, Johan Heinrich	b. 9-12-1854 bapt. 12-26-1854	Peter Haus wife Anna Margaretha

CHILD	BIRTH AND BAPTISM	PARENTS
RICKER, Luisa Sophia	b. 11-23-1854 bapt. 1-1-1855	George Ricker wife Katharina
DIETHER, Regina Christina Lidia	b. 11-30-1854 bapt. 1-16-1855	Friedrich Diether wife Carolina
KOCH, Rebecka	b. 1-11-1855 bapt. 1-21-1855	Gothardt Koch wife Friedrika
KOCH, Sophia	b. 1-11-1855 bapt. 1-21-1855	Gothardt Koch wife Friedrika
SCHNEIDER, Ludwig Jefferson	b. 11-23-1854 bapt. 2-18-1855	Georg Schneider wife Maria
METZ, Maria Luisa	b. 10-12-1854 bapt. 3-4-1855	Friedrich Metz wife Christina
BIEHLER, Adam	b. 8-7-1854 bapt. 3-16-1855	Barnhardt Biehler wife Margaratha
SCHUPP, Simmon Friedrich	b. 5-27-1854 bapt. 3-16-1855	Samuel Schupp wife Rosina Elizabetha
EBERHARDT, Christina Doratha	b. 10-30-1854 bapt. 3-16-1855	Friedrich Eberhardt wife Katharine
GAHN, Luisa	b. 12-16-1854 bapt. 4-10-1855	Conrad Gahn (Minister) wife Margaretha
EDINGER, Wilhelm	b. 4-20-1854 bapt. 4-15-1855	Johannes Edinger wife Christina
EDINGER, Maria	b. 11-5-1853 bapt. 4-15-1855	Johannes Edinger wife Christina
ECKERT, Wilhelm	b. 1-30-1855 bapt. 7-15-1855	Burkhardt Eckert wife Barbara
HORLE, Isak	b. 3-27-1855 bapt. 4-15-1855	Johanas Horle wife Anna
ZIMMERMAN, Georg Heinrich	b. 9-15-1854 bapt. 4-25-1855	Daniel Zimmerman wife Charlotte
LUST, Jacob	b. 3-17-1855 bapt. 6-10-1855	David Lust wife Katharina
MECK, Conrad Friedrich	b. 2-15-1854 bapt. 6-10-1855	Johannes Friedrich Meck wife Christina
MECK, Elizabetha	b. 2-20-1855 bapt. 6-10-1855	Adam Meck wife Christiana
HARSHBERGER, Elizabetha	b. 5-24-1840 bapt. 7-8-1855	Jacob Harshberger wife Magdalina
KRONENWET, Elisa	b. 3-18-1855 bapt. 7-15-1855	Friedrich Kronenwet wife Elisa
GARDNER, Katharina	b. 4-5-1855 bapt. 7-15-1855	Jacob Gardner wife Christina
ZIMMERMAN, Heinrich	b. 5-29-1855 bapt. 7-15-1855	Peter Zimmerman wife Barbara
SEIF, Samuel	b. 11-25-1854 bapt. 7-15-1855	Michael Seif wife Katharina
GROHS, Susanna Dortha	b. 8-15-1854 bapt. 7-22-1855	Friedrich Grohs wife Barbara

CHILD	BIRTH AND BAPTISM	PARENTS
HURR, Sarah	b. 5-29-1855 bapt. 7-22-1855	Jacob Hurr wife Katharina
HURR, Maria	b. 1-17-1841 bapt. 7-22-1855	Georg Hurr wife Christina
WEIS, Emanual	b. 4-15-1846 bapt. 7-29-1855	Israwl Weis wife Atalia
WEIS, Samuel	b. 12-25-1851 bapt. 7-29-1855	Israel Weis wife Atalia
BAINER (BAIER?) Regina Katharina	b. 11-15-1854 bapt. 7-29-1855	Philipp Bainer (or Baier) wife Lavina
ROHRIG, Samuel	b. 6-30-1855 bapt. 7-29-1855	Heinrich Rohrig wife Katharina
FINK, Heinrich Franz	b. 6-30-1854 bapt. 7-29-1855	Samuel Fink wife Maria Katharina
STINEHELFER, Elizabetha	b. 8-13-1855 bapt. 9-7-1855	Christoph Stinehelfer Lidia nee Strack
STARK, Heinrich Franklin	b. 1-3-1855 bapt. 9-7-1855	Franklin Stark wife Juliana
SHAAL, Georg Wesley	b. 6-30-1855 bapt. 9-7-1855	Gottlieb Shaal wife Diana
QUANDT, Ludwig Daniel	b. 8-13-1855 bapt. 10-21-1855	Ludwig Quandt wife Maria nee Gerth
SCHNEIDER, Sophia Maria	b. 8-28-1855 bapt. 10-21-1855	Wilhelm Schneider wife Sophia nee Eichhorn

342

CRAWFORD COUNTY, OHIO - BIRTH AND BAPTISMAL RECORDS 1856-1860
ST. MARK METHODIST CHURCH, FORMERLY GERMAN METHODIST, GALION, OHIO

Contributed by: Mrs. Ira R. (Mary Louise) Rizor, 410 Cherry St., Galion, Ohio 44833

CHILD	BIRTH AND BAPTISM	PARENTS
FOHL, Losinte	b. 10-9-1855 bapt. 1-1-1856	John Fohl wife Julianna nee Schneider
SCHMIDT, Elisa Margaretha	b. 9-27-1855 bapt. 1-1-1856	Johann Schmidt wf. Margaretha nee Schneider
SEIF, Franklin Pierce	b. 1-16-1854 bapt. 1-7-1856	Phillip Louis Seif wife Henrietta nee Althaus
SEIF, Phillip Louis	b. 9-23-1855 bapt. 1-7-1856	Phillip Louis Seif wife Henrietta nee Althaus
NELSON, Susanna Elizabeth	b. 10-2-1855 bapt. 2-10-1856	Georg Nelson wife Carolina nee Ernst
LAGER, Jacob	b. 6-9-1854 bapt. 2-11-1856	Heinrich Lager wife Cethrina nee Heinle
HEINLE, Sara Climer	b. 6-17-1854 bapt. 2-17-1856	Ludwig Heinle wife Mary Jane nee Finn
HEINLE, Heinrich Franklin	b. 9-23-1855 bapt. 2-11-1856	Ludwig Heinle wife Mary Jane nee Finn
HEINLE, Maria Allen	b. 9-28-1855 bapt. 2-11-1856	Johann Heinle wife Elisabeth nee Winter
STABE, Johann Heinrich	b. 2-10-1856 bapt. 3-26-1856	Wilhelm Stabe wife Elisabeth nee Rainharr
GIEGER, Emile Carolina	b. 12-8-1855 bapt. 7-20-1856	Daniel Gieger wife Elisabetha
SEIF, Adam	b. 12-3-1855 bapt. 8-17-1856	Jacob Seif wife Sophia nee Tauer
KUNSI, Heinrich	b. 12-10-1855 bapt. 8-17-1856	Christian Kunsi wife Maria nee Yenge
BITSCH, Louisa	b. 12-22-1855 bapt. 9-14-1856	Friedrich Bitsch wife Elisabetha nee Bucker
KROHNENWIRTH, Anna Catharina	b. 8-8-1856 bapt. 10-12-1856	Friedrich Krohnenwirth wife Elisabeth nee Bucker
NEIER, Linus Heinrich	b. 11-25-1849 bapt. 9-26-1856	Isack Neier wife Ester nee Yetzel
FINK, Allen Adleine	b. 4-15-1856 bapt. 12-20-1856	Samuel Fink wife Maria Catharina nee Weis
BOHMER, Daniel	b. 11-28-1856 bapt. 2-6-1857	Gottlieb Bohmer wife Scharlotte nee Lichte
NEFF, Samuel	b. 3-2-1856 bapt. 3-2-1857	Gottlieb Neff wife Rosina nee Mutchler
YEICHNER, Jacob	b. 1-17-1857 bapt. 3-3-1857	Martin Yeichner wife Barbara nee Schmidt
RICKER, Maria Dorthea	b. 1-5-1857 bapt. 4-10-1857	Georg Ricker wf. Anna Catharina nee Schneider
SULZER, Jacob	b. 3-7-1857 bapt. 5-17-1857	Jacob H. Sulzer wife Elisabeth nee Bruck
FÖHL, Susanna Anna	b. 9-5-1856 bapt. 5-19-1857	John Fohl wife Julianna nee Schneider
SCHOLEY, Susanna Sophia	b. 1-3-1840 bapt. 5-31-1857	John Scholey wife Maria nee Dotz

343

CHILD	BIRTH AND BAPTISM	PARENTS
ECKART, Samuel	b. 1-30-1857 bapt. 6-21-1857	Burghardt Eckart wife Barbara nee Dufler
GADNER, Christina	b. 1-29-1857 bapt. 6-21-1857	Jacob Gadner wf. Christina nee Krohnenwirth
SEIF, Catharina Elisabetha	b. 2-22-1857 bapt. 6-21-1857	Michael Seif wf. Anna Catharine nee Fliser
ELDER, Leve Maria	b. 4-7-1839 bapt. 6-28-1857	Samuel Elder wife Abigail nee Neuer
NACHTRIEB, Heinrich Franz	b. 5-11-1857 bapt. 6-28-1857	Christian Nachtrieb wife Friedrika nee Diether
HOFSTATTER, Johnnes	b. 5-21-1857 bapt. 9-6-1857	Jacob Hofstatter wife Margretha nee Hocker
LEMMLER, Esa	b. 12-2-1857 bapt. 12-14-1857	Peter Lemmler wife Barbara nee Ganshorn
NEFF, Regina	b. 12-23-1851 bapt. 12-6-1857	Johan Neff wife Sahra nee Young
NEFF, Maria Christina	b. 7-21-1853 bapt. 12-6-1857	Johan Neff wife Sahra nee Young
NEFF, Susanna Johanna	b. 11-8-1854 bapt. 12-6-1857	Johan Neff wife Sahra nee Young
STEINHELFER, Joseph	b. 3-6-1857 bapt. 2-21-1858	Christoph Steinhelfer wife Lidia nee Strack
GUNTHER, Rosina	b._____ bapt. 2-21-1858	Abraham Gunther wife_____
GUNTHER, Catharina	b._____ bapt. 2-21-1858	Abraham Gunther wife_____
LAIER, Sara Regina	b. 1-21-1857 bapt. 2-28-1858	Johan Heinrich Laier wife Catharine nee Heinle
NELSON, Jacob	b. 3-3-1858 bapt. 3-7-1858	Georg Nelson wife Carolina nee Wilhelm
BACKER, Johannes	b. 7-31-1856 bapt. 3-15-1838	Jacob Backer wife Charlotte nee Kahn
TROPF, Louisa	b. 11-6-1857 bapt. 3-15-1858	Jacob Friedrich Tropf wife Philipina nee Maus
TROPF, Heinrich	b. 2-10-1858 bapt. 3-15-1858	Reinhardt Tropf wife Louisa nee Backer
TROPF, Catharina	b. 2-10-1858 bapt. 3-15-1858	Reinhardt Tropf wife Louisa nee Backer
PLETCHER, Georg Wilhelm	b. 10-5-1857 bapt. 3-7-1858	Israel Pletcher wife Lena nee Schneider
SCHAFER, Maria Catharina	b. 1-22-1857 bapt. 8-22-1858	Conrad Schafer wf. Catharina nee Schneider
BURKHARDT, Samuel Wesley	b. 3-5-1858 bapt. 9-5-1858	Abraham Burkhardt wife Carolina nee Schafer
QUANDT, Johanes Theophilus	b. 8-24-1858 bapt. 9-11-1858	Ludwig Quandt wife Maria nee Garth
QUANDT, Maria Catharina	b. 8-24-1858 bapt. 9-11-1858	Ludwig Quandt wife Maria nee Garth
STRAAS, Thomas Alfred	b. 9-13-1857 bapt. 6-18-1858	Wilhelm Straas wife Susanna nee Seifert

344

CHILD	BIRTH AND BAPTISM	PARENTS
POMMERT, Charles Levieth	b. 5-16-1854 bapt. 10-2-1858	Adam Pommert wife Sarah nee Burkhardt
POMMERT, John Joseph	b. 1-5-1856 bapt. 10-2-1858	Adam Pommert wife Sarah nee Burkhardt
POMMERT, Josephine Rosella	b. 1-5-1856 bapt. 10-2-1858	Adam Pommert wife Sarah nee Burkhardt
SEIF, Christina	b. 6-27-1857 bapt. 10-3-1858	Jacob Seif wife Sophia nee Neyer
SCHWEINFIRTH, Katharina	b. 8-5-1858 bapt. 12-17-1858	Phillip Schweinfirth wife Magdalena nee Echart
MINGERSDORF, Atna Catharina	b. 9-10-1858 bapt. 12-17-1858	Lanhardt Mingersdorf wf. Katharina nee Schweinfirth
SEIF, Wilhelm Heinrich	b. bapt. 1-31-1859	Phillip Seif wife Harriet
RÜCKER, Wilhelm Heinrich	b. 2-6-1859 bapt. 4-19-1859	Georg Rucker wf. Katharina nee Schneider
HERZER, Emma Emilie	b. 6-21-1859 bapt. 7-13-1859	L. G. Herzer wife Maria nee Droudt
NEFF, Christina Catharine	b. 8-11-1858 bapt. 7-24-1859	Gottlieb Neff wife Rosina nee Mutchler
WINTER, Johnnes	b. 3-29-1859 bapt. 7-24-1859	Tobias Winter wife Maria nee Gieszer
GUGLER, Anna Maria	b. 4-10-1859 bapt. 8-7-1859	L. Gugler wife Louisa
SCHNEIDER, John Samuel	b. 12-31-1859 bapt. 1-7-1860	John Schneider wife Mary nee Mutchler
KROCK, Jacob	b. 3-4-1855 bapt. 2-2-1860	Tobias Krock wife Mary nee Heinli
KROCK, Georg Franklin	b. 9-18-1858 bapt. 2-2-1860	Tobias Krock wife Mary nee Heinli
NELSON, Catharina Sarah Jane	b. 6-3-1859 bapt. 2-2-1860	John Nelson wife Catharina nee Aug
BALYARD, Charles Wesly	b. 10-30-1857 bapt. 4-20-1860	Samuel Balyard wife Mahala nee Neyer
RÖSH, Salome Louisa	B. 10-26-1859 bapt. 4-1-1860	Carl Wilhelm Rosch wife Dorotha nee Nake
SCHMITT, John Wilhelm	b. 2-2-1860 bapt. 5-2-1860	Johannes Schmitt wf. Margaretha nee Schneider
SULZER, Maria Barbara	b. 10-11-1859 bapt. 12-25-1860	Jacob Sulzer wife F. Elisabetha nee Bruck
STRICKLER, Mary Ann	b. 5-23-1855 bapt. 3-31-1860	John Strickler wife Margaretha nee kepler
STRICKLER, Margaretha Lucinda	b. 9-6-1857 bapt. 9-31-1860	John Strickler wife Margaretha nee Kepler
NELSON, Lucyndia	b. 9-3-1859 bapt. 11-10-1860	Georg Nelson wife Carolina nee Wilhelm
BURKHARDT, Mary Louisa	b. 10-15-1857 bapt. 5-27-1860	Johnnes Burkhardt wife Elisabetha nee Schaffer
BURKHARDT, George William	b. 2-1-1860 bapt. 5-27-1860	Abraham Burkhardt wife Carolina nee Schafer

CHILD	BIRTH AND BAPTISM	PARENTS
GUNTHER, Catharina	b. 5-24-1845 bapt. 1-26-1860	
GUNTHER, Elisabetha	b. 8-11-1845 bapt. 1-26-1860	
" GUNTHER, Anna Maria	b. 4-30-1847 bapt. 1-26-1860	
BOLYARD, Daniel	b. 8-23-1848 bapt. 6-4-1860	John Bolyard wife Sarah nee Mumey
BOLYARD, John Wesly	b. 10-4-1859 bapt. 6-4-1860	John Bolyard wife Sarah nee Mumey
BOLYARD, Mary Jane	b. 10-16-1854 bapt. 6-4-1860	John Bolyard wife Sarah nee Mumey
BOLYARD, Samuel	b. 8-1-1851 bapt. 6-4-1860	John Bolyard wife Sarah nee Mumey
ZIMMERMAN, Jacob	b. 7-25-1857 bapt. 6-24-1860	Peter Zimmerman wife Barbara nee Miller
TROPF, Georg Friedrich	b. 2-27-1859 bapt. 6-24-1860	Jacob Friedrich Tropf wife Philipina nee Maus
TROPF, Reinhart	b. 3-2-1860 bapt. 6-24-1860	Reinhart Tropf wife Louisa nee Baker
FINK, James Eli	b. 4-2-1858 bapt. 6-24-1860	Samuel Fink wife Mary nee Weis
FINK, John Albert	b. 2-20-1860 bapt. 6-27-1860	Samuel Fink wife Mary nee Weis
WEIDEMAIR, Samuel Franklin	b. 3-29-1860 bapt. 6-10-1860	Peter Weidemair wife Christina nee Dingel

Pastors and Circuit Riders of the old German Methodist Church in Galion, Ohio. Their salary is listed as $200.00 for the year.

LEVERDIGE, Benjamin	1820	NACHTRIEB, Gottlob	1850-1851
SCHARROCK, Benjamin		REUTER, Georg A.	1851-1852
BIGELOW, Russell	1827	REUTER, G. A.) DIETER, F.)	1852-1853
NAST, Dr. Christian	1836		
SCHNEIDER, John Sr.		GAHN, Christian) JACOBSMUEHLER, Herman)	1853-1854
BIER, John	1846-1847		
HAEFNER, C.H.) BALDUFF, E.B.)	1847-1848	GAHN, Christian) GRILL, H.)	1854-1855
HAEFNER, C.H.) WESTERFIELD, John H.)	1848-1849	WUNDERLICH, E.	1855-1856
		NACHTRIEB, Christian	1856-1857
SCHNEIDER, P.F.)		HEITMAYER, C.F.	1857-1858
NUHF, Nik) RUF, M.)	1849-1850		

Contributed by Mrs. Ira R. Rizor, 410 Cherry St., Galion, Ohio 44833

MARGARETHA BUEHLER, nee Bohl, b 14 Dec. 1817 in Nussloch, Oberamt Heidelberg, Baden; d 14 May 1875. J. A. Schulze, Pastor.

WIDOW ELINORA FUCHS, nee Winkles, b 2 April 1800 in Bautsch, Kingdom of Sachsen; d 6 Aug. 1875.

ELISABETH HESS, nee Kaeffer, b 21 Feb. 1840 in Mansfield, Ohio; married 10 Mar. 1861 to Heinrich Hess; d 17 Sept 1875.

MATTHIAS RAUCH, b 3 March 1842 in Voeringen, Oberrict Sulz, Wurttenberg; d 8 May 1876.

ANNA ELISABETH DINKEL, nee Steinhilber, b 13 Dec. 1795 in Reichenstatt, Wurz-burgischen; married Johann Christof. Dinkel and was mother of 15 children, 2 living; d 8 Sept 1875 in Olentancy Village.

JOHANN JACOB MOHRENHAUT, b 22 May 1807 in Amsterdam; married in 1850 to Louise Noll; d 27 Oct. 1875.

WILHELM FR. FOHL (FAIL). b 19 Jan. 1797 in Klein Aspach, Wurttenberg; twice married --1st to Ana Maria (no last name given) and 2nd to Caroline Sophia Rabe; he died of a chest cold 17 Dec. 1875.

LOUISE MOHRENHAUT, nee Noll, b 20 June 1800 in Hohensolms, Kreis Wetzlar, Germany; married in 1854 to Johann Mohrenhaut; Louise died on 13 Oct. 1876.

ANNA MARIA LUDWIG, nee Rettig, b 20 Nov 1835 Leesville, Ohio; married 6 July 1841 to Johann Ludwig; d 8 Nov. 1876.

ELISABETHA BARBARA MUTH, nee Lorz, b 1 Jan. 1818 in Klein Bieberan, Hessen Darmstadt; married 4 Dec. (no year given) to George Muth; d 5 Dec. 1876.

HELENA SOPHIA KUHN, nee Stollen, b 9 Jan. 1806 in Obstadt, Wurttenberg; married 24 Oct. 1829 to Christian Kuhn; died in Olentancy Village 27 Jan. 1877.

GEORGE HEINRICH STOTZEL, b 9 Jan. 1795 in Reimerswidler, Canton of Sulz, Elsass; married Anna Maria nee Studer. They came to America in 1836. Anna d 16 Sept. 1873 leaving 3 sons and 4 daughters. George died 16 Feb. 1877 leaving 2 sons and 3 daughters.

ADAM TRACHT, b 31 Dec. 1785 in Reidelbach, Hessen Darmstadt; married 24 Aug. 1817 to Elisabetha Diegeldeyn. They came to America in 1831 with 19 children, 7 sons and 12 daughters. Adam died 14 May 1877.

WM. FAIL, b 5 Oct. 1833 in Stark Co., Ohio; confirmed 4 June 1854; married 3 Dec. 1857 to Marie Christine nee Pfau; Wm died 30 May 1877.

JOHANN GEORGE RAUSCH, b 31 Oct. 1798 in Reichenbach, Hessen Darmstadt, baptized 4 Nov. 1798. Twice married--1st to Dorathea Horn and 2nd to Margaretha Weyra ch. Came to America in 1873. He died 11 Oct. 1877.

347

JACOB HELLINGER, b 3 Feb. 1809 in Abstadt, Oberamt Heilbronn, Wurtenberg; married Catharine Lang; came to America in 1847; d 29 Oct. 1877

ANNA CATHARINE NESS, nee Schisler, b 2 May 1799 in York Co., Pa., baptized 5 June 1799; married in 1817 to Johann Michael Ness. Came to Ohio in J. 1834. She d 31 Jan. 1878 leaving 3 sons and 1 daughter.

HEINRICH PEISTER, b 16 April 1820 in Nussloch Grossherztum Baden; married Elizabeth Transkoph; Heinrich d 21 Nov. 1878.

ANNA ELISABETH SCHAEFER, nee Ness, b 24 Oct. 1833 in Battanfeld, Hessen Darmstadt. Twice married--1st to Wm H. Kreater in J. 1852 (he died 30 Dec. 1857) and 2nd to Johan Jakob Schaefer on 18 Sept. 1859. She d 15 Apr. 1879.

PETER HAUS, b 1804 in Grossaltanstattan, Kreis Wetzlar, Kingdom of Preaussau (Prussia); married Marg. Neumann. Came to America in 1847. Peter d 1 Oct. 1879.

SOPHIA CAROLINE FAIL (FOHL)", nee Rabe. b 19 June 1807 in Kleingschwenda, sovereign of Schwarzbach Rudelstadt; d 25 Nov. 1879.

WIDOW ELISABETH PEISTER, nee Transkoph, b 27 Apr. 1816 in Koenigoberg in Giesen Grossherztum, Hessen; d 23 Dec. 1879.

CATHARINE ELISABETH FLATTISH, nee Scheider, wife of Christ. Flattish, b 2 Feb. 1845 in Dodenau, Hessen Darmstadt, baptized 15 Sept. 1856; married 4 Oct. 1864. She d 21 Feb. 1881.

CARL TROSTEL, b 21 Sept. 1828 in Rossweg, Oberamt Fecingen, Wurttenberg; 1st married Lena Ott who preceded him in death leaving 5 children; 2nd married Rebecca Delp of Hessen Darmstadt. He died 3 Aug. 1881 of sunstroke.

MICHAEL THOSTEL, father of Carl Trostel, b 16 Jan. 1795, came to America in 1848. His wife died at sea. He died 15 Aug. 1881.

CATHARINE SINGER, nee Beinhauer; married on 31 May 1807 to Johan Singer. She died 25 July 1880 leaving 6 sons and 3 daughters. Burial in Ruggles in Ashland Co., Ohio.

MARIA ANA GERMANN wife of Gared Germann, born 16 Nov. 1818 in Hamerville, Schuylkill Co., Pa., she d 5 Dec. 1880.

CATHARINE SPIEGEL widow of H. Spiegel, b 31 Oct. 1809 in Northhampton Co., Pa., she d 28 Dec. 1880.

CATHARINE HELLINGER, nee Lang, b 17 Oct. 1809 in Abstadt, Wurttenberg, German; married 2 Feb. 1837 to J. J. Hellinger (he d 29 Oct. 1877). They came to America in 1847. Catharine died 9 Nov. 1881.

GEORGE HAUS, b 28 Mar. 1823 in Oberling, Preussen(Prussia), came to America in 1852; married Elisabeth nee Poister. He d 6 Feb. 1882 leaving 3 sons and 3 daughters.

ST. JOHNS LUTHERAN AND GERMAN REFORMED CHURCH RECORDS - DARKE COUNTY, OHIO

Contributed by: Kenneth Ketring, P.O. Box 910, Fairborn, Ohio 45324

This church located in German (now known as Liberty) Township was one of the early churches in the area. The church, no longer in existence was located in the southeastern corner of Section 22, Township 11, Range 1.

BAPTISMS

Date of Bapt. Date of Birth	Parents	Child	Sponsors
Oct 31 1835 Oct 17 1835	William W. KESTER Elizabeth C.	John A.	the parents
Aug 13 1837 June 30 1837	William W. KESTER Elizabeth C.	Sarah	the parents
June 16 1839 Mar 21 1839	William W. KESTER Elizabeth C.	Catharin Maria	the parents
Jany 16 1839 Jany 3 1838	Carl Christian LOSH Julyanna	John Ludwig	the parents
June 16 1839 May 14 1839	David KETRING	Jonethan	Esther Siniard
May 21 1839 --- 2 1838	Abraham BOWMAN Maria	Mariann	the parents
May 21 1839 Mar 8 1839	Abraham COX Hannah	Luvena Jane	Maria Waggoner
Dec 30 1838 Dec 19 1838	Lewis KIMMERING Katharine	William	the parents
Apr 18 1838 Sept 9 1837	Wm WAGGONER Elizabeth	Daniel	the parents
Mar 3 1838 Jany 5 1838	Abraham KIMMERLING and wife Ka.	Susannah	the parents
Apr 29 1838 Mar 12 1838	Ludwick TEFORD Susanna	Elizabeth	the parents
Aug 12 1838 June 24 1838	Jacob TEFORD Elizabeth	Jacob	the parents
Aug 12 1838 June 16 1838	George TEFORD Molly	Aaron	the parents

349

Date of Bapt. Date of Birth	Parents	Child	Sponsors
Apr 19 1840 Nov 18 1839	George KESTER Eve	Solomon	the parents
Apr 19 1840 Apr 3 1840	Abraham KIMMERLING Katherine	Katharine	the parents
Apr 19 1840 Jany 23 1839	Jacob BENDER Nelly	Eli	the parents
Oct 2 (1840) Oct 8 1839	Lewis KIMERLING Catharine	Henry	the parents
Oct 2 1840 Aug 22 1840	Stephan WAGNER	Maryan Julyan	Parents
Oct 2 1840 July 5 1840	Henry BOWMAN Matilty	John	Henry Bowman Matilty
Oct 2 1840 Aug 23 1839	Henry BOWMAN Matilty	Wm Henry	the same
Sept 6 1840 Sept 7 1839	John BOWMAN Marchel	Catharine	Parents
Sept 6 1840 July 14 1840	Jacob BOWMAN Catharine	Daniel	Parents
Sept 6 1840 July 10 1840	Peter LANTZ Sarah	Israel	Parents
Sept 6 1840 May 18 1840	Cristophar FAYLER Carolina Lantz	Anna	Peter Lantz Sarah
Sept 6 1840 Dec 7 1839	Benjamen GERST Rebeca	Rebeca	Anna Gerst
Feb 5 1841 Dec 7 1840	Wm W. KESTER & Elizabeth	Mary	Wm W. Kester and wife
July 4 1841 Jany 16 1841	Abra. BOWMAN and Mary	David	Abra. Bowman and wife
(not given) Oct 7 1841	David_____(?) Anna	Johannes	Parents
(not given) Oct 22 1841(?)	John BOWMAN	Mary	Parent

350

Date of Bapt. Date of Birth	Parents	Child	Sponsors
(not given) Jany 3 1842	John HAUSENFOES Margaret	Mary Ann	Parents
(not given) Aug 26 1841	Henry BOWMEN	Catharine	Parents
Oct 17 1842 Sept 6 1842	Johannes HENNING Christina	Isaac	the parents
Oct 17 1842 Sept 1 1842	Johannes LINDEMUTH Catharina	Maria Catharina	Jacob Henning Catharina
Mar 27 1842 Sept 6 1841	Tobias WAGGNER Lydia	Lydia	Jacob Henning Barbara
Mar 27 1842 Dec 18 1841	Jacob KOHLMAN Sara	Philip	the parents themselves
Mar 27 1842 Aug 30 1841	Peter SCHEFER(?) Elizabeth	Willhelm	Christian_____?
Dec 2 1838 Oct 3 1838	Jacob KOHLMAN Sara	Maria Catharina	Maria Catharina _____?
Nov 6 1842 Sept 2 1842	David SCHLECTY Scharlot	Maria	the parents themselves
Nov 6 1842 Sept 9 1842	William KESTER Elizabeth Catharina	Paul _____ ?	the parents themselves
Nov 6 1842 Nov 24 1841	Jacob TEFORD Elizabeth	Jain (in pencil- Sarah Lantz)	the parents themselves
Aug 3 1845 June 1 1845	Jacob TEFORD Elizabeth	Daniel	the parents
Aug 3 1845 Nov 3 1844	Christopher SCHWILLE Anna Maria	Jacob	the parents
Aug 3 1845 Sept 30 1844	George KESTER Eve	Lucetta Ann	the parents
(not given) June 24 1844	Jacob (AGNE or AYRES) Elizabeth	Gertrude	the mother

351

COMMUNICANTS - June 16, 1839

Henry H. SMELCHER
John KETRING
Wm W. KESTER
George KIMMERLING
Abraham KIMMERLING
Michael FAILOR
Leonard HEIGHBARGER
John HOSSENFOOIS
John BOWMAN
Charles C. LUSH

David KETRING
George WAGGONER
Peter LANTZ
Christtina SMELCHER
Katharine KETRING
Elizabeth C. KESTER
Katharine KIMMERLING
Katharine KIMMERLING
Katharine FAILOR
Katharine HEIGHBARGER

Margaret HOSENFOOES
Sarah KETRING
Esther SINIARD
Juliana LUSH
Maria SLECHTY
Barbara KETRING
Sarah LANTZ
Maria WAGGONER
Elizabeth LINTERMOOTE
Elizabeth DENNER

COMMUNICANTS - Dec. 1, 1839

Jacob H. SMELCHER
John KETRING
Wm W. KESTER
Abraham KIMMERLING
George KIMMERLING

Michael FAILOR
David KETRING
Peter LANTZ
George WAGGONER

Mary BUTT
Sarah FOX
Katharine FAILOR
Katherine KIMMERLING
Katharine KIMMERLING

Sarah KETRING
Elizabeth DENNER
Katharine KETRING
Julian WAGGONER

COMMUNICANTS - April 20, 1840

John KETRING
Abraham KIMMERLING
Michael FAILER
Jacob H. SMELCHER
John HOSSENFOOSE
John BOWMAN
Abraham BOWMAN
George KIMMERLING

John BOWMAN
Leonard HEIGHBARGER
Jacob BOWMAN
Wm W. KESTER
Peter LANTZ
Michael LINTHAMOOTE
David KETRING
Katharine KETRING

Elizabeth BOWERS
Mary WAGGONER
Katharine FAILER
Christena SMELCHER
Marg. HOSSENFOOSE
Sarah KETRING
_____? BOWMAN
Katharine KIMMERLING

Elizabeth WILLCOX
Mary BUTT
Marg. HEIGHBARGER
Katharine BOWMAN
Eliz. C. KESTER
Sarah LANTZ
Barbara KETRING
Elizabeth DENNER

COMMUNICANTS - (not dated)

Wm KESTER, Elizabeth
J. H. SMELKER, Dene
George KIMERLING, Catharine
John BOWMAN
Jacob BOWMAN
David KETRING
Peter LANTZ, Sarah
Elizabeth DENNER
John KETRING, Catharine
Sarah KETRING
Michael FAYLER, Catharine

Jacob BENDER, Nelly
Catharine BOWMAN
Samuel BOWMAN, Deane
Christian SCHLECHTY, Susan
Samuel NOGLE
John SCHLECHTY, Mary
Mary WAGNER
Abraham BOWMAN
Michael LINDERMUDE, Elizabeth
Mary BOWMAN
John BOWMAN

COMMUNICANTS - November 6, 1842

Jacob TEFORD
Christian SCHLECHTY
George WAGONER
David KETRING
Johannes KETRING
George KIMMERLING
Abraham KIMMERLING

Jacob SMELCHER
William KESTER
Michael LINDERMUTH
Johannes _____?
Johannes BOWMAN
Michael FAILER

Elicabeth TEFORD
Maria WAGONER
Esther SINIARD
Ellen(?) KETRING
Sarah KETRING
Catharine KETRING
Catharine KIMMERLING

Catharine KIMMERLING
Christina SMELCHER
Elizabeth KESTER
Elizabeth LINDERMUTH
Marchel BOWMAN
Catharine FAILER

352

The following records were copied from "Naturalization Record, First Papers, No. 1" which was originally located in the Common Pleas Court (Clerk of Courts's Office) in Darke County, but has since been removed to the Archives Division, Wright State University, Dayton, Ohio. Page on which record may be found in the original book is given in parenthesis. It should be explained that the first papers refer to the Declaration of Intention, while second papers refer to the actual Naturalization itself. However, quite often the first papers give more genealogical data than the second papers.

12-3-1856 - Frederick SELBER, a native of Hassel, Germany, aged 46 yrs., emigrated from Bremen in July 1853, arrived New York in August 1853. (1)
12-5-1856 - Frederick LANFER a native of Prussia, aged 28 yrs., emigrated from Prussia 9-14-1853 and arrived in New York 12-5-1953. (2)
12-19-1856 - Michael MORRIS a native of Lower Canada, aged 24 yrs., emigrated from Lower Canada 8-20-1852 and arrived in Buffalo, New York 8-20-1852. (3)
12-22-1856 - Jacob SLOTTENBECKER, a native of Wertemburgh, aged 55 yrs., emigrated from Wertemburgh April 1845 and arrived in New York in May 1845. (4)
12-22-1856 - Henry BOTENHEIFER a native of Wertimburgh, aged 46 yrs., emigrated from Wertenburgh in May 1831 and arrived in Baltimore 11-26-1831. (5)
12-25-1856 - Henry WISE a native of Hessen, aged 19 yrs., emigrated from Hesson 10-5-1853, arrived in New York 1-17-1854. (6)
1-14-1857 - Christian STRENCH a native of Wirtemburgh, aged 35 yrs., emigrated from Wirtemburgh Sept. 1853 and arrived in New York Sept. 1853. (7)
1-16-1857 - William ALLAN a native of Ireland, aged 55 yrs., emigrated from Ireland Nov. 1852 and arrived New York 12-24-1852. (8)
2-2-1857 - Michael MURRY a native of Ireland, aged 28 yrs., emigrated from Ireland 1-1-1849 and arrived in New Orleans 2-20-1849. (9)
2-3-1857 - John KAHLI (KOHLI) a native of Austria, aged 52 yrs., emigrated from Austria July 1853 and arrived in New York 8-27-1853. (10)
4-14-1857 - Christian Frederick KARN a native of Baden, aged 22 yrs., emigrated from Baden 10-20-1853 and arrived in New York 12-20-1853. (11)
4-15-1837 - John G. STAPF (or SLOPF) a native of Wirtemburgh, aged 21 yrs., emigrated from Wirtenburgh 4-4-1854, arrived New York 5-4-1854. (12)
4-16-1857 - Charles SEIFERT a native of Saxony, aged 25 yrs., emigrated from Saxony Nov. 1853 and arrived in New York 11-18-1853. (13)
5-30-1857 - Henry WEITZEL a native of Hessia, aged 50 yrs., emigrated from Bremen Nov. 1852 and arrived in New Orleans in Jan. 1853. (14)
6-1-1857 - Frederick ENDORFF a native of Hessia, aged 52 yrs., emigrated from Hessia 5-15-1852 and arrived in New York 7-8-1852. (15)
7-4-1857 - R4qncis M. KATZENBERGER a native of Baden, aged 81 yrs., emigrated from Baden in Mar. 1845 and arrived in New York 4-21-1845. (16)
7-28-1857 - Charles REINHART a native of Saxony, aged 28 yrs., emigrated from Hamberg in 1844 and arrived in New York in 1844. (17)
9-29-1957 John CASHMAN a native of Ireland, aged 37 yrs., emigrated from Liverpool in 1846 and arrived in New York in 1846. (18)
10-5-1857 - Frederick KIRCHERT a native of Wertinburgh, aged 43 yrs., emigrated fr om Wertinburgh 3-1-1857 and arrived in New York 4-28-1857. (19)
10-5-1857 - Jacob ROLLER a native of Wertinburgh, aged 41 yrs., emigrated from Wertinburgh 11-13-1853 and arrived in New York 1-15-1854. (20)
10-5-1857 - James LYNCH a native of Ireland, aged 50 yrs., emigrated from Ireland 12-25-1848 and arrived in New Orleans 2-1-1849. (21)

10-5-1837 - Patrick RYAN a native of Ireland, aged 23 yrs., emigrated from
    Ireland in Feb. 1841 and arrived in New York in Mar. 1841. (22)
10-8-1857 - Joseph SMITH a native of Ireland, aged 29 yrs., emigrated from Ireland
    10-19-1849 and arrived in New Orleans 12-18-1849. (23)
10-8-1857 - Patrick KEOGH a native of Ireland, aged 30 yrs. (written over-35 yrs.),
    emigrated from Ireland 4-27-1851 and arrived in New York 5-30-1851. (24)
10-5-1857 - Henry COOMBS a native of England, aged 23 yrs., emigrated from England
    3-9-1851 and arrived in New York in April 1851. (25)
10-9-1857 - Henry KREMME a native of Hesse Cassel, aged 29 yrs., emigrated from
    Hesse Cassel July 1852 and arrived in New York August 1832. (26)
10-17-1857 - Peter HERBERT a native of Prussia, aged 36 yrs., emigrated from Prussia
    8-24-1857 and arrived New York 10-4-1857. (27)
11-3-1857 - John Christian SCHMIDT a native of Prussia, aged 31 yrs., emigrated
    from Prussia 8-26-1852 and arrived in New York 10-4-1857. (28)
11-5-1837 - Andrew HILDENBRANT a native of Baden, aged 29 yrs. emigrated from Baden
    9-8-1845 and arrived in New York 10-20-1845. (29)
12-24-1857 - Jacob MILROON a native of Baden, aged 36 yrs., emigrated from Baden
    9-25-1854 and arrived in New York 12-24-1854. (30)
3-20-1858 - Cornelious CASHMAN a native of Ireland, aged 23 yrs., emigrated from
    Liverpool in 1845 and arrived in New York in 1846. (31)
4-10-1858 - John MURPHEY a native of Ireland, aged 22 yrs., emigrated from Ireland
    in 1852 and arrived in New York in 1852. (32)
4-10-1858 - Jeremiah FRALEY a native of Ireland, aged 30 yrs., emigrated from
    Ireland in 1846 and arrived in New York in 1846. (33)
4-17-1850 - Frederick Poller a native of Wertemburgh, aged 25 yrs., emigrated from
    Wertemburgh in Mar. 1858 and arrived in New York in Apr. 1858. (34)
5-18-1858 - Michael CUNNINGHAM a native of Ireland, aged 29 yrs., emigrated from
    Ireland in 1853 and arrived in New York in 1853. (35)
6-15-1858 - Isaac POLLACK a native of France, aged 21 yrs., emigrated from Havre
    France in 1854 and arrived in New Orleans in 1854. (36)
6-24-1858 - Sebastian WORCH a native of Hesse Cassel, aged 25 yrs., emigrated from
    Germany in 1853 and arrived in New York in 1853. (37)
8-13-1858 - Frederick EHRMANN a native of Bavaria, aged 37 yrs., emigrated from
    Bavaria in 1853 and arrived in New York in 1853. (38)
9-27-1858 - John LANG a native of Baden, aged 43 yrs., emigrated from Baden
    10-24-1854 and arrived in New Orleans 12-22--1854. (39)
10-2-1858 - Frederick BLACKMAN a native of Baden, aged 44 yrs., emigrated from
    Baden 9-25-1854 and arrived in New York 12-24-1854. (40)
10-6-1858 - Frederick KOENING a native of Wertenburgh, aged 24 yrs., emigrated from
    Wertenburgh in Sept. 1852 and arrived in New York in Oct. 1852. (41)
10-9-1858 - Michael SHEA a native of Ireland, aged 30 yrs., emigrated from Ireland
    7-1-1850 and arrived in New York 8-17-1850. (42)
10-11-1858 - Michael CURRY a native of Ireland, aged 39 yrs., emigrated from
    Ireland 5-5-1849 and arrived in New York 8-17-1850. (43)
10-11-1858 - Alexander McALPIN a native of Scotland, aged 30 yrs., emigrated from
    Scotland 7-27-1854 and arrived in New York 8-24-1854. (44)
10-14-1858 - George ROESSER a native of France, aged 32 yrs., emigrated from
    France 8-11-1853 and arrived in New York 9-12-1853. (45)
10-22-1858 - Henry JACOBY a native of Hessia Hamburg, aged 44 yrs., emigrated from
    Germany 4-1-1853 and arrived in New York 5-20-1853. (46)

10-25-1858 - Frederick KERMMER a native of Switzerland, aged 30 yrs., emigrated
    from Switzerland in May 1852 and arrived in New York 7-25-1858. (47)
11-20-1858 - Michael ROHLAND a native of Bavaria, aged 42 yrs., emigrated from
    Germany 3-2-1847 and arrived in New York 5-14-1847. (48)
12-2-1858 - George WISE a native of Hesse Dannstadt, aged 25 yrs., emigrated
    from Germany 9-21-1834 and arrived in New York 10-22-1854. (49)
12-2-1858 - John WISE a native of Hesse Darmstadt, aged 31 yrs., emigrated from
    Germany 3-1-1851 and arrived in New Orleans 5-10-1851. (50)
12-20-1858 - Frederick SCHATZER a native of Baden, aged 32 yrs., emigrated from
    Germany 11-7-1846 and arrived in New York 11-30-1846. (51)
3-18-1859 - Francis John FRANCIS a native of France, aged 34 yrs., emigrated
    from France 11-7-1854 and arrived in New York 1-1-1855. (52)
3-18-1859 - Jule FRANCIS a native of France, aged 21 yrs., emigrated from France
    11-10-1856 and arrived in New York 1-5-1857. (53)
3-18-1859 - John Nicholas ALEXANDER a native of France, aged 33 yrs., emigrated
    from France 3-12-1854 and arrived in New York 4-22-1854. (54)
4-4-1859 - Joseph WEBER a native of France, aged 38 yrs., emigrated from France
    10-5-1857 and arrive in New Orleans 11-16-1837. (55)
6-21-1859 - Joseph HARMAN a native of Baden, Germany, aged 42 yrs., emigrated from
    Germany 5-16-1853 and arrived in New York 7-4-1853. (56)
7-12-1859 - Ira TRIPP a native of Canada, aged 31 yrs., emigrated from Canida
    10-3-1853 and arrived at Wilson Village, New York in Oct. 1853. (57)
7-19-1859 - William STUCK a native of Leppe Detmold, aged 53 yrs., emigrated from
    Germany 4-19-1854 and arrived in New York 6-29-1854. (58)
7-19-1859 - William GROTE a native of Leppe Detmold, aged 45 yrs., emigrated from
    Germany 4-19-1854 and arrived in New York 6-29-1854. (59)
8-10-1859 - Thomas DOOLY a native of Ireland, aged 23 yrs., emigrated from England
    3-26-1857 and arrived in New York 4-20-1857. (60)
8-10-1859 - Michael COSTOLO a native of Ireland, aged 23 yrs., emigrated from
    England 10-10-1856 and arrived in Philadelphia in Nov. 1856. (61)
8-10-1859 - James RYEN a native of Ireland, aged 30 yrs., emigrated from England
    6-3-1857 and arrived in New York 7-15-1837. (62)
8-29-1859 - Robert KIRKLEY a native of England, aged 49 yrs., emigrated from
    England in Feb. 1850 and arrived in New York 3-31-1850. (63)
9-17-1859 - Jacob STRIENZ a native of Wertemburgh, aged 67 yrs., emigrated from
    Germany 9-28-1852 and arrived in New York in Oct. 1852. (64)
9-21-1859 - Peter HERBELET a native of France, aged 36 yrs., emigrated from France
    5-1-1853 and arrived in New York 7-1-1853. (65)
9-21-1859 - Nicholas HUNBERT a native of France, aged 56 yrs., emigrated from
    France 3-27-1852 and arrived in New York 5-28-1852. (66)
9-21-1859 - Christopher NAGOTOUX (MAGOTOUX) a native of France, aged 47 yrs.
    emigrated from France 3-27-1852 and arrived in New York 5-28-1852. (67)
9-21-1859 - Charles BRANDT a native of Germany....(rest not filled in). (68)
9-21-1859 - Adam KIPP a native of Wertemburgh, Germany, aged 37 yrs., emigrated
    from Germany 4-1-1857 and arrived in New York 5-28-1857. (69)
9-23-1859 - John STUBY a native of Prussia, aged 47 yrs., emigrated from Prussia
    7-25-1854 and arrived in New York in Sept. 1854. (70)
9-24-1859 - Jacques ANDREWS a native of France, aged 25 yrs. emigrated from France
    5-20-1853 and arrived in New York 6-28-1853. (71)
Sept. 1859 - John N. HENRY a native of France, aged 65 yrs., emigrated from France
    5-1-1852 and arrived in New York 7-1-1852. (72)
Sept. 1859 - Stephen PEQUIGNOT a native of France, aged 35 yrs., emigrated from
    France 5-3-1850 and arrived in New York 7-12-1850. (73)
9-24-1859 - Francis H. CHAPPIUS a native of Switzerland, aged 35 yrs., emigrated from
    Switzerland in Mar. 1853, and arrived in New Orleans (date not given). (74)

9-24-1859 - John B. HENRY a native of France, aged 31 yrs., emigrated from France
3-10-1853 and arrived in New York 6-1-1853. (75)
9-24-1859 - Lewis MANGIN a native of France, aged 36 yrs., emigrated from France
3-14-1854 and arrived in New York 4-21-1854. (76)
9-24-1859 - Lewis NEYSON a native of France, aged 49 yrs., emigrated from France
4-21-1838 and arrived in New Orleans 7-7-1838. (77)
9-28-1859 - August DEPPORE a native of France aged 29 yrs., emigrated from France
in Jan. 1855 and arrived in New York in Mar. 1855. (78)
10-1859 - John PRACHTER a native of Hessia, Germany, aged 31 yrs., emigrated from
Germany in July 1847 and arrived at Baltimore in Sept. 1847. (79)
10-4-1859 - Joseph ALEXANDER a native of France, aged 29 yrs., emigrated from France
in Feb. 1853 and arrived in New York 3-28-1853. (80)
10-4-1859 - Louis WILLIAM a native of France, aged 24 yrs., emigrated from France
3-9-1853 and arrived in New York 4-28-1853. (81)
10-4-1859 - Peter BUDVIE (BUDVIO) a native of France, aged 30 yrs., emigrated from
France 3-15--1854 and arrived in New York 5-1-1854. (82)
10-4-1859 - Francis MALLER a native of France, aged 24 yrs., emigrated from France
5-10-1853 and arrived in New York in Aug. 1853. (83)
10-5-1859 - John Nicholas DIDOT a native of France, aged 40 yrs., emigrated from
France 5-11-1853 and arrived in New York 7-12-1853. (84)
10-5-1859 - John MURPHY a native of Ireland aged 28 yrs., emigrated from Ireland
4-8-1850 and arrived in Boston 5-16-1850. (85)
10-5-1859 - John B. MILLER a native of France, aged 46 yrs., emigrated from France
4-23-1840 and arrived in New York 6-24-1840. (86)
10-5-1859 - James SHELLY a native of Ireland, aged 47 yrs., emigrated from Ireland
10-8-1847 and arrived in New Orleans 11-20-1847. (87)
10-8-1859 - James HOGEN a native of Ireland, aged 23 yrs., emigrated from Ireland
5-23-1855 and arrived in New York 6-23-1855. (88)
10-10-1859 - Christopher WENNER a native of Germany, (no age given), emigrated from
Wertenburgh, Germany 9-10-1853 and arrived in New York 11-10-1853. (89)
10-11-1859 - John KIRKLEY a native of England, aged 26 yrs., emigrated from England
in July 1853 and arrived in New York 9-3-1853. (90)
10-11-1859 - Henry AHLES a native of Hanover, Germany, (no age given), emigrated
from Germany 5-1-1854 and arrived in New York 6-24-1854. (91)
10-11-1859 - John KESLAR a native of Hessen Darmstadt, Germany, aged 51 yrs.,
emigrated from Germany 4-1-1847 and arrived New York 5-22-1847. (92)
10-21-1859 - Joseph DINTNER a native of Bavaria, Germany, aged 43 yrs., emigrated
from Germany 6-9-1859 and arrived in New York 8-14-1859. (93)
10-24-1859 - Lewis SCHICKENDANCE a native of Hanover, Germany, aged 30 yrs., emigrated from Germany 10-1-1856 and arrived New York 11-30-1856. (94)
12-9-1859 - Celeste BRUEY a native of France, aged 40 yrs., emigrated from France
3-11-1844 and arrived in New York 5-5-1844. (95)
2-4-1860 - Henry CARON a native of Bayern, Germany, aged 30 yrs., emigrated from
Germany 9-26-1854 and arrived in New York 10-26-1854. (96)
2-4-1860 - Franz Johann Melchoir MUELLER a native of Prussia, Germany, aged 45 yrs.,
emigrated from Prussia 9-16-1853 and arrived New York 1-4-1854. (97)
2-4-1860 - John BELGER a native of Germany, aged 25 yrs., emigrated from Germany
8-28-1857 and arrived in New York 9-19-1857. (98)
2-28-1860 - Nicholas PLEGNEY a native of France, aged 45 yrs., emigrated from France
3-22-1839 and arrived in New Orleans 6-1-1839. (99)
4-2-1860 - George BONNORONT a native of France, aged 34 yrs., emigrated from France
3-31-1860 and arrived New York 5-9-1860. (100)

4-25-1860 - Jacob WARNER a native of Wertemburgh, Germany, aged 22 yrs., emigrated
        from Germany 4-12-1858 and arrived in New York 7-3-1858. (101)
6-11-1860 - George KELLER a native of Wertemburgh, Germany, aged 40 yrs., emigrated
        from Germany 4-2-1857 and arrived in New York 5-18-1857. (102)
7-9-1860 - James WELSH a native of Ireland, aged 33 yrs., emigrated from Ireland
        3-13-1854 and arrived in New York 4-25-1854. (103)
7-31-1860- Henry GIMBLE a native of Hesse Cassel, Germany aged 68 yrs., emigrated
        from Germany 4-1-1860 and arrived New York 5-6-1860. (104)
8-4-1860 - Adam WOLFEL a native of Hesse Kassel, Germany, aged 44 yrs., emigrated
        from Germany in 1842 and arrived in Baltimore in 1842. (105)
9-3-1860 - James McGLAUGHLIN a native of Ireland, aged 40 yrs., emigrated from
        Ireland 11-14-1847 and arrived in New York 4-12-1848. (106)
9-10-1860 - John REICHTER a native of Bavaria, Germany, aged 51 yrs., emigrated
        from Germany 10-5-1839 and arrived in New Orleans 1-2-1840. (107)
9-22-1860 - John COSTOLO a native of Ireland, aged 45 yrs., emigrated from Ireland
        10-13-1851 and arrived New York 12-26-1851. (108)
9-22-1860 - John CAULFIELD a native of Ireland......(rest not filled in). (109)
10-1-1860 - Philip WISE a native of Hesse Darmstadt, aged 24 yrs. emigrated from
        Germany 9-21-1854 and arrived New York 10-22-1854. (110)
10-3-1860 - John SWAIN a native of Canida, aged 30 yrs., emigrated from Canida
        12-10-1832 and arrived in Buffalo in Dec. 1832. (111)
10-5-1860 - Timothy HONNEL (HORMEL) a native of Ireland, aged 46 yrs., emigrated
        from Ireland 11-1-1850 and arrived in New Orleans 3-1-1851. (112)
10-5-1860 - Miles GILRAIN a native of Ireland, aged 21 yrs., emigrated from Ireland
        3-1-1858 and arrived in New Orleans 5-2-1858. (113)
10-10-1860 - Henry LARNRINACH a native of France, aged 56 yrs., migrated from
        France 3-31-1852 and arrived New York 5-20-1852. (114)
11-6-1860 - Michael GALVIN a native of Ireland, aged 36 yrs., emigrated from
        Ireland 4-18-1847 and arrived at Burlington 6-13-1847. (115)
11-19-1860 - Christopher ZACHARIAS a native of Saxe Weimar, Germany, aged 22 yrs.,
        emigrated from Germany 5-1-1860 and arrived New York 5-30-1860. (116)
1-1-1861 - Martin HOFACKER a native of Wertemberg, Germany, aged 31 yrs., emigrated
        from Germany 2-11-1852 and arrived New York 4-23-1852. (117)
2-2-1861 - William Frederick ADAM a native of Prussia, aged 61 yrs., emigrated from
        Prussia 3-9-1856 and arrived New York 5-10-1856. (118)
4-4-1861 - Michael MAGHER a native of Ireland, aged 37 yrs., emigrated from Ireland
        4-1-1854 and arrived Burlington, Vermont in Sept. 1854. (119)
6-19-1861 - William ILIGAN a native of Sax Weimar, Germany, aged 45 yrs., emigrated
        from Germany 5-16-1859 and arrived in Philadelphia 6-4-1859. (120)
6-19-1861 - Laurence SIMON a native of Sax Weimer, Germany, aged 49 yrs., emigrated
        from Germany 5-16-1859 and arrived Philadelphia 6-4-1859. (121)
Nov. 1861 - George WENGER a native of Baden, Germany, aged 32 yrs., emigrated from
        Germany 3-29-1849 and arrived New York 5-3-1849. (122)
11-18-1861 - Justine SIMON a native of Saxhan Waimer, Germany, aged 22 yrs.,
        emigrated from Germany 1-12-1860 and arrived New York 3-3-1860. (123)
11-25-1861 - John TRIESCHMAN a native of Hesse Kassle, Germany, aged 29 yrs.,
        emigrated from Germany in July 1850 and arrived Baltimore in Oct. 1850.(124)
11-28-1861 - John Christian FISHER a native of Wertenberg, Germany, (no age given),
        emigrated from Germany 11-6-1849 and arrived New York 12-3-1849. (125)
12-4-1861 - Peter SCHIELDS a native of Belgium, aged 35 yrs., emigrated from Belgium
        3-20-1852 and arrived New York 5-6-1852. (126)
4-10-1862 - Gustav HORNNING a native of Prussia, aged 37 yrs., emigrated from Prussia
        6-26-1859 and arrived New York in July 1859. (127)

357

4-19-1862 - Charles GOBLEN a native of Sheps Arms Hartz, Germany, aged 39 yrs.,
emigrated from Germany in June 1861 and arrived New York in Aug. 1861.(128)
5-21-1862 - Charley BRANDT a native of Hesse Kassle, Germany, aged 22 yrs., emigrated from Germany 4-15-1859 and arrived New York 5-1-1859.   (129)
6-2-1862 - George SINNAMAN a native of Ireland, aged 36 yrs., emigrated from Ireland
in Sept. 1847 and arrived in New York in Oct. 1847.   (130)
6-21-1862 - Francis KUSNACK a native of Switzerland, aged 25 yrs., emigrated from
Switzerland 9-14-1858 and arrived New York 12-28-1858.   (131)
6-24-1862 - Geodlobe SUMMER a native of Wertemburgh, Germany, aged 24 yrs., emigrated from Wertemburgh 6-10-1860 and arrived New York 7-23-1860.   (132)
8-1-1862 - John Andrew ARNOLD a native of Prussia, Germany, aged 41 yrs., emigrated
from Prussia 5-10-1862 and arrived Baltimore 6-25-1862.   (133)
9-29-1862 - Conrad SMITH a native of Hesse Cassle, Germany, aged 32 yrs., emigrated
from Germany 4-1-1861 and arrived in New York 5-24-1861.   (134)
7-27-1863 - Echhardt FLACK a native of Car Hessen, Germany, aged 54 yrs., emigrated
from Germany 4-12-1853 and arrived in Baltimore 5-25-1853.   (135)
8-18-1863 - Christipher BERRICE a native of Saxhon Waimer, Germany, aged 48 yrs.,
emigrated from Germany 5-1-1861 and arrived in New York 5-30-1861.   (136)
9-18-1863 - Hermin HORIN a native of Hesse Kassle, Germany, aged 46 yrs., emigrated
from Germany 10-3-1860 and arrived in Baltimore 11-25-1860.   (137)
10-7-1863 - Edward HOME of Hertzog, Sae Memigen, Germany, aged 36 yrs., emigrated
from Germany 3-10-1856 and arrived New York 5-26-1856.   (138)
10-10-1863 - Stephen CONNER a native of Ireland, aged 36 yrs., emigrated from
Ireland in Mar. 1852 and arrived in New York 5-27-1852.   (139)
10-9-1863 - Christopher HOLCAPLE a native of Kurhessen, Germany, aged 26 yrs.,
emigrated from Germany 3-15-1860 and arrived New Orleans 5-29-1863.   (140)
11-7-1864 - Conrad BAKER a native of Hessia Darmstadt, Germany, aged 24 yrs.,
emigrated from Germany (no date given) to United States 10-17-1859.   (141)
5-1-1865 - Gottlieb ZIEGLER a native of Saony, Germany, aged 50 yrs., emigrated
from Germany 4-11-1861 and arrived in New York 5-1-1865.   (142)
8-15-1865 - Michael McCARTY a native of Ireland, aged 45 yrs., emigrated from
Ireland 4-4-1846 and arrived in New York 5-3-1846.   (143)
8-31-1865 - Thomas HARRINGTON a native of Ireland, aged 36 yrs., emigrated from
Ireland 8-15-1852 and arrived New York 10-1-1852.   (144)
10-9-1865 - Michael BAIRNAS a native of Ireland, aged 55 yrs., emigrated from
Ireland 4-6-1859 and arrived New York 5-12-1859.   (145)
11-27-1865 - Conrad BAUSS a native of Wertemberg, Germany, aged 68 yrs., emigrated
from Germany 8-5-1859 and arrived New York 9-30-1859.   (146)
11-27-1865 - Frederick MARTIN a native of Saxon Weimer, Issemach, Germany, aged 48
yrs., emigrated from Germany 5-1-1860 and arrived New York 6-1-1860.   (147)
7-28-1866 - George ROMBARG (ROUSBARG) a native of Hanover, Germany, aged 22 yrs.
emigrated from Germany (no date given) and arrived New York 5-6-1865.(148)
8-28-1866 - James AGAN a native of Ireland, aged 29 yrs., emigrated from Ireland
4-29-1865 and arrived New York 5-12-1805.   (149)
9-3-1866 - Daniel COSTELO a native of Ireland, aged 40 yrs., emigrated from Ireland
about 1846 and arrived Port Huron 11-28-1861.   (150)
9-7-1866 - Frederick THEIS a native of Byron, Germany, aged 29 yrs., emigrated
from Germany about 1857 and arrived New York (no date given).   (151)
9-24-1866 - William CRAIG a native of Scotland, aged 44 yrs., emigrated from
Scotland 3-25-1847 and arrived New York 5-19-1847.   (152)
9-24-1866 - John MOORE a native of Saxon Weimer Issemach, Germany, aged 29 yrs.
emigrated from Germany 5-7-1860 and arrived New York 5-29-1860.   (153)

10-5-1866 - Winebald WAHL a native of Baden, Germany, aged 25 yrs., emigrated
  from Germany 4-2-1861 and arrived New York 5-13-1861. (154)
10-3-1866 - James MARSHALL a native of Ireland, aged 46 yrs., emigrated from
  Ireland 6-2-1846 and arrived Alexandria, Va. 7-6-1846. (155)
10-5-1866 - Sebastian SWARTZ a native of Baden, Germany aged 32 yrs., emigrated
  from Germany 4-2-1861 and arrived New York 5-13-1861. (156)
10-8-1866 - David JOHNSON a native of Ireland, aged 29 yrs., emigrated from
  Ireland 5-17-1862 and arrived in Philadelphia 7-9-1862. (157)
2-15-1867 - Michael MAHAR a native of Ireland, aged 40 yrs., emigrated from Ireland
  3-25-1847 and arrived in New Orleans, La. (no date given). (158)
9-7-1867 - Conrad BIESNER a native of Hesse Kassel, Germany, aged 72 yrs., emigrated
  from Germany 4-8-1859 and arrived New York 5-1-1859. (159)
12-11-1867 - Gottleib DIESINGER a native of Hesse Cassel, Germany, aged 52 yrs.,
  emigrated from Germany 4-15-1861 and arrived New York 5-1-1861. (160)
1-18-1868 - William REED a native of Ireland, aged 35 yrs., emigrated from Ireland
  4-28-1855 and arrived New York City 6-5-1855. (161)
4-4-1868 - Philip HABIG a native of Hesse Cassel, Germany, aged 38 yrs., emigrated
  from Germany 4-15-1861 from New York (no date given). (162)
4-7-1868 - Henry TRIEBOLDT a native of Hessa Cassel, Germany, aged 27 yrs., emigrated from Germany 11-2-1867 and arrived New York 11-20-1867. (163)
4-7-1868 - Conrad HAGDORN a native of Hessia Kassel, Germany, aged 52 yrs., emigrated from Germany 9-14-1867 and arrived New York 9-28-1867. (164)
4-8-1868 - Conrad RENTZ a native of Germany, aged 25 yrs., emigrated from Germany
  4-4-1867 and arrived in New York 4-7-1868. (165)
8-24-1868 - J.J. BEGIE a native of France, aged 74 yrs., emigrated from France
  4-11-1839 and arrived New Orleans in May 1839. (166)
8-24-1868 - John N. SIMONS a native of France, aged 78 yrs., emigrated from France
  4-11-1839 and arrived in New Orleans in May 1839. (167)
9-11-1868 - Mathias RENTZLER a native of Wirtembergh, Germany, aged 45 yrs., emigrated from Germany 3-4-1868 and arrived New York 3-25-1868. (168)
9-26-1868 - Henry HORN a native of Hessia Kassel, Germany, aged 22 yrs., emigrated
  from Germany 8-11-1865 and arrived New York 9-28-1865. (169)
9-26-1868 - Christian STICKLE a native of Wirtemburgh, Germany, aged 34 yrs.,
  emigrated from Germany 5-13-1867 and arrived New York 5-24-1867. (170)
10-7-1868 - Andrew WACHTON (WACHTOR) a native of Baden, Germany, aged 27 yrs.,
  emigrated from Germany 1-13-1867 and arrived New York 2-25-1868. (171)
10-12-1868 - Conrad LAEBER a native of Baden, Germany, aged 55 yrs., emigrated
  from Germany 3-12-1848 and arrived New York 5-2-1848. (172)
10-14-1868 - William MEYER a native of Hesse Kassel, Germany, aged 27 yrs., emigrated from Germany 5-17-1863 and arrived New York 6-8-1865. (173)
5-14-1870 - Louis HOFFMANN a native of Prussia, Germany, aged 30 yrs., emigrated
  from Germany 10-10-1867 and arrived New York 11-4-1867. (174)
3-30-1872 - William RISMILLER a native of Prussia, Germany, aged 25 yrs., emigrated
  from Germany (no date given) and arrived New York (no date given). (175)
3-25-1873 - Francis C. IHLE a native of Baden, Germany, aged 39 yrs., emigrated
  from Bramen (no date given) and arrived New York (no date given). (176)
12-23-1873 - Jacob SCMIDT a native of Wirtembergh, Germany, aged 33 yrs., emigrated from Germany (no date given) and arrived New York about 4-21-1868.
  (177)

The following records were abstracted from Comon Pleas Court Record A-1, page record is listed on, is given in parenthesis ().

February Term 1818

Honorable Judge Joseph H. CRANE with Enos TERRY, John PURVIANCE and James RUSH, Associated Judges - Linus BASCOM, Clerk - M. SCOTT, Sherrif.

COMPTON, John vs. Anthony RECHARD (RECART), 10-3-1817, Damages. (1)
RUSH, Peter - Petition to made deed, 2-19-1818 - Peter RUSH of Picaway Co., Ohio about 6-1-1811 together with Andrew Rush, late of Darke Co., now dec'd, tenants in common of NW¼ Sec. 31, Twp. 12, Range 2, Darke Co.; land sold about same time to John HILLER (3)

REEDER, Jesse & Sharp D. BALDWIN as firm of REEDER & BALDWIN assignees of Robert & William N. HOOD vs. Abraham FREEMAN, 1-10-1818, Debt (5)

RUSH, Peter vs. Heirs of Andrew RUSH - Petition of Peter Rush of Pickaway Co. & Andrew Rush late of Darke Co., dec'd whereon or about 5-1-1812 were tenants in common of the S½ Sec. 31, Twp. 12, Range 2 east. That Andrew Rush died on or about 5-1-1812 leaving John Westley RUSH and Cynthia RUSH his only children and heirs, under 21 yrs. and Isabella, his widow, entitled to dower in estate - Petition for Partitions of lands: Peter Rush guardian of heirs, 5-12-1818, 113 acres assigned to widow and heirs, 108 acres to Peter Rush (6)

August Term 1818

WILSON, vs. James I. NESBIT, 5-12-1818, Debt   (13)

Jury selected as follows: John SNELL, George FRESHOUR, William MARTIN, Stephen PERRINE, John NOFFSINGER, James WILLIAMSON, James BRYSON, John WHITACRE, Alexander SMITH, John RYERSON, Daniel POTTER and Daniel HOLLY.

LENHAM, Philder G. vs. John RYERSON, 5-10-1818, Debt   (17)

December Term 1818

LUCAS, David vs. Robert & William N. HOOD firm of R. & W. N. HOOD, 8-25-1818, Damages   (20)

MILEY, Abraham, Sr. - Petition to complete payment on United States Lands: 12-1-1818 - Abraham Miley, Sr., adms. of the estate of Abraham Miley, Jr. who in his lifetime purchased SE¼ Sec. 10, Twp. 12, Range 1 east and NE¼ Sec. 27, Twp. 11, Range 2 through Cincinnati Land Office at rate of $2.00 per acre. Abraham, Jr. paid for half of first purchase and one-fourth of second - Petitioner has completed payments.   (22)

VAN AUSDOL, Cornelius vs. Zachariah HOLE 2-9-1818, Debt   (25)

CONNER, David vs. Samuel KELSO, Dec. 1818, Appeal   (28)

May Term 181C

Henry STODDARD, Esq., Prosecuting Attorney

HOLT, Joseph assignee of Josiah GRIFFITH who was assignee of Samuel LAMB vs. Robert BARNET, 3-20-1819, Damages.   (31)

GREGORY, James vs. Nathan PIPEJOY, 2-18-1819, Slander. (33)

September Term 1819

SCOTT, Eliza, under 20 yrs. by next friend William SCOTT vs. David BUCHANAN, 2-22-1819, Slander. (38) SCOTT, Eliza, under 20 yrs by next friend Willaim SCOTT vs. Benjamin THOMAS, 2-22-1819, Slander. (39)

DEAN, Aaron vs. David WILLIAMSON 5-13-1819, Slander (40)

FREEMAN, Abraham vs. Robert & William N. HOOD, partners, 8-6-1818, Damages - Appeal to Supreme Court. (40)

Jury selected as follows:- James ROLFE, Job WESTFALL, Sr., David ARNOLD, Alexander FLEMING, Samuel COLE, James McDO ELL, Job DeCAMP, David WILLIAMSON, Charles SUMPTION jr. and Asa SPENCER.

MILLER, Jacob vs. John DEVOR, 3-23-1819 - Jacob Miller filed petition setting forth that he is about to erect a grist and saw mill propelled by water on Greenville Creek below the town of Greenville near where TERRY's mill formerly stood and that he had partially erected a dam on said creek where Terry's dam stood being part of Sec. 36, Twp. 12, Range 2 east, and water will overflow dam on Devor land - Petition to pay damages. (49)

Jury selected as follows:- Alexander SMITH, Nathan TERRY, William WILLSON, John BEERS, Charles SUMPTION, Jr., George WESTFALL, Felder G. LANHAM and Abraham MILLER.

DEVOR, John vs. Jacob MILLER 12-1-1818, Damages. (52)

COLE, David vs. James and David WILLIAMSON 8-20-1819, Debt. (55)

December Term 1819

William J. THOMAS, Prosecuting attorney - Eastin MORRIS, Clerk and Alexander SMITH, Sheriff.

SCOTT, William vs. William THOMPSON 8-27-1818, Slander (58)

April Term 1820

BEMIS, Jonathan vs. Samuel KELSO, Late of Darke Co., 6-21-1819. Damages. (61)

McMAHON, William vs. Samuel KELSO, Peter O. HELPHENSTINE, Philip HELM and Henry MONFORT, 9-6-1819, Debt. (65)

SUMPTION, Chas. Jr. vs. Henry CREVISTON 9-6-1819, Slander (69)

CREVISTON, Henry vs. Charles SUMPTION, Jr., 12-6-1819, Slander (72)

SCRIBNER, Abraham vs. John BEERS, 8-23-1819, Debt. (75)

HELM, Philip vs. Samuel KELSO, (no date - 1819), Damages (80)

SCOTT, Eliza, under 21 yrs. by her next friend William SCOTT vs. Easton MORRIS, 5-10-1819, Slander (81)

Jury selected as follows:- Moses RUSH, Mark T. MILLS, George WILT Jr., John
WATSON, James PERRY, Jacob WINEGARDNER, Jonathan HOLE, Thomas HATHAWAY, John
CHINO ETH, William ARNOLD, John CLARK and David IRWIN.

Second Jury selected as follows:- Samuel COLE, Levi ELSTON, James HOLE, George
ADAMS, Isham ATKINSON, Henry CREVISTON, Jacob CARLOCK, James CURRY, Abraham MILLER,
Joseph McDONALD, Andrew W. INGRAM and James CLOYD.

September Term 1820
WHITACRE, John constable of Greenville Twp.

HUNTSMAN, Jane vs. William THOMPSON, 3-23-1820, Paternity.   (86)

GRIFFY, John vs. Joseph ADAMS 9-20-1819, Damages   (89)
KENNEDAY, James vs. Amos SMITH, 12-14-18-19, Damages   (91)

WILLIS, Lucy, under 21 yrs. by next friend, James C. KENNEDAY vs. Amos SMITH
(date not given - 1819), Damages.   (92)

ANDREWS, Margaret vs. R. & W. N. HOOD, 4-28-1820, Debt   (95)

AMNIS, David vs. George W. HIGHT, 9-4-1819, Damages.   (98)

December Term 1820
William SCOTT, sheriff.
SCHLECHTY, Mary vs. Daniel EDWARDS 4-22-1820, Paternity.   (101)

Jury selected as follows:- David COLE, John DEVOR, Richard FISHER, Nathan POPEJOY,
Jonathan THOMS, Jacob HARTER, James BRYSON, William LEMAN, Moses SCOTT, Daniel
BUMGARDNER, David BRIGGS and Mark T. MILLS.

CRAIG, John vs. Robert HOOD, James WILLIAMSON and Andrew HOOD, 9-7-1820, Slander(103)

ARMSTRONG, John vs. Robert HOOD, Samuel WILLIAMSON and James I. NESBIT, 9-7-1820,
Slander.   (105)

SCRIBNER, Azor vs. Henry LOW, 7-24-1820, Slander.   (107)

HOOD, Robert & Wm. N., partners under firm of R. &. W. N. Hood vs. Azor SCRIBNER,
(no date given - 1820), Debt.   (109)

ATCHISON, Silas vs. Jacob MILLER, 9-7-1820, Damages. (114)

PATTON, James assignee of Margaret ANDREWS vs Robert and William HOOD, partners,
9-8-1820, Debt.   (116)

NEITHERCUTT, William - Petition for pension, 12-19-1820, aged 58 yrs, resident of
Preble Co., Ohio - Enlisted for the term of 12 months on the 25 day of May 1781 in
North Carolina in company commanded by Capt. Dougherty in regiment commanded by Col.
Armstrong who was either killed or went home from Eutau Springs when Col. James
LITTLE or LYTLE took the command of the regiment - Discharged in South Carolina
after serving five or six tours in the militia of several months. Was in the battle
of Eutau Springs - Family consists of wife, aged 60 yrs., eight children who are all
of age and away from home except for one daughter, age 17.   (119)

BASCOM, Linus vs. David W. Halsted and Stephen PERRINE, 9-7-1820, Halsted sold NW¼ of Lot 33, Greenville, which he claimed he owned. (123)

FOUNTAIN, Stephen - Petition for continuance of Pension, 12-16-1830, aged 66 yrs., resident of Darke Co. - Served in Revolutionary War in Company commanded by Capt. Warner and after his death by Capt. Lord in the 2nd Regt., 2nd Brigade in the Massachusetts line. Pension certificate #14049 - Occupation was that of farmer - Family is wife, aged 55 yrs., one girl (not named) aged 11 yrs. and one grand child (not named) aged 2 yrs. (128)

April Term 1821
John EMBREE, constable of Greenville Twp.

GRAY, Robert, adms. of Francis INNIS vs. John DEVOR, 10-27-1819, continued to 12-14-1820, continued to 4-7-1821, Damages. (132)

SUMPTION, Charles Jr. and Mary, his wife vs. Daniel HARTER 6-4-1820, continued to 12-14-1820, continued to 4-20-1821, Slander - Depositions atken Ohio Co., Va.(134)

SUMPTION, Charles Jr. & Mary, his wife vs. Barnebas BURNS and Mary, his wife, adms. of estate of John EMBREE, 12-18-1819, Debt - Mary BURNS, late Mary EMBREE - Mary SUMPTION late Mary EMBREE one of the heirs at law of John EMBREE, dec'd - Settlement, 4-17-1821. (136)

Treasurer, Miami Co., Ohio for use of James Armstrong, a minor heir of Rachel ARMSTRONG, dec'd by his guardian and next friend, James ARMSTRONG vs. John DEVOR and Mary GRAY, 9-7-1820. (140)

HAYS, James vs. Hezekiah VIETS, 4-27-1821, Debt. (141)

CONNER, David vs. Samuel & James MITCHELL, adms. of John MITCHELL, 4-27-1821, Discontinued. (143)

MATHERS, Ruth vs. James DEVOR, 4-27-1821, Premissory Note. (144)

JONES, Hudson vs. Thomas McKEE, 4-27-1821, Damages, Discontinued. (146)

VANGORDEN, Benj., adms. of Joseph DUNLAP, dec'd vs. John DEVOR, 4-27-1821, Debt. (147)
Jury selected as follows: Michael WILTFONG, Abraham MILLER, James MILLER, Timothy MOTE, Aquella LOVEALL, James FYERS, George W. HIGHT, Jacob F. MILLER, James CURRY, Jacob WESTFALL and Abraham STUDEBAKER.

RIFFLE, David vs. Silas ATCHISON, 4-27-1821, Debt, for Lot #3 in town of Jacksonville - David Riffle having dec'd after continuance 8-1-1820 and prior to 4-27-1821, Jacob RIFFLE, adms. comes into court. (151)

McCLUER, Nathaniel S. & Samuel, Executors of Samuel McCLUER, dec'd vs. George HIGHT & Dennis HART, 4-27-1821, Debt. (153)

HARTER, Conrad vs. Chas. SUMPTION, Jr., 4-27-1821, Damages. (156)

MORRIS, Eastin, appointed by court as Comissioner in Chancery of the United States, 4-27-1821. (160)

SCRIBNER, Azer vs. William Wilson, 4-27-1821, Slander. (161)

Jury selected as follows: James MILLS, Timothy MOTE, James FYERS, James DOUGLASS, Alexander SMITH, John WHITACRE, William ARNOLD, Amos P. BALDWIN, Stephen PERRINE, John McNEEL, Aquella LOVEALL and Michael WILLFONG.

ATCHISON, Silas vs. Robert HOOD, 4-27-1821, Debt. (166)

SCRIBNER, Azor vs. Samuel WILSON, 4-27-1821, Slander. (174)

SPENCER, Asa vs. William Wilson, 4-27-1821, Slander. (179)

Jury selected as follows: David IRWIN, Timothy MOTE, James FYERS, George W. HIGHT, Charles SUMPTION, Jr., Samuel LORING, Archibald BRYSON, James BRYSON, Henry CREVISTON, James MASH, William R. JONES and David COLE

FLEMING, John vs. George WARD & Thomas HATHAWAY, 4-27-1821, Debt. (182)

GUESS, Joseph vs. Asa SPENCER, 4-27-1821, Slander. (183)

HARTER, Conrad vs. Charles SUMPTION, Jr., 4-27-1821, Damages (184)

VIETS, Hezekiah vs. Daniel DEETER, 4-27-1821, Debt. (187)

DEADER, Daniel vs. Hezekiah VIETS, 4-27-1821, Debt. (188)

DUGAN, William - Petition for continuance of Pension, 4-30-1821, aged 58 yrs. resident of county. That he served in the Revolutionary war in the company commanded by Capt. Anderson in the Third New Jersey Regt. Pension Certificate #10399. That occupation was that of farmer. His family who reside with him consists of his wife Jane Dugan about forty or forty five yrs., their children, one son James aged 11, one daughter aged 11, one other son Ross aged 5 or 6 yrs.
(189)

December Term 1821
GREGORY, John vs. Nathan POPEJOY & Alexander SMITH, 12-14-1821, Debt. (192)

PERRINE, Stephen vs. David W. HALSTEAD, 12-14-1821, Attachment. (195)

FISHER, Richard vs. James WOODEN, 12-14-1821, Damages. (199)

Jury selected as follows: James STEPHENSON, John W. BORDERS, James BRYSON, Benjamin EAKEN, John PHILLIPS, James CLOYD, James PERRY, Stephen PERRINE, Dennie HART, John SNELL, John ARMSTRONG and George WAGGONER.

PERRINE, Stephen vs. Linus BASCOM, 12-14-1821 - Attachment of articles of David HALSTEAD which are believed in possession of Linus BASCOM. (203)

PERRINE, Stephen vs. David W. HALSTEAD, late of Darke Co., now of parts unknown, 12-4-1821, Bill in Chancery. (206)

364

The following estate records are among the Probate Court records which are kept in the third floor attic of the Darke County Court House. Many are not included in the index to intestate estates and those that are, are listed with case numbers which they can not be found under. All of the following estates are filed under the first letter of the surname with no case number being applied to them.

ADAMS, Caleb dec'd - Jane Adams and Aaron Hiller, adms. - Bond dated 3-9-1842 of $100 by James Adams and Aaron Hillwer with Alexander Hays and Abraham Scribner as sureties. - Mentions articles set aside for support of widow and two children. - Mentions real estate described as S½ SE¼ Section 28, Township 10, Range 3, with map showing location of land.

ANDERSON, Benjamin dec'd - John Cassel, adms. - Bond dated 9-24-1849 of $1000. by John Cassel with A. M. McKibbin and David Light as sureties. - 9-22-1849, Sarah Ann Anderson widow of said Benjamin relinquishes right to administer in favor of John Cassel who was appointed administrator.

ANDERSON, James of Jacksonville, dec'd - James Fenner and David Miller, adms. - Bond dated 12-5-1836 by James Fenner and David Miller of Miami County, Ohio with William Jordon and David Angel sureties, $3200. - Receipt dated 3-16-1838 "for $50.00 for support of myself and children for one year (Signed) Abigail Anderson". - Receipt "medicine and attendance during last sickness Nov. 26, 1836...$4.50, (Signed) James C. Wood" ...

ARNOLD, Aaron dec'd - Wm. Arnold Jr. and Aaron Fleming, adms. - Bond dated 9-4-1839 for $800. by William Arnold and Aaron Fleming with Hugh Lourimore and Henry Arnold sureties. - $100.00 allowed for support of widow, Edna Arnold. Disbursement to heirs: $43.69 to Henry Arnold and $145.00 to Edna Arnold. Among persons purchasing items at public sale held 12-9-1839 were George Arnold and Henry Arnold.

BAMFIELD, John dec'd - Inventory dated 7-12-1837 by Joshua Edwards, Phillip Williams and Aaron Phleming, with certain articles being allowed for widow's support, Public sale held (no date given with Martha Bamfield being among purchasers.)

BANTA, Jacob dec'd - Jacob Horine, executor - Bond dated 4-8-1840 of $800. by Jacob Horine with Thomas Marshall and Samuel Cablentz as sureties. Jain (mark) Banta, widow relinquishes dower in land on which she resides in Butler Township, dated 1-2-1851. - Allowance for support to Mary Banta, widow and minor children; Rachel, Elizabeth and Daniel Banta. Mentions estate coming to Jacob Banta, dec'd from his father, Albert Banta, dec'd. - Appraisement dated 4-25-1850 mentions 100 acres SE¼ Section 34, Township 10, Range 2 in Darke County, Ohio and 33 acres N½ of E½ NE¼ Section 3, Township 9, Range 2 in Preble County, Ohio.

BURDGE, Joseph Sr. dec'd - John Burdge, adms. - Bond dated 4-7-1846 of $600 by John Burdge with William McKhan and Hugh Reed as sureties. Mentions support to widow but does not name. Among persons purchasing items at public sale held 4-29-1846 were Anthony Burdge, James Burdge, John Burdge and Joseph Burdge.

BYRAM, Ebenezer of Adams Twp. - Polly Byram, adms. - Bond dated 11-23-1821 of $1200. by Polly Byram with George Adams and Abraham Scribner as sureties. Tax receipt for 1827, heirs of Ebenezer Byram, 320 acres SW¼ Section 29, Township 12, Range 2 and SW¼ Section 26, Township 10, Range 3. - deposition by Samuel Robinson (Robeson) dated 8-28-1827 stating he has intermarried with Mary late Mary Byram who is the adms. of Ebenezer Byram, dec'd and that deceased at the time of his death had two children who survived him being James and Susan Byram, and that said children resided with their mother and were supported by her until their death. - Deposition dated 8-27-1827 by Mary Robison stating that at the time of his death, Ebenezer Byram was indebted to Wm. Byram for $5.50. (Editor's note: Montgomery County, Ohio marriages, Mary Byram to Samuel Robertson - 4-21-1824.)

BYRAM, Nath'l L. dec'd - Silas C. Byram, adms. - Bond dated 9-20-1841 of $400. by Silas C. Byram with Ebenezer Byram and Thomas Barns as sureties. Widow, Mary Byram. - Receipt dated 3-28-1846 signed by Nancy Ann Byram, widow of Silas Byram, dec'd.

BYRAM, H. J. M. dec'd - Ebenezer Byram, adms. - Bond dated 2-10-1849 of $200. by Ebenezer Byram with Ralph A. Cooper and Richard Chenoweth as sureties. One acre of land near or in Mill Grove sold at public sale for $50.00, 6-2-1849.

CARNAHAN, John dec'd - Norman Sumner and William T. Carnahan, adms. - Bond dated 3-8-1847 of $2000. by Norman Sumner and William T. Carnahan with Henry Arnold and Abraham Scribner as sureties. Inventory 3-23-1847 by Joseph Cole, Nathan W. Perry and John Chenoweth with allowance to widow Sarah Carnahan and children (not named).

FLEMING, Alexander dec'd - Christopher Martin, adms. - Bond dated 9-2-1831 of $600. by Christopher Martin with Aaron Fleming and Abolom Fleming as sureties. Appraisement 9-7-1831 by Henry D. Williams, Richard Gower and Samuel Culbertson. - Note of Alexander Fleming to Merba (Marybe) Westfall.

GRANDSTAFF, Thomas of Wayne Twp. - Joseph Taylor, adms - Bond dated 10-3-1836 of $100. by Lucinda Grandstaff and Joseph Taylor with Modest R. Taylor and George Ward as sureties. - Allowance for support of widow, Lucinda Grandstaff and children (not named). - Note dated 12-6-1834 Hartford Twp., Licking County, Ohio to J. Rice signed by Thomas (his mark) Grendstaff. - Note dated May 1835 to John Umstatte Harford Twp. signed by Thomas (mark) Grenstaf.

LIVENGOOD, Isabella dec'd of Greenville Twp. - Aaron Hiller, adms. - Bond dated 3-12-1842 of $300. by Aaron Hiller with John S. Hiller and Joseph Crowell as sureties. - Public sale held 3-31-1842 with G. W. Hamilton, Henry Hiller, Oliver Jenness, William Livengood and Jacob Wise purchasing all items.

LIVENGOOD, Peter dec'd of Greenville Twp. - Jacob Livengood and John S. Hiller, adms. - Bond dated 3-15-1836 of $400. by Jacob Livengood and John S. Hiller with Archibald Bryson and James Devor as sureties. Appraisement 3-25-1836 by Benjamin Murphy, James Brady and Henry S. Juday with personal property set aside for support of widow and three children (not named). Public sale held 5-2-1836 with Isabella Livengood being among the purchasers.

McINTOSH, John J. dec'd - David Putman, adms. - appraisement sets off personal property for support of widow, Elizabeth McIntosh and minor children, Rue, James M. and Melinda McIntosh.

MARK, Margaret dec'd — John Mark and Jesse Mark, adms. — Bond dated 9-5-1834 of $600. by John Mark and Jesse Mark with John N. Mark and Henry D. Williams as sureties. — Appraisement dated 9-6-1834 by Jos. Burdg, James Brady and Philip Manuel with $40. allowed for support of two minor heirs, Lavina and Amanda Mark. — Among purchasers at public sale held 9-27-1834 were Jesse Mark, John N. Mark and Nicholas Mark — Receipts dated 10-20-1835 and 4-2-1836 signed by John N. Mark for keeping minor child, Amanda M. Mark. — Account of John N. Mark for boarding deceased and family for years 1833 and 1834, also for hauling deceased and family from Pennsylvania to Darke County, 25 days at $1.25 a day.

MARTIN, Christopher Sr. — Inventory dated 9-22-1818 by James Gregory, William T. Carnahan and Daveirn Clary — Receipts of heirs; 4-21-1821 signed by William Martin and 4-21-1821 signed by Christopher Martin Jr. for cash received by him from William Taylor of Pennsylvania — Distribution made to balance shares to Christopher Martin, William Martin and Thomas Martin. — Receipt (no date) of Samuel Martin to Christopher Martin Sen. for 13 harrow teeth and 1 handsaw.

MILLS, James dec'd of Neave Twp. — Mark T. Mills, adms. — Bond dated 9-21-1833 of $800. by Mark T. Mills with William Edger and John McGriff as sureties. Appraisement dated 9-28-1833 by Joseph Bloom, Thomas McGinnis and James Davis mentions property set off for support of widow (not named) and minor child, William Mills. — Mentions suit in the Common Pleas Court of Butler County, Ohio dated 3-13-1830 of Williard M. Smith vs. James Mills.

MITCHELL, John dec'd of Greenville Twp. — Samuel Mitchell, adms. — Bond dated 9-9-1819 by Samuel Mitchell of Preble County, Ohio and James Mitchell of Greenville with James Williamson and Robert Hood of Darke County as sureties, $1000. Personal property set off for support of widow (not named). Public sale held 11-26-1819 and among purchasers were Samuel Mitchell and Samuel Mitchell Sr.

OVERHOLSER, Abr. dec'd of Adams Twp. — John Miller, adms. — Bond dated 11-9-1819 of $400. by John Miller of Montgomery County, Ohio with Moses Scott and David Miller as sureties. Receipt (not dated) of Jacob Overholser for halling.

OVERHOLSER, Jno. dec'd — Henry Overholser, adms. — Bond dated 9-7-1840 of $400. by Henry Overholser with Benjamin Overholser and David Linn(?) as sureties. — Mentions trips made by adms. to sell estate: Shawtown, Indiana to get property; also to Montgomery, Green and Clark Cos., Ohio.

RECK, William dec'd — John Reck, adm. — Bond dated 11-13-1839 of $1000. by John Reck with Samuel Reck and Thomas McCun as sureties. Jacob B. Hershey guardian of Mary Ann Reck and for widow (not named). Tax receipt for 1841 on land in Section 30, Township 9, Range 4. Public sale held 11-27-1839 and among persons purchasing items were: David Reck, John Reck, John Reck, Jr., Magdelene (Madlana-Malana) Reck, Michael Reck, Samuel Reck, Sarah B. Reck and William Reck.

ROBBINS, Richard dec'd of Twin Twp. — Hezekiah Phillips, executor — Inventory dated 4-18-1825 by Joseph Colvill, George Francis and Frazy Doty. Receipts of heirs: 4-18-1825 Elam Rebbins and 4-18-1825 Teney Robbins

REED, Sarah dec'd - Geo. Reed, adms. - Bond dated 5-20-1844 of $400. by George Reed with Donavan Reed and William Wilson sureties. - Receipt of George Reed for $100. for keeping and boarding deceased from 8-1-1838 to the time of her death 8-13-1843.

RARICK, Daniel dec'd of Washington Twp. - Nathan W. Perry, adms. - Bond dated 2-17-1847 of $800. by Nathan W. Perry with Henry Arnold and Abraham Scribner as sureties. $125. in personal property set off for support of widow and children for one year (not named). - Receipt dated 4-3-1849(?) for $17.54 "my share of estate" (Signed) Sarah (mark) Rarrick. - Tax receipt for 1848 for 120 acres E½ SW¼ Section 30, Township 12, Range 1. - Accounting mentions Sarah Rarick and Philip Rarick.

ROBERTS, Samuel dec'd of Butler Twp. - Hiram Bell, adms. - Bond dated 5-10-1839 of $1000. by Hiram Bell with Wm. W. Jordan, J. C. Potter and James Hall as sureties. - Mentions money due from the executor of Daniel Roberts. - First bond dated 3-12-1842 of $200 by Ellis Thomas with James Polly and Jacob A. Roberts as sureties for Thomas' guardianship of George Roberts aged 14 years, Sarah Roberts aged 11 years, Conrad Roberts aged 13 years, David Roberts aged 8 years, Samuel Roberts aged 3 years and Isaac Roberts aged 1 year, children of Samuel Roberts, dec'd. - Second bond dated 10-4-1845 of $2000. by Rebecca Roberts with Ellis Thomas and Jacob Roberts as sureties for Rebecca's guardianship of George, Conrad, Sarah, David, Samuel and Isaac Roberts, children of Samuel Roberts, dec'd.

ROSS, Joseph dec'd - Jane E. Ross, adms. - Bond dated 10-22-1838 of $400. by Jane E. Ross with Josiah D. Farrar and William M. Wilson as sureties. - Tax receipt for 1838 and 1839 for lot 42 and SE½ lot 167 of Jane E. Ross and out-lot 8, all in Greenville.

RUPEL, Martin dec'd - John Rupel and Archibald Bryson, adms. - Bond dated 10-25-1823 of $1000. by John Rupel and Archibald Bryson with John Devor and James Bryson as sureties. Allowance made for support of widow (not named). Tax receipt for 1824 for E½ Section 7 and east part Section 8, Township 11, Range 2. - Tax receipt for 1827 for 26 acres W½ Section 7, Township 11, Range 2 and SW¼ Section 1(?), Township 11, Range 2.

RUSH, Abel dec'd - James Rush, adms. - Bond dated 4-17-1826 of $200 by James Rush with John Rush and Abraham Studabaker as sureties - receipt dated 11-27-1827 of John Rush for boarding Able Rush during his last sickness from June 27 to Dec. 24, 1825.

RUSH, Jacob dec'd of Greenville Twp. - Isaac Rush and Isaac House, adms. - Bond dated 8-28-1841 of $1000. by Isaac Rush and Isaac House with Abraham Scribner and Abraham House as sureties - Appraisement dated 10-9-1841 by Linus Bascom, Henry House Jr. and John Beers(?) allows support for widow Mary Rush - Receipt dated 11-23-1844 for dower signed by Jemima Rush.

RUSH, Jacob dec'd of Wayne Twp. - Solomon Christian, adms. - Bond dated 3-9-1842 of $200. by Solomon Christian with Daniel R. Davis and Daniel Morgan as sureties.

368

RUSH, John Sr. dec'd - John Rush Jr., executor - Inventory 6-25-1819 by Solomon Brodrick; Jacob Miller and William Curry; mentions widow and family but names only daughter, Barbara. Public sale held 8-2-1819 and among purchasers were: Christopher Rush, James Rush, John Rush Jr. and Mrs. Rush.

SEBRING, Abraham dec'd - Aaron Fleming, adms. - Bond dated 4-11-1846 of $600. by Aaron Fleming with Andrew Sebring and Israel Sebring as sureties. - Tax receipts for 1846 and 1847 for north part E½ NW¼ Section 17, Township 9, Range 3 and 40 acres and 11 acres SE part NW¼ Section 36, Township 12, Range 2 - Account dated 10-23-1846 for rent of farm by Firman Sebring. Receipts of heirs: 8-16-1848 for $175. by Laura (mark) Sebring; 8-19-1848 for $47.15 by Amniel G. Briggs and 8-12-1848 for $47.15 by Andrew Sebring.

STUDABAKER, Mary dec'd - Abraham Studabaker and David Miller, adms. - filed 5-6-1828; settled Sept. 1828 - Bond dated 12-15-1821 of $100. by Abraham Studabaker and David M. Miller with William Arnold and Dennis Hart as sureties. Receipt for coffin April 1821, $6.00 = Inventory Dec. 1821 by Eli Edwards, Eastin Morris and Caleb Neal; among items were "3 Dutch Books".

WESTFALL, Job dec'd - George Adams, adms. - Bond dated 1-4-1823 of $300. by George Adams with William Scott and John Beers as sureties - Receipt "Received the 17th, 1824 from George Adams, adms of the estate of Job Westfall, dec'd $5.50 for making two coffins (signed) John Craig", - Public sale held 1-21-1823 and among purchasers were Pegey Westfall, John Westfall, Jacob Westfall, Enos Terry, Eligah Tenney, Thos. Smith, James Stephenson, James Rush, William Martin, Richard Lyon, William Hays, James Hays, James Grage and Joseph Abbitt. - Deposition: Darke Co., Ohio Common Pleas Court, Nov. Term 1826 . . . George Adams deposeth that NE¼ Section 31, Township 10, Range 3 was originally entered by Job Westfall, dec'd who made first payment of $80.00, and afterwards assigned section to Adams who agreed to reconvey the farm on being repaid the principal and interest; the reconveyance to be as follows: the west half to William Westfall son of said Job Westfall, the east half to the children of said Job Westfall by his second wife .....dated 11-17-1826 (signed) George Adams.

WESTFALL, Joel dec'd - George Willis, adms. - Bond dated 10-6-1843 by George Willis. Witn. Amville(?) Briggs and Isaac House as sureties. Several items were set aside for minor children including clothing of their deceased father and mother. - $150. set off for support of minor children: John Westfall, Job Westfall, Elizabeth Westfall and absalom Westfall all under age of 15 yrs., minor children of Joel Westfall, dec'd. - Public sale held 10-27-1843 and among purchasers at sale were Andrew Westfall and Levi Westfall.

WESTFALL, Margaret dec'd - Job Westfall, adms. - Bond dated 8-29-1830 of $200. by Job Westfall with Jacob Westfall and H. D. Williams as sureties. Public sale held 9-30-1831 and among purchasers were: Andrew Westfall, Eli Westfall, Jacob Westfall, Joel Westfall, Simpson Westfall.

WORLEY, John dec'd - Nathan Worley, adms. - Bond dated 1-5-1820 of $600. by Nathan Worley of Montgomery County, Ohio with George Adams and Ebenezer Byram of Darke Co. as sureties. - Inventory dated 1-19-1820 by Ebenezer Byram, Christopher Martin and James Gregory; mentions widow (does not name), mentions account due from Caleb Worley; grave dug by Caleb Worley with James Stakehouse making coffin.

The boundaries of surveyed townships and ranges are not always the
same as named townships. The name of the township in which sections
are located will be given in ( ) parenthesis. Sections 1-2, 11-16,
21-28 and 33-36 are in Adams Twp. Sections 3-10 in Richland Twp.
Sections 17-20, and 29-32 in Greenville Twp.

(ADAMS TOWNSHIP)

Name	Sect.	Area	Acres	Date	Vol. & Page
MITCHELL, David	1	NW¼	107	11-7-1837	U-1/151
of Miami County, Ohio					

(RICHLAND TOWNSHIP)

PLAYSINGER (PLESSINGER) Jacob	3	W½ NW¼	80	2-18-1826	I-1/484
of Montgomery County, Ohio					
COPPESS, Adam	4	E½	320	9-20-1825	80/390
HART, Jacob of Pennsylvania	4	NW¼	60	12-8-1823	94/414
OLIVER, William	4	SW¼	160	12-20-1820	154/4
of Clermont County, Ohio					
OLIVER, George	5	E½ SE¼		12-2-1830	K-2/66
of Clermong County, Ohio					
FRAMPTON, Hugh	5	E½ SW¼	80	8-1-1821	0-2/253
OLIVER, George	5	W½ SE¼	80	8-14-1834	194-227
McLAUGHLIN, Robert	6	E½ SW¼	80	3-1-1836	74/193
HARLOS, Jacob	6	SW¼ SW¼	40	3-1-1836	T-1/165
SCHAR, John & Jacob	7	NE¼		8-17-1833	K-1/570
of Warren County, Ohio					
HERBSTRAIT, George	7	SW¼	160	10-16-1835	X-1/8
of Hamilton County, Ohio					
SMITH, Thomas	8	E½ NE¼		8-14-1834	73/300
SMITH, William	8	W½ NE¼	82	8- 14-1834	194/227
ALBERT, Frederick William	8	NW¼	164	8-4-1834	G-1/556
of Warren County, Ohio					
PERINE, Stephen	8	SE¼	164	6-8-1824	N-1/396
FARMER, William	9	W½NE¼	82	9-20-1825	U-1/342
CURTNER, George	9	SW¼		8-11-1817	W-1/584
of Montgomery County, Ohio					

(ADAMS TOWNSHIP)

MILLER, Peter	11	NE¼		4-8-1819	0-1/600
of Montgomery County, Ohio					
OVERLY, William	11	E½ SW¼	81	8-14-1834	K-1/150
FURNEY, Emanuel	11	W½ SW¼	81	10-16-1835	K-1/37
BOWMAN, David)					
KIMMEL, George) of Ohio	12	Whole	394	5-20-1825	F-2/417
MILLER, John	14	E½ NE¼	80	7-10-1852	L-2/428

(GREENVILLE TOWNSHIP)

WESTFALL, John	17	NW¼	160	4-4-1833	H-1/101
of Greene County, Ohio					
CUMMING, Alexander	18	NE¼	160	10-16-1835	0-1/285
of Warren County, Ohio					
BROWN, William	18	NW¼	160	4-4-1833	Q-1/73
SCOTT, James	18	E½ SE¼	80	10-17-183?	143/46
of Montgomery County, Ohio				(Year not given)	
WILLS, Daniel	18	W½ SE¼	80	8-14- 1834	P-1/56
WILLS, Abraham	19	W½ NE¼	80	11-26-1827	143/23
of Warren County, Ohio					
MEYERS, Francis	19	W½ NW¼	80	10-16-1835	R-1/230
of Hamilton County, Ohio					

Greenville Twp. continued:

Name	Sect.	Area	Acres	Date	Vol. & Page
LAFETRA, Robert E.	19	W½ SE¼	80	5-2-1827	M-1/83
assignee of John Earnheart					
BUHLER, Augustin	19	E½ SW¼	80	10-16-1935	M-1/82
of Montgomery County, Ohio					
THOMPSON, William	19	W½ SW¼	80	10-10-1831	69/416
SMITH, John	20	E½ NE¼	83	3-20-1828	107/449
assignee of Daniel Davis					
SMITH, John	20	NW¼ NE¼	41	4-4-1833	107/448
SUCKER, Bartholomew	20	SW¼ NE¼	41	10-16-1835	T-1/433
of Montgomery County, Ohio					
SEFFERMAN, George) of					
ZINK, Jacob)Pennsylvania	20	E½ NW¼	93	10-16-1835	F-2/298
(ADAMS TOWNSHIP)					
CUNNINGHAM, William	26	NE¼	160	3-5-1832	87/341
BOLTIN, William	26	NW¼	160	3-23-1821	112/345
of Montgomery County, Ohio					
NOGGLE, Jacob	26	SE¼		3-8-1817	100/91
assignee of Samuel Boyd					
BYRAM, Ebenezer	26	SW¼	160	11-10-1848	98/491
of Warren County, Ohio					
McCANLES, James Jr.	27	E½ NW¼	83	2-18-1826	99/470
of Montgomery County, Ohio					
HORNER, Heirs of John dec'd	27	SE¼	159	4-26-1847	U-1/306
assignee of Nathaniel Bonner					
ADAMS, George	27	SW¼		9-9-1824	185/497
of Montgomery County, Ohio					
ADAMS, George	28	SE¼	160	2-21-1821	125/472
of Montgomery County, Ohio					
KAYLOR, David	28	SW¼	160	6-8-1824	192/238
of Montgomery County, Ohio					
(GREENVILLE TOWNSHIP)					
WESTFALL, John	30	NE¼ SE¼		10-16-1835	K-2/143
WESTFALL, W.	30	S½ SE¼	80	12-16-1833	145/443
WILLIS, George	31	SE¼	164	9-20-1825	G-2/236
assignee of Nathan Popejoy					
SAWYER, Jacob	31	SW¼	164	11-3-1830	O-1/378
assignee of William Hays					
WESTFALL, Jacob	32	NE¼		4-1-1825	G-1/490
of Montgomery County, Ohio					
(ADAMS TOWNSHIP)					
ADAMS, George	33	NE¼		9-9-1824	185/ 497
of Montgomery County, Ohio					
ADAMS, George	33	NW¼	160	4-27-1819	192/237
of Montgomery County, Ohio					
FLEMING, Alexander)					
ROLFE, James)	33	SE¼		5-6-1819	I-1/203
HORNER, John, dec'd	34	NE¼	159	4-26-1847	U-1/306
assignee of Nathaniel Bonner					
WESTFALL, Absolem	34	NW¼	160	5-27-1824	E-1/337
of Montgomery County, Ohio					
MICHAEL, Jacob	34	SE¼	159	1-17-1826	87/572
of Preble County, Ohio					

Adams Twp. continued:

Name	Sect.	Area	Acres	Date	Vol. & Page
JENKINS, William	34	SW¼	159	5-2-1821	69/385
of Preble County, Ohio					
HARNELL, John	35	NE¼	162	2-24-1820	89/88
of Warren County, Ohio					
WILSON, William	35	E½ NW¼	81	11-1-1830	69/551
RECK, John	35	W½ SW¼	81	6-3-1831	69/552
STEWART, William	36	NE¼		4-27-1819	V-1/558
of Cincinnati, Ohio					
HUNT, Jesse	36	SE¼	114	10-2-1832	91/164
assignee of Henry Livengood					

Persons 50 years of age and over

DEATH RECORDS
DARKE COUNTY, OHIO

Name	Death date and Age	Residence at Death	Marital Status	Place of Birth
GRIMES, James	d. 8-11-1867 a. 69-7-4	Dallas	Widower	Fred. City, Md.
WOLFE, Joseph	d. 11-6-1867 a. 68-5-3	Wayne Twp.	Married	Franklin Co. Pa.
LECKNER, Anna Maria	d. 12-16-1867 a. 62-3-14	Webster	Married	Baden, Germany
LECKNER, Barnhard	d. 12-7-1867 a. 66-2-28	Webster	Married	Baden, Germany
ARNET, Jacob	d. 8-26-1867 a. 85 years	-------	Widower	--------------
HEFFNER, Jacob	d. 2-18-1868 a. 72-6-3	Greenville	Married	Pennsylvania
SWINGER, Jacob	d. 8-11-1867 a. 62y 5m	Franklin Twp.	Married	Germany
WAGNER, Eliz	d. 12-1-1867 a. 61y 24d	Adams Twp.	Widow	--------------
SCHUK, Ragena	d. 8-30-1867 a. 59 years	Greenville	Married	Werternburg
CADY, Joseph	d. 10-27-1867 a. 73y 10m	Greenville	-------	Ohio
DOWLER, Thomas	d. 11-15-1867 a. 57-7-11	Harrison Twp.	Married	Ohio
GRAMM, John B.	d. 1-2-1868 a. 59-9-20	Franklin Twp.	Married	Pennsylvania
WOGOMAN, Joseph	d. 10-5-1867 a. 56 years	Richland Twp.	Married	Montgomery Co., Ohio
RUDY, Isaac	d. 11-28-1867 a. 56-6-17	Richland Twp.	Married	Pennsylvania
BLOCKER, Susannah	d. 2-3-1868 a. 50y 9d	Washington Twp.	Married	Adams Co., Pennsylvania
	Parents: John and Susanna Warner			
BRAND, Conrad	d. 1-27-1868 a. 72-11-28	Greenville	(?)	Germany
RAIRICK, Elizabeth	d. 6-3-1868 a. 79-1-27	Adams Twp.	Widow	Virginia

Contributed by: Mrs. Cecile Montgomery, Box I-D, R. R. 1, Flat Rock, Ind. 47234

The following records were copied from a fly-leaf in one of the Darke County, Ohio Atlases found in Salt Lake City. The writing was faded and could not be read in some places. Information or parts of names in parenthesis has been added by Anita Short with inscriptions from Old Rose Hill, New Rose Hill, Pleasant Ridge and Mt. Zion Cemeteries as references.

1867 BIRTHS

_____ G. Suman	Apr 14
Hatta Hooper	July 14
C. Behymer	Oct 9, 1866
Ele Max	July 1
G. Fuller	January 13, 1867
Boy of G. Harper	24 Apr 1869
Boy of C. Mellhouse	18 March 1867
Girl of James Behymer	April 25
Boy of Frank Hooper	Dec 22 1868
Boy of J. Yongman	Febr 24 1869
Boy of J. Whitacre	Dec 26 1868
Boy of Lew Horine	Nov 10 1868
Boy of Lida Wolf	Febr 27 1870
Boy of Frank Harper	March 15 1870
Boy of Orth Meeker	Apr 9 1870
Girl of J. Reproghe	April 12 1870
(Replogle)	
Boy of G. Stu_	Dec 27 1869
Girl of Allen Masslich	Jan 26 1870
Girl of Sam Johnson	July 2 1870
Boy of Dan Snyder	August 12 1870
Boy of J. J. Whitacre	August 25 1870
Boy of Abi Skiner	Sept 7 1870
Girl of Frank Fr_p	Sept 22 1870
Girl of Lou Horine	Sept 29 1870
Girl of J. A. Whitacre	Nov 4 1867
Girl of Goodyear	Nov 13 1870
Girl of Wm. Hill	No 25 1870
Girl of Dan Dutr_	Aug 24 1871

1867 MARRIAGES

F. Hooper & E. McCornic	October 17
M. Shoyer & S. Knox	Nov 7
John May & Kit Bricker	December 8
George Charles & M. Bricker	Dec 29
Bellz Fact & F Watensfird	Dec 25
Zac Stomer & S _ockerage	Jan 1 1868
Miner Arming & R Stockley	Dec 25 1865
J Whitacre & C. Suman	October 25 1866
James Behymir & E Oswalt	September 6 1868

1867 DEATHS

Johnny Hagg	August 13
Burus Brown	Aug 31
Lu(isa) Barnheart	Nov 3 1866
(wife of James-Old Rose Hill Cem.)	
Mrs. Manning	Aug 13 1866
Sapa (Sofa?) Brown	Sept 15 1869
Sam Keller	Sept 13
Lizza Whitacre	Feb 1 1870
Cnond? Yost	March 6 1870
G. Dutre	March 16 1869
Mrs. W(interrowd)(a.57y 21d)	Feb 22 1870
(Sarah J. w/o David-Old Rose Hill)	
Elizabeth Bowers	June 25 1870
(a. 26y-Old Rose Hill)	
Mrs. Emmons	Sept 9 1870
Eaby Child	Sept 9
Mrs. Bowers	Sep 27 1870
(William Bowers-a. 29-2-1-Old Rose Hill)	
Mrs. Johnson (a. 31y)	Oct 4 1870
(Mary A. w/o S.M. Johnson-Pleasant Ridge)	
Mrs. Scranton	Oct 11 1870
Sara Johnson child	
Malena? Clinger	No 26 1870
Enme Price	No 25 1870
Kalla Wolf	Dec 15 1870
(Catharine w/o W. H.-Old Rose Hill)	
Isaac Wilson	Dec 30 1870
(b. 1824-Old Rose Hill)	
Nancy Gonbert?	Apr 15 1871
John Wiles	June 14 1871
J Wiles child	June 20 1871

G Hooper & C Wilbourn	May 14 1866
B Massligh & P Watkins	March 17 1867
Miles Br____ & Miss Painter	April 22 1869
Abe Mot & Mrs. Wagoner	April 15 1869
All__ Snyder & Be___ Dutri (Dutro)	Sept 16 1869
Albai__ Skiner & Be___ Peters	Dec 5 1869
John Dritre (Dutro) & Miss __aler	Dec 9, 1869
Hiram Wilson & Lizz Mathews	Oct 13 1868
Eafron Hall & Clen Watkins	Mar 20 1870
Dan Snyder & Bell Wint(erowd)	Oct 31 1869
Kirt Richardson & Margaret Rep(logle)	Apr 10 1870
Frank Hall (or Wall?) & Louisa Watkins	Aug 28 1870
M____ Dutre(Dutro) & Miss Crabe	Oct 4 1870
John Miller & ____ ____ingman	Dec 22 1870
Oscar Petis & Miss Skiner	Feb 5 1871
____ Peters and Bell __igh__	Mar 9 1870
Jessa Devin and Ellen Peters	April 2 1871

374

DEFIANCE COUNTY, OHIO - WILL ABSTRACTS 1845-1852

The following records were taken from Will Record 1845-1852, as found in the Probate Court of the Court House at Defiance. Page on which the record may be found in the original book is given in parenthesis.

PERKINS, Simon of Warren, Trumbull Co., Ohio - dated 4-20-1844; recorded Trumbull Co., Ohio 12-3-1844; recorded Defiance Co. 5-13-1850. Wife, Nancy. All children except Henry, who is not of age, have already received $5000.00 each. Much real estate is mentioned--owned land in Trumbull Co. (Warren and Howland)and in Cleveland, Cuyahoga Co. Executors: sons, Simon Perkins, Joseph and Jacob Perkins and nephew, Frederick Kusman. Signed: Simon Perkins. Witnesses: Thomas D. Webb, Henry Lane and Charles White. (1)

SUTHERLAND, Alexander of Steubenville, Ohio - dated 2-25-1840; recorded Jefferson Co., Ohio 4-3-1840; recorded Defiance Co., Ohio 9-13-1847. Wife, Jane. Son, John H. Sutherland. Two daughters, Mary Jane and Rebecca Elizabeth with Doctor John Andrews to serve as their guardian. Bequeath to Rebecca Howard (no relationship if any is stated) a 1½ acre lot in Steubenville. Owned land in Henry and Williams Counties. Executors: wife and brother, William Sutherland. Signed: A. Sutherland. Witnesses: W. Spencer and James Trumbull. (7)

TITTLE, Jacob of Henry Co., Ohio - dated 7-30-1839; recorded Henry Co., Ohio 5-21-1846; recorded Defiance County 11-12-1850. Wife, Rachel to have farm where now live of 200 acres in Henry Co. Jonas who is unable to provide for himself; James to have 80 acres W½ NW¼ Section 27, Township 5N, Range 5E; Jefferson to have E½ NE¼ Section 28, Township 5N, Range 5E; and Peter to have SE¼ SE¼ Section 21, Township 5N, Range 5E. Daughters: Polly Perkins, Elizabeth Perkins and Rachael Davidson. Wife to serve as guardian of minor sons. Executors: Peter Tittle and Jacob Davidson. Signed: Jacob (his mark) Tittle. Witnesses: Pearce Evans and Wm Mosher. (10)

EVANS, John of Allen Co., Indiana - dated 8-10-1842; recorded Allen Co., Indiana 8-16-1842; recorded Defiance Co. (not given). Requests that he be buried in Fort Wayne. Wife, mentioned but not named. Sons, Carey and Rush to continue the mercantile business. Daughters: Merica (Evans?) and Eliza Hill. Executors: sons, Carey and Rush Evans; Allen Hamilton, Hugh McCulloch and Pierce Evans. Witnesses: L. G. Thompson and A. G. Evans. (12)

POCOCK, Jesse of Delaware twp. - dated 9-11-1845; recorded (not given). Sons: Eli Pocock, Israel Pocock, James Pocock and Jesse P. Pocock. Daughters: Jemina Bond, Charity Burrel, Anner Eaton, Thirza Simpson and Mary Rutledge. Signed: Jesse Pocock. Witnesses: Joseph Miller and Charles Gardner. (13)

KINTIGH, Daniel of Tiffin twp. - dated 11-17-1845; recorded (not given). Wife, mentioned but not named. Sons: William F. Kintigh. Adam Kintigh, John Kintigh and Jacob Kintigh. Daughter, Katherine Kintigh. Wife to serve as guardian of daughter and in case of her death, son, William F. to serve as guardian. Executors: Jacob and Wm F. Kintigh. Signed: Daniel Kintigh. Witnesses: Jacob Smith and Wm C. Porter. (14)

HIVELY, Adam of Richland twp. - dated 3-6-1847; recorded (not given). Wife, mentioned but not named. Son, John Hively. Brothers, Isaac and Thomas Hively. Executor: Benjamin B. Abell. Signed: Adam (his mark) Hively. Witnesses: John Wilson and G. M. Wilson. (16)

BIXBY, Adam - dated 8-27-1847; recorded (not given). Wife, Maria. Sons: Lewis W. Bixby and Jonas E. Bixby. Daughters: Mary, Rachael Martin Bixby and Matilda S. Bixby. Executors: wife, Maria and son, Lewis. Signed: Aaron Bixby. Witnesses: H. Sessions and George T. Carpenter. (17)

HILL, John C. - dated 11-22-1847; recorded (not given). Nephew, James Chauncey Jackson, not of age, son of sister, Margaret Jackson with Luther C. Jackson as his guardian. Brother and sister, Luther C. and Margaret Jackson. Executor: Luther C. Jackson. Signed: John C. Hill. Witnesses: A. M. Woodcox and Peter Snook. (18)

ACUS, John - dated 9-1-1847; recorded (not given). Heirs of Eldest son, Daniel Acus to have one dollar. Heirs of 2nd son, James Acus to have one dollar. Heirs of 4th son, Hiram Acus to have one dollar. Third son is dead leaving no heirs. Heirs of 3rd daughter, Mary Ann Carzatt to have one dollar. Second daughter, Nancy Karine, she being living, to have one dollar. Eldest daughter, Hannah Dawson and her heirs to have plantation where testator now lives being NW fraction NE¼ Section 29 Township 5N, Range 4E containing 32.10 acres. Signed: John (his mark) Acus. Witnesses: Enos (his mark) Purtee and John P. Cameron. (19)

RICE, Oney Jr. of Farmer twp. - dated 7-3-1848; recorded (not given). Wife, Lydia. Two sons, Hiram F. and Aaron A. Rice, both not of age. Two daughters, Uretta M. Rice and Ellen A. Rice, both not of age. John C. Rice and Darius Allen to serve as guardians of two sons and two daughters. Executors: wife, Lydia; John C. Rice and Darius Allen. Signed: Oney Rice. Witnesses: John C. Rice, Darius Allen and Martin Thrall. (20)

ARNEL, Catharine of Aurora, Dearborn Co., Indiana and now at Mr. Brechbill's in Defiance Co., Ohio - dated 9-16-1849; recorded (not given). Sister, Susan. Bequeath to Sarah Elizabeth Lose, daughter of George Lose of Blairsville, Indiana Co., Pa. (no relationship if any is stated). Brother, Nathaniel Arnel to have money coming from father, Daniel Arnel's estate, he being dec'd and lately of Pleasant Amity, Westmoreland Co., Pa. Signed: Catharine Arnel. Witnesses: John Brech ill and Susan Brechbill. (21)

JOBEREN, Frederick of Tiffin twp. - dated 10-7-1850; recorded (not given). Wife, Elizabeth, to have farm of 75 acres where now reside. Daughter, Sarah. Youngest child, Christiann Mary, not of age. Wife is now pregnant and said child to be educated and supported. Wife to serve as guardian of daughters. Executrix; wife, Elizabeth Joberen. Signed: Frederick (his mark) Joberen. Witnesses: John N. Meyer and Coonrod Rourke. (22)

SELLINGER, Volentine of Defiance - dated 8-2-1848; recorded (not given). Wife, Sophia. Executor, William Carter. Signed: Volentine Sellinger. Witnesses: Henry Miller and Joseph Grossell. (23)

POOL, Frederick - dated 4-17-1851; recorded (not given). Children: Zebadiah, Elizabeth, Mary Ann and Frederick. Executor and guardian of children: Hector R. Major. Signed: Frederick (his mark) Pool. Witnesses: Mary A. McDorman and Hector R. Major. (24)

GARDNER, Joshua of Farmer twp. - dated 2-1-1850; recorded (not given). Wife, Margaret. Daughter, Nancy Gardner. Second son, William Gardner. Third son, James Gardner. Executors: wife, Margaret and son, William. Signed: Joshua Gardner. Witnesses: Wm O. Ensign, Eli W. Tharp and Henry Ruse. (24)

MANN, William - dated 11-9-1851; recorded (not given). Sons: Thomas, William, George, Robert, Alexander, Joseph and Archibald. Adopted daughter, Elizabeth Davidson. Executors: son, William and friend, Nathan Smith. Signed: William (his mark) Menn. Witnesses: Thomas Cheyney and A. C. Biglow. (26)

ZEIGLER, Philip of Farmer twp. - dated 5-31-1851; recorded (not given). Wife, Gartrude. Sons: eldest, John Zeigler, Henry Zeigler; George Zeigler; and Philip Zeigler. Daughters: Harriet McQuilling, Eliza Bays, Sarah Roberson and Catherine Dustine. Executors: son, Henry and friend, Thomas Cheyney. Signed: Philip Zeigler. Witnesses: Thomas Cheyney and Isaac L. Tharp. (27)

CHAMBERS, Benjamin of Richland twp. - dated 5-1-1852; recorded (not given). Wife, Catharine. Executors: wife, Catharine and John Flory. Signed: Benjamin Chambers. Witnesses: Jacob Moyer and William B. Morse. (28)

NOFFSINGER, Hannah of Richland twp. - dated 12-26-1851; recorded (not given). To Jonathan Lengle all property both real and personal except $100.00 to Eliza Heck, Joseph Heck and William Francis Heck, heirs of Lewis Heck. Executor: son-in-law, Jonathan Lengle. Signed: Hannah (her mark) Noffsinger. Witnesses: B. B. Abell and Jacob Hire. (29)

MOREHEAD, John of Henry Co., Ohio - dated 11-1-1842; recorded Henry Co., Ohio 12-8-1842; recorded Defiance Co. 9-30-1852. Mother, Elizabeth Morehead. Sisters: Catherine Armstrong, Emeline Morehead, Elizabeth Morehead, Maria Morehead and Amanda Morehead. Elizabeth Morehead to choose executor. Signed: John Morehead. Witnesses: Joseph Moss and James Morehead. (30)

LOWREY, Chancey P. of Milford twp. - dated 12-12-1851; recorded (not given). Wife, Bloomy, also to serve as executrix. Sons: eldest, Talman Lowrey; 2nd son, Oscar Lowrey, not of age; 3rd son, Henry C. Lowrey. Daughters: eldest, Lydia Lowrey; 2nd dau., Almira Lowrey; 3rd dau., Martha C. Lowrey; 4th dau., Levina C. Lowrey. Signed: Chancey P. Lowrey. Witnesses: Isaac Lowrey and James Marshall. (32)

MOCHIMER, John of Milford twp. - dated 9-14-1852; recorded (not given). Wife, Nancy to have farm where testator now resides. Sons: eldest, John Mochimer; two youngest sons, George and William Mochimer, not of age. Five daughters: Lydian Bowers, Sarah Wartenbee, Elizabeth Mochimer, Mary Mochimer and Rachel Mochimer. Executor: John G. Thompson. Signed: John (his mark) Mochimer. Witnesses: James Marshall and John H. Havenstock. (34)

DEFIANCE COUNTY, OHIO - MARRIAGES 1845-1849

The following marriages were copied from Marriage Record 1, located in the Probate
Court of the court house at Defiance.

ALLEN, Aaron W. to Eliza P. Ryan	12-27-1849
ALLEN, Harvey to Matilda Morse	10-4-1845
ALLEN, Joseph to Jane M. Hall	1-20-1847
ALLEN, William to Betsey Brownlie	1-11-1848
ASH, David to Elizabeth Maxwell	11-29-1847
AUSTIN, Franklin to Harriet Hively	10-30-1847
AVERY, Elish Jr. to Nancy Hurt	9-8-1846
BARBAGE, Wm to Betsy T. Johnson	4-23-1846
BAKER, Andrew to Anne Bostian	3-19-1846
BALE, William to Matilda Britton	6-16-1849
BANKS, Henry to Emily Morse	10-21-1845
BARBER, Esquire D. to Sally Swank	3-26-1848
BASSETT, Edward to Sarah Ann Mortimor	8-23-1847
BATES, John to Barbary Kisling	6-2-1849
BEERUSS (BURUSS), John to Judith Kerr	12-23-1847
BELLINGER, Philip to Margaret Wilson	3-25-1849
BLACKBURN, Samuel to Mary Ann Pool	3-27-1846
BLAIR, Peter to Sarah Gordon	11-3-1847
BLUE, Barnabus D. to Catherine Whitcomb	6-23-1846
BOURTON, Darling H. to Anna L. Thompson	2-28-1847
BOUTON, Henry C, to Juliet Holgate	8-4-1846
BOWER, Grant to Lydia Mochmar	8-23-1847
BOWMAN, Wendlin to Elizabeth Rath	10-28-1849
BREMER, Peter to Modalina Slagal	11-12-1848
BRETCH, Philip to Margaret Hessker	11-22-1847
BRITTON, Finley to Margaret Gardner	10-4-1849
BROWN, Wesley to Eliza Doll	10-30-1845
BURNET, Ephraim James to Lydia Walker	12-7-1849
BURRELL, Silas to Louisa Hoffman	2-2-1849
CALLENDER, John C. to Elvira Sisco	3-25-1847
CAMPBELL, David to Phebe Ann Billieu	8-20-1848
CAMPBELL, McDonald to Lucinda Boyles	8-30-1846
CAREY, David E. to Sarah L. Talbot	5-22-1848
CARMAN, Jason A. to Clarissa Heatly	10-8-1848
CARPENTER, Reuben to Hannah Bricklew(Brickler?)	4-18-1849
CARY, Isaac to Aurel Sessions	11-21-1847
CASE, Samuel S. to Nancy Kepler(or Kessler)	12-24-1846
CHAPMAN, Lyman to Hannah Rice	4-3-1848
CHEYNEY, Daniel to Sarah Immell(Imnsell)	12-28-1848
CHURCHMAN, Thomas to Elizabeth Sullivan	10-25-1849
CHURCHMAN, William to Sarah Ann Hall	10-21-1847
COFFMAN, Zachary to Emeline Osborn	10-4-1849
CRAIG, Jonathan to Catherine Limber	11-23-1846
CROCKER, Calvin to Nancy Partee	12-28-1846
CROSSLAND, Cyrus to Nancy Nelson	4-15-1849
DAURVE, John to Barbara Speaker	12-17-1846
DAVIS, Hiram to Huldah Skiver	9-28-1845
DAVIS, John W. to Ann Eliza Ellen Evans	1-4-1849

```
DAY, Eli W. to Elizabeth F. Smith                       4-4-1847
DEAL, Samuel to Hannah Lucina Fields                    8-19-1846
DEARDORFF, John to Mary Heatly                          10-16-1849
DECRASS, Christian to Catharina Daums(?)                4-24-1847
DELLETT, Charles to Elizabeth Clark                     7-20-1845
DILLON, John to Roxy Rose                               9-27-1846
DONLEY, Levi to Elizabeth Beard                         8-16-1846
DONLEY, Levi to Alvina Hougland                         10-29-1848
DUNKELBERGER, Daniel to Hannah Peterson                 10-12-1846
ELKINS, Alfred to Elizabeth McAnally                    12-3-1848
ENOS, William E. to Esther M. Wasson                    9-2-1849
EVANS, Eli B. to Jane E. Slocum                         4-20-1848
EVANS, William R. to A. Minerva Root                    4-13-1848
FAY, Elam G. to Cyntha Haymaker                         10-29-1848
FENDESS, John to Christina Deitsch                      7-29-1849
FIELDS, Anson to Emily Grundy                           12-13-1849
FISHER, John to Catherine Hammer                        4-28-1846
FISHER, John Jr. to Nancy Cheney                        11-24-1846
FRANKS, Peter to Polly Kolebecker                       9-23-1847
FREEMAN, James to Margaret Beerbower                    1-14-1846
GARDNER, James to Elizabeth C. Hartman                  11-11-1845
GARDNER, James to Susan Miller                          11-30-1848
GILBERT, Smith to Mary Long                             12-11-1849
GINTER, Casper to Ann Campbell                          4-5-1849
GINTER, John Q. to Mary M. Boyls                        6-17-1849
GLEASON, Elias to Keziah Decker                         12-15-1849
GORDEN, William to Sarah Jane Platter                   5-18-1848
GORDON, James to Sarah J. Woodcox                        6-21-1849
GRASSER, Deidrich to Nancy Wells                        10-12-1848
GREEN, Jacob to Lavina Green                            1-17-1847
GUITER, John S. to Elizabeth J. Boyles                  2-7-1847
GUNN, Edward M. to Jane Stone                           6-6-1847
HALEY, James G. to Mary A. Conkling                     8-12-1845
HALEY, Thomas to Ann Meriahan                           4-23-1849
HALL, Lorenzo D. to Mary Ann Wines                      5-18-1848
HALTERMAN, Henry to Louisa Lautenschlager               2-23-1847
HARPER, James to Gracy A. Hively                        8-6-1849
HATFIELD, Edward to Ruth Donley                         12-23-1847
HAYES, James to Caroline Skeen                          10-25-1848
HAYFORD, James H. to Hannah J. Chapman                  4-7-1846
HAYMAKER, Frederick to Eliza Ann Butenbaugh             3-26-1849
HAYMAKER, William D. to Elmira Brancher                 4-12-1848
HILBERT, Samuel to Mary Ginter                          5-28-1848
HOBERGER, John Kilian to Mina Herold                    11-5-1848
HOLLINGER, William H. to Louisa Rose                    2-10-1848
HOOVER, Isaac to Hannah McFarlin                        9-7-1846
HORNISH, John Jr. to Eve Freize                         12-27-1846
HUDSON, Jacob to Eliza Ann Kibble                       10-24-1847
HUSTON, John R. to Margery Ann McFaddin                 8-5-1845
JOHNSON, Charles E. to Rachael Potts                    12-19-1846
JOHNSON, James to Elizabeth _____(not given)           12-8-1848
JOHNSON, John to Marcia Hulburt                         3-15-1848
```

```
JUSTUS, David to Elizabeth J. Collins              8-23-1849
KETCHAM, Andrew J. to Lena A. Campbell             6-7-1848
KIMBALL, James M. to Arvilla Stone                 4-12-1848
KIMMEL, Timothy to Elvira Sweet                    6-1-1848
KINGERY, Perry to Charlotte _____(not given)      1-14-1846
KITCH, Solomon to Susan Benner                     9-10-1848
KNISELY, Philip to Lydia Fellows                   5-23-1849
KOCHEL, Isaac to Elizabeth Black                   12-17-1848
KOLEBECKER, Bartle to Polly Shaffer                5-9-1846
KUHN, John Julius to Rachel Bixby                  3-14-1848
LAHMAN, Henry to Mary Jane Williams                2-1-1846
LAHMAN, Jacob to Philapena Freas                   11-15-1846
LAMMONTON, Hiram to Ellen O'Nail                   9-25-1845
LANGDON, William to Sarah Goodson                  6-4-1846
LOURY, Geo. W. to Rachel R. Barnhart               3-1-1849
LUCE, Hayes G. to Harriet Daggett                  1-21-1848
LUITZ, Eli to Nancy Fisher                         12-30-1847
McCAULY, Philip to Mary Wessler                    4-2-1846
McCORD, Samuel M. to Lavina Taylor                 6-8-1848
McCULLY, Philip to Clarissa Bellinger              3-11-1847
McDOWELL, James to Sarah Fisher                    9-11-1845
MAJOR, Stephen to Mary Ann Hall                    7-7-1846
MANN, William to Elizabeth E. Tharp                3-19-1846
MASON, John Jr. to Mary F. Hudson                  12-3-1848
MAVIS, Abraham to Christianna Kintner              5-27-1847
MERIHUE, Gideon to Diana Daggett                   11-28-1848
MILLER, Frederick I. to Margaret Gardner           5-22-1848
MILLER, Henry Wise to Barbara Starr                12-29-1846
MOORE, Samuel A. to Harriet M. Barnum              2-8-1849
MORRIS, Richard to Alexander Mooninger             2-11-1849
MORSE, George to Eliza Ann Haymaker                5-31-1846
MORTIMORE, Adam to Sally Gardner                   1-18-1848
MULLIGAN, Josiah J. to Hannah A. Gordon            6-21-1849
MYERS, Henry Peter to Elizabeth Richmauns          12-19-1845
NAGLE, Frederick to Mary Lehman                    11-1-1846
NAGLE, John to Mary Elizabeth Koons                4-22-1847
NEER, Samuel to Sarah M. Figley                    9-2-1849
NEHER, John George to Wilhelmina Schall            7-13-1847
NOBLE, Leander C. to Laura Biglow                  5-17-1849
NOE, David to Harriett Goodenoe                    5-31-1846
PARTEE, James A. to Eliza M. Hood                  11-2-1848
PETERSON, Christian to Elizabeth Moyer             2-25-1847
PORTER (or PORTEE), William to Mary E. Sanford     3-12-1846
POTTERF, Samuel to Mary Ann McCauley               3-15-1849
POTTS, William to Sabrina Hopkins                  3-16-1848
PRICE, Wm to Sarah Ann Tharp                       6-30-1846
PURTEE, James H. to Rebecca Bennard                11-11-1849
RAGNER, Francis to Martha Gardner                  2-5-1849
REGER, Daniel to Lucinda Landis                    4-1-1849
REID, Thomas Jr. to Joanna Brown                   8-30-1849
RICHARDS, John to Catharine A. Miller              11-20-1849
ROBBINS, Joseph to Mary A. Reppetoe                7-6-1845
```

ROBINSON, George Jr. to Mary Sellinger   6-18-1846
ROMINE, Andrew to Margaret Kibble   2-1-1846
ROSE, James to Orpha Wood   9-9-1848
RUSSELL, John to Catherine Acus   12-9-1847
SALES, Lorenzo H. to Mary Ann Wartenbee   8-31-1845
SEGEN, William B. to Ann M. McCurdy   11-13-1849
SHERMAN, William to Chloe Ann Benner   3-25-1849
SHIRLEY, John J. to Lucinda C. Pefly   1-20-1848
SHOCK, Adam to Elizabeth Freize   5-4-1848
SIMPSON, Evans to Permelia Travis   12-23-1847
SKEEN, Andrew to Sarah Partee   8-2-1846
SKIVER, Isaac to Mary Ann Wheeler   6-6-1847
SNOOK, Peter to Caroline Whetstone   10-28-1849
SPERGEN, Samuel to Elizabeth Colwell   12-20-1849
STARK, Philip to Elizabeth Bremer   5-27-1849
STEER, George to Frederiko Holborn   7-12-1847
STITES, Henry N. to Rebecca Clark   9-23-1848
STOCKMAN, George to Rachel Davison   10-30-1845
STONE, Nelson to Laura M. Crary   1-6-1848
STOUT, Joseph to Martha E. Barnhart   12-29-1847
STOW, Solomon to Elizabeth Wood   8-21-1847
STOY, Joseph to Rebecca Kintner   10-31-1849
SULLINGER, Rolla D. to Martha Rathmal   8-5-1847
SULLIVAN, Samuel C. to Elizabeth Williams   6-12-1845
THAKER (THACKER), John to Elizabeth Brechbill   5-20-1848
THARP, Eli W. to Susannah Snook   4-16-1845
THOMPSON, Matthew to Ann Kellington   7-27-1846
THRALL, Martin to Ellen M. Barny   12-6-1849
TITTLE, James M. to Sarah M. Dodd   2-22-1846
TITTLE, Thomas I. to Phebe Dodd   2-6-1848
TROXEL, Elijah to Eliza Justus   8-21-1849
WAIT, Tracy L. to Sarah Washburn   6-24-1849
WANK, Jacob to Elizabeth Collins   12-4-1848
WANK, Michael to Eve Lintz   10-26-1848
WATERS, Mason to Mary Martin   4-14-1847
WEBSTER, David to Maria Henry   2-22-1847
WELLS, Henry to Ellen I. Coleman   5-21-1848
WESSLER, Solomon to Nancy M. Partee   2-19-1846
WESTERN, John to Hannah See   12-25-1845
WILSON, William to Lydia Hess   12-29-1848
WILSON, Wm C. to Eley Groves   11-12-1845
WIRNER, Everhart to Elizabeth Hoffman   10-15-1845
WISEMILLER, William to Sarah A. Dickinson   2-18-1847
WISSNER, George to Charlotte Lee   2-3-1848
WOODWARD, John C. to Mary A. Evans   4-20-1848
YEARGER, John to Elizabeth Shasteen   6-9-1846
YORKEY, Adam to Sally Mader   12-16-1847
YORKEY, William to Katherine Wirts   11-9-1848
YOUNG, Peter to Martha Clow   3-22-1849

DEFIANCE COUNTY, OHIO - HUGHES CEMETERY

Contributed by: Mrs. Roger D. Yeider, Jr., 1238 Kinsmoor Ave., Fort Wayne,
Indiana 46807

This cemetery is located on north side of Highway #24 about a quarter mile from
the road, between Gier and Burns Roads, probably in Section 33 of Delaware township. It is on the bank of the river, but well nowed and fenced in. Inscriptions
were taken May 13, 1971 by Betty Yeider and Mary Ellen Bowman.

DRENNING, Elizabeth 1844-1921
RIGEL, Barbara Ann d. Jan. 3, 1868 a. 55y 11m 2 (or 9)d
POOL, Jemima d. Jan. 14, 1873 age 38y 11m 2d
HUGHES, Rosabell b Oct. 8, 1822 d Feb. 4, 1884
    Emma dau. of W. H. & C. Huahes d. Sept. 1, 1880 aged 17d
    Idela A. dau. of W. H. & C. Hughes d July 21, 1875 aged 3m
    Jonas M. son of W. H. & C. Hughes d. Sept. 15, 1876 aged 9d
    Ida A. dau. of W. H. & C. Hughes d. Jan. 1, 1877 aged 3y & 16d
    Ada M. dau. of W. H. & C. Hughes d. Sept. 7, 1879 aged 1m 15d
    Jesse d 9 May 1886, 73y 10m 9d (same stone as Nancy E.)
        Nancy E. d 14 May 1883, 24y 1m 3d
COULDSBERRY, Howard son of A. & L. d Sept. 7, 1881 aged 1y 6m 12d (ss as Evert)
    Evert son of A. & L. d. Jan. 12, 1881 aged 1y 7m 26d
BALDWIN, Esther d Feb. 7, 1896 aged 32y 5m 16d
    Thomis d. Dec. 21, 1913 aged 52y 9m 25d
    Elizabeth d. Apr. 1, 1899 aged 71y 1m 22d
    Lucas d. June 21, 1898 aged 78y 9d (Note: Last four on same stone)
    Floyd son of __(?) &__(?). A. Baldwin d Mar. 11, 1900 aged 7m 14d

DEFIANCE COUNTY, OHIO – ORPHANS HOME CEMETERY

Contributed by: Mrs. Roger D. Yeider, Jr., 1238 Kinsmoor Ave., Fort Wayne,
Indiana 46807

This cemetery is very close to the road, although not quite visible from the road
(marked by a lone pine tree), on the south side of the Schick Road between Evans-
port and Trinity Roads in Tiffin Township. From present day plat maps this appears
to be the southeast corner of Section 32 of Tiffin Township. From the Griffing,
Gordon & Company Atlas of Defiance County (1890 copyright), the Orphans Home was
located on 67.10 acres at this site and it appears the County still owns this land
as well as an adjoining 160 acres upon which the airport is located.
Inscriptions taken Oct. 25, 1971 by Roger and Betty Yeider.

MITCHELL, Carrie 1878-1886
ANDERSON, Verner 1891-1893
JACKSON, Bessie 1892-1892
COLE, Stella 188 7-1893
SLOCUM, Bertha 1894-1904
LANGDAN, Loby 1881-1893
LANGDON, Sarah 1884-1893
McCRACKEN, Clara "come home"
(Note: Evidenced remained that at least one stone had been broken off at ground
    level, but no pieces of it remained.)

382

DELAWARE COUNTY, OHIO - WILL ABSTRACTS 1812-1825

The following abstracts were taken from Will Book 1, pages on which record may be found are given in parenthesis.

WILLIAMS, John of Radnor twp. - dated 6-17-1811; recorded 1-14-1812 - Wife, Margaret. Eldest son: Joseph. Daughters: Jane, Tena(?) and Catharine. Executors: Wife, Margaret and friend, Joseph Smart. Signed: John Williams. Witnesses: Joseph Shoup and Zechariah Williams. (1)

CARPENTER, Nathan of Liberty twp. - dated 8-26-1813; recorded 10-22-1814. Wife: Naoma, mentions furniture she brought with her at time of marriage. Sons: Ira, Alfred, Nathan and James. Daughters: Lucy Swinerton, Irena, Sally and Lorry Carpenter. Executor: James Carpenter. Signed: Nathan Carpenter. Witnesses: Reuben Lumb, and Amaza Case. (2)

CELLAR, Thomas - dated (no date); recorded 4-24-1816. Wife: Sarah. Sons: Thomas, Robert McCoy, John Flanigan, George, James and Joseph; last three not of age. Daughters: Margaret, Jane and Hannah. Mentions; Betty Fisher who makes home with testater. Executors: Sons, Robert McCoy and Thomas. Signed: Thomas Cellar. Witnesses: Joseph Cronkleton, Sr., Joseph Cronkleton, Jr. and Elizabeth Craig Cronkleton. (4)

STEPHEN, Zachariah of Sciota twp. - dated 9-11-1815; recorded 4-23-1817. Present wife, Nancy Steven. Five living sons: Alexander, Andrew, who will be of age on 28 Apr. 1822; Zachariah; Hugh; and Ephraim. Four daughters: Anna, Nancy, Polly and Rebecca. Mentions: Sawmill on property. Executors: Wife, Nancy; David Mark and Samuel Cooper of Radnor Twp. Signed: Zachariah Stephen. Witnesses: Samuel Weaver and Joseph Decker. (6)

WELCH, Aaron of Delaware, Ohio - dated 4-21-1818; recorded 4-21-1818. Wife, Content. Son-in-law, Francis Bebee. Children: Luther Welch, Aaron Welch, William Welch, Ruth Shaw, Susanna Beebe, Philina Smith and Loretta Welch. Executors: Josiah M. Smith and Francis Bebee. Signed: Aaron (mark) Welch. Witnesses: Jacob Drake, Noah Spalding and David Thomas, Jr. (10)

DAVID, Richard - dated 6-20-1818; recorded 11-10-1818. Wife, Elizabeth. Sons: David David and John David; also to serve as executors. Daughters: Ginny Persy and Sally David; Sally not of age. Signed: Richard David. Witnesses: Reuben Lamb, Nicholas Whitingin and Evan Jenkins. (8)

LUDWIG, Elenor of Radnor twp. - dated 8-25-1818; recorded 11-9-1818. Sons: Thomas and John. Daughter: Lettice, a single woman. Signed: Elenor (mark) Ludwig. Witnesses: Evan Jenkins, Robert Warren and John Philips (12)

RILEY, John of Berkshire twp. - dated 12-25-1818; recorded 1-7-1820. Wife, Mary. Sons: John and Henry; also to serve as executers. Daughters: Margaret and Mary. Mentions: William Riley eldest son of Henry Riley. Signed: John Riley. Witnesses: David Gregory, Joseph Crunkletin and George Cowgill. (13)

SHOUP, Joseph - Verbal Will - dated 9-28-1819; recorded 1-7-1820. Wife, Mary Magdelena. Sons, (in order of birth) David, Sebastian and Joseph. Daughters, (in order of birth), Margaretta Martin, Catharine Dilsaver, Elizabeth Wilson, Susannah Swartz, Nancy Shoup, Magdelena Shoup, Sarah Shoup and Hester Shoup. Mentions: That sons, David and Sebastian, are to complete building of the mill on Fulton's Creek. Executors: Wife, Mary Magdelena and sons, David and Sebastian. Witnesses: Jas. W. Crawford and John J. Swartz.   (14)

BLACK, Andrew - dated 6-2-1820; recorded 3-8-1821. Wife, Esther. Mentions that Nancy Hare and Mary Hare are to have equal shares with lawful heirs. Executors: Wife, Esther and John Worline. Signed: Andrew Black. Witnesses: John Elliott and David Elliott.   (16)

BUTLER, Nathaniel - dated 12-3-1820; recorded (No mo. & da. given) 1821. Bequeaths to Widow Orr living near Seneca Town on the Sandusky River. Executor: James Lumbert. Signed: Nathaniel Butler. Witnesses: Edmund Buck, Cyrus Benedict and Noah White.   (17)

BENEDICT, Sylvester of Bennington twp. - dated 16th day, 3rd month, 1821; recorded (No da. or mo. given) 1821. Children: Cyrus, Allen, Gidson, Ira, Mary, William, Jane and Amos Benedict. Executors: Reuben Benedict and Daniel (or David) Wood. Signed: Sylvester Benedict. Witnesses: Aaron Benedict, Wm. Benedict and Maurice Pleas.   (18)

BROWN, Moses of Radner twp. - dated 12-11-1819; recorded 11-5-1821. Daughters: Jean Flemin and Sally, wife of Humphrey Mounts. Grandson: James Wallis Brattin. Executors: Samuel Cooper and Robert McIlvain. Signed: Moses (mark) Brown. Witnesses: John F. Dunlap and Adam Cooper.   (19)

FARNAM, Douglas of Marion attached to Delaware Co. and town of Green Camp. - dated 11-28-1821; recorded 1-23-1822. Wife, Susan. Wife's father: John Lendenberger. Children by first wife: Erastus, Floreet and Adaline Farnam. Daughter: Lucy Louisa Farnam. Mentions: Daniel Butler, Betsy Morse and Polly C. Black (also called Clark) being "three children of God now living with me". Signed: Douglas Farnam. Witnesses: James Gooding and David Tipton. Codicil dated 11-13-1821 names wife Susan as guardian of daughter Lucy Louisa. Administrator: William Justice. Witnesses: James Gooding and Aaron Hill. Witnesses oaths taken Big Rock twp., Marion County attached to Delaware Co., Ohio.   (20)

CARPENTER, James of Sunbury twp. - dated 10-5-1821; recorded 1-23-1823. Wife, Betsey, also to serve as executrix. Sons: Benjamin Own and John Carpenter. Daughters: Esther, Eliza, Harriet and Mary. Signed: James Carpenter. Witnesses: John Kerr, Stephen Hennington and Gideon McMillon.   (22)

EIMAN, Jacob of Marion Co., Ohio - dated 3-31-1823; recorded July 1823. Wife, Barbara. Sons: Eldest son, John Eiman, dec'd, his heirs (not named); Jacob Eiman. Daughters: Katherine Dunmire, Betsey Hancock, Barbara Brown, Mary Eiman, Sally Eiman and Anna. Executors: Son, Jacob and Daniel Jones. Signed: Jacob Eiman. Witnesses: John Reed, George (mark) Hancock and Samuel Ferrill. (23)

WILLIAMS, Mary - dated 5-2-1822; recorded 11-18-1822. Sons: James and Elijah to have "all property willed to me by their father, Nehemiah Williams". Daughters: Margaret Martin, Sarah Main, Rebecca Main, Mary Main and Grace Sill. Executors: Timothy Main and Benjamin Martin. Signed: Mary (mark) Williams. Witnesses: David Carter and Lyman Main. (26)

ROBERTS, Hezekiah of Sunbury - dated 9-13-1821; recorded 11-18-1822. Wife, Jemima. Only son: Hezekiah Roberts. Daughter: Catherine Rogers. Grandsons: Jonah (or Josiah), Hezekiah Thompson and Simon Ford Rogers and Hezekiah Roberts. Grand-daughters: Deliverance Chaffar Rogers now Prindle and Catherine Rogers now Brunson. Mentions: Asenath Rogers and Hezekiah son of James Roberts, relationship not given. Executors: Son, Hezekiah, Jr.; grandson, Hezekiah Roberts, the third; grandson, Hezekiah Thompson Rogers and James Roberts. Signed: Hezekiah Roberts. Witnesses: Thomas W. Wigton and David Welch. (27)

HUMPHREY, Lemuel G. of Liberty twp. - dated 10-26-1822; recorded (not given, 1822-23). Wife, Dorcas. Sons: Lemuel, Aaron C. and Eber. Daughters: Arminda M. C. Master, Laura Humphrey, Lorinda Plum, Eliza Hall and Sarah. Grandson: Richardson the youngest son of Ralph Richardson. Executors: Wife, Dorcas and son, Lemuel. Signed: Lemuel G. Humphrey. Witnesses: Isaac Case, Abner P. Kinney and Joseph M. Gardner. (28)

DILSAVER, George - dated 3-17-1823; recorded March 1823. Wife, Elizabeth. Sons: John B., Zachariah, George, William Henry, Adam and Jeremiah. Daughters: Sarah, Mary and Barbary. Executors: John B. Dilsaver, John S. Swartz and Roswell Field. Signed: George Dilsaver. Witnesses: Henry Swartz and David Shoup. (30)

ADAMS, Abraham of Harlem twp. - dated 9-29-1822; recorded 3-30-1823. Wife, Susannah. Children: Elijah, Hannah, Susannah, Sarah, Mary, Martha, Margaret and John. Executors: Elijah Adams and Susannah Adams. Signed: Abraham Adams. Witnesses: John Caney, David Adams, Jr. and Susannah Bennet. (32)

CARPENTER, Benjamin of Sunbury - dated 1-28-1820; recorded Oct. 1823. Wife, mentioned but not named. Children: James, Elizabeth, Benjamin, Robert, Lolla, Polla (also named as Mary) and Charles. Executors: Ezekiel Brown and son, Robert Carpenter. Signed: Benjamin Carpenter. Witnesses: Jedediah Collins, David Sheels, Jr. and Lovina Collins. (33)

DODDS, Andrew - dated 8-21-1823; recorded Oct. 1823. Wife, Hannah.
Sons: Joseph, James, Thomas, John, William C. and Andrew. Daughter:
Margaret. Executors: William Crathy and William C. Dodds. Signed:
Andrew Dodds. Witnesses: John Elliot and John Dodds. (35)

WALKER, William of Upper Sandusky, Crawford Co., Ohio - Verbal Will -
dated 1-1-1823; recorded (not given-1823). Wife, Catherine. Children:
John Walker of Territory of Michigan, William Walker, Nancy Walker, Maria
Walker, Mathew Walker, Joel Walker and Isaac Walker; Isaac to have house
known as "Britain". Mentions: Land being 500 acres in Territory of Mich-
igan on Detroit River; land in Upper Canada which is property of wife,
Catherine. Executors: John R. Walker of Michigan and William Walker.
Witnesses: Jno. Shaw, John Lewis and Isaac Walker. (36)

NETTLETON, Nathan of Orange twp. - dated 8-25-1821; recorded Oct. 1823.
Wife, Hannah. Eldest son, John. Executors: Wife, Hannah and son, John.
Signed: Nathan Nettleton. (38)

QUICK, Mathew of Sunbury - dated 6-3-1820; recorded 4-13-1822. Wife:
Rhoda, also to serve as executrix. Sons: Jesse and Benjamin. Daughters:
Elizabeth and Mary. Signed: Mathew (mark) Quick. Witnesses: Nathan
Dustin, Benjamin Carpenter, Jr. and Moses Carpenter; (39)

WILLIAMS, Nehemiah of town of Troy - dated 8-6-1821; recorded 4-15-1822.
Wife, Mary. Sons: James and Elijah Williams; also to serve as executors.
Signed: Nehemiah Williams. Witnesses: Sabeers Main, John Main and
Benj. Martin. (41)

SCOTT, Asa - dated 3-4-1822; recorded 4-16-1822. Wife, mentioned but not
named. Sons: Oldest son, Harvey, to have "all land property which belonged to my father at his decease"; 2nd son now living, Elias Scott;
3rd son now living, Lewis Scott; youngest son, Thomas J. Scott. Daughters:
Betsey, wife of W. G. Sturdevant and Ruth, wife of John Lewiss. Executors:
Wife, (not named) and son, Lewis. Signed: Asa Scott. Witnesses:
John Lewis, Joseph Cronkleton and James Eaton. (42)

BUCK, Phebe - dated 30th day, 8th month, 1822; recorded Oct. 1823. Sons:
Gideon, Edmund and Andrew. Daughter: Phebe Allen. Grandson: Israel
Buck, now living in the State of New York. Grand-daughter: Philena Buck.
Executors: Andrew Buck and William Benedict. Signed: Phebe Buck.
Witnesses: Aaron Benedict of Westfield twp. and Daniel Osborn. (44)

ELLIOTT, David - dated 8-29-1823; recorded 11-19-1823. Wife: Elizabeth,
also to serve as Executrix. Sons: Joseph, David Wilson and James S.
Daughters: Jane, Catharine W., Elizabeth S. and Margaret. Signed:
David Elliott. Witnesses: John Elliott and David Mitchell. (45)

386

SMITH, David - dated 10-1-1823; recorded 11-24-1823. Wife, Chloe. Son: James. Mentions other sons and daughters, but does not name. Executors: Wife, Chloe and son, James. Signed: David Smith. Witnesses: William Sharp and Nehemiah Smith. (46)

BLACKMER, Rufus - dated 10-10-1823; recorded 12-3-1823. Wife, Rachael. Executors: Wife, Rachael and Owen Owens. Signed: Rufus Blackmer. Witnesses: James W. Larrabee, Amos Sack and Samuel Lewis. (47)

McCOY, Ephraim of Sunbury twp. - dated 6-19-1820; recorded April 1824. Wife: Sarah, also to serve as executrix. Daughters: Mary McCoy and Sarah, wife of James Marvin. Signed: Epraim (mark) McCoy. Witnesses: Elizabeth Perfect and William Perfect. (48)

LEWIS, William of Marlborough twp. - dated 2-7-1824; recorded April 1824. Wife, Elizabeth. Mother, Amelia Justice. Stepsons: William and John Justice. Step-daughter: Rhoda Justice. Sister, Elenor, her son Levi. Executor: John Moses, Jr. Signed: William Lewis. Witnesses: Amos Wilson and Noah Spalding. (50)

MOREHOUSE, Stephen of Bennington twp. - dated 4-30-1823; recorded April 1824. Wife, mentioned but not named. Sons: Seth and Ebenezer. Daughters: Joanna B. Meekeer to have "land to include house Enoch Meekeer built"; Mary. Two grandsons: Abraham and Abner S. Morehouse and also their brother Charles R. Morehouse. Executors: Ebenezer E. Morehouse and Thomas Hance. Signed: Stephen (mark) Morehouse. Witnesses: Thomas Hance, Augustus Ayres and Amos McNames. (51)

JONE, John of Radnor twp. - dated 8-1-1822; recorded July 1824. Wife: Margaret, also to serve as executrix. Only son: John. Daughters: Susannah, Margaret and Polly; Polly not of age. Signed: John (mark) Jones. Witnesses: James Davis and William Williams. (53)

WRIGHT, Mary of Sunbury - dated 5-5-1824; recorded July 1824. Brothers: William A. Nelson to have land and Family Bible; Robert Nelson. Sisters: Esther Nelson, Jane Nelson, Anna Randal and Elizabeth. Nieces: Mary Anne Smith and Ann Eliza Nelson. Nephew: Thomas Wright Randal, a son of my sister Anna Randal. Executor: William A. Nelson of Sunbury. Signed: Mary Wright. Witnesses: Thomas Young, Elijah Young and Eleazer Copeland. (54)

HATCH, Joseph of Harlem twp. - dated 7-30-1824; recorded 9-30-1824; recorded 9-30-1824. Wife, Abigal. Four sons: Nathaniel, Waterman, Alfred and Jonathan. Executors: Wm. Budd and John Caney. Signed: Joseph Hatch. Witnesses: John Budd, Jr., Richard H. Randall and Eli Budd. (56)

CUNNINGHAM, Hugh - dated 4-8-1824; recorded Sept. 1824. Wife: Sarah, also to serve as executrix. Sons: William and Barnet. Oldest daughter: Margaret Cunningham. Signed: Hugh Cunningham. Witnesses: Hugh Lee and J. J. Smith. (57)

JENKINS, Evan - dated 9-16-1824; recorded 1-15-1825. Wife, Isabella.
Daughters: Mary Johnson and Magdalen David. Stepson: David David.
Stepdaughter: Jane David. Bequeaths money to Baptist Church.
Executors: John Philips and Henry Perry. Signed: Evan Jenkins.
Witnesses: Solomon Smith and Eva Griswold.   (59)

CRONKLETON, Joseph - dated 11-30-1822; recorded 11-22-1824. Wife, Mary.
Sons: Robert, Joseph, Samuel and John. Daughters: Elizabeth Taylor,
Ann Cronkleton and Margaret Cronkleton. Mentions: Son, William's widow
and their two daughters, to have "land south of farm where I now live....
reserve for the use of my family, two perches square on said 200 acres
where my son William is buried for use of burying ground...being in Town-
ship 4, Range 19 of United States Military lands on Whetstone River."
Executors: Son, Joseph and James Gillis. Signed: Joseph Cronkleton.
Witnesses: Joseph Eaton, Robert McCoy and Joseph Cunningham. Codicil
dated 9-18-1824 mentions daughter-in-law, Jane Cronkleton, now Jane
Harter and her two children she had by son William. Witnesses: Robert
McCoy, Joseph Cunningham and Joseph McKinnie.   (61)

WILLCOX, Isaac formerly of Wilkesberry twp., Luzerne Co., Pa. now of
Kinston twp., Delaware Co., Yeoman - dated 11-27-1820; recorded Feb. 1825.
Sons: Isaac, dec'd, and Crandal. Daughters: Lucy Green, dec'd, her
children (not named), Desiah, wife of Phasris Lake; Sarah Sprag, her heirs;
Thankful Rosecrans. Mentions: Cornelia, Mariah and Newcom Wilcox, possibly
children of son Isaac. Executors: Daniel Rosacrans of Kingston twp. and
Samuel Willcox of Pittstown, Luzerne Co., Pa. Signed: Isaac (mark)
Willcox. Witnesses: Crandall Rosecrans, Jemima Rosecrans and Joseph
Rosecrans, third.   (65)

LEWIS, Chester of Berlin twp. - dated 12-11-1824; recorded 3-1-1825.
Wife, Catharine. Brother: Isaac Lewis, dec'd. Children: Thomas,
Sylvester, William, Alonzo and Alney. Executors: Wife, Catherine and
friend, John Johnson. Signed: Chester Lewis. Witnesses: David Lewis,
Benonia Dirkerman and Florilla Lewis.   (66)

MURPHY, Andrew - dated 3-24-1814; recorded 3-1-1825. Wife, Jane.. Sons:
John, to have Bible in which his name is written; James. Daughters:
Mary, wife of James McWilliams and Jane, wife of David Pugh. Mentions
555 acres in Flemon Co., Kentucky. Mentions: His carpenter's, wheel-
wright and cooper's tools. Executors: Wife, Jane and son, James.
Signed: Andrew (mark) Murphy. Witnesses: Reuben Lamb, John Minter
and Samuel Cooper. (68)

KEEN, Ezra of Bennington twp. - dated 7-29-1824; recorded 5-9-1825.
Wife, Hannah. Sons: Sanford and Peter. Daughters: Nancy Keen.
Executors: Wife, Hannah and friend, John Lewis. Signed: Exra Keen.
Witnesses: Joseph Keen, Abiah Ann Keen and Zirah Smith.   (69)

388

CLARK, George D. of Sunbury twp. - dated 2-26-1824; recorded 5-10-1825.
Wife, Deborah. Son: Jonathan. Two daughters: Sally and Miram Clark.
Executors: Wife, Deborah and David Armstrong. Signed: George D. Clark.
Witnesses: John Keer and Cyrus Longshare. (72)

BENEDICT, Aaron - dated 26th day, 7th month, 1825; recorded Oct. 1825.
Wife, Esther. Son: Aaron L. Daughters: Sarah, Elizabeth and Esther L.
Executors: Wife, Esther; son, Aaron L. and Daniel Osborn. Signed:
Aaron Benedict. Witnesses: Joseph Riley and Daniel Benedict. (74)

BRUNDICE, William of Marlborough twp. - dated 10-31-1823; recorded 12-30-
1825. Sons: Nathaniel, Stephen, Thomas and John. Daughters: Anna Wyatt;
Sarah Ter Boss; Elizabeth Mitchell; Mary Darke, dec'd, her heirs (not named).
Executors: Sons, Nathaniel and John. Signed: William Brundige.
Witnesses: William Little, Platt Bush and John Bush. (75)

DELAWARE -COUNTY, OHIO - WILL ABSTRACTS 1826-1835

BLACK, Isaac of Orange twp. - dated 12-24-1825; recorded 2-25-1826. Sons: 3rd son,
Nathan; 4th son, Calvin; 5th son, John; 6th son, George W.; other sons not named.
Daughter: Julia Ann. Signed: Isaac Black. Witnesses: Silas C. McCamp and Chester
Campbell. (76)

MAIN, Hannah of Troy twp. - dated May 1826; recorded 5-22-1826. Sons: Jonas, Lyman
and Thomas. Daughters: Hannah Wilson and Dorcas Martin. Executor: son, Thomas
Main. Signed: Hannah Main. Witnesses: Sabeers Main and Eleazer Main. (77)

DUNCAN, John - dated 4-19-1826; recorded 5-25-1826. Wife: Mary, also to serve as
executrix. Niece: Sally Sharp; her children Mary, Sarah, Betsey and John Sharp.
Mentions: that if he has any other living kin, that they are in southern states and
he bequeaths them $1.00. Signed: John (mark) Duncan. Witnesses: Wm. G. Norris
and Sarah Williams. (79)

LOUP, Christian of Berkshire twp. - dated 9 20-1826; recorded 11-6-1826. Sons:
George Loup and John Rouse. Daughter: Grace Filkey. Grand-daughter: Catherine
Rouse. Executors: John Rouse and George Loup. Signed: Christian Loup. Witnesses:
Amos Utley and George Fisher. (82)

HOMAN, Magdalen - dated 9-26-1827; recorded Feb. 1828. Heirs: John Ligh. Susannah
Hyre, Benjamin Scott, George Coberly, Martin Powers and Jane Lewis. Executor:
George Coberly. Signed: Magdalen (mark) Homan. Witnes ses: John Luckenbell,
William Norman and Joseph Coberly. (84)

McLEAN, Lauchlin of Sunbury twp. - dated 9-15-1824; recorded 10-6-1828. Wife, Amy,
also to serve as executrix. Sons: Mordock, Alexander and Allen. Daughters: Mary
Atherton, Betsey, Susan, Eunice and Amy. Signed: Lauchlin McLean. Witnesses:
B. Carpenter, Rufeet Atherton and John B. Grist. (86)

WARREN, Robert of Radnor twp. - dated 8-21-1828; recorded 10-6-1828. Wife; Elizabeth also to serve as Executrix. Sons: Thomas, Wm. P. and Benjamin. Five daughters: Mary Margaret, Sally, Eliza, **Perry** and Issabella. Signed: Robert Warren. Witnesses: James H. Hills, Henry Perry and Henry Van Deman. (88)

MOREHOUSE, John of Bennington twp. - dated (not dated); recorded 10-6-1828. Wife, Matilda. Brother: Stephen Morehouse, to ,have all interest left by will of father. Executors: Thomas Hance and Stephen Morehouse. Signed: John Morehouse. Witnesses: Justin Dewey and Stephen Barneby. (90)

CLARK, Charles of Liberty twp. - dated (not dated); recorded 11-12-1828. Wife, Deborah. Children: Nancy wife of Marques L. Plum. Alsunous, Mary Clarissa, Jackson, Charles, Hannah, James R. and Elijah. Signed: Charles Clark. Witnesses: Josiah McKinnie, Nancy Clark and Assenth Travis. (91)

FANCHER, William of Harlem twp. - dated 6-5-1828; recorded 3-16-1829. Wife, Lucy. Children: Nehemiah Fancher, David Fancher, Rebecca Fancher, Henry Fancher, Samuel Fancher, William Fancher, Nancy Davison, Aney Fancher and Polly Billings. Signed: William Fancher. Witnesses: Nicholas (mark) Budd and Catherine (mark) Budd. (94)

FELKEY, Craft of Berlin twp. - dated 2-4-1829; recorded June 1829. Sons: Jacob, Henry, Daniel, William and Samuel. Executor: son, Samuel. Signed: Craft (mark) Felkey. Witnesses: David Eaton, John Wateman and Andrew Heaverlo. (96)

TAYLOR, Nathan of Kingston twp. - dated 11-27-1828; recorded June 1829. Wife, Lucy. Brothers: Ira and Siles. Sisters: Polly, Sarah and other sisters mentioned but not named. Children, mentioned but not named. Executors: wife, Lucy and brother, Ira. Signed: Nathan Taylor. Witnesses: Almon Stark, Jacob Rosecrans and Daniel Wiloman, Jr. (98)

WILLIAMS, Thomas - dated 10-24-1825; recorded 3-16-1829. Wife, Catherine. Son: Job Williams. Grandsons: Thomas Williams, son of Robert Williams; Robert Williams Jr. Signed: Thomas (mark) Williams. Witnesses: Elias Murray and Dustin H. Cooke. (99)

BEAKLEY, Samuel - dated 9-4-1828; recorded 3-18-1829. Wife, Susannah. Sons: Hiram, Henry and John. Daughters: Matilda, Polly, Peggy, Jane and Elizabeth. Executors: John Beakley and Solomon Smith. Signed: Samuel Beakley. Witnesses. E. Griswold and Benj'n Powers. (101)

FINKHAM, Abel - dated 2-15-1828; recorded 3-16-1829. Wife, mentioned but not named. Son: Noah. Daughters: Elizabeth and Hannah. Signed: Abel Finkham. Witnesses: Marshal Black, Nathan Black and M. H. Sackett. Codicil dated 4-18-1828 names son, Isaac. Same witnesses. (103)

WYATT, Nathaniel of Marlborough twp. - dated (not dated); recorded 3-3-1830. Wife: Sarah, also to serve as executrix. Four children: Charlotte, Leonard, Ezra and Mary Ann. Guardians of four children are to be Ezra Wyatt of Cuyahoga Co., Ohio and John Brundrige of Delaware Co. Signed: Nathaniel Wyatt. Witnesses: T. D. Wyatt, L. S. Heull and Nathaniel Wyatt. (106)

MOSES, William of Delaware twp. - dated 10-12-1820; recorded 4-2-1831. Bequeaths to: Abraham Williams, "man I have long lived with" and his wife Polly Williams; Winslow Birce; Mara Chester, "she being an inmate of family with me from her youth". Executor: Hosea Williams. Signed: William (mark) Moses. Witnesses: T. Boardman and Adeline Campbell. (108)

KILBOURN, Susan of the town of Delaware - dated 1-29-1827; recorded 7-21-1831. Sisters: Mary Kimball; to have land in town of East Hartford, Hartford Co., Conn.; Anna Williams. Sister-in-law; Eunice Kilbourn, also to serve as Executrix. Nephew; Alexander Kilbourn. Nieces: Mary Kimball, Jane Niersted and Emily Hiersted. Signed: Susan Kilbourn. Witnesses: Solomon Smith, Keturah Steward and Sarah Steward. (111)

THOMPSON, Samuel of Liberty twp. - Oral Will - will made 4-29-1831; recorded July 1831. Samuel Thompson died 4-30-1831. Wife, Elizabeth Thompson. Witnesses, Elizabeth Crookshanks and Azuba Myric made deposition 5-5-1831. (113)

VANLOON, Nicholas - dated 8-10-1831; recorded 11-7-1831. Wife: Experience. Sons: 3rd son mentioned but not named; Isiah. Executors: wife, Experience and son, Isiah. Signed: Nicholas (mark) Vanloon. Witnesses: B. Carpenter, Alpheus Bigelow and Edw. S. Randall. (116)

MURRAY, Lyman of the town of Delaware late of Bellefontaine - dated 2-24-1829; recorded 11-11-1831. Wife: Ann C. Brothers: Eli; Richard, to have tract of land in Cuyahoga Co., Ohio. Sisters: Clarissa and Emely. Sisters-in-law: Maria and Isabelle Gunn. Brother-in-law: John Gunn Jr. Bequeaths to: Robert Gunn (no relationship stated)and friend, Dr. J. H. Hills. Executors: wife, Ann C. and brother, Richard. Signed: Lyman Murray. Witnesses: Calvin Cobell and Reuben Hills. (114)

WATKINS, Evan of Radnor twp. - dated 7-18-1831; recorded Nov. 1831. Wife: Mary, also to serve as executrix. Signed: Evan (mark) Watkins. Witnesses: David Evans Jones and Humphrey Humphreys. (117)

HEAVERLOW, Andrew of Berlin twp. - dated 7-11-1826; recorded April 1832. Wife, Rachael. Children: Andrew; Reuben; Polly; Martha; Barton; William; James; Rachael Martin; Sarah. Executors; sons, James and Andrew. Signed: Andrew Heaverlow. Witnesses: David Eaton, John Rouse and Atwood Smith. (119)

TAYLOR, Joel of Marlborough twp. - dated 5-18-1832; recorded 6-18-1832. Wife; Elizabeth, also to serve as executrix. Sons: Elam, James E., Eli, Arthur and Joel. Daughters: Eliza, Harriet, Mary and Emilia Taylor. Mentions: money due Sophia Taylor and the heirs of Anna Taylor (no relationship given). Signed: Joel Taylor. Witnesses: John Brundridge and Levi Hinton Jr. (121)

WEAVER, Samuel - dated 7-23-1831; recorded 11-15-1832. Wife, Elizabeth. Children: John, George, Beth Solomon, Samuel, Mary, Carah and Catherine. Executors: wife, Elizabeth and two friends, John Philips and Ober Taylor. Signed: Samuel Weaver. Witnesses: Jas. W. Crawford and Michael Dilsaver. (125)

391

WOOD, Desire of Marion Co., Ohio - dated 13th day 6th month, 1832; recordëd 5-16-1833. Bequeaths to: Charles Osborn son of Henry Osborn, dec'd; Mary Davis; Daniel, Azar, Dorcas, Jabid Jr. and Charles Osborn; Esther widow of Henry Osborn (no relationships given). Executor: Daniel Osborn. Signed: Desire Wood. Witnesses: Jonathan Wood Jr. and Griffeth Lewis. (125)

COYKENDALL, Harmon of Kingston twp. - dated 9-11-1826; recorded 8-27-1835. Wife, Catherine. Son: Peter. Daughters: Elizabeth Finch and Charlotte Decker. Executor: Isaac Finch. Signed: Harmon Coykendall. Witnesses: John Vansickle and Silas C. McClary. (127)

BOUSH, John of Brown twp. - dated 3-18-1834; recorded 4-21-1834. Wife. Abby. Two youngest children: James and John; James being blind; other children mentioned but not named. Bequeath to Cornelius Sickles. Executor: Thomas Arnold. Signed: John Boush. Witnesses: Eli Mead. Robert Jones and James Lombert. (128)

DAVIES, William of Harmony twp. - dated 2-3-1834; recorded 9-1-1834. Wife, Mary. Children: Benjamin, Eleanor, Mary Ann and John Davies. Executors: Charles McCracken and George Burns. Signed: William Davies. Witnesses: Robert Jones and David Davies. (131)

EVANS, Thomas late of Wales, now of Delaware County - dated 9127-1834; recorded 11-26-1834. Uncle: John Williams of Radnor twp. Sister: Eleanor Evans living near City of Utica, New York. Executors: David Cadwallader and John Owens. Signed: Thomas Evans. Witnesses: Chas. H. Pricket, Thomas Jones and Edward Evans. (134)

SPONG, Samuel - dated 7-24-1834; recorded 11-27-1834. Wife, Mary Eve. Son: Uriah, not of age. Brother: Absolem Spong, also to serve as executor. Signed: Samuel Spong. Witnesses: Israel Carpenter and William Fulton. (135)

BURROUGHS, Thomas - dated 8-31-1832; recorded 3-4-1835. Wife, Margaret. Sons: John W., Thomas H. and Stephen G. Daughter: Rebecca wife of Amos Fuller. Executors; wife, Margaret and son, John W. Signed: Thomas (mark) Burroughs. Witnesses: Milo D. Pettibone and Francis Horr. (137)

DIX, David of Troy twp. - dated 5-6-1833; recorded 9-3-1834. Wife, Mary. Sons: David, Elijah, Stanton Clark, Peres Main to have land from maternal grandfather, and Stephen. Daughters: Matilda wife of Joseph Eagon, Drusilla wife of Aaron Redman, Polly Dix. Mentionsi land in Marion Co., Ohio. Executors; son, David Dix. Signed: David Dix. Witnesses: Thos W. Powell. Wilder Jay (or Joy), James Smith and Asahel Welch. (139)

ERIE COUNTY, OHIO - RUGBY CEMETERY - VERMILION TOWNSHIP

Contributed by Mrs. LeRoy A. Harris, #2, Vesta Rd., Box 156, Wakeman, Ohio 44889
Cemetery is located on North Ridge Road in Vermilion twp., near Axel, Ohio on
Route 60 to Lake Erie. Complete inscriptions copied.

HARRIS, Thomas died Jan. 14, 1879 aged 80y 10m 4d
    Charles son of Thomas & Sarah died Nov. 8, 1853 aged 12y
    Ella wife of Royal Harris died May 5, 1878 aged 22y 1m 28d
    Earl R. 1883-1940; Cynthia wife of earl R. Harris 1889-19--(not engraved)
SKINN, Father 1842-1913; Mother 1851-1952
    Nellie 1888-1941; Eliza Feb. 15, 1876 - June 17, 1894
PEASE, Lewis died Nov.20, 1878 aged 72y 6m
    Zilpha wife of Lewis Pease died May 17, 1892 aged 74y 7m
ZEGLER, George 1828-1914; Christina wife of Geo. Zegler 1825-1913
SHROEDER, Gustas H. 1840-1919
    Otto son of G. Y. & E. Oct. 12, 1876 - March 9, 1880
NORMANEAU, Joseph 1832-1909
    Louisa Johnson wife of Joseph Normandeau Aug. 5, 1835 - Aug. 19, 1906
MORSE, George C. born Feb. 15, 1819 Great Barrington, Mass., died Aug. 24, 1886,
    Brownhelm, Erie Co., Ohio
    Eliza J. Ball April 9, 1832 - Aug. 26, 1911
    George B. died Dec. 1, 1871 aged 4y 1m 26d
COOLEY, Jennie E. Morse wife of C. E. Cooley April 4, 1865 - March 19, 1893
MORSE, Edward died Sept 17, 1854 aged 45y
    Emma dau. of E. & A. died Aug. 25, 1867 aged 21y
    George T. son of E. & A. died Dec. 16, 1851 aged 5m
    James R. Jan. 2, 1817 - Sept. 12, 1897
    Mahala Brown wife of James R. Morse June 27, 1823 - Feb. 22, 1912
    Mary Elgiva dau. of J. R. & M. died July 7, 1874 aged 28y
BROWN, Stephen Feb. 7, 1800 - Aug. 25, 1867, native of Skaneteles, N.Y.
    Sally Nye wife of Stephen Brown Dec. 1, 1802 - Dec. 31, 1881
    Stephen son of S. & S. died Feb. 6, 1844 aged 18y 6m
    John son of S. & S. May 17, 1828 - Feb. 20, 1889:
    Liva 1830-1909; Clara Harris wife of Liva Brown 1832-1915
    Adaline wife of Daniel Brown (date gone)
    Charles son of D. & A. (date gone) age 15m
    Hannah wife of J. Brown died Oct. 2, 1836 aged 64 years
    Charles R. died Dec. 13, 1856 aged 56y 24d
    Sarah Root wife of C. R. Brown died Jan. 22, 1902 aged 86y 11m 13d
    Clara 1869-1914; Liva 1896-1901; Burton 1905-1909; Howard 1913-1920
NYE, Frances died Nov. 18, 1888 aged 31y
AUSTIN, Lodemia died April 1, 1867 aged 84y
GEGENHEDNER, G.W. 1849-1918; Anna B. wife of G.W. Gegenheimer 1846-1912
    Fred H. 1870-1945; Amy A. wife of Fred H. Gegenheimer 1879-19--
    Maria C., daughter, 1870-1945
HILL, Henry died Feb. 9, 1886 aged 62y 3m 14d
    Betsey wife of Henry Hill died March 1, 1868 aged 40y
    Roxana dau. of Henry & Betsey died Oct. 26, 1879
MILLER, Jacob Feb. 11-1821 - Dec. 5, 1910
    Catherine wife of Jacob Miller Sept 29, 1823 - Dec. 15, 1904

REYNOLDS, Sherman M. 1872-1947; Bertha E. wife of S. M. Reynolds 1878-1930
    Rufus 1835-1900, 15th Ohio Battery, Civil War
    Rebecca wife of Rufus Reynolds 1844-1929
BODFISH, Charles H. 1836-1897
DEAN, Cooper, died Jan. 1, 1867, infant
BALDWIN, Thomas died May 14, 1868 aged 82y 6m 7d
    Esther wife of Thomas Baldwin died Jan. 1, 1880 aged 86y
    Joseph H. Jan. 6, 1824 - Feb. 14, 1902
    Sarah M. wife of Joseph Baldwin July 17, 1832 - Sept. 5, 1864
    Adeline H. wife of Joseph Baldwin Jan. 16, 1833 - April 21, 1890
    May E. wife of Joseph Baldwin Oct. 14, 1843 - Sept. 19, 1906
    William A. Jan. 2, 1859 - July 7, 1883
    Charles son of Joseph H. died Nov. 9, 1863, infant
FRISBE, Myra R. died Sept. 3, 1877 aged 5y, son of W. & H.
GROVER, S. B. 1819-1906; Mary wife of S. B. Grover died Mar. 21, 1875 aged 52y
    Sarah I. dau of Shepherd & Mary died May 17, 1845 aged 2y 6m 19d
HOLL, Clarence son of J. & A. died July 1, 1887 aged 8m.
    Bertie Brown wife of J. J. Holl died June 23, 1890 aged 21y 1m 7d
HILL, Louisa died Dec. 29, 1853 aged 23y, wife of Austin
OPFER, Jacob died July 6, 1905 aged 63y 6m 15d
    Elizabeth wife of Jacob Opfer died Mar. 19, 1880 aged 38y 5m 17d
WYLDE, William died Oct. 30, 1880 aged 63y 1m 24d
    Elizabeth wife of Wm Wylde died Dec. 31, 1877 aged 57y
    Benjamin fied May 21, 1865 aged 84y 3m 17d
    Sarah H. wife of Benj. Brown died Jan, 5, 1860 aged 69y
    Hannah Worcester dau. of Benj. & Sarah June 27, 1819 - July 3, 1888
BASSETT, Thomas died April 21, 1856 aged 61y 1m
    Nancy H. wife of Thomas Bassett died March 11, 1838 aged 33y 1m 21d
    Thomas son of Thomas & Nancy died March 4, 1852 aged 11y 3m 10d
    Edward son of Thomas & Nancy died March 10, 1835 (no age)
    Edgar S. son of Nathan & M. died March 22, 1851 aged 22d
    Ketusak dau. of Thomas & Nancy died Mardh 5, 1835 aged 19y 7m 6d
McGREGOR, T. M. died Oct. 1, 1888 aged 78y 3m 22d
    Jane wife of T. M. McGregor died Dec. 20, 1879 aged 70y 7m 21d
    Daughter of A. & J. died Oct, 1864 aged 3y 6m
    Julia wife of Adolphus1832-1912; Adolphus 1832-1894
    Charles 1852-1903; James 1859-1907; Andrew, Co. F, 88th O.V.I.
OPPERMAN, Mary E. dau. of P. & M. died Feb. 28, 1886 aged 6m 17d
STERMEN, Charles W. son of G. M. & S. A. died Sept 14, 1841 aged 4m 17d
NEWBERRY, John died Nov. 8, 1851 aged 36y; Sally died April 16, 1876 aged 85y 6m 10d
GOODRICH, Timothy L. May 10, 1836 - Feb. 3, 1896, Co. K, O.V.C.
    Lois E. wife of T. L. Goodrich April 21, 1835 - Feb. 2, 1892
    Esther A. wife of Stephen Goodrich died Feb. 20, 1845 aged 27y 11d
    Henrietta L. wife of J. D. Goodrich died April 9, 1866 aged 21y 8m 28d
BRADLEY, William May 10, 1826 - Dec. 1, 1901
    Alvira Washburn wife of Wm Bradley Feb. 3, 1838 - Feb. 22, 1921
    John B. Lent son of Wm & A. died July 2, 1871 aged 24y 3n
    Julia April 16, 1832 - Feb. 15, 1899
    Leonard died May 3, 1875 aged 82y 6m
    Roxie wife of Leonard Bradley died Feb 25, 1858 aged 67y

BRADLEY, Emily T. wofe of Leonare Bradley died Sept. 21, 1885 aged 83y
ALLEN, Robert 1842-1921, Co. H., 103rd OLV.I.; his wife 1848-1934
SCHUSTER, Gust 1855-1928; Mary 1861-1926
HEWITT, Leeds M. died May 26, 1838 aged 41y 2m 6d
    Sally L. wife of L. M. Hewitt Jan. 26, 1796 - June 9, 1836
    William E. Son of L. M. & S. L. died March 3, 1847 aged 16y 1m 9d
DALZELL, Ran 1847-1908; Sarah wife of Ran. March 18, 1857 - March 30, 1901

ERIE COUNTY, OHIO - OLD BERLIN HEIGHTS CEMETERY - BERLIN TOWNSHIP

Cbntributed by: Mrs. LeRoy A. Harris, #2, Vesta Rd., Box 156, Wakeman, Ohio 44889

Cemetery is located in back of an old unused church in Berlin Heights. All
inscriptions copied.
MEEKER, Leah Elson 1835-1917   Lucy L. 1859-(not engraved)
KING, Hiram 1818-1900; Sarah H. wife of Hiram King 1820-1914
    Chester died March 12, 1861 aged 77y 1m 8d
    Louisa C. died Jan. 3, 1832, age......
    Elizabeth died Nov. 15, 1823 age 78y
    Jemina wife of Chester King died......(unreadable)
    Joseph S. Aug 15, 1827 - Jan. 30, 1910
    Melona V. wife of Joseph S. King July 20, 1831 - Sept. 5, 1891
    Charles W. son of Joseph S. & N. V. Aug. 3, 1853 - Aug. 5, 1866
SMITH, Jemima King wife of Steven Smith died April 21, 1850 age 80y
CASE, Willie W. died Aug. 18, 1860 age 17y, son of H. & A. Case
    Almera W. whife of A. Case died May 9, 1878 aged 72y 2m 21d
DAVIS, Charles M. 1866-1920
SMITH, Steven 1835-1890
    Charley son of J. & M. died Aug. 5, 1866 aged 13y 2d
    Turner M. died May 21, 1869 aged died May 21, 1869 aged 73y 9m 4d
    Amy wife of Turner M. Smith died June 30, 1863 aged 68y 4m 4d
    Horace C. 1822-1911; Susan Johnson 1828-1912
    Lucius B. died July 13, 1864 aged 40y 1m 22d, 7th Regt. U.S.T.
    G. W. 18__(?); Nancy wife of G. W. Smith 1829-1882
    Esley, Co. F, N.S.S.T.
    Sophonia wife of D. H. Smith Nov 14, 1824 - March 23, 1872
    Marcia E. wife of D. H. Smith died Oct. 13, 1860 age 22y 4m 10d
    Amanda H. dau. of J. C. & S. L. Smith died Oct. 18, 1856 aged 6y 4m 18d
BEACH, Isaac 1793-1858; Hannah 1814-1888
BQILEY, Marvin April 2, 1822 - May 19, 1899; Susan June 13, 1818 - Oct. 20, 1907
NICHOLS, Curtis 1826-1903; Mary wife of Curtis 1825-1876; Maria wife of Curtis
                                1837-1906
    Clara A. dau. of C. & M. 1861-1863
SHELDON, Myrtle O. dau. of C. & M. Nichols and wife of Mr. Sheldon 1863-1939
PHILLIPS, Dr. Xenophon died June 16, 1874 aged 60y 10m 16d
    Betsey Ruggles wofe of Dr. X. Phillips 1812-1882
    Emily A. June 1, 1884 - March 10, 1924
    Lina dau. of X. & B. died June 11, 1864 aged 15y 11m 20d

PHILLIPS, Almon P. son of X. & B. died June 11, 1813 (?1843?) aged 3y 3m 14d
Paul J. Sept. 9, 1880 - April 3, 1950; Elizabeth M. wife of Paul J.
     Nov. 10, 1877 - (not engraved)
Capt. S. S. 1816-1898; Nancy L. Rathbun wife of S. S. Phillips 1820-1886
Leslia S. died Sept. 29, 1856 aged 3y
Alice A. 1813-1903
Rebecca widow of Elder J. Phillips died Aug. 2, 1872 aged 92y
Elder Joshua died May 21, 1815 (1845?) aged 60y 1m 21d
Capt Zebah son of J. Y R. died Aug. 21, 1834 aged 27y 10m 28d
Spencer - Dec. 24, 1840, Pvt., Porter's Mass. Mil. Rev. War.
Henry C. Jan. 2, 1842 - March 25, 1894
Z. May 8, 1804 - March 31, 1882; Eunice Cobb wife of Z Phillips 1814-1898
Hattie Louise dau. of H. C. & B . C. Phillips Dec. 11, 1888-March 9, 1894
Infant dau. of H. C. & B. C. Phillips died 1885 aged 5 weeks
ROOT, Polly Reynolds dau. of Daniel & Phebe Reynolds and wife Mr. Root died
     Sept. 15, 1875 aged 62y 5m 2d
GOODSELL, Benjamin 1837-1908; Catharine wife of Benj. Goodsell 1838-1920
GREEN, Herbert 1848-1906; Sarah wife of Herbert Green 1858-19--(not engraved)
     Calvir 1885-1939; Freddie 1885-1889
CLAPHAN, Ulysses S. 1876-1912; French, Co. B. 28th U. S. C. I.
KELLOGG, Chester died July 16, 1809 (1869?) aged 72y 7m 11d
     Martha wife of C. C. Kellogg died Oct. 10, 1857 aged 62y aged 62y 6m 21 d
L. O. died Mar. 25, 1866 aged 63y 4m 16d
Caroline died Jan 2, 1877 aged 49y 5m 6d
MINARD, Alice M. died Jan. 10, 1853 aged 8m 21
Callie died Sept. 8, 1863 aged 16y 5d
Mamie S. died Oct 9, 1878 aged 22y 9d
S. W. 1825-1953
MILES, Homer son of H. B. & L. M. died Oct. 7, 1862 aged 21y 10 22d
Elizabeth wife of J. Miles died July 2, 1872 aged.....
Dea. Jasper died Mar. 11, 1849 aged 66y 2m 14d
BURDUE, Nathaniel, Capt. in Delop's Co., Pa. Mil. Rev. War
FISK, Leonard Aug. 1, 1811 - Feb. 9, 1900
     Caroline W. wife of L. Fisk Mar. 11, 1816 - Sept. 10, 1881
WHITNEY, Eliza died Dec. 12, 1875 aged 89y
George Jan. 11, 1783 - July 30, 1866
Clarissa: wife of Geo. Whiteney May 10, 1788 - Jan. 28, 1835
LOWRY , William died Nov. 25, 1855 aged 36y 4m 17d
Joseph S. 1806-1885
Rebecca Phillips wife of J. S. Lowry 1810-1891
Sarah L. wife of Pallt J. Lowry died Aug. 25, 1858 aged 24y 8m 26d
William, Co. E. 7th O.V.I.
J. C. Jan. 4, 1842 - March 17, 1890, Co. I. 45th S.C.I.
GROVER, Curtis T. 1827-1801; Maria M. 1836-1913; Frank B. 1858-1919
WILBUR, George M. 1855-1926; Cora B. 1856-1936
ALGER, Cyrus born Aug. 24, 1813 Columbia Co., N.Y. died Jan. 16, 1855
     Ethan A. 1807-1897; Rachel A. Stamler wife of E. A. Alger 1830-1907
SKINNER, Mary B. wife of H.G. Skinner died April 21, 1841 aged 35 years
BIRD, Joseph died July 24, 1861 aged 37 years
SLOAT, Maria dau of H. & M. Stewart and wife of John Sloat died May 21, 1884
     aged 61y 5d

SIMPSON, Ella Sloat wife of James Simpson died May 14, 1879 aged 21y 9m 8d
BUCKLEY, Medad H. July 29, 1844 - June 5, 1901
    Julia A. wife of M. H. Buckley May 1, 1844 - Dec. 17, 1877
    Julia A. dau. of Joseph Elson died Dec. 17, 1877 aged 32y 7m 17d
ELSON, Joseph April 1, 1795 - Aug. 14, 1883
    Lutecia wife of Joseph Elson Feb. 27, 1809 - Nov. 10, 1882
GOODRICK, Margaret Elson wife of Geo. Goodrick died Feb. 15, 1880 aged 33y 4m 4d
TURNER, Caroline wife of F. B. M. Turner Dec. 7, 1822 - May 9, 1865
DANIELS, Elias L. died May 1, 1866 aged 17y 6m 17d
BUTLER, C. W. April 12, 1817 - Sept. 15, 1858; Charles Jan 15, 1835 - Aug. 17, 1856
    Euebia April 6, 1818 - (not engraved); Willie Aug. 10, 1852 -(not engraved)
WALKER, David died Feb. 18, 1842 aged 25 years
    Hannah died Sept..9, 1857 aged 73y 6m
    Frances Ann wife of Perry G. Walker died Dec. 28, 1857 aged 21y 10m
OTIS, Frances Ann youngest dau. of Joseph & Nancy Otis (note: no dates)
REED, Margaret died Feb. 5, 1870 aged 53y 5m
    I. N. 1811-1900
    Georgiana dau. of N. & M. died May 28, 1857 aged.........
    Willie P. died Oct. 26, 1862 aged 10y
    Howard N. died Oct. 10, 1836 aged 1y 20d
    Ellen A. 1839-1924
OTIS, Joseph born Sept. 10, 1792 Montville, Conn., died April 16, 1844
    Nancy Billings born Dec. 26, 1792 Montville, Conn., died Jan. 2, 1858
    Mary dau. of J. & Nancy died Oct. 2, 1852 aged 25y 1m
ELLIS, Cornelius died April 6, 1861 aged 66y 1m
    Elizabeth wife of Cornelius Ellis died Aug. 9, 1865 aged 63y 26d
    Monanda dau. of Cornelius & E. died Dec. 8, 1842 aged 6y 10m 23d
WEATHERLOW, Daniel R. died Nov. 13, 1865 aged 23y 4 m enlisted in 7th O.V.I.,
        June 3, 1861, wounded at Antietam, Md., Sept. 17, 1862, discharged
        Feb. 18, 1863, re-enlisted 101st O.V.I., Dec 3, 1863, wounded
        at Kennesaw Mountain, Ga., June 20, 1865, mustered out Nov. 2
    Zebah P. died Oct. 4, 1865 aged 28y 9m 11d, son of Samuel & Polly
POWERS, Alanson died Aug. 16, 1855 aged 50y 9m 6d
SQUIER, Eli died Sept. 26, 1848 aged 83 years
    Sally died April 6, 1830 aged 73y 9m 26d
LUCAS, Hiram G. son of Ira 1828-1898; Mary Trumble wife of Hiram G. Lucas 1844-1901
    Ira 1800-1882; Infant son of H. & M. died 1868 aged 11 days
CHAPMAN, Corwin C. son of T. C. & E. P. died Jan. 8, 1848 aged 3y
    T. C. 1820-1894; E. P. wife of T. C. Chapman 1821-1901
    Clara R. dau. of T. C. & E. P. died Aug. 7, 1873 aged 15y
    Tal S. died Aug. 1, 1849 aged 21y
    Samuel died Dec. 12, 1851 aged 65y
    Rachel wife of Samuel Chapman died Dec. 25, 1879 aged 90y
MORGAN, Emma Chapman wife of F. W. Morgan died July 21, 1892 aged 77y 11m 17d
    F. W. died Dec. 17, 1892 aged 81y 7m 21d
    E. J. died Oct. 10, 1857 aged 7y
CORNWELL, Sargt F. H., Co. I, Wisconsin Inf.
DAY, Anna S. wife of Wm Day May 5, 1827 - Oct. 18, 1897
    William Dec. 5, 1817 - Dec. 23, 1893
    William July 16, 1855 - 1855 - April 6, 1880
    Nina dau. of Wm & A. S. Sept. 14, 1881 - May 10, 1898

397

ERIE COUNTY, OHIO - JIM WOOD CEMETERY - FLORENCE TOWNSHIP

Contributed by:- Mrs. LeRoy Harris, #2 Vesta Rd., Wakeman, Ohio. 44889

Cemetery is on Carter Road off Route 60; it is back in field near the Vermilion
River. Some inscriptions were very had to read. Transcribed by LeRoy and Stella
Harris.

PARKER, Ormel, died 6 July 1868 age 71y
    Adline, 10 Jan 1829 - 9 April 1889, wife of C. Ames
    Elexander 1823-1893   Mary H. 1835-1917 wife of Elexander
    Frank V. 1862-1864   Otha O. 1877-1881   Nellie 1873-1881
    Ashel, died 16 May 1841 age 76y 1m 16d
    Jemima, died 3 Sept 1823 age 53y, wife of Ashel
    Benjamin, died 7 Dec. 1821 age 15y 3m.
    Joanna, died 23 Aug 1838 age 42y 6m 24d, wife of Lucius C.
    Salvina Higgins, died 12 Aug. 1857 age 45y 7m 1d, wife of Z.
    Ruth, died 26 April 1821 age 27y, wife of Z.
    Zachariah, died 11 Jan. 1845 age 56y 10m
    Elbert, died 18 Dec 1850 age 11y 6m, son of Z. & S.
    George C. died ___(date gone) age _____
    Maria, died ___(date gone) age ___
    Sylvia, 13 June 1883 age 1y 29d, dau. of I. & M.
    Ella J. 17 July 1886 age 30y 2m 27d.
    Austin, Killed 11 May 1841 age 15y 9m 4d, son of Wm. & Sarah
    Eunice, died 28 Feb. 1863 age 97y 8m 17d, wife of Levi
BATES, Henry, (note:- date gone—died a very old man)
BENTLEY, William died 7 July 1867 age 83y 7m
    Lydia, died 10 Sept. 1861 age 72y 1m, wife of Wm.
    Wm. I. U. died 30 March 1848 age 21y 27d, son of Wm. & Lydia
    Benjamin, died 25 July 1842 age 50y 9m 16d
    Margaret, died 9 Dec. 1822 age 65y, wife of Benj.
    John, died 29 March 1859 age 76y 11m 21d
    Anna, died 28 April 1862 age 69y 7m 27d, wife of John
WOOD, James died 31 March 1877 age 77 years
    Minnie J. 1856-1904   F. H.   1856-1891
    Phebe died 16 Nov 1894 age 84y, wife of James
    Daniel, died 12 Nov 1854 age 86y 7m 6d
STARKS, Betsey E. died 30 Nov 1858 age 53y 7m 27d wife of Jeramiah
HATINGER, William died 6 July 1864 age 32y 2d
    Annis died 1 May 1881 age 52y wife of Wm.
CRAWFORD, A. D. died 8 Sept 1884 age 84 years
    Martha died 26 Oct 1842 age 42 years wife of A. D.
FREEMAN, Lucy M.   1834-1915
    Jemima died 7 April 1864 age 59y 9m
JOHNSON, Polly died 28 April 1850 age 57y 5m 26d
PALMETIER, Lydia died 15 March 1875 age 49y 7m 22d wife of W. M.
CLOUGH, William died 14 March 1860 age 12y 6m 3d son of L. & C.
BARBER, George W., died 16 April 1863 age 28 years
TAYLOR, Theresa died 18 April 1852 age 24y 11m 23d wife of J.
MOOTERS, William S. died 31 Aug 1851 age 1y 22d son of P. & L.
ALDRICH, John died 6 March 1864 age 3y 9m son of P. & J. K.

RICE, Elizabeth died 2 Dec. 1872 age 56y 6m 24d
COLE, Andrew J., died 11 Feb. 1883 age 17y, son of Cyrus & Rebecca
HOPKINS, Ebenezer, 23 June 1825 - 18 Feb. 1876
   Ebenezer, 1858-1923
TUMBLE, Daniel, died 14 Jan. 1836 age 48y 5m
   Daniel, died 16 Aug. 1846 age 25y
   Isaac, died 24 Jan. 1832 age 19y (or 89y?)

ERIE COUNTY, OHIO - JUSTICE OF THE PEACE BOOK 1881-1907

Contributed by Mrs. Patsey A. Read, 15862 Hocking Blvd., Cleveland, Ohio 44142

(Explanation: The following records were abstracted for names only and titles if listed, from a book salvaged by Mrs. Read's husband about twenty years ago from rubbish when the town hall in Berlin Heights, Berlin township was remodeled into a township Fire Hall. Mrs. Read states that if any names were not clear or if she had any doubt about spelling, she indicated it either with the alternate possibility or by a question mark (?) after the name. Page number is indicated in parenthesis (). Pages are numbered so when the book lies open, both pages facing the reader have the same number.)

Samuel F. (or L.) REED, of Niles, Michigan to Betsy E. BARNS of Berlin Twp., Erie Co., Ohio. October 20, 1881. Sayres N. Lemmon, J.P. (3)

Henry NELDING vs. Oscar GREEN. November 15, 1884. Lowell M. Eaton, Justice of the Peace, Chester Daniels, Constable; H. G. Miller, G. R. McConnelly, E. N. Street, N. G. Sarr, Katie Knott, Joshua Driver, Albert Coleman (or Holman), Dwight Rathburn, John Brown, and Curtiss Nickols. (17)

L. D. Allen vs. Charles THOMPSON. January 3, 1881. Sayres N. Lemmon, J.P. (19)

M. KLIMAN vs. Wm. BARTLETT. October 20, 1882. S. N. Lemmon, J.P. Eaton. (20)

Mrs. Julia MEEKER vs. Wm. BARTLETT. Dec. 29, 1882. S. N. Lemmon, J. P. Geo. Meeker (son of Mrs. Julia Meeker), M. L. Eaton, John Wilson, P. J. Clark, Dan Fox, Geo. Bons(?), Amos Meeker, Geo. Bartlett. (21)

Jacob HILDEBRAND vs. Gertrude MILLER and Henry MILLER. February 23, 1883. S. N. Lemmon, J.P. Eaton. (22)

James DOUGLASS vs. H. H. WILLARD. Feb. 26, 1883. S. N. Lemmon, J.P. L. M. Eaton, J. S. Douglass. (23)

William N. BARTLETT vs. William and Henry MINKLER. Sept. 25, 1886, Jacob Sarr, J.P. Mentions "Monroe Black farm", John Sarr. (24)

T. D. MOFFAT vs. Curtiss NICKOLS. Nov. 15, 1886. Jacob Sarr, J.P. M. B. Lemmon, Atty for Pltf., Clyde, Ohio; John Sarr, Constable, A. J. Nickols. (25)

R. REITTER vs. Jacob KRISS. Dec. 13, 1886. Jacob Sarr, J.P.; John Sarr, Constable. (26)

James ANDERSON vs. Charles THOMPSON. June 20, 1884. Jacob Sarr, J.P. (28)

E. P. FISHER vs. Gertrude KOCH, Administratrix of Bernhard KOCH, deceased. March 28, 1887. Jacob Sarr, J.P. F. A. Barnes, James Fisher, Alic Davis, Wm. Weaver, C. A. Hardy, M. Bailey, G. M. Austin, Willis Youngs, Geo. Chapin, John Wilson, H. S. Miller, Otto Paulhorn(?), Curtiss Nickols, W. Stone, James Bell, C. Curth (or Custh), Charles Becker, Watson Belle. (29)

Frank STANG vs. J. NEWBERGER. March 19, 1887. Jacob Sarr, J.P. (30)

Mary E. DAVIS vs. John HOFFMAN. July 20, 1887. Jacob Sarr, J.P. Mary E. Davis, executrix of deceased Henry Davis. (31)

May LEWIS vs. P. K. LOOMIS. July 26, 1887. Jacob Sarr, J.P. (32)

George W. BARTLETT vs. William H. BARTLETT. Sept. 28, 1887. Jacob Sarr. J.P. Mentions "Monroe Black farm", George H. Bartlett, F. A. Barrows, Constable; Monroe Black, T. C. Chapman, Notary Republic. (33)

A. H. RUPLE vs. Emarilla DRIVER. October 5, 1887. Jacob Sarr, J.P.; J. M. Stahl, Henry Hine, Hiram Lucus. (35)

Albert CONGDON vs. J. W. GUNN. Oct. 12, 1887. Jacob Sarr, J.P. John M. Gunn, F. A. Barrows, mentions "Gunn, the Deft. being a non resident of Erie Co." (36)

F. A. BARROWS vs. Fredrick HUTTENLOCKER. October 26, 1887. Jacob Sarr. J.P. Fred Huttenlocker. (37)

Charles PEAKE vs. Edward HINDE. Oct. 27, 1887. Jacob Sarr, J. P. (38a)

STRAY NOTICE. July 20, 1887. James E. DRIVER declares rightful owner may claim animal by "calling and paying all charges thereon." Charles H. Becker Twp. Clerk; Eugene Peak, and Gust Wetzle, Appraisers. (38b)

Henry GRENZEBACH vs. Eugene SCHUMER. Nov. 15, 1887. Jacob Sarr, J.P. A. Grenzebach, son of Henry; F. A. Barrows, Constable; John Coven, resident of Cleveland, Cuyahoga Co., Ohip; Gust Wetzel, resident of Cleveland, Cuyahoga Co., Ohio, R. Shoff, Eugene Schorner (or Schumer), Frank Schorner, John Willson, C. Williams, C. A. Hardy, M. Finton, A. Hardy, H. Knott, Gust Wetzel, John Coven, R. Champer (?), C. A. Heald, John Kelly, F. Schumer. (39)

John B. NETSCHER vs. John HOFFMAN. Nov. 1887. Jacob Sarr, J.P.; F. A. Burrows, Constable; James Douglas, P. J. Clark, George Peak, F. Meeker, A. W. Bartholenew, G. R. McConnelly, Chester Daniels, Lucy Daniels, I. B. (or J. B.) Poyer, Charles Kock John Getz, Mart Daniels, W. Young, James Douglass, Anson Hoffman. (41)

W. B. BARTLETT vs. William H. BARTLETT. Dec. 20, 1887. Jacob Sarr, J.P.; F. A. Barrows, Constable. (42)

Chester DANIELS vs. Daniel FOX. Feb. 4, 1884. Jacob Sarr, J.P. Mrs. Lucy Daniels, E. H. Chandler, Constable. (43)

John FOX vs. Lant HUTCHMAN, Marsh 10, 1888. Jacob Sarr, J.P. Lant Hitsman, James Brundage. (44)

John BURTON vs. Ira LEWIS. Oct. 19, 1888. Jacob Sarr, J.P. E. Chandler, Constable; James Hogan, I. W. Wright, Frank Allgood, John Allgood, Charlott Berton. (45)

H. J. MASON vs. George BRUNDAGE. Oct. 26,1888. Jacob Sarr, J.P. F. A. Barrows, Constable; b. Finley and John Borman (or Bowman). (46)

Charles A. MORTON vs. W. S. HOWARD. Nov. 14, 1888. Jacob Sarr, J.P. (47)

Henry HULL and Horace W. RAND vs. Leonidis CHAPIN. Jan. 15, 1889. Jacob Sarr, J.P.;
F. A. Barrows, Constable; B. Finley, John BOWMANN, H. Miller, T. C. Chapman, atty.(48)

Theodore ALVARD vs. Leonidas CHAPIN. Feb. 29, 1889, Jacob Sarr, J.P. F. A.
Barrows, Constable. (49)

Horace ANDREWS and A. V. ANDREWS partners as Andrew Bros. vs. Leonidis CHAPIN.
Dec. 24, 1889, F. A. Barrows, J.P. Andrew Bros. of Norwalk, Huron Co., Ohio; A. C.
(or W.C.) Wright, L. B. Chapin. (50)

Jacob CLAY vs. Eugene Schorner. May 3, 1890, F. A. Barrorws, J.P.; E. H. Chandler,
Constable. (51)

Aultman MILLER & Co. vs. John HOFFMAN. Jan. 3, 1892. F. A. Barrows, J.P. B. B.
Walker, general agent for Aultman Miller & Co.; E. H. Chandler, Constable; Frank
Meeker, Wm. Fenton, Milton Schepley, Geo. Sage, Isaac Freemen (or Fruman), Frank
Haley, John Fenton, Sidney Macomber, John Harp (or Harss) and Henry Sprinkle. (52)

E. W. HUGHES vs. John MELZER. Jan. 13, 1891. F. A. Barrows, J.P.; E. H. Chandler,
Constable. (53)

J. S. BERGER vs. New York, Chicago & St. Louis Rail Road Company. March 23, 1891.
F. A. Barrows, J.P.; E. H. Chandler, Constable; Solomon Phillips, John Peak, agent
at Berlin Heights Station. (54)

Fred BOHRER and infant by Jacob BOHRER his appointed guardian vs. Mathew CARROLL.
Sept. 2, 1892. John H. Poyer, J.P. "said infant being fourteen years of age". (55)

The Berlin Heights Banking Co. vs. I. W. WRIGHT and D. A. JAMES ----1893. J. H.
(Jno. H.) Poyer, J.P. (56)

Joseph HYDE vs. Isaac W. WRIGHT. Sept. 8, 1893. Jno. H. Poyer, J.P.; W. Youngs,
Constable. (57)

Thomas BELLANY vs. Isaac WRIGHT. (no date given). H. Hitsman, Constable. (58)

Mrs. N. W. LOCKWOOD, L. L. STODARD as the Milan Banking Co. vs. John MADDOX, Issaac
W. WRIGHT and J. D. FISHER. Feb. 3, 1894. John H. Poyer, J.P.: H. (Henry) Hitsman,
Constable; Lizzie Maddox, W. J. Poyer, O. C. Tillinghast, Richard Jarrett, D. A.
James, Ira Saunders, Wm. E. Andrews, Joseph Maddox, John Maddox a resident of Huron
Co., Ohio; Marvin Bailey, A. Phinney, R. J. Jarrett, Mary W. Lockwood, Joseph
Strickford(?). (58-59)

Mary W. LOCKWOOD and L. L. STODARD, Partners of Milan Baking Co. vs. I. W. WRIGHT.
Feb. 10, 1894. John H. Poyer, J.P.; H. Hitsman. Constable; Marvin Bailey, M.B.
Peck. (60)

John BURTON vs. William LAWRENCE, April 10, 1894. John H. Poyer. W. J. Poyer,
Constable; Rosewell Derby. (61)

402

Arthur J. NICKOLS vs. Mrs. Ellen STAHL. June 4, 1894. John H. Poyer. W. J. Poyer, Constable; Spencer M. Stahl, Moses J. Jenkins, Curtiss Nickols, mentioned as resident of Erie Co., Ohio removed to Henry Co., Missouri; A. E. Penney, H. T. Smith, Mrs. H. T. Smith, S. M. Stahl, Mrs. Dora Dirlew. (62)

H. J. SHANNON vs. Isaac W. WRIGHT. July 6, 1894. John Poyer, J.P.; Wm. Terry, W. J. Poyer, Constable. (63)

Fristram HARDY vs. Henry B. BLAKE. Oct. 29, 1894. John H. Poyer, J. P. Statira Blake, "Henry B. Blake is a non-resident of Erie Co., Ohio", W. J. Poyer, Constable; Geo. W. Close, Tristram Hardy. (64)

Lake Erie Tobacco Co. vs. James P. Huntrip (or HUNTRESSO. March 23, 1895. John H. Poyer, J.P. (66)

Robert JARRETT vs. J. W. BERNBOWER (or DENBOWER). Apr. 8, 1895. John H. Poyer, J.P.; W J. Poyer , Constable; A. H. Pearl. (67)

A. H. PEARL, administrator; Mrs. J. H. LAWRENCE and Emma ROHRER (or ROEHRER) vs. William RUSE. May 10, 1897. W. R. Frailey, J.P. A. H. Pearl, a resident of Berlin twp.; mentions "estate of John H. Lawrence dec'd and Mrs. John H. Lawrence of Florence Twp., widow"; S. M. Marsh, Constable; Grant Miller, John Algood, Neil Grunzelbauch, Coon Grunzelbauch, Forey Ennis, Frank Barrows, Edwin Brown, Mrs. Finch, Gertrude Finch, Mrs. Ruse, David (Daril or Dan'l) James, Mrs. John Smith, H. P. Minkler, Palmer James, Geo. Drudage, Zip Calibel(?), Thomas Lee, H. D. Fisher, James Corgin, Willard Youngs, Curtis Nichols, C. C. Johnson, Grant Miller. (68)

Norton SMITH vs. H. H. SMITH. Oct. 10, 1899, W. R. Frailey, J.P. H. S. Smith, S. M. Marsh, Constable. (70)

W. R. MARSH vs. John KEILBRIDE. Jan. 29, 1901. W. R. Frailey, J.P.; S. M. Marsh, Constable; John Kilbride. (71)

Henry C. SPAULDING vs. B. L. SHAW as constable of Berlin twp. and the Eclipse Stove Co. Oct. 15, 1901. W. R. Frailey, J.P. J. J. Spaulding, J. E. Penny, Constable. (72)

Norton SMITH vs. Fred BOOTH. May 17, 1902. W. R. Frailey, J.P. H. T. Smith, G. F. Marsh, Constable; Jessie Vail, Bookepper of Baille Stone Co. (73)

Philip SPRANKEL vs. Conrad SPRANKEL. Aug. 12, 1902. W. R. Frailey, J. P. Phillip Sprankel, Geo. F. Marsh, Constable. (74)

Harlon STEWART vs. R. W. JARRETT. Nov. 28, 1906. W. R. Frailey, J.P.; J. A. Heys, Constable; William E. Sidnall, Willi m Johnson, A. Heys, Elmer Wasem. Robert Hum, J. E. Penny, T.C. Johnson. (77)

S. M. MARSH vs. Jack FALLON. Dec. 6, 1907. W. R. Frailey, J.P. Mentions "Wm. Rice property", and "land owned by A. Heys". (78)

(note: scrap of paper between pages dated August 5, 1884 appears to be bill for "hauling, Sawing and piling on tack" bears name of John Riley and C. Daniels.)

The following marriages are recorded in Volume "A" of the Deed Records:-

AKERT, Abraham to Katherene SMITH	6-13-1801
BRIDGES, John to Mary JOHNSON	10-22-1801
GASELL, Jacob to Elizabeth LETHERS	5-11-1802
HARDY, James to Isabella MARTIN	6-25-1801
HARPER, William to Sarah GOLDEN	12-25-1801
HART, Thomas to Elizabeth McCLALLAND	6-7-1802
INKS, John to Nelly COMPTON	6-4-1801
JOHNSTON, Evan to Catharine ASHBAUGH	8-19-1802
McCART, Henry to Belly TUMBLSON	2-18-1802
McMULLEN, Joseph to Margaret LUSK	3-15-1802
MAXWELL, James to Mary HUGHES	3-11-1802
MURPHY, Edward to Sarah MURPHY	1-7-1802
RATLIF, John to Hannah STATTEN	10-21-1802
TEAL, Edward to Rebecca MURPHY	3-11-1802
TURNER, James C. to Rachel JIMES	8-5-1802
WATSON, James to Martha HURNEL	8-25-1801
WERTWINE, Henry to (net given)	5-25-1802
WILLIAMSON, Peter to Rebecca GREEN	6-29-1801
WILSON, Jacob to Sarah McCAWLEY	9-2-1802
YOUNG, Edward to Rachel MILLER	4-15-1802

The following marriages are recorded in Marriage Record 1803-1835:-

_____?, John to Mary THOMPSON		3-5-1804
BARRACK, William to Betsey THOMPSON		3-4-1805
both of Licking Twp.		
BARTON, Jacob to Susanna WERSTENBERGER	Lic.	-1805
BEARD, John to Peggy BRADLY		5-3-1804
BETT, Apela to Mary INSCHO		2-29-1804
BIXLER, John to Margaret SEDAPENDER		8-13-1804
BLACK, James to Jane GELLESPIE alias WALLACE		7-16-1804
both of Licking Twp.		
BRADLEY, John to Johanna FETTSGERALD		5-25-1804
BROTHERS, Francis to Polly HOWE		6-14-1804
COLSON, William to Jane DUGAN		3-24-1805
CUNNINGHAM, Joseph to Catharine WARD		10-30-1804
DALTON, Amos to Polly McCALLA		2-1-1803
DRURY, Isaiah to Prusella REYNOLDS		6-7-1804
ELLIOTT, Samuel to Margaret PARR		May 1803
ENGMAN, Edmond (Edw'd-lic.) to Kitty HANESON		7-4-1805
FOLEY, Stephen to Elizabeth GARDNER	Lic.	1-21-1805
FUNK, Jacob to Nancy BUSH		4-10-1804
GEORGE, John to Polly MARTIN		7-26-1804
GRAY, Thomas B. to Sarah SHADLEY	Lic.	8-30-1805
GREEN, George to Deademy WILLISON		12-18-1805
HEAVENS, Jesse to Rebecca HENTHORN		9-17-1805
HEISTAND, Abraham to Mary SHISLER		2-5-1805
HELM, John to Mary MYERS		7-5-1804
at house of Jacob HELM, father of John		
HERREN, David to Elizabeth HORNET		7-8-1804
both of Licking Twp.		
HITE, John to Barbara PEBLER		12-4-1803

```
HOUK, Jacob to Roda JENNINS                         1-5-1803
HOW, James to Mary Ann DELSOVER                     2-18-1805
        at house of George DELSOVER, father of Mary Ann
HUMMEL, Thomas to Mary HYNES                        5-18-1804
HUTCHENS, Bradberry to Susan JADEN                  7-4-1805
IJAMS, Wm. to Catherine REEFNER (or Rufner)         6-20-1805
IRWIN, William to Nancy PURSLEY                     (5?)-8-(1803?)
JENNINS, Joseph to Rebecca HUNTER                   12-22-1803
JOHNSTON, John to Mena(?) KELLY                     9-22-1805
LAMB, George to Peggy BRANN                         4-17-1804
LENTON, Zachariah to Catharine GEGER                7-9-1805
McCALLA, Andrew to Rebecca LEWES                    1-2-1804
McCALLA, Edward to Elenor NELSON                    12-19-1803
MAYSE, Wm. H. to Hannah WILLETS                     12-10-1802
MERRET, Levi to Elizabeth SCOTT                     8-16-1804
MILLER, Peter to Polly TENFT(?)                     6-27-1805
MORE, John to Jane PORTER                           10-27-1802
MOYER, Abraham to Mary WOLFEN                       7-30-1805
MULFORD, Joab to Uphems THOMPSON           Lic.  2-12-1805
            both of Licking Twp. - Consent by
            Benjamin Thompson, her brother
NORTH, Zachareah to Dolly MARKS                     12-13-1804
PAGE, Jermiah to Sarah SMITH                        9-15-1803
PARR, Richard to Mary ELLIOTT                       May 1803
PECAH(?), Abram to Polly COFFENLENY(?)     Lic.  Jan. 1805
PENCE, Frederick to Mary HARP                       6-1-1804
PIATT, John to Margret ELDER                        7-3-1803
PORTER, James to Trecy LESSLY                       12-17-1805
POWLES, Jacob to Mary BEARD                         3-15-1804
PRICE, Joseph to Hannah PRICE                       6-1-1805
REAM, Simpson to Anny STOOKEY                       11-20-1803
REYNOLDS, William to Sarah DRURY                    6-25-1804
RICKETS, Jeremiah to Polly COLE            Lic.  4-15-1805
ROBENSON, Robert to Elizabeth McMEAN                5-9-1805
ROBESON, John to Jamima EDGAR                       1-17-1804
ROUGH, George to Nancy COLEMAN                      2-8-1804
RUSSEL, Thomas to Catherine JOHNSTON                10-14-1805
SCOTT, George to Mary MOORE                         10-3-1805
SHEERE, John to Rebecca SCRIFT                      6-27-1801
SHIELD, John to Peggy BUNN                          3-7-1804
SLEEMER, Fredr'k to Kitty WALTERS                   4-18-1805
            (Lic. gives names as Fred'k SEAMORE and
            Catherine Walters)
SLOOKEY, Christian to Peggy HERSH                   7-21-1805
SMITH, Henry to Clary WOLFEN                        11-24-1805
STANFORD, James to Elizabeth STANBERRY         Lic.4-18-1805
STONERSPRING, Henry to Solema WARTWEINE             11-25-1804
STOOKEY, Peter to Eve HERON                         10-6-1805
SWISSER, Jacob to Phebey GREEN                      1-1-1805
            both of Licking Twp.
TAILOR, Henry to Elizabeth KEPLER                   12-25-1805
            at house of Elizabeth Tailor
            Elizabeth Kepler dau of Benjamin
```

```
TEAL, Walter to Mary IJAMS                          11-29-1804
TONG(TOUG?), William to Rabecca WILSON               5-12-1805
VANBUSKIRK, Thomas to Ruth HEUS                      3-10-1805
          both of Licking Twp.
VICARS, James to Polly HOOVER                       11-3-1805
WAGNER, Alrich to Barbara SLATTELY                   1-29-1804
WAGNER, Andrew to Mary SATTELY                       1-29-1804
WARD, William to Barbarra HERRING                    8-26-1805
WHITSEL, Henry to Elizabeth TAILOR                  12-25-1805
          at house of Elizabeth Tailor, widow and mother
WORDNER, Thomas to Elizabeth BIBLER                  4-21-1805
```

FAIRFIELD COUNTY, OHIO - MARRIAGES 1805-1809

The following marriages were copied from "Marriage License Book 1803-1835." Both marriage licenses and returns are found in this book. It should be noted that there is an unusually high number of licenses for which no returns were filed. Also, in many cases the names are highly questionable with different names being found on the license from those on the return. These have been given in parenthesis. However, if there is any question as to whether these are the same people--both the license and the return are then given as two entries.

ABRAMS, Joseph to Nelly Davis	lic. 1-31-1807
ALGIR (ALGAN on lic.) John to Ann Counts (Curtz on lic.)	2-15-1807
ALSPACH, Adam to Mary Barber	8-11-1809
ALSPACH, George to Elenor Glesson	12-30-1809
ALSPACH, Sabastian to Elizabeth Runkle	11-24-1809
ARNOLD, Jacob to Rachel Creamer	9-19-1807
AUSPACK (AUSBAUGH on lic.), Christian to Christina Overmire	8-23-1808
AUSPAUBH (or ANSPAUGH), Andrew to Easter Rhea	5-21-1807
AUSBAUGH, Jacob to Elizabeth Sphon	4-5-1807
AUSPCK, (AUSPAUGH on lic.), Benjamin to Mary Dubler	5-11-1808
BACHER, Frederick to Susanna Rough	3-5-1810
BAILY, Thomas to Barbary Hite	5-19-1809
BANCROFT, Samuel to Clarissa Rose, Both of Granville	5-18-1807
BARK, Jacob to Mary Boyle	10-21-1807
BARNHART, David to Elizabeth Cole	12-20-1807
BARNHART, Simon to Sally Cole	1-5-1808
BARR, Thomas to Jane Scott	lic. 1-7-1808
BARTON, William to Ann Done (Dunn on lic.)	1-26-1809
BAUGHER, Henry to Christ'a Gl_____(.)	lic. 3-16-1809
BEAR, Joseph to Elizabeth Shirek	9-6-1808
BEBLER, David to -?- Bear	10-24-1809
BEBLER, John to Eln'r Wilson	lic. 8-13-1808
BECHELDERFER, Zury to Nancy Buzzard	12-26-1809
BECKER (BAKER on lic.) Henry to Polly Binkley	12-25-1808
BEEREY, Isaac to Polly Ruddlebaugh	5-13-1806
BENNETT (BURNETT on lic.), William to Elener Bennett	7-23-1808
BIRD, Samuel to Nancy Cliner	11-30-1809
BIXLER, Henry to Killy (Kitty?) Gunder	9-2-1806
BLACK, John to Gemima Benjamin	3-29-1808
BLACK, Phillip to Kelly(Kitty?) Bear	lic. 1-13-1807
BLY, John to Elizabeth Breakbile	7-28-1807
BOND, Joseph to Hannah Bearnhart	lic. 3-8-18-8
BOUGHER, Henry to Christena Glick	3-17-1809
BOWDEL, Henry to Elizabeth Miller	10-8-1807
BOWMAN, Bernard Hy. to Elizabeth Wagoner	10-23-1809
BRIGHT, John to Easter Bowman	11-10-1807
BRIGHTBILL, Benjamin to Mary Evans	lic. 7-26-1809
BROMBACK, Sam'l to Elizabeth Funkhous(er)	lic. 8-3-1809
BROWN, David to Jane Merrit	11-17-1807
BROWN, James Junr. to Emele Green	2-16-1808
BROWN, Joshua to Rebecca Scothorn	5-4-1809
BRYAN, David to Nancy Stevens - Amanda twp.	9-8-1808
BRYAN, James to Nancy Hardesty	4-7-1808

BULLENHAM*, Solomon to Leathe Brown   2-25-1806
        *surname indexed as BRITTENHAM
BURKET, George to Mary Fox   lic.5-12-1807
BUSH, Christian to Jane -?- (not given)   lic. 2-13-1806
BUSH, George to Elizabeth Smith   lic. 1-28-1808
BUSH, Richard to Margerit Kaiger   11-21-1807
CARPENTER*, George to Barbara Wilson   8-25-1808
        *(Lic. gives George's surname as "McCOURAN or CARPENTER").
CARPENTER, Sabesten (Solomon on lic.) to Polly Gonder (Gunder)   1-20-1807
CASEY, Cornelies to Mary Kennedy   11-30-1809
CAUNLEE (CONOLEY on lic.), Joseph to Delila Mackrel   8-14-1808
        Benjamin Mackre, father of Delila attested to her
        age on license.
CHAPMAN, William to Elizabeth Mires   5-5-1807
CHRISLY, Laurance to Kitty Spone   10-20-1806
CLARK, Alpheus to Elizabeth Loyd   4-19-1809
CLENDENAN, Robert to Martha Friend   1-5-1809
CLOAE, Adam to Susanna Rodebaugh - Liberty twp.   9-6-1808
COAPLAND, William to Polly Means   10-15-1807
COFFMAN (KAUFMAN on lic.), John to Elizabeth Beery   8-16-1808
COLE, John to Betsy Cole - Amanda twp.   10-5-1806
COLE, Joshua to Margaret Long   2-16-1808
COLLINS, James Hatten to Charity Bright (Due or Doe on lic.)   9-23-1806
COLLINS, William to Lucy Brown   1-26-1808
COMPTON, Joab to Rebecca Inks   7-19-1808
CONE (KOONS on lic.) George to Mary North (Mary Burket North   11-4-1808
        on lic.) - both of Clear Creek twp., married at home
        of Thomas North, father of Mary
COOK, John to Lucy Senter   lic. 11-23-1809
COOPER, Levi to Marget Wilson   5-31-1807
CRAWFORD, Samuel to Sarah Vanmeter   6-11-1807
CREGER, And'w (Richard on lic.) to Rachel Chamberlane   12-27-1808
CROCKET, Andrew to Margret Pitcher   12-10-1807
CROOK, John to Polly Crossan   4-11-1809
CROSSIN, Wm R. to Sally Lott   lic. 11-26-1809
CUTRIGHT (COURTRIGHT on lic.), Richard to Sarah Rickets   12-25-1806
DAVIS, John to Mary Young   5-5-1808
DEFENSBACH, Daniel to Hannah Culp   12-23-1806
DELSAVOUR, John to Kitty Shoup   6-13-1808
DENNICK, Daniel to Rachel Leonard   4-5-1806
DERBIN, Samuel to Rebecca Collins   4-5-1806
DICK, Charles to Hanna Mannen - black people   7-4-1807
DRAKE, Wm to Elizabeth Denquinn   9-16-1809
DRURY, Samuel to Ann Reynolds   2-8-1808
EAGLE (ENGLE on lic.), George to Mary Hensel   2-3-1807
EBRIGHT, William to Betsey Bird   11-16-1809
ECKERT, Jaob to Nelly (or Kitty?) Shellenberger   lic.11-9-1807
EDMONSON, William to -?- Lowe   9-5-1808
ELENGTON (ELLINGTON on lic.), William to Prissella Duvall   8-20-1807
ELLIOTT, Corn. to Eliz'th Evins   lic. 11-28-1806
ENGLAND, Asa to Prudence Mackrel   3-10-1809

```
ENGLAND, Isaac to Prudence Chilcote                          7-16-1809
ENGLER, Henry to Rachel Poling                             10-5-1809
ENTRICKS, Frederick to Patty Stolts                         7-11-1809
FELLER, Phillip to Betsey Cent (Ceut)                       6-3-1807
FETTER, Henry to Catharine Robenhold                       10-4-1808
FIERBAUGH, Phillip to Barbara Gunder                       11-12-1806
FILL, Henry to Sarah Shellenberger                          4-11-1809
FISHER, Adam to Barbara Miller                       lic,   3-29-1806
FISHER, Jacob to Mary Gorton (Girten on lic.)               2-15-1809
FLETCHER, Roleson (or Robeson) to Kitty Woodring           11-13-1807
FOGELSONG, John to Ruth Neal                               12-25-1806
FOLEY, Stephen to Elizabeth Gardner                         1-23-1806
FORD, Adam C. to Elizabeth Nelson          2 dates         (9-20-1807
                                                           (9-21-1807
FOSTER, Andrew to Mary Macklin                              1-20-1809
FOX, John to Nancy Julin - mar. at house of John Julin      4-1-1806
                    father of Nancy
FOX, John to Mary Foster                                    8-7-1809
FRAKER, John to Peggy Neveling                              3-21-1809
FREEMAN, Benjamin to Elizabeth Lamb                   lic. 12-29-1806
FUNK, Daniel to Mary Phillips (marriage return filed,  lic. 6-7-1806
                    but no date given)
GARDNER, Jacob to Elizabeth Kistler                   lic. 4-9-1808
GASTER (GARTER), John to Betsey Lansbaugh                  12-26-1807
GAU, William to Polly Cunningham                            6-30-1807
GILKESON, James M. to Nancy Casenberry                     11-17-1808
GILKERSON, John to Sally Coffenberry                        2-4-1808
GOLDTHREAD (GOODHEART on lic.), John to Mary Crawford       7-30-1807
GOOD, Christ'n to Mary Hufman                         lic.10-1-1808
GOOD, Peter to Barbara Hesler (Foster on lic.)             4-19-1807
GRABELL, Gabriel to Rebecca Bush                            9-12-1809
GRAY, Thomas to Sarah Evins                           lic. 9-18-1806
GREEN, John to Elizabeth Holsberry                          6-25-1807
GREEN, Requal to Mary Maxwell (Maxan on lic.)               5-28-1806
GYGAR, David to Catharine Winegardner                      10-28-1808
HANSEL, John to Peggy Zerby                                 4-23-1809
HARRIS, James (Amus on lic.) to Susannah McEntruff          8-11-1807
HARRISON, James to Hannah Crumley (Crowley on lic.)         8-13-1808
HAYMAN, Jacob. to Susan Shoup                               7-31-1806
HAYS, Jonathan to Elizabeth Hooker (no date given-1809      ----(1809)
HEDGES, Joseph to Maria Rice                               12-26-1809
HEISTAND, Samuel to Margaret Reedebach                      9-23-1809
HELMS, John to Betsey Spangler                              2-24-1807
HENSEL, George to Kitty Shisler                             5-31-1808
HERRON, Cook to Polly -?- (not given)                 lic.4-25-1808
HERRON, David to Mary Wilson                                6-25-1807
HELSER, John to Polly Rising                                9-9-1807
HIDELBACH, Peter to Kitty Stookey (Stoker on lic.)          9-25-1806
HITE, Abr'm to Barbara Pew                                  6-25-1808
HITE, Conrad to Elizabeth Frey (Frye on lic.)              1-9-1808
```

```
HITE, Isaac to Maetalan Pratz (Poals on lic.)                          2-1-1807
        lic. states her brother, Valentine attested to her age
HOCKER, Richard to Nancy Talmon                                        1-16-1806
HOLLACHER, Christian to Molly Kritz                                    2-3-1808
HOLMES, Thomas to Rachel Wells (Wills on lic.)                         7-30-1807
HOLLINS, Isaac to Christiena Shitz                                     6-1-1809
HOLT, William to Susanna Lane                                          1-15-1807
HOLTS, George to Elizabeth Shafer                                      8-17-1807
HOOD, Frederick to Mary Ann Quinn                                      4-28-1806
HOOK, John to Catherine Sith - Licking twp.                           3-13-1808
HOUCK, James to Kath(?) Shadley                                        2-6-1806
HOVER (HOOVER on lic.), john to Mary Darst        2 dates   (11-7-1807
                                                            (11-8-1807
HOW, James to Mary Ann Delsover - married at house                     2-18-1806
        George Delsover, father of Mary Ann.  John Delsover,
        brother of Mary Ann attested to her age on license.
HOWE, David to Sally Babb                                             10-17-1809
HUBER,  John to Magdalena Corpman                                      4-27-1809
HUDDLE, Henry to Elenor Murphy                                         2-27-1806
HULL, John to Sarah Taylor                                      lic. 1-23-1808
HULLER, Warden to Kitty Hanshew                                 lic. 3-14-1807
HUME, John to Sarah McCleland                                          4-20-1809
HUNRICKHOUSE, Peter to Dorathy Campbell                         lic. 11-22-1806
HUNTER, William to Susan Barkshire (Berkshire)                        7-13-1806
HUREN 'HERRON on lic.), John to Ginney Pool                           6-16-1806
JAMES, Abner to Nancy Turner                                          2-20-1806
JEMISON, James L. to Samaneth(?) Reese                          lic. 1-13-1808
JOHNS, George to Polly Moyer                                          1-22-1809
JOHNSTON, Barnabas to Mary Clymer                                     8-21-1807
JOHNSTON, John to Elizabeth Save (Sive)*          2 dates   (10-7-1806
        *Elizabeth's surname not clear on either              (10-16-1806
        return or lic., it may be LANE
JOHNSTON, John B. to Rebecca Knode                                    4-27-1809
JONES, Samuel to Margaret Hughes                                      3-3-1807
JULIAN, Stephen to Hannah Berry                                     12-29-1808
JULIEN, Stephen to Zane Lewis                                         5-5-1809
JULIEN, William to Susanna Noggle                                     9-23-1806
KARR, William to Hannah Good (?)                                lic. 4-18-1808
KEREY, John Jacob to Elizabeth Loloway(?)                            11-7-1808
KEY, Moses (Amos on lic.) to Ann Becket                              5-20-1806
KIRK, George to Sarah Death                                     lic. 4-9-1808
KIRTZ, Law to Barbara Glick                                          4-16-1809
KISTLER, Peter to Eliz'th Bowman                                lic. 4-22-1808
KITE (HITE on lic.), Adam to Sary Parson (Parr on lic.)              3-17-1808
KITTSMILLER, Wm to Polly Clouse                                 lic. 3-20-1807
KNOFF, George to Rebecca Julian                                      8-23-1808
KNOYER, George to Mary Herod                                         6-8-1809
KNOYER, Jacob to Betsey Palmer                                      11-8-1808
KNOYER, John to Susana Kittsmiller                                   1-3-1806
            Ulrick Knoyer attested to age on lic.
KOONTZ, Isaac to Sarah (Shel?)lenbarger                             2-22-1809
```

410

```
LABAKER, John to Elizabeth Stinnbrin(?) (Stainbring on lic.)   2-9-1808
LAMB, George to Lydia Black                                    5-17-1806
LAMB, Jacob to Magdalina Culp                                  8-19-1806
LAMB, Phillip to Kitty Bear                                    1-14-1807
LANCE, Martin to Betsey Bebler                              lic7-25-1808
LANE, David to Sarah Swairy(?)                                 2-8-1808
LANE, Jacob to Sally Kyzer                                     4-2-1807
LANE, William to Martha Wheeler                                2-20-1809
LANFORD (SANFORD), John to Mary Drum                           4-13-1809
LAPE, Nicholas to Polly Longbreak                              12-6-1808
LARREMORE, James to Jane Love                                  4-10-1806
LARREMORE, Robert to Margaret Ray (Mary Rhay on lic.)          6-30-1808
LITTLE, John to Kitty Kirrans                            lic.  11-5-1808
LIVESTON (LIVINGSTON on lic.), John to Betsey Clutter          4-30-1806
LOATHERS, John to Maria Fensler, widow of Martin Fensler,dec'd 5-4-1809
LOFLAND, Thomas to Sarah Lee           (no day given)          5-?-1807
LONABAGH, Jacob to Nelly Shoup                           lic.  5-14-1806
LONG, Thos. to Mary Jiles                                      2-4-1808
LONGBREAK, Daniel to Mary Lepe                                 1-3-1809
LOSSLEY, William to Biddy Boyles                               7-3-1806
LOSTPEACH, Ra(1)ph to Amelia Rigby (Emelia Rigly on lic.)      4-26-1808
LOVE (LANE on lic.), James to Polly Marshall                   6-29-1809
        her age attested to on lic. by her gdn, Hugh McCormack
McBRIDE, William of Ross Co. to Letty McBride of Fairfield Co. 1-9-1806
McCABE, Jostenus(?) to Mary Owins                              12-4-1809
McDOLE, Joseph to Jane Carron                                  2-12-1807
McFARLAND, John to Mary Cambel (Campbell on lic.)              12-31-1807
MACKLIN, Jacob to Kitty Foster                                 1-29-1807
MANLEY, Samuel to Charlotta O'Niel(?)                    lic.  2-5-1807
MANLEY, Samuel to Elizabeth Devall                             2-10-1807
MARK, Peter to Christina Myers                                 11-30-1809
MARQUAT, John to Katherine (Kitty) Morrow                      11-2-1806
MAY, Iazam (Chesum on lic.) to Elizabeth Humphries             7-3-1806
MEAN, John to Anny Smith                                       5-22-1806
MEEKS, Samuel to Deliley Simpson - Licking twp.                3-20-1808
MERCHANT, Isaac to Rachel Rues                                 5-18-1809
MERVIN, Elijah B. to Sophia Reed                               10-2-1808
MIDDLETON, Joseph to Lilly Linsey                              7-12-1806
MILES, Mich'l to Moity -?- (surname not given) (no day given)  5-?-1807
        both black people of said county
MILLER, Abraham to Sarah Grubbs                          lic.  12-11-1806
MILLER, Abraham to Ester Long                                  6-14-1807
MILLER, Henry to Mary Maque (Wagoner on lic.)                  8-9-1806
MILLER, Jacob to Barbara Lynn                                  2-7-1807
MILLER, John to Mary Grubbs                                    12-16-1806
MILLER, John to Kelly (Kitty) Grove                           9-5-1809
MILLIGAN, William to Ann Crawford (recorded with 1809 marriages)1-2-1801
MONGOLD, Henry to Betsey Culp                            lic.  2-8-1806
MOREHEAD, Alexander of Ross Co. to Elizabeth Iles of Fairfield 4-4-1809
MORGAN, B_ger(?) to Elizabeth Lerick (Lorick on lic.)         9-27--1808
```

MORRIS, James to Mary Mattes - both of Clear Creek twp.,   2-19-1807
    married at house of Henry Matley, father of Mary.
MORRES, Thomas to Elizabeth Malla (Matta) - both of Clear Creek 10-7-1806
    twp., married at house of Henry Mattas.
MOURTZ (MOUNTZ), Abner to Catherine Mumma   8-17-1809
MURATER(?), Charles to Catherine Burl   12-4-1806
MURPHEY, John to Rebeckah Vanbuskirk   11-1-1807
MURPHY, Benjamin to Nelly Gardner   2-3-1809
MURPHY, William to Hester Lettieer(?)   lic. 1-22-1808
MUSSELMAN, Jacob to Susana Bebler   5-8-1808
NASH, Abraham to Barbary Shallenberger   5-4-1809
NAUGLE, Andrew to Nancy Hedges   9-9-1806
NAUGLE, Benjamin to Nancy Julian   11-2-1809
NEELEY, Daniel to Sarah Thompson   8-25-1807
NEFF, George to Mary Peters - both of Clear Creek twp.; her   2-23-1808
    brother, Isaac Peters attested to age on lic.
NELSON, Samuel to Jane Rawson   6-23-1807
NEVELIN, Christian to E. Siviler (?)   (no day given) lic. 4-?-1806
NOGGLE, Isaac to Jane Moyer   lic. 1-23-1808
NOGLE, Isaac to Kitty Prough   2-23-1808
NORTON, Thomas W. to Rebeca Young   1-20-1808
ORRE, Thomas to Kitty Arnold   5-5-1808
OVERMIRE, Geo. to Eve Huffman   lic. 9-30-1808
OVERMIRE, Jacob to Barbara Kester   4-7-1807
PAUEL (POWEL on lic.), Thomas to Phoebe Graham   1-14-1808
PEERRY (BERRY on lic.), Abraham to Barbara Pebler(Bibler on lic)12-23-1806
PERRIN, William to Rachel Patterson   8-29-1809
PLUMMER, George to Mary Cote (Cole on lic.)   6-1-1808
POLING, Robert to Betsey Fast   4-18-1809
PONTIUS, George to Mary Lore (Line on lic.)   6-14-1807
PROUGH, George to Sally Winter   7-8-1806
RANKEN, James to Mary Oldfield   3-30-1808
RAY, Abraham to Patsey Asbaugh - Rush Creek twp.   3-9-1808
RAY, Samuel to Mary Ashbaugh   2-20-1808
READING, George to Susanna Wright   2-8-1808
REAM. William to Liddy Swisher   11-9-1806
REED, James. to Lee R(e)ynolds   8-17-1807
REESE, Lewis to Polly Reese   1-20-1808
REYNOLDS, Joseph to Mary Starey   8-17-1809
RICE, James to Barbara Strickler   9-13-1807
RICHARDS (RICHARDSON on lic.), John to Polly or Mary Hornet   10-27-1807
                              (Harnet on lic.)
RIDENHOUR, John to Hannah Uptoon(?)   lic. 2-24-1807
RIDENHOUR, Lewis to Catharine Auspach   7-26-1808
RIDONHOUR, Jacob to Magdelena Lesler (Lefler on lic.)   1-19-1808
RINEHART, Jonas to Peggy (Elizabeth on lic.) Baker   2-28-1809
ROBERTS, Thomas to Mary Freeman   2-18-1806
RODEBACK, John to Eve Kemerer(?)   5-21-1809
RUFFNER, Jacob to Magaline Bebler (Belder on lic.)   6-14-1807
RUDEBAUGH (RAUDEBAUGH on lic.), Nicholas to Kitty Wagoner   6-21-1806

```
RUMBAUGH, John D. to Elizabeth Kline                        11-5-18-5
        Elizabeth dau. of Coonrad Kline of Clearcreek twp.
RUNKLE, Dan'l to Polly Hushour(Henshour on lic.)           12-3-1808
RUNKLE, Jacob to Eve Plotner (or Clesson)                   1-7-1806
RUSBAUGH, Jacob to Elizabeth Sphoon                         3-31-18-7
SAILOR, Henry to Elizabeth Kepler - both of Clear Creek twp.  12-25-1805
        Elizabeth dau. of Benjamin Kepler
SCOLEY (SEELEY on lic.), John to Polly Bennett              8-6-1807
SELLEY, -?- (not given) to Kelly (Kitty) Hayes        lic. 3-24-1806
SELLEY, Ralph to Peggy Carpenter                      lic. 3-27-1806
SEUY (SPERRY on lic.), Abraham to Elizabeth Conard         3-10-1808
SEYMORE, Adam to Elizabeth Channel - Licking twp.          4-14-1808
SHAW, John to Rachel Stewart                               11-2-1809
SHEAFFER, John to Hannah Prough                            9-15-1807
SHELLENBERGER, John to Mary Patten                    lic. 2-10-1807
SHIPS, Nathan to Elizabeth Hull                            9-24-1807
SILLE(?), John to Caty Keenan                             11-6-1808
SKILLMAN, William to Nancy Henton (Inston)                3-19-1807
SLAUGHTER, Robert F. to Sarah Bond                         4-6-1807
SPANGLER, Samuel to Susanna Taylor                         8-17-1807
SPELMAN, Timothy Esq. to Mary Avery                       12-24-1807
SPITLAR, Warner to Kitty Hendshue                          3-15-1807
SPHOON, Daniel to Elizabeth Bashore                        4-21-1807
SPITLER, Jacob to Caterina Litz                            8-22-1809
SPRAGER, John to Delilah Clark                             1-4-1808
SREEVES, Joshuaway to Amy Stark                       lic. 11-25-1809
STATLER, Mahal to Polly Simpaon                       lic. 7-(?14)-1806
STEPHENS, Thomas to Sarah Hall                             5-2-1809
STEVENSON, George to Rebeckah -?- (not given)             4-11-1809
STEVENSON, Thomas to Rachel Hooper                       12-6-1807
STONE, George to Elizabeth Holmes                        12-20-1807
STOOKEY, John to Catherine Eatert(?)                      4-14-1809
STULL (STUTTS on lic.), Jacob to Catharine Thorn.         1-13-1807
SUNDERLIN, John to Elizabeth Williams                 lic. 2-5-1807
        (note: return filed but no date given)
SWARTZ, J n : to Eve Crisman (Cuffman on lic.)           11-13-1808
SWEARINGEN, Thos. V. to Theedosia Good*le (no day given)  lic. 4-?-1806
SWITZER, Fr__ack(?) to Barbara Stookery                   1-15-1808
TALLMAN, James to Polly Bell                              3-16-1809
TEAL, Nathaniel to Elisabeth Murphy     (no day given)   11-?-1806
THOMAS, Jacob to Elizabeth Hile                           9-25-1806
THOMMES, Fr'drick to Catherine Wickel                 lic. 1-15-1808
THOMPSON, John to Pruseilla -?- (not given)           lic. 2-12-1809
THOMPSON, Samuel to Betsey Morehart                      10-17-1809
TICKEL, William to Ann Thompson                           3-24-1808
TOMSON, John to Prisilla Murphy  (probably same as John   6-14-1809
                                   Thompson above)
TROUT, Abr'm to Jane McFarland                        lic. 3-30-1807
TURNER, Jos. to Elizabeth Layman                         11-9-1808
VANATTA, Aron to Nancy Murphy                            11-19-1807
VANNATTA, John to Mary Murphy                        lic. 11-16-1807
```

413

```
VAN COURTRIGHT, Abraham to Betsey McFarlan                        3-30-1809
WAGGONER, George to Judith Wettsbough                             5-19-1807
WALLSON, William to Mary Miller                                  12-15-1809
WALTERS, Henry to Nancy Mills                                     9-12-1809
WARDEN, James to Eve Darling (Darland on lic.)                   1-31-1808
WEIRTS, John to Eliz'th Smith                           lic. 2-25-1807
WELLS, Hugh to Sarah Wills                                       6-16-1807
WELSH, George to Sarah Inks                                      9-8-1807
WHETSTONE, George to Ester Custard                       lic. 10-9-1809
WHITE, George to Susanna Bibler (Bebler on lic.)                1-12-1808
WHITE, John to Mary Green - both of Clearcreek twp., married    2-18-1806
        at house of Jacob Green, father of Mary.
WHEALLY, Thomas to Nancy Peddegrew                               5-23-1809
WHITSEL, Henry to Elizabeth Sailor - married at house of       12-25-1805
        Elizabeth Sailor widow and mother of said Elizabeth.
WILLIAMS, Thomas to Piercy Bell                                  3-24-1807
WILLIAMSON, John to Rachael Wilson                               4-27-1809
WILLIAMSON, Peter to Kaziah Low                                  7-17-1806
(WILLISON), George to Deademy Willison (note: George's surname  1-20-1806
        not given in record, but indexed as Willison)
WILSON, John to Barbara __ary(?)                                 4-12-1808
WILSON, Joseph to Sarah Wilde                                    4-12-1808
WINTER, Alexander to Susan Slegal                               12-17-1806
WINTERMOOT, Daniel to Kitty Bochart                             4-29-1808
WISELY, George to Elizabeth Green (return filed but no    lic. 7-18-1809
        date given--lic. states consent by Henry Green)
WISELY, William to Sarah Cole (Cote on lic.)                   12-3-1807
WISHARD, Abr'm to Sally Byrod                                    3-22-1806
WISLEY, Edward to Leah Tombleson                               10-21-1806
WITSLOW, George to Ester Coster                                10-17-1809
WOODS, Moses to Elizabeth Shaw - Elizabeth's age attested       2-25-1808
        to on lic. by her brother, John.
WOOTRING, Peter to Polly Fletcher                               7-2-1807
WORK, Robert to Sarah Neeley                                    8-27-1807
YORK, William to Fanny Utzler                                   1-31-1807
YOST, Abraham to Sally Brown                                    1-19-1808
ZUEGG, John to Hannah Ford - on lic. consent given by her
        father, John Ford
-?-, -?- (no names given) to Mary Smith                       10-11-1807
```

414

The following marriages were taken from "Marriage Record #1" located in the Probate Court at the court house in Lancaster. Page on which record may be found is given in parenthesis.

METTS, John to Mary SULLIVAN		4-24-1835	(1)
SPRANER, Andrew to Barbara BINDE	lic.	4-18-1835	(1)
HILT, Moses to Mary DAVIS*		4-23-1835	(1)
*Age certified by John DAVIS, tne father			
HILARDS, Shadrick to Mary FAIRCHILD		4-30-1835	(1)
CHERRY, James H. to Harriet TAYLER*		4-30-1835	(1)
*Age certified by the father			
SAMUEL, James to Mary Ann McELROY		4-30-1835	(1)
ALSPACH, John H. to Caroline CRANE		4-30-1835	(1)
POLAND, Pete to Margaret WOOD (cer. by Mose Wood)		4-30-1835	(1)
KUCHERBARGER, Geo. to Sarah WOLF	lic.	5-1-1835	(1)
YOUNG, James P. to Harriet RICE		5-3-1835	(1)
HANNA, Henry to Mary RADER		5-5-1835	(1)
McNEIL, Sam'l to Maria TURNER		5-_(?)-1835	(1)
NIGH, Jacob to Catharine CLIPPINGER	lic.	5-4-1835	(2)
SMITH, John to Eliza FANSNAUGHT		5-7-1835	(2)
HALL, Phillip to Susan BAUGHER	lic.	5-6-1835	(2)
CARPENTER, Gabriel to Matilda Va. CONNELL	lic.	5-6-1835	(2)
HILLIS, Thos. to Kezia SEALOCK		5-17-1835	(2)
HILLER, Henry to Margaret POWERS*		5-17-1835	(2)
*Age certified by H. Heller & Wm. Powers-fathers			
HITE, Joseph to Sarah REEDLE		5-17-1835	(2)
DOVE, Elijah to Mary SMALL		5-21-1835	(2)
HEDGES, Isaac to Maria NEELEY		5-17-1835	(2)
THORP, Miles to Mary E. WILSON	lic.	5-18-1835	(2)
GREEN, William to Margaret DUTTON	lic.	5-21-1835	(2)
SAIN, Christian H.* to Rebecca KENNAND		5-21-1835	(2)
*Age certified by Jacob Sain his father			
TRIPP, Calvin T. to Nancy CALANDINE	lic.	5-20-1835	(3)
REINHARDT, Geo. to Mary STUDY		5-20-1835	(3)
DAVIS, Thos. to Sarah McGINNIS		5-28-1835	(3)
EARHART, Isaac to Mary Ann EVANS	lic.	5-23-1835	(3)
COFFMAN, Martin to Nancy COLLINS		5-24-1835	(3)
BEATTY, John to Delila BEERY*	lic.	5-23-1835	(3)
*Age certified by N. Beery, the father			
JOHNSON, Chas. K. to Rebecca LELAND	lic.	5-30-1835	(3)
REAM, Geo. to Elizabeth GOSS		5-7-1835	(3)
CLARK, Thos. to Amelia MEEKS		5-31-1835	(3)
ROLAND, David to Elizabeth TURNER		6-7-1835	(3)
BECK, Henry to Susanna SMITH		6-4-1835	(3)
KIRKENDALL, James to Delila GILMON		6-7-1835	(4)
SHERRICK, Henry* to Rebecca STEAMER		6-4-1835	(4)
*Age certified by John Sherick, his father			
RUFF, John P. to Julia COMER	lic.	6-5-1835	(4)
ENGLAND, Amos to Rebecca HUFMAN	lic.	6-5-1835	(4)
KONRAD, Adam to Carolina Philippina KULL	lic.	6-5-1835	(4)
MILLER, Christian to Susan STARNER		6-6-1835	(4)

```
SHAFFER, Joseph to Anna MELCHI                              6-11-1835    (4)
GRIFFITH, John to Mary SWEYER                    lic.       6-6-1835     (4)
ALLEN, Thomas C. to Catharine DABLER            lic.       6-6-1835     (4)
RUGH, Christian to Eleanor SPOHN                           6-11-1835    (4)
KYGER, Bennet to Elizabeth LARNOTT                         6-13-1835    (4)
BUMBGARDENER, John to Anna GOOD                            6-18-1835    (4)
YOUNG, Nicholas to Caroline LITTLE                         6-13-1835    (5)
IMEROT, Geo. to Hester ALSPACH (order of father)          6-21-1835    (5)
WOLTERS, Sam'l to Christiana KRAMER             lic.       6-13-1835    (5)
WHITEHURST, John to June Eliza McCONNELL                   6-16-1835    (5)
ROTH, Adam to Christiana GOOD                    lic.      6-8-1835     (5)
KISLER, Sam'l to Louisa FRASER       lic. 6-13-1835       3-20-1836    (5)
RABURN, John to Magdaline LEATHER                         7-2-1835     (5)
GROVES, David to Nancy ALSPACH                            6-25-1835    (5)
GROVE, Lewis to Elizabeth KRUTSCH                         6-25-1835    (5)
BROOK, Benjamin to Elizabeth WICKIZER                     6-30-1835    (5)
WHITEHUNT, John to Hannah HARRISON              lic.       6-20-1835    (5)
MILLER, Jacob to Sarah TIGNER                             6-30-1835    (5)
FRIZZLE, John to Martha Ann HOWELL              lic.       6-26-1835    (6)
HUFER, Michael to Anna NEISWANER                          7-2-1835     (6)
TUTWEILER, Thos. to Esther B. AGLESHIRE                   7-2-1835     (6)
FRIZZLE, John to Martha Ann HOWELL                        7-5-1835     (6)
KERRNARD, Wm. L. to Martha BLACK                          7-2-1835     (6)
HAYNIE, Geo. W. to Susan MILLER                           7-2-1835     (6)
CUSHING, Stephen to Margaret Ann HOLLAND*                 7-9-1835     (6)
       *Age certified by her father
DIXON, Wm. to Hannah Jane HALL                            7-18-1835    (6)
SWARTZ, Andrew* to Jane HARPER                            7-19-1835    (6)
       *Age certified by Nathaniel Swartz, father
MILLER, Thomas to Sophia ROBINSON                         7-21-1835    (6)
MORIT, Michael to Elizabeth HOOVER                        7-25-1835    (6)
BOWEN, Wm. to Lydia CARTY                                 7-26-1835    (7)
BOTHEL, Benjamin to Ann GRIFFMAN                          7-26-1835    (7)
GLICK, Lewis* to Polly SCHWANDER                lic.       7-27-1835    (7)
       *Age certified by Glick's father
HARBAUGH, Wm. to Leah DEEDS                               8-6-1835     (7)
DEFENBAUGH, Washington to Lydia McCONNELL                 8-6-1835     (7)
GRIGSBY, Wm to Elizabeth KERNS                  lic.       8-6-1835     (7)
KRANER, Wm to Elizabeth MULLEN                            8-6-1835     (7)
HUBER, Henry to Arianne WILLIAMSON                        8-13-1835    (7)
LOWMASTER, John to Hannah NEELY                           8-13-1835    (7)
DECKER, Isaac D. to Sarah FRENCH                          8-14-1835    (7)
CULLENS, Michael to Rebecca CULP                          8-13-1835    (7)
SIVERY, Wm to Elizabeth MANN                              8-16-1835    (7)
ALLOIS, Etli to Christina KAESTER               lic.       8-18-1835    (8)
CARPENTER, Wm to Sarah SHOEMAKER                          8-23-1835    (8)
HAUSER, Josiah to Elizabeth McGROVEY                      8-25-1835    (8)
LACY, Amos to Margaret GRIZZLE                  lic.       8-22-1835    (8)
NEVILL, Joseph to Barbara BIBBS                           8-23-1835    (8)
KLANEROTH, Wm to Mary SMITH                               8-23-1835    (8)
NEIWINGER, Munehardt to Barbara SCHETZLER                 8-23-1835    (8)
```

```
HUSTON, Andrew to Ann Elizabeth RICHANAN                     8-27-1835   (8)
BAUGHMAN, John to Catharine BOWMAN                           8-30-1835   (8)
HARVEY, Thos. to Jane MOTRING                                8-27-1835   (8)
PRATT, Daniel to Catharine LATIMORE                  lic.    8-26-1835   (8)
GILE, John to Clarisey B. HOTTLE                             8-27-1835   (8)
RUHLEN, John to Christiana BRITIGHAM                         8-28-1835   (9)
BACHTEL, Jacob to Rebecca STEPLETON                  lic.    8-29-1835   (9)
BORN, Jacob to Elizabeth SHOUB                               9-3-1835    (9)
BRIGHT, Joseph to Catharine LEOHNARD                        9-11-1835    (9)
STITH, John to Delilia HITE                                  9-6-1835    (9)
BUFFINGTON, Richard to Ellsey CRAWFORD               lic..   8-29-1835   (9)
MILLER, Abraham to Elizabeth BLASOR*                (Sept.?) 8-3-1835    (9)
     *Age certified by, Isaac Blasor, the father
DITZLER, Jacob to Christina Elizabeth WALKER         lic.    9-3-1835    (9)
WILDERMUTH, David to Christina HAVENS                        9-6-1835    (9)
COUNTS, Low to Elizabeth WOODRUFF                    lic.    9-5-1835    (9)
TOWNSEND, Reed to Elizabeth SHEPLER                         9-10-1835    (9)
INMAN, Dulin to Ann JEFFERIES                               9-6-1835     (9)
PFIFER, Jacob to Maria FRIEND                        lic.    9-6-1835   (10)
HARMON, Chas. to Almira McBAFFERTY                         9-10-1835    (10)
KELTNER, Anderson to Catharine POPE                 lic.    9-7-1835    (10)
KOMRATH, Phillip to Mary Magdaline SIEGLER                  9-8-1835    (10)
FALL, John C. to Sarah CONNELL                              9-9-1835    (10)
SHOEMAKER, Jacob to Elizabeth GARRETT*                     7-10-1835    (10)
     *Age certified by Henry Garrett, the father
KUKNS, John to Barbara LEBERT                              9-13-1835    (10)
HART, Barney to Maria WOOSTER                       lic.    9-12-1835    (10)
EWING, Thomas E. to Eliza ARNOLD                          9-22-1835    (10)
SPERRY, James to Levina BONHAM                      lic.    9-16-1835    (10)
MIDDLESWORTH, Joseph to Harriett HAMILTON                 9-20-1835     (10)
SOLIDAY, Samuel to Elizabeth GRESY                         9-20-1835    (10)
HOWELL, John T. to Margaret RUTHERFORD                    9-20-1835     (11)
MILLER, Daniel to Lucinda KEMP                            9-22-1835     (11)
PICKERING, Washington to Margaret SWAYZE*                 9-24-1835     (11)
     *Age certified by Daniel Swayze
FEHLER, Benjamin to Margaret HALE                   lic.    9-24-1835    (11)
COFFMAN, John to Eliza LIGHTNER                           10-1-1835     (11)
NEINWANDER, Chas. to Sarah SMITH                           9-30-1835    (11)
NEFF, John to Catharine HARVEY                      lic.    9-29-1835    (11)
MITCHELL, Benjamin G. to Angeline MATTHEWS               10-1-1835     (11)
MOISER, Henry to Catharine DAVIS                         10-4-1835      (11)
FETTEROW, Elias L. to Ann CLARK                          10-3-1835      (11)
LEIS, Robt. to Priscilla CRISTY                     lic.   10-3-1835     (11)
RARICK, Jacob to Franeena BAKER                          10-25-1835     (11)
MURPHY, Wm. to Rebecca HOLMES                            10-7-1835      (12)
KROUSE, Philip I. to Rebecca LELAND                 lic.   10-6-1835     (12)
CRUMER, Jacob to Elizabeth SWIRCK                        10-8-1835      (12)
HARMON, John to Magdaline LUDWICK                   lic.   10-13-1835    (12)
REESE, David to Mary OWENS                               10-18-1835     (12)
BRODY, Wm. to Sarah FRASIER                              10-17-1835     (12)
CLYMER, Fountain to Susanna HARRIS                  lic.   10-15-1835    (12)
```

```
BROWN, Zedekiah to Eleanor MONTGOMERY                        10-22-1835  (12)
REES, Abner to Jane SMITH                                    10-22-1835  (12)
HUNSAKER, Isaac to Sarah FREEZNER             lic.          10-22-1835  (12)
GINDERT, John to Barbara SCHANK                              11-3-1835   (12)
LITTLE, John N. to Margaret DRUNA             lic.          10-22-1835  (12)
BROWN, Zedekiah to Ellen MONTGOMERY           lic.          10-23-1835  (13)
NORTH, Thos. to Eve HAMMEL                                   10-29-1835  (13)
HECKMAN, Lewis to Elizabeth NIGH              lic.          10-23-1835  (13)
                                              mar.          3-20-1836   (13)
HOWRYHOUSER, Wm. to Caroline BELOTE                          11-3-1835   (13)
WELLER, Henry to Sophia CONRAD                lic.          11-1-1835   (13)
                                              mar.          10-25-1836  (13)
COKELEY, Jacob to Jane PAUL                                  10-27-1835  (13)
HUBER, Martin to Sarah LAMB                                  10-29-1835  (13)
CAMPBELL, Harvey to Mary COWAN                               11-5-1835   (13)
LAMB, Washington to Mary McCREA               lic.          10-31-1835  (13)
EVANS, Solomon to Mary PEPPLE                                11-5-1835   (13)
ALSPACH, Jacob to Caroline BRIDVILL                          11-30-1835  (13)
WHITMAN, Henry to Elizabeth LYONS                            11-3-1835   (13)
MATHIAS, Jacob to Julian D. HART                             11-5-1835   (14)
CRUTCHEN, Wm. to Rebecca WALKER                              11-5-1835   (14)
HUNTWORK, Geo. to Barbara HALEY                              11-12-1835  (14)
BROOKS, John to Margaret HOCKER                              11-8-1835   (14)
PICKERING, James to Catherine SMITH                         11-18-1835  (14)
HAY, Peter to Polly STUMP                     lic.          11-7-1835   (14)
YOUNGHOSES, Jastin to Caroline MYER           lic.          11-9-1835   (14)
STROLL, Nicholas to Elizabeth JOHNSON                       11-12-1835  (14)
POLING, John to Elizabeth LAPLY                             11-12-1835  (14)
LIGHTER, Henry to Martha FRIZZLE                            11-26-1835  (14)
BROWN, Edward to Emina OWENS                                11-23-1835  (14)
WERTZ, John to Mary ANDERECK                                11-12-1835  (14)
GOOD, Joseph to Harriet TAYLOR                             11-12-1835  (15)
SPOON, John to Catharine AWL                               11-17-1835  (15)
FOLTZ, Peter to Elizabeth POWEL                            11-17-1835  (15)
SHARP, Jacob to Ruth CULTON                                11-17-1835  (15)
TAUNAHILL, James to Keyla HOLLOWAY                         11-16-1835  (15)
SPRINGER, John to Susannah FRAZEY                          11-17-1835  (15)
REED, John to Joan W. SANFT                                11-17-1835  (15)
BACLL (or BUCLE, Hiram to Rebecca PARRISH                 11-20-1835  (15)
TROUT, Noah to Margaret KIGER                              11-19-1835  (15)
HARRIS, Thomas to Sarah GREEN                              11-19-1835  (15)
HOLMES, Wm. to Mary BEERY                                  11-19-1835  (15)
MURRAY, Reuben I. to Harriet KNOX                          11-22-1835  (15)
SEITZ, Jacob to Elizabeth DEETZ                            11-23-1835  (16)
BENEDUM, Wm. to Mary Ann EBRIGHT                           11-29-1835  (16)
DEAN, John to Rachael HITE                                 11-29-1835  (16)
APPLEGATE, Harrison to Margaret CRAWFORD                   12-1-1835   (16)
WELKER, Joseph to Frances OTINI               lic.          11-27-1835  (16)
MEYERS, Frederich to Elizabeth BIZER          lic.          11-27-1835  (16)
JOSEPH, John to Permelia PETERS                            12-4-1835   (16)
PARKERSON, George to Elizabeth HENDERLICK                  12-3-1835   (16)
```

```
BLANK, Michael to Salome OZENBACH                              12-16-1835 (16)
RICHARDSON, Solomon to Eleanor LOWMASTER          lic.  12-4-1835  (16)
MILLER, Michael to Mary FAULEY                    lic.  12-5-1835  (16)
ROLEY, Isam to Mary WILLIAMS                            12-8-1835  (16)
HITE, Lewis to Dorothy RUFFNER                         12-10-1835 (17)
RUNKLE, John to Hannah HEDRICK                    lic.  12-9-1835  (17)
FETTERS, Thos. to Sarah BRIGHT                         12-10-1835 (17)
TOBIN, James to Catharine FRANK                   lic.  12-16-1835 (17)
HEFT, George to Elizabeth BEERY                        12-24-1835 (17)
ZIMMERMAN, Valentine to Eliza BRANDT                   12-27-1835 (17)
BAKER, John to Susanna SNIDER                          12-19-1835 (17)
CRICK, Jacob A. to Lydia LANTZ                         12-24-1835 (17)
KISTLER, David to Margaret FOLTZ                  lic.  12-21-1835 (17)
ALLEN, Geo. to Nancy CARLISLE                          12-24-1835 (17)
SIMON, Wm. to Sarah TROVINGER                     lic.  12-22-1835 (17)
BUSBY, Sam'l S. to Rachel FETTER                       12-22-1835 (17)
LOCHART, Jacob to Harriet HERRING                      12-24-1835 (18)
WAGNER, John to Elizabeth TIPPLE                  lic.  12-22-1835 (18)
SHOOP, Geo. to Mary Ann VAUKIN                         12-24-1835 (18)
HINTERLICH, Jacob to Rachel LYONS                      12-25-1835 (18)
RUFF, Jacob to Christiana SCHUSTER                lic.  12-25-1835 (18)
JACKSON, Samuel to Mary STREETS                        12-24-1835 (18)
MILLER, Elijah to Lydia LEOHNER                        12-31-1835 (18)
FOOR, Wm. to Mary WARD                            lic.  12-28-1835 (18)
PEPPLE, Ipe to Mary Ann TIPPLE                         12-30-1835 (18)
CORNWILL, Willis to Sarah Ann COOK                     12-31-1835 (18)
WESTENBARGER, John, Jr. to Mary Ann DERICKSON          1-3-1836   (18)
SCOTT, James to Betsy SMITH                       lic.  12-31-1835 (18)
WELTZ, Christian to Salome BLOSSER                     12-31-1835 (19)
THOMPSON, John to Mary FISHER                     lic.  12-31-1835 (19)
CHEN, Sylvester W. to Maria ARNOLD                     12-31-1835 (19)
RITTGERS, John to Elizabeth HOCKE                      1-1-1836   (19)
SHAW, Joseph S. to Eleanor G. BEATTY                   1-4-1836   (19)
ECKART, Wm. R. to Anna Maria COC                 lic.  1-1-1836   (19)
STALL, Geo. to Catharine AKER                          1-7-1836   (19)
GLASSER, Geo. G. to Dorcas HUFFORD                     1-7-1836   (19)
STOUTER, David to Catherine MARSHALL*                  1-12-1836  (19)
       *Age certified by Benuel Marshall, her brother
GROVE, Andrew to Sarah ALSPACH                         1-10-1836  (19)
MILLER, Isaac to Sally KNEPPER                         1-10-1836  (19)
WYCLOFF, Matthew to Nancy FINKBONE                     1-14-1836  (20)
FALL, Jacob to Elizabeth HOCKMAN                       1-14-1836  (20)
SIPLE, Geo. W. to Mary Ann NEIBLING                    1-17-1836  (20)
NEWSTATE, Henry to Nancy MORGAN                   lic.  1-13-1836  (20)
DAUT, Jefferson to Sarah WILSON                        1-13-1836  (20)
RUTHERFORD, Archibald to Elizabeth L. REED       lic.  1-13-1836  (20)
BICHTEL, Andrew to Magdalen GARDNER                    1-14-1836  (20)
GOUBLE, John to Rebecca HOSSROD                        1-21-1836  (20)
VARNEL, Joseph to Catharine WOODS                      1-17-1836  (20)
TRUMP, P. Van to Mariah Louisa BEECHER                 1-17-1836  (20)
SMITH, Samuel to Magdaline FOELLER                     1-24-1836  (20)
```

```
RECKER, Wm. to Hannah SHOEMAKER                          1-21-1836   (20)
MAST, John to Rachel TIPPLE                       mar.   12-31-1835  (21)
                                                  1ic.   Dec. 1835   (21)
DOUVEMIRE, Peter to Susan RICHEY*                        1-24-1836   (21)
     *Age certified by her father
RUNKLE, John to Catharine FELLER                         3-29-1836   (21)
CLUM, Geo. to Elizabeth RADER                            1-24-1836   (21)
BROWN, Henry to Mary Ann JOSEPH                          1-28-1836   (21)
FREEZNER, Samuel to Mary KAUFFMAN                        1-28-1836   (21)
BLOSSER, Isaac to Lydia FREEZNER                         1-25-1836   (21)
LEIB, Elises to Delilia HILL                             1-26-1836   (21)
BENSON, Joel to Anne COONS                        lic.   1-26-1836   (21)
LUTZ, Geo. to Rebecca FREISNER                           1-28-1836   (21)
BEERY, Joshua to Catharine HUNSAKER                      1-28-1836   (21)
HENSEL, Charles to Christine HENSEL                      1-30-1836   (21)
HEAVER, John to Mary CLY                                 2-4-1836    (22)
LAMBS, Joseph to Chorolotte THOMDN(?)             lic.   2-1-1836    (22)
BULL, Geo. F. to Maria WILSON                     lic.   2-3-1836    (22)
LANDIS, Martin to Salome KUNTZ                           2-4-1836    (22)
RANK, Philip to Polly SHIMP                              2-7-1836    (22)
SIPLE, Solomon to Lydia SPITLER                          2-11-1836   (22)
WHITE, Samuel to Rachel HEMPWHITE                 lic.   2-8-1836    (22)
RITTGERS, Daniel to Eve FOGHT                            2-11-1836   (22)
SCOTT, I. P. to Henrietta DOAN                           2-11-1836   (22)
MILLER, Michael to Louisa GAREY                   lic.   2-15-1836   (22)
KENSON, Christopher to Catharine GIBSON                  2-15-1836   (22)
RIFFNER, Michael to Sarah NICHOLS                        2-18-1836   (22)
SMITH, Wm. to Lyia CULP                                  2-18-1836   (23)
FOUTCH, Jonathan to Rebecca COWDEN                lic.   2-18-1836   (23)
CHANNELL, Alpheus to Julia WILLIAM                       2-23-1836   (23)
FAIRCHILD, Moses to Eve SHRIEVE                          2-25-1836   (23)
DILLON, Thomas to Margaret SHIRLEY                       2-25-1836   (23)
McCRITTON, John to Eliza Ann MOCK                        2-25-1836   (23)
CLIPPINGER, Solamon to Rebecca C. PRUDEN                 2-21-1836   (23)
NEWKIRK, John to Juliann STANBERY                        3-3-1836    (23)
GREEN, John to Martha Ann COKE                           2-25-1836   (23)
WILEY, Joseph to Nancy BROWN                             3-17-1836   (23)
SWAYER, Amos to Catharine FELLERS                 lic.   2-27-1836   (23)
WOOD, Gilbert to Elizabeth McFARLAND                     3-17-1836   (23)
BOHN, Frederick to Elizabeth RICKLEY                     3-30-1836   (24)
GOLLOHER, Wesley to Sarah MIDDLESWORTH                   3-2-1836    (24)
BOURER, Jacob C. to Delila CLICK                         3-15-1836   (24)
COLMAN, John to Sarah BARNHART                           3-1-1836    (24)
KUHNS, David to Polly HIVELY                             3-1-1836    (24)
HOFFMAN, John to Magdoline BRUNNERS                      3-8-1836    (24)
HENSEL, Geo. to Sally BILLING                            3-3-1836    (24)
JULIEN, Ormon to Rachel CLARK                            3-21-1836   (24)
DRAKE, Wm. to Susan CUPP                                 3-5-1836    (24)
GEARHART, Henry to Susannah RODER                        3-10-1836   (24)
HOLMES, Joshua to Mary M. FOUNTAIN                       1-8-1836    (24)
WORD, Benjamin to Naomi MORGAN                           3-6-1836    (24)
```

```
DELONG, John to Catharine SMIVES            lic.    3-7-1836    (25)
SAMUEL, Paul to Mary EGBERT                          3-20-1836   (25)
BAUMGARDNER, Samuel to Eleanor GREEK                 3-17-1836   (25)
KELLEY, John to Priscilla CLARK                      3-12-1836   (25)
MOREHART, Adam to Elizabeth DUNKEL                   3-14-1836   (25)
SWARTZ, John to Mary BRIGHT                          3-20-1836   (25)
PLUMMER, Henry to Phebe McFARSEN                     3-20-1836   (25)
BILMAN, Richard to Maria BENTON             lic.    3-23-1836   (25)
RANDOLPH, Wm. to Elizabeth RUDOLPH                   3-27-1836   (25)
SIDENER, Henry to Sarah BOYER                        3-31-1836   (25)
LEITH, James to Barbara RANK                         3-31-1836   (25)
GALLAGHER, Henry to Sarah LONG                       3-31-1836   (25)
BROWN, John to Otillia SHAFER                        3-31-1836   (26)
BOLENBARRGH, Peter to Olive NEWKIRK                  3-31-1836   (26)
SHAEFFER, Samuel to Amy BUZZARD                      3-31-1836   (26)
COATES, Nelson to Catharine Mary WACHTER            4-3-1836    (26)
POWELL, John to Melinda TAYLOR                       3-31-1836   (26)
BINKLEY, Christian to Rosanna CLUM                   3-31-1836   (26)
HOLMES, Wm. to Mary Ann BIRD                lic.    3-30-1836   (26)
PITY, John to Anna CLY                               4-5-1836    (26)
KELLER, Jacob to Nancy NELSON                        4-17-1836   (26)
HIPSHEAR, Christian to Margaret SHARP               4-7-1836    (26)
MORING, Christopher to Marith WOLFANA       lic.    4-2-1836    (26)
GEADLEB, Thorn to Mariah KELLER             lic.    4-2-1836    (26)
SPEIRER, A_____ to Hortensia KELLER               4-6-1836    (27)
BAUGHMAN, Emanuel to Mary SOLES                      4-28-1836   (27)
CLY, Jacob to Rebecca BEERY                          4-3-1836    (27)
HAGLER, John to Susan ECKERT                lic.    4-6-1836    (27)
CLINE, David to Rebecca SHRODER                      4-10-1836   (27)
BRAY, Daniel to Catherine DECKER            lic.    4-9-1836    (27)
LONG, David D. to Mary TOOL                          4-14-1836   (27)
JONES, A. Ream to Hannah E. PHILLIPS  lic. issued Feb. last 2-21-1836  (27)
PATRICK, Thos. to Emily BROCINS                      4-27-1836   (27)
LOWES, Benjamin to Eliza SYFORD             lic.    4-13-1836   (27)
WILSON, Geo. W. to Honor TALLMAN                     4-14-1836   (27)
SAGAR, Christian to Catharine LONGBROKE             4-21-1836   (27)
SANNS, Georg to Mary JUDA                            4-28-1836   (28)
SMALTZ, George to Mary Ann DARRK            lic.    4-19-1836   (28)
FRIZZLE, Jason to Barbara BAUGHMAN                  4-20-1836   (28)
CUTSHALL, James to Ellen STRADER                    4-26-1836   (28)
RISLEY, David to Charlotte KOCH             lic.    4-21-1836   (28)
MONTGOMERY, Joshua to Susannah TANNER               4-21-1836   (28)
ALLEN, Lyman to Eliza REBER                          4-28-1836   (28)
FOWLER, Zadich to Susan WOLF                         4-24-1836   (28)
DUBBLE, Henry to Catharine STURN                    4-24-1836   (28)
BURRELL, Henry A. to Brayeda WHEATLEY               5-8-1836    (28)
SPRINGER, George to Lena FOUTZ       lic. 5-6-1836  4-14-1836   (28)
WARNER, Wm. to Catherine BAKER                      5-8-1836    (28)
GEPHART, Peter to Polly BAKER               lic.    5-6-1836    (29)
BOYLE, Michael to Mable SMITH                        5-8-1836    (29)
SOLIDA, Jacob to Mary DARING                         5-12-1836   (29)
MORRIS, Joseph H. to Lavinia PHELPS                 5-15-1836   (29)
```

```
HOLIDAY, John to Magdaline RUFFNER                               5-12-1836   (29)
RUFF, John Martin to Barbara WEIDNER                             5-15-1836   (29)
MILLER, John to Susan SIGLEY                                     5-26-1836   (29)
DAGON, Chas. to Susana WERNER                                    5-15-1836   (29)
HANNA, James to Emily HAVENS                                     5-17-1836   (29)
DAVIS, Wm. L. to Susanna COPP                                    5-22-1836   (29)
STEVENSON, James to Mary CALDWELL                                5-26-1836   (29)
SWEYER, John to Sary WORTHMAN                          lic.      5-26-1836   (29)
CRAWFORD, James to Susannah GESSLLE                    lic.      5-28-1836   (30)
TALBOTT, Paul to Rosanna SMITH                                  5-29-1836   (30)
SHUPE, Abraham to Mary ABRAMS                                   5-31-1836   (30)
LAPE, George to Christiana BECHTEL                              5-5-1836    (30)
APT, Henry B. to Eve ROLEY                                      5-31-1836   (30)
SMITH, David N. to Sophia COONRAD                     lic.      5-31-1836   (30)
PRICE, Samuel to Jane HUNTER                                    6-2-1836    (30)
LYTLE, John to Hannah JOHNSON                                   6-2-1836    (30)
GERKEN, Frederick to Sophia RAVER                     lic.      6-3-1836    (30)
Le BORENCHON, Felic George to Rose Anna GALLIGHER               6-5-1836    (30)
FINNELL, Elijah to Susan BOLING                                 6-9-1836    (30)
HAY, Peter to Catharine YORK                                    6-9-1836    (30)
BATESON, Wm. to Rebecca MINER                                   6-9-1836    (31)
SHAFFER, Isaac to Rosanna HOFFMAN                     lic.      6-7-1836    (31)
MEAD, David to Eliza COLLINS                          lic.      6-10-1836   (31)
MILLER, Phillip to Catharine SPEAR                             6-15-1836   (31)
LAKIN, I. O. to Eliza WHITE                                     6-12-1836   (31)
DOUGLAS, Wm. H. to Jane Frances BOLING                         6-23-1836   (31)
KITSMILLER, Elijah*to Elizabeth ROADS                          6-16-1836   (31)
        *Age certified by Benj. Kitsmiller, father
MILLER, Jacob to Hannah SEVER                         lic.      6-15-1836   (31)
SNYDER, John to Maria PHIFER                                    6-16-1836   (31)
STORY, James to Harriet I. SITES                               6-17-1836   (31)
CARR, John to Marilda NEIGHBOR                                 6-17 1836    (31)
SHANG, John M., Jr. to Jane WILLIAMS                           6-21-1836   (31)
LASLEY, Andrew E. to Catherine MILLER                         6-23-1836   (32)
DECKER, John to Sarah ZIMMER                                   6-28-1836   (32)
McCABE, Isaiah to Maria REED                                   6-29-1836   (32)
STEVENSON, Henry to Mary MILLER                       lic.     7-3-1836    (32)
DEORTH, Randolph to _rena HILLMAN                              7-17-1836   (32)
KELLER, David to Elizabeth RODEBAUGH                           7-3-1836    (32)
FLOOD, W. W. to Frances A. McDORMITH                  lic.     7-12-1836   (32)
TEAL, Eli M. to Sarah TEAL                                     7-13-1836   (32)
STUDER, George to Elizabeth GASTER                             7-20-1836   (32)
SPIELMAN, Christian to Mary GIESY                     lic.     7-19-1836   (32)
ANGLE, Joseph to Emily McVEY                                   7-21-1836   (32)
STRADER, Albert to Alice Ann HOKE                              8-15-1836   (33)
TURNER, McPherson to Ienpia(?)                                 7-21-1836   (33)
SMETHERS, Joseph E. to Sarah RAUCH                             7-23-1836   (33)
ALSPACH, Philip to Mary Ann HARING                             7-28-1836   (33)
BIBLER, John to Eliza HOARD                                    7-26-1836   (33)
BRUNNER, Henry to Maria Finetta WHILESY              lic.      7-28-1836   (33)
FREEZE, John to Catharine LUTZ                        lic.     7-30-1836   (33)
```

FAIRFIELD COUNTY, OHIO - NEWSPAPER DEATH NOTICES AND OBITUARIES 1849-1850

The following records were taken from the original copies of the newspapers which are located in the library in City Hall at Lancaster.

OHIO EAGLE, published Lancaster, Ohio on Thursday
(all newspapers from Mar. 8, 1849 through Dec. 27, 1849,inclusive were checked)
4-12-1849 - DIED on 6th inst. at his residence in this place of consumption, Henry SHULTZ aged 37 years.
4-26-1849 - DIED near Lancaster on Wednesday, April 8, 1849, Jane Wilson DRUM wife of Chas. D. Drum, aged 29 years and 3 months.
6-14-1849 - DIED on Wednesday morning, the 6th inst. in this town, Eliza daughter of William P. and Emily GREED, aged 7 years.
6-28-1849 - DIED in Lancaster, Ohio on Saturday morning, June 23rd, 1849, Mrs. Sarah A. TALLMADGE, wife of Mr. D. Tallmadge...daughter, wife and mother...25 year member of M.E. Church....left aged father, husband and two sons.
6-28-1849 - DIED at his residence near Lancaster, on the 13th inst., Mr. George SEE, in the 62nd year of his age. The deceased was born in Hardin County, Virginia and emigrated to this county in 1804 where he has remained since.
7-5-1849 - DIED June 29th, Mrs. Eliza Jane LEVERING, aged 37 years, consort of Mr. Maris Levering occupying Prospect Hill farm near this city.
7-26-1849 - DIED on the morning of the 19th inst., Marsella, youngest child of William P. and Emily CREED, aged 15 months.
8-16-1849 - DIED at the residence of his father-in-law, Mr. James Russell in Columbus on the morning of Sunday last, James H. EWING, in the 38th year of his age....represented Hamilton County in Congress.
8-16-1849 - DIED August 9th, Albert Williamson, son of Marish LEVERING, aged 3 months and 3 weeks.
8-16-1849 - DIED on yesterday morning at the residence of John Reber, Esq. in Lancaster, Work GALBRAITH, aged about 32 years.
9-6-1849 - DIED on 8th August at his residence in Columbus, Ohio, Capt. Henry S. MALLORY late of the United States Army. Capt. Mallory resided for a time in this place previous to going to Columbus.
10-11-1849 - DIED on the 4th of October at his residence on the farm of Wm Latta, Esq., near Etna, Ohio, John RINEHART, aged 45 years.
11-1-1849 - DIED on Tuesday the 16th ult., Mr. James DUNGAN at the advanced age of 84 years. Mr. Duncan was one of the early settlers of this county and was one amongst the first members of the First Presbyterian Church in Lancaster.
11-1-1849 - DIED at the residence of Mr. John Work on the 26th inst., Mr. James WILSON, in the 27th year of his age. The deceased was the last child of the late Dr. Wilson who practiced medicine in this community.
11-1-1849 - DIED on the 20th October at Ashland, Catharine A. wife of the late David RUFFNER, and formerly of Charleston, Virginia.

LANCASTER GAZETTE published Lancaster, Ohio on Friday
(all newspapers from May 11, 1849 through Dec. 27, 1850 inclusive were checked)
5-25-1849 - DIED at his residence one mile east of Lancaster on Friday morning last, Mr. John S. WALTERS. He leaves relatives and friends to mourn.

5-25-1849 - DIED at his late residence in Hocking township on the 17th inst., Mr.
David BROOMFIELD, at the advanced age of 87 years, 6 months and 13 days,
leaving a large family of children, grandchildren and great grandchildren.
The deceased migrated to this county in the fall of 1819 from Virginia
and has resided here since that time in this township.

6-8-1849 - ANOTHER REVOLUTIONARY SOLDIER GONE. Died at his residence in Twin
township near this city on the evening of the 27th ult. after a decline
of health of 3 months, Mr. Casper PLYLY in the 90th year of his age.
This aged father when a youth, entered the Army of the Revolution,
fought the battles of his country unto victory, was one of the first
settlers in the vicinity of Chillicothe, raised a large family of
children; gave each a piece of the soil for which he fought....tender
father and true friend. (Scioto Gazette)

6-15-1849 - DIED on Wednesday morning, the 6th inst., Eliza daughter of William
P. and Emily CREED, aged 7 years.

6-29-1849 - DIED, Mrs. Sarah A. TALLMADGE (note: same as in OHIO EAGLE)

7-6-1849 - DIED, Eliza Jane LEVERING (note: same as in OHIO EAGLE)

7-13-1849 - DIED on the 5th day of July 1849 in Good Hope township, Hocking
County, Ohio, John DELONG, aged 32 years, formerly of this place.

7-27-1849 - DIED, Marsel A. CREED (note: same as in OHIO EAGLE)

8-17-1849 - DIED in this town on Friday, August 10th, 1849, Mary youngest daughter
of Samuel and Ann BEERY, aged 1 year and 10 days.

8-17-1849 - DIED, Albert Williamson LEVERING (note; same as in OHIO EAGLE)

8-17-1849 - DIED, Work GALBRAITH (note: same as in OHIO EAGLE)

8-17-1849 - DIED at his residence in this town, on the 15th inst., Mr. William
HUTCHINS, aged 39.

8-24-1849 - DIED at the residence of his son in Bern township on the 20th inst.,
Mr. William JACKSON aged 89 years. The deceased emigrated to this
county from Frederick County, Virginia in 1805, where he continued
to reside until his death. Consistent member of the Baptist Church
for nearly 40 years, kind neighbor and good citizen.

8-24-1849 - DIED on Wednesday, August 15, 1849, James Moore son of E. and Amanda
Ann VAN DYKE of Greenfield township, aged 3 years, 8 months and 25
days.

8-24-1849 - DIED in Rushville on Saturday the 18th inst., Mr. Joseph Thomas
HILLARD, of the firm of Wise and Hillard of this place, aged 24.

8-24-1849 - DIED Albert Lewis son of Lyman H. and Sarah M. GUTHRIE, aged about
5 years.

9-14-1849 - DIED on Sunday morning the 9th inst., after an illness of two weeks,
Mrs. Adeline wife of Mr. Eli ASHBROOK

9-28-1849 - DIED at Elyria, on the 4th inst., Mr. Francis KENDALL formerly a
merchant at this place. Leaves wife and two children.

9-28-1849 - DIED on 22d inst., Rufus William infant son of Jones and Rebecca
GIBBONY, aged 4 months and 26 days.

10-12-1849 - DIED on 21st of September 1849, Mr. Charles REBER, aged 38 years
3 months and 1 day. He was born in Amanda township, Fairfield County.

10-12-1849 - DIED, John Rinehart (note: same as in OHIO EAGLE)

10-26-1849 - DIED in Cincinnati on 30th of September 1849, Mr. Philip FETTERS, formerly a resident of this town, aged 23 years 4 months and 17 days.

11-2-1849 - DIED, James WILSON (note: same as in OHIO EAGLE)

11-2-1849 - DIED, Catharine A. RUFFNER (note: same as in OHIO EAGLE)

11-2-1849 - DIED on 20th September last, near Decatur, Indiana, Mrs. BEERY wife of John M. Beery, also on 24th of same month, Mr. John M. BEERY, leaving two small children. They formerly resided in this county and leave a large number of relations and friends.

12-7-1849 - DIED in Madison township on the 24th ult., Mrs. Mary Ann wife of Mr. John WYLIE in the 42nd year of her age.

12-14-1849 - DIED at the residence of Mrs. Effinger, on Tuesday morning the 14th inst., Miss Isabella NOBLE, aged 23 years only daughter of Robert A. Noble, late of Tarlton, dec'd.

12-14-1849 - DIED at his residence in Amanda, this county on Tuesday evening December 4th in the 43d year of his age, Dr. John I. DAUGHERTY, formerly of Maryland but for 16 years a resident of Ohio.

1-18-1850 - DIED at Marietta, Ohio, December 24, 1849, Susan consort of Mr. William P. DANA, formerly residents of this place.

1-25-1850 - DIED in this village on morning of the 16th inst., Mrs. E. A. DUTWILER, consort of Mr. Eli Dutwiler in about the 37th year of her age. Born in Franklin County, Pennsylvania and late of Lancaster this state. Left a husband and four small children to mourn. The early part of her life was spent as a member of the German Reformed church and rest of her life as member of the Evangelical Lutheran Church. (Hancock Whig)

2-1-1850 - DIED on Friday 25th inst. in this county, Malinda youngest daughter of John STONEBURNER, aged 4 years and 11 months.

3-1-1850 - DIED on Wednesday morning, February 13th, 1850, Ellen M. daughter of George and Mary CARLISLE of this place aged 3 years 5 months and 18 days.

3-8-1850 - DIED on Sunday evening last at 3 o'clock at her residence near this place, Mrs. Alice WILSON, relict of the late Nathaniel Wilson, deceased, at the advanced age of 80 years. Mrs. Wilson came to this county, in connection with her husband in the year 1800....Mrs. Wilson became a member of the Presbyterian church in the early part of her life before she left Pennsylvania.

3-29-1850 - DIED on Saturday morning the 23d inst., Mary Jane youngest daughter of Dr. G. K. and Maria MILLER of this place.

3-29-1850 - DIED on Thursday evening at 9 o'clock at her residence in Auburn township, Mrs. Ann Maria BURY, relict of Rev. Isaac Bury. Mrs. Bury came to this country in 1806 shortly after her marriage. She lived with her husband for 44 years. Mother of 13 children of which 3 are dead, 50 grandchildren of which 7 are dead and 4 great grandchildren. Mrs. Bury, a member of the Dunkart Church died at the age of 66 years and 8 days.

4-26-1850 - DIED on Thursday the 18th inst., at about noon, Mrs. Nancy consort of Mr. Joseph WORK, Sen., in the 46th year of her age, leaving both husband and children.

5-3-1850 - DIED in Lancaster on Monday, April 15th, Mrs. Sarah Elizabeth BARKER in the 25th year of her age, wife of Charles A. Barker, Esq. and a daughter of Horatio Hatch, Esq, formerly a resident of Lancaster, now of this place. (Athens Messenger)

5-24-1850 - DIED on the 18th May 1850 at his residence in Baltimore, Fairfield County, Ohio, Dr. Silas Smith CEOHEGAN, in the 43d year of his age. A native of Kentucky, but emigrated to this state in early life. He was a printer by trade until 1322 when he abandoned this to study medicine with Dr. Luckey of Circleville and in 1825 located in Baltimore.

6-7-1850 - DIED in Rushcreek township, Fairfield County, Ohio on Friday evening the 31st of May 1850, Mr. John BEERY in the 85th year of his age. Mr. Beery was one of the pioneers of Ohio; he was a native of Rockingham County, Virginia and in the year 1805 settled in Been township, six miles east of Lancaster. Here he resided for 5 years when he was called to part with the companion of his youth, since that time he has recided mostly in Rushcreek township. He was a member of the Dunkard church for 50 years prior to his death.

6-21-1850 - DIED at his residence in Lancaster on Thursday, 13th inst., Mr. William KNIGHT in the 61st year of his age. The deceased was a native of Kent, England, emigrated to this country about 13 years since--11 last past in this town.

8-9-1850 - DIED at Keokuk, Iowa, July 16, Mrs. Elizabeth wife of Mr. Henry LITTLER, formerly a merchant of Circleville.

8-30-1850 - DIED at Keokuk, Iowa, August 27th at noon, Mrs. Margaret M. wife of Mr. P.D. FOSTER formerly of this place, and daughter of the late Henry Dubble.

9-20-1850 - DIED at Mount Auburn on the morning of the 7th inst., Eliza B. concort of John MACCRACKEN and daughter of Moses Brooks, in the 26th year of her age, also on the 9th inst., John B. youngest son of John and Eliza B. MCCRACKEN. (Cincinnati Chron.)

11-8-1850 - DIED on Sunday the 3d inst., at the residence of her daughter, Mrs. Wilkinson in Lancaster, Mrs. Jane SPRINGER relict of the late William Springer, dec'd, aged 77 years. The deceased with her family emmigrated from Fayette County, Pennsylvania in the spring of the year 1800.

11-8-1850 - DIED on the 6th inst., Mr. George WILLHITE aged 66 years.

11-15-1850 - DIED on the 11th inst., Henry Clinton son of Frederick A. and Mary SHAEFFER, aged 9 years 4 months and 12 days.

12-13-1850 - DIED at his residence near West Rushville, Fairfield County, Ohio on the 11th inst., Mr. David KERR in the 50th year of his age.

426

FAIRFIELD COUNTY, OHIO - NEWSPAPER DEATH NOTICES May 1869 to May 1870

Abstracted from the "Ohio Eagle", Lancaster, Ohio - published on Thursdays.

5-6-1869 - Obituary - Dr. E. L. MINOR was born June 9th, 1797 in Middletown, Vermont. Attended Cartleton Medical College. In 1820 emigrated to Ohio and located at Royalton. In 1825 removed to Lithopolis where he practiced for more than 50 years. Died April 8th, 1869.

6-17-1869 - Died June 12, 1869, Mrs. Susan GRAHAM wife of Wm. Graham. The deceased was 82 years and 9 ms. of age. She and her husband settled near Lancaster in the fall of 1822. Joined the United Presbyterian Church in 1837. Left an aged companion, 3 sons, 27 grandchildren and 9 great-grandchildren.

7-15-1869 - Died July 10, 1869 near Lancaster, Terese Ellen dau. of David and Hannah Ewing. Five summers of age.

7-29-1869 - Died July 13, 1869, Robert Clarke youngest son of K. & P. FRITTER, aged 19 months and 5 days.

7-29-1869 - Died July 7th, 1869 near Hebron, Licking Co., Ohio, Joseph PENCE aged 56 years. His remains now rest beside the loved forms of a wife, five daughters and one son, all except one of whom he has followed to their graves during the last six years.

8-5-1869 - Died at his residence at the corner of Columbus and Wheeling Sts. in this city, Adam W. GUSEMAN aged 58 years. The deceased was a native of Martinsburg, Virginia, emigrated to this county with his parents and family in 1817. Forty years a blacksmith on Columbus Street. Never married. Member of the City Council.

8-5-1869 - Died Sat. morning, July 31st, Elijah TOBIN aged 35 yrs. 7 mos. and 28 ds. Clerk of Probate Court. Husband and father.

8-5-1869 - Miss Alice M. SPRINGER daughter of Henry Springer, Esq. died July 16, 1869 aged 19 yrs. 3 mos. and 4 days. Less than a year ago her mother died. Member of the M. E. Church. Leaves father and sisters.

8-12-1869 - Obituary, Mrs. Thalia Lochard wife of Thomas Lockhart, Esq.; born April 11, 1832, died July 28th, 1869. Daughter of Dr. M. Z. Kreider. Married 22 December 1857 to Thomas Lockhart, Esq. After their marriage they went to the Pacific coast near Marysville, California and returned in Dec. 1866. Member M. E. Church.

9-16-1869 - Died in Berne Twp., Mrs. Phebe Ann wife of Aaron ANESHENSEL in the 36th year of her age.

9-16-1869 - Died, Lancaster, Ohio, Thurs. Aug. 5th, Mrs. Mary Jane RUDOLPH wife of John RUDOLPH, aged 27 years. Wife, mother and sister. Member of the Catholic Church.

10-7-1869 - Died, Amanda Twp. on 24th Sept. 1869, Andrew youngest son of John H. and Sarah YOUNG aged 2 yrs. 2 mos. and 25 days.

427

9-30-1869 - Died, Mrs. Eliza EWING wife of Samuel EWING, Esq. of this city on the 4th September 1869 aged 65 years. Mrs. Ewing was the oldest daughter of John Myers, was born in Berkeley.County, Virginia on th 1st day of January 1804' and with her parents emigrated to Fairfield County in 1803. She married Samuel Ewing in January 1824. Left husband and children.

10-7-1869 - Died, John HARMON born 1 November 1803 departed 21 September 1869 aged 65 years 10 months and 20 days. Member of the U. B. Church for about 28 yrs.

10-21-1869 - Died, Oct. 12, 1869 at the residence of her father in Lancaster, Sarah daughter of John G. and Ann Myer, aged 22 years and 8 months. Member of the Lutheran Church. Leaves father, mother and three sisters.

10-21-1869 - Died on 14th inst., Robert son of Henry L. and Julia M. BECK of Hocking Twp., aged 9 months and 5 days.

11-4-1869 - Another Pioneer Gone to Rest. Died in Huntington Co., Indiana Sept. 27, 1869 at the residence of his son-in-law, Jacob D. Hite, Mr. John DAVIS aged 77 years 5 months and 18 days. The deceased moved from Pennsylvania when a boy ten years old with his father to Fairfield Co., Ohio. At the age of 19 years he enlisted in the War of 1812 under Capt. George Sanderson of Fairfield County and served six months. He lived in Fairfield County 62 years then moved five years ago this fall with his son-in-law, Wm. Guseman to Huntington Co., Indiana.

11-18-1869 - Died Nov. 1, 1869, John E. only son of John S. and Mary A. Feeman, ef Pleasant Twp.

11-25-1869 - Died at her residence near New Salem, Perry Co., Ohio on 17 Nov. 1869, Mrs. Ann Stinchcomb wife of George Stinchcomb, aged 77 years and 11 months. Mrs. S. was the daughter of Rev. John Wiseman of the M. E. Church, who moved from Virginia to Ohio in 1818 and she was married on 24 August 1819 to George Stinchcomb who survives her. Mother of eight children, four of whom are still living; James W. at Logan, Ohio, Elizabeth W. Pugh in Morrow Co., Ohio, George F. at Ft. Wayne, Indiana and Susan H. who lives with her father. Funeral 19th at M. E. Church.

12-2-1869 - Died at his residence near Crystal Spring, Copiah Co., Mississippi on 30 Oct. 1869, Wilson Latimor in the 68th year of his age. Native and many years a resident of Fairfield Co., Ohio.

12-9-1869 - Died Dec. 5, 1869, Mrs. Sarah J. wife of George Eversole, aged 33 yrs. and 4 months. Member of the Presbyterian Church. Leaves husband and two children.

12-30-1869 - Died at his residence in Dumontsville, Sat. 18th inst., George Stump aged 46 years. Born Chambersburg, Pennsylvania but for many years a resident of Fairfield County. In the fall of 1861 he enlisted under Capt. Brown, Co I, 43d Regt., Ohio Vols. and served with General Sherman.

12-16-1869 - Died on Dec. 11th, Mrs. Clara E. wife of James P. Hall. Sister and wife. Christian for 23 years.

12-16-1869 - Died Dec. 13th, Henry B. infant son of Dr. D. N. Kinsman.

1-13-1870 - Died Dec. 15, 1869 at residence of Mrs. Jonas Hite in Pleasant Twp., Silas W. Hite in the 23rd year of his age.

1-13-1870 - Died in this city January 4th 1870, Maggie Skillman aged 19 years 4 months and 4 days.

1-20-1870 - Died at the residence of her parents in Amanda Twp., Essie Witt Murphy infant daughter of Benjamin and Hannah Murphy aged 2 yrs. 4 mos. and 28 ds.

1-20-1870 - Died on 10th inst., Mr. Wm. Jenkins Sr. of Pleasant Twp. at the advanced age if 90 years 1 month and 6 days. Faithfully served his country in the War of 1812. Resident of Pleasant Twp. for 53 years.

2-24-1870 - Died in Pleasant Twp. on 31st ult., Mrs. Eve Spangler wife of Jacob Spangler in the 53d year of her age.

3-3-1870 - Died near Pleasantville Feb. 25, 1870, Elmore Levering infant son of Christian and Sallie B. Levering. Gone to join his brother Frankie in the happy home above.

3-10-1870 - Died Amanda Twp. on Feb. 24th, 1870, John H. Young, Esq. aged 49 years 9 months and 6 days.

3-10-1870 - Died a little son of Mr. William Vorys, living on Broadway, Monday eve., Johnnie aged about 4 years.

4-7-1870 - Died on March 28, Charles D. Dunbar in the 52d year of his age. Husband and father.

4-21-1870 - Obituary, John Odel Woolard died near Pleasantville aged 16 years 1 month and 15 days. He was the only remaining member of a large family of six children. His father has also followed him to the spiritual world leaving only a mother to mourn her great loss. Funeral New Salem.

4-28-1870 - Died at the residence of her son Samuel Showley in Fulton Co., Indiana on Mon. eve., April 10, 1870, Ursilla Showley aged 76 yrs. 3 mos. The deceased was born in Canton Basel in Switzerland in 1794 and in 1802 came to the United States with her parents and settled in Liberty Twp., Fairfield Co., Ohio. She married Jacob Showley on 7th April 1814 with whom she lived upwards to half a century. Buried Wed. April 20, 1870.

4-28-1870 - Died on 20th inst., at the residence of his son-in-law, Mr. Henry Welker, Lawrence Strayer of Berne Twp., aged 82 years.

429

Persons 50 years of age and over. The following information was taken from Volume I, Death Records. Some of the names were recorded twice, and as the information differed, they are also recorded twice on these pages.

Name	Death Date & Age	Marital Status	Place of Death	Place of Birth
CREMMER, Otto	9-17-1867 55-5-12	mar.	Lancaster	Hanover, Germany
FRIEDLEY, John	8-2-1867 74y 7d	wid.	Liberty twp.	Switzerland
	Parents: John & Anna Maria Friedley			
JOSEPH, Benjamin	8-26-1867 68-7-2	mar.	Liberty twp.	Virginia
	Parents: John & Catharine Joseph			
SCHAUB, Anna	9-2-1867 77y	mar.	Liberty	Switzerland
	Father: Daniel LEONARD			
FRIEDLEY, John	8-2-1867 77-7-8	wid.	Liberty	Germany
SCHAUB, Anna	8-31-1867 77y	wid.	Liberty	Germany
FEATHERBY, Old Mr.	9-23-1867 75y	---	Lancaster	Fairfield Co.
GRIFFITH, James	7-30-1867 79-1-6	wid	Amanda twp.	----------
POTTS, Rachel	8-2-1867 61y 11m	mar.	Amanda twp.	----------
MORLOCK, Jacob	5-17-1867 72y	mar.	Lancaster	Germany
KRAEMER, O. W.	9-17-1867 55y	---	Lancaster	Goettingen, Germany
TEAGARDIN, Elizabeth	2-4-1867 66-1-27	mar.	Pickaway County	----------
GRUE, Mary	3-10-1867 51-3-9	single	Fairfield County	----------
SCHIRM, Margaret	4-28-1867 83-8-8	mar.	Fairfield County	----------
PARKER, Mary	11-19-1867 50y	single	Amanda twp.	Wigtownshire, Scotland
LONG, Wesley	12-3-1867 55-3-30	mar.	Amanda twp.	Amanda twp.
REA, Catharine	12-6-1867 61y	mar.	Baltimore, Ohio	Somerset Co., Pennsylvania
GRIFFITH, Martha	9-2-1867 68y 4	single	Richland twp.	York Co. Pennsylvania
CISCO, Ann	12-26-1867 50-6-22	wid.	Violet twp.	Lithopolis
MOUTZ, Peter	10-30-1867 55y	mar.	Lancaster	Baden, Germany
McGEE, Martha	11-21-1867 72y 6m	mar.	Circleville	Pennsylvania
ARNEY, Mary	11-23-1867 65y	mar.	Lancaster	Prussia
NICHOLS, John	12-20-1867 85y	mar.	Pleasant	---------

430

RICHARDS, William	10-4-1867	mar.	Lancaster	Wales
	68-2-14			
LONG, Frederick	12-28-1867	wid.	Lancaster	Pennsylvania
	64-11-24			
RICHARDS, Wm.	10-5-1867	mar.	Lancaster	Wales
	68-2-4			
BEERY, Samuel	11-15-1867	mar.	Lancaster	Rockingham Co.,
	67-9-22			Virginia
ARNEY, Joanna M.	11-22-1867	mar.	Lancaster	Prussia
	61-11-8			
ROCKEY, Anna B.	10-20-1867	mar.	Amanda	Pennsylvania
	71-1-7			
GEISER, Joseph	12-7-1867	wid.	Lancaster	Germany
	77y 3m			
LANG, Fredeeic	12-25-1867	mar.	Lancaster	Germany
	64-11-24			
HELLER, Catharine	11-26-1867	wid.	Bloom twp.	----------
	55y			
FERRIER, John	8-8-1867	mar._	W. Rushville	----------
	63-7-5			
NICHOLS, John	12-19-1867	wid.	Lancaster	Maryland
	84-4-11			
REED, Elizabeth	1-5-1868	mar.	Rushville	Virginia
	75-3-15			
GIRSY, Elizabeth	10-6-1867	wid.	Basil,	Switzerland
	80-8-17		Liberty twp.	
LEFEVER, William	12-8-1867	mar.1	Liberty twp.	Chester Co.
	55-9-25	Parents: Jacob & Rebecca Lefever		Penna.
BROWN, Wm. G's	8-22-1867	wid.	Lancaster	---------
mother-in-law	--------			
ALT, Frederick	2-21-1868	wid.	Licking Co.	---------
	73-3-28	Parents: Joseph and Anna Alt		
WEAVER, Jacob	3-7-1868	mar.	Liberty twp.	---------
	64-11-28			
HALL, James	2-5-1868	mar.	Bremen	Maryland
	64-11-28			
DICKSON, David	3-11-1868	wid.	Perry Co.	Fayette Co.
	81-6-9			Pennsylvania
DUSTMAN, Salome	1-21-1868	mar._	Clear	Lancaster Co.
	83-2-3	Father: Peter STERN		Pennsylvania
REY, Catharien	12-6-1868	mar.	Baltimore	Pennsylvania
	61-7-4			
HAMPSON, Leah	2-21-1868	wid.	Pleasant-	Maryland
	87-10-24		ville.	
HALL, James	2-5-1868	mar.	Rush Creek	Maryland
	77y		twp.	
RHODES	1-12-1868	mar.	Lancaster	Maryland
	72-10-1			
KNIERIEHMEN, Jacob	1-31-1868	wid.	Hocking twp.	Germany
	86y			
BECK, Martin	3-2-1868	mar.	Greenfield	Germany
	60y 1m		twp.	

431

WORK, Ann	1-30-1868 76-11-25	wid.	Hocking	Virginia
NEWMAN, Lucy	2-13-1868 78y 3m	wid.	Lancaster	Oswego, New York
CI'LUMBER, Wm. M.	4-8-1868 73y 2m	---	Lancaster	Virginia
CULLUMBER, Catharine	4-9-1868 69-11-2	---	Lancaster	Virginia
HITCHCOCK, Sarah	1-12-1868 74-6-6	wid.	Amanda twp.	--------
DODD, Mary	3-22-1868 55-10-27	single	Madison twp.	Sussex Co., Delaware
HOFER, Jacob	5-9-1868 64-7-13	mar...	Pleasant twp.	Europe
PUGH, John H.	3-16-1868 65y	mar.	Walnut twp.	-------
ROADS, Elizabeth	7-14-1868 68y	wid.	Quincy, Illinois	Pennsylvania
HOOD, Susannah	7-15-1868 95-4-12	wid	Lancaster	Frederick, Maryland
SHELLENBARGER, Jonas	7-18-1868 74y 8m	mar.	Fairfield County	Lancaster Co., Pennsylvania
LEATHERS, Magdalene	4-13-1868 67-1-15	wid.	Clear Creek Twp.	Center Co. P nnsylvania
MYERS, Matilda	8-10-1868 55y	mar.	Pickaway County	--------
WHITE, James	9-26-1868 69-3-16	mar..	Lancaster	Philadelphia Pennsylvania
BASHORE, David	8-22-1868 54-1-7	mar.	Lancaster	Pennsylvania
BURMAN, Anna Mary	9-28-1868 87-3-1	mar..	Greenfield twp.	Pennsylvania
PIERCE, Lewis	5-13-1868 68y	mar.	Lancaster	----------
GIFFORD, Effie	7-13-1868 55y	mar.	Lancaster	----------
WHITEHOUSE, Hannah	8-1-1868 77y	wid.	Fairfield County	----------
' 'EING, Margaret E.	9-17-1868 56-3-16	mar.	Pleasant twp	----------
DISINGER, Catharine	7-13-1868 94-7-26	mar.	Amanda twp.	Virginia
CARPENTER, Wm.	7-25-1868 57-11-13	mar.	Lancaster	----------
KEMP, Henry	8-1-1868 90-9-3	mar.	Fairfield County	Virginia
WEAVER, Elizabeth	7-28-1868 73y 11m	wid.	Liberty twp.	----------
LEONER, Michael	9-20-1868 68-8-16	wid.	Lancaster	Virginia
BROWN, David	11-28-1868 90-8-2-	mar.	Pleasant twp.	Miflin Co., Pennsylvania

432

GRANT, Jesse	12-24-1868 84y	mar.	Oakland	Virginia
SMITH, Michael	10-9-1868 74y	mar.	Berne	Germany
POWERS, Mrs.	12-3-1868 70y	wid.	Lancaster	--------
SHUPE, Daniel	10-3-1868 68-2-1	mar.	Clearcreek twp.	Maryland
FOSNAUGHT, Christian	11-14-1868 82-5-29	mar.	Clearcreek twp.	Maryland
STOUT, Benjamin	8-10-1868 64-4-9	mar.	Stoutsville	Berks Co. Pennsylvania
PETERS, Elizabeth	8-18-1868 83--7-13	wid.	Clearcreek twp.	Lancaster Co., Pennsylvania.
BAUGHMAN, Isaac	9-24-1868 68y	mar.	Baltimore	-------
CULLUMBER, Wm.	4-7-1868 74y	mar.	Greenfield	-------
CULLUMBER, Mrs. Wm.	4-8-1868 71y	mar.	Greenfield	-------
McKEE, Dennis	5-3-1868 65y	lid.	Lancaster	Ireland

FAIRFIELD COUNTY, OHIO - DIVORCES 1833-1842

The following records are recorded in "Supreme Court Record 3" which may be found in the Common Pleas Court (Clerk of Courts Office). Pages on which record may be found are given in parenthesis.

Nov, 1833 - Charlotte LOOKER vs. Joseph LOOKER. Divorce. Filed 7-16-1833. Charlotte in her petition states that there were six children. Joseph in his answer states seven children, that he owned land in Pickaway Co., Ohio, with his statement being signed in Franklin Co. (1)

Nov. 1833 - Thomas PATTON vs Sally PATTON. Divorce. Filed 8-1-1832. Married about four years ago, Sally's maiden name was McCarhen. (7)

Nov. 1833 - Amelia CARPENTER vs. Samuel CARPENTER. Divorce. Filed 7-22-1833. Amelia has been a resident of the county for ten years. (9)

Nov. 1833 - Magdalena BURNSIDES vs. Nicholas BURNSIDES. Divorce. Filed 8-9-1833. Married in January 1811. (11)

Nov. 1833 - Mary Ann MORROW vs. Benjamin MORROW. Divorce. Filed 3-4-1833. Married 7-17-1828 in Fairfield Co., Mary Ann's maiden name was Stadt. Issue: John Morrow near four years of age. (15)

Nov. 1833 - Barbara PHILLIPS vs. Jonas PHILLIPS. Divorce. Filed 7-12-1832. Married 4-20-1818. (18)

Nov. 1834 - Jacob PLIEFFER (or PHEFFER) vs. Mary PLIEFFER (or PHEFFER). Divorce. Married in 1801 in Pittsburg, Pennsylvania. Mary's maiden name was Ellinger. Moved to Ohio in 1806. (21)

Nov. 1834 - Sarah ASHER vs. John ASHER. Divorce. Filed 9-3-1834. Married 1-1-1827. John of Muskingum County. (23)

Nov. 1835 - George C. BEERY vs. Susan BEERY. Divorce. Filed 7-10-1835. Married on 2-22-1830 in Pickaway County, Ohio. (32)

Nov. 1835 - John HOUDESEL vs. Ann HOUDESEL. Divorce. Filed 3-7-1835. John a resident of Fairfield County. Married 11-18-1829 in Logan County. Ann's maiden name was Franciscoe. They resided in Logan County for three years. (35)

Nov. 1835 - Mary FETTERLY vs. Jacob FETTERLY. Divorce. Filed 8-17-1835. Married in Feb. 1832. Mary's maiden name was Walker. (39)

Nov. 1835 - Elizabeth THOMPSON vs. Samuel THOMPSON. Divorce. Marriage date not given. Lived in Pickaway and Fairfield Counties. Children, not named. Elizabeth daughter of John Morehart. (42)

Nov. 1837 - Elizabeth BUCKINGHAM vs. Ellick W. BUCKINGHAM. Divorce. Filed 4-7-1837. Married more than twenty years. Seven children. Lived last two or three years in Violet Township. (44)

Nov. 1837 - Jonas BAUGHMAN vs. Dersha Ann BAUGHMAN. Divorce. Filed 2-6-1837 Married June 1829 in Northampton County, Pennsylvania. Dersha Ann's maiden name was Cramer. Lived Northampton for fifteen months then emigrated to Pleasant Twp., Fairfield Co. (49)

Nov. 1838 - Mary FITCH vs. John FITCH. Divorce. Filed 9-7-1837. Married May 1824. (53)

Nov. 1838 - Juliann MILLER vs. John MILLER. Divorce. Filed 8-20-1838. Married 1-12-1834 in Frederick County, Virginia. Juliann lived in Frederick Co. until December 1835 when she moved with her mother to Fairfield Co. and has resided in this county with the exception of eight months in Hocking Co., Ohio. John Miller went to Millerstown, Pennsylvania. Children (mentioned but not named). (55)

Nov. 1838 - Susan WOLF vs Andrew WOLF. Divorce. Filed 8-4-1838. Married about thirty years ago in Washington Co., Pa. Nine children, seven living,with five children living with petitioner and three of these being minors. Henry Eversole son-in-law of Andrew Wolf. (60)

Nov. 1838 - Julian LAKEN vs. Lewis S. LAKEN. Divorce. Filed 7-3-1838. Married 6-10-1834 Fairfield Co. Julian states that in March last Lewis married Clarissa Fitzgerald in Madison Co., Ohio and that they are now living in Pickaway Co., Ohio. Lewis S. Laken is son of Daniel Laken. (64)

Nov. 1839 - Mary BOWERS vs. Volentine BOWERS. Divorce. Filed 6-3-1839. Married twenty years ago. Mary's maiden name being Raver. Volentine supposedly has since married Lizza or Elizabeth Kistler. (69)

Nov. 1839 - Sarah WHITE vs. Josiah WHITE. Divorce. Filed 5-11-1839. Married in Oct. 1833 in Fairfield Co. Lived at Chillicothe until 2-11-1836. Two children. (73)

Nov. 1839 - Elizabeth JOHNSON vs. John JOHNSON. Divorce. Filed 9-9-1839. Married thirteen years ago. (75)

Nov. 1839 - Elizabeth MILLER vs. John MILLER. Divorce. Filed 7-19-1838. Married 10-14-1832. One child. Elizabeth's father has died since her marriage by which certain real estate descended to her. (77)

Nov. 1839 - Jacob BOWSER vs. Sally BOWSER. Divorce. Filed 7-23-1839. Married 2-12-1832. Sally's maiden name was Cleak. (80)

Nov. 1839 - Sophia MONINGER vs. Mahlon MONINGER. Divorce. Filed 9-9-1839. Sophia's maiden name was Nigh. Married in Feb. 1831. Children. (82)

Nov. 1839 - Sarah OSFORD vs. Richard OSFORD. Divorce. Filed 6-26-1839. Married in May 1835 in Franklin Co., Ohio. One child, Edward aged 3 yrs. 4 mos. (84)

435

Nov. 1839 - Ann CUNNINGHAM vs. John CUNNINGHAM. Divorce. Filed 5-10-1839.
Married in Dec. 1830. Lived Fairfield Co., then Columbus, then Chillicothe
until 1837 when Ann returned to relatives in Fairfield Co. (88)

Nov. 1839 - Sarah FAUSNAUGHT vs. Windle FAUSNAUGHT. Divorce. Filed 8-11-1839.
Married 1-8-1833. Two surviving children, Andrew aged five years last April
and James aged three years last June. (91)

Nov. 1839 - Maria BENNET vs. Samuel S. BENNET. Divorce. Filed 7-21-1838.
Maria a native of Fairfield Co., her maiden name being Courtright. Married in
1833 in Pickaway Co., Ohio and lived at Darbysville, Pickaway Co. until 1834.
One child. (94)

Nov. 1839 - Jacob MEEKS vs. Abigale MEEKS. Divorce. Filed 1-29-1838.
Married 12-20-1829, Abigale's maiden name being Reynolds. (98)

Nov. 1840 - Susannah CRAWFORD vs. James CRAWFORD. Divorce. Filed 8-13-1840.
Married 5-31-1836. On 10 June 1837 James left for Pennsylvania to get money
from his father and never returned; Susannah heard he was living in Logansport,
Indiana. One child, Margaret Jane born May 4, 1837. (104)

Nov. 1840 - James McCRORY vs. Mary Ann McCRORY. Divorce. Filed 9-10-1840.
Married 2-26-1835. (107)

Nov. 1841 - Philip YOUNG vs. Susan YOUNG. Divorce. Filed 7-26-1841.
Married in fall of 1838. (110)

Nov. 1841 - Mary Elizabeth LOMAN vs. Joseph LOMAN. Divorce. Filed 7-26-1841.
Married in 1826 at Logan, Hocking Co., Ohio. (112)

Nov. 1841 - Maria MORRIS vs. Isaac MORRIS. Divorde. Filed 9-10-1841.
Married in 1820 in York Co. Pa. Two minor children, Carolina and Ellen
Morrison. Maria received land from the estate of her father and mother, both
deceased. (115)

Nov. 1842 - Charlotte ALLEN vs. Thomas C. ALLEN. Divorce. Filed 9-10-1842.
Married in Feb. 1841. Charlotte states that Thomas had a wife at the time of
their marriage, who he had married in 1828 in Dauphin Co., Pennsylvania. (119)

Nov. 1842 - Mary Ann CLUTTER vs. Benjamin CLUTTER. Divorce. Filed 9-10-1842.
Mary Ann's maiden name was Sidenn. (122)

FAIRFIELD COUNTY, OHIO - WILL ABSTRACTS 1812-1815

The following abstracts were taken from "Will Book 2" located under the juris-
diction of the Probate Court in the Hall of Justice (beside the court house)
at Lancaster. Number of page on which will may be found in original record
is given in parenthesis.

THOMPSON, William - dated 10-31-1811; recorded 1-27-1812. Wife, Hannah. Sons:
William, John, Robert and Samuel. Daughters: Sarah Neeley, Rachel Neeley,
Elizabeth and Jane. Mentions money coming from Pennsylvania. Conveys 3 acres
land to Rush Creek Congregation on which meeting house stands. Executors: wife,
Hannah and brother-in-law, John Karr. Signed: William (his mark) Thompson.
Witnesses: David Neeley and James Neeley. (1)

REYNOLDS, Thomas - dated 9-14-1810; recorded 5-25-1812. Sons: Benjamin, Reynolds,
Deckison Reynolds and Thomas Reynolds; Thomas not of age. Mentions personal
property belonging to testator in the state of Delaware. Executors: sons, Benjamin
and Deckison. Signed: Thomas Reynolds. Witnesses: John Leeliger, Elisabat
Leeliger and Sam'l Carpenter. (2)

WILLIAMSON, Peter Jr. of Hocking twp. - Verbal Will - deposititio made by witnesses 1-25-1812; recorded 1-27-1812. Wife, Kesiah. Two eldest sons, Abraham
and William. Two oldest girls: Sidney and Polly. Other children mentioned but
not named. Witnesses: Peter Williamson Sr. and Ann Cross. (3)

BEERY, Nicholas - dated 5-15-1811; recorded 5-28-1812. Wife, Mary. Sons: Joseph
Beery, Jacob Beery and Christian Beery. Daughter, Rebecca. Mentions land owned
by testator on which Abraham Beery Sr. now lives. Executors: John Beery and William
Trimble. Signed: Nicholas Beery (German signature). Witnesses: George Hensel
and Nicholas Tipple. (5)

STRODE, Margaret, a widow - dated 12-7-1811; recorded 1-28-1812. She held mortgage deed of Isaac Woodruff, a black man for place on Main Street in Lancaster
where said Isaac resides and that mortgage is to be released and Isaac is to have
land. To Betsy Strode wife of son, Edward Strode. To Nancy Strode natural daughter of son, Edward, who she brought up and educated. Daughter, Polly Evans who
resides with her husband near Urbana. William Strode natural son of son, William,
he not of age and his uncle, Edward Strode to serve as his guardian. Executor,
Edward Strode. Signed: Margaret (her mark) Strode. Witnesses: George Hood,
and Charles R. Sherman. (6)

BUBB, John Christian - dated 9-11-1812; recorded 10-10-1812. Two grandsons,
George Bubb and Jacob Bubb being two eldest sons of my son, Abraham Bubb, to
have Bible. Sons: Abraham, Frederick, Henry and Adam. Daughter, Elizabeth, dec'd,
late wife of John Bare. Executors: sons, Abraham and Frederick. Signed:
J. Christian (his mark) Bubb. Witnesses: Adam Weaver and John Feemen. (11)

WEAVER, Leonard - dated 5-9-1812; recorded 10-10-1812. Wife, mentioned but not
named. Mentions eight children but only names son, Jacob who is to have Large
Dutch House Bible and daughter Mary. Mentions that he has sold land to son,
Jacob in Virginia. Executors: John Hampson and son, Jacob Weaver. Signed:
Leonard (his mark) Weaver. Witnesses: John Hampson, Faney (her mark) Miers and
George Goss. (12)

437

BIXLER, Christian - dated 11-5-1812; recorded 2-2-1813. Wife, Elizabeth.
Mentions owning land in Licking Co., Ohio. Executor: Abraham Miller who is
to serve as guardian of sons, Abraham and Joseph. Mentions other children, but
does not name. Signed: Christian (his mark) Bixler. Witnesses: Joseph Heestend,
Samuel Heestend, Elizabeth (her mark) Young. (13)

KEITH, Edmon - dated 3-29-1813; recorded 5-31-1813. Wife, Agness Keith. Oldest
brother, William Keith. Youngest brother, Zachariah Keith. Oldest sister, Hannah
Keith, Second sister, Margret Keith. Third sister, Elizabeth Keith. Fourth sister,
Jane Keith. Executors: wife, Agness Keith and Daniel Snider. Signed: Edmon Keith.
Witnesses: Mathias (his mark) Renebold, Henry Foster and Samuel Henderson. (13)

BOUSEY, Ludwick of Pleasant twp. - dated 2-24-1812; recorded 9-27-1813. Wife,
Mary Bousey. To Jacob Macland and his heirs, 100 acres land purehased from Samuel
Kreitzer. To Theopheles Mackland, 150 acres of land. That Theopheles Macland
is to support John Bousey son of Christian Bousey, during said John's natural
life. To Peter Macland the survey made to testator's sister's son, William Jones
in Section 26, Township 15, Range 18, being 20 acres. To Michael Brichman who
now lives with testator and who testator raised from a child SW¼ Section 4,
Township 15, Range 16 entered in testator's name on 3-26-1811 at the Chillicothe
land office. Mentions Molly Anderson and Mary Foster, daughters of testator's
wife, Mary Bousey. Mentions Christian Bousey's heirs but does not name. Sisters:
Mary Christiana Hines, Charlotta Thompson, Williamena Fry and Mary Elizabeth Prewe.
Executors: wife, Mary and Frederick Harman. Signed: Lucwick Bousey (German signature). Witnesses: Henry Hockman, John Flick and Thomas Cissna. (15)

WELLS, James - dated 1-6-1814; recorded 2-7-1814. Sons, James and John. Mentions
two youngest daughters, but does not name. Nephew, Thomas Wells. Executors:
George Tong and Samuel Tolman. Signed: James Wells. Witnesses: George Wells and
James Wilson. Codicil (same date) mentios oldest children: Mary McCall, Sally
Tolman, Rachel Wilson and Honor Reaves who have previously had their portions.
Witnesses (same). (18)

REDENHOUR, John - dated 12-29-1813; recorded 2-7-1814. Wife, Christeana. Sons:
John, Michael, Henry, George and Peter; son, George to have saw mill in SE¼
Section 21, Township 13, Range 20. Daughters: Elizabeth, Caty, Christianna, Mary,
Sarah, Easter and Susanna. Executors: wife, Christeanna and Moses Sowers. Signed:
John (his R mark) Redenhour. Witnesses: Moses Sowers and Eli Barker. (19)

LANE, Wilkeson of Bloom twp. - dated 11-29-1813; recorded 2-7-1814. Wife, Jane.
Only son, John. Daughters: Elizabeth and Mary Rabecca. Grandsons, James Cole
and Elisha Cole. Grandson and grand-daughter, Wilkeson and Nancy Barr, son and
daughter of Rachel Barr. Executors: sons-in-law, Horatio Clark and James Kelly.
Signed: Wilkeson (his mark) Lane. Witnesses: John Serl, Robeson Fletcher and
Jeremiah Williams. (20)

WEAVER, Jacob of Liberty twp. - dated 8-21-1813; recorded 2-7-1814. Wife, Mary
Weaver. Heirs: Jacob, John, Christian and Mary Weaver. Executor, Samuel
Hiestend. Signed: Jacob Weaver (German signature). Witnesses: Joseph Heistend
and Jacob Dooney. (21)

RENGLESPAUGH, Christian - dated 1-11-1814; recorded 2-8-1814. Sons: Christian and Abraham; Abraham is youngest son and not of age. Daughters: Barbara; Susanna Develer; and Easter Hennings. Signed: Christian (his mark) Renglespaugh. Witnesses: Adam Weaver and Elizabeth (mark) Pitcher. (22)

RUBLE, George - dated 1-15-1812; recorded 9-27-1813. Sons: John Ruble; Jesse Ruble's Heirs (not named); George Ruble. Daughter, Jane Strobredge. Executor, Marshell Pugh Sr. Signed: George Ruble. Witnesses: Daniel Rees, Wm Crook and John Copland. (23)

HUNTER, Robert - 1-19-1814; recorded 5-31-1814. Wife, Jane. Sons: David, Robert, James and William. Daughter, Mary. (note: no executor named). Signed: Robert Hunter. Witnesses: John Michel and Samuel Michel. (23)

IERICH, Jacob - dated 12-26-1813; recorded 9-7-1814. Wife, Catharina. Five children: son, George Ierich, son, Jacob Ierich; daughter, Beatha Margarete wife of Peter Glick; daughter, Eve; daughter, Magdaline. Executors: wife, Catherina; David Rees and Thomas Frecker. Signed: Jacob (his mark) Ierich. Witnesses: Adam Weaver and Michal Hensel. (24)

JULIAN, Stephen - dated 9-25-1813; recorded 5-30-1814. Wife, Azenah Julian. Children: John, Alexandrew, Jesse, Isaac, Susannah, Mariah, Sarah and one child that wife is now pregnant with. Witnesses: James Reat Jr., John Jackson and Hugh Roat Jr. Executors: wife, Azenah and John Augustus. (26)

SALATHE, John Adam - dated 4-14-1812; recorded 9-7-1814. Wife, mentioned but not named. Eight children, mentioned but only ones named are oldest son, Frederick and youngest son, John Jacob who is not of age. Mentions also that youngest daughter is not of age. No executor named. Signed: John Adam Salatha. Witnesses: Samuel Carlenter and Samuel Hiestand. (27)

COUPLAND, Margret - dated (not given); recorded 5-30-1814. Son, William Coupland, also to serve as executor. Mentions money coming from Pennsylvania. Signed: Margret (her mark) Coupland. Witnesses: Jacob Dittoe and Joseph Wigdon. (29)

BOWSER, Jacob - dated 3-30-1814; recorded 5-30-1814. Wife, Freena. Heirs: Jacob, John, Frederick, Barbara and Sally. Mentions that son, Frederick is not of age. Executors: Andrew Wagner and Joseph Hiestand. Signed: Jacob (his mark) Bowser. Witnesses: John Wintermote and Daniel Faell. (30)

PIERSE, Stephen - dated 4-23-1814; recorded 5-30-1814. Brothers: James Pierse and William Pierse. Signed: Stephen Pierse. Witnesses: Prescella Pierse and James Gobin. (31)

WILSON, Nathaniel Sr. - dated 3-4-1814; recorded 5-30-1814. Wife, Elizabeth. Sons: Robert Wilson; Nathaniel Wilson Jr.; Samuel Wilson; William Wilson; James Wilson, dec'd, his heirs--John Wilson and two daughters (not named). Daughters: eldest daughter, Sarah Crocket--her son, Nathaniel Crocket; Polly Lattimore. Grandsons: John and Nathaniel Lattimore; Josiah Wilson son of Samuel Wilson; Nathaniel Wilson son of William Wilson. Mentions that three head stones are to be placed on graves of testators three sons buried in the Lancaster burying ground. Executors: William Wilson and William Trimble. Signed: Nathaniel Wilson. Witnesses: Mich'l Garaghty and William King. (32)

BIBLER, Francis - dated 12-14-1813; recorded 2-7-1814. Wife, mentioned but not named. Sons: Joseph, John, Abraham and Jacob. Daughters: Barbara, Mary, Elizabeth, Anna and Catharine; Catherine not of age. Executors: son, John Bibler and Christian Cagey. Signed: Francis (his mark) Bebler. Witnesses: Joseph Hiestand and Paul Hively. (34)

DARST, Paul - dated 11-15-1814; recorded 1-23-1815. Wife, Nancy. Mentions cabin and land in Hubersburgh, Licking Co., Ohio being 80 acres. Executors: wife, Nancy and Jacob Schleich. Signed: Paul (his mark) Darst. Witnesses: John Smith, Andrew Proudfoot and Jacob Schleich. (35)

CRAWFORD, William - dated 10-9-1810; recorded 1-23-1815. Sons: James, Samuel, Robert and John: the last two named are not of age. Daughters: Mary, Anney and Margret. Son-in-law, Andrew Stull. Mentions Thomas son of daughter Mary, his share to be held in trust by John Goldthread. Executor: son-in-law, John Goldthrait. Signed: William Crawford. Witnesses: James Holmes, Eli Whitaker, and Samuel Stroud. (35)

BLACK, John - dated 8-29-1814; recorded 1-23-1815. Wife, Sarah. Son, James Black. Three daughters: Mary, Sally and Lydy. Executors: Robert Black and Jesse Pew. Signed: John (his mark) Black. Witnesses: John Hampson and Valentine Cup. (37)

REESE, John - dated 3-27-1814; recorded 10-17-1814. Wife, Abena. Daughters: Lydia, Elizabeth, Ruth, Shelome, Mary, Albena, Rachel and Hannah. Executors: wife, Albena Rees and daughter, Rachel Merchant. Signed: John Rees. Witnesses: George Hardesty, Peter Williamson and William Regby. (38)

RAIRTON, Michael Sr. of Amanda twp. - dated 10-16-1814; recorded 1-24-1815. Wife, Nancy. Son, Michael. Daughter, Margret. Mentions that four youngest children are not of age, but does not name. Executors: wife, Nancy and son, Michael. Signed: Michael (his mark) Rairiton. Witnesses: Esa England, John McFerson and Isaac England. (38)

RITHELBACH, Johannes - dated 11-1-1809; recorded 1-16-1810; in German. Wife, Dorothea. Son-in-law, Rev. Biry. Sons: Fridrich; Andre, not of age, Rev Biry to be his guardian; Jacob, not of age, to live with Rev. Biry. Daughter, Maria Biry. Executors: wife, Dorothea and son-in-law, Rev. Biry. Witnesses: Johannes Weli and Heinrich Stemen. (39)

LARY, Margretha - dated 8-9-1810; recorded 11-4-1811; in German. Brother, Friedrich Lary. Rest of estate to Johannes Gebrung Sr. with him to pay to building fund when they build a new church. Witnesses: Friedrich Horn, Johannes Gehrung. (40)

EINSEL, Heinrich of Bern twp. - dated 2-22-1814; recorded 1-23-1815; in German. Wife, Barbara. Youngest son, Ludwig Einsel, not of age, he being born Oct. 22, 1813. Mentions other children but does not name. Executors: Josef Leib and Ludwig Fritz. Witnesses: George Swarts, Heinrich Bauman, Heinrich Steinbrink. (41)

BRETZ, Johannes of Bern township - dated 2-6-1808; recorded 10-6-1812; in German. Wife, Christina. Sons: Philip; Valentine; Johannes; Anthony, oldest son; Jacob; Conras; Martin; Heinrich. Daughters: Margret Millerin; Catarina Furmann, Elizabeth Benter, Magtalena Hestin, Executors: sons, Philip and Valentine Bretz. Witnesses: Lewis Seitz, Jacob Meyers, Johannes Bretz Jr. (42)

BOLLENBACH, Nichlaus - dated 3-5-1811; recorded 5-31-1813; in German. Sons, Abraham and Johannes, with Abraham to have 80 acres which includes home place. Wife, Anna Maria. Daughters: Katrina and Magareta still in Pennsylvania; Elizabeth and Gertraud. Mentions that his book, "The True Christendom" is to go to Peter Rauch. Executors: wife, Anna Maria and son-in-law, Jacob Rauch. Witnesses: Daniel Moyer and Jacob Brumback. (44)

STOTTS, John of Clear Creek twp. - dated 4-22-1815; recorded 5-17-1815. Wife, Margret. Sons: Abraham, eldest son; Arthur; Uria; Hiram. Daughters: Polly wife of Frederic Andrake, eldest daughter; Betsey, not married; Margaret, not married; Maria, not married; Rebecca, not married. Executors: wife, Margaret and son, Abraham. Signed: John (his mark) Stotts. Witnesses: John Leist, Martin Smith, and Peter Swineford. (47)

CLEINER, Charles F. - verbal will made 4-25-1815 before George Needles and Masse Clyner Sr.; recorded 11-3-1815 (note: surname is given as both Cleiner and Clyner.) Wife, Nancy, now pregnant. Sons: John, Masse, Francis and Charles. Daughters: Susanna Nieleson, Nancy Clyner and Anna. Mentions Mary Johnston and also Sally; they may be daughters, but does not specifically name them as such. Mentions property coming from Allegeny County, Maryland. Witnesses: (named above). (48)

HODGE, John of Reading township - dated 7-8-1815; recorded 10-2-1815. Wife, Elizabeth, also to serve as sole executrix. Children: Charity Garrison, dec'd, her children not named; John Hodge, dec'd, his children not named; Catherine Angle; Elizabeth Stiff; Joseph Hodge; Elenor Wolf; Isaac Hodge; Mary Hodge; Sarah Hodge; and Levi Hodge. Signed: John Hodge. Witnesses: Daniel Lydy, John Lydy and Roswell Mills. (49)

HEDGES, Jesse - dated 7-1-1815; recorded 10-2-1815. Wife, Rachel, to serve as sole executrix. Mentions, Elizabeth King "now living with me". Daughters: Alse and Rebecca Hedges, not of age. Sons: Joshua, Isaac, Jesse, Abraham and Silas, not all of age. Signed: Jesse Hedges. Witnesses: Jacob Benton, Joseph Mergan and Charles (his mark) Lemar. (51)

KEATH, Nancy - dated (no month and day given) 1815; recorded 10-2-1815. Mother, mentioned but not named. Brothers: James Henderson; John Henderson; Samuel Henderson; Joseph Henderson, youngest brother. Sisters: Sarah Keith, Mary Herron and Matty Henderson. Niece, Nancy Heron. Executors: William Heath and Matty Henderson. Signed: Nancy Keith. Witnesses: Henry Boyer and Mathias Renebolt. (53)

FOSTER (FORSTER), William, Preacher of Thorn township (German signature) - dated 4-5-1815; recorded 10-2-1815. Wife, Magdelena. Sons: William, Andrew, Daniel, John, Henry, Samuel, George, Benjamin and Christian. Daughters: Mary, Catherine (German signature). Witnesses: Henry Bowman and Daniel Snider. (53)

CHAMBERS, Alexander Sr. - dated 8-23-1815; recorded 10-4-1815. Wife, Agness. Sons: John, William, James and Alexander. Daughters: Sarah Chambers, to have silver watch; Aby Chambers; Rebecca wife of Jacob Marks; Mary Ann Connell. Executor: John Marks. Signed: Alexander (his mark) Chambers Sr. Witnesses: James McClelland and Andrew Clandenen. (56)

BARR, Andrew - dated 11-27-1815; recorded 12-14-1815. Children: James Barr, William Barr, John Barr, Thomas Barr and Nancy wife of John Owens. Mentions two grandchildren, not named, sons of Thomas Barr. Executors: sons, John Barr and Thomas Barr along with William Hamilton. Signed: Andrew Barr. Witnesses: Wm Hamilton, Martin Smith and Alexander Deniston. (57)

The following records are from Will Book A, page on which record may be found is given in parenthesis. A Court House fire destroyed records prior to 1828.

MILLER, Michael - concerning will made December 1819, but destroyed by court house fire; deposition recorded 9-23-1828. Widow, mentioned but not named. Son, Daniel Miller. Mentions other heirs but does not name. Executors: Robert Burnett and Henry Coil. Witnesses: Leonard Bush Sr., Thomas Turnett now 39 years of age and Abraham Bush now 48 years of age. (1)

MOON, Thomas - dated 10-6-1824; recorded 2-23-1828. Sons: Thomas, Jacob, David and William. Daughters: Christian, Jane now a widow, Margaret Rees. Mentions land in Highland County, Ohio. Executor: son, David Moon. Signed: Thomas Moon. Witnesses: John How and James Crothers. (2) Inventory of Thomas Moon of Green twp. dated 3-2-1828. (4)

BLUE, Michael - dated 2-16-1826; recorded May 1828. Wife, Mary. Sons: John, Michael, Isaac, Daniel, Garret and Uriah. Daughters: Elizabeth wife of William Lees, Mary Campbell, Ann wife of George Lees, and Kiziah Lambert. Grandson, Ephraim Herriot son of daughter Elizabeth Lees. Executors: sons, Garret and Uriah. Signed Michael (mark-M.B.) Blue. Witnesses: Samuel Dew, P. B. Dodridge, Oliver Kile, James Gunning and John Sinsabaugh. (7)

ROTROCK, Daniel - dated 3-18-1828; recorded 10-6-1828. Son, Benjamin Rotrock. Executors: Jacob Rankin and Samuel Allen. Signed: Daniel Rotrock. Witnesses: John Hill, Moz Allen and Susana Lattimer. (12)

YEOMAN, Stephen of Wayne twp. - dated 2-20-1826; recorded 9-19-1829. Wife, Abigail, also to serve as executrix. Signed: Stephen (mark) Yeoman. Witnesses: Aaron Archer and James Adams. (40)

MASSIE, Henry of Jefferson Co., Kentucky - dated 2-6-1830; recorded 3-9-1830 Jefferson Co., Ky. Wife, Helen, also to serve as executrix. Brother, Thomas Massie. Nieces: Constance Massie, Elizabeth Thompson and Sally Hawes. Nephews: Heath Jones Miller of Louisville and Nathaniel Massie of Ohio son of testators deceased brother Nathaniel. Mentions Henry Bullett son of Cuthbert Bullett and Alexander Scott Bullett son of William C. Bullett, relationship is not clearly stated--may be nephews. Mentions interest at Portsmouth, Ohio and other Ohio property. Signed: H. Massie. Witnesses: N. Bullett and Edw. Johnson. (53)

ARMSTRONG, John of Mercer Co., Kentucky - dated August 1830; recorded 11-16-1830 Mercer Co., Ky. Bequeathes estate to brothers, but does not name. Signed: John Armstrong. Witnesses: John J. Allin, Wm. H. McCown and James Armstrong. (55)

CUMERFORD, George - dated 6-10-1830; recorded 6-29-1830. Wife, Lydia, also to serve as Executrix. Children, John, Sarah Ann, Elizabeth, Mary and Lydia Ann Cumerford. Signed: George (mark) Cumerford. Witnesses: Abel Lloyd and Daniel Davis. (67)

DAVIS, Zorababel of Wayne township - Noncupative Will - will made 12-4-1830 at house of Benjamin Davis; deposition given 12-4-1830 by witnesses; recorded 3-16-1831. Sister, Esther Rowe. Witnesses: Benjamin (mark) Davis, John Davis, Jacob Davis, Charles (mark) Stafford and Sarah (mark) Vandevirt. (74)

DAWSON, Ann of Washington - dated 9-19-1831; recorded 3-2-1832. Daughter, Harriett Clayburn Dawson. Sixth daughter, Mariah Louisa Dawson. Mentions other daughters but does not name. Executors: James Henton and Henry Clinton Phelps. Signed: Ann Dawson. Witnesses: Sam'l Loofbourrow and Mary Loofbourrow. (88)

COLEMAN, Ann Christena - dated 4-1-1831; recorded 6-1-1832. Husband, Henry P. Coleman. to have 100 acres land deeded by Cadwalder Wallace and wife Ruth on 12-30-1822 which is part of survey #11,026 which was patented to said Wallace. Signed: Ann Christena (mark) Coleman. Witnesses: Samuel Myers, Daniel Gilmer. and Moza Allen. (91)

EDGE, Obadiah of Campbell County, Virginia - dated 6-20-1826; recorded 12-18-1832. Sons: Elam, Asa, Edward Wels, Obediah, Bacon. Daughters: Elizabeth Edge, Nancy Edge, Betsy Barker. Mentions land on Shugar Creek of Ohio. Executors: Richard Mann and James Curdwell. Signed: Obadiah Edge. Witnesses: James Ausstin, Richard Mann and Samuel Martin. (92)

McCAY, Job - dated 4-26-1830; recorded March 1833. Wife, Ann. Signed: Job McCoy. Witnesses: Joel Rogers and Clary (mark) Newland. (94)

WRIGHT, John - dated 4-1-1833; recorded June 1833. Wife, Ann, also to serve as executrix. Sons: Anthony, Amos and Allen. Daughters: Susannah, Isabella, Margaret and Rachel. Signed: John Wright. Witnesses: Robert Iron and James Crothers. (95)

HOPKINS, Mathew - dated 7-25-1833; recorded 9-7-1833. Wife, Mary, also to serve as executor. Sisters son, Matthew Jamison. In case wife has no heir by testator estate is to go to child of Susan Blackmore reported to belong to testator provided it is proven that child is his. Signed: Matthew Hopkins. Witnesses: Benjamin Henton and Jacob Jamison. (144)

JOHNSON, William - dated 4-29-1833; recorded 9-7-1833. Wife, mentioned but not named. Son, Thomas. Remainder of estate to minor children, not named. Executors: wife and James Crothers. Signed: William (mark) Johnson. Witnesses: Elijah Harbour, John King, Alfred B. Noble, and T. McGarraugh. (146)

McADAMS, Isaac - dated 4-4-1835; recorded 9-29-1835. Wife, mentioned but not named. Heirs, James Lurey(?) of Warren County, Ohio, a boy bound to testator; Nancy wife of John McAdams, a girl testator raised; and William Woodward son of Isaac M. Woodward of Highland County, Ohio. Signed: Isaac McAdams. Witnesses: John Priddy, James Crothers and Evelina (mark) Wright. (155)

OCHELTREE, John - dated 11-14-1833; recorded 10-9-1834. Wife, Elinor, Mentions children but does not name. Signed: John Ocheltree. Witnesses: Alex M. McCoy and Maryann Parker. (156)

WATTS, John of Bedford County, Virginia - dated 8-27-1829; recorded 7-27-1830 Bedford Co., Va. Wife, Betsy. Sons: William W. and Arthur. Daughter, Elizabeth R. wife of Joseph Scott. Mentions John and Sarah, son and daughter of William. Mentions land in Campbell Co., Kentucky and bank stock in Chillicothe, Ohio. Signed: John Watts. Codicil dated 5-2-1830 names Nephew Edward Watts and sons William W. and Arthur as Executors. Witnesses: Wm. Radford, Lerard Alexander and Joel Yancy.   (158)

BRANNON, William - dated 5-4-1834; recorded 7-1-1834. Mother of his children, Perina Bartless. Sons: William, James and Thomas; Thomas to be bound out. Daughter, Elizabeth, to be bound out. Mentions lots in Waterford, Loudon County, Virginia. Executors: Daniel McLean and William Mooney. Signed: William (mark) Brannon. Witnesses: Norman J. Jones, Nancy Boyd and George Boyd.   (162)

CLARK, Isabella - dated 9-8-1832; recorded 10-3-1832. Bequeaths of the children of Juli Ann Hill wife of William Hill. Mentions all real estate she holds by will of James Clark for deceased husband. Executor: Z. W. Hagler. Signed: Isabella(mark) Clark. Witnesses: Robert Robinson and Wm. Stockdale.   (166)

HUKLE, Richard of Wayne township - dated 8-2-1834; recorded 6-27-1836. Wife, Letticia. Children: Hiram Hukill, David Hukill, Niomi Resler (or Kesler), Polly Landon, Stephen Hukill, Elsy Hukill, Noah Hukill, Seth Hukill and Nancy Hukill. Grandson, Samuel Hukill son of Polly Landon late Hukill. Mentions that Nathan and Zebulon Hukill are to be barred from any part of estate. Executor: friend, William Edwards. Signed: Richard Hukill. Witnesses: John Dewitt, Henry Dewitt and John Barker.   (167)

HIXON, Elijah - dated 5-2-1836; recorded 7-2-1836. Bequeaths to Rachel Hixon, William Hixon wife and Reubin Hixon (note: not chear as to whether Rachel Hixon and William Hixon's wife are two individuals or if Rachel is wife of William Hixon). Signed: Elijah (mark) Hixon. Witnesses: John Surber and John Painter.   (169)

The following records were taken from Will Book A and consist primarily of inventories, appraisals, sale bills, etc. Only minimal information of a genealogical nature is given. If an ancestor is listed on the following list an effort should be made to check the estate packet for possible receipts of heirs or an accounting in which heirs are named.

Name	Date	Page
MOUSER, Benjamin	1828	15
of Madison twp.		
McCAFFERTY, William	1828	18
RUNNELS, Joseph	1828	24
of Union twp.		
widow, Nancy Runnels		
MYERS, Jacob	1829	26
of Paint twp.		
WADDLE, Samuel	1829	50
McCORMACK, John	1829	52
BOSTWICK, William	1830	57
BARGER, Christian gdn	1830	61
of John, Philip & Lewis Barger		
heirs of Philip Barger, dec'd		
CORE, Christian Jr.	1830	68
GOODNIGHT, Leonard	1831	76
Martha Goodnight adms.		
SMITH, Matthias	1830	78
ALLEN, Samuel gdn. of	1831	83
Susanna Lattamore now wife		
of John Hill & heir of		
Samuel Lattamore		
CLARK, John	1830	84
of Concord twp		

Name	Date	Page
OGDEN, Abner	1829	32
of Madison twp.		
Margaret Ogden, adms.		
JONES, Nathaniel	1829	35
widow, catharine Jones		
adms.		
ROSS, Levin	1829	36
McGARRAUGH, Joseph	1829	37
RODGERS, Hamilton Sr.	1832	89
gdn of Isabella and		
Joseph Patterson heirs of		
Joseph Patterson, dec'd		
SHOBE, Edward	1830	97
SLAUGHTER, George	1832	120
BUZZARD, Michael	1831	138
of Concord twp.		
widow, Sarah Buzzard		
BUSH, Jacob	1832	132
BRADY, John	1830	134
of Union twp.		
WILSON, Joshua	1833	138
of Green twp.		
McCOY, Rebecca	1833	148
WILFONG, Christopher	1833	148
HAGLER, Isaac	1836	170

446

FAYETTE COUNTY, OHIO - WILLS, ESTATES AND GUARDIANSHIPS 1838-1842

The following records were taken from "Record of Wills A" located in the Probate
Court at the court house in Washington Court House. Page on which record may
be found in the original book is given in parenthesis.

Will of John WILSON Sr., will made in 72nd year of testators life; dated
8-28-1838; recorded 10-8-1838. Sons: Lewis F., Adam B., James N. and John.
Three daughters: Mary, Fanny and Hannah. Executors: sons, John, Lewis F. and
James N. Signed: John Wilson Sr. Wit: John C. Wilson and Eliza H. Smith. (316)

Will of Archibald STEWART of the town of Bloomingburg - dated 7-23-1838;
recorded 10-10-1838. Wife, Sarah, to have one third of farm in Madison Co.;
also tract of 150 acres adjoining Bloomingsburg purchased from testator's
brother James; also lots 12,29,30,47 & 48 in Bloomingsburg. Daughters: Margaret
Mary and Sarah Linton. Nephew, Robert Fullerton, not of age. Brother, Hugh.
Aged mother, Margaret Stewart. Sisters, Mary and Margaret. Bequeaths to Mrs. Burman Martin. Executors: wife, Sarah and brother, Hugh. Signed: Arch'd Stewart.
Wit: James Stewart, Geo. S. Fullerton and Wm Davis. (318)

Will of William MORRISON - dated 9-14-1837; recorded 10-10-1838. Wife, Affia.
Natural daughter, Anna Jane, to have all land where testator now resides.
Signed: William Morison. Wit: H. C. Stewart and W. A. Ustick. (320)

Will of George MILLER - dated 7-17-1838; recorded 10-9-1838. Wife, Polly, also
to serve as executrix. Children, mentioned but not named. Signed: George (his
mark) Miller. Wit: George Glase Sr. and Wm H. Blakemore. (321)

Will of Joseph SHARP - dated 8-24-1838; recorded 10-13-1838. Brothers: George
and William to have property where testator now lives including land, mills
and distillery; James C. Sharp, Andrew G. Sharp and Thomas K. Sharp. Sisters:
Mary Ann and Nancy Jane Sharp. Signed: Joseph Sharp. Wit: E. Crosby and G.
Hewitt. (322)

Estate of Johb SMITH, Appraisement dated July 1837. Public Sale held 7-29-1837.
Accounts filed Oct. 1838. (324)

Estate of Thomas MARPLE. Inventory 4-13-1836. Property set off to widow (not
named) 4-13-1836. Account filed Oct. 1838. (327)

Estate of Elizabeth CARR. Inventory 11-21-1833; Public Sale held 11-22-1833.
Account filed 6-12-1838. (332)

Estate of George HEAGLER. Inventory 10-16-1829; Public Sale 10-17-1829.
Account filed 6-18-1838. (338)

Estate of Joshua HOLMES. Inventory 7-27-1836. Account filed Oct. 1838. (343)

Will of Richard CORSON - dated 10-8-1838; recorded 10-27-1838. Sons: Thomas,
Benjamin and Henry. Daughters: Margaret wife of James E. Stanferd and Hannah.
(note: may be other heirs not named.) Executors: sons, John and Henry. Signed:
Richard (his mark) Corson. Wit: Samuel Myers. John Fisher and Isaac T. Cook. (347)

Estate of Moses WILLIAMS. Inventory 4-6-1831. Public Sale 4-7-1831. Account filed Oct. 1838. All records indicate Moses Williams was late of Concord twp., Ross Co., Ohio. (348)

Estate of George DUNKLE. Inventory 10-7-1833; Sale Bill 10-9-1833; Account filed Oct. 1838. (353)

Will of Samuel LOOFBOURROW - dated 11-1-1838; recorded 11-14-1838. Wife, Polly. At wife's death, all estate to go to Mary Jane Doron and Nicholas Hay. Executors: Jared Plumb and L. D. Willard. Signed: Samuel Loofbourrow. Wit: Jas. Heuton and A. H. Eaton. (357)

Will of William SANDFORD - dated 3-21-1801; recorded Hampshire Co., Va. 5-18-1801; recorded Fayette Co., Ohio -----1839. Wife, Penelope. Son, Thornton, not of age. Mentions seven daughters, but does not name. Mentions four negro slaves: George, Daniel, Jacob and Moses. Executors: wife, Penelope; Elijah Guithen and William Nayler. Wit: Edw'd Dyer, J. Bighill(?) and Peter Engle. (359)

Will of Jacob BUSHONG - dated 8-15-1838; recorded 7-15-1839. Wife, Esther. Three sons: Joseph, Benjamin and James. Daught rs: Betsy, Rachel and Margaret. Executors: wife, Esther and brother-in-law, Abraham Windle. Signed: Jacob Bushong. Wit: George H. Creamer and John Wilson. (361)

Will of Joseph SHOUGH - dated 7-28-1835; recorded 9-9-1839. Estate to be divided among children (not named),"with Jacob Ott to do justice among them, three in Indiana have their share and to have no more"--three in Indiana are named as: Poly, Peggy and Sarah. Signed: Joseph Shough. Wit: James Stewart and Jane C. Stewart. (363)

Estate of Henry DRAIS. Inventory 10-16-1835. Account filed July 1839. (364)

Estate of David M. GAFF. Account filed July 1839. Hannah Calhoun guardian of minor heirs. (366)

Estate of Martin HOPKINS. Appraisement 4-1-1837. Public Sale 4-1-1837. Account filed July 1839. (370)

Estate of Hugh PAUL. Public Sale 2-10-1837. Account filed Sept. 1839. (372)

Estate of George CONNER. Inventory 9-6-1837. Property set off to widow (not named) 9-6-1837. Accounty filed Spet. 1839. (376)

Estate of Austin HUSTON. Account of John McKilip guardian of Tyrantus R. and Austin C. Huston, minor heirs of Austin Huston, filed Sept. 1839. (384)

Estate of Daniel ALLEN. Account filed Spet. 1839. (386)

Estate of Aquilla JAMISON. Inventory 9-27-1837. Public sale 902801837. Account filed Sept. 1839. (387)

Estate of Jacob CAYLOR of Concord twp. Inventory 8-17-1837. Public sale
8-18-1837. Account filed Sept. 1839. (391)

Will of Valentine POST - dated 10-26-1839; recorded 4-27-1840. Wife, Margaret.
Sons: Andrew Post, Jacob Post, Wesley Post, Eli Post, John Nelson Post and
Abraham Post. Daughters: Sarah Berry and Barbary Ann Post. Executors: wife,
Margaret and son, Andrew. Signed: Valentine Post. Wit: Stephen Yeoman and
Eli West Sr. (395)

Estate of William BAKER of Paint twp. Inventory 5-15-1837. Account filed
Sept. 1839. (397)

Estate of Richard WILSON. Appraisement 2-2-1835; Public sale 2-3-1835; Account
filed Sept. 1839. (401)

Estate of Isaiah ROWE. Inventory 8-12-1837, includes Family Bible. Account
filed April 1840. (409)

Estate of James NUTT. Inventory 8-28-1832; property set off to widow and
children (not named) 11-3-1832; Public sale 8-30-1832; account filed Apr.
1840. (416)

Robert Robinson and James Beaty guardians of Harriet Ann McCOY, a minor.
Account filed Apr. 1840. (428)

Estate of Elijah HIXON. Account filed April 1840. (429)

Estate of Isaac FANSHER. Appraisement 3-10-1837; public sale 6-29 1837. Account
filed April 1840. (430)

Estate of John WRIGHT. Inventory 8-1-1833; account filed April 1840. (433)

Estate of Benjamin S. YEOMAN. Inventory 9-29-1836; Public sale 10-14-1836; Account
filed April 1840. (436)

Estate of Henry CHRISTOPHER. Inventory 10-6-1834; public sale 10-22-1834;
Account filed April 1840. (439)

Estate of Henry PHELPS. Inventory 4-12-1833; public sale 4-29-1833; Account
filed April 1840. (444)

Will of Thomas GHORMLEY of Wayne twp. - dated 6-21-1836; recorded 8-10-1840.
Wife, Judith. Sons: Hugh, David, and William Logan Ghormley; with son, William
Logan Ghormley to have land where testator resided containing 206 acres. Daughters:
Sarah, Jane and Eleanor. Grand-daughter, Margaret Bigham. Mentions house and
lot in Greenfield. Executor: son, William L. Ghormley. Signed: Thomas Ghormley.
Witnesses: Benjamin Rogers and Wm Rogers. Codicil dated 8-29-1839 states daughter,
Eleanor is wife of Rev. William Dickey. (454)

Will of Joseph FARMER of Madison twp. - dated 5-5-1839; recorded 8-10-1840.
Wife, Catharine. Sons: John to have farm where he now resides and William
to have half of land where he now resides. Daughters: Susan, Lydia wife of
Hugh Roebuck and Betsy wife of Joseph Warner. The small house formerly occupied
by Moses Stitt as a tailor shop to be fitted up with a fireplace for wife,
Catharine and daughter, Susan. Executors: sons, William and John. Signed:
Joseph Farmer. Wit: H. C. Stewart and Eleaser Martin. (456)

Will of Daniel DAVIS of Wayne twp. - dated 4-4-1840; recorded August 1840.
Wife, Malinda, at her death estate to be divided among testator's heirs (not
named). Executors: wife, Malinda and Henry Sayers. Signed: Daniel (his mark)
Davis. Wit: Stephen Yeoman and Wm Mooney. (457)

Estate of Wilson A. DAVIS. Account filed August 1840. (458)

Estate of Joseph SHOUGH. Inventory 3-30-1840. Account filed August 1840. (460)

Will of Jacob SNIDER - dated 9-17-1839; recorded 11-13-1840. Wife, mentioned
but not named, to have farm where now live being 112 acres. Sons: John, to
have farm where he now lives of 100 acres; William, to have farm where he now
lives of 140 acres; Jefferson to have farm where he now lives of 112 acres;
Hewy, at death of wife to have homested farm of 112 acres. Daughter, Sarah
wife of William Boggs to have farm where they recently reside containing 50 acres.
Mentions Catharine Boggs and Joseph Boggs daughter and son of Sarah Boggs.
Signed: Jacob Snider. Wit: Nelson Bush, Robert Irion, John King and James
Pursell. (461)

Estate of Thomas MOON. Account filed November 1840. (463)

Will of John LARRIMER - dated 7-9-1840; recorded 3-8-1841. Wife, Elizabeth,
to have 100 acres where now live. Sons: Thomas, to have 100 acres where he
now lives; hugh to have 115 acres where he now lives; Robert to have land now
being purchased from widow Smith; James and John to have all residue of land
being about 300 acres. Daughter, Elizabeth. Executors: sons, James and John.
Signed: John Larrimer. Wit: James Stewart and Adam Steel. (464)

Will of Isabel(la) KNOX - dated 1-23-1841; recorded (not given)-1841. Son,
James William Knox. Daughters: Mary Jane Lunbeck, Nancy Ann Knox and Hannah
Frances Knox. Executor: brother, James Rodgers of Highland Co., Ohio. Signed:
Isabel (her mark) Knox. Wit: Wm Ross, James Harper and Hamilton Rodgers. (466)

Will of James SANDERSON Sr - dated 11-17-1835; recorded 3-9-1841. Wife,
Barbarah, to have where now live being 100 acres. Daughter, Mary wife of William
Moorman. John R. Sanderson, dec'd (note: no relationship given but indication is
that he was testator's son), his children--Elizabeth, Barbarah, Sythe, Jane, Mar-
garet, John, Mary, Lathey Jane and Martha. Son, Alexander Sanderson. Son, James
Sanderson. Bequeath to Marey Wittey heir of ___(left blank) Wittey, daughter of
Rachel Sanderson who was daughter of James Sanderson (note: testator). Daughter,
Hannah wife of William Ryan. Son, Harvey Sanderson. Signed: James Sanderson.
Wit: Joseph Straley and David Creamer. (467)

Will of William IRWIN of Wayne twp. - dated 5-10-1841; recorded 7-19-1841. Wife, Elizabeth, also to serve as executrix. Signed: William Irwin. Wit: Nathan Coffman and Sarah C. Coffman. (469)

Will of Daniel ARNOLD of Concord twp. - dated 7-23-1841; recorded 7-26-1841. Wife, Eleanor L. Arnold. Child (not named), not of age. Mentions father but does not name. Executors: wife, Eleanor and Robert McWhorter. Signed: Daniel (his mark) Arnold. Wit: John S. Burnett and Elias M. Sparks. (470)

Estate of Thomas MOON. Deceased left will dated 10-6-1824. Deposition filed July 1841. (471)

Estate of William TITSWORTH. Inventory 3-18-1837. Account filed July 1841. (472)

Estate of David HANKINS. Appraisement 12-20-1838. Account filed July 1841. (475)

Estate of John McMAHAN. Inventory 11-2-1838. Account filed July 1841. (479)

Will of James HAYS - dated 3-2-1836; recorded (not given)-1841. Wife, mentioned but not named. Daughters: Jane Thompson, dec'd and Mary Buck. Son, James. Executors: sons, John Hays and William Hays. Signed: James Hays. Wit: Chandler Tuttle, John Parker and John Baker. (481)

Estate of John WILSON. Inventory 10-24-1838. Public sale 10-26-1838. Account filed October 1841. Deceased owned lot in Gallipolis. (482)

Isaac HEAGLER's minors. John Hankins, guardian. Account filed October 1841.(486)

Estate of Hiram JENKINS of Jefferson twp. Inventory 6-23-1837; public sale 7-3-1837 and 7-6-1837. Account filed October 1841. (487)

Estate of Samuel EDWARDS. Inventory 1-13-1840; property set off to widow and four children under 15 years (not named) 1-13-1840; public sale 1-23-1840; Account filed October 1841. (497)

Estate of William SNODGRASS. Inventory 12-3-1838; public sale 12-11-1838; Account filed October 1841. (503)

Estate of Anslem IRION. Inventory 8-7-1839; Property set off to widow and children (not named) 8-7-1841; Account filed October 1841. (505)

Estate of John HARPER. Inventory 10-12-1838; public sale 11-3-1838. Account filed October 1841. (509)

Estate of Solomon SALMON. Inventory 9-14-1837; account filed October 1841. (513)

Will of John BROWN of Frankfort, Kentucky - dated 5-4-1836; recorded Franklin Co., Ky. 10-16-1837; recorded Fayette Co., Ohio 10-6-1841. Wife, Margaretta. Sons: Mason Brown and Orlando Brown. Grandson, Benjamin Gratz Brown. Granddaughter Euphemia Helen Brown. Servants, Mary Stepney, Miles Stepney and wife Hannah and their unfortunate daughter, Mourning, also their son James Stepney.

Negro boys, George and Edward, to be free at 25 years of age. Executors: sons, Mason and Orlando. Signed: J. Brown. Codicil dated 8-22-1837. Two grandsons: Mason Preston Brown and John Brown. Mentions suit filed by representatives of testator's brother, James Brown and Nancy his wife against John B. Humphreys, dec'd of Lousiana's representatives--that if they recover, testator's portion which will be one moiety is to be divided between his three nieces, Mary Ann Sproull, Margaretta B. Sproull and Elizabeth Humphreys, daughters of James Humphreys, dec'd. Nephew, David C. Humphreys is to serve as executor with testator's sons, Mason and Orlando. Signed: J. Brown. Wit: A. S. Parker and J. P. W. Brown. (517)

Estate of Charles MADDUX. Inventory 2-16-1839; widow, Nancy Maddox received personal property set off to her. Account filed October 1841. (521)

Estate of George SEAVER. Public sale 3-31-1837; account filed October 1841. (526)

Guardianships of James H. GAFF, Sarah Jane GAFF and Joanna GAFF. Account filed July 1841 by Hannah Calhoun late Hannah Gaff, their guardian. (528)

Will of William ADDISON formerly of Chesterfield County now of Richmond, Va. - dated 1-14-1837; recorded Richmond, Va. 4-11-1841; recorded Fayette Co., Ohio 7-11-1842. Uncle, Francis Graves of Goochland Co., Va. to have one dollar. Rest of estate to go to friend James Jenks of Richmond, Va. who is also to serve as executor. Signed: William (his mark) Adison. Wit: Joseph C. Haley, Wm Taylor and John Cullen. (529)

Will of Henry LIMES - dated 9-7-1841; recorded 7-14-1842. Wife, Hannah. Sons: John; 2nd son, Hiram. Daughters: oldest daughter, Julia Ann; 2nd daughter, Maria Crooks; daughters, Margaret and Rebecca. Executors: wife, Hannah and son, Hiram. Signed: Henry Limes. Wit: Isaac Depery, Daniel Lucas and William Smith. (532)

Estate of George RODGERS. Public sale 11-5-1838; property set off to widow (not named) 11-5-1838; account filed March 1842. (534)

Estate of Isaac SELLERS. Inventory 12-1-1830; account filed March 1842. (540

FAYETTE COUNTY, OHIO - COMMON PLEAS MINUTE BOOK E - 1828-1831

The following records were taken from "Minute Book E" located in the Common Pleas Court (Clerk of Court's Office) at the court house in Washington C.H. Page on which record may be found in original book is given in parenthesis. References to papers being burned refers to the court house fire which took place Jan. 19, 1828.

1-24-1828 - Estate of Benjamin MOUSER, dec'd. Widow, Susannah Mouser appointed admsx. (1)

1-31-1828 - Estate of William McCAFFERTY, dec'd. Widow, Sarah McCafferty appointed admsx. (1)

2-23-1828 - Will of Thomas MOON, dec'd produced and proven in court. (2)

5-12-1828 - Lurana LATTIMORE over age of 14 yrs., daughter of Samuel LATTIMORE, dec'd, chose Samuel Allen as her guardian. (4)

5-12-1828 - Will of Michael BLUE, dec'd produced and proven in court. (4)

5-12-1828 - Aaron JOHNSON granted license to keep tavern at his house in Washington. (4)

5-12-1828 - Andrews GREGORY granted license to keep tavern at his house in Madison twp. (4)

5-12-1828 - Samuel WILSON granted license to keep tavern at his house in Bloomingburg. (5)

5-13-1828 - Nancy Jester admsx. of estate of Thomas W. JESTER, dec'd vs. Thomas JESTER. Petition to sell land. (7)

5-13-1828 - Ambrose TORBET a minor aged 18 yrs. chose John Torbet as his guardian. William S. TORBET a minor aged 16 yrs. also chose John Torbet as his guardian. (7)

5-13-1828 - Robert Waddle and Norman F. Jones adms. of the estate of Samuel WADDLE, dec'd vs. the heirs. Petition to sell land. (8)

5-13-1828 - Eliza P. DAWSON aged 19 yrs., Charoline A. DAWSON aged 16 yrs. & 10 mos., Sarah C. DAWSON aged 14 yrs. & 10 mos., Harriet C. DAWSON aged 12 yrs. & 11 mos. chose Robert Robinson as their guardian and he to also serve as guardian of Maria L. DAWSON aged 8 years. (8)

5-13-1828 - Mary WRIGHT vs. Thomas MADDUX. Bastardy. (10)

5-14-1828 - James B. Webster adms. of the estate of Joseph McGARRAUGH, dec'd filed account, papers destroyed by fire to be substituted. (12)

5-15-1828 - Robert R. Wilson appointed adms. of the estate of Rebecca McCOY, dec'd as Andrew Gibson former adms. is now dec'd. (16)

5-15-1828 - Robert Robinson guardian of the minor heirs of Benjamin DAWSON, dec'd vs. Thomas Buck and others. (17)

5-15-1828 - Nancy Hawkins appointed guardian of her two minor daughters, Rebecca HAWKINS aged 10 yrs. and Jane HAWKINS aged 5 yrs. & 6 mos., heirs of Thomas HAWKINS, dec'd. (17)

5-15-1828 - Catharine BLOOMER former JONES admsx. of the estate of Nathaniel JONES, dec'd filed account. (19)

5-15-1828 - Robert Irion executor of will of Joseph MARKS, dec'd filed account for settlemen. (19)

9-22-1828 - Will of Daniel ROTROCK, dec'd, produced and proven in court. (20)

9-22-1828 - Estate of Joseph REYNOLDS, dec'd. Norman F. Jones appointed adms. (21)

9-22-1828 - Frederick BYERLY granted license to keep tavern at his house in Washington. (21)

9-22-1828 - Frederick BYERLY granted license to retail merchandize at his store in Washington. (21)

9-22-1828 - David Creamer adms. of the estate of George CREAMER, dec'd vs. George H. CREAMER. (24)

9-23-1828 - Henry Core adms. of the estate of Christian CORE, dec'd granted further time to settle accounts. (26)

9-24-1828 - Jesse MATLE aged 16 yrs. chose George Mantle as his guardian. (32)

9-24-1828 - Benjamin ADAMSON, minister of the Baptist Church of Christ granted license to solemnize marriages. (32)

9-24-1828 - Humphrey Warring appointed guardian of his son, James K. WARRING, aged 16 yrs. (32)

9-24-1828 - Thomas Williams adms. of the estate of Levin ROSS, dec'd filed accounts for settlement. (32)

9-24-1828 - William MINSHIN native of England makes his declaration of intention to become citizen. (33)

9-24-1828 - Noah Evans guardian of Elizabeth, Louis, Wright and Calvin McCORMICK vs. William McCormick and Joseph S. Gillespie adms. of the estate of John McCORMICK, dec'd. To settle accounts. (33)

9-24-1828 - Robert Waddle and Norman F. Jones adms. of the estate of Samuel WADDLE, dec'd file sale bill with affadavit from clerk of court showing loss of petition, appraisement, etc. made earlier. (33)

2-26-1829 - Samuel Myers adms. of the estate of Mathias SMITH, dec'd, late of this county, filed accounts. (38)

2-26-1829 - Estate of Jacob MYERS, dec'd. Christiana Myers and Samuel Myers appointed adms. (39)

2-26-1829 - Estate of Abner OGDEN, late of this county, dec'd. Widow, Margaret Ogden appointed adms. (39)

2-26-1829 - Daniel GILMER aged 14 yrs. chose David Gilmer as his guardian. (39)

2-26-1829 - John Rankin appointed guardian of Lewis JONES, Mahala JONES, Rachel JONES, John JONES and William JONES, all minors under 12 and 14 years. (40)

2-27-1829 - Lewis NELSON aged 14 yrs. chose Philip B. Dodridge as his guardian. (44)

2-27-1829 - Jacob HUGHETT and Nancy HUGHETT aged 12 and 14 yrs. respectively chose John Smith as their guardian. (44)

2-27-1829 - Benjamin Bloomer and Catherine Bloomer formerly Catharine Jones adms. of the Estate of Nathaniel JONES, dec'd, accounts examined and accepted. (44)

2-27-1829 - John B. MOORE a minister of the Baptist Church granted license to solemnize marriages. (44)

2-28-1829 - James B. Webster adms. of the estate of Joseph McGARRAUGH, dec'd given permission by court to substitute papers which were destroyed by fire. (48)

2-28-1829 - Aaron JOHNSON granted license to keep tavern at his house in Washington. (50)

2-28-1829 - Thomas Williams Adms. of the Estate of Levin ROSS, dec'd, filed accounts which were recorded by court. (51)

2-28-1829 - Naomi HARPER vs. Peter DRACE. Petition for Dower. (52)

2-28-1829 - Estate of Thomas W. JESTER, dec'd. Samuel Loofbourrow appointed adms. of said estate in place of Nancy JESTER former admsx. who is now deceased. (52)

5-21-1829 - Herman L. AKIN granted license to keep tavern at his house in Washington. (54)

5-21-1829 - Robert ABERNATHY granted license to keep tavern at his house in Madison. (54)

5-21-1829 - Samuel LIDY granted license to keep grocery at his house in Washington. (54)

5-21-1829 - Messrs. LARRICKS and SHARTLE granted license to keep grocery at their house in Washington. (54)

5-21-1829 - On affidavit of Benjamin R. DAVIS, Lawrence Paine and Mildred Paine his wife late Mildred Davis executors of the estate of James N. DAVIS, dec'd are ordered to show cause. (55)

5-22-1829 - Estate of Robert WILSON, dec'd, late of said county. Joseph Parret, Jr. appointed adms. (59)
5-22-1829 - Estate of John TWAY, dec'd, late of said county. John Tway appointed adms. (59)
5-22-1829 - Samuel Sollers appointed guardian of Nathaniel JONES aged 5 yrs. and Nancy JONES aged 7 yrs., children of Nathaniel Jones, dec'd. (59)
5-22-1829 - Samuel WILSON granted license to keep tavern at his house in Blooming-burg. (59)
5-23-1829 - James B. Webster adms. of the estate of Joseph McGARRAUGH, dec'd filed accounts. (62)
5-23-1829 - John Wilson adms. of the estate of Archibald G. WILSON, dec'd granted further time to file accounts. (65)
6-2-1829 - Estate of George SLAUGHTER, late of said county, dec'd. James Baker appointed adms. (70)
6-29-1829 - Estate of Jacob RINTZEL, late of said county, dec'd. William Wibright appointed adms. (72)
9-17-1829 - Aaron JOHNSON granted license to keep a tavern at his house in Washington. (72)
9-17-1829 - Christian Barger guardian of John BARGER, Philip BARGER and Lewis BARGER filed accounts for settlement. (73)
9-17-1829 - Jonathan McCafferty adms. of estate of William McCAFFERTY, dec'd granted further time to file accounts. (73)
9-17-1829 - Samuel Myers adms. of the estate of Matthias SMITH, dec'd, allowed by court to substitute sale bill of estate heretofore filed and destroyed by fire. (73)
9-17-1829 - Estate of William REED, dec'd, late of said county. Widow, Polly Reed appointed adms. (74)
9-18-1829 - Messrs. BOGGS and STAGGS granted license to keep grocery at their house in Washington. (75)
9-19-1829 - Estate of George HAGLER, dec'd, late of said county. Zebedee Hagler appointed adms. (80)
11-5-1829 - Estate of Daniel MILLER, dec'd, late of said county. Jacob Jamison appointed adms. (85)
2-22-1830 - Sally WHITE and Elizabeth WHITE minors over 12 yrs., children and heirs of William WHITE late of Caroline Co., Maryland, dec'd, chose Philip B. Dodd-ridge as their guardian. (86)
2-22-1830 - Estate of Jefferson FERREL, dec'd, late of said county. Widow, Mary Ferrel appointed admsx. (87)
2-23-1830 - Andrews GREGORY granted license to keep tavern at his house in Madison twp. (90)
2-23-1830 - Estate of Eden CLEVENGER, dec'd, late of said county. Amos Hankins and Hezekiah Brown appointed adms. (91)
2-26-1830 - Accounts of Robert Waddle and Norman F. Jones adms. of the estate of Samuel Waddle, late of said county, dec'd, examined and recorded. (105)
2-27-1830 - Accounts of Samuel Allen and Jacob Rankin executors of estate of Daniel ROTROCK, dec'd, examined and recorded. (107)
5-17-1830 - Elizabeth REED, William REED and Mary REED minors over the age of 12 and 14 yrs., chose David Harper as their guardian and he to also serve as guardian of John REED, Sarah REED, Rachel REED, Charity REED and David REED minors under 12 and 14 yrs., call children of William REED, dec'd. (111)
5-17-1830 - Matthew SIMPSON granted license to keep grocery at his house in Wash-ington. (111)

455

5-17-1830 - Walter Yeoman adms. of the estate of Jared BENJAMIN, dec'd filed
    petition on behalf of heirs to complete contract made by dec'd in his lifetime
    to sell John Linch land. (111)
5-17-1830 - Estate of Joshua CLARK, dec'd, late of said county. Jonathan Mark
    appointed adms. (112)
5-18-1830 - Benjamin Leach and Adoniram Bostwick appointed guardians of Adley
    BOSTWICK and Oliver BOSTWICK minors under 14 years. (116)
5-19-1830 - Harriet MOON over the age of 12 yrs., daughter of William MOON chose
    William Moon as her guardian. (121)
5-19-1830 - Bartholomew FUEL a minor over 14 yrs., heir of James FUEL, dec'd, late
    of said county, chose Joseph Bloomer as his guardian. (121)
5-20-1830 - STODARD and MERREL granted license to keep tavern at their house in
    Washington. (124)
5-20-1830 - Robert R. Wilson adms. of the estate of Rebecca McCOY, dec'd granted
    further time to file accounts. (125)
5-20-1830 - Benjamin Henton appointed guardian of Robert James WILSON a minor under
    14 years, son of Robert WILSON, dec'd, late of said county. (125)
5-20-1830 - Accounts filed by Wm McCormick and Joseph S. Gillespie adms. of the
    estate of John McCORMICK, dec'd, on file since Feb. term 1829 examined and
    ordered recorded. (126)
5-20-1830 - James FUEL and Henry FUEL minors over 14 yrs. of age chose Joseph Bloomer
    as their guardian and he to also serve as guardian of Lewis FUEL, Jeruch FUEL
    and Lucy FUEL minors under 12 and 14 years, all children of James FUEL, dec'd.
    (129)
5-21-1830 - Henry CORE adms. of the estate of Christian CORE, dec'd file accounts
    for settlement. (130)
5-21-1830 - Accounts of Abner Seers adms. of the estate of Wm BOSTWICK, dec'd,
    on hand from Feb. term 1830 passed and recorded. (132)
5-21-1830 - Accounts of Garret M. Blue adms. of the estate of Michael BLUE, dec'd,
    late of said county, on file since Sept. term 1828 passed and recorded. (132)
6-4-1830 - James Pollock appointed guardian of Nancy POLLOCK a minor aged 8 months,
    daughter of Joseph POLLOCK, dec'd, late of said county. (134)
6-29-1830 - Will of George CUMERFORD, dec'd, Joseph Parret, Jr. appointed adms. in
    place of Susannah Hagler, widow and former admsx. (136)
8-17-1830 - Estate of Edward SHORE, dec'd. William Campbell and Martin Peterson
    appointed adms. in place of Sarah Shobe widow and former adms. (137)
8-17-1830 - Alva YEOMAN and Jared YEOMAN minors over 14 yrs. chose Walter Yeoman
    as their guardian and he to also serve as guardian of Lydia YEOMAN an idiot,
    Minerva YEOMAN and Samantha YEOMAN the last two under 12 yrs., call children
    of James YEOMAN, dec'd, late of said county. (137)
11-8-1830 - Samuel F. YEOMAN granted license to keep grocery at his house in Wash-
    ington. (140)
11-8-1830 - James Baker adms. of George SLAUGHTER, dec'd, granted further time to
    file accounts. (140)
11-8-1830 - Estate of Isaac SOLLARS, dec'd. John Sollars appointed adms. (140)
11-9-1830 - Lawson P. REID granted license to keep tavern at his house in Washing-
    ton. (145)
11-9-1830 - James BURNET a minor over 14 yrs. chose George Miller as his guardian
    and Miller to also serve as guardian of Fleming BURNET a minor under 14 yrs.,
    both children and heirs of Robert L. (or S.) BURNET, dec'd, late of said county.
    (145)

11-9-1830 - Edward Smith appointed guardian of Phebe SMITH his minor daughter under the age of 12 yrs. (145)
11-9-1830 - Abraham Blue appointed guardian of Hannah LINDSLEY a minor under 12 yrs. (145)
11-11-1830 - Alexander SELLARS and Martha SELLARS minors over 12 and 14 yrs. chose Samuel Sollars as their guardian and he to also serve as guardian of Lucy Ann SOLLARS, Julia Ann SOLLARS and Ruth Jane SOLLARS minors under 12 yrs., all children and heirs of Isaac SOLLARS, dec'd, late of said county. (151)
11-11-1830 - Samuel WILSON granted license to keep tavern at his house in Bloomingburgh. (151)
11-12-1830 - James WOODS, Jr. a minor over 14 yrs., son and heir of William WOODS, dec'd chose James Woods as his guardian. (156)
11-12-1830 - Estate of John BRADY, dec'd. Thomas Coil appointed adms. in place of Caty Brady, widow and former admsx. (157)
11-12-1830 - Joseph Bloomer guardian of James FEWELL, Henry FEWELL and other minors files petition to court to sell interest of said minors in tract of land of their dec'd father. (157)
11-12-1830 - Accounts of Henry Core, Adms. of estate of Christian CORE, dec'd, on file since May term 1830 passed and recorded. (158)
11-12-1830 - Accounts of Jesse Barten and Andrews Gregory, adms. of estates of Jehiel GREGORY and Sarah GREGORY, both dec'd on file since May term 1828 passed and recorded. (158)
3-14-1831 - Polly Reed adms. of the estate of William REED, dec'd, granted further time to file accounts. (160)
3-14-1831 - Samuel Myers adms of estate of Jacob MYERS, dec'd, granted further time to file accounts. (161)
3-14-1831 - Elizabeth Turnipseed appointed guardian of Henry TURNIPSEED, George TURNIPSEED, Elizabeth TURNIPSEED and Morgan TURNIPSEED, her children being minors under 12 and 14 yrs. (161)
3-14-1831 - John NEWMAN granted license to keep tavern at his house in Madison twp. (161)
3-15-1831 - Aaron JOHNSON granted license to keep tavern at his house in Washington. (165)
3-15-1831 - William WESTLAKE a minister of the Methodist Episcopal Church granted license to solemnize marriages. (165)
3-16-1831 - Estate of Henry JANES, dec'd. Edward Janes appointed adms. (169)
3-16-1831 - Estate of Moses WILLIAMS, dec'd. William S. Williams appointed adms.(169)
3-16-1831 - Jehiel B. GREGORY a minor over 14 yrs., son of Nehemiah GREGORY late of said county, dec'd, chose Andrew Gregory as his guardian. (169)
3-16-1831 - Andrews GREGORY granted license to keep tavern at his house in Madison twp. (170)
3-16-1831 - Edmund Clarridge appointed guardian of Deborah OGDEN, Albert OGDEN and Dorothy OGDEN aged under 12 and 14 yrs., children of Abner Ogden. (170)
3-16-1831 - Noncupative will of Zarobabee DAVIS, dec'd, produced and proven by oath of Jacob Davis and Benjamin Davis. (170)
3-16-1831 - Accounts of Margaret Ogden admsx of the extate of Abner OGDEN late of said county, dec'd, passed and recorded. (170)
3-16-1831 - Accounts of Martha Goodnight admsx. of the estate of Lenoard GOODNIGHT, late of said county, dec'd, passed and recorded. (170)
3-17-1831 - Lettitia MILLER vs. Heirs of Daniel MILLER. Petition for dower. (174)
4-25-1831 - Estate of Philip MOORE, dec'd, late of said county. Katherine Moore and Anthony Moore appointed adms. (176)

5-23-1831 - Mary DAVISSON and Margaret DAVISSON minors over 12 yrs. chose their
    father, James Davisson as their guardian. (177)
5-23-1831 - Christian Turnipseed appointed guardian of Jackson TURNIPSEED, a minor
    under 14 yrs. (178)
5-23-1831 - James Nutt appointed guardian of Eliza McCAFFERTY and David McCAFFERTY
    minors under 12 & 14 yrs., children and heirs of William McCAFFERTY, dec'd.(178)
5-23-1831 - David C. Eastman appointed guardian of his minor daughter, Betsy
    EASTMAN under 12 yrs. of age. (178)
5-23-1831 - Accounts of Samuel Myers adms. or estate of Matthias SMITH, late of
    said county, dec'd, passed and recorded. (178)
5-23-1831 - Elizabeth GREGORY a minor over 12 yrs. chose Isaac Cook as her guardian.
    (179)
5-23-1831 - Annas GREGORY a minor over 12 yrs. chose John Leavell as her guardian.
    (179)
5-23-1831 - Henry WALKER granted license to keep a tavern at his house in Union twp.
    (179)
5-25-1831 - Mary KRUSEN vs. Jacob House and Nicholas Devault. Petition for dower.
    (190)
5-25-1831 - Estate of Michael BUZZARD, dec'd, late of said county. Robert Burnet
    appointed adms. (190)
8-9-1831 - Estate of John McMANIS, dec'd late of said county. George McManis and
    Daniel Radcliff appointed adms. (193)
8-19-1831 - Estate of John THOMAS, dec'd, late of said county. Benjamin Thomas and
    Hiram Barker appointed adms. Widow, Elizabeth Thomas relinquishes right to
    adms. estate. (194)
10-3-1831 - William STOCKDALE granted license to keep tavern at his house in Wash-
    ington. (196)
10-3-1831 - Thomas Thompson appointed guardian of William Thompson REYNOLDS aged
    11 yrs. on 3 Nov. next. (196)
10-3-1831 - James B. Webster guardian of minor heirs of James PATTERSON filed
    accounts for settlement. (196)
10-3-1831 - John Wilson adms. of estate of Archibald G. WILSON, dec'd, late of said
    county, granted further time to file accounts. (196)
10-3-1831 - Joseph Young adms. of the estate of Rees YOUNG, dec'd, late of said
    county granted further time to file accounts. (196)
10-3-1831 - Robert ABERNATHY granted license to keep tavern at his house in Madison
    twp. (196)
10-3-1831 - Authenticated copy of will of Henry MASSIE, dec'd, of Jefferson Co.,
    Ky. produced and recorded in this court. (197)
10-3-1831 - Nancy Reynalds appointed guardian of Joseph REYNALDS, John REYNALDS,
    William REYNALDS and Mary REYNALDS minors under 12 and 14 yrs. (197)
10-3-1831 - Estate of William McCAFFERTY, dec'd. Edmund Clarridge appointed adms.
    de bonis non. (197)
10-3-1831 - Estate of John HALTERMAN, dec'd, late of said county. Edward Janes
    appointed adms. (197)
10-4-1831 - Horation Walker appointed guardian of John B. CUMMERFORD, Sarah Ann
    CUMMERFORD, Elizabeth CUMMERFORD, Mary CUMMERFORD and Lydia Ann CUMMERFORD
    minors under 12 and 14 yrs., children of George CUMMERFORD, dec'd. late of
    said county. (200)
10-4-1831 - Accounts filed by Benjamin Rodgers guardian of the heirs of William
    RODGERS, dec'd. (202)

10-5-1831 - This day satisfactory evidence was produced in court to prove that Patsy WISEMAN late Patsy TROTTER and now the wife of John WISEMAN and Polly TROTTER are the daughters and only heirs at law in fee of Christian TROTTER, late a soldier of Armands corps of the revolutionary war and afterwards a pensioner for Ohio, who died near Cincinnati, Ohio, about two years ago leaving no widow and no other heirs but those above named Patsy and Polly. (204)

10-5-1831 - This day satisfactory evidence was produced in this court to prove that William WALLACE, Levi WALLACE, Thomas WALLACE, David WALLACE, John WALLACE and Tuften WALLACE are the sons and only heirs at law in fee of John WALLACE late a private in the Revolutionary war in the New Hampshire line who died at Sandwich in New Hampshire about eighteen years ago leaving a widow who died about three years ago. (204)

10-5-1831 - Authenticated copy of the will of John ARMSTRONG, dec'd, late of Mercer Co., Ky. produced in court and recorded. (204)

10-5-1831 - Estate of Joshua WILSON, dec'd, late of said county. William Limes appointed adms. (205)

10-6-1831 - Accounts of Adley Gregory guardian of the minors, heirs of Jehiel GREGORY filed for settlement. (210)

10-6-1831 - Accounts of Garret M. Blue and Uriah Blue executors of Michael BLUE filed and recorded. (210)

10-26-1831 - Estate of Christopher WILFONG, dec'd, late of said county. Daniel Thompson appointed adms. (212)

The following records were taken from Marriage Record Book A, located in the Probate Court.

ADAMS, Thomas to Patience McKay	11-6-1817
ALDRIDGE, Azel to Mrs. Martha Barton	9-11-1817
ARCHER, William to Barbary Boots	8-15-1816
ARMON, George to Elizabeth Rosel	6-10-1811
ARMSTRONG, John to Elizabeth Parret	3-25-1817
BAKER, Jos. to Mary Hankin	6-20-1813
BALDWIN, Benjamin to Margret How	11-14-1816
BARKER, James to Aley Hubbard (no mo. given)	(?)-28-1814
BARTLESON, Peter to Nancy Parker	10-15-1812
BELL, Joseph to Sally Young	3-28-1811
BELL, Joseph to Peggy Young	12-31-1812
BERRY, John to Elizabeth Clark	3-30-1815
BINEGAR, David to Jean Draper	5-29-1817
BLACKMON, Joseph to Elizabeth Young	4-11-1816
BLAIR, Thomas to Margaret Job	5-9-1816
BLOCHER, Matthias to Sarah Clark	12-12-1811
BLOOMER, Jesse to Sarah Bevington	10-9-1817
BOCKSHIRE, Teboias to Jane Guimer	1-7-1812
BONNER, Nathaniel to Jane Gormely	11-29-1814
BOOTS, John to Rhody Man	7-28-1816
BOWERS, Jacob to Charity Carder	10-31-1815
BOYCE, William to Miram Hollis	11-25-1813
BOWLIN, Isaac to Mary Niebarger	7-18-1816
BROOMHEAD, Jos. to Rachel Aller	1-24-1815
BROOMHEAD, Joseph to Catharine Hanes	9-4-1817
BRYAN, James to Catherine Eyman	12-24-1812
BUCK, John to Polly Heys; mar. within past 30 das.(not dated 1813?)	
BURNET, Robert to Susan Bush	8-24-1813
BURNETT, Thomas to Rachel Bush	10-15-1812
BUSH, Jacob to Sarah Bouhan	4-13-1813
CAMBELL, Runey to Winne Grubb	7-25-1813
CARTOR, Isaac to Elizabeth Davis	3-17-(1814)
CAILOR, Jacob to Catherine Snider	8-20-1811
CHAPMAN, John to Betsy Myers	4-10-1817
CHENOWORTH, Thomas to Rachel Morgan	9-19-1811
CLARK, Henry to Mrs. Ker	7-27-1815
CLARK, Jos. to Lydia Hurley	1-19-1815
CLARK, Thos. to Aveinda Robinson	3-14-1814
COIL, George to Hannah Jones	7-16-1812
COON, Adam to Elenor Dickinson	8-27-1812
COON, Michael to Abigail Soward	9-20-1812
COX, Elias to Hannah Ayre	8-1-1811
CRABE, James to Peggy Blew	1-4-1814
CREAMER, Jos. to Margaret Miller	12-22-1814
CRUMER, David to Betsy Smith	5-18-1815

```
CUEKESS(?), Lewis to Martha Baldwin                         2-27-1817
CULVER, Daniel to Jemima Boots                              12-25-1817
CULVER, Gardner G. to Elizabeth Carter                      12-1-1817
DAVIS, Charles to Betsy Hays                                8-8-1813
DAVIS, Henry to Catherine Emberling                         7-4-1816
DAVIS, John to Hannah Hays                                  5-8-1814
DAY, Addison to Elizabeth Compton                           4-30-1812
DILLY, John to Mary Lock                                    3-5-1817
DWIGGINS, Joseph to Rebecca Leaverton                       10-22-1817
ELLIS, Henry to Charity Harper                              6-26-1810
FERRELL, Edward to Mary Wright                              12-13-1810
FERREL (or TERREL), John to Maris Martha Kimble             2-27-1817
FLESHER, Henry to Susannah Popejoy                          12-20-1810
FULTON, William to Eliza Loofbourrow                        11-19-1811
FUNK, Jacob to Susannah Popejoy                             4-20-1813
FUNK, John to Margaret Carr                                 5-15-1814
GARRISON, Mahershall Charles to Sally Richards              12-28-1813
GILMORE, John to Nancy McCormick                            2-11-1817
GILMORE, William to Nancy Squires                           10-17-1816
GILMORE, Wm. to Ade Vandolph                                6-22-1815
GOLDIES, George to Magdelene Bowers                         1-2-1817
GREGORY, Jehiel to Sarah Vandolah                           6-9-1816
HAINES, George to Mrs. Harriet Sowards                      4-1-1815
HANKINS, Amos to Polly Clevenger                            6-24-1813
HANNAMAN, George to Polly Hannaman                          11-26-1812
HARRIS, Joseph to Lewe Stinson; mar. 3 mos. last
                                    past; dated             6-12-1811
HARRISON, William to Elizabeth Hendrix                      11-10-1814
HARROD, Samuel to Elizabeth Carder                          3-10-1811
HARTMAN, Isaac to Jane Rowe                                 8-6-1812
HAYMAKER, Joseph to Phebe Myers                             11-13-1817
HAYS, David to Theodocia Wolf                               7-17-1810
HEIBEIGH (HUBEIGH), Peter to Polly Roweboth (Rowe)          7-18-1813
HILL, Asa to Nancy Clark                                    1-19-1815
HINKSON, John to Betsy Keely                                4-27-1816
HOFKINS, John to Mary Bevington                             2-4-1813
HOW, John to Elizabeth McVay                                10-17-1816
HUGHES, James to Polley Williams                            10-1-1814
HUKILL, Zebulon to Jane Harper                              2-4-1817
HULLINGER, George to Mary Bowser                            8-31-1817
HURLEY, Wm. to Lucy Kendle                                  11-22-1810
HUSHAW, Jacob to Rachel Foster                              3-31-1814
JACKSON, Uriah to Ann Allen                                 3-12-1812
JAMISON, Jacob to Drucilla(?) Harrison                      3-25-1815
JEFFERS, Isaac to Nancy Faul (Fant)                  (no date-1816)
JOHNSON, Isaac to Sarah Kervan(?)                           7-22-1815
JONES, Mathus to Elizabeth Allen                            3-9-1815
KENDALL, Jos. to Phebe Hincle                              1-20-1814
```

461

```
KENDLE, Wm. to Elizabeath McCaliss                          8-1-1815
KERRAN, John to Abigail Clemmons                            1-23-1817
KILGORE, John C. to Elizabeth Horney                        1-13-1817
LEAR, Edward to Betsey Anderson                             8-4-1814
LEAVERTON, John to Mary Thurman                             9-2-1813
LEE, John to Polly Richards; mar. within 30 days
                              past;        dated            4-20-1813
LEVERTON, Daniel to Isabella Barker                         8-15-1816
LEWS, Thomas to Juliana Scwartz                             12-5-1811
LOOFBORGH, Wade to Mary Pancost                             5-15-1813
LOOFBOURROW, Nathen to Hannah Pancost                       3-26-1815
LOVE, William to Ann Holladay                               3-4-1813
McCALESS, Wm. to Peggy Robinson                             8-20-1815
McCANDLES, Hugh to Sally Parrot                             1-24-1815
McCARTNY, Isaac to Elizabeth Heath                          9-5-1816
McCLURE, Henry to Mary Toothaker                            12-25-1817
McCOY, Jesse to Martha Sanders                              1-2-1812
McCOY, John to Sally Casebolt                               6-28-1814
McDORMAN, Riston to Elizabeth Killgore                      1-2-1812
McGOWAN, James to Saray Carder                              4-22-1812
McGOWAN, John to Polly Rian                                 3-10-1811
McKAY, Robert to Sophia Mendinghall                         11-19-1817
McLAUGHLIN, William to Elizabeth Hannaman                   12-31-1812
MARSHALL, Sam'l to Nancy Barber                             1-14-1814
MARTIN, Charles to Elizabeth Parker                         7-8-1813
MAXWELL, Ephraim to Nancy More                              6-4-1814
MILLER, Henry to Sally Powers                               8-18-1812
MILLER, HUGH to Hannah Fansher                              9-19-1816
MILLER, Sollomon to Mary Glase                              6-11-1816
MONOHON, Samuel to Caty H obsugh                            12-4-1812
MOON, David to Mary Ellis                                   1-7-1812
MOON, Jos. to Mrs. Bendaa Dawson                            3-2-1815
MORE, Ezekiel to Priscilla Newland                          1-12-1815
MORRIS, Samuel to Jane Moor                                 10-30-1817
NEELY, Nicholas to Rhoda Hankins           two             (6-1-1815
                                           dates            (6-2-1815
NEWLAND, George to Mary Pendergrass                         4-20-1816
PAGE, Edmond to Rachel McDormen                             8-12-1813
PANCOST, Shreves to Polly Myres                             8-3-1812
PARIS, Hiram M. to Nancy Baker                              5-2-1816
PARKER, James to Jeane Powel                                2-14-1817
PARKER, Thos. to Mary Thompson                              1-20-1814
PATTERSON, James to Isabella Rodgers                        12-17-1812
PATTERSON, Jos. to Isabella Caldwell                        11-29-1814
PAXSON, Nathen to Hannah Davis (Davison)                    4-28-1814
POPEJOY, William to Polly Thompson                          9-26-1811
POPEJOY, William to Nancy Wiley                             10-2-1817
PRICE, John to Catherine Murley                             10-15-1814
RANKIN, John to Sarah Smith                                2-17-1814
```

```
RANKIN, Thomas to Barbary Fultz                          2-25-1813
REECE, Owen to Margaret Moon                            12-23-1813
RICHARDS, Saul to Nancy Pendergrass                      9-28-1815
RIDDLE, Abner to Sarah Thomas                            8-1-1816
RITTENHOUSE, Richard to Susannah Rowe                    1-21-1813
ROMIND, Noah to Hannah Clavenger                         2-21-1813
ROWLEY, Alpeus to Seley Keller                           8-23-1812
ROZETT, James to Susanah Jemison                        12-31-1814
RUDE, James to Mary Trenany                              9-4-1815
SALMAN, William to Polly Moore                          11-24-1817
SANDERSON, Harvy to Ruth Higgins                         3-14-1816
SCOTT, David to Sarah Archer                             2-6-1817
SEAMAN, John to Elesabeth Harroson                       2-16-1812
SHANER, Peter to Polly Boyd                             11-23-1816
SHRANGER, George to Margaret Bennett                     6-1-1815
SILLUK(?), Isaac to Lydia Upp                            6-13-1816
SKIDMORE, Jeremiah to Melly Sonard (Soward)              5-16-1813
SKILES, James to Catherine Smith                         6-23-1813
SMALLEY, Jos. to Polly Rogers                            4-20-1815
SMITH, John to Elenour Ellis                             2-26-1815
SMITH, John to Lydea Skiles                              4-16-1815
SOWARD, Daniel to Sarah Connelly                         2-14-1813
SPRAY, James to Charity Sanders                          3-12-1816
STEBBLEFIELD, Robt. to Sarah Funk                        5-14-1814
STINSON, Thos. to Sarah Benegar                          5-2-1815
STOUT, William to Mary Vandolah                          9-27-1812
SUTHERLAND, Robert to Hannah Ross                        5-7-1811
          License issued Fayette Co., Mar. in Ross Co.
SWEET, Joseph to Polly Popejoy                           8-1-1816
TALIMAN, Isiach to Mary Newman                           3-26-1815
TARENTON(?), William to Elizabeth Newby                 10-15-1812
TAULGHMAN, Jacob to Eppe West                            1-30-1814
TEAQUIS, Neddy to Elizabeth Bush                        12-20-1812
THOMPSON, Jacob to Nancy Carder                         12-8-1811
THOMPSON, John to Susannah Pursley                      10-25-1814
TIMMONS, Jesse to Susannah Blue                          2-27-1817
          License issued Fayette Co., mar. Pickaway Co.
TROTHERGILL, Eliziah to Betsy Carpenter                  6-28-1814
WADDLE, Robert to Eleanor Orr                            1-10-1812
WEBSTER, Samuel to Peggy King          (1814?)          11-1-1815
WHITSTONE, Abraham to Mary Hincle                       12-2-1813
WICK, John to Elizabeth King                             4-18-1811
WICKS, Wm. to Peggy Redman                               4-10-1817
WILCOX, Wm. to Alys Blue                                 6-4-1816
WILKIN, William to Rebecca Windle                        8-13-1812
WILKINS, George to Susannah Windel                       9-15-1814
WILLIAMS, George to Nelly Riel                     (Not dated-1817)
WILLIAMS, John to Sarah Dungan                          12-26-1816
WILSON, BENJAMIN to Ann Heath                           11-25-1817
WINGET, Luther to Pheby Rude.                            6-29-1813
WITTY, Jonathan to. Rachel Sanderson                     5-15-1814
WOOD, Joel to Sarah Price                                5-8-1814
WOODERD, Isaac W. to Margaret Todhunter                 12-4-1817
```

463

The following marriages were taken from Marriage Record A. All of the marriages prior to the year 1818 were recorded with the marriages recorded in 1819 and 1820.

ALLEN, Samuel to Sophia Lattimer	8-10-1823
ALLOWAYS, Joseph to Hannah Hankins	2-11-1816
ANDERSON, Robert to Sarah Rowe	9-16-1819
ARCHER, John to Sarah Smith	1-24-1822
ARNOLD, Elijah to Rebecca Bush	2-12-1823
ARNOLD, John to Rachel Gilbert	1-27-1820
BAILEY, Burton to Harriet Timmons	9-18-1820
BANNAN, William to Betsy Redding	2-25-1819
BARGER, Philip to Jane Andrews	3-7-1824
BARKER, James to Jane Simpson	4-21-1824
BARKER, John to Christena Curl	12-1-1822
BARNET, Hiram to Mary McArthur	4-1-1823
BEATY, James to Margaret Gibson	5-25-1820
BELL, Rev. Wm. to Catherine Dickerson	7-13-1824
BENTLEY, Caleb to Rebecca Bingar	12-19-1822
BIGELOW, Hiram to Abigail Yeoman	1-28-1818
BINEGAR, John to Elizabeth Parker	8-12-1819
BINEGAR, Samuel to Sarah Larkins	2-9-1820
BLACK, William to Mariah Dougan	11-7-1815
BLACK, William to Sarah Davis	8-20-1822
BLEW (BLUE?), Benjamin to Margaret Wileg (or Wiley)	8-1-1824
BLOOMER, Joseph to Mary McDonald	7-10-1823
BLUE, David to Zelpah Bohrer - dated Pickaway Co., Ohio	6-12-1823
BLUE, Uriah to Fanny Scott	2-12-1824
BLUE, William to Margaret Hamilton	6-4-1818
BOETWICK, Adoriran to Roxanna Buckley	12-10-1822
BOHRER, Peter to Eliza Needham	12-21-1822
BOSTWICK, William to Sarah Gillispie	7-22-1823
BOUGHAN, Zachariah to Rebecca Keran	2-19-1824
BOXLEY, William to Mary Row	3-23-1823
BOYD, George to Nancy Beard	5-2-1816
BRIENT, Benjamin to Susannah Harper	10-14-1819
BRILEY, John to Lydia Thornton	9-7-1824
BRITON, Joseph to Elizabeth Denham	9-2-1824
BROWN, Hezekiah to Marey Williams	4-27-1823
BRUIN, Martin to Priscilla Denny	3-28-1822
BRYAN, Jonathan to Polly Johnson	11-29-1821
BURBRIDGE, Robert to Sarah Hays	6-10-1818
BURNET, Henry to Magdalene Bush	11-26-1818
BUSH, Daniel to Susana J. Boughan	2-7-1816
BUSH, Philip to Rebecca Parret	8-16-1820
CAHILL, Isaac to Polly Popejoy	9-28-1822
CAHILL, Joseph to Elizabeth Crabb	5-14-1818
CANON, Byard to Sarah Blue	2-20-1823
CARPENTER, Elisha M. to Mary Busick	12-10-1822
CARR, Jacob to Elizabeth Thompson	8-1-1824

```
CARR, Solomon to Rebecca Price                                    3-18-1819
CHENOWETH, William to Elizabeth Morgan                            2-26-1824
CHORN, John L. to Nancy Davis                                     9-16-1819
CLARK, Benjamin to Sarah Gilbert                                  3-23-1818
COCKERILL, William S. to Phebe Mooney                             2-22-1824
COEN, John to Margaret Baldwin                                   11-16-1815
COIL, Andrew to Elizabeth Foster                                  1-1-1823
COIL, Isaac to Betsy Hesser                                      10-30-1823
COIL, Peter to Catharine Hesser                                   3-12-1824
COOPER, Isaac to Polly Carder                                    10-29-1820
COOPER, Wm to Clory Bonner                                        4-10-1823
CORE, Christian to Catharine Glass                               11-29-1824
COX, Andrew to Nansey Thomas                                     12-6-1824
CREAMER, Simeon to Elizabeth Conner                               4-24-1823
CRISTY, Sml. to Rosana Creamer                                    3-14-1822
CRUSENBERRY, William to Milley Chew                              12-18-1823
CUNNINGHAM, John to Peneny Henkle                                 2-14-1822
CUTTER, Thomas to Margaret Bowhur                                10-1-1818
DAVIS, Benjamin R. to Jane Compton                                9-7-1819
DAVIS, Edward to Fanny Burson                                    11-16-1823
DAVIS, James to Sarah Brownfield                                  3-21-1816
DEVAULT, Noah to Elizabeth Pendergrass                            2-9-1824
DOSTER, Lewis to Joanah Hand                                      1-17-1822
DRAPER, John to Martha Moon                                      10-16-1822
DRAPER, Simson to Nancy Larkins                                   1-3-1822
DUNBAR, George to Elizabeth Barrett                               6-28-1821
DYE, Harrison to Leathy Thomas                                    1-15-1824
EMERLING, George to Elizabeth Lewis                               2-28-1822
EVERTSON, Caleb to Mary Mantle (note: no date recorded)         -----(1821)
EYRE, Robert to Elizabeth Cockaril                                6-22-1819
EYRE, Samuel to Elizabeth Stout                                  12-27-1821
FAINT, Phillip to Polly McGill                                   10-11-1821
FEAGINS, Absalam to Margaret Cook                                 4-29-1819
FENT (FEUT), James to Ann Rose                                    7-26-1821
FIELDS, Gilbert to Rhoda Soward                                  10-18-1818
FISHER, John to Mary Hanes                                        6-4-1818
FISK, Jesse to Regana Henkle                                      4-13-1824
FLICK, William to Sarah Thurman                                   2-18-1816
FLOOD, Obediah to Jane How                                        4-22-1819
FOSTER, Nathan to Ann Boyd                                       11-6-1823
FREE, Frederick to Susanah Mark                                  11-27-1823
FREEMAN, Henry to Catharine Gaskill                               3-2-1820
(GARINGER), Alexander to Elizabeth Boots                        (8-1)-1818
GARRINGER, John to Elizabeth Johnson                             5-1-1823
GASSON, William to Patsey Burbridge                              1-13-1820
GAZE, Jacob to Jane Worthington                                  8-26-1824
GELLER, George to Phebe Hathaway                                 5-1-1821
GELLER, Jacob to Mary Willson                                    7-10-1823
GILMORE, John to Rebecca Vandolak                                7-16-1822
```

```
GRACY, Samuel to Rachel Snivly                              11-2-1824
GRUBB, James to Mary Bowhur                                 10-1-1818
GRUBB, Stephen to Diana Halland                            8-6-1818
GUNNING, John to Lavinia Stitt                             9-9-1819
HAGLER, George to Tabitha Dickins                          12-28-(1820?)
HAIGER, John to Ann Hanson                                 6-17-1823
HALL, John to Polly Timmons                                6-11-1824
HAND, Robert O. to Sally Cohran                            7-1-1819
HANER, John Jr. to Elsy Kikendall                          5-20-1823
HARPER, William to Rachel Truax                            3-8-1822
HARRISON, Michael to Rachel Rupart                         8-27-1822
HEATH, George to Sarah Rosebrook                           3-11-1823
HENDERSON, Daniel to Sarah Smith                           9-30-1819
HENKLE, Elen to Sally Rowe                                 1-15-1824
HENKLE, Jacob to Phebe Smith                               10-10-1815
HENKLE, Salem to Elizabeth Haulk                           5-8-1824
HENTON, Benjamin to Rachel Stinson                         4-17-1821
HEYNE, William to Jane Steel                               9-10-1818
HIDY, William to Barbary Hinkle                            12-27-1822
HILL, William to Jane Brown                                4-3-1823
HINKLE, Elan to Sally Rowe(recorded twice-see Henkle above)  1-15-1824
HIZER, Richard to Jemimah Brown                            7-12-1821
HOPPIS, Jacob to Hannah Davis                              10-25-1824
HOTEMAN, Jesse to Mary Twitchel                            3-7-1822
HOW, Jacob to Sarah Matlock                                1-19-1813
HUGHS, David to Emily Whitsell                             5-23-1818
HUKEL, Hiram to Nancy Harper                               3-1-1821
HUKLE, Stephen to Anna Beaty                               1-2-1823
HUNT, Joseph to Nancy McKillip                             7-27-1824
IMAN, Abraham to Phebe Harper                              12-12-1822
JEFFRIES, Isaac to Nancy Faut (note: no date recorded)     ----(1816?)
JENKINS, Jacob to Ruth Creamer                             8-28-1823
JOHNSON, Thomas to Elizabeth Armon                         5-27-1817
JOHNSTON, Macajah to Rhoda Johnson                         9-16-1811
JONES, Amos to Elizabeth Hillard                           12-27-1821
JONES, Norman F. to Polly McLean                           5-27-1819
JONES, Thomas to Sarah Karson                              12-28-1814
KEARNS, Azariah to Mary Blue                               10-27-1824
KEE, Samuel to Elizabeth Greathouse                        2-20-1824
KERKPATRICK, John to Elizabeth Bush                        4-19-1824
KERR, William to Betsey Baker                              12-14-1815
KEY, Martin to Ruth Merryman                               8-17-1823
KINDEL, Wm to Elizabeth McCaless                           8-1-1815
KIRKENDALL, Moses to Tene Malot                            10-15-1818
KNIGHT, William C. to Eleanor Vanvaulkingburg              3-1-1823
KROUS, John to Rebecca Bowers                              2-20-1824
LARKIN, John to Polly Smith                                9-7-1823
LAWYER, Jacob to Phebe Carr                                2-4-1816
```

466

```
LAWYER, William to Catherine Emerick                          1-18-1822
LEACH, Benjamin to Sarah Bostwick                             2-1-1822
LEVALLY, Joseph to Eve Hushaw                                 10-10-1819
LEVALLY, Joseph to Betsy Hamilton                             8-10-1824
LEVEE, Lewis to Elizabeth Levally                             11-4-1815
LINDSEY, Samuel to Nancy Young - dated Pickaway Co., Ohio     4-12-1821
LITTLER, Seth to Fanny Brown                                  4-15-1824
LOCKRIDGE, William to Margrit Benson                          10-17-1822
LOWDERMAN, Henry to Mary Thompson                             12-20-1818
LOWDERMAN, Henry to Elizabeth Burnett                         6-17-1824
McCAFFERTY, David to Varicissa Black                          8-20-1818
McCAFFERTY, William to Sarah Nutt                             4-25-1820
McCALESS, Wm to Peggy Robinson                                8-22-1815
McCARTY, Andrew to Nancy Kilgore - both of Ross Co., Ohio     11-26-1822
McCAY, Robert to Betsy Myers                                  5-9-1819
McCLURE, James to Mary Todhunter                              10-10-1822
McCONNELL, John to Margaret Byers                             12-30-1818
McDANIEL, George to Henrietta Milbourn                        12-25-1823
McDONALD, William to Susanah Smith                            1-31-1822
McHENRY, Isaac to Jamima Everston                             11-20-1815
McKEE, James to Emly Chew                                     4-18-1822
McMAHAN, George to Mary Mobley                                4-10-1823
McMULLEN, William to Catherine Myers                          2-5-1824
MADDUX, Severn to Elizabeth Hill                              1-18-1818
MAN, John to Matilda Allegre                                  4-10-(1823)
MAN, Warner to Nancy Pavey                                    11-4-1823
MARK, Joseph to Amy Buxh                                      1-9-1823
MARKS, Jonathan to Susannah Plaugher                         9-10-1818
MARTIN, Josiah to Sus nah How                                2-22-1816
MASON, Owen to Elizabeth Vanvaltingburg                      5-22-1822
MERCHANT, William to Elizabeth Smith                         5-19-1822
MERPHEY, John to Sahry Newlan                                2-25-1823
MILLER, Absolam to Polly Grim                                12-17-1818
MILLER, George to Mary Pool                                  9-18-1823
MILLER, Leonard to Mary Handley                              3-30-1820
MILLER, Robert to Nancy Hill                                 3-15-1821
MOON, Aaron to Rosannah Powel                                2-14-1822
MOON, John to Mary Clemming  (note: no day given)            8- -1818
MOON, Jonathan to Katherine Davis                            4-7-1824
MOON, Thomas to Anny Ellis                                   2-18-1819
MOORE, Anthony to Mary Thompson                              11-21-1822
MOORE, Ephraim R. to Ann Dyer                                2-5-1824
MORRIS, William to Sarah Allen                               9-1-1822
MORRIS, William to Peggey Right                              12-19-1822
MORRISS, Isaac to Jane Rich                                  1-24-1820
MORTEMORE , William to Julia Ann Noland                      2-24-1822
MOUSER, George to Sarah Gilmore                              11-23-1821
MURPHY, James to Jain Morris                                 1-18-1823
NEWLAND, John to Nancy Newland                               4-16-1824
NEWMAN, Isaac to Margaret Slaughter                          1-16-1823
NUN, Joseph to Mary Olinger                                  1-29-1824
OGDEN, Benjamin to Sarah Stretch                             3-4-1824
```

```
OLIVER, Andrew to Christiana Myers                              3-25-1824
PAINTER, John to Deborah Heath                                  12-25-1822
PARIS, Daniel to Elisa Mills                                    2-1-1821
PARROTTE, Thomas to Elizabeth Coil                              5-20-1821
PATTERSON, Joseph to Jane Rodgers                               12-20-1818
PAUL, Alx'r to Eliza Smith                                      2-21-1822
PENDERGRASS, John to Ann Davis                                  11-1-1818
PERSON, William to Ann Hanes                                    7-9-1823
PETERSON, Jesse to Jemimah Bush  (note:  no year given)         9-9-(1819-20?)
POTER, William to Elizabeth Keller                              1-8-1818
POWEL, Philip Jr. to Mary McCaleb                               2-27-1823
POWEL, Robert to Polly James                                    11-14-1822
PRIDDY, George to Jane McDonald                                 9-28-1819
RAMSEY, Alexander to Tabitha Scissel                            11-20-1820
RAMSEY, Andrew to Clarisa Toothaker                             4-1-1824
RANKIN, Jacob to Jane Paul                                      3-5-1820
RANKIN, Jacob to Elizabeth Carr                                 3-29-1821
REED, Manlove to Dianna Johnson                                 5-11-1820
RIBHT, Jonathan to Joana Davis                                  3-27-1823
RILEA, John to Pegay Bevington                                  3-21-1816
ROEBUCK, Abner to Naomi Thompson                                10-11-1821
ROSEBROOK, John to Nancy McDaniel                               11-16-1815
ROWE, Jonathan to Lucretia Vanvaulkingburg                      2-14-1816
ROWE, Thos. to Prudence Marpole (Marple)                        3-14-1824
RYEN, Thomas to Nancy Depew                                     3-1-1824
SANDERS, John to Betsey Goodheart                               9-28-1815
SANDERS, Samuel to Jean Jones                                   5-20-1821
SCOTT, Joseph to Patience Gregory                               4-13-1818
SHACKLEFORD, William to Mary House                              4-1-1823
SHIPLEY, Peter to Nancy Keller                                  2-11-1816
SHOOK, Henry to Barbary Kimble                                  11-27-1823
SIEES, Abraham to Polly Bartlow                                 6-30-1819
SNIDER, John to Delila Beard                                    6-13-1820
SQUIRE, Justus to Jane Gilmore                                  12-16-1819
STAFFORD, Young to Polly Heath                                  10-6-1818
STERIT, Charles to Tena Henkle                                  4-4-1822
STEWART, James to Mary Berriger                                 8-7-1818
STINSON, David to Elenor Haney                                  9-14-1819
STOUT, Peter to Ann Eyrs                                        5-3-1819
STROPE, Wm to Nancy Blue                                        3-16-1824
STUBBLEFIELD, John to Tabitha Funk                              11-2-1823
STUBBLEFIELD, Robert to Dorathy Funk                            7-29-1822
SWANEY, Robert to Catherine Hatfield                            9-26-1819
TAYLOR, William to Hannah Sanderson                             2-13-1818
TERREL, John to Lydia Hays                                      2-17-1819
THOMPSON, David to Nelly Pendergrass                            5-26-1822
THOMPSON, David to Hannah Car (note:  this entry cross out)     9-17-1823
THOMPSON, James to Rhoda Boyd                                   1-5-1821
```

468

THURMAN, Johnson to Rosannah Boots	5-30-1816
TIMMONS, Lewis to Susannah Mouser	12-20-1821
TODHUNTER, Jacob to Rebecca Douston	6-4-1818
TOMLINSON, Jesse to Catherine Gaskill	8-31-1822
TRACEY, John to Levina Henderson	12-2-1821
TURNER, Andrew to Christena Allen	3-13-1823
TURNIPSEED, Benjamin to Rebecca Glase	4-28-1823
TWAY, Nathaniel to Sophia Salmon	10-6-1822
WABULL, Adam to Ann Person	4-3-1821
WARDEN, Timothy to Saray Taynor	7-19-1820
WARNER, John to Rachel Farmer	2-6-1823
WATKINS, Moses to Mary Kee	12-2-1819
WELLS, Wm to Mary Maybeery	2-22-1821
WHITE, Andrew to Moddy Rankin	8-11-1822
WHITE, Samuel to Nancy How	5-9-1819
WILCOX, Zeno W. to Martha Elis	2-20-1823
WILLIAMS, Calven to Poly Pursley	11-27-1823
WILLIAMS, James W. to Elizabeth Marks	11-30-1820
WILLIAMS, Joseph to Mary Davis	3-8-1823
WILLIAMS, William to Nancy Roebuck	11-20-1823
WILLSON, William to Anny Hill	4-5-1821
WILSON, George to Phebe Coliss	3-28-1822
WILSON, George to Sarah Miller	3-16-1824
WILSON, Henry to Polly Burbrige	8-16-1821
WILSON, Lewis P. to Eleanor Bodkin	8-5-1824
WILSON, Samuel to Sarah Heath	1-16-1821
WILSON, William to Margaret Hoskins	10-13-1819
WINDLE, Abraham to Sarah Smith	7-25-1822
WINDLE, Joseph to Caty Harper	10-8-1818
WITSON, Thomas to Nancy Philips	11-25-1824
WOODARD, Isaac M. to Jane Fisher	1-29-1824
WORKMAN, Joseph to Sarah Carr	12-23-1820
WRIGHT, Hosea to Mary Rankin	4-23-1820
WRIGHT, Jacob to Anna Caylor	2-28-1822
WRIGHT, Josiah to Amy Atcher	1-2-1823
ZIMMERMAN, Eli to Polly Smith	9-2-1823

The following records were taken from "Death Record 1" located in the Probate Court of the court house at Wauseon. They include only records for persons 40 years and older. The page on which the record may be found in the original book are given in parenthesis. Abbreviations used are : d=died; a=age; w=widow or widower; m=married; s=single; pd=place of death; pb=place of birth; res=residence. Residence is given only if it is different than place of death.

WISE, Polly - d 9-1-1867; a 74; w; pd Clinton; pb------. (1)
WISE, Mary - d 9-2-1867; a 67; m; pd Clinton; pb Pickaway Co. (1)
SALTZGABER, John - d 9-29-1867; a 60; m; pd Gorham; pb----------. (1)
KILBOUM (KILBOURNE), Stephen - d 10-6-1867; a 80; w; pd Clinton; pb-------(1)
BOSTOPH, _____(not given) - d 10-15-1867; a 63; s; pd Clinton; pb-------(1)
CHAMPLIN, Martin - d 11-18-1867; a 58; m; pd Pike twp.; pb Jefferson Co., N.Y. (2)
SEYMOUR, Effa Ann - d 12-12-1867; a 45½; m; pd York twp.; pb Reading, Burk Co.,
          Pa.; father, Geo. Markel. (2)
KELLER, Elizabeth - d 12-12-1867; a 58; m; pd Clinton; pb Born(?), Burk Co., Pa.;
          parents, Jno. & Margaret Bender. (2)
SOUTER, Barbara - d 2-23-1868; a 53; m; pd German twp.; pb Germany. (3)
OLMSTEAD, Austres - d 1-30-1868; a 63; m; pd Chesterfield; pb R.I.; name of
          father and mother, Hopkins. (3)
VASS, Frederick - d 1-13-1868; a 49; m; pd Henry Co.; pb Werden, Prussia. (3)
LEWIS, John - d 3-1-1868; a 62; m; pd Royalton; pb--------(3)
KELLAR, Sarah - d 5-20-1868; a 75; m; pd Fulton, Fulton Co.; pb Lavunand(?) Co.,
          Pa. (3)
NIXON, _____(not given) - d 9-6-1868; a 51; pd York; pb Beaver Co., Pa. (3)
BROWN, Henry L. - d 8-28-1868; a 67; m; pd Wauseon; pb Wauseon. (4)
MAUGER, George - d 8-8-1868; a 76; w; pd Royalton; pb-------. (4)
MARKLEY, John - d 7-29-1868; a (50); m; pd Clinton; pb--------. (4)
BROWN, Henry H. - d 8-28-1868; a 67; w; pd Clinton; pb N.Y. (4)
ROUSH, Jacob - d 11-27-1868; a 54; m; pd Swan Creek twp.; pb Penn. (4)
AUSPACH, Elizabeth - d 10-19-1868; a 74; w; pd Clinton twp.; pb Hagerstown, Md. (4)
KUTZLY, Elizabeth - d 12-29-1868; a 68; m; pd Fulton Co.; pb-------(4)
WHITE, Robert - d 10-17-1868; a 67; m; pd Pike twp.; pb New York. (4)
WATKINS, Thomas - d 8-22-1868; a 55; m; pd Delta; pb-------. (4)
NIXON, John - d 9-7-1868; a 56; m; pd Delta; pb Penn. (4)
MARTIN, Thomas - d 9-28-1868; a 50; m; pd Delta; pb------. (4)
SALSBERRY, Susan - d 11-1-1868; a 86; w; pd Delta; pb----------. (5)
FUNK, Joseph E. - d 1-4-1869; a 41; m; pd Wauseon; pb Philadelphia Co., Pa. (6)
CARPENTER, Richard - d 1-15-1869; a 77; m; pd Clinton twp.; pb Ballston, Saratoga
          Co., N. Y. (6)
DUNCAN, Mariah - d 2-28-1869; a 45; pd Amboy twp; pb-------. (6)
ECHART, Peter - d 3-9-1869; a 70; pd Amboy twp.; pb-------. (6)
BURR, Charles - d 1-14-1869; a 64; m; pd Clinton twp.; pb Plymouth, Bridgewater
          Co., Mass.; Parents, Elijah & Olive Burr. (6)
DAVALL, Job - d 3-26-1869; a 54; m; pd Amboy twp.; pb-------. (6)
WIEMANN, Maria A. - d 2-6-1869; a 82; w; pd Williams Co., O.; pb Hanover. (6)
NIESERAUER, Barbara - d 3-15-1869; a 61; m; pd Bryan, William Co.; pb-----. (6)
HERRICK, William D. - d 2-6-1869; a 60; m; pd Swanton, Lucas Co.; pb N.Y. (6)
MARSH, Julius N. - d 2-18-1869; a (50); m; pd Swanton, Lucas Co.; pb-------; res.
          Ottokee, Fulton Co. (6)

HALL, Reuben - d 6-30-1869; a 74-8-4; m; pd Amboy twp.; pb Connecticut. (7)
ALDRICH, Thomas - d 10-24-1869; a 77-1-25; m; pd Royalton twp; pb Adams, Mass. (7)
ROBB, Nathaniel - d 3-10-1870; a 60; m; pd Royalton twp.; pb New Hampshire. (7)
CARPENTER, Jos. B. - d 11-18-1869; a 49-10-3; m; pd Royalton twp.; pb N.Y. (7)
BUTLER, Mary - d 11-19-1869; a 66-11-2; m; pd Chesterfield; pb Bloomfield,
        Ontario Co., N. Y. (7)
HATHAWAY, Elizabeth - d 3-18-1870; a 46y 20d; m; pd Chesterfield; pb Romnus,
        Seneca Co., N. Y. (7)
STANTON, Elizabeth - d 1-1-1870; a 84; w; pd Chesterfield; pb Penn. (7)
PERSONS, Samuel - d 11-23-1869; a 71-4-26; m; pd Gorham twp.; pb Penn. (7)
GAMBER, Margaret Jane - d 7-7-1869; a 46-6-18; m; pd Gorham twp.; pb Penn. (7)
VANARSDALEN, Catharine - d 7-7-1869; a 5903017; m; pd Gorham twp.; pb N. J. (7)
GUILFORD, Phoebe - d 8-8-1869; a 48; m; pd Dover twp.; pb London. (8)
HOFFMIRE, Johanna - d 3-31-1870; a 71y 6m; w; pd Spring Hill; pb Md. (8)
HERRICK, Hughey - d 9-19-1869; a 69y 3m; m; pd Spring Hill; pb N. Y. (8)
PATTERSON, George - d 9-12-1869; a 78y 10m; m; pd Dover twp.; pb N. H. (8)
RITTENHOUSE, Mary - d 9-9-1869; a 71-3-4; w; pd Spring Hill; pb Penn. (8)
SHAFFER, Sally - d 4-25-1870; a 53; m; pd Dover twp.; pb Penn. (8)
VINE, John - d 5-7-1869; a 54-4-11; m; pd Dover twp.; pb N. Y. (8)
CRISPIN, Francis - d Sept. 1869; a 54y 11m; pd Fulton twp.; pb Lincolnshire,
        England. (8)
NOBBS, John - d 2-17-1870; a 74; m; pd Fulton twp.; pb England. (8)
RITTENHOUSE, H. S. - d 1-29-1870; a 74-7-9; m; pd Fulton twp.; pb Philadelphia,
        Penn. (8)
WATKINS, Wesley - d 9-24-1869; a 57-7-1; m; pd Fulton twp.; pb------. (8)
WITT, John - d 3-2-1870; a 76-5-15; m; pd Fulton twp.; pb Germany. (8)
FRAKER, Rebecca - d 5-10-1869; a 71-8-24; w; pd Swan Creek twp.; pb New Lisbon,
        Ohio. (8)
RAKER, Sarah - d 3-12-1870; a 81-9-2; w; pd Swan Creek twp.; pb Northumberland
        Co., Pa. (8)
SNYDER, Lovina - d 7-7-1869; a 46-6-29; m; pd Swan Creek twp.; pb Stark Co., Ohio.(8)
CRILE, Margaret - d 1-26-1870; a 44; w; pd York twp.; pb-----. (9)
CONSTABLE, Eliza - d July 1869; a 57; m; pd Delta; pb Entland. (9)
GARWOOD, Jesse - d 5-25-1869; a 77y 6d; m; pd York twp.; pb Lafayette Co., Pa. (9)
TRASK, Orville C. -d 3-3-1870; a 65-10-10; m; pd York twp.; pb Conn. (9)
ASHBACK, John - d 6-23-1869; a 41; m; pd Clinton twp.; pb Germany. (9)
BAYES, Mary - d 6-7-1869; a 53-2-18; m; pd Clinton twp.; pb Penn. (9)
BARTLETT, Calvin - d 9-15-1869; a 74-1-15; m; pd Clinton twp.; pb Mass. (9)
CRONINGER, Mary - d 3-9-1870; a 79-8-13; s; pd Wauseon; Pb Penn. (9)
FREY, Christian - d 12-30-1869; a 42y 17d; m; pd Clinton twp.; pb France. (9)
HOLLISTER, Philemon - d 11-15-1869; a 79y 11m; w; pd Wauseon; pb Conn. (9)
HARRISON, Nancy L. - d 8-7-1869; a 78y 10m; w; pd Clinton twp.; pb N. Y. (9)
MERRILL, Samuel S. - d 6-30-1869; a 50; s; pd Clinton twp.; pb England. (9)
MIKESELL, Catharine - d 12-26-1869; a 55-3-11; m; pd Clinton twp.; pb Jefferson
        Co., Ohio. (9)
MUNN, Russell - d 11-25-1869; a 82-9-8; w; pd Wauseon; pb Conn. (9)
SWAN, Theodore - d 12-6-1869; a 42-1-7; m; pd Wauseon; pb Wayne Co., Ohio. (9)
WILLEY, Margaret - d 8-9-1869; a 54-5-1; m; pd Clinton twp.; pb Penn. (9)
EIKER, Jacob - d 12-13-1869; a 82-7-15; m; pd German twp.; pb France. (10)

FIDLER, Sarah - d 7-7-1869; a 76-8-3; m; pd German twp.; pb Penn. (10)
GEARICH, Joseph - d 10-2-1869; a 40y 11m; m; pd German twp.; pb France. (10)
KLOPPENSTINE, Peter - d 3-17-1870; a 52-4-15; m; pd German twp.; pb Franc. (10)
MILLER, Paulina - d July 1869; a 44; m; pd German tqp. pb Penn. (10)
PERNEY, Josephine - d 10-31-1869; a 50; w; pd German twp.; pb France. (10)
ROTH, Mary - d 2-10-1870; a 65; m; pd German two.; pb France. (10)
RUPP, Peter - d 6-19-1869; a 64y 8d; m; pd German twp.; pb Baden. (10)
SHIBELER, Henry - d 10-14-1869; a 80; m; pd German twp.; pb Penn. (10)
WINGLER, John - d 8-22-1869; a 62-1-10; w; pd German twp.; pb Switzerland. (10)
WYMER, Sally - d 11-8-1869; a 86y 17d; w; pd German twp.; pb France. (10)
KREIZER, Samuel - d 8-25-1869; a 74; m; pd German twp.; pb Penn. (10)
BLACK, Camilla - d 2-2-1871; a 88; w; pd Swan Creek twp.; pb Mass. (11)
RAKER, George - d 2-2-1871; a 50; m; pd Swan Creek twp.; pb Swan, Fulton Co. (11)
STATES, Sarintha - d 11-25-1870; a 45; m; pd Swan Creek twp.; pb Ohio. (11)
WRIGHT, William - d 11-19-1870; a 70; m; pd Swan Creek twp.; pb Penn. (11)
STINE, Catharine - d 8-11-1870; a 53; m; pd Pike twp.; pb Virginia. (11)
SCHOF, John - d 10-24-1871; a 56; pd Pike twp.; pb Witsmber(?), Germany. (11)
BROWN, Abram Westbrook - d 7-23-1870; 60; m; pd Ottokee; pb Great Bend, N.Y. (11)
HIBBARD, Jane Eliza - d 2-19-1871; a 47; m; pd Ottokee, pb N.Y. (11)
NOLAN, Sallie - d 11-3-1870; a 59; m; pd Ottokee; pb Portage Co., O. (11)
TIFFANY, Lydia - d 3-8-1871; a 85; w; pd Ottokee; pb N.Y. (11)
BARBAR, Weiler - d Jn. 10, 1870; a 55; m; pd Dover twp.; pb Baden, Germany. (11)
KIBLES, Susanna - d 12-8-1870; a 82; m; pd German twp.; pb Switzerland. (12)
HUTZMAN, David - d 10-23-1870; a 79; m; pd German twp.; pb Summerset Co., Ohio. (12)
DODGE, Warren - d 11-14-1870; a 66; m; pd Royalton twp.; pb Rudess, Seneca Co.
                N.Y. (12)
POWEL, Stephen - d 8-21-1870; a 89; m; pd Royalton twp.; pb-------(12)
SPENCER, Sarah - d 12-15-1870; a 59; m; pd Royalton twp.; pb Gorham twp., Fulton
                Co. (12)
VANARSDULEN, Gilbert - d 6-25-1870; a 68; m; pd Royalton twp.; pb N. Jersey. (12)
BARTON, Sarah Jane d 6-28-1871; a 43; m; pd Franklin twp.; pb Vermont. (12)
BIRBER, Barbara - d 6-3-1870; a 44; m; pd Franklin twp.; pb Germany. (12)
KARR, Sarah - d 2-19-1871; a 65; m; pd Franklin twp.; pb Penn. (12)
STORRES, Sebastian - d 7-25-1870; a 63; m; pd Franklin twp.; pb Germany. (13)
LEWIS, Rhoda - d 3-20-1871; a 74; w; pd Amboy twp.; pb Amboy, N.Y. (13)
ANDREWS, Sarah A. - d 10-12-1870; a 81; w; pd York twp.; pb Baltimore, Md. (13)
CREW, Lucy - d 5-7-1870; a 65; m; pd York twp.; pb Charles City, Pa. (13)
RUPERT, Henry - d 6-18-1870; a 83; w; pd York twp.; pb Burks Co., Pa. (13)
TAYLOR, Calvin - d 4-14-1870; a 65; m; pd Delta; pb Hartford, Conn. (13)
GILLIS, Samuel - d 2-9-1871; a 81; m; pd Chesterfield; pb Argile, N.Y. (13)
HARRIS, Joseph - d 7-15-1870; a 41; m; pd Chesterfield; pb Ross River, N.Y. (13)
STANTON, Elizabeth - d 1-8-1870; a 84; s; pd Chesterfield; pb Penn. (13)
BROWN, Gustavus - d 3-2-1871; a 41; m; pd Wauseon; pb Maine. (14)
CATELY, John - d 3-15-1871; a 58; m; pd Wauseon; pb N.Y. (14)
CARTER, Susanna - d 12-18-1870; a 70; w; pd Clinton twp.; pb Erie Co., Penn. (14)
DOUGHERTY, Elizabeth - d 5-16-1870; a 40; s; pd Clinton twp.; pb unknown. (14)
GORSUCH, Catharine - d 11-12-1870; a---; w; pd Clinton twp.; pb Penn. (14)
HUNTINGTON, Elisha - d 4-8-1870; a 73; m; pd Clinton twp.; pb Conneticut. (14)
McCLAREN, Robert - d 11-5-1870; a 61; s; pd Wauseon; pb Wauseon. (14)
MIKESELL, James Wilson - d 7-21-1870; a 53; m; pd Clinton twp.; pb Penn. (14)
BERRY, Arminda - d 4-8-1871; a 41; m; pd Fulton; pb not known. (14)

DAVIS, Harriett J. - d 6-11-1870; a 62; w; pd Fulton; pb Ross Co., Ohio. (14)
SPANGLER, Margaret - d 2-26-1872; a 72; pd,Franklin twp.; pb Switzerland. (17)
SEILER, Margaret - d 7-27-1871; a 50; m; pd Franklin twp.; pb Switzerland. (17)
MOWEY, Jenks - d 11-15-1871; a 74; m; pd Royalton twp.; pb Rhode Island. (18)
KINNEY, Jacob - d 2-9-1872; a 60; m; pd Royalton twp.; pb Penn. (18)
DRAKE, Elisha F. - d 8-27-1871; a 60; m;.pd Royalton twp.; pb Hampshire, Mass. (18)
THORNTON, George H. - d 8-23-1871; a 42; pd Newburh; pb Wayne Co., Ohio. (18)
VANSCODER, Hannah - d 3-5-1872; a---; m; pd Swan Creek twp.; pb Coshocton, Ohio.(19)
BRAILEY, Gideon - d 6-9-1871; a 78; m; pd Swan Creek twp.; pb N.Y. (19)
NEWCOMB, Esther H. - d 6-27-1871; a 40; m; pd Swan Creek twp.; pb Canada. (19)
HOYLE, Jane E. - d 3-10-1872; a 58; m; pd Swan Creek twp.; pb N.Y. (19)
SHEFFIELD, Margaret E. - d 12-14-1871; a 67; w; pd Swan Creek twp.; pb N.Y. (19)
LEWIS, Joshua - d 9-9-1871; a 90; w; pd Swan Creek twp.; pb Connecticut. (19)
PERRY, Fanny - d 2-18-1872; a 78; w;.pd Swan Creek twp.; pb Mass. (19)
KNAPP, Henry - d 11-5-1871; a 75; m; pd German twp.; pb Bavaria. (20)
KNAPP, Christian - d 1-6-1872; a 70; m;. pd German twp.; pb Bavaria (20)
KEEFFER, Martin - d 9-2-1871; a 79; m; pd German twp.; pb Elsos, Europe. (20)
MARKLEY, Catharine - d 3-4-1872; a 87; w; pd German twp.; pb Penn. (20)
WEBER, Barbary - d 12-31-1871; a 43;.m; pd German twp.: pb Germany. (20)
WARD, Hannah - d 2-18-1872; a 43; m; pd Ottokee; pb N.Y. (21)
PEIRCE, Mary - d 10-5-1871; a 62; w; pd Ottokee; pb N.Y. (21)
HAGERMAN, Mary J. - d 12-22-1871; a 44; m; pd Dover twp.; pb Wayne Co., Ohio. (21)
MARKLEY, Emma - d 11-17-1871; a 53; m; pd Dover twp.; pb N.Y. (21)
CARTER, William - d 2-14-1872; a 81; m; pd Dover twp.; pb N.Y. (21)
SWARTOUT, Amy - d 1-26-1872; a 72; w; pd Dover twp.; pb Orange Co., N.Y. (21)
HAMPSHIRE, Joseph - d 2-4-1872; a 50; m; pd Ottokee; pb Highland Co., O. (21)
YOUNGS, Marella - d 6-15-1871; a 47; m; pd Ottokee; pb Berlin, Erie Co., O. (21)
HOLBEN, Catharine - d 12-13-1871; a 88; w; pd Amboy twp.; pb Penn. (22)
BAILEY, William - d 11-19-1871; a 85; w; pd Amboy twp.; pb England. (22)
CRAFT, Ann - d 8-24-1871; a 82; w; pd Amboy twp.; pb N.J. (22)
CARUGHER, Thomas - d 4-26-1871; a 63; pd Amboy twp.; pb Ireland. (22)

ADAMS, Philip T. to Elizabeth Bird	5-23-1809
ALESHIRE, David to Peggy Scott	3-30-1809
ALLEN, William to Lucy Stark	3-31-1808
ALLISON, Benjamin to Susannah Cutliss	3-24-1807
BALLARD, Harris to Sally Hatcher - Union twp.	2-23-1810
BARKER, Eleazer Jr. to Theresa O. Smith	5-9-1809
BEARE, Henry to Dready Curre - Union twp.	10-1-1810
BEEBE, Joseph to Margaret Persons - Letart twp.	8-3-1809
BING, James of Kiger twp. to Polly Vanzandt of Gallipolis twp.	3-31-1808
BOGGIS, Elisha to Nancy Daniel	11-22-1804
BOOTON, John to Anne Humphreys Stratton	2-1-1808
BRADFORD, Joseph to Martha (alias Patty) Wright	9-11-1807
BRAHAM, John to Mary Pancake - Union twp.	11-27-1810
BROWN, Robert to Elizabeth Messinger	10-3-1809
BROWNFIELD, John to Martha Entsminger	2-14-1804
BUCK, Thomas to Hannah Lasley	2-4-1807
BUCK, Thomas to Susannah Cherrington	11-15-1810
BUFFINGTON, Jacob to Mibar Harvey - Letart twp.	6-26-1804
BUFFINGTON, Philip to Elizabeth Stouts	10-30-1804
BURRAGE, Benjamin to Achsah Barker	10-30-1810
BURRIL, George to Lydia Ewing	7-27-1809
BUTLER, Syms to Nancy Robinson	11-9-1809
BUTLER, Thomas to Polly Robinson	8-26-1808
BUYERS, Edward to Sarah Rion	2-26-1806
BYERS, George to Rebeckah Gillispie	5-6-1807
CARTER, John to Barbara Wales	2-19-1807
COLLISON, James to Isabella Jones	7-3-1806
CRISTTIN, David to Polly Blankenship - Ohio twp.	10-25-1810
CROW, John to Polly Reed	7-15-1804
DANIEL, Robert to Dolly Erwin	12-20-1803
DARST, Abraham to Catharine Rife	6-24-1806
DARST, Jacob to Elizabeth Farr	8-30-1810
DARST, Martin to Isabell Scott	4-26-1806
DAY, John to Betsey Smith	3-21-1809
DIGGIN, Basel to Delia Gibson	8-22-1809
DODDRIDGE, Josiah to Margaret McCoy	8-15-1805
DONALLY, Dominicke to Christina Rackaback	12-8-1807
DYER, Jasper to Sarah Hoppes	12-24-1806
ELLIS, William to Elizabeth Adams - Union twp.	2-6-1810
ENTSMINGER, John to Rebecca Picket	5-28-1805
ERWIN (IRWIN), John to Milly Johnson	2-21-1809
ERWIN, Robert to Patsey Scurlock	12-6-1810
EVANS, Aldrige to Nancy Fulton	12-8-1810
EVANS, Richard to Elizabeth Branham - Union twp.	2-7-1810
EWING, Andrew to Jannat Glenn	8-23-1809
FARR, John to Rebecca Zin (Zen)	7-2-1808
FEE, Thomas to Sarah Collins	8-11-1803
FEE, William to Margaret Collins - both of Gallipolis twp.	12-8-1807
FIFER, John K. to Catharine Rupe	12-7-1810

```
FRAZEE, John to Hannah Martin                                    5-7-1807
FREDERICK, Mr. to Miss Sailor (given names not stated)           3-22-1807
GILLASPY, Moses to Susannah Burris                               1-29-1807
GILLMORE, Samuel of Letart twp. to Rhoda Davis                  10-21-1806
GLASSBURN, George to Lucy Russel                                 6-24-1810
GRANT, David to Mary Boggs - Gallipolis twp.                     7-13-1807
GREENLEE, James to Deborah Carrol                                7-23-1807
GREENLEE, Morris to Nancy Kimberling                             9-20-1809
GRIFFITH, Adam to Jane McCloud                                   3-27-1810
HALSEY, Jesse to Nancy Danis (or Davis?) of Letart twp.        10-19-1806
HARMSTRONG, Andrew to Susannah Snider                          10-4-1803
HARRELL, Robert to Mary Entsminger                              8-7-1810
HARRISS, Isaac to Betsey Buyers                                 4-25-1808
HAWK, John to Rebecka Switzer                                  12-20-1810
HAWK, Joseph to Nancy Cutliss                                  11-28-1807
HEDRICK, Leonard to Betsey Loucks                               4-25-1809
HEIGBY, Elim to Jane McMillion                                  6-18-1806
HEPLER (HESSLER?), Jacob to Christena Miller - Union twp.       9-2-1810
HIDE, William to Martha Tanner of Letart twp.                  3-18-1805
HOLMES, John to Margaret James                                 4-6-1806
HOPPAS, George to Elizabeth Hisle                              4-15-1807
HOPPES, Daniel to Susannah Booco                              10-20-1807
HOWELL, Levi to Jane Ewing                                     1-12-1804
HUBBALL, Abijah Jr. to Lucretia Merrill                        9-15-1809
HUBBELL, Abijah to Elizabeth Case                             10-18-1810
HUGHES, Jonathan to Elizabeth McNigh                           8-30-1807
HUMPHREY, Henry to Nancy Russle                                7-23-1807
HUMPHRIES, William to Clary Lott                               1-25-1809
HYSEL, Edward to Jemima Hysel                                  3-5-1809
HYSELL, Hedgeman to Anzila Perkins                             8-7-1810
JAMES, John to Ruamy Allison                                   8-7-1806
JOHNSON, Court to Sarah Byram                                 10-11-1807
JONES, Philip to Polly Heigby                                  5-7-1806
KERR, John, Esq. to Chestena Niswanger                         3-8-1804
KINCAID, George to Theresa Sheward - Rackoon twp.              4-27-1809
KING, Leonard to Sarah Dunlap                                  4-1-1807
KOKEMORE, John to Susanna Darst - Kyger twp.                   5-28-1810
KOONTZ, John to Mary Reckaback                                10-4-1803
KOONTZ, John to Sally Boyles                                   3-12-1808
KOONTZ, Martin to Lydia Rickaback                              1-4-1807
LASLEY, Abraham Jr. to Nancy Runnells                         12-24-1807
LASLEY, David to Dolly Switzer                                 9-23-1806
LEVISAY, Thomas to Mrs. Winfield Nicewonger                    7-15-1805
LITTLE, George to Nancy Ward                                  12-26-1810
LOGUE, Samuel to Elenora Vanzant                               5-1-1809
LONG, Peter to Dolly Blazer                                    9-22-1808
LYND, John to Betsey Pancake - Union twp.                      3-1-1810
McCARLEY, William to Rachel Totten                             9-13-1810
McCORMACK, James to Rachel Nisewonger                         12-29-1807
```

475

```
McCORMACK, William to Jemima Osburn                          4-5-1807
McDONALD, James to Sibby McCarley                          12-19-1805
McKINNEY, William to Hannah Frazee                           9-8-1805
McKINNY, Thomas to Polly Hamilton - Union twp.              9-3-1810
McKINSEY, Alexander to Unity Jones                          3-20-1804
McMURTY, Samuel to Elsy Reed                                 8-9-1808
MADDER, Dennis to Mary Glaseo - Union twp.                 11-13-1810
MAGNET, Anthony Rene Robert to Adle LeClerc                 1-27-1806
MARRET, Peter to Alexandrine Louisa Genevieve Magnet       (8-7-1803
                                             2 dates       (9-19-1804
MARTIN, William to Elizabeth Rickaback                      2-13-1806
MASON, William to Mary Martin                               1-9-1810
MATHEWS, Thomas to Nancy Buck                                7-7-1808
MERIFIELD, James to Hannah Hains                            9-11-1803
MERRIFIELD, John to Martha Hazelet                         7-27-1806
MILLAR, Benjamin to Priscilla Hatcher - Union twp.        12-26-1810
MILLER, Abraham to Rebecka Hughes                          3-31-1807
MILLER, Isaac to Susanna McCoy                             5-18-1807
MILLER, Jacob to Anna McNight                              5-27-1809
MILLS, Benjamin to Nancy Ewing                              3-2-1806
MOORE, Samuel to Mary Ann Manring                         10-25-1810
NELSON, John G. to Polly Arbuckel                         5-22-1806
NEWNHAM, Shadrack C. to Nancy Callison                    4-29-1806
NEWMAN, Walter of Mason Co., Va. to Wanaford Levesay of GalliaCo6-5-1808
NEWSOM, John to Sally McClung                             2-19-1809
NISCWONGER, John to Winney Buck                            2-9-1804
NORTHRUP, Hampton E. to Elizabeth Dean                    10-18-1807
NORTHRUP, Thomas to Margaret Syler                        10-1-1804
NOX, Wm. to Mary Glesbay of Rackoon twp.                  7-30-1806
PENCE, William to Eve Roush                                1-11-1810
PERRO, Lewis to Antonette Berthe                          5-27-1806
PHELPS, Boswell to Elizabeth Aleshire                      7-9-1808
PICKENS, Thomas to Hannah Parsons                        10-23-1804
PIERCE, Enos to Sarah Byers                                8-3-1806
POOR, George to Caty Hopper                              10-23-1806
RALSTON, Andrew to Betcey Bing                           12-20-1804
RAY, John to Mrs. Sally Deuy          (no day given)      March 1806
RICHARDSON, John to Elizabeth Manring                    12-17-1807
RICKABACK, Adam to Mary Koontz                            5-22-1807
RIFE, Jacob to Mary Darst                                4-20-1809
RIFE, Joseph to Betsey Howard                            6-24-1806
RIGG, Thomas to Polly Hobbs                              8-13-1809
ROADAMER, John to Barbara Syler                           1-28-1810
ROBINSON, George to Elizabeth Claypool                    5-31-1810
ROBINSON, James to Ruth McMullin                         10-18-1808
ROBINSON, Robert, Esq. to Marieannie R. Marret both of Gallipolis6-24-1804
ROUSH, Henry Jr. to Anney Sayre                           1-15-1804
RUSSELL, William to Susanna Denny                         9-13-1810
RUSSLE, Reuben to Polly Ridder                            7-23-1807
```

476

SANBORN, Richard S. to Eunice Knapp - Ohio twp.   4-22-1810
SAWYERS, Thomas to Cathrine Lastley   9-3-1805
SAYRE, Daniel to Sarah Hall   6-19-1806
SAYRE, Daniel Jr. of Mason Co., Va. to Sinah Harnan
    (or Haman?) of Gallia Co., Letart twp.   10-15-1807
SCOTT, Andrew to Mary Weese   7-15-1804
SCOTT, Charles to Mary Darst   8-10-1807
SHAW, Cusing of Waterford twp., Washington County to
    Polly Parker of Kiger twp., Gallia County   5-9-1805
SHEPARD, Luther to Margaret Entsminger - Gallipolis twp.   5-6-1810
SIMONIN, Francis to Athalia LeClerc   10-5-1809
SIMS, James to Martha Prayton   10-15-1805
SLEATH, David to Catharine Butcher   9-20-1808
SMITH, James to Sarah Hubbel   2-9-1808
SMITH, Lewis to Patse Cradle   11-30-1809
SOUTH, John B. to Eunice Knop   10-17-1808
STONE, Anster to Jane Smith   9-27-1803
STRONG, Daniel to Prudencia Wells   4-30-1809
STRONG, Stephen to Nancy Parker - both of Salisbury   3-9-1808
THOMAS, Jason to Catherine Hisel   7-24-1806
TYLER, Isaac to Elizabeth McDaniel   2-10-1810
VANDENVENDEN, John to Jane Betts   1-28-1808
WEBB, David to Elizabeth Hayman - Letart twp.   9-10-1809
WEESE, Daniel to Sarah Shoards - Raccoon twp.   10-16-1806
WELDON, James to Lety Stout   5-17-1810
WILLARD, Jacob to Polly Runnells   3-13-1808
WILLIS, Joshua to Mary Blankenship   7-28-1807
WILSON, Jacob to Nancy Adams   6-29-1809
WILSON, William to Sarah Koontz   7-4-1809
WOLF, Peter to Elizabeth Rousch   9-13-1803
WOOD, Mathew to Nancy Eve (or Ene?) - Union twp.   2-2-1810
WOOTEN, Thomas to Polly Russell   11-23-1808

The following marriages were taken from "Marriage Record 1" as found in the Probate Court of the court house at Gallipolis.

ADAMS, Philip to Polly Mills	2-18-1813
ALESHIRE, Ephrain to Betsey Williams	7-7-1813
ALESHIRE, John to Jane Dodson	6-16-1814
ALISON, Jesse to Rachel James	8-1-1813
ALFERD, Roy to Mary Ann Vonschriltz	2-16-1814
ALLISON, John to Becca Carter	1-3-1815
BARKER, Amos to Nancy Russel	2-2-1815
BEELY, David to Rhody Nysel	5-10-1812
BENNET, Gilbert to Margaret Holmes	7-17-1813
BERRINGER, William to Elizabeth Buffington	2-2-1812
BERRY, Daniel to Charlotte Knight	2-2-1815
BILLUPS, Edward to Polly Neel	5-13-1814
BINGHAM, Ralph to Fanny Mapples	7-6-1814
BLANKENSHIP, Andrew to Hanna Kinne	1-9-1812
BLANKENSHIP, Lodewick to Betsey Sharp	4-1-1813
BLAZER, Peter to Frances Adkinson	2-14-1815
BOGGS, David to Elizabeth Blagg	1-10-1815
BOGGS, Ezekiel to Elizabeth Bowen	2-28-1813
BOWEN, Joel to Keziah Allen	4-16-1815
BOWMAN, Jacob to Polly Buffington	2-14-1813
BOYLES, Jacob to Sally Wooten	11-5-1812
BRADBURN, Ignatius to Sally McCoy	11-26-1811
BRADFORD, Joseph D. to Lucinda Griffith	11-28-1813
BULLER (BUTLER), Isaac to Clarissa Sargent	3-11-1813
BUMGARDNER, John to Polly Miller	9-14-1813
BURRELL (BURNETT), Nathan to Polly Petit John	3-9-1813
CAMPBEL, George to Lydia Lambert	2-2-1812
CASHAT, John to Isabella Falkner	12-29-1814
CASTER, Hezekiah to Susannah Graham	1-12-1815
CHAPDU, Peter Francis to Julia Renard	3-15-1814
CHERRINGTON, William to Elizabeth Switzer	1-5-1813
CLARK, Samuel to Phebe Sayre	3-2-1815
COPELAND, Isaac to Nancy Langford	2-21-1815
COVIN, William to Aglac Clarissa LeClerc	4-27-1814
DANFORTH, Samuel to Phebe Knight	1-25-1813
DARST, David to Polly Sheller	4-29-1812
DAZIER, James to Elizabeth Forbes	7-14-1813
DeFESTARD, Adrun to Annette Pittan	6-9-1813
DURST, Benjamin to Nancy Scott	12-24-1812
EBLEN, John to Margaret Riffe	1-1-1815
EDWARDS, William to Relief Everton	12-8-1814
ENTSHINGER, John to Anna Stephens (Stevens)	9-20-1812
EVERETT, Samuel to Sally Kerr	3-8-1814
FLETCHER, Joseph Jr. to Mary Chapman	3-19-1815
FLIN, Thomas to Betsey Thorinton	11-18-1813
GALASPY, Robert to Sarrah Rice	8-14-1814

```
GANDEE, Eli to Mary Bibbee                                          4-3-1814
GEORGE, William to Nancy Hazlett                                    3-30-1815
GILMORE, Samuel Jr. to Elizabeth Ralph                             3-12-1815
GRAHAM, David to Ann Robnet                                       12-19-1813
GRAHAM, Gabriel to Mary Bickle                                      4-2-1815
GRAVES, Thomas to Rebecca Lawless                                   1-29-1814
GRAYUM, Joseph to Polly Entsminger                                 1-22-1815
GRIFFIN, Abraham to Polly Spurlock                                  2-9-1815
GUTHRIE, William to Sarrah Switzer                                  9-6-1812
GUY, Andrew to Ailey Lawridge                                     12-24-1812
HALL, Samuel to Jane Smith                                          2-4-1813
HANA, Peter to Sally French                                       11-11-1813
HANDSHAW, John to Rebecka Gandee                                   3-12-1814
HARPOLE, Adam to Dolly Roush                                       1-23-1812
HARRISON, Jacob, a black man to Katy Kecler, a black woman         7-26-1813
HAYMAN, James to Sarrah Sayre                                     11-10-1814
HAYMAN, John Jr. to Mary Wellbarger                                1-12-1815
HAYWARD, Solomon to Elizabeth Philips                              3-19-1813
HEISS (HASS), Jacob to Mary Breno (Brems)                          9-16-1813
HENSON, John to Catharine Weaver                                   2-16-1815
HOGE, Robert to Debourk Flower                                     8-15-1813
HOLDSBERRY, Jacob to Betsey Entsminger                             4-22-1813
HUBBELL, Jesse to Nancy Smith                                      2-15-1815
HUCKS, Benjamin to Jane McBean                                    11-22-1814
HUGHES, Silas to Catharine Neal                                    4-8-1813
HYSEL, Anthony to Margaret Hysel                                   1-16-1813
HYSELL, Francis to Nancy Dodson                                    3-24-1814
JEFFERS, Joseph to Delia Higingbottom                             6-25-1812
JEFFERS, William to Sally Fuller                                   3-14-1812
JOHNSTON, William to Betsey Ward                                    3-8-1814
JONES, Elias to Charlotte Smith                                   10-30-1814
JONES, James to Elizabeth Pine                                     5-20-1814
JONES, Thomas to Jane McMullin                                    11-24-1812
JONES, Thomas to Sarrah Cammel                                     5-6-1813
KINGERY, Abraham to Fanny Deviney                                  1-23-1814
KOONTZ, Jacob to Sarrah Fee                                        9-22-1814
KOONTZ, John L. to Elizabeth Rion                                 12-13-1812
LASLEY, Jonathan to Mary Ann Hickle                              10-20-1814
LOURY, John to Margaret Gilmore                                    3-15-1815
LYMAN, Samuel to Phebe Vining                                      3-24-1814
McCARLEY, John to Anna Glenn                                        7-1-1813
McCARTY, David to Sally Farr                                       8-27-1812
McCARTY, George to Nancy Orbough                                   11-9-1813
McDADE, Edward to Hannah Sayre                                     1-22-1815
McDANIEL, Caleb to Patsey Williams                                 9-4-1812
McDANIEL, John to Elizabeth Boggs                                10-14-1813
McGEE, John to Priscilla Ratcliff                                 12-3-1812
MAPLES (MAPLER), Asa Spencer to Fanny Smith                        7-5-1812
MARION, Clavin to Jane Devinney                                   12-30-1813
```

```
MARTIN, Benjamin Jr. to Rhoda Blankenship                    7-11-1813
MARTIN, David to Nancy Wilson                                1-9-1814
MASURE, Michael Desire to Angelique Ferrard                  11-8-1813
MATHEWS, James to Elizabeth Roock                            11-17-1812
MATHEWS, Nathaniel to Pamillia McNeel                        6-25-1812
MAY (McCOY), Benjamin to Polly King                          8-12-1813
MAYS, Joseph to Betsey Atkinson                              7-28-1812
MILLER, Brison to Mary Marshal Burrel                        4-9-1813
MILLER, Frederick to Louisa Petts                            12-31-1814
MILLER, John the third to Polly McCoy                        1-16-1814
MILLER, Luke to Eleanore McCoy                               7-30-1812
MORE, Joseph to Polly Molder                                 3-25-1813
NEAL, John to Kitty Hall                                     1-28-1814
NIBERT, Thomas to Betsey Day                                 7-9-1812
NORTHRUP, Vernon to Elizabeth Ewing                          12-24-1812
NYE, Horace to Fanny Safford                                 8-24-1813
PAULK, Cyrus to Armillia Sweet                               5-4-1815
PECK, Peter to Rebecka Vanmater                              2-9-1815
PEWSY, William to Susanna King                               7-25-1812
PICKENS, Robert to Elizabeth Anderson                        8-26-1812
PICKENS, William to Polly Commins                            3-14-1814
POOR, Alexander to Nancy Burris                              4-29-1813
POOR, Martin to Polly Barton                                 4-15-1813
PRATT, Abraham to Lucy Drake                                 6-27-1813
RADER, Michael to Catherine Roush                            2-23-1813
RALPH, Stephen to Ann Gilmore                                4-9-1815
RATHBURN, Daniel Jr. to Laura Higley                         5-21-1812
REED, Thomas to Mary Russel                                  7-11-1813
REED, William to Polly Morrow                                12-29-1811
REES, John to Margaret Campbell                              5-20-1813
RICE, Allan to Nancy Corn                                    3-25-1815
RICE, James to Zeletty Keeton                                2-21-1815
RICHARD, Jacob to Nancy Oliver                               7-11-1814
RICKABAUGH, Adam to Catharine McCoy                          9-30-1813
RICKABAUGH, John to Tabitha Shelton                          1-20-1814
RICKMAN, John to Susannah Lee                                7-25-1814
ROADAMER, George to Susannah Holmes                          3-10-1812
RODENBOUGH, George to Polly Smith                            3-17-1812
RODGERS, Moses to Margaret Claypool                          3-15-1814
ROOS, William to Nancy Nowlen                                2-8-1814
ROUSH, Abraham to Susannah Roush                             9-24-1812
ROUSH, Michael to Polly Weaver                               12-20-1811
ROX, Nehemiah to Mary McCloud                                4-25-1813
RUCKER, Robert to Eliza Vermillion                           2-27-1814
RUNNER, Isaac to Catharine Miller                            6-2-1811
RUSH, James to Elizabeth Justice             (1813?)         1-31-1812
RUSSELL, George to Elizabeth Hysel                           6-3-1812
RUSSELL, Isaac to Rhoda Hoppas                               3-12-1815
RUTHERFORD, John to Sally Scott                              7-15-1813
SANNS, John to Julia LeMoyne                                 11-8-1813
```

```
SAYRE, John Jr. to Hannah Jones                              8-18-1814
SAYRE, Robin to Patty Jones                                 3-12-1812
SCOTT, Thomas to Charlotte Weaver                           11-17-1814
SHARP, John to Betsey Keller                                2-2-1812
SHARP, Richard to Nancy Blankenship                         12-29-1814
SHASTEEN, John to Hanna Whitten                             4-8-1813
SHAW, Peter to Clarissa Parker                              11-5-1812
SHELTON, Henly to Hannah Rice                               7-21-1814
SKINNER, Isaac W. to Sally Denham                           6-20-1815
SMITH, Eli to Barbary Ney                                   12-7-1814
SMITH, John to Elizabeth Monroe                             9-24-1812
SMITH, Ruben to Christina Durst                             5-1-1815
SMITH, Samuel Sr. to Sarah Neal                             1-1-1815
SMITH, William to Peggy Waugh                               3-24-1814
SOUVERAIN, Francis to Antonette Berthe                      2-11-1814
STATTS, Jacob to Nelly Evans                                2-22-1815
STORTS, Abraham to Sally Fillman                            12-31-1812
SUMPTER, Richard to Isa Smith                               2-4-1813
SYMS, John B. to Ellice Castle                              4-13-1815
TAYLOR, Abraham to Betsey Walfenbarger                      1-15-1815
THOMAS, David to Mary Ann Bradford                          8-29-1813
VANDENBENDEN, Joseph to Mary Randle                         12-25-1814
VANZANT, James to Peggy Guy                                 6-9-1814
VINING, Josiah to Sally Reed                                10-12-1814
WALFINBARGER, John to Mary Shoemaker                        1-13-1814
WARD, Robert to Polly Rickaback                             1-20-1814
WARMAN, Francis to Anne Barlow                              3-1-1815
WAUGH, John to Sarrah Hall                                  10-31-1813
WAUGH, Solomon to Nancy Ross                                1-20-1814
WAUGH, Sylas to Sarah Warigh                                6-30-1812
WESE (WERSE), Leonard to Susy Rose                          7-6-1813
WHEELER, William to Betsey Floyd                            6-13-1813
WHITTEN, Ranson to Sally Riggs                              9-4-1814
WILLIAMS, Ezekial to Rhoda Sharp                            2-9-1812
WILLIAMS, William to Eva Long                               5-1-1815
WILLIS, Henry to Polly Tucker                               1-6-1814
WILLIS, Hugh to Polly Delly                                 5-23-1815
WILLIS, Isaac to Saney Blankenship (note: no date given)    -----(1812?)
WILLS, (WELLS), Zemariah to Sally Sargeant                  1-12-1815
WILSON, Henry to Sarah Martin                               12-12-1813
WIMMER, Jacob to Jane Galaspy                               4-28-1814
WOLF, Peter to Rebeccka Baty                                1-15-1815
WOMELSDORFF, Michael to Jane Waddle                         10-27-1812
```

481

GALLIA COUNTY, OHIO - WILL, ESTATE AND GUARDIANSHIP RECORDS 1803-1815

The following records were abstracted from what is now known as Will, Estate and Guardianship Book 1 & 2 as found in the Probate Court of Gallia County. The period of 1803-1815 included here constitutes what was originally Book 1 or A. Pages on which record may be found are given in parenthesis.

8-1-1803 Estate of Joseph Basil MARRET, dec'd, late of Gallipolis. Peter Marret, Jr., adms. (1)

8-18-1803 Estate of Nathaniel EDDY, dec'd, late of Gallipolis. Hannah Eddy, widow, adms. (1)

10-28-1803 Estate of Rebecca BOILS, dec'd, late of Gallipolis. Patrick Reed, adms. (2)

10-28-1803 Estate of John BUYERS, dec'd, late of Gallipolis. Edward Buyers, adms. (3)

12-24-1803 Estate of Emil LEFEBVRE, dec'd. Joseph Winox Devacht, adms. (9)

7-5-1804 Will of Stephen WILSON of Northwest Territory. Dated, 10-27-1801 Wife, Gane. Sons:- Thomas, Robert, Charles and James. Two daughters; Elizabeth Smith and Margret Alford. Mentions blacksmith tools and also, land on Jackson in Bath Co., Va. sold to David Grier (Guir). Mentions that he owned land in partnership with Thos. Buffington and Thos. Worthington. Executors:- Wife, Gane and son, Thomas. Signed:- Stephen Wilson. Witnesses:- Thomas Buffington and Martin Hull. (11)

7-6-1804 Will of Stephen BARTIER of Gallipolis, Washington Co., Northwest Territory. Dated, 10-8-1801. Bequeathes to three children of the late Claudius Cadot, dec'd (not named) and to Franket Blin wife of Francis Davors. Executor, John Baptist Ferard. Signed:- Stephen Bartier. Witnesses:- Peter Ferard and C. Etienne. (13)

11-9-1804 Estate of Andrew MEALMAN, dec'd, late of Letart twp. Fuller Elliot, adms. (18)

11-10-1804 Estate of Remy Thurry QUIFFE, dec'd, late of Gallipolis. Peter Robert Magnet, adms., appointed by the Probate of Washington Co., Ohio, now prays for authority to sell real estate. (19)

11-10-1804 On motion of Hannah Eddy, widow of Nathaniel EDDY, dec'd, George Worthington Putnam appointed guardian of Nathaniel EDDY aged 8 yrs. son of the late Nathaniel Eddy and Hannah. (22)

4-4-1805 Estate of Thomas ALEXANDER, dec'd, late of Letart twp. His son, Robert Alexander, adms.; widow relinquishes her right to adms.(24)

4-5-1805 Betsey Case widow of John CASE, dec'd, appointed guardian of Elisa Case, daughter of John and Betsey. (25)

4-6-1805 Estate of Henry MINGUY, dec'd. John Prix Minguy, adms. (26)

4-6-1805 Jonathan VOWEL aged 16 yrs. chose Robert Safford his guardian. (29)

4-8-1805 Peter Lalance of Letart twp. appointed guardian of Adam MEALMAN aged 16 yrs., John Mealman aged 15 yrs., Margaret Mealman aged 13 yrs., Betsy Mealman aged 12 yrs., Polly Mealman aged 9 yrs., Jacob Mealman aged 7 yrs. and Nancy Mealman aged 5 yrs. all children of Andrew Mealman, dec'd. (36)

4-8-1805   Gabriel LEWIS natural son of Hannah LARQUILHEN begotton before
marriage of said Hannah to Francis Larquilhon; chose Francis Le
Clereg as his guardian. (38)

7-1-1805   Will of Adam WOLF of Letart twp. Dated, 4-15-1805. Brother,
Peter Wolf. Two sisters, Rebecca Wolf and Elizabeth. Executors:
Brother, Peter and sister, Elizabeth. Signed, Adam Wolf.
Witnesses:- Thomas Whittaker, Daniel Sayre and Henry Roush. (39)

7-2-1805   Estate of Michael CRAUSAZ, dec'd. Michael Chanterelle, adms. (42)

3-22-1806   Will of John NISEWONGER, Jr. of Gallipolis twp. Dated, 1-19-1806.
Wife, Winny. Son, Charles Buck Niscewonger. Mentions brothers and
sisters but does not name. Executors, Charles Mills and Charles
Buck. Signed, John Nisewonger. Witnesses:- Wm. Harvey, James
Boggs and William Waddel. (51)

3-20-1806   Estate of William PETIT JOHN (PETTIJOHN), dec'd, late of Gallipolis. John Petit John (Pettijohn), adms. (53)

8-29-1806   Estate of William CLAYTON, dec'd. Christopher Etamore, adms. (55)

7-3-1806   John Peter Romain Bareau and John Savary appointed guardians of
Sophia DROZ daughter of the late Peter DROZ and Marguerite
BOURDON, both dec'd. (59)

7-3-1806   Estate of Margarette Bourdon FERARD, dec'd, late of Gallipolis.
John Peter Romain Bareau, adms. (59)

3-17-1807   Winnifield NISEWONGER widow of the late John NISEWONGER, dec'd,
appointed guardian of Charles Buck NISEWONGER son of said John,
dec'd, and herself. (65)

3-16-1807   Estate of Jether BAILEY, dec'd, late of Letart twp. Peter Lalance,
adms. (66)

6-20-1807   Estate of Marit DAPORT, dec'd, late of Gallipolis. John Baptist
Ferard, adms. (67)

6-20-1807   Will of Guy Soussigne Marin DUPONT native of Melan in the Seine
living in Gallipolis, Gallia Co., Ohio. Dated, 3-20-1804.
Bequeath to Jean Baptiste Ferard, who is also to serve as executor. Witnesses:- Pierre Le Clerc, Peter Marret, Jr., Pierre
Ferard and F. Larquillion. (73)

8-10-1807   Estate of Benjamin ALLISON, dec'd. Widow, Rachel Allison, adms.;
also to serve as guardian of Samuel Allison 13 yrs., John Allison
aged 14 yrs., Jemima Allison 11 yrs., Thomas Allison aged 9 yrs.
and James Allison aged 7 years, all children of Benjamin Allison,
dec'd. (75)

8-12-1807   Estate of William PETIT JOHN, dec'd. John Petit John, adms.
Account. Disbursement of estate:- Widow (not named) $150.00;
George Martin and wife $65.00; William Crow and wife, Isaac But-
ler and wife, Andrew Freed and wife, and William Petit John Jr.,
$55.00 each; John Petit John $53.75. (77)

8-12-1807   Lewis BERTHE a minor aged 14 yrs. son of Lewis BERTHE and Hannah
Thevenin formerly the wife of said Lewis Berthe; chose his father-
in-law, Nicholas Thevenin and Christopher Etienne as his guardians. (77)

8-12-1807   Orasha Strong appointed additional guardian to Elisa CASE daughter
of John CASE, dec'd. (78)

8-12-1807 Estate of Patrick G. FORDE, dec'd, late of Gallipolis. Thomas Rogers, adms. (79)

8-12-1807 Francis Le Clereg guardian of Gabriel LEWIS binds said Gabriel, a minor, to Thomas Rodgers to learn the trade of carpenter. (81)

8-12-1807 Robert Safford guardian of Jonathan VOWELL, a minor, binds said Jonathan to Thos. Rodgers to the trade of carpenter. (82)

8-12-1807 Agreement between Jeane Prix MINQUY and his son, Antonine Henry MINGUY, dated 1798 Philadelphia, Pa.; that should one die first, the survivor is to have all property. Witnesses:- Francois Miveut and Pierre Simonet. (87)

9-26-1807 Estate of Thomas LIVESAY, dec'd, late of Gallipolis twp. Widow, Winnefield Livesay. (88)

11-13-1807 Robert Safford and Eleanor Vanzant widow of Elijah VANZANT, dec'd, appointed adms. of his estate and also to serve as guardians of James Vanzant aged 18 yrs., Nancy Vanzant aged 14 yrs., Betsy Vanzant aged 10 yrs., Matty Vanzant aged 7 yrs., Sally Vanzant aged 5 yrs. and Lorenzo Vanzant aged 3 yrs., children of said Elijah Vanzant, dec'd. (106)

3-28-1808 Estate of Elizabeth ALEXANDER, dec'd, late of Letart twp. Daniel Sayre of Mason Co., Virginia, adms. (112)

3-29-1808 Estate of Samuel GELSTON. Widow, Martha Gelston, adms. Martha Gelston and Robert Safford appointed guardians of William Gelston aged 18 yrs., Elizabeth Gelston aged 16 yrs., Samuel Gelston aged 12 yrs., Martha Gelston aged 9 yrs. and Margaret Gelston aged 19 months. (119)

3-29-1808 Will of John Henry ENTSMINGER late of Gallipolis. Dated, 3-29-1806. Son, Michael. Executors:- John Ewing and David Rees. Signed, John Entsminger. Witnesses:- John Bing, Andrew Ralston and Samuel Logue. (122)

3-29-1808 Estate of John BUYERS, dec'd. Edward Buyers, adms. Account. Mentions money paid by Jacob Snider of Montgomery Co., Va. as per agreement.with dec'd. Mentions Sarah Buyers mother of dec'd; also James Burford. Disbursement to heirs:- George Buyers $24.09, William Buyers $24.09, Sally Burford $24.09, Elizabeth Buyers $24.09, David Buyers $24.09, Isaac Buyers $24.09, and Edward Buyers $19.35. (123)

9-5-1808 Estate of Rebecca BOILES. Account. Mentions that said Rebecca moved to Gallia County from Rockbridge Co., Va. and owned land there at time of her death. Also, that adms. made trip to Kentucky to meet with lawyers of said Rebecca. (131)

3-28-1808 Estate of Thomas ALEXANDER. Account. Mentions bond due from John Steware of Rockbridge Co., Virginia. (132)

4-10-1809 Estate of John SEISIE, dec'd, late of Letart twp. Widow, Sarah Seisle, adms., also to serve as guardian of Nancy Seisle aged 11 yrs., James Seisle aged 10 yrs., William Seisle aged 6 yrs. and Polly Seisle aged 3 yrs., children of said John Seisle, dec'd. (152)

4-10-1809 Estate of Stephen WILSON, dec'd. Account. Heirs:- Son, Robert Wilson of Gallia Co.; son, James Wilson of Gallia Co.; daughter, Elizabeth Smith of Kanawha Co., Va.; son, Charles Wilson of Gallia Co. (153)

4-12-1809   Estate of James BOGGS, dec'd. Son, David Boggs, adms. (155)
4-13-1809   Estate of James LAURENT. John Peter Romain Bureau, adms. (157)
9-13-1809   Estate of Patrick G. FORDE. Account. Heirs:- Son, Thimothy G.
             Forde; son, Patrick Forde; daughter, Elizabeth G. Forde. (168)
9-3-1810   Estate of Eleazar BARKER, dec'd. Widow, Mehetable Barker and
             Samuel R. Holcomb, Esq., adms. (178)
9-3-1810   Mehetable BARKER appointed guardian of Permilla Barker aged 5 yrs.,
             daughter of Eleazar Barker, dec'd. (179)
9-3-1810   James BOGGS 19 yrs. and Elizabeth Boggs 15 yrs., minors of James
             Boggs, dec'd, chose William Waddle as their guardian. (179)
12-24-1810   Amos BARKER aged 17 yrs. and Daniel Barker aged 14 yrs., children
             of Eleazer Barker dec'd, chose Benjamin Burrage as their guardian.(183)
12-24-1810   Estate of Abraham BUCCO, dec'd. Widow, Mary Ann Bucco and
             Masquil Manring, adms. (184)
4-22-1811   Will of James BUTLER of Huntington twp. Dated, 9-29-1810. Wife:-
             Anne, also to serve as executrix. Sons:- William, John, James,
             Sims, Thomas and Isaac. Two daughters:- Eleanor Claypool and
             Anne Shintopher. Signed, James (his mark) Butler. Witnesses:-
             Samuel R. Holcomb, William Glenn and James Glenn. (189)
4-24-1811   Verbal Will of Michael CROZIER of Natchez, Mississippi. Dated,
             1-26-1804. Bequeath to friend, Capt. William Nichols of Natchez.
             Witness:- J. B. Hart. (192)
12-24-1811   Will of Daniel NORTHUP. Dated, 3-7-1808. Sons:- Henry, Hampton,
             Thomas and Vernon; Vernon to have land formerly in Delpre twp.,
             Washington Co., Ohio now in Athens Co., Ohio. Two daughters:-
             Sarah Painter and Jane McCaull. Grandson, Thomas Jefferson North-
             up, son of Henry, to have 100 acres in forks of Duck Creek, Salem
             twp., Washington Co., Ohio. Executor, Thomas Northup. Signed,
             Daniel Northup. Witnesses:- Robert Safford and Mosses Everett.(197)
5-12-1812   Will of John Baptist LETALLIEUR of Gallipolis. Dated, 5-5-1812.
             Daughter, Mary Frances Charlotte, not of age. Brother, Peter
             Letallieur's children (not named) who reside in France. Friends:-
             Christopher Etienne, G. W. Tupper, Lewis Newson and Nathaniel
             Gates to serve as guardians of daughter, Mary Francis Charlotte.
             Executor, Christopher Etienne. Signed, John Baptist Letallieur.
             Witnesses:- W. Devacht, Thos. Rodgers and Tosessainh Schowman.(199)
9-8-1812   Will of Richard Blankenship. Dated, 4-13-1812. Mentions wife
             but does not name; also mentions children but does not name ex-
             cept for Lodwick Blankenship. Signed, Richard R. Blankenship.
             Witnesses:- Isom Blankenship and George Willis. Widow,
             Margaret Blankenship appointed adms. (202)
12-23-1812   Will of John Baptist FERARD native of Rumiquy, Champaigne Pro-
             vince, France, residing in Gallipolis. Dated, 12-19-1812.
             Brother, Peter Ferard of Gallipolis. Testator was Godfather of
             and bequeathes to:- Charlotte Letailleur dau. of the late John
             Baptist Letailleur; Madelaine Tillaye dau. of John Baptist Nic-
             kolas Tillaye of Gallipolis; and John Claudius Caveau son of late
             Claudius Caveau. Wife, Marie Madelaine Angeline Boutdeville,
             also to serve as executrix. Signed, John B. Ferard. (221)

12-21-1812   Estate of Isaac MILES, dec'd. Henry Coonts, adms. Widow,
Rosey Miles declined adms.   (228)
9-8-1812   Will of William DAVIDSON. Dated, 6-20-1810. Wife, Barbara.
Sons:- John, Lewis, David, Abraham A. M., Thomas, William,
Jesse and Joseph. Daughters:- Comfort McCourtney, Mary Williams,
Peggy Francis, Betty Lyne, Sarah McKee and Cinthia. Executors:-
Wife, Barbara; son, Abraham A. M.; and nephew, Joseph Davidson.
Signed, William Davidson. Witnesses:- David McCoy and Richard
(his mark) Sharp.   (232)
4-5-1813   Estate of Isaac BUTLER, dec'd. Widow, Mary Butler and Andrew Boggs,
adms.   (238)
12-23-1812   Will of George HOPPES. Dated 11-18-1812. Wife, Elizabeth.
Children:- John, Daniel, George, Henry, Jacob, Anna, Caty, Sarah,
Hannah, Barbara, Rhoda and Elizabeth; with Barbara, Rhoda, Elizabeth, Henry and Jacob being unmarried. Executors:- Wife, Elizabeth and Samuel W. Blagg. Signed, George Hoppes. Witnesses:-
George (mark) Poor, John H. (mark) Stanley and Samuel W. Blagg.
4-5-1813   Estate of James JARDIN, dec'd. Widow, Isabel Jardin and William
Callison, adms.   (242)
4-5-1813   Estate of John K. HOLMES, ded'd. Widow, Margaret Holmes, adms.(244)
4-6-1813   Estate of Francis WAUGH, dec'd. George Waugh, adms.   (246)
8-16-1813   Mary BUTLER appointed guardian of Butler CROW aged 4 yrs. from 15
January last.   (250)
8-16-1813   Will of Peter FERARD of Gallipolis. Dated 7-11-1813. Wife, Anne
Marie Vonschriltz Ferard. Brother, Jacques Nicholas Ferard residing in France. Bequeathes to Peter son of testator's wife,
Peter not of age; also to Mary Madelaine Angeline Bouteville
Ferard to have two lots in Gallipolis bequeathed to testator by
his brother, John Baptiste Ferard. Executor:- Lewis Victor
Vonchrilitz. Signed:- Peter Ferard. Witnesses:- John Sanns,
Francis Le Clerog and F. Simonin.   (251)
8-17-1813   Estate of Peter MARRET late of Gallipolis. John Peter Romain
Bureau, adms.   (256)
8-17-1813   Estate of Robert HUMPHREYS, dec'd, late of Huntington twp.
Brother, Morris Humphreys, adms.   (257)
11-29-1813   Estate of McCoy RALSTON, dec'd. Brother, Andrew Ralston, adms.(266)
11-29-1813   Estate of Jesse FLESHMAN, dec'd. Widow, Rachel Fleshman and
George Washington Putnam, adms.   (267)
11-30-1813   Estate of Eleazer BARKER, Jr., dec'd. Widow, Theresa Owen Barker
and James E. Phelps, adms.   (273)
4-11-1814   Estate of John DONNALLY, dec'd. Father, Andrew Donnally, adms.(283)
4-12-1814   Will of John BLAZER. Dated 10-22-1813. Wife, Dorotha. Son
and daughter, Peter and Elizabeth. Executors:- Philip Blazer
and Jacob Roadarmer. Signed:- Jacob (his mark) Blazer.
Witnesses:- John Carrell, John Rader and Adam Rader.   (284)
4-11-1814   Estate of David McCOY, dec'd. Widow, Ann McCoy and Edward
Simmons, adms.   (286)
4-12-1814   Estate of Elnathan BARLOW, dec'd. Widow, Ann Barlow; Andrew
Johnson and Nathaniel Gates, adms.   (287)

4-12-1814 Estate of Francis LARQUILHON, dec'd. Widow, Hannah Larquilhon, adms. (288)
9-5-1814 Estate of Levi MOORE, dec'd. Widow, Margaret Moore, adms. (295)
9-6-1814 Theresa Owen Barker widow of Eleazer Barker, Jr., dec'd appointed guardian of Gideon Barker aged 4 yrs., Sally Barker aged 2 yrs. and Eleazer Owen Barker aged 1 year. (298)
11-8-1814 Will of John SAVARY born in Lyon, France, came to America in year 1783 and became a citizen by oath of allegiance at Morganstown, Virginia; now established in Millersburg, Bourbon Co., Kentucky being on the starting point for New Orleans. Dated, 2-6-1808. Friend, Robert Alexander of Woodford County, president of the State Bank to have all lands in Virginia, Pennsylvania and Ohio. Executor:- Friend, Lewis Vimont of Millersburg, Kentucky. Signed, J. Savary. Witnesses:- George Madison, John T. Pendleton and John P. Thomas. Recorded Bourbon Co., Kentucky 11-8-1814. (303)
12-1-1814 Will of Moses EVERET of Gallipolis. Dated, 11-29-1814. Bequeathes to Nathaniel Gates and to Julia Ann Gates daughter of said Nathaniel. Executor, Edward White Tupper, Esq. Signed, Moses Everett. Witnesses:- Mathew Buell, Peter Marret and John Ralph. (314)
11-8-1814 Estate of Joseph TOWNSEND, dec'd. Samuel Everett, adms. upon request of widow, Eunice Townsend. (316)
4-10-1815 Will of Patrick REED. Dated 5-31-1814. Wife, Mary Reed. Sons:- Charles Reed and youngest son, James Reed. Daughters:- Mary Crow and Elsey McMurty. Executors:- Wife, Mary and son, James. Signed, Patrick Reed. Witnesses:- Sam'l R. Holcomb and David Boggs. (319)
4-10-1815 Will of Jesse GEORGE. Dated, 2-9-1815. Sons:- Isaac, James, William and Enock. Daughters:- Elizabeth Holt, Mary Prator, Phebe wife of Moses Hazlett, Elsey Graham and Nelly Nelson. Executor:- Son, James George. Signed, Jesse (his mark) George. Witnesses:- David Robertson, Mitchel Ware and Jacob Ward. (323)
4-10-1815 Will of John McCARLEY. Dated, 9-21-1814. Sons:- William, John, Samuel and Moses. Three daughters:- Elizabeth, Margaret and Zebiah. Executors; John McCarley, Joseph W. Ross and John Cherington. Signed, John McCarley. Witnesses:- Sam'l W. Blagg and William Blagg. (333)
4-10-1815 Estate of Henry DELAY, dec'd. Mother, Elizabeth Delay, adms. (335)

All lots were granted by Paul Fearing and Return Jonathan Meigs, Jr. in execution
of a trust for the Ohio Company dated Marietta January 7, 1796; with the deeds being
executed to the lot owners on December 26, 1796.

It would be useful at this point to explain how this list, as well as those for the
following lists of lots, has been compiled. First, a page by page search of the various early deed books in both Gallia and Washington Counties was completed for the
original deeds from Fearing and Meigs to the lot owners. Secondly, the abstract book
of the Gallipolis City (or town) lots was then checked for each lot. This resulted
not only in serving as a cross-check on the first search results; but through the
first sale of land by the lot owner or his heirs, additional lot owners were confirmed as having received their lots from Fearing and Meigs. There remained a few
lots whose owners could not be confirmed and in the latter instance, the name of the
lot owner is given in parenthesis based on the first sale of land, with the date of
this first sale also being added in parenthesis. In all instances, the deed book
and page on which confirmation of record may be found, has been given.

Lot No.	Name of Owner		Book & Page
1	MARION, Francis		2-111
2	THEVNIN, Nicholas		2-319
3	MARION, Francis		2-111
4	MINGUY (MINGEY, MINGAY), Henry		2-32
5	MINGUY (MINGEY, MINGAY), Henry		2-32
6	DEVACHT, Francis Joseph Winox		2-130
7	DEVACHT, Francis Joseph Winox		2-130
8	DEVACHT, Francis Joseph Winox		2-130
9	MARION, Francis		2-111
10	MARION, Francis		2-111
11	MINGUY, (MINGEY, MINGAY), Henry		2-32
12	MINGUY (MINGEY, MINGAY), Henry		2-135
13	BARA, Vincent		2-251
14	(DUDIET, William)	(1813)	(8-440)
15	DEVACHT, Francis Joseph Winox		2-130
16	LARQUILHON, Francis Alexander		2-178
17	MARION, Francis		2-111
18	(THEVININ, Nicholas)	(1800)	(2-113)
19	THEVININ, Nicholas		2-319
20	MARION, Francis		2-111
21	CRAUSAZ, Michael		2-219
22	(LeCLERCQ, Francis)	(1832)	(16-176)
23	(THEVININ, Nicholas)	(1800)	(2-113)
24	(DUDUIT, William)	(1813)	(8-440)
25	JACQUMIN, Anthony Nicholas		8-96
26	MICHAU, John		1-4
27	(LeCLERCQ, Francis)	(1832)	(16-176)
28	CRAUSAZ, Michael		2-219
29	MARION, Francis		2-111
30	MINGUY (MINGEY, MINGAY), Henry		2-135
31	(D'HEBECOURT, Francis)	(1796)	(13-37)
32	(D'HEBECOURT, Francis)	(1796)	(13-37)
33	*DEVACHT,Jeanne Francoise(wife of Fran.Jos.Win. (Devacht)		2-128
34	(D'HEBECOURT, Francis)	(1799)	(2-180)

*(See next page)

Lot No.	Name of Owner		Book & Page
35	SAUGRAIN, Anthony Francis		8-105
36	SAUGRAIN, Anthony Francis		8-105
37	MAGNIER, Peter		2-107
38	MAGNIER, Peter		2-107
39	(VALODIN, Francis)	(1826)	(10-39-#34)
40	SAUGRAIN, Anthony Francis		8-105
41	PETIT JEAN, James	(Common Pleas)	I-592
42	ETIENNE, Christopher		2-17
43	*DEVACHT, Jeanne Francoise		2-128
44	*DEVACHT, Jeanne Francoise		2-128
45	QUESTEL, Nicholas		5-110
46	*DEVACHT, Jeanne Francoise		2-128
47	*DEVACHT, Jeanne Francoise		2-128
48	BASTIDE, Stephen		2-201
49	PETIT, Nicholas		2-165
50	PETIT, Nicholas		2-165
51	(LeCLERCQ, Francis)	(1832)	(16-176)
52	WILLEMY, Stephen		2-164
53	DAVOIUS, Francis		2-202
54	DAVOIUS, Francis		2-202
55	SERROT, Heirs of Peter		9-206
56	SERROT, Heirs of Peter		9-206
57	SERROT, Heirs of Peter		9-206
58	(D'HEBECOURT and PETIT)	(1815)	5-419
59	QUIFFE, Heirs of Remy Theiry		10-238
60	DUC, Anthony Bartholomew		2-152
61	DEVACHT, Francis Joseph Winox		2-130
62	MARRET, Mary Madelane Ferrand(wife of Peter Marret)		B-52
63	ETIENNE, Christopher		2-17
64	ETIENNE, Christopher		2-17
65	GERVAIS, John Gabriel		2-38
66	(D'HEBECOURT and PETIT)	(1815)	(5-419)
67	(D'HEBECOURT and PETIT)	(1815)	(5-419)
68	DROZ, Heirs of Peter		2-341
69	(LAFORGE, Peter Anthony)		(6-90)
70	(LAFORGE, Peter Anthony)		(6-90)
71	MARRET, Mary Madelane Ferrand(wife of Peter Marret)		B-52
72	DEVACHT, Francis Joseph Winox		2-130
73	SAUGRAIN, Anthony Francis		8-105
74	SAUGRAIN, Anthony Francis		8-105
75	(LAFORGE, Peter Anthony)		(6-90)
76	(D'HEBECOURT and PETIT)		(5-419)
77	DROZ, Heirs of Peter		2-341
78	(D'HEBECOURT and PETIT)		(5-419)
79	(D'HEBECOURT and PETIT)		(5-419)
80	(D'HEBECOURT and PETIT)		(5-419)
81	(D'HEBECOURT and PETIT)		(5-419)

*Jeanne Francois Devacht was the daughter of Joachim Pignolet who died in 1796 and her first husband was John Parmentier who also died the same year; her second husband was F. J. W. Devacht; thus some of her lots may have been obtained by her being daughter of Pignolet and widow of Parmentier.

Lot No.	Name of Owner		Book & Page
82	(D'HEBECOURT and PETIT)		(5-419)
83	(LAFORGE, Peter Anthony)		(6-90)
84	(LAFORGE, Peter Anthony)		(6-90)
85	(D'HEBECOURT and PETIT)		(5-419)
86	(D'HEBECOURT and PETIT)		(5-419)
87	(D'HEBECOURT and PETIT)		(5-419)
88	LETAILLEUR, John Baptist		5-182
89	(D'HEBECOURT and PETIT)		(5-419)
90	(D'HEBECOURT and PETIT)		(5-419)
91	(D'HEBECOURT and PETIT)		(5-419)
92	(D'HEBECOURT and PETIT)		(5-419)
93	LaCIRER (LaCOUR), Ambrose		B-78
94	CHABEAU, Peter		2-169
95	CHABEAU, Peter		2-169
96	LETAILLEUR, John Baptist		5-182
97	DUC, Anthony Bartholomew		2-152
98	DUC, Anthony Bartholomew		2-152
99	DUC, Anthony Bartholomew		2-152
100	DUC, Anthony Bartholomew		2-152
101	CHANTERELL, Michael		1-46
102	CHANTERELL, Michael		1-46
103	LETAILLEUR, John Baptist		5-182
104	VINCENT, Anthony		B-79
105	LeMOYNE, John Julius		1-60
106	LETAILLEUR, John Baptist		5-182
107	CHANTERELL, Michael		1-46
108	(DEVACHT, Francis Joseph Winox)	(1797)	(1-47)
109	DUPORT, Marin		2-250
110	DUPORT, Marin		2-250
111	DesKOYERS, Peter John		2-117
112	LeMOYNE, John Julius		1-60
113	LeCLERC(Q), Lewis		2-121
114	LeCLERC(Q), Lewis		2-121
115	DUPORT, Marin		2-250
116	DUPORT, Marin		2-250
117	GERVAIS, John Gabriel		2-38
118	VIOLETTE, John Lewis		2-343
119	LETAILLEUR, John Baptist		5-182
120	VINCENT (VIMONT), Lewis		B-55
121	GINET, Peter		2-106
122	GINET, Peter		2-106
123	(MALDON, Lewis)	(1796)	(2-321)
124	(SERROT, Peter)	(1796)	(1-64)
125	VINCENT, Lewis		B-55
126	(LAFORGE, Peter Anthony)	(1816)	(6-128)
127			
128	(LAMBERT, Nicholas)	(1797)	(2-199)
129			
130	MAGUET, Anthony Rene Robert, Jr.		2-139
131			
132	(TREVININ, Nicholas)		(6-408)

Lot No.	Name of Owner		Book & Page
133	(LeCLERCQ, Francis)	(1832)	(16-176)
134	QUESTEL, Nicholas		5-110
135	VALODIN (VALLEN), Francis		3-253
136	VANDENBLENDEN, Martinus.		2-83
137	FRESIN, John		2-242
138	FRESIN, John		2-242
139	D'HEBECOURT, Francis		3-183
140	D'HEBECOURT, Francis		3-183
141	(BRUNIER, Francis)		(6-244)
142	VANDENBEMDEN, Martinus		2-83
143	VALODIN (VALLON), Francis		3-253
144	VALODIN (VALLON), Francis		3-253
145	MAGUET, Peter Robert		2-137
146	DesNOYERS, Peter John		2-117
147	DesNOYERS, Peter John		2-117
148	CADOT, Claudius		2-258
149	DAZET, Joseph		2-157
150	DAZET, Joseph		2-157
151	DAZET, Joseph		2-185
152	FRISON (FRESIN), John		2-242
153	D'HEBECOURT, Francis		3-183
154	D'HEBECOURT, Francis		3-183
155	D'HEBECOURT, Francis		3-183
156	D'HABECOURT, Francis		3-183
157	MENAGER, Claud Romain		2-42
158	BASTIDE, Stephen		2-201
159	LeCLERCQ, Augustin		2-31
160	DALLEZ, Maria Josephine		3-45
161			
162	FERARD, John Baptist		2-88
163	DALLEZ, Maria Josephine		3-45
164	LeSEREC (LeSOUR), Heirs of Peter		5-181
165	MENAGER, Claude Romain		2-42
166	MENAGER, Claude Romain		2-42
167	BERTHELOT, Claudius		2-206
168	BERTHELOT, Mathew		2-207
169	GERVAIS, John Gabriel		2-38
170	LeCLERCQ, Augustin		2-31
171			
172	LAFORGE, Peter Anthony		B-101
173	LAFORGE, Peter Anthony		B-101
174	LAFORGE, Peter Anthony		B-101
175	LAFORGE, Peter Anthony		B-101
176	LAFORGE, Peter Anthony		B-101
177	LeSUERE, Heirs of Peter		5-181
178	LeSURERE, Heirs of Peter		5-181
179	DUTIEL, Francis Charles		2-257
180	LeCLERCQ, Augustin		2-31
181	FERARD, John Baptist		2-88
182	PRADEL, Heirs of Julien		5-112
183	VIOLETTE, John Lewis		2-343

491

Lot No.	Name of Owner		Book & Page
184	VIOLETTE, John Lewis		2-343
185	FERARD, Peter		1-8
186	FERARD, Peter		1-8
187	VANDENBEMDEN, Martinus		2-83
188	VANDENBEMDEN, Martinus		2-83
189	LAFORGE, Peter Anthony		B-101
190	LAFORGE, Peter Anthony		B-101
191	(SARAZIN, Abel)		(12-297)
192	(SARAZIN, Abel)		(12-297)
193	DEVACHT, Francis Joseph Winox		2-130
194	DEVACHT, Francis Joseph Winex		2-130
195	DEVACHT, Francis Joseph Winex		2-130
196	(SARAZIN, Abel)		(12-297)
197	LAFORGE, Peter Anthony		B-101
198	VANDENBENDEN, Martinus		2-83
199	FERARD, Peter		1-8
200	VONSCHRILTZ, Lewis Victor		B-138
201	VONSCHRILTZ, Lewis Victor		B-138
202	FERARD, Peter		1-8
203	VILOMAID (VILOMAIN), Francis	(Common Pleas)	I-592
204	LAFORGE, Peter Anthony		B-101
205	MARRET, Peter, Sr. and Peter, Jr.		B-53
206	MARRET, Peter, Sr. and Peter, Jr.		B-53
207	MARRET, Peter, Sr. and Peter, Jr.		B-53
208	MARRET, Peter, Sr. and Peter, Jr.		B-53
209	MARRET, Peter, Sr. and Peter, Jr.		B-53
210	MARRET, Peter, Sr. and Peter, Jr.		B-53
211	VANDENBEMDEN, Martinus		2-83
212	VANDENBEMDEN, Martinus		2-83
213	BAUDOT, John		2-168
214	DEU (DUC), Anthony Bartholomew		2-152
215	MARRET, Peter, Sr. and Peter, Jr.		B-53
216	MARRET, Peter, Sr. and Peter, Jr.		B-53
217	PETIT JEAN, James	(Common Pleas)	I-592
218	GERVAIS, John Gabriel		2-38
219	GERVAIS, John Gabriel		2-38
220	GERVAIS, John Gabriel		2-38
221	PETIT JEAN, James	(Common Pleas)	I-592
222	PETIT JEAN, James	(Common Pleas)	I-592
223	MARRET, Peter, Sr. and Peter, Jr.		B-53
224	MARRET, Peter, Sr. and Peter, Jr.		B-53
225	MARRET, Peter, Sr. and Peter, Jr.		B-53
226	MARRET, Peter, Sr. and Peter, Jr.		B-53
227	DEU (DUC), Anthony Bartholomew		2-152
228	DEU (DUC), Anthony Bartholomew		2-152
229	(PITHARD or PITHOUD, Philip Augustus)		(B-138)
230	(PITHARD or PITHOUD, Philip Augustus)		(B-138)
231	MARRET, Peter, Sr. and Peter, Jr.		B-53
232	MARRET, Peter, Sr. and Peter, Jr.		B-53
233	(PRIOUX, Nicholas)		(2-13)
234	(PRIOUX, Nicholas)		(2-13)

Lot No.	Name of Owner	Book & Page
235	MARION, Francis	2-111
236	MARION, Francis	2-111
237	LeCLERC, Lewis	2-121
238	LeCLERC, Lewis	2-121
239	LeCLERC, Lewis	2-121
240	LeCLERC, Lewis	2-121
241	DEVACHT, Jeanne Francoise	2-128
242	DEVACHT, Jeanne Francoise	2-128
243	GERVAIS, John Gabriel	2-38
244	GERVAIS, John Gabriel	2-38
245	LeCLERC, Lewis	2-121
246	LeCLERC, Peter	2-51
247	LeCLERC, Lewis	2-121
248	LeCLERC, Lewis	2-121
249	MAGUET, Peter Robert	2-137
250	(PRIOUX, Nicholas)	(2-13)
251	MARRET, Peter, Sr. and Peter, Jr.	B-53
252	(MARRET, Basil Joseph)	(2-142)
253	(PRIOUX, Nicholas)	(2-13)
254	MAGUET, Peter Robert	2-137
255	LeCLERC, Lewis	2-121
256	LeCLERC, Lewis	2-121
257	LeCLERC, Lewis	2-121
258	LeCLERC, Peter	2-51
259	LeCLERC, Lewis	2-121
260	LeCLERC, Peter	2-51
261	LeCLERC, Peter	2-51
262	LeCLERC, Peter	2-51
263	ETIENNE, Christopher	2-17
264	(PRIOUX, Nicholas)	(2-13)
265	(MARRET, Basil Joseph)	(2-142)
266	(MARRET, Basil Joseph)	(2-142)
267	(PRIOUX, Nicholas)	(2-13)
268	ETIENNE, Christopher	2-17
269	LeCLERC, Peter	2-51
270	LeCLERC, Peter	2-51
271	MARION, Francis	2-111
272	MARION, Francis	2-111
273	LeCLERCQ, Augustin	2-31
274	LeCLERCQ, Augustin	2-31
275	LeCLERCQ, Augustin	2-31
276	LeCLERCQ, Augustin	2-31
277	LeCLERC, Peter	2-51
278	LeCLERC, Peter	2-51
279	LeCLERC, Peter	2-51
280	LeCLERC, Peter	2-51
281	ETIENNE, Christopher	2-17
282	ETIENNE, Christopher	2-17
283		
284		
285	FERARD, Peter	1-8

Lot No.	Name of Owner		Book & Page
286	FERARD, Peter		1-8
287	DAVOIUS, Francis		2-202
288	DAVOIUS, Francis		2-202
289	QUESTEL, Nicholas		5-110
290	QUESTEL, Nicholas		5-110
291	QUESTEL, Nicholas		5-110
292	QUESTEL, Nicholas		5-110
293	PERROT, Peter		2-299
294	PERROT, Peter		2-299
295	PERROT, Peter		2-299
296	PERROT, Peter		2-299
297	VANDENBEMDEN, Martinus		2-83
298	VANDENBEMDEN, Martinus		2-83
299	VANDENBEMDEN, Martinus		2-83
300	VANDENBEMDEN, Martinus		2-83
301	VANDENBEMDEN, Martinus		2-83
302	VANDENBEMDEN, Martinus		2-83
303	BIDDON (BELDEN), Augustus	(Common Pleas)	I-592
304	BERTRAND, John Baptist		2-79
305	BERTRAND, John Baptist		2-79
306			
307			
308			
309	BERTRAND, John Baptist		2-79
310	BERTRAND, John Baptist		2-79
311	BERTRAND, John Baptist		2-79
312	CA(R)LERON, Francis		3-252
313	VANDENBEMDEN, Martinus		2-83
314	VANDENBEMDEN, Martinus		2-83
315	MENAGER, Claude Romain		2-42
316	MENAGER, Claude Romain		2-42
317	LaCAISSE, Mary Margaret		2-147
318	LeMOYNE, John Julius		1-60
319	LeMOYNE, John Julius		1-60
320	LeMOYNE, John Julius		1-60
321	VONSCHRILTZ, Heirs of Mathurin		5-123
322	VONSCHRILTZ, Heirs of Mathurin		5-123
323	VONSCHRILTZ, Heirs of Mathurin		5-123
324	VONSCHRILTZ, Heirs of Mathurin		5-123
325	LeMOYNE, John Julius		1-60
326	LeMOYNE, John Julius		1-60
327	LeMOYNE, John Julius		1-60
328	LaCAISSE, Mary Margaret		2-147
329	MENAGER, Claude Romain		2-42
330	MENAGER, Claude Romain		2-42
331	MENAGER, Claude Romain		2-42
332	MENAGER, Claude Romain		2-42
333	MENAGER, Claude Romain		2-42
334	MENAGER, Claude Romain		2-42
335	LaCAISSE, Mary Margaret		2-147

Lot No.	Name of Owner		Book & Page
336	LaCAISSE, Mary Margaret		2-147
337	LeMOYNE, John Julius		1-60
338	LeMOYNE, John Julius		1-60
339	LeMOYNE, John Julius		1-60
340	LeMOYNE, John Julius		1-60
341	LeMOYNE, John Julius		1-60
342	MARION, Francis		2-111
343	VONSCHRILTZ, Heirs of Mathurin		5-123
344	VONSCHRILTZ, Heirs of Mathurin		5-123
345	VONSCHRILTZ, Heirs of Mathurin		5-123
346	VONSCHRILTZ, Heirs of Mathurin		5-123
347	VISENIOR (VISINIOR), Nicholas Charles		2-184
348	VISENIOR (VISINIOR), Nicholas Charles		2-184
349	VISENIOR (VISINIOR), Nicholas Charles		2-184
350	VISENIOR (VISINIOR), Nicholas Charles		2-184
351	MICHAU, John		1-4
352	MICHAU, John		1-4
353	MICHAU, John		1-4
354	MICHAU, John		1-4
355	LeMOYNE, John Julius		1-60
356	SERROT, Heirs of Peter		9-206
357	SERROT, Heirs of Peter		9-206
358	SERROT, Heirs of Peter		9-206
359	MATRY, Peter		3-47
360	MATRY, Peter		3-47
361	MATRY, Peter		3-47
362	MATRY, Peter		3-47
363	MATRY, Peter		3-47
364	SERROT, Heirs of Peter		9-206
365	LeMOYNE, John Julius		1-60
366	MICHAU, John		1-4
367	MICHAU, John		1-4
368	VISINIOR, Nicholas Charles		2-184
369	VISINIOR, Nicholas Charles		2-184
370	VISINIOR, Nicholas Charles		2-184
371	VISINIOR, Nicholas Charles		2-184
372	MICHAU, John		1-4
373	MICHAU, John		1-4
374	LeMOYNE, John		1-4
375	LeTURE, Joseph	(Common Pleas)	I-592
376	MATRY, Peter		3-47
377	MICHAU, John		1-4
378	LeTURE, Joseph	(Common Pleas)	I-592
379	BASTIDE, Stephen		2-201
380	LaCAISSE, Mary Margaret		2-147
381	PETIT JEAN, James	(Common Pleas)	I-592
382	PETIT JEAN, James	(Common Pleas)	I-592
383	PETIT JEAN, James	(Common Pleas)	I-592
384	VIOLETTE, John Lewis		2-345
385	PETIT JEAN, James	(Common Pleas)	I-592

Lot No.	Name of Owner		Book & Page
386	LaCAISSE, Mary Margaret		2-147
387	LaCAISSE, Mary Margaret		2-147
388	BASTIDE, Stephen		2-201
389	LeTURE, Joseph	(Common Pleas)	I-592
390	MICHAU, John		1-4
391	MICHAU, John		1-4
392	MICHAU, John		1-4
393	WILLENNY, Stephen		2-164
394	WILLENNY, Stephen		2-164
395	CADOT, Claudius		2-258
396	CADOT, Claudius		2-258
397	DUPORT, Marion		2-250
398	DUPORT, Marion		2-250
399	PETIT JEAN, James	(Common Pleas)	I-592
400	PETIT JEAN, James	(Common Pleas)	I-592
401	PETIT JEAN, James	(Common Pleas)	I-592
402	PETIT JEAN, James	(Common Pleas)	I-592
403-408	(no entries listed)		
409	LeSERERE, Heirs of Peter		5-181
410	LeSERERE, Heirs of Peter		5-181
411			
412			
413	THOMAS, Peter Thomas		2-148
414	THOMAS, Peter Thomas		2-148
415	THOMAS, Peter Thomas		2-148
416	THOMAS, Peter Thomas		2-148
417	DROZ, Heirs of Peter		2-341
418	DROZ, Heirs of Peter		2-341
419	MATRY, Peter		3-47
420	MATRY, Peter		3-47
421			
422	(D'HEBBERCOURT, Francis)		(1-34)
423-428	(no entries listed)		
429	(D'HEBBERCOURT, Francis)		(1-31)
430	LeMOYNE, John Julius		1-60
431	MATRY, Peter		3-47
432	MATRY, Peter		3-47
433	(SARAZIN, Abel)		(14-434)
434			
435	LeMOYNE, John Julius		1-60
436-443	(no entries listed)		
444	(VIBERT, Anthony)		(14-627)
445			
446	(SARAZIN, Abel)		(11-246)
447	(SARAZIN, Abel)		(11-246)
448	(SARAZIN, Abel)		(11-246)
449-472	(no entries listed)		
473	(VALODIN, Francis)		(3-61)
474	(VALODIN, Francis)		(3-61)
475	LETAILLEUR, John Baptist		5-182

GALLIA COUNTY, OHIO - SMALL LOTS IN TOWN OF GALLIPOLIS

All lots were deeded to the first owners on December 26, 1796 by Paul Fearing and
Return Jonathan Meigs, Jr. as has been previously explained preceding the list of
town lots.

Lot No.	Name of Owner	Book & Page
1	FERARD, Peter	1-8
2	LeCOUR, Ambrose	2-25
3	BUREAU, John Peter Romain	1-30
4	VONSCHRILTZ, Heirs of Martherin	5-123
5	CHANDIVERT, Mary Magdelean LeBrun	5-113
6	MINQAY, Henry	2-32
7	(RICHEU, Perre)	(6-151)
8	MICHAU, John	1-4
9	CHANDIVERT, Peter Mathew	6-128
10	GERVAIS, John Gabriel	2-38
11	CHANDIVERT, Stephen	6-413
12	LAFFILLARD, Peter	1-48
13	DAVOUIS, Francis	2-202
14	VONSCHRILTZ, Lewis Victor	13-59
15	(VALODIN, Francis)	(3-52)
16	VANDENBEMDEN, Martinus	2-83
17	WILLENNY, Stephen	2-164
18	CARLERON, Francis	3-252

The small lots were the lots adjoining "The Place" on its east and west sides.
Lots 1-9 were on the west side and lots 10-18 were on the east side.

GALLIA COUNTY, OHIO - GARDEN LOTS, TOWN OF GALLIPOLIS, FIRST OWNERS

All lots were deeded to the first owners on December 26, 1796 by Paul Fearing and
Return Jonathan Meigs, Jr. as has been previously explained preceding the list of
town lots.

Lot No.	Name of Owner		Book & Page
1	MARION, Francis		2-111
2	BARA, Vincent		2-251
3	(LeCLERCQ, Francis)	(1832)	(16-176)
4	ETIENNE, Christopher		2-16
5	SAUGRAIN, Anthony Francis		8-105
6	MAGNIER, Peter		2-107
7	DUC, Anthony Bartholomew		2-151
8	DEVACHT, Francis Joseph Winox		2-130
9	THEVININ, Nicholas		2-319
10	(LAFORGE, Peter Anthony)		(6-90)
11	(MENAGER, Claude Romain)		(21-390-1)
12	CHANTERELL, Michael		1-46
13	SAFFORD, Robert		B-40
14	DUPORT, Marin		2-250
15			
16	DEVACHT, Jeanne Francoise		2-128
17	(D'HEBECOURT, Francis)		(3-183)
18	BERTHELOT, Mathew		2-207
19	GERVAIS, John Gabriel		2-38
20	VANDENBEMDEN, Martin		2-83

21	BUREAU, John Peter Romain	1-30
22	LeCLERC(Q), Lewis	2-121
23	TILLAYE, John Baptist Nicholas	1-56
24	MARION, Francis	2-111
25	LeCLERCQ, Augustin	2-31
26	VANDENBEMDEN, Martin	2-83
27	MENAGER, Claude Romain	2-42
28	MATRY, Peter	3-47
29	MICHAU, John	1-4

Garden Lots were those lots lying between city lots and the river.

GALLIA COUNTY, OHIO - GARDEN LOTS, TOWN OF GALLIPOLIS, OWNERS IN 1819

The following list of owners of Garden Lots located along the river and in front of the city lots, for the year 1819 was found glued to the first inside page of Deed Book 8 in the Recorder's Office.

Lot No.	Name of Owner
1	MARION, Francis
2	RENARD, Mitchel
3	LEFEVER, Emulus
4	RENARD, Mitchel
5	SOUGRAIN, Anthony
6	MAGNIER, _____(not given)
7	NEWSOM, Lewis
8	DEVACHT, Joseph W.
9	GATES & CHAPDU
10	VALODIN, Francis
11	MENAGER, Claude R.
12	NEWMAN, Walter
13	SAFFORD, Robert
14	SAFFORD, Robert
15	DEVACHT, Joseph W.
16	DEVACHT, Joseph W.
17	BALTZELL & HOLDER
18	CAREL, Rene
19	RODGERS, Thomas
20	VANDENBEMDEN, Mar.
21	LeCLERC & BODAT
22	LeCLERC & BODAT
23	CHANTRELLE, Michael
24	GOULD, William R.
25	GOULD, William R.
26	DAMERIN, _____(not given)
27	(not given)
28	(not given)

The following records were taken from records found in the Recorder's Office of the court house at Xenia. Book and page on which record may be found are given in parenthesis.

William CURRIE and Agnes his wife late Agnes Winter, James WADE and Elizabeth his wife late Elizabeth Winter, William WINTER and Elizabeth his wife, Adam WINTER and Elizabeth his wife, John WINTER and Nancy his wife, Joseph C. WINTER and Margaret his wife, heirs of James WINTER, dec'd, late of Greene Co., Ohio to Hugh HAMILL of Greene Co., Ohio; 5-19-1834; $300.00; Quit Claim to all interest in fractional lots 197, 198, 199 and 200 in Xenia. Witnesses: James C. Johnson, Andrew Heron, Albert Galloway and James Galloway Jr. Recorded 3-20-1835. (Deed Book 15, page 708)

Robert WATSON and Catharine his wife formerly Catharine McCormick, John McCORMICK and Eliza his wife and Philey McCORMICK all of Hamilton Co., Ohio to David HUSTON of Greene Co., Ohio; 12-17-1833; $440.00; Quit Claim all interest in SE¼ Section 10, Township 3, Range 8. Witnesses: Thomas Smith and Abraham Huston. Recorded 2-4-1834. (Deed Book 15, page 51)

Betsey INGLE of Scipio twp., Seneca County, Ohio power of attorney to her husband, Isaac INGLE of same place; 8-24-1832; Betsey grants power of attorney to Isaac to convey undivided part of land in Beever Creek twp. of Greene Co., Ohio willed to her in common with heirs of John KISER, dec'd late of Beever Creek twp., Greene Co., Ohio. Witnesses: Ira Pennock and Ezra Gilbert. Recorded 4-12-1833. (Deed Book 14, page 94)

William (his mark) POLEN of Greene Co., Ohio, Peter (his mark) POLEN, Daniel (his mark) POLEN, Rebeckah (her mark) POLEN, Elasha DEWIT and Nancy his wife, all of Union County, Ohio to Benjamin KISER of Montgomery Co., Ohio; 12-18-1829; $25.00; Quit claim to land of their grandfather, John KISER, dec'd late of Greene Co., Ohio who died seized of north part NW¼ Section 7, Township 2, Range 7. Witnesses: Henry H. Brandenburg and Joseph Kruzen. Recorded 4-12-1833. (Deed Book 14, page 91)

Abraham KISER of Tippecanoe Co., Indiana, Lewis KISER and Sarah his wife of Greene Co., Ohio to Benjamin KISER of Montgomery Co., Ohio; 9-29-1829; $50.00; Quit claim interest in 100 acres of land which dec'd in north part NW¼ Section Co., Ohio died seized, as heirs and legatees of dec'd in north part NW¼ Section 7, Township 2, Range 7. Witnesses: David Huston and Samuel Kiser. Recorded 4-12-1833. (Deed Book 14, page 92)

Samuel KISER and Mary (her mark) his wife, Daniel KISER and Catharine (her mark) his wife all of Montgomery Co., Ohio to Benjamin KISER of same place; 8-4-1830; $50.00; Quit Claim interest in 100 acres of land which John KISER, dec'd, late of Greene Co., Ohio died seized of as his heirs in north part NW¼ Section 7, Township 2, Range 7. Witnesses: M. Patton and John Folkerth, Recorded 4-12-1833. (Deed Book 14, page 92-93)

John (his mark) SELLERS and Elizabeth (her mark) his wife, Jacob (his mark)
SELLERS and Lydia (her mark) his wife, Henry SELLERS and Barbary (her mark)
his wife and Elizabeth WEAVER all of Greene Co., Ohio (note: Henry and Barbary
attested to deed in Logan Co., Ohio) to John BLAKELY of Greene Co., Ohio;
4-19-1830; $425.00; Quit Claim 100 acres in Clement Biddles Military Survey
No. 1378. Witnesses: N. Z. McCollock, Sol. McCollock, Harbert Harris and Henry
Kealofer Jr. (Deed Book 12, pages 163-164)

John READ and Cynthia (her mark) his wife, Samuel C. MITCHELL and Susannah
his wife, all of Miami Co., Ohio, Simeon DUNN and Sophia his wife, James READ
and Matilda his wife, all of Greene Co., Ohio, Eliphalt READ and Sarah his wife
of Fayette Co., Indiana, heirs of Andrew READ, dec'd to William READ of Greene
Co., Ohio; 3-15-1830; $750.00; Quit Claim with incumbrance of two other heirs
of Andrew Read, dec'd viz. Mary Read and Jemima Katherine Reyburn to 210 acres
part NW corner Section 14, Township 3, Range 8. Witnesses: Wm Mitchell and
George Mitchell. Recorded 6-29-1830. (Deed Book 12, pages 193-194)

Margaret CLATON, Reuben (his mark) CLATON and Elizabeth (her mark) his wife,
John CLATON and Phebe (her mark) his wife, Jacob TINGLEY and Elizabeth (her
mark) his wife, George COST and Drusilla (her mark) his wife, Henry (his mark)
MARTIN and Mary (her mark) his wife, Lewis CLATON and Sarah CLATON by John
Cost her guardian, heirs of Wm CLATON, dec'd late of Greene Co., Ohio to
Jonathan CLATON of Greene Co., Ohio; 3-3-1830; $130.00; Whereas Thomas CLATON
Sr. late of Greene Co., Ohio, dec'd father of said Wm CLAYTON, dec'd, with said
William Clayton, dec'd being father of above parties--Reuben, John, Elizabeth,
Drusilla, Mary, Lewis and Sarah and the husband of Margaret; Quit Claim to
land Wm Clayton died seized of interest in being 109½ acres part Sections 30 & 36,
Township 3, Range 7. Witnesses: Wm Low and Samuel Woodward. Recorded
7-13-1830. (Deed Book 12, pages 201-202)

Robert KENDALL Jr. of Greene Co., Ohio to James KENDALL, Sarah GIBSON formerly
Sarah KENDALL, Joseph W. KENDALL, Thomas L. KENDALL, being heirs of Wm KENDALL,
dec'd; (no date--1826?); Quit Claims all right to personal or real estate of
Wm Kendall, dec'd (note: not described). Witnesses: Joseph Hamill and S.W.
Reeder. Recorded 9-9-1830. (Deed Book 12, page 262)

John KENDALL Sr of Greene Co., Ohio to Jane KENDALL, James KENDALL, Sarah
KENDALL, Wilson KENDALL, Thos. L. KENDALL all of Greene Co., Ohio, heirs of
Wm KENDALL, dec'd; 4-2-1826; Quit Claims all right to personal and real estate
of Wm Kendall, dec'd (note: not described). Witnesses: S. W. Reeder and Joseph
Hamill. Recorded 9-10-1830. (Deed Book 12, pages 262-263)

Francis KENDALL and Elizabeth his wife to Heirs of Wm KENDALL; 5-15-1830;
Whereas Wm Kendall late of Greene Co., Ohio died intestate seized of tract
of 266 acres in Xenia twp. and that said land descended to James Kendall,
Sarah wife of James Gibson late Sarah Kendall, Joseph W. Kendall, Thomas
Kendall, John Kendall, Robert Kendall and Vrancis Kendall, children and heirs
of Wm Kendall, dec'd, and whereas Francis Kendall at time of his father's
death was indebted to him, now said Francis Kendall of Montgomery Co., Ohio

(Francis KENDALL cont'd) quit claims to said other heirs as named above, said land (note: no further description given). Witnesses: James Steele, Ira I Fenn. Recorded 9-10-1830. (Deed Book 12, pages 263-264)

Jacob RUSH and Nancy his wife of Clark Co., Ohio to John CIMMERMAN, Jacob CIMMERMAN, Betzy CIMMERMAN, Sally CIMMERMAN, Polly CIMME MAN, Catharine CIMMERMAN and Nancy CIMMERMAN, heirs of Geo. CIMMERMAN, dec'd late of Greene Co., Ohio; 5-24-1821; $250.00; Quit Claim to 50.48 acres SW corner Section 2, Township 3, Range 8. Witnesses: Melyn Baker and Joseph Tatman. Recorded 6-21-1821. (Deed Book 8, page 139)

Elizabeth TURNBULL of Warren Co., Ill. widow of Wm. TURNBULL, dec'd. Alexander TURNBULL and Sarah his wife of Greene Co., Ohio, Gilbert TURNBULL and Ann Lowry his wife of Warren Co., Ill., David TURNBULL and Nancy his wife of Warren Co., Ill., John TURNBULL and Margaret his wife, James TURNBULL and Susanah his wife, Thomas TURNBULL and Mary Ann his wife, Elizabeth STERRETT widow of Joseph STERRETT, John CHALMERS and Isabell his wife, all of Greene Co., Ohio, children and heirs of William TURNBULL late of Warren Co. (Ohio?), dec'd to Samuel HOWELL of Greene Co., Ohio; 9-6-1834; $4468.00; 248½ acres being resurvey of part of Military Survey No. 2272 originally made for Warner and Addison Lewis. Witnesses: Wm (his mark) Scott, Jonathan Flood, Samuel Murray, John Barnes, Jacob Rush and Geo. S. Pierce. Recorded 10-25-1834. (Deed Book 15, pages 447-449)

George CONFER and Elizabeth his wife of Washington Co., Md., Adam WOLF and Catharine his wife late Catharine CONFER of Greene Co., Ohio, John CONFER and Elizabeth (her mark) his wife of Clark Co., Ohio, Michael CONFER and Elizabeth his wife of Clark Co., Ohio, Solomon CONFER and Jane W. his wife of Greene Co., Ohio, Elizabeth CONFER, Hannah CONFER and Barbara CONFER all of Greene Co., Ohio to Jacob CONFER of Greene Co., Ohio; 4-1-1830; $1600.00; Quit Claim to 200 acres part NW corner Section 30, Township 4, Range 7. Witnesses: Chas. Ohlwine and Richard (his mark) Maitland. Recorded 3-13-1833. (Deed Book 14, pages 49-50)

George ALEXANDER and Priscilla (her mark) his wife, Zachariah FURGESON and Polly (her mark) his wife, William FREEMAN and Sarah his wife and Elizabeth JOHN all of Greene Co., Ohio to John JOHN of same place; 12-25-1815; $2480.00; Quit Claim to all interest in Section 1, Township 2, Range 7. Witnesses: David Huston and James John. Recorded 6-8-1826. (Deed Book 10, page 142)

Elizabeth (her mark) JOHN, James JOHN and Anna (her mark) his wife, Lemuel JOHN and Rebecca his wife of Greene Co., Ohio, Jeremiah JOHN and Mary his wife of Montgomery Co., Ohio to William JOHN of Greene Co., Ohio; 6-5-1826; $1300.00; Quit Claim to all interest part SW corner Section 1, Township 2, Range 7 being 174 acres and 133 poles, lines--James John. Witnesses: Abraham Huston and Israel Huston. Recorded 6-8-1826. (Deed Book 10, page 143) (note: for additional John deeds for same parties see Deed Book 10, pages 144, 209, 222 and Deed Book 11, page 565)

Samuel KYLE and Rachel his wife, William ANDERSON and Jane his wife, David M.
LAUGHEAD and Elizabeth his wife, John KENDALL and Catharine his wife all of
Greene Co., Ohio to Joseph KYLE of Greene Co., Ohio; 2-14-1822; Whereas Joseph
Kyle Sr. late of Greene Co., Ohio, dec'd on or about 2-23-1821 by his last
will devised land on which he last lived containing 400 acres to Joseph Kyle Jr.
his youngest son and said heirs of dec'd quit claim their interest in said
land for consideration of natural love and affection for said Joseph Kyle
Jr.; said land is bordered by lands of Isaac and Jacob McFarland, Daniel Murphy,
George Galloway, Wm Turnbull, Wm Buck, James Bull, Wm Anderson and James Morrow.
Witnesses: Joseph Hamill and James Benjamin. Recorded 6-14-1823. (Deed Book 9,
pages 23-24`

Jacob RUS of Berkely Co., Virginia grants power of attorney to Elijah ELLIS of
Greene Co., Ohio to receive rent due from James Cooper for rented tract of
land in Greene Co. that was conveyed to Jacob Rus by James Russel; 4-14-1825;
recorded 8-10-1825. (Deed Book 9, pages 455-456)

David ECKMAN of Greene Co., Ohio, heir of Jacob ECKMAN, dec'd late of Greene
Co., Ohio to Jacob ECKMAN, Daniel ECKMAN, Henry ECKMAN, John ECKMAN and Joseph
ECKMAN, sons and Mary ECKMAN, daughter, all heirs of Jacob ECKMAN, dec'd; 5-23-1831;
Quit Claim because of property advanced to David Eckman by his father during his
lifetime, to all property in any part. Witnesses: John Shannon and David Huston.
Recorded 12-1-1831. (Deed Book 13, page 89)

Catharine ECKMAN widow of Jacob ECKMAN, dec'd late of Greene Co., Ohio, Jacob
ECKMAN Jr., Daniel ECKMAN, Henry ECKMAN and Mary ECKMAN to David ECKMAN;
11-5-1831; Quit Claim to all amount standing against said David Eckman; David,
Jacob Jr., Daniel, Henry and Mary being heirs of Jacob Eckman, dec'd. Witnesses:
Samuel D. Kirkpatrick and John Westfall. Recorded 12-1-1831. (Deed Book 13,
page 90)

Jacob ECKMAN and Mary his wife, Henry ECKMAN and Mary his wife, of Greene Co.,
Ohio, children and heirs of Jacob ECKMAN, dec'd, late of Greene Co., Ohio to
Mary ECKMAN and John ECKMAN, two other children and heirs of said Eckman, dec'd;
2-23-1833; $200.00; Quit Claim all interest in 87 and 3/4 acres W½ Section 27,
Township 3, Range 7. Witnesses: David Huston, David Eckman. Recorded 4-13-1833.
(Deed Book 14, page 99)

Jacob ECKMAN and Mary his wife, Henry ECKMAN and Mary his wife, Mary ECKMAN
and John ECKMAN, children and heirs of Jacob Eckman, dec'd late of Greene
Co., Ohio to Catharine ECKMAN; 2-23-1833; in consideration of quit claim deed
this day received from Catharine Eckman widow and relict of said Jacob Eckman
dec'd and guardian of Joseph ECKMAN another child and heir of dec'd for all
of that part of Section 27, Township 3, Range 7 that Jacob Eckman died seized
off and in return this deed is quit claim to Catharine for all that part of
Section 33, Township 3, Range 7 of which Jacob Eckman was possessed at the time
of his death. Witnesses: David Huston, David Eckman, Sarah Huston. Recorded
4-16-1833. (Deed Book 14, page 100)

Henry ECKMAN and Mary his wife, Mary ECKMAN and John ECKMAN, children and heirs of Jacob ECKMAN, dec'd late of Greene Co., Ohio to Jacob ECKMAN, another child of said Jacob ECKMAN, dec'd; 2-23-1833; $150.00; Quit claim all interest in part Section 27, Township 3, Range 7 being 32.88 acres. Witnesses: David Huston, David Eckman and Sarah Huston. (Deed Book 14, page 101)

John BATES and Nancy (her mark) his wife, Henry BATES and Sarah his wife, Jacob BATES and Margaret his wife, Jacob KOOGLER and Catharine his wife formerly Catharine BATES and Conrod WOOLF, said John, Henry, Jacob and Catharine being children and Conrad Bates being a grandson of Conrad BATES, dec'd, late of Greene Co., Ohio, all parties of Greene Co., Ohio to Henry ECKMAN who is married to Mary BATES another child and heir of Conrad Bates, dec'd; 3-9-1833; $481.47 2/3; Quit Claim interest to part of Sections 5 and 6, Township 2, Range 7 which Conrad Bates was seized at time of his death. Wit: David Huston, Valentine Frybarger and Adam Koogler. Recorded 8-7-1833. (Deed Book 14, page 296)

Eleanor COLLINS of Greene Co., Ohio to James C. COLLINS of Greene Co., Ohio; 3-20-1832; $230.00; Quit Claim to that part of land in Section 5, Township 3, Range 7 of which William COLLINS died seized. Witnesses: Sarah Galloway, James GALLOWAY Jr. Recorded 3-26-1832. (Deed Book 13, page 263)

Eleanor COLLINS of Greene Co., Ohio to Josepn COLLINS of Greene Co., Ohio; 3-17-1832; $200.00; Quit Claim to NE corner Section 5, Township 7, Range 7. Witnesses: Sarah Galloway, James Galloway Jr. Recorded 3-26-1832. (Deed Book 13, page 264)

Catherine CRUMRINE of Perry Co., Ohio to Jacob CRUMRINE of Perry Co., Ohio; 2-13-1832; $250.00; uit Claim 100 acres on head waters of Caesars Creek being part of Peter Pelhams survey #6367, lines--Thomas Poseys survey #3080 and Thomas Crowders survey #4621; said part being conveyed is one equal half with heirs of Michael Crumrine as conveyed by deed of 4-29-1831 from Mathias Winans and wife, this deed for half being 50 acres. Witnesses: John M. Davis and Peter Odlin. Recorded 3-26-1832. (Deed Book 13, page 262)

William C. ROBESON and Sarah his wife of Greene Co., Ohio to John GOWDY of Greene Co., Ohio; 10-7-1831; Whereas by death of George Foglesong and Catharine his wife of Warren Co., Ohio their being father and mother of said Sarah Robinson, William and Sarah are entitled by descent to an equal undivided 1/5th part being lot set apart on petition of partition amongst the heirs of John STNAVELY, dec'd late of Greene Co., Ohio who was the father of said Catharine Foglesong, dec'd and is 145.08 acres and designated as lot 4 in said partition which took place at the Oct Term 1820 Common Pleas Court of Greene Co., Ohio (note: no further description given). Witnesses: Henson Robison and David Douglass. (Deed Book 13, pages 39-40)

Jacob SNAVELY and Christina his wife of Washington Co., Md. to George FOGELSONG of Warren Co., Ohio; 10-9-1829; $150.00; Whereas by the death of Margaret Snavely only child of Samuel Snavely one of the children and heirs of John Snavely late of Greene Co., Ohio, dec'd, the aforesaid Jacob Snavely hath become entitled to by descent to one equal undivided fifty part, said Jacob being a son of John Snavely, dec'd and uncle of said Margaret, and George Fogelsong in the right of his wife, a daughter of John Snavely to one undivided fifth part, being lot 8 in partition among Snavely heirs at the October term 1820 Common Pleas Court of Greene Co., Ohio. Recorded 2-25-1830. (Deed Book 12, pages 39-40_

Ann Mariah NICODEMUS, Henry NICODEMUS and Catharine his wife, Andrew NICODEMUS and Rachel his wife, Levi DEVILBLISS, Sarah DEVILBLISS, Isaac CASSELL, Lydia CASSELL, Frederick CRONICE, Ann CRONICE, John NICODEMUS and Hana his wife all of Frederick Co., Md., John PROUGH and Rebecca PROUGH of Montgomery Co., Chio to John HARSHMAN of Greene Co., Ohio; 10-11-1832; $1593.76; Quit Claim to 147.23 acres part Section 5, Township 2, Range 7. Recorded 12-8-1832. (Deed Book 13, pages 558-559)

Samuel H. WILLIAMSON and Mercy his wife, Moses HALL and Nary his wife of Greene Co., Ohio to William COZAD of Greene Co., Ohio; 7-2-1832; Quit Claim on 11 acres being par SE¼ Section 27 and part SW¼ Section 21, Township 3, Range 8. Witnesses: Wm. Low and Jonathan Davis. Recorded 9-13-1832. (Deed Book 13, page 446)

Samuel H. WILLIAMSON and Mercy his wife, William COZAD and Mariah his wife of Greene Co., Ohio to Moses Hall of same place; 7-2-1832; $1000.00; Quit Claim to 11 acres part SW¼ Section 21, Township 3, Range 8 (note: Section 27 not mentioned). Witnesses: Wm Low, Jonathan Davis. Recorded 9-29-1832. (Deed Book 13, page 480)

James GALLOWAY Jr. and Martha his wife, Damuel GALLOWAY and Elizabeth his wife, George Galloway and Rebecca his wife, Andrew GALLOWAY and Mary his wife, John JACOBY and Ann his wife and Anthony GALLOWAY, heirs of William GALLOWAY, dec'd, late of Greene Co., Ohio to Martin Kershner of Greene Co., Ohio; 12-10-1829; $800.00; Quit Claim 166 acres SW¼ Section 26, Township 4, Range 8 which was patented to Wm Galloway by U. S. Witnesses: Henry P. Galloway, David Douglass. Recorded 5-11-1830. (Deed Book 12, page 144)

James GALLOWAY Jr. and Martha his wife, Samuel GALLOWAY and Elizabeth his wife, George Galloway and Rebeckah his wife, Andrew Galloway and Mary his wife, John JACOBY (no wife given in this deed) and Anthony GALLOWAY all of Greene Co., Ohio, heirs of William GALLOWAY, dec'd to Amos QUINN of Greene Co., Ohio; 1-1-1830; $720.00; Quit Claim to 160 acres NW¼ Section 35, Township 4, Range 7 which William Galloway died seized of. Witnesses: John Dodd and Josiah Davisson. Recorded 4-13-1830. (Deed Book 12, page 97)

David HOLMES and Margaret his wife late Margaret BAIN, Ebenezer BAIN and Matilda his wife, Isaiah McCONNELL and Ann his wife late Ann BAIN, Sarah BAIN and Mary BAIN, said Margaret, Ebenezer, Ann, Sarah and Mary being devisees of James BAIN, dec'd late of Greene Co., Ohio to William BIGGER of Greene Co., Ohio; 9-16-1833; $1500.00; Quit claim to tract James Bain late of Greene Co., Ohio, dec'd died seized and on which he resided at the time of his death being whole pre-emption lot 1 of Section 32, Township 3, Range 6. Witnesses: William Bain and Abner G. Luce. Recorded 2-6-1834. (Deed Book 15, pages 54-55_

Simon KENTON and Phebe his wife of Greene Co., Ohio to Joseph HARBISON of Greene Co., Ohio; 1-9-1830; $570.00; E½ of in-lots 90 & 104 and whole of in-lot 103 in Xenia. Witnesses: Wesly Boyles and Josiah Davisson. Recorded 5-11-1830. (Deed Book 12, pages 142-143)

John Lambert, Amos Lambert, Hannah Davis late Lambert, Robert Parks and Lucina his wife late Lambert, Thomas Holden, Jemima Holden, Isaac Stout and Hannah his wife late Hannah Fullens children and heirs of Anna Holden of which said John, Amos, Hannah Davis, Lucina Parkes and Anna Holden are and were brothers and sisters and the true heirs of William Lambert, dec'd, late of Greene Co., Ohio to Aaron Lambert of Greene Co., Ohio - 12-12-1833 - $166.00 - Lot #4 in Fairfield- Deed Book 15, pages 263-4

William Kirkpatrick of Greene Co., Ohio to Rebeckah Stull formerly Rebeckah Kirkpatrick of Greene Co., Ohio - 2-23-1825 - consideration of one dollar and love and affection he has for his daughter - Lot #1 of Section 33, Township 3, Range 7, 65 acres - Deed Book 9, pages 393-4

Asahel Martin and Margaret (her mark) his wife of Logan Co., Ohio; Henry Martin and Mary (her mark) his wife of Clark Co., Ohio; William Stevens and Sarah his wife and Indiana Martin of Greene Co., Ohio to Isaac Phillips of Greene Co., Ohio - 2-21-1837 - $941.86 - two-thirds part of land in Bath twp. on waters of Madriver being SW¼ Section 33, Township 3, Range 8 - Deed Book 18, page 296

Roda (her mark) Martin to Isaac Philips, both of Greene Co., Ohio - 4-1-1837 - $706-26 pt. SW¼ Section 33 and 80 acres south side Section 33, Township 3, Range 8, Bath twp. on waters of Madriver being land deeded from Asahel Stiles and Raney his wife to Uri Martin on 12-2-1822 - Deed Book 18, page 298

Stephen Martin of Lagrange Co., Indiana to Isaac Phillips of Greene Co., Ohio- 6-7-1837 - pt. SW¼ and south side Section 33, Township 3, Range 8, Bath twp. on waters of Madriver being land deeded from Asahel Stiles and Raney his wife to Uri Martin on 12-2-1822 - Deed Book 18, Page 299

John M. Bull and Eliza his wife, David Bull and Elizabeth his wife, Wm. H. Bull and Isabella his wife, Hiram Bull and Elizabeth his wife, all of Shelby Co., Ohio to John Clark - 1-15-1846 - $4.00 - Quit Claim - west side little Miami 24 acres pt. NE¼ Section 30, Township 4, Range 5; lines—line between land former- ly 24 acres pt. NE¼ Section 30, Township 4, Range 5; lines—line between land formerly owned by William Tanner and Nathan Bull, Aaron M. Crumleys line.—Deed Book 24, page 172

Zacariah Walker's Heirs to Francis Brock - 4-3-1849 - $15.00 - John W. Walker and Cintha his wife, Samuel L. Walker and Elizabeth C. his wife, William H. Walker and Mary P. his wife, Joseph C. McFarland and Mary his wife - 205 acres on waters of Massies Creek in Military Survey #516 originally entered in name of Wm. Washington; subject to widows dower. - Deed Book 26, page 196

David Monroe's Heirs to John W. McBeth - 4-14-1849 - George Monroe and Martha his wife, James B. Monroe and Henrietta his wife, John Chartens(?) and Margaret his wife, John Moore and Mary Ann his wife and Barbary Monroe, all of Greene Co., Ohio. - Quit Claim - Lot #4 in Lauman's addition to Xenia. - Deed Book 26, page 4

Charles McCristy and Phebe his wife of Warren Co., Ohio and Jesse McChristy and Nancy his wife of Greene Co., Ohio to John Hale of Greene Co., Ohio - 11-7-1829 - $86.05 - Lots 70 & 78 in Bellbrook - Deed Book 14, pages 146-7

Timothy Searl Jr. and Elizabeth his wife formerly Hosier, Brown Searl and Anna Barbara his wife formerly Anna Barbery Hozier all of Greene County, Ohio to John Hozier - 6-3-1825 - $50.00 - Quit Claim - 2/8ths part NW¼ Section 27, Township 3, (no range given), Bath twp., 77.60 acres being part of real estate of Frederick Hosier, dec'd of Bath twp. - Deed Book 9, page 514

James McCoy and Nancy his wife, David McCoy and Polly his wife, Alexander McCoy and Abigail his wife, Elizabeth Jamison, Samuel Cristy and Jane his wife, Alexander Turnbull and Sarah his wife, William McCoy and Amelia his wife, heirs of Alexander McCoy, dec'd, all of Greene Co., Ohio to John McCoy at same place - 2-25-1825 - Quit Claim - "consideration of natural love and affection" - 109½ acres in Military Survey #606 & # 616 originally entered in name of James Culbertson; lines--Frances Whitring and David Lawhead - Deed Book 9, page 451

George Harshman and Catharine his wife, John Harshman and Anna Mariah his wife, Jacob Harshman and Catharine his wife, Jonathan Brown and Mary his wife, John Sipe and Elizabeth his wife, all of Greene Co., Ohio to William Higgins - 5-23-1850 - $60.00 - 1.44 acres being undivided 6/8ths part of Section 32, Township 3, Range 7 - Deed Book 26, pages 559-60

Ann Mariah Nicodemus, Henry Nicodemus and Catharine his wife, Andrew Nicodemus and Rachel his wife, Levi Devilbis and Sarah his wife, Isaac Cassell and Lydia his wife, Frederick Cronice and Anna his wife, John Nicodemus and Hannah his wife, all of Frederick Co., Maryland and John Prough and Rebecca his wife of Montgomery County, Ohio to Samuel Miller of Greene Co., Ohio - 10-11-1832 - $553.00 - 100.70 acres part of S½ Section 36, Township 3, Range 7

Richard Bull's Heirs to Bently Bull - 10-3-1849 - Rachel Bull, James Bull and Amelia A. his wife, David P. Baldwin and Julia A. his wife, William Bull and Mariah S. his wife all of Greene Co., Ohio, widow and heirs of Richard Bull, dec'd, late of Greene Co., Ohio to Bently Bull - $510.00 - Quit Claim - 102 acres part of Military Survey #605 originally entered in name of George Gray; lines--John Marshall - Deed Book 26, pages 231-2

John Weaver's Heirs to Martha Weaver - 1-22-1849 - Jacob L. Weaver and Amanda his wife, John M. Weaver and Elizabeth his wife, Felix Peterson and Mary his wife, Jesse Peterson and Eleanor A. his wife, Abel Peterson and Alivia his wife, Clarrissa H. Weaver, Martha C. Weaver and Nancy J. Weaver - grantee, Martha Weaver is widow of John Weaver - Quit Claim - $5.00 - 112 acres part Military Survey #2234 on waters of Caesars Creek; lines--Charles Wells and Jacob Sellers - Deed Book 26, page 74

Elizabeth (her mark) Kingery of Franklin County, Indiana to Henry Shank of Greene Co., Ohio - 4-24-1849 - $1.00 - Quit Claim - 1/9th part NE¼ Section 10, Township 2, Range 6 - Deed Book 26, page 21

506

Jonathan Clayton's Heirs to Samuel Koogler - 4-2-1849 Catharine Clayton, George
Clayton and Mary Ann his wife, David Clayton and Elizabeth his wife, Samuel
Durnbaugh and Elizabeth his wife, Peter E. Hardman and Mariah his wife, Wm.
Mercer and Huldah his wife and Cynthia Clayton all of Greene Co., Ohio - $3500.00
- 109¼ acres part of Section 36, Township 3, Range 7 - Deed Book 26, page 50.

John Scarff, Sarah L. Scarff, Rachel L. Scarff and Minerva Scarff of Greene Co.,
Ohio, James C. Scarff, William D. Scarff of Bellfontaine, Logan Co., Ohio, George
Sweny and Margery Jane his wife formerly scarff of Kenton, Hardin Co., Ohio to
John Anderson of Fayette Co., Ohio - 3-1-1849 - $3000.00 - land on waters of
Caesars Creek south-east of Tract belonging to James Anderson and bounded on
north by tract of 100 acres owned by John Scarff being residue of tract of land
willed to John H. Anderson by will of John Anderson which was sold by Benjamin
Norford to aforesaid John Scarff the father of first mentioned parties and devised
by his will to them - Deed Book 26, page 3

Michael Gunckel and Sarah (her mark) his wife of Montgomery Co., Ohio to Jacob
Eley - 8-15-1829 - Quit Claim - $100.00 - SE¼ Section 10, Township 2, Range 7 -
Sarah being a daughter of Isaac Eley, dec'd - Deed Book 14, page 165

John Aley and Susannah his wife of Greene Co., Ohio to Jacob Aley of same place -
4-3-1832 - Quit Claim - $232.00 - SE¼ Section 10, Township 2, Range 7 - John Aley
being a son of Isaac Eley, dec'd - Witnesses: David Huston and Abraham Aly -
Deed Book 14, page 166

Jacob (his mark) Fox and Elizabeth (her mark) his wife to Jacob Eley, all of
Greene Co., Ohio - 8-10-1818 - Quit Claim - $175.00 - SE¼ Section 10, Township
2, Range 7 - Elizabeth being a daughter of Isaac Aley (Eley), dec'd - Deed Book
14, page 167

Isaac Aley of Greene Co., Ohio, a son of Isaac Eley, dec'd to Jacob Aley -
2-25-1829 - Quit Claim - $100.00 - SE¼ Section 10, Township 2, Range 7 - Deed
Book 14, page 168

David Cosler and Mary (her mark) his wife to Jacob Aley, all of Greene Co., Ohio
- 8-15-1829 - Quit Claim - $100.00 - SE¼ Section 10, Township 2, Range 7 - Mary
being a daughter of Isaac Aley, dec'd - Deed Book 14, page 168 :

Jacob Gerst and Catharina (her mark) his wife of Montgomery Co., Ohio to Jacob
Aley of Greene Co., Ohio - 3-15-1819 - Quit Claim - $175.00 - SE¼ Section 10,
Township 2, Range 7 - Catharina being a daughter of Isaac Aley, dec'd - Deed
Book 14, page 169

Samuel Staley and Catharine Staley adms. of Daniel Staley, dec'd, late of Greene
Co., Ohio to David Cosler and Abraham Ely - 11-17-1832 - petition filed in Common
Pleas Court 6-15-1832 atainst Jonathan Staley, Daniel Staley Jr., Mary Staley,
Peter Staley, Catharine Staley Jr. and Sophiah Staley children and minor heirs of
Daniel Staley, dec'd and Jacob Rike their guardian - NW¼ Section 9, Township 2,
Range 7 which Daniel Staley died seized - $500.00 - Deed Book 14, page 171

507

Abraham Aley of Greene Co., Ohio, a son of Isaac Aley, dec'd to Jacob Aley of same place - 8-15-1829 - Quit Claim - $100.00 - SE¼ Section 10, Township 2, Range 7 - Deed Book 14, page 170

Mary Fogle widow of Michael Fogle, dec'd, late of Greene Co., Ohio, Peter Fogle and Elizabeth his wife, Henry Harshman and Magdalena his wife and Margaret Fogle of Greene Co., Ohio, Roman Mason and Susanna his wife of Montbomery Co., Ohio, George Shegley and Barbary his wife of Clark Co., Ohio, John Fogle and Mary his wife, Anthony Hyres and Mary his wife of Wayne Co., Indiana children and heirs of Michael Fogle, dec'd to Uacob Fogle of Miami Co., Ohio, also one of the heirs of Michael Fogle, dec'd - 1-14-1829

George Junkin and Martha his wife, James Criswell (Creswell) and Anh (her mark) his wife, Arthur McFarland and Jane (her mark) his wife to Lancelet Junkin, all of Greene Co., Ohio - 8-31-1833 - consideration of natural love and affection and one hundred dollars - 30 acres part of Military Survey #4502 originally entered in name of Thomas Browder being lands conveyed by Lancelot Junkin Sr. to Lancelot Junkin Jr. and from him to Silas Roberts; lines—Moffit Brownlee, John Mitchell, Joseph Cooper and McGuire Survey - Deed Book 15, page 57

GREENE COUNTY, OHIO - LAND GRANTS

VAN EATON, Abraham of Hamilton Co., Ohio - NE¼ S6, T3, R5; 10-3-1806; rec. 4-29-1808; Deed Book 1, page 482

VAN EATON, Abraham of Hamilton Co., Ohio - 41.44 ac. S end E½ S1, T2, R6; 10-3-1806; rec. 5-7-1808; Deed Book 1, page 485

TINGLE, John Philip assignee of Ralph PHILLIPS - S½ S22, T5, R8; 1-18-1811; rec. 6-22-1811; Deed Book 2, page 294

TINGLE, John Philip assignee of Ralph PHILLIPS - N½ S22, T5, R8; 1-18-1811; rec. 6-22-1811; Deed Book 2, page 295

FUNDERBURGH, Daniel assignee of John JUDAH - NE¼ S13, T3, R8; 3-12-1812; rec. 8-7-1813; Deed Book 3, page 303

HARTEN, Edward of Greene Co., Ohio - SW¼ S35, T5, R8; 3-5-1812; rec. 10-21-1813; Deed Book 3, page 357

TORRENCE, George P. assignee of Matthias CROW - Fractional So, T3, R7; 1-29-1811; rec. 12-25-1813; Deed Book 3, page 401

DEWITT, Peter assignee of John CALLAWAY - SE¼ S23, T5, R8; 7-13-1812; rec. 2-9-1814; Deed Book 3, page 457

McCUNE, Joseph; IRWIN, John; and HUNTER, John assignees of John BLUE - all S32, T4, R8; 1-4-1814; rec. 8-19-1814; Deed Book 4, page 161

LESLEY, Elisha of Greene Co., Ohio - NW¼ S27, T5, R8; 6-1-1814; rec. 9-20-1814; Deed Book 4, page 201

CURRY, David of Hamilton Co., Ohio - NW¼ S36, T4, R5; 7-20-1812; rec. 20-4-1814; Deed Book 4, page 223

VANCE, Joseph and CLENSEY, James - 404 ac. Send Fractional S32, T3, R6; 2-18-1812; rec. 9-21-1815; Deed Book 5, page 26

BURROWS, Joseph assignee of William SNODGRASS - NE¼ S11 T2 R7; 5-20-1810; rec. 6-26-1816; Deed Book 5, page 188

BURNETT, Jacob of Cincinnati, Ohio - NE¼ S9, T3, R8; 3-17-1818; rec. 6-3-1819;
Deed Book 7, page 156
BURNETT, Jacob of Cincinnati, Ohio - NE¼ S15, T3, R7; 2-22-1813; rec. 6-4-1819;
Deed Book 7, page 157
BURNETT, Jacob of Cincinnati, Ohio - SE¼ S15, T3, R7; 2-22-1813; rec. 6-4-1819;
Deed Book 7, page 158
BURNETT, Jacob of Cincinnati, Ohio - NW¼ S15, T3, R7; 2-22-1813; rec. 6-4-1819;
Deed Book 7, page 158
RIDDLE, James and FINDLAY, James - Survey 1 in S13 & SE¼ S14, T4, R8; 6-27-1817;
rec. 10-5-1819; Deed Book 7, page 271
MUIR, Francis - for military service performed by said Muir as Capt for 3 years in
Virginia Line, Cont'l establishment; Military Warrent #1474 granted in favor
of said Muir on Glady Run a branch of Little Miami, by survey dated 11-14-1794,
lines--Survey #1000, Churchill Jones survey #417; 10-9-1804; rec. 10-6-1819;
Deed Book 7, page 273
McCULLY, Solomon of Greene Co., Ohio - Fractional S34, T4, R7 except 159.61 ac.
in NE corner; 9-4-1807; rec. 1-10-1822; Deed Book 7, page 524
BAKER, Thomas assignee of Ralph PHILLIPS - 85.57 ac. Fractional S1, T4, R8;
12-6-1821; rec. 1-10-1822; Deed Book 8, page 234
WOOLF, George of Hamilton Co., Ohio - 195.26 ac. West end S½ S18, T3, R7;
9-23-1812; rec. 10-31-1823; Deed Book 9, page 92
WOOLF, George of Greene Co., Ohio - Survey #1 in NW¼ and Survey #4 in SE corner
S18, T3, R7; 8-28-1813; rec. 10-31-1823; Deed Book 9, page 93
FULTON, William assignee of Wm BARR and Geo. P. TORRENCE - Survey 1, S3, T2, R8;
2-7-1817; rec. (not given); Deed Book 12, page 126
NICODEMUS, John - SE¼ S5, T3, R7; 6-22-1810; rec. 11-29-1831; Deed Book 13,
page 83
NICODEMUS, John - NE¼ S5, T2, R7; 6-22-1810; rec. 11-29-1831; Deed Book 13, page 83
NICODEMUS, John - NW¼ S5, T2, R7; 6-22-1810; rec. 11-29-1831; Deed Book 13, page 84
NICODEMUS, John - SW¼ S5, T2, R7; 6-22-1810; rec. 11-29-1831; Deed Book 13, page 84
NICODEMUS, John - SE¼ S5, T2, R7; 6-22-1810; rec. 11-29-1831; Deed Book 13, page 85
NICODEMUS, John - SW¼ S36, T3, R7; 6-22-1810; rec. 11-29-1831; Deed Book 13,
page 85
TINGLEY, John A. assignee of Ralph PHILLIPS - NE¼ S32, T3, R8; 8-20-1810 rec.
1-20-1832; Deed Book 13, page 194
BELFIELD, Winefred B., heir at law of John BELFIELD - for service by John Belfield
as a Major for 3 years in Virginia Line, Cont'l Establishment; 1333 1/3 ac.
survey dated 10-25-1798, Military Warrant #1849, waters of Little Miami,
lines--corner George Baylors survey #1188; 5-29-1801; rec. 3-13-1832; Deed
Book 13, page 252
HUNT, Jesse assignee of John ANDREWS - all S28, T3, R7; 8-3-1814; rec. 8-30-1832;
Deed Book 13, page 435
HUNT, Jesse assignee of John HIGHWAY - all S34, T3, R7; 8-13-1814; rec. 8-30-1832;
Deed Book 13, page 435
HERSHMAN, John assignee of Martin BAUM - SW¼ S3, T2, R7; 7-30-1812; rec.12-7-1832;
Deed Book 13, page 557

509

The following records were abstracted from Volume 1803-1813. Pages on which record may be found are given in parenthesis. Book begins in 1808.

9-29-1808 – John EATON appointed guardian of Peter PRICE minor of David PRICE, dec'd. (10)

9-27-1808 – Elizabeth CURRY and William CURRY appointed adms. of Walter CURRY, dec'd. (1)

9-29-1808 – Petition of John WILLIAMS one of the heirs of Charles WILLIAMS, dec'd and William Bozel in the right of Polly his wife who is also one of the eight heirs of said deceased. Andrew Read and David Huston guardians of Nancy, William, James, Sally and Eli Williams and eight heirs of said deceased praying that certain lands may be conveyed to Jeremiah YORK and Ann his wife formerly Ann WESTFALL. (11)

1-24-1809 – Nathaniel BELLIS appointed guardian of Rebecca Garretson minor daughter of Richard GARRETSON, dec'd. (21)

1-24-1809 – Nancy BOYD and James MORROW appointed adms. of John BOYD, dec'd. (21)

1-24-1809 – Will of John MORGAN proven by oath of John Morgan and Jonathan Morgan. Evan Morgan, Executor. (22)

1-24-1809 – John HEATON appointed guardian of John Price minor of David PRICE, dec'd. (28)

5-23-1809 – Isaac SPINNING appointed adms. of Andrew YOUNG, dec'd. (34)

5-25-1809 – Hugh DICKEY vs. Heirs of Wm. TOMPKINS, dec'd. In Chancery. Defendants: Peter McArthur and Mary his wife, Aron Stockton and Elizabeth his wife, Mary Thompkins, Henry Tompkins, John Tompkins, William Tompkins, Sarah Tompkins and James Tompkins; not residents of the State of Ohio. (43)

9-26-1809 – Nancy MAXWELL appointed adms. of William MAXWELL, dec'd. (48)

9-27-1809 – Ministers license granted to David JONES. (54)

9-28-1809 – Mary STERRETT appointed adms. of Joseph STERRETT, dec'd. (58)

1-25-1810 – William MORGAN appointed guardian of Peter BOYD minor son of John BOYD, dec'd. (70)

5-22-1810 – James CURRIE and James ANDREW, Sr. appointed guardian of George Currie, Isabella Currie and James Currie minors of William CURRIE, dec'd. (80)

5-22-1810 – John JOHNSTON appointed adms. of estate of John JOHNSTON, Sr., Dec.'d.(82)

5-25-1810 – William GALLOWAY appointed guardian of Jacob, Rebecca and Effy CASY, orphans. (91)

5-28-1811 - Michael SWIGERT appointed guardian of Eave and John NAVE minors of Leonard NAVE, dec'd. (93)

5-28-1811 - William Berry and Isabella Berry appointed adms. of John BERRY, dec'd. (94)

5-28-1811 - Elizabeth Andrews and George NUCOM appointed adms. of Hugh ANDREWS, dec'd. (94)

9-30-1811 - Simeon DUNN appointed adms. of John DUNN, dec'd. (101)

9-30-1811 - Celista WESTFALL aged 15 yrs. chose David HUSTON as her guardian. William VAN CLEVE appointed guardian of Elbert Westfall aged 12 yrs. and Cynthia Westfall aged 10 years, minors of James WESTFALL, dec'd. (101)

9-30-1811 - Elizabeth TATMAN and Joseph TATMAN appointed adms. of James TATMAN, dec'd. (102)

9-30-1811 - Mary FARMER appointed adms. of William FARMER, dec'd. (102)

10-4-1811 - Petition of John R. STOKES heir at law of John STOKES, dec'd late of Rowan County, North Carolina for redemption of sundry parcels of land in Greene County on the waters of the Little Miami; and said John R. Stokes on producing sufficient evidence to this court that he was born on the 27th day of June 1789 and that he is the sole surviving heir of the said John Stokes, dec'd; and that 100 acres of land in the Virginia Military District was sold in the name of John Stokes to James SMITH for taxes. John R. Stokes entitled to redemption. (116)

1-28-1812 - Will of William BULL proven by oath of William McFARLAND and James COWAN. Executors, John Bull and James Bull. (122)

1-29-1812 - On motion of Magalene GARLOUGH, Solomon SHOUP is appointed guardian of Daniel PUTERBAUGH aged 18 yrs., Jacob Puterbaugh aged 16 yrs. and Andrew Puterbaugh aged 13 yrs. on January 1812; minors of David PUTERBAUGH, dec'd. (127)

1-29-1812 - On motion of Magdaline PUTERBAUGH, Solomon SHOUP is appointed guardian of Samuel PUTERBAUGH aged 11 yrs. on Jan. 1812, Henry Puterbaugh aged 9 yrs. in Feb. 1812 and David Puterbaugh aged 7 yrs. on 15 March 1812; minors of David PUTERBAUGH, dec'd. (128)

1-30-1812 - Aaron MENDENHALL appointed guardian of Deborah HORNEY aged 15 yrs., Anderson Horney aged 12 yrs., Rhoda Horney aged 10 yrs., Esther Horney aged 6 yrs. and Paul Horney aged 11 yrs. (131)

2-1-1812 - Settlement of the estate of John LOVE, Mary LOVE adms. Account filed for boarding and schooling of: Katherin Love aged 7 yrs., Polly Love aged 8 or 9 yrs., Thomas Love aged 10 yrs., Margaret Love aged 11 yrs., Elener Love aged 13 yrs., Richard Love aged 15 yrs. and Joseph Love aged 16 yrs. (139)

2-1-1812 - Nancy WEST vs. John McDANIEL. Bastardy. (141)

5-25-1812 - David JOHN and Margaret Petro appointed adms. of Paul PETRO, dec'd.(146)

5-27-1812 - John McCULLOUGH appointed adms. of the estate of Alexander McCULLOUGH, dec'd. (156)

5-29-1812 - William L. PIERCE heir at law of William PIERCE, dec'd; redemption of 95 acres which was sold to James McNIGHT for taxes. (160)

9-28-1812 - John KNOX appointed adms. of estate of Margaret BRADFORD, dec'd. John KNOX appointed guardian of John Bradford aged 15 yrs. and William Bradford aged 2 years; minors of Margaret BRADFORD, dec'd. (168)

9-28-1812 - Ephraigm MENTHOW, native of Prussia, makes his declaration of intention to become citizen. (169)

9-28-1812 - Will of Samuel GRIMES proven by oath of John STEELE and John WINSWORTH. (169)

1-26-1813 - Will of John SANDERS proven by oath of Henry BURK and Samuel STEELE. Christian SANDERS, admrs. (181)

1-27-1813 - Will of Nicholas PETRO proven by oath of Acey JOHN and Maxom CLAYTON. (183)

1-27-1813 - Will of George SHARP proven. Solomon SHARP, executor. (183)

1-27-1813 - Will of Joseph TINGLEY proven by oath of William CLAY TON and Joseph ALLEN. Andrew READ, executor. (185)

5-25-1813 - Jacob SMITH appointed adms. of the estate of Thomas LOWE, dec'd. (195)

5-25-1813 - Thomas GLYNN aged 19 yrs. chose David LOUGHEAD as his guardian. (195)

5-25-1813 - Petition of Jonathan CAMPBELL and Henry CAMPBELL to have Nathaniel ALEXANDER of Sugar Creek township declared insane. (196)

5-26-1813 - Will of Jonathan WALLACE proven by oath of Robert GOWDY and John R. ROLLINS. (198)

5-26-1813 - Mitchell GLENN aged 14 yrs. chose Christopher SROWFE as his guardian. (198)

5-26-1813 - John BULL appointed adms. of the estate of Asaph BULL, dec'd. (198)

9-27-1813 - Will of William BURT proven by oath of Samuel Steele, Forris SANDERS and Samuel Perry. Executors, Wm. STANFIELD and Jemima BIRT. (202)

9-28-1813 - Robert MERCER aged 18 yrs., minor of Jonathan MERCER, dec'd, chose John COX as his guardian. (205)

9-30-1813 - Will of Jonathan WESTFALL proven by oath of Joel Westfall and Thomas Cottrell. Samuel D. Kirkpatrick, executor. (213)

The following records were taken from Will Book A-B, pages on which record may be found are given in parenthesis. In the case of estates, occasionally additional information may be obtained from the estate packet.

LOWRY, Archabald - dated 12-12-1803; recorded 12-22-1803. Wife, Elizabeth. Sons, James and David, not of age, to be gound to testator's brother, Thomas Lowry. Daughters, Lettis and Queen. Mentions that there may possibly be a child born after his decease. Mentions lots in Springfield. Executors: Thomas Lowry and Elizabeth Lowry. Signed: Arch'd Lowry. Witnesses: John Crosley, Jr. and John Vorts. (1)

ALLEN, Henry - estate - 9-16-1806 appraisal by Thomas Cully, Aaron Cozad and James Tatman. Mentions notes on Thomas Frasair, Adam Cooglar, Samuel Josiah Holly, Dumes Dann, Jacob Allen and John Taylor. Public sale held 10-2-1806 with a Bible being sold to Geo. Kuhendall. (3 & 38)

LOWE, John - estate - Inventory 4-2-1805. Thomas Halson one of the adms. Mary Lowe purchased a number of items at auction. (7)

ADAMSON, Elisha - estate - Appraisal 4-8-1805 by Joseph Layton, John Dawson and James Robinson. Nancy Adamson, adms. (9)

SANDERS, Jesse - dated 1-23-1806; recorded 5-14-1806. Wife, Sarah. Sons: Jesse, Ferris (Farris), and John. Daughters: Jemimah, Jane and Susannah. Executors: wife, Sarah and James Sanders. Witnesses: Thos. Spain and William Therney. Codicil dated 1-23-1806, no further information and same witnesses. (15)

RAMSEY, James - estate - 8-2-1806 appraisal by James Cunningham, John Vance and William Tanner. Mary Ramsey purchased numerous items at public auction. (18 & 49)

ROBINSON, Joseph - dated 3-3-1800; recorded 9-10-1806. Sons, Joseph and Edward. Daughters, Priscellar Armstrong and Elizabeth. Mentions land in Wilson County, Kentucky. Executors: Joseph Robinson and Alexander Armstrong. Signed: Joseph Robinson. Witnesses: Nathan Lamme and John Marshall. (22)

PRICE, David - dated 5-26-1806; recorded (not given). Wife, Susanna. Sons: David, William, John, Peter and Joseph. Daughters: Esster Yates and Susanna Price. Executors: wife, Susanna and David Forkner. Signed: David Price. Witnesses: Theo. Spain and James Spain. (23) Inventory 1-31-1807. (45)

McCLELLAN, John - dated 8-23-1806; recorded (not given). Mother, Sarah Wilson. Brother, Abraham McClellan. Sisters: Peggy Sterritt and Polly McClellan. Executors: brother-in-law, John Sterritt. Mentions land in Breckenridge County, Kentucky. Signed: John McClellan. Witnesses: Jno. Wilson and Samuel Wilson. (25) Inventory 5-7-1808. (26)

WILSON, Peggy - dated 12-10-1806; recorded (not given). Brothers: Joseph, John and Samuel Wilson. Sister, Sally Wilson. Executor: mother, Sarah Wilson. Signed: Peggy Wilson. Witnesses: John Sterritt and John Hoop. (26)

MERCER, Jonathan - dated 12-17-1805; recorded (not given). Requests to be interred beside Thomason his late wife. Sons: Henry, Robert, Jonathan, Moses and Aaron. Daughter, Mary Mercer. Appoints Joseph Tatman and Andrew Read as guardians of children and estate until they come of age. Signed: Jonathan Mercer. Witnesses: James Benefield and Jonathan Flood. (26) Inventory 12-1-1807. (58)

GOWDY, John - dated 10-21-1807; recorded (not given). Wife, Ann. Sons: Andrew, William and John. Grandson, John son of Andrew. Requests that remainder of property be divided between all his children. Executors: James Barret, Esq. and John Begger, Sr. of Montgomery Co., Ohio. Signed: John Gowdy. Witnesses: Moses Mills, Lucy (mark) Webb and Fanny (mark) Kingery. (27) Inventory 12-7-1807 mentions money in hands of William Hamilton for sale of land in York Co., Pa. (43)

QUINN, Nicholas - dated 1-15-1808; recorded (not given). Brother, Matthew Quinn to have land in SW¼ Section 5, Township 3, Range 7; also to serve as executor. Signed: Nicholas Quinn. Witnesses: James Galloway, Jr., William Galloway, James Downey and Nathan (mark) Lane. (29)

JENKINS, Aaron of Greene twp. - dated 11-7-1807; recorded (not given). Wife, Charity and specifies that she is to have all moveables brought with her when they married. Sons: Aaron; Hiram and Nimrod to have 20 acres of land in Tennessee; Baldin to have saw mill; James to have grist mill. Daughters: Elizabeth Springer and Lydia Mason. Grand-daughter: Rebecca Mann. Mentions Rachel Garwood his present wife's daughter. Executors: John Guthry, Esquire at Peapee on Scioto and son, Baldin Jenkins. Signed; Aaron Jenkins. Witnesses: John Woolman, Amos Compton and Phinius Heston. (30) Inventory (not dated-1807?) mentions 706 acres lying in Anderson Fork of Caesar Creek and 395 acres on waters of little Whitey Creek. (47)

ALEXANDER, Agnes of Cincinnati, Ohio - dated 7-25-1807; recorded (not given). Daughters: Ruehema and Mary Margaret. Sons: William and James Nichols. Mentions Amos Nicholas, not of age, relationship not stated. Executors: William Nichols. Signed: Agnes Alexander. Witnesses: James Miller and Thos. Fream. (31)

WILLIAMS, Charles - estate - 1-24-1807 appraisement by Henry Martin, Jacob Coy and Timothy Green. Elizabeth Williams, adms. (32)

HORNEY, Paris - dated 29th day, 2nd month, 1808. Wife, Lida. Mentions two sons but does not name—youngest, Parris, not of age. Daughters: Deborah, Rody and Esther Horney. Executors: wife Lyda and John Anderson. Signed: Paris Horney. Witnesses: William Stanfield and James Anderson. (35) Public sale held 5-28-1808. (144)

BONE, Jacob - estate - 6-9-1806 Martha Bone, adms. Martha Bone and Valentine Bone purchased items at public auction. (37)

DEWIT, Peter of Bath twp. - dated 8-23-1807; recorded (not given). Wife, Mercer. Sons: Peter, Isaac, Squire, Daniel and Elisha. Daughters: Rachael, Fields, Elizabeth, Pracella and Nancy Dewit; the last two not of age. Executors; wife, Mercy, and son, Peter. Signed: Peter Dewit. Witnesses: Martin Judy and Sam'l Stewart.(41)

HOUK, Felix - estate - 12-3-1807 appraisement by Edward Messer, Josiah Elam and Adam McConnell. (51) Settlement by John Houk, adms. Mentions debt due from North Carolina. No heirs named. (161)

WEBB, James - estate - (not dated 1807-8) appraisement by Jno. McClane, James Snowden and Wm. Irwin. Martin Kingery and Lucy Webb, adms. (54)

BOYER, John - estate - 10-2-1807 appraisement by James Snowden and Robert Marshall. (62)

BARTON, John - estate 11-2-1807 appraisement by Reuban Wingey and James Galloway.(64)

HOWARD, George - estate - 10-27-1808 appraisement by Jacob Hanes, Jacob Coy and Isaac Ely. (65)

CURRIE, Walter - estate - 11-2-1808 appraisement by James Galloway, Sebastian Sroufe and Jacob Real. Eliza Currie and Wm. Currie, adms. (67)

PUTTERBAUGH, David - estate - 12-16-1808 appraisement by Jacob Hanes, Robert Marshall and Isaac Miller. Magdalena Putterbaugh, adms. (71)

BOYD, John - estate - 2-3-1809 appraisement by David Laughhead, John Gregg and Thomas Simpson. Mentions tax, clerk and sheriff fees from Kentucky. Nancy Boyd and James Morrow, adms. (83)

WILSON, John - being between 23 and 24 years of age - dated 1-13-1809; recorded (not given). Mother, Sarah Wilson. Brothers, Samuel and Joseph Wilson. Sister, Sarah Townsley to have land on Todds Fork. Executor: brother, Samuel Wilson. Signed: John Wilson. Witnesses: David McCoy, Alexander Townsley and John Sterrett. (85) Appraisement 4-25-1809. (86)

WILSON, Sarah, alias McClelland, Alias Lowrey - dated 3-1-1809; recorded (not given) Children: Abraham McClelland, Peggy Sterrett alias McClelland, Polly McCoy alias McClelland, Joseph Wilson, Jno. Wilson, Samuel Wilson and Sarah Townsley alias Wilson. Grand-daughter, Sally Sterrett. Executor: youngest son, Samuel Wilson. Mentions land on Todds Fork. Signed: Sarah Wilson. Witnesses: Jno. Hoop, Matthew Alexander and James Hays. Codicil 3-1-1809, no further information, same witnesses. (87) Appraisement 4-25-1809. (89)

NOWE, Leonard of Beaver Creek twp. - estate - 4-18-1809 appraisement by Jacob Harner, Jacob Shingledecker and Paul Petro. (89)

WILSON, Samuel - dated 10-19-1809; recorded (not given). Brother, Joseph Wilson. Sister, Sarah Townsley. Executors: brother, Joseph Wilson and brother-in-law, George Townsley. Signed: Sam'l Wilson. Witnesses: Jno. Hoop, Matthew Alexander and Richard Thornburgh. (97) Appraisement 12-15-1809. (113)

MORGAN, John - dated 9-22-1808; recorded 9-15-1809. Wife, Sallie (Sally). Daughters: Nancy, Martha, Sally and Peggy. Executors: William Morgan and Evin Morgan. Signed: John Morgan. Witnesses: Jno. McLane, John Morgan and Jonathan (mark) Morgan. (98)

MAXWELL, William - estate - 10-23-1809 appraisement by Robert Marshall, James Popenoe and John Hivling. Personal property set off to Nancy Maxwell. (99)

STERRETT, Joseph - estate - 10-12-1809 appraisement by Wm. A. Beatty, John Sull and Joseph Hammil. Public auction held 11-14-1809 with Mary Sterret purchasing numerous items. (108)

BELL, John - estate - 5-29-1809 James Collins, adms. Appraisement 6-19-1809 by Jno. Watson, Bennett Moxey and Isaiah McDaniel. (115)

JOHNSTON, John - estate - 5-24-1810 appraisement by John Bell, James Butler and Bennet Maxey. Mentions 100 acres of land in Boone County, Kentucky. (118)

TEMPLETON, John - estate - 11-10-1811, widow mentioned but not named. Mentions money due estate from Hamilton County. (119)

BERRY, John - estate - 6-26-1811 appraisement by Moses Miller, Jacob Hubble and Benj. Whiteman. (122)

TATMAN, James - estate - 10-7-1811 appraisement by Jno. Heeth, Alexander Heeth and Jno. Carpenter. Personal property allowed to Elizabeth Tatman. Public sale held 11-12-1811 with Joseph Tatman Jr. purchasing items. (124)

FARMER, William - estate - 11-11-1811 appraisement by Rueben McDaniel, Thos. Moorman, Jr. and Benj. Harner. Widow, mentioned but not named. (128)

ANDREW, Hugh of Bath twp. - estate - 6-7-1811 appraisement by Jno. Cox, Jno. McKaig and Richard Hall. (131)

BAIN, Jno. - estate - (not dated-1811?) appraisement by Richard Hall, Jno. Cox and Jno. McKay. (133)

BURROWS, Joseph - estate - 10-15-1811 appraisement by Jno. McKaig, Moses Miller and David Humfreville. (134)

DUNN, John of Bath twp. - estate - 10-15-1811 appraisement by Nimrod Hadix, Shaphet McCray and Sam'l Stiles (Stites). (138)

BULL, William - dated 10-10-1811; recorded (not given). Sons: Asaph, John, James, Thomas, Richard and William. Daughters: Ann Marshall and Mary. Grandson, Amos Shaw. Grand-daughter, Mary Shaw. Mentions land sold to John Marshall. Mentions money due from Virginia. Executors: sons, John and James. Signed: William Bull. Witnesses: William McFarland and James Cowin Jr. (144) Appraisement 3-6-1812. (167)

McKNIGHT, John - estate - Appraisement 4-8-1812 by James Snodgrass, William Tanner and Sam'l Steele. Mentions cash left at Zanesville. (148)

HUSSEY, Christopher - estate - 8-1-1812 appraisement by Martin Mendinghall, William Galloway and James Stewart. (152)

516

PETRO, Paul - estate - 5-20-1812 appraisement by Sam'l Kirkpatrick, Tobias Ritter and James Popenoe. Personal property set off to widow, Margaret. (153)

GRIMES, Samuel - dated 8-12-1812; recorded (not given). Wife, Betsey, to have all property left to her by her father, also balance due testator from sale of land in Virginia. Executors: wife, Betsey; uncle, John Grimes and George Newcome of Montgomery Co., Ohio. Signed: Samuel Grimes. Witnesses: John Steele, John Aimesworth and Moses Kirkwood. (160)

Tingley, Joseph of Bath twp. - dated 10-3-1812; recorded (not given). Brother, John. Niece, Sally Tingley daughter of Jno. Tingley. Nephews, Anthony Cozad and Jno. Winans, not of age. Executor: Andrew Read. Signed: Joseph Tingley. Witnesses: Wm. Cayton and James Allen. (162) Appraisement 2-4-1813. (171)

SANDERS, John - dated 7-20-1812; recorded (not given). Wife, Christian, also to serve as executrix. Sons, Jesse Sanders. Mentions Carpenter tools. Signed: John Sanders. Witnesses: Henry (mark) B urk and Samuel Steele. (163)

PETRO, Nicholas of Bath twp. - dated 11-2-1812; recorded (not given). Children: Paul, Phillip, Elizabeth, Susanna, Sarah, Mary and Margareta. Daughter-in-law, Mary Shall. Executor: David John. Signed: Nicholas Petro. Witnesses: Maxon Clayton, Thomas Cayton and Asa John. (164)

BRADFUTE, Margaret of Miami twp. - estate - 10-27-1813, Jno. Knox, adms. sale of personal property. (173)

PAULIN, Uriah - estate - 10-27-1812 appraisement by Lancelot Jenkins, Thomas Moorman and Wm. McClelland. Rebekah Paulin and Jacob Paulin purchased items at the public auction. (175)

HADDEN, Jacob - estate - 10-24-1812 appraisement by David Henor(?), Andrew Garlaugh and Andrew Sevelier(?). (180)

BULL, Asaph - estate - 6-3-1813 appraisement by William McFarland, David Langhead and James Stevenson. Mentions cash of $174.57½ coming from estate of William Bull, dec'd. (185)

SHOUP, George - dated 10-4-1812; recorded (not given.) Wife, Charlotty. Sons: David, not of age; George; Solomon, to have land including grist mill in Section 32, Township 3, Range 7, which mill was sold to testator by Sam'l Huston of Hamilton County on 1-11-1808; Moses, not of age, to have still and distillery. Daughter, Mary Houke live in Tecomseh, Frederick County, Maryland. Mentions land in Montgomery Co., Ohio owned in partnership with George Fryberger. Mentions a stone quarry. Executor: son, Solomon Shoup. Signed: George Shoup. Witnesses: David Harris and George Cinnamon. (192) Appraisement 3-26-1813. (197)

LOWE, Thomas - estate - 9-23-1813 appraisement by David Hains, Zech. Ferguson and James Popenoe. (198)

ADAMS, Eli to Elizabeth BECKS	8-2-1810
AGIN, William to Catherine SHOVES	5-3-1805
ALIEN, Edward to Mary BENSON	6-28-1810
AMES, William to Polly McDONNEL	2-9-1805
ANDERSON, David to Nancy CURRIE	6-25-1809
ANDERSON, James to Priscilla COFFIN	11-16-1809
ANDERSON, John Horney to Hannah Panter	2-19-1806
ANDERSON, Seth to Anne Cotrell	7-14-1807
ARCHIBALD, David to Rachael McCORMECK	1-17-1809
ASH, Adam to Jane McCAULY	7-31-1806
BAIRD, John to Sidney DAVIS	11-17-1808
BARRETT, James to Nancy MENTON	9-17-1806
BARRETT, Philip to Elizabeth BARNES	9-1-1808
BARTON, John to Ann CHAMBERS	6-13-1805
BARTON, Thomas to Masse LOYD	10-16-1806
BEASON, Isaac to Jane SANDERS	12-25-1806
BEASON, Joseph to Susannah BOANE	4-13-(1805?)
BECK, Samuel to Betsey TRUE	1-9-1806
BELL, John to Mary BEALS	6-23-1807
BELL, John to Lydia SMITH	9-15-1808
BELL, Nathaniel to Rebeckah GARRETSON	1-24-1809
BISHOP, William to Nancy FREED	1-29-1806
BLAYLOCK, Brewer to Elizabeth KENNEDY	2-21-1810
BLAYLOCK, George to Elizabeth McKENNEY	11-1-1808
BONE, George to Nancy MULLENIX	9-20-1809
BONE, Samuel to Abetha BEASON	11-8-1803
BONNER, Chapell H. to Anne PELHAM	4-14-1809
BONNER, Chapell H. to Polly DAVIS	10-12-1809.
BOYER, John to Ruth MORGAN	3-13-1806
BREWIN, Luther to Susanna BARNETT	6-14-1810
BROWN, Jonathan to Delilah SPENCER	1-1-1807
BROWN, William to Mary GUFFY	4-5-1810
BRUCE, James to Rebeckah HARRIS	10-9-1806
BUCKLES, Abraham to Jenny CARMAN	11-8-1803
BUCKLES, John to Elizabeth SMITH	6-27-1810
BULL, James to Ann GOWDY	11-8-1804
BURRELL, John to Elenor MARSHALL	10-29-1807
BUSHELL, Samuel to Sarah MORGAN	9-13-1810
BUTCHER, Joseph to Mary ALLEN	8-23-1810
CAMPBELL, John to Polly GRIEVS	12-1-1806
CAMPBELL, John to Polly CARON	11-9-1809
CARVER, Jacob to Elizabeth HOOVER	12-8-1808
CHAMBERS, Elijah to Abigal STEWART	-----1807
CHEIN, John to Elizabeth BLACKBURN	12-1-1806
CLEVENGER, Enos to Susannah MARTIN	9-11-1805
COLLIER, James to Rachel SMITH	6-5-1805
COLLIER, Moses to Elizabeth SMALL	9-19-1810
COMPTON, William to Jemima DOTY	7-4-1809
COMWELL, Richard to Mary Anderson GROVER	10-25-1810
CORY, James to Patty SHOUG	4-17-1806
COY, John to Mary JONES	9-18-1804
COZARD, John to Rosannah KUYCKEMDAL	10-21-1806
COZARD, Samuel to Mary MERSER	1-25-1806
CRIEM, John to Mary LEE	4-10-1806
CROMWELL, John to Mary MILLER	9-8-1806

```
CUMPTON, Matthew to Rachel CAMPBELL        9-1-1803
CURRIE, William to Jane TORRENCE           10-24-1810
CURST, Christian to Easter STALEY          11-12-1805
CURTIS, Thomas to Lydia TUCKER             9-13-1810
DARLINGTON, Samuel to Nancy McDONALD       3-18-1804
DARST, Abraham to Polly WOLF               9-21-1809
DAVISSON, Andrew to Rebeckah TODD          6-15-1807
DELLIN, Jesse to Mary JAY                  2-9-1804
DONNEL, Jonathan to Sally NEWLAND          - - 1803
DROMGOOLE, Edward to Sarah Creese PELHAM    3-28-1810
DUNCAN, Amos to Elizabeth BELL             5-5-1808
DUNN, Dennis to Polly PETRO                3-19-1807
EDGE, William B. to Dorcas MILLER          2-2-1809
ENNIS, Samuel to Polly DUNWIDDIE           2-7-1809
FAULKNOR, William to Polly B. TRUE         12-6-1810
FAQUIER, Jonah to Elizabeth BELL           7-15-1808
FERRELL, Daniel to Elizabeth FIFE          3-12-1806
FOLK, George, Jr. to Susannah WYLAND       3-27-1810
FORGER, John to Margaret DENNY             4-20-1804
FORGEY, James to Polloy MITCHEL            3-16-1809
FORGUSON, Elijah to Mary RUE               12-13-1804
FRAKES, Robert to Margaret ORR             5-2-1805
FUNDERBURG, Daniel to Mary WILSON          11-3-1810
GALLOWAY, James to Patsey TOWNSLEY         1-16-1806
GARLOUGH, Adam to Katharine HAINES         2-26-1808
GIBSON, Andrew to Jenny STEVENSON          9-18-1806
GIBSON, Montittran to Sarah EMBREE         9-13-1810
GIBSON, William to Mary CHAMBERS           3-8-1808
GILLUM, Jesse to Kesiah MERRYMAN           9-5-1810
GOODMAN, Aaron to Polly CHAPMAN            8-23-1803
GOOLDY, John to Margaret PUNCE             4-1-1808
GOWDY, Andrew to Polly McCONNEL            2-27-1806
GRAY, Samuel to Sarah WALLACE              3-1-1810
GREENE, Timothy to Haldy WELL              1-15-1804
GREGG, John to Lucy MILL                   9-14-1807
GRIFFIN, Daniel to Lydia PERRY             3-22-1810
HAIL, James to Sarah GARRISON              11-6-1806
HAIL, Josiah to Eve DEVORE                 11-13-1807
HAINER, Jacob to Polly Hfley(?)            6-17-1806
HALL, Jacob to Ann McGUIN                  3-26-1805
HANBEY, Elisha to Mary ROGERS              3-11-1810
HARDWICK, William to Elizabeth PARMER      11-15-1806
HATFIELD, Moses to Catherine JOHN          11-12-1805
HEATON, Jonah to Lydia HEATON              11-20-1808
HENDCOCK, Joseph to Susannah MILLMAN       7-27-1808
HEVISTON, William to Peggy SEST            - - (1807?)
HORNEY, Daniel to Margaret COFFIN          7-15-1808
HORNEY, William to Rhody ANDERSON          2-20-1806
HOOVER, John to Elizabeth SHINGLEDECKER    11-30-(1809?)
HOPPING, John to Polly WOODARD             2-17-1809
HUBBLE, Sampson to Polly ROSEGRANT         10-19-1809
HUME, Robert to Isabella DAVIS             10-6-1808
HURLEY, Leven to Susannah BIRT             3-26-1810
INDICOTT, Jesse to Sarah LOU               3-2-1809
INGLE, Isaac to Susanna SWIGART            4-19-1810
```

```
INMUN, John to Lucy FIRES                        6-27-1809
IRVIN, John to Polly ANDERSON                    9-7-1809
JAMISON, John to Elizabeth McCOY                 8-10-1809
JOHN, John to Jenny McFARLAND                    4-30-(1807?)
JOHNSON, James to Margaret JOHNSTON              2-15-1808
JOHNSON, William to Deborah COFFIN               8-5-1808
JONES, Joseph to Rebeckah MOONEY                 8-16-1804
JONES, Stephen to Jemima JONES                   12-6-1810
JUDY, Martin to Sally PETRO                       12-8-1803
KELLY, John to Charity McKENNY                   5-15-1806
KEMPT, Joseph to Elizabeth HERRING               7-5-1810
KENGREY, Michael to Betsey WEBB                  2-7-1805
KENNADY, James to Mary BRIGDMAN                   11-28-1809
KIRKPATRICK, Samuel to Blancy DEROUGH            10-6-1805
KIZER, William to Mary WILLLAMS                   3-16-1807
KUGLER, Jacob to Kelly HORNER                     3-6-1804
LAMBERT, Aaron to Mary TURNER                     10-6-1805
LAMME, Josiah to Nancy CANNON                     9-25-1806
LAMME, William to Ruth BOYER                      1-12-1809
LANGSTRETH, Harnet to Nancy YORK                  6-24-1806
LAUGHEAD, David M. to Elizabeth KYLE             2-7-1810
LAYTON, Arthur to Susannah McHENRY               10-16-1803
LEAMAN, John to Betsey FOX                        5-10-1810
McBRIDE, Henry to Betsey TODD                     10-25-1810
McCABE, Armstrong to Eleanor BARRETT             4-12-1805
McCLURE, William to Margaret MITCHELL            12-20-1810
McCONNEL, William to Polly McCUNE                9-6-1810
McCORD, Joseph to Mary HALL                      11-10-1803
McCOY, David to Polley McCLELAND                 3-31-1809
McCULLY, James to Rebecca JUNKIN                 5-11-1809
McDANIEL, James to Betsey READ                    12-7-1804
McDANIEL, Levitt to Susannah STRONG             10-24-1808
McFERSON, Samuel to Betsey FORGEY                11-19-1306
McKENNEY, William to Anne BLAYLOCK               1-12-1809
McNAMEE, John to Elizabeth TRUBY                 12-9-1805
MALTBY, Amos to Rachael CARMAN                   9-25-1806
MAN, Charles to Lydia JENKINS                    10-4-1805
MARSHALL, John to Ann SHAW                        9-1-(1803?)
MARSHALL, John to Fanny MARTIN                    8-11-1808
MARTIN, John to Elizabeth PRICE                   9-6-1304
MATTHEWS, John to Polly HUSSEY                    1-4-1809
MENDENHALL, John to Rachael SUTTON               2-18-1808
MENDINGHALL, Aaron to Lydia HORNEY               3-2-1809
MERCER, Edward to Elizabeth WILLIAMS             7-14-1807
MILLER, Aron to Jane SMITH                       11-19-1807
MILLER, Benjamin to Sarah SHANNON                1-14-1808
MILLER, Martin to Mary FROST                      5-8-1809
MOCK, Daniel to Ruth LINDSEY                      5-10-1810
MOONE, William to Nancy FLOOD                     9-4-1806
MORGAN, William to Sarah VANCE                    1-29-1305
MORRISON, Ephraim to Letty Gibson                11-29-1804
MOSER, John to Elizabeth BUFBARGER               2-22-1808
MYRE, Marlin to Hannah ADBY                       6-27-1804
NAVE, Jacob to Catharine GARLACH                 8-23-1808
NILE, Laurence to Polly MILLER                    11-5-1809
```

```
OWENS, George to Deborah MARSHALL            5-17-1810
OWENS, James to Deborah MARSHALL             8-15-1805
OWENS, Jonathan to Lany MARSHALLON           5-22-1806
PAINTER, Jacob to Mary DEVORE                6-26-1810
PAUL, John to Sally Griffin GROVER           9-29-1808
PELHAM, Samuel to Martha BONER               9-30-1807
PELVEY, James to Mary JACKSON                4-24-1805
PENATTOE, Thomas M. to Mary LEWIS            11-25-1803
POWERS, William D. to Sally BECKS            4-26-1810
PRICE, John to Hannah DAVIS                  7-12-1804
PRICE, John to Anny WILSON                   6-11-1807
PRICE, John to Elizabeth BROCK               5-10-1810
PRICE, Peter to Hannah TURNER                2-15-1809
RECTOR, Daniel to Esiah REECE                3-2-1805
ROBERTSON, Jacob to Easter McKINNEY          7-9-1804
ROBERTSON, Thomas to Lydia HORNEY            8-15-1805
ROBINSON, William to Hannah HORNEY           8-11-1808
ROCK, Philip to Mary KELLY                   8-4-1803
RODGERS, William to Rebeckah LEWIS           1-12-1809
ROGERS, Henry to Susannah HURLEY             8-15-1805
ROWEN, Edward to Elizabeth LUZE              10-6-1809
RUTH, John to Polly LAIN                     9-17-1810
RUTH, Samuel to Jane WILSON                  5-10-1804
RYAN, Jacob to Hannah BUSH                   3-18-1804
SAIL, John to Nancy BONNER                   7-7-1804
SALINGER, Andrew to Sally BORDERS            8-12-1810
SALSBURY, Jeffrey to Jemima SANDERS          9-8-1806
SANDERS, John to Christian CANE              1-18-1808
SERVER, Jacob to Nancy ROBERTSON             7-9-1804
SHEGLEY, Adam to Isabella CHAMBERS           12-6-1810
SHEGLEY, Frederick to Tamer BAILEY           12-29-1803
SHELEY, Michael to Louis DUFFY               5-17-1807
SHROFE, Sebastian to Catherine TOWNSEND      11-9-1808
SMITH, Josiah B. to Margaret BORDERS         8-31-1809
SNODGRASS, James to Elizabeth TAYLOR         10-9-1806
SNOWDON, Benjamin to Sally CAMAN             11-1-1810
SROFE, David to Rebeckah TOWNSEND            6-23-1810
STANDLEY, Abraham to Mary HORNE              10-3-1805
STANFORD, Hector to Elizabeth DAVIS          10-30-1810
STAPLETON, John to Sally VANEATON            7-23-1807
STEVENS, James to Melinda WHITE              8-20-1807
STEVENS, John to Lanes HAINES                9-13-1810
STEVENSON, James to Anna GALLOWAY            4-3-1805
STEVENSON, John to Kitty KIRKPATRICK         10-27-1807
STEVENSON, William to Peggy SCOTT            11-19-1808
STEWART, James to Mary STEWART               2-15-1808
STRONG, Geo. Washington to Sarah MENDINGHALL 3-29-1810
STRONG, Reuben to Anna WILSON                4-19-1804
SUTTON, William to Sarah BRAY                8-20-1807
TAYLOR, George to Polly SMITH                12-29-1803
TAYLOR, Henry to Hannah McCOLOUGH            11-5-1807
TOD, John to Elizabeth EKEBERGER             2-12-1809
TOWNSEND, Levy to Martha MARTIN              6-23-1808
TOWNSLEY, Alexander to Nancy CONWELL         3-2-1809
TOWNSLEY, George to Sally WILSON             11-10-1809
```

```
TRADER, Moses to Elizabeth McDONNEL          9-2-1804
TRUBY, Jacob to Elizabeth NAVE               9-1-1809
VANEATON, Abraham to Elizabeth MILLS         10-31-1809
WALLACE, Jonathan H. to Isabella GUFFEY      12-25-1810
WARFIELD, Richard to Elizabeth Ennis         4-11-1805
WARTON, Jonathan to Rachel GARWOOD           9-7-1807
WATSON, Jesse to Rachael BAILS               1-19-1809
WATSON, John to Polly LINDSEY                12-28-1809
WHICKAR, Matthew to Catharine HOUK           4-26-1810
WILLIAMS, John to Elizabeth OWENS            1-14-1805
WILSON, Daniel to Elizabeth PRICE            2-17-1807
WILSON, George to Anne BARTON                12-6-1810
WILSON, Jeremiah to Elizabeth DAVIS          12-9-1810
WILSON, John to Nancy DUNWIDDY               10-30-1806
WILSON, Joseph to Joanna TOWNSLEY            11-10-1807
WILSON, Joseph to Asenith SUTTON             3-15-1810
WILSON, Michael to Temperance JUDY           3-1-1810
WILSON, Valentine to Elenor JUDY             12-4-1806
WILSON, William to Catharine HEFLEY          7-7-1808
WILSON, William to Rachel MILLS              3-8-1810
YATES, William to Maryann MASLANDOS          6-4-1807
YORK, Jeremiah to Ann WESTFALL               4-7-1805
YOUNG, William to Polley McKNIGHT            1-26-1810
```

ADAMS, John to Margaret MOORLAND	6-27-1811
AKINS, James to Jane McCLANE	12-16-1813
ALBAUGH , John to Eley MUSGROVE	9-3-1815
ALLEN, Joseph to Elizabeth CADWALADER	4-29-1815
ALSOP, John to Mary ROBINSON	9-22-1814
ASBERRY, Lowery to Jane MORGAN	12-24-1812
BAIN, James, Jr. to Polly McCLELLAND	1-3-1815
BAKER, Jesse to Rebeckah CASE	12-31-1812
BALDWIN, DAVID Jr. to Elenor McLUGHLIN	8-4-1814
BARKER, Joseph to Sarah MOOREMAN	9-7-1815
BARLOW, Edward to Polly LAWRENCE	3-12-1815
BARNEY, James to Nancy McCONNELL	5-28-1812
BATES, Coonrod to Catharine TRUBEE	3-9-1815
BEAL, Jonathan to Margaret DRISCAL	2-13-1814
BEALES, John to Sally LUCUS	9-9-1813
BEALL, George to Rachel DRISCAL	12-21-1815
BEASON, Nathan to Sarah TURNER	12-10-1812
BEASON, Thomas to Kesiah TURNER	8-11-1814
REASON, William to Mary STANBURY	2-28-1811
BELL, Thomas to Elizabeth TANNER	10-27-1814
BIGGER, Thomas to Hannah SNOWDEN	3-16-1815
BINGAMAN, Lewis to Temperance KAIN	12-29-1814
BISHOP, Solomon to Elizabeth FORBES	8-11-1814
BLACK, Nathan to Mary CRUZAN/COZAN	4-8-1813
BLOOKE, Neathan to Mary TEMBELTON	7-28-1814
BONE, Henry to Mary GRAYHAM	4-23-1812
BONE, Thomas to Eleanor TURNER	8-6-1812
BOOKER, John to Rhoda BRIKBACK	12-30-1811
BRAKE, John to Kesiah STILES	7-4-1813
BRANSON, Eli to Anne TURNER	10-5-1811
BRENNON, Thomas to Dorcas FREINT	5-5-1815
BRIDGES, William to Patsey MARTIN	1-29-1812
BROCK, Evan to Elizabeth (Betsey) BROWN	12-25-1812
BROCK, Frances to Sarah HARPER	1-4-1813
BROWN, William to Mary SPILLARS	8-31-1815
BRUMIGEM, Simon to Sarah CRISWELL	10-21-1814
BRYAN, David to Mildred JOHNSON	4-16-1815
BRYAN, James to Polly JOHNSTON	5-2-1813
* BULL, Thomas to Margaret MILL	7-18-1811
BUTLER, Thomas to Margaret HERRNETT	12-30-1811
BUTT, Samuel to Elenor TYLER	3-5-1811
CAIN, Daniel to Sarah KNIGHT	9-5-1814
CAIN, Samuel to Jane LINSEY	5-28-1812
CAFNEY, Sherm to Anne ALLISON	5-8-1814
CARSON, Abraham to Polly PERSON	5-28-1811
CHAMBERS, Adam to Mary KIRKWOOD	9-28-1813
CHAMBERS, John to Ann BLUE	9-3-1812
CHAMBERS, William to Elizabeth KIRKWOOD	5-3-1815
CLAYTON, Menon to Margaret GASTON	7-24-1812
CLIFFORD, Thomas to Nancy HEATH	3-7-1812
COLE, William R. to Susannah ELAM	7-15-1813

*For *Margaret Mill* read *Margaret Miller.* GATEWAY TO THE WEST, Vol. 3: No. 3 (July-Sept. 1970).

```
CONKELON, Samuel to Nancy HOBBS              2-2-1815
CONKLEAN, Joseph to Rachel CASEY             3-7-1815
CONWELL, Abraham to Sarah BELL               6-20-1811
COOGLAR, Jacob to Catharine BATES            12-27-1812
COSSLER, Abraham to Elizabeth WOLF           6-13-1815
COSTLER, Henry to Polly MIRES                12-19-1811
COTRELL, Lemuel to Catharine REVES           6-21-1814
COTRELL, Thomas to Sarah GATE                9-26-1811
COZAD, John to Sophia SHOUP                  8-4-1814
CRISWELL, James to Ann JUNKINS               1-23-1812
CRUMLEY, Steven to Jane STANFIELD            5-30-1813
CURRIE, William to Nancy WINTER              2-11-1813
CURRY, John to Mary LEONARD                  5-4-1815
DASHIELL, Charles to Nancy MASTEN            4-20-1815
DAVIS, Jacob to Sarah DAVIS                  1-30-1812
DAVIS, John to Loulla KING                   5-20-1811
DAVIS, Thomas to Caroline PELHAM             1-13-1814
DAY, Peter to Margaret RUE                   2-20-1811
DEAM, Adam to Magdaline WOLF                 3-24-1814
DEWYT, Elisha tp Nancy PLEN                  9-4-1814
DOUGLAS, David to Margaret WATSON            9-26-1811
DOWNEY, Andrew to Elizabeth WYLAND           1-25-1814
DRAKE, Richard to Elizabeth STRAIN           1-29-1811
DRISKALL, John to Mary JONES                 9-5-1813
DUNLAP, James to Eliz. McCLELLAN             ----1814
DUNN, Simeon to Sophia READ                  8-30-1815
EDGE, Obediah to Mary MOORLAND               9-2-1812
ELKIN, William F. to Elizabeth CONSTANT      12-5-1813
ELLIOTT, Ebenezer to Margaret GILLISPIE      7-4-1815
ELLIS, Abraham to Sarah OGLESBY              1-21-1812
ELLIS, Joel to Elizabeth SHELENGER           8-25-1811
ELSBERRY, William to Elizabeth McKee MILLER  12-31-1812
ESPY, Josiah to Margaret MITCHELL            10-25-1814
EWING, Samuel to Katharine BECKS             9-29-1814
FAIR, Thomas to Elizabeth MOORLAND           5-6-1813
FARMER, William to Sophia HIBBENS            12-29-1814
FIELDS, Allison to Mary CLINE                7-23-1815
FIELDS, John to Maryann HITE                 11-3-1814
FIFER, John to Deborah ALLEN                 2-16-1815
FIRES, James to Ruth BORDERS                 12-31-1813
FORMAN, Robert D. to Olive HAINES            12-28-1815
FORT, John to Alice WRIGHT                   2-12-1815
FOX, Jacob to Elizabeth ELY                  10-3-1815
FULLER, James to Mary SMITH                  7-23-1812
FUNDERBURGH, John to Ann SIMMONS             12-12-1814
GALLOWAY, George to Rebeckah GALLOWAY        12-3-1812
GARST, Jacob to Catharine ELEY               4-18-1815
GARVIN, John to Ann VANCE                    6-23-1814
GIBSON, John to Jane CLEVSEY                 9-2-1811
GOWDY, James to Jonanna TOWNSLEY             1-25-1814
GRANT, Robert to Jane BANES                  5-19-1814
```

524

GRAY, William to Lucy RICE	9-23-1814
GREER, John C. to Eleanor McCLELLAN	3-26-1812
GREY, Henry to Ann BURRIS	6-2-1812
GUTHRIE, James to Elizabeth ANDREW	4-20-1813
HAEL, John to Louisa WHITE	7-27-1815
HINS, Henry to Nancy WEST	9-2-1813
HALE, John to Sally LEWIS	6-29-1815
HEFFLEY, Charles to Elizabeth WILSON	1-26-1815
HENRY, William to Nancy STEPHENSON	7-3-1812
HERDMAN, Peter to Sarah EDGE	10-261815
HIERS, Anthony to Mary FOGLE	3-12-1811
HOSIER, Jacob to Anny ROBINSON	11-10-1813
HUGHY, William to Prudy LAW	11-4-1813
HUSSEY, Jacob to Sally COPELAND	6-9-1814
HUSSEY, Steven to Rebeckah DAMTS	12-24-1812
INLOW, Abraham to Margaret FALY	12-24-1813
JACKSON, Samuel to Susannah BEST	11-26-1812
JINKINS, Daniel to Elizabeth MOON	6-30-1813
JOHNSON, Gavin to Margaret RUFF	4-9-1811
JOHNSON, James to Anna CRUSAN	1-14-1812
JOHNSON, Joseph to Polly MOORMAN	5-2-1813
KEFFER, Jacob to Polly HERSHMAN	8-23-1812
KELSO, John to Sarah WIRE	12-23-1812
KENNADY, John to Nancy CAMPBELL	3-10-1814
KERSHNER, Daniel to Susanna HOWARD	12-21-1815
KEY, James to Polly DOWNY	10-29-1812
KIZER, Jesse to Rachel GRIFFING	2-9-1815
KYLE, Joseph to Jane GOWDY	11-19-1811
KYLE, Samuel to Rachel JACKSON	12-13-1814
LAMBERT, Aaron to Eley KIRKENDALL	6-14-1814
LAMBERT, John to Nancy TURNER	12-15-1811
LAMBERT, John to Nancy LEE	6-10-1813
LAMME, Samuel to Elizabeth MARTIN	12-31-1811
LAW, William to Margaret HUGHY	11-4-1813
LAY, Jesse to Nancy GOWDY	8-14-1811
LAUGHEAD, James to Ann MORTON	11-2-1815
LAURENCE, Samuel to Ann McCONNEL	4-13-1815
LAVRE(?), George to Ann STEWARD	9-14-1815
LOYD, James to Polley MAXEY	11-14-1811
LOYD, John to Sophia WRIGHT	7-27-1815
McCLELLAN, Robert to Patsey McCONNEL	3-29-1814
McCLELLAND, Joseph to Nancy McCONNEL	1-11-1814
McCULLOUGH, John to Harriet DAYLE	10-5-1813
McFARLAND, Arthur M. to Jane JUNKEN	8-12-1813
McKAIG, James to Jane HOWARD	2-21-1811
McKINNEY, Anthony to Elizabeth BRACKIN	2-2-1815
MACMAN, Moses to Patsey WILLIAMSON	12-22-1813
MACOLM, Samuel to Mary MATHEWS	7-21-1814
MALONE, Leslie to Elizabeth WESTFALL	9-26-1815
MARSHALL, James to Ibby BOYD	1-28-1813
MARTIN, Jacob to Elizabeth FOLLICE	2-21-1815

525

```
MAXWELL, David to Elizabeth McCASHON            8-25-1814
MAXWELL, William to Patsy MORGAN                9-14-1815
MELVIN, Charles to Rebecca IRWIN                3-16-1815
MENDENHALL, Stephen to Jane DAVIS               4-20-1815
MILL, Lewis to Rebeckah FEESPATRICK             8-6-1812
MILLER, Isaac to Sarah SEARL                    12-19-1815
MINICK, George to Catharine SHOVES(widow)       12-7-1816(1815?)
MOODLE, Samuel to Mary ALLEN                    7-8-1815
MOORE, William Camm to Orepenia WESTFALL        11-21-1815
MOORMAN, James to Elizabeth JOHNSON             6-18-1815
MOORMAN, Zachariah to Katharine ELLIS           4-14-1811
MORGAN, Jonathan to Lydia BENGAMAN              3-19-1812
MORGAN, Thomas to Nancy MORGAN                  10-28-1813
MORROW, John to Abigal BOYLSTON                 4-5-1814
MOSS, Charles A. to Temperance SHIPARD          8-10-1813
MULLENIX, John to Unice TOWNSEND                1-2-1814
MULLIN, William to Christiana JONES             6-15-1815
MURRAY, James to Margaret BUSKER                11-4-1813
MYERS, Samuel to Mary TURNER                    10-30-1814
NAGLEY, Henry to Phebe BRIGGS                   4-15-1813
NEWPORT, William to Margaret McFARLAND          12-28-1815
NIMERICH, Peter to Jane WEST                    8-29-1814
NIMERICK, John to Porthena BEALL                12-13-1812
OGLESBY, Asa to Phebe MOCK                      3-28-1815
OMMERMAN, Henry to Elizabeth MACKY              6-12-1813
OSHALL, John to Mary MARSHALL                   7-29-1813
OWENS, Samuel to Elizabeth MAXWELL              7-30-1815
OWENS, Thomas to Jane MARSHALL                  4-18-1815
PALMER, Joseph to Juliana BUTLER                3-3-1814
PARKER, Peter to Mary MURPHEY                   5-2-1815
PATTEN, William to Elizabeth GOWDY              3-30-1815
PAVEY, Samuel to Heathy DENNY                   3-25-1813
PAYNE, John to Letticia WHITEMAN                3-25-1813
PERKINS, Jeremiah to Ann DRISKIL               10-16-1814
PERRY, Allen to Elizabeth GRIFFEY               8-29-1811
POLAN, Peter to Ruanna KRUZAN                   7-27-1815
PRICE, George to Jane HUSSEY                    6-10-1813
PRINGLE, Robert to Elizabeth SMITH              9-21-1815
QUINN, James to Sarah ANDERSON                  10-7-1813
QUINN, James to Mary SCOTT                      1-20-1815
READ, William to Polly TALMAN                   3-3-1814
REEVES, Jonathan to Susana EKER                 8-25-1814
REUBEL, Owen to Rachel MARTIN                   1-6-1814
RICH, Jacob to Silvia WOMBLE                    1-19-1813
ROBERTS, Silas to Cassander SPARKS              2-24-1814
ROGERS, Isaiah to Ann THOMAS                    8-12-1814
ROMIN, William C. to Sarah GOLDSBY              5-9-1811
ROSS, Alexander E. to Hannah PETERSON           1-30-1812
ROSS, John to Polly STRANE                      6-13-1815
SEARLS, Swedland to Elizabeth STEVENSON         9-12-1815
SHEATH, Thomas to Rachel CANYELL                2-24-1812
```

526

SHELEY, Benjamin to Milley STRONG   0-7-1814
SHILLIBARGER, Eprian to Rebecca WINGET   1-5-1815
SHINGLEDECKER, Abraham to Rebeckah HOOVER   8-9-1812
SHINGLEDECKER, Isaac to Jemima   10-19-1813
SHINGLEDECKER, John to Catharine KNAVE   6-16-1814
SHOCKLEY, Clement to Elizabeth SCOTT   10-10-1815
SHOUP, Moses to Elizabeth SMELZER   9-15-1814
SIDENSTICKER, Henry to Catharine FROST   11-10-1811
SIPE, William to Elizabeth MORNINGSTAR   6-6-1813
SLEETH, James to Catharine BAZE   10-26-1813
SLEETH, Jonah to Margaret SKIDMORE   3-2-1814
SMITH, George M. to Lovey MITTEN   9-19-1814
SMITH, Jeremiah to Mary MARSHALL   11-18-1813
SMITH, William to Katharine STIFY   6-30-1814
SNIDER, Henry to Sally SMITH   11-25-1813
SNODGRASS, Joseph to Nancy KIRKPATRICK   1-13-(1813?)
SNODGRASS, Robert to Sarah WHICKER   2-3-1814
SOWARD, Mahlon to Katharine RUMBOUGH   12-9-1813
SPARKS, Andrew to Jane TEMPLETON   1-12-1813
SPARKS, Simon to Catharine TEMPLETON   4-2-1813
SPENCER, Asa to Mary WILSON   9-3-1814
SROFE, Lewis to Hannah BATCHALOR   10-6-1812
STANLEY, William to Sarah MILLER   9-22-1814
STEPHENSON, William to Elenor SUTTON   1-25-1812
STERETT, Joseph to Ann BOYD   5-19-1812
STERRET, John to Margaret CHAMBERS   12-28-1815
STEVENSON, Robert to Sarah COHAGAN   2-3-1814
STEWART, John to Ann ELDER   3-2-1815
STIP, Frederick to Catharine BRANSON   ?-24-1812
STRONG, Benjamin to Elizabeth WILSON   3-19-1815
SUTTON, Ezra to Lydia CANADY   7-22-1813
SUTTON, Jesse to Keziah BRANSON   7-3-1815
SUTTON, William to Jane JACKSON   7-8-1813
TAYLOR, John A. to Elizabeth McKNIGHT   1-19-1811
TAYLOR, Matthew to Ann McKNIGHT   1-16-1812
TAYLOR, Peter to Catharine HOLLENGER   3-18-(1811?)
THOMPSON, Jeffery to Lettitia MERIDEN   2-7(or 17)-1814
THORNBURGH, John to Mary DAVIS   7-23-1815
THORNBURGH, Uriah to Sarah HITE   6-1-1815
THORNBURY, Asahel to Rebekah STANBURY   3-9-1815
TINGLEY, Joseph to Amy GARDNER   10-22-1815
TORRENCE, William to Jane LAWRENCE   1-2-1812
TOWNSLEY, Alexander to Peggy EWIN   1-12-1813
TOWNSLEY, John to Hannah MARSHALL   1-16-1812
TRUBEE, John to Rebecca LIPPINGCOTT   2-9-1815
TURNBAUGH, Samuel to Margaret HOLVERSTOT   10-26-1815
TUTTOR, Amos to Phebe DAVIS   4-3-1812
VANCE, James to Margaret ENOS   6-9-1814
VANCE, Joseph to Jane HOBLET   1-31-1814
WADE, James to Elizabeth WINTER   10-26-1812
WARNER, William to Mary BLOCKSAN   9-22-1813

527

```
WATSON, James to Nancy LINSEY                    10-16-1813
WATSON, Lewis to Rebeckah BAILES                 6-25-1815
WEBB, James to Elizabeth SMITH                   12-24-1812
WEST, William to Eliza BLAIR                     9-23-1814
WESTFALL, John to Polly ALLESON                  10-6-1814
WESTFALL, Jonathan to Margaret KIRKPATRICK       11-26-1811
WHICKER, John to Sarah BINGAMAN                  7-14-1814
WHITE, Joseph to Dinah J. Miller                 8-31-1815
WILLIAMS, Remembrance to Jane OWENS              1-31-1813
WILLIAMSON, James to Rebeckah WINANS             1-10-1813
WILSON, George to Effy CASEY                     6-12-1815
WILSON, Isaac to Amilia JONES                    7-6-1815
WINGET, Caleb to Anny SHILLEBARGER               6-24-1814
WOLF, John to Catharine YANTS                    5-25-1815
WOMBLE, Edward to Polly JOHNSTON                 12-5-1811
```

The following marriages were taken from Marriage Book A, located in the Probate
Court of the court house at Xenia, Ohio.

ADAMS, Esbon to Martha Galloway	12-31-1818
ALDRIDGE, Littlebury to Rebecca Read	7-19-1817
ALLEN, John to Susanna Kirkpatrick	11-6-1817
ALLEN, Reuben to Lydia Penny weight	1-1-1818
ALLEN, Solomon to Anney Moodle	------1818
ANDERSON, Daniel to Jane Dinsmore	9-4-1817
ANKENY, Henry to Ester Petro same persons,	(12-31-1816
ANKENY, Henry to Hesther Petro 2 dates	(1-1-1817
ARNEST, John to Mary Mackey	7-4-1816
AURENTINE, Richard to Ann Newkirk	3-20-1817
BABCOCK, Jacob to Lydia Maxen	5-22-1817
BAILIS, Elisha to Elizabeth Shook	7-25-1816
BAIRD, Thomas to Sarah Currie	6-3-1818
BAKER, Daniel to Nancy Snodgrass	3-20-1817
BAKER, Stephen A. to Effe Low	1-22-1818
BALES, Jacob to Dolly Hickman	9-25-1817
BARBER, John to Sarah Martin	10-16-1817
BATS, Henry to Sarah Hooglen	10-22-1818
BAYNARD, John to Elisabeth Dill	7-2-1816
BEALL, George to Rachel Driscal	12-21-1815
BEALL, Isaac to Susannah Shepherd	2-20-1817
BEER, John to Elizabeth Elifretze	5-7-1818
BELL, George to Vincey J. Heath	8-20-1818
BELL, John to Margaret Marten	3-28-1816
BELL, William to Margaret Farmer	11-5-1818
BEST, George to Elizabeth Hite	2-13-1817
BEST, John to Elizabeth Berry	2-19-1816
BLACK, David to Christiana Sanders	4-18-1816
BOND, Joseph to Elizabeth Robison	1-15-1818
BORDERS, Henry to Jane Stare	12-1-1818
BRASILTON, Benjamin to Alice C. Moore	6-18-1816
BRATTON, James to Sarah Edwards	9-5-1816
BREARLEY, Lewis to Caroline Knott	2-12-1818
BRIGGS, Levi to Catharine Hadden	2-21-1817
BROMEGEM, Samuel to Catharine McClelland	9-10-1818
BROWGER, James to Betsy Hays	7-4-1816
BRUNER, Michael to Elizabeth Heffley	3-7-1816
BRYAN, Garner to Sarah Hutson	8-14-1817
BRYAN, John to Agness Galloway	4-4-1816
BUCKLES, Henry to Elizabeth Heaton	4-25-1816
BUCKLES, James to Sarah Perkins	10-30-1817
BUNNEL, Daniel to Alice Albaugh	3-12-1818
BURRIS, William A. to Elizabeth Gray	1-29-1818
CAIN, Abner to Elisabeth Paulin	9-3-1818
CAMPBELL, Hugh to Jennet Dean	12-31-1816
CAMPBELL, James to Elizabeth Dean	7-3-1817
CARGDOLL, George to Margaret Meallon	12-24-1818

```
CARSON, William to Mary Johnston                          6-3-1818
CARTER, Samuel to Elcy (or Eley) Mendenhall              12-9-1816
CHAMBERS, David to Elizabeth Sirlott                     12-25-1817
CLARK, Robert to Elizabeth Jenkins                       1-22-1818
CLOSSER, Jacob to Susanna Heffley                        1-2-1817
COHAGEN, John to Sarah Costant                          12-26-1816
COMPTON, Henry to Mary Horner                            8-20-1818
CONFER (COUFER), Jacob to Martha Graham                 10-24-1816
CONRAD, Henry to Sarah Smith                             8-2-1817
CONWELL, Stephen to Martha Mills                         5-30-1816
COPELAND, Joseph to Elizabeth Wikiel                    12-24-1818
COPPRESS, (COPPESS), Devaul to Sarah Horney             10-1-1818
COX, David S. to Nancy S. Tingley                        2-5-1818
COYNER, Michael to Phebe Peterson                        1-22-1818
COZAD, Aaron Jr. to Mary Hall                           10-26-1818
CRAWFORD, David to Ann Sterrett                         11-12-1817
CRAWFORD, Matthew to Eliza Irvin                         1-2-1818
CRAWFORD, William D. to Elizabeth Andrew                 8-13-1816
CROWELL, John to Ally Bishop                             9-15-1818
CROY, Jacob to Catharine Davis                           2-15-1816
CULBERTSON, Robert H. to Rhoda I. Lamson (Lawson?)       9-30-1818
CUMTON, Aaron to Sarah Cozad                             8-27-1817
DALSTON, Peter to Sarah True                             2-8-1816
DAVIS, Japheth to Polly Troxel                          11-13-1817
DAVIS, Joseph to Catharine Leppencott                    7-24-1817
DEAN, Robert to Elizabeth Campbell                       1-8-1818
DEWITT, Daniel to Rebeckah Thornburgh                    1-12-1817
DOWNEY, John to Celia Shepherd                           5-26-1816
DRAKE, Thomas to Elizabeth Fields                        3-4-1817
DRAPER, Edward to Barsheba Helm                         12-29-1818
EDGAR, William to Rebecca Travis                         8-27-1817
EDWARDS, Emanuel to Sarah Lowe                          12-24-1818
ELLENWORTH, David to Sarah Hardman                       4-17-1817
ELLIS, John to Susanna James Wright                     10-29-1817
ELMORE, Providence to Lydia Salisbury                   11-6-1817
ENNIS, Samuel to Elizabeth Elanson                       7-2-1818
FAULKNER, Robert to Phebe Scott                          4-3-1816
FIELDS, Thomas to Jane Morgan                           11-1-1818
FLETCHER, James to Isabella Blue                         1-15-1818
FORSMAN, Hugh to Elizabeth Jacoby                        6-11-1816
FOX, John to Tenney Kirkendall                          12-11-1816
FRAKES, Nathan to Susannah Russle                        8-14-1817
FRAZIER, James to Christena Hare                         9-19-1817
FULLER, James to Margaret Weeks                          4-25-1816
GAFF, John S. to Margaret McCracken                     12-24-1818
GALLOWAY, James Sr. to Tamer Wilson                      2-13-1817
GALLOWAY, John to Isabella Wilson                        6-28-1816
GARRETT, John to Lettitia Quinn                          8-1-1816
GARTRELL, Richard to Orpha Logan                         9-19-1816
```

530

```
MASON, Rhoman to Nancy Downey                          12-18-1817
MENDENHALL, Aaron to Lavinia Westfall                   8-5-1816
MENDENHALL, William to Sarah Peterson                  11-20-1817
MENDENHALL, Joseph to Cloe Bargdoll                    10-1-1818
MILHOLLIN, McClintick to Mary Kelly                    10-24-1816
MILLER, Augustus C. to Mary Williamson                  6-23-1818
MILLER, William to Rachel Drake                         2-15-1816
MILLER, William to Esther Ross                          7-15-1817
MILLER, William to Sarah Johnson                       10-16-1817
MILLS, John to Elizabeth Stephenson                     2-8-1816
MINICK, George to Catharine Shover, widow      (1815?)12-7-1816
MOORE, John A. to Prudence Ferguson                     2-6-1816
MOORE, Samuel to Rachel Ewing                          10-11-1816
MOORMAN, Charles to Matilda Watson                     11-24-1816
MORELAND, William to Nancy Frazier                      2-15-1816
MORGAN, Jonathan to Nancy Bloxum                       10-17-1816
MURPHY, John to Ann Laurence                            1-29-1818
PANCER, Francis I. to Margaret Flatcher                 6-23-1818
PAULIN, Enos to Polly Mauzey                           11-18-1817
PELHAM, Jesse B. to Martha Butler                       1-15-1818
PILCHER, Enoch to Susanna Grant                        11-10-1818
PENDRAY, Jacob to Margaret Boots                        2-16-1817
POWERS, Snowden to Rebecca Wickiel                     12-29-1818
PUTERBAUGH, Jacob to Hannah Hittle                      5-26-1816
RAY, William M. to Nancy Rue                            1-7-1817
READ, John to Sally Sterrett                            3-4-1817
REAVES, George to Mary Lee                              7-31-1817
RICE, Silas to Esther Richey                            8-19-1817
RICHARDS, William to Mary Mayberry                      5-30-1816
RICHARDSON, Aaron to Nancy Perry                       11-5-1818
ROBERTS, Conrad to Sarah Cook                          11-12-1816
ROBERTS, George to Sarah Beal                           7-9-1818
RODEHAMMELL, Henry to Sarah McAffee                    11-14-1816
RUBLE, Henry to Mahaly Martin                          12-24-1818
RUTLEDGE, William to Rebecca Inlow                      6-12-1817
SACKETT, Joseph to Anna Vandolah                        5-28-1816
SCOTT, Adam to Susannah Ewing                           7-21-1817
SEARL, Brown to Barbary Hoschar                         2-13-1817
SELLERS, Jacob to Nancy Beatty                          8-26-1817
SHAUL, Aaron to Anna Evans                              2-1-1816
SHAW, George to Jane Rhodes                             8-24-1817
SHOUP, Daniel L. to Judy Wentermote                     9-20-1818
SIPE, Christian to Catharine Carpenter                 10-22-1817
SIRLOTTE, Samuel to Sarah Harper                       12-1-1818
SKILLINGS, Lewis to Anna Craig                         10-31-1816
SMILEY, William to Nancy Pennington                    11-26-1817
SMITH, George M. to Catharine Beeks                     10-2-1817
SMITH, Jacob to Sarah Kerkendall                        6-3-1818
SPAHR, Matthias to Susannah Hagler                      8-8-1818
```

```
GIBSON, John to Martha Campbell              7-4-1816
GILL, Hugh to Malinda Forrest                5-6-1818
GILL, John to Elizabeth Carson               2-27-1817
GILLESPIE, Henry T. to Elenor Laughead       11-11-1817
GOODHEART, Frederick to Martha Moreland      4-10-1816
GRENDAL, Henry to Elizabeth McMichael        12-27-1817
HACKER, John to Susanna Creyell              5-12-1818
HADDIX, John to Sarah Cox                    3-29-1817
HADDIX, Philip to Isabella Hughey            6-23-1816
HAINES, Zimri to Elizabeth Compton           11-23-1817
HAND, Benjamin to Sarah Sackett              4-16-1816
HANES, Nathan to Elizabeth Woolmen           4-10-1818
HARE, Daniel to Phebe Horner                 9-18-1817
HARLAN, Eli to Maria Wallace                 11-5-1816
HARMAR, William to Hannah H. Lawson          2-6-1816
HARPER, John to Harriet Strong               4-3-1817
HARPER, Thomas to Mary Serlott               5-24-1818
HENDERSON, Joseph to Catharine White         2-15-1816
HIERS, Abraham to Uranah Peterson            1-4-1816
HIXON, Enoch to Phebe Edwards                3-6-1816
HIXON, Reuben to Catharine Borders           4-29-1817
HOLVERSTAT, John to Elizabeth Crowl          10-31-1816
HORNER, Nathan to Nancy Hipes                9-16-1817
HOWARD, John to Hannah Welsh                 1-23-1817
HUNTER, Jonathan to Mary Shaw                1-25-1816
HUTCHINGS, Benjamin to Tamer Izard           9-5-1817
HUTCHINSON, George to Martha Clancy          3-19-1818
INSLEY, Zard to Jane Ash, widow              12-30-1817
JOHNSON, James to Mary R. Burgess            1-22-1818
JOURDAN, George to Elizabeth Coffman         12-26-1816
JUDY, John to Christian Hittle               4-9-1818
KERSHNER, Daniel to Susanna Howard           12-31-1815
KIRKENDALL, Joseph to Polly Kirkendall       1-25-1817
KIRKWOOD, William to Julia Ann Shover        1-11-1816
KITTEMAN, Jonathan to Mary Peterson          10-8-1818
KNOTT, David to Margaret Brearly             12-30-1818
LAURENCE, John B. to Armillia Vickers        2-8-1816
LAURENCE, William to Jane McConnel           1-11-1816
LEWIS, William to Mary Stiles                1-3-1817
LONG, William to Phebe Purgett               9-19-1816
LUCAS, Simon to Elizabeth Sutton             7-14-1816
McALESTER, Joseph to Elizabeth Goodnight     11-9-1817
McANLESS, William to Nancy McClelland        3-7-1816
McFARLAND, John K. to Mary Clymer            4-16-1816
McINTIRE, Joseph to Caroline Boyd            7-4-1816
McKNIGHT, Daniel to Mary Powers              8-24-1818
McPHERSON, John G. to Margaret Hivling       9-21-1817
MARSHALL, John to Nancy Hays                 1-18-1816
MARSHALL, Robert to Mary Smith               6-25-1818
```

```
SROUFE, Andrew to Mary Bachelor                          10-6-1817
STALEY, Jacob to Lydia Bell                              6-9-1816
STANFIELD, John to Ruth Mendenhall                       8-30-1818
STARE, Abraham to Mary Stanfield                         10-15-1818
STEELE, John to Mary Porter                              4-9-1816
STEELE, Thomas to Maria Gaff                             10-22-(1818)
STEPHENSON, Robert W. to Abigail Gowdy                   9-23-1818
STERRETT, Robert E. to Eliza Boyd                        9-18-1816
STERRETT, William to Mary McCoy                          3-31-1818
STIP (or STISS), David to Mary McClure                   9-12-1816
STRONG, Reuben to Barbary Boots                          2-15-1816
SUPPINGER, Alexander P. to Elizabeth Shaner              11-20-1817
SUTTON, Amos to Sarah Lippingcutt                        3-27-1817
SUTTON, Isaiah to Elizabeth Handley                      5-26-1816
SWEADLER, Jacob to Margaret Cramer                       2-12-1818
SYNIP (SYNISS), Jacob to Mary Trubey                     12-5-1816
TATE, Hugh to Mary Torrence                              6-20-1816
TANNER, William to Mary Ramsay                           11-7-1816
TANNSLEY (TOWNSLEY?), William to Sarah Baker             11-16-1816
THOMAS, George to Elizabeth Beck                         10-3-1818
THORNBURGH, Thomas to Ann Gowdy                          3-28-1816
TOWNSLEY, George to Mary Lowry                           1-18-1816
TOWNSLEY, Thomas to Margaret Barber                      4-15-1816
TOWNSLEY, William to Elizabeth Beard                     1-15-1818
TURNBULL, Alexander to Sarah McCoy                       12-29-1818
TURNER, Robert to Elizabeth Lucas                        8-11-1818
VANCE, Abraham to Mary Ennis                             7-29-1816
VICKREY, Christopher to Mary Airy                        9-12-1818
WATSON, John to Nancy Humphries                          1-30-1817
WATSON, Robert to Nancy Stanford                         8-29-1816
WEAVER, Martin to Susan Jordan                           7-21-1818
WELCH, Andrew to Martha Baker                            4-18-(1818?)
WELLS, Perequin to Charlotte Miller(no other date) Tues., July 1817
WESTFALL, John to Mary Weaver                            8-28-1817
WHITE, John to Tabitha McFarland                         9-5-1816
WHITE, John to Mary Davisson                             6-12-1817
WHITE, William to Elenor Marshall                        12-27-1816
WIFORD, Jacob to Catharine Tingley                       10-8-1817
WIKIEL, Daniel to Ruth A. Willis                         12-24-1818
WILLIAMS, Seabury to Susan Parker                        6-3-1818
WILLIAMSON, Samuel H. to Mercy Cozad                     7-22-1817
WILSON, James to Elizabeth Replogle                      10-10-1816
WILSON, James to Lydia Warner                            1-1-1817
WILSON, John to Nancy Scott Campbell                     5-1-1817
WILSON, Seth to Sarah Hussey                             11-7-1816
WILSON, William to Jane Johnson                          10-9-1818
WINGET, Robert to Sarah Rynearson                        8-28-1817
WINTER, William to Elizabeth Cochron                     1-29-1818
WOLF, Jacob to Elizabeth Kershner                        2-9-1817
```

```
WOLF, John to Mary McNear                         8-6-1818
WOLF, John to Polly Hauker                        12-31-1818
WOODARD, Joseph to Sarah Tatman                   2-15-1816
WOOLMAN, Abraham to Ruth _____(not given)         1-29-1818
(note:  the following marriage was recorded with the 1818-1819 marriages)
WATSON, James to Nancy Linsey                     8-4-1813
```

GREENE COUNTY, OHIO DEATH RECORDS 1869-1871

Persons 50 years of age
    or over

Name	Date of Death	Age	Place of Death	Marital Status
BARRETT, Mahala	d. 1-30-1870	64	Spring Valley Twp.	mar.
RADER, Christian	d. 3-24-1870	79	Spring Valley Twp.	widower
RADER, Adam	d. 10-30-1869	82	Spring Valley Twp.	mar.
HANSFORD, Squires	d. 7-15-1869	71	Spring Valley Twp.	widower
WHITE, Mary	d. 8-17-1869	73	Spring Valley Twp.	widow
COMPTON, Juda	d. 11-9-1869	53?	Spring Valley Twp.	single
COX, Joseph D.	d. 9-15-1869	65	Spring Valley Twp.	mar.
CROSS, Matilda	d.10-26-1869	56	Cedarville	mar.
CORBIN, Jeremiah	d. - - 1870	100	Cedarville	widower
LANGHEAD, David M.	d. 1-27-1870	81	Cedarville	widower
MILLER, Sarah	d. 3-20-1870	67	Beaver Creek	mar.
LITTLE, John	d. 3-23-1870	86	Ross Twp.	widower
McFARLAND, Robert	d. Sept.1869	85	Cedarville Twp.	widower
CARRUTHERS, John	d. 3-15-1870	83	Cedarville Twp.	widower
KYLE, John G.	d. 3-4-1870	50	Xenia	mar.
McGAREY, Elizabeth	d. 10-15-1869	68	Xenia	mar.
BERRYHILL, Sidney	d. 9-8-1869	67	Sugar Creek	mar.
HAYSLIT, Thomas K.	d. 8-8-1869	68	Jamestown	mar.
KAVANAUGH, Thomas	d. 6-18-1870	75	Silver Creek Twp.	mar.
MOORMAN, Manson	d. 9-13-1869	51	Silver Creek Twp.	mar.
PRICE, Mary	d. 4-17-1870	59	Xenia	widow
LEWIS, Nancy	d. 2-10-1870	68	Xenia	widow
ALLEN, John	d. 8-6-1869	71	Xenia	mar.
ALLEN, Wesley Davisson	d.6-13-1869	66	Clifton	mar.
BRADLUTE, John	d. 2-4-1870	73	Miami Twp.	widower
ELLIOTT, Sarah	d. 2-15-1870	73	Clifton	single

534

Name	Date of Death	Age	Place of Death	Marital Status
CHARLES, John	d. 1-6-1870	67	Xenia Twp.	mar.
GOWDY, Rev. John	d. 8-4-1869	80	Xenia Twp.	mar.
STEVENSON, Samuel	d. 3-9-1870	89	Xenia Twp.	widower
SHIELDS, Kesiah	d. 7-23-1869	82	Xenia Twp.	widow
COX, Ruth	d. 10-17-1869	57	Bath Twp.	mar.
CONIES, Wm. C.	d. 3-8-1870	68	Bath Twp.	widower
COZAD, Scharlotte	d. 7-9-1869	67	Fairfield, Ohio	widow
MILLER, John	d. 1-5-1870	61	Bath Twp.	mar.
HOSIER, John	d. 12-24-1869	81	Bath Twp.	mar.
MORAN, Johanna	d. 4-6-1870	75	Bath Twp.	widow
NELSON, Jacob	d. 3-5-1870	63	Bath Twp.	single
PRUDEN, Mary A.	d. 4-3-1869	50	Bath Twp.	mar.
SHOHN, Margaret	d. 12-8-1869	50	Bath Twp.	mar.
TROLLINGER, Jacob	d. 2-13-1870	71	Bath Twp.	mar.
WHITE, Elizabeth	d. 10-7-1869	86	Jefferson Twp.	widow
CHANEY, Thos.	d. 8-22-1869	84	Bowesville	mar.
SMITH, Mary	d. 1-31-1870	69	New Jasper Twp.	widow
ARY, John	d. 11-10-1869	75	Caesars Creek	mar.
COPSY, Nancy	d. 6-25-1869	77	Caesars Creek	mar.
CURL, Mary	d. 1-31-1870	63	Caesars Creek	mar.
GARRETT, Wells	d. 8-26-1869	61	Paintersville	mar.
SMITH, Thomas B.	d. Nov. 1869	57	Caesars Creek	mar.
WRIGHT, Thomas C.	d. 2-25-1871	73	Xenia	mar.
JOHN, Rebecca	d. 6-2-1870	77	Xenia	widow
DIXON, Nathaniel	d. 10-31-1870	79y 11m	Xenia Twp.	mar.
HOOLI, James Samuel	d. 10-14-1870	67y 5m	Xenia Twp.	mar.
STEWART, Elizabeth	d. 10-4-1870	87	Xenia Twp.	widow
HAWKINS, Reuben	d. 9-16-1870	59y 4m	Xenia Twp.	mar.
VAN ELTON, Sarah	d. 4-25-1871	77	Xenia Twp.	widow
FRY, Jacob	d. 2-15-1871	66	Xenia Twp.	mar.
RYAN, John	d. 7-1-1870	58	Infirmary	single
FROCK, Joann	d. 8-15-1870	55	Osborn	widow
GALLOFS, Sarah	d. 2-12-1870	71	Osborn	widow
STOUT, Henry	d. Feb. 1871	66y 4m	Osborn	mar.
JOHNSTON, Arthur	d. 5-6-1870	86	Fairfield	widower
JOHNSTON, Sarah	d. 11-2-1870	54	Bath Twp.	single
PIERCE, Hannah	d. May 1870	73	Bath Twp.	mar.
DUNLAP, Jane Maria	d. 1-21-1871	52	Cedarville	mar.
POLLOCK, Mary	d. 12-1-1870	89	Cedarville	widow
REID, William	d. 8-12-1870	68	Cedarville	mar.
MILLER, Margaret	d. 4-27-1870	63	Cedarville	mar.
McMILLAN, Matilda	d. 11-25-1870	73	Miami Twp.	widow
ALEXANDER, John A.	d. 12-24-1870	83	Yellow Springs	mar.
ALEY, Fanney	d. 9-15-1870	75	Yellow Springs	widow
COLLIER, Elizabeth	d. 1-6-1871	79	Miami Twp.	widow
FOGERTY, James	d. 4-9-1870	65	Yellow Springs	mar.
JOHNSON, Mary C.	d. 9-18-1870	62	Yellow Springs	widow
SHEELY, William B.	d. 5-21-1870	53	Jefferson Twp.	mar.
OXLEY, Elizabeth	d. 7-15-1870	75y 2m	Jefferson Twp.	mar.
BAKER, Mary D.	d. 10-11-1870	85	Jamestown	widow
DAVISON, John	d. 3-28-1871	88	Jamestown	widower
GRAY, Phillip	d. 10-12-1870	79	Jamestown	widower
MOORMAN, Childs	d. 1-12-1871	84	Jamestown	widower
MOORMAN, Matilda	d. 12-31-1870	71	Jamestown	mar.
SNODGRASS, Abigal	d. 7-6-1870	66	Jamestown	mar.

535

Name	Date of Death	Age	Place of Death	Marital Status
TURNER, Levi	d. 12-15-1870	73	Jamestown	mar.
TURNER, Elizabeth	d. 1-9-1871	68	Jamestown	mar.
WICKERSHAM, Catharine	d. 2-21-1871	55	Jamestown	widow
CUPER, Manani	d. 2-2-1871	52-4-18	Ross Twp.	mar.
KIRKPATRICK, Hugh	d. Feb.1871	57	Ross Twp.	mar.
FARMER, Wm.	d. 2-14-1871	80	Ross Twp.	mar.
GOINGS, Lucretia	d. 4-2-1871	68-6-29	Ross Twp.	mar.
CLEMENS, Susan	d. 3-9-1871	74	New Jasper Twp.	widow
MULLON, John	d. 6-13-1870	84	New Jasper Twp.	single
PEERMAN, Anna	d. 1-4-1871	64	New Jasper Twp.	widow
YOUNG, Lorenzo Daw	d. 12-15-1870	56	New Jasper Twp.	mar.
GIDEON, Baynard	d. 11-15-1870	53	Caesars Creek	mar.
WEAVER, George	d. 3-28-1871	68y 8m	Caesars Creek	widower
BELL, Franklin J.	d. 9-12-1870	51-8-17	Spring Valley	widower
ELLIS, Elizabeth	d. 2-10-1871	80	Spring Valley	widow
MASON, Joseph	d. 1-30-1871	70-3-9	Spring Valley	mar.
SHEPHERD, Mary	d. 11-16-1870	65	Sugar Creek	mar.
TALBERT, Sarah E.	d. 9-6-1870	50	Sugar Creek	mar.
KOOGLER, Jacob	d. 1870-1871?	80	Beaver Creek	mar.
BURROWS, John	d. 1870-1871?	70	Beaver Creek	widower
AUKENY(ANKENY?),Henry	d.1870-1871?	90	Beaver Creek	mar.
COY, Peter	d. 1-1-1871	58	Beaver Creek	mar.
BEALL, Alexander	d. 12-14-1871	62	Xenia	mar.
CONFER, Elizabeth	d. 12-6-1871	81	Xenia	widow
CAREY, Nancy	d. 8-22-1871	76	Xenia	single
LANMAN, Geo. C.	d. 11-13-1871	70	Xenia	mar.
FERGUSON, Charles	d. 9-1-1871	56	Xenia Twp.	widower
ADAMS, Samuel	d. 10-14-1871	71	Spring Valley	mar.
LAMME, Alonzo	d. 12-11-1871	77	Sugar Creek	mar.
LANTZ, John	d. 11-14-1871	66y 10d	Beaver Creek	mar.
HAWKER, Abraham	d. 11-23-1871	53y 5m	Beaver Creek	mar.
GRINER, Elizabeth	d. 10-15-1871	71	Beaver Creek	widow
SHILT, Peter	d. 5-23-1871	83	Beaver Creek	widower
GRIMES, Thomas	d. 3-4-1871	80	Beaver Creek	widower
SNYDER, Rosana	d. 12-23-1871	89	Beaver Creek	widow
KIRKWOOD, Robert	d. 7-1-1871	70	Bath Twp.	mar.
BARE, John	d. 5-25-1871	80	Clifton Twp.	mar.
DILLE, Sarah	d. 6-10-1871	80	Cedarville Twp.	widow
McHATTER, Sarah	d. 10-17-1871	77	Cedarville Twp.	widow
PATTERSON, Catharine	d.7-30-1871	67	Cedarville Twp.	widow
REID, John	d. 10-29-1871	81	Cedarville Twp.	mar
SHENDECKER, Nath'l	d. 8-18-1871	65	Cedarville Twp.	mar.
SPENCER, Thomas	d. 5-18-1871	88	Cedarville Twp.	mar.
SWENY, Margaret	d. 2- 3-1871	80	Cedarville Twp.	widow
BLAIR, Mary Ann	d. 11-17-1871	68	Ross Twp.	widow
LAWRENCE, John B.	d. 10-12-1871	80	Ross Twp.	mar.
GASTON, Margaret	d. 10-5-1871	69	Jamestown	mar.
HIBBEN, James	d. 8-22-1871	77	Jamestown	mar.
ELLIOT, Patience	d. 5-21-1871	66	Jamestown	widow
SAVILLE, Ann	d. 5-18-1871	79	New Jasper	widow
KIRLER, Fred	d. 8-11-1871	74	Greene Co.	mar.

GUERNSEY COUNTY, OHIO - COMMON PLEAS COURT RECORDS 1822-1824

The following records were taken from Minute Book C, pages on which record may be found are given in parenthesis.

Feb. 1822 - Archibald DODS a native of Scotland. Declaration of intention to become citizen. -- Hugh BROOM a native of Scotland. Declaration to become citizen. (7)

Feb. 1822 - Philip CARTER a native of Ireland, has resided in the United States since 18 June 1798. Naturalization. (15)

Apr. 1822 - Thomas JOHNSTON a native of Ireland, filed declaration of intention on 21 Aug. 1812 in Common Pleas Court of Lancaster County, Penna. Naturalization. (19)

Apr. 1822 - Robert JAMISON a native of Ireland, resided in United States prior to 29 January 1795. Naturalization. (20)

Apr. 1822 - James GILLILAND and Hannah GIFFEE appointed adms. of estate of Benjamin GIFFEE, dec'd. (20)

Apr. 1822 - Isaac WARDEN a native of Ireland, in the United States prior to Jan. 29, 1795. Naturalization. (21)

Apr. 1822 - John RUSSELL filed his petition for permanent lease of NE¼ Section 10, and SE¼ Section 1, Township 3, Range 1 in U. S. Military land appropriated for use of schools. (28)

Apr. 1822 - Archibald McGIFFIN aged 14 yrs. child and heir of James Mc-GIFFIN, dec'd, chose Jehu FINLEY as his guardian. (31)

Apr. 1822 - Henry VICTOR appointed guardian of William Washington COOKE, aged 3 yrs., child of Joseph COOK, Jr. late of Muskingum County, Ohio, dec'd. (31)

Sept. 1822 - Michael BRADY a native of Ireland made his declaration of intention to become citizen. (41)

Sept. 1822 - Benjamin SMITH, aged 17 yrs. on the 24th Sept. last, child of George Smith, dec'd, chose Amos Smith as his guardian. (42)

Sept. 1822 - John HENDERSON appointed adms. of William MOORE, dec'd. -- Margaret St. CLAIR and Benjamin St. CLAIR appointed adms. of John St. CLAIR, dec'd. (42)

Sept. 1822 - Charles HAMMOND adms. of the Estate of Dennis CASSAT of the State of Virginia; deceased, presented his petition setting forth that Dennis Cassat, a citizen of Virginia, died in Wheeling, Virginia, in March 1808, leaving business in the State of Ohio, that Cassat died seized of lots 2, 3, 8, 10, 11, 14, 27, 30, 40, 48 & 50 in town of Frankford, Guernsey County. (42)

Sept. 1822 - Sarah NEILL and Turner G. BROWN appointed adms. of estate of
Peter NEILL, dec'd. — Thomas HIDE appointed adms. of the estate of John
HIDE, dec'd.   (44)

Sept. 1822 - George WALKER aged 16 yrs. on 4 Feb. last, child of George
WALKER, dec'd, chose Amos SMITH as his guardian.   (45)

Sept. 1822 - John TURNER presented to the Court his declaration of his
services as a soldier in the Revolutionary War and schedule of his property made under oath in Open Court, and the court being satisfied of the
truth of his declaration and schedule are of opinion that the property of
the declarant is worth eighty-nine dollars and fifty-five cents and the
Court order that the same be certified agreeably to law.   (47)

Sept. 1822 - Andrew WILKIN appointed adms. of the estate of Nathan SPURGEON,
dec'd. Sufficient proof submitted to court that James, George R., Jeremiah,
Elizabeth, Susan and Catharine SPURGEON are brothers and sisters and heirs-
at-law of Nathan SPURGEON, dec'd, who enlisted in the army of the United
States during the late war and who died while in the service of said United
States.   (50)

Sept. 1822 - Will of George SMITH produced and proven. Phebe SMITH, aged
15 yrs. and 4 mos., child and heir of George SMITH, dec'd, chose Amos
SMITH as her guardian.   (51)

Sept. 1822 - The court appointed Amos SMITH as guardian of Anna WALKER,
aged 7 yrs., 8 mos. and 26 days, child and heir of George WALKER, dec'd.
                                                                    (51)
Sept. 1822 - Nathan SMITH appointed guardian of George B. SMITH, aged 8
yrs. and 10 mos. and Amos SMITH aged 2 yrs., 11 mos. and 19 days, children
of William SMITH, dec'd.   (52)

Sept. 1822 - James LeRETILLEY a native of Scotland made his declaration of
intention to become citizen.   (52)

Oct. 1822 - Henry HITE and David JOHNSON appointed adms. of the estate of
Andrew HITE, dec'd. — Will of Samuel MATHERS, dec'd, produced and proven.
                                                                    (59)
Oct. 1822 - Joseph SMITH who was appointed adms. of the estate of Rev'd
James SMITH, dec'd, has since departed this life and his legal represent-
ative is residing in another state, therefore Joshua ROBB appointed adms.
                                                                    (59)
Mar. 1823 - Will of Moses SHUMAN presented and proven.   (59)

Mar. 1823 - Will of William HILL presented and proven. — Mary WINE
appointed adms. of the estate of George WINE, dec'd. — Thomas LEVINGTON
and John HAINES appointed adms. of the estate of Thomas HAINES, dec'd.(60)

Mar. 1823 - John WINE aged 15 yrs. in July last, chose Andrew DARNER as his guardian and Darner to also serve as guardian of Emanuel Wine aged 13 yrs. July last, both children of George WINE, dec'd.   (61)

Mar. 1823 - John St.CLAIR aged 16 yrs. on 25 March last, child of John St. CLAIR, dec'd, chose Benjamin St. CLAIR as his guardian.   (64)

Mar. 1823 - Edward LAWN a native of Ireland made his declaration of intention to become citizen.   (64)

Mar. 1823 - William GIBSON, James CARR and James GALLAGHER, all natives of Ireland made their declarations of intention to become citizens. (65)

Mar. 1823 - Will of Joshua W. SATTERTHWAITE of Berlington, New Jersey ordered to be recorded in Guernsey County.   (76)

Mar. 1823 - On application to the court a new township has been set off by the name of Liberty.   (79)

June 1823 - Will of John CRANSTON presented and proven. — Will of John KACKLEY presented and proven.   (81)

June 1823 - Rev. John M. JONES a minister of the Episcopal Church granted license to solemnize marriages.   (86)

June 1823 - Margaret St. CLAIR appointed guardian of Jane Davis St. Clair aged 7 yrs. on 8 Sept. last, Rebecca St. Clair aged 6 yrs. on 17th July next and Lester St. Clair aged 4 yrs. on 17th April last, all children of John St. Clair, dec'd.   (92)

June 1823 - William COWDEN a native of Ireland. Naturalization. Made declaration of intention on 1 July 1818.   (94)

Oct. 1823 - Will of Peter SARCHET, Senior presented and recorded.   (102)

Oct. 1823 - William ARNOLD appointed adms. of the estate of Anthony ARNOLD, dec'd. — George METCALF and Sarah METCALF appointed adms. of the estate of Thomas METCALF, dec'd.   (103)

Oct. 1823 - James OLDHAM and Stuart SPEER appointed adms. of the estate of Robert BROWN, dec'd.   (104)

Oct. 1823 - Samuel BROWN aged 18 yrs. on 19 Dec. next, Andrew Brown aged 17 yrs. on 8 March next and Robert Brown aged 14 yrs. on 6 Oct. instant, all children of Robert BROWN, dec'd, chose James CLEMENTS as their guardian.   (107)

Oct. 1823 - Esther BROWN appointed guardian of William Brown aged about 12 yrs., Isabella Brown aged about 9 yrs., James Brown aged about 6 yrs. and Joseph Brown aged about 2 yrs., children of Robert BROWN, dec'd.(107)

Oct. 1823 - Francis DUSOUCHET appointed adms. of the estate of Peter TORODE, dec'd.   (111)

Oct. 1823 - Aaron KIRKPATRICK aged 16 yrs. child of Andrew KIRKPATRICK, dec'd, chose Thomas Kirkpatrick as his guardian.   (111)

Oct. 1823 - John DIXON a native of Ireland made his declaration of intention to become citizen.   (112)

Oct. 1823 - Matilda SARCHET aged 15 yrs. chose Catharine Sarchet as her guardian and Catharine also to serve as guardian of Peter T. Sarchet aged 13 yrs. and Theophilius Sarchet aged 12 yrs., children of Peter Sarchet, Jr., dec'd.   (115)

Nov. 1823 - Zadock LUALLEN eldest son of Francis LUALLEN, dec'd, declines adms. of the estate of Said Francis, deceased, and court appointed James LUALLEN as adms.   (139)

Jan. 1824 - David TULTER and Sarah WITTEN appointed adms. of the estate of Thomas WHITTEN, dec'd, his brother within the state having declined.   (140)

Mar. 1824 - Will of Nathan WEBSTER produced and proven. -- Will of James CAMPBELL produced and proven.   (141)

Mar. 1824 - Hannah TORODE appointed guardian of Mary TORODE aged 17 months, child of Peter Torode, dec'd.   (142)

Mar. 1824 - Robert ADAIR aged 15 yrs. child of John Adair of Guernsey County and legatee of John TEMPLETON late of Cumberland County, Pa., dec'd, chose John Adair, his father, as his guardian. Court appointed John Adair guardian of Michael Adair aged 13 yrs. and Nancy Adair aged 10 yrs. children of said John Adair and legatees of John Templeton late of Cumberland County, Pa., dec'd.   (142-143)

Mar. 1824 - James WARNACK aged 15 yrs. on 17 Sept. last, child of Robert Warnack, dec'd, chose Edward BRATTON as his guardian.   (143)

Mar. 1824 - Daniel BICHARD a native of the Island of Guernsey in Europe. Naturalization. Declaration of intention made 30th Oct. 1819.   (145)

Mar. 1824 - Will of Robert CALDWELL produced and proven. -- Will of Thomas FULLER produced and proven.   (156)

Mar. 1824 - Francis DUSOUCHET a native of France. Naturalization. Declaration of intention made 18 Nov. 1820.   (157)

540

Mar. 1824 - Anne KIRKPATRICK aged 13 yrs. child of John Kirkpatrick chose said John Kirkpatrick as her guardian and court appointed John to also serve as guardian of John Kirkpatrick aged 11 yrs., Martin Kirkpatrick aged 9 yrs., Samuel Kirkpatrick aged 7 yrs. and Martha Kirkpatrick aged 3 yrs., children of said John Kirkpatrick. (160)

Mar. 1824 - William BLAIR a native of Ireland, made his declaration of intention to become citizen. (163)

Mar. 1824 - William BRYAN appointed adms. of the estate of Cornelius BRYAN, dec'd. (168)

Mar. 1824 - Sufficient proof offered to court that William Bryan, James Bryan, Lewis Bryan, Sarah Newell wife of David Newell, Aaron Bryan, Amos Bryan, Thomas Bryan and Elizabeth wife of John Dixon, are brothers and sisters of Cornelius Bryan, dec'd, who enlisted in the Army of the United States during the late War and died while in service. (169)

June 1824 - Frederick DICKERSON appointed adms. of the estate of William SHEPHERD, dec'd, widow (not named) declines. — Will of Thomas HARDIN presented and recorded. — Margaret WILSON, widow, appointed adms. of Benjamin WILSON, dec'd. (173)

June 1824 - Will of Henry JACKSON presented and recorded. (179)

Sept. 1824 - Esther BROWN widow of Robert BROWN, dec'd, appointed guardian of Maria WARDEN, Sanins(?) Warden and Hannah Warden, children of Benjamin WARDEN, dec'd. (211)

Sept. 1824 - David BALLANTINE, a native of Ireland. Naturalization. Declaration of intention made 15 November 1820. (211)

Sept. 1824 - Elisha PLANFRIED a native of the Island of Guernsey in Europe. Naturalization. Declaration of intention made on 30 October, 1819. (212)

Sept. 1824 - James BREEZE and Samuel ORR natives of Ireland made their declarations of intention to become citizens. (213)

541

GUERNSEY COUNTY, OHIO – U.S. LAW ENTRIES, 1800-1820

The following records were copied from the Index in the Recorder's office. The first column is name of person entering land. Second column is date. Third column is Section (or Lot), Township and Range. Fourth column, the letter designates volume and number is page where complete record may be found.

Patent To	Date	S.T.R.	Bk. & page	Patent To	Date	S.T.R.	Bk. p.
ECKLES, William	1817	23-4-1	O-627	ADAIR, John	1817	13-3-1	C-152
ROBE, Josiah	1812	25-2-1	P-202	CLARY, Henry	1817	33-10-7	C-165
BARNES, Ford	1817	17-9-10	P-206	CROY, Richard	1816	4-8-7	C-169
SHELY, John	1815	11-4-4	P-208	LUZADER, Abraham	1817	2-2-2	C-180
TETERICK, Jacob	1818	19-3-1	P-228	MORRIS, Isaac	1817	36-7-8	C-182
BOGGS, Rice	1808	6-9-10	A-10	SPEER, Robert	1817	22-2-4	C-189
SPEER, Robert	1810	21-2-4	A-10	CROUSE, Jacob	1817	6-2-1	C-192
MOORE, David	1811	1-1-2	B-77	RANNELS, William	1817	5-8-10	C-195
MILLER, John	1802	22-4 ?	B-173	ARCHIBALD, James	1816	18-6-9	C-237
YOHO, Jacob	1811	12-8-8	B-169	ARCHIBALD, James	1815	18-6-9	C-237
DAY, Ezekiel	1812	32-8-10	B-188	BELL, William	1816	17-6-9	C-238
COWGILL, Isaac	1811	22-4-4	D-209	BOYD, Thomas	1815	17-6-9	C-277
WOODSIDE, John	1806	30-1-1	B-243	THOMPSON, Jacob	1818	17-8-8	C-299
WOODSIDE, John	1806	35-1-1	B-243	THOMPSON, Abrah'm	1818	28-8-9	C-300
TITERICK, Jacob	1812	15-3-1	B-253	THOMPSON, Abrah'm	1818	28-8-9	C-301
BRYANT, John	1805	1-2-2	B-265	SHRIVER, Elijah	1818	17-1-5	C-320
HAYS, Thomas	1813	28-9-7	B-275	SHRIVER, Adam	1818	17-1-3	C-320
JOHNSTON, John	1810	28-8-10	B-283	EDGAR, James	1818	2-2-4	C-323
SHRIVER, Elijah	1811	19-1-3	B-331	SAVAGE, Henry	1818	29-10-7	C-333
SHRIVER, Adam	1811	19-1-3	B-331	CROY, Richard	1818	10-8-7	C-367
CALDWELL, James	1813	13-10-7	160-230	EDGAR, William	1818	11-8-7	C-369
				CROY, John	1818	10-8-7	C-369
TETIRICK, Dan'l	1814	26-11-7	B-397	MURPHY, James	1815	15-2-4	C-378
WILKIN, Robert	1813	20-11-7	B-398	JEFFERS, John S.	1818	3-8-7	C-379
PAXTON, John	1815	10-3-2	B-416	CROUSE, Jacob	1818	5-2-1	C-381
TETRACK, Jacob Jr.	1815	15-3-1	B-445	LONG, Frederick	1814	4-2-4	C-391
COWGILL, Isaac	1814	21-4-4	B-449	BEATTY, Zacheus A.	1809	34-1-3	C-408
BEATTY, Cyrus P.	1813	3-2-3	C-6	BEATTY, Zacheus A.	1809	35-1-3	C-408
BEATTY, Cyrus P.	1816	4-2-3	C-6	LANNING, Robert	1818	10-4-2	C-456
RANDALL, Annanias	1815	1-4-2	C-16	ELLIOTT, John	1818	1-2-3	D-30
MILNER, Edward	1815	10-4-2	C-16	BOWER, William	1817	8-4-1	D-52
RANDALL, Annanias	1816	1-4-2	C-18	BROWN, Jesse	1817	8-8-8	D-89
HARRIS, Daniel	1815	31-8-7	C-24	MORRISON, William	1819	9-8-8	D-90
DULTY, John	1814	9-2-2	C-65	BOYD, Daniel	1820	20-3-1	D-93
HAYS, Thomas	1814	34-9-7	C-75	BOYD, Thomas	1820	20-3-1	D-93
SPEER, Stewart	1815	18-2-4	C-81	MEREDITH, George	1819	24-10-7	D-138
THOMPSON, James	1815	11-8-9	C-88	PHILLIS, Charles	1819	23-1-4	D-165
THOMPSON, James	1815	27-8-9	C-88	DUGAN, James	1818	2-2-4	D-224
SCHOFF, Philip	1814	19-4-4	C-90	SHERRARD, Robt. A.	1820	24-2-4	D-272
SCHUMAN, Moses	1816	20-3-1	C-111	SHIPLEY, Ezekiel	1818	19-11-7	D-335
CULVER, Asa	1817	6-9-10	C-115	HARRIS, James	1819	13-8-8	D-386
ENOCKS, Elisha	1815	1-6-3	C-116	MATTHEWS, Paul	1817	17-4-1	D-388
ARCHER, Joseph	1816	27-7-8	C-116	ST CLAIR, John	1819	19-9-10	D-605
ARCHER, James Jr.	1816	27-7-8	C-116	KIRKPATRICK, Thos.	1814	24-3-2	D-643

Patent To	Date	S.T.R.	Bk.& p.	Patent To	Date	S.T.R.	Bk.&p.
FORD, Charles E.	1807	18-2-2	E-435	BIGGS, Zaccheus	1804	31-3-2	L-194
FORD, Charles E.	1807	19-2-2-	E-435			32-3-2	
BAY, Thomas Sr.	1816	33-9-10	E-485	KELSO, George	1819	26-10-7	L-195
FORSYTH, Elijah	1818	25-2-4	E-687	LITTLE, Nicholas	1819	16-2-4	L-211
PRESTON, Silas	1819	6-8-9	H-122	ORR, William	1820	30-9-7	L-231
MORGAN, David	1800	--1-2	H-660	LINSLEY, Noah	1808	7-10-7	L-248
SARCHET, Thomas	1806	24-3-3	I-533	SMITH, David	1819	32-10-7	L-499
BALL, Moses	1813	21-8-7	I-692	BAXTER, William	1818	26-10-7	L-527
BINGHAM, Eli	1817	32-9-10	I-608	BEAHAM, James	1801	38-2-2	L-545
CARPENTER, John	1814	9-8-7	I-640	TETERICK, Michael	1818	6-3-1	L-569
RITCHIE, Thomas	1814	7-8-8	I-663	BAXTER, Robert	1818	29-10-7	M-10
FORDICE, Samuel	1820	4-8-7	J-11	MARSH, Henry	1819	23-4-1	M-94
FULLOR, Thomas	1812	18-4-4-	J-23	HANNA, Robert	1816	25-4-3	N-260
NOURSE, Michael	1805	4-3-1	J-70	FINLEY, Ebenezer	1818	12-8-9	M-250
STULL, Henry	1814	18-3-2	J-275	FINLEY, Ebenezer	1816	7-8-8	M-250
WATERS, John	1817	13-3-1	J433	LOWRY, William	1814	8-8-8	M-263
THOMPSON, William	1812	8-8-8	J-510	RENFREW, James	1817	25-4-3	M-404
JOHNSON, James	1802	--2-1	J-526	RICH, Samuel	1801	29-2-2	M-450
COLEMAN, John	1804	7-3-2	J-568	BEYMER, George	1805	15-2-2	M-457
McELROY, John	1802	12-3-1	K-69			16--2-2	
CONNER, Patrick	1802	11-3-1	K-70			17-2-2	
WALLER, Jesse	1812	20-1-5	K-71	LeFEIVRE, John	1811	7-8-9	M-507
BELT, John S.	1804	35-3-2	K-74	MARSH, Enoch	1816	7-10-7	N-18
		36-3-2		SMITH, George	1818	8-11-7	N-191
		37-3-2		SMITH, Nathan	1818	2-11-7	N-191
ADAIR, Arthur	1808	4-2-1	K-125	HIBBS, Valentine	1818	9-11-7	N-220
CALDWELL, James	1810	3-1-2	K-178	REYNOLDS, William	1812	18-9-10	N-306
WILSON, James	1820	4-2-3	K-223	ATKINSON, Robert	1815	21-4-4	N-419
ROBB, John	1819	6-2-4	K-262	HIBBS, William	1816	1-11-7	N-561
ROBERTS, Patrick	1802	13-3-1	K-332	LAW, Matthew	1813	17-10-7	N-574
CARLILE, William	1818	17-3-1	K-607	PORTER, John	1817	3-3-3	N-630
THOMPSON, Robert	1817	6-8-8	K-614	FRAME, William	1820	7-1-2	O-50
RITCHIE, George	1809	6-8-8	K-615	LANTZ, George	1817	24-3-2	O-76
Ritchie, Thomas	1809	6-8-8	K-615	LANTZ, Andrew	1812	23-3-2	O-78
FERBRACHE, Daniel	1817	2-2-3	K-628	ARNELL, John	1819	24-4-1	O-447
BAY, John	1816	28-9-10	K-640	HAYS, Thomas	1818	35-9-7	O-471
COLE, Abner	1801	28-3-3	K-641	SWIFT, James	1817	22-2-2	W-240
BICHARD, Nicholas	1819	16-1-3	K-645	SARCHET, Thomas	1806	24-3-3	W-283
McGINNIS, Robert	1816	25-10-7	K-647	THOMAS, Jacob	1812	1-1-2	W-376
McPEEK, John	1815	33-10-7	K-686	McCRAREN, Christ'r	1812	11-9-7	W-361
WOOD, Abraham H.	1817	3-8-8	L-26	GRAHAM, Hugh	1813	2-1-2	P-489
STRONG, Joseph	1805	19-1-3	L-50	BELL, James	1814	18-3-3	P-572
		20-1-3		KERSHAW, Mitchel	1805	33-2-2	Q-104
		29-1-3		TETRICK, Daniel	1817	23-3-1	S-177
		30-1-3		TETRICK, Michael	1817	23-3-1	S-177
MORRISON, Abrah'm	1815	19-2-1	L-94	ORR, John	1819	5-10-7	S-235
DELONG, James	1812	22-1-1	L-130	WILLIAMS, Levi	1818	24-4-1	S-475
BIGGS, Zaccheus	1804	30-3-2	L-194	BAY, Benjamin	1815	27-9-10	V-397

Patent To	Date	S.T.R.	Bk.&p.	Patent To	Date	S.T.R.	Bk.p.
HAMMOND, Eliza'beth	1815	11-8-8	V-444	FRAME, Wm. Sr.	1818	24-2-1	1-330
BEATTY, Zacheus A.	1811	8-2-3	T-297	SCOTT, John	1819	20-2-1	1-399
ADAIR, John	1807	5-3-1	T-471	BAILY, Jesse	1820	1-9-7	1-476
STEEL, William	1817	3-2-4	U-17	HANNA, John	1815	12-3-3	2-27
BAY, Thomas	1816	29-9-10	V-52	WILKINS, Francis	1816	15-2-1	2-120
McCOMB, Hugh	1813	23-10-7	V-53	SARCHET, Peter	1808	13-2-3	2-358
McCOY, James	1812	17-10-7	V-326	CUNNINGHAM, Wm.	1811	25-2-1	2-393
JACKSON, Henry	1812	17-8-9	V-458	SLATES, John	1817	12-2-3	3-223
JACKSON, Jacob	1812	17-8-9	V-458	PARKINSON, Thomas	1816	21-3-3	3-425
WILSON, Isaac	1820	33-8-7	W-94	HOLT, James	1815	23-2-1	4-152
MILLS, Nathan	1815	33-8-7	W-94	STEWART, William	1815	21-2-1	4-159
WINE, Christian	1815	11-9-7	W-397	STEWART, Robert	1815	21-2-1	4-159
SEGAR, Ebenezer	1806	8-1-1	W-515	SARCHET, Thomas	1806	23-3-3	4-181
BLACKSHIRE,				SARCHET, Thomas	1806	23-3-3	4-181
Benezer	1806?	7-1-1	W-516	McPEEK, Daniel	1813	33-10-7	4-347
ASKINS, William	1816	17-2-1	X-10	McPEEK, Daniel	1816	34-10-7	4-347
REED, John	1819	12-8-7	X-56	LAW, John	1818	25-3-4	5-303
MITCHELL, George	1813	19-4-4	X-105	SPENCER, John W.	1820	1-4-1	6-231
EDWARDS, Isaac	1818	20-4-1	X-188	McCOLLOUGH, Robt.	1820	24-4-2	6-236
STEWART, John	1811	14-3-1	X-196	HANNA, John	1815	25-3-1	7-41
STEWART, John	1811	14-3-1	X-197	HANNA, John	1811	25-3-1	7-42
KACKLEY, John	1817	34-8-9	X-209	HANNA, John	1819	18-3-1	7-49
WELLS, Robert T.	1815	20-1-1	X-257	CRAMER, Henry	1820	16-3-1	7-139
JACKSON, Henry	1815	11-1-3	X-446	STOKELEY, Joseph	1810	7-3-1	8-455
UMSTOT, Peter	1812	18-2-2	X503			11-3-1	
HENDERSON, John Jr.	1813	17-9-7	X-503			12-2-2	
BOYER, Adam	1816	1-4-1	X-519	SLATS, John	1817	6-2-3	13-482
BELL, Joseph	1812	12-2-2	X-550	SMITH, Joseph	1809	2-1-1	15-713
WARRACK, James	1813	14-3-1	X-550	STEWART, Galbreath	1812	23-2-1	16-461
SCOTT, Abraham	1817	17-4-1	X-570	SMITH, Andrew	1819	9-2-2	16-541
HANNA, John	1812	4-2-1	X-632	GRAHAM, William	1819	4-9-7	16-605
STATEN, David	1812	14-2-1	X-676	PEDAN, John	1820	2-2-2	26-576
VANCE, Ezekiel	1811	5-9-7	Y-18	LANG, John	1817	31-9-7	32-430
VANCE, Ezekiel	1811	11-9-7	Y-18	HALL, Benjamin	1817	9-9-7	33-544
CRANSTON, John	1819	5-9-7	Y-18	SMITH, Joseph	1807	19-2-1	34-388
HANNA, John	1817	19-3-3	Y-19	BIGGS, Zaccheus	1800	--1-1	36-124
BEATTY, Zacchaus A.	1810	24-1-1	Y-88	BARRY, Benjamin	1818	18-3-1	36-451
BEEMER, George	1806	28-2-2	Y-217	PRICE, Joel	1819	33-11-7	36-581
BAIRD, John	1815	24-3-2	Y-321	GIBSON, Wm. Sr.	1813	23-4-3	38-446
SATTERTHWAITE,				THOMPSON, William	1820	4-1-2	39-15
Joseph W.	1807	3-8-9	Y-333	MONROE & COMERS	1815	3-1-2	39-16
DWIGGINS, James	1819	18-4-1	Y-416	STONE, Noyce	1815	3-1-2	39-16
TETRACK, John Jr.	1815	14-3-1	Y-531	WEBSTER, John	1808	19-9-7	40-341
LAUGHLIN, John	1814	22-2-2	Y-560	LARROW, James	1811	8-1-1	43-316
BEATTY, Zaccheum A.	1811	13-2-3	Z345	FRAME, Thomas	1812	18-2-1	48-16
CROOKS, Henry	1817	7-2-4	Z-416	FRAME, Thomas	1819	18-2-1	48-17
LEEPER, James	1812	8-3-3	Z-446	CALDWELL, John	1810	2-1-1	52-552
LEEPER, James	1814	8-3-3	Z-447	CARPENTER, Edw'd	1812	26-11-7	55-322
FRAME, James	1820	23-2-1	Z624	PATTERSON, Joseph	1820	1-2-4	57-156
WILLIAMS, Joel	1819	2-1-1	1-287	MOSER, Conrad	1820	13-1-2	62-470
MACKEY, William	1819	8-9-10	90-353	OGIER, William	1808	7-2-3	86-282

544

First column is name of person entering land. Second column is date. Third column
is Section (or Lot), Township and Range. Fourth column, the letter (or first
number) designates volume and number is page where complete record may be found

McKINNIE, Sam'l F.	1830	27-11-7	O-540	LEWIS, Morgan	1825	74-4-1	I-486
VORHIES, Isaac	1828	10-8-8	P-120	BAY, Thomas	1826	33-9-10	I-533
SMITH, John	1825	22-3-1	P-201	McGREW, Jacob	1828	13-4-1	I-534
LEAMON, Reuben	1823	19-1-4	P-208	McPEEK, Richard	1824	21-3-1	I-545
WHITEHILL, Thos.				GLASS, Thomas	1825	11-4-2	I-596
Jr.	1824	6-3-2	P-211	STEWART, Robert	1827	30-8-7	I-641
WILKIN, Robert	1827	20-11-7	P-222	CARPENTER, Thos.	1825	26-8-7	I-652
MAYHEW, Richard	1821·	21-4-2	D-169	BAY, Archibald	1828	30-9-10	J-86
FERBRACHE, Judith	1821	12-3-4	D442	DOWNEY, Walter	1825	31-8-9	J-125
WALKER, Heirs of				JEFFRIES, William	1822	32-8-7	J-140
George L.B.	1823	12-4-1	D-504	MOORE, Andrew	1829	32-10-7	J-147
PRATT, Rufus	1821	12-1-1	D-580	MOORE, Robert B.	1829	32-10-7	J-147
VORHIES, Aaron	1824	28-8-8	D-633	MARSH, Joseph	1830	21-9-7	J234
WARREN, George	1824	24-3-2	D-690	REEVE, William	1826	10-8-8	J-277
FERBRACK, Thomas	1825	9-2-3	E-37	COOPER, Caleb	1826	15-11-7	J-306
FERBRACHE, Thos.	1824	12-3-4	E-38	LAWRENCE, Samuel	1827	7-3-1	J-336
REED, Hezekiah	1825	6-1-2	E-182	SPEERS, Peter	1828	1-2-3	J-347
WARREN, George	1824	24-3-2	E-191	PHILLIPS, John Sr.	1827	10-4-3	J-359
COCHRAN, William	1827	30-9-7	E-429	NELSON, Archibald	1823	22-3-3	J-381
CARPENTER, Thos.	1822	14-8-7	E-479	McCORKLE, Joseph	1825	9-2-4	J-416
BUMGARDNER, Jac.	1827	6-2-1	E-511	LARROW, John	1825	13-1-1	J-479
HUFFMAN, Jacob	1825	9-3-2	E-559	DELONG, John	1826	3-8-7	J-506
WINDELL, William	1826	12-8-7	E-560	BROWN, Turner G.	1821	33-11-7	J-570
LINDLEY, Davidson	1826	22-9-10	E-686	BROWN, Turner G.	1825	11-4-1	J-571
FLEMING, Alexd'r	1825	7-2-2	E-704	COCHRAN, William	1821	21-3-4	J-636
WATSON, Joseph	1829	38-3-2	F-75	SARCHET, Peter	1827	19-3-3	J-671
CARY, Abel	1828	11-10-7	F-205	SARCHET, Peter	1829	19-3-3	6-7672
RUDOLPH, John	1826	9-1-1	F-220	ROSE, Robinson	1826	12-1-2	K-21
		23-1-1		CAMPBELL, Moses	1826	12-1-2	K-21
LINDSEY, Joseph	1825	19-2-4	F-225	WALKER, Heirs of			
McCREA, David	1825	31-10-7	F-270	Geo. L. B.	1824	8-11-7	K-47
BLACK, Joseph	1828	14-2-4	F-364	WALKER, Geo. L.B.	1825	.12-4-1	K-58
BARNES, Hannah	1826	5-1-1	F-462	MORRIS, Heirs of			
HANNA, James	1826	12-1-3	F-498	Benjamin	1829	24-3-2	K-119
STEWART, William	1826?28-10-7		F-591	SMITH, Wm. C.	1824	35-9-7	K-128
ROUSE, George	1827	6-10-7	G-167	JONES, Enoch	1825	22-3-4	K-234
IRWIN, George	1825	22-2-2	H-168	JONES, Enoch	1827	22-3-4	K-235
MORRIS, Jonathan	1824	21-8-8	H-206	RUBERT, Vincent	1821	22-4-4	K-285
BLACKBURN, Anth'y	1821	25-3-2	H-292	BEATTY, Zaccheus A.	1827	17-1-3	K-556
STEPHENS, Anth'y	1821	25-3-2	H-292			20-4-4	
STEPHENS, John	1825	19-8-8	I-15	KELL, John	1823	6-2-2	K-571
THOMAS, Josiah	1830	21-9-7	I-168	BLAIR, John	1823	6-2-2	K-571
BROWN, Robert	1824	19-2-4	I-389	KELL, John	1827	6-2-2	K-572
REED, George	1827	4-4-1	I-479	BLAIR, John	1827	6-2-2	K-572
REED, George	1825	4-4-1	I-480	McFARLAND, Robt C.	1829	39-3-2	K-592
HEDGE, Israel	1826	13-4-3	I-483			40-3-2	

MARSHALL, Mary	1830	12-2-3	K-602
WILSON, Isaac	1830	16-1-3	K-622
BAY, John	1828	28-9-10	K641
HARDEN, Thomas	1823	12-3-1	L-166
MITCHELL, George	1825	19-4-4	L-250
DELONG, John	1830	3-8-7	L-252
BURT, John	1825	5-1-2	L-253
MOORE, William	1826	5-8-7	L-277
MAPLE, Isaac	1830	6-1-3	L-572
WILSON, Thomas	1824	13-8-9	L-572
BLAIR, James	1825	11-2-3	M-132
BURNSIDE, William	1823	15-11-7	M-168
LEMON, William	1823	20-1-4	M-175
LEAKE, John	1826	1-8-7	M-187
LOWRY, William	1824	8-8-8	M-263
ANNET, Arch'd	1824	20-2-4	M-341
BOGLE, John	1825	25-3-3	M-370
ROBB, James	1821	14-2-4	M-410
HART, Joseph	1827	14-8-9	M-448
REDD, Daniel	1824	26-9-10	M-464
ABLESS, John	1825	21-3-1	N-11
BROWN, John	1824	1-2-4	N-70
KRITZWIZER, John C.	1823	22-1-1	N-96
KIRTZWIZER John C.	1823	22-1-1	N-96
SMITH, James	1824	25-10-7	N-176
THEAKER, Heirs of William C.	1824	20-10-7	N-195
HAVENS, James	1827	10-2-2	N-306
ARMSTRONG, Wm.	1825	22-3-3	N-336
BAIRD, Thos. F.	1827	3-3-2	N-414
RUSSELL, James	1825	20-3-3	O-27
BIRD, Daniel	1825	27-1-1	O-81
CLARY, Nathaniel	1825	15-9-7	O-124
McCONN, Thomas	1826	7-2-2	O-192
MASTERS, Henry	1824	8-3-1	O-193
PORTER, Moses	1821	19-2-2	O-320
McGREW, James W.	1824	13-4-1	O-407
SCOTT, Abraham	1829	16-3-2	O-523
ARMSTRONG, Jos.	1829	16-3-2	O-523
SCHOOLEY, Joseph	1825	3-4-1	O-532
CAMPBELL, James	1825	1-2-2	W-237
ADAMS, Mordecai	1823	22-4-4	W-360
WARD, William	1823	3-8-8	W-38-
TETIRICK, William	1823	18-3-1	P-259
McCOLLUM, Isaac	1826	7-2-2	P-455
BELL, James	1825	18-3-3	P-572
FRAZIER, Alex	1828	13-2-4	Q-243

ROSE, John	1827	9-2-4	Q-431
LINTON, Joseph	1825	32-8-9	R-253
HAGER, Kelion	1826	1-9-7	S-38
WILLIAMS, William	1823	32-8-9	S116
PATTON, Jane	1826	3-3-2	S-168
		9-3-2	
		20-5-3	
REASONER, William	1825	23-2-4	S-327
WATSON, Alexd'f	1825	7-3-1	T-16
STEVEMS, Chas. A.	1826	22-1-4	T-33
ROSS, Robt. A.	1825	4-2-4	T-49
McCLENNAHAN, John	1824	22-10-7	T-79
SCOTT, James	1824	2-9-10	T-156
SCOTT, James	1828	2-9-10	T-156
PATTERSON, Jos.	1830	5-2-2	V390
WILLIAMS, Rebecca	1825	20-8-7	V-404
ST CLAIR, Marg't	1823	18-9-10	T-221
ST CLAIR, John	1825	19-9-10	T-221
OGIER, Thomas	1823	11-9-10	T-298
OGIER, Thomas	1823	14-9-10	T-299
OGIER, Thomas	1827	15-9-10	T-300
OGIER, Thomas	1824	10-9-10	T-301
BEAL, John	1828	13-4-2	T-500
COWEN, William	1827	15-3-3	U-99
CRUSER, Henry	1827	4-10-7	U-192
MARQUAND, John	1825	6-3-3	U-490
JACKSON, Henry	1825	19-8-9	V-89
MOORE, Joseph	1830	21-8-9	V-263
COULTER, Elizb'h	1821	21-1-4	V-287
MARTIN, John	1827	22-8-7	V-459
HOUSE, John	1827	28-8-7	W-95
FREEMAN, Simeon	1827	9-1-2	W-210
COLLIFLOWER, Sam'l	1828	23-8-7	W-236
MASTERS, Richard	1826	24-10-7	W-392
MASTERS, William	1826	24-10-7	W392
CAMPBELL, Alex.	1825	18-4-2	W-400
DOUGLAS, William	1825	13-11-7	W-462
McCOMB, Hugh	1824	24-10-7	W-533
BLAIR, John	1830	15-2-2	W-597
JOHNSTON, James	1824	8-2-4	227-536
HAWTHORN, James	1830	16-3-4	271-529
EVANS, Henry H.	1825	1-2-2	X-43
EVANS, Henry H.	1826	1-2-2	X-43
REED, John	1826	6-8-7	X-57
WILLIAMS, Sarah	1824	19-4-1	X-156
COULTER, Eliz'th	1824	21-1-4	X-198
DILLEY, Robert	1824	19-1-2	X-209
SHERLOCK, James	1821	10-9-7	X-253
LEECH, Matthew	1828	17-2-4	X-273

STINER, Nicholas	1827	14-4-3	X-307	GIBSON, William	1823	23-4-3	38-447
CAREY, John	1822	24-10-7	X-524	BOTTS, John	1823	8-1-2	42-472
BOLINGER, John W.	1828	13-8-7	X=535	WOODROW, Henry	1823	19-1-3	44-396
ATKINSON, Wm.	1826	1-8-7	X-653	MACK, John	1825	30-10-7	45-159
ATKINSON, Wm.	1829	7-8-7	X-654	DUFF, David	1824	16-2-4	46-459
REASONER, John	1827	35-9-10	X-708	SCOTT, Charles	1828	23-3-4	48-42
CARPENTER, Thomas	1825	26-8-7	Y-37	COATS, Charles	1831	4-2-2	H-227
BOGLE, John	1828	25-3-3	Y-254	LAWRENCE, Jacob	1832	2-3-4	I-297
WELLS, Levi	1822	15-10-7	Y-352	ASKINS, Polly	1834	11-2-3	I-327
JOHNSON, Edmund	1825	10-1-2	Y-353	READ, John	1833	3-4-1	I-494
ADAMS, John	1824	5-3-2	Z-216	STEWART, Robert	1832	30-8-7	I-641
CROOKS, Henry	1824	7-2-4	Z-416	RICHIE, Thomas	1833	6-8-8	I-633
PARKINSON, Wm.	1830	5-2-2	Z-436	ROE, Robert S.	1831	32-8-7	J-144
CLARK, John	1823	13-3-4	Z-445	ROBE, David	1831	19-1-2	J-243
COX, Church	1824	10-3-2	1-265	PRATT, James B.	1831	23-8-7	J-265
FREEMAN, James	1824	13-1-3	1-321	REEVE, Stephen	1835	10-8-8	J-278
BELL, George	1821	4-3-2	1-497	POLAND, Wm. H.	1832	8-4-3	J-424
NICHOLSON, Robt.	1821	39-3-1	1-546	DELONG, Thomas	1833	7-8-7	J-497
FRAME, David Jr.	1828	6-2-1	2-107	DELONG, John Jr.	1831	7-8-7	J-507
WHARTON, John	1825	21-9-10	2-441	DELONG, John Jr.	1833	13-8-7	J-508
HANNA, And'w Jr.	1826	32-3-1	3-77	DELONG, Thomas	1833	13-8-7	J-508
HANNA, James	1826	31-3-1	3-78	BOWERSOCK, Daniel	1831	20-8-7	J-666
BAKER, John	1823	12-1-1	3-477	SECRIST, John	1835	9-8-9	K-29
BOGLE, Samuel	1826	20-3-4	4-455	PAXTON, MargaretF.	1831	14-9-10	K-45
BOGLE, Samuel	1827	20-3-4	4-456	LEEPER, John	1835	9-3-3	K-47
DOUGLAS, Samuel	1827	12-4-3	5-330	DEPEW, James	1831	1-8-8	K-218
DILLEY, Abraham	1829	11-1-2	6-65	WILSON, Henry	1835	12-4-4	K-265
McLAUGHLIN, Pat'k	1823	14-2-1	6-281	WILSON, Hwnry	1835	12-4-4	K-265
WITTEN, Thomas	1826	15-1-2	6-459	ROSE, Elisha	1835	4-9-10	K-278
YOUNG, William	1825	24-3-4	6-523	ALLEN, Francis B.	1835	L26-3-2	K-365
HILL, Richard	1830	10-2-3	9-390	ALLEN, Francis B.	1835	L25-3-2	K-365
DENNISON, Henry	1826	15-1-3	10-447	ROE, Robert S.	1831	20-8-7	K-397
PATTEN, William	1829	17-2-4	10-449	FULLER, Thos. R.	1835	23-4-4	K-417
WAGSTAFF, John	1830	20-3-4	11-256	SMITH, Adam	1835	29-8-8	K-426
MISKIMINS, James	1826	8-4-4	12-51	SMITH, Adam	1835	32-8-8	K-426
KECKLEY, Benj.	1826	9-8-9	15-46	WILLIAMS, Isaac	1835	9-2-3	K-436
JOHNSON, John	1825	15-9-10	15-713	MULLEN, Isaac	1835	21-1-1	K-456
KIRKPATRICK, John	1821	8-2-2	15-790	BRITTON, John	1835	7-3-3	K-482
LINN, John	1830	8-3-2	16-139	McILYAR, Wm.	1835	11-2-4	K-489
PATTERSON, Sam'l	1824	31-11-7	19-572	MILONE, John	1832	9-4-3	K-579
COWDEN, William	1824	27-9-7	35-54	SMITH, Joseph R.	1832	8-4-1	K-609
McCORMICK, Robt.	1824	27-9-7	35-54	SHOFF, Philip	1832	12-1-3	K-622
OVERLEY, John	1823	22-9-7	35-55	WILSON, Isaac	1835	16-1-3	K-625
REASONER, Solomon	1825	18-1-4	35-110	BURT, David Jr.	1835	16-1-3	K-654
REASONER, Solomon	1824	18-1-4	35-111	DENNIS, Samuel	1835	16-1-3	K-655
McBURNEY, John	1826	12-1-1	37-83	DENNIS, Joseph	1835	15-1-3	K-656
DYSON, Thomas	1824	22-2-2	37-580	McILYAR, William	1835	10-2-4	K-668
HANNA, Thomas	1824	22-2-2	37-580	FIELD, Reuben	1836	L17,18	
BRADEN, Ezekiel	1824	22-2-2	37-50			19-1-1	K-671

547

STEWART, Charles	1831	8-1-2	L-29
JEFFRIES, John	1835	26-8-8	L-73
JEFFRIES, John S.	1835	34-8-8	L-74
JEFFERIES, John S.	1835	35-8-8	L-74
JEFFRIES, John S.	1835	35-8-8	L-75
JEFFRIES, John S.	1835	34-8-8	L-76
JEFFRIES, John S.	1835	33-8-8	L-76
McILYAR, William	1835	11-2-4	L-170
BRUSH, Daniel	1835	5-3-4	L-184
DUFF, James	1835	6-3-4	L-184
COLLINS, Wm. R.	1835	5-8-8	L-232
SIGMAN, John	1835	5-1-2	L-255
MAPLE, Isaac	1835	21-3-4	L-357
ARCHER, Henry	1835	24-9-10	L-385
GILPIN, Elijah	1835	1-4-3	L398
GILPIN, Elijah	1835	1-4-3	L-399
ATCHISON, David R.	1835	25-3-4	L-401
ACHESON, James	1835	25-3-4	L-401
ACHESON, David R.	1835	25-3-4	L-402
FORSYTHE, Thomas	1835	24-3-4	L-407
LAKE, John	1835	14-3-2	L-409
THOMPSON, Martin	1835	10-4-3	L-413
THOMPSON, John	1835	9-4-3	L-414
BUCKINGHAM, Alvah	1835	6-2-2	L-416
BOYD, Jonathan	1832	19-3-1	L-440
PEDWIN, Nicholas	1835	25-1-3	L-561
WALLER, Joseph	1835	20-1-4	L-562
HUFF, John	1831	13-2-2	L-616
FRAZIER, David	1831	13-2-4	L-628
GALLACHAR, Patrick	1835	3-8-7	L-635
DELONG, James Jr.	1835	2-8-8	M-2
FORSYTHE, John	1831	24-3-4	M-8
PULLY, Henson	1835	11-3-2	M-101
OBNEY, John	1835	6-1-3	M-121
JORDON, Joshua	1835	4-9-10	M-140
JORDON, Joshua	1835	4-9-10	M-141
WILLIAMS, John	1835	11-2-3	M-143
LONG, Charles	1832	2-4-3	M-144
SHRIVER, Adam	1835	19-1-3	M-221
ACHESON, John	1835	25-3-4	M-238
BUCHANNAN, John	1837	25-3-4	M-238
BUCHANAN, John	1837	25-3-4	M-239
BUCHANAN, John	1837	25-3-4	M-239
FINLEY, Joseph	1835	12-8-9	M-248
FINLEY, Joseph	1835	12-8-9	M-249
LYLE, Robert	1835	25-9-10	M-338
MACKEY, Robert	1831	9-2-4	M-344
HARDESTY, Lewis	1837	5-4-2	M-373
JOY, James	1835	21-1-1	M-419
HAMERSLEY, Isaac	1835	2-4-4	M-420
MARSHALL, Elizabeth	1837	73-9-10	M-481
SPAID,Michael	1837	9-8-9	M-523
THARP, James	1837	15-1-3	M-539
CLEGG, Matthew	1831	4-2-2	M-551
ROBERT, Paul	1835	lot 9	
		1-1-3	M-596
ROBERT, Paul	1835	lot 8	
		1-1-3	M-597
LEACH, Thomas	1835	8-4-4	M-610
BAY, William C.	1835	21-9-10	M-617
FERBRACHE,JacobN.	1837	12-3-4	N-19
FERBRACHE,JacobN.	1837	12-3-4	N-20
McKINNEY, Sam'l F.	1832	20-4-1	N-57
COCHRAN, Alexander	1832	1-2-4	N-109
MILLS, John	1837	23-8-9	N-166
BUCKINGHAM, Alvah	1837	22-8-9	N-167
McDONALD, Daniel	1835	5-1-3	N-229
DOUGLASS, David	1837	5-3-3	N-374
BRUSH, Daniel	1838	9-3-4	N-512
MISKINNIS, Isaac	1837	20-4-4	N-515
SIMKINS, Amos	1832	3-4-3	N-587
McGUIRE, Patrick	1837	21-3-4	N-619
FORSYTHE, John	1831	24-3-4	N-619
McGUIRE, Patrick	1838	21-3-4	N-620
WILLSON, Jesse	1835	15-1-3	N-629
RANKIN, James	1835	7-3-4	N-632
SAYRE, David	1832	19-1-1	O-5
DRAKE, David	1835	26-8-8	O-11
WILSON, David	1837	7-4-3	O-16
WALLER, Margaret	1835	4-1-3	O-95
SMITH, Joseph B.	1837	9-4-3	O-98
SMITH, Nathaniel	1837	2-4-3	O-98
CHAPMAN, John	1837	3-1-3	O-199
GRIFFITH, William	1832	9-4-1	O-323
PICKERING, Lot	1835	7-3-2	O-529
CARTER, William A.	1832	2-4-3	O-530
SCHOOLEY, Joseph	1832	2-4-1	O-532
MITCHELL, Alexander	1837	20-4-4	O-547
RODGERS, John	1840	6-4-3	O-549
LEACH, Thomas	1835	33-8-8	O-561
SHUFF, Philip	1835	20-4-4	O-571
PALMER, Benjamin	1832	36-8-7	O-616
VORHIES, Isaac	1835	15-8-8	P-119
DOUGLAS, David	1837	25-4-3	P-173
ROBERTSON, Samuel	1837	6-3-3	P-181
HEDGE, Israel	1837	1-3-4	P-209

HEDGE, Israel	1837	1-3-4	P-209		HALL, John	1840	7-3-4	S-415
WALGAMOT, David	1835	16-4-3	P-227		DUFF, David Jr.	1840	7-3-4	S-415
BUCHANAN, John	1840	5-3-4	P-253		GOODREL, George	1831	12-1-1	S-525
LAKE, John	1840	14-3-2	P-323		MAPLE, Abraham	1835	12-4-4	S-537
HURST, Aaron	1837	7-2-3	P-353		MAPLE, Abraham	1835	12-4-4	S-537
McCUNE, James	1837	3-4-4	P-455		STANBERY, Jonas	1840	12-4-4	S-540
WARDEN, Isaac J.	1835	12-1-2	P-460		HOFFMAN, George	1835	21-4-2	T-77
HAMILTON, Joseph	1840	6-4-3	P-494		SCOTT, James	1835	2-9-10	T-157
BELL, James	1837	13-3-3	P-572		ROBINS, John	1837	2-9-10	T-157
DOUGLAS, David	1835	3-3-3	P-575		BRUSH, Daniel	1842	4-3-4	T-190
PATTERSON,Robt M.G.	1837	3-3-3	P-575		STURGES, Solomon	1844	17-4-3	T-193
DOUGLASS, Samuel	1837	25-4-3	P-579		MORRIS, James	1831	20-8-7	V-404
GRIFFIN, Thos. W.	1837	3-4-3	Q-135		LAW, Ada	1835	2-8-8	V-405
RANKIN, James	1837	7-3-4	N-633		LAW, Ada	1835	2-8-8	V-406
EDIE, Rosana	1835	3-4-3	Q-4		BRUSH, Daniel	1835	3-3-3	V-420
ASHER, Abraham	1835	2-9-10	Q-57		SHAFFER, Christopher	1840	2-4-4	V430
WHEELER, Rezin	1832	2-4-3	Q-150		SHAFFER, Samuel	1840	2-4-4	V-430
BRUSH, Daniel	1837	20-4-4	Q-261		STANBERY, Jonas	1844	5-4-3	T-243
SHAFFER, Samuel	1840	2-4-4	Q-280		STURGES, Solomon	1844	9-4-4	T-260
COOK, Robert	1840	11-4-4	Q-349		STILES, Thomas	1837	14-3-3	T-344
COOK, Robert	1840	1-3-4	Q-349		DRAKE, David	1837	1-3-3	T-421
COOK, Robert	1840	25-4-3	Q-350		NEVIN,John Duffin	1837	14-4-3	T-442
TROTT, John	1835	19-3-1	Q-406		NEVIN,John Duffin	1837	4-1-3	T-443
BELL, Joseph	1837	15-1-2	Q-490		LOWRY, Samuel	1835	8-1-2	T-482
ATCHISON, David	1837	4-3-4	Q-559		STEWART, Charles	1837	8-1-2	T-483
ATCHISON, David	1837	5-3-4	Q-559		FERBRACHE, John S.	1840	8-3-4	T-498
STANBERRY, Jonas	1840	12-4-4	Q-571		CLARK, William	1835	12-3-4	U-36
WICOFF, Jacob	1832	32-8-7	R-63		BUCKINGHAM, Alvah	1837	13-3-4	U-37
SHAFFER, George	1837	33-8-8	R-273		CLARK, Wm. H.	1837	13-3-4	U-37
SAYRE, Ezekiel	1842	19-1-1	R-302		BLISS, Washington	1840	13-3-4	U-38
KACKLEY, Isaac	1837	23-8-9	R-332		WINN, William	1837	36-9-10	U-45
RODGERS, John	1840	7-4-3	R-415		STANBERY, Jonas	1840	14-3-4	U-82
RODGERS, John	1840	7-4-3	R-416		PATRICK, John	1835	13-3-4	U-97
WILSON, William	1835	26-8-8	R-593		PATRICK, John	1837	12-3-4	U-98
WILSON, William	1831	26-8-8	R-594		STANBERRY, Jonas	1837	15-3-3	U-100
WILSON, William	1831	26-8-8	R-595		TEEL, Alexander	1837	25-9-10	U-216
SCOTT, Samuel	1837	24-3-4	S-3		TEEL, Alexander	1837	25-9-10	U-216
MALOY, Alford	1844	6-3-4	S-52		BRYSON, Abraham	1837	5-1-3	U-258
ATKINSON, James	1842	8-3-4	S-99		PICKERING,Greenbury	1835	7-3-2	U-356
DYSON, John B.	1835	29-8-9	S-136		PICKERING,Greenbury	1835	7-3-2	U-356
THOMAS, William	1844	16-3-2	S-138		DAVIS, Benjamin	1844	11-3-4	U-383
EVANS, David	1844	16-3-3	S-138		BOYD, James	1840	16-4-3	U-390
MANYPENNY, Geo. W.	1832	2-3-4	S-201		WARDEN, Isaac	1844	15-3-3	U-395
ALDRICH, Martin	1837	20-1-1	S-304		STANBERRY, Jonas	1844	11-3-4	U-437
DUFF, John	1835	7-3-4	S-313		HELLYER, John	1844	11-3-4	U-438
MAPLE, William	1837	22-4-4	S-323		MISKIMINS, Nelson	1835	2-3-4	U-488
DEW, David	1837	4-3-4	S-414		MISKIMINS, Nelson	1835	2-3-4	U-488
HALL, John	1840	7-3-4	S-415		MARQUAND, John	1835	6-3-3	U-190
DEW, David	1840	7-3-4	S-415		MARQUAND, John	1838	15-3-3	U-491

GRIFFIN, James	1835	10-3-3	V-81	BORROUGH, Thomas W.	1834	13-8-7	X535
GRIFFIN, James	1835	11-3-3	V-81	BISHOP, Samuel	1834	13-8-7	X-536
GENTZLER, John	1840	5-3-3	V-160	BORROUGH, Thomas W.	1834	13-8-7	X-536
GENTZLER, John	1840	5-3-3	V-160	BATSTONE, Sarah	1834	13-8-7	X-536
BUCKINGHAM, Alvah	1835	21-8-9	V-264	SWEARINGEN, Thomas	1838	23-4-4	X-526
GASKILL, Charles	1835	3-4-3	V-283	KEEN, Jesse	1840	23-4-4	X-525
BUCKINGHAM, Alvah	1837	7-4-3	V-297	KEEN, Jesse	1840	23-4-4	X-525
CASNER, John	1835	23-8-8	V328	STANBERY, Jonas	1835	18-1-3	X-639
CASNER, John	1837	23-8-8	V-329	LYONS, Robert	1835	13-1-3	Y-50
WEASER, John	1838	23-8-8	V-330	FOSTER, Jonathan	1840	8-3-4	Y-92
STANBERY, Jonas	1844	17-4-3	V-349	BRUSH, Daniel	1840	8-3-4	Y-93
LANNING, James	1844	17-4-3	V-349	JACKSON, Hosea	1844	10-3-4	Y-121
DAVIS, Benjamin	1844	20-3-4	V-480	BURT, Daniel	1836	12-1-3	Y-156
CONAN, Caleb	1835	13-3-2	V-497	DISALLUMS, John	1840	9-3-4	Y-170
CONAN, Caleb	1837	13-3-2	V-498	BRUSH, Daniel	1835	9-3-4	Y-179
DAVIS, Jabez	1840	19-3-4	V-508	FERBRACHE, John S.	1840	9-3-4	Y-179
LAWRENCE, David	1832	6-1-2	W-1	WEIR, Thomas	1831	3-3-4	Y-198
ACHESON, Robert	1837	5-3-4	W-44	HERST, Aaron	1837	1-2-4	Y-198
LEECH, Thomas	1844	17-3-7	W-81	CARTER, Andrew	1844	19-4-3	Y-239
JACKSON, Hosea	1844	11-3-4	W-92	STEVENS, John	1835	24-1-3	Y-249
McCONAUGHY, Wm.	1835	8-1-3	W132	STEPHENS, John	1834	24-1-3	Y-250
McCONAUGHY, Jas.	1835	7-1-3	W-133	BELLEW, Joseph	1835	10-9-10	Y-251
BUCKINGHAM, Alvah	1837	23-8-8	W-199	WINE, George	1832	6-3-1	Y-339
CAMPBELL, John	1844	4-3-4	W-214	MONTGOMERY, Mitchell	1840	17-4-3	Y-374
COLLIFLOWER, Sam'l	1832	23-8-7	W-237	STANBERY, Jonas	1835	18-1-3	Y-428
HALL, John	1837	4-1-3	W-352	KELL, Robert	1835	26-9-10	Y-462
STANBERY, Jonas	1837	36-9-10	W-564	STURGES, Solomon	1844	10-4-4	Y-510
WAGSTAFF, James	1837	10-3-4	W-582	HAWES, Wells	1840	9-4-4	Y-544
STEVENS, James	1832	19-8-8	W-598	BUCHANAN, Thomas	1835	15-4-2	Z-9
STEVENS, James	1835	24-8-9	W-598	BRADFORD, James	1835	12-2-4	Z-116
LAUGHLIN, Joseph	1837	23-8-9	W-633	SIMPSON, Joseph	1835	11-2-4	Z-121
MORRIS, Jonathan J.	1835	20-8-8	X-102	STANBERRY, Jonas	1844	16-4-3	Z-131
LAUGHLIN, Joseph	1837	23-8-9	X-102	ADAMS, --?-----	!*#!	4-3-2	Z-217
STURGES, Solomon	1844	12-4-4	X-103	CRAWFORD, John	1835	13-3-2	Z-285
WINN, William	1837	31-8-9	X-122	McDONALD, William	1838	6-3-4	Z-320
STANBERRY, Howard	1844	17-3-4	X-134	SNODGRASS, James	1840	6-3-4	Z-320
COULTER, Elizabeth	1849	22-1-4	X-199	BRUSH, Daniel	1838	2-3-4	Z321
KACKLEY, John	1837	33-8-9	X 210	ATKINSON, Robert	1837	2-3-4	Z-322
HELLYER, Robert	1835	33-8-9	X-210	SHERRARD, William	1835	10-2-4	Z-357
HELLYER, Elijah	1837	33-8-9	X-211	BUCKINGHAM, Alvah	1840	8-3-4	Z-365
HELLYER, Elijah	1837	33-8-9	X-212	ATWOOD, Cornelius	1838	13-3-4	Z-366
STURGES, Solomon	1837	25-4-2	X-217	SMITH, Mary	1837	13-1-2	Z-376
RICH, Jacob	1835	2-8-8	X-258	STURGES, Solomon	1838	7-3-2	Z399
ROSITER, Thomas	1839	3-8-8	X-258	JENKINS, Edward	1837	15-1-3	Z-411
DUFF, Oliver	1837	18-3-4	X-334	LINCH, James	1835	14-3-4	Z-417
INGLEHART, Adam	1844	9-4-4	X336	STURGES, Solomon	1835	13-3-4	Z-444
BUCKINGHAM, Alvia	1837	24-9-10	X-338	STURGES, Solomon	1835	13-3-4	Z-445
TORODE, John	1837	4-1-3	X-397	CLARK, Samuel	1838	4-1-2	Z-621
SWEARINGEN, Thomas	1838	23-4-4	X-524	McKNIGHT, Samuel	1835	11-2-4	1-21

McELHEREN, Joseph	1838	11-3-4	1-144
STANBERY, Howard	1844	13-3-4	1-149
REED, William	1837	21-4-4	1-170
OLIVER, Thomas	1835	25-4-1	1-439
KILBRIDE, Michael	1844	7-3-4	1-459
RANNELLS, David	1835	26-9-10	2-1
ZIMMERMAN, John	1844	10-3-4	2-63
McCULLEY, Matthew	1835	14-3-4	2-90
McCULLEY, Matthew	1835	14-3-4	2-92
BROWN, John	1837	3-3-4	2-184
BUCKINGHAM, Alvah	1837	3-3-4	2-185
BRUSH, Daniel	1837	21-4-4	2-185
FRAME, John	1835	14-1-2	2-231
BRADSHAW, James	1837	10-3-3	2-331
BRADSHAW, James	1838	10-3-3	2-332
KELL, John	1831	16-3-2	2-392
DULL, David	1854	5-3-3	2-497
LISLE, Robert	1831	3-2-4	3-31
HAMMOND, David P.	1835	6-2-3	3-93
MORRISON, Alex.	1842	2-3-4	3-273
MORRISON, Alex.	1842	3-3-4	3-274
SMYTHE, William	1851	2-3-4	3-313
GANT, Richard	1837	20-3-4	3-430
GANT, Richard	1838	20-3-4	3-431
MISKIMINS, Isaac	1835	5-4-3	4-80
MISKIMINS, Isaac	1835	5-4-3	4-81
STANBERY, Howard	1840	5-4-3	4-81
PALMER, John	1844	5-4-3	4-82
PALMER, John	1844	5-4-3	4-83
MITCHELL, Hance	1837	4-3-3	5-301
BYE, Jonathan	1837	6-1-2	5-128
McGOWAN, George	1838	3-3-4	5-261
McGOWAN, George	1840	3-3-4	5-262
BRITTON, Robert	1837	20-4-3	5-330
KINKEAD, David	1840	1-3-3	5-582
STURGES, Solomon	1844	17-3-4	5-594
STANBERY, Jonas	1837	6-1-3	6-206
STANBERY, Jonas	1837	15-1-3	6-206
HUFFMAN, Robt. F.	1837	10-3-2	6-273
DAVIS, Jos. G.	1853	9-4-4	6-326
DAVIS, Jos. G.	1853	6-3-3	6-327
REED, Hezekiah B.	1837	5-1-2	6-583
FULLER, Abel	1837	11-4-4	7-224
MUSKIMINS, Harrison	1840	12-4-4	7-225
JONES, Asbury	1838	2-4-3	7-305
EMERSON, John	1831	11-1-1	8-321
CHANDLER, Isaac	1837	4-4-3	10-345
DENNISON, Henry	1835	15-1-3	10-447
DENNISON, Henry	1835	15-1-3	10-448
HOLCOMB, James	1844	15-3-4	245-51
HAWTHORN, John Mc.	1837	16-3-4	271-530

STURGES, Solomon	1844	10-4-4	11-405
STURGES, Solomon	1840	10-4-4	11-405
STURGES, Solomon	1844	10-4-4	11-406
BRATSHAW, Jos. B. H.	1840	6-4-3	12-10
SUNNAFRANK, Jacob	1831	20-2-4	12-42
MISKIMINS, James	1837	8-4-4	12-50
STANSBERY, Jonas	1844	15-4-2	13-481
MORROW, William	1832	18-3-4	13-718
WILLIAMS, Nehemiah	1835	3-1-3	13-728
SILLS, David	1837	22-4-3	14-471
REEVES, Menasseh	1831	10-2-3	14-544
EVANS, John C.	1837	1-4-3	15-112
GREGORY, John	1837	10-4-3	15-113
MAXWELL, Joseph	1838	4-1-3	15-224
MAXWELL, David	1835	4-1-3	15-225
MARLATT, Abraham	1837	2-4-4	16-354
SMITH, John	1831	8-4-2	17-328
SMITH, John	1831	8-4-2	17-328
JONES, John L.	1844	8-4-2	17-565
PRESTLEY, Joseph	1837	21-4-3	19-189
PRESTLEY, Joseph	1835	21-4-3	19-238
BEADENHEAD, Coonrod	1844	10-4-4	20-321
MORROW, James	1844	16-3-4	22-1
DISSALUMS, John	1835	12-3-4	23-16
LENT, Ludlow	1835	13-3-4	23-317
STEWART, James	1835	10-2-3	27-308
STEWART, James	1835	10-2-3	27-309
SMITH, Henry	1837	14-1-2	31-31
BLAIR, William	1837	12-2-4	35-39
HALL, David	1831	23-8-7	35-228
ENGLE, Job	1832	24-8-7	35-228
GOSSET, Jacob	1831	26-9-7	35-410
GREEN, Jacob	1835	5-1-2	37-361
MITCHELL, Hance	1832	3-3-3	37-480
HAMMERSLY, Isaac	1835	2-3-3	38-431
LUCCOCK, Nephtali	1831	23-4-3	38-432
WYRICK, Peter Jr.	1837	2-3-3	38-433
THOMPSON, David	1832	8-1-2	38-506
MAGEE, James	1838	13-1-4	39-23
MAGEE, James	1835	13-1-4	39-24
CHANEY, William	1840	4-4-3	39-501
BOTTS, John	1835	8-1-2	42-473
McCANN, Thomas	1835	13-1-2	42-474
NORRIS, Joseph	1840	12-4-4	43-301
RUSSELL, Thomas	1835	23-1-3	44-543
BLACK, Samuel	1833	7-2-2	59-136
NELSON, Robert	1837	14-1-3	93-256
NORRIS, John	1831	8-2-4	229-536
BRUSH, Daniel	1844	6-3-4	245-51
HAWTHORN, John Mc.	1838	16-3-4	271-531
HAWTHORN, John Mc.	1844	16-3-4	271-532

The following records were abstracted for genealogical information and are
to be used as a finding aid. Due to the fact that many were quite detailed,
land descriptions have not been included. It should be remembered that at
this early date (prior to 1803), Hamilton County's boundaries included a
large portion of southern Ohio. Many of the mortgages to John Cleves
Symmes were levied on at a suit of Gashom Gard vs. John C. Symmes on October
19, 1803; however, some mortgages were assigned to others. Terms followed
by Symmes in disposing of his land were that each purchaser was bound to begin improvements within two years, or forfeit one-sixth of the land to whom-
soever would settle thereon and remain seven years.

    Abbreviations used are: P of A = Power of Attorney.

                   Mtg. = Mortgage.

Page on which record may be found is given in parenthesis.

12-16-1794 - John MAHONEY to Samuel OSBURN. (1)

5-30-1795 - Oliver SPENCER and Anne, his wife, to Caleb HALSTED, Jr. (4)

8-30-1794 - Jonathan DAYTON of Elizabethtown, N. J. to Israel LUDLOW,
           P of A. (7)

8-7-1795 - Elias D. GRIFFITH to Samuel WILLIAMS. (8)

11-17-1795 - William PETERSON, license to operate Ferry opposite to Ferry
           established on Kentucky shore known as Wilson's Ferry. (10)

3-12-1796 - William TAIT to William STOTHART, both of Davidson Co., Tenn.,
           P ef A. (11)

3-12-1796 - Andrew EWING of Davidson Co., Tenn. to John GORDON, P of A. (13)

11-24-1792 - Samuel ROBINSON to Daniel DUFFIE, late of Pennsylvania. (14)

4-29-1796 - Jacob WICKERSHAM to John and Samuel ARMSTRONG. (16)

6-11-1789 - John Cleves SYMMES of North Bend to Maj. Benjamin STITES of
           Columbia and Capt. John Stites GANOE of Washington in Kentucky;
           recorded 5-4-1796. (21)

4-22-1796 - William WALLACE of Ohio Co., Va. to David EDIE, P of A. (26)

5-11-1796 - Wm. WARD and Simon KENTON of Mason Co., Ky. to Reuben CLARKE,
           P of A. (28)

1-15-1795 - Joel WILLIAMS to Israel LUDLOW. (30)

6-13-1796 - John EGEAN, aged 29 yrs. binds himself as a servant for five
           years to Doctor John SELLMAN. (31)

9-23-1795 - John N. CUMMINGS of New Arkin, Essex Co., N. J. to William C.
           SCHENCK and Israel LUDLOW; P of A. (33)

7-23-1794 - Will of Richard GRAHAM of Tyrone Twp., Fayette Co., Pennsylvania,
           yeoman. Wife, Elizabeth to have 200 acres being Military Warrant
           #2311. Sons: Noble, Thomas and Richard Graham. Daughter, Sarah
           Graham. Executors: Wife, Elizabeth and sons, Richard and Noble.
           Signed: Richard (mark) Graham. Witnesses: Jacob Stewart, Sam-
           uel Cochran, Thomas Grimes and Sarah Grimes. Recorded 8-2-1796. (35)

8-16-1796 - Thomas COCHRAN to Abraham KIRKPATRICK, Esq. of Pittsburgh, Pa. (38)

8-15-1796 - Thomas COCHRAN to Benjamin STITES, Sr. (42)

8-17-1796 - Thomas COCHRAN, innkeeper to Benjamin STITES, Sr.; Bill of Sale. (45)

2-15-1792 - William LYTLE of Fayette Co., Ky., agent or attorney for
           Robt. TODD to Jno NEALY. (47)

4-12-1796 - Bennet TOMPKINS of Caroline Co., Va. to Wm. CLARK of Jefferson
    Co., Kentucky, P of A. (49)
5-19-1795 - Hugh GASTON of Washington Twp., Northumberland Co., Pa. to Bro-
    ther John GASTON; P of A. (50)
10-15-1796 - Ann WILSON, James BRISON and Andrew BOGGS, executors of the will
    of William WILSON, late of Pittsburgh, Allegheny Co., Pa., to
    James ROBINSON; P of A. (52)
8-7-1797 - David ACHESON of Washington, Pa. to Daniel DUFFY; Agreement. (54)
9-23-1791 - Jonathan DAYTON of Elizabethtown, N. J., to Isaac FREEMAN;
    Agreement. (55)
1-26-1797 - Robert ADAMS and James LAWSON; Bond to establish Ferry opposite
    to Ferry now established at mouth of Cabin Crick on Kentucky
    shore. (56)
1-12-1797 - Nathaniel MASSIE to George PORTER and Joshua PORTER, jr. of
    Baltimore Co. Maryland. (58)
11-24-1796 - Elizabeth CLEMENTS, widow of Forgerson Clements to her child-
    ren: James, Alexander, Forgerson, Elizabeth, John, Joseph,
    Grier, Isaac and Jesse who she had by her deceased husband,
    Forgerson Clements. Consideration of her love for said chil-
    dren. (59)
11-12-1796 - Dafney HOGSET, a negro girl bound as an apprentice to Owen TODD. (61)
6-26-1796 - Thomas DOYLE to Charles VITIER. (63)
7-8-1797 - Robert MITCHELL, Merchant, and Frances, his wife, to Thomas
    GIBSON and Arthur ST. CLAIR, Jr., agents or executors of the
    estate of Henry REED, dec'd. (64)
2-17-1797 - Isaac ANDERSON to Samuel RIDDLE and Willoughby Washington
    LANE, Merchants, of Franklin County, Pennsylvania. (66)
8-17-1797 - William CHRIBBS, Merchant, and Elizabeth, his wife. to Charles
    WILKINS of Kentucky, agent of John and Charles WILKINS Company
    of Allegheny Co., Pennsylvania. (69)
8-15-1797 - Jesse HUNT to Rose, a slave woman aged 22 years. Her Freedom. (70)
8-15-1797 - Rose, a free negro bound to Jesse HUNT. (71)
5-8-1797 - George O'HARA of Morristown, Morris Co., N. J., to Daniel C.
    COOPER; P of A. (72)
5-21-1796 - George W. BURNET of Newark, Essex Co., N. J., to Jacob BURNET:
    P of A. (75)
6-10-1796 - John MERCER and wife Susanna to Abijah and Jesse HUNT,
    Merchants; Mtg. (77)
3-17-1795 - Peter GREEN to Kennedy MORTON. (82)
2-1-1798 - Robert FLACK to Samuel DICK. (83)
2-1-1798 - John BROWN to Alexander McLAUGHLIN & Oliver ORMSBY,
    Merchants; Mtg. (84)
8-10-1796 - John C. SYMMES to Daniel C. COOPER; Agreement. (86)
3-29-1798 - James FISHER to Joel WILLIAMS. (87)
8-13-1796 - John C. SYMMES to William C. SCHENCK; Agreement. (89)
4-15-1798 - Andrew CHRISTY to John Cleves SYMMES; Mtg. (90)
1-24-1791 - Joel WILLIAMS to Richard BENHAM. (92)
11-18-1797 - Francis L. COOCH of Philadelphia, Pa., Merchant, to Samson
    McCULLOUGH; P of A. (93)
3-14-1798 - Jesse and Abijah HUNT to John Cleves SYMMES; Mtg. (94)

553

7-25-1798 - John S. GANO to John C. SYMMES. (96)
7-16-1798 - John BRINEY (Johann BRINNIG) to John C. SYMMES; Mtg. (97)
2-10-1796 - John Cleves SYMMES and wife Susan to David McGAUGHEY. (99)
11-13-1797 - Fredereck DELOW (DEELO) and Elizabeth, his wife, to Jacob
    Stewart. (100)
2-10-1798 - John C. SYMMES and Susan, his wife, to John HOLLANDS. (101)
10-15-1798 - Israel SHREEVE to James COON and Charles COON. (102)
4-30-1798 - James and Samuel ARMSTRONG to John VAN NUYS. (103)
1-7-1799 - William T. CULLUM to John C. SYMMES; Mtg. (104)
1-7-1799 - George CULLUM, Sr. to John C. SYMMES; Mtg. (106)
11-1-1798 - Silas HOWELL to John C. SYMMES; Mtg. (107)
1-25-1799 - James COX to John C. SYMMES; Mtg. (109)
2-2-1799 - James LOWES to James MOORE. (110)
12-18-1798 - John McCHESNEY to William H. HARRISON. (113)
4-27-1799 - James COLWELL to Archibald HOOD of Washington Co., Pa, Mer-
    chant; P of A. (114)
5-13-1799 - John GREER to Wm. Patrick DICKEY; Bill of Sale. (115)
5-5-1799 - Thomas COCHRAN of Campbell Co., Ky. and Phebe, his wife, to
    John C. SYMMES. (115)
9-17-1796 - John C. SYMMES to Wm. James BYARS. (118)
2-9-1799 - Derick LOWE of Somerset Co., N. J. to son, Jacob LOWE, P of A. (118)
6-15-1797 - Willis WILSON and Elizabeth, his wife, of Cumberland Co.,
    Va. to George NICOLSON of Richmond, Virginia. (120)
4-22-1799 - Robert McCLELLAN of Mason Co., Ky. to Daniel VEITNER. (122)
2-28-1799 - Mary PHIBBS to James ADAMS. (124)
1-4-1799 - John BROWN of Frankfort, Franklin Co., Ky. by James BROWN, his
    attorney, to Jacob SPEARS of Bourbon Co., Ky. (124)
9-9-1799 - Thomas GIBSON to Oliver ORMSBY of Pittsburgh, Allegheny Co, Pa. (127)
8-16-1799 - John RADLEY of Mill Creek, Miami Purchase to John C. SYMMES;
    Mtg. (129)
12-16-1798 - Christian WALLSMITH of Highbottom on Little Miami to John C.
    SYMMES: Mtg. (131)
6-5-1799 - Asa HINKLE to John C. SYMMES: Mtg. (133)
12-9-1798 - Brice VIRGIN to John C. SYMES; Mtg. (135)
6-25-1799 - David BRICOURT to John C. SYMMES; Mtg. (137)
8-7-1799 - Cornelia PARSELL, widow of Richard PARSELL, dec'd, to John C.
    SYMMES; Mtg. (139)
6-24-1799 - Joseph CATTERLIN to John Cleves SYMMES; Mtg. (141)
8-8-1799 - John PARSELL to John Cleves SYMMES; Mtg. (143)
8-8-1799 - Richard PARSELL to John Cleves SYMMES; Mtg. (146)
8-8-1799 - Samuel BAXTER to John Cleves SYMMES; Mtg. (148)
12-16-1798 - George HAMER to John Cleves SYMMES; Mtg. (150)
9-8-1797 - Elias BONDINOT to Cornelius R. SEDAN and Abijah HUNT; Agreement
    and P of A. (152)
8 -16-1799 - John EWING to John Cleves SYMMES; Mtg. (154)
3-10-1798 - James BENNET to John Cleves SYMMES. (156)
10-5-1799 - John Cleves SYMMES to Doctor Evan BANE; Mtg. (159)
10-5-1799 - John Cleves SYMMES to John SMITH. (162)
10-5-1799 - John Cleves SYMMES to Samuel HEIGHWAY of Waynesville. (166)
6-11-1799 - John HERVEY late of Kentucky to John Cleves SYMMES; Mtb.(169)

554

6-11-1799 - Joseph PEAK of Kentucky to John Cleves SYMMES; Mtg. (171)
6-11-1799 - Peter MURPHY of Kentucky to John Cleves SYMMES; Mtg. (173)
9-12-1799 - John SEWARD to John Cleves SYMMES. (176)
7-6-1799 - John CASSIDY to John Cleves SYMMES; Mtg. (178)
6-22-1799 - Peter MURPHY of Kentucky to John Cleves SYMMES; Mtg. (179)
12-29-1798 - George FITHIAN to John Cleves SYMMES. (183)
8-16-1799 - Hugh EWING lately of Berkeley Co., Va. to John Cleves SYMMES;
           Mtg. (185)
6-11-1799 - Thomas VIRGIN, son of Brice VIRGIN, to John Cleve SYMMES; Mtg.
11-1-1799 - Levi JENNINGS and Elizabeth, his wife, to John Stites   (187)
           GANO. (190)
12-2-1799 - John Cleves SYMMES to Miss Ferguson, daughter and heiress of
           Wm. Ferguson, dec'd. (192)
11-11-1790 - James HENRY of Somerset Co., N. J. to Israel LUDLOW. (194)
9-17-1792 - James HENRY of Lamberton, N. J. to Israel LUCLOW. (196)
6-4-1799 - John BROWN to Jacob BROADWELL; Brown received Virginia Military
           Warrant #2294 of 200 acres for consideration of 3 years service
           as Sgt. in Va. Cont'l Line, surveyed 10-21-1792, with Brown
           assigning his title and interest to same, to Broadwell. (196)
6-4-1799 - John BROWN to Jacob BROADWELL; Robert BROWN received Virginia
           Military Warrant #2296 of 100 acres for serving 3 years as
           soldier in Va. Cont'l Line, surveyed 10-21-1792, with John
           Brown as heir of his brother, Robert Brown, assigning title
           and interest to Broadwell. (198)
10-3-1799 - John HOLLANDS to John KIDD; Mtg. (199)
6-3-1799 - Nicholas JOHNSTON of Greenwich Twp., Cumberland Co., N. J. to
           Abraham ROGERS of Downs, Cumberland Co., N. J.; P of A. (201)
9-20-1799 - David DENMAN to John Cleves SYMMES; Mtg. (203)
9-12-1799 - Ziba WINGENT to John Cleves SYMMES; Mtg. (205)
11-5-1799 - Allen CULLUM to John Cleves SMMMES; Mtg. (208)
9-13-1799 - John McGILLAND to John Cleves SYMMES; Mtg. (210)
9-10-1799 - John BRAND to John Cleves SYMMES; Mtg. (213)
10-5-1799 - George VANNOSTRANT to John Cleves SYMMES; Mtg. (215)
8-4-1799 - Samuel WILLIAMS to John Cleves SYMMES. (218)
11-28-1799 - John INGRAM to John C. SYMMES; Mtg. (220)
5-28-1799 - James WHITE to John Cleves SYMMES; Mtg. (223)
6-5-1799 - Michael BROKAW to John Cleves SYMMES; Mtg. (225)
1-16-1799 - John WALLACE to John Cleves SYMMES; Mtg. (228)
11-22-1799 - Christian REMLY, late of Kentucky, to John Cleves SYMMES;
           Mtg. (231)
12-23-1799 - John ARMSTRONG to Aaron FOFORTH; P of A as Territorial
           Treasurer. (233)
8-5-1799 - Aaron CADWELL to John SHAW. (235)
2-6-1800 - William LOWES to John McCORMICK; Mtg. (237)
2-7-1800 - Stephen OSBORNE to John Cleves SYMMES; Mtg. (239)
2-7-1800 - Wm. John JONES to John Cleves SYMMES; Mtg. (241)
12-18-1799 - John SEWARD to John Cleves SYMMES; Mtg. (242)
2-5-1800 - John HUMES to John Cleves SYMMES; Mtg. (246)
8-26-1799 - John EARNEST, late of Mason Co., Ky., to John Cleves SYMMES; Mtg. (249)

9-17-1799 - Joseph FOOR of Brackin Co., Ky. to John Cleves SYMMES; Mtg.(251)
9-17-1799 - Conrad COOK of Mason Co., Ky. to John Cleves SYMMES; Mtg. (254)
8-26-1799 - Patrick BRODERICK to John Cleves SYMMES; Mtg. (256)
8-1-1799 - Thomas YOUNGBLENDE to John Cleves SYMMES; Mtg. (259)
8-8-1799 - Archibald McCREARY of Redstone, Fayette Co., Pa. to John C.
          SYMMES; Mtg. (261)
2-25-1800 - Robert PLATT and Nancy, his wife, of Boone Co., Ky., to David
          E. WADE. (264)
3-15-1800 - Thomas GOUDY and Sarah, his wife, to David E. WADE. (266)
6-22-1799 - John HERVEY to John Cleves SYMMES; Mtg. (268)
2-5-1800 - Darius C. ORCUTT to John Cleves SYMMES; Mtg. (270)
2-11-1800 - Samuel ERWIN to John Cleves SYMMES; Mtg. (272)
2-12-1800 - Samuel LINE to John Cleves SYMMES; Mtg. (275)
2-5-1800 - William BRODRICK to John Cleves SYMMES; Mtg. (277)
1-16-1799 - James MORRIS to John Cleves SYMMES; Mtg. (279)
1-16-1799 - Samuel SERRING to John Cleves SYMMES; Mtg. (281)
2-25-1800 - James McCLELLAND of Kentucky to John Cleves SYMMES; Mtg. (283)
1-16-1799 - James KAMPER to John Cleves SYMMES; Mtg. (284)
3-28-1800 - Oliver SPENCER to Doctor Richard ALLISON. (287)
2-17-1800 - Samuel JAMES to Michael BROKAW. (288)
3-1-1799 - William HUSE to John THARP. (290)
11-16-1797 - John Stites GANO and Mary, his wife, to Peter DRAKE, yeoman; (291)
1-28-1800 - George ROBERTSON and Elleanor, his wife, to Dominious
          ABBETT. (293)
5-3-1799 - John Cleves SYMMES to Jeremiah BRANN; Brann, a volunteer settler
          being the first applicant who has duly entered for forfeiture,
          lands (under terms for forfeiture of land under Symmes origin-
          al papers), said forfeited lands originally entered by Nehemiah
          TUNIS of N. J., who has not complied with terms. (295)
7-12-1799 - John Cleves SYMMES to James WHITE; Agreement. (297)
2-5-1800 - John Cleves SYMMES to John HUMES. (298)
12-25-1798 - William RUFFIN; Ferry license. (300)
8-26-1795 - Joel WILLIAMS; Ferry license. (302)
1-1-1800 - Amos HARRIS to Thomas WILLIAMS. (302)
8-27-1799 - James TAIMAN; Ferry license. (304)
3-27-1799 - William FEE; Ferry license, from mouth of Bullskin to that
          established on opposite shore in Kentucky. (305)
6-4-1800 - Matthew TOMSON of Clark Co., Ky., to Jase VONDSLAH. (306)
3-30-1798 - John Cleves SYMMES to David FLINN; forfeited land entered by
          John Joseph HENRY. (307)
5-1-1800 - John S. GANO and William STANLEY to John FIELDS and Son,
          Merchants. (310)
12-3-1795 - James GILLESPIE to Joseph PRINCE. (313)
2-26-1800 - John CASSIDY and Sally, his wife, to James HARDIN. (315)
1-15-1799 - John CORELY and Elizabeth, his wife, to Stephen DAVIS. (317)
7-5-1800 - Archibald McMILLEN binds his son, James McMILLIN, as an
          apprentice in farming for a period of five years from date,
          to Lieut. Col. David STRONG of the 2nd U. S. Regiment. (319)
6-9-1800 - Wm. McFARLAND and Nancy, his wife, to George HOWARD. (321)

11-7-1795 - Jonathan DAYTON to Benjamin SCUDDER. (322)
11-7-1795 - Jonathan DAYTON to Benjamin SCUDDER. (325)
11-7-1795 - Jonathan DAYTON to Benjamin SCUDDER of N. J. (327)
10-1-1796 - Jonathan DAYTON to Benjamin WILLIAMS of Elizabethtown, N. J. (329)
7-15-1800 - David STRONG, Lt. Col. of the Armies of the U. S. to
        Doctor Richard ALLISON. (330)
5-31-1800 - George LEWIS and Mary, his wife, of Mason Co., Ky., to John
        McKIBBIN of same place. (332)
7-31-1799 - Jacob D. LOWE of Somerset Co., N. J., to William CHEESMAN of
        Mason Co., Ky. (337)
1-17-1800 - John MAN and Mahitabel, his wife, to Richard COLIVER. (337)
7-29-1800 - Gersham GARD to Justus GIBBS. (338)
8-7-1799 - John Cleves SYMMES to Sophia ERTILL, widow of Valentine ERTILL. (340)
4-1-1800 - David CUMMINGS to William M. KINSTON. (342)
7-19-1800 - William GOFORTH and Catherine, his wife, to Nathaniel Shepherd
        ARMSTRONG, late of Virginia, now of Ohio. (343)
8-11-1800 - Samuel DICK and Martha Allen, his wife, to Thomas WILLIAMS.(346)
5-26-1800 - John T. HALL of Beaver Creek near Pittsburgh, for Jacob LOWE
        and Derick LOWE to Jesse NEWPORT, Sr. (347)
8-5-1800 - John BALDING to Joseph MOSS. (349)
5-24-1800 - Job GARD and Elizabeth, his wife, to James FISHER. (351)
12-18-1798 - John Cleves SYMMES to Joseph MEEKER, assignee of Silas HALSEY. (353)
4-9-1800 - Dr. William WILES and Nancy Wiles of Norfolk Co., Va. to
        George MARTIN of same place; P of A. A military warrant was
        issued to Nancy GRIMES, now Nancy WILES wife of Wm. Wiles who
        is the legal representative of Wm. GRIMES, dec'd. (354)
9-1-1800 - Thomas ALSTON to James HENRY of Somerset Co., N. J. (356)
7-8-1800 - Adam WINN of Fayette Co., Ky. to Wm. FORD: P of A. (358)
2-16-1800 - Deposition of David CRITCHLEY as a witness. (360)

The following deed records were abstracted from Deed Book F-1. The pages of this deed book were not numbered; however, a number precedes each deed and these numbers have been given in parenthesis. These records have been abstracted primarily as a finding aid and for genealogical items—the land descriptions, which many times were long in length have not been given.

6-13-1801 - James CONN, Charles CONN and Patty his wife to James MAGINNIS. (1)
5-4-1804 - Ethan STONE to Jacob SHEELER. (1)
8-17-1804 - Jacob WHEELER and Joanna his wife to William CASTO. (2)
3-31-1798 - John Cleves SYMMES and wife Susan to James McCLELLAN. (3)
9-6-1803 - James MACHIR and Rebecca his wife of Hary Co., Va. to Moses BROADWELL.(3)
10-1-1800 - William WOODWARD to Cornelius VOORHEES. (4)
3-10-1804 - John S. GARNO and Mary his wife to Samuel HILDITCH. (5)
7-26-1804 - Nath'l TERWILLEGAR to Sam'l HILDITCH. (6)
12-31-1798 - Wm. GOFARTH Sr. and his wife Catharine to Wm. GOFARTH Jr. of Mason Co.,
                                Ky. (6)
12-31-1798 - Wm. GOFARTH Sr. and Catharine wife to Wm. GOFARTH Jr. of Mason Co. Ky.(8)
12-31-1798 - William GOFARTH Sr. and Catharine wife to John ARMSTRONG. (9)
8-2-1804 - Wm. GOFARTH to Alexander STEWART, Samuel DELAPHANE and Comfort SANDS;
                last three all of New York City, N. Y. (10)
12-26-1801 - Nath'l TERWILLEGAR and his wife Ann to John W. BROWNE. (12)
8-27-1804 - John EARNEST and Jane his wife to Josiah GWALTNEY. (12)
7-1-1795 - John Cleves SYMMES to Thomas RICH. (13)
11-20-1799 - Israel LUDLOW and Charlotte Chambers his wife to Patrick DICKEY.(14)
10-10-1798 - James BRADY and Jane his wife to Patrick DICKEY. (15)
6-28-1800 - William STANLEY and Sally his wife to Patrick DICKEY. (15)
6-23-1803 - John Cleves SYMMES to Patrick DICKEY. (16)
5-17-1804 - Joel WILLIAMS and Phebe his wife to Patrick DICKEY. (15)
4-9-1804 - Benjamin STILES and Hannah his wife to Wm. VAN HORNE of N. J. (17)
11-25-1803 - Hezekiah PRICE to Jacob FELTER. (18)
11-26-1787 - Peter PELSER to Hermann PARSONS. (19)
7-1-1795 - John Cleves SYMMES to Thomas RICH of Fayette Co., Pa. (20)
9-1-1804 - John Cleves SYMMES to McKEARN of Warren Co., Ohio. (20)
8-8-1799 - John Cleves SYMMES to Andrew WILSON. (21)
6-24-1799 - John Cleves SYMMES to John WINGENT. (22)
3-16-1803 - James SMITH, Sheriff to Moses MITCHELL. (22)
9-4-1804 - Nath'l DENMAN and Susanna his wife to Edward SMITH. (24)
7-8-1804 - Albin SHAW and Eunice his wife to Jeremiah BUTTERFIELD. (24)
8-31-1804 - Jeremiah BUTTERFIELD and Polly his wife to Stephen CAMPBELL. (25)
7-23-1804 - Albin SHAW and Eunice his wife to Noah WILLEY. (26)
7-23-1804 - Noah WILLEY and Elizabeth his wife to Alexander SIMPSON. (27)
7-23-1804 - Albin SHAW and Eunice his wife to Knowles SHAW. (28)
5-16-1803 - Wm. LUDLOW and Elizabeth his wife to Anthony HIGHLAND. (29)
4-23-1804 - Edward COEN and Margaret his wife to Wm. TERRY. (29)
5-1-1804 - Wm. TERRY and Rebecca his wife to Edward COEN. (30)
7-23-1804 - Abraham VOORHEES and Mary his wife to Samuel FRAZY. (31)
9-14-1802 - John HUMES and Margaret his wife to Chas. VATTIER. (32)
9-12-1804 - Samuel KITCHELL and Margaret his wife to John FULLER. (33)
3-10-1803 - James SMITH, Sheriff to John SMITH. (33)
4-10-1803 - James SMITH, Sheriff to John SMITH. (35)
9-10-1803 - James SMITH, Sheriff to John SMITH. (38)

9-10-1802 – James SMITH, Sheriff to John SMITH. (39)
6-1-1803 – Ethan STONE and Abigail M. his wife to Samuel STITT. (40)
2-10-1804 – James SMITH, Sheriff to Chas. VATTIER. (41)
3-3-1801 – John Cleves SYMMES to John COCHRAN. (43)
1-10-1801 – John Cleves SYMMES to Andrew SPEARS. (44)
6-13-1801 – Andrew SPEARS to John C. SYMMES Jr. (45)·
8-1-1804 – Abraham VOORHEES and Mary his wife to John LUDLOW. (45)
10-1-1804 – Frederick COONSE and Catharine his wife to Betsey DEXTER. (46)
5-19-1803 – William STEWART and Sarah his wife to Henry JENNINGS. (47)
8-13-1803 – Benjamin STITES and Hannah his wife to John McADAMS. (47)
6-1-1804 – Cornelius R. SEDAM and Eliza his wife to Edward COEN. (48)
6-15-1804 – Isaac MORRIS and Rebecca his wife to John SMITH. (49)
9-19-1804 – Jonathan STITES to John SMITH. (50)
6-16-1798 – Thomas DOYLE and Margaret his wife to Nancy CHRISTY. (50)
7-3-1804 – Albin SHAW and Eunice his wife to Asa HARVEY. (51)
10-8-1804 – Chas. FARREN to James RUSSELL. (52)
10-6-1804 – Conrad FEAGUE and Eve his wife to Felty ANDREWS. (53)
8-29-1803 – David GRUMMORE (or Greenmore) and Rachel his wife to David NICHOLS. (54)
3-1-1802 – Isaac FERRIS, Sr. and Mary his wife to Joseph CLARK. (54)
6-1-1803 – Joseph REEDER and Anne his wife to Jonah HEATON. (55)
10-20-1804 – Jonah HEATON Sr. and Margaret his wife to Jonah H EATON Jr. (56)
7-20-1801 – Israel LUDLOW to Christopher CARY. (57)
10-15-1804 – John Cleves SYMMES to Conrad FEAGUE. (57)
10-29-1804 – John STEELE of the City of Natchez by Wm. STEELE his attorney of
              Woodford Co., Ky. to John BETTS. (58)
10-29-1804 – John STEELE of the City of Natchez by Wm. STEELE his attorney of
              Woodford Co., Ky. to Stephen DAVIS. (59)
10-29-1804 – John STEELE of the City of Natchez by Wm. STEELE his attorney of
              Woodford Co., Ky. to Joseph Williamson. (60)
6-25-1795 – John Cleves SYMMES and Susan his wife to Hezekiah STITES. (61)
8-30-1804 – Benjamin STITES and Hannah his wife to Hezekiah STITES. (62)
7-23-1804 – Patrick DICKEY and Peggy his wife to James FERGUSON. (63)
3-29-1804 – Asa RICHARDSON and Margaret his wife to James FERGUSON. (63)
4-17-1804 – Asa RICHARDSON and Mary his wife to James FERGUSON. (64)
11-6-1804 – Manassa BROWNE and Mary his wife to Garrit VOOHEES. (65)
10-18-1801– John C. SYMMES to Horatio R. DAYTON; Horation R. Dayton being the
              husband of Cornelia the daughter of Doctor Jonathan I.
              Dayton of Elizabethtowne, New Jersey. (66)
10-29-1804 – Peter SMITH and Catharine his wife to Samuel SMITH. (67)
8-2-1802 – Isaac FERRIS, Sr. and Mary his wife to John FERRIS. (68)
12-18-1802 – Isaac FERRIS and Mary his wife to Abraham FERRIS. (68)
10-9-1804 – Conrad KOTTS, Sheriff to Christ'r CAREY. (69)
11-5-1804 – Chas. AVERY to Conrad FEAGUE. (70)
12-5-1804 – Chas. AVERY to Conrad FEAGUE. (71)
9-20-1804 – Mathias CROW to Nath'l DENMAN. (71)
11-15-1804 – John C. SYMMES to James BLACKBURN. (72)
11-12-1804 – James McGINNIS and Lucy his wife to R. MERRIE and P. McNICHOL. (72)
11-16-1804 – James BLACKBURN of Warren Co., Ohio to George HOWARD. (73)
8-6-1804 – Asa S. RICHARDSON to George CHAMBERLAIN. (74)
11-5-1804 – Conrad FEAGUE and Eve his wife to Chas. AVERY. (75)
2-17-1803 – Israel SHREVE by Sheriff, James SMITH to James CONN. (76)

559

6-19-1804 - Peter DAVIS and Catharine his wife to Henry VANZANT. (77)
11-24-1804 - Jeremiah MILLS and Abigail his wife to Nathaniel BRIANT. (78)
5-24-1804 - David LAYMON and Susan his wife to Joseph COX; both of Butler Co., Ohio(78)
5-25-1799 - John C. SYMMES to Ephraim KILBY. (79)
11-28-1804 - John C. SYMMES to Josiah HARMER, Brig. General U. S. Command. (80)
11-18-1804 - Abijah WARD and Esther his wife to Chas. VATTIER. (81)
11-18-1804 - Calvin KITCHELL and Mary his wife to Chas. VATTIER. (82)
12-13-1803 - Alexander McKee to Joseph COLBY. (82)
12-12-1798 - John C. SYMMES to Isaac WINANTS of New Jersey. (83)
3-15-1803. - John R. MILLS, Collector to Thomas CARTER. (84)
12-17-1804 - John FISHER of Butler Co., Ohio to Joseph LANG. (85)
11-13-1804 - Matthew G. WALLACE and Deborah his wife to David CONNER. (85)
8-18-1804 - Benjamin STITES and Hannah his wife is Elijah INMAN. (86)
11-26-1787 - John C. SYMMES to Daniel CAMMEION. (87)
11-19-1804 - Jesse HUNT to Abijah HUNT of Natchez in the Mississippi Territory.(88)
5-1-1795 - John C. SYMMES and Susan his wife to Daniel HOWELL. (89)
9-13-1804 - Moses HUTCHINGS and Sarah his wife to Levy ESTILL. (90)
12-13-1804 - Conrad TEAGUE and Eve his wife to Hugh MOORE. (91)
11-16-1804 - Calvin KITCHELL and Mary his wife to Piercy KITCHELL. (91)
12-26-1803 - Jonathan MUNDLE and Catharine his wife to John Whetstone. (92)
9-14-1804 - Levi ESTIL to James McCLELLAND. (93)
12-28-1804 - Isaac FERRIS and Mary his wife to Archibald HOSBROOK. (94)
6-19-1804 - Peter DAVIS and Catharine his wife to Hamilton BLACKBURNE. (94)
2-4-1804 - Josephus GARD and Sarah his wife to Levi GARD. (95)
10-15-1788 - Jonathan DAYTON to Ephraim KILBY. (96)
5-14-1799 - Jonathan DAYTON to Ephraim KILLEY. (97)
8-8-1799 - John C. SYMMES to John HOLE, of Westfield, Essex Co., N. J. (98)
12-10-1804 - Barnabus (Barney) McCARRAN to Thomas CISSNA; both of Butler Co., O.(99)
————1804 - Asa Harvey, Christopher HARVEY, Charles CONE and Jane his wife, Richard
         MACK and Betty his wife, Samuel HUSTON and Elizabeth his wife, John
         RAMSEY Jr. and Lucy his wife, all of Hamilton County, and Jabez WARNER
         and Sarah his wife of East Hadden, Hartford Co., Conn. to John CAMPBELL.
         (100)
10-10-1804 - Esther HARVEY to John CAMPBELL. Quit Claim. (101)
11-26-1804 - Albin SHAW to Knowles SHAW, John SHAW, Salla SHAW, Rueben ROOD and
         Huldah ROOD his wife, heirs of John SHAW, Esq. of Hamilton Co.,
         dec'd. (102)
9-27-1804 - Knowles SHAW and Sophia his wife to Isaac OGG. (103)
6-23-1804 - Auditors by attachment of Robert PARK to Culbertson PARK. (104)
3-23-1798 - John Cleves SYMMES to Elizabeth WINDSOR. (105)
3-20-1801 - Elizabeth WINSOR to Joseph BLACKBURN. (106)
12-4-1804 - Marsh WILLIAMS and Nancy his wife to Abraham CHASE. (106)
1-15-1805 - Ezekiel HUTCHINSON and Elizabeth his wife to Jonathan HUTCHINSON. (107)
9-7-1804 - Joel WILLIAMS and Phebe his wife to John MAHARD. (108)
9-7-1804 - Joel WILLIAMS and Phebe his wife to Daniel CONNER. (109)
9-5-1804 - Joel WILLIAMS and Phebe his wife to Edward H. STALL. (110)
1-23-1805 - Lewis LAING and Claresy his wife to John DILL & Co. (110)
1-25-1805 - Alexander KING and Olivia his wife to Patrick COYLE. (111)
1-29-1805 - Joel WILLIAMS and Phebe his wife to Doctor John CRAMMER. (112)
3-30-1804 - Ethan STONE and Abigail his wife to Stephen WHEELER. (113)
6-22-1803 - Ethan STONE and Abigail his wife to Stephen WHEELER. (114)

12-1-1798 - John Cleve SYMMES to Philip MASON. (115)
10-1-1804 - United States, Thomas Jefferson, President to Ezekiel HUGHES. (116)
8-5-1800 - Michael BROKAW and Esther his wife to John BALDWEN of Springfield twp.(117)
2-26-1803 - John McGLAUGHLIN and Pheby his wife to Dennis DUSKEY. (118)
2-4-1803 - Dennis DUSKEY and Rachel his wife to Nathan BARKLEY. (119)
12-20-1804 - John Cleves SYMMES to Francis MINISSIER. (119)
12-28-1799 - John RIDDLE and Mary his wife to Moses MILLER. (120)
2-12-1805 - Charles VALTIER and Pamela his wife to Andrew GILL. (121)
3-10-1804 - Michael AYRES, Daniel PAUGH, Daniel PRINE (PRYNE), James THOMPSON and
            Joseph McMAHON all of Butler Co., Ohio to David LEMMON of same. (122)
2-13-1797 - Joel WILLIAMS and Phebe his wife to Henry PICKLE. (123)
2-14-1805 - Henry PICKLE to Joel CRAIG. (124)
2-14-1805 - Charles VALTIER and Pamela his wife to Andrew DUNSETH. (125)
11-24-1804 - Daniel C. COOPER of Dayton, Montgomery Co., Ohio to Mary CHRIEST of
            Hamilton Co., Ohio. (126)
2-16-1805 - Matthew NIMMO and Mary his wife to John NIMMO and Sarah his wife. (127)
2-16-1805 - Matthew NIMMO and Mary his wife to John NIMMO and Sarah his wife. (129)
-----1805 - Peter KEENE of Colerain twp. to Gersham GARD. (131)
2-23-1805 - Gershem GARD and Phebe his wife of Springfield twp. to Peter KEENE. (132)
12-4-1795 - Gersham GARD and Phebe his wife of Miami twp. to Seth GARD. (133)
2-23-1805 - John CRAMMER to Conrad TEAGUE. (134)
2-26-1804 - Conrad TEAGUE and Eve his wife to Doctor John CRAMMER. (134)
2-27-1805 - Thomas STEAD and Margaret his wife to Robert COMPTON. (135)
8-29-1801 - Hans LECKIE to Benjamin SEARS. (136)
1-16-1805 - William COWAN to Benjamin SEARS. (137)
2-22-1805 - Moses MILLER and Phebe his wife to Jacob SKILLMAN. (138)
3-6-1805 - Henry BALSOR and Margaret his wife to Abraham YOST. (139)
1-8-1804 - Matthias DENMANN and Phebe his wife of Springfield twp. to Daniel C.
            COOPER. (140)
1-31-1805 - Taber WASHBURNE and Nancy his wife to Andrew DUNSETH. (141)
2-2-1798 - John Cleves SYMMES to James HAMILTON. (142)
9-4-1804 - William C. SCHENCK, Esq. late coroner of Hamilton Co. to James SMITH and
            James FINDLAY, Esq. (143)
8-20-1804 - Ebenezer Ward FENNEY of Springfield twp. to David SIMMONS of same. (144)
4-9-1805 - John BLACKBURN to David MORGAN. (145)
4-21-1798 - John WINAN to Lewis WINAN. (146)
11-10-1804 - Samuel SMITH and Elizabeth his wife to William JONES. (147)
2-25-1800 - Ichabod Benton MILLER and Sarah his wife of Anderson twp. to William
            MILNNER (or HILNNER). (148)
4-2-1804 - Nathaniel TERWILLEGER to Elis DUSKEY. (148)
4-1-1805 - Abraham VOORHEES and Mary his wife to Joseph MORSE. (149)
4-2-1805 - Charles AVERY to Joseph WILLIAMS. (150)
11-24-1803 - Uzal BEATS and Elizabeth his wife of Sycamore twp. to Uzal Bates FOX
            of same. (151)
-----1805 - Henry KER to Tabar WASHBURN; Notice of Patent Rights of Improved
            Stills. (151)
4-24-1805 - Henry KER of Shake, New York by Tabar WASHBURN to Betsey DEXTER of
            Cincinnati. (152)
3-25-1803 - James SMITH, Sheriff HCO to Jonathan SEELY, William McMILLAN and
            Charles AVERY. (152)
3-17-1796 - John CUMMINS, blacksmith and Jean his wife to Clark BATES. (154)

561

4-1-1799 - Isaac BATES to Clark BATES. (155)
4-8-1805 - John MILLER and Susanna his wife and James MILLER of Warren Co., Ohio
          to Robert COMPTON. (156)
2-17-1800 - John Cleves SYMMES of North Bend to Samuel JAMES. (157)
5-10-1805 - Nathaniel TERWILLEGER of Sycamore twp. to John CAMPBELL. (158)
2-25-1805 - Matthias SCUDDER and Sarah his wife of Bourbon Co., Kentucky to
          Alexander MARTIN of Hamilton Co., Ohio. (158)
8-12-1797 - John DIXON to Jesse and Abijah HUNT; Articles of Agreement. (159)
1-26-1787 - John Cleves SYMMES to John Dixon. (160)
11-13-1804 - Abijah HUNT formerly of Cincinnati now of Natchez, Mississippi to
          Jesse Hunt of Cincinnati. (161)
11-13-1804 - Abijah HUNT formerly of Cincinnati now of Natchez, Mississippi to
          Jesse Hunt of Cincinnati. (161)
3-26-1805 - John MILLER and Hannah his wife of Mill Creek to Jonathan HUTCHINSON
          of same. (162)
5-10-1805 - Daniel PIERCE and Elizabeth his wife to Thomas STEAD. (163)
5-9-1805 - Clark BATES and Rachel his wife to Matthias NIMMO. (164)
4-13-1799 - Clark BATES and Rachel his wife to Joshua WILLIAMS. (164)
5-20-1805 - Jonathan DAYTON of New Jersey to Hugh MOORE of Cincinnati. (165)
1-1-1805 - Daniel SYMMES and Eliza his wife to Electra OLIVER of Hamilton Co.,
          Ohio daughter of Col. Alexander OLIVER of Marietta, Ohio. (166)
5-13-1805 - John S. GANO and Mary his wife and William STANLEY and Sally his
          wife to Oliver SPENCER. (167)
5-13-1805 - James SMITH, Esq. late Sheriff of HCO to Ezekiel HUTCHINSON. (168)
5-25-1805 - Charles VALTIER and Pamela his wife to Felix CHRISMANN. (169)
5-28-1805 - James HAMILTON of Butler Co., Ohio to William McCLUNEY. (170)
9-5-1804 - Henry JENNINGS and Sally his wife to Edward COVINGTON. (171)
8-29-1804 - Jacob BROADWELL and his wife to John DAY of Clermont Co., Ohio (172)
4-15-1805 - John CARLISLE, Collector to Henry LUDLOW. (173)
5-4-1805 - Alexander KIRKPATRICK and Kasanna his wife to Christopher Hayden. (174)
4-1-1805 - Abraham NOORHEES, Sr. to John DODSON Jr. (175)
2-10-1804 - James SMITH, Esq., Sheriff HCO to James FERGUSON. (176)
2-8-1807 - David McCASH in consideration of his moving, to James FERGUSON. (177)
6-11-1805 - James FERGUSON and Jane his wife to Christopher ERENFIGHT. (178)
4-25-1805 - Job DeCAMP and Mary his wife to John BALDWIN. (179)
6-21-1802 - James SMITH, Esq., Sheriff HCO to John KITCHELL. (180)
5-29-1805 - Thomas McFARLAND and Hannah his wife to William McFARLAND. (182)
2-2-1805 - Moses BROADWELL and Jeany (Jenny) his wife of.Clermont Co., Ohio to
          John ROSE of Hamilton Co., Ohio. (183)
2-7- 1799 - Matthew WINTON to Thomas GOUDY. (184)

The following records were abstracted for genealogical information and as a finding aid from Deed Book D-1. Pages on which record may be found are given in parenthesis.

11-14-1801 - Daniel GRIFFING to John BARNET and William CRANE. (1)

12-23-1801 - Calvin MORRELL to Samuel MUCHMORE. (3)

1-26-1784 - John McDOWEL. Military Warrent #2300. Surveyed for John McDowel, his heirs and assigns consisting of 200 acres for his services in the Virginia Continental Line. Recorded 1-20-1802.

3-9-1801 - Daniel STOUT and Ann his wife of Monmouth County, New Jersey to Ralph PHILLIP of Hunter County, New Jersey. (6)

12-14-1801 - William TURDALL (TINDALL) of Trenton, New Jersey to Jesse HUNT. (8)

1-15-1802 - Samuel MARTIN of Waynesville, HCO to Samuel HIGHWAY of same. (9)

6-12-1801 - Will of James BRADY of Franklin township, Hamilton County, Ohio. Wife, Jane. Daughter, Polly. Bequeathes to Ester Cambell (no relationship stated). Son, John Brady. Mentions William Murry, not of age, who is living with family. Executors: James Barret and John Brady. Signed, James Brady. Witnesses: And'w Ches and Benjamin Gee. Recorded 2-3-1802. (11)

3-24-1801 - Nancy SANSON, a mulatto woman vs. Thompkins BARLOW. Suit brought in Paris District Court, Bourbon County, Kentucky. Writ issued. (12)

7-6-1801 - Robert POLLARD and Jael his wife of Richmond, Virginia to Thomas RICHARDSON and Elizabeth C. RICHARDSON. (14)

3-7-1801 - Samuel WOODS to Stephen FOX. (17)

4-3-1802 - Zachariah HOLE to William McMILLAN, James FINDLAY and Jacob BURNET. (19)

12-25-1801 - John HOLE to James FINDLAY and William McMILLAN. (20)

3-19-1788 - John Cleves SYMMES to Thos. KINNY of Morristown, New Jersey. (21)

5-10-1802 - Patrick PRESTON of the Army of the United States places his son George PRESTON as an apprentice to Zebulon Montgomery PIKE of the Army of the United States until 4-19-1819 when said apprentice is of full age. (22)

9-1-1801 - Edmond a poor boy aged 1 year son of Lewis a black man and Barbary a black woman is bound to Griffin YEATMAN. (23)

7-20-1802 - Samuel SEWARD of HCO to David PEEK of New Jersey. (25)

-----1802 - Elizabeth STEPHENS widow and relict of John STEPHENS late of Kentucky, dec'd to Charles BRITTON (alias BRETTON). Quit Claim. (26)

June 1802 - Suit filed in Lexington (Kentucky) District Court by James a black man against Isaac WILSON for Trespass, Assault and Battery. (27)

2-10-1798 - John MERCER and Susanna his wife to Abijah and Jesse HUNT, merchants. Mortgage. (29)

4-1-1802 - David McCASH of Springfield township to Oliver SPENCER for and in behalf of Major Mahlon FORD. (32)

Aug. 1802 - Charles a black boy aged 7 months, son of Lewis a black man and Barbary a black woman indentured to Griffin YEATMAN. (34)

6-5-1795 - Jonathan DAYTON to Capt. Cornelius R. SEDAM of the Army of the United States. (36)

6-24-1802 - Benjamin SCUDDER of Springfield twp., Essex Co., New Jersey, millwright to Jonathan SPINNING. (38)

12-31-1802 - Benjamin INYARD to John Townsend BRIDGE. Mortgage. (39)

4-25-1802 - John Briney (Dutch signature) to Daniel SYMMES. (40)

8-5-1802 - Noah CRANE to Daniel SYMMES. (41)

-----1802 - Isaac ZANE of Ross County, Ohio to William WARD of Hamilton County, Ohio. Power of Attorney. (43)

12-7-18-2 - Isaac ZANE of Ross County, Ohio to William WARD. Agreement. (44)

9-25-1802 - John N. CUMMING of Newark, Essex County, New Jersey, in consideration of his moving to William C. SCHENCK of Franklin, HCO. Power of Attorney. (45)

1-25-1803 - Jacob BURNET, William McMILLAN and James FINDLAY to John Noble CUMMING of Essex, New Jersey. (46)

7-26-1802 - Peter WILLCOCKS to John BADWIN. (47)

2-1-1793 - John Cleves SYMMES agent for 24 proprietors of Miami township to W. John WALKER. Agreement. (48)

Dec. 1802 - Steven BURNET and Robert ROSS to John Cleves SYMMES. (50)

-----1802 - John FIELD and John FIELD Jr. of Philadelphia, Pa. to George W. FIELD. Power of Attorney. (51)

3-15-1803 - Elmor WILLIAMS to Stephen WHEELER. (52)

12-7-1802 - Isaac ZANE to William WARD. Agreement. (53)

--------- - Robert PIATT and Thomas SMITH of HCO to John JONES of Boone Co., Kentucky. (note: not dated, recorded 3-23-1803). (54)

3-3-1803 - Samuel JAMES to David ZEIGLER. (54)

4-8-1803 - Benj. VAN HOOK to Charles VATTIER. (55)

5-12-1803 - John HUMES to William JONES. Mortgage. (56)

3-8-1803 - Jonathan DAYTON of Elisabeth, Essix Co., New Jersey to wife, Susan DAYTON; brother, Elias B. DAYTON; and son Elias I. DAYTON. Power of Attorney. (57)

6-24-1803 - Samuel HEIGHWAY of Waynesville, Warren Co., Ohio to Jacob MILLER of Virginia. (59)

6-24-1803 - Samuel HEIGHWAY of Waynesville, Warren Co., Ohio to John JONES, Esq. of Columbia township. (59)

4-25-1800 - Edward MEEKS Sr. of New York, New York to Col. Edward MEEKS of Virginia. Power of Attorney. (60)

8-8-1803 - Nathan HATFIELD to David ZEIGLER. (61)

8-6-1803 - David GRUMMAN to Charles VATTIER. Mortgage. (62)

-------- - Uriah GATES to John CHICK. (note: not dated, recorded 8-16-1803). (63)

10-27-1798 - Will of Stephen BRANT of Hanover township, Morris County, New Jersey. Wife, Sarah. Bequeathes to Samuel Kitchel and Phebe Flint children of late sister, Rachel Kitchel. Executors; David Cory and Noah Young. Signed, Stephen Brant. Witnesses: John Darey, Cornelius Ball, John Ball and John Beaty. Recorded Hamilton County, Ohio 10-1-1803. (63)

8-25-1788 - Matthias DENMAN of Essex County, New Jersey to Robert PATTERSON and John FILSON of Lexington, Fayette County, Kentucky. Agreement. (65)

10-18-1803 - Gersham GARD to Jacob BURNET and William McMILLAN. (66)

5-28-1803 - James POLLOCK to John Cleves SYMMES. (67)

9-24-1803 - John Cleves SYMMES on behalf of Bane Heighlway & Co. to Francis DUNLEAVY. (68)

9-12-1803 - Benjamin SEARS Jr. of Sycamore twp. to Hans LERKIE. (68)

11-25-1803 - Aaron GOFORTH to John SUNDERLAND. (70)

9-15-1803 - John Cleves SYMMES to Rev'd John SEWARD. Receipt. (71)

6-24-1803 - Samuel HEIGHWAY of Waynesville, Warren Co., Ohio to Isaac BUSH of
Columbia twp., HCO. (71)
12-17-1802 - Frederick FISHER to John GASTON. Mortgage. (72)
12-27-1803 - Deposition of Robert PATTERSON of Kentucky concerning land in Cincinnati commonly described as "the Common". (73)
12-27-1803 - Deposition of Melyn BAKER of HCO concerning land in Cincinnati
commonly described as "the Common". (75)
12-27-1803 - Deposition of John R. MILLS, Esq. of Springfield, HCO concerning land
in Cincinnati commonly described as "the Common". (76)
12-27-1803 - Deposition of Israel LUDLOW of Cincinnati concerning land in
Cincinnati commonly described as "the Common". (77)
8-25-1803 - Deposition to certify that Peter LOTT a young man of color was born
in the family of Mr. Jacob BRIANT in Springfield, Essex Co., New
Jersey and that Mr. Samuel MEEKER, merchant of Philadelphia having
married a daughter of Mr. Briant, that Peter Lott was given by Mr.
Briant to Mr. Meeker in 1797, and that said Peter Lott has now become
a free man. (78)
1-7-1804 - Deposition by Abraham VOORHEESE Jr. stating that on 8-1-1786 he was present with Gerrit Voorheese the debtor of amounts existing between Abraham Voorheese the father of deponent and said Gerrit Voorheese. (78)
2-1-1802 - Patrick MOORE to Charles MOORE. Agreement. Patrick Moore of Cincinnati
agrees to give his brother Charles Moore free use of his land which
is adjoined by Maj. Ludlow and Mr. Riddle's land. (79)
11-30-1799 - Jonathan HUTCHINSON to John HERMAL. (79)
1-17-1804 - Jacob WHITE Jr. of Springfield twp. to Jeremiah FRENCH. Bill of
Sale for chattels and household goods. (80)
1-18-1804 - Lewis LAING to John DILL & Co. (80)
9-10-1801 - Adam MENCH (or MEUCH?) to John Cleves SYMMES. (81)
6-24-1803 - Samuel HEIGHWAY of Waynesville, Warren Co., Ohio to Aquila NORRIS of
Columbia twp., HCO. (83)
4-3-1804 - John LYON of Springfield twp. to John LUDLOW. Mortgage. (83)
7-25-1795 - Samuel FREEMAN, Israel LUDLOW and Joel WILLIAMS proprietors of
Cincinnati to Francis WILSON, Agreement. (84)
4-10-1804 - Thomas CARNEAL to Daniel GREENHAM, distiller. Agreement. (85)
8-17-1803 - William VAN HORNE to Maj. Wm. GOFORTH and Maj. John Stites GANO.
To revoke Power of Attorney. (85)
8-29-1803 - William VAN HORNE of Essex Co., New Jersey to Aaron GOFORTH. Power of
Attorney. (86)
11-1-1797 - James COX to John S. GANO. Bond. (86)
8-30-1803 - William DRAKE to David SPONG. (87)
4-24-1804 - Patrick MOORE to Bustard MOORE. Mortgage. (88)
4-25-1804 - George WILLIAMSON to William McFARLDND. (89)
4-17-1804 - James McGURNES to Patrick MOORE. Mortgage. (90)
5-14-1803 - John CLEVES SYMMES to Samuel LINES. Cancellation of Mortgage. (91)
4-13-1804 - William SYMMES to Peter MURPHY. Cancellation of Mortgage. (91)
5-1-1804 - James SMITH, Sheriff HCO to James KAMPER. (91)
5-1-1804 - James SMITH, Sheriff HCO to Thomas AUTOR. (91)
5-1-1804 - James SMITH, Sheriff HCO to James WHITE. (92)
5-3-1804 - Deposition of James SILVER concerning partnership of Israel Ludlow
in land. (92)

5-3-1804 - Deposititon of John Cleves SYMMES concerning partnership of Israel LUDLOW in land. (93)

9-10-1801 - Christian REMLEY (Dutch signature)to John Cleves SYMMES. Mortgage.(95)

5-9-1804 - Peter Legris BELISLE of the Republic of France to Payton SHORT of Woodford Co., Kentucky. Agreement. (96)

5-10-1804 - Deposition of Peter Legris BELISLE a citizen of France concerning his departure for a visit to France. (97)

--------- - William DICKERSON, William GRANT, John GRANT and Barnet STEWART of Campbell Co., Kentucky to John and Mathew NIMMO of HCO. Bond. (note: not dated, recorded 5-25-1804). (98)

5-8-1804 - William WALLACE to John BROWNE. Mortgage. (98)

5-31-1804 - John HUMES of Cincinnati to Loyd OGG of Colerain twp. (100)

1-24-1804 - Joseph CATERLON of Springfield twp. to David PRECOUNT of same; Bill of Sale for goods and chattels. (101)

6-14-1804 - Emanuel VANTREES of Whitewater twp. to John and Mathew NIMMO. Mortgage to be paid by goods in an Orlean Boat at Lawrence burgh. (102)

3-6-1804 - Will of John JESSUP of Springfield twp. Wife, Judith, all lands, horses and chattels to use for benefit of younger children of testator's family. Eldest son, Stephen Jessup. Daughter, Judith Jessup now wife of Eberzer Miles residing in Bruch Valle, North Cumberland Co., Pa. Son, John Jessup. Two sons, Daniel and David. Mentions three daughters who are all 18 and over, and in another place refers to 3 youngest daughters, but does not name or clarify. Executors; son, Stephen Jessup and friend, Ephraim Brown. Signed: John Jessup. Witnesses: John W. Browne, Doctor John Crammer and Ephraim Brown. Recorded 3-6-1804 with original copy of will on file and recorded in Will Book 1, pages 81 & 82. (102)

5-1-1804 - James SMITH, Sheriff HCO to Josiah GWALTENEY. Assignment. (104)

6-21-1804 - Daniel STOUT of the west side Little Miami HCO to John Cleves SYMMES, Jur. Mortgage. (104)

10-7-1803 - Deposition of William McMILLAN who deposeth that he was one of those who founded the settlement of Cincinnati on 12-28-1788 and that a few days afterward a plan of the town was drafted by Israel Ludlow with advise of Robert Patterson, both of whom were considered joint proprietors with Mathias Denman of New Jersey with Ludlow acting as agent for Denman. That the town was laid out and surveyed except part which lies south of Front St. and west of Main St., which was not laid out until sometime later. That Patterson and Ludlow declared that all ground lying between the front of the lots which lie between Vattiers and Gibsons corner that is to say, all south of the two upper squares on Front St. should be a perpetual Common for the use of the Inhabitants of said town provided no Commoner in virtue of his right of Common should be entitled to a right of keeping a Ferry on the Ohio. In 1793 Robert Patterson was reported to have sold his right of property in the Town of Cincinnati to Samuel Freeman. That deponent in conversation with Joel Williams in 1792, said Williams agreed that common should be maintained as stated. (104)

6-20-1803 - Oath of Alliegence by Matthew NIMMO. (106)

566

7-4-1804 - B. CHAMBERS to James FINDLAY of Cincinnati. Assignment of land. Dated
at Lawrenceburgh. (106)
7-7-1804 - James ARMSTRONG of HCO to Samuel BORDEN and Rachel his wife of HCO.
Lease for consideration of $1.00, that Borden's should hold lease during
their natural lives and at their decease to revert back to Armstrong or
his heirs. (106)
2-18-1793 - John VANCE of Cincinnati to Levi WOODWARD. (106)
7-24-1804 - Samuel AYRES to Charles VATTIER. Mortgage. (107)
7-26-1804 - Manassa BROWN of Cincinnati to Jacob WHEELER of same. Mortgage. (108)
8-3-1804 - James SMITH, Sheriff HCO to Abraham SKINNER. Assignment of Mortgage.(109)
-------- - Matthias DENMAN, Jonas WADE, Israel LUDLOW, John ARMSTRONG, Sam'l
MEEKER, Jona. DAYTON, GALBREATH & ELMSS, Thomas SALTER and John L. NORTON
to William WELLS, John MATTHEWS, Israel LUDLOW, Zacheus BIGGS and John
ARMSTRONG. Power of Attorney to contract land to persons who shall
actually settle, improve and reside in said land. (Recorded 1804).(109)
7-30-1804 - John S. GANO of Cincinnati to Griffin YEATMAN of same and William
goforth, Junr. Articles of Agreement. (110)
8-17-1804 - William CASTO of Cincinnati to Jacob WHEELER. Mortgage. (111)
7-23-1804 - Samuel FRAKEY of HCO to Aaron SACKET of same. Mortgage. (112)
9-10-1804 - Daniel C. COOPER of Montgomery Co., Ohio to Peyton SHORT of Woodford
Co., Ky. (113)
5-25-1804 - Robert STEEL of Springfield twp. to Peyton SHORT of Woodford Co., Ky.
(113)
2-11-1804 - Jacob MINTURN of Butler Co., Ohio to Oliver SPENCER attorney for
Major Mahlon FORD of HCO. (114)
2-11-1804 - Justus JONES of Butler Co. Ohio to Oliver SPENCER attorney for
Major Mahlon FORD of HCO. (115)
5-1-1804 - James SMITH, Sheriff HCO to Gershom GARD. Assignment. (117)
6-27-1804 - William FELTER to GERSHOM GARD. One horse in payment of mortgage. (117)
5-27-1803 - Abraham SKINNER to Symmes HARRISON, son of William H. HARRISON, Esq.
Quit Claim. (117)
3-8-1804 - John (his mark) COCHRAN to William HARRISON, second son of William
Henry HARRISON, esq. of Vincennes. Quit Claim. (117)
----1804 - John JONES, Esq. of HCO to Peyton Short SYMMES of Cincinnati. (118)
1-23-1804 - James COLWELL to Adam LEE of Sycamore twp. Assignment of grain
and farming utensils. (119)
9-21-1804 - Notification by Andrew BRANNON, Constable of Cincinnati twp. to
Charlotte Chambers LUDLOW, admrs., James FINDLAY, John LUDLOW and
Sineas(?) PIERSON, adms. of the Estate of Israel LUDLOW late of HCO,
dec'd, that on Oct. 5th deposition of John Cleves SYMMES and Samuel
FREEMAN will be taken. (119)
10-5-1804 - Deposition of John Cleves SYMMES taken in regard to title of Lot
No. 401. (120)
10-5-1804 - Deposition of Samuel FREEMAN taken in regard to title of Lot
No. 401. (121)
10-11-1804 - Mary McNAMOR wife of Morris McNAMOR late of Miflin Co., Pa., dec'd,
said Mary now of HCO to Thomas KAIN of HCO, her son-in-law. Power
of Attorney. (123)

567

10-22-1804 - John WHITWORTH of HCO to Samuel HILDITCH of Columbia, HCO. Power
of Attorney. (123)
6-10-1796 - Jonathan DAYTON of New Jersey to Israel LUDLOW formerly of N. J., but
now of HCO. Power of Attorney. (124)
3-15-1790 - Matthias DENMAN of Elizabeth twp., Essex Co., N.J. to Israel LUDLOW
of Losantville, Northwest Territory, Surveyor. Power of Attorney. (125)
10-26-1804 - Asa S. RICHESON of Cincinnati to Charles VATTIER of same. Mortgage.
(125)
10-28-1802 - John Cleves SYMMES, Joseph GIBSON and Return J. MEIGS Jr. Judges of
General Court of Territory certify that John W. BROWN, Esq. an inhabitant
of Cincinnati and admitted to become citizen of the United States and
naturalized. Dated at Marietta. (126)
10-25-1804 - Oath of Allegience of Thomas RAWLINS. (126)
4-17-1804 - James McGINNIS of Cincinnati to Patrick MOORE of same. Mortgage. (127)
11-6-1804 - Garret VOORHEESE of Cincinnati to Jacob WHEELER of same. Mortgage.(127)
10-26-1804 - Asa S. RICHARDSON of Cincinnati to Charles VATTIER of same. Mortgage. (129)
11-22-1804 - Samuel GULICK, Jacob REYNEARSON, Peter MILLS, Amos MILLS and Samuel
REDENBAUGH, being children and heirs of Tunis GULLICK, late of HCO,
dec'd to Luke FOSTER of HCO. Power of Attorney to act as agent
relative to "our grandfather Samuel Gulick, dec'd's estate in
Somerset Co., N.J. as by provision of will of said Samuel Gulick."(129)
1-16-1804 - Cornelius VOORHEESE of HCO to Isaac MARTIN of Green Co. Mortgage.(130)
12-6-1804 - Jesse DODD of HCO to William McCLAIN of HCO. Bill of Sale for a
horse. (131)
9-15-1804 - Ralph PHILIPS of Hunterdon Co., N.J., Gentleman to Jesse HUNT of Ohio.
Power of Attorney. (131)
6-15-1804 - Abijah HUNT of Natches, Mississippi Territory, Merchant to Jesse HUNT
of Cincinnati, Merchant. Power of Attorney to sell land in HCO.
Abijah Hunt's signature attested to Philadelphia, Pa. (132)
10-3-1804 - William P. MEEKER and Samuel DENMAN of Philadelphia, Pa., Merchants to
Jesse HUNT of Cincinnati, Merchant, Power of Attorney. (133)
9-3-1804 - John PHILIPS and Mary his wife of Marden twp., Hunterdon Co., N. J.
to Abijah HUNT. (133)
11-12-1804 - Abijah HUNT assignee of John PHILIPS to Jesse HUNT. Assignment.(135)
12-12-1804 - Abigal LONG widow of the late Daniel LONG, dec'd of Springfield twp.,
HCO to Isaac STERRET of HCO. Whereas a marriage is intended between
Isaac Sterret and Abigail Long, contract to secure estate and effects
for said Abigail Long and her children by Daniel Long. (136)
------1804 - John PHILIPS of Hunterdon Co., N.J. to Jesse HUNT of Ohio. Power
of Attorney. (137)
11-27-1804 - Deposition of Eden BURROWS concerning forfeiture of S32, T3, R2.(137)
11-5-1804 - Deposition of William HUNT concerning forfeiture of S32, T3, R2. (138)
11-5-1804 - Deposition of Abijah HUNT concerning forfeiture of S32, T3, R2. (139)
10-10-1804 - John CAMPBELL of HCO to Stephen CAMPBELL of HCO. Mortgage. (140)
10-15-1804 - Matthias DENMAN of Springfield twp., Essex Co., N.J. to Daniel G.
COOPER of Dayton, Ohio. Power of Attorney. (141)
1-5-1805 - Joseph BLACKBURN of HCO to Ephrain KIBBEY, James MERANDY and Benjamin
STITES as adms. of Benjamin STITES late of Columbia, dec'd. (141)

12-4-1804 - Abraham CASE and Elizabeth his wife of HCO to Marsh WILLIAMS of HCO. Mortgage. (144)

11-20-1804 - Heirs of John CUTLER to William WOODWARD of Cincinnati. John Cutler of Cincinnati, Northwest Territory, dec'd died intestate leaving two lots #20 & #92...Whereas Isaac Weatherly of Boston, Mason and Hannah his wife; William Dixon, Yeoman and Rachel his wife of Charleston; and Martha Gardner, widow, of Medford, all in the State of Mass., being three lawful heirs of John Cutler, dec'd. (145)

1-31-1805 - Samuel HILDITCH of Columbia, HCO to Samuel W. DAVIS of Williamsburgh, Clermont Co., Ohio. Power of Attorney. (145)

8-18-1804 - Deposition of Elijah INMAN concerning deed by Benjamin Stites to said Inman. (146)

8-21-1804 - Ellis JOHN and Margaret his wife to Edward MEEKS of HCO. (148)

2-19-1805 - Deposition by John NIMMO stating that he came to United States in Sept. 1801 and in the month following came to Ohio and founded a partnership of John and Matthew Nimmo which remains in force and also gives Oath of Allegience. (149)

2-12-1805 - Andrew GILL of Cincinnati twp. to Charles ATTIER. Mortgage. (149)

6-2-1804 - Elias B. DAYTON and Isaac H. WILLIAMSON, esqs of Elizabethtown, N. J. to Jonathan DAYTON of same. (150)

1-22-1805 - John W. BROWNE of Cincinnati to Ezekiel HUGHES of White Water twp. Mortgage. (151)

1-22-1805 - John W. BROWNE of Cincinnati to Ezekiel HUGHES of White Water twp. Mortgage. (152)

4-13-1805 - Alexander KING and Oliva KING of Cincinnati to David ZEIGLER of HCO. (154)

7-8-1803 - Abijah HUNT of Natchez, Mississippi Territory to Jesse HUNT, his brother, of Cincinnati. Power of Attorney. (154)

11-17-1804 - Abijah HUNT of Natchez, Mississippi Territory to Jesse HUNT of Cincinnati. Power of Attorney to transact business for Abijah in States of Pa., Ky. and Ohio and Territories of Indiana and Louisiana.(155)

5-6-1805 - Thomas LINDSLEY, Archer DICKERSON, John B. LINDSLY and William DICKERSON of Campbell Co., Ky. to John and Matthew NIMMO of HCO. Mortgage. (156)

9-4-1804 - Deposition of Joel WILLIAMS concerning notes. (156)

4-9-1805 - Jabez WARNER, 2nd and Sarah his wife of East Haddam, Middlesex Co., Conn. being heirs of estate of Asa HARVEY late of Colerain, HCO, dec'd to Judah WILLEY, Esq. of Colerain. Power of Attorney. (157)

4-30-1795 - Israel LUDLOW of HCO to James DUMENT of HCO. (158)

5-22-1802 - James DEMINTT of HCO to Delzil KEASLY of Cincinnati, Hatter. Assignment. (158)

2-9-1805 - Abel AMIDEN, Aseal AMIDEN, Cloe THOMAS, Rhoda RUSSEL, Hannah CHAPMAN, Cheney AMIDEN and Amasa CHAPMAN of Onondaga Co., New York, heirs at law of Abner AMIDEN late of Cincinnati, HCO, dec'd to Caleb AMIDEN of Onondaga Co., New York. Power of Attorney. (158)

2-15-1805 - Horatio R. DAYTON and Cornelia DAYTON late of Elizabethtown, N.J.,
now of New York City to Jonathan DAYTON, Senator of the United States
and their brother. Power of Attorney. (159)
6-1-1805 - William TERRY of Cincinnati twp. to Jonathan DAYTON of Elizabethtown,
New Jersey. Mortgage. (160)
6-1-1805 - Enos TERRY of Cincinnati twp. to Jonathan DAYTON of Elizabethtown,
New Jersey. Mortgage. (161)
7-9-1805 - Deposition of William JONES concerning Lot #86 in Cincinnati. (162)
8-7-1804 - Henry KER of Supio, Cayuga Co., New York to Dudley AVERY of same.
Power of Attorney. Ker's signature attested to Franklin Co., Vermont.(162)
7-20-1805 - Robert CALDWELL of Cincinnati to William McFARLAND. Mortgage. (162)
7-20-1805 - William McFARLAND of Cincinnati to Robert CALDWELL of same. Mortgage.
(163)
4-9-1805 - John Conrad KOTTO of Trenton City, Hunterdon Co., N.J. to Sylvanus
HUTCHINSON and John ARMSTRONG. Power of Attorney. (164)
11-19-1803 - Cancelation of indenture of Samuel BROWNE, son of Jno. W. BROWNE
of Cincinnati, Ohio to N. WILLIS of Chillicothe, Ohio. (165)
3-30-1805 - John MILLER of HCO to Daniel SYMMES. (165)
8-5-1805 - John CAMPBELL of Crosby twp. to James WILSON of Springfield twp. (166)
8-13-1805 - David PIERSON of HCO to Ralph ELSTUN of HCO. (168)
7-13-1805 - William Henry Harrison, Gov. of Indiana Territory authorized by
President of United States to decide upon claims of persons whose
property had been taken or destroyed by Indians examined claims of:
Aaron Richardson for Bay mare stolen by Shawnees in year 1796 from HCO;
Samuel Gregory for bay mare and Daniel Richardson for a Sorrel mare
stolen by Shawnees in Spring 1796; Zachariah Hole for a Roan Horse;
Henry Hutchinson for a black horse; William Hole for a brown horse;
John Dogherty for a bay horse; and Abraham Richardson for a bright bay
mare stolen by Shawnees in month of Dec. 1795; All claims allowed and
substantuated by evidence except Zachariah Hole who is not entitled as
by his own confession he received $20.00 from an Indian Trader who
purchsed horse. (169)
3-7-1805 - James BRUNTON of HCO to William HARVEY of HCO. Mortgage. (169)
8-14-1805 - Deposition of Aaron GOFORTH concerning land issued to Mr. Henry
MYERS. (170)
8-21-1805 - Jacob WHITE and Joseph DELAPLAIN, Esqs. of HCO to John NIMMO, Esq. of
HCO. Mortgage. (172)
8-14-1805 - Robert CAMPBELL to Jonathan DAYTON of Elizabethtown, New Jersey;
mortgage. (174)
10-7-1799 - Suit filed Lexington, Kentucky District Court. George, a pauper,
pltf. vs Peter McKEARNAN, deft. Plaintiff a free man and not a
slave, set at liberty. Recorded 9-5-1805. (174)
Oct. 1791 - Robert TODD to Martin VARNER and Wm MOUNTS. (175)
--------- - Jacob WHITE and Joseph DELAPLAINE, Esq. to John NIMMO; mortgage;
(no date given); recorded 9-20-1805. (175)
7-24-1805 - Caleb AMIDON of Cincinnati by Power of Attorney dated 2-9-1804 given
by Heirs of Estate of Abner Amidon, dec'd, late of Cincinnati,
Hamilton Co., Ohio to Jacob WILLIAMS of Cincinnati; Power of Attorney
to collect money from David Grummon. (176)

570

11-28-1804 - John SARGANT (SERGEANT) and Prudence wife of West Bethlehem twp., Washington Co., Pa. to Sampson SARGENT of Hamilton Co., Ohio: Power of Attorney. (176)

8-10-1805 - Robert CALDWELL to William McFARLAND; note. (177)

8-15-1805 - Asa PEEK (or PECK) to David ZEIGLER and Jacob BURNET. (177)

5-13-1802 - Deposition of Lewis KERR attorney for H. CADBURY including letter dated 5-1-1802 concerning 12 paintings seized at house of Mr. Charles Avery believed to be goods of George Turner in suit of George Gordon, but not goods of Turner but property of Henry Cadbury.(178)

9-10-1805 - John JONES to Jonathan DAYTON of Elizabethtown, New Jersey; mortgage. (179)

10-18-1805 - Dayton IRELAN(D) to Jonathan DAYTON of Elizabethtown, N.J.; mortgage. (180)

10-18-1805 - Aaron IRELAN(D) to Jonathan DAYTON of New Jersey; mortgage. (181)

---------- - James GOUDY to Moses BROADWELL; note; recorded 10-31-1805. (182)

---------- - Joseph B. LEIBERT to John NIMMO; note; recorded 11-5-1805. (183)

11-4-1805 - William HOWARD to John HORNER; note. (183)

---------- - George WILLIAMSON of Hamilton County to Peter SMITH of Champayne Co., Ohio; mortgage; recorded 11-29-1805. (183)

9-7-1802 - William PETERS late a Major in the Army of the United States to William STANLEY of Cincinnati; Power of Attorney to sell lands purchased from Mahlon Ford late a Major in United States Army on 10-12-1797. Recorded 11-29-1805. (184)

12-12-1805 - Andrew WILSON of Hamilton Co. to John WILSON of Belmont Co., Ohio; Power of Attorney to collect money from the estate of James Wilson, dec'd, late of Annvil, Rockingham twp., West Jersey; residence of James Wilson, dec'd also given as Cranbury Town in Middlesex Co., New Jersey. (185)

8-7-1805 - Matthew NIMMO and John NIMMO; assignment to each other of bonds, judgment notes and due bills. (187)

5-10-1805 - Joseph B. LEIBERT to John NIMMO; note. (189)

12-13-1805 - David VAN GILDER to Jacob BURNET; mortgage. (190)

12-13-1805 - William GOFF to Jacob BURNET; mortgage. (190)

_____ - Alexander SMITH to Joseph DELAPLAINE; mortgage; recorded 1-6-1806.(191)

11-3-1802 - Court of Quarter Sessions held at Woodford Co., Kentucky. Suit of Job, pltff. vs. John TANNER, deft; jury found plaintiff entitled to freedom. (192)

1-11-1806 - Joseph CROSLEY and Polly wife to Benjamin MULFORD of Warren Co., Ohio. (193)

1-25-1806 - Elizabeth GILMAN to Thomas MATTHEWS. (194)

1-6-1806 - Evi MARTIN to Ralph PHILLIPS of New Jersey; mortgage. (194)

8-19-1805 - Jonathan DAYTON late of New Jersey to James GREER of Ohio. (195)

1-28-1806 - Deposition to certify that contract papers dated 8-21-1805 between John NIMMO to Jacob WHITE and Joseph DELAPLAINE were destroyed by fire. (196)

12-6-1805 - Charles VATTIER to John CRAIL; mortgage. (197)

1-24-1806 - James CONNER to Thomas RUSK; sale of personal property. (198)

2-13-1806 - George WILLIAMSON to Charles VATTIER; mortgage. (198)

1-28-1806 - Adam MOORE to John WALL; Articles of Agreement. (200)

12-10-1802 - John HUMES to William WOODWARD; mortgage. (200)
3-14-1806 - Deposition by Samuel HILDITCH revoking Power of Attorney given to
Samuel W. DAVIS of Williamsburgh, Clermont Co., Ohio on 1-31-1805. (201)
3-22-1806 - Henry LORE(?) of Colerain twp. to Thomas MATTHEWS; sale of personal
property. (202)
-----1806 - Robert GARDNER, an orphan boy by consent of Samuel FOSTER his guardian
binds himself as apprentice to John WALL, sadler of Cincinnati, to
serve until 9-27-1811. (203)
3-12-1806 - Charles VATTIER to David DUNCAN. (203)
3-8-1806 - Robert CALDWELL to Charles VATTIER; mortgage. (204)
3-15-1806 - Isaac VAN NUYS and Thomas BEST, co-partners of Cincinnati to Charles
VATTIER; mortgage. (206)
3-25-1806 - Andrew BURT to Charles VATTIER; mortgage. (207)
3-26-1806 - Felix CHRISTMAN (CHRISMAN) of Columbia twp. to Charles VATTIER. (208)
3-13-1806 - John JOHNSON to John R. GASTON; mortgage. (209)
9-28-1804 - T. WASHBURN to William McFARLAND; receipt for $60.00 for "field piece"
Washburn purchased in Luisianna Country and brought to Cincinnati. (210)
12-31-1805 - John WOOLEY and Martha wife of Edward COVINGTON. (210)
4-5-1806 - William TORRENCE to James RIDDLE of Chambersburg, Franklin Co., Pa.;
Whereas Albert Torrence late of Franklin Co., Pa. by will bequeathed
to Albert, William B., Samuel H. and Sophia Torrence children of
William Torrence of Hamilton Co. a portion of his estate and whereas
William Torrence appointed guardian of said children, said William
now gives Power of Attorney to Riddle to obtain same from executor
of the will. (211)
4-5-1806 - Barton LEONARD to William TOSSH. (212)
2-8-1806 - Francis MINNESIER and Maria Rose wife to Philip PRICE; articles of
agreement. (212)
4-18-1806 - Jacob MOORE to Charles VATTIER; mortgage. (213)
5-3-1806 - Aaron GOFORTH to Alexander STEWART, Samuel DELAPLAINE and Comfort
LANDS of New York City; mortgage. (214)
4-4-1806 - Deposition of Daniel VORHEES relative to land purchased by Vorhees from
John Cleve Symmes. (215-216)
10-29-1805 - Daniel HARAGAN of New Orleans, La., merchant to Thomas DUGAN of
Cincinnati twp.; Power of Attorney to dispose of all his lands
in Ohio and Kentucky. (217)
5-9-1806 - Henry GIMBLE of Cincinnati to Jacob FOWBLE of same; Power of Attorney
to collect money due from John Winn of Baltimore Co., Md. (218)
4-2-1805 - Samuel DICK of Butler Co., Ohio and Samuel BEST of Cincinnati, clock
and watch maker; articles of agreement. (218)
5-10-1806 - Thomas BEST to William McFARLAND. (219)
5-30-1806 - John JONES to Ethan STONE; mortgage. (220)
6-17-1806 - Robert SAMPLE of Davidson Co., Tenn. to John ARMSTRONG, Esq. of
Hamilton Co.; Power of Attorney to sell land being 300 acre tract part
East of Scioto River for satisfying military warrants being lot 5, 4th
quarter, Township 3, Range 17. (221)
10-2-1804 - Barton LEONARD to David NICHOLS and Uriah GATES; one still containing
88 gallons, etc. (221)
12-1-1805 - Robert DAVIS to Jos. B. LEIBERT; note. (221)

7-13-1806 - Robert TOWNLY to James McCLELLAND; receipt. (222)
7-13-1806 - John SMITH to James McCLELLAND; receipt. (223)
4-22-1806 - James FORDISE to Solomon LORING; articles of agreement. (223)
10-19-1805 - John RIPPY to Ephraim KIBBEY; mortgage. (223)
7-24-1806 - Will of Joseph Bowman LEIBERT of Cincinnati; dated 7-14-1806; recorded
7-24-1806. Wife, Sidney Leibert. Son, John Stapler Leibert. Father,
John Leibert of Germantown, Pennsylvania. Executors: wife, Sidney;
friend, James W. Sloan formerly of Baltimore, Md. now of Cincinnati;
and John Nimo. Witnesses: Peter McNicoll, _____(not given) Mennessier,
and Robert Merrie. (224)
4-4-1806 - John Cleves SYMMES, Esq. of North Bend to Doctor Evan BANE of Miami
Purchase; deed in sonsumation of mortgage between above two parties
dated 10-5-1799. (225)
4-4-1806 - Evan BANES of Waynesville, Warren Co., Ohio Phisician to John Cleves
SYMMES of Cincinnati. (226)
4-3-1806 - Evan BANES of Waynesville, Warren Co., Ohio to John Cleves SYMMES. (227)
4-3-1806 - Evan BANES of Waynesville, Warren Co., Ohio to John Cleves SYMMES. (228)
7-19-1806 - John SMITH to Charles VATTIER; mortgage. (230)
10-6-1806 - William BETTS of Hamilton Co. to Peyton SHORT, Esq. of Kentucky. (231)
2-19-1806 - Mathew ANDERSON of Glocester Co., Va. to his brother, Richard C.
ANDERSON and Benjamin ANDERSON; Power of Attorney to sell 2 tracts
land in Ohio, one on waters of Little Miami containing 1000 acres
and other on Clough Creek containing 1333 acres, also part of another
tract in Kentucky on waters of Highland Creek containing 2000 acres,
said tracts held by Mathew and brother, Richard C. as tenants in
common. (232)
7-9-1806 - Richard C. ANDERSON of Kentucky to Benjamin ANDERSON; Power of Attorney
to sell tracts owned by himself and brother Mathew, in Ohio. (233)
8-28-1806 - Adam HURDUS to wife, Hannah HURDUS; Power of Attorney to receive
possession of land recently purchased. (233)
11-28-1805 - William LEMMON(D) of Cincinnati to Robert KYLE of Kentucky;
mortgage. (234)
8-14-1806 - Joel WILLIAMS to Andrew BRANNON. (236)
9-5-1806 - John McKINNEY of Bourbon Co., Ky. to John ARMSTRONG, Esq. of Hamilton
Co.; Power of Attorney to sell 612½ acres, 4th quarter, Township 6,
Range 19 in Franklin Co., Ohio. (236)
3-1-1803 - Mathias DENMAN of Springfield twp., Essex Co., N.J. to Jonathan DAYTON
of same; Power of Attorney to dispose of land. (237)
3-1-1803 - Jonathan DAYTON of Elizabethtown, Essex Co., N.J. by Power of Attorney of
Mathias DENMAN of Springfield, Essex Co., N.J. to Jacob BURNET of
Cincinnati; Power of Attorney to dispose of Denman's land. (238)
12-6-1806 - Elias BOUDINOT of Philadelphia but now of Burlington, New Jersey to
Jacob Burnet of Cincinnati; Power of Attorney to sell or lease land.(238)
-------- - Catherine STOCKTON and Elias BOUDINOT executors of will of Philip
STOCKTON to William C. SCHENK and Jacob BURNET, Esq. of Ohio; Power
of Attorney. (239)
11-12-1799 - Henry MYERS to Jacob BURNET and William McMILLAN; recorded
9-10-1806. (240)
9-8-1806 - Deposition of Elizabeth CLEMENTS stating that she drew an instrument
reserving land for herself during her lifetime and at her decease
to be divided between her children and now makes said instrument void.
(241)

9-9-1806 - Jacob WHISLER and John HART to Jacob WHEELER; mortgage. (241)
1-16-1805 - Cornelius VOORHEES to Isaac MARTIN; note. (242)
1-10-1805 - Cornelius VOORHIS to Isaac MARTIN of Greene Co., Ohio; note. (242)
1-16-1804 - Cornelius VOORHES to Isaac MARTIN of Greene Co., Ohio; note. (243)
--------- - William PACK to Robert CALDWELL; mortgage, with mortgage assigned
            by Caldwell to William McFarland. (243)
9-4-1802 - John EDWARDS Sr. of Bourbon Co., Kentucky to Jacob WHITE and Johannah
            his wife of Hamilton Co.; a negro woman named Rosanna. (244)
-------- - James MARANDA and Ephrain KIBBEY of Warren Co., Ohio adms. of estate
            of Benjamin STITES, dec'd to Benjamin STITES of Warren Co., Ohio;
            bond; recorded 10-16-1806. (245)
4-19-1806 - Lewis RUE and Christianna wife to Thomas RUE of Delaware Co., harness-
            maker; Agreement, whereas Lewis and Christianna agree to live apart
            from each other the remainder of their lives, that bequest Christianna
            received under will of her father John Taylor to be hers alone; agree-
            ment also recorded Delaware Co. in Book H, page 542. (246)
6-25-1806 - Benjamin ANDERSON agent for Mathew ANDERSON and Richard C. ANDERSON
            to Vincent SHINN; bond. (247)
10-14-1806 - Peter KEENE of Colerain twp. to Moses LAUGHLIN of same; lease;
            assignment of lease to Ben Spencer in Book F, page 138. (248)
8-1-1806 - Christopher SMITH to Charles VATTIER; mortgage. (249)
9-22-1806 - Francis CARR to Charles VATTIER; mortgage. (250)
9-11-1806 - George ST CLAIR to Charles VATTIER; mortgage. (251)
8-1-1806 - Herman LONG to Charles VATTIER; mortgage. (252)
11-11-1806 - Certification of Richard MARTIN of Cincinnati that he sold Joseph
            DELEPLAIN 100 acres of land near Lebanon, with deed given to Deleplain
            by Samuel Stites and wife Martha. (252)
11-14-1806 - William STRATTON, Treasurer to Nehemiah HUNT; receipt for $10.00
            for one share in Cincinnati Academy. (253)
3-19-1806 - Mary CUTTER of Metford, Middlesex Co., Mass., single woman to Samuel
            FOSTER of Cincinnati, tanner; Power of Attorney to lease lands in
            Cincinnati. (253)
8-21-1806 - Samuel STUBENS to Jonathan HARPER; assignment. (253)
10-25-1806 - Casper STONEMIT (or STONEWIT) to Enos TERRY. (254)
10-22-1806 - Casper STONEMIT (or STONEWIT) to William TERRY. (254)
11-25-1806 - John CRAIL to Jacob MOORE (255)
(note: at this point the mechanically printed numbers were scratched out--for no
apparent reason--and different page numbers were inserted by hand. The numbers
used from here on will be the inserted numbers. For the mechanically printed
number, add two pages--example: page 254 inserted number = 256 mechanical
number)
12-3-1806 - William COLHOUN to Jacob MOORE; mortgage. (254)
11-21-1806 - Hugh BRACKEN to John W. BROWNE. (256)
12-3-1805 - Jesse NEWCOMBE to Jacob MOORE; mortgage. (255)
12-8-1805 - Summons issued to Pallas P. STEWART to appear at court at house
            of Joseph Conn relative to a land dispute. (257)
12-13-1806 - James LOWES, John LUDLOW and William McMILLAN to James SMITH,
            Sheriff; bond. (258)

12-17-1806 - Isaac CANNON of Cincinnati to James EWING, Esq.; Power of Attorney
            to dispose of land. (259)
9-6-1806 - William GREEN to William TERRY; mortgage. (259)
9-16-1806 - Samuel DOUGLAS of Bernard twp., Somerset Co., New Jersey to William
           CAIN of same; Power of Attorney to dispose of Ohio land. (260)
12-10-1806 - Joel CRAIG to Hiram YOUNG; receipt. (261)
7-2-1806 - Thomas VANDERRON (VANDEARON) to John VANDERRON; sale of personal
          property and chattels. (261)
1-15-1807 - Sarah BROWNE and Mary Ann BROWNE to Uriah GATES. (262)
1-15-1807 - Uriah GATES of Cincinnati twp. to Sarah BROWNE and Mary Ann BROWNE;
           Gates binds his daughter Polly Gates aged 8 yrs. on 22 Sept. last, as
           an apprentice to Brownes for term of three years. (262)
2-13-1807 - James KIRBY to William HICKS; bond. (262)
2-13-1807 - James KIRBY to Daniel HELEY; bond. (263)
6-15-1807 - David GOLDEN to Samuel GAMBLE; receipt. (263)
1-15-1807 - Barnabas HEGENS of Whitewater twp. to Urban BUNNEL; sale of personal
           property. (264)
4-5-1807 - Hyram YOUNG to Joel CRAIG; receipt. (264)
4-10-1807 - Jacob DETERLY of Cincinnati to Harman LONG of same; Power of Attorney
           to receive all sums bequeathed by Deterly's father. (265)
4-15-1807 - James McGINNIS of Cincinnati to Lebulon FOSTER; Power of Attorney
           to receive money from Evi Martin. (265)
4-29-1807 - Oral Will of William JONES. Deposition of Henry Andrews stating he
           was at house of James Jones of Colerain twp. on night of 21st instant
           when William Jones son of James Jones was on his death bed and told him
           his property was to be left to his father, James Jones. Recorded
           4-29-1807. (265)
5-7-1807 - John RIPPEY of Warren Co., Ohio to Edward MEEKS; assignment of interest
          in mortgage. (265)
5-9-1807 - Ephrain KIBBY of Warren Co., Ohio to Edward MEEKS; Power of Attorney
          to convey land. (266)
-------- - Will of Peter Legris BELISLE in original French (see page 97 of
          this book for translation). (266)
5-1-1807 - Francis Menessier by Power of Attorney from Pierre Le Gris BELISLE
          to Peyton SHORT; Whereas agreement entered at Cincinnati 5-9-1804 between
          Pierre Le Gris Belisle then a citizen of France and Peyton Short whereas
          Belisle on 5-10-1804 about to descend to New Orleans to embark to pass to
          France did grant Power of Attorney to Francis Menessier of Cincinnati to
          dispose of his land if he did not hear from Belisle in 18 months or 2 years
          and Menessier being unable to determine fate of Belisle is now selling
          land to Short. (267)
5-11-1807 - Charles VATTIER of Cincinnati to Nicholas LONGWORTH, Esq. of same;
           Power of Attorney to sell land; schedule of real estate annexed. (269)
4-27-1807 - Daniel WOODWORTH of Columbia twp. to Henry BALSOR Jr. of Sycamore
           twp. (270)
10-2-1806 - John DILL to Andrew BURT. (270)
3-2-1807 - Ezra CLARK of Columbia twp. to Joseph EDWARDS of same. (272)
5-15-1805 - Jonathan JOHNSON of Washington twp., Berlington Co., N. J. to
           Cornelius McCOLLOM of Williamsburgh twp., Clermong Co., Ohio; bond. (272)

575

11-5-1805 - Daniel THEW and Elizabeth THEW of Rockland Co., New York to Jacob
            BURNET of Ohio; Power of Attorney to sell land in Colerain twp. (273)
5-2-1807 - John WILKINS Jr. of Pittsburgh, Pa. to Jacob BURNET of Hamilton Co.;
           Power of Attorney to sell lot in Cincinnati. (273)
11-25-1807 - Casper HOPPLE to Samuel NEWALL; assignment of lease. (272)
7-17-1807 - Deposition of Elias GLOVER concerning mistanken William McFarland
            for Col. Burr in November of 1806. (274)
7-17-1807 - Deposition of Jesse HOOK concerning his statements which were
            mis-represented into story that Aaron Burr was seen in Cincinnati in
            November 1806 after he had actually left town. (274)
9-13-1806 - Deposition that whereas B. Stites late of Hamilton Co., dec'd
            did in the year 1791 lay out the town on Banks of Ohio known as Columbia
            consisting of a number of lots, streets, etc. and whereas the Legislature
            of the Territory by act passed 19 December 1799 did delegate that all
            houses in said town be valued at $200.00 and upwards and whereas Stites did
            on 8-19-1801 relinquish the idea of the place called Columbia. Signed by
            the proprietors of Columbia: John Armstrong, William Goforth, John Seaman,
            John McAdams, O. M. Spencer, Samuel Hilditch, James Mathis, John Young for
            Clover Spencer and C. M. Spencer, Morris Witham, Samuel Armstrong, Conrad
            Tergue, James Witham, Thaddeus Hanford, Thomas Frazea and Eph. Kibby. (274
8-1-1792 - Ann HENDERSON with consent of her mother, Elizabeth Henderson is bound
           as an apprentice to Frederick ALTER of Baltimore town to learn mystery
           of sewing, spinning and being a housewife for period of 10 years and
           seven months from date. (276)
7-10-1807 - Paul MICHAEL to James McCLELLAN; personal property and chattels. (276)
9-2-1807 - Maria CAMPBELL by consent of her mother, Mary Ann Campbell, both of
           Cincinnati is bound as apprentice to James H. LOOKER and Lydia wife of
           same, to serve from date to 12-29-1815. (276)
10-6-1805 - Robert BENHAM to Jesse HUNT; assignment of interests in lots. (277)
6-12-1807 - Sylvester LYONS to James ANDREWS; personal property and chattels. (277)

ENON VALLEY PRESBYTERIAN CHURCH CEMETERY- HANCOCK COUNTY, OHIO

Located in Big Lick Township on the south side of State Route 224 about five miles
west of the Hancock-Seneca County Line. Church is on east side of cemetery.

WEIMER, Sarah Jane daughter of C. & M. J. died Nov. 19, 1856 ag'd 14 yrs. 4 mo.
                                                                10 d's.
SHIRLEY, Elisabeth died Aug. 29, 1850 aged 70y 6m 25d
DOUGHERTY, John died Jan. 11, 1870 aged 63y 3m & 12d
THOMPSON, Nancy wife of Wm. Thompson died Apr. 10, 1850 aged 39 years
WILSON, Phebe daughter of A. & E. died_____(Note: Cemented in base)
        Susan wife of Wm. M. Wilson died Oct. 27, 1856 ag'd 25 yrs. 23d
        Robert died Oct. 4, 1865 aged 56y 9m 7ds.
        (Note: Next stone is cemented in base, probably a Wilson stone, all that
              can be read is) Sarah wife of_____
        Isabel wife of A. Wilson died Jan. 2, 1856 AE. 54 years
        Mary I. dau. of R. M. & I. J. died Aug. 27, 1856 AE. 2 mo 20d
        Mary Ann wife of R. M. Wilson died Sept. 2, 1853 aged 20y 4m 2d
LEONARD, In memory of Elisabeth daughter of R. & F. died Oct. 27, 1857 aged 44 yrs
        Frances wife of Robert Leonard____(Note: Cemented in base)
        Robert died May 4, 1867 aged 75y & 27d
THOMAS, Olive dau. of W. & S. died Apr. 17, 1860 aged 7y 9m 13d
COBB, Mary Ann wife of Foster Cobb died Apr. 23, 1881 aged 60, 7m 12d
BEAR, Mary wife of Jacob Bear died Aug. 20, 1856 aged 71 yrs. 9 mo. & 6 ds.
        Jacob died Aug. 2, 1864 aged 80 yrs. 7 mos. & 28 ds.
BINGER, Michael died Aug. 22, 1848 AE. 39 yrs. 10 mos. 14 ds.
MYRES, Sarah J. wife of Samuel Myres died July 8, 1865 aged 39y 11m & 12d
WINDLER, Henry son of J. & E. S. died Dec. 1, 1844 aged 2 yrs 6 mos. 25 ds.
McBRIDE, Sarah wife of Wm. McBride died May 5, 1862 aged 82 yrs. & 9 mos.
THOMAS, Infant son of S. & M. A. died Oct. 28, 1858
        Jane wife of Henry Thomas died Nov. 22, 1851 aged 71 ys. 10d.
        Henry died Oct. 14, 1863 aged 81 ys. 11 mo. 2 ds. (Note: Stone cracked)
MOORE, Wm. died May 6, 1867 aged 73y 3m 21d - WAR of 1812
BAYLESS, Jehu 1825-1919 Isabella C. his wife 1839-1922 (same stone)
        In memory of Richard Bayless who died Nov. 16, 1845 aged 44 years & 6 mo.
        Children of E. J. & A. C. Bayless (on same stone)
        Mary B. died Nov. 25, 1879 aged 2y 6m 27d
        Louella D. died Nov. 20, 1887 aged 19y 2m 21d
        Amos R. son of A. & M. died Apr. 21, 1853 ag'd 1 yr. 14 ds.
WILSON, Margaret dau. of A. & L. died May 13, 1854 AE. 24 ys. 6 M's 23 ds
MARTIN, Kezia dau. of R. L. & P. died Dec. 14, 1848 aged 1 mo. & 26 ds.
WILSON, Miles B. son of A. & L. died March 19, 1854 AE. 27 yrs. 8 mos. 13 d's
(Note: Old yellow slate stone with initials) B. B.
WHITAKER, Catharine wife of Peter S. Whitaker died Sep. 5, 1858 AE. 58 y's 1 m 18d
HENRY, William died Feb. 6, 1891 aged 87y 4m 10d
        Jane his wife died Nov. 8, 1856 aged 39y 4m 5d
        Isabella dau. of Wm. & J. died Sep. 8, 1855 aged 1m 5d
        William son of Wm. & R. died Sep. 6, 1865 aged 4y 11m 16d (all same stone)
Henderson, Andrew died July 6, 1858 AE. 81 y. 10 m. & 8 d.
DEATSMAN, Our mother Mary E. Deatsman formerly wife of Samuel Schwab died Apr. 7,
        1855 aged 59 years
SCHWAB, Samuel died Dec. 12, 1855 aged 61 yrs. 4 ms.

577

WEISBROD, Minerva dau. of J. C. & Mary died Oct. 22, 1861 aged 1y 8m & 2d
        Children of J. C. & M. Weisbrod (same stone)
            Cecelia died Aug. 27, 1864 aged 1y 7m 16d
            Clement L. died Aug. 27, 1864 aged 3m & 14d
SCHWAB, Gottlieb A. died Apr. 27, 1865 aged 19 yrs. & 11 mos.
MOFFET, John died Feb. 24, 1872 aged 65y 27d
WILSON, Zelma Ardella dau of J. & M. died Mar. 6, 1872 aged 7y 9m 13d
LEONARD, Mary A. dau. of A. & P. died Sept. 21, 1871 aged 17y & 5m
        David Brown son of A. & P. died Oct 14, 1866 aged 18y 5m & 13d
        Alice Margaret dau. of A. & P. died Sept. 2, 1866 aged 3y 9m 5d
        Harvey son of A. & P. died Mar. 17, 1867 aged 2 days
        Melissa J. dau. of A. & P. died Dec. 15, 1858 aged 2 years
        Effie M. Dau. of A. & P. died Mar. 10, 1854 aged 2 years
        Margaret A. dau. of S. & S. died Aug. 20, 1851 aged 1 month
BAYLESS, T. Hughs 1823-1894 Cassie J. his wife 1829-1921 (same stone)
THOMAS, Elizabeth wife of H. B . Thomas born Feb. 4, 1826 died Apr. 1, 1897
        H. B. born Nov. 6, 1819 died Oct. 3, 1891 (Note: Same stone Elizabeth)
        David 1855-1929 Frances Ella wife of D. Thomas 1856-1933
LEONARD, Phebe Melissa 1859-1920
        Children of W. K. & M. J. Leonard (same stone)
            Maggie M. died Sept. 13, 1865 aged 1y 2m 14d
            Samuel M. died Sept. 9, 1859 aged 4m 27d
            Mary Alice died Sept. 24, 1862 aged 3m 12d
        W. K. died Oct. 22, 1890 aged 69y 8m 29d (same stone as Martha J.)
            Martha J. wife of W. K. Leonard died Nov. 2, 1904 aged 78y 10m 27d
CREIGHTON, Isabella dau. of S. & A. died Aug. 31, 1847 aged 8 yrs. 10 mos. 26 ds.
        Infant son of S. & A. died Mar. 8, 1849 aged 18 ds.
        John son of S. & A. died Mar. 18, 1861_____(cemented in base)
LONG, George W. died Feb. 1, 1897 aged 49y 4m 13d Nancy A. 1851-1930
        Children of C. W. & N. A. Long (same stone as above)
        Mary E. died May 6, 1883 aged 1y 3m 25d Infant son died Feb. 6, 1893
STININGER, Amos died Sept. 26, 1877 aged 58y 6m 10d
        Eleanor his wife died July 12, 1902 aged 77y 8m 17d
        Children of A. & E. Stininger
        Samuel W. died Nov. 30, 1860 aged 6y 10m 17d
        Leannah J. died Nov. 30, 1860 aged 2y 22m 2d (Note: Stiningers
            all on same stone and on same stone as LONGS)

HANCOCK COUNTY, OHIO - MARRIAGES 1828-1838

The following records were taken from Marriage Record 1, located in the Probate Court, Hancock County, Ohio.

ALSPACH, Daniel to Catharine Ann Vanlue	9-15-1836
ALSPAUGH, George to Selizabeth Sull	2-14-1835
ANDERSON, Elijah R. to Mary Heistan	9-21-1834
ANDREWS, Elis to Phebe Hough	2-25-1836
ANTISDALE, Martin to Margaret Baker	10-20-1835
ATEN, Aaron to Mary Wagner	6-14-1836
ATEN, John M. to Margaret Redfearn	9-29-1836
AULTMAN, George to Tena Mooma	6-30-1835
BAKER, Aaron to Mary Hartley	1-29-1833
BAKER, Elisha to Mary Bell	5-1-1836
BAKER, Levi to Sarah Deph	10-27-1834
BAKER, William to Hannah Lambert	5-8-1834
BALDWIN, William H. to Mary Jane Patterson	4-21-1835
BALL, James to Mary Young	2-1-1836
BALLENTINE, James to Catharine Anna Vaneuon	9-15-1836
BAXTER, George to Margaret Fox	5-8-1834
BEARD, Adam to Delight Smith - consent; brother, Justin Smith	10-11-1830
BEARD, Elijah to Martha Egbert	3-27-1834
BEARDSLY, Hill of Licking Co. to Ann Strother	6-1-1830
BEESON, Elisha S. to Eliza Trout	4-2-1835
BENNETT, William to Polly Cole	12-6-1836
BISHER, Samuel to Mary Ann Albertson	11-12-1836
BISHOP, John D. to Sidney Williamson.	3-26-1837
BLIZZARD, Wesley to Sally Colclo	8-22-1833
BLOOM, Frederick to Nancy Miller	10-13-1836
BOLENBAUGH, Philip to Nancy Clymer	11-12-1835
BOMAN, Thomas of Pike Co. to Nancy Powel	7-26-1829
BONHAM, Robert to Hester Douglas	8-7-1836
BOWEN, Thomas to Margaret Fisher	9-19-1833
BRICKET, Jacob to Mary Phillips	8-27-1835
BRYAN, James to Mary Johnson	7-19-1836
BURGES, William to Sarah Ann Clark	1-1-1835
BURKHART, Jacob to Sally Kramer	7-28-1833
BUSHONG, Jacob to Susannah Rodebaugh	4-26-1836
CARLIN, James to Sarah Foster	3-22-1835
CARLIN, Parlee to Sarah Dewit - consent: father, Joseph Dewit	7-28-1830
CHAMBERLIN, Job to Sarah Craner	1-7-1830
CHAMBERLIN, Norman to Elizabeth Baker	3-20-1834
CHAMBERLIN, Norman to Eliza Watson	7-28-1836
CLAPPER, Henry to Melesa Jones	7-28-1836
COATS, James to Caroline Smith -consent: father, Stephen Smith	10-10-1830
COLCLO, Wm. M. to Louisa Patrick	5-18-1834
COLE, John W. to Henrietta Hall	3-22-1836
COLE, Thomas to Sarah Litsenberger	9-22-1831
CONDRON, John to Mary Williams - consent: Nathaniel Williams	12-24-1829
COOPER, Amos to Elizabeth Poe	11-20-1834
COOPER, Henry to Mary Powell	9-13-1832
COOPER, Jacob G. to Judith Wood	9-27-1835
COPLIN, Robert to Lucinda Cox	8-6-1835

579

```
CORBIN, William to Amanda Sallee                              10-30-1836
CROSSER, Daniel to Nancy Archer                              2-15-1836
DAILY, David J. to Elizabeth Hales                          7-10-1834
DAVIS, Daniel to Jane Blair                                 12-8-1836
DAVIS, James to Lovina Morrell                              10-15-1835
DAY, Lewis M. to Calista Fairchild                          3-20-1834
DEEMER, Peter to Lydia Johnson                              4-22-1832
DORSEY, William to Louisa Bryan                             4-3-1835
DRAKE, Joseph to Mary Sweany                                4-12-1835
DUBAL, William to Elizabeth Punches                         7-13-1834
DUDLESON, James to Rozella Moore                            3-12-1835
DUKES, John to Jane Houch                                   11-19-1830
DULIN, Sanford to Mary Hedges                               3-14-1833
EBERSOLE, John to Nancy Baker                               4-17-1836
ELDER, Jeremiah to Delia Miller                             5-17-1832
ELIOT, George to Darias Ecles                               7-4-1833
ENGLAND, Enoch L. to Christin Ackles                        2-19-1834
FAIRCHILD, Acton H. to Hariet Day                           10-23-1836
FISHEL, John to Sarah McKinnis                              5-1-1828
FISHER, John to Catharine Braucht                           12-13-1836
FLENNER, George to Massy Wolford                            4-10-1830
FOLK, Jacob to Sally Iler                                   5-21-1835
FOSTER, Jacob Jr. to Adaline Dewitt                         1-5-1932
FOWLER, William to Susan Slight-consent: father, Thomas Slight 10-23-1830
FOX, William to Margaret Mull                               1-10-1836
FRANKS, Michael to Priscilla Bowers                         4-1836
FREEMAN, Jacob to Hariet Bryan                              7-21-1836
FREEMAN, Job to Eveline Baird                               2-9-1834
FREEZE, John to Mary Ann Richardson                         2-12-1835
GARDNER, William of Michigan Territory to Eliza Johnson
                    consent:  Isaac Johnson                 7-4-1829
GEORGE, Peter to Mary Ann Woodruff                          5-8-1831
GIBSON, Charles to Sarah Beard                              11-15-1833
GILBERT, Aquilla to Lorrain Hamblin                         6-28-1829
GILPIN, William to Anner Smith                              10-6-1836
GOIT, Edson to Jane Patterson                               2-1-1833
GORSUCH, Silas A. to Martha Norris                          10-17-1833
GREER, James to Delila Hashberger                           6-30-1833
GREER, John H. to Mary Brown                                8-16-1835
HADDIX, Enoch to Ann Mariah Colclo                          7-13-1832
HAGERMAN, Richard to Sarah George                           1-15-1832
HATE, Reuben to Emiline Wickham                             12-20-1828
HALES, Joel to Rebecca Thomas                               2-19-1835
HALL, Aron to Abalina Vanemon                               11-10-1836
HALL, Samuel to Hester Corbin                               1-1-1833
HAMBELTON, Blewford to Sibella Baird                        12-30-1830
HAMBLIN, Don Alonzo to Isabel Slight                        2-12-1829
HANCOCK, Van R. to Lucinda Grant                            9-6-1835
HANCOCK, Warren to Malinda Bates                            12-27-1829
HANCOCK, William to Emily Shephard                          4-24-1834
HARTLY, Benjamin to Eliza Fox                               1-1-1835
HASHBERGER, Samuel to Anna Rader                            8-28-1834
```

580

HATEN, Alexander to Margaret Beam   8-7-1834
HELEM, Samuel to Barbara Ebright   2-11-1834
HELMICK, Nicholas to Sarah Ward   3-16-1834
HELMS, Jacob to Sally Ebright   10-3-1833
HELMS, Joseph to Eveline Ransbottom   5-27-1832
HELMS, Joseph to Harriet Tanner   8-10-1836
HELMS, Samuel to Lucinda Ebright   4-4-1833
HEMRY, George to Julian Geady   7-7-1836
HOOBLER, John to Barbara Moona   8-4-1835
HUFF, Thomas to Ann Walker   1-1-1835
HULL, Hiram to Lucinda Latta   3-27-1835
ILIFF, Joshua to Eve George   1-1-1832
ISHAM, Edward to Sarah Ann Day   3-12-1834
JAMES, George to Nancy Ward   8-2-1835
JAQUA, Amborse to Letitia Egbert   3-10-1836
JOHNSON, Joseph to Susan George   5-30-1830
JOHNSON, Miller to Hannah Cayton   6-14-1832
JONES, Isaiah to Sarah Wade   8-26-1834
JONES, Samuel to Edith Jones   2-15-1836
JUD, William to Sarah Clymer   12-6-1835
JULIEN, Samuel E. to Henrietta Byal   4-13-1835
KELLY, Daniel R. to Margaret Watson   9-13-1835
KELLY, Joshua to Nancy Hobbs   7-28-1833
KELLY, Moses to Hannah Keedy   5-22-1834
KIMMEL, John to Elizabeth Clark   8-16-1836
KRAMER, Adam to Eliza Schabb   4-5-1836
KRAMER, Philip to Polly Cotsmyre   9-8-1833
KRAMER, Simon to Sally Robenaught   9-15-1833
LIGHTEL, Martin to Elizabeth Mull   9-3-1835
LINCOLN, Wm. to Matilda Clark   12-28-1836
LITSENBERGER, Henry to Margaret Bell   11-19-1834
LITSENBERGER, Isaac to Sarah Beard   12-23-1830
LOCKWOOD, Peter to Charlotte Brown   8-30-1835
LOMAN, Thomas to Delila Ingland   1-2-1834
LONG, John to Marzilla Poulson   2-2-1832
LONG, Robert to Mary Essex   1-16-1832
LONG, William to Catharine Ann Cherry   12-31-1835
LUCE, Freeman to Louisa Horton   3-29-1835
McANALLY, Moses to Mary Roller   7-10-1834
McGEE, John to Eliza McKinnis - consent: Robert McKinnis   3-3-1831
McKINNIS, James to Lucy Wickham   3-11-1830
MACKRELL, Joshua to Martha Thomas   2-13-1834
MARTIN, Robert to Lovina Drake   12-14-1834
MEAD, John to Elizabeth Jones   7-12-1832
MECIMON, John to Rachel Hammond   12-24-1835
MILLER, Thomas to Temperance Picket   10-4-1832
MOFFITT, Charles to Elizabeth Davis   12-22-1836
MOORE, Aron to Nancy Walker   5-15-1834
MOORE, James to Hannah Aultman   9-4-1834
MOORE, James B. to Rachael Trude   11-13-1828
MOORHEAD, William to Mary Thompson   2-25-1836
MORGAN, Joseph to Elizabeth Lytle   8-27-1835

581

```
MULLEN, Thomas to Katharine Decker                              9-18-1834
MYERS, Wm. to Elizabeth Parish                                  6-21-1832
NICHOLS, John M. to Hannah Woodruff                             1-15-1833
OSENBAUGH, Abraham to Susan Spracher                            2-20-1836
PARKER, Jonathan to Elizabeth Hambelton                         10-31-1833
PARKER, Jonathan to Lucinda Workman                             9-5-1835
PELTIER, James of Allen Co. to Jane Clark                       9-25-1831
PERRIN, William to Martha Sallee                                10-30-1836
PICKET, William to Nancy Simmons                                6-8-1834
PINKERTON, William to Rosand Jones                              1-28-1836
PLOTNER, George to Rachel Lee                                   8-21-1836
POWEL, Philip to Betsy Fellows                                  3-8-1836
PRESSLER, George to Elizabeth Miller                            3-3-1836
PUNCHES, Elias to Catherine Punches                             1-1-1835
QUINN, Moses A. to Calista Cole                                 7-7-1836
RANSBOTTOM, Simeon to Rosanna Greer                             3-22-1834
READFEARN, Francis to Elizabeth Phillips                        12-27-1832
REDFEARN, Joseph to Ann Philips                                 1-8-1835
RHAMY, George to Barbary Wagoner                                3-2-1834
RICHARDSON, Joseph R. to Sarah Nigh                             11-12-1835
RICKETS, Resin to Mary Marce Hess                               8-14-1836
RISING, Benjamin to Mary Cox                                    10-24-1836
ROBERTS, John to Abagail Wickisson                              12-3-1834
ROBERTSON, Samuel to Zebella Hambelton                          6-5-1834
ROBINSON, Jacob to Elizabeth Studley                            8-7-1834
ROBINSON, James to Delilah Bohart                               ?-5-1835
ROSE, Jesse to Martha Lake                                      3-21-1833
ROSE, Jesse to Eliza Ulin                                       9-29-1836
ROSMAN, Peter to Catharine Hechler                              8-18-1836
ROYER, James to Margaret Archer                                 11-24-1836
RUMER, Isaac to Mary Daugherty                                  9-1-1836
RUMMEL, Frances to Caroline Ensminger                           9-10-1833
RUTE, William to Sarah Green                                    6-12-1834
SARGENT, Joseph A. to Elizabeth Dewit -consent: Joseph Dewit    9-24-1829
SHANKS, Hiram to Elizabeth Jones                                5-29-1834
SHANNON, Joseph of Crawford Co. to Vesta Chamberlin             12-13-1829
SHARP, Jacob to Julia Ann Whitman                               1-25-1835
SHAW, Thomas to Catharine Wolford                               12-25-1836
SHEPHERD, Thomas M. to Eliza Fisher                             4-16-1835
SHIPPY, Lorenzo D. to Mary Thomas                               11-15-1832
SHOCKEY, Philip to Susan Swisher                                2-16-1836
SKINNER, Morris to Mary Gorsuch                                 10-3-1833
SLIGHT, Thomas to Dulcinea Ward                                 9-1-1835
SLIGHT, Thomas Sr. to Sarah Cooper                              2-12-1832
SMITH, Charles D. to Mary Ann Cooper                            3-27-1834
SMITH, Harvey to Nancy Carpenter                                5-25-1834
SMITH, John to Rebecca Moore                                    11-28-1833
SMITH, Justin to Sarah Beard                                    5-31-1829
SMITH, Reason to Nancy Robinson                                 8-7-1834
SOWERS, Paul to Lea Gise                                        12-19-1835
SPANGLER, Daniel to Hannah Myers                                4-11-1835
SPURGEON, Jeremiah to Eliza Bates                               1-30-1834
```

```
SPURGEON, Richard to Matilda Roberts                              8-22-1833
STEWART, Charles to Mary Ann G. Stradley                         7-14-1836
STONE, Lewis E. to Sophronea Trask                               9-1-1836
STOTT, Teagle to Catharine Anderson                              10-9-1836
STRADLEY, Daniel to Elizabeth Bell                               5-15-1834
STRADLEY, Thomas to Mary Picket                                  2-27-1834
STRATTON, Thomas to Selah Jones                                  6-21-1835
SWIHART, Aaron to Susanna Thomas                                 9-18-1836
SWIHART, Mathias to Mary Thomas                                  10-23-1836
THOMAS, Jacob to Rebecca Eddington                               6-26-1834
THOMPSON, Enoch to Mary Swaggart                                 10-28-1830
TILLIS, Griffin to Diana Ransbottom                              3-23-1831
TRAVIS, John to Rachael Wilson                                   11-22-1832
TULLIS, John to Eveline Tanner                                   11-21-1829
TWINING, Jacob to Elizabeth Adams                                6-18-1835
VALENTINE, John to Elizabeth Williams                            1-21-1836
VANLUE, Fredrick to Margaret Farthing                            8-27-1835
VANLUE, William to Presachey Tiding Brown                        2-25-1836
WALTER, Jacob to Atha Ann Price                                  9-25-1834
WATSON, Elisha to Amanda Hill                                    10-16-1834
WATSON, George to Mary Rogers                                    12-8-1836
WEBSTER, David to Ann Elizabeth Teatsorth                        10-29-1835
WIANS, George to Mary Ann Dunbar                                 2-23-1836
WILLIAMS, Elijah to Sarah Anne Watson                            4-20-1834
WILLIAMS, John W. to Elizabeth Hall                              12-18-1836
WILLIAMS, Nathan to Ann Hamblin                                  5-27-18;
WILLIAMSON, Levi to Mary Bibler                                  6-7-1836
WILLIAMSON, Peter to Rachel Pinkerton                            5-26-1836
WILSON, Isaac S. to Ann Coen                                     12-19-1833
WISELY, Allen to Amela Bright                                    11-2-1830
WISELY, William to Lourenna Bright                               6-7-1831
WOLFORD, Andrew to Charlotte Corben                              7-4-1833
WOLFORD, Jeremiah to Derusia Hancock                             11-23-1834
WOLFORD, Washington to Lydia Lake                                7-25-1829
WOODRUFF, Elijah to Sarah Walters                                10-16-1836
ZIMMERMAN, John to Catharine Heaston                             3-29-1835
_____, Robert (Surname not given) to Elizabeth Redfearn       12-28-1836
```

The following wills were abstracted from Will Book 1, located in the Probate Court. Pages on which record may be found are given in parenthesis.

WOLFORD, John - dated 6-26-1829; recorded 5-28-1830 - Wife, Mary S. Sons: George W., Andrew, Jeremiah, Absalom W., John and Abraham. Daughter: Elizabeth Elen. Grandsons: John W. Elder, son of daughter Mary Ann Elder; John W. Elder son of daughter Sarah Elder. Executor: Absalom W. Wolford. Signed: John Wolford. Witnesses: Mordecai Hammond and John Rose. (1)

SARGENT, Eli of Finley twp. - dated 3-7-1830; recorded 5-29-1830. Mother, Nancy Sargent, also to serve as executrix. Signed: Eli (mark) Sargent. Witnesses; J. E. Wickham and Bass Rawson. (3)

RABB (ROBB?)/-dated 9-9-1830; recorded 10-27-1830 - Wife, Margaret. Son, John, not of age. Signed: Andrew Rabb. Witnesses: Henry Reel and Aquilla Gilbert. (5)

TANNER, Abel - dated 2-22-1835; recorded 7-27-1835. Wife, Mary. Eight children, mentioned but not named; some are married and some are not of age. Executors: wife, Mary and Benjamin Spar. Signed: Abel Tanner. Witnesses: Elihu Smith and Charles O. Bradford. (6)

LONG, John - dated 1-20-1835; recorded 2-13-1836. Wife, Sebena. Son, Robert Long. Executors: wife, Sebena and son, Robert. Signed: John (mark) Long. Witnesses: William Roller and Andrew Foulson. (8)

RICHESON, Philip - dated 11-14-1836; recorded 4-4-1837. Wife, Elizabeth, "mother of six children of mine". Children: Mary Ann wife of John Friese, Joseph Richeson, Michael Richeson, Hannor Richeson, James Richeson and Henry Richeson. Step-daughter: Barbara wife of William Preston. Executors: wife, Elizabeth and neighbor, Michael Battenfield. Signed: Philip Richeson. Witnesses: Abraham Huff and Thomas N. SHepherd. (11)

ROSE, James - dated 4-22-1837; recorded (not given). Wife, Sarah. Sons: David James, John, Jesse, Thomas, Jonathan and Levi. Daughters: Rachael Taylor, Hannah Nelson, Mary Clark, and Sarah Rose. Executor: son, John Rose. Signed: James Rose. Witnesses: Felix Miller and Thomas Miller. (15)

HOISINGTON, John S. of Canaan - dated 3-30-1834; recorded 2-10-1838. Wife, Elizabeth. Sons: SmEth and Saniel. Daughters: Rhoda Shaw, Triphene White, Polly Washburn, Betsy Steele, Lucy Tay(?), and Elvira Jones. Signed: John S. Hoisington. Witnesses: John Miles, Hiram Powers and Earl Moulton. (16)

SHEPHERD, Jacob - dated 1-18-1838; recorded 4-10-1838. Wife, mentioned, but not named. Son: Thomas H. Shepherd. Son-in-law: Wm. Hancock and Emily his wife. Mentions two grandchildren, daughters of Emily, but does not name. Executors: Thomas Thompson and John Long. Signed: Jacob (mark) Shepherd. Witnesses: Noah Wilson and Andrew Thompson. (19)

GILLCHRIST, Susan - dated Sept. 1C37; recorded 4-11-1838. Sister: Mary Gillchrist. Sister-in-law: Sarah H. Gillchrist widow of brother Hugh Gillchrist. Heirs of brother, Hugh Gillchrist: Thomas, Steward, Amanda and John Ebenezer Gillchrist. Signed: Susan Gilchrist. Witnesses: David Dorsey and Joseph Hardy. (21)

LITZENBERGER, George - dated 4-29-1834; recorded 5-6-1839 - Sons: mentioned not named except two names as executors; may be more. Four Daughters: Mary Hushour, Katherine Myers, Susan Van Truce and Sarah Cold. Grandson: Samuel Orwig, to have share his mother Mary Hushour would be entitled. Mentions a piece of land in Pennsylvania which was sold to Henry Orwick. Executors: sons, Isaac and Henry. Signed: George (mark) Litzenberger. Witnesses: Frederick Benner and Henry (mark) Treece. (23)

NELSON, Margaret - dated 10-18-1837; recorded 2-7-1840. Sons: William, James, John, Robert, Joseph and Daniel. Eight daughters: Margaret, Agnes, Jannet, Mary, Elizabeth, Ester, Ann and Sally Nelson. Mentions: John Nelson son of Robert Nelson. Mentions: bonds in the hands of Robert Adams of Perry County, Pennsylvania. Executor: son, Daniel Nelson. Signed: Margaret Nelson. Witnesses: Isaac Wiseman and James T. Caywood. (25

COLCLO, Jeremiah - dated 1-19-1839; recorded 1-4-1840. Five unmarried children: Polly, Betsey, Hiram S., James H. and Emily Colclo. Married children: William, Ann and Sally. Executor: son-in-law, Enoch Haddox. Signed: Jeremiah Colclo. Witnesses: Reuben Oliver, Samuel Bardin and James Fleming. (27)

BYAL, William - dated 1-4-1840; recorded 4-22-1840. Wife, Mentioned, but not named. Sons: William, Samuel A., Absolem, John and Peter. Daughters: Sarah Jane Byal, Amy Byal, Martha Getlis, Ann Myers, Henrietta Julian, wife of Wm. Grubb, and Delia Stanley. Mentions: Heirs of Charles Byal, not of age. Mentions one share to Jane Byal, no relationship given. Mentions: one share to William Byal son of John Byal; one share to William Byal Grubb son of William Grubb and my daughter the wife of Wm. Grubb. Executors: sons, John and Peter; also to serve as guardians of Wm., Samuel A. and Sarah Jane. Signed: William Byal. Witnesses F. Henderson and Price Blackford. Codicil dated 1-17-1840, additional mention of daughter Ann Myers. Same witnesses. (30)

BRANDEBERRY, Rudolph of Cass twp.- dated 8-12-1840; recorded 10-12-1840. Sons: Adron, Andrew, Jacob, Isaac and John. Six daughters: Katherine Dephenbaugh, Delia, Susannah, Margaret, Anna and Elizabeth. Signed: Rudolph Brandeberry. Witnesses: Philip Condit and Charles J. Eckles. (36)

McCLELLAN, Robert of Eagle twp. - dated 3-10-1841; recorded 5-17-1841. Wife, mentioned, but not named. Sons: Alexander, James, George, David, Forges, Thomas and John. Daughters: Margaret Hughs and Nancy. Executors: son, John and William L. Henderson. Signed: Robert McClellan. Witnesses: George W. Alspach and George Nimrod. (37)

CAZIER, Abraham of Cass twp. - dated (not given); recorded (not given-1841). Brother: Murry Cazier, to have 80 acres in DeKalb Co., Indiana and also to serve as executor. Signed: Abraham (mark) Cazier. Witnesses: A. B. Brandeberry and John Eckels. (40)

COLE, Abraham Senior - dated 10-8-1841; recorded 10-21-1841. Wife, Verlinda. Sons: William, Samuel, Joshua and Thomas. Daughters: Athaliah Bell and Melinda Chilson. Grand-daughters: Mary Jane Hagerman, Margaret Hagerman and Sarah Cole. Executor: son, Thomas. Signed: Abraham (mark) Cole. Witnesses: Harvey Smith and John H. Green. (41)

RIDER, Reuben - dated 12-23-1841; recorded 5-17-1842. Wife, Christina. Son: Silas H. Rider. Daughters: Sarah H. Rider and Marinda P. Rider. Executors: wife, Christiana and Allen Wisely; also to act as guardians of son and daughters. Signed: Reuben Rider. Witnesses: William Wickham and George B. Price. (45)

HULSE, Israel - dated 7-7-1842; recorded 11-7-1842. Brother: Ambrose Hulse of New York. Sister: Mary Murry. Niece: Nancy Jane Morrison. Nephews: Aristeus Hulse, Eaton (also given as Cayton) Murry and Zelatus Murray. Mentions: "I give and bequeath to Albert P. Hulse a piece of land in Section 31, Township 14, where his father was buried as per deed recorded in land office at Bucyrus, being E½ NW¼ Section 13 and NE¼ SW¼ Range 12E". Signed: Israel Hulse. Witnesses: Jonathan Church and Richard Y. Massey. (47)

FOUST, John of Cass twp. - dated 1-17-1842; recorded 11-9-1842. Wife, Rebecca, also to serve as executrix. Four children: Catharine, Margaret, Daniel and Anthony. Requests that Samuel Hunnington serve as guardian of minor children. Signed: John (mark) Foust. Witnesses: Paul Adams, David Dorsey and Joseph Hardy. (50)

MATHEWS, James J. of Union twp. - dated 6-14-1842; recorded 11-8-1842. Brothers and Sisters: John K. Mathews, Nathan N. Mathews, Elizabeth M. Davidson, William Mathews, Mary J. Mathews, Sarah T. Mathews, Mariah Mathews and Joseph Mathews. Executors: William Mathews and Henry Mathews. Signed: John J. Mathews. Witnesses: John McKinley, William McConnell, and James T. McConnell. (53)

HARDIN COUNTY, OHIO
Marriages 1833-1842

Kindly note that in several instances the names given on the marriage application differs in spelling from the names given on the marriage return. In some
cases a completely different surname was given. Whenever this occurs, the alternate spelling, surname etc. is given in parenthesis.

AMY, Charles to Rebecca RICHISON	8-4-1834
ANDERSON, John to Patina SAXTON	5-5-1836
AWNCHIDE, Charles to Mary CASPER	8-6-1840
BADLEY, Lewis W. to Rebecca B. Davis	10-3-1835
BAIRD, John H. To Llance DINWIDDIE	12-5-1835
BAKER, Alexander to Sarah FARNAMAN	10-8-1842
BAKER (BACKER), John to Catharine BOLENBAUGH	12-28-1837
BALCH (BATCH), Israel to Sarah McDONALD	10-11-1842
BALES, Thomas to Elenor GREEN	12-2-1833
BALTZELL, John C. to Mary Ann HOLLY	7-26-1835
BARNES, Andrew C. to Almeda EVANS	4-1-1835
BARNES, Joseph to Sarah FITCH	12-28-1837
BARRET, George to Polly PRICE	5-15-1836
BEAGS, Robert to Mariah CANDLER	1-7-1841
BENSON, Chancy to Nancy A. HUGHEY	9-20-1839
BORTEN, John to Ruth BAZEL	1-5-1839
age proven by Bethard BORTEN	
BOSSERMAN, Samuel to Lavina PRICKERPRILES	4-4-1841
BOWDLE, Samuel P. to Harriett RUTLEDGE	2-24-1842
BOWYER, Charles to Lucretia LYLES	6-27-1833
BOYNTON, Benjamin L. to Mary FARNAM	2-14-18
BROWN, Amos to Agnes MILLER	10-20-1842
BROWN, Richard J. to Jane MILLER	3-23-1842
BUTCHER, Alfred to Elizabeth CASTOR	2-27-1842
BUTCHER, Jacob to Evilina S. SHOW	7-28-1842
BUTCHER, John G. to Dianna SPITZER	7-11-1839
CAMPBELL, Samuel to Matilda ALEXANDER Iss.	3-27-1839
CANAN, John to Rebecca POE (HAAS)	2-7-1830
CANDLER, General Washington to Elizabeth WEAVER	12-8-1842
CANNON, Westley to Allean CUMSTON (CUMPSTON)	2-14-1839
CARPENTER, John to Susannah COLE	3-30-1837
CASTOR, Paul to Ellenor HINTON	12-29-1836
CHARLTON, Henry to Janett THOMSON	12-27-1838
CHURCH, Collins to Nancy WORREL	9-20-1842
CLARK, Avery to Harriet HAYS	1-1-1842
CONNER, Patrick to Margaret F. SMITH	12-19-1841
COOLY, William to Catharine CANNAN	7-5-1835
COOPER, John to Mary ADAMS	7-20-1837
COREY, Enos Ayres to Eliza Ann FOUGHT	1-13-1841
COTTERIL, John to Mariah BROWN	2-17-1842
COULTER, David W. to Rebecca COLLINS	7-1-1841
CROW, Jacob to Mary EMERT	12-16-1841(
CUMMINS, John to Mary DALLAST	2-17-1842
DANIALS, John to Sarah SHOW	11-27-1841
DARRINGER, Jacob to Mary HANNAH	12-22-1840
DAVIDSON, Patrick to Elizabeth MATHEWS	9-30-1841
DAVIS, Elijah to Mary HASTINGS	11-11-1841
DAVIS, John G. to Isabel McCRACKEN	6-7-1838

587

```
DAYTON, Lucius to Catharine PINE                    12-2-1835
DEEM, James to Christinna RYNN                      10-24-1841
DILLE, Cephas to Mary Ann FOUGHT                    3-6-1838
DOLLY, Charles to Elizabeth McELROY                 9-14-1838
DOLLY, Milford to Mary McELROY                      1-31-1839
DOLSON, Hugh to Jane HERRON                         3-23-1837
DRAPER, Isaac to Susannah TETTER                    2-9-1837
DUNHAM, Jonathan to Elizabeth HARDIN                8-20-1840
EMERY, Ellis to Betsy Ann MARKS                     3-31-1842
ERNEST, George Jur. to Mary FRY (FREY)              10-21-1837
FARNAM, Amasa to Hannah COSSE (COPE)                11-28-1833
FISHER, Edwin to Rachel BANNING                     10-27-1841
FOSS, Lyman to Minerva HASSEY                       2-19-1837
FOUGHT, James to Sarah BIRD               Iss.      6-5-1838
FOUGHT, Preston to Lanough PUGH                     1-24-1839
GARDNER, John to Susanah PEAVER                     1-18-1838
GAREY, John H. to Almira Jane HINELIN               4-20-1840
GARLOCK, Ulric to Mary PIPHER                       10-7-1839
GARWOOD, Beni to Ruth KELLY                         5-3-1838
GARWOOD, Fenton to Mary LYON                       (6-15-1842
                             2 dates               (11-15-1842
GERROD, Lewis to Anna Mary STIVER                   10-27-1842
GIBSON, Joseph to Barbary PIXLER                    9-23-1841
GILLESPIE, James M. to Elcy GARDNER                 3-13-1834
GILLILAND, Ambrose B. to Catharine EDE              7-7-1842
GLOVER, John O. to Elizabeth WOLF                   9-3-1835
GOODIN, George B. to Lydia Ann LETSON               4-29-1838
GOSS, Westly to Elizabeth EVANS                     3-17-1836
GOSSAY, William to Margaret DENWEDIE                3-12-1835
GRANT, Thomas to Mariah PEAL                        11-14-1839
GRAVES, Huron to Ulrana ARBUCKLE                    9-12-1839
GRAY, Thomas to Sarah Ann HOWSER                    9-21-1841
GRIMBLEBECK, John to Elizabeth SHEAF                4-12-1841
GUM, John to Catherine WILLIAMSON                   8-4-1840
HALEY, George to Rachel H. GARY                     1-1-1835
HALSTEAD, Hiram to Anna CROSS                       4-6-1837
HALSTEAD, Ira to Atemessa SALES                     3-16-1837
HALSTED, John B. to Mitina WILLIAMS       Iss.      4-7-1836
            Returned same day and not married
HAMBLIN, Reuben to Ann PARKER                       10-21-1837
HAMILTON, James to Mary Ann ROUTSAN                 2-28-1836
HAMILTON, Richard to Mary LYNCH                     7-12-1836
HARDMAN, Michael to Charity MOUREY                  7-2-1838
HARVEY, Ephraim to Nancy HUBBARD                    11-16-1837
HARVEY, James to Elisabeth ffOLSE                   6-16-1842
HARVEY, John to Margaret SLOANE                     8-10-1837
HATFIELD, Nelson to Susan HITES                     12-7-1839
HATFIELD, Noah to Nancy BAILEY                      10-5-1841
HATTERY, David to Mary RUTHLEDGE                    11-17-1842
HAYES, Orlando to Eliza CLARK                       1-25-1842
HAYS, William O. to Mary CESSNCO                    3-21-1841
HECKATHORN, Henry to Ester HARTLE                   9-30-1837
HENDRICKSON, Harvy to Cynthia BLAND       Iss.      8-12-1836
HENRY, John H. to Isabella ZIMMERMAN                11-26-1836
```

588

HILL, Samuel to Elizabeth ANDERSON   10-1-1835
HILL, Samuel to Prescella SCOTT   Iss. 4-6-1839
HINDMAN, Robert to Matilda KIRTLAND   3-11-1841
HINTENE, William to Anny HOUSER   Iss. 4-11-1839
HITCHCOCK, Erastus to Lucinda WESTBROOK   2-13-1842
HITES, John to Margaret HUBBARD   11-11-1841
HOLMES, Ellis to Matilda FOX   4-15-1841
HOLMES, James F. to Mariah E. SCHOONOVER   5-27-1841
HOLMES, Thomas to Lavina EWING   11-19-1840
HOLT, Morgan to Caroline COYLE   6-17-1841
HOUGHAN, Aaron C. to Pillettia (Potite) DOTSON 1-20-1839
HOUSER, George H. to Elizabeth WILLMUTH   11-3-1842
HOUSER, Isaac to Julia Ann WIL(L)MOUTH   1-23-1839
HOUSER, John H. to Margaret McBRIDE   6-10-1841
HOW, Lelden to Elenor RICESON   9-29-1835
HOWEY, John to Salome BARNES   7-21-1836
HURD, Euri P. to Margaret M. MASSES (MOSSES)   9-16-1835
HUSTON, Thomas to Ann HARVEY   2-6-1836
HUSTON, William to Lucinda JOHNSTON (JOHNSON) 12-14-1841
INGMAN, George P. to Martha JOHNS   7-1-1838
INGRAM, John to Sarah CLAPPER   10-2-1842
IRWIN, William to Eliza Jane ZIMMERMAN   3-8-1838
JACKSON, William to Rachel HOSEMAN   1-11-1838
JACOBS, Isaac to Rachel PAVER   6-26-1834
JENKINS, Joseph to Martha Ann Kellough   1-10-1839
JOHNSON, Benjamin to Mary JOHNSON   10-2-1836
JOHNSTON, William to Susannh MYERS   4-12-1838
JOHNSTON, William H. to Amanda HUSTON   1-30-1837
JOHNSTON, William W. to Sarah Ann HINDBAUGH Iss. 4-26-1841
JONES, Isaiah to Sarah BARNES   12-5-1839
JONES, Jesse to Francis BAKER   5-12-1842
JONES, Joseph to Martha ADKINS   5-7-1836
JONES, William to Amer (Omer) LIGHTNER   12-25-1838
KALER, Lewis to Margaret ORTH   9-4-1842
KARNS, Harry to Betsy SALMON   11-3-1842
KEIFER, Benedict to Mary OBENOUR   5-17-1840
KELLOG (KELLOUGH), William to Mary JENKINS   4-18-1837
KING, William to Nancy Ann LYNE   7-2-1835
KINNEAR, Isaac to Seraphina WISONG   6-29-1842
KIRKLAND, Samuel to Nancy McBRIDE   2-25-1841
KIRKPATRICK, Joseph to Elizabeth MOORE   Iss. 5-3-1836
KOUTZE, Christopher to Margaret MILLER   8-13-1837
KRAFT, Johann Friedrick Wilhelm to Johanna Louise
         KRAFSMANN (KRASSMANN)   7-31-1836
KYLE, Henry L. to Rebecca CESSNA   3-25-1838
LAMBERT, Isaac to Harriet CLAYTON   11-10-1839
LATIMORE, Francis to Aramenta RICHASON   7-27-1837
LAWRENCE, Lin. to Elisabeth CONNOR   10-14-1841
LETSON, C. B. to Jane Hueston   3-22-1840
LEWIS, Chester to Catharine HOWEY (HEWEY)   9-1-1840
LOMBARD, Eli to Dorcas KYLE   12-14-1837
LOUGHTON, W. (or U.) P. to Ellen HOUSER   1-19-1840
McAFEE, Robert W. to Caroline CONKLIN   10-31-1836

589

```
McCAMBER, Charles to Hulda R. LAIN                    12-4-1836
McCLOUD, William to Martha DILLE                      11-1-1835
McCOY, Moses to Rebecca BOWDLE                        7-2-1835
McCRACKEN, Robert to Nancy HOUSTON                    12-20-1835
McFARLAND, Wm. H. to Mariah SEIG                      9-20-1842
McHENRY, John to Margaret SEWARD                      1-4-1841
McINTIRE, Joseph C. to Rebecca PINE                   2-6-1834
McKINNON, John M. to Sarah HILE (HILL)                11-1-1841
McMILLEN, Robert to Aelena SMITH                      2-14-1841
McQUOWN, John S. to Rath Ann (Sarah A.) PUW (PEW)     1-13-1839
McQUEN, Robert to Catharine SIMMS                     1-31-1837
MARLOW, Judson to Rachel MARSH                        5-12-1839
MASON, Francis to Mary Ann WAGGONER                   6-10-1842
MATHEWS, Samuel to Hannah LYNCH                       6-26-1842
MAYNARD, James to Harriet GOSS                        6-22-1836
MEADS, Lewis to Nancy RUTLEDGE                        2-3-1842
MENTZER, Samuel to Eliza WHITEMAN                     11-17-1836
MENTZER, Samuel to Sophia BENJAMIN                    4-23-1838
MIDDAUGH, George to Isabel CLAYPOOL                   3-7-1841
MILLER, Lewis A. to Margaret A. STEVENSON             1-16-1840
MINARD, James M. to Pheby GOHEGGIN                    5-21-1835
MONROE, Isaac to Sarah COLLINS                        7-14-1842
MOORE, Benjamin to Sarah RANDLE                       11-17-1842
MOORE, George G. to Polly POE                         1-26-1837
MORE, George W. to Abigail RANDEL (RANOLDS)           7-31-1841
MORE, Samuel to Charlotte SHOW                        3-11-184,
MORGAN, Calvin to Karah LOVER                         9-1-1836
MOURY, George to Margaret FROY                        9-12-1839
MOURY, George to Sarah CROW (CROSS)                   9-10-1840
MOURY, Jacob to Margaret McELROY                      7-29-1841
MOURY, John to Elizabeth ERNAST                       12-14-1837
MOURY, Joseph to Phebe Ann CURNS                      5-22-1842
MYERS, Adam to Dorotha RAMSEY                         12-24-1840
MYERS, Elias to Pamilla A. TAMANY                     6-24-1841
NEWLAND, John S. to Mary HILL                         8-20-1840
NEWTON, Willas to Mary Ann WOLF                       2-8-1838
OBENOUR, Frederick to Mary WYANT               Iss.  12-21-1837
OSBERN, Samuel to Sarah MOOD                          8-11-1842
OTIS, Stephen to Rosannah HASTINGS                    6-24-1841
PATTERSON, Thomas to Kurnhopeth LUPEE                 3-17-1842
PAVER, John to Sarah THOMAS                           1-11-1836
PENTZER, Henry to Deborah CROSS                       11-27-1839
PEW, Day to Elizabeth DAVIS                           9-22-1841
PIFFER, John to Eva ELSASSER                    Iss. 7-21-1838
PIMPERTON, Jasper M. to Charlotte COPELAND            10-20-1842
PITTINGTON, Sylvester to Elisabeth MARSH              6-10-1842
PLUMER, John to Vesti SWAIN                           2-25-1841
POE, Andrew to Levina SAMMERMAN(?)*                   2-11-1836
POST, John to Mary Ann CROSSAN                        2-5-1835
POST, John to Eliza BAKER                             10-18-1839
PRESTON, John to Hannah PEAL                          10-11-1839
PRESTON, William to Aseneth GARWOOD                   5-15-1842
PUGH, Hugh to Philinda CROSS                          7-15-1841
```

*For *Levina Sammerman* read *Levina Zimmerman*. GATEWAY TO THE WEST, Vol. 3: No. 2 (Apr.-June 1970).

```
PUGH, Thomas to Rebecca BACKER                              3-16-1837
QUINN, Charles to Cleressa CHAMBERLAIN                      10-26-1837
QUNE, Geo. W. to Eliza SWEET                        Iss. 1-4-1840
RANGE, George to Elisabeth PIPHER                          10-13-1841
REAMS, John Jordan to Matilda SCOTT                        5-31-1842
RICE, George to Jane CAILE                                 3-8-1839
RICE, Robert to Mary STUART                                4-25-1842
RICE, William to Polly SCOTT                               12-23-1841
RILEY, John F. to Susanna PACKARD                          12-16-1841
RINE, George to Edey BEAM                                  4-5-1837
RITCHEY, Jeptha to Cynthia NEWLAND                         6-2-1835
RITCHEY, Jeptha to Lucinda TIDD                            1-5-1836
RITCHEY, Samuel to Andey (Anssly) DAVIS                    7-9-1835
ROBINSON, George R. to Parthenia MORE                      6-24-1833
ROBY, Hanson to Delila E. JOHNSON                   Iss.4-11-1839
ROBY, John to Nancy LATIMORE                               7-30-1841
ROEMACK, William to Cynthia Ann G. PURDY                   12-21-1842
ROSEBROOK, John to Mary RICHISON                           10-4-1836
RUNKLE, Ralph E. to Eliza E. SEIG                          12-20-1840
RUTLEDGE, Samuel to Margaret ZIMMER                        12-15-1842
SARM, Levi to Sarah SHUSTER                                11-17-1842
SCHYLER, Vansler (Van Sauseler) to Cynthia NICHOLS         5-24-1834
SCOTT, Lynn Sterling to Marinda BENNET                     12-30-1842
SEIG, Kinnon to Rebecca VANMETER                           10-6-1841
SHANKS, Henry to Elizabeth LATTIMORE                       11-10-1838
SHANKS, Samuel to Lana VALENTINE                           6-19-18
SHARP, Benjamin W. to Margaret SCOTT                       6-26-1838
SIMMS, William to Martha BALIS                             4-8-1841
SMITH, Agustus to Louisa FLEMMING                          9-21-1842
SMITH, John George to Susannah WEYANT                      10-27-1837
SMITH, Joshua to Sarah Ann DENWIDIE                        3-5-1835
SMITH, Robert to Katharine HOUSER                          5-27-1834
SMITH, Robert to Aelena SMITH                              2-14-1841
SNELLING, John to Cynthia Baroel (Beroel)                  4-16-1836
SNODDY, John to Margaret BLAIR                             11-24-1836
SPENCER, George to Elizabeth RABBY (ROBBY)                 11-22-1838
SPENCER, Watson to Ellenor RUTLEDGE                        5-28-1836
SPIKES, David S. to Catherine BOWAN (LOWER)                12-19-1839
SPITZER, Ephriam to Sarah PETERS                           2-20-1840
SPITZER, John to Sarah COTTERAL                            9-25-1838
STEEL, Daniel to Mary MARSH                                2-21-1841
STEINSON, Harmon to Mary OTIS                              9-2-1841
STERN, John to Lydia YOUNG                                 4-12-1841
STEVENSON, Eli to Mary McCOY                               4-1-1835
STEVENSON, Homer P. to Mary HULINGER                       11-25-1840
STROUD, Geo. K. S. to Catharine SOMERVILLE                 6-29-1841
STROUD, Samuel H. to Catharine DERRINGER                   8-25-1842
TELLER, Edwin S. to Martha THOMPSON                        7-14-1842
THARP, Alexander to Sophiah HARRISON                Iss.3-9-1835
THOMAS, Joel to Rachel LEONARD                             7-2-1838
THOMPSON, Stephen to Martha KIRKPATRICK                    12-16-1841
THOMSON, Alexander to Katharine CANADY                     6-28-1835
```

591

```
THOMSON (THOMAS), James W. To Elizabeth
                HAIVEBAUGH (HEVBAUGH)                    10-15-1837
THOWARD, Emanuel to Jane JOHNS                   Iss. 3-16-1839
TIDD, John to Polly Ann NEIL                          8-15-1835
TODD, Martin H. to Sarah J. CONNER                   2-14-1839
TRUMP, Andrew Jackson to Sarah DRAPER                12-16-1841
ULIN, John to Betsy OBENHOUR                          5-16-1841
ULIN, John P. to Elizabeth LYNCH                      6-24-1842
VANOSDOL, Eli to Lavina SNIDER                       12-31-1840
VANSKY, Samuel P. to Elizabeth Ann LITTLETON         11-7-1841
VOZEY, James to Jane D. MOSS                          2-16-1837
WAGNER, Samuel to Mary Ann HOSEMAN                   12-24-1834
WAGGONER, Barney to Barbary EMERTS                   10-6-1839
WAGGONER, Francis to Elizabeth McELROY               8-18-1842
WAGONER, Anthony to Mary Ann EMERTS                   9-1-1839
WALLACE, William to Lydia MOORE                      10-18-1838
WARNER, Edward to Mary ADAMS                          8-19-1841
WETSON, Robert to Meribah JOHNSON                    12-31-1835
WHEELER, H. N. to Matilda McCOY                      12-10-1837
WHEELER, Joseph to Sophrony FARNUM                   10-10-1837
WHITE, William to Delilah ROGERS                      1-17-1836
WHITHARTT (WHITEHARTS), John to Lodices COLDWELL      2-28-1836
WILLCOCKS, John A. to Elizabeth MEAR                 12-25-1839
WILLMUTH, Lemuel to Mary DAVIS                        5-27-1840
WILLMUTH, William to Mary FOGLESONG                   6-30-1841
WILLSON, David to Mary Ann ROBEY                     10-16-1842
WILLSON, James to Elizabeth HOPKINS                   1-19-1840
WOLFORD, Gideon to Eliza RAPP                         2-20-1840
WOOD, Isaac S. to Mary Jane MOORE                    11-17-1842
YOUNG, David H. to Eve Ann PENCER                    10-27-1836
YOUNGS, William to Love SOLMAN                       12-30-1837
ZIMMERMAN, George to Sarah Ann ROPP                   3-6-1842
```

Persons 50 years and over.

Name	Date of Death	Age	Marital Status	Place of Death	Place of Birth
SHOEMAKER, Peter	8-8-1867	75y 8m	mar.	Buck Twp.	Virginia
MYRES, John	8-25-1867	58y	wid.	Kenton	Germany
INGMAN, Ruth	9-5-1867	71y 13d	wid.	Goshen Twp.	Penna.
HOLMES, Mary	7-2-1867	73y 2m	mar.	Hardin Co.	Wash. Co. Pa.
MERCER, Susan	11-1-1867	57-1-25	mar.	Hale Twp.	- - - - - -
CHURCH, Horace	12-24-1867	64-3-25	mar.	Kenton	Mass.
CALHOON, Lucy H.	12-31-1867	77-8-8	wid.	Troy, Ohio	Conn.
ZEIGLER, Rebecca	11-9-1867	55-7-28	mar.	Hardin Co.	Penna.
SEIG, Jonathan H.	2-9-1868	52-9-1	mar.	Ridgway	Virginia
KIPFER, Benedict	3-3-1868	70y	mar.	Kenton	Germany
KELLERHAUS, John U.	3-15-1868	68y	wid.	Cessna Twp.	Germany
WAGNER, Ann	2-5-1868	60y 14d	wid.	Pleasant Twp.	Wash. Co. Md.
GLENN, Martha	2-8-1868	74-10-28	mar.	Pleasant Twp.	Wash. Co. Pa.
HOLMES, Enos H.	3-1-1868	76-2-24	wid.	Pleasant Twp.	Virginia
STEINER, Mary B.	2-7-1868	71-10-19	mar.	Cessna Twp.	Wertemburg
WARD, Sarah	3-8-1868	68y 29d	—	Round Head	- - - - -
ATKINSON, John	5-21-1868	69-4-7	mar.	Hale Twp.	Virginia
WALKER, Margaret	8-8-1867	69-10-13	wid.	Dudley Twp.	Penna.
FRY, John	4-25-1868	61-9-22	mar.	Pleasant Twp.	- - - - -
BAILS, George N.	4-30-1868	76y 1m	wid.	Buck Twp.	Virginia
SUTENNISLER, Jacob	8-25-1868	58y	mar.	Buck Twp.	Switzerland
McGorif, Patrick	9-3-1868	58y	mar.	Buck Twp.	Ireland
WILLIAMS, Isaac G.	9-16-1868	58-3-17	mar.	Kenton	Virginia
RAMGEE, Lewis	9-25-1868	58-5-6	mar.	Goshen Twp.	Germany
COPELAND, Wm.	7-16-1868	83y	mar.	Jackson Twp.	England
STEWART, Sarah	9-8-1868	87-11-29	wid.	Mt. Victory	Penna.
STANSELL, Zady P.	11-20-1868	59y	wid.	Jackson Twp.	Conn.
WALKER, Lucinda	10-12-1868	75y	wid.	Ridgway	Vermont
COLBERT, Rachel	11-9-1868	63y	wid.	Hale	Virginia
GROVER, Sam'l	10-16-1868	69-11-1	mar.	Pleasant	Bucks Co., Pa.
CESSNA, Jonathan	10-17-1868	79-7-17	mar.	Pleasant	Bedford Co. Pa.
LEOFFERT, Nicholas	10-19-1868	59y 8m	mar.	Pleasant	Germany
NEWCOMB, Fred.	10-30-1868	66-2-28	mar.	Kenton	Switzerland
STEVENS, Justin	12-28-1868	78-9-15	wid.	Dudley	Syraense Co.
RANGER, Lewis	9-25-1868	58y	mar.	Goshen	Germany
FLEMING, Abraham	12-8-1868	53	sing.	McDonald	Trumbull Co.
BORDERS, Nancy	3-8-1869	61y	mar.	McDonald	Maryland
MILLER, Fanny	3-24-1869	52y 14d	mar.	Buck	Switzerland
ROGERS, James	3-25-1869	67y	wid.	Pleasant	Penna.
BOLENBAUGH, John	3-25-1869	94-9-23	wid.	Goshen	Penna.
GLENN, Alex	4-7-1869	78-6-12	wid.	Hardin Co.	Penna.
KING, Rebecca	5-8-1869	66-6-6	mar.	Kenton	Penna.
DEHL, George	5-9-1869	82y 1m	wid.	Pleasant	Germany
KING, James	5-10-1869	70-2-26	wid.	Kenton	Penna.

PFEIFFER, Michael	6-4-1869	85-4-12	wid.	Pleasant	Germany
WROTEN(?), Westly	8-6-1869	65y	mar.	Taylor Creek	- - - -
WOOD, Wm.	7-10-1869	56y	mar.	- - - -	- - - -
KARNEK, Amanuel	8-12-1869	52-7-12	mar.	Washington	Penna.
SHOW, Rev. E. W.	11-12-1869	79y	wid.	Blanchard	Virginia
FIELDS, Susan	3-12-1870	64y	wid.	Blanchard	Virginia
WHETSEL, Sarah	2-23-1870	61y 7m	—	Blanchard	Ohio
SWARTZ, Elizabeth	2-12-1870	77y	wid.	Pleasant	Europe
WABEL, Margaret	6-29-1869	56y	wid.	Pleasant	Hardin Co.
SHOPP, Thos.	3-28-1870	75y	wid.	Pleasant	Germany
LANBERT, Jos.	3-11-1870	59y 3d	mar.	Pleasant	- - - -
ALLEN, David	2-11-1870		mar.	Pleasant	Sharlot Co. Va.
		Mother:-	Catharine Allen		(Charlotte Co.)
WADDLE, Charles	5-9-1870	80y	—	Pleasant	Fulton Stalion
HOVER, John B.	2-10-1870	60-1-28	mar.	Marion	Penna.
GOULD, Elizabeth	3-21-1870	71-5-10	wid.	Marion	Franklin Co.
MOON, John	11-13-1869	73-10-12	mar.	McDonald	Virginia
GRAVES, Sarah	9-14-1869	74y	mar.	Roundhead	- - - -
HUNT, Thomas C.	2-6-1870	54-7-14	mar.	Ridgway	Hale Twp.
SMITH, William R.	8-10-1870	64-1-6	mar.	Hardin	Warren Co.
DIJE, Deborah	4-5-1869	66y	mar.	Hale	Washington Co.
CAHL, Margaret	10-29-1869	54-2-8	mar.	Hardin Co.	Logan Co.
WILLIAMS, Sarah	12-8-1869	69-5-23	wid.	Hardin Co.	Virginia
STUART, Thomas	4-22-1870	54-2-1	mar.	Hardin Co.	Penna.
YOUNG, Jaushua	3-7-1870	62-2-8	wid.	Hale	Penna.
SACERTGER, Eve	1-9-1869	66y	wid.	Hale	Penna.
COLE, Mary E.	12-3-1869	55-11-14	sing.	Cessna	Hardin Co.
MATHWS, Jacob	8-26-1869	57-2-3	mar.	Cessna	- - - -
MUSTARD, Malisa	4-18-1869	64-10-27	mar.	Ada, Ohio	Hardin Co.
POST, John	11-28-1869	59y	mar.	Blanchard	Penna.
COPELAND, William	8-16-1869	73-3-9	mar.	Jackson	England
BELUGAR, John	8-4-1869	50y 8m	mar.	Jackson	Fayette Co. Ohio
ZIMMELMAN, Amanda	12-2-1869	51y 6m	mar.	Jackson	- - - - -
WILLIAMS, Mary E.W.	8-26-1869	62-6-18	wid.	Forest, Ohio	New Jersey
McFARLAND, Rebecca	11-7-1869	86 yrs.	—	Buck	Virginia
McCONNELL, Mary	4-14-1870	58-8-29	wid.	Buck	Buck Twp.
TAYLOR, Obed	1-21-1870	73y 9m	mar.	Hardin Co.	Franklin Co. Pa.
ROBINSON, Wm.	9-30-1869	78-1-1	wid.	Goshen	Ireland
PFEIFFER, Susan	10-6-1869	58y	mar.	Goshen	Germany
WHEELER, Amos	Sept.1870	50y 9m	mar.	Dudley	Scioto
		Father:-	P. Wheeler		
WILLIAMS, Ardella	6-10-1870	63y	wid.	Kenton	Delaware
McHLAKEN(?), Sagas	7-5-1870	53y	wid.	Taylor Creek	- - - -
NORMAN, Mary	9-29-1870	58y	—	Taylor Creek	- - - -
GALLAGHER, Levina	9-4-1870	63y	wid.	Hale	Harrison Co.
CURL, E. E.	5-13-1870	51y 5m	mar.	Hale	Logan
SHAFFER, Elizabeth	5-3-1870	72-5-18	mar.	Hale	- - - -
McGALAN, Susan	11-21-1870	70y	—	Roundhead	- - - -
GUIELER, Augustus	12-23-1870	61y	mar.	Washington	Germany

KRIDLER, Andrew	10-2-1870	62-10-18	mar.	Washington	Trumbull
FRANK, Michael	12-22-1870	76y 6m	mar.	Washington	Germany
ORTH, Adam	12-22-1870	76y 6m	mar.	Washington	Germany
McCOY, Elizabeth	11-2-1870	60-2-21	mar.	Cessna	Columbus
McCOY, Sam'l	12-27-1870	59y 16d	mar.	Cessna	Penna.
MATHEWS, Nancy	11-29-1870	82-3-14	mar.	Cessna	Washington, P.
NELSON, Elizabeth	6-22-1870	60y	mar.	Liberty	Trumbull

HARDIN COUNTY, OHIO - Death Records - 1871-1872

Persons 50 years of age and over.

Name	Date of Death	Age	Marital Status	Place of Death	Place of Birth
PHILLIPS, Hannah	1-31-1871	66-7-7	mar.	Blanchard	Belmont
Father: Moses Parker - Mother: Eva Packer					
HANNAN(?), George W.	- - -1871	71y	mar.	Dudley	Ky.(?)
KERCT, Jacob	6-2-1871	73-11-12	wid.	Pleasant	Switzerland
CESSNA, Cosh	5-5-1871	70y	----	Pleasant	Penna.
BOWENBAUGH, C.	5-4-1871	65y 7m	----	Pleasant	- - - - -
TAYLOR, Joseph	3-2-1871	58y	----	Taylor Creek	- - - - -
KENSEY, Elinora	2-27-1871	88-3-9	wid.	Hale	Penna.
MARMAN, Martin	1-9-1871	71-?-5	mar.	Hale	orth Caro
HORNER, Isam	3-19-1871	71y	----	Roundhead	- - - - -
REESE, Jesse	1-26-1871	77y	----	Roundhead	- - - - -
ELENSING, Charles	2-25-1871	54y	mar.	Washington	Rusa
NELSON, John	Mar. 1871	65y	mar.	Liberty	Virginia
FREMAN(?), Daniel	Apr. 1871	55y	----	Liberty	- - - - -
LOPPER, Lavina	- - -1871	66y	----	Liberty	- - - - -
GREEN, Rebaca	9-24-1871	63y 9m	----	Dudley	Ciago Co.
KELLY, Martha	8-15-1871	70y 5m	wid.	Dudley	Penna.
HIAMMAN(?), George	5-6-1871	76y	mar.	Dudley	Virginia
CLEMENT, David	7-26-1871	75y	mar.	Dudley	Vermont
BOSERT, Frederick	9-24-1871	65-4-24	mar.	Washington	- - - - -
STROUD, Solomen (or Saloma)	9-19-1871	56y ?m	wid.	- - - - -	Bucks Co. Pa.
ALLMAN, Rebaca	Sept. 1871	82y 8m	wid.	Logan Co.	Louthan Co. V.
Parents: Samuel and E. Allman					
LOUTHEN, Henry	11-1-1871	72y 20d	mar.	Blanchard	Washington P.
Parents: Moses and E. Louthen					
MASON, Anna Sophia	2-11-1872	67-8-1	mar.	Goshen	Maryland
PELLEN, James E.	5-11-1871	52y	mar.	Buck	Green
SCOTT, Joseph	10-27-1871	72y	wid.	Buck	Franklin
LYNCH, John	4-21-1871	57y	mar.	Buck	Ireland
RECHARDS, Malinda	3-31-1872	74y	wid.	Buck	Virginia
FULTZ, Anna	6-14-1871	72y 5d	wid.	McDonald	Virginia
Father: Samuel Forote - Mother: Barba Allen					
DOLPH, Benjamin	5-11-1871	80-2-11	----	Roundhead	- - - - -
CALVERT, Robert	3-10-1872	58y	----	Roundhead	- - - - -

Name	Date	Age	Status	Township	Origin
HUSTAN, Thomas	3-14-1872	59y	mar.	Jackson	- - - - -
HARRIS, Catharine	- - -1872	62y	mar.	Jackson	- - - - -
GARDNER, John	2-18-1872	68-5-3	sing.	Patterson	- - - - -
WEAVER, George	6-22-1872	70y	mar.	Patterson	Penna.
GUME, Isabel	8-7-1871	70-2-8	wid.	Lynn	Penna.
NORMAN, N.	2-8-1872	65-8-6	mar.	Lynn	Virginia
ROUNSBURY, Cathrine	2-23-1872	50-3-2	—	Lynn	Carrol Co.
COONEY, Nancy	9-9-1871	64-6-10	mar.	Marion	- - -.- -
CLOSE, Margaret	1-20-1872	61-6-2	mar.	Pleasant	Tuscarawas
	Father: Wm. Close				
NEWCOMB, CROMWELL	9-10-1871	81-11-2	mar.	Pleasant	New York
BURKHOLDER, Mary	12-19-1871	54-3-6	mar.	Pleasant	Switzerland
BORN, Elizabeth	4-25-1872	59-10-11	mar.	Pleasant	Fairfield Co.
COOK, Isaac	12-28-1871	69y 8m	sing.	Kenton	New Jersey
CLARK, Edward A.	4-8-1872	56-8-4	mar.	Kenton	Ceront(?)
BORET, Andrews	3-18-1872	61-3-6	mar.	Kenton	Germany
CROPER, Isaac	6-17-1872	74y 21d	mar.	-. -- - -	..rginia
REED, Manley	7-3-1871	80y 5m	mar.	Hardin	New York
REID, Michal Mag.	3-23-1872	82-2-18	wid.	Hardin	Maryland
MARTIN, Anna	4-14-1872	74y 25d	wid.	Hardin	Penna.
ABLEFIELD, Rinehart	5-28-1872	76-3-6	mar.	- - - -	- - - - -
SHANKS, Thomas	10-5-1871	101y	wid.	Liberty	- - -.- -
	Parents: William and Catharine				
MILLER, Sarah	5-4-1872	78y	wid.	Liberty	-.- - - -
TURNER, Thos.	11-25-1871	52-8-1	mar.	Liberty	- - - -.-
DEBELL(?), Jane L.	12-13-1871	50y	mar.	Liberty	- - - - -
BIRD, A. N.	8-6-1872	54y	wid.	Buck	Marion
RULL, Nancy	11-10-1872	64y	mar.	Hale	Virginia
EDWARDS, R.	9-8-1872	55y 6m	mar.	Dudley	Penna.
ALTHAUSER, Bar.	4-27-1872	73y 6m	wid.	Goshen	- - - - -
ROBY, Mary	6-5-1872	56-11-26	mar.	Goshen	Virginia
SHILEMENTLE, A.	- - -1872	51y	—	Kenton	Germany
KAHLER, Nicholas	5-15-1872	72y 11d	mar.	Kenton	Germany
RAGAN, Julia	6-17-1872	73y	mar.	Kenton	- - - - -
BLEM, Jacob	8-13-1872	86-11-14	wid.	Cessna	Penna.
REID, C.	6-30-1872	52y 1m	mar.	Cessna	Germany
AUSPACH, Lydia	5-24-1872	59-2-4	mar.	Marion	Penna.
WILSON, J. D.	11-25-1872	67-6-20	mar.	Liberty	- - - - -

The following wills can be found in Will Book A. Date given is date will was recorded unless recording date was not given, then date is date will was made and is so designated by a "d" following date.

Name	Date	Page	Name	Date	Page
ANDERSON, William	1822	86	ECKLEY, Mary	1826	143
ATKINSON, George of			EVANS, Alexander	1831	270
Brooke Co., Va.	1831	279	EVANS, Mary	1830	247
BANE, Mary	1830	242	EYRE, Robert	1828	211
BARGER, Valentine	1828	214	FINNEY, James	1829	229
BARKHURST, Lewis	1823	100	FINNEY, Phebe	1821	75
BARNHILL, Margaret	1817	44	FISHER, Elizabeth	1828	209
BARR, William	1818	55	FISHER, George	1821	78
BAXTER, John	1815	26	FISHER, George	1823	105
BECK, Samuel	1821	82	FISHER, John	1815	22
BECKLEY, Jacob	1832	284	FISSEL, Anthony	1828	207
BEKNAP, David	1832	287	FITZ SIMMONS, Chas.	1830	248
BIGGART, Samuel	1831	269	FORD, Ann	1821	79
BLAIR, Runnell of			FORD, Isaac	1831	278
Brooke Co., Va.	1818	52	FORNEY, Abraham	1824	118
BREDEN, David	1815	18	FOOS, William	1831	266
BROKAW, Abraham	1825	125	FRANCE, John	1826	154
BROWN, Ann	1825	122	FRANCIS, John	1813	5
BROWN, Daniel	1823	110	FULTON, James	1825	135
BROWN, Hugh	1822	94	FULTON, John of		
BROWN, William	1831	263	Fayette Co., Pa.	1825	145
BURROWS, Benjamin			GALEHER, William	1832	304
aged 66 years	1822	93	GATCHEL, John	1815	17
BUSBY, Edith	1830	254	GEARY, James	1820	68
CADWALADER, Isaac of			GILBERT, Joseph	1832	298
Tuscarawas Co., O.	1813	7	GOODSON, Jacob	1815	15
CANNON, Erasmus	1814d	14	GREER, Valentine	1827	196
CAREN, Thomas	1826	165	GUNDY, Joseph	1823	97
CAROTHERS, Samuel	1831	131	GUTTERY, Robert	1815	23
CECIL, Joshua, Sr.	1814	8	HALEY, Thomas	1832	291
CHICKEN, Daniel			HANES, John	1824	121
aged 54 years	1824	115	HANNA, James of	1828	221
COALTRAP, William	1821	83	Washington Co., Pa.		
COOKE, James	1815	16	HANNA, William	1830	245
COUZENS, Sarah	1822	92	HARMAN, John	1830	239
COX, Zebediar	1825	129	HAUN, John	1828	218
CRABTREE, Peter	1827	204	HEDGE, Solomon of		
CRAIG, John	1825	135	Brooke Co., Va.	1815	21
CRAIG, Susanna	1826	168	HEMRY, John, Sr.	1827	198
CRAWFORD, Edward	1831	274	HENDRICKS, John Sr.	1818	51
CRAWFORD, Thomas	1826	171	HILBERT, Peter	1815	19
DAVIS, John F.	1827	202	HINES, Rudolph	1823	107
DAVIS, Nicholas	1826	185	HITCHCOCK, Thomas	1829	223
DAVIS, William	1829	228	HODGE, Robert	1827	200
DICKS, John	1830	240	HOOEY (HUEY), John	1822	90
DUNLAP, Adam	1830	237	HUMPHREY, James	1826	182
EAGELSON, William	1829	226	HURLESS, George	1826	174

Name	Date	Page
INSKEEP, John	1822	89
JEFFERS, John	1819	65
KAIL, John	1821	75
KARNACHAN, George	1816	36
KELLY, Daniel	1831	264
KENT, Joseph	1829	231
KENT, Joseph	1829	232
KERR, James, Sr.	1825	127
KIMMEL, Henry	1826	183
KIMMEL, Lenard	1826	156
LAYPORT (LEPORT), Isaac	1825	137
LEE, John	1813	3
LEEPORT, George	1814	12
LEZEAR, John	1819	58
LOWDEN, Joseph	1832	297
LYNN, John	1814	11
McCLEARY, Darcus	1819	61
McCONNELL, John	1831	273
McCOY, John of		
Washington Co., Pa.	1824	162
McCULLOCH, Robert	1823	102
McCULLOUGH, William	1831	261
McDOWELL, James	1815	29
rec. Fayette Co., Pa.		
McKAIN, William, Sr.	1828	213
McNUTT, James, Sr.	1822	85
MARSHALL, Jacob	1824	117
MARSHALL, William	1816	37
MAXSON, Jonathan	1825	131
MAXWELL, Thomas	1832	294
MELTON, William	1820	69
MERRYMAN, Caleb		
of Baltimore Co., Md.	1827	193
NEWHIRTER, Barr	1826	164
MILLER, Hannah	1817	45
MILLER, John	1832	289
MILLER, John, Sr.	1826	176
MILLIKIN, Jane	1831	265
MOFFET, John	1830	252
MORGAN, Michael	1829	225
NICHOL, John of		
Belmont Co., Ohio	1831	255
OGLEVEE, John	1815	28
OLDSHOE, John	1823	112
OLER, Peter	1832	296
PARRISH, Mordecai, Sr.	1826	178
PATTON, Thomas	1832	292
PAULSON, James	1816	31
PHILLIPS, William	1816	41
POLLOCK, John, Sr.	1820	66
POLLOCK, Sarah	1821	77

Name	Date	Page
PORTER, John	1831	276
POULSON, Samuel	1831	267
PROVINES, Matthew	1827	187
of Washington Co., Pa.		
RANKIN, Thomas	1832	285
RILEY, John	1823	109
ROBERTS, James	1828	217
ROGERS, Catharine	1832	288
SABLE, Adam	1826	158
SCOTT, John	1830	251
SHARP, Thomas	1826	148
SHAWVER, Christopher	1818	50
SHULTZ, George	1828	208
SIMPSON, John	1815	24
SMITH, William	1820	67
SMOOT, Solomon	1828	206
SNEDAKER, John	1816	39
SPEER, John	1831	271
SPIKER, Christian	1821	71
STEPHEN, Hester	1830	236
SWAYNE, Joshua	1832	303
TARBET, William	1818	47
rec. Clermont Co., Ohio		
TAYLOR, Jonathan of	1832	300
Jefferson Co., Ohio		
TEAS, Hugh	1828	210
TEDROW, George	1819	57
THOMAS, Isaac	1826	139
THOMPSON, Daniel	1816	35
THOMPSON, John	1831	259
THOMPSON, Josiah	1826	166
TIMMONS, Eli	1829	227
TIPTON, Aquilla	1826	173
TIPTON, John	1832	295
TIPTON, Mary	1827	194
widow of Samuel		
URQUEHART, Alexander	1814	10
WALLS, John	1826	160
WALRAVEN, William	1813	1
WATTERS, Allen	1823	99
WEAVER, Thomas	1827	189
WELCH, Daniel	1819	62
WELLING, John, Sr.	1821	72
WILEY, John	1816	33
WILLIAMS, Thomas	1816	43
WILSON, Charles	1830	250
WILSON, John	1819	61
WILSON, Thomas, Sr.	1830	234
WOOD, William	1831	260
WOOD, Zachariah	1831	275
YOUNG, Denton	1832	282
YOUNG, William	1813	4
of Brooke Co., Va.		

The following records are from the Recorder's Office at the court house in Napolson. Book and page of original book in which record may be found is given in parenthesis.

Dorothy PALMER to John Scofield, both of Henry Co., Ohio; 12-22-1860; $25.00; 1 acre NE¼ Section 35, Township 6N, Range 5E, Ridgeville twp. (Deed Book 7, page 563)

Francis A. PALMER of Fulton Co., Ohio, Cordelia STOUT and Joseph A. STOUT, her husband, John O. PALMER, David Henry PALMER and Charles B. PALMER, all of Henry Co., Ohio, heirs of Barten PALMER, dec'd to John SCOFIELD; 12-22-1860; $1.00; S½ W½ NE¼ and SE½ E½ NW¼ Section 35, Township 6N, Range 5E. (Deed Book 7, page 564)

Dorothy PALMER and David Henry PALMER to John SCOFIELD; 12-22-1860; Whereas Barton PALMER, dec'd executed his will dated 3-4-1853 and that Dorothy and David Henry Palmer as executors of same now deed S½ W½ NE¼ Section 35, Township 6N, Range 5E and also S½ E½ NW¼ Section 35, Township 6 N, Range 5E except 1 acre used as a family burying ground of Palmer Family and now fenced in with the public cemetery. (Deed Book 7, page 565)

Milton CROCKET and Sarah his wife, Nelson CROCKET and Sarah A. his wife to Abner LEMART all of Henry Co., Ohio; 2-12-1857; Power of Attorney to sell land being W½ SW¼ Section 22, Township 5N, Range 7E. (Deed Book 6, page 477)

Abraham KNISELY and Catharine his wife, George ROGERS and Content E. his wife, Commodore ROGERS and Adelia L. his wife, Humphrey ROGERS and Eliza his wife all of Winnebago Co., Wisconsin to John PITTMAN; 10-22-1855; $160.00; Quit Claim to undivided 4/10ths share as heirs of Thomas ROGERS, dec'd in 118.41 acres E½ and NW¼ NW¼ Section 1, Township 3N, Range 7E; deed recorded 3-7-1859. (Deed Book 6 page 466)

John ROGERS and Catherine his wife, Mary FRALICK, David WHITE and Orream his wife all of Crawford Co., Ohio to John PITTMAN; 6-16-1855; $120.00; Quit Claim to undivided 3/10ths share as heirs of Thomas RODGERS, dec'd in 118.41 acres E½ and NW¼ NW¼ Section 1, Township 3N, Range 7E; deed recorded 3-7-1859. (Deed Book 6, page 467)

John EARLY and Hannah his wife of Allen Co., Ohio to Susan EBY wife of Amos ERY; 9-5-1857; $435.00; 80 acres E½ SE¼ Section 4, Township 4N, Range 7E. (Deed Book 6, page 258)

Oliver A. CROCKETT and Laura his wife, William WICKWINE and Olive H. his wife, Emily CROCKETT and Frank CROCKETT all of Seneca (Co.?), Ohio to Milton CROCKETT and Nelson CROCKETT of Henry Co., Henry Co., Ohio; 2-5-1857; $310.00; Quit Claim W½ SW¼ Section 32, Township 5N, Range 7E being 80 acres, also NE¼ NE fraction quarter Section 6, Township 4N, Range 7E being 44 acres; deed recorded 8-17-1857. (Deed Book 5, page 587)

Leroy CROCKET of Henry Co., Ohio to Milton CROCKET and Nelson CROCKET of same; 2-6-1857; $77.00; Quit Claim 45 acres NE¼ NE¼ Section 6, Township 4N, Range 7E, also 80 acres W½ SW¼ Section 32, Township 5N, Range 7E; deed recorded 8-18-1857. (Deed Book 5, page 588)

K. L. ECKRIDGE and Rosanna his wife of Henry Co., Ohio to Milton CROCKET and Nelson CROCKET of same; 3-5-1857; Quit Claim 80 acres W½ SW¼ Section 32, Township 5N, Range 7E deed recorded 8-18-1857. (Deed Book 5, Page 588)

The following marriages were taken from "Marriage Record A" located in the Probate Court House at Napoleon.

ABBOT, Joel to Sylva Harris	7-4-1850
ABOTT, Darius to Clarissa E. Bellinger	7-4-1851
ADAMS, Carlisle to Sebschi Erwin	lic. 9-21-1850
ALTS, Harmon to Catherine Ross	10-23-1850
ALVERY, Jno. N.(George N. on lic.) to Delila Wells	6-18-1848
ANDREW, Aman B. to Elizabeth Wells	2-5-1848
BABCOCK, Alanzo to Jane Curtis	10-18-1848
BABCOCK, Lorenzo to Sarah Ann Patrick	4-4-1849
BABCOCK, Solomon to Nancy Ann Kinslar	1-23-1851
BACK, Lyman to Eunice L. Gunn	4-1-1849
BACK (or BOCK), William to Lucy (Eunice L. on lic.) Back (or Bock	7-17-1851
BAKER, John to Elizabeth Knapp	5-14-1848
BARLOW, Bradford to Jane Jameson	7-6-1850
BAUDENHAL (BADENHOP on lic.) Dederick to Maria Wichers (Wiechens on lic.)	10-23-1849
BECK, Paul to Sally Jane Mitchel	12-26-1850
BIXBY, Lewis H. to Maria Essea	4-20-1848
BLETTER, John to Providence, Lucas Co. to Sarah Ann Fuller of Ridgeville, Henry Co.	8-9-1849
BOYLES, Daniel to Sarah Ann Knapp	5-23-1850
BRICKLIN, Osman to Nancy N. Price	5-1-1849
BUCHANNON, G.W. to Ann E. Cowdrick	12-10-1850
BURRELL, Silas to Henrietta Bollie	lic. 1-12-1849
CARPENTER, David to Martha Jane Karshner	2-7-1850
CHAPMAN, Clark to Matilda Hardin (2 dates given)	(5-14-1850 (7-14-1850
CLAPP, Rusel K. to Amilia Catherine Clough	lic. 3-26-1851
CLAY, Coonrod to Julia Stodard	10-9-1851
CONDIT, Cyrinus to Rebecca Jane Rowland	5-1-1851
COOLMAN, Frederick Wilhelm to Frederica Weeber (Vaber on lic.)	4-15-1849
COWDRICK, J. E. to Sarah E. Clapp	9-9-1850
CROCKETT, Benjamin A. to Jane Reid	lic. 11-27-1847
CROCKETT, George to Harriet N. Emery	3-15-1851
CROCKETT, Nelson to Sarah Ann Hoffman	4-25-1850
CROSBY, G. P. to Jane M. Pratt	6-12-1850
CROSBY, John C. to Sylva B. Harris	10-13-1850
CULVER, William to Catharine Belinda Stevins	3-2-1851
DAMAN (DAYMAN), Edward to Catharine Mitchel	3-9-1848
DAVIDSON, Jonathan to Eliza Lowery	7-12-1847
DAY, William to Esther Mitchel	9-21-1848
DELONG, Columbus S. to Sarah Ann Musgrove	11-29-1849
DOWENN, Jacob to Margaret Elizabeth Coulter	9-12-1847
DURBIN, Thomas W. Jr. to Lucinda King	5-22-1850
DURBIN, William Esq. to Rachael Officer	11-24-1850
EASTMAN, Guy C. to Mrs. Allis Lamphire	5-23-1850

```
EDING, Jared to Sarah Stephan (Stephens)                        3-8-1848
EDWARDS, Samuel E. to Rachael Hill                              4-12-1849
ELDER, John to Amanda M. Hiy                                   12-13-1847
EMORY, Judson to Lucinda Mead                                   6-10-1848
ESKRIDGE, Kendell to Rosina Shastzer                            5-4-1851
FAUGHT, Charles to Rosina M. Grace                              1-19-1851
FERGUSON, Andrew to Mary Parker                                 9-14-1848
FOWLER, Robert to Rebecca Van Fleet                            3-23-1850
FOX, John O. to Elizabeth Quilliman                            6-22-1851
FREYBERGER, John to Elizabeth Bowman                          10-14-1850
FULLER, Sanford W. to Permelia Jane Halsey                     1-13-1851
FURGERSEN, Nelson to Ann Elizabeth Jones                       5-25-1847
GARDNER, Charles to Catharine Grau                             4-14-1851
GLORE, John to Mary Siters (Ziter on lic.)                     7-13-1851
GRAMLING, John to Sylvania Snell                               3-29-1851
GRIM, Peter to Caroline Hoffman                                7-20-1848
GUNN, Nelson to Harriet Bucklin (Bricklin)                     9-13-1848
HAGGERTY, John P. to Susanna Boldon                            4-28-1848
HALSEY, Harvey to Mary Parlin                                 10-13-1850
HANLIN, John D. to Elizabeth Rhodes                           12-14-1848
HARLEY, David to Martha E. Scofield                            3-2-1851
HARRISON, John to Sarah Durbin                                10-25-1849
HEATH, John T. (P. on lic.) to Elizabeth A. Cole               9-14-1851
HEIGHT, Jesse to Lydia C. Doremus                              6-20-1850
HINCKLE (HINKLE), George W. to Katherine Mansfield             6-6-1850
HOLLY, Anderson to Mary Ann Buller (or Butler)                 9-21-1848
HOPKINS, Phineas to Joanna Huffman                             4-3-1851
HUGHS, Patrick to Margaret Merter                             12-30-1850
JEFFREY, John M. to Lucy A. Farrand                            2-12-1851
JOHNSTON, Lewis to Mary Edwards                                1-17-1851
KARSNER, Isaac, Esq. to Mrs. Sarah Ann Bowen                   4-8-1849
KARSNER, John to Rachael Durham                                3-30-1851
KEYZAR, Jacob R. to Mary B. Austin                            10-16-1851
KLINE, Joseph to Marinda Austin                               10-16-1851
LAMPHIRE, Aaron to Allice Kitchen                              3-8-1848
LEAP, Christian to Mary Rayl                                  10-21-1848
LEEDERMAN, Peter to Mrs. Sophia Leederman                     10-12-1850
          (note: lic. gives both names as LUDERMAN)
LONG, Levi to Sarah Bortel                                     5-23-1850
LOOMIS, B. S. to Laura A. Hart                                11-28-1849
LUDERMAN, William to Mara(h) Hases (Hawes)                     2-14-1850
LYMAN, Edward to Jane Downing                                  3-8-1851
McCARTY, Jared to Louisa H. Stoors                             1-30-1850
MARGUARSTEN, Jacob to Mary Lonsman                            11-21-1851
MARKWORTH, Henry to Catherine Brigger                         11-21-1847
MATCH, William to Elizabeth Hull                              11-19-1851
MIER, Christopher to Maria Cours                               6-12-1848
MIDDLETON, James to Druzella Chaney                            4-4-1850
MILLER, Daniel to Rachael Inman                                4-22-1847
```

```
MITCHEL, Andrew to Elizabeth Preston                              3-10-1851
MITCHEL, Orris to Margaret J. Jackson                            7-27-1848
MOHLER, David to Mariah Shriver (River on lic.)                 12-19-1850
MORSE, Orrin D. to Ann Kelsby                                    6-10-1848
MURPHY, Cornelius to Eliza Knapp                                 5-16-1847
MURR, William to Nancy Avery                                     7-15-1849
NEWELL, Ira to Nancy Newell                                     11-9-1851
PALMER, Francis A. to Elizabeth Jane Armstrong                   5-8-1849
PARKER, Orrin to Zintha Curles                                  5-23-1847
PAULES, Samuel to Cornelia Willcox                              4-26-1849
PEARCE, Martin to Sally E. Earl                                  6-21-1851
PERCEVAL, Franklin to Mary Wells                                 8-4-1850
PERNING, Henry to Doris Othmar                                   1-18-1851
POWER, Ahart to Netta Polish                                     8-24-1851
PRATT, Abraham to Nancy Carter                                   1-8-1850
PRATT, Silas to Louiza Farley                                    7-7-1851
PREGE (PRIGGIN on lic.), Henry to
              Mary Hilberg (Hielbear on lic.)                  12-22-1850
PRICE, Seth to Mary Ann Andlemir                          lic. 9-15-1849
REDFIELD, Albert to Harriett Hudson                            12-19-1851
REED, Benjamin to Clarinda Morse                               12-24-1848
RICE, Owen to Mary Sweney                                 lic. 9-18-1847
RICHARDSEN, George A. to Phebe H. R. Herring                    4-26-1849
ROBERTS, Robert L. to Sarah Davis                               4-3-1851
ROBINS, George to Susan Lightner                                7-23-1850
ROBINSON, George W. to Catherine Ward                           3-28-1850
ROCKWELL, Samuel K. to Sarah Ann Skates                         6-10-1849
ROWEN, John P. to Susan S. I. Stout                             7-7-1850
SCHOULTER, Henry to Sophia Ludeman (Gudiman on lic.)           5-2-1850
SCOFIELD, James E. to Catharine E. Leork                        9-16-1849
SCOTT, John to Jane Murdock                                    12-9-1847
SHASTEEN, Jackson to Sarah Larue                          lic. 7-31-1851
SHASTEEN, James M. to Nancy Jane Butler                        11-9-1848
SHEFFIELD, Edward to Phebe Brownell                             6-16-1850
SHELDENBERGER, Nicholas to Eliza Jane(Eliza Ann on lic.)Keyzer 10-15-1848
SHELLINGBERGER, Aaron to Elizabeth Knapp                       11-2-1851
SHELLINGBERGER, Solomon to Mary Ann Nogle                       5-4-1851
SHILT, John to Catherine Trisler (Tressler)                     3-21-1850
SHINAMAN, John to Rosina Inman                                  2-10-1848
SHOCK, Josiah (Isaih on lic.) to Sarah Ann Yauger              2-14-1850
SHOTTS, John Henry to Margaret Sowerman                         9-16-1847
SHRIVER, Lewis to Lucy Ann Mohler                              10-4-1849
SHULL, Charles G. to Rebecca Jane Lovery                        6-4-1851
SHULL, Jacob to Delilah Sturgeon                                3-15-1851
SIMMONS, Ephrain to Mary Ann Mansfield                         12-10-1851
SISTY, James H. to Mary E. Crockett                            11-20-1848
SLACK, Ralph to Catherine Wollett                         lic. 4-19-1847
SMITH, Christian F. to Margareta Lougman                       11-21-1851
SMITH, Daniel C. to Elizabeth Dorakon                           9-16-1849
```

```
SMITH, S. S. to Mary Jane Officer                          4-13-1851
SORRICK, Levi to Orintha Herkimer                           6-8-1851
SPAFFORD, Amexicus M. to Maria Glass                  lic. 4-26-1847
STEEL, George to Caroline Wait                             6-11-1851
STEVENS, Jacob G. to Matilda Spring                   lic. 1-5-1850
STEVENSON, Enoch G. to Susan Sisty                         3-15-1849
STRUBLE, Alfred to Sarah Knapp                            12-23-1848
SULLINGER, John to Lutitia M. Walls                      11-27-1851
TRUBY, John to Sarah Jane Daugherty                        3-23-1851
VEERS (VIERS), James Madison to Elizabeth Smith            7-18-1847
WALTON, Richard R. to Mrs. Mary Andrews                    4-24-1850
WATERMAN, George to Catherine Lowery                        1-4-1849
WEELHAM, Jacob to Christiana Deryimer                 lic. 4-19-1847
WILLSON, Henry to Eliza Beckwith                      lic. 11-4-1851
WELLS, Joseph to Louisa Avery                              7-29-1848
WELSTED, David F. to Rosana Hughs                           3-8-1849
WISE, Daniel to Catharine Jane Lingle                     12-30-1847
WOLERY (WOLLERY), Henry G. to Amanda Robinson               6-5-1849
WOLF, George N. to Elizabeth Wolf                     lic. 4-1-1850
WORTH, John A. to Doratea Elizabeth Rungen                11-17-1850
YARNAL, Thomas to Anna E. Hannon                            5-2-1848
```

HIGHLAND COUNTY, OHIO - INDENTURE RECORDS 1825-1832

The following records were abstracted from a book called "Indenture Record" as found in the Common Pleas Court (Clerk of Court's Office) at the court house at Hillsboro. Page on which record is given in original record is given in parenthesis.

This indenture made 13 Nov. 1824. Hugh I. McGRAW son of Hugh McGraw, dec'd, aged 10 years, 4 months and 9 days with consent of his mother, Juliann McGraw, now July Ann Kelson and of his own free will is bound as a servant to William Morrow of Highland County, Ohio until he is 18 years of age. Recorded 2-6-1825. (1)

This indenture made 13 Nov. 1824. That Adam McGRAW son of Hugh McGraw, dec'd, aged 12 years, 6 months and 1 day by consent of Juliann Kelso late July Ann McGraw, his mother and of his own free will binds himself as a servant to John Morrow of Highland County, Ohio until he is 18 years of age. Recorded 2-6-1825. (2)

This indenture made 19th Feb. 1825 between John R. Strain and Phillip McWilliams trustees of Madison twp., Highland County, Ohio with consent of Isaac Smith acting trustee of said township and county of one part and Samuel McConnell of same place of the other part, do bind out John Westley LEE a poor boy aged 6 years and 1 day, son of Edward Lee to serve McConnell for term of 14 years and 29 days from date until he is 21 years of age which will be 18 Feb. 1839. Recorded 4-25-1825. (3)

This indenture made 16 July 1825 between Mary Huffstutter of Fairfield township, Highland County, Ohio and William HUFFSTUTTER her son, aged 3 years, 4 months and 1 day of one part to James Carver of same place of the other part. That William Huffstutter with consent of his mother, Mary, is bound as an apprentice in farming to James Carver until he is of the age of 21 which will be 15 March 1843. Recorded 8-22-1825. (5)

This indenture made 24 Sept. 1825 between Amos Wilson of Highland County, Ohio of one part and Archibald Brown of same place of other part. That Amos Wilson binds as an apprentice for term of 8 years and 9 months from this date, his son, Alexander WILSON to said Brown to learn the art of wagonmaking. Recorded 12-31-1825. (6)

This indenture made 24 Sept. 1825 between Amos Wilson of Highland County, Ohio of one part and Archibald Brown of same place of the other part. That Amos Wilson does bind his son, Jacob L. WILSON until he is 21 years of age to said Brown as an apprentice in wagonmaking. Recorded 12-31-1825. (7)

This agreement made 29 Dec. 1825 between William Marsh and Zacharias Harper of the one part and Nathan Baker of the second part. That Poleman HARPER aged 19 years on 6th August last shall serve said Baker in Blacksmith business. Recorded 12-29-1825. (8)

This indenture made 9 Aug. 1826 between Richard Barrett, James Young, and Moses H. Gregg trustees of Paint township, Highland County, Ohio with consent of Phillip W. Spanger, J.P. for said township of one part and John Davis of same place of the other part. Said trustees do bind out Esther TRIVET a destitute girl aged 11 years 1 month, daughter of Joseph Trivet late of this township and supposed to be deceased, as an apprentice to said Davis for six years and eleven months

605

from date until she is of age of 18 years which will be 19 July 1833. Recorded 11-7-1826

This indenture made 18 Oct. 1826 between William Scott and William Murphy overseers of the poor for Jackson township, Highland County, Ohio with the consent of Zadock Bundy, J.P. of said township of one part and Jacob Weaver Jr. of same place of the other part. Said overseers do bind out Edmond MATHES a poor boy aged 3 years, 1 month and 23 days, son of Sally Mathes late of said township who is unable to support said child as an apprentice to Weaver in the art of farming for the term of 17 years, 10 months and 7 days until he is 21 years of age which will be 27 August 1844. Recorded 12-2-1826. (12)

This indenture made 12 Aug. 1826 between James Young and Moses H. Gregg trustees of Paint township, Highland County, Ohio with consent of David Reese, J.P. of said township of one part and Reese W. Barnes of same place of the other part. Said trustees do bind James CARTER a destitute boy of colour whose parent, Hannah Carter has absented herself from this township and county, aged 2 years and 6 months to said Barnes until he is 21 years of age which will be 12 August 1844. Recorded 1-27-1827. (15)

This indenture made 13 Jan. 1827 between Joel Brown, Thomas Mullenix and John Woolis trustees of Liberty township, Highland County, Ohio with consent of George Shinn, J.P. of said township and county on one part and Elizabeth Carroll of same place on the other part. Said trustees to bind Amanda Ann a black girl aged 8 years old on 15 November last of said township as an apprentice to said Elizabeth Carroll to learn the art of cooking and serving until she is 18 years of age which will be on 15 Nov. 1836. Recorded 4-10-1827. (17)

This indenture made 11 June 1827 between Lucy Summers of one part and Armwted Doggett of the other part, both of Highland County, Ohio. That Lucy Summers does bind her son, William SUMMERS aged 15 years on 9 May 1827 as an apprentice to said Doggett in the saddlery business until he is 21 years of age. Recorded 6-11-1827. (20)

This indenture made 28 Apr. 1827 between Pleasant Arthur, Jonathan Sunday and Elijah Wilkinson trustees of Fairfield township, Highland County, Ohio with consent of David Terrell, J.P. of said township and county of one part and William Chalfant of same place of other part. Said trustees do bind George GILLASPIE a destitute boy of said township aged 17 years, 6 months and 20 days as an apprentice to learn the trade of wagon making to said Calfant until he is 21 years which will be on 15 Oct. 1830. Recorded 5-20-1827. (21)

This indenture made 26 Mar. 1827 between Nancy Pool of Highland County, Ohio of one part and John Boyd of same place on other part. Said Nancy Pool gives consent to bind her son, Jesse BROWN aged 9 years as an apprentice to Boyd to serve until he is 21 years of age in the occupation of farmer, said Jesse having no father able to make this indenture. Recorded 3-26-1828.   (25)

606

This indenture made 4 Sept. 1828 between Andrew Lear of one part and James A. Trimble of the other part. That Andrew Lear binds his son, John LEAR aged 16 on 29th day last March to Trimble as an apprentice in the tanning business until he arrives at 21 years of age. Recorded 9-6-1828. (26)

This indenture made 18 Aug. 1828 between William Murray, Stephen Cary and Nathaniel Campbell trustees of Condord township, Highland County, Ohio with the consent of William Miller, J.P. for same township and county of one part and Abner Musgrove of the other part. Said trustees bind Julianna FULETON a poor girl aged 1 year, 3 months, daughter of John and Nancy Fuleton of said township who are unable to support their child, as a servant girl for the term of 16 years and 9 months from date until she is 18 years of age. Recorded 10-22-1828. (27)

This indenture made 25 Dec. 1827 between Richard Barrett and Moses H. Gregg trustees of Paint township, Highland County, Ohio with consent of David Rees, J.P. for said township and county of one part and James Young of the other part. Said trustees do bind out Elijah MILLS a destitute boy aged 10 years as an apprentice to said Young for 11 years from date until he is 21 years of age which will be 24 Dec. 1838, to learn the art of farming. Recorded 12-22-1828. (29)

This indenture made 14 Nov. 1828 between James Lunn of Cearmong township, Brown County, Ohio who has bound his son, Esquier LUNN who also by his own free will is bound to Joseph McFadden of Whiteoak township, Highland County, Ohio to serve said McFadden for 11 years 1 month in the business of farming. Recorded (not given). (31)

This indenture made 10 Nov. 1828. Andrew DAVIDSON aged 16 years, 1 month and 4 days, son of Margaret Davidson a widow of Scott township, Adams County, Ohio and of his own free will and with his mother's consent apprentices himself until Joseph Woodrow of Highland County, Ohio in the occupation of tanner for 4 years from 6 Oct. last. Recorded 1-21-1829. (32)

This indenture made 6 Jan. 1829. Stephen BAILES aged 15 years, 8 months and 21 days, son of Thomas Bailes of Paint township, Highland County, Ohio of his own free will and with consent of his father binds himself as an apprentice to John Fidler of Hillsborough, this county in the occupation of wagonmaker to serve 5 years, 3 months and 9 days until 15 April 1834. Recorded 2-9-1829. (33)

This indenture made 10th day 1st month 1829. Pleasant Arthur, Elijah Wilkinson and Jonathan Sanders trustees of Fairfield township with consent of David Terrell, J.P. of said township do place Jonathan BLIZZARD a destitute boy of said township aged 14 years, 10 months as an apprentice to Jacob Horton of said county until he is 21 years of age being a term of 6 years, 1 month and 23 days to expire on 3rd day, 3rd month 1835. Recorded 4-10-1829. (35)

This indenture made 8 May 1828 between Alexander Buntain and Robert Stewart overseers of the poor of Liberty township, Highland County, Ohio with consent if Stuart J. Buntin, J.P. of said township of one part and Samuel Gibson of same place of the other part. Said trustees do bind a poor girl, Mary JOHNSON aged 9 years 29 Dec. 1827 until she is 18 years of age to said Gibson. Recorded 7-20-1829. (37)

607

This indenture made 23 July 1829 between John Lewos(?) of Buckskin township, Ross County, Ohio and david LEWOS(?) his son aged 19 years, 3 months and 3 days of one part and Zimri Mauker of Hillsborough, Liberty twp., Highland County, Ohio of the other part. That David with consent of his father has boundhimself as an apprentice to said Mauker in the occupation of blacksmith until 20 July 1832. Recorded 7-23-1829. (38)

This indenture made 16 Oct. 1829. John M. TRIPLETT of Highland County, Ohio of his own free will and with the consent of his father, John Triplett binds himself as an apprentice to James A. Trimble, Tanner of Hills borough, Liberty township in aaid county in the occupation of tanner for term of 4 years from 16th of this month or 16 Oct. 1833. Recorded 10-23-1829. (40)

This indenture made 18 Sept. 1819, Greenfield, Highland County, Ohio. That Nancy Owens of her own free will has bound her son Balser KENSY aged 13 years, 8 months and 13 days as an apprentice to Zephaniah Bryan, Blacksmith of same place for the term of 7 years, 4 months and 10 days until he is 21years of age. Recorded 12-12-1829. (42)

This indenture made 2 Dec. 1829 between John Gossett of the one part and James A. Trimble of the other part, both of Highland County, Ohio. That John Gossett has bound his son, Abraham GOSSETT aged 17 yea rs on 26 July last to said Trimble as an apprentice to the tanning business until he is 21 years of age. Recorded 12-3-1829. (44)

This indenture entered 6 Dec. 1829 between Susannah Simpson widow of Stephen Simpson, dec'd and William R. SIMPSON son of the said Stephen and Susannah Simpson, of Fayette County, Ohio of the one part and Daniel Pavey of Highland County, Ohio of the other part. That Susannah Simpson with conse rt of her son, William R. Simpson binds him to Pavey to learn the occupation of farmer until he is 21 years of age which will be on 6 May 1839, said William R. having been born 6 May 1818. Recorded 3-1-1830. (55, page mis-numbered should be 45)

This indenture made 8 Mar. 1830. That Burgess W. BROWN aged 14 years, 11 months and 3 days, son of Elizabeth McLoud of Hillsborough, Highland County, Ohio of his own free will and with consent of his mother apprenticed himself to George W. Doggett, Shoemaker of Hillsborough same county to learn occupation of shoemaker for the term of 5 years and 27 days from date. Recorded 3-8-1830. (47)

This indenture made 23 Jan. 1830. William JOHNSON aged 18 years, 7 months and 25 days, son of James Johnson of Madison township of his own free will and with consent of his father apprentices himself unto Elijah Fletcher a Blacksmith of Paint township to learn occupation of blacksmith for term of 2 years, 4 months and 7 days until he is 21 years of age which will be on 29 May 1832. Recorded 4-26-1830. (49)

This indenture made 15 Feb. 1830 between Elizabeth Smith of Paint township, Highland County, Ohio of one part and Jonathan Shaw of Concord township, same county of the second part. That Elizabeth Smith of her own will does bind her son John SMITH to said Shaw for term of 12 years, 10 months and 24 days. (note: no age given) Recorded 4-30-1830. (50)

608

This indenture made 15 Mar. 1830; That John W. SINCLEN aged 16 years, 6 months and
18 days son of Sarah Sinclen of Highland County, Ohio of his own free will and with
consent of his mother apprentices himself to George W. Tucker, Taylor of Hillsborough,
Highland County, Ohio to learn the occupation of Taylor for term of 5 years from
date. Recorded 5-7-1830

This indenture made 30 Dec. 1830. That John SUMMERS of Hilsborough, Highland
County, Ohio of his own free will and with consent of his mother, Lucy Summers
has apprenticed himself to Zimri Mauker, Blacksmith of Hillsborough, same county
in the occupation of Blacksmith for 4 years from 22 Nov. last until 22 Nov. 1834.
Recorded 1-1-1832. (54)

This indenture made 25 Oct. 1831. That John DORMAN aged 16 years, 11 months and
16 days, step-son of Jacob Roads of Highland County, Ohio hath of his own free will
and with consent of his step-father, Jacob Roads binds himself to Tucker and White,
Taylors of Hillsborough, same county to learn occupation of Tailor for term of 4
years and 14 days which will be 7 Oct. 1835. Record d 12-6-1831. (55)

This indenture made 9 Mar. 1831 between Samuel Dalton and Drury DALTON his son
of Highland County, Ohio of one part and Joseph Worthington of same place of the
other part. That Drury Dalton of his own will and with consent of his father
apprentices himself to Worthington until he is 21 years of age which will be
for a term of 14 years. Recorded 1-6-1832. (57)

This indenture made 10 Apr. 1830. Lewis DAVIS son of Fanny Davis aged 9 years and
9 days with consent of his mother, Fanny Davis of Brown County, Ohio and of his own
will apprentices himself to Samuel Murphy of Highland County, Ohio to learn the
Tanning business until the year 1843. Recorded 10-8-1831. (58)

This indenture made 1 Sept. 1830, Greenfield, Madison township, Highland County,
Ohio. That Thomas Jones of his own will has bound his son, James JONES aged 13
years, 3 months and 7 days as an apprentice to Zepheniah Bryan, Blacksmith of
aforesaid place to learn trade of blacksmith for term of 7 years, 9 months and 7
days or until he is 21 years of age. Recorded 10-14-1831. (60)

This indenture made 10 Apr. 1831. Tarlton DAVIS son of Fanny Davis, 12 years of
age with consent of his mother said Fanny Davis of Brown County, Ohio and of his
own free will apprentices himself to John Eakins of Highland County, Ohio to learn
the art of farmer until the year 1840. Recorded 10-5-1832. (61)

This indenture made 14 April 1831 between Lewis Lewis and Jarrett Long overseers
of the poor of Concord township, Highland County, Ohio with the consent of William
Miller, J.P. of same place of the one part and William Storer of Jackson township,
same county of the second part. Do bind Stacey BEARD a poor boy aged 8 years,
son of George Beard of said township who is unable to support him as an apprentice
to said Storer to be taught the art of farmer for term of 13 years from date until
he is 21 years of age which will be in 1844. Recorded 6-27-1831. (63)

609

ROADS, Heirs of George to John Smith - 9-29-1823 - George Roads and Rachel his wife of Preble Co., Ohio; Abraham Roads; Jacob Roads; Joseph Roads; Andrew Lear and Caty his wife, late Roads; James Doherty and Susannah his wife, late Roads; William Titsworth and Elizabeth his wife, late Roads; Jacob Slow and Mary his wife, late Roads; Peter Houseman and Peggy his wife, late Roads, all of Highland County, children and heirs of George Roads, deceased. Part of Survey #2335 - Volume P, page 471

AULT, Heirs of Henry to Susanna Ault - 1-1-1825 - Christianna, widow of Henry Ault, dec'd of Highland Co.; Christian Ault and Phebe his wife; Henry Ault and Demaris his wife; Adam Ault; Jonathan Barfield and Betsy his wife, formerly Ault; heirs of Henry Ault, dec'd. Susanna Ault, party of the second part, legal heir of Henry Ault, dec'd. Tract on Plumb Run, a branch of Paint Creek being 301 acres - Volume R, page 130

BRAUGHER, Heirs of Frederick to Reuben Pennywait - 7-18-1828 - Frederick Braugher late of Highland County, died intestate leaving Nancy Braugher his widow and the following heirs: Isaac Braugher; Mary Ann Braugher now Mary Ann Evans intermarried with Peirce Evans; Margaret Smith wife of William Smith, formerly Braugher; Christopher Braugher; Allen G. Braugher; Hester Ann Braugher; Sarah Ann Braugher and Frederick Cary Trimble Braugher. 466 acres being part of Survey #3321 and #3909 - Volume T, page 432

SMALL, Jesse etal. to John Vanpelt - 4-16-1833 - Jesse Small, Reuben Small, Aaron Milles (or Miller) and Rebecca his wife, Daniel Jones and Elizabeth his wife; all of Wayne County, Indiana; land in Paint Township now in the occupancy of Able Roberts and in which Clarky Small has dower for life; claim rights they derived from legacy of Joseph Small, Jr. deceased. - Volume 1, page 693

LEWIS, Heirs of Charles to Lewis Lewis, Jr. - 10-29-1832 - Lewis Lewis Sr., Abigail Lewis, Judah Lewis, Alfred Lewis, Simon Lewis, William Lewis and Truit(?) E. Lewis; also Milton and Amelia Lewis, minors of their guardian Able Roberts; Elizabeth Lewis widow of James Lewis, dec'd for herself and as guardian of Harrictt, Mariah (?) and Alfred Lewis, children of James Lewis, dec'd; all heirs of Charles Lewis, deceased. Lewis Lewis Jr., executor of the will of Charles Lewis. 44 acres part of Survey #1996 on Brush Creek - Volume 1, page 515

COOL, Barbara etal. to Daniel Cool of Highland Co. - 6-6-1830 - Barbara Cool, William Cool and Elizabeth his wife, Peter Cool and Malinda his wife, Catharine Bennett formerly Catharine Cool, Elizabeth Cool all of Highland County and Emanuel Cool and Mary his wife of Lewis County, Virginia. Out-lots 20,21,31,32,34 and 35 in Greenfield. - Volume 1, page 202

CROW, Heirs of Irial to John E. Starns - 6-29-1833 - Thomas Crow, Irial Crow, Thomas Denison and Margaret his wife formerly Crow all of Ross Co. Ohio and Thomas McClain and Elizabeth his wife formerly Crow of Highland County; heirs of Irial Crow, deceased. Part of Survey #1049 - Volume 1, page 757

FITZPATRICK, Heirs of James to James Kemper - 8-5-1833 - John Fitzpatrick and Margaret his wife of Sciota County, Ohio; Mary Richards, Nancy Fitzpatrick, Elizabeth Fitzpatrick, Easter Fitzpatrick along with Fitzpatrick and James Fraley, children and heirs of Jane Frailey, deceased, formerly Fitzpatrick and sister of the above; all of Highland County; heirs of James Fitzpatrick, deceased. Part of Survey #1700. - Volume 1, page 708

GIBLER, Heirs of Lewis to Phillip Gibler - 8-4-1832 - John Gibler and Ann his wife, Matthias Gibler and Easter his wife, Lewis Gibler and Margaret his wife, Samuel Gibler and Jane his wife, William Gibler and Rachel his wife, Abraham Gibler and Nancy his wife, William Davidson and Sarah his wife, all of Highland County, heirs of Lewis Gibler, deceased. Part of Survey #4201 - Volume 1, page 70

BROCK, Benjamin and Lettie Ann his wife to Asseneth Brock, all of Highland County - 11-30-1832. Land on Clear Creek in Paint Township which was sold to said Benjamin Brock by Josiah Vanpelt. - Volume 1, page 201

BOWMAN, Heirs of John to Abraham Lowman - 7-17-1841 - Adam Miller and Matilda his wife, Levi Chaney and Lydia his wife, Lewis W. Bowman and Matilda his wife, James A. Bowman, Moses T. Bowman, Elizabeth Bowman and Mary Ellen Bowman; legal heirs of the estate of John Bowman, deceased of Highland County. Tract on Clear Creek being part of Augustus Davis Survey #2517. - Volume 9, page 57 - RACHEL BOWMAN widow of John Bowman, deceased to Abraham Lowman 7-17-1841 - Rachel's right, title and interest in above described land - Volume 9, page 58

SHULZE, Mary etal to Edward L. Shulze - 6-6-1844 - Mary Shulze, widow; J. E. Shulze; Samuel S. Rex and Lucretia S. his wife; Edward Vanderslice and Clementia E. his wife; all of the City of Philadelphia, children and son-in-law of the late Peter Shulze son and heir-at-law of Rev. Christopher Shulze late of Berks Co., Penna., deceased. Part of Peter Muhlenberg's tract conveyed to him by Emanuel Shulze, deceased. - Volume 11, page 258 - SHULZE, Edward L. and Elizabeth his wife of Lebanon Co. Penna. to Margaretta Ege of South Lebanon Twp., Lebanon Co., Penna.; Undivided 1/8th part of the above described tract of land - 6-10-1844 - Volume 11, page 260. - ALBRIGHT, John and Sarah his wife to Margaretta Eage - 5-31-1844 - Interest in above described land as heirs of Revd. Emanuel Shulze late of Berks Co., Penna., deceased - Volume 11, page 257 - CAMERON, Mary Magdalene to Margaretta Ege - 6-1-1844 - Mary Magdalene of Lancaster Co., Penna., her interest in above described tract of land as daughter and heir of Rev. Emanuel Shulze, deceased - Volume 11, page 253 - SHULZE, Andrew and Susan his wife of Lycoming Co., Penna. to Margaretta Ege - 6-14-1844 - Andrew's interest in above described tract as son and heir of Rev. Emanuel Shulze, dec'd - Volume 11, page 254 - SHULZE, Catharine E. and Maria Elizabeth of Berks Co., Penna. - 5-29-1844 - Their interest in above described tract as daughters and heirs of Rev. Emanuel Shulze, deceased - Volume 11, page 256

BUFORD, Executors of A. to Margaret Nutt - 11-4-1844 - Charles Buffard and Wm. S. Buford of Scott and Woodford County, Kentucky, executors of will of A. Buford, deceased - tract of 35 acres on north fork of White Oak Creek in A. Buford's Survey #3186. - Volume 11, page 622

FOX, Susannah by Sheriff to John Fox - 8-30-1842 - On Jan. 20, 1840, John Fox of Highland Co., Ohio filed his petition in the Common Pleas Court against Susanna Fox, Hiram Hodson and Maria his wife, John Owens and Margaret his wife, Andrew H. Fox, William Fox, Emily Eliza Fox and Hannah Fox; demanding partition of real estate described as 100 acres on waters of the East Fork of the Little Miami River and adjoined by Surveys #753 and #2351. - Volume 11, page 621

GASTON, Heirs of Mary to Thomas M. Boyd of Highland Co. - 9-12-1844 - William Boyd Jr. of McDonough Co., Illinois, William W. Thompson and Sarah J. his wife; Mitchell H. Murray and Lavina his wife and Samuel Murray of Highland County; William Collier and Eleanor his wife; Thomas Murray of Ross Co., Ohio; heirs at law of Mary Gaston, deceased. Out-lot #16 Greenfield which was conveyed to said Mary Gaston on Jan. 21, 1817 by Duncan McArthur. - Volume 11, page 477

LANICK, Ausman etal to Josiah M. Duvall - 8-26-1844 - Ausman Lanick and Mary Ann his wife, Allen W. Spurgon and Elizabeth his wife formerly Elizabeth Wade, Samuel Wolf and Sarah his wife formerly Sarah Wade, Jane Wade and Sanford Wade of Highland County. 300 acres part of Survey #1520 and #1521 made in name of John Marks on waters of Brush Creek. - Volume 11, page 391 - WADE, Josiah of Jay County, Indiana to William Harrison Wade - 6-8-1844 - Power of Attorney to receive all moneys, etc. derived from Josiah's interest in above described land. - Volume 11, page 390

HIGHLAND COUNTY, OHIO - COMMON PLEAS RECORDS

The following records were abstracted from Supreme Court Record and Journal #1. Although there were a number of pages in this book, very few were written upon. The majority of the items were appeals on judgments concerning debts and contained no genealogical information; however, the following gave this type of information:

SHOEMAKER, Simon vs. Elizabeth SHOEMAKER - Petition for Divorce - 10-14-1809 - On June 22, 1807 Simon Shoemaker married Elizabeth Medzher in Highland County. Elizabeth has since been absent for some length of time. (page 7)

TRIMBLE, Allen vs. Others - Petition for Partition - 10-12-1810 - Allen Trimble, Wm. A. Trimble, James A. Trimble and James A. McCue; children and heirs of James Trimble deceased, who died intestate and being seized of lands in Ross, Adams, Highland and Scioto Counties. Also with an heir's interest are; Carry A., Polly L., Cyrus and John A. Trimble, minor children and heirs of James Trimble, deceased. James A. McCue intermarried with Margaret C. Trimble one of the children and heirs of James Trimble, deceased. Land described as: 520 acres part of Survey #538 in Ross Co., Ohio; 560 acres part of Survey #1270 in Scioto Co., Ohio; 230 acres part of Survey #2586 in Adams County, Ohio; 1200 acres part of Survey #2586 and #3029 and 2000 acres part of Survey #2508 in Highland County, Ohio - (page 14)

HIGHLAND COUNTY, OHIO - Common Pleas Records
June 1834 - July 1837

The following records were abstracted from Journal "1834". Only items giving information of a genealogical nature were abstracted; items not abstracted were proceedings concerning debts, criminal etc. Page on which record may be found is given in parenthesis.

6-23-1834 - Isaac Greathouse adms. of estate of Robert Glass for use of Jonathan Allison vs. the widow and heirs of Robert Glass, dec'd - Petition to sell land.(3)

6-24-1834 - This day came into court, Mathew Wilson an applicant for a pension, stating he was a Soldier of the Revolution. Also, came into court to testify to Wilson's age were: John Duvall, a minister; Joel Wolf and Joshua Burnet(?). Court is of the opinion that applicant was a Soldier of the Revolution. (16)

6-24-1834 - Rev. Andrew Kuhn, a minister of the Lutheran Church granted license to perform marriages - Rev. Samuel Steel, a minister of the Presbyterian Church granted license to solemnize marriages. (17)

6-24-1834 - Court is satisfied that Thomas Bernard, late deceased, was a Revolutionary Pensioner and that he died on the 12th day of June 1833 and left Polly Bernard his widow. (17)

6-27-1834 - Butcher's Executors vs. Butcher Heirs - Ann Butcher, widow. (24)

6-27-1834 - Court is satisfied that William Morris Sr. was a Revolutionary soldier and that he departed this life on 12th May A. D. 1834 without leaving a widow, but leaving the following children and heirs, to-wit: William Morris, Jr., Sally Brown wife of Soverighn H. Brown, Polly Shockley wife of John Shockley, Catherine wife of John Driskill, Thomas Morris, Rollif Morris, Joshua Morris, John Morris and Nancy Morris. That Nancy Morris is dead and that Thomas, Rolliff, John and Joshua Morris are non-residents of Ohio, but others are residents. (28)

6-27-1834 - Proved to the courts satisfaction that Jacob Fishbach a soldier of the Revolution departed this life intestate about the month of March A. D. 1826 and that John Fishbach and Rosanah Fishbach are the children and only heirs of said Jacob Fishbach. (29)

6-27-1834 - William Triggott vs. Heirs of Robert Johnson - Minor heirs are: Margaret, Virginia, Martha, Alexander, Mary and John Johnson. (36)

10-14-1834 - John Stevens, a native of Scotland files declaration to become citizen. Has lived in Highland County thirteen years. (56)

10-17-1834 - Stephen Ogden an applicant for a pension appeared in court and presented his declaration in writing. At the same time came Charles B. Smith, a minister and John Smith who each testified under oath to their belief of his age and being a Soldier of the Revolution. Court ordered to be certified. (65)

10-17-1834 - Reuben Plumer, a minister of the Methodist Episcopal Church granted license to solemnize marriages. (69)

10-17-1834 - This day came into court William Boatman an applicant for a pension; also came Charles B. Smith, a minister and George W. Barrere who testified to age of applicant and their belief in his services as a Revolutionary soldier. Court ordered to be certified. (69)

10-18-1834 - William Roush and wife vs. heirs of George Wilkins - Petition for Partition. Abraham Wilkins is to have 70 acres out of 230 acres agreeable to the will of Philip Wilkins, deceased. Sarah Wilkins, 1/5th part; Rebecca Wilkins, 1/5th part; Rachel Wilkins, 1/5th part; Polly Ann Wilkins, 1/5th part. (72)

3-9-1835 - Rev. Joseph Simpson, a Methodist minister, granted license to solemnize marriages. (82)

3-9-1835 - Jeremiah Fenner vs. Sarah Ann Fenner and others - Petition for Partition. Mary Ann Fenner, 1/3rd part as her dower right; Jeremiah Fenner, 4/7th part; Sarah Ann Fenner, 1/7th part; Mary W. Fenner 1/7th part; Rachel Fenner, 1/7th part. (84)

3-10-1835 - Perry Collier, guardian vs. Christopher Johnson Heirs - Petition for Partition. Harriett Johnson, 1/6th part. (Note: No further division given).(86)

3-14-1835 - Yesterday John Baker and Alexander Bunteun(?) made oath that they were acquainted with Samuel Gibson a reputed Revolutionary Soldier late of said county, deceased. That Samuel Gibson departed this life in this county on the 20th day of February, 1835, as well as said deponents recollect. That they had for several years been well acquainted with Elizabeth Gibson reputed wife, now widow of said Samuel Gibson and that said Elizabeth Gibson is still living in this county. Court is satisfied to same. (117)

3-17-1835 - Benjamin Eakins, adms. vs. Benjamin Eakins Widow and Heirs - Petition for Partition. Nancy Eakins, widow has dower interest. (129)

7-27-1835 - Samuel Cary and others vs. Daniel McPherson and others - Partition. 1/3rd part set off to Mary McPherson as dower estate; David South and Mary his wife, 1/14th part; Samuel Carey and Ann his wife, 1/14th part; Thomas Leavin(?) and Elizabeth his wife, 1/14th part; Harmen Davis and Martha his wife, 1/14th part; Ruth McPherson, 1/14th part; Daniel McPherson, 1/14th part; to Stephen, John, Joseph Meral(?) and Benjamin McPherson 1/14th part; David Crisim and Rachel his wife, 1/14th part; John Smith and Charlotte his wife, 1/14th part; Jonathan Hayworth, 1/14th part during his life and after his death share to Daniel, Mary and George Hayworth. (137)

7-29-1835 - This day came into court Peter Snider an applicant for a pension. Also coming into court were Frederick Acre, William Davidson, Thomas Colvin and Jeremiah Walker having testified as to age and belief of Peter Sniders services as a Revolutionary Soldier. Court satisfied. (155)

7-29-1835 - Thomas E. Teter appointed guardian of Benjamin and Catherine Teter his wife who are deaf and dumb and incapable of managing estate. (152)

8-4-1835 - Jonathan Harrison, a foreigner, filed his declaration of intention to become citizen. (182)

10-5-1835 - Mahlon Branson vs. Branson Heirs - Petition for Partition. One-third part to petitioner, assigned to said Mahlon Branson by Beulah Branson, it being her dower interest; John, Isaac, Robert, Jacob, Lot and Rebecca Branson, Sarah Barker late Sarah Branson, John Holman and Lois his wife late Lois Branson each to have 1/11th part; Mary and Nathan Branson only children of Nathan Branson, deceased 1/11th part; Mahlon Branson, 1/11th part. (199)

10-5-1835 - This day Patsey Beard widow and relict of John Beard, deceased, proved to the satisfaction of the court that the said John Beard late of this county departed this life on the 30th day of August 1835 leaving said Patsey Beard his widow and that said John Beard was a Revolutionary pensioner of the United States. Court orders to be certified. (201)

10-6-1835 - Christopher Crosier, a foreigner presented his declaration of intention to become citizen. (205)

10-7-1835 - Jesse Barker and wife vs. Richard Beeson and wife - Petition for Partition. Jesse Baker and Nancy his wife, ¼th part; John Beeson, ¼th part; Amasa Beeson, ¼th part; Rebecca Beeson, ¼th part. (207)

10-15-1835 - Deposition of Allen Gulliford who made oath that he was acquainted with Spencer Wilson formerly of this county for several years. That Allen Gulliford first became acquainted with said Wilson about 24 or 25 years ago, a few weeks before the said marriage of said Spencer Wilson to Sarah Ann Hague daughter of John Hague. That Spencer Wilson departed this life about 16, 17, or 18 years ago in Highland County leaving John T. Wilson, Ann Barbara Wilson and Spencer Wilson his children and heirs. Said Allen Gulliford attended the funeral of said Spencer Wilson and that he never understood nor does he suppose that Spencer Wilson left other children. Said Gulliford has been informed that said Ann Barbara Wilson has since the death of her father been married in the State of Indiana.(235)

3-14-1836 - This day it was proved to the satisfaction of the court that Joseph Moller a Revolutionary pensioner of the United States departed this life the 27th day of January 1836 leaving the following children, to-wit: John Moller and Lewis Moller who reside in Highland County; Isaac Moler, Esther wife of Job Mace and Mary wife of Daniel Keithler who have gone to parts unknown. That Joseph Moller left no widow and that said John Moller is the sole executor of the last will and testament of said Joseph. (250)

3-14-1836 - This day came into open court, James Humphrey who being duly sworn proved to the satisfaction of the court that Benjamin Williams a Revolutionary pensioner departed this life in the County of Highland Ohio on the 17th day of January 1836 leaving Aramenta William s his widow who is now living. Which is ordered to be certified. (250)

3-14-1836 - Rev. Robert Calvert, a German Baptist minister is granted license to solemnize marriages. (251)

615

3-15-1836 - Jesse Barker and wife vs. Beeson Heirs - Petition for Partition. Amelia Beeson widow of Richard Beeson, deceased is granted $50.; Jesse Barker and Nancy Barker former Nancy Beeson, ¼th part; Samuel Bond guardian of John, Amasa and Rebecca Beeson, minors 3/4th part. (254)

3-16-1836 - Catharine Roads vs. Heirs of Roads - Petition for dower. (264)

3-16-1836 - Scott Douglas vs. Holliday Heirs - Partition. Abraham Penington and Mary Penington late Mary Holliday, dower estate; Scott Douglas, 1/3rd part; David, Samuel, Jane, Mary Ann, Isabella, Nancy and Elizabeth Holliday, 1/11th part each; Joseph, William J. and Hoinlas(?) H. Holliday and Phillip Wilson and Sarah his wife late Holliday, 1/32nd part each. (269)

7-11-1836 - Rev. John J. Rennisnider, a minister of the German Evangelical Lutheran Church is granted license to solemnize marriages. (289)

7-12-1836 - Christian Mattiell, a foreigner makes declaration of intention to become citizen. - John Sayer, a foreigner makes declaration of intention to become citizen. (298)

9-27-1836 - John Stokes and wife vs. Nathan Henderson's Heirs - Partition. One third part to Mary Henderson as dower estate; John Stokes and wife, 1/5th part; Charles Henderson, 1/5th part; Thompson Henderson, 1/5th part; Elijah Henderson, 1/5th part; Susan Saum late Susan Henderson, 1/5th part. (336)

3-14-1837 - Rev. Rene Wolf, a Methodist Episcopal minister is granted license to solemnize marriages. (360)

7-11-1837 - Rev. William W. Davis, a United Brethren minister is granted licence to solemnize marriages. (409)

7-11-1837 - Samuel E. Snider vs. Heirs of Adam Snider, dec'd - Partition. One-third part to Rachel Snider as her dower estate; Samuel E., Jacob, Henry, David, Adam George and David Snider, 1/10th part each; Thomas Williamson and Nancy his wife, 1/10th part; James Wolf and Eliza his wife, 1/10th part; to the Heirs of Thomas Snider—Elizabeth, George, James, Daniel, William and Peter Snider and one other childs share for child whose name is unknown, 1/10th part. (404)
(Note: The name of David is given as in the records and was REPEATED, possibly one name may be DANIEL, but the writing was plain and both names could only be deciphered as David.)

7-12-1837 - Pharoah A. Ogden, a minister of the M. E. Church granted license to solemnize marriages - James Frazier, a minister of the Baptist Church granted license to solemnize marriages. (410)

7-14-1837 - John Triplett, etal. vs. Alexander Bartley, etal. - Partition. John Triplet Sr., John Triplet Jr., Wm. M., Christopher C., Elizabeth and James Triplett and Nelson Franklin and wife, 1/11th part; Heirs of Alexander, Daniel, John and William McIntire, 1/11th part each; Alexander Bentley and wife, John, William and Christopher Moxley, 1/11th part; Catharine Bentley widow of Joseph Bentley, 1/11th part. (421)

Contributed by: Mrs. Carrie Purtell, Box 85, Leesburg, Ohio 45135

Persons 40 years of age and over. Information taken from Death Book #1, Hillsboro, Ohio.

Name	Death Date & age	Marital Status	Place of Death	Place of Birth
FELLERS, Samuel	1867 July 26 45y	m.	Greenfield	
ARNETT, Mary	1867 Aug. 5 76 y	s.	Highland Co.	Pennsylvania
BELL, Charles	1867 Sept. 27 73 y	w. Parents:	Greenfield William & Mary Bell	New Jersey
WATKINS, Johnson	1867 Sept. 28 67 y	m.	Highland County	
HIXON, Rebecca McClure	1867 July 2 57 y		Fairfield Twp.	
ROLER, Mrs. S.	1867 Sept. 16 72y		Dodsonville	
MARCHANT, Susan	1867 July 30 45y	Parents:	Leesburg John & Susan Binegar	Tennessee
BLAIR, James	1867 Aug. 20 43y	Parents:	East Monroe Thomas & Dinah Blair	Virginia
STEED, Nathan	1867 Sept. 4 68y	Parents:	East Monroe John & Susan Steed	Virginia
MYERS, Lucy	1867 Sept. 8 67y		East Monroe	
STRATTON, Albert	1867 Sept. 3 48y 3m		Greenbush	Clay Twp.
HARRISON, William	1867 Sept. 6 54y	s.	Clay Twp.	Pennsylvania
PUGSLEY, Ruth	1867 July 3 40y	m. Parents:	Brush Creek Jacob & Rachel Kirby	Hillsboro, O.
FERGUSON, Sarah	1867 Nov. 2 71y	w. Parents:	Rainsboro William & Elizabeth Patton	Kentucky
DEEPH, Paton	1867 Oct. 23 53y	m. Parents:	Madison Twp. Moses & Mary Deeph	Virginia
PITZER, John C.	1867 Dec. 6 58y		Lynchburg	Virginia
HUSTON, Thomas	1867 Nov. 8 67y	Parents:	Concord Twp. John & Mary Huston	Antrim, Ireland
DWYER, Mary	1867 Nov. 23 74y 6m 23ds	Parents:	Greenfield Dwyer	Franklin Co. Va.
NEWELL, William	1867 Nov 21 70y	s.	At Home	Liberty Twp.
DUCKWALL, Sally	1867 Dec. 19 47y	m.	At Home	Liberty Twp.
JOHNSON, Edith	1867 Dec. (?) 67y	s. Parents:	Penn Twp. Elisha & (?) Johnson	

617

Persons 40 years of age and over. Taken from Death Book #1, Hillsboro, Ohio

Name	Death Date & age	Marital Status	Place of Death	Place of Birth
STOOP, Rebecca	1867 July 28 48y	s.	Madison Twp.	
CLYBURN, Charles D.	1867 Dec. 26 49y	m.	Paint Twp.	
ESHELMAN, Samuel	1868 Jan 6 66y	w.	Greenfield, O.	Shenandoah, Va.
CAMPTON, James	1868 Feb. 2 52y 11m 26d	m.	Washington twp.	Adams County, O.
RILEY, Bridget	1868 Mar. 10 40y	m.	New Lexington twp.	Ireland
MASSEY, William B.	1868 Feb. 21 52y	m. Parents: J. M. Massey	Jackson Twp.	Jackson Twp.
AUCHENLECK, George	1868 Feb. 10 67y	m.	Greenfield	Ireland
ROBINSON, James	1868 (?) 86y	s.	Greenfield	Ireland
VANPELT, Eleanor	1868 Mar. 20 81y 2m 5d	w.	New Market Twp.	Maryland
MORROW, Elizabeth	1868 Mar. 28 75y 6m 9d	w. Parents: Teneror Tence?	Dodson Twp.	Maryland
KENADY, Jane	1868 Jan. 8 47y 6m 21d	m.	Highland Twp.	Ireland
HOMAN, Christan	1868 Jan 1 48y 5m 21d	m.	Highland Co.	Va. Res. Clay twp.
MURRIAN, Charlotte	1868 May 4 80y	w.	Brushcreek Twp.	New Jersey
ZUCK, Jesse	1868 May 27 55y	m.	Brushcreek Twp.	Pennsylvania
REED, George O.	1868 May 29 64y	m.	Brushcreek Twp.	Ohio
MILLER, Jacob	1868 June 29 86y	w.	Brushcreek Twp.	Virginia
HOWARD, James	1868 May 21 85y	m.	Hillsboro, O.	Ireland Penn Twp.
PAGE, Letitia	1868 June 23 57y 3m	m.	Salem Twp.	Virginia
KINZER, Eliza David	1868 May 14 50y 21d	m. Parents: Thornton Davis	Fairfield Twp.	Fairfield Twp.
FINLEY, Margaret	1868 May 23 70y		Greenfield, O.	Greenfield
MILLER, Sarah	1868 Apr.(?) 75y	w.	Highland	Kentucky
MEOSKER(?), Susan	1868 June 29 74y 3m	w.	Hillsboro	Frederick Co. Va.
ROADS, David	1868 Apr. 18 70y	m.	Paint Twp.	Virginia

618

Persons 40 years of age and over. Taken from Death Book #1, Hillsboro, Ohio

Name	Death Date & age	Marital Status	Place of Death	Place of Birth
FERNEAU, Henry	1868 June 16 75y	w.	Brushcreek	Virginia
MITCHEL, Samuel	1868 July 12 54y	s.	Concord Twp.	Ohio
McQUILTY, Elizabeth	1868 July 15 52y	m.	White Oak Twp.	Ohio
St. CLAIR, Benz Alex	1868 Aug. 25 48y	s. Parents:	Hillsboro, O. Wm. Benz & Jane (?)	Stanton, Va.
NAKEN, Lucy Richman (or NUKES?)	1868 July 21 54y	m.	Penn Two	(?) Highland Co.
SMALLEY, Phillip W.	1868 Sept. 13 44y 10m 21d	m.	Highland Co.	Highland Co.
ROUSH, Ellen	1868 Sept. 14 40y	w.	Highland Co.	Highland Co.
SHARP, Esther	1868 Sept. 14 44y	m. Parents:	Paint Twp. Lecke Vandllon	Virginia
TEDRON(?), Naomi	1868 Sept. 14 45y	m.	Marshall Twp.	Ohio
LONG, John	1868 Dec. 1 86y	m.	Fairfield Twp.	Virginia
COWGILL, Rachel	1868 Dec. 9 49y	m.	Paint Twp.	(?)
GADBERRY, Samuel	1868 Dec. 6 41y 7m 24d	m.	Greenfield, O.	Ross County
STINE, Josiah C.	1868 Dec. 29 57y 9m 9d	m.	New Market Twp.	Pennsylvania
WORKMAN, Rachel	1868 Dec. 13 53y	m.	Salem Twp.	Kentucky
SPARGUR, Anthony W.	1868 Nov. 8 41y 2m 29d	m. Parents:	Washington Twp. John & Marie Sparger	Jackson Twp.
FENNER, Joseph	1869 Sept. 13 65y	m. Parents:	Liberty Twp. Felty & Nancy Fenner	Liberty Twp.
GLAZE, John	1869 Dec. 20 84y 6m 22d	m. Parents:	Brush Creek Twp. John & Elizabeth Glaze	
LYLE, Finley	1869 Mar. 27 61y	m.	(Illegible)	Virginia
DAILY, Mary	1869 June 15 83y	w.	White Oak Twp.	Virginia
BYRD, S. O.	1869 Apr. 4 47y	w.	Sinking Springs	
GAIN, Soloman	1869 Aug 27 58y	m.	Liberty Twp.	Virginia
BOYD, John	1869 Nov. 1 66y 3m 12d		Greenfield	Pennsylvania

Persons 40 years of age and over. Taken from Death Book #1, Hillsboro, Ohio

Name	Death Date & age	Marital Status	Place of Death	Place of Birth
ANDERSON, John	1869 Apr. 20 77 yrs.	m.	Highland Co.	Pennsylvania
WILSON, Joseph	1869 Aug. 28 73 yrs.		Greenfield	
GIBSON, Warren	1869 Apr.(?) 70y	m.	Union Twp.	
DAVIS, Martha P.	1869 Apr. 22 75y	w.	Penn Twp.	Virginia
APPLEGATE, John P.	1869 May 3 69y	s.	Fairfield Twp.	New Jersey
STOOP, Jacob	1869 June 27 89y	m.	White Oak Twp.	Virginia
McCARTHY, James	1869 Jan. 24 75y	m.	Hillsboro, O.	(Illegible)
BROPHY, Margaret	1869 Feb. 16 (Note: no age)	w.	County Infirmy	Killkenny(?)
_____, Henry (Illegible)	1869 Feb. 1 96y		County Infirmy	Hillsboro, Ohio
BOWMAN, John	1869 Jan. 27 54y 1m 17d	m.	Greenfield, O.	Rochbridge Co. Va.
WILCOX, Mrs. Jane	1869 Feb. 26 46y 2m 29d	w.	Greenfield	Ross Co.
HUGHEY, Catherine C.	1869 Feb. 22 53y	s. Parents:	Hillsboro, O. Isaac & Kate Hughey	Highland Co.
WEST, Elizabeth	1869 Mar. 28 74 yrs.	w.	Brush Creek Twp.	Highland Co.
BROOKINGS, Lydia	1869 June 7 48y	m.	Allenburg, O.	Dodson Twp.
COCHRAN, Mary	1869 Dec. 14 74y 3m 2d	m. Parents:	New Market Twp. John Faris	Virginia
STAIN, John	1869 Sept. 3 80y	m.	New Market Twp.	Kentucky
DUCKWALL, Samuel	1869 Apr. 23 74y	m. Parents:	Danville, O. Lewis & Susan Duckwall	
WRIGHT, John D.	1869 June 21 65y	m.	Penn Twp.	
BURNETT, William	1869 June 21 55y	m.	Boston, O.	
HOPKINS, Malinda	1869 Apr. 23 79y	s.	Washington Twp.	Maryland

620

HIGHLAND COUNTY, OHIO - REGISTER OF BLACKS 1827-1859

The following records were copied from a book "Indenture Record" as found in the Clerk of Courts Office at the court house at Hillsboro. Page on which record may be found in original book is given in parenthesis.
(Note: This record has recently been microfilmed by the Ohio Historical Society, Columbus, Ohio)

Certificate of Freedom. Ross County, Ohio. I certify that Benjamin WEST a man of colour was brought out to this state from Virginia by my father, that Ben is now Free and that my father is not present or he would sign said certificate. That Ben is 22 years old in April next, dated 18 Feb. 1823. (Signed) Pleasant Thurman. Recorded 7-10-1827 Highland Co., Ohio. (19)

Free Paper. I certify that on arrival of Benjamin WAGGONER he produced a paper declaring him a free man now living with David Swain in whose family the aforesaid paper was ashed to pieces, the remains now in my possession, dated Leesburgh, O. 8th month 16th, 1825. (Signed) Gersham Bordner. I certify that when I employed Benjamin WAGGONER in my service he was in possession of a free paper which he lost, it being washed to pieces by some of my family, dated Aug. 25, 1825, Leesburg, O. (Signed) David Swain. Rec. 7-19-1827 Highland Co., Ohio. (23)

Highland County, Ohio. This day appeared before me, Moses H. Kirbey being sworn deposeth that he for many years has been acquainted with Joseph KING, a coloured man and knows he was born of free parents and is at present a free black citizen of Ohio, dated 27 Sept. 1827. Recorded 10-3-1827. (14)

Perquimans County, North Carolina. I, David White of said county one of the Trustees of the yearly meeting of Friends of North Carolina by power vested in me by Sampson Lawrence of same county, have removed to Highland County, Ohio a negro man named Smith WHITE, dark complexion, middle size, about 27 years of age and his wife, Louisa and her child, Elizabeth, all who belonged to Sampson Lawrence above named, Louisa about 20 years of age. That these persons have been manumitted to manage themselves. 12th day, 10th month, 1825. (Signed) David White. Wit: Nathan Hunt. Rec. 7-15-1836, Highland Co., Ohio. (65)

Jane WHITE. Perquimans County, North Carolina. I, David White of said county and state as agent or trustees for the yearly meeting of Friends of North Carolina and by authority vested in me, manumit and set free a negro woman, Jane, dark complexion, about 49 years of age and her daughter, Louisa about same colour, aged 20 years, and her son, Bartlet about 10 years old. Also, Louisa's child, John. That they are now in Highland County, Ohio having left this county in 1834 under control of Thaddeus White and William Nixon, dated 13th day, 10th month, 1835. (Signed) David White. Wit: Nathan Hunt. Recorded 7-15-1836 Highland Co., Ohio. (66)

Perquimans County, North Carolina. I, David White of said county and state, agent or trustee of the yearly meeting of Friends of North Carolina by authority vested in me, do manumit and set free a woman of colour named Winney LAMB and her three children: Elizabeth, Thomas and Louisa; also, Theophelus WINSLOW now in Wayne County, Indiana, he is about 27 years old, 6 feet high, tollerably dark complexion and is the son of Betty Winslow of Highland County, Ohio. Said Winney Lamb is a low woman of yellow complexion about 42 years old and with her children are now in Highland County, Ohio. That they left this state in 1834 under the care of Thaddeus White and William Nixon, dated 13th of 10th month, 1835. (Signed) David White. Wit: Nathan Hunt. Recorded 7-15-1836 Highland Co., Ohio. (67)

Perquimans County, North Carolina. I, David White of said county and state, as trustee or agent of the North Carolina Friends Yearly Meeting and by power as their agent have removed to Highland County, Ohio, a negro woman, Edith RUTCLIFF, aged about 40 years and her son, Amzel, commonly called Amzel WATKINS aged 20 years, middle size swings himself greatly when he walks, have manumitted these persons with full liberty to do for themselves. 12th of 10th month, 1835. (Signed) David White. Wit: Nathan Hunt. Rec. 7-15-1836. (69)

Perquimans County, North Carolina. I, David White, of said county and state as agent or trustee for the yearly meeting of Friends of North Carolina by power as their agent manumit and set free the following people of colour now in Highland County, Ohio, namely: Betty WINSLOW aged about 50 years, her sons: Joseph Winslow, Robinson, Henry, Alfred and John and daughter Mary Ann, they having left this state in 1834 under the care of Thaddeus White and Wm Nixon. Said Joseph is about 24 years, very dark in colour, middle size. Robinson is of middle size, of dark complexion and 22 years old. Henry is tall, thin and yellow complexion, about 20 years of age. Alfred is about 15 years of age. John is about 8 years old and Mary Ann is about 14 years old. Dated this 13th day of 10th month 1835. (Signed) David White. Wit: Nathan Hunt. Rec. 7-14-1836. (71)

Perquimans County, North Carolina. I, David White, of said county and state as agent and trustee for the yearly meeting of Friends of North Carolina by power as their agent have removed to Highland County, Ohio, a certain negro woman named Patience the wife of Daniel WHITE and their five children--Nancy, Wiley, Smith, Peter and Mary; also, the above named Daniel WHITE whom I bought of Jonathan White of Perquimans Co., North Carolina and do manumit all said persons from slavery. Daniel White is aged about 35 years, yellow complexion and a stout make; his wife, Patience, is about 30 years of age and a shade darker than her husband, 12th of 10th month, 1835. (Signed) David White. Wit: Nathan Hunt. Rec. 7-15-1836. (72)

Hastings Court of Staunton, Virginia. James MARTIN, son of Joseph Martin, of dark brown complexion about 19 years of age on 5th April 1827 and born free as appears by the register of his freedom in said office 5 Sept. 1823. Dated 27 Oct. 1837, Walter H. Papp, C.C. Recorded 1-28-1837, Highland Co., Ohio. (74)

That Robert Peele and Thomas I. Outland of Northampton County, North Carolina being legally authorized and impowered by trustees of the yearly meeting of the Society of Friends of North Carolina take charge and convey to the State of Ohio, Indiana and Illinois, Turner PEELE together with a number of other colored people held by said trustees, said Robert Peele and Thomas I. Outland having removed and placed said Turner Peele together with a number of others in Highland County, Ohio and that said Turner Peele is a free man,/dated this 1st day of 12th month, 1836. Recorded 8-11-1837.(75)

Perquimans County, North Carolina. Before me, Jonah Perry one of the Justices of the Peace for said county came Nathan Wislow and deposeth that he knew Harrison WINSLOW a man of color of said county to be free born about 21 years of age, rather of a dark complexion, 5 feet 6 inches high with a small scar over the right eye. Dated 10th January 1838. Recorded 1-2-1842. (76)

622

Highland County, Ohio. Personally appeared before me Augustus Brown a Justice of the
Peace for said county, John Bolt who saith that he was well acquainted with Jerry
OLDHAM and Asa, his son, both men of color of the state of North Carolina and that
they were the property of his father, Charles Bolt, and that he gave them their freedom and they have been set free from Nov. 28, 1826 as by certificate, dated Jan. 17,
1840. Certificate: This is to certify that I gave the negroes Jerry and Asa Oldham
liberty to go with my son, William, to Ohio, dated Nov. 28, 1826. (Signed) Charles
Bolt. Rec. 2-28-1840.   (80 & 81A)

Highland County, Ohio. Leesburgh. That Samuel White and Osmond White by power of
attorney executed to them by David White of Perquinmans County, North Carolina and
Joseph Parker of Pasqotank County, North Carolina trustees of the yearly meeting of
the Society of Friends, brought and set at liberty, Luke WISLOW and Levina his wife
to enjoy freedom of the state of Ohio as may appear more fully by records of Henry
County, Indiana where the power of attorney is recorded, dated this 12th day, 10th
month, 1841. Rec. 10-23-1841.   (81)

Patrick County, Virginia. That on April 12, 1821, Jariessa GOING, Polly GOING and
Andrew GOING free people of colour appeared in the Clerk's office of this county and
made exhibit that Jariessa GOING aged 62 years of age, a female of dark complexion
with straight and well proportioned stature residing on Little Daun River, Polly
GOING aged 28 years, female of light complexion and of close and low stature also
residing on Little Daun River and Andrew GOING 9 years of age, son of the above
named Polly Going, of dark complexion with a small scar over and above the left eye
and residing with his mother. Dated 15 April 1821. Rec. 2-28-1840.

Augusta County, Virginia. Know all men by these presents that my negro man, Lewis
MEETIN (or MUTIN) and Fanny, his wife, the first about 34 and the latter about 35
years of age are emancipated and set free together with their five children, to-wit:
--Julia about 12, Hezekiah about 10, James about 7, Zacariah about 4 and Lucy Jane
about 1. Dated 16 Sept. 1843. (Signed) James Nelson. Rec. 10-23-1843.   (86)

Owen County, Kentucky. I, Samuel D. Fisback, of said county and state do manumit
and set free and emancipate all my slaves namely--William and Martha and her child,
Thomas Davis, also Susan. That I wrote a deed of emancipation for said William
15 or 18 years ago to take effect when he would be 28 years of age, but it was lost,
and now make this deed. That they are free as long as they live with me as long as
I live and they are to have 100 acres of land a piece. That they are none of them
21 years of age except William. Dated 22 July 1841. Rec. 1-22-1845. (96 & 100)

Washington County, Kentucky. Nov. 23, 1849. John, a negro man emancipated by the
last will and testament of Barnabas Hughes, dec'd, came into court with Thomas B.
Hughes executor of said will, who acknowledged his freedom. Said John is 22 years
old, slender made, 5 feet 7 inches high, black complexion, no scars. Recorded (not
given).   (97)

Albemarle County, Virginia. Charlottesville June 3, 1845. Fayette SIMS a free man
of colour was this day registered in this office, that he was emancipated by Col.
Joseph Wyath by deed dated 13 March 1819 and recorded in this court 6 March 1843.
That he is of bright mulatto complexion, has a small scar on the forehead and another
between the shoulders produced by a burn, that he is 28 years of age, 5 feet and
3/4ths inches high in shoes. Recorded 4-28-1847.   (99)

Brown County, Ohio. That Isaiah Dent and William S. Dudley of Fleming County, Kentucky for $595.00 to us paid have emancipated and set free, Jacob EMMONS, a negro man about 25 years of age being same negro man sold to us by Elijah Emmons of said county and state by bill of sale dated 2 Jan. 1840, dated this 29 July 1841. Recorded 11-23-1850. (101)

Halifax County, Virginia. Nov. 22, 1858. That Jacob, emancipated by last will and testament of Philip E. Voss, dec'd, was this day registered in my office. That Jacob is 52 years old, 5 feet 8 inches high, dark mulatto, black kinky hair, has a scar on the wrist of the right arm, one on the back of the left hand, one of his thighs has been broken. Clerk of Court, Halifax Co., Va. Recorded (not given). (110)

Highland County, Ohio. Hissborough Aug. 23, 1859. Martha FOWLIS now the widow MITCHELL and sister-in-law of Biddy FOWLIS the mother of Mary HUGHES wife of John HUGHES who applies for free papers says that Biddy FOWLIS who was the wife of her brother, Winston FOWLIS were both at the time and prior to their marriage in the possession of their freedom and that Mary FOWLIS, daughter of Winston and Biddy FOWLIS, now wife of John HUGHES was born a free child of free parents in Halifax County, Virginia. (Signed) Martha (her mark) Mitchell. Wit: Jn. (mark) Hughes, J. W. Tucker. Recorded (not given). (111)

The following marriages were taken from "Marriage Record A (1818-1839)" as found in the Probate Court at the court house at Logan.

ALEXANDER, Andrew to Mary Ann Claxton		8-1-1829
ALEXANDER, Samuel to Elizabeth Eckhart		1-2-1825
ANDERSON, John to Martha Roult	lic.	1-17-1829
ANDERSON, Joseph to Kisiah Friend		4-12-1827
ASHTON, Reuben to Joanna Von (Vann)		5-21-1826
BARTER, Enoch to Rebecca Swinhart		7-7-1822
BEAGLE, Wm to Rosanna McCarty	lic.	1-31-1827
BELL, James to Barbary Bitcher		6-3-1819
BENCE (PENCE?), Daniel to Jane Clark		9-25-1823
BENN, John to Polly Francis		1-4-1824
BERNHILL, David to Mary Shaffer		7-14-1829
BLAKESLEE, Lorin to Rachael Shoemaker		11-26-1820
BLANE, Joseph to Caty Pence		4-13-1823
BOUGH, George W. to Margaret Inbody		5-17-1825
BREWER, William to Sabra Johnson		5-22-1823
BRITON, Elijah to Betsey Carey		9-6-1825
BROWN, John to Susannah Barnet		6-20-1824
BUMGARNER, John to Polly Bumgarner - on application of John Gross		10-9-1828
BUMGARNER, William to Eve Shrekingast		4-10-1828
BUSH, David to Betsy Moor		2-7-1824
BUTIN, Anthanas to Rebecca Coleman (note: see 1821 Butin marriage)		10-7-1822
BUTIN, Anthonias to Rebecca Coleman		10-7-1821
BYERLY, Jacob Jr. to Susannah Hosse		12-7-1820
CALDWELL, Walter to Margaret Clark		9-26-1822
CAMPBELL, Henry to Nancy White		2-9-1819
CAREY, John to Fanny Johnson		7-10-1825
CARPENTER, Jacob to Elizabeth Yates		8-28-1821
CARPENTER, Peter to Catharine Duple		4-20-1826
CARPENTER, Sampson to Catharine Walters		5-30-1822
CARY, James to Francia Wycuff		2-6-1822
CAVE, John to Elizabeth Steel	lic.	12-14-1826
CENTER, Ashley W. to Kissiah Hyatt		2-15-1821
CHAPMAN, Casper to Polly Inbody		4-13-1826
CLARK, Benj. to Eliza (or Elza) Donaldson		4-2-1823
CLARK, Benj'n to Mary Swazy		8-30-1821
CLARK, Benj'n to Mary Sweany (note: see 1821 Ben'n Clark marriage)		8-30-1822
CLARK, Elias to Betsey Woolsy		1-30-1827
CLARK, Henry to Elizabeth Morrison		7-24-1828
CLARK, Isaac to Nancy Francis		9-20-1827
CLARK, Robt. to Elizabeth Davis	lic.	2-15-1825
CLARK, William to Rachel Starkey		3-3-1824
CLOPP, John to Mary Every		10-30-1824
COBLIN, James to Sarah (Sally) Webb		12-25-1826
COFFINBERRY, J. W. to Nancy Gallagher		3-23-1826
COKELY, William to Sarah Clark		1-18-1821
COOK, Abraham to Mary Filson		8-14-1828

```
COOK, Thomas to Brady Low                                              9-8-1822
CONRAD, Felix to Matilda Cave                                          9-6-1829
CONRAD, George to Milley Rinolds                                       12-24-1829
COONROD, Wollery to Hulda Purtee                                       8-23-1823
COZAD, Henry to Margaret Colwell                                       11-9-1827
CRAGELER, Solomon to Elizabeth Bussard                          lic.   6-20-1826
CROTHERS, James to Catharine Kensser (Kinson)                          12-25-1828
CULLINS, Samuel to Nancy Davis                                      (12?)-27-1823
CULVER, Reuben to Mary Beadle                                          8-12-1824
CUSHING, Gilbert to Nancy Boys                                         12-19-1822
DAVIS, Moses to Modaline Davis                                         2-1-1827
DAVIS, Thomas to Catharine Kokeley - both of Green twp.               3-11-1824
DAVIS, William to Betsy Shirker                                        5-1-1827
DEFENBAUGH, John to Caty House                                         11-28-1819
DEVALT, Abraham to Sarah Starkey                                       1-22-1829
DIXON, Silas to Mrs. Mary Vanderford                                   2-20-1828
DIXSON, Elias to Lucinda Anderson                                      12-25-1828
DODD, Peter to Eliza Donley                                            8-25-1825
DONALDLY, Jesse to Margaret Oneil                                      8-3-1823
DONALLY, John to Elizabeth McKee                                       3-20-1828
DONALSON, Henderson to Johannah Sweasey                         lic.   4-28-1828
DORMAN, James D. to Polly Jonston                                      11-3-1827
DOWD, Alexander to Nancy Vanderford                                    9-21-1821
DUCENBURY, Nathaniel to Eliza Meeker                                   9-30-1821
DUPLER, John to Elizabeth Dupler                                       7-17-1828
DUSENBERRY, Nathan to Eliza Meeker (note; see 1821 Ducenbury mar.)     9-30-1822
EBERT, Benj'n to Elizabeth Kniss                                       10-26-1824
EBERT, Daniel to Mary Goul - on application of George Goul             2-28-1828
EBY, George to Elizabeth Hill                                          4-23-1826
EBY, Joseph to Elizabeth Dorman                                        1-13-1822
ELDRIDGE, Walter to Polly Pence                                        3-14-1819
ENGLAND, Titus to Katharine Bussard                                    1-1-1829
ENGLE, William to Rachel Hostetter                                     2-5-1829
ERAKES, William to Sarah Jones                                         12-9-1823
ETTENTON, George to Mary Brown                                         7-7-1826
EWENS, James to Sarah Demoss                                           11-21-1824
FINNEY, Solomon to Catharine Bartlett                                  1-8-1825
FRANCESKA, William to Rachael Pixler                                   1-27-1824
FRANCESKO, Abraham to Polly Roads                                      10-22-1826
FRANCIS, William to Betsey White                                       8-3-1826
FRANCISCO, Aaron to Catharine Crothers                                 8-17-1828
FRIEND, Andrew C. to Zuriah Jackson                                    7-21-1825
FRIEND, Andrew to Maria Plotner                                        2-11-1826
GARRET, George to Lydia Saters (Salves?)                               5-30-1822
GARRET, Isaac to Sally Fine                                            4-19-1826
GARVIN, James to Prudence Powell                                       1-18-1829
GIBSON, John to Betsy Prough                                     lic.   4-2-1828
GIBSON, Benjamin to Polly Newhouse - both of Laurel twp.              2-19-1829
GIBSON, Joel to Elizabeth Friend of Laurel twp.                       3-13-1828
```

GLASSBURN, John of Gallia Co. to Jane Fee of Hocking Co.   3-9-1829
GREEN, Richard to Mary Blank   4-25-1822
GREGORY, James P. to Sarah Patton - both of Green twp.   3-1-1829
GRIM, Henry to Hannah Francisko   9-24-1820
GRIMES, Ephraim to Hannah Pence   2-10-1829
GRIMES, William to Nancy Cobbin   3-26-1829
HAGERLY, Jacob Frederick to Elizabeth Ponsious   5-16-1822
HARPER, John to Betsy Spencer   4-30-1822
HARRISON, William to Hannah Beaver   6-27-1819
HARSH, David Esq. to Nancy Woolf   9-5-1819
HARSH, John to Christina Stivason   10-17-1819
HARSH, Samuel to Elizabeth Keyse   8-12-1819
HART, Elijzh to Margaret Brown   2-23-1828
HART, George to Polly Brown   8-16-1827
HASTLER, Isaac to Sally Ebert   11-17-1824
HASTLER, Jacob to Polly Ebert   4-30-1826
HATCH, Horatio to Harriet Cushing   9-19-1824
HATHAWAY, Nimrod to Jane O'Neill   2-15-1821
HECOCKS, James to Mary Ann Meeker   10-13-1821
HEFT, Peter to Chloe Smith   624-1825
HENSEL, George to Mary Pontius   3-17-1829
HERMAN, John to Mary Ann Carrell   6-24-1823
HICKOX, James to Maryann Meaker (note: see 1821 Hecocks marriage)   10-13-1822
HOSS, Abraham to Donhua Eby   10-14-1826
HOSS, Jacob to Catharine Shriver   9-15-1825
HOWDESHALL, John to Ann Francisco   11-18-1829
HUBER, Elijah to Catharine Chriver   lic. 8-11-1829
HUNTER, James to Barbara Beck   7-4-1829
HURLBERT, Henry to Ruth Thannihill   11-30-1823
ILER, Jacob to Fanny Walters   1-14-1827
ILLICK, Frederick to Barbara Housman   2-21-1825
INBODY, Daniel to Lydia Hastler   3-1-1827
INBODY, George to Mary McKinsey   3-16-1826
INBODY, John to Mary Hasler   6-1-1819
JOHNSON, James to Darcus Rains   12-12-1826
JONES, John of Salt Creek twp. to Rebecca Demoss   4-20-1824
JONSTON, Enoch to Sally Tanninhill   3-5-1826
JUSTICE, John to Nancy Rees   6-2-1827
KALER, Joseph to Mary Ann Engle   6-8-1828
KEASEY, Christian to Elizabeth Roads   12-18-1825
KEASY, Joseph to Elizabeth Bitcher   1-15-1824
KEETON, Martin to Mary Fee   11-23-1819
KIMBLE, Solomon to Mary Yates - on application of John Kimble   2-18-1829
KIMBLE, William to Elizabeth Smyers   7-21-1825
KINSER, Jacob to Hannah Jackson   5-30-1824
KITCHEN, John to Mary Clapp   3-18-1826
KLINE, Henry to Sofiah Eugh   11-19-1826
LEE, George to Martha O'Neill   5-24-1819
LITTLE, John to Polly Roby   12-5-1824

```
LONG (or DeLONG), Samuel D. to Mary Kimble            8-14-1825
LOOMAN, Joseph to Elizabeth Preesley                  1-16-1825
LOWER, Adam to Catharine Coonrod                      11-27-1827
LOWERY, John to Beers (or Burs) Johnston              2-29-1823
McDONALD, John to Nancy Watts                         5-26-1822
McFARLING, Jesse to Mary Shad                         1-12-1825
McKEE, Albin to Polly Walters                    lic. 8-19-1827
McKEE, Arthur to Polly Picken                         12-6-1821
McMANUS, Henry to Mary Kaler                          11-26-1824
MACKLIN, John to Sally Francisco                      11-7-1824
MARTIN, William to Elizabeth Plank                    3-29-1823
MATTHIAS, Abraham to Christian Zeller                 10-10-1824
MILLER, Flemming to Betsey Himes                      3-21-1829
MILLS, Allen to Elizabeth Rager                       8-20-1829
MOLLENHOWER, John to Margaret Tester                  9-28-1828
MONTGOMERY, William to Susan E. Claxton               6-1-1826
MORRISON, James to Elizabeth Picken                   1-4-1826
MORRISON, John to Sarah Wyckoff                       5-7-1824
MORRISON, John to Margaret Wilkinson                  11-1-1827
MOURY, John A. to Rachael Dunkle                      9-27-1827
NIXON, Jasper to Sarah McGee                          9-8-1829
OLAM, Peter to Elizabeth Coonrod                      10-30-1827
O'NEILL, Thomas to Nancy Lee                          5-4-1818
PENCE, John Jr. to Kitty Keasy                        6-28-1821
PETERSON, John to Jane Claypool                  lic. 12-29-1826
PHILLIPS, Abram to Hetty Luis                         1-29-1829
PHILLIPS, Anthony to Polly England                    2-2-1826
PONSLER, John to Ann Shadd                            5-1-1827
POTTER, John to Margaret Gustin                  (12?)-30-1823
POX, John to Batterna Friend                          8-16-1827
PRENIER (or PREMER), John to Polly Matthias           12-22-1822
PRIMMER, Henry to Nancy Keahy                         6-18-1826
RAINS, George to Nancy Berch                          12-14-1828
RAINS, Nathaniel to Ruth Wilkinson                    1-12-1826
RATCLIFF, Ezekiel to Nancy White                      9-23-1824
RATCLIFF, Ezekiel to Charity Francis                  10-5-1826
RATCLIFF, Miles to Nancy Groves                       11-29-1827
RATCLIFF, Thomas to Rebecca Rains                     7-20-1826
REEVES, Griffis to Olivia Strong                      2-7-1827
RELSA, John to Katy Swim                              2-22-1820
RENCY, William S. to Margaret Bomgarner               3-31-1825
RENSHE, William S. to Elizabeth Culberson             2-24-1828
RICE, Abner to Susanna Whittesey                      7-23-1826
ROADS, Abraham to Catharine Hines                     4-22-1824
ROADS, Jacob to Nancy Byerly                          5-4-1820
ROADS, John to Catharine Zeller                       3-4-1822
ROBINSON, Benjamin to Sarah Robey                     4-26-1829
ROBY, Jesse to Pleasant Hurlburt                      1-1-1826
ROBY, John to Nancy Roby                              4-4-1826
```

628

ROGERS, Samuel M. to Ruth Jones	3-11-1829
ROHN, John to Margaret Hall	2-24-1825
ROUSH, George to Catharine Ettion	6-5-1825
RUSH, Sam'l to Sarah Powell	lic. 11-28-1827
SCIVENER, David to Elender Warien	8-31-1820
SEELEY, Henry to Susan Congrave	lic. 9-11-1829
SEELEY, John D. to Permela Corrick	6-15-1828
SELF, Obadiah to Elizabeth Sweasy	6-23-1822
SELF, Obediah to Elizabeth Clark	lic. 2-21-1829
SHARP, John to Margaret Anderson - both of Perry twp., Fairfield County, Ohio	2-17-1829
SHERK, Jacob to Lucy Davis	2-3-1828
SHRINER (SHRIVER?), Peter to Leah Dunkle	lic. 2-5-1827
SHRIVER, Francis to Kisiah Hill	5-3-1827
SIMANS, Samuel to Malinda Shagler	1-6-1822
SKIVERS, Isaac to Cossa Roby	7-4-1824
SMITH, Absalom to Mehaly M Carty	12-24-1822
SMITH, Henry to Hannah Pence	3-7-1820
SMITH, Jacob H. to Elizabeth Hanes	11-17-1822
SMITH, Robert D. to Maria C. Bitcher	3-21-1822
SMYERS, John to Christina Kimble	8-23-1825
SPEAKMAN, Ebenezer to Patty Morrison	6-3-1824
SPEAKMAN, Jacob to Margaret Jonston	9-19-1822
SPENCER, Charles W. to Athelinda Beadle	6-7-1822
SPENCER, James to Eleoner Kershner	6-9-1829
STANDCLIFF, David to Leah Burch	11-1-1829
STEEL, James to Polly Scherick	lic. 4-7-1827
STEPHENS, Alfred to Belinda Drake	5-27-1828
STEWART, John to Jane McCabe	9-8-1825
STIVERSON, Barney to Eve Mathias	12-8-1818
STIVERSON, John to Elizabeth Hensel	6-26-1825
STONE, Horace to Betsey Ramsey	4-30-1824
STRAIT, Peter to Sophia Jane Sweasey	lic. 11-18-1829
STRAWSER, David to Rhoda Starkey	12-22-1818
SUGENCOURT (SERGENCOURT), George to Hannah Enochs	11-10-1825
SWESY, Henry to Jamime Clark	12-21-1824
SWIFT, Thomas to Rebecca Rise	5-14-1826
TANNIHILL, Zachariah to Sarah Fowler	8-1-1824
TEATS, George to Pheaby Starky	7-21-1822
THROGMORTON, Thomas to Margaret Shaffer	3-26-1829
TRIPP, William to Nancy Roby	4-24-1821
VAN VALTENBURGH, John to Redy Strong	12-16-1826
VICORS, John to Aquitiah Yates	5-15-1823
WALTER, David to Elizabeth Dupler	2-15-1824
WALTERS, John to Fanny Plunk	5-9-1824
WARTHMAN, Matthias to Sally Funk	3-25-1827
WATT, Joseph to Polly McFarland	lic. 4-18-1827
WEBB, George to Rachel Peterson	10-17-1819
WEBB, Joseph to Milla Farlen (also given as Permilla Farber or Farver)	5-10-1821

```
WEBB, Joseph to Permilly Pharber (note: see 1821 Joseph Webb mar.)      5-10-1822
WESTHAVER, John to Mary Orr                                            12-12-1822
WILKINSON, John to Tabithe Grove                                        6-3-1819
WILKINSON, John to Rachael Demas                                      11-29-1821
WILKINSON, Ratcliff to Rebecca Rains                                   12-5-1820
WILKINSON, William to Susanna Swim                                      9-23-1819
WILKISON, Jacob to Mary Demoss                                         3-24-1825
WILL, J. G. to S. Swinhart                                    lic. 7-2-1828
WISWELT, John to Sarah Spencer                                        12-13-1824
WOOD, Mr. ____(not given) to Rebecca Roby                              5-8-1821
WOODWARD, Isaac to Mary Ann Owens                                     12-6-1828
WRIGHT, John 3rd to Elizabeth Tannihill                               10-29-1829
WRIGHT, Joseph to Levinia Carver                                       7-25-1827
WRIGHT, William to Polly Myers                                        11-2-1826
WYCOFF, John to Sally White                                          10-31-1826
WYCOFF, Samuel to Elizabeth Cooper                                     9-28-1828
YOUNG, Charles to Ann Donly                                            6-10-1827
ZELLER, Benjamin to Sarah Matthias                                    2-6-1825
ZELLERS, Jacob to Caty Goss                                           5-12-1822
ZIMMERMAN, Michael to Dorcas Davis                                    8-12-1828
```

630

The following records were taken from Marriage "Book A" located in the Probate Court of the court house at Logan, Ohio.

ANDROM, Aaron to Nancy Chilcoat	7-19-1831
BECK, Frederick to Mary Wilkison	3-13-1832
BENJAMIN, Elisha to Mary Smith	7-18-1832
BEEREY, Daniel to Mary Hensel	9-13-1830
BIRD (BYRD), John T. to Mary Ann Conrad	9-12-1830
BOSTON, Michael to Jane Stant	4-23-1831
BOUCHER, William to Sarah Painter	3-27-1832
BRADFORD, Ward to Margaret Martin	12-15-1831
BREWER, Isaac to Margaret Fee	4-14-1831
BREWER, Nathan to Sarah Fee	3-4-1832
BROWN, Elijah to Elizabeth C. Tilton	8-12-1832
BUCHER, John to Polly Binkley	10-4-1832
BURCH, William to Elizabeth Wykoff	3-27-1831
BUZZARD, Christian to Sally Watts	4-6-1830
BUZZARD, William to Rachel Garrett	4-6-1830
CALDWELL, Pressly to Ruanna Dawson	9-29-1831
CAREY, Maurice to Joanna Butin	10-27-1831
CARTER, Alexander to Margaret H. Whitney	4-22-1830
CARTLICK, Elijah to Harriet Johnson	6-19-1832
CAVE, Benjamin E. to Susanna Routh	7-5-1832
CAVE, Ezekiel to Nancy Barnhill - lic. only	9-20-1830
CHINOWETH, Absalom to Sarah Burgess	1-6-1832
CHINOWETH, William to Morelaes Ann Burgess lic. only	4-18-1831
CLARK, James to Mary Marbel	4-19-1832
CLEMONTS, Thomas to Margaret Ealtz	9-11-1831
COLEMAN, Hartwell to Elizabeth Engle	10-20-1831
COLWELL, Washington to Rebecca Devault	3-10-1831
COOK, George to Catharine Bucher	9-8-1831
COONRAD, Woolery to Olive Brown	2-6-1831
CORRAN, Samuel to Lucy Cartlick	6-17-1830
CROTHERS, John to Caroline Davis	5-21-1831
CUSHING, Robert W. to Elizabeth Orr	12-11-1832
DAVIS, Seth L. to Sally Ann Smith	10-3-1830
DAWSON, William to Milley Dorman	8-26-1830
EBBERT, Ruben to Margaret Haynes	7-3-1831
EBERT, Jesse to Elizabeth Stucky	1-6-1831
EBY, Christian to Cinderilla Dawson	1-21-1830
ENGLE, Joseph to Barbara Hoss	1-6-1831
ENGLE, William to Anne Catharine Bitcher	6-10-1831
FINEY, Sylvenus to Myra Washburn	4-18-1830
FINNEY, Caleb M. to Polly Briggs	11-9-1830
FINNEY, Harvey to Maria Bartlett	7-4-1830
FINNEY, Sylvanus to Jerusha Bingham	11-15-1832
FUNK, Abraham to Martha Crook	10-25-1832
GARRETT, James to Claraissa Lacey	9-29-1830
GARRETT, Wells to Maria Misener	4-3-1831
GIGER, Samuel to Fanny Howdeshall	12-16-1832
GODFREY, Elijah to Jane Seymore Jones	10-2-1831
consent given by both fathers (not named)	

```
GONDER, Daniel to Sarah Roads                    12-2-1832
GOSS, George to Priscilla Clutter                12-16-1830
GOSS, John to Sarah Bougher                      1-31-1830
GRAVES, Jesse to Ruth Ratcliff                   1-19-1830
GREENE, Joseph A. to Sarah Ann Davis             6-17-1832
GREGARY, James P. Elizabeth Kuder                11-18-1830
HANCUKER, Samuel to Nelly Web                    3--25-1830
HANSON, Samuel C. to Elizabeth Kinser            8-9-1832
HEDGES, Silas A. to Sarah Cushing                4-6-1831
HITT, Peter R. to Rebecca Nye                    11-11-1832
HOLDERMAN, Christopher to Susan Kershner         2-8-1832
HOOD, George W. to Lydia Cramer                  12-19-1830
HOOVER, Valentine to Polly Miller                4-8-1830
HOSTETTER, John to Mehela Ramsby                 10-21-1830
HOWDESHALL, Michael to Sarah Howdeshall          3-8-1832
HUFMAN, Andrew to Sarah Loy                      1-26-1832
ILER, John to Maria Hampton                      12-9-1832
KALER, Samuel to Amelia Slotterback              1-11-1831
     oath to age by Gideon Schlotterback
KELLER, Jacob to Mary Clark                      12-8-1830
KIGER, William to Lydia Cox                      2-3-1831
KIMBLE, Jacob to Adah Peters                     2-16-1832
LINTON, William to Elizabeth Chidester           11-8-1832
LOWE, Edin to Sarah Godfrey                      5-29-1831
LYONS, John to Mary Lyman                        11-16-1831
MANNON, Samuel to Betcy Inbody                   12-22-1831
MATTHIAS, Abraham to Mary Foy                    9-25-1832
MOORHEAD, Thomas to Patty Peterson lic. only     2-29-1832
MORRISON, James to Franky Anderson               10-22-1831
NIHISER, Jacob to Phebe Kitchen                  7-11-1830
NUTTER, John to Christeen Sweesey                12-6-1832
NUTTER, William to Elizabeth Rice                12-13-1832
OZEBAUGH, Henry to Sarrah Tannehill              2-10-1831
PATTERSON, Lawson B. to Saville Dunkle           1-9-1832
PATTON, Abraham to Rosanna Hamilton              6-10-1832
PONTIUS, George to Elizabeth Engle               6-15-1830
PROUGH, John to Catharine Confall                5-3-1832
PROUGH, Samuel to Sarah Confare                  9-13-1832
RATCLIFF, Elias to Elias Dutcher                 3-1-1832
RAUDERBAUGH, Nicholas to Catharine Stukey        8-26-1832
RAYBURN, John to Maria Brant       (1832?)       12-1-1833
RICHARDS, William to Margaret Enocks             11-13-1831
ROADS, Matthias to Rebecca Coonrod               4-1-1830
ROBINSON, Barney J. to Parmelia Webb             12-19-1831
SANDERSON, Alexander to Maria Kimble             4-1-1830
SEELEY, Henry to Susanna Congreave               4-4-1830
SEKENGOSS, Michael to Betcy Pixler               12-2-1831
SELF, William to Catharine Robey                 9-18-1831
SEYMOUR, William to Anna C. Bartlett             11-15-1832
SHADD, John to Catharine Shaffer                 7-22-1832
SHAFFER, Abraham to Elizabeth Swinehart          11-15-1832
```

632

```
SHOEMAKER, Ahimaez(Amos?) H. To Samantha Bennett  5-20-1830
SLAGLE, Joseph to Polly Dawson                     8-9-1832
SMITHBY, Casper to Mary Beck                       4-1-1832
STALL, Hugh to Wida Vincent                        9-8-1832
STAUNT, John to Maria Raider                       8-2-1832
STINE, Jacob to Line Shaffer - lic. only           9-3-1832
STUKEY, Jacob to Catharine Francisco              10-20-1832
SWEASEY, Henry to Sally Nutter                     12-2-1832
THOMPSON, John to Rachel Clark                    11-9-1831
TILTON, Simeon H. to Eliza Brown                   8-19-1830
UTSLER, Henry to Elizabeth Turner                  8-16-1832
VANDERFORD, John to Jane Hobson                    3-3-1831
VANDERFORD, William Jr. to Mary MGree             11-17-1831
WARFORD, Lot to Sibbel Briggs                      4-22-1830
SANDERSON, William to Martha Bartlett              4-7-1831
SMITH, B. F. to Nancy Orr - lic. only              May 1830
TURNER, George Washington to Lydia Elleson         1-28-1830
WALKER, William to Matilda Claxton                 9-8-1831
WATERS, David to Catharine Miller                  5-24-1832
WATKINS, Benjamin to Almira Lane                  12-20-1832
WHITE, David to Delila Francis                     6-7-1832
WHITE, James to Sally Winders                      3-11-1830
WILCOX, Robert to Elizabeth                       12-27-1832
WILKINSON, Baldwin to Jane Boggs                  12-27-1832
WILL, Joseph K. to Phebe Dunkle                    1-9-1832
WINE, Linza to Elizabeth Correck                   8-11-1831
WOLTZ, Silas to Mary Ann Duhurst                  11-23-1831
WRIGHT, David to Margaret Wilkinson                9-13-1832
YOUNG, Abijah R. to Rachel Beck                    1-9-1831
ZELLER, John D. to Mary Wolf                       3-10-1831
```

The following records were copied from a book "Transcribed Will Record From C.P.C. 1820-1851". This book is located in the probate Court. A few of the earlier wills are also recorded in a small book called "Will Book 1", but the majority of the wills have apparently been brought from the Common Pleas Court as there is no other will book or books for the period prior to 1852. Pages on which record may be found are given in parenthesis.

COX, Solomon - dated 9-9-1819; recorded July 1820. Wife, Hannah. Sons: Absalom, Christopher, Thomas, Stephen and Solomon Cox. Daughters: Martha Cox, Mary Cox, Ann Perkins, Amy Mahon and Ruth Johnston. Executors: son, Solomon Cox and William Dixon. Signed: Solomon Cox. Witnesses: Nicholas Cox, Alexander H. Greave and John Ratliff. (1)

SMITH, Susannah - dated 9-15-1821; recorded May 1822. Sons: John Adams, George W. Smith, Banjiman F. and Robert D. Only daughter, Sally Ann; to have likeness (note; apparently refers to pictures or silhouettes) of father and uncle, also $50 in hands of Geo. W. Smith. Grand-daughter, Susan. Step-daughter, Jane. Executors: sons, George W. and Benjamin F. Smith. Signed: Susannah (her mark) Smith. Witnesses: Samuel H. Ramsey and Betsy Ramsey. (2)

PENCE, John - Verbal Will - will made Thursday night 29th last month; deposition given 9-4-1822; recorded (not given). Wife, mentioned but not named. Witnesses: Walter Eldridge and George Clark. (3)

PICKEN, Joshua - dated 9-6-1823; recorded (not given). Wife, Mary. Sons: Robert, John, Samuel, Joshua and William. Daughters: Margaret Cook, Mary McKee, Lizzie Plen (or Pleu), Elizabeth Picken and Julian Picken. Executors: oldest son, Robert Picken and John Ratcliff. Signed: Joshua Picken. Witnesses: James Carter and Samuel (his mark) Wykoff. (3)

RAINES, Lawrence of Ross Co., Ohio - dated 5-21-1817; recorded (not given). Wife, Ann. Sons: Isaac, Lawrence, John, Nathan and Benjamin; son John to have land deeded by William Gregg including mill seat. Daughters: Hannah Cox, Ruth Dixon, Catharine Moffitt, Ann Comer, Elizabeth Raines and Rebecca Raines. Wife, Ann to serve as guardian of daughter, Rebecca and youngest sons Nathan and Benjamin. Executors: sons, Isaac and John. Signed: Lawrence Raines. Witnesses: John Ratcliff, Eli Vanderford and Jacob Cox. (5)

RAMSEY, Robert of Falls twp., Yeoman - dated 6-22-1822; recorded Oct. 1823. Wife, Mary. Sons: William, Samuel M. John and James B. Daughters: Charity Boyce, Nancy Beans, Jean Ramsey, Mary Ramsey and Betsy Ramsey. Executors: wife, Mary and son, Samuel M. Signed: Robert Ramsey. Witnesses: Robert Stewart and Sarah Stewart.(6)

WEBB, Benjamin of Green twp. - dated 2-9-1826; recorded Nov. 1826. Wife, Anna Webb to have property in her possession that she brought when she came to testator with all that is coming to her by her former husband. Sons: Ralph Webb, Garrett Webb, John Webb, Joseph Webb to have W½ SW¼ S25 T14 R16, and Thomas Webb to have NE¼ S13 T14 R16. Daughters: Rachael Griffin; Nancy Rice, her heirs; Betsey Starr; Mary Thompson; three youngest, Sarah, Elendor and Patty to have household furniture their mother left. Executor: son, Thomas Webb. Signed: Benjamin Webb. Witnesses: W. Wallace, Mead Bowen and James Calhoun. (7)

634

WORTHINGTON, Thomas of Ross Co., Ohio - dated 3-5-1827; recorded Ross Co. 10-25-1827.
Wife, Eleanor, to have dwelling house in which testator now lives with farm attached
to it on the hill usually called Adenia. Sons: James, Albert, Thomas, William and
Francis. Daughters: Mary McComb; Sarah King—her son Thomas King, not of age; Eleanor; Margaret; and Elizabeth. Grandson, Thomas Macomb. Executors: wife, Eleanor and
sons, James T., Albert G. and Thomas Worthington. Will includes large list of land by
description owned by testator in Hocking, Franklin, Ross, Clinton, Adams, Delaware and
Madison Cos., Ohio. Signed: T. Worthington. Witnesses: John Renshaw, James G.
Harrison and George J. Milligan. (9)

O'NEILL, Henry - dated 7-11-1828; recorded ----1829. Wife, Nancy O'Neil. Sons: John,
Charles, Stiles, James and Thomas O'Neil; each to have 60 acres in Section 25, Township 12, Range 16 with exception of Thomas who is to have the homestead farm of 167
acres. Daughters: Jane O'Neil now Jane Hathaway to have 60 acres in Section 25,
Township 12, Range 15; Martha; Peggy; and Nancy. Grand-daughter, Laura. Six grandchildren which have been named Henry after testator are to have land in Washington
and Athens County, Ohio. Son, Stiles and daughter, Jane are both deceased and their
share is to go to their heirs as they became of age. Executors: wife, Nancy; Joseph
Ludlow and Zena Ferris. Signed: Henry O'Neil. Witnesses: David Clapp, Isaac Buckingham and Isaac Lewis. (14)

KRIDER, Peter of Logan - dated 5-5-1829; recorded (not given). Wife, Elizabeth.
Mentions indentured girl live in testators family named Elizabeth Richter. Executors:
John A. Smith, Reuben Culver and Sumner L. Cushing. Signed: Peter Krider. Witnesses:
William Orr and Mary Jane Claxton. (17)

BIRD, Clarence of Troy - dated 12-1-1825; recorded 12-29-1828 Rensselaer Co., N. Y.
and 12-1-1830 Washington Co., Ohio. Devises all property both real and personal to
David Bird Jr. of Troy, William A. Bird of Black Rock and David Bird, not of age with
August Bird his guardian. Executors: David and William Bird. Signed: Clarence Bird.
Witnesses: D. Buel, Edw'r H. Coe and Henry F. Bayens. (18)

RAMSBY, John - dated 5-9-1830; recorded June 1830. Wife, Elizabeth. Children, mentioned but not named, not of age. Executor: Henry Hostetter. Signed: John (his mark)
Ramsby. Witnesses: Perry Cliphant and Jonathan Kimble. (20)

O'NEILL, Nancy - dated 3-22-1830; recorded Jan. 1831. Sons: Charles, Thomas, John
and James; James to have large Bible. Daughters: Martha, Nancy and Margaret. Grand-
daughter, Laura O'Neill, not of age, George Lee to serve as her guardian. Executor:
Joseph Ludlow. Signed: Nancy O'Neill. Witnesses: Zina Ferris and David Clapp. (21)

SANDERSON, William of Washington twp. - dated 2-11-1831; recorded 2-28-1831. Sons:
Robert, George William, Alexander and James Elliott; James Elliott to have home farm.
Daughters: Peggy, Sally, Elizabeth and Nancy. Executors: sons, Robert and William.
Signed: William Sanderson. Witnesses: David Cox, Joseph Wright and Lewis Cox. (22)

COYKENDALL, Jacob of Salt Creek twp. - dated 5-28-1831; recorded April 1832. Wife,
Elizabeth to have land and farm lying in Hocking and Fairfield Cos.; she is also to
serve as executrix. Youngest son, William Coykendall, not of age. Signed: Jacob
Coykendall. Witnesses: John Moss and Emanuel (his mark) Cave. (25)

SCHREIVER, Lewis - dated 9-14-1830; recorded April 1831. Wife, Susannah, also to serve as executrix. Sons: Frederick William, Philip, John Luckhart and Thomas Schreiver. Daughters: Catharine Schreiver now Huber, Margaret Schreiver and Elizabeth Schreiver. Signed: Lewis Schreiver. Witnesses: Samuel Fetherolf and Anthony Swinhart. Codicil dated 11-27-1830 states that testator has conveyed part of land bequeathed in will to Sarah Bixler. Witnesses: Samuel Fetherolf and William (his mark) Francisco. (24)

DORMAN, Elias - dated 3-18-1832; recorded April 1832. Wife, Leanah. Mentions sons and daughters but only names sons, John and William. Grand-daughter, Clarenda Eby. Executors: wife, Leanah and son, John. Signed: Elias (his mark) Dorman. Witnesses: A. Coonrod, Precella (her mark) Caldwell and Walter (his mark) Caldwell. (27)

FARRIS, Edward Sr. of Washington, Mason Co., Kentucky = dated 4-8-1824; recorded Mason Co., Ky 5-12-1825. Wife, Margaret to have house in Washington. Sons: John Farris, dec'd, his children and heirs (not named) to have land in Ohio part of Ohio Company Purchase; Edward Farris, dec'd, his heirs. Daughters: Nancy Greely wife of Reverend Allen Greely to have land in Ohio in Ohio Company purchase; Elizabeth Wilson; Sally Baldwin; Abigail Johnston, dec'd, her heirs. Executor: grandson, Edward A. Farris. Signed: Edward Farris, Senior. Witnesses: John Chambers and B. Boyles.(31)

SAUNDERS, Peter - dated 10-21-1831; recorded March 1835. Son-in-law, John Iles to have W½ Section 13, Township 14, Range 17. Son-in-law, Charles Wright and wife Nancy being daugher of testator. Executor: John Iles. Signed Peter (his mark) Saunders. Witnesses: Hocking H. Hunter and Henry Stansbury. (34)

LIGHT, David of Logan - dated 4-1-1835; recorded (not given). Wife, Magdalena. Children mentioned but not named. Executor; son-in-law, William J. Crook. Signed: David Light. Witnesses: W. Wallace and C. W. Jones. (37)

ORR, John Sr. - dated 3-27-1833; recorded Oct. 1833. Sons: Jackson, John and William; William to have land purchased from United States. Daughters: Jane, Margaret and Sarah; other married daughters mentioned but not named. Executor: son, William. Signed: John Orr. Witnesses: W. Wallace and Meed Bowen. (38)

COX, John - dated 3-9-1835; recorded June 1835. Three brothers: George, Daniel and Joseph Cox. Executors: George and Daniel Cox. Signed: John Cox. Witnesses: Benjamin Johnston and James Harden. (39)

DAVISON, Zachariah of Falls twp. - dated 7-8-1835; recorded Sept. 1835. Requests that his body be interred on Francis Davison farm. Mentions land in Bedford County (state not given) to be divided between Comfort Riglet and Zachariah Davison Jr. and after death of Comfort Riglet, her share to go to Sary Hamilton. Mentions money in hands of John Elik to be divided between Nalky McLane and Elizabeth Davison. Wife, mentioned but not named. Rest of real and personal estate divided between Liddy Lowe, Levi Davison, Sary Hamilton and Frances Davison. Rifle gun to Perry Davison son of Francis Davison. Executors: Richard Burgis and William Davison. Signed: Zachariah (his mark) Davison. Witnesses: Jacob Huss, James (his mark) Vanhorn and David (his mark) Davison. (40)

FEE, Abram - dated 6-27-1835; recorded March 1836. Wife, mentioned but not named. Sons: Moses, Hamilton and John; to have land in Hocking County. Four daughters: Nancy, Esther, Mary and Rachel; to have real estate in Athens Co., Ohio. Signed: Abram Fee. Witnesses: John Keeton and Isaac Rogers. (42)

HUBER, William - dated 4-1-1835; recorded March 1836. Wife, Anne Elizabeth, also to serve as executrix. Signed: William Huber. Witnesses: Daniel Kershner, Elijah Kershner and James Spencer. (44)

WYLLIS, Samuel of Hartford, Hartford Co., Ct. - dated 9-30-1809; presented Hartford Co., Ct. 7-12-1823 and recorded same 12-26-1836. Sons: Oliver St. John Wyllis and William Alfred Wyllis. Daughter, Mary W. wife of John M. Gammet. Brother, William Wyllis. Executor: John M. Gammet, Esqr. Signed: Samuel Wyllys. Witnesses: A. Kingsburry, Elizabeth Colt and Ralph Pomeroy. (45)

GAMMET, Mary W.; wife of John M. Gammet, Esq. of Hartford, Ct. - dated 2-12-1825; presented Hartford Co., Ct. 4-18-1825 and recorded same 12-26-1836. Bequeaths entire estate to William Falcott of Hartford in trust for her children: Samuel Wyllys Gammet, John Polsgrave Gammet, Catharine Wendell Gammet, George Alfred Gammet and Caleb Thornton Kirkland Gammet. Executor, William Falcott. Signed: Mary H. Gammet. Witnesses: James Ward, John Williams and James Dodd. (47)

MOORE, Samuel - dated 5-16-1837; recorded June 1837. Daughters: Mary wife of John Web, Elizabeth Bush and Sarah Myers. Grandsons: Samuel Webb, Samuel M. Bush and Horace M. Bush. Executor: Joseph Whipple. Signed: Samuel Moore. Witnesses: Conrad Bryan and Bailey Fritter. (49)

FLINN, Joseph of Perry Co., Ohio - dated 12-25-1831; recorded Hocking Co. Sept. 1838. Wife, Magdalena to have land in Hocking Co. Executors: David Stuky and Henry Dittoe. Signed: Joseph Flinn. Witnesses: John Woolfe and George Keigler. (50)

COAKLEY, John of Green twp. - dated 2-17-1825; recorded 4-20-1838. Wife, Barbara to have east end fractional Section 30, Township 13, Range 16 of Ohio Company Purchase. Sons: Daniel, Solomon, Isaac, William and Jacob. Signed: John (his mark) Coakley. Witnesses: James Jones and William Long. (51)

BEOUCHER, Benjamin - dated 1-8-1838; recorded 11-20-1838. Wife, Elizabeth, also to serve as executrix. Children: mentioned but not named except for two youngest sons, Henry and Daniel. Signed: Benjamin Berigher. Witnesses: Robert McBroom, Peter Mathias and Henry Goss. (52)

KINGSBURY, Jacob of Franklin, London Co. Ct. - dated 3-17-1828; recorded New London Co., Ct. 7-30-1837; recorded Hocking Co. Sept. 1837. Wife, Sally P., to have land in Ohio. Children: James Wilinson Kingsbury, Julia Ann Ellis Hartshorn, Thomas Humphrey Cushing Kinsbury, William Eustis Kingsbury, Sarah Hill Kingsbury and Charles Ellis Kingsbury. Executors: wife, Sallie T.; Jarred Hyde and Henry Strong, Esq. Signed: Jacob Kingsberry. Witnesses: Jesse Lathrop, William Ladd and Fredric Land. (53)

JOHNSTON, Benjamin - dated 4-30-1838; recorded July 1838. Wife, Catharine. Children mentioned but not named. Executors: wife, Catharine and John Anderson. Signed: Benjamin Johnson. Witnesses: Ephrain Chapman and James Harden. (55)

WIGGINS, Mary - dated 12-29-1837; recorded April 1838. Daughter, Mary wife of James Towers. Executor: son, Moses Wiggins. Signed: Mary (her mark) Wiggins. Witnesses: Jacob Karshner Jr. and William Alexander. (56)

HUKROM, Aaron - dated 8-1-1837; recorded July 1838. Wife, Nancy, also to serve as executrix. Three children: William, Polly and Elizabeth to have real estate in Jackson twp. Father, William Aukrom not to have control over children. Signed: Aaron (his mark) Aukrom (or Huckrom). Witnesses: Samuel R. Chilcote, John Carrick Jr. and Frederick Carrick. (57)

WELDON, John of Falls twp. - dated 5-22-1838; recorded Sept. 1838. Wife, Ruhannah. Children: Susannah and John. Executors: Reuben Culver and Levi Davison. Signed: John Weldon. Witnesses: Jacob Snyder and Abram McCollester. (58)

WHITNEY, Elisha of Beverly, Essex Co., Mass., Physician - dated 1-20-1807; presented Essex Co., Mass. 4-1-1807; recorded same 3-6-1839. Wife, Eunice, also to serve as executrix. Children, mentioned but not named. Signed: Elisha Whitney. Witnesses: Josiah Page, Robert Brookhouse and Guiger Leach. (59)

CASE, Ambrose of Hocking Co., Ohio, late of Hartford, Ct. - dated 6-22-1839; recorded 7-2-1839. Wife, Esther. Sons: Chester, Solon, Richard, Lucius, Flavius, Albert and Oakly. Daughters: Julia, Amanda, Electa, Ursula, Emeratte and Sally Ann. Executor: son, Flavius Case. Signed: Ambrose Case. Witnesses: D. W. James, Dr. Wm. Albers, Sam'l Doty and E. Martin. (61)

PENCE, John of Falls twp. - dated 5-13-1840; recorded 9-21-1840. Wife, mentioned but not named; to have farm and reside on E½ SW¼ Section 12, Township 14, Range 17 being 78 acres. Sons: Willia, Peter and Cashon Pence. Daughters: Heirs of daughter Polly Eldredge, Heirs of daughter Hannah Smith, Rebecca Pence, Eliza Tennerbill, Sarah Powell and Jane Pence. Executor: son, William Pence. Signed: John (his mark) Pence. Witnesses: John Rochester, Meed Bowen and John A. Smith. (63)

BROOKS, William - dated 6-5-1840; recorded 9-21-1840. Wife, Mary. Sons: John, Dorcee, Samuel, William and Joel Brooks. Executors: wife, Mary Brooks and John Rochester. Signed: William Brooks. Witnesses: Alexander White and Benjamin Clinger. (64)

LOW, John P. - dated 11-17-1839; recorded 12-5-1839. Wife, Rachael. Children, mentioned but not named, not of age. Shedrick John, wife's father, to be guardian of children. Executor: John Abrams. Signed: John P. Low. Witnesses: Thomas Cook, Christopher Hiles and William Moore Jr. (65)

The following records were taken from "Transcribed Will Record From C.P.C. 1820-1851" which located in the Probate Court at the court house at Logan. Page on which the record may be found in the original book are given in parenthesis.

HANKINSON, James - dated (not given); recorded 3-8-1861 (note: date of recording is given as stated, however this will appears between a will recorded in 1839 and a will recorded in 1842). Wife and children mentioned but not named. Executors: wife (not named), Thomas Taylor and Brice W. Wallace. Witnesses: Johnathan Kimble and Thomas Underwood. (66)

BOYCE, John - dated 3-28-1842; recorded 4-4-1842. Wife, Charity, farm where now reside being 43 acres S29 T13 R16. Son, John Boyce. Executors: wife, Charity and son, John. Signed: John (mark) Boyce. Witnesses: Horace Stone and Barnet Kepler. (67)

'OUGH, Peter - dated 9-29-1841; recorded 4-4-1842. Wife, Sarah, also to serve as executrix, plantation where now live and 80 acres. Three children: Peter, Mary Ann and Frederick Raugh. Signed: Peter Rough. Witnesses: Thomas Taylor, Brice W. Wallace and Oliver Kimble. (68)

WOODS, George - dated 9-17-1841; recorded 4-4-1842. Wife, Elizabeth. Children: Hannah, Nancy, Isabella, Amos J., James H. and Lonidas H.; not all are of age. Executors: Samuel S. Bright and testator's wife, Elizabeth. Signed: George Woods. Witnesses: Obediah Self and Elizabeth K. Self. (69)

FRANTZMAN, Peter of Falls twp. - dated 10-3-1842; recorded 10-24-1842. Wife, Mary, to have 117 acres where now live. Son, Nicholas Jacob Frantzman. Daughter, Susannah wife of Jacob Ringiser. Two grandchildren: Mary Plumer and Caroline Plumer with Gottleib Plumer to have use of their property until they are of age. Executors: wife, Mary and Thomas B. Jones. Signed: Peter Grantzman. Witnesses: Abraham Hockman and Ann Mary Hockman. (70)

MYERS, John P. - dated 10-21-1842; recorded 11-14-1842. Mentions five children all unmarried, but does not name. Signed: John P. (his mark) Myers. Witnesses: J. Whipple and B. J. Robison. (72)

GROSS, Barbara - dated 4-28-1843; recorded 8-7-1843. Devises to Abraham and Susan Gross 10 acres W½ E½ SW¼ SW¼ S33 T12 R19. Devises to Elizabeth Strouse wife of Philip STROUSE formerly Elizabeth Gross E½ E½ SW¼ SW¼ S33 T12 R19. Signed: Barbara (her mark) Gross. Witnesses: James Spencer and Eleanor Spencer. (74)

WYKOFF, Samuel - dated 11-16-1842; recorded 10-23-1843. Wife mentioned but not named, to have farm where live of 50 acres in Green twp., and at her death property to be divided between lawful heirs (not named). Signed: Samuel (his mark) Wykoff. Witnesses: William Cole and Gilbert Hosier. (75)

BIERLY, Mathias - dated 6-24-1843; recorded 10-23-1843. Wife, Catharine, plantation where now reside of 40 acres. Son, Mathias Bierly. Two daughters: Catharine Fisher and Mary Bierly. Son, Mathias to serve as adms. Signed: Mathias Bierly. Witnesses: John S. Good, Samuel Clayton and John Leffler. (76)

RAMSEY, James B. - dated8-14-1841; recorded 10-23-1843. Brothers and Sisters: Samuel Mc. Ramsey, John Ramsey, Mary Ramsey and Jane Ramsey. Bequeath to James Horace Stone who is also to serve as executor. Signed: James B. Ramsey. Witnesses: C. B. Guthrie and John Jourdan. (77)

FEDEROLF, Philip of Saltcreek twp. - dated 12-5-1840; recorded 5-27-1844. Wife, Catherine Federolf born Leslier, farm where now live of 357 acres. Son, Samuel to have 357 acres after death of testator's wife. Son, Benjamin and his eleven children--William, Mary, Samuel, Anna, Rebecca, David, Susan, Elizabeth, Benewell, Peter and Isaac; with Mary dau. of Benjamin having lived with testator. Daughter, Elizabeth born Federolf now wife of Samuel Lutz. Executors: son, Samuel and Minerva Jane daughter of Mary Federolf. Signed: Philip (his mark) Federolf, Witnesses: Samuel F. Shock, Conrad (mark) Miller and Jacob (mark0 Miller. (78)

SHOFF, Otho - dated 6-22-1844; recorded 9-23-1844. Wife, Nancy to have farm where reside of 80 acres in Laurel twp. Mentions heirs, but does not name. Executors: Joel Giberson and Thomas Whitcraft. Signed: Otho Shoff. Witnesses: John G. Doyle and Daniel Giberson. (81)

MACKLIN, Philip pf Pleasant twp., Fairfield Co., Ohio - dated 9-22-1842; recorded Fairfield Co. 9-22-1843; recorded Hocking Co. (not given). Wife Katharine. Sons: Peter, John and Jacob Macklin. Daughters: Salome wife of John Weaver; Mary wife of Jacob Hansel; Elizabeth, dec'd, her children--Mary and Catharine Kline (Cline); Susanna, her daughter--Catharine Wagner. Mentions Philip and Mary, Children of son, Peter Macklin. Executors: son, Peter and son-in-law, Jacob Kline. Signed: Philip (his mark) Macklin. Witnesses: Joseph Heistand, Nicholas Radebaugh and Samuel Hiller. (82)

BIRD, John of Troy, New York, counsellor at law - dated 4-20-1805; recorded 3-13-1836 Rensselaer Co., N.Y.; recorded Hocking Co. (not given). Wife (not named), if she relinquishes dower to following named trustees to receive $175.00 yearly. Sons: John Hampden Bird and Clarence Bird. Mentions that second son (not named and not stated if it is one of the foregoing) living in Burlington, Vermont and under 14 years of age. All property both real and personal to go to Col. Albert Pawling, Ebenezer Wilson and Benjamin Smith in trust for the heirs named above, with these men to also serve as guardians of sons, Hampden and Clarence. SSigned: John Bird. Witnesses: Thed. Drake, Isaiah Marble and Howard Houlton. Codicil dated 1-27-1806. Mentions two negro servants and mulatto boy, Dick to be paid and Dick to receive two years schooling. Also request to be buried on Van Buren farm belonging to testator. Witnesses: Moses Hale, Stephen Barnes and Isaiah Marble. (84)

BIRD, Dr. Seth of Litcnfield, Conn. - dated 11-27-1804; recorded Litchfield 10-9-1805; recorded Hocking County (not given). Son, John Bird, also to serve as executor. Daughters: Minerva wife of James Stoddard and Sarah Bird; Sarah being disabled from taking care of her own estate and her estate in trust to James Morris and Roger Newton Whittlesy, Esqs. Signed: Seth Bird. Witness: Rhoda Tarram and Uriah Homes Jr. Codicil dated 11-30-1804 bequeaths to Angelina Sperry who has lived with testator since infancy. Witnesses: James Morris and William Woodruff. Codicil dated 2-8-1805 gives Black Boy servant his freedom at age 25 years. Witnesses: James Morris, Michael Sterling and Betsy Morris. (85)

COLES, Thomas of Providence, Rhode Island - dated 6-30-1828; recorded 11-19-1844.
Wife, Sarah Coles, to have estate in Westminster St. commonly known as Starry Estate.
Sister, Flora Bowley, dec'd, her two sons (not named). Sister, Susan Comely, her
seven children (not named), with Samuel Comely husban d of sister Susan to have
all lands in Ohio for use of testator's father's grandchildren. Bequeaths to:
Thomas Coles Happin, Thomas Coles Harlstrom, Thomas Coles Peckham, Sarah Coles
Stanton and Thomas Happin son of Thomas Coles Happin, the last named to have
8 acre lot adjoining town of Cranston. Wife's niece, Sarah Ann Walker to have
all estate where she now lives on Westminster Street. Wife's niece, Elizabeth Lyman.
Executors: wife, Sarah Coles; Thomas Coles Happin; and Thomas Peckham. Signed:
Thomas Coles. Witnesses: Samuel Brown, John B. Barton and Richard M. Field.
Codicil dated 6-1-1841. Wife, Sarah is now dec'd. Bequeaths to: Thomas C. Lyman,
Mr. Benj. Gardner, Mrs. Bernard Eddy's children consisting of four daughters,
Thomas C. Hartshorn, late wife's sister Mrs. Mary Walker, Frederick Street Happin
son of William W. Happin, Sarah Coles Lyman and Sarah Ann Walker. Witnesses:
Benj. Happin, David Barton and Geo. Grinnett. (87)

WOLF, Christopher - Dated 9-19-1845; recorded Oct. 1845. Sons: Joseph, William,
Jonathan, Mathew, Barrick, Edmund and Andrew Wolf. Daughters: Lydia Moore and
Elizabeth Wolf. Bequeath to Elizabeth Funk, no relationship if any is stated.
Rodie and Lydia, daughters of dau., Lydia Moore. Executors: Joseph Brett, Robert
Wright and Robert D. Wolf. Signed: Christ'r Wolf. Witnesses: J. Whipple and
James Conn. Codicil dated 9-19-1845. Son, Jonathan Wolf and Josiah H. Moore to have
testator's saw mill for six months and son, Edward to have mill for six months.
Witnesses: same as above. (92)

COONEY, Frederick of Green twp. - dated 11-13-1846; recorded 3-17-1847. Wife,
mentioned but not named, also to serve as executrix. Four children mentioned but
not named. Signed: Frederick Cooney. Witnesses: Caleb Arnold and George Dyson.(95)

STROUS, Jacob - dated 2-8-1845; recorded 4-19-1845. Sons: Allen, John and Samuel
Strous. Daughters: Elizabeth Strous and Mary wife of Hiram Flanagan. Executors:
sons, John and Samuel. Signed: Jacob Strous. Witnesses: K.H. Dunkle, John Frey,
S. Lutz and George Dunkle. (96)

RAMSEY, Jane of Falls township - dated 10-18-1843; recorded 10-7-1845. Brothers
and Sister: Samuel L. Ramsey, John Ramsey and Mary Ramsey, all to share in farm
where they and testatrix now live as left by their father, Robert Ramsey's will
being in Falls twp., S3 T14 R17. Bequeaths to: Mary Stone, Jane Stone and Sarah
Eliza Stone. Executor: Horace Stone. Signed Jane Ramsy. Witnesses: John Jordan,
Barbara Jordan and Francis Judy. (98)

DILL, John - dated 6-7-1843; recorded Oct. 1845. Wife, Elizabeth. Grand-daughter,
Elizabeth Dixon. Executor, Andrew Curry. Signed: John Dill. Witnesses: Jeremiah
Redfearn and Archibald O. Russel. (99)

FEE, Thomas - dated 5-25-1844; recorded Oct. 1845, Wife, Sarah. Sons: John and
William. Daughters: Margaret, Jane, Salley and Christina. Grandchildren: Ann,
Eave, William, Davis and Elizabeth, children of daughter, Mary. Executor, John
Fee. Signed: Thomas Fee. Witnesses: Moses J. Fee and N. S. Jordon. (100)

STACKHOUSE, Amos - dated 8-20-1844; recorded Oct. 1845. To Caleb Williams my certificate due me on 9-4-1844 from the United States Government as a pension for my services in the Revolutionary War. Calico Quilt or Bedspread to Sally Slane. Large Bottle to Hugh Slane's wife. Tin Truck to Jane Slane. Two dollars to Amos Stackhouse Slane son of Hugh Slane. Signed Amos Stackhouse. Witnesses: Richardson Williams and Hiram Benson. (101)

RICE, Abner - dated 2-12-1844; recorded 6-29-1846. Son, James. Daughters: Prudence Nancy, Sarah, Susannah and Elizabeth. Mentions "Land I now dwell known as New England Purchase on which I hold patent and 87 acres". Executors: Samuel Jones and Susannah Rice. Signed: Abner Rice. Witnesses: James O'Neil Jr. and John Slane.(102)

TONE, Jacob Sr. - dated 4-12-1846; recorded 5-18-1846. Wife, mentioned but not named. Children: Jacob Jr., Josiah, Bennet, Henry, Catharine, Mary Ann and Susan. Executors: wife (not named) and son, Josiah, Signed: Jacob (his mark) Tone Sr. Witnesses: Lemuel F. Drake and James Dow. (103)

COOK, John of Falls township - dated 3-27-1846; recorded May 1846. Wife, Catharine. Two daughters, Sarah Cox and Fanna Cox. Signed: John (his mark) Cook. Witnesses: William D. Wolf and Samuel Stultz. (104)

BRADFORD, Moses - dated 4-7-1845; recorded March 1846. Wife, Anna. Three sons: Ward, Duffie and William Bradford. Daughter, Nancy Bradford, not of age. Signed: Moses Bradford. Witnesses: Moses B. Cherry and Abraham Chapman. (105)

FINNEY, Solomon Sr. - dated 8-1-1846; recorded 9-23-1846. Sons: Solomon Finney Jr., Joseph W. Finney, Silvanus Finney, Alvan Finney and heirs (not named) of Harvey Finney, dec'd. Executor; son, Alvan Finney. Signed: Solomon Finney. Witnesses: George Payne and Solomon Finney Jr. (106)

PONTIUS, John - dated 5-11-1846; recorded 2-15-1847. Wife, Margaret to have 70 acres S8 T14 R17 in Falls township and at wife's death to go to testator's brothers and sisters children (not named). Signed John Pontius. Witnesses: John (his mark) Sherren and A. White. (107

STONEBURNER, Philip - dated 10-20-1846; recorded 2-15-1847. Wife, Christiana. Son, Philip. Daughter, Elizabeth wife of Daniel Lowry. Granddaughter, Elmira, daughter of daughter, Elizabeth. May be other children not named. Executrix: son, Philip and Samuel Hoffert. Signed: Philip Stoneburner. Witnesses: John Hansacker and Saloman Welty. (108)

LEE,, James Sr. - dated 1-25-1843; recirded (not given-1847). Wife, mentioned but not named. Grandchildren, heirs of son George: Samuel, Nancy, Washington, Boss, Elijah and Julian to have 78 acres off land where testator now lives in NE¼ S2 T12 R17. Grand-daughter, Anna wife of George Payne and child of son James Lee, 100 acres off farm where testator now lives in NE¼ S2 T12 R17. Daughters, Nancy wife of Thomas O'Neil and Rosannah Childs. Executor, Joseph Keelor. Signed James (his mark Lee Sr. Witnesses: Robert Payne and George W. Johnston. (109)

DEXTER, John Luiger age 88 years, of Cumberland, Providence Co., Rhode Island -
dated (not dated); recorded Providence Co., R. I. 8-5-1844. Recorded Hocking Co.
(not given). Son, John Pearce Dexter. Daughter Eliza Nightengale. Grandsons:
George Edward Nightengale, land in Ohio and Frederick Auboynean Eddy. Grand-daughters:
Mary Dexter Nightengale; Ellen Evans Dexter, her father being son of testator and
now dec'd and her mother remarried a few years ago to an officer of the Army of the
United States who holds rank of Field Officer. Executors: John P. Dexter and
Frederick A Eddy. Signed John L. Dexter. Witnesses: Ira Kent and Manning Rawson.
(111)

WARD, Eliza, a widow of Providence, Rhode Island - dated 6-30-1841; recorded
Providence Co., R. I. 4-8-1845; recorded Hocking Co. (not given). Niece, Harriet
E. Ward. Bequeaths to: daughters of Rev. Stephen Gano except Dornelius Helroyd,
John Brown Benedict, John Brown son of Hugh H. Brown, Phyllis Church a colored
woman living with testatrix. Real estate to kinsman, Moses Brown Ives in trust
for niece Eliza B. Rogers. Executors: Moses Brown Ives and Joseph Rogers. Signed:
Eliza Ward. Witnesses: Franklin Greene, Richard W. Greene and Lemuel W. Peckham.
Codicil dated 10-2-1844 mentions Eliza B. wife of Joseph Rogers. Witnesses:
Franklin Greene, Mary D. Crandell and R. W. Greene. (112)

RODGERS, John of Swan township - dated 2-12-1839; recorded May 1845. Wife,
mentioned but not named. My own children: John Rogers, Catharine Rogers, Polly
Rogers and Eve Rogers. Grandchildren: Polly Rogers daughter of testator's son
George Edward Rogers, dec'd; John Rogers; William Rogers; Elizabeth Rogers; Polly Rogers;
Sophia Rogers; Barbara Wright; Julian Wright; Henry Wright; Catharine Miller;
Elizabeth Miller and Polly Morris. Executor, David Johnson. Signed: John (his
mark) Rogers. Witnesses: George Payne and Robert Payne. (117)

VANCUREN, Cornelius - dated 10-7-1846; recorded June 1848. Wife, Catharine.
Sons: William, Andrew, Paul, James, John and Isaac; Isaac is not of age. Daughters:
Hannah, Magdalena, Elizabeth, Rebecca, Mary Ann and Delilah. Mentions that Peter
Vancuren to have 50 cents, no relationship stated if any, may be son. Executors:
John Weltner, Joseph C. McBroom and George Bear. Signed: Cornelius Vancuren.
Witnesses: Joseph Kaler, John Weltner and George Bear. (119)

EDDY, Frederick A., physician of Boston, Suffolk Co., Mass. - dated 5-8-1847;
recorded Hocking Co. June 1848; recorded Suffolk Co., Mass. 1-8-1848. Lands in
Ohio to be sold. Uncle, John P. Dexter. Wills to: Eliza wife of John G.
Whipple of Providence, R. I.; to Joel Scott of Boston; to Mrs. Charlotta Leach wife
of Ezekial W. Leach; to Nathaniel Gree e of New York, merchang. Executor, Joel
Scott. Signed: Frederick A. Eddy. Witnesses: H. G. Tenny, Francis M. Mitchell
and N. T. Dow. (120)

MOORE, William of Green township - dated 3-15-1848; recorded June 1848. Wife,
Nancy, 80 acres where now live. Youngest son, Johnathan Limerick Moore farm where
now resides of 40 acres in Green twp. Daughter mentioned but not named.
Executor: oldest son, David Moore. Signed: William Moore. Witnesses: Benjamin
Webb and John Nutter. (123)

ELLICK, Christopher Frederick - dated 3-12-1847; recorded 4-21-1847. Wife, mentioned but not named. Children, names only Jacob Ellick, Sarah and Catharine, but also states that youngest child was not of age. Signed: Christopher Ellick. Witnesses: Gottleib Brodt and Benjamin C. Beougher. (124)

SLANE, James 2nd - dated 11-15-1848; recorded 12-13-1848. Daughter, Mary Ann Slane to have farm where I now live being 79 acres in School Lot 4 of S16 T12 R16. Executor: Samuel Jones, also to serve as guardian of Mary Ann Slane. Signed: James Slane. Witnesses: John (mark) Crosby and Isaac Lewis. (125)

O'NEILL, Charles - dated 1-31-1849; recorded March 1849. Grand-daughter, Catharine Schrader, daughter of testator's daughter, Charlotta Scheereden, to have farm of 162½ acres S15 T12 R16. Executor, Samuel Jones, also to serve as guardian of Catharine Schrader. Signed: Charles O'Neill. Witnesses: Isaac Lewis and Nathan L. Goodwin. (126)

AIKINS, John of Morgan Co., Ohio - dated 9-17-1846; recorded Morgan Co. 3-3-1847; recorded Hocking Co. (not given). Wife, Jane Lydia Aikins. Sons: Daniel, George W., Charles, Eli and William H. Aikins. Daughters: Nancy Spurrier, Sarah Jane Aikins and Almira Aikins, to have proceeds of land in Hocking Co. which is to be sold. Executor: Isaac Williams of Deerfield twp. Signed: John Aikins. Witnesses: Samuel Aikins, Mary Allard and William Aikins. (127)

JOHNSTON, Thomas - dated 8-21-1849; recorded 9-17-1849. Wife, mentioned but not named. Children: Thomas Johnson, Nancy Brown, Margaret Dittoe, Mary Kinsel, Andrew Johnston and James Johnston. Mentions Elizabeth Hoghen a girl now living with testator's family. Executors: sons, Andrew and James. Signed: Thomas (has mark) Johnston. Witnesses: George Mauk and John Crawford. (129)

DAWSON, Nancy - dated 5-7-1849; recorded 9-18-1849. Three sons: John, David and Edmond Dawson. Signed: Nancy (her mark) Dawson. Witnesses: Joseph Eby and Elizabeth (mark) Eby. (131)

LOW, John - dated 6-5-1849; recorded 10-30-1849. Wife, Lydia, farm where now reside in Green twp. being 80 acres W½ NE¼ S24 T13 R16. Son, Henry Low. Mentions other children but does not name. Executor, Richard Adcox. Signed: John Low. Witnesses: John Williams, Wm Williams and Wm M. Price. (132)

CASE, Esther of Logan - dated 8-7-1849; recorded 10-30-1849. Requests that grave marker be erected, not to exceed $25.00. Sons: Oakley Case to have in-lot 70 in Logan and all family pictures and Family Bible, Albert Case, Lucius Case and Flavious Case. Daughter, Sally Ann. To Amanda wife of John Brown (note: may be daughter, but if so, it is not clearly stated). Daughter, Emiraetta, dec'd. Executor: son, Flavias Case. Signed: Esther (her mark) Case. Witnesses: C.W. James and W. H. Haines. Codicil dated 10-2-1849 gives no additional information.(134)

RUNNER, Michael of Mount Vernon, Knox Co., Ohio - dated 7-10-1850; recorded Knox Co. 9-12-1850; recorded Hocking Co. Nov. 1850. Wife, Sarah, also to serve as executrix. Sons: Frelin Alexander Runner to have one-fourth part of real estate in Delaware Co., Ohio known as Olentangy Mills including Grist Mill, Saw Mill and

(Runner con't) two dwelling houses which property was conveyed to Runner by Edward Pratt; Rheuben Runner, to have farm in Licking Co. known as Bancroft farm on Mt. Vernon Rd.; Milton Runner to have lot 4 in Logan, Hocking Co., Ohio and land in Wood Co., Ohio. Daughters: Mary Ann, lot in Lancaster, Fairfield Co., Ohio including dwelling house and carriage shop opposite the Broadway Hotel; Emeline, to have 60 acres in Green twp. and 120 acres in Laurel twp., Hocking Co., Ohio; Margarette Ann Smedley, to have 80 acres now in Blackford Co. formerly in Jay Co., Indiana. Signed: Michael Runner. Witnesses: R. C. Hurd, James Black and James Hutcheson. (137)

RAMSEY, John - dated 10-15-1848; recorded 11-26-1850. Bequeathes to: John Ramsey McVicker, William McKendrie Iles, Sarah Iles and Henry Iles, no relationship, if any, is stated. Son, Nelson Ramsey, not of age. Executors: David Iles and John Crawford. Signed: John Ramsey. Witnesses: George Iles and Margaret Iles. Codicil dated 10-19-1849 names wife, Rebecca and mentions children but does not name. Witnesses: John Crawford and Daniel Tracy. (140)

MORRIS, Isaac - dated 4-15-1845; recorded 4-21-1851. Son, Moses Morris, also to serve as executor, to have farm where now live NE¼ S5 T12 R18. Daughter, Anna Cost. Mentions other children but does not name. Signed: Isaac Morris. Witnesses: Robert McBroom and Nancy V. McBroom. (142)

KEPLAR, Andrew of Green township - dated 12-3-1850; recorded 4-26-1851. Wife, mentioned but not named and under a former contract son, Barnet to keep her during her natural life. Sons: John, Andrew Jr., David, barnet and Samu :. Kepler. Daughters: Nelly wife of Samuel Price, Polly wife of Jacob Tom, Peggy wife of Hugh O'Hare and Elizabeth Price. Signed: Andrew (his mark) Keplar. Witnesses: A. White and S. L. Julian. (143)

CLENDENEN, Andrew - dated 8-14-1850; recorded 4-21-1851. Wife, Mary. Six children: David, James, Mary, William, Anderson and Elenor. Grand-daughter, Mary Margaret daughter of Andrew Clendenen Jr. Requests that when property is sold that to reserve one half acre land in SW corner for purpose of a burying ground and it is to remain for that purpose forever. Executor, Andrew Forest. Signed: Andrew (his mark) Clendenen. Witnesses: George Mayes and John Grubb. (145)

COLLFASS, Jacob - dated 1-2-1851; recorded 7-7-1851. Wife, Elizabeth, also to serve as executrix. Signed: Jacob Collfass. Witnesses: Thomas England and John (his mark) Hurand. (147)

DEETS, Henry - dated 6-3-1851; recorded 7-8-1851. Wife, mentioned but not named. Lawful Heirs: Joseph Deets, Alson Deets and Sarah Deets. Requests that executor sell 28 acres of land in Preston Co., Virginia. Executor: Christopher Kinser. Signed: Henry (his mark) Deets. Witnesses: John V. Clutter and Levi Mathias.(148)

WEST, John of Laurel township - dated 5-2-1851; recorded 7-12-1851. Wife, Mary, to have farm where now reside being 40 acres S½ W½ NW¼ S23 T12 R18. Sons: William and Benjamin West, Benjamin not of age. Susan Reed, Elizabeth Peach and Rose Ann Campbell "to have five dollars as their full share out of my estate at their mother's decease." Executor: son, William. Signed: John West. Witnesses: Thomas Whitecraft, Benjamin Crane, and A. C. Friend. (150)

SPONSLER, John - dated 8-27-1851; recorded 9-20-1851. Wife, Sarah. Children: Agnes wife of Abner Beegle to have large Family Bible, John J. Sponsler, Sarah C. wife of John Rising and Harriett wife of John Shaw. Executor, Abner Beegle. Signed: John Sponsler. Witnesses: Moses R. Cherry and Henry Meldrum. (152)

BUSSARD, Mary - dated 8-29-1851; recorded 11-12-1851. All property to Oner Sharp. Signed: Mary (her mark) Bussard. Witnesses: George Sell, Jacob (mark) Bowman and C. Murray. (153)

ILES, John - dated 8-23-1851; recorded 11-22-1851. Wife, mentioned but not named, to have farm where now live in SE¼ S10 T12 R18. Mentions children but does not name except youngest son, William who is not of age. Executors: Jacob Iles and Robert McBroom. Signed: John Iles. Witnesses: John K. McBroom and Magdalena Rach. (154)

WRIGHT, Barbara - dated 10-3-1846; recorded March 1847. Son, Charles H. Wright, to collect all balance coming to testatrix from father's estate. Daughter, Polly Calhoun, to have large Family Bible. Signed: Barbara Wright. Witnesses: E. T. Brown and H. S. Wright. (155)

HOLMES COUNTY, OHIO – DIVORCE RECORDS, 1826-1842

Contributed by: Carol Willsey Flavell, C.G., 4649 Yarmouth Lane, Youngstown, Ohio 44512
The following records were copied from "Supreme Court Record Volume 1" as found in the Clerk of Court's Office at the court house in Millersburg. The page on which the record may be found in the original book is given in parenthesis.

HUM, Sarah vs. John, filed 5-15-1826; married 1-16-1823 at Millersburg, Holmes Co.; wilful absence for 3 years. (2)

POULSON, Thomas vs. Elizabeth, filed 6-1-1827; married Sept 1816 in Holmes Co. to Elizabeth THOMPSON; lived together 2 years and she left. (4)

ACKISON, Henry vs. Ruth, filed 5-19-1828; married 10-20-1825 in Holmes Co. to Ruth FOUCH; charged with adultery with John ODELL and others. (9)

BIRD, Harriet vs. Thomas, filed 4-2-1828; married 11-15-1827 at Millersburg; charged with assault and battery. (11)

BIRD, Thomas vs. Harriet, filed 6-15-1832, cross petition; married 11-15-1827 to Harriet BURROW of Hardy twp.; charge, absent and adultery. (48)

WELLS, Susan vs. Calvin, filed 6-23-1834; married 6-17-1828 in Holmes Co.; charge, wilful absence for more than 3 years. (51)

MIKESEL, Adam vs. Nancy, filed 7-15-1835; married 7-20-1829 to Nancy ARTES at Turkeyfoot twp., Somerset Co., Penna.; now residents of Paint twp., Holmes Co., Ohio; charge, wilful absence. (86)

MATTOCKS, Harriet vs. Samuel, filed 6-15-1836; married 2-21-1832 in Prairie twp., Holmes Co.; charge, left her with an infant child. (118)

KIRKPATRICK, Ariel vs. Samuel, filed 5-26-1836; for divorce and alimony; married Jan. 1834 in Knox twp., Holmes Co.; on 6-1-1835 he took her only child a female about 7 months old; she recovered it in Jefferson Co., Ohio; while she was at her brother's,......(not given) HUGHES, in Knox twp., said Samuel became abusive. (123)

HARRIOTT, Nancy vs. James E., filed 9-27-1837; married 4-19-1831 in Wooster, Wayne Co., Ohio; has 2 children, a male about 3 yrs. and a female about 2 yrs.; mention of a girl by his previous marriage; charge, illicit affairs with one Sarah SMITH. (132)

GIBSON, Margaret vs. George, filed 8-27-1836; married 3-17-1825 in Monroe twp., Holmes Co. (143)

FOREMAN, Conrad vs. Barbara, filed 7-12-1838; married 6-27-___(not given) at Entrim twp., Franklin Co., Pa. to Barbara BARGER; they had no children; charge, adultery. (173)

BURNIE, Mary vs. William, filed 6-29-1840; married 2-4-1817 at Erie Co., Penna.; has had 9 children now living: John 21, Alexander 19, Esther 17, William 14, Rachel 12, George M. 9, Holmes 7, Samuel 4, and Robert 3. (note: more data. in record). (224)

McELROY, John vs. Margaret, filed 4-11-1840; married 3-22-1836 in Monroe twp., Holmes Co. to Margaret SIMPSON. (325)

BILLINGER, Jacob vs. Hannah, filed 6-10-1842; married 6-21-1835 at Oswego., New York; charge, adultery. (479)

STILES, Elizabeth vs. Jonathan W., filed 7-15-1842; married 6-3-1838 in Holmes Co.; he left her children, and is in Michigan. (481)

BERRY, Thomas vs. Margaret, filed 7-25-1842; married 4-1-1841 at Wooster, Wayne Co., Ohio. (488)

Contributed by: Catharine F. Fedorchak, 7590 West 85th Ave., Crown Point,
                 Indiana 46307

Mrs. Fedorchak states that the following marriages were found recorded in the
front of a book containing Civil Suits from Dec. 1855 to Jan. 8, 1861 kept
by the Greenfield Township Trustees; this book now being in her possession.
Mrs. Fedorchak further states that the book is for sale.

Marraige Registry

Feb. 18, 1857 - Joseph Graham and Mary Bare was given in marriage by at the hose
of J. Howard in Greenfield Township Co. Ohio
Joseph Graham, age 30   Mary Bare age 24
Joseph Graham born in Dunham Co. England   Mary Bear born in Seneca Co. N.Y.
                                    /s/ J. Noggle, J.P.

March 19, 1857 - I solemenized the marraige of Wm Zarr*, age 30 years of
Greenefield Township, place of birth Cumberland Co. Pa. single to Miss
Elizabeth Smith of same place, age 21 years, place of birth Europe, Single
                                    /s/ J. Noggle. J.P.

*(could be Zurr)

Jan. 6, 1858 - I solemenised the marraige of Wm. Parrott of Greenfield Township
at the house of Wm. Parrot. He was aged 28, residence Greenfield Township,
place of birth Somersett Co. England, single, parents William & Hannah Parrott
to Catharine Holmes of Riple Township aged 18. Place of birth Cumberland Co.
England, parents Wm. Holmes and Isabel Holmes of Ripley, Ohio
                                    /s/ J. Noggle, J.P.

HURON COUNTY, OHIO - DEATH RECORDS 1867-1868

The following death records were copied from Death Record 1, located in the Probate Court at Norwalk. The page on which the original record may be found is given in parenthesis. Only persons 40 years of age and over were copied. Abbreviations used are: d=died; m=married; s=single; w=widow or widower; a=aged; pb=place of birth; pd=place of death; r=residence. Residence is the same as place of death unless otherwise stated.

McKIM, James - d 7-7-1867; a 75y; m; pd Belleven; pb Penn. (1)
McKIM, Mrs. Elizabeth - d 7-30-1867; a 73y; w; pd Belleven; pb----- (1)
PLATZ, Peter - d 8-25-1867; a 78y; m; pd Norwalk; pb Germany. (1)
MEFFORD, Abyel - d 9-2-1867; a 74y; w; pd Norwalk; pb New Jersey; parents, Wm and Pheeby Mitchell. (1)
RULE, John Henry - d 7-17-1867; a 73y; m; pd Norwalk; pb Headington, Scotland. (1)
CASHNER, Leonard - d 7-11-1867; a 76y; m; pd Norwich; pb---; r Havana. (1)
DRURY, Sallie - d 8-18-1867; a 86y; w; pd Townsend; pb Conn. (1)
ELLS, Sarah - d Aug. 1867; a 84y; w; pd Fairfield; pb New York. (1)
BALWICK, Peter - d 10-28-1867; a 83y; m; pdPeru; pb----- (1)
BILLS, Elijah - d 10-30-1867; a 67y; m; pd Hartland; pb-----(1)
BOOKMAN, Anna - d 11-22-1867; a 67y; m; pd Lyme; pb Germany. (1)
HAFFNER, Anny - d 10-7-1867; a 56y; m; pd Sherman; pb Europe. (1)
MILLER, Frank - d 10-14-1867; a 95y; w; pd Sherman; pb Bavaria. (1)
STEBBINS, Roswell - d 12-31-1867; a 75y; m; pd Lyme; pb Huron Co. (1)
MEFFORD, Abigal - d 9-3-1867; a 73y; w; pd Norwalk; pb Essex Co., N. Y. (1)
BUCHANNAN, Jane - d 9-3-1867; a 85y; w; pd Norwalk; pb Essex Co. N. J. (2)
HARRIS, Rachel - d 12-14-1867; a 55y; w; pd Townsend; pb Pa. (2)
SHAW, Mary E. - d 1-8-1868; a 54y; w; pd Townsend; pb Vt. (2)
AUSTIN, Caroline E. - d 1-31-1868; a 56y; m; pd Townsend; pb Stanford, Fairfield Co., Conn. (2)
STEVENS, Sophia - d 2-11-1868; a 57y; w; pd Fairfield; pb Hamden, Mass. (2)
LEE, Mary - d 3-20-1868; a 78y; w; pd Ripley; pb N.Y.; parents, Solomon and Thankful (note: no surname given). (2)
SMITH, Erastus - d 3-27-1868; a 55y; m; pd Greenfield; pb Trumbull Co., Ohio; parents, Erastus and Fanny. (2)
McFARLAN, Archabald - d 3-29-1868; a 46y; m; pd Fairfield; pb Sandusky, Erie Co., Ohio; parents, George and Ann. (2)
PALMER, Elizabeth d. 10-6-1867; a 64y; w; pd New London; pb N. Y. (2)
TWINMON, Laura - d 10-8-1867; a 46y; s; pd Dubuke City, Dubuke Co., Iowa; pb N. Y.; r Iowey. (2)
CARON, Achsah A. - d 3-19-1868; a 64y; w; pd Lyme; pb Auburn, Dayuga Co., N.Y.(2)
SLATER, Paul - d 2-27-1868; a 79y; s; pd Norwalk; pb R.I. (2)
SMITH, Fanny - d 3-14-1868; a 79y; w; pd Norwalk; pb New London Co., Ct. (2)
BARNUM, Ebenezer M. - d 3-4-1868; a 75y; m; pd Clarksfield; pb Danbury Co., Ct.(2)
PRENTISS, Gran - d 11-5-1867; a 101y; w; pd Rubyfield; pb New London, Conn. (2)
GURLEY, Jane d 1-12-1868; a 67y; m; pd Bunsen; pb Ireland. (2)
BALWIG, Peter - d 10-30-1867; a 84y; m; pd Peru; pb Germany. (2)
GRISS, Crescentia - d 10-30-1867; a 66y; pd Bunson; pb Peru, Huron Co.; parents, A. and Mary Bishop. (2)
FITCH, Thomas - d 3-24-1868; a 43y; m; pd Lyme; pb Lyme. (2)
COLLINS, John - d 10-6-1867; a 40y; s; pd Norwalk; pb Ireland. (2)
SMITH, Jones - d 10-10-1867; a 60y; s; pd Norwalk; pb N. Y. (2)

SLATER, Paul - d 2-28-1868; a 80y; m; pd Norwalk; pb R.I. (2)
CURTIS, Harriet - d 3-13-1868; a 75y; m; pd Norwalk; pb N.Y. (2)
KEELER, Rebecca - d 4-26-1868; a 65y; m; pd Huron Co.; pb---- (2)
PENNWELL, Louisa - d 1-14-1868; a 72y; m; pd Norwalk; pb Hagerstown, Md. (2)
GRANT, Ann C. - d 9-25-1868; a 49y; m; pd Lyme; pb Ireland. (2)
STEEL, Abigail - d 6-24-1868; a 58y; m; pd Richmond; pb N.Y.; parents, Geo. and
     Sarah Lane. (2)
OWEN, Permelia - d 9-8-1868; a 59y; m; pd Norwalk; pb N.Y. (4)
GREEN, James - d 9-15-1868; a 63y; m; pd Norwalk; pb England. (4)
STANCHAK, Phoeb - d 5-12-1868; a 80y; w; pd Royalton, Fulton Co., Ohio; pb N.Y.(4)
EATON, Alvin C. - d 10-23-1868; a 51y; m; pd Peru; pb N.Y. (4)
HOSKINS, Marie S. - d 11-13-1868; a 56y; w; pd Peru; pb V.I. (4)
HAYNES, Asa - d 10-15-1868; a 49y; m; pd Richmond; pb Greenfield, Huron Co. (4)
KONZELMANN, Catharine - d 11-7-1868; a 40y; m; pd Lynn; pb Germany. (4)
SEYMOUR, Hart - d 8-18-1868; a 70y; m; pd Plymouth; pb------ (4)
PARKER, Seth C. - d 10-18-1868; a 66y; m; pd Greenfield; pb N.Y. (4)
GRANNELLS, Ellen - d 11-20-1868; a 71y; w; pd Greenfield; pb Ireland. (4)
HAAS, John I. - d 4-30-1868; a 72y; s; pd Sherman; pb Germany. (5)
PARKER, Seth C. - d 10-19-1868; a 66y; m; pd Greenfield; pb Benton, Cayuga Co.,
     N. Y. (5)
BURTON, Wm - d 10-13-1868; a 54y; w; pd Hartland; pb Qunsty, Washington Co., N.Y.;
     parents, David and Lydia Burton. (5)
HALL, Betsey - d 6-13-1868; a 80y; w; pd Wakeman; pb Granville, Hamilton Co.,
     Mass.; parents, Israel and Artenesia Coe. (5)
ADAMS, Betsey - d 11-19-1868; a 78y; w; pd Fairfield; pb Fairfield Co. Ct.;
     parents, Joseph and Lois Lyons. (6)
CAMPBELL, Joseph N. - d 7-23-1868; a 59y; m; physcian; pd Fairfield; pb Geneva,
     N. Y.; parents, John L. and Anna Campbell. (6)
DAVIS, Sarah - d 10-14-1868; a 58y; s; physcian; pd Fairfield; pb Camillas,
     Onondaga Co., N.Y.; parents, Solomon and Margaret Davis. (6)
KNAPP, Rheda - d 7-21-1868; a 50y; m; pd Fairfield; pb Osnego, Jefferson Co.,
     N.Y.; parents, R. and Nora Jewett. (6)
BAKER, Abijah - d 12-2-1868; a 66y; m; pd Fitchville; pb Onondaga Co., N.Y.;
     parents, Abijah and Mary Jane. (6)
BARAHART, Henry - - - - - d 8-12-1868; a 80y; w; pd Fitchville; pb Washington Co.,
     N.Y.; parents, Henry and Betsy. (6)
HINKLEY, Horace - d 10-8-1868; a 70y; m; pd Fitchville; pb Schoharie Co., N.Y.;
     parents, Joshua and Hannah. (6)
ULMSTED, John - d 12-22-1868; a 42y; m; pd Fitchville; pb Frederick Co., Md.;
     parents, Aaron and Elizabeth. (6)
GOLDING, John - d 12-16-1868; a 68y; m; pd Port, West Chester Co., N.Y.; pb
     Weschester Co., N.Y.; r Fitchville; parents, Joshua and Hannah. (6)
SNYDER, Benjamin - d 11-9-1868; a 75y; w; pd Richmond; pb Buck Co., Pa. (6)
STEELE, Abigail - d 8-18-1868; a 49y; m; pd Richmond; pb Richmond. (6)
ATHERTON, Samuel - d 12-21-1868; a 58y; m; pd Peru; pb Attleborough, Bristol Co.,
     Mass.; parents, Rufus and Content. (6)
EATON, A. C. - d 10-24-1868; a 51y; m; physician; pd Peru; pb Boonville, Herkimer
     Co., N. Y.; parents, Comfort and Mary. (6)

HASKINS, Maria S. - d 11-13-1868; a 56y; w; pd Peru; pb Barnard, Windsor Co., N.Y.:
    parents, Dynes and Deborah Lawton. (6)
HEPP, Rosa - d 10-5-1868; a 54y; m; pd Peru; pb Hantham, Welkhan, Baden; parents,
    Thomas and Mary Bower. (6)
KLISNER, Sebastian - d 5-20-1868; a 68y; w; pd Peru; pb Baden. (6)
BURGER, Anthony - d 11-16-1868; a 86y; m; pd Peru; pb Fallburg, France; parents,
    Christopher and Mary. (6)
KAKELER, Mary Ann - d 4-11-1868; a 73y; w; pd Peru; pb Walsh, France, parents,
    Asa P. and Pamelia (note: no surname given). (6)
JACK, Harriet E. - d 12-27-1868; a 62y m; pd Norwalk(?); pb Windsor Co., Vt.(6)
STEPHENS, Hezekiah - d 1-23-1868; a 61y; m; pd Peru; pb N.Y.; parents, Hezekiah
    and Tamer. (6)
HAYNES, Asa - d 10-14-1868; a 49y; m; pd Norwich; pb Greenfield, Huron Co.;
    parents, Nathaniel and Elizabeth. (6)
WELCH, Abbey Jane - d 6-25-1868; a 52y; w; pd Norwich; pb Kingsbury, Washington
    Co., N. Y.; parents, Ambrose and Polly Guy. (7)
PARMER, Elizabeth - d 9-4-1868; a 81y; w; pd Norwich; pb Rockland Co., N. Y.;
    parents, John and Temperance (note: no surname given). (7)
MARSH, Marvin M. - d 6-9-1868; a 56y; m; physician; pd Ripley; pb Pompey, Onondaga
    Co., N. Y.; parents, David and M. Marsh. (7)
EDWARDS, Clarissa - d 9-5-1868; a 73y; w; pd Ripley; pb Mass.; parents,_____
    and _____White. (7)
CARPENTER, Abbey - d 7-7-1868; a 71y; s; pd Ripley; pb Covert, Seneca Co., N. Y.;
    parents, John and Lucy (note: no surname given). (7)
SHAYES, Elizabeth - d 11-26-1868; a 50y; m; pd Clarksfield; pb Danberry, Conn.;
    parents, Horace and Elizabeth Porter. (7)
HAYES, Sturges - d 6-3-1868; a 71y; m; pd Clarksfield; pb Hartford, Conn.;
    parents, Nathaniel and Phebe. (7)
THAYER, Naomi - d 8-8-1868; a 70y; w; pd New London; pb Otsego Co., N.Y. (7)
HOSNER, John - d 5-7-1868; a 75y; m; pd New London; pb Conn. (7)
PARMENTER, Sally - d 9-20-1868; a 78y; m; pd New London; pb Rensselaer Co., N.Y.(7)
POND, Mabel - d 12-6-1868; a 83y; m; pd New London; pb Putney, Rutland Co., Vt. (7)
BOND, Stephen - d 12-6-1868; a 89y; w; pd New London; pb Leonix, Mass. (7)
RICHARD, Martha - d 11-11-1868; a 56y; m; pd New London; pb Franklin Co., Pa. (7)
SAWERS, John - d 6-3-1868; a 80y; m; pd Ridgefield; pb Little York, Maryland;
    parents, John and Mary Ann Sawers. (8)
PRENTISS, Turner - d 5-8-1868; a 67y; m; pd Ridgefield; pb Chesterfield, New
    London Co., Conn.; parents, Samuel and Grace Prentis. (8)
GIBSON, Bersheby S. - d 10-30-1868; a 50y; w; pd Greenfield; pb Amberland, R. I.;
    parents, Isaac and Joannah. (8)
LEWIS, Betsey - d 5-25-1868; a 45y; m; pd Townsend; pb-----. (8)
GIBBS, Stephen - d 4-27-1868; a 81y; m; pd Norwalk; pb Conn. (8)
JACKSON, Charles - d 6-1-1868; a 46y; m; pd Norwalk; pb N.Y. (8)
GREEN, James - d 9-15-1868; a 63y; m; pd Norwalk; pb England. (8)
HAWKS, John - d 11-20-1868; a 77y; pd Norwalk; pb N.H. (9)
WHITNEY, A. M. - d 5-20-1868; a 44y; m; pd Norwalk; pb Conn. (9)

The following death records were copied from Death Record 1, located in the Probate Court at Norwalk. The page on which the original record may be found is given in parenthesis. Only persons 40 years of age and over were copied. Abbreviations used are: d=died; m=married; s=single; w=widow or widower; a=aged; pb=place of birth; pd=place of death; r=residence. Residence is the same as place of death unless otherwise stated. Page numbers begin with page 4. If there were any 1867 or 1868 deaths, they are not found in book at the present time.

WHITNEY, Margaret - d 1-13-1869; a 80y; w; pd Norwalk; pb-------(4)
HOLLOWAY, Lowania - d Jan. 1869; a 60y; w; pd Havanna; pb-------(4)
HOLLISTER, Lewis - d Feb. 1869; a 57y; m; pd Norwalk; pb--------(4)
BURNHAM, Asa - d 2-7-1869; a 63y; w; pd Greenfield; pb New Hampshire. (4)
CUNNINGHAM, Emma - d 3-9-1869; a 63y; w; pd Clarksfield; pb Erie Co., N.Y. (4)
BROOKS, Wm - d 2-12-1869; a 68y; pd Greenfield; pb Huron Co. (4)
DAVIS, Daniel - d 7-1-1869; a 78y; pd N. Haven; pb-------- (4)
OSBORN, Ebenezer - d 3-19-1869; a 65; w; pd Fitchville; pb N.Y. (4)
MILLER, William - d 2-3-1869; a 47y; m; pd Bronson; pb England; parents, C. & E. Miller. (5)
PECK, Annis - d 3-21-1869; a 80y; s; pd Bronson; pb N.Y.; mother. Abigail Peck.(5)
DAVIS, Daniel - d 4-1-1869 a 62y; m; pd New Haven; pb N.Y. (5)
FURGASON, Mary - d 3-6-1869; a 80y; w; pd New Haven; pb N.Y. (5)
WYKLE, Jacob - d 1-5-1869; a 49y; m; pd Sherman; pb Germany. (5)
BROOKS, William - d 2-14-1869; a 60y; m; pd Greenfield; pb Marble, Benington Co., Vermont. (5)
BURNHAM, Asa - d 2-7-1869; a 64y; w; pd Greenfield; pb Milford, Hilsborough Co., N.H. (5)
BAKER, Williams - d 2-11-1869; a 71y; m; pd Fairfield; pb R.I.; parents, Obigjah and Mary Baker. (5)
McCORD, Louisa - d 1-21-1869; a 40y; m; pd Fairfield; pb Huron Co.; parents, A. & M. Brundage. (6)
CURTISS, Hiram - d 2-25-1869; a 71y; m; pd Fitchville; pb Penn.; parents, Johann W. and Susanna. (6)
FAIRCHILD, Cyntha - d 3-2-1869; a 68y; m; pd Fitchville; pb Southerton, Conn.; father, John Root. (6)
MARTIN, Jas. W. - 3-20-1869; a 56y; m; pd Fitchville; pb Ulster Co., N.Y.; parents, Gilbert and Hannah. (6)
OSBORN, Ebenezer - d 3-18-1869; a 67y; m; pd Fitchville; pb Greene Co., N.Y.; parents, Ebenezer and Clorinda. (6)
TILLSON, Azuba - d 1-27-1869; a 84y; w; pd Peru; pb Seedburg, Mass.; parents, Moses and Dina Vois. (6)
LINDER, Mary Lana - d 3-30-1869; a 72y; m; pd Peru; pb Augsteen, New Stadt, Bavaria; parents, Henry and Barbara Sitzler. (6)
GAUNGS, William - d 1-24-1869; a 59y; m; pd Peru; pb Norfolk Co., England. (6)
HOLLOWAY, Loranna - d 2-6-1869; a 59y; w; pd Norwich; pb Trenton, Oneida Co., N.Y.; parents, Barnard and Barbara (note: no surname given). (7)
JENNINGS, Rhoda - d 3-12-1869; a 66y; s; pd Ripley; pb Easton, Fairfield Co., Conn.; parents, Daniel and Phebe Jennings. (7)
SATTISON, Elizabeth - d 3-1-1869; a 71y; m; pd Ripley; pb Penn.; parents, _____Restor. (7)

CUNNINGHAM, Dunice - d 3-9-1869; a 63y; w; pd Clarksfield; pb Vt.; parents,
          Brown. (7)
FERRIS, Polley A. - d Jan. 1869; a 42y; w; pd New London; pb------(7)
SMURE, John - d 2-29-1869; a 69y; w; pd New London; pb Va. (7)
SLAGLEY, Anthony - d 1-27-1869; a 70y; m; pd Monroeville; pb-------(7)
BRECKENRIDGE, Geo. W. - d 2-26-1869; a 56y; m; minister; pd Ridgefield; pb
          Charlot, Chittenden Co., Vermont; parents, James and Lovina Breckenridge. (8)
RICE, Hannah - d 2-2-1869; a 78y; m; pd Ridgefield; pb Virginia; parents, Adams
          and Mary Myers. (8)
FROYLEY, Richard - d 3-5-1869; a 43y; m; pd Norwalk; pb England. (8)
HOLESTER, L. P. - d 2-8-1869; a 49y; pd Norwalk; pb N.Y. (9)
WATKINS, John - d 2-23-1869; a 40y; m; pd Norwalk; pb England. (9)
HERTER, Martin - d 1-31-1870; a 83y; w; pd Bronson; pd Morgantown, Green Co.,
          Pa.; parents, John and Elizabeth. (9)
HAGAMAN, John - d 1-29-1870; a 68y; m; pd Bronson; pb Cayuga Co., N.Y.; parents,
          Thomas and Nelley. (9)
CULLIFF, Nathan - d 2-22-1870; a 46y; m; pd Bronson; pb----- (9)
HEMBROW, Charles - d 3-12-1870; pd Bronson; pb----- (9)
STRATTON, James - d 8-9-1869; a 43y; m; pd Hartland; pb N.Y.; father, Richard
          Stratton. (9)
GRAINGER, Trumble - d 5-14-1869; a 69y; m; pd Hartland; pb N.Y. (9)
PIERCE, Lucinda - d 12-21-1869; a 44y; m; pd Hartland; pb Hartland. (9)
WESTFALL, Harvey - d 8-25-1869; a 73y; m; pd New Haven; pb Beverly, Randolph
          Co., Virginia. (9)
CULP, Eloner - d 2-23-1870; a 79y; w; pd New Haven; pb New Haven, Huron Co. (9)
KNIFFIN, Salley - d 9-30-1869; a 53y; m; pd Greenwich; pb N.Y.; father, James
          S. Collins. (9)
BRENNEMAN, Adam - d 10-7-1869; a 80y; m; pd (Greenwich?) Huron Co.; pb Pa.;
          parents, John and Mary. (9)
ST JOHN, Edward - d 9-3-1869; a 82y; w; pd Greenwich; pb N.Y. (10)
BATES, Sarah - d 6-11-1869; a 62y; m; pd Wakeman; pb N.Y. (10)
WAUGH, Gideon - d 5-12-1869; a 71y; m; pd Wakeman; pb Conn. (10)
WELCH, Samuel - d 9-28-1869; a 73y; m; pd Wakeman; pb N.Y. (10)
WHELER, Martha D. - d 3-16-1870; a 45y; pd Wakeman; pb N.Y. (10)
GREEN, Lucinda - d 6-9-1870; a 41y; m; pd Wakeman; pb Florence (?), Erie Co.,
          Ohio; parents, Abner and C. L. Green. (10)
BENTLEY, Hesse P. - d 2-22-1870; a 40y; m; pd Wakeman; pb Wakeman; parents,
          W. & C. L. Bentley. (10)
KELLOGG, Asher Porter - d 11-3-1869; a 61y; m; pd Fairfield; pb Cayuga, N. Y.;
          parents, Solomon and Rebecca. (10)
WHITNEY, Maranda S. - d 2-19-1870; a 64y; m; pd Fairfield; pb Fairfield Co.,
          Conn.; parents, Justin and Ruth Tilleman. (10)
BUCKMAN, Sarah - d 3-13-1870; a 92y; w; pd Fairfield; pb Hampshire Co., Va.;
          father, Levi Lee. (10)
WELCH, Jane - d 11-25-1869; a 99y; pd Fairfield; pb Dutchess Co., N.Y. (10)
CHERRY, John - d 4-8-1870; a 72y; m; pd Fairfield; pb Seneca Co., N.Y. (10)
PRIER(?), Abigail - d 12-14-1869; a 64y; m; pd Fairfield; pb Onondaga Co., N.Y.(10)
MANN, Lydia Ann - d 11-9-1869; a 53y; m; pd Fairfield; pb Conn. (10)
SMITH, Walter B. - d 11-15-1869; a 54y; m; pd Fairfield; pb Cayuga, N.Y. (10)

CALKINS, Margaret - d 5-5-1869; a 40y; pd N. London; pb----; parents, M. & A. Dunn. (10)

WARNER, Mary P. - d 2-13-1870; a 46y; m; pd N. London; pb-----; parents, Cyrus and _enna(?) Turner. (10)

AMES, Ambrose - d 9-28-1869; a 69y; m; pd N. London; pb-------. (10)

PERRINE, Elizabeth - d 4-14-1869; a 66y; m; pd N. London; pb------; parents, James and Mary Furgeson. (10)

CARPENTER, Giles - d 3-25-1870; a 71y; w; pd Clarksfield; pb Dover, Dutchess Co., N.Y.; parents, Fredrick and Betsy Carpenter. (10)

CHAMBERLAIN, Elizia - d 10-27-1869; a 84y; w; pd Clarksfield; pb Rich, Berkshire Co., Mass.; parents, Alex and Huldah CGarton. (10)

WASHBURN, Jonathan - d 6-21-1870; a 61y; m; pd Clarksfield; pb Putnam Co., N.Y. (10)

NEWMAN, John - d 6-16-1870; a 84y; m; pd Clarksfield; pb Trenton, N.J. (10)

BURDEN, Mary G. - d 12-22-1869; a 59y; m; pd Townsend; pb Canada. (10)

LOVE, Andrew - d 7-21-1869; a 71y; m; pd Townsend; pb Caro, Green Co., N.Y.; parents, John and Sarah Love. (10)

WALDRON, Cynthia - d 4-13-1870; a 82; w; pd Townsend; pb Mass.; parents, Conston and Seline(?) Simmons. (11)

DRAPER, Clarisa - d 11-11-1869; a 66y; pd Townsend; pb N.Y.; parents, P. & B. Cole. (11)

GEROW, Daniel D. - d 1-7-1870; a 72y; m; pd Townsend; pb N.J.; parents, Isaac and Sarah Grow. (11)

LOCKWOOD, Alvah - d 7-8-1869; a 67y; pd Townsend; pb West Chester, N.Y.; parents, T. & U. Lockwood. (11)

GFILL, Kunegmda - d 5-25-1869; a 56y; w; pd Peru; pb Baden. (11)

SANDERS, John - d 5-21-1869; a 69y; m; pd Peru; pb N.Y. (11)

ROE, Corrinna - d 10-22-1869; a 59y; m; pd Peru; pb N.Y.; parents Daniel and Eunice Caner. (11)

WOODRUFF, Geo. H. - d 6-2-1869; a 73y; m; pd Peru; pb Germany; parents, Chauncey and Eunice Woodruff. (11)

SAUER, Philip - d 5-27-1869; a 46y; m; pd Peru; pb----; parents, Clement and Mary. (11)

HAWKINS, Eleaser - d 12-28-1869; a 84y; m; pd Ripley; pb-------; parents, Samuel and Polly Hawkins. (11)

BELDIN, Elizabeth - d 10-17-1869; a 73y; pd Norwalk; pb------ (11)

BENNINGTON, Sarah - d 10-13-1869; a 80y; pd Norwalk; pb------ (11)

BISHOP, Amos - d 1-3-1£ ; a 83y; pd Norwalk; pb------ (11)

PERRIN, Oliver H. - d 6-7-1869; a 41y; m; pd Norwalk; pb Plymouth, Luzerne Co., Pa.; parents, Raymond and M. Perrin. (11)

DELAMATER, James Vanness - d 8-7-1869; a 41y; m; pd Norwalk; pb Hyde Parke, Dutchess Co., N.Y.; parents, Benj. and Almira Delamater. (11)

HITCHCOCK, Elisha - d 8-28-1869; a 88y; w; pd Norwalk; pb Vt. (11)

BUCHY, Martin - d 10-30-1869; a 56y; m; pd Norwalk; pb Switzerland. (11)

FOX, John - d 1-22-1870; a 81y; m; pd Norwalk; pb New Hampshire. (11)

Note: The following marriages were copied from Marriage Book A, as found in the Probate Court at the court house at Jackson. It should be noted that there were only three marriages found for the year 1821, one marriage for the year 1822 and 3 marriages for the year 1823 recorded in the proper chronological order. Possibly these marriages were recorded later, but in leafing through the book I did not find any additional listings for these three years. Anita Short, C.G.

ACORD, Valantine to Elizabeth Oliver	9-1-1825
ANDERSON, David to Jane Scott	12-14-1824
ANTHONY, Phillip to Hannah Timberman	7-28-1825
ARMSTRONG, Henry to Polley Barrett	8-7-1817
ARTHUR, Amos to Anna A. Elliott	10-10-1820
ARTHUR, Benjamin to Catharine Radabaugh	2-14-1817
ATHERTON, Ashael to Elizabeth Adams	6-23-1820
BARTON, Thos. to Charlotte Haile	12-24-1816
BEARDSLEE, Bennet to Evalina Meeker	11-24-1825
BEMELTON, Richard to Jemima Hill	8-19-1819
BENNETT, John to Anne Stockham	1-17-1816
BICKLE, Henry to Clarissa Merrill	3-17-1824
BOGARD, Gasper to Rebecca Nickels	3-30-1825
BOGGS, Anthony to Mary Friend	9-17-1816
BORER, Peter to Rheabe Vanskey	3-15-1818
BOWEN, William to Margaret Stinor	2-6-1825
BOWERS, Jacob to Peggy Reed	1-17-1820
BREWER, Willis to Catharine Hoffman	6-16-1824
BROWN, Reuben to Sarah Jones	4-2-1818
BROWN, Solomon to Elizabeth Vernon	6-5-1817
BROWN, Wm to Patsey Burris	9-30-1819
BUNN, Peter to Tacy How	2-25-1824
BUNN, Samuel to Elizabeth Nelson (note: no day given)	Jan. 1819
BURRIS, William Jr. to Charlotte Ross	11-18-1819
CADEY, Elias to Elizabeth Hughs	4-13-1825
CAHILL, John to Elizabeth Wiles (note: no day given)	Nov. 1818
CANTER, Henry to Rebecca Canter	12-29-1825
CASEL, Henry to Polley Wiles	2-8-1819
CLEMMONS, John Jr. to Ruth Peterson	8-10-1820
CORN, Jesse to Uley Hammon	10-8-1818
CORN, John Jr. to Anna Miller	12-15-1825
CORN, William to Mary Massie	12-23-1824
COZAD, Abraham to Charity Davis	4-3-1820
CRABTREE, James to Alsay Throckmorton	11-23-1819
CRABTREE, Lewis to Anna Dixon	8-21-1817
CRABSTREE, Samuel to Elizabeth Murphy	4-1-1825
CRAIG, Samuel to Elizabeth Jenkins	1-25-1819
CRAIG, Samuel to Patsy Ann McCray	2-5-1824
CRAIG, Thomas to Elizabeth Deavor	3-12-1818
CRAIGO, James to Sarah Climons	8-17-1816
CRAY (or ORAY), Francis to Fanky Hughbanks (Eubanks)	2-11-1818
CROW, Isaac to Louisa James	1-3-1825

```
DARBY, William to Margaret Davis                                      8-18-1824
DAVIS, Luther to Mary Brewer                                          6-7-1820
DAVIS, William to Nancy Jenkins                                       3-31-1825
DELAY, James to Mary Forney otherwise called Mary Hoover             3-31-1825
DIXON, Henry Junr. to Elizabeth Rickabaugh                           (8-9-1816
                                                          2 dates (8-24-1816
DIXON, Jacob to Nancy Derby                                           1-6-1820
DIXON, John (or Jehu) to Frances Ray                                 4-13-1820
DIXON, Joseph to Rachel Wilkinson                                    2-4-1819
DIXON, Lemuel to Rosanna Graves                                      3-2-1825
DIXSON, Nathan to Rachel Graham                                      3-20-1817
ELLIOTT, James to Margaret McCray                                    12-14-1820
EUBANKS, Joseph to Catharine Nally                                   12-11-1818
EUBANKS, Joseph to Dolly Craige                                      2-11-1819
EUTSLER, George to Betsy HOLLINGSHEAD                                10-22-1820
FAULKNER, Andrew to Mary Crump                                       7-30-1818
FLACK, Benjamin to Polly Dever                                       1-27-1819
FLORA, John to Sarah Findley                                         10-30-1817
FLORA, Robert to Elsy Detty                                          2-20-1817
FRAZEE, Augustus to Sarah McCray                                     1-6-1825
FRENCH, Bartemeus to Elizabeth Cooley                               2-11-1819
FULLET, William to Rachel Wishong                                   10-28-1819
GIBSON, James B. to Hester R. Cochrane                              11-18-1818
GILLELAND, John B. to Sarah Johnston                                6-25-1820
GORDEN, William to Mary Keller                                       9-9-1824
GRAHAM, John to Elenor Leach                                        11-4-1824
GRANT, George to Anna Stancliff                                      7-6-1825
GRAVES, William to Elizabeth Waldren                                3-25-1824
GREAVES, Joseph to Jane McVey                                       4-20-1820
GREAVS (GREAVES), Henry to Alice Greavs (Graves)                   3-3-1825
GREGORY, William to Frances Long                                     5-20-1820
GUTHRIE, James to Nancy -----(not given)                            12-17-1817
HALE, William to Jane Fullerton                                     12-30-1819
HALL, James to Sarah Wilkins                                         9-14-1820
HALTERMAN, Henry to Mary Dixon                                       9-16-1823
HANNA, Christopher to Sarah Poor(no day given-rec. 10-2-1818)      Sept. 1818
HARTLEY, Thomas to Prudence Newel                                   2-6-1817
HIGGONBOTTOM, John to Nancy Pemetton                                5-13-1818
HIX, John to Mary Thompson                                          5-18-1820
HORTON, Isaac C. to Rosanna Funston                                 6-14-1820
HOWARD, William to Margary Whitsel (Whetzel)                       12-16-1819
HUFFMAN, Daniel to July James                                       8-28-1818
HURST, Hooper to Elizabeth James                                    12-9-1818
JAMES, Thomas to Elizabeth Burns                                    12-7-1817
JENKINS, James to Margaret Rodabaugh                               11-27-1823
JOHNSON, Samuel R. to Susan Ward                                    1-13-1825
KEATH, Christian to Martha Wilson                                   9-16-1823
KEETON (KEYTON), William to Sophia Jeffreys                         7-13-1819
LAKE, Silas to Eliza Schellenger                                    1-18-1820
```

LANTZ, Aaron to Leah Claypool	5-4-1819
LEACH, Ambrose to Mrs. Tabitha Westfall	9-10-1818
LEACH, Archibald to Rosan Wheatley	4-21-1825
LEACH, Thomas W. to Nancy Rose	3-14-1819
LEVISAY, Jefferson to Elizabeth Varian	2-24-1825
LOCKARD, Joseph to Mary Law	11-18-1818
LONG, James to Alse Boggs	11-19-1820
LONG, Joel to Jane Boggs	1-29-1818
LOVE, John to Jenny Blake	2-12-1824
McCUNE, Joseph to Orlinda Cuting	2-17-1820
McCOLLISTER, John to Feeby McNutt	2-12-1819
McDOWELL, John to Elizabeth Bowen	10-30-1817
McKEEL, Moree to Sabra Hanson	9-28-1820
McKINNIS, Joseph to Louisa Shearer	12-2-1824
MADDOX, Hiram to Mary Whaley	5-19-1819
MARTIN, Joel to Sarah Beatty	3-22-1825
MARTIN, William to Hannah Deaver	3-15-1817
MARTIN, William to Jane McIntire	9-13-1824
MEEKER, Taundy to Ruthy Hubel	11-7-1824
MERCER, Thomas to Sabrann Mercer	8-7-1820
MILLER, Alexander to Marmoen James	8-21-1825
MONROE, Moses to Elizabeth Johnston	1-14-1819
MOOT, Aaron to Polley McDaniel	2-25-1819
MOTES, Abraham to Barbary Nicholas	5-18-1820
MOTZ, John to Elizabeth Crow	10-11-1816
MURDOCK, John to Nancy South	12-24-1818
NICHOLSON, James to Mary Ann Pickle	12-30-1818
NULL, Isaac to Jane Snodgrass	1-13-1825
OLIVER, William to Nancy Smith	8-6-1818
PALMER, Layton to Catharine Whetsel	1-14-1819
PETERSON, James to Mary F. Caron	10-22-1819
PHILLIPS, Jenkin to Elizabeth Funston	8-20-1820
POTTER, Peleg to Nancy Cutwright	1-1-1817
POWERS, Hickman to Harriet Douthet	10-28-1819
PRAITHER, John to. Deborah Clemons	5-20-1818
PRAUSE, Daniel to Elizabeth Sprause	1-5-1821
RADABAUGH, Henry to Lydia Henson	7-28-1825
RAMBAUGH, William to Anna Aldridge	1-28-1819
RATHBURN, John W. to Roanna	7-24-1821
RAWLES, David to Misses Margaret Johnston	12-28-1819
RAY, John to Dinah Dixon	6-13-1824
REED, Jeremiah R. to Sarah Smith	2-23-1819
REILY, Hugh to Peggy Devere	3-20-1825
RICHARDS, Joseph to Matilda Gillespy	3-16-1824
RICKABACK, Reuben to Mary Martin	1-2-1817
RIDER, Mathew to Nancy Rollins (no day given-rec. 10-14-1816)	Oct. 1816
ROBERTS, Ezekiel W. to Elizabeth Cozad (note: no day given)	Nov. 1818
RODABAUGH, John to Mary Elliott	3-11-1825
SCOTT, Hugh to Susana McCune (note: no day given)	Nov. 1818
SCOTT, James to Nancy White	1-16-1825
SCOTT, Nathaniel to Anny McDowell	12-31-1818

```
SCURLOCK, George to Elizabeth Hanna                              5-26-1825
SCURLOCK, James to Margaret Jenkins                              1-28-1819
SCURLOCK, Joseph to Elenor Stephenson                           6-10-1822
SCURLOCK, Joshua to Martha Long                                 7-29-1819
SEEMONS, Thomas to Margaret Hoffman                             1-19-1825
SHARP, John to Mary Jones                                       8-25-1825
SHEWARD, Nathan to Martha E. Boggs                              3-3-1819
SHIELDS, James to Eliza Moredock                                1-21-1819
SHOEMAKER, John to Mary Burnsides                               3-22-1825
SHRECK, Paul to Bethany Moss                                    3-10-1825
SNOOK, Henry to Susanah Cune                                    1-28-1821
SNOOK, John to Purlina Newton                                   5-20-1824
SNOOK, Matthias to Sarah Creige                                 10-5-1820
SOUTHARD, Vincent to Elenor O'Neil                              12-21-1819
STAR, John to Mary Weas                                         12-25-1820
STEPHENSON, Alexander to Nancy Jenkins                          7-26-1818
STEPHENSON, Alexander to Rhoda Hale                             4-13-1819
STEPHENSON, John S. to Mary Shumate                             5-26-1825
STEPHENSON, Joseph to Elizabeth Bowen  (note: no day given)     Aug. 1818
STEPHENSON, Samuel to Martha McClure                            1-15-1824
STEPHENSON, William to Milley Hale                              2-8-1825
STROUPE (STROUSS), Henry son of John to Tamer Nelson            1-8-1824
STROUPES, Isaac to Nancy Nelson                                 9-18-1825
THOMPSON, Joseph to Sarah Suitor                                3-7-1817
THOMPSON, William to Jane Suitor                                3-2-1817
THRUM, George to Mary Fareling                                  11-16-1820
TIMBERMAN, Paul to Mary Anthony                                 1-23-1825
TURNER, Caleb to Sylvy Bradley                                  9-26-1816
TURNER, William to Mary Dixon                                   4-7-1825
VERNIN, Elisha to Elizabeth Kinnison                            7-25-1816
VERNON, William to Jane Martin                                  7-26-1820
VINSON, Malachi to Catharine Brown                              8-18-1825
WALDEAN, George to Charlotte Morley                             2-17-1825
WALDREN, Phillip to Bythama Moss                                4-29-1824
WALDREN, Solomon to Susanna Cassill                             8-26-1824
WALLES, John to Jane Nelson                                     10-5-1820
WARE, William to Mary Vernon                                    12-1-1825
WELLMAN, James to Peggy Wetsel                                  10-20-1825
WESTFALL, Eli to Ruth Jones                                     9-20-1818
WHETSEL, John to Massee Braley                                  12-29-1825
WHITE, James to Nancy Masters                                   11-25-1825
WHITE, John to Elizabeth Clark                                  10-8-1818
WILSON, James to Michal Gilem                                   7-6-1825
WILSON, Joseph to Jane Hanna                                    2-10-1820
WINTERS, William of Athens Co. to Anne Shook of Jackson Co.     8-14-1825
WOODEN, Samuel to Hathander hughes                              10-28-1820
WYMAN (WIMAN), John to Nancy Johnson                            1-23-1820
```

JACKSON COUNTY, OHIO - DEATH RECORDS 1867-1871

The following records were taken from "Death Record Book A" located in the court house at Jackson. Page on which the original record may be found is given in parenthesis. Only persons 40 years of age and over were copied. Abbreviations used: d-died; a-aged; m-married; w-widow or widower; s-single; pd-place of death; pb-place of birth; res-residence. Residence is same as place of death unless stated.

HARRIS, Hannah - d 7-25-1867; a 50y; w;pd Jackson Co.; pb-------. (2)
WILLIAMS, Jane - d 9-21-1867; a 56y; m; pd Lawrence Co.; pb Wales; res. Washington twp., Lawrence Co., Ohio. (2)
WILLIAMS, David - d 7-19-1867; a 80y; pd Jackson Co.; pb Wales. (2)
JONES, Jane - d 9-28-1867; a 56y; m; pd Lawrence Co.; pb Wales; res. Washington twp., Lawrence Co., Ohio. (2)
SCOTT, Abijah - d 8-1-1867; a 54-8-2; m; pd Jackson Co.; pb Virginia. (2)
SILVY, Netty S. - d 12-12-1867; a 45y; m; pd Jackson Co.; pb--------. (2)
EVANS, Reece - d 1-31-1868; a 91y; pd Bloomfield; pb Wales. (2)
MORGAN, David D. - 6-5-1868; a 64y; m; pd Jefferson twp.; pb Wales. (4)
HUGHES, Elizabeth - d 8-17-1868; a 50y; w; pd Madison twp.; pb Wales. (4)
LEWIS, Jane - d 9-6-1868; a 70y; w; pd Madison twp.; pb Wales. (4)
HARRIS, Elizabeth - d 8-10-1868; a 48y; m; pd Milton twp.; po Virginia. (4)
DAVIES, Mary - d 10-1-1868; a 48y; pd Jefferson twp.; pb Wales. (4)
MORGANS, Peter - d 10-29-1868; a 67y; pd Jefferson twp.; pb Wales. (4)
SCURLOCK, J. - d 12-6-1868; a 65y; pd Bloomfield; pb-----. (4)
VANDIVERT, Martin - d 9-27-1869; a62y 1m; pd Liberty; pb Jackson Co. (6)
BEHEM, John - d 12-9-1869; a 74y 3d; m; pd Lick twp.; pb Virginia. (6)
HILL, John J. - d 1-18-1870; a 59-5-11; m; pd Liberty twp.; pb Jackson Co. (6)
COPELAND, Minor A. - d 2-8-1870; a 66y 4m; m; pd Liberty twp.; pb Virginia. (6)
HOWELL, Moses A. - d 11-17-1869; a 51-11-12; m; pd Liberty twp.; pb Gallia Co., O. (6)
GORDON, James - d 4-11-1869; a 68-11-5; m; pd Liberty twp.; pb Liberty twp., Jackson Co. (6)
SCANTILIA, Dalilah - d 8-16-1869; a 56-8-17; w; pd Washington; pb Guernsey Co. (6)
JOHNSON, William J. - d 10-23-1869; a 42-8-19; m; pd Jackson Co.; pb Jackson Co. (6)
CARTER, Benjamin F. - d 8-3-1869; a 89y; pd Jackson Co.; pb Virginia. (6)
DAVIS, David D. - d 3-22-1870; a 75-7-17; m; pd Jackson Co.; pb Wales. (6)
SULLIVAN, Margaret H. - d 7-20-1869; a 74y; a 74y; m; pd Jackson; pb Jackson. (8)
DICKERSON, Lydia - d 7-22-1869; a 46-2-22; m; pd Gallia Co.; pb Virginia; res. Jackson Co. (8)
RICHARDSON, Jane - d 3-22-1870; a 78-1-22; w; pd Jackson Co.; pb Virginia. (8)
WIDNER, John G. - 5-2-1870; a 70-8-3; w; pd Jackson Co.; pd German. (8)
WILLIAMS, Jeremiah O. - d 3-28-1870; a 74-2-21; m; pd Jackson Co.; pb------. (8)
HUNT, James - d 12-1-1869; a 41-7-20; m; pd Madison twp.; pb Ohio. (8)
GRIFFITH, Hannah - d 4-20-1870; a 70y; w; pd Madison twp.; pb Wales. (8)
EVANS, Elizabeth - d 2-5-1870; a 60y; m; pd Madison twp.; pb Wales. (8)
JONES, Thomas Y. - d 6-11-1869 a 85y; m; pd Madison twp.; pb Wales. (8)
JONES, Ann - d 2-27-1870; a 65y 1d; w; pd Madison twp.; pb Wales. (8)
McCULGAN, William - d 1-20-1870; a 71y 1m; m; pd Madison twp.; pb not known. (8)
DAVIS, Samuel - d 5-1-1870; a 54y; m; pd Madison twp.; pb Virginia. (8)
HERBERT, Thomas - d 7-27-1869; a 40-2-15; m; pd Madison twp.; pb Madison twp. (8)
COMER, Nancy Ann - d 5-11-1870; a 60y; w; pd Madison twp.; pb Madison twp. (8)
CANTER, Isaac - d 12-6-1869; a 64-3-10; m; pd Jefferson twp.; pb Jefferson twp. (8)

659

DAVIS, Mary C. - d 8-21-1869; a 62-4-21; m; pd Jefferson twp.; pb Wales. (8)
HORTON, John - d 6-6-1869; a 83-2-12; m; pd Jefferson twp.; pb Virginia. (10)
JENKINS, David - d 7-30-1869; a 77-1-14; m; pd Jefferson twp.; pb Wales. (10)
GRIFFITHS, Elisabeth - d 12-10-1870; a 76-7-26; m; pd Jefferson twp.; pb Wales. (10)
CAMPBELL, Jane - d 3-28-1870; a 61-2-12; m; pd Jefferson twp.; pb Virginia. (10)
MORGAN, Mary - d 7-15-1869; a 64y 15d; m; pd Jefferson twp.; pb Wales. (10)
PHILLIPS, Daniel - d 3-25-1870; a 75y; m; pd Bloomfield twp.; pb South Wales,
    G. B. (10)
SCURLOCK, Elizabeth - d 12-12-1869; a 69-1-15; m; pd Bloomfield twp.; pb Greenbier
    Co., Va. (10)
KERR, Robert - d 6-30-1869; a 76-2-15; m; pd Bloomfield twp.; pd Washington Co.,
    Pa. (10)
HALE, Permelia - d 9-12-1869; a. 33y 2m; m; pd Bloomfield twp.; pb Gallia Co.,
    O. (10)
EVANS, Margaret H. - d 12-20-1869; a-?-; pd Bloomfield twp.; pb South Wales, G. B.
    (10)
BUTLER, Henry - d 12-12-1869; a 46y 9m; m; pd Bloomfield twp.; pb Pennsylvania. (10)
McCOY, Michael - d 11-8-1869; a 69y; m; pd Hamilton twp.; pb Lawrence Co., O. (10)
CAUTER, Catharine - d 6-4-1869; a 58y; m; pd Hamilton twp.; pb Penn. (10)
STEELE, William B. - Mar. 1870; a 59y; w; pd Jackson Co.; pb Virginia. (12)
LAW, Martha - d March (1869-70?); a 48y;m; pd Jackson Co.; pb Jackson Co. (12)
HUNSINGER, Samuel - d June 1869; a 76y; m; pd Lick twp.; pb Switzerland. (12)
UMPHRIES, Elizabeth - d June 1869; a 76y; w; pd Lick twp.; pb East Virginia. (12)
McCLUNG, Alice - d Jany 1870; a 65y; m; pd Lick twp.; pb Pa. (12)
McGHEE, Gaston - d Feby 1870; a 68y; m; pd Lick twp.; pb East Virginia. (12)
NAIL, Mary - d Jany 1870; a 87y; w; pd Lick twp.; pb East Virginia. (12)
KEES, Thomas - d Feb. 1870; a 95y; m; pd Lick twp.; pb Ireland. (12)
BEHEM, John - d Dec. 1869; a 74y; m; pd Lick twp.; pb East Va. (12)
RITCHIE, Mary - d Oct. 1869; a 75y; w; pd Lick twp.; pb Pa. (12)
GRIFFITH, Edward - d Feb. 1870; a 41y; m; pd Lick twp.; pb Wales. (12)
BURKE, Walter U. - d Jany 1870; a 43y; m; pd Portsmouth, O., pb Ohio; res.
    Lick twp. (12)
WALKER, Elizabeth - d Mar. 1870; a 84y; w; pd Lick twp.; pb Maryland. (12)
EASTMAN (or CASTMAN), Emma - d Feby 1870; a 40y; m; pd Lick twp.; pb Bavaria. (12)
LONG, Andrew - Nov. 1869; a 59y; m; pd Lick twp.; pb Ohio. (12)
NEAL, John - d Aug. 1869; a 45y; m; pd Milton twp.; pb Pa. (14)
LONG, Isaac M. - d Aug. 1869; a 60y; pd Milton twp.; pb Ohio. (14)
CAUTER, Nancy - d 7-3-1870; a 43y; m; pd Hamilton twp.; pb Lawrence Co., O. (18)
HAVENS, Sarah - d 3-9-1871; a 58y 11m; m; pd Hamilton twp.; pb Tyrrel Co., Va. (18)
McCORKLE, Andrew - d 1-21-1871; pd Hamilton twp.; pb Virginia. (18)
CALL, John - d-----1870; a 49-2-3; m; pd Madison twp.; pb Penn. (18)
DAVIS, Samuel - d 5-1-1870; a 54y 6m; m; pd Madison twp.; pb Virginia. (18)
DAVIS, Morgan - d 7-18-1870; a 58-7-15; m; pd Madison twp.; pb Wales. (18)
DAVIS, Sarah - d 7-18-1870; a 55-10-11; m; pd Madison twp.; pb Wales. (18)
DAVIS, Evan J. - 9-30-1870; a 40y; s; pd Madison twp.; pb Wales. (18)
DAVIS, John B. - d 10-3-1870; a 70y 8m;m ;pdMadison twp.; pb Wales. (18)
EDWARDS, Evan J. - d 12-7-1870; a 58y 17d; m; pd Madison twp.; pb Wales. (18)
GILBERT, John R. - d 10-13-1870; a 45y; 10m; m; pd Madison twp.; pb Virginia. (18)
VAUGHTERS, Nancy - d 8-8-1870; a 52-11-8; m; pd Washington twp.; pb Virginia. (20)
CLUAR(?), Mary - d 10-26-1870; a 73-10-1; m; pd Franklin twp.; pb Penn. (20)
CLUAR(?), Lydia - d 7-25-1870; a 63-10-1; pd Franklin twp.; pb Penn. (20)

FRENCH, Abraham - d 7-27-1870; a 62-7-27; m; pd Jackson twp.; pb Virginia. (20)
HANNA, James - d 10-1-1870; a 48-9-26; m; pd Bloomfield twp.; pb Jackson Co.,
   O. (20)
HAINSEY, Michael - d 12-1-1870; a 65-10-12; m; pd Bloomfield twp.; pb Westmore-
   land Co., Pa. (20)
HAINSEY, Elizabeth - d 1-16-1871; a 64-6-12; w; pd Bloomfield twp.; pb Blair
   Co., Pa. (20)
EVANS, Elijah - d 7-3-1870; a 70-4-11; m; pd Scioto twp.; pb Virginia. (22)
EMLER, Margaret - d 2-17-1871; a 65y; m; pd Scioto twp. - pb Pennsylvania. (22)
LESSER, Anna - d 8-15-1870; a 41-9-15; pd Scioto twp.; pb Ohio. (22)
SHRIVER, Elizabeth - d 3-20-1871; a 77-7-10; m; pd Scioto twp.; pb Maryland. (22)
JOPE, John - d 2-28-1871; a 73-11-11; m; pd Scioto twp.; pb Ohio. (22)
WILLIAMS, Jeremiah - d 4-19-1871; a 75-7-7; m; pd Scioto twp.; pb Virginia. (22)
ZINSMASTER, Margaret - d 2-15--1871; a 76-8-10; w; pd Scioto twp.; pb Germany. (22)
CULP, Mary - d 10-7-1871; a 80-2-11; w; pd Scioto twp.; pb Pennsylvania. (22)
ELLIOTT, John - d 12-17-1871; a 81-1-18; w; pd Milton twp.; pb West Va. (22)
WILSON, John T. - d---1871; a 50y; m; pd Buckeye furnace; pb------. (22)
DAVIS, John G. - d 1-8-1871; a 84y; m; pd Jefferson twp.; pb Cardigan Shire,
   Wales. (22)
HORTON, James - d 3-29-1871; a 62-5-22; m; pd Jefferson twp.; pb Virginia. (24)
HAMER, John Sr. - d 1-12-1871; a 59-2-25; m; pd Jefferson twp.; pb England. (24)
LLOYD, Mary D. - d 9-25-1870; a 82y; w; pd Jefferson twp.; pb Wales. (24)
NEFF, Elizabeth - 11-10-1870; a 60y; w; pd Jefferson twp.; pb Pennsylvania. (24)
SLATER, Young - d 7-14-1870; a 80-5-3; m; pd Jefferson twp.; pb Jefferson twp. (24)
DUDLEY, Elizabeth - d 2-10-1871; a 70-1-6; m; pd Jackson C.H.; pb Virginia. (24)
McKITTERICK, Thomas - d Jan. 1871; a 80y; m; pd Lick twp.; pb Ireland. (24)
STEELE, William - 4-1-1870; a 58-9-26; s; pd Jackson C.H.; pb Virginia. (24)
TILLEY, Foster - d 12-3-1870; a 80y; w; pd Lick twp.; pb North Carolina. (24)

The information below includes the name of the person receiving the land patent, book and page on which record may be found--Example: C-317=Deed Book C, page 317. If a number in parenthesis follows the page number, it indicates that more than one record is included on the page for the same person.--Example: H-357[(2)]=two land patents found on this page for the person named.
Location: Recorder's Office, Court House, Jackson, Ohio.

665

The following wills are all recorded in Will Book A located in the Probate Court. It should be noted that no wills were recorded vetween approximately 1819 and 1829, possibly there weren't any as all estates may have been intestate. The first column refers to testator, second column to date will was recorded (unless date of recording was not given, then date will was made is given preceded by a "d"), third column is page on which record may be found in Will Book A.

ADAMS, Richard	1841	43	DONNALLY, Andrew	d1815	3
ALBANS, Alban	1847	76	of Gallia Co., Ohio		
ALESHIRE, Peter	1847	77	EAGON, Hannah	1849	95
ANDREWS, James	1846	70	EDWARDS, Rees	1845	61
ANTHONY, Elizabeth	1834	20	ELDER, Robert	1836	23
ANTHONY, George	1833	15	ERVIN, James	1831	13
ANTHONY, Jacob	1853	145	of Greenbrier Co., Va.		
BAKER, Abraham	1819	1	ERVIN, Thomas	1836	52
BAMBOROUGH, Allen	1841	44	EVANS, Rees	1851	118
BARTON, Sharp	1841	41	FARLEY, Matt	1854	158
BEARDSLEE, Nehamiah	1834	17	FARRAR, Peter	1850	115
BECK, John	1851	123	FAULKNER, Absalom M.	1829	4
BOLLES, David C.	1840	38	FEERCE, John	1845	62
BORIER, Peter	1839	33	FLEMING, Andrew	1849	108
BROWN, George	1849	94	FORD, Isaiah N.	1851	127
BROWN, Jane	1850	111	FOWLEY, John	1847	80
BROWN, Nathan	1844	50	GILLELAND, John Berrisford	1849	105
BROWN, Robert Sr.	1845	58	GILLELAND, Samuel	1852	134
BUCK, Charles J.	1852	140	GRIFFETH, Elias	1849	92
CALLAGHAN, John	1852	142	HALTERMAN, Christian	1851	122
CASSILL, Henry Sr.	d1811	2	HALTERMAN, Daniel Sr.	1849	97
of Ross Co., Ohio			HAMILTON, William	1852	141
CHERINGTON, Lorenzo D.	1852.	139	HANK, Thomas P.	1847	84
CLARK, John	1851	128	HARKLESS, Aaron	1848	125
CORN, John R.	d1828	4	of Morgan Co., Ohio		
CRABTREE, Thomas	1850	110	HENRY, John	1848	85
CROUCH, Amy	1848	90	HOW, John	d1817	1
CROUCH, Joseph	1837	91	JAMES, John	1854	159
CUTTER, William	1851	126	JOHNSON, James	1837	25
DANIELS, Kelley	1849	109	JOHNSTON, Robert	1850	109
DARLING, Thomas	1831	9	JONES, Owen	1852	131
DAVIS, Jane D.	1853	168	JONES, William	1849	96
DAVIS, John	1849	99	KELLY, John	1842	45
DAVIS, Lewis	1838	30	KENNADY, Ambrose	1847	82
DAVIS, Mary	1854	156	KENNADY, Ezekiel	1851	117
DAVIS, Samuel	1841	41	KIPP, John D. W.	1844	53
DELONG, Isaac	1852	136	LACKEY, James	1853	152
DEVER, James	1845	57	LEACH, Lewis	1838	29
DILL, Andrew	1830	8	LIVESY, Sterling	1833	11
DIMICK, Erastus	1853	150	LLOYD, Edward	1844	54
DIXON, Abraham	1853	151	LOTT, Abel	1839	34
DOANE, Francis E.	1849	104	LUCUS, Robert	1838	35
			McCLURE, Samuel	1846	68

McGHEE, Lively	1843	48	SCHELLENGER, Joseph	1840	39
McGILLURAY, Daniel	1853	166	SELL, Adam	1849	100
McKINNIS, Charles	1837	24	SHEARER, Patrick	1847	74
MACKLEY, John Sr.	1848	86	SHOEMAKER, Jacob	1846	69
MARTIN, Hugh	1853	146	SILVESTER, John	1842	46
MARTINDILL, Moses	1849	106	SMITH, Elizabeth	1846	71
MAYNARD, Luther	1847	78	SMITH, James	1849	102
MERCER, Joseph	1834	19	SPRIGGS, Daniel Sr.	1846	64
MERCER, Robert	1851	124	SPURLOCK, Andrew	1847	81
MINCKS, Hiram	1854	173	STEPHENSON, Andrew	1834	16
MORGAN, Morgan	1854	171	STEPHENSON, James	1846	67
MORRIS, Morris	1845	56	STRAIN, Elihu W.	1846	73
MURRAY, Thomas J.	1848	88	SWANEY, John	1851	121
MUSGROVE, Elijah	1854	169	THOMAS, John	1854	154
NEWELL, Albert (Hilbert)	1829	7	VANXCOY, Jonathan	1852	132
OGIER, James	1841	39	WALL, Elizabeth	1848	89
OLIVER, Thomas	1844	51	WEBER, Melcher	1853	148
PARY, David	1841	42	WELLS, John	1845	63
PHILLIPS, John	1843	49	WEST, John	1839	34
PHILLIPS, Thomas M.	1846	72	WHETSELL, John	1829	5
PHIPP, Nathaniel	1852	138	WHETSTONE, John	1849	93
POYNTON, William	1854	175	WHITE, John	1835	27
PYLES, Ayres	1845	55	WILLIAMS, John	1851	119
RADENBAUGH, Jesse	1846	66	WISHON, William	1847	79
READ, Downey	1830	8	WOODS, William	1854	161
REED, William.	1839	31	of Holmes Co., Ohio		
RICE, George	1851	113	YEAGER, Philip	1847	84
RICHARDS, John	1850	112			

BAPTISMS - First Presbyterian Church formerly Indian Short
Creek Church, Mt. Pleasant, Jefferson County, Ohio 1833-1870

The following records were taken from "The First Presbyterian Church Mt. Pleasant,
Ohio formerly The Indian Short Creek Congregation 1798-1948". Located in Jefferson
County, Mt. Pleasant lies just a short distance north of the Jefferson-Belmont
County line. Although the above mentioned church history and records is in published form, but not copyrighted, it seems that copies are not too numerous. We offer
our sincere thanks to Julie Overton of Yellow Springs, Ohio for her assistance,
through which we are able to share these records. Although not specified, the
asterisk (*) appears to indicate adults.

Name	Date	Parents
ALAWAYS, Alexander	5-28-1860	
ALAWAYS, Ann Florence	5-28-1860	
ALLAWAYS, Emily	10-24-1857	
ALEXANDER, Alonza Jane	10-26-1842	Nancy Alexander
ALEXANDER, Alphenon Americas	10-26-1842	Peter Alexander
ALEXANDER, Elvy May	1-11-1866	Athelbert Alexander
ALEXANDER, Elvira Isabella	10-26-1842	Peter Alexander
ALEXANDER, Ethelbert Janus	10-26-1842	Nancy Alexander
ALEXANDER, James Wilson	Dec. 1844-45	Peter Alexander
ALEXANDER, Josephine Catherine	10-26-1842	Peter Alexander
ALEXANDER, Lucinda Adalade	10-26-1842	Peter Alexander
ALEXANDER, Martha Melissa	6-4-1847	Peter Alexander
ALEXANDER, Rachel	Mar. 1833	
ALEXANDER, Rachel Ann	10-26-1842	Peter Alexander
ALEXANDER, Revanda Austin	5-12-1870	A. J. Alexander
ALEXANDER, Smiley Ross	Sept. 1838	John Alexander
ALEXANDER, William Humphrey	11-20-1837	Thomas Alexander
ALLIN, Rolin Leroy	5-15-1865	
AMRINE, Esther Maria	8-28-1840	Henry Amrine
AMRINE, Henry Hosak	10-19-1842	Henry Amrine
AMRINE, Mary Angeline	May 1833	Henry Amrine
AMRINE, Nancy Isobel	8-28-1839	Henry Amrine
AMRINE, Nannee Loretta	6-9-1862	Robits (Robert) Amrine
AMRINE, Robert Frederic	Sept. 1837	Henry Amrine
BECK, Anthony	8-19-1849	Martha Beck
BECK, Elizabeth	8-19-1849	Martha Beck
BECK, John Brown	8-19-1849	Martha Beck
BENNET, Harriet*	2-15-1864	
BLACKFORD, James Mitchell	5-26-1837	Joseph Blackford
BLACKFORD, Jane E.*	9-7-1842	
BLACKFORD, John Hosac	5-26-1835	Joseph Blackford
BLACKFORD, Joseph Anderson	10-31-1854	W. H. Blackford
BLACKFORD, Robert Allin	Nov. 1833	Joseph Blackford
BLACKFORD, William Paden	11-1-1856	W. H. Blackford
BLAIR, Joseph	5-25-1839	Robert Blair
BRACKEN, Joseph P.*	2-15-1864	
BRACKEN, Joseph Willard	5-7-1866	J. Plummer Bracken
BRACKEN, Oliver Morton*	2-15-1864	

Name	Date	Parents
BRACKEN, Sarah Emma*	2-15-1864	
BROWN, Bell*	10-19-1867	
BROWN, Elizabeth*	6-6-1864	
BROWN, Sarah	----1833	Simon Brown Jr.
CAROTHERS, Minerva	2-23-1867	E. J. Carothers
CHAMBERS, Catherine Ann*	3-5-1858	
CHAMBERS, Elizabeth K.*	5-28-1860	
CHAMBERS, John*	2-15-1864	
CHAMBERS, Robert W.*	5-28-1860	
COLWELL, Ella Elizabeth	6-9-1867	
COLWELL, John Logan	6-9-1867	
COLWELL, Margaret Ann	6-9-1867	
DEAN, David Robinson	9-21-1840	Abram Dean
DEAN, Marjerty*	-----1833	
DEAN, Soffia*	-----1833	
DESSEL, Gertrude*	2-15-1864	
DICKEY, Kezia*	5-16-1840	
DICKEY, Margaret J.	10-1-1869	D. L. Dickey, M.M. Dickey
DRENNEN, Eugene James Alex.	5-14-1849	J. H. Drennen
DRENNEN, Genetta Ezilbella	5-13-1845	James Drennen
DRENNEN, Isabella*	5-13-1843	
DRENNEN, Lycurgas John Clark	10-5-1846	James Drennen
DRENNEN, Mary	10-26-1842	James Drennen
DRENNEN, Jane	10-26-1842	James Drennen
DRENNEN, Margaritta	10-26-1842	James Drennen
DRENNEN, Miney Lawretta	1-28-1859	James H. Drennen
DRENNEN, Peter Ross Jefferson	1-28-1859	James H. Drennen
DUTTON, Mary Lizzie*	2-15-1864	
ENOCH, Alexander Campbell*	2-15-1864	
EWING, Lyddia*	Mar. 1833	
FINLEY, Celestina Caroline*	2-15-1864	
FOGLE, Sarah Ann*	2-26-1869	
GIFFEN, Albert Elsworth	10-6-1862	James Giffen
GIFFEN, Elizabeth*	10-26-1857	
GIFFEN, James*	10-24-1857	
GIFFEN, Martha	11-6-1835	John Giffen
GIFFEN, _____(not given)	Sept. 1838	John Giffen
GILMORE, Anna Virginia	9-19-1858	
GILMORE, Feeby Jane	10-21-1850	
GILMORE, Hannah Sophia	5-14-1849	
GILMORE, James Dunlap	5-14-1849	
HAGENE, Edward	Nov. 1833	Edward Hagene
HAMILTON, Thomas	5-24-1847	James Hamilton
HANES, Benjamin Mitchell	6-10-1856	Samuel Hanes
HANES, Harriet Luisa	10-5-1846	Samuel Hanes
HANES, James Clark	10-5-1846	Samuel Hanes
HANES, Jemima Angaline	4-25-1853	Samuel Hanes

Name	Date	Parents
HANES, John Thomas Bracken	10-21-1850	Samuel Hanes
HANES, Rebecca*	5-10-1845	
HANES, Samuel*	10-3-1846	
HANLEY, Martha Ellen	6-1-1868	
HAPKIRK, Ann	7-30-1840	William Hapkirk
HAPKIRK, William	8-10-1839	William Hapkirk
HARISON, Benjamin Mitchell	12-5-1853	William Harison
HARPER, Ann Cooper	Mar. 1833	Joseph Harper
HAWTHORNE, Mary Ann*	3-5-1858	
HAWTHORNTWAIT, Mary Isabell	10-31-1858	Smithson Hawthorntwait
HAWTHORNTWAIT, William Alex.	10-31-1858	Smithson Hawthorntwait
HICKS, Henrietta Hone	9-19-1858	Josephine Hicks
HIGGINS, Maria	6-2-1834	Edward Higgins
HIGGIN, _____(not given)	Mar. 1838	Edward Higgins
HIGGINS, John	9-1-1839	Edward Higgins
HIGGINS, Susanna	5-16-1836	Edward Higgins
HOGG, Miriam*	Mar. 1833	
HOOPER, John	Nov. 1833	Frances Hooper
HOPE, Charles Duncan	9-26-1864	Richard Hope
HOPE, William Stringer	6-9-1862	Richard Hope
HUMPHREVILLE, Julianna*	3-5-1858	
HUMPHREVILLE, Susana*	5-12-1851	
JONES, Mrs. Hariet*	5-23-1839	
JONES, Leander	5-25-1839	Amos Jones
JONES, Mary Anne	5-25-1839	Amos Jones
JONES, Martha Jane	5-25-1839	Amos Jones
JONES, Robert Wiley	10-19-1842	Amos Jones
JONES, Samuel Woodmancy	5-18-1840	Amos Jones
JORDEN (JORDAN), Alex. Ross	6-29-1862	P.(Potter) Jorden (Jordan)
JORDEN, Mary Ann Augusta	10-31-1854	Potter Jorden
JORDEN, Thomas Steel	4-16-1859	J. P. Jorden
KING, Charles Rufus*	2-15-1864	
KING, Robert*	2-15-1864	
KINNARD, Elenor*	3-7-1856	
KINSEY, Alphis I.*	6-6-1864	
KINSEY, Amos*	6-6-1864	
KITHCART, Catherine (Kate)*	1-28-1859	
KITHCART, Elizabeth Ann*	1-28-1859	
KITHCART, Elizabeth Jane	5-28-1860	
KITHCART, Anna Catherine	Sept. 1862	
KITHCART, Henry Comings	11-8-1852	Elizabeth Kithcart
KITHCART, Jessie Bertha	5-16-1865	
KITHCART, Joseph A.*	2-15-1864	
KITHCART, Mary	11-26-1855	
KITHCART, Mary Elizabeth	5-13-1845	Joseph Kithcart
KITHCART, Rebecca	5-13-1845	Joseph Kithcart
KITHCART, Robert Sherrard	10-21-1850	Elizabeth Kithcart

Name	Date	Parents
KITHCART, Sara Louisa	5-13-1845	Joseph Kithcart
KITHCART, Sarah K.	2-15-1864	
KITHCART, William Smiley	2-23-1867	
KITHCART, Martha Ellen*	2-15-1864	
KITHCART, Martha Ellen	Nov. 1867	
KITHCART, Martha Hellen	5-13-1845	Joseph Kithcart
KITHCART, Mary Althiza*	10-19-1867	
LATTIMER, John Calvin	7-8-1836	James Lattimer
LATTIMER, Nancy Brown	7-8-1836	James Lattimer
LATTIMER, William Henry	7-8-1836	
LAWSON, Henrietta A.*	5-13-1843	
LENNING, Hannah Maria	7-27-1845	Margaret Lenning
LIGHTNER, Rachel*	9-15-1843	
LINDSAY, Carson	7-30-1840	
LINDSAY, George	7-10-1842	
LINDSEY, Susan Mary	10-18-1845	
LYLE, Alfred	Mar. 1834	John Lyle
LYLE, Elizabeth	Mar. 1834	John Lyle
LYLE, Elizabeth*	5-23-1839	
LYLE, Jacob*	5-23-1829	
LYLE, Frances	9-4-1840	Jacob Lyle
LYLE, Hannah	9-4-1840	Jacob Lyle
LYLE, Jacob	9-4-1840	Jacob Lyle
LYLE, John	Mar. 1834	John Lyle
LYLE, Katherine*	Mar. 1833	
LYLE, Mary Ann	9-4-1840	Jacob Lyle
LYLE, Sarah Jane	9-4-1840	Jacob Lyle
LYLE, William	Mar. 1834	John Lyle
MADIUS, Andrew McMahan	May 1833	Jeremiah Madius
MAJOR, Adison	5-24-1847	Thomas Major
MAJOR, Archibald Cooper	10-31-1854	John Major
MAJOR, Clarissa Jane	10-18-1867	John A. Major
MAJOR, Elizabeth Clark	5-18-1840	John Major
MAJOR, Erastus	5-20-1850	Thomas Major
MAJOR, James Francis	6-26-1854	Thomas Major
MAJOR, John McCoy	6-4-1847	John Major
MAJOR, Maggie Hannah	6-1-1863	John A. Major
MAJOR, Mary	5-31-1852	Thomas Major
MAJOR, Mary Catherine	1-11-1866	John A. Major
MAJOR, Mary Jane	----1844	Arch Major
MAJOR, Martha Bogs	5-12-1854	John A. Major
MAJOR, Rebecca Jane	10-24-1857	Thomas Major
MAJOR, Robert Lemon	5-25-1839	Arch Major Jr.
MAJOR, Ruth Ann	7-15-1842	Arch Major
MAJOR, Samuel Hawthorne	8-29-1858	John Major
MAJOR, Sarah Adeliza	5-16-1836	John Major (Elder)
MAJOR, Thomas Carson	5-16-1843	John Major

671

Name	Date	Parents
MAJOR, Thomas Ramsey	11-1-1856	John A. Major
MAJOR, William Alexander	9-23-1861	John Major
MAXWELL, Franklin Collins*	2-15-1864	
MEDILL, Elizabeth Ellen	Sept. 1843	Nancy Medill
MEDILL, Fleming	7-15-1842	
MEDILL, George Washington	7-15-1842	
MEDILL, Joseph	7-30-1840	
MEDILL, Margaret Ann	7-15-1842	
MEDILL, Mary Jane	7-15-1842	
MEDILL, Nancy Caroline	10-18-1845	
MEDILL, Thomas	1-9-1861	
MEDILL, William	7-15-1842	
MILLER, Mary Adaline	9-18-1843	R. H. Miller, Esq.
MILLER, Robert Hughs	9-18-1843	R. H. Miller, Esq.
MILLIGAN, Anna Mary	6-13-1862	George Milligan, Mary Milligan
MILLIGAN, George Francis	6-13-1862	George Milligan, Mary Milligan
MILLIGAN, Mary Isadore	6-13-1862	George Milligan, Mary Milligan
MILNER, Anna M.*	5-28-1860	
MILNER, William Alexander*	2-15-1864	
MILNER, Lizzie*	2-2-1868	
MITCHELL, Albon	10-3-1853	
MITCHELL, Andrew Dinsmore	-----1833	Rev. B. Mitchell
MITCHELL, ____(?)	8-4-1834	John Mitchell
MITCHELL, Catherine	1-6-1839	Mary Mitchell
MITCHELL, Catherine*	9-7-1842	
MITCHELL, Demaratus Benjamin	10-26-1842	Thomas Mitchell
MITCHELL, Eleanor Beatty	10-19-1842	Jane Ann Mitchell
MITCHELL, Elizabeth Leanore	5-28-1860	
MITCHELL, Emedatha Catherine	5-13-1845	Thomas Mitchell
MITCHELL, George Smith	5-12-1857	
MITCHELL, Hariot	1-6-1839	Mary Mitchell
MITCHELL, James Algernon	Sept. 1838	Jane Ann Mitchell
MITCHELL, James Clark	9-30-1839	Mary Mitchell
MITCHELL, James Clark	9-15-1845	John Mitchell
MITCHELL, James Smiley	8-28-1840	Martha Mitchell
MITCHELL, John	10-5-1846	Jane Ann Mitchell
MITCHELL, John Americas	8-18-1839	Martha Mitchell
MITCHELL, John Thomas Porter	8-22-1848	John P. Mitchell
MITCHELL, John F. Hogg	5-15-1846	Vincent Mitchell
MITCHELL, Joseph Ethin	9-21-1840	Jane Ann Mitchell
MITCHELL, Lavinia	5-26-1837	Jane Ann Mitchell
MITCHELL, Maadell	11-26-1855	Jane Ann Mitchell
MITCHELL, Margaret Alexander	5-16-1836	Mary Mitchell
MITCHELL, Mary Angeline	1-6-1839	Mary Mitchell
MITCHELL, Mary Melisa	4-20-1836	John Mitchell
MITCHELL, Matthew Clark	7-4-1841	John P. Mitchell
MITCHELL, Myrtilla Ella	3-12-1851	John Mitchell

Name	Date	Parents
MITCHELL, Nancy Marion	5-25-1839	Vincent Mitchell
MITCHELL, Rachel Jane	8-28-1839	Martha Mitchell
MITCHELL, Rachel Jane	10-19-1841	Vincent Mitchell
MITCHELL, Robert Nelson	10-7-1838	John Mitchell
MITCHELL, Ross Andrews	9-19-1858	Jane Ann Mitchell
MITCHELL, Samuel Martin	9-25-1836	Rev. B. Mitchell
MITCHELL, Susanna*	2-5-1838	
MITCHELL, Thomas Jefferson	5-13-1845	Jane Ann Mitchell
MITCHELL, William	5-14-1849	
MOOR, John McCormick	5-15-1843	Andrew Moor
MOOR, Samuel Alexander	5-13-1845	Andrew Moor
MURDOCK, Abigal Ann	5-14-1849	Thomas Murdock
MURDOCK, Arch Major	9-30-1839	George Murdock
MURDOCK, Arthur	10-26-1842	Thomas Murdock
MURDOCK, Arthur James	7-4-1841	George Murdock
MURDOCK, Elizabeth Hubbert	10-18-1845	Thomas Murdock
MURDOCK, George*	9-28-1839	
MURDOCK, George	9-30-1839	Thomas Murdock
MURDOCK, James Fleming	7-4-1841	Thomas Murdock
MURDOCK, Robert Thomas	5-28-1860	Thomas Murdock
MURDOCK, Thomas*	9-28-1839	
McCLURE, James	11-8-1852	Lewis McClure
McCLURE, Lewis*	11-8-1852	
McCLURE, Louisena	11-8-1852	Lewis McClure
McCLURE, Martha Lewellen	11-8-1852	Lewis McClure
McCLURE, Mary E. Brown	11-8-1852	Lewis McClure
McCLURE, Samuel Lewis	11-8-1852	Lewis McClure
McCLURE, Sarah*	11-8-1852	
McCLURE, William Mitchell	11-8-1852	Lewis McClure
McCONAHEY, Margaret McCune	Sept. 1843	Samuel McConahey
McCONAHEY, Nancy Clark	7-4-1841	Samuel McConahey
McCONAHEY, Thomas Mitchell	9-15-1845	Samuel McConahey
McCONNEL, William Thomas	6-1-1863	James McConnel
McCORMICK, Hanah Maria	11-18-1835	Hannah McCormick
McCUNE, Elizabeth	6-2-1834	James McCune, Esq.
McCUNE, James	9-2-1834	Thomas McCune
McCUNE, Mary	before 1833	James McCune
McCUNE, Agness Adeline	8-22-1848	James McCune
McCUNE, Albert Elsworth	9-23-1861	
McCUNE, Caroline McCormick	5-15-1846	Joseph McCune
McCUNE, Catherine Ann	9-18-1843	James McCune
McCUNE, Emiline Whitely	5-18-1840	James McCune
McCUNE, George Gillespie	3-27-1842	James McCune
McCUNE, Henry Russel	10-31-1854	Adam McCune
McCUNE, Jessie Ellen	10-1-1865	
McCUNE, Joseph Addison	1-28-1859	Joseph McCune
McCUNE, Joseph Mitchell	10-21-1850	Joseph McCune

Name	Date	Parents
McCUNE, Josephine	7-27-1845	James McCune
McCUNE, Karenhappuch	1-28-1859	Joseph McCune
McCUNE, Maria Ella	8-22-1848	Joseph McCune
McCUNE, Marcus	5-28-1838	Joseph McCune
McCUNE, Mary Brady	8-22-1848	
McCUNE, Rose Ellen	6-1-1868	William R. McCune
McCUNE, Sarah Jane	9-18-1843	James McCune
McCUNE, Samuel	before 1833	Thomas McCune
McCUNE, Samuel	9-26-1836	Joseph McCune
McCUNE, Sarah Jane	7-20-1838	James McCune
McCUNE, Thomas Benton	5-25-1839	Thomas McCune
McCUNE, Thomas Fleming	5-12-1851	
McCUNE, Valinia	9-30-1839	Joseph McCune
McCUNE, William	9-26-1836	Thomas McCune
McCUNE, William R.*	10-1-1869	
McCUNE, William Robison	8-22-1848	
McCUNE, William Washington	7-16-1836	James McCune
McFARLAND, George Bates	11-1-1856	Susana McFarland
McFARLAND, James Read	11-1-1856	Susana McFarland
McFARLAND, Joseph Hardesty	9-19-1858	Susana McFarland
McFARLAND, Joseph Smith	9-19-1858	Susana McFarland
McGEE, Ellen Emma	10-21-1850	Robert McGee
McGEE, Elizabeth Jane	9-21-1840	Robert McGee
McGEE, Eliza Jane	5-25-1839	James McGee
McGEE, James	5-24-1847	Robert McGee
McGEE, John Chambers	5-13-1845	Robert McGee
McGEE, Lucrettia Ann	5-13-1845	William McGee
McGEE, Margaret*	2-5-1838	
McGEE, Martha	5-25-1839	James McGee
McGEE, Martha Ann	5-25-1839	Robert McGee
McGEE, Martha Cornelia	5-14-1849	William McGee
McGEE, Mary Lucinda	10-19-1842	William McGee
McGEE, Mary Luisa	10-19-1842	Robert McGee
McGEE, Samuel Hare	5-25-1839	James McGee
McGEE, Watson Huze	10-5-1846	William McGee
McHAFFEY, Mary Jane*	4-22-1848	
McHUGH, Elva Retta*	2-27-1837	
McKIM. Thomas*	5-31-1852	
McKIM, Sarah*	5-20-1850	
McMANNIS, Margaret Jane	Sept. 1837	Jacob McMannis
McMANNIS, Sarah*	11-6-1847	
McWILLIAMS, Alexander	9-18-1834	James McWilliams
McWILLIAMS, David	9-18-1834	James McWilliams
MxWILLIAMS, Elizabeth Jane	9-18-1834	James McWilliams
McWILLIAMS, John	9-18-1834	James McWilliams
McWILLIAMS, Rachel	9-18-1834	James McWilliams
NOBLE, Charles*	1-28-1859	

674

OSBORNE, Alexander	5-25-1839	Alexander Osborne
OSBORNE, Amos James	5-25-1839	Alexander Osborne
OSBORNE, Elias James	5-25-1839	Alexander Osborne
OSBORNE, George*	5-23-1839	
OSBORNE, Henry*	5-23-1839	
OSBORNE, James	5-25-1839	Alexander Osborne
OSBORNE, Martha*	5-23-1839	
OSBORNE, Martha Ann	5-25-1839	Alexander Osborne
OSBORNE, Mary Elizabeth	5-25-1839	Alexander Osborne
OSBORNE, Rachel Caroline	5-25-1839	Alexander Osborne
OSBORNE, Thomas	5-25-1839	Alexander Osborne
OSBURN, Arabella	7-4-1841	Alexander Osburn
PASCO, Elizabeth	11-20-1837	Eliza Pasco
PASCO, Martha	5-28-1838	Eliza Pasco
PASCO, Rebecca Ann	11-20-1837	Eliza Pasco
PASCO, William	11-20-1837	Eliza Pasco
PASTERS, John Westley	Nov. 1833	
PASTERS, Silvia	Nov. 1833	
PASTORS, Frances	3-27-1842	Mary Pastors
PASTORS, Stacisa(?) Maria	10-24-1835	
PICKENS, Benjamin Mitchell	Nov. 1833	James Pickens
PICKENS, Dorothy Ellen	before 1833	James Pickens
PICKENS, Hugh Clark	4-24-1836	Thomas Pickens
PICKENS, Hugh Clark	6-9-1862	W.(William) Pickens
PICKENS, Bartley Jamison	11-28-1867	Hugh Pickens
PICKENS, Hugh McConahey	Mar. 1834	John C. Pickens
PICKENS, John Calwell	5-28-1860	William Pickens
PICKENS, John Ross	1-11-1866	Hugh Pickens
PICKENS, Margaret	5-16-1836	James Pickens
PICKENS, Margaret Elizabeth Jennett	5-18-1840	William Pickens
PICKENS, Martha Ada	5-28-1860	Hugh Pickens
PICKENS, Martha Ann Clark	9-1-1839	James Pickens
PICKENS, Mary Genetta	5-13-1845	James Pickens
PICKENS, Robert Harold	6-9-1867	William Pickens
PICKENS, Samuel Alexander Clark	8-22-1848	John C. Pickens
PICKENS, Sarah Martha	6-6-1864	Hugh Pickens
PICKENS, Sarah Moor	7-4-1841	James Pickens
PICKENS, Thomas McCune	5-18-1840	John C. Pickens
PICKENS, William	Nov. 1833	John C. Pickens
PICKENS, William	Nov. 1833	James Pickens
PICKENS, William Clark	1-11-1866	Hugh Pickens
PICKENS, _____(?)	Sept. 1838	John C. Pickens
PICKENS, _____(?)	5-15-1843	John C. Pickens
REID, James Lafayette	9-18-1843	Rachel Reid
REID, John Washington	9-30-1839	Rachel Reid
REID, Lafe Catherine	6-10-1856	Rachel Reid
REID, Lucinda Mitchell	10-5-1846	Rachel Reid

Name	Date	Parents
REID, Lyman	11-8-1852	Rachel Reid
REID, Mary Alma	5-14-1849	Rachel Reid
REID, William Henry	10-19-1842	Rachel Reid
RICHARDS, Debora*	2-8 1862	
SCHOOLY, Emily*	6-6-1864	
SCOTT, Jane Elizabeth	10-19-1842	Merch(?) Scott
SHANON, Caroline*	5-20-1850	
SHANNON, Samuel	11-3-1851	Caroline Shanon
SHARON, Joseph*	2-5-1838	
SHARON, Juliet*	2-15-1864	
SHARON, Martha Ellen*	2-2-1868	
SHARON, Sarah J.*	9-23-1861	
SHIVELY, Forgus Ratchel	5-14-1849	
SIMERAL, Elizabeth Hogg	12-5-1853	Sarah Ann Simeral
SIMERAL, George Hogg	12-5-1853	Sarah Ann Simeral
SIMERAL, James Vincent	12-5-1853	Sarah Ann Simeral
SIMERAL, Mary Ann	12-5-1853	Sarah Ann Simeral
SISLY (LISBY?), Maria	5-25-1839	Solomon Sisly (Lisby)
SISLY, Solomon	10-24-1835	Solomon Sisly
SMITH, Robert	May 1833	Rosanah Smith
SMITH, Susanah Baxter	May 1833	Rosanah Smith
SPENCE, James Alexander	10-24-1835	James Spence
SPENCE, Sarah Jane	9-1-1839	James Spence
SPENCE, Thomas Pickens	7-16-1837	James Spence
STEEL, Mary Abigal	10-18-1867	William A. Steel
STEEL, Wesley Andrew*	2-15-1864	
STEER, William*	2-15-1864	
TEMPLETON, Mary	6-16-1845	John Templeton
THEAKER, George Albert Parks	11-3-1851	John Theaker
THEAKER, George Whitfield	5-26-1835	George M. Theaker
THEAKER, Hugh Albert	7-15-1842	Thomas Theaker
THEAKER, Mary Elizabeth	5-28-1860	John Theaker
THEAKER, Mary Isabella	11-4-1849	John Theaker
THEAKER, Matilda Jamimah A.	9-6-1846	Robert L. Theaker
THEAKER, Matthew Clark	9-15-1845	Robert P. Theaker
THEAKER, Nancy Elizabeth	7-4-1841	Robert P. Theaker
THEAKER, Nancy Jane	-----1833	George Theaker
THEAKER, Robert Nelson	7-2-1837	George M. Theaker
THEAKER, Thadius Newton	1-6-1839	Thomas Theaker
THOBURN, Anna Lyle	11-1-1856	Catherine Thoburn
TILTON, Anna Cornelia	9-19-1858	
TILTON, Edgar Disberry	9-19-1858	
TILTON, Noah Augustus	9-19-1858	
WATERSON, James Gordon	7-16-1837	Alexander Waterson
WATERSON, Jenet Irabella Alexander	7-16-1837	Alexander Waterson
WATERSON, Thomas	7-16-1837	Alexander Waterson
WATERSON, David Gardner	9-30-1839	Alexander Waterson

Name	Date	Parents
WATTERSON, William Thoburn Scott	7-4-1841	Alexander Watterson
WATSON, George Albert	11-3-1851	Margaret Watson
WATSON, James*	5-12-1851	
WATSON, Levina Jane	6-26-1854	Levina E. Watson
WATSON, Margaret*	5-12-1851	
WELLS, Alexander	6-19-1845	Levi Wells
WELLS, Alice	6-19-1845	Levi Wells
WELLS, Ann	6-19-1845	Levi Wells
WELLS, Eleanor*	10-6-1841	
WELLS, George Mitchell	5-14-1849	Cadwalader Wells
WELLS, John	6-19-1845	Levi Wells
WELLS, Levi*	10-6-1841	
WELLS, Margaret Jane	6-19-1845	Levi Wells
WELLS, Maria*	9-16-1845	
WELLS, Merca Cass Ander	10-18-1845	Cadwalider Wells
WILEY, Alexander	7-31-1840	James Wiley
WILEY, Andrew	4-20-1836	John Wiley
WILEY, Catherine	7-31-1840	James Wiley
WILEY, Elizabeth	7-31-1840	James Wiley
WILEY, Hannah*	5-7-1866	
WILEY, James*	5-16-1840	
WILEY, Jane	10-7-1838	John Wiley
WILEY, Joseph	8-6-1834	John Wiley
WILEY, Mary Ann	before 1833	John Wiley
WILEY, Matthew	7-31-1840	James Wiley
WILEY, William	Mar. 1834	James Wiley
WILEY, William	7-31-1840	James Wiley
WILKINSON, Benjamin Mitchell	Dec. 1844-45(?)	Thomas Wilkinson
WILKINSON, Geo. Henry Comings	Dec. 1844-45(?)	Thomas Wilkinson
WILKINSON, John	7-15-1842	
WILSON, Adde Bell	10-1-1865	Catherine Wilson
WILSON, Elizabeth Ann	5-28-1860	
WILSON, John Watson	6-10-1856	
WILSON, Joseph Ross	10-3-1853	Catherine Wilson
WILSON, Martha Agnes	6-13-1862	
WILSON, Mary Alexander	10-3-1858	Catherine Wilson
WILSON, Rachel Jane	9-19-1858	
WILSON, Sarah M.*	3-5-1858	
WILLIAMS, Sallie E. R.*	2-15-1864	
WILLIAMS, Sarah*	2-15-1864	

The following records were taken from "Common Pleas Court Record Book LA".
This book can be found in the Archives Room in the basement of the Jefferson
County Court House. Only partition suits, petitions to sell real estate, etc.
have been abstracted; suits for debts, trespass etc. were not included.
Page on which record may be found is given in parenthesis.

James Westley LYNCH vs. Lloyd RAMSEY et al. Petition for Partition. Filed
6-20-1834. Land, Lot 40 Steubenville. Partition: 1/6th part, James Westley
Lynch of Jefferson Co.; 1/6th part, Lloyd Ramsey and Maria his wife, late Lynch
of Jefferson Co.; 1/6th part, Jeremiah Alexander and Fanny his wife, late Lynch
of Jefferson Co.; 1/6th part, Solomon Lynch of Hamilton Co., Ohio; 1/6th part,
Bezaleel Wells Lynch of Hamilton Co., Ohio; and 1/6th part, Mary Elizabeth
Lynch of Hamilton Co., Ohio. (82)

Robert GEORGE adms. of Daniel ANDERSON, dec'd vs. John TWADDLE, et al. Petition
to sell real estate. Filed 9-3-1834. Land, 42 acres S½ W½ NW¼ Section 12,
Township 12, Range (not given) in Steubenville Land District, purchased from
John Miller. Widow, Mary Anderson now the wife of John Twaddle. Children:
Martha and Margaret Anderson, both minors. (86)

Margaret HOUT vs. Henry HOUT, et al. Petition for dower. Filed 9-2-1833.
Land, 112 and 3/4 acres part Section 35, Township 7, Range 2 on waters of
Island Creek, Jefferson Co. in Steubenville land district; also lot 26 in
Shelleys addition of town of Richmond. Adam Hout, dec'd, late of Jefferson
County died 7-18-1833 without issue. Widow, Margaret Hout. Brothers and
Sisters: Henry Hout of Jefferson Co.; George Hout of Jefferson Co.; Peter
Hout of Jefferson Co.; John Hout of Richland Co., Ohio; Jacob Hout of Richland
Co., Ohio; Mary wife of William Albert of Tuscarawas Co., Ohio; Elizabeth wife
of John Minnich of Tuscarawas Co., Ohio; Catherine wife of Samuel Simpson of
Richland Co., Ohio; and Sarah wife of Robert Pettis of Harrison Co. Ohio. (90)

Henry H. LEAVETT and Judith CARREL adms. of the estate of Robert CARREL, dec'd,
vs. James M. CARREL, et al. Petition to make deed. Filed 8-25-1835. On
7-31-1817 Robert Carrel contracted to sell Adam Wise lots 227 and 228 in Steubenville. Children: James M. Carrel, Thomas Carrel, Harriet Carrel, William
Carrel, and Rachel Carrel; the last four being minors. (185)

Aaron ALLEN and John GLENN executors of James GLENN, dec'd vs. David McCUTCHEN,
et al. Petition to make deed. Filed 5-19-1835. James Glenn in his lifetime
on 3-27-2834 contracted to sell William Morrow the NE¼ Section 33, Township 8,
Range 2 in Jefferson Co. James Glenn made will dated 4-11-1827 and died 3-19-
1835. Heirs: David McCutcheon and Jane his wife; Calvin Morehead and Sarah
his wife; David Glenn, John Glenn; and Aaron Allen and Mary his wife. (194)

John CLINTON of Carroll Co., Ohio adms. of Abel CLINTON vs. Edward CLINTON,
et al. Petition to made deed. Filed 5-16-1835. Abel Clinton of Columbiana
Co., Ohio now dec'd, in his lifetime contracted on 11-9-1826 to sell Abel Grant
Lot 26 in town of New Summerset Jefferson County. Abel Clinton died 8-1-1828.
Widow, Eve Clinton now the wife of Edward Clinton. Children: Peter and Pris-
cilla Clinton, minors, of Carroll Co., Ohio. (196)

Samuel STOKELY and Catherine JUDKINS executors of Anderson JUDKINS, dec'd vs. Elizabeth JUDKINS, et al. Petition to make deed. Filed 9-16-1835. Anderson Judkins contracted on 1-3-1834 to sell James O'Neal one half of lot (lot number not given) in Steubenville. Children: Elizabeth, Martha and Maria Judkins, all minors. (199)

Maria NIXON vs. Robert CARR, et al. In Chancery. Filed 7-1-1834. Land, SE¼ Section 24, Township 10, Range 3 Jefferson Co. John Nixon late of Jefferson Co. died on 5-10-1824. Widow, Maria Nixon. Children: John Nixon, Cillian Nixon, Andrew Nixon, Mary Nixon, Nancy Nixon and Fanny late Nixon wife of Robert Norton. (200)

                    * * * * * * * * * * * *

The following records were taken from "Common Pleas Court Record Book L". This book is also found in the Archives Room in the basement of the court house. Pages on which record may be found are given in parenthesis.

Andrew BURNS by his guardian John BURNS vs. Abram LITTEN and Elizabeth his wife. Petition for Partition. Filed 5-13-1836. Land, 100 acres NE¼ Section 32, Township 5, Range 2. Thomas Burns, dec'd. Widow, Elizabeth Burns. Children: Robert Burns, Elizabeth Burns now wife of Abram Litten, Lettice Burns now wife of John Chew, Thomas Burns, Mary Burns now wife of William Sprague, John Burns, William Burns and Andrew Burns by his guardian; each entitled to 1/8th part. (51)

James McCOY adms. of the estate of James McCORMICK, dec'd, late of Jefferson Co. vs. Mary Jane McCORMICK, et al. Petition to sell real estate. Filed 4-11-1835. Land, 80 acres part of a larger tract of 180 acres formerly conveyed by Thomas and Elizabeth James to James McCormick Sr. of which James Sr. conveyed 100 acres to John McCormick. James McCormick Sr. dec'd. Widow, Martha McCormick. Heirs: Mary Jane McCormick, Elizabeth McCormick, Priscilla McCormick and James McCormick. (59)

James McCUNE adms. of James McCAUGHEY, dec'd, late of Jefferson Co. vs. William McCAUGHEY, et al. Petition to sell real estate. Filed 1-3-1835. Land, SE¼ Section 35, Township 17, Range 21, Crawford Co., Ohio in Wooster Land District. Children: William McCaughey, a minor, of Jefferson Co.; Joseph McCaughey a minor of Jefferson Co.; Cyrus McCaughey a minor of Jefferson Co.; Thomas McCaughey of Jefferson Co.; Robert J. Boggs and Margaret his wife late McCaughey of Belmont Co., Ohio; Elizabeth McCaughey a minor of Belmont Co., Ohio; Jackson McCaughey a minor of Belmont Co., Ohio; Mary Ann McCaughey of Belmont Co., Ohio; and Marshall Drury and Jemima his wife late McCaughey of Washington Co., Pennsylvania. (63)

Sarah FOWLER vs. John HANLON. Petition for dower. Filed 5-26-1835. James Fowler, dec'd, died 11-18-1834 and at the time of his death was seized by inheritance of an interest in S½ Lot 6 on High Street in Steubenville. Widow, Sarah Fowler, the petitioner. (66)

Martha AULD and John R. SUTHERLAND adms. of Samuel AULD, dec'd vs. John AULD, et al. Petition to sell real estate. Filed 3-30-1836. Land, N½ Lot 403 in Ross's addition to town of Steubenville. Widow, Martha Auld. Heirs: John Auld, Samuel Auld, William Auld, Robert Irwin and Mary his wife, David Love and Gracey his wife, Robert Auld, Benjamin Paisley and Elisa his wife, and Stewart Auld. (111)

John C. BAYLESS adms. of David B. BAYLESS, dec'd, of Wheeling, Ohio Co., Virginia vs. Maria E. BAYLESS. Petition to sell real estate. Filed 4-15-1836. Land, 51½ acres S part SE¼ Section 18, Township 9, Range 3 in Jefferson Co., on waters of Cross Creek, conveyed to said David B. Bayless in 1827 by John McKown. Heir: Maria E. Bayless, a minor. (116)

John WATSON adms. of James TAYLOR, dec'd vs. Dorothy TAYLOR, et al. Petition to sell land. Filed 11-26-1836. Land, 3 acres, lines—State Road and lot of James Updegraff. Widow, Dorothy Taylor. Children: Sarah Ann wife of Stark McMasters, Nancy wife of William McMasters, Susannah Taylor, Eliza Taylor, Harriet Taylor, John Taylor, James H. Taylor and William H. Taylor; the last six named being minors. (274)

John TILTON adms. of Nathan DURRANT, dec'd vs. John DURRANT. Petition to sell land. Filed 7-15-1836. Land, lot 42 in Tiltonville. Only known heirs being John Durrant of Jefferson County. (283)

Aquilla KIRK adms. of Caleb KIRK, dec'd vs. Lydia KIRK, et al. Petition to sell real estate. Filed 12-8-1836. Land, lot 69 in town of Smithville. Widow, Lydia Kirk. Heirs: Augustus, Elmer, Erastus, Aquilla, Josiah, Eli and Henry Kirk. (286)

Robert LESLIE adms. of Moses HANLON, dec'd vs. Elizabeth HANLON, et al. Petition to sell real estate. Filed 11-3-1835. Land, lots 10 and 11 in New Amsterdam. Widow, Elizabeth Hanlon. Heirs: Richard Morrow and Charlotte his wife; John Hanlon; Thomas Hanlon; Moses Hanlon; James Hanlon; Sarah Hanlon; Wabrantz Hanlon; Nancy, Daniel, William and Benjamin Hanlon. (287)

Phineas ASH and Louisa Caroline his wife vs. James ASH, et al. Petition for Partition. Filed 7-21-1836. Land, SE¼ and SW¼ Section 23, Township 11, Range 3, also lot 130 in Steubenville; also lot 88 in Cadiz, Harrison Co., Ohio. Phineas Ash, dec'd of Lancaster Co. Pa. Widow, Eleanor Ash of Lancaster Co., Pa. Partition: 1/8th part, Phineas Ash and Louisa Caroline his wife of Lancaster Co., Pa.; 1/8th part, Rachel Ash wife of James Ash; 1/8th part, Amanda wife of Morgan I. Thomas; 1/8th part, Martha Eleanor Ash; 1/8th part, Julia Ann Ash; 1/8th part, Phinias Washington Ash; 1/8th part, Ann Elizabeth Ash; 1/8th part, Harriet Ash; the last five named being minors and all of Lancaster Co., Pa. (290)

John LANTZ vs. Abraham LANTZ, et al. Petition to sell real estate. Filed 5-27-1837. Peter Lance, dec'd late of Jefferson Co. died seized by inheritance of 1/11th part and by purchase of 2/11th part in 85 acres, lines—Thomas Elliott, Charles Elliott, George Day, Ephraim Johnston, James Porter. Widow, mentioned not named. Children: Christopher, John, William, Sally, Polly, Abraham aged 17 yrs. 16th last July and Abigail aged 15 yrs. 21 June last; the last two named of Harrison Co., Ohio. (341)

Jacob SHULTZ adms. of John SHULTZ, dec'd, late of Jefferson Co. vs. George SHULTZ, et al. Petition to sell real estate. Filed 3-24-1836. Land, lots 12, 45, 47 in town of Annapolis; also undivided one-half of NE¼ Section 8, Township 11, Range 4 in Harrison Co., Ohio. Widow, Mary Shultz. Heirs: George Shultz of Pennsylvania; Jacob Shultz; Margaret Shultz; and Samuel Shultz, a minor. (344)

William CAMPBELL and wife vs. William JACKMAN, et al. Petition for Partition. Filed 9-16-1836. Land, 143½ acres Section 30, Township 3, Range 1 on Ohio River, said land being conveyed by Isaac White to William White, dec'd. Partition: 1/5th part, William Campbell and Polly his wife; 1/5th part, Eleanor wife of William Jackman; 1/5th part, Jane Skinner; 1/5th part, Nancy wife of Thomas Stein; 1/5th part, Isaac Hukill a minor, son of James and Elizabeth Hukill, both dec'd and ward of John Stoakes. (355)

John EDINGTON vs. Daniel EDINGTON, et al. Petition for Partition. Filed 12-9-1836. Land, 96 acres SW¼ Section 10, Township 7, Range 2. Asahel Edington Sr., dec'd, late of Jefferson Co., Ohio. Partition: 1/8th part, John Edington of Rock Island Co., Illinois; 1/8th part, Daniel Edington of Rock Island Co., Illinois; 1/8th part, Martha wife of William Patterson of Ashland Co., Ohio; 1/8th part, Diana wife of Samuel Douglas of Ashland Co., Ohio; 1/8th part, Nancy Patterson, dec'd, her children—Martha, Cassandra, Lucinda, James and John Patterson, the last two being minors and all of Franklin Co., Ohio; 1/8th part, Drusilla Miser, dec'd, her children—Alexander and Eleanor Miser, both minors of Jefferson Co.; 1/8th part, James Edington, dec'd, his children—Mary Ann and Harriet Edington of Portage Co., Ohio; 1/8th part, Brice Edington, dec'd, his children—Rachel M., Nancy P., Abraham M. and Martha Edington, all minors and all of Jefferson Co., Ohio. (358)

Margaret HENDERSON vs. George W. ROBINSON, Mathew M. LAUGHLIN and James WALLACE. Petition for Dower. Filed 6-1-1837. Thomas Henderson late of Jefferson Co., dec'd, died 1-1-1837. Land, part lot 216 and N½ lot 215 in Steubenville. Widow, Margaret Henderson of Posey Co. Indiana. (424)

The following records were taken from "Common Pleas Court Record MN". This book can be found in the Archives Room in the basement of the Jefferson County Court House. Only partition suits, petitions to sell real estate, etc. have been abstracted; suits for debts, trespass, etc. were not included. Page on which record may be found is given in parenthesis.

May 1838 - Roswell MARSH guardian of the children and heirs of Hugh THOMPSON vs. Samuel THOMPSON, et al. Petition to sell real estate. Filed 9-11-1837. Land, lot 342 in Wells addition to town of Steubenville. Children: Samuel Thompson, Margaret Jane Thompson, James W. Thompson and John R. Thompson; all minors. (13)

May 1838 - Margaret THOMPSON vs. Samuel, Margaret Jane, James W. and John R. THOMPSON, minor children and heirs of Hugh THOMPSON, dec'd. Petition for Dower. Filed 9-13-1837. Land, lot 342 Wells addition to Steubenville. Hugh Thompson, dec'd, died 6-1-1833. Widow, Margaret Thompson of Jefferson Co. (15)

May 1838 - William SHIELDS vs. Robert SHIELDS, et al. Petition for Partition. Filed 7-12-1836. Land, 70 acres NE corner Section 30, Township 6, Range 2, Jefferson Co. William Shields, dec'd, late of Scioto Co., Ohio. Widow, Leah Shields of Portsmouth, Scioto Co., Ohio. Partition: 1/8th part, William Shields of Carrollton, Carroll Co., Ohio; 1/8th part, Alexander Shields of Licking Co., Ohio; 1/8th part, John Shields, dec'd, his heir--Elizabeth Shields a minor of Muskingum Co., Ohio; 1/8th part, Robert Shields; 1/8th part, Jane Shields; 1/8th part, Anne Shields; 1/8th part, Samuel Shields; 1/8th part, Sarah wife of Eli M. Pyle; the last five named all of Jefferson Co. (18)

May 1838 - Nathan SIDWELL vs. Plumer SIDWELL. Petition for Partition. Filed 3-8-1837. Land, W pt. S6, Township 8, Range 3, 138 acres adjoining land of William Purviance. Sarah Sidwell late Sarah Purviance, dec'd. Her children: Nathan Sidwell, Plumer Sidwell, Phebe Sidwell, Sinah Sidwell, Elmira Sidwell and Henry Sidwell; all of Jefferson Co. and the last five named being minors. (24)

May 1838 - Sarah DAY vs. Joseph DAY, et al. In Chancery. Filed 3-7-1837. John Day, dec'd, late of Jefferson Co., died 7-1-1836. Widow, Sarah Day. Heirs: Joseph Day; Rachel wife of____(not given) Shaw; Nancy wife of William Hunter; Joseph D. Williams; Sarah Clendening, her children--Margaret, Jane and Joseph D. Clendening by Joseph Day their guardian. (40)

May 1838 - Elizabeth CROW vs. Samuel CROW, et al. In Chancery. Filed 7-3-1837. John Crow, dec'd, late of Jefferson Co., died 3-29-1836. Widow, Sarah Crow. Heirs: Samuel Crow, William Crow, Robert Crow, John Crow, Mary wife of Hugh Johnston, Elizabeth wife of Joel Fisher, Christena wife of David Davis, Margaret wife of John Hess, and Ann wife of Peter Hess. (45)

May 1838 - Delilah SHANNON adms. of James SHANNON, dec'd, late of Jefferson Co. vs. Elizabeth SHANNON, et al. Petition to sell real estate. Filed 9-1-1835. Land, 2 acres, out-lots 35 & 36, Wells and Helmicks addition to town of New Salem. Widow, Delilah Shannon. Children: Elizabeth and James W. Shannon, both minors. (67)

682

August 1838 - Isabella HUSTON adms. of John HUSTON, dec'd vs. Jane HUSTON, et al. Petition to complete contract. Filed 10-21-1837. Wodow, Isabella Huston. Children: Jane and James Huston. John Huston in his lifetime contracted to sell William Kerr the NE¼ SE¼ Section 15, Township 12, Range 3. (125)

August 1838 - Henry M. SOOK and John COOPER adms. of Robert WARE, dec'd vs. Ellen WARE, etal. Petition to sell real estate. Filed 7-27-1835. Land, lots 38 & 39 in town of New Somerset, Jefferson Co. Widow, Ellen Ware. Heirs: Catharine wife of James McElroy of Jefferson Co.; George S. Ware of Jefferson Co.; Lucinda Jane Ware of Jefferson Co.; Samuel A. J. Ware of Columbiana Co., Ohio; Beal R. Ware of Columbiana Co., Ohio; Hiram Ware of Columbiana Co., Ohio; William Ware of Stark Co., Ohio; Anne wife of George Smith of Pennsylvania; Robert C. Ware of Pennsylvania; Nathan H. Ware of Maryland; Rezin Ware of the Territory of Michigan. (127)

August 1838 - Ann KREPPS, et al. by their next friend vs. Mordecai MOORE. Petition for Partition. Filed March 1837. Land, part NW¼ Section 27, Township 11, Range 3. Partition: 1/4th part jointly--Ann, Mary, Bolivar, John, Rebekah and Ellen Krepps all minors and all of Fayette Co., Pennsylvania by Cassandra S. Krepps their next friend. Mordecai Moore being seized of 3/4ths part. (132)

August 1838 - John WATSON and George MITCHELL adms. of Samuel CAROTHERS, dec'd vs. Hannah CAROTHERS, et al. Petition to sell real estate. Filed 11-26-1836. Land, undivided moiety or half part Lot 36 Mount Pleasant, E part lot 33 Mount Pleasant and SE¼ Section 11, Township 7, Range 3 in Jefferson Co.; also Lot 64 in Morristown, Belmont Co., Ohio. Widow, Hannah Carothers. Children: Samuel Y Carothers of Wassington Co., Pennsylvania; Jane C. wife of Robert Kerlin of Jefferson Co.; Mary Carothers of Jefferson Co.; John Carothers of Washington Co., Pennsylvania; Hugh W. Carothers; Sarah A. Carothers; William F. Carothers; Barbara A. Carothers; and Johnson C. Carothers; the last five named of Jefferson Co. and the last six named being minors. (154)

August 1838 - James DILLON adms. of the estate of Joseph HARFORD, dec'd vs. William STARR, et al. Petition to sell real estate. Filed May 1837. Land, 54 acres part SW¼ Section 12, Township 9, Range 3. Widow, Ann Harford. Heirs: Ann wife of Thomas Wright of Carroll Co., Ohio; Anna Matilda wife of William Starr; Naoma wife of Hugh Starr; Sena wife of John Harford; Hiram Harford; Allen Harford; and Louiza Harford; the last six named all of Jefferson Co. and the last three named being minors. (161)

August 1838 - John HAMMOND adms. of Joseph W. PLUMMER, dec'd, late of Jefferson Co. vs. Kinsey TALBOT, et al. Petition to make deed. Filed 7-19-1838. Joseph W. Plummer in his lifetime on 15th of 12th month 1829 contracted to sell John Hamond two parcels of land being 218 acres part of Sections 11 & 12, Township 9, Range 3. Children: Mary wife of John Hammond; Deborah wife of Kinsey Talbot; Rachel wife of Joel Norris; Sarah wife of George Earnshaw; Ann wife of Amos Pidgeon, Mahala wife of Alexander Shelley; Thomas Plummer, dec'd, his children--Mary wife of Henry Teeples, Joseph, John, Caleb and Thomas Plummer. (169)

November 1838 - William TWEEDY vs John TWEEDY, et al. Petition for Partition.
Filed 3-10-1838. Land, 42 acres part of Section 8, Township 8, Range 3 on waters of
Pine Fork of Short Creek. John Tweedy, dec'd. Widow, Sarah Tweedy of Jefferson Co.
Partition: 1/7th part, John Tweedy of Jefferson Co.; 1/7th part, Margaret Anguish
late Tweedy, dec'd, her children--James and David Anguish of Morgan Co., Ohio; 5/7ths
part, William Tweedy of Jefferson Co.--part of William's interest being by purchase
of other interests. (291)

November 1838 - Abram MYERS vs. William WRIGHT and others. Petition for Partition.
Filed 3-2-1838. Land. SW¼ Section 34, Township 8, Range 2 except 27½ acres conveyed
y Jacob Wright in his lifetime to Abner Moore and also except 34 acres conveyed to
Abram Myers--parcel partition being 87 acres. Partition: 2/9ths part, Abram Myers;
2/9ths part, William Wright; 1/9th part, Martha Wright; 1/9th part, Sarah Wright a
minor; 1/9th part, Nancy Culp, dec'd, late wife of Adam Culp, her children--Jacob,
George, Samuel, William, Margaret, Nancy, Adam and Benjamin Culp of Jefferson Co.;
1/9th part, William Stoakes and John Stoakes; 1/9th part, Jacob Myers, dec'd, his
children--Susannah, Rachel, Martha, Eliza, George F. and Jacob Myers, all minors. (295)

November 1838 - Benjamin Walker vs. Madison WALKER and others. Petition for Partition.
Filed 11-23-1837. Land, 33 acres part of Section 32, Township 3, Range 1 in Steubenville Land District. William Walker, dec'd. Partition: 1/4th part, Benjamin Walker
of Jefferson Co.; 1/4th part, Madison Walker; 1/4th part jointly or 1/24th part each,
Elizabeth, Mary Ann, Emily, Jonathan, Isaac and Martha Ann Walker, minors; 1/4th
part jointly or 1/8th part each, John and David Walker. (301)

November 1838 - Joseph NESBET and Joseph McCONNELL adms. of John WOODS, dec'd vs.
James FERGUSON, et al. Petition to make deed. Filed 10-27-1831. John Woods in his
lifetime on 9-27-1824 contracted to sell Edward Weir 10 acres part of Section 21,
Township 6, Range 2 in Cross Creek twp., Jefferson Co. Children: Sally wife of
James Ferguson, Mary Woods, Elizabeth Woods, Catharine Woods, William Woods, Rebecca
Woods and Margaret Woods; the last three named being minors. (305)

March 1837 - This day it was proved to the satisfaction of the Court in Open Court by oath of Roswell Marsh, Esq. and John Millegan two respectable and disinterested witnesses, that Mrs. Abagail Prior late of Steubenville, Jefferson County and widow of Abner Prior departed this life on or about the 17th of September last at the residence of her daughter, Mrs. Abagail W. Hening, it is thereupon ordered that a copy of the foregoing be certified by the Clerk of Court. (Common Pleas Journal H, page 428)

9-28-1841 - This day proof was made on oath in Open Court by John H. Chambers that Joseph Chambers formerly a Sargeant in the army of the Revolution and late a Revolutionary pensioner of the United States departed this life on the 12th day of January A.D. 1841 at Warren township in Jefferson County and left as his widow who survives him Rachel Chambers now resident of Smithfield township in said county. And the Court being satisfied with the said proof orders the same to be recorded and certified to the War Department. (Common Pleas Journal 11, page 303)

9-29-1841 - This day proof was made on oath in Open Court by James Irvine and Thomas McElroy that John Humphrey Sr. formerly a Sargeant in the Army of the Revolution, and late a Revolutionary Pensioner of the United States departed this life on the 30th day of June A.D. 1841 at Warren township in Jefferson County and left leaving Robert Humphrey of Scott County, Iowa Territory, John Humphrey Jr., David Humphrey, Elizabeth McElroy wife of Thomas McElroy and Mary Trimble wife of John Trimble of Jefferson County, Ohio and George Humphrey of Fulton County, Illinois his children and heirs at law. And the Court being satisfied with said proof ordered the same to be recorded and certified to the War Department. (Common Pleas Journal 11, page 306)

November 1842 - This day proof was made by witnesses in Open Court. That Thomas McCune of Jefferson County in the State of Ohio was a private during the War of the Revolution and was a Revolutionary Pensioner and died on the 12th day of March A.D. 1842 holding at the time of his death a certificate from ;the war department dated the 23rd day of November 1838 . . . that Thomas McCune died on the 12th day of March aforesaid leaving five children to wit: Sarah intermarried with Elisha Brown, Mary intermarried with Alexander Mutchmore, Jane intermarried with Alexander McConnell and James McCune and Joseph B. McCune, that the above named persons are the only children of said Thomas McCune and that he left no widow and that his children are of full age. And the court being satisfied with the proof of said facts ordered the same to be recorded and certified to the War Department. (Common Pleas Journal 11, page 592)

Pages on which record may be found are given in parenthesis. These records have been abstracted primarily as a find aid and for genealogical items--land descriptions, which many times are quite lengthy have not been given. KCO=Knox Co. Ohio

1-2-1808 - Joseph WALKER & Nancy wife of Mt. Vernon, Fairfield Co. to Robert ANDERSON. (1)

6-10-1808 - James CRAIG Sr. & Mary wife of Ohio Co., Va. to James CRAIG, KCO. (2)

1-5-1808 - George HOLCOMBE of Trenton twp., Hunterdon Co., N.J. to David MOORE OF Belmont Co., Ohio. (3)

10-1-1800 - James KIRKPATRICK, soldier American Army of United States & Heziah wife to George HOLCOMBE of Trenton twp., Hunterdon Co., N. J. (3)

12-23-1806 - Thos. Bell PATTERSON & Barbary wife to James PYLE. (4)

6-21-1808 - John KERR to Thomas Bell PATTERSON of Franklin Co., Ohio. (5)

6-22-1808 - Thos. Bell PATTERSON of Franklin Co., Ohio to Gilman BRYANT, KCO. (6)

6-22-1808 - Plat of town of MANSFIELD, Richland Co., Ohio (6)

6-22-1808 - Thos. Bell PATTERSON of Franklin Co., Ohio to John CLICK, KCO. (7)

6-12-1808 - Benjamin BUTLER & Leah wife of KCO to Robert THOMPSON of Pa. (8)

6-9-1808 - Calvin SHEPHERD & Mahala wife to Enoch HARRIS. (9)

4-8-1808 - John MATHEWS & Sally wife of Muskingum Co., Ohio to John LASH, KCO. (10)

5-13-1808 - Samuel KRATZER & Affunity wife to George LINN. (10)

6-9-1808 - Abraham JOHNSTON & Lucy wife of Licking Co., Ohio to Stepehen CHAPMAN, KCO. (11)

4-22-1808 - Samuel KRATZER & Affunity wife to Stephen CHAPMAN. (13)

7-11-1808 - John BIGGS to George SPURGEON. (14)

6-23-1808 - Joseph WALKER & Nancy wife to Thos. DURBIN. (14)

5-9-1808 - Samuel KRATZER & Affunity wife to William Wallace. (15)

4-11-1807 - Aaron BROWN of Clinton twp., Fairfield Co., Ohio to Alexander WALKER of same. (16)

8-4-1808 - Joseph WALKER & Nancy wife of KCO to Nathan CONNARD of Licking Co., Ohio. (17)

2-9-1808 - Lucas SULLIVANT of Franklin Co., Ohio to Samuel H. SMITH of Fairfield Co. Ohio. (18)

6-8-1808 - Coonrth of GOODNER of Tennessee to Samuel Hay SMITH. (19)

4-1-1806 - Thos. B. PATTERSON of Mt. Vernon, Fairfield Co., Ohio to John Johnston of same. (20)

4-5-1808 - Robert WOODBURN & Sarah wife of Trumbull Co., Ohio to Mary BALDWIN wife of Ellis BALDWIN of same. (20)

6-9-1808 - Abraham JOHNSTON & Lucy wife of Licking Co., Ohio to James WALKER Jr., KCO. (21)

8-12-1808 - William WELLS of Zanesville, Collector for State of Ohio to Samuel H. SMITH. (22)

7-28-1808 - Daniel of Washington, Columbia to Michael MOURSE of same. (23)

8-12-1808 - Wm. WELLS of Zanesville, Collector State of Ohio to Hauerours TAULMAN assignee of Samuel H. SMITH. (25)

9-1-1808 - Benj. BUTLER & Leah wife to Isaac RODGERS. (25)

4-8-1808 - John MATHEWS & Sally wife of Muskingum Co., Ohio to John GREEN. KCO. (26)

9-7-1808 - Joseph WALKER & Nancy wife KCO to Samuel LEWIS of Richland Co., Ohio. (27)

9-7-1808 - Joseph WALKER & Nancy wife to Wm. WALLACE. (28)

3-7-1808 - Benj. BUTLER & Leah wife of Mt. Vernon, Fairfield Co., Ohio to Calvin SHEPHERD OF same. (29)

9-9-1808 - George GIBSON to Jesse SMITH, both of Muskingum Co., Ohio (30)
5-13-1808 - Wm. WALLACE & Patience wife of KCO to Jesse PROCTOR of Beford Co., Pa.(30)
9-15-1808 - James CRAIG, KCO to James LOGAN of Belmont Co., Ohio. (31)
8-17-1807 - Ziba LEONARD & Martha wife of Clinton twp., Fairfield Co., Ohio to Benj-
               amin LEONARD of same. (32)
10-22-1808 - Joseph WALKER & Nancy wife to David MILLER. (33)
3-18-1808 - James WILLIAMS of Anapolis, Md., Merchant to John MATHEWS, Surveyor,
               Muskingum Co., Ohio. (34)
10-24-1808 - Benj. BUTLER & Leah wife of KCO to Gasper EICHLEBERGER of Frederick
               Co. Md. (35)
10-24-1808 - Wm. WALLACE and Patience wife of KCO to Christian SHOWLTS of Rocking-
               ham Co. Va. (36)
11-10-1808 - Jos. WALKER & Nancy wife of Wm. McBRIDE. (37)
7-6-1808 - Samuel H. SMITH agent for Wm. C. SCHENCK of Warren Co., Ohio to Thomas
               McKEE for benefit of Wm. C. SCHENCK. (38)
12-22-1800 - John MATHEWS of Marietta, Col. in Army of United States to John F.
               HAEUTRAUCK. (39)
11-17-1808 - Thomas MERRILL & Susannah wife to Robt. WALKER. (40)
6-3-1808 - John KERR & Sarah wife to Amariah WATSON. (41)
12-9-1808 - John CLICK & Sally wife of KCO to Christian SHOUTTS of Rockingham
               Co., Va. (42)
11-16-1808 - Benj. BUTLER & Leah wife of KCO to Valentine KENDLE of Washington Co.,
               Pa. (43)
12-5-1808 - Jos. WALKER & Nancy wife of KCO to Samuel LEWIS of Richland Co., Ohio.(44)
8-22-1808 - John MATHEWS & Mahala wife of Muskingum Co., Ohio to James DUNLAP. (45)
8-22-1808 - John MATHEWS & Mahala wife of Muskingum Co., Ohio to Samuel DUNLAP of
               KCO. (46)
11-9-1807 - Jonas STANBERRY & Ann Lucy wife of New York, N.Y. to John VANCE of
               Rockingham Co., Va. (47)
12-23-1808 - Solomon COCHRAN to Thos. McBRIDE. (48)
2-2-1809 - Wm. PERINE of Belmont Co., Ohio to Gilman BRYANT of KCO. (49)
2-4-1809 - Thos. B. PATTERSON of Franklin Co., Ohio to Gilman BRYANT of KCO. (50)
2-4-1809 - James PELL to Thos. B. PATTERSON. (51)
6-21-1808 - John KERR to James PELL. (52)
2-4-1809 - James PELL of KCO to Thos. B. PATTERSON of Franklin Co., Ohio. (52)
2-2-1809 - Samuel KRATZER & Affunity wife to Selah SIMPKINS. (53)
2-8-1809 - Joseph WALKER & Nancy wife to Gilman BRYANT. (54)
2-25-1809 - Joseph WALKER & Nancy wife to George LYBERGER. (55)
2-27-1809 - Isaac BONNETT of KCO to James STARKEY of Bedford Co., Pa. (56)
2-27-1809 - Isaac BONNETT to Christopher JOB, blacksmith, of Bedford Co., Pa. (57)
2-27-1809 - Isaac BONNETT to John McNEIL of Bedford Co., Pa. (58)
12-6-1807 - Jos. WALKER & Nancy wife of Mt. Vernon, Fairfield Co., Ohio to Michael
               CLICK of same. (59)
4-16-1808 - Michael CLICK of KCO to Isaac BONNETT of ,Pa. (60)
3-1-1809 - Wm. McBRIDE to George LYBARGER. (61)
3-13-1809 - Gasper EICHELBARGER to George LYBERGER. (62)
11-7-1804 - Capt. Aaron DOUGLASS of Chester twp., Morris Co., N. J. to William
               DOUGLASS of Fairfield Co., Ohio. (63)
3-21-1809 - Benj. BUTLER & Leah wife of KCO to Jesse PROCTER of Pa. (64)
3-21-1809 - Erkareas BEATY of N. J. & Samuel H. SMITH of Ohio to Benj. BUTLER. (65)
12-31-1802 - Thos. JEFFERSON, President United States to Asa SENTER, a Capt. in
               late Army of United States. (66)

12-31-1802 - Thos. JEFFERSON, President United States to George REID, a Col. in
            late Army of United States. (67)
10-24-1808 - Asa SENTER of Wardham, Rockingham Co., N. . to Alexander WILSON of
            Boston, Hillsborrough Co., N.H. (68)
10-24-1808 - Geo. REID of Londondary, Rockingham Co., N.H. to Alexander WILSON of
            New Boston, Hillsborough Co., N.H. (69)
3-4-1809 - Jos. WALKER & Nancy wife of KCO to Montgomery NOWTURE of Richland Co.,
            Ohio. (69)
12-13-1809 - Samuel KRATZER & Affinity wife to Wm. PETTEGREW. (71)
6-18-1808 - Enoch BALL and Joanna wife of Springfield, Essex Co., N. J. to Richard
            LEVERIDGE of Randolph, Morris Co., N.J. (72)
3-31-1809 - Jesse PROCTOR of Pa. to Samuel H. SMITH & Erkereas BEATY. (73)
3-10-1809 - Lucas SULLIVANT of Franklin Co., Ohio to John KERR of KCO. (74)
5-1-1809 - John KERR & Sarah wife to John LEWIS. (75)
Will of William PORTER of Pittsburgh, Allegheny Co., Pa. - dated 9-12-1808;
recorded Pa. 11-14-1808. Wife, Jane to have $7000. to bring up children. To
Robert Steele, not of age, son of Christian Steele, 1000 pounds Pa. currency. To
Eliza Steele, not of age, daughter of Christopher Steele, $200. To the children
of my brother Moses Porter $50. To Sisters, Margaret and Hannah each $100. To
William Cochran, not of age, son of sister Sophia, $100. My children; Eliza, Mary,
Jane and Sophia, all personal and real estate excepting above bequests. Executors:
Anthony Beeler, Alexander McLaughlin and Zachariah Tamehill. Mentions real
and personal estate in Kentucky, Tennessee, Ohio and Pennsylvania. Signed: William
Porter. Witnesses: Robert Steele, C. Cowan and Wm. Hamilton. (76)
3-29-1806 - John ADAMS, President of United States to Alexander McLAUGHLIN. (77)
3-29-1800 - John ADAMS, President of United States to Isaac CRAIG of Pittsburgh.(78)
10-11-1808 - Isaac CRAIG of Pittsburg, Allegheny Co., Pa. & Amelia wife to Joseph
            TAGGERT, Edward GRAY, Robert TAYLOR all of Philadelphia and
            Alexander McLAUGHLIN of Pittsburgh. (78)
3-17-1809 - Anthony BEELER, Alexander McLAUGHLIN and Zachariah A. TANNEHILL,
            executors of will of William PORTER of Pittsburgh, Alleghany Co.
            Pa. to Henry Haslet. (80)
3-18-1809 - Henry HASLET and Eliza wife of Pittsburgh, Pa. to Edward GRAY & Robert
            Taylor of Philadelphia. (82)
3-21-1800 - John ADAMS, President United States to James WILLIAMS. (83)
1-20-1809 - Robert PATTON & Anna wife of Fairfax Co., Va. to Joseph TAGGERT,
            Alex. McLAUGHLIN, Edw. GRAY and Robert TAYLOR. (84)
3-16-1800 - Stephen CHAPMAN & Polly his wife of Licking Co., Ohio to Benjamin
            Tupper of Licking Co., Ohio and Ichabod NYE of Washington Co.,
            Ohio. (86)
5-14-1809 - Gilman BRYANT and Elizabeth wife to James NEWELL. (87)
8-5-1809 - Samuel H. SMITH OF Fairfield Co. as agent of William C. SCHENCK of
            Warren Co., Ohio to George DAVIS of Fairfield Co., Ohio. (88)
5-26-1809 - Thos. McBRIDE to Philip WELKER. (89)
4-5-1809 - Benj. BUTLER & Leah wife to James SMITH. (90)
4-11-1801 - Enoch BALL & Joanna wife of Essex Co., N.J. for natural love and
            affection to Davis CRANE son of Benjamin and Rachel CRANE. (91)
4-11-1803 - John MATHEWS of Washington Co., Ohio to James WALKER of Fayette Co.,
            Pa. (92)

6-19-1809 - Jos WALKER & Nancy wife of KCO to Gasper CRAMER of Trumbull Co., Ohio(93)
6-19-1809 - Jos. WALKER & Nancy wife of KCO to Michael CRAMER of Trumbull Co.,
        Ohio. (94)
6-19-1809 - Samuel H. SMITH of Ohio in his own right and for Erkerias BEATY of N.J.
        to Azariah DAVIS of KCO. (95)
722-1808 - Thomas LINE of Belmont Co., Ohio to Wm. SMITH of same. (96)
6-10-1806 - Thos. B. PATTERSON of Mt. Vernon to Robert THOMPSON of Allegheny Co.,
        Pa. (97)
7-3-1809 - Calvin BAFFETT & Rachel wife of Ohio Co., Va. to Enoch HARRIS, KCO.(98)
7-12-1809 - John KEER & Sally wife of KCO to Elias DELASHMENT of Franklin Co.,
        Ohio. (99)
1-1-1807 - Israel CANFIELD & Rachel wife of Morris Co., N.J. to Aliza CONGER &
        Stephen CONGER of Morris Co., N. J. (100)
1-31-1809 - Elijah CONGER & Phebe wife of Morris Co., N.J. to Jehiel DAY of same.
        (102)
7-11-1809 - Enoch HARRIS to John CLICK. (103)
6-19-1809 - Sylvenus LAWRENCE & Jemima wife of Morris Co., N.J. to Samuel T.
        LAWRENCE of same. (104)
7-19-1809 - Lucas SULLIVANT of Franklin Co., Ohio to William MITCHELL, KCO. (105)
8-15-1809 - Enoch HARRIS of KCO to John WELCH of Somerset Co., Pa. (106)
8-14-1809 - Jos. WALKER & Nancy wife of John WELCH of somerset Co., Pa. (107)
8-15-1809(rec.) - Zeba LEONARD & Martha wife to Samuel H. SMITH. (108)
6-1-1809 - John KERR & Sarah wife to Joseph MOORE. (109)
7-25-1809 - George LYBERGER & Caty wife to Michael CLICK. (110)
8-21-1809 - Benj. BUTLER & Leah wife to Enoch HARRIS. (111)
4-9-1800 - John MATHEWS OF Marietta to Edward OWEN of Somerset Co., Pa. (112)
8-6-1800 - Edward OWEN of Philadelphia, Pa. to Thomas W. JONES of Somerset Co.,
        Pa. (114)
9-14-1809(rec) - Joseph WALKER to John CHAPMAN. (116)
9-19-1809 - John ARMSTRONG of Hamilton Co., Ohio by Samuel H. SMITH to John ARNOLD
        of KCO. (117)
10-5-1809 - Enoch HARRIS to Gilman BRYANT. (118)
10-5-1809 - James SMITH & Rebecca wife to Enoch HARRIS. (119)
10-5-1809 - Enoch HARRIS to James SMITH. (120)
10-23-1809 - Elias ARNOLD & Rachel wife to George SAPP Jr.; Power of Attorney to
        recover part of estate of George PAYNE, dec'd late of
        Alleghany Co., Md. (120)
10-23-1809 - John MATHEWS & Sally wife of Muskingum Co., Ohio to Abraham SPERRY
        of same. (121)
10-26-1809 - Abraham SPERRY & Elizabeth wife of KCO to Peter SPERRY of Hardy Co.,
        Va. (122)
11-17-1809 - Enoch HARRIS of KCO to Thomas VENNUM of Washington Co., Pa. (123)
11-14-1808 - Zeba LEONARD & Martha wife of KCO to Noah COOK of Washington Co., Pa.
        (124)
11-28-1809 - Jos. WALKER & Nancy wife of KCO to Vachel KIRK of Fayette Co.,Pa.(125)
7-3-1809 - Calvin BABBETT & Rachel wife of Ohio Co., Va. to James CRAIG. (126)

KNOX COUNTY, OHIO - DEED AND INDENTURE RECORDS

8-9-1811 - Subscribers to a Petition concerning Presbyterian Church of Clinton, show Inhabitants of the town of Clinton to be:-

John BARNEY	John WHEELER	N. C. BOALS	Oliver STRONG
S. H. SMITH	Joseph TARRENTS	Roye N. POWERS	Seely SIMKINS
Benjamin BARNEY	Benjamin CORWIN	Ichabod MARSHALL	Abel COOK
Gabriel WILKINS	Joseph RICKEY	Samuel NYE	Richard FISHBACK
Richard AYERS	Ichabod NYE	(Deed Book B, page 228)	

12-26-1823 - Wm. WATTS aged 16 yrs. on 1st December by Gilman BRYANT his guardian is bound as an apprentice for 3 yrs. and 4½ months to learn the trade of tinner to Charles SAYER. (Deed Book F, page 148)

12-9-1824 - Samuel HOFFMAN and Henry WIDER, trustees of Middleberry twp. bind Mary SHEPHERD a poor girl of said township, aged 11 yrs. and 29 days as a servant until she reaches 18 years of age in about 1831 to Mary LEVERING of said township. (Deed Book F, page 162)

3-22-1825 - John ELDER of Knox Co., Ohio, Thomas ELDER of Brook Co., Va. and Thomas ELDER and Margaret his wife of Washington, Penna. to Hugh NEWEL of Mt. Vernon, Knox Co. - $700. - In-lots 129 & 130 in Mt. Vernon. Signatures of Thos. Elder, Sr. and Thos Elder, Jr. attested to in Jefferson Co., Ohio. (Deed Book F, page 252)

3-3-1825 - Enos JONES son of Nathan JONES and Betsy his wife, aged 15 yrs. on 30 August last by consent of Betsy JONES his mother of Milford township is placed as an apprentice in farming to Samuel POPPLETON of Liberty township for 5 years, 4 months and 27 days. (Deed Book F, page 253)

1-29-1825 - George BRICKER, Jr. and Hannah his wife of Fairfield Co., Ohio, William FRY and Catharine his wife formerly BRICKER, Sarah BRICKER, Elizabeth BRICKER and Jacob BRICKER children of John BRICKER, dec'd and Margaret BRICKER widow of John BRICKER, dec'd; all of Knox County to Solomon BRICKER of Knox Co. - $500. - part of 1st quarter, 6th township, 14th range, U. S. military tract being 150 acres, lines—George Bricker; said land being conveyed by G. Bryant and Elizabeth his wife to John Bricker on 8-2-1817. (Deed Book F, page 267).

4-30-1825 - John BUTLER and George H. SCOLES, trustees of Pike twp. bind Hannah McLAUGHLIN daughter of Nancy TAYLOR to Robert KENEDY. Said Hannah formerly having been found to Daniel ELWELL. (Deed Book F, page 286)

1-18-1821 - Hiram BALL and Betsy his wife of Richland Co., Ohio, Lenas BALL and Sarah his wife, Timothy Ball and Sally his wife, all of Morris twp., Knox Co. to Cyrus BALL and Elizabeth his wife of Morris twp., Knox Co. - $500. - being pt. of land conveyed to our father David Ball by Lemuel Coble by deed dated 9-4-1800 and lying in 3rd quarter, 7th township, 8th range, military tract. Said land being in Morris township and lines in 1821 were—David Jackson, Wm. Mitchell and Timothy Ball. (Note:- In some instances the surname appears as BALE, however it is primarily given as BALL). (Deed Book F, page 413)

10-25-1825 - Jacob MARTIN and Ann his wife, Margaret MARTIN, Isaac VORE, Jr.
and Mary his wife formerly MARTIN, John DWIRE and Sarah his wife formerly
MARTIN, David MOORE and Elizabeth his wife formerly MARTIN, James MARTIN and
Ruhamah his wife, Margaret LAIN formerly MARTIN; Heirs of George MARTIN, dec'd
late of Knox Co. to Joseph S. MARTIN of Knox C. - $150. - Lots 90 & 96 in Mt.
Vernon. (Deed Book G, page 8).

2-26-1827 - Calvin CORBIN, Lyman CORBIN, Lucretia CORBIN, Clarissa CORBIN,
Artimas CORBIN, Schyler CORBIN and Mary DISBROW; Heirs of Jedediah CORBIN,
dec'd of Knox Co. to Alvin CORBIN of Knox Co. - $1000. - Land on East fork
Owl Creek Section 2, Township 7, Range 13, military tract consisting of 220
acres, lines—Abner Ayres, John Eversole, Thos. Doolittle, Jas. Doolittle,
Ziba Benedict, Schuyler Corbin. (Deed Book G, page 30)

5-28-1826 - Laura STEVENS aged 11 yrs. on 28 September last, daughter of Amiza
STEVENS, with consent of Amiza her father is bound to John STEVENS of Knox
County until said Laura is 18 yrs. of age. (Deed Book G, page 43)

3-16-1827 - James MONTGOMERY and Elizabeth his wife, Andrew MORRISON and Margaret his wife of Green Co., Pennsylvania to Thomas MORRISON of Knox County.
Power-of-Attorney. (Deed Book G, page 61)

5-21-1828 - George Washington RUNYAN aged 16 yrs. and 16 dys., son of Hill
RUNYAN is bound to Adam PYLE of Mt. Vernon to learn the trade of Tailor for
4 yrs. 10 mos. and 15 dys. (Deed Book G, page 380)

8-5-820 - Samuel GEDDES aged 18 yrs. on 21 November next, son of John GEDDES
is bound to William SMITH of Mt. Vernon to learn the trade of Hatter for
3 yrs (Deed Book G, page 399)

4-17-1825 - Daniel LEWIS by consent of his guardian, Wm. MEFFARD, is bound to
Richard and Nathan HOUSE to learn the trade of house joiner and cabinet maker
until he is 21 yrs. which will be 5 January 1832. (Deed Book G, page 433)

4-17-1825 - Richard BLAKE with consent of William BLAKE his father is bound
to Richard and Nathan HOUSE to learn the trade of house joiner and cabinet
maker until he is 21 yrs. which will be on 19 December 1831. (Deed Book G,
page 433)

6-8-1825 - Elias HILL of Jefferson Co., Ohio to Thomas P. HILL of Jefferson
Co., Ohio, Josiah HILL and Stephen HILL of Washington Co., Pennsylvania; sons
and heirs of John HILL, dec'd, late of West Bethlehem twp., Washington Co.,
Penna. - 150 acres part of Section 3, Township 6, Range 13 in Knox County.
(Deed Book G, page 457)

Nov. 1827 - Henry SMITH aged 6 yrs. last Sept. by Hosner CURTIS his guardian
is bound to William IRVINE until said Henry is 14 years of age.
(Deed Book G, page 542)

3-20-1829 - The Trustees of Clinton township bind William TELAFERO aged 10 yrs. 6 mos. and 9 dys., the illegitamate son of Harriet STEELE of said township to Jesse B. THOMAS to learn the trade of farmer. (Deed Book G, page 668)

Feb. 1829 - Philemon PIERSON, Jr. and Robert HENRY overseers of the poor of Clay township bind Daniel I. RUSSELL a poor boy aged 13 yrs. 11 mos. and 5 dys., son of Isaac RUSSELL whose residence is unknown to Peter BARNES for 7 yrs. 1 week and 4 days. (Deed Book G, page 678)

6-21-1831 - Mary SHEPHERD, John McGOWAN and Susan his wife, Elizabeth McGOWAN and Phebe McGOWAN of Knox Co., William McGOWAN of Richland Co., Ohio, Martin McGOWAN and Hannah his wife of Marion Co., Ohio; Heirs of Charles McGOWAN, dec'd to Isaac and Thomas McGOWAN of Knox County - $1.00 - Lot 11 in 4th quarter 8th township, 15th range, U. S. military tract. (Deed Book J, page 133)

12-29-1831 - George McGOWAN and Elizabeth his wife of Guernsey Co., Ohio, Heirs of Charles McGOWAN, dec'd to Isaac and Thomas McGOWAN of Knox Co. - $1.00 - Lot 11 in 4th quarter, 8th township, 15th range, military tract. (Deed Book J. page 134)

3-21-1832. - James McGOWAN of Sandusky Co., Ohio, heir of Charles McGOWAN, dec'd to Isaac and Thomas McGOWAN of Knox Co. - $1.00 - Lot 11 in 4th quarter, 8th township, 15th range, military tract. (Deed Book J. page 135)

9-1-1832 - William HANNAH and Barbara his wife of Knox Co. to Anthony JONES, Elizabeth JONES, Sabina JONES, Eleanor JONES, Nathan JONES, Christiana JONES, Mary JONES, William JONES and George JONES; Heirs of William JONES, dec'd, late of Jackson twp., Knox Co. - $127.50 - part SW¼ Section 4, Township 5, Range 10. (Deed Book J, page 333)

8-23-1831 - George WOLFE and Sarah his wife to Obediah HALL and others. Obediah Hall of Knox Co. and Amos Hall late of Knox Co., dec'd did in the lifetime of said Amos become purchasers and tenants in common. Said Amos departed this life before deed of conveyance could be executed leaving heirs:- Obediah Hall, Joel Hall, Anna wife of Samuel Wheeler, formerly Hall, Mary wife of Israel Dillon formerly Hall, Elizabeth wife of James Griffith formerly Hall, Samuel L. Hall and Ruth Hall - $800. - NW¼ Section 8, Township 5, Range 10 of lands sold at Zanesville. (Deed Book J, page 320)

4-10-1832 - Will of William BALDWIN of New Haven, Connecticut - dated 2-15-1831. Wife, Ann, also to serve as executrix. Children mentioned but not named. Signed, William Baldwin. Witnesses:- Rogers S. Baldwin, Amos Baker and Virgil M. Dow. (Deed Book J, page 94)

6-19-1833 - Mary BIGGS, Ephraim BIGGS, Noah BIGGS, Jeremiah BIGGS, Rezin BIGGS, Eleazer BIGGS and Davis BIGGS and Sarah his wife, Heirs of Noah BIGGS, dec'd to John. SHAFER - $1630. - SW¼ Section 25, Township 6, Range 11. (Deed Book K, page 367)

692

7-15-1833 - Philip DeWALT and Catharine his wife, George DeWALT and Christiann his wife, Isaac HARTER in his own right and by Power-of-Attorney of
Henry HARTER, all of Canton, Stark Co., Ohio, to Jacob SWITZER - $2500. -
90 acres 3rd quarter, 8th township, 13th range, U. S. military tract.
(Deed Book K, page 392).

11-20-1811 - Lodowick BRICKER (German Signature) and Elizabeth his wife of
Green County, Pennsylvania to Jacob BRICKER, John BRICKER, George BRICKER,
George LEWIS and Peter BRICKER, all of Knox Co.; various land descriptions.
(Deed Book B, pages 233-237)

6-21-1825 - Isaac RIDER aged 16 yrs. on 1st January last of Jonathan MILLER
his guardian is bound to James HUNTSBERRY to learn the trade of Chairmaking
until said Isaac is 21 years of age. (Deed Book F, page 272)

The following Death Notices were taken from the OHIO TIMES, MOUNT VERNON, OHIO Published on Tuesday morning.

9-25-1849 – DIED on 21st inst. at the Mansion House in Mt. Vernon, Mr. Samuel Hildreth of Frederickstown, Knox Co., Ohio.

10-9-1849 – DIED at the house of David Potwin, Esq. in Mt. Vernon, on Sabbath Sept. 30th 1849, Jefferson Hildreth son of Miner Hildreth, Esq. of Miller Twp., aged 20 yrs. and 5 ds.

10-9-1849 – DIED on Monday last at his residence near Newark, Mr. George Baker aged 55. He was a native of England, lived a short time in Brownsville, Penna. and moved to Newark, Ohio in 1822 (Newark Advocate Sept. 29)

10-16-1849 – DIED on 2d inst. in Bloomfield Twp., Morrow County, Mrs. Ann Potter wife of Captain Lemuel Potter, aged 63 yrs. 8 mo. and 17 days. The deceased was a native of New York state, emigrated with husband and family to this state in 1818. Was a member of the Baptist church for 30 years.

10-23-1849 – DIED on Sunday morning, Sept. 30th in Frederickstown, Knox County, Ohio, Mary Ellen Lewis aged 22 yrs. 9 mo.

10-23-1849 – DIED on Monday, Oct. 1st, George H. Kellam in the 30th year of his age.

10-23-1849 – DIED on Monday evening, Oct. 1st, Mrs. Eleanor Miller, in the 22d year of her age.

10-23-1849 – DIED on Sunday evening, Oct. 7th David M. Amadon in his 30th year.
(Bellville, O.)
10-30-1849 – DIED in Mt. Vernon on 8th inst. Miss Selviny Wright wife of Mr. Isaac Wright and only daughter of Mr. Richard Philips, aged 26 years.

11-6-1849 – DIED at the residence of her father in Clinton Twp. on Saturday the 3d inst., Miss Novina, third daughter of Mr. Joseph BEENY in the 18th year of her age.

11-27-1849 – DIED in Ankenytown, Knox Co., Ohio on 3d inst., Sherman Holister, aged 39 yrs. 8 mo. and 11 days. (Ind. and Ill. papers please copy)

12-11-1849 – DIED in Clinton Twp., 26th Nov. Ult. at the late residence of her son, James Newell, deceased; Mrs. Margaret Newell, formerly of Washington Co., Penna. aged about 90 years.

1-15-1850 – DIED in Clinton Twp. on the 6th of January 1850, Harvey Clark son of Harvey and Jeanette Lambert aged 6 months lacking 1 day.

1-22-1850 – DIED on 28 Dec. 1849 in Morris Twp., Mary Elizabeth daughter of Alfred and Elizabeth Hamblin aged 2 years and 10 months.

2-12-1850 - DIED at her residence in Morris Twp., Knox County, Ohio, on the 5th inst., Mrs. Sarah Trimble relict of James Trimble.

2-12-1850 - DIED on Thursday morning, Mr. Bradley Buckingham in the 65th year of his age. He settled in Newark at an early period after the town was laid out.

2-12-1850 - DIED on Wednesday last in the 30th year of her age, Mrs. Mary Haynes. Member of the Baptist Church.

2-19-1850 - DIED on the 8th inst. in Berlin Twp., Knox Co., Ohio, Joseph L. Richardson son of Hon. Isaac N. Richardson; aged 24 yrs.

3-12-1850 - DIED at New Castle, Coshocton Co., Ohio on Sunday 3d inst., Daniel W. Osborn of Licking County, aged 35 yrs. 5 mo. and 21 days.

4-30-1850 - DIED in Howard Twp. on Tuesday the 24th April inst., Miss Louisa, second daughter of Hon. Nicholas Spindler in the 24th year of her age.

4-30-1850 - DIED in Mt. Vernon on the 13th April inst., Cinthia S. only daughter of L. B. and Charlotte Gardner aged 3 yrs. 7 mos. and 13 ds.

4-30-1850 - DIED on the 20th inst. at her residence in Harrison Twp., Mrs. Ruth Veatch in the 87th year of her age. Also Mrs. Smylie of Clay Twp. on the same day aged about 87.

4-30-1850 - DIED at her residence in Clinton Twp. on Monday the 15th inst., Mrs. Polly Newell widow of James Newell, deceased, aged 58 yrs. 8 mos. and 28 days.

4-30-1850 - DIED in Burlington, Licking County on the 8th inst., Wm. H. Cooley aged 58 years.

4-30-1850 - DIED March 31st on board the steamboat Cincinnatus on a trip from New Orleans, Micajah W. Munson aged 24 years, youngest son of Gen. S. Munson of Licking Co., Ohio. (Newark Gazette)

4-30-1850 - DIED at his residence in Middlebury Twp., Knox Co., Ohio on 2d of 3d mo., Wm. W. Wright aged 58 yrs. and 21 days. Member of Society of Friends.

5-28-1850 - DIED in Clinton Twp., April 22d, Mr. Asabel Allen, Sr. aged 80 years. He was a native of Bridgewater, Mass. but resided for some years in Knox Co.

5-28-1850 - DIED in Morris Twp. on Friday morning, May 24th, Mrs. Elizabeth Wiley, aged 48 yrs. and 5 mos. Member of Church of Christ.

6-4-1850 - DIED at his residence three miles north-west of Mt. Vernon on Wednesday 29th May, James M. Hughes in the 25th year of his age. A brother of Dr. J. C. Hughes of this place, deceased was a native of Washington Co., Penna., which he had been a resident of until early in March when he removed to this county. (Washington Penna. papers please copy)

6-25-1860 - DIED at his residence in Morris Twp., Knox Co., on Friday the 14th inst. after a brief illness, Mr. William Bartlett in the 66th year of his age.

6-25-1850 - DIED at the residence of her son Wm. Bartlett in Morris Twp., Knox Co., on 21st of May ult., Mrs. Elizabeth Bartlett aged 85 years.

8-20-1850 - DIED in the city of Columbus on Friday the 16th inst., Mrs. Elizabeth D. wife of Amos Hall and daughter of James Osborne, Esq. of Knox County, aged 24 years; leaving husband, infant son and father.

9-10-1850- DIED in Mt. Vernon, Ohio on Tuesday morning Sept. 3d, 1850, Mr. Michael Runner, formerly of Granville, Licking County, aged 49 years and 4 months.

10-1-1850 - DIED in Miller Twp. on the____ _____(note: left blank), Arminta A. eldest daughter of Dr. Wm. Beardslee aged 12 years 3 months 17 days.

10-15-1850 - DIED at Mt. Vernon on 9th inst. Mrs. Mary Reed aged 46 yrs. Member of Associate Reformed Church.

10-15-1850 - DIED in Marion, Ohio on evening of 4th inst., Dr. R. H. Cochron aged 25 years 5 months & 10 days. (Marion Mirror)

2-4-1851 - DIED in the city of New York, Jan. 20, 1851, Rev. Edward Weed, formerly Paster of the Congregational Church, Mt. Vernon, Ohio.

3-4-1851 - Another REVOLUTIONARY Soldier gone - DIED at his residence in Union Twp., Knox County, Ohio on Sunday, February 9th, 1851, James McElroy, Sen'r. aged 86 years, 1 month and 15 days. He was born in Orange County, New York, Dec. 25, 1764. In the fall of 1779 when scarcely 15 years of age, he enlisted in Col. Washington's Dragoons and served in the far famed contest for American Liberty and Independence. He participated in several distinquished conflicts of these times such as the battle of Cowpens, Eutaw Springs &c. For some 20 years past he has shared the Pension bounty.

The following records were abstracted from Will Book A. Pages on which original record may be found are given in parenthesis.

LEONARD, William - dated 3-5-1806; recorded 5-3-1808. Eldest son, Amos. Daughter, Rachel. Signed, William (his mark) Leonard. Witnesses: John Mills, Thompson Mills, and Benj'm Brown. (1)

BOYLE, Jonathan of Clinton twp. - dated 11-24-1807; recorded 5-3-1808. Wife, Elizabeth. Sons: John, James and Thomas. Daughters: Christiana, Hannah, Sarah and Mary; all not of age. Executors: Mathew Merrit and John Mills. Signed, Jonathan (his mark) Boyle. Witnesses: Jonathan Hunt, Zeba Leonard and Daniel Demmick. (1)

SAPP, George of Union township - dated 1-6-1811; recorded 5-1-1811. Children: Daniel, Joseph, William, John, Margaret Critchfield, Catharine Critchfield, Mary Myers, Elizabeth Waide, and George. Signed: George Sapp (German signature). Witnesses: John Greer and William Robinson. (3)

HILLIER, Richard of Zanesville twp. Muskingum Co., Ohio - dated 12-18-1807; recorded 10-2-1811. Wife, Ann, also to serve as executrix. Five sons: Franklin, Anthony, John, Thomas and William; all not of age. Signed, Richard Hillier. Witnesses: Samuel Herrick, Luke Walpole and D. Harvey. (4)

WALKER, James Jr. - dated 11-9-1812; recorded 12-12-1812. Wife, Hannah. Sons: Philip, John, Joseph, Alexander, James, Robert and Jesse; Jesse to have larg Bible. Daughters: Polly and Sarah. Executor, Azariah Davis. Signed, James Walker. Witnesses: Solomon G. Mor and James Smith. (7)

JOHNSTON, William of Chester twp. - dated 9-10-1813; recorded 10-22-1813. Sons, mentioned but not named other than Daniel and Emsley who were to serve as executors. Five daughters, mentioned but not named. Signed, William Johnston. Witnesses: Joseph Denman, Robert Dalrymple and John Lewis. (9)

FISHBACK, Richard of Clinton - dated 5-21-1814; recorded August 1814. Wife, Mary. Sons, William Parker Fishback. Executors: Samuel H. Smith, Benj. Barney and Ichabod Marshall, all of Clinton. Signed, Richard Fishback. Witnesses: Ichabod Nye, Freeman Fishback and John P. McArdle. (10)

LINDSLY, John of Chester twp. - dated 8-15-1814; recorded Dec. 1814. Wife, Susanah. Sons, Elias and John. Daughters, Mary, Abigail, Lorana and Serena. Executors: Elias Lindsley and John Lewis. Signed, John Lindsley. Witnesses: John Lewis, Isaac Hoffman and Uriah Denman. (11)

LEONARD, Ziba - dated 7-23-1813; recorded 4-18-1815. Sons: Amos, Ziba, Michael and Joseph. Daughters, Martha and Lydia. Wife, not mentioned or named but note signatures. Signed, Ziba Leonard and Martha (mark) Leonard. Witnesses: Smith Hadley, Benjamin Brown, Wesley Spratt, Benjamin Leonard and Jonathan Burch. (12)

697

HUNTER, James - dated 9-12-1816; recorded Dec. 1816. Wife, Catharine, also to serve as executrix. Sons, George and Richard. Grandsons, George and William Freshwater sons of George Freshwater and Mary his wife. Signed, James Hunter. Witnesses: Mathew Davidson and Jacob Draper. (13)

SIMPKINS, John - Noncupative Will - dated 8-5-1809; recorded (1816-1817?). Wife, Pheaby. Two sons, Sealy and Benjamin. (14)

HINTON, John - dated 9-16-1817; recorded Oct. 1817. Wife, mentioned but not named. Sons, George and Thomas. Two youngest daughters, Mary and Malinda Hinton. Executor, Joseph Jennings. Signed: John (his mark) Hinton. Witnesses: John Borden, James Houck and Joseph Jennings. (15)

HARDISTY, Francis - dated 4-9-1817; recorded 5-5-1820. Wife, Sarah. Two sons, Hugh and Francis, also to serve as executors. Daughters: Mary wife of Philip Hawkins, Hannah wife of Barney Dewitt, Rachel wife of Francis Plakney (or Hakley?), Elizabeth wife of Charles McBride, Sarah wife of Alex'r Dallis (Dallas) and Ruth wife of Benjamin Austin. Signed, Francis Hardisty. Witnesses: John Davidson and James Smith. (15)

COOPER, George of Morgan twp. - dated 8-5-1817; recorded Oct. 1817. Wife, Jane. Two sons, John and William, not of age. Daughters, mentioned but not named, not of age. Executors, James Pollock and Jacob Hanger. Signed, George Cooper. Witnesses: Abner Brown, Jr. and James H. Smith. (17)

MAGERS, Lawrence - dated 8-21-1818; recorded May 1819. Sister, Henrietta Magers. Mentions other brothers and sisters, but does not name. Executor, John Arnold. Signed, Lawrence (his mark) Magers. Witnesses: John Furniss and William (his mark) Magers. (18)

DOTY, John of Miller twp. - dated 4-23-1819; recorded May 1819. Wife, Esther. Sons: Jeremiah, John and Samuel; Samuel not of age. Daughters: Elizabeth Crawford, Esther Farmer, Polly Myers, Ann and Sarah Doty; the last two not of age. Executors, John Doty and Jonathan Hunt, Jr. Signed, John (his mark) Doty. Witnesses: Timothy Colopy, Daniel Baxter and Elizabeth Boyle. (19)

DENMAN, William of Chester twp. - dated 6-26-1819; recorded Aug. 1819. Wife, Prudence. Children: Jonathan Denman, Joseph Denman, Rachel Clutter, Sarah Corwin, Margaret Parcel, Phebe Hathaway, Lydia Kimble, Electa Hathaway and Prudence Denman. Grandsons, Abner Trowbridge and William Denman son of Joseph. Executor: daughter, Prudence until Abner Trowbridge comes of age and then he is to serve as executor. Signed: William (his mark) Denman. Witnesses: Isaac Norton, Bartlett Norton and David Norton. (20)

SPEAKMAN, James - dated 1-29-1820; recorded May 1820. Brother, Joseph Wilson, also to serve as executor. Nephew, James Speakman, not of age. Signed, James Speakman. Witnesses: Wm. W. Farquher, Samuel Wilson and John Cook. (22)

COLVILLE, Jennet - dated 8-25-1821; recorded 10-2-1821. Sister, Martha Colville to have legacy left by will of their father, Joseph Colville; with Martha also to serve as executrix. Brother-in-law, John Adams. Signed, Jennet Colville. Witnesses: James Park and William Reeder.   (23)

WILSON, Samuel - dated 21st of 11th mo. 1821; recorded Apr. 1822. Wife, Hannah. Son, Joseph, not married. Grand-daughter, Hannah Townsend, not of age. Three grandsons: William Townsend, James Townsend and James Speakman. Executors: wife, Hannah and son, Joseph. Signed, Samuel Wilson. Witnesses: Wm. W. Farquhar, Thomas Townsend and W. W. Wright.   (25)

CRAMER, Joseph of Clinton twp. - dated 7-3-1821; recorded (not given-1822?). Wife, Mary. Five children: Levi, Rosana, George, Catherine and Rebecca. Mentions interest in estate of testator's late father, Gasper Cramer. Executor: friend, John Shaw of Mt. Vernon. Signed, John Cramer. Witnesses: Alex'r Elliott, Daniel D. Stevenson and John Roberts.   (26)

DURBIN, Samuel - dated 4-17-1822; recorded 4-29-1822. Wife, Rebecca, Sons: Thomas, James and John. Other children mentioned but not named. Brother, Scott Durbin. Executors: wife, Rebecca and brother-in-law, John Collins of Fairfield Co., Ohio. Signed, Samuel Durbin. Witnesses: John Trimble, Benjamin (his mark) Selvy and Scott Durbin. (27)

LEWIS, John of Wayne twp. - dated 4-5-1823; recorded 6-15-1822. Children, mentioned but not named, youngest not of age. Signed, John Lewis. Witnesses: Noah Willson, Nathan M. Young and James Bryant.   (29)

COOK, John Sr. - dated (not given); recorded 4-27-1822. Wife, Rachel to have Family Bible so long as she remains widow. Children: Polly, Dinah, John, Eliza, Idah, Stephen, Joseph, William, Nathan and Ruth. Executors: son, John Cook of Richland Co., Ohio and William Lavering of Knox Co. Signed, John Cook. Witnesses: John Ockerman and Obadiah Stillwell.   (30)

MELKER, Wendal of Morgan twp. - dated 10-4-1822; recorded 4-21-1823. Wife, Elizabeth. Only son, Abraham. Daughters: Elizabeth, Mary, Charlotte, Molly, Ann and Barbara. Executors: son, Abraham and brother, Philip Melker. Signed, Wendal (his mark) Melker. Witnesses: Peter Veatch and Jacob Cook. (32)

STRONG, Jane of Chester twp. - dated (not given); recorded 4-22-1823. Four sons: Josiah, Harley, Arvin C. and Orange. Two grand-daughters: Matilda and Cynthia Adelia daughters of son, Josiah Grant. Daughter, Orfella Strong. Son, Niles Strong. Executors: Darius Strong and Thomas Extol. Signed, Jane Strong. Witnesses: Reubin Clark and Moses George. (35)

LAVERING, Daniel - dated (not given); recorded 6-5-1821. Wife, Mary. Seven children: Grace, Henry, Charles, Nathan, John, Noah and Joseph; the last two not of age. Niece, Fanny Maxfield, not of age. Mentions grist and saw mill. Executors: son, Nathan; son-in-law, William Rambo. Signed, Daniel Lavering. Witnesses: John Cook and Thomas Mitchell. (36)

LEWIS, Elisha of Wayne twp. - dated 4-28-1823; recorded 5-22-1823. Wife, Charlotte. Sons, Daniel and John. Mentions two daughters but does not name. Executors, Nathaniel M. Young and Daniel Conger. Signed, Elisha Lewis. Witnesses: Noah Wilson, Wm. Lewis and David Lindsley. (39)

BLAIR, John - dated 9-13-1822; recorded 8-13-1823. Wife, Elizabeth, also to serve as executrix. Son, James. Mentions that there possibly may be another child on way. Signed. John Blair. Witnesses: Robert Giffin, Martin Engle, James Rightmire and Joseph Staats. (40)

BRIGHT, Nicholas of Zanesville twp., Muskingum Co., Ohio - dated 1-25-1817; recorded 11-24-1823. Wife, Nancy, also to serve as executrix. Son, David. Son-in-law, William Jones. Signed, Nicholas (his mark) Bright. Witnesses: James Lane, John Campbell and Hemphrey Campbill. (41)

McCARDLE, Peter - dated 8-13-1823; recorded 11-25-1823. Wife, Nancy. Daughter, May (Mary?). Grand-daughter, Nancy Murphy. Signed, Peter McCardle. Witnesses: Timothy Collopy and Jacob Collopy. (42)

SHAW, William Sr. of Chester twp. - dated 2-10-1824; recorded 3-15-1824. Brothers, Andrew and Samuel Shaw. Sisters: Margaret White, Jenner Oveats(?) and May (Mary?) Shaw, her heirs. Nephews, Robert and David Shaw. Bequeath to David Peoples, relationship if any, not stated. Executor, David Shaw. Signed, William Shaw. Witnesses: Martin McGown and Mary Sheapard. (43)

DUNN BARR, James - dated 12-8-1824; recorded 5-16-1825. Sons: Joseph D. Barr and Robert D. Barr. Bequeathes to Susannah McMillen and Jane wife of George Hunter, relationship, if any not stated. Executor, Abraham Doty. Signed, James Dun Barr. Witnesses: Jacob Draper and Thomas McDonnal. (45)

YOAKAM, Michael of Liberty twp. - dated 6-21-1825; recorded 8-20-1825. Wife, Drusilla. Children: Elizabeth Hornback, William Yoakam, Jacob Yoakam, John Yoakam, Michael Yoakam, Jr., Absalom Yoakam, Morgan Diether (? ink blot) and Ruth Shinberry. Executor, Gilman Bryant. Signed, Michael Yoakam. Witnesses: Stephen Chapman and Joseph Higgins. (46)

KEMMERER, John of Butler twp. - dated 9-8-1825; recorded 10-17-1825. Wife, Nancy. Son, Samuel. Mentions other children, but does not name. Executors: wife, Nancy and son, Samuel. Signed, John (his mark) Kemmerer. Witnesses: Dan'l Campbell and Adam Mosholder. (47)

HERROD (HARROD), Levi of Pleasant twp. - dated 9-24-1825; recorded 10-17-1825. Wife, Rachel. Five sons: Levi, Michael, James, William and Samuel. Four daughters: Jemima Biggs, Racheal Biggs, Elizabeth Bell and Sarah Dun. Executors: sons, Michael and Levi. Signed, Levi Harrod. Witnesses: Peter Veach and Andrew Casto. (49)

MILLER, John - dated 11-18-1825; recorded 1-21-1826. Wife, mentioned but not named. Children: Mary, Sarah, Joseph, Jesse, John, Isaac, Ire and Silas. Executors: wife (not named) and James McGibbany. Signed, John Miller. Witnesses: Solomon Geller and Abner Ustick. (52)

DARTING, William - dated 8-2-1825; recorded 10-17-1825. Son, Abraham Darting, also to serve as executor; mentions his daughter but does not name. Daughter, Jane. Grandsons: Patrick Morgan Darting, William Darting, Adam Hider Darting, William Darting Beaty, Jeremiah Beaty, Milan P. Darting. Mentions land owned by testator in Virginia. Signed, William (his mark) Darting. Witnesses: William Parker, Jehu Dailey and Wofford Vithy. (50)

WILSON, James of Jackson twp. - dated 12-17-1824; recorded 3-13-1826. Wife, Rebecca. Executors: wife, Rebecca and two sons, William and Michael. Signed, James Wilson. Witnesses: William Bawdon(?) and George Melick. (54)

SEVERN, Daniel Sr. of Union twp. - dated 8-10-1823; recorded 3-13-1826. Sons: Joseph, Absolom, Daniel Jr. and John. Daughters: Sarah wife of James Conner, Mary wife of Joseph Sovern, Abigail wife of Joseph Butter, Elizabeth wife of Thomas Butter and Rebeca wife of Oliver Jones. Grand-daughters: Jane Sovern and Mary Severn. Executors: sons, Joseph and Daniel Severn. Signed, Daniel Severn. Witnesses: Jesse Simpson, John Severns and Stephen (his mark) Severn. (55)

WILLIAMS, John - dated 2-17-1826; recorded 3-18-1826. Wife, Rachel. Sons: Dan, to have tract of land in Richland Co., Ohio where he resides; William, to have farm in Knox Co. where he resides; Gist, to have tract of land in Richland Co., Ohio containing saw mill; John P., land in Knox Co.; Abraham, land including Mill; Thomas; and Independance. Daughters: Rachel Williams now Prater (Prather), Eliza Williams and Emeline Williams. Grand-daughter, Elanor daughter of Wm. Williams. Mentions slaves to be released to Frederick Co., Maryland. Executors: wife, Rachel and son, John P. Signed, John Williams. Witnesses: Joseph Baker, Syvester Clark and John Byres. (57)

MURPHEY, Abner of Middlebury twp. - dated 2-25-1826; recorded 6-21-1826. Wife, Sarah. Sons: William, Basel, Elias and Hiram. Daughters: Rachel, Sarah, Mary Jackson and Ealinor Murphey. Nephew, Abner Shuman. Mentions tanyard. Executors: wife, Sarah and son, William. Signed, Abner Murphey. Witnesses: Hiram Murphey, Catharine Kirby and W. Spear. (62)

TURNER, Thomas - dated 5-9-1826; recorded 6-26-1826. Wife, Chloe. Bequeathes to Otis Warren and his two sons, Samuel and Thomas Warren. Executors, James Miller and Emor Haris. Signed, Thomas Turner. Witnesses: James Miller, Cyrus Gates and Emor Harris. (65)

McBRIDE, Charles of Pike twp. - dated 8-27-1826; recorded 3-6-1827. Wife, Elizabeth. Three sons: Thomas, William and Hugh. Daughters: Sarah, Jane, Ruth, Elizabeth, Mary and Nancy McBride; the last four not of age. Executors: wife, Elizabeth and Vom(?) Smith. Signed, Charles McBride. Witnesses: Hugh Bleakley and Benjamin Austin. (64)

BUTLER, James - dated 2-27-1827; recorded 6-2-1827. Sons: John, Levy, Charles S. and Isaac. Daughters: Prudence Butler now Harris wife of Warren Harris, Delila and Betsey Butler. Mentions land in Holmes Co., Ohio. Executor: brother, Benjamin Butler. Signed, James Butler. Witnesses: John Breer and James Henderson (66)

BROWN, Abner - dated 8-28-1827; recorded 10-29-1827. Wife, mentioned but not named. Son, Eleaser. Daughters: Mary and another daughter mentioned but not named. Executors: sons, Jeremiah and Aaron. Signed, Abner Brown. Witnesses: John Carmichael and Silas Brown.   (68)

SIMONS, Royal D. - dated 8-25-1826; recorded 11-1-1826. Wife, Levia. Daughters: Delean (Deleamias), Louisa, Emily, Caroline, Augusta, Nancy, Eliza and Mary. Executors: wife, Levia and James McGibeny. Signed, Royal D. Simons. Witnesses: Gideon Mott and John B. Jewett.   (69)

NYE, Samuel of Clinton twp. - dated 1-8-1828; recorded 3-15-1828. Father and Mother, Ichabod and Mary Nye. Brother, Ebenezer Nye. Two sisters, Assenath Yeoman and Mariah C. Nye. Executor; father, Icahabod Nye. Signed, Samuel S. Nye. Witnesses: Thomas Sprague and Stephen Chapman. (70)

ROSS, Abner of Chester twp. - dated 10-22-1827; recorded 3-10-1828. Wife, Anna, also to serve as executrix. Sons: Samuel, John and William. Daughters: Elenor, Deborah, Mary, Phebe, Hannah, Rachel, Sarah and Martha. Signed, Abner Ross. Witnesses: I. B. Packard and L. D. Mozier. (71)

HATHAWAY, Samuel of Jefferson twp., Green County, Pennsylvania - dated 3-23-26-1823; recirded 10-19-1827. Father, Simeon Hathaway. Two brothers, Uriah and Elijah. Mentions other brothers and sister. Wm. and Stephen Huss to be kept until 14 yrs. of age. Mentions land near Mt. Vernon, Ohio. Executor, Jacob Harry of Morkin twp. Codicil dated 4-14-1823. Brother, John Hathaway's three children. Sister, Sarah. Bible to Mary Cruir(?). New Bible to sister, Ruth. Signed, Samuel Hathaway. Witnesses: John Andrane. Lot Leonard Jr. and Samuel Smith.   (72)

EWING, Sarah of Chester twp. - dated July 1825; recorded (no no. & da. given) 1827. Son, John. Step-son, Edward Evans. Executors, Morris Morris and Wm. W. Evans. Witnesses: John Smith and Theophilus Rees.   (76)

DAY, Abraham - dated 6-20-1826; recorded 11-1-1826. Wife, Deborah. Children: Abraham, Elizabeth Garnren(?), Isaac and Jacob. Executors, Abrham Day and Ebenezer Condict. Signed, Abraham Day. Witnesses: James Porter and Joseph Kercue(?).   (78)

WORKMAN, Isaac - dated 10-3-1827; recorded 3-12-1828. Wife, Lydia. Sons: Stephen, Joseph, John, Levi, Abraham and Solomon; the last three not of age. Daughters: Hannah Workman now Porter, Elizabeth Workman now Robeson, Nancy Workman now Wells (or Wills), Susannah Workman now Waddle, Eve Workman now Graham, Rebecca Workman now Robeson, Margaret Workman now Graham, Mary Workman, Abigail Workman, Jane Workman and Sarah Workman. Executor, Solomon Robeson. Signed, Isaac Workman. Witnesses: Isaac Draper and Solomon Workman.   (79)

CARMICHEL, John of Morgan twp. - dated 9-16-1828; recorded 10-27-1828. Children: Rody; Mary; Pheby; Hannah; Sarah; Stephen; Anne, her children; Jacob; Elizabeth; Meribah. Grand-daughter, Catherina McClain. Executors, Jacob Hanger and Joseph Robinson. Signed, John Carmichal. Witnesses: Jacob Robb and Aaron Davis. (82)

The following marriages were copied from Marriage Record 1-2-3, located in the
Probate Court of the court house at Ironton. This book appears to be a transcript
of the original three books.

ADAMS, Richard to Fanny Murrel Creedle	6-20-1817
ADAMS, Solomon to Susannah Overstreet	4-15-1818
ADKINS, Littlebay to Delfy Adkins	7-1-1821
ALFORD, James to Mary Hatfield	2-15-1821
ARTHER, Jechonias to Franney Brown	1-23-1823
BABER, John to Elizabeth Maxey	4-21-1821
BAKER, Jacob to Polly Yingling	12-29-1822
BAKER, Squire to Polly Switzer	12-21-1823
BALL, Robert to Sarah Wilson	10-17-1817
BECKET, John to Nancy King	2-21-1821
BECKET, Josiah to Henrietta King	11-23-1820
BECKLEY, Solomon to Laura Scovell	5-8-1821
BELL, Benjamin to Lavina Webb	5-28-1822
BELL, Isaac to Elizabeth Jones	10-13-1822
BILLUPS, Edward to Dosha Wilgus	10-24-1822
BILLUPS, John to Hetty Wilgus	6-29-1820
BLACK, Lewis to Leandra Lambert	2-23-1823
BLANKENSHIP, Isham to Moody Keeney	11-26-1820
BLANKENSHIP, Isam to Hannah Collins	5-11-1820
BLANKENSHIP, Isam Sr. to Elizabeth Dilley	6-13-1820
BLANKNELL, Jacqu Eetter Theadore to Florida Harson	4-23-1820
BLOWERS, Pairpoint to Sarah Piles	1-14-1821
BOWEN, George to Lettishe McFan	10-7-1819
BOYD, John to Sarah Moore	1-27-1820
BRADSHAW, Skelton to Mary Violet McCoy	9-16-1819
BRAMMER, Edmund to Nancy Hatfield	8-28-1823
BRAMMER, Jesse to Anna Lambert	8-2-1822
BRAMMER, Joseph to Nancy Collins	7-13-1817
BRAMMER, William to Elizabeth Clarke	10-20-1818
BROWN, George to Lucy Minerva Gillet	10-6-1822
BRUMFIELD, John to Rachel Haskins	7-28-1823
BUMGARNER, Abraham to Rebecca Lambert	11-20-1823
CAMPBELL, James to Mary Stewart	5-28-1821
CANTER, Thomas Jr. to Anny Canter	7-19-1821
CARPENTER, Thomas to Nancy Ertes	7-15-1818
CARTER, James to Elizabeth Scarborough	9-11-1817
CHAFFIN, John H. to Susannah Wolf	1-16-1821
CLARKE, James to Martha Lambert (1818?)	10-13-1819
COLLIER, James 2nd to Mary Hisey	4-4-1822
COLLIER, William to Hannah Snider	2-24-1822
COLLINS, Patrick to Nancy Griffy	12-8-1818
COMER, Emanuel to Patsy Smith	2-3-1820
COMPSTON, John to Salley Triggs	4-30-1821
CONWAY, Charles to Mary Collins	3-5-1819
CONWAY, Richard to Tenney Pancake	12-11-1823

```
COOPER, Thos. to Mary Nelson                        4-18-1822
COPENHAVEN, John to Elizabeth Bumgardner            7-20-1818
COX, James to Nancy Noble                           12-28-1820
CULRIGHT, George to Caulina Walbridge               8-28-1820
DAVIDSON, Joseph to Betsey Westcott                 3-8-1821
DAVIDSON, Thomas to Polly Creedle                   1-19-1820
DAVIDSON, William to Sarah Short                    5-31-1821
DAVIDSON, William to Hannah Ross                    8-7-1823
DAVIS, Joseph to Elizabeth Bowers                   10-30-1817
DAVIS, Zacariah to Margat McCullough                8-24-1823
DIX, James to Eleey (or Elecy) Bivins               1-7-1819
DREWYER, Simon to Cynthia Billups                   5-10-1818
DROUILLARD, Joseph to Sally Bowen                   8-31-1820
DUNKEL, William to Elisibeth Lee                    8-7-1823
DUNN, Armstrong to Polly Brandon                    12-30-1819
EARLS, Martin to Elizabeth Sumpter                  10-15-1820
EDMUNDS, Thomas to Nancy Leftwich                   1-25-1820
ERWIN, John to Eliza M. Chadwick                    10-5-1822
FALKNER, John to Susannah Spears                    12-27-1818
FAULKNER, William to Thirsey Creedle                3-23-1823
FERRIS, John to Polly Murphy                        3-5-1822
FISHER, Martin to Lovey W. Tunnell                  7-22-1821
FITZER, John to Polly Woods                         9-20-1822
FITZER, Joseph to Sary Woods                        12-31-1822
FORGEY, Hugh to Elizabeth Kneff                     7-20-1817
FORGY, Alexander to Lucy Elkins                     6-18-1820
FRAD, John to Zibia Blowers                         8-15-1822
FRAMPTON, Elijah to Rebecca Clark                   10-28-1822
FRANCIS, Elihu to Sarah Radford                     6-16-1822
FUDGE, Jacob to Margret Taitt                       7-26-1821
FUDGE, John to Prescilla Porter                     1-22-1818
FURGUSON, John to Elizabeth McCoy                   4-11-1817
GANDY, David to Olivia Vanbibber                    3-6-1821
GARDNER, Thomas to Chloe Gillett                    9-5-1818
GARRETT, Leroy to Elizabeth Allison                 7-4-1819
GILLETT, Joel to Julia Risley                       6-18-1820
GILRUTH, Wim to Rebeckah Austin                     10-3-1822
GLOVER, Thos. to Betsey Burn                        9-13-1820
GOLDEN, Martial to Peninah Dilley                   9-11-1823
GOLDEN, Thomas to Christianne Brammer               3-14-1822
GRAVES, George to Lucy Childers                     6-29-1820
HALL, Pheneas D. to Sally Baerdaley                 12-28-1823
HARRISON, John to Frances Howard                    5-25-1820
HATCHER, Charles to Sally Melvin                    4-17-1823
HATFIELD, Isaac to Polly Clark                      2-7-1822
HELVESON, William to Jane Bradshaw                  12-19-1822
HELVISSON, James to Sary Fittspatrick               4-6-1823
HENSLEY, Samuel to Katharine Leftridge              5-4-1817
HENWOOD, Joshua to Anna Knight                      11-16-1820
```

704

HEWETT, Ira to Rebecca Bardsley	7-11-1819
HOBBS, Ephergn to Ellender Doderedge	4-13-1823
HOLADAY, Andrew to Mary Stover	3-1-1821
HOLLADAY, George to Agnes Huddleston	5-2-1819
HOLTEN, George to Sarah Holley	6-13-1820
HUGHS, Asa to Sarah Neal	7-19-1818
IRWIN, George to Jemima Russell	7-5-1821
JAMS, Peter to Jemina Bagley	1-1-1822
JAYNES, Zopher to Catharine Baker	12-24-1823
JOHNSTON, James to Mary McGinnis	9-26-1822
JOHNSTON, Lewis to Polly French	7-24-1823
JONES, David to Barbary Brumfield	6-25-1821
JONES, James to Margaret Crane	11-13-1817
JONES, William to Martha Howard	5-12-1819
JOURDON, Pleasant to Anna Burchet	4-27-1821
KELLY, John to Anny Dilley	6-5-1823
KELLY, Joseph to Elizabeth Stitth	10-20-1817
KENNELL, Isaac to Rhoda Webb	10-13-1822
KILGORE, Jeremiah to Nancy Fullerton	3-16-1821
KING, John to Catharine McCormas	7-22-1822
KINNEY, Eleazer to Caroline Clark	9-26-1821
KOONS, Andrew to Hannah Hysey	10-25-1821
LAMBAUGH, Joseph to Lydia Virdin	8-12-1823
LAMBERT, Isaac to Nancy Sperry	11-3-1817
LAMBERT, Josiah to Elizabeth McIntire	2-15-1821
LANE, William R. to Sally Frampton	12-17-1819
LANGDON, Joseph to Arthametta Brammer	3-13-1823
LEWIS, Samuel to Mary Burcham	10-14-1819
LEWIS, William to Elizabeth Oxer	11-19-1817
LIGAN, Jacob G. to Elizabeth Moman	4-20-1821
LOVEJOY, John to Sarah Wilson	5-4-1821
LOVEJOY, John to Sarah Coal	5-21-1821
LUCAS, Burton to Elizabeth Stith	12-2-1817
McAMBUS, Benjamin to Sarah Loar	7-29-1819
McCARTNEY, Andrew to Mary Warren	2-6-1822
McCORKLE, Samuel to Elizabeth Seemans	9-9-1819
McCORMUS, George to Katharine McConnell	3-11-1818
McCORMUS, Sartin to Henrietta Howard	1-6-1820
McCORNAS, Ammon to Polly Brumfield	1-23-1823
McCOY, John to Jame Cambell	2-12-1822
McGINNIS, John to Mercy Lockhart	3-14-1822
McGLAUGHLIN, David to Phebe Gillet	10-11-1821
McINTIRE, Joseph to Lucy Pine	1-30-1823
McKEE, John to Nancy Ankrim	1-11-1821
McMAHAN, James to Elizabeth Monahon	12-30-1817
McMAHAN, Stephen to Polly Lunsford	2-21-1820
McMAN, John to Susannah Burcham	4-15-1819
McSORLEY, James to Polly Price	8-12-1820
MALONE John to Eunice Neff	1-6-1819
or	1-7-1819

MANNEN, Moses to Polly Simmons	1-10-1822
MANNEN, Wilson to Sinthy Mannen	1-23-1823
MARKIM, Thomas to Francis Sumpter	7-24-1817
MARKIMS, Charles to Nancy Sampson	11-30-1820
MARTAIN, John to Steny Fudge	7-31-1818
MARTIN, Oty to Elizabeth Earls	8-4-1822
MARTIN, William to Mrs. Nancy Watts	9-14-1820
MELVIN, Nathan to Barbara Jenkins	12-11-1823
MILES, Martin to Betsey Smith	3-21-1822
MILLER, Abraham Jr. to Nancy Lowsey	6-28-1821
MORGAN, Asa to Elizabeth Blankenship	11-24-1822
MORRISON, Joseph to Rebecca Stephenson	3-20-1818
NANCE, Banester to Barshaba Wells	9-26-1821
NANCE, Eliger to Polly Mannen	1-23-1823
NANCE, Richard to Betsy Dodd	2-27-1820
NANCE, Richard to Genny Wells	8-28-1822
NEAL, Asael to Polly Hall	1-9-1820
NEWBERRY, John to Ebee Night	6-30-1819
NIXON, William to Jane Hopkins	2-4-1822
PATON, Charles to Jane Paton	11-27-1823
PEAS, Samuel E. to Harriet Gillett	6-17-1819
PERKINS, Joseph to Ruth Walls	1-18-1821
PERKINS, William to Ebby Veel	5-2-1822
PETTERY, Sinkler to Elizabeth Higgins	6-11-1818
PIERCE, James to Betsey Lambert	4-3-1823
POAGE, James A. to Sarah C. Campbell	5-3-1820
POUGE, Robert W. to Ann Johnston	12-12-1822
POWELL, William to Franey Yingling	1-25-1821
PRESTON, Moses to Elizabeth Harvey	6-11-1818
PRICHET, Luis to Lucy Toler	12-29-1821
RADER, Charles to Elizabeth JOHNSTON	3-11-1819
RESE, Archibald to Cincerella Rice	11-29-1818
RICE, George to Isabel Knight	4-27-1820
RICE, James to Elizabeth Kinner	2-17-1822
RIDDLE, John to Susannah Colyer	6-5-1817
RIPLEY, David to Esther Griswald	1-13-1819(?)
ROBERSON, Samuel to Elizabeth Marsh	12-15-1823
ROSE, Robert to Hannah Coneway	3-28-1818
ROSS, Joseph to Rhody Kelley	2-8-1823
ROWLEY, Isham to Katharine Snell	12-18-1817
RUSSELL, Samuell to Mary Irwin	2-13-1823
RUSSELL, Sandford to Barbary Losey	5-10-1821
SAMPSON, Valentine to Nancy Higgins	1-18-1821
SHERMAN, James G. to Nancy Hankins	7-13-1820
SHORT, James to Nancy White	9-14-1823
SHUTE, John C. to Nancy Koons	9-13-1821
SIMMONS, Joel Jr. to Nancy Mannen	3-7-1822
SKITMORE, Andrew to Elizabeth Martin	11-19-1823
SMITH, Abraham to Alia Clark	3-14-1821
SMITH, William to Tabitha Haws	10-22-1820

SOWARDS, Griffin to Elizabeth Purkins	10-9-1823
SOWARDS, James to Phebe Chapman	9-28-1820
SOWARDS, Thomas to Rosannah Spears	7-26-1821
SPROUSE, Lewis to Cynthia Doolittle	4-21-1822
SPROUSE, William A. to Matilda Graham	7-7-1822
STERNS, John W. to Miomi McCane	5-29-1820
STEWART, Edward to Jane McCoy	8-10-1820
STEWART, John to Sally McCartney	3-16-1820
STUCK, Jacob to Betsey Baird	7-29-1821
SUITER, Philip to Sally Shour	11-19-1819
SUITER, Wiliam M. to Elizabeth Sparling	10-14-1819
TACKETT, Thomas to Winney Sampson	3-30-1819
TAITT, James Skelton to Sarah Fudge	12-5-1819
TAITT, John A. to Docia Breeding	12-3-1823
TAYLOR, Horatio to Anna Francis	12-3-1823
TEMPLETON, James to Jane Morrison	2-13-1823
THOMAS, James to Eliaabeth Miller	6-28-1822
THUMBO, George to Polly Austin	6-22-1817
TULL, William to Hannah Cyle	12-7--1817
VANCONEY, Samuel to Jane Thurston	6-28-1821
VERMILLION, John to Elizabeth Compston	1-23-1820
VERMILLION, Reuben to Rebecca Compton	2-10-1820
WARD, Charles to Amey Kelley	3-8-1818
WARPLEY, Henry to Elizabeth McKinsey	11-11-1817
WATTERS, Joel to Keziah Miller	10-22-1822
WEBB, Elias to Jane Gillelum	3-8-1818
WEBB, George to Genne Coleman	6-24-1822
WHITE, David to Sarah Parsons	6-13-1817
WHITE, James to Wealthy Faulkner	10-29-1819
WILLIAM, James to Rebecca Davidson	1-31-1821
WILLIAMS, Enoch to Sarah Keller	3-4-1818
WILSON, Terry to Artey Nance	6-12-1820
WOOD, Paulus Emelius to Adaline Augusta Fuller	7-4-1822
YATES, Benjamin to Ann Delong	6-15-1820

The following records were copied from "Journal 3-4" as found in the office of the Clerk of Court at the court house at Ironton. Only records of genealogical value have been included. Civil actions have not been copied. Page on which record may be found in the original record is given in parenthesis.

9-9-1830 - Will of Robert BAIRD late of Burlington produced 4-19-1830 and proven this court. Widow, Leah Baird. (4)

9-9-1830 - Thomas Hatfield appointed guardian of William HOWARD jr., minor son of William Howard Sr. (9)

9-9-1830 - William DAVIDSON granted license to keep grocery and retail spiritous liquors at his stand at mouth of Davidson Street in Burlington. (9)

9-9-1830 - Settlement by Charles Hatcher executor of will of Farley HATCHER. (9)

9-9-1830 - Peter KINGRA declared insolvent. (9)

11-29-1830 - Will of John McCORKLE produced. John Layne, executor. Robert McCorkle brother of deceased contested will. (10)

3-8-1831 - Samuel LANGDON granted license to keep ferry across Syms Creek at his usual landing in Union twp. (16)

3-8-1831 - George JONES granted license to keep ferry across the Ohio River at his usual landing near the Hanging Rock. (16)

3-8-1831 - Sarah Horner and Joshua Horner appointed administrators of the estate of Moses HORNER, dec'd. (16)

3-8-1831 - Leah BAIN granted license to keep tavern in Burlington. (16)

3-9-1831 - Rev. John FORBUSH minister of Presbyterian Society granted license to solemnize marriages. (21)

3-9-1831 - Sally Boyd widow and relict of John BOYD appointed guardian of Malinda BOYD aged 10 yrs. 11 mos., Polly BOYD aged 8 yrs. 11 mos. & Matilda BOYD aged 6 yrs. 9 mos., minor children of John Boyd, dec'd. (22)

3-10-1831 - Marinda Wakefield and Elnathan W. Wakefield appointed adms. of the estate of Timothy WAKEFIELD, dec'd. (23)

3-11-1831 - Will of John DAVIDSON produced. John Davidson, executor. (25)

3-11-1831 - Susana DAVIDSON, widow of John Davidson relinquishes dower in estate.(26)

3-11-1831 - Jesse Dollarhide and Mary Dollarhide adms. of estate of Allen DOLLARHIDE file settlement. (26)

3-11-1831 - Reuben Kelly appointed guardian of Thomas DOLLARHIDE age 11 yrs., Sarah DOLLARHIDE aged 8 yrs. and Washington DOLLARHIDE aged 6 yrs., children of Allen Dollarhide, dec'd. (26)

3-11-1831 - Abraham MILLER granted license to keep ferry across the Ohio at his usual landing in Rome twp. (34)

3-11-1831 - William DAVIDSON granted license to keep ferry across the Ohio River at his usual landing at mouth of Davidson St. in Burlington. (34)

3-11-1831 - Reuben KELLY granted license to keep ferry across the Ohio River at his landing at his house in Upper twp. (34)

3-11-1831 - Katherine Hughs adms. of estate of Silas HUGHS files settlement. (34)

3-11-1831 - Samuel Huff adms. of estate of Ezekiel ALDRIGE files settlement. (34)

3-11-1831 - Asa Kimball appointed guardian of Joseph DAVIDSON aged 12 yrs., minor heir of Asa KIMBALL, dec'd. (34)

3-11-1831 - Charles KELLEY and John H. CHAFFIN granted license ti jeeo taverb at house at forks of road near bridge across Hales Creek at Charles Kelley Mill in Elizabeth twp. (34)

6-9-1831 - Final settlement by Leah Baird and Curtis Scovill executors of Will of Robert BAIRD. Widow, Leah Baird. Children: Leah wife of John Charlton, Rufus Baird, Abner Baird, Moses Baird, Maria Baird, Robert Baird and Susanna Baird. (36)

9-7-1831 - Esther Austin widow of George AUSTIN, dec'd relinquishes dower. Will
of George Austin proven at May term of court 1827. (46)
9-9-1831 - Curtis Scoville and Leah Shields formerly Leah Baird executors of will
of Robert Baird resign as executors and Leah resigns as guardian of minors. (52)
9-9-1831 - Leah SHIELDS and William Shields her husband appointed guardians of
Moses BAIRD aged 13 yrs., Mariah BAIRD aged 8 yrs., Robert BAIRD aged 6 yrs.
and Susanna BAIRD aged 4 yrs., heirs of Robert Baird, dec'd. (52)
9-9-1831 - Abner BAIRD aged 16 yrs., heir of Robert Baird chose William Miller
as his guardian. (53)
9-9-1831 - Leah SHIELDS formerly guardian of Rufus BAIRD ordered to pay court
$342. 17 being share of said Rufus Baird. (53)
9-9-1831 - Elisha B. Greene adms. of estate of William BAIRD files settlement. (53)
9-9-1831 - Preston Moore appointed guardian of Melinda BOYD aged 9 yrs., Polly
BOYD aged 7 yrs. and Matilda BOYD aged 6 yrs., heirs of John Boyd, dec'd.(53)
9-9-1831 - Joseph McNignt adms. of the estate of Charles McNight files settlement.
Widow and four minor children mentioned but not named. (54)
9-15-1831 - Stephen Stewart appointed adms. of the estaste of Richard CONDON,
dec'd. (54)
10-19-1831 - Jacob Bumgardner appointed adms. of the estate of Daniel CONDON,
dec'd. (55)
2-29-1832 - Maria V. F. Vintroux Herson adms. of estate of William VINTROUX,
dec'd presents account to-wit: Francis Leclerq guardian of Lewis Edward
Vintroux minor of William Vintroux, paid $266.00 for boarding said Lewis
Edward from Nov. 11, 1824 to Nov. 11, 1828. Francis Leclerq guardian of
Maria V. Camella Vintroux, Helen Matilda Eugene Vintroux, William Vintroux,
Celestine Vintroux, Clarissa Vintroux, Alphonzo Vintroux and Alphonsine
Vintroux, minors of William Vintroux, dec'd, paid $250.00 for each for
boarding, clothing and schooling each from Nov. 11, 1824 to Feb. 28, 1832.(61)
2-29-1832 - Abraham D. DAVIDSON granted license to keep ferry across Ohio River at
his usual landing at his house in Fayette twp. opposite mouth of Big Sandy.(63)
3-1-1832 - William WATTS granted license to keep tavern at his house in Burlington
formerly occupied by Elisha B. Greene as a tavern house. (66)
3-1-1832 - Settlement of estate of William VINTROUX, dec'd filed at August term
1827 by Maria Viryile Fanny Vintroux Herson, adms. with order at June term
1825 directing sale of real estate of which William Vintroux died seized.
At this term Maria Viryilia Vintroux paid $444.08 belonging to Lewis Edward,
Maria V. Camilla, H. M. Eugene, William, Celestine, Clarissa, Alphonso and
Alphonsine, children and heirs of dec'd. (66)
6-4-1832 - Isaac Davisson executor of John DAVISSON, dec'd who was guardian of
Harriet STOVER files settlement. (71)
6-4-1832 - Isaac DAVISSON executor of John DAVISSON, dec'd files settlement.(71)
6-4-1832 - Thomas Campbell guardian of Joseph DAVISSON files settlement. (71)
6-4-1832 - Abraham MILLER granted license to keep ferry across Ohio River at his
usual landing in Rome twp. (71)
6-4-1832 - Andrew Wolf Sr. and John Clark, witnesses prove will of Andrew WOLF Jr.(72)
6-6-1832 - Titan Kimble and Alexander Campbell, witnesses prove will of John
McCANE, dec'd. (75)
6-6-1832 - Charles Riggs guardian of Thomas RIGGS and Malinda wife of Alfred
Haden files settlement. (75)
6-7-1832 - Reuben KELLY granted license to keep ferry across Ohio River at usual
landing in Upper twp. (76)

6-7-1832 - John COLLIER granted license to keep ferry across Ice Creek at usual
landing. (76)

8-27-1832 - Charles KELLEY granted license to keep tavern at a house at the forks
of the road near bridge across Hales Creek at said Kelley Mill in Elizabeth
twp. (80)

8-27-1832 - William DAVIDSON granted license to keep ferry across Ohio River at
his landing at mouth of Davidson St. (Burlington). (80)

8-28-1832 - This day appeared in open court Nathaniel PRITCHARD who made and filed
his Declaration to obtain the benefit of the act of congress of the 7th June
1832 granting pensions for service rendered in the revolutionary war and the
court does hereby declare their opinion after the investigation prescribed by
the war department and from their personal acquaintance with said applicant
he having been some years a member of the court that he was a revolutionary
soldier and served as he states and the court further certify that Elisha B.
Greene and William G. Robinson there being no clergyman residing in the neighborhood of applicant who have signed the above certificate, are residents in
this county and state and are personally known to the court to be creditable
persons and that their statements are entitled to credit. (85)

8-28-1832 - This day appeared in open court William GILLELAN who made and filed his
declaration to obtain the benefit of the act of congress of the 7th June 1832
granting pension for services rendered in the revolutionary war and the said
court does hereby declare their opinion that the above named applicant was a
revolutionary soldier and served as he states. (85)

8-28-1832 - This day appeared in open court Anthony CLARKE who made and filed his
Declaration to obtain the benefit of the act of Congress of the 7th June 1832
and the said court does hereby declare their opinion after the investigation of
the matter and after putting the interrogation prescribed by the war department
that the above named applicant was a revolutionary soldier and served as he
states and the court further certifies that Peter Wakefield and Edward Mumahan
who have signed the preceding certificate there being no clergyman residing in
the neighborhood are creditable persons and that their statements are entitled
to credit. (85)

8-28-1832 - This day appeared in open court John ELLISON who made and filed his
Declaration to obtain the benefit of the act of congress of the 7th June 1832
and the said court does hereby declare their opinion after the investigation of
the matter and after putting the interrogation prescribed by the war department
that the above name applicant was a revolutionary soldier and served as he
states and the court further certifies that William Miller and Elisha B. Greene
who have signed the preceding certificate there being no clergyman having any
acquaintance with said applicant being resident in the neighborhood reside in
Burlington as stated and are persons well known to the court as creditable
persons and that their statements are entitled to credit. (85)

8-28-1832 - This day appeared in open court Robert McCORKLE who made and filed his
Declaration to obtain the benefit of the act of congress of the 7th June 1832
granting pensions for services rendered in the revolutionary war and the said
court does hereby declare their opinion that the above named applicant was a
revolutionary soldier and served as he states. (85-86)

8-29-1832 - This day appeared in open court Joseph LUMBAUGH who made and filed his
Declaration to obtain the benefit of the act of congress of the 7th June 1832
granting pensions for services rendered in the revolutionary war and the said
court does hereby declare their opinion that the above named applicant was a
revp;itopmaru sp;doer amd served as je states/ (86)

710

8-29-1832 - This day appeared in open court John ROBERTS who made and filed his
Declaration to obtain the benefit of the act of congress of the 7th June 1832
granting pension for services rendered in the revolutionary war and the said
court do hereby declare their opinion that the above named applicant was a
revolutionary solder and served as he states. (86)

8-29-1832 - This day appeared in open court Frederick STUMBAUGH who made and filed
his declaration to obtain the benefit of the act of congress of the 7th June
1832 granting pensions for services rendered in the revolutionary war and the
said court having examined the applicant find that by reason of an infirmity
occasioned by a paralytic shock he is unable to give any direct or intelligible
testimony of his services or the names of officers except by an interpreter,
his son John Stumbaugh and by this help a very imperfect testimony is obtained
but from the evidence of said John Stumbaugh and the applicant and Judge
Reuben Kelley and Preston Moore who were acquainted with the applicant witnesses examined before us the court are of the opinion that the above named
applicant was a revolutionary soldier that he enlisted in March 1781 and served
to the conclusion of the war. Yet as to the term of service or the time
when he was discharged the court gives no opinion except that he served from
March 1781 till after the surrender of Cornwallis at York Town. (86)

8-29-1832 - This day appeared in open court Samuel LEYNE who made and filed his
Declaration to obtain the benefit of the Act of Congress of the 7th June 1832
granting pension for service rendered in the revolutionary war and the court
do hereby declare their opinion after the investigation of the matter and
putting the interrogations prescribed by the war Department that the above
named Samuel Leyne was a revolutionary soldier and served as he states and the
court further certifies that it appears to them that Robert McCorkle and John
Stumbo who have signed the preceding certificate, there be no clergyman
residing in the neighborhood, reside in said county and township near the said
Leyne and that they are creditable persons and their statements are entitled
to credit. (86)

8-29-1832 - Nathan LEEDOM declared insolvent. (87)

8-29-1832 - Isaac Suitor son of Jacob SUITOR, dec'd appointed adms. of the estate
said Jacob SUITOR, dec'd. (87)

8-29-1832 - Isaac Davidson executor of John DAVIDSON, dec'd who was guardian of
Harriet Colmes formerly Harriet STOVER files settlement. (87)

8-29-1832 - Isaac Davidson executor of John DAVIDSON, dec'd who was guardian of
Elizabeth LAMBERT formerly Elizabeth STOVER makes settlement. (88)

8-29-1832 - Richard Lambert makes settlement June 1831 of guardianship of Barbara
HATFIELD formerly Barbara STOVER and of Joel STOVER. (88)

8-29-1832 - E. W. Wakefield and Marinda Beams formerly Wakefield adms. of estate
of Timothy WAKEFIELD, dec'd, ask for more time to make accounting. (88)

8-29-1832 - Charles Riggs guardian of Malinda HASTINGS formerly Malinda RIGGS
and of Thomas RIGGS makes settlement. (89)

10-26-1832 - Nancy Shute, widow and George Koons appointed adms. of the estate
of John C. SHUTE, dec'd. (89)

11-29-1832 - Amherish S. KIMBALL aged 20 years, heir of Asa Kimball, dec'd, chose
his brother, Asa Kimball as his guardian. (90)

11-29-1832 - Will of Reuben BRUMLETT, dec'd produced by John McKea and William
Freeman, executors. (90)

711

3-11-1833 - This day appeared in open Court Henry MANNON who made and files his
Declaration in order to obtain the benefit of the act of congress of the 7th
June 1832 granting pensions for service rendered in the Revolutionary War
and the court does hereby declare their opinion after the investigation of
the matter and putting the interrogations prescribed by the war department
that the above named applicant was a Revolutionary soldier and served as he
states and that it appears to the court there being no clergyman residing in
the neighborhood of the applicant and that William Holderby and Joseph
Davidson who signed the above certificate are creditable persons and their
statements are entitled to credit. (95)

3-11-1833 - Samuel LANGDON granted license to keep ferry across Symmes Creek at his
usual landing. (95)

3=11=1833 - Abraham D. DAVIDSON granted license to keep ferry across the Ohio River
at his usual landing. (95)

3-11-1833 - Overseers of the poor of Rome twp. file inventory of property of Robert
SETLAMD a lunatic and David McLaughen appointed guardian of said Setland.(96)

3-12-1833 - This day appeared in open court Zachariah DAVIS who made and filed
his declaration in order to obtain the benefit of the act of Congress of the
7th of June 1832 granting pensions for service rendered in the revolutionary
war and the court does hereby declare their opinion that the above named
applicant was a Revolutionary soldier and served as he states. (96)

3-12-1833 - This day appeared in open court William LOCEY who made and filed his
Declaration in order to obtain the benefit of the act of Congress of the
7th of June 1832 granting pensions for service rendered in the revolutionary
war and the court does hereby declare their opinion that the above named
applicant was a Revolutionary Soldier and served as he states. (96)

3-12-1833 - This day appeared in open court Isaac RIEL who made and filed his
declaration in order to obtain the benefit of the act of Congress of the 7th
of June 1832 granting pensions for service rendered in the revolutionary war
and the said court do hereby declare their opinion after the investigation
of the matter and after putting the interrogation prescribed by the War
Department that the above named applicant was a Revolutionary Soldier and
served as he states and that it further certifies that it appears to them
that George Sparling is a resident of Upper township as he states and is a
creditable person and that his statement is entitled to credit. (96)

3-12-1833 - In will of Rosanna BRYANT, dec'd court issues commission to Common
Pleas Court of Marion County, Ohio to take deposition of Horatio N. Wheeler
a subscribing witness. (101)

4-6-1833 - Robert McCorkle, son, appointed adms. of estate of Robert McCORKLE, dec'd.
(101)

6-17-1833 - Will of Charles MARKIN produced in court by Lucinda D. Markin,
executrix. (106)

6-18-1833 - Will of William C. JOHNSTON produced by Benjamin Johnston and Thomas
Campbell, executors. (111)

6-19-1833 - This day in open Court William LOCEY who made and filed his amended
Declaration in order to obtain the benefit of the act of Congress of the 7th
of June 1832 granting pensions for service rendered in the revolutionary war
here set out the Declaration and the court does hereby declare their opinion
after the investigation of the matter and after putting the interrogation prescribed by the War Department that the above named applicant was a Revolutionary Soldier and served as he states and the court further certifies that it

712

appears to them that Samuel Haskell who has signed the preceding certificate is a clergyman resident in Rome township in Lawrence County and that Thomas Walton who signed is a resident of the same township and are creditable persons and their statements entitled to credit. (114)

6-19-1833 - This day in open court Zachariah DAVIS who made and filed his amended Declaration in order to obtain the benefit of the act of Congress of the 7th of June 1832 granting pensions for service rendered in the revolutionary war here set out the Declaration and the court do hereby declare their opinion after the investigation of the matter and after putting the interrogation prescribed by the War Department that the above named applicant was a Revolutionary Soldier and served as he states and the court further certifies that it appears that James Haskell who has signed the preceding certificate is a clergyman resident of Rome township aforesaid and Thomas Walton who signed is a resident of the same township and are creditable persons and their statements are entitled to credit. (114)

6-19-1833 - Will of Rosannah BRYANT produced by John Bryant, executor. (115)

6-20-1833 - Israel L. Suiter appointed adms. of the estate of Hiram G. SUITER, dec'd Widow, Lettie Sparling late Lettie Suiter. (115)

9-17-1833 - William DAVIDSON granted license to keep ferry across the Ohio River at his usual landing at the mouth of Davidson St. in Burlington. (122)

9-18-1833 - Pleasant ELLINGTON granted license to keep ferry across the Ohio River at or near Hanging Rock in Upper township. (124)

1-28-1834 - Will of Andrew ELLISON, dec'd produced by Jane G. Ellison, Dyre Burgess and Joseph Riggs, executors. (125)

3-10-1834 - Abraham MILLER an ordained deacon of the Methodist Episcopal Church granted license to solemnize marriages in absence of an Elder. (131)

3-11-1834 - Samuel LANGDON granted license to keep ferry across Symmes Creek at his usual landing. (132)

3-11-1834 - Abraham D. DAVIDSON granted license to keep ferry across the Ohio River at his usual landing in Fayette township. (132)

3-12-1834 - This day appeared in open court Joseph L. ROWLEY who made and filed his declaration in order to obtain the benefit of the act of congress of the 7th June 1832 granting pensions for service in the Revolutionary War and the court does hereby declare their opinion after the investigation of the matter and after putting the interrogation prescribed by the War Department that the above named applicant was a revolutionary soldier and served as he states and the court further certifies that it appears to them that Joseph Davidson and Asa Kimble who have signed the certificate reside in Union township in said county and are both creditable persons and that their statement is entitled to credit and that there is no clergyman residing in the neighborhood acquainted with Joseph Rowley or who can testify as to the reputation of his serving as a Revolutionary Soldier. (135)

3-12-1834 - Asa KIMNSLL vs. Thomas W. WAKEFIELD, et al. Bill in Chancery. Timothy Wakefield, dec'd. Widow, Marinda now the wife of George W. Beams, she had an infant son after Wakefield's death, which died but was his child. Children: Thomas L. Wakefield of Granville, New York; Harriet Wakefield of Vermont; Rebecca wife of Joel Howe of Vermont; Sarah wife of Rufus Ewens of New Jersey; Auratha wife of Michael Johnston of New York. (131)

713

3-13-1834 - Sarah Brood appointed admsrx of the estate of Henry H. BROOD, dec'd.(141)
3-13-1834 - Louisa MYERS daughter of John Myers of German chose Henry Verdant of
    Lawrence County as her guardian. (141)
3-14-1834 - Thomas Hatfield resigned as guardian of William HOWAN. (142)
3-14-1834 - Jane G. ELLISON widow of Andrew Ellison, dec'd files for dower under
    will of deceased. (142)
7-15-1834 - Judeth M. PRATT daughter of William Pratt, dec'd, chose Joshua Pratt
    as her guardian. (152)
7-15-1834 - Anna Miller widow of Jacob MILLER, dec'd relinquishes right to adms.
    estate in favor of Oliver Miller and Charles Wilgus who were appointed adms.
    (152)
7-15-1834 - Abraham MILLER granted license to keep ferry across the Ohio River at
    his usual landing in Rome twp. (152)
7-18-1834 - Edward Morse appointed adms. of the estate of James TUMLINSON, dec'd.(157)
8-28-1834 - Lawrence Gillet, brother of dec'd appointed adms. of the estate of
    Fidelis GILLET, dec'd as deceased left no widow or children of age. (159)
8-28-1834 - Bartemus Bardsley appointed guardian of Perceval GILLET aged 6 yrs.
    and Harriet GILLET aged 15 months, minor children of Fidelis GILLET, dec'd.
    (159)
11-12-1834 - William HOWAN aged 14 yrs. on 28 August last, heir of William HOWAN,
    dec'd, chose Martha HOWARD, his mother as his guardian. (166)
11-12-1834 - John STOVER aged 16 yrs., heir of John Stover, dec'd chose Walter
    Whitten as his guardian. (166).
11-12-1834 - Joseph WHEELER granted license to keep tavern at his house in Burl-
    ington. (166)
11-12-1834 - A. H. FRIZELL produced his credentials proving him an attorney. (166)
11-14-1834 - William DAVIDSON granted license to keep ferry across the Ohio River
    at his usual landing. (170)
11-14-1834 - Samuel STOVER aged 18 yrs., son of John STOVER, dec'd chose William
    Lambert as his guardian. (170)
11-14-1834 - Pleasant ELLINGTON granted license to keep ferry across the Ohio
    River at landing near or at Hanging Rock. (170)
11-14-1834 - Marcus Hopkins appointed adms. of estate of William NIXON, dec'd. (173)
1-19-1835 - Rebecca Russell, widow and Lewis Singres appointed adms. of the estate
    of Jeremiah RUSSELL, dec'd. (175)
3-30-1835 - In the matter of Robert McCORKLE's Pension an application made in open
    court it is ordered that the following facts be certified as satisfactory form,
    Viz. That Robert McCorkle of Lawrence County Deceased died on the tenth March
    1833 and that he was a pensioner that he has left no widow that the following
    named persons are children and lawful heirs of said Robert McCorkle Deceased
    to-wit: Robert McCorkle, Andrew McCorkle, James McCorkle, John McCorkle, Jacob
    McCorkle, Betsey wife of Thomas Templeton, Catharine wife of Rolen Brammer,
    Sally wife of John Cantwell, Polley wife of John Morrison, also that Samuel
    McCorkle a child of said Robert deceased is dead leaving Robert F. Davis and
    Joel his lawful children and heirs. (180)
3-30-1835 - William W. DAVIDSON granted license to keep ferry across the Ohio River
    at or near his landing opposite the mouth of Big Sandy. (180)
3-31-1835 - Daniel McCORKLE aged 15 yrs. son of Samuel McCorkle, dec'd, chose Rolen
    Brammer as his guardian. (183)
4-1-1835 - Thomas ASHMORE declared insolvent. (186)

4-2-1835 - William Churchill appointed guardian of William CHURCHILL aged 12 yrs.,
Melissa CHURCHILL aged 7 yrs., Mendall CHURCHILL aged 6 yrs., Julia CHURCHILL
aged 3 yrs. and Solomon CHURCHILL aged 1 yr., children of Solomon Churchill,
dec'd. (192-193)
4-3-1835 - Mary Jane ELLISON aged 13 yrs. past daughter of Andrew Ellison, dec'd
chose Robert Patterson as her guardian with said Patterson also appointed to
serve as guardian of Andrew Jackson ELLISON aged 10 yrs., Marcissa P. ELLISON
aged 7 yrs., John A. ELLISON aged 4 yrs. and Archibald B. Ellison aged 1 yr.,
children of Andrew Ellison, dec'd. (196)
4-3-1835 - On application of the overseers of the poor of Rome twp., Johnston Bell
appointed guardian of Thomas HOWAN. (196)
4-3-1835 - William WARD granted license to keep ferry across the Ohio River at or
near his landing. (196)
4-3-1835 - Elizabeth CHURCHILL aged 14 yrs. past, daughter of Solomon Churchill
chose William Churchill as her guardian. (196)
4-3-1835 - Samuel LANGDON granted license to keep ferry across Symmes Creek at
his landing in Union twp. (196)
4-3-1835 - Charles Wilgus appointed adms. of estate of Jacob MILLER, dec'd. (197)
7-1-1835 - Abner SMITH granted license to keep ferry across the Ohio River near his
usual landing opposite town of Guyandotte in Union twp. (209)
7-1-1835 - Request that accounts be returned to court by Daniel Winters guardian
of John Bumgarner, Mary Ann Bumgarner and Eliza Jane Bumgarner heirs of
Abraham BUMGARNER, dec'd. Winters relinquishes guardianship. (209)
7-1-1835 - Jesse COON a minister of the Regular Baptist Church granted license to
solemnize marriages. (210)
7-1-1835 - Lucius TAYLOR declared as insolvent. (210)
7-1-1836 - Will of Robert MASSIE proven by John Higgins and Jesse Coon two witnesses. (210)
7-24-1835 - Margaret WARD declared prisoner on charge of murdering a male child.(216)
10-26-1835 - Sarah Singers, widow and Mark Singers, son of dec'd appointed adms.
of the estate of Thomas SINGERS, dec'd. (217)
10-26-1835 - William McKee and Curtis Scovill appointed adms. of the estate of
William McKee Jr., dec'd. (217)
11-24-1835 - Jacob Bumgarner appointed guardian of John BUMGARNER aged 10 yrs. and
Mary Ann BUMGARNER aged 8 yrs., children of Abram Bumgarner, dec'd. (229)
11-25-1835 - William DAVIDSON granted license to keep ferry across the Ohio River
at his usual landing. (232)
11-26-1835 - Petition for Dower in 100 acres Section 19, Township 1, Range 18.
1/3 part, Daniel Winters and Rebecca his wife; the remaining part to
John Bumgarner and Mary Ann BUMGARNER minors by Jacob Bumgarner their guardian.
(235)
11-26-1835 - Pleasant ELLINGTON granted license to keep ferry at or near Hanging
Rock. (236)
11-26-1835 - John DUNLAP declared an insolvent. (236)
11-26-1835 - Garland W. MEEKS granted license to solemnize marriages. (236)
11-26-1835 - Peter Ionbarger guardian of Susanna STOVER, John STOVER and Samuel
STOVER filed accounts. (237)
11-26-1835 - David K. COCHRANE granted license to keep tavern in Burlington. (237)

The following records were copied from "Journal 3-4" as found in the office of the Clerk of Court at the court house at Ironton. Only records of genealogical value have been included. Civil actions have not been copied. Page on which record may be found in the original record are given in parenthesis.

4-19-1836 - William WARD granted license to keep ferry at his usual landing across the Ohio River. (250)

4-19-1836 - William W. DAVIDSON granted license to keep ferry across the Ohio River at his usual landing. (250)

4-19-1836 - Samuel HARVEY a minister of the Methodist denomination granted license to solemnize marriages. (260)

4-19-1836 - James H. Heban appointed guardian of Harris HEBAN aged 9 yrs., child of P. M. HEBARD, dec'd. (260)

4-20-1836 - Micajah DILLON declared an insolvent. (261)

7-26-1836 - Abner SMITH granted license to keep ferry across the Ohio River at his usual landing near opposite town of Guyandotte. (275)

7-26-1836 - Russell SMITH granted license to keep tavern without retailing ardent spirits at his dwelling house at Burlington. (275)

7-26-1836 - John JOHNSTON, native of Ireland. Naturalization. Has resided in United States for 15 years and upwards last past and in United States for three years prior to his arriving at age of 21 years. (275)

7-27-1836 - Will of Philip FOUT produced by Ann Fout, widow and Sherman Fout, executors. (279 & 289)

7-27-1836 - John KYLE native of Ireland. Naturalization. Oath by Solomon Beckly. Kyle has resided in United States 17 years past and 3 years prior to his arriving at 21 years of age. (279)

7-27-1836 - William KYLE native of Ireland makes his declaration of intention to become citizen. (280)

9-8-1836 - Oliver C. Hanley, son of dec'd, appointed adms. of the estate of Cornelius HANLEY, dec'd. (281)

10-5-1836 - Will of Matthias WINTERS produced and proven by Rebecca Winters, widow and David Brubaker two of the witnesses. (281)

10-5-1836 - Ruth Combs, widow and Rhodes Westcott appointed adms. of the estate of John COMBS, dec'd. (281)

11-7-1836 - William MILLER granted license to keep a tavern at the Bunk House in Burlington formerly occupied by Russell Smith. (288)

11-8-1836 - Harrison WOLF aged 17 years in Dec. next, son of Jesse Wolf, dec'd, chose James H. Gholson as his guardian. (296)

11-8-1836 - Pleasant ELLINGTON granted license to keep ferry across the Ohio River at his usual landing at Hanging Rock. (296)

11-8-1836 - Samuel S. Branch appointed adms. of the estate of Henry BRANCH, dec'd. (296)

11-8-1836 - Ruth Combs appointed guardian of John COMBS born 1st April 1832, Amanda COMBS born 16 March 1834 and Helen COMBS born 10 September 1836, children of John Combs, dec'd. (296)

11-9-1836 - Will of Anthony CLARK produced for probate. (298)

4-24-1837 - Diana Payne and Moses Payne appointed adms. of the estate of William PAYNE, dec'd. (307)

4-24-1837 - William W. DAVIDSON granted license to keep ferry across the Ohio River at his usual landing near opposite of Big Sandy. (307)

4-24-1837 - William WARD granted license to keep ferry across the Ohio River at his usual landing. (307)

4-26-1837 - Sherman Fout resigns as executor of will of Philip FOUT. (316)

4-26-1837 - James White appointed adms. of the estate of Joseph McNIGHT, dec'd. (316)

4-27-1837 - William DAVIDSON granted license to keep ferry across the Ohio River at his usual landing. (318)

7-24-1837 - Abner SMITH granted license to keep ferry across the Ohio River opposite town of Guyandotte. (332)

8-13-1837 - Hiram D. Hull, brother of dec'd, appointed adms. of the estate of David McL. HULL, dec'd. (342)

10-23-1837 - Pleasant ELLINGTON granted license to keep ferry across the Ohio River at his usual landing near Hanging Rock. (352)

10-24-1837 - Will of Isaac DELONG produced for probate. (358)

10-24-1837 - James BURGESS granted license to keep tavern at his dwelling house in Elizabeth twp. (358)

10-25-1837 - Sheldon PARKER a deacon of the Methodist Episcopal Church granted license to solemnize marriages. (361)

10-26-1837 - William MILLER granted license to keep tavern at the Brick house in Burlington now occupied by him. (364)

11-27-1837 - Jane Stewart widow of dec'd and Charles W. Simmons appointed adms. of the estate of Edward STEWART, dec'd. (364)

4-2-1838 - William WARD granted license to keep ferry across the Ohio River at his usual landing. (379)

4-2-1838 - Be it remembered that on this day Lydia LAMBAUGH widow of Joseph LAMBAUGH Deceased came into open court and made proof to the court by the oaths of William Johnston and William G. Robinson that Joseph Lambaugh was a pensioner of the United States at the rate of twenty one dollars and fifty five cents per annum, that he was a resident of the County of Lawrence in the state of Ohio and died in the said county and state aforesaid in the year of our Lord one thousand eight hundred and thirty eight on the twentieth day of January, that he left a widow whose name is Lydia Lambaugh. (379)

4-2-1838 - William McCANE granted license to keep tavern at his dwelling house in Burlington formerly occupied by William Miller as a tavern stand. (380)

4-2-1838 - Will of John CUTRIGHT produced for probate. (380)

4-2-1838 - Authenticated copy of the will of Thomas BUFFINGTON late of Cabell County, Virginia produced to be recorded by the court. (380)

4-3-1838 - Will of John BALL produced and proven by David Ball and Mary K. Ball, witnesses. John Ball Jr. is one of the executors. (387)

4-3-1838 - Elizabeth BALL widow of John BALL, dec'd elects not to claim dower under said will of John Ball, dec'd. (387)

4-3-1838 - Elizabeth Sparling, widow appointed adms. of the estate of Stephen SPARLING, dec'd. (387)

4-3-1838 - Andrew Dempsey appointed adms. of the estate of William WILLIAMS, dec'd who died leaving no widow or other persons of near akin to him. (388)

4-4-1838 - Be it remembered that this day Lucy MANNON widow of Henry MANNON Deceased came into court and made proof to the court by the oath of Peter Wakefield that Henry Mannon was a pensioner of the United States at the rate of forty five Dollars and ninety seven cents per annum, that he was a resident of the County of Lawrence in the State of Ohio and died in said county and state aforesaid in the year one thousand eight hundred and thirty eight on the twelfth day of February, that he left a widow whose name is Lucy Mannon. (390)

4-6-1838 - @ill of Thomas WILSON produced to court for Probate. (393)

7-30-1838 - Nancy COLLIER aged 17 yrs., daughter of Ambrose Collier, dec'd
chose Ambrose H. Collier as her guardian. (409)

7-30-1838 - Hamilton SMITH aged 19 yrs. and Harvey SMITH aged 16 yrs., sons of
William Smith chose Washington Smith as their guardian and he also appointed
to serve as guardian of John SMITH aged 11 yrs., child of William Smith. (409)

7-30-1838 - Francis Russell appointed adms. of the estate of Manoah Bostick RUSSELL,
dec'd. (409)

7-30-1838 - Ambrose H. Collier appointed adms. of the estate of John N. KEMP,
dec'd. (410)

7-30-1838 - Lydia Austin appointed admsrx. of the estate of Isaac AUSTIN, dec'd.
(410)

7-30-1838 - William W. DAVISSON appointed adms. of the estate of John DAVIDSON,
dec'd. (410)

7-30-1838 - Will of Eli LOPER, dec'd produced for probate. (411)

8-1-1838 - Jeremiah Knox appointed adms. of the estate of Hamilton H. SMITH,
dec'd. (420)

8-1-1838 - Whitfield Kelly appointed adms. of the estate of Joseph LAMBERT, dec'd.
(420)

8-1-1838 - Will of Katharine CLARK produced for Probate by William Brammer,
executor. (420)

8-1-1838 - Rolen Hankins appointed adms. of the estate of William Smith, dec'd.(421)

8-1-1838 - Solomon B. Simpson appointed adms. of the estate of Henry MANNON, dec'd.
(421)

8-1-1838 - Bartemus BARDSLEY granted license to keep ferry across the Ohio River
at his landing in Rome twp. (421)

8-1-1838 - William W. DAVIDSON granted license to keep ferry across the Ohio River
at his usual landing opposite Big Sandy. (421)

8-1-1838 - William DAVIDSON granted license to keep ferry across the Ohio River at
his usual landing. (421)

8-1-1838 - Abner SMITH granted license to keep ferry across the Ohio River at his
usual landing near opposite of the town of Guyandotte. (421)

8-1-1838 - Tallaferro WALLACE granted license to keep ferry at his usual landing
in Rome twp. (422)

8-1-1838 - Benjamin EVANS a native of Wales files his declaration of intention to
become citizen. (423)

8-1-1838 - William KYLE a native of Ireland. Naturalization. His declaration of
intention was filed at the July term 1836 of this court. (423)

9-15-1838 - Elizabeth Halteman, widow appointed admsrx. of the estate of Henry
HALTEMAN, dec'd. (434)

11-13-1838 - Will of William DAVIDSON produced for probate. (437)

3-7-1839 - Harriet Launtz, widow of dec'd relinquishes her right to adms. estate
in favor of Simon Woods who is appointed adms. of the estate of Leonard LAUNTZ,
dec'd. (438)

3-7-1839 - Solomon Isaming appointed guardian of James LAUNTZ aged 11 yrs. on 8
April 1839 and Solomon LAUNTZ aged 8 yrs. in December 1838, children of Leonard
Launtz, dec'd. (439)

5-14-1839 - Daniel Beller appointed adms. of the estate of Elisha BELLER, dec'd.(456)

5-14-1839 - Be it remembered that on this day in open court proof was made to the satisfaction of the court by the oaths of Richard Adams, Harrison Ellis and Caleb Wilshire that Robert ADAMS was a pensioner of the United States that he was a resident of the County of Lawrence in the State of Ohio and died in said county and state aforesaid in the year one thousand eight hundred and thirty nine on the fourteenth day of March, that he left children whose names are Solomon Adams, Richard Adams, Elizabeth Ellis and Nancy Wilshire. (456)

5-14-1839 - William WARD granted license to keep ferry across the Ohio River at his usual landing in Union twp. (456)

5-14-1839 - James RODGERS granted license to keep ferry across the Ohio River at his usual landing at the mouth of Normans Runn in Upper twp. (462)

5-14-1839 - Joseph TODD a native of Wales aged about 27 years shipped from port of Liberpool and landed in New York in August 1830 and resided in United States since and now a resident of Elizabeth twp. makes his declaration of intention to become citizen. (464)

5-14-1839 - George DISTERDICK a native of Germany born in the dutchy of Hanover aged 33 yrs., shipped from port of Bremen and landed at port of Baltimore 15 June 1832 and resided in United States since, now a resident of Elizabeth twp. makes his declaration of intention to become citizen. (464)

5-14-1839 - Godfrey ERNST aged 21 years on 17 January 1839 born in Kingdom of Hanover, Germany from which he emigrated arriving at Baltimore, Maryland in June 1832 and has resided in United States since makes his declaration of intention to become citizen. (464)

5-14-1839 - Henry SPILLMAN Jr. a native of Germany born in the dutchy of Hanover aged about 22 years, shipped from port of Bremen and landed in Baltimore about 1st October 1835 and resided in United States since and now a resident of Elizabeth twp. makes his declaration to become citizen. (464)

5-15-1839 - Nicholas RITTER aged 32 yrs. of Elizabeth twp., native of Germany makes his declaration of intention to become citizen. (465)

5-15-1839 - Henry SPILLMAN aged 48 yrs. of Elizabeth twp., native of Hanover, Germany makes his declaration of intention to become citizen. (465)

5-15-1839 - Ernest SHRADER a native of Hanover, Germany aged about 40 years shipped from port of Breman and landed in New York in April 1834, has resided in United States since and is a resident of Elizabeth twp. makes his declaration of intention to become citizen. (465)

5-15-1839 - John Conrad FREDE a resident of Elizabeth twp. and native of Hanover, Germany makes his declaration of intention to become citizen. (465)

5-15-1839 - John VOUGHAN a native of Wales aged about 30 yrs. shipped from port of Liverpool and landed in New York in August 1830 and resided in United States since and now a resident of Elizabeth twp. makes his declaration of intention to become citizen. (466)

5-15-1839 - Henry BISERE a native of Germany born in the Dutchy of Hanover aged about 34 yrs. shipped from port of Bremen in 1832 and landed in Baltimore in June of same year, has resided in United States for seven years makes his declaration of intention to become citizen. (466)

5-15-1839 - Francis FISHER born in Dutchy of Hanover aged about 34 yrs. now a resident of Elizabeth twp. makes his declaration of intention to become citizen. (466)

5-15-1839 - Frederick FINK a native of Germany born in the Dutchy of Hanover aged
about 28 years shipped from port of Bremen and landed in New York 25 July 1835
and resided in United States since a resident of Elizabeth twp. makes his
declaration of intention to become citizen.   (466)
5-15-1839 - Will of Nathaniel TROBRIDGE produced by Abraham Miller, executor.   (470)
5-15-1839 - William WARNER aged 20 yrs. last Sept. past, chose Aaron H. Richardson
as his guardian.   (470)
5-15-1839 - Will of Joseph LAMBOUGH produced for probate.   (471)
5-17-1839 - Elisha F. GREENE granted license to keep tavern without retailing ardent
spirits at the Brick house in Burlington.   (481)
8-5-1839 - Bartemus BARDSLEY granted license to keep ferry across the Ohio River
at his landing in Rome twp.   (494)
8-5-1839 - Abner SMITH granted license to keep ferry across the Ohio River at his
usual landing near opposite of town of Guyandotte.   (494)
8-5-1839 - Tallaferro WALLACE granted license to keep ferry at his usual landing
in Rome twp.   (494)
8-5-1839 - Authenticated copy of will of William EDGER, dec'd late of New York
City recorded in this county.   (499)
8-8-1839 - William Kelly appointed guardian of Charles R. AUSTIN aged 12 yrs. on
10 Sept. 1838, Lycurgus C. AUSTIN aged 10 yrs. on 27 Dec. 1838 and Philonise
AUSTIN aged 5 yrs. on 25 May 1838, heirs of Isaac Austin, dec'd.   (513)
8-9-1839 - Thomas W. MACKEREL a native of Londonderry, Ireland aged 22 yrs. makes
his declaration of intention to become citizen.   (515)
8-9-1839 - This day appeared in open court Mary EASTMAN who made and filed her
declaration to obtain the benefit of the Act of Congress passed July 7, 1838,
an act granting half pay and pensions to widows in the words and figures
following, to-wit: State of Ohio, Lawrence County, to-wit:--Court of Common
Pleas August Term 1839 on this 9th day of August in the year 1899 personally
appeared Mary Eastman a resident of Lawrence County aged 72 years having been
born 13th January 1767 being sworn....that she is widow of Peaslee EASTMAN who
was a soldier in the American army during the Revolutionary War but unable to
state the particular service in which her husband engaged but relies upon the
Records of the War office for that evidence, he the said Peaslee Eastman having
been placed on the pension list and been such a pensioner at the time of his
death. She further declares that she was married to the said Peaslee Eastman
the 1st day of November 1786 and that her husband the aforesaid Peaslee Eastman died on the 14th day of September 1823, that she was not married to him
prior to his leaving service but that marriage took place previous to 1st June
1794. (Signed) Mary (her mark) Eastman. Sworn to in open court before me
August 9th 1839 (Signed) Joseph Wheeler, Clerk. At time aforesaid came into
open court Mary G. Proctor, Jacob Proctor and B. T. Miles and made affidavits
in the words following, to-wit: At Court of Common Pleas sitting in and for
the County of Lawrence in the State of Ohio personally appeared in open court
Mary G. Proctor who made oath...that said Mary G. Proctor is daughter of Peaslee and Mary Eastman....that her mother now resides with her and attests to
statement made by her mother, Mary Eastman. Jacob Proctor certifies that he is
husband of Mary G. Proctor and knew Peaslee Eastman. B. T. Miles states he
knew Peaslee Eastman for 25 years and is still acquainted with Mary Eastman.
(518-519)

9-10-1839 - John Mann appointed adms. of the estate of John PINKENNAN, dec'd as widow, Jane Pinkennan relinquishes her right to adms. estate. (521)

9-10-1839 - Esther Shattuck, widow appointed admsrx. of John H. SHATTUCK, dec'd.(521)

10-28-1839 - Charles Cooper, Jr. aged 20 yrs., heir of Charles Cooper, Sr. chose Andrew Dempsey as his guardian. (534)

10-28-1839 - Authenticated copy of will of Charles WILKS, dec'd late of New York City produced and recorded in court. (535)

10-28-1839 - William W. DAVIDSON granted license to keep ferry across the Ohio River at his usual landing opposite the mouth of Big Sandy. (535)

10-28-1839 - Augustine M. ALEXANDER a minister of the Methodist church granted license to solemnize marriages. (535)

10-28-1839 - James HASKELL a minister of the Baptist church granted license to solemnize marriages. (535)

10-29-1839 - Daniel K. COCHRANE granted license to keep tavern at the Brick House in Burlington occupied by him. (545)

10-29-1839 - Abner SHOCKLEY aged about 17 years, son of John Shockley, dec'd chose Richard Morrison as his guardian. (546)

10-29-1839 - Francis RUSSELL adms. of Manoah B. RUSSELL, dec'd vs. Samuel RUSSELL, William RUSSELL, Sanders RUSSELL, Thomas RUSSELL, James RUSSELL, George IRVIN and Jemima his wife, William NELSON and Jane his wife, Abner DILLY and Annieda his wife, Elizabeth Jane infant heir of John and Anne COMPTON representative of said Anne deceased, Virginia infant heir of Jeremiah RUSSELL, dec'd representative of Jeremiah, John RUSSELL, Lawrence RUSSELL, Rachel ROBUCK, Elizabeth ROBUCK and Esther RUSSELL. In Chancery. That William, John, Lawrence, Rachel, Elizabeth and Esther are half blood brothers and sisters of intestate and the residue are whole blood brothers and sister of said intestate, all children of John Russell, dec'd. Suit filed to deliver deed. (546)

The following records were copied from Death Record 1, pages on which record may be found in this book are given in parenthesis. Only persons 40 years of age and over were copied. Abbreviations used: d=died; m=married; s=single; w=widower; pb= place of birth; pd=place of death; r=residence. Residence is same as place of death unless stated otherwise.

MILLER, Mary Anne - d 7-6-1867; m; a 62y 8m 4d; pd Ironton; pb Ironton; parents, Filey Day and Emma Day. (2)
BOWMAN, Jacob - d 8-19-1867; m; a 74y; pd Fayette twp.; pb --------. (2)
YOUNG, Andrew - d 11-21-1867; m; a 56y 7m 18d; pd Elizabeth twp.; pb Scotland. (4)
UNGER, Henry - d 12-6-1867; m; a about 60y; pd Elizabeth twp.; pb Germany. (4)
HUGHS, Absalum - d 11-4-1867; m; a 84y; pd Perry twp.; pb ----. (4)
RODGERS, Lemuel - d Nov. 1867;m; a supposed 58y; pd Lawrence Co.; pb Va. (4)
TINDER, Lucinda - d 12-4-1867; s; a 65y; pd Ironton; pb Rockingham, Va. (4)
STRONG, Emily Caroline - d 12-3-1867; m; a 54y 8m; pd Coal Grove, Upper twp.; pb New Hampshire. (4)
SULLIVAN, Mary - d 3-17-1868; m; a 47y 2m 11d; pd Ironton; pb Ireland. (4)
MARTIN, Margaret - d 1-28-1868; m; a 43y; pd Lawrence Co.; pb Delaware. (4)
MOORE, Bridget - d 3-30-1868; w; a supposed 55y; pd Lawrence Co.; pb----- (4)
SHARP, Louisa - d 3-9-1868; m; a 42y 2m 21d; pd Vesuvius Furnace; pb Lawrence Co. (6)
MAYS, Jonathan - d 3-9-1868; m; a about 44y; pd Clinton Fce.; pb Scioto Co. (6)
CLARK, Anthony - d 1-25-1868; m; a 49y; pd Decatur twp.; pb Greenup, Ky. (6)
CASPELMAN, William - d 1-26-1868; m; a 63y 9m 13d; pd Burlington, O.; pb Tellensted, Germany. (6)
BURGE, Drusy - d 3-28-1868; m; a 70y 27d; pd Hamilton twp.; pb Stokes Co., N.C.(6)
SHERIDAN, Mrs. M. - d 3-3-1868; m; a about 40y; pd Ironton; pb Ireland. (6)
MARKHAM, Sarah - d 4-17-1868; m; a 44y; pd Washington twp.; pb Greenup Co., Ky. (6)
MULLIGAN, James - d 8-24-1868; a 87y; pd Lawrence Co.; pb Ireland. (8)
McGARVY, Eunice - d 8-24-1868; m; a 70y; pd Lawrence Co.; pb Ireland. (8)
WILLIAMS, William - d 8-3-1868; m; a 67y; pd Ironton; pb Wales. (8)
CLIFFORD, John - d 10-9-1868; w; a about 68y; pd Ireonton; pb Scotland. (8)
DUTCHELL, _____ - d 11-24-1868; m; a 59y 9m 8d; pd Washington twp.; pb Germany.(10)
GRINSON, Frank - d 10-12-1868; s; a 102y; pd Infirmary, Lawrence Co.; pb Virginia. (10)
SMITH, Rice - d 10-7-1868; m; a 45y; pd Union twp.; pb Union twp. (10)
EVERLY, Mrs. Jos. - d 6-27-1868; m; a 63y; pd Upper twp.; pb Germany. (10)
BOMER, John - d 9-16-1868; m; a 54y; pd Hamilton twp.; pb Ohio. (10)
McCULLOUGH, Eliza A. - d 12-18-1868; m; a 51y; pd Ironton; pb West Union, O. (10)
THOMAS, Thomas - d 3-23-1869; m; a 49y; pd Ironton; pb South Wales. (12)
WAITES, Joseph - d 5-16-1869; m; a 47y; pd Ironton, O.; pb Germany. (12)
McCOMAS, Mary Ann - d 6-6-1869; m; a 45y 5m; pd -----; pb------. (12)
WELLS, Elizabeth - d-----1868; w; a 73y; pd ------; pb -------. (12)
KELLEY, Aramatha - d 10-24-1868; m; a 58y; pd Ironton; pb Russell Co., Va.; r 2nd Ward. (14)
KELLEY, James - d 10-19-1868; m; a 56y; pd Lawrence Co.; pb----; r 1st Ward. (14)
SMITH, Ruth - d 4-10-1870; w; a 83y; pd Ironton; pb Ironton; r 2nd Ward. (14)
MARTIN, Patrick - d Feb 1870; s; a 48y; pd Ironton; pb Ireland; r 2nd Ward. (14)
STICH, Peter - d 9-14-1869; m; a 44y; pd Ironton; pb France; r 4th Ward. (16)

BUHR, Frank - d 6-17-1869; m; a 62y; pd Ironton; pb Germany; r 5th ward. (16)
WHITE, John - d 8-13-1869; m; a 65y 4m 9d; pd Washington twp.; pb Pike Co., Ky.;
    r Aid twp. (16)
LAMBERT, Mary - d 1-20-1870; m; a 71y 3m 21d; pd Aid twp.; pb Va. (16)
SPEARS, Charles - d 2-7-1870; m; a 65y 9m 3d; pd Aid twp.; pb Scioto Co. (16)
MARTIN, Wm. - d Dec. 1869; m; a 82y; pd Aid twp.; pb Aid twp. (16)
BURKE, Thomas - d 3-7-1870; m; a 70y; pd Decatur twp.; pb Ireland. (18)
BAUMER, Henry - d 8-23-1869; m; a 53y 5m 9d; pd Elizabeth twp.; pb Germany. (18)
JONKEY, Elizabeth - d 5-4-1869; w; a 89y 8m; pd Elizabeth twp.; pb Wales. (18)
WOLF, John - d 3-28-1870; w; a 71y 7m 19d; pd Elizabeth twp.; pb Pa. (18)
STEPHENS, Nancy J. - d 1-25-1870; m; a 40y 3m 5d; pd Elizabeth twp.; pb Ohio. (18)
WELSH, Hannah - d 10-28-1869; m; a 40y; pd Elizabeth twp.; pb Ireland. (20)
SKELTON, Wm - d 3-30-1870; m; a 67y 7m 29d; pd Fayette twp.; pb N. Carolina. (20)
BEAMS, Marinda - d 2-26-1870; m; a 59y 1m 26d; pd Fayette twp.; pb Ohio. (20)
BURDETT, Samuel - d 12-10-1869; m; a 50y 1m 5d; pd Fayette twp.; pb England. (20)
SNELL, Albert - d 8-12-1869; m; a 44y 11m 16d; pd Fayette twp.; pb Va. (20)
TEMPLE, Francis - d 3-18-1870; m; a 60y 2m 17d; pd Fayette twp.; pb Ireland. (20)
MOORE, Polly - d 12-19-1869; w; a 91y 8m 4d; pd Fayette twp.; pb Va. (20)
STORY, Sarah - d 1-23-1870; m; 52y 11m 16d; pd Hamilton two.; pb Va. (20)
ROSS, James - d 1-15-1870; m; a 53y 10m 4d; pd Lawrence twp.; pb Ireland. (22)
PANCAKE, Joseph - d 3-5-1869; m; a 43y 15d; pd Lawrence twp.; pb Ohio. (22)
PLATT, Jane - d 4-15-1869; w; a 60y 11m 23d; pd Lawrence twp.; pb Ohio. (22)
NEAL, Thomas - d 2-2-1870; m; a 74y; pd Lawrence twp.; pd W. Va. (22)
OSBURN, Mary - d 2-10-1870; m; a 66y; pd Lawrence twp.; pb Ohio. (22)
HINNEMAN, Sarah - d 7-30-1869; m; a 62y 11m 15d; pd Mason twp.; pb Ohio. (22)
RUCKER, Elizabeth - d 1-13-1870; w; a 76y; pd Mason twp.; pb Va. (22)
NEAL, Mary - d 9-19-1869; m; a 41y 3m; pd Mason twp.; pb Va. (22)
RAPP, John - d Apr. or Aug. 16, 1869; m; a 75y; pd Mason twp.; pb Europe. (22)
McCOMAS, Mary A. - d 1-6-1870; m; a 42y; pd Mason twp.; pb Ohio. (22)
HAINES, Arthur - d 12-9-1869; m; a 74y 9m 1d; pd Mason twp.; pb Ohio. (22)
MASSIE, Mary - d 6-22-1869; m; a 46y; pd Mason twp.; pb ------ (22)
STEAD, Harriet - d 1-7-1870; m; a 40y; pd Perry twp.; pb Ohio. (22)
AMOS, Margaret - d 2-12-1870; w; a 69y 9m 12d; pd Perry twp.; pb------. (22)
WALLER, Catherine - d 4-14-1869; m; a 46y; pd Perry twp.; pb Ohio. (22)
ISRAEL, Wm P. - d 7-12-1869; a 52y 6m; pd Perry twp.; pb Pa. (22)
WYLIE, Elizabeth - d 3-10-1870; w; a 69y 9m; pd Rome twp.; pb Ohio. (24)
FRAMPTON, _____ - d. 10-15-1869; born 1801; pd Union twp.; pb Pa. (24)
POLLY, George - d 9-7-1869; s; a 85y; pd Upper twp.; pb Ohio. (26)
CALL, Rhoda - d 1-14-1870; s; a 75y; pd Upper twp.; pb------. (26)
SHARP, John - d 3-15-1870; m; a 101y; pd Upper twp.; pb Va. (26)
TOWNSEND, Catharine - d 4-18-1869; a 46y; pd Washington twp.; pb Va. (26)
HOSKINS, Elizabeth - d 12-9-1869; a 87y 11m 26d; pd Washington twp.; pb Va. (28)
MANNON, James - d 3-23-1870; m; a 58y 14d; pd Windsor twp.; pb W. Va. (28)
THACKER, Reuben - d 2-21-1870; w; a 105y 4m 6d; pd Windsor twp.; pb W. Va. (28)
PAYTON, Charles - d Apr. 1870; w; a 82y; pd Aid twp.; pb E. Virginia. (30)
PAYTON, Isaac - d 6-17-1870; m; a 72y 11m; pd Aid twp.; pb Scioto. (30)
RUTER, Jacob - d 4-6-1870; m; a 55y; pd Elizabeth twp.; pb Germany. (32)
WOOD, Anna M. - d 6-5-1870; m; a 44y; pd Elizabeth twp.; pb Va. (32)
ALEXANDER, An Jane - d 12-22-1870; w; a 50y; pd Fayette twp.; pb Ireland. (32)

723

BANKS, Samuel - d 4-24-1870; m; a 58y 21d; pd Fayette twp.; pb North Carolina. (32)
DRURY, James H. - d 7-12-1870; m; a 63y 1m 10d; pd Fayette twp; pb New Hampshire.(32)
SCOVILLE, Curtis - d 7-9-1870; w; a 75y 7m 9d; pd Fayette twp.; pb Conneticut. (32)
NEWMAN, Elizabeth - d 8-6-1870; w; a 74y 9m 3d; pd Fayette twp.; pb Va. (32)
LAMBESON, Richard - d 5-3-1870; w; a 67y 9m 16d; pd Hamilton twp.; pb Pa. (34)
McHASTERS, John - d 6-17-1870; w; a 79y; pd Hamilton twp.; pb Washington D.C. (34)
KELLEY, Isam - d 12-1-1870; m; a 51y 4m 10d; pd Lawrence Co.; pb Lawrence Co. (34)
CORN, Henry H. - d 12-22-1870; s; a 50y 5m 2d; pd Lawrence Co.; pb Lawrence Co.
          (34)
WOLFE, John - d 11-29-1870; m; a 58y 6m; pd Perry twp.; pb Germany. (36)
THOMAS, Archeble - d 12-30-1870; m; a 70y; pd Rome twp.; pb Va. (36)
DAVIS, David - d 10-25-1870; m; a 85y; pd Lawrence Co.; pb Wales. (36)
SMITH, William - d 4-5-1870; m; a 59y 5m pd Lawrence Co.; pb Va. (36)
KEENEY, William H.C. - d 10-20-1870; w; a 81y 5m 10d; pd Union twp.; pb
           Greenbriar Co., W. Va. (38)
GRIFFETH. Sarah - d ------1870; a 45y; pd Upper twp.; pb Ohio. (40
HENRY, Morris - d 10-3-1870; m; a 50y 5m 2d; pd Upper twp.; pb Ohio. (40)
JONES (JANES?), Sarah A. - d 7-22-1870; m; a 51y 8m; pd Upper twp.; pb Wales. (40)
HORTON, William - d 10-5-1870; a 42y; pd Upper twp.; pb Ohio. (40)
MORRIS, J. - d 6-26-1870; m; a 40y; pd Infirmary; pb Ireland. (40)
PARTLOW, Mary - d 6-29-1870; m; a 63y 4m 9d; pd Coal Grove; pb Cabel Co., Va. (40)
RUCKER, Adaline - d Oct. 1870; m; a 51y 7m; pd Windsor twp.; pb Monroe Co.,
          Ohio. (40)
DAY, John - d 10-25-1870; m; a 77y 9m; pd Washington twp.; pb Quincy. (40)
EVANS, Mary - d ------1870; s; a 88y; pd Wash. Fur.; pb Wales. (40)
PENROD, Jacob - d 6-22-1870; m; a 82y 9d; pd Symmes twp.; pb Penna. (42)
AMES, William - d 10-14-1870; m; a 50y; pd Ironton; pb Ireland; r 2nd ward. (42)
GRINSHAW, William - d 9-2-1870; m; a 84y 2d; pd Ironton; pb Europe; r 2nd ward.(42)
WARD, Edward - d 8-5-1870; m; a 49y 23d; pd Ironton; pb Rome twp.; r 3rd ward. (42)
WILSON, Henry - d 4-12-1870; m; a 58y; pd Ironton; pb Morgantown; r 3rd ward. (44)

LICKING COUNTY, OHIO - PARTITION RECORDS 1816-1830

The following records are from Partition Record A. Pages on which record may be found are given in parenthesis.

1-24-1816 - George AVERY and others. Filed May 1815. George Avery, dec'd, departed this life 27 Sept. 1807 intestate. Widow, Mary Spelman, late Avery, now wife of Timothy Spelman. Land, 100 acres Lot 17, Section 3, Township 2, Range 13 and 100 acres lot 37, Section 4, Township 2, Range 14 in U. S. Military District. Children: George, Christopher, Simeon, Alfred, Polly and Synthia Ayery; the last three not of age with Mary Spelman guardian of Polly and Synthia. (1)

12-19-1816 - David MOREY and Hariet MOREY vs. Other Heirs of REYNOLDS, dec'd. Filed Dec. 1816. William Reynolds, dec'd. Land, Lot 13, Section 4, Township 2, Range (not given) in Military tract. Heirs: Harriet wife of David Morey; Theodose late Reynolds wife of Enos Hurlbut; William Reynolds; and Laurey Reynolds; the last two being minors by Enox Hurbut their guardian. (5)

6-20-1817 - John N. CUMMING, James W. BURNET, Harriet BURNET and William SCHENCK. Petition for Partition. Filed Dec. 1816. William C. Schenck of Franklin, Warren Co., Ohio; John N. Cumming and John Burnet, both of Newark twp., Essex Co., New Jersey were tennents in common in undivided tract of land in Licking co. being 4220 acres 4th quarter, 2nd township. 12th range, military tract. That prior to 7-11-1811 William C. Schenck served as agent for John N. Cumming and John Burnet. That John Burnet died on or about 7-11-1811 intestate leaving children--James W. and Harriet Burnet. Included is plat of town of Newark with above parties being partitioned many lots in Newark. (7)

10-9-1817 - Isham SENNET vs. Elizabeth SENNET, et al. Filed 6-18-1817. James Sinnet, dec'd, died intestate Dec. 1809. Land, 100 acres Lot 6 Section 2, Township 2, Range 13 and Lot 11 Section 4, Township 2, Range 14 in military district; also in-lot 8, Block 22, Granville. Ten children: Isaac, Elizabeth, Peggy, Anna wife of Titus Knox, John, Allen, James, Allanson, Lathrop, Willard and Mary. (note: says ten but eleven named with commas between all); John James and Lathrop all died since death of their father without marrying and without heirs; Allen a minor under 21 by Grove Case his guardian; Allanson, Willard and Mary all minors by Sylvanus Mitchell their guardian. (10)

7-10-1818 - Robert DAVIDSON and William TRINDLE vs. Heirs of William LEEPER, dec'd. Filed Oct. 1817. William Leeper, late of Pennsylvania, dec'd. Land, 916 and 2/3 acres E side Section 3, Township 2, Range 12 in U. S. military lands. Heirs: Samuel W. Leeper of Pennsylvania; Mary late Leeper wife of Joseph Arthur; William Leeper, both ofdWoodstock, Virginia; Elizabeth late Leeper wife of John Herron of Pennsylvania; Jane Leeper of Pa.; George Leeper of Pa. Also, that the heirs of Mathew Scott or Samuel Kirk have undivided 3/8ths interest. Davidson and Trindle hold interest by purchase. (16)

10-29-1818 - George SHRUM, John KUHN, Henry LAUTZENHISER and Christian BRENNEMAN, all of Westmoreland Co., Pa. Filed 10-10-1817. That the above parties are tenants in common with parties unknown in 3rd Section, Township 3, Range 14 of U. S. Military tract and ask partition of same. (21)

725

10-31-1818- James JOHNSTON vs. James E., SMITH. Filed 10-28-1818. That James Johnston of Columbus, Ohio and James E. Smith of Philadelphia, Pa. each hold 1/2 interest in NE corner Section 1, Township 2, Range 14, U. S. Military District and ask partition of same. (24)

5-19-1819 - HOLLENBACK vs. HOLLENBACK. Filed 3-19-1817. Thomas Hollenbach, late of Hampshire Co., Virginia, dec'd. Widow, Margaret. Land, 1912 acres part W part 3rd quarter, Township 4, Range 14. Children and heirs; George Hollenback of Fairfield Co., Ohio; Thomas Hollenback of Pike County, Ohio;Daniel Hollenback of Hampshire Co., Va.; Jacob Hollenback of Muskingum Co., Ohio; Sarah wife of Jacob Leece of Hamshire Co. Va.; Abraham Hollenback of Hampshire Co., Va.; John Hollenback of Hampshire Co. Va.; Catharine Young, dec'd, her son--George Young, a minor by Frederick Shutz his guardian, of Hampshire Co., Va.; Elizabeth wife of John Bently of Hardy Co., Va.; Margaret wife of John Jones of Fairfield Co., Ohio; William Hollenback of Washington, D.C., Amos Hollenback of Washington, D.C.; Mary wife of Oakly Johnson of Hampshire Co., Va.; and Isaac Hollenback of Hampshire Co. Va. (28)

May 1819 - William SMITH and wife vs. Samuel CAMPBELL and others. Filed 7-11-1818. James Campbell, dec'd. late of Christiana Hundred, New Castle Co., Delaware. Land, 3rd quarter, 34d township, range 13 in Military tract, being 320 acres; lines-- Peter Jacqueth, George Monro and Thomas H. Thompson. Brother and Sisters: Samuel Campbell, dec'd who died before his brother James, leaving children--Samuel and David Campbell of New Castle Co., Del.; Elizabeth wife of William Smith; and Margaret Campbell of Christiana Hundred, New Castle Co., Delaware. (32)

5-12-1820 R. DAVIDSON vs. TRINDLE.'s Heirs. Filed ------1819. William Trindle, dec'd, late of Licking Co., died in 1819, being a tennent in common in land (not described) with Robert Davidson, each having 1/2 interest. Children: Hannah Trindle, William Trindle, Sally late Trindle wife of James Young, Peggy Trindle, Ruth Trindle, Ann Trindle, Elizabeth Trindle, Matilda Trindle and Rebecca Trindle. (35)

5-12-1820 - Joseph MORTON and others. In Partition. Filed Dec. 1819. John ARMSTRONG, dec'd, Land, part of Quarters 1 & 4, Township 3, Range 13, in Military District being 1429 acres as exhibited in division of lands between William Wells, John Armstrong and the Heirs of Israel Ludlow in Sept. Term 1809; also 240 acres pt. 3rd quarter, Township 4, Range 13 Military District, Children: Ann wife of Joseph Morton of Hamilton Co., Ohio; Catharine wife of Henry Morton of Hamilton Co., Ohio; William G. Armstrong of Clark Co., Indiana; Mary G. wife of William C. Drew of Franklin Co., Indiana; Eliza Armstrong; Thomas Pool Armstrong; Viola Jane Armstrong and John H. Armstrong; the last four named being minors of Tabitha Armstrong their guardian and all of Clark Co., Indiana. (39)

5-12-1820 - Charles MARSTILLER of Licking Co., Ohio vs. James E. SMITH of Philadelphia, Pa. Filed Aug. 1819. Parties named above are each holders of 1/2 interest and tennets in common. in NW corner 1st quarter, Township 2, Range 11 of U. S. Military District. (44

10-27-1820 - Joseph and Mercy FASSETT, et al. In Partition. Filed (not given).
Moses BOARMAN, late of Licking Co., dec'd, died Sept. 1816. Widow, Abigail Boardman
died Feb. last. Land: lot 39, S1, T4, R15, 167½ acres; Lot 34, Sw,T4, R13, 167½
acres; Lot 28,S2, T2, R14, 167½ acres; lot 27, S1, T4, R15, 100 acres; Lot 6, S 4,
T2, R14, 167 acres; Lots 15, 25 & 26, S2, T2, R14, 100 acres each; and numerous other
land descriptions. Children: Mercy wife of Joseph Fassett; Hiram Boardman; Emily
Boardman; Moses Boardman; Lewis Boardman, a minor by Samuel Bancroft his guardian;
Jane Boardman, a minor, by Joseph Fassett her guardian. (48)

May 1821 - Henry Dana WARD of Marietta, Washington Co., Ohio vs. Theodore FOSTER,
Esqu. of Rhode Island. Filed 2-7-1821. The above parties are tennets in common
in 4th quatter, Township 1, Range 14 of Military tract; Foster having 1240.68
acres and Ward having 639 acres. (52)

5-9-1822 - Mary DECAMP vs. Benjamin A. BROWN and others. Filed 10-26-1820.
Daniel MARSH, dec'd, late of Rahway, Essex Co., New Jersey, died intestate in 1802.
Land, 4000 acres, 1st quarter, Township 2, Range 15, military lands; that Daniel
Marsh in his lifetime with wife Esther, deeded on 6-2-1800 one-third part to
Benjamin A. Brown of Woodbridge, Middlesex Co., New Jersey and one-third part to
Ralph Marsh of New Jersey. Daniel Marsh left six children: Mary wife of Job
DeCamp, Job being dec'd, of Middlesex Co., N.J.; Anna wife of Thomas Edger of
Middlesex Co., N.J.; Sarah wife of Robert Clarkson of Middlesex Co., N.J.; Daniel
Marsh Jr., dec'd, his three children--Elias Marsh, George Taylor Marsh (res. unknown)
and Rachel Barnet Marsh of New York City; William Ralph Marsh, dec'd, his four
children--Anna Marsh, John Ralph Marsh, Noah Marsh and Daniel Marsh (res. unknown);
Elizabeth Marsh wife of Jacob Marsh, both dec'd, her four children--Mary Shute, a
widow of New York City, Noah Marsh, Ester wife of Lewis Prall, both of Bridgetown,
Essex Co., N.J. and Anna Eliza wife of John Payne of Middlesex Co., N.J. (55)
(note: see also pages 66, 97 and 104; some of the data does not agree, but has been
given as given in the record.)

5-9-1822 - Luther WETHERILL and others. Filed 5-29-1821. Daniel Wetherill, dec'd,
died intestate about 10 years ago. Widow, Hannah. Land 100 acres lot 38, Section 4,
Township 2, Range 14 in U.S. Military tract. Ten children: Luther Wetherill;
Amelia Wetherill; Phebe wife of Elvin Smith of Connecticut; Marquis Wetherill of
Connecticut; Comfort Wetherill of Conn.; Calvin Wetherill of Conn.; Clement Wetherill
of Conn.; Ada wife of Harlon Dickinson; Polly wife of Roger Fox of Conn.; and Daniel
Wetherill. (59)

5-9-1822 - Oliver DICKINSON and others. Filed 8-16-1821. Timothy ROSE, dec'd, late
of Licking Co. Widow, Lydia Dickinson, late Rose, now wife of Oliver Dickinson.
Land, 100 acres Lot 1, Township 2, Section 4, Range 13, U.S. Military tract; 100
acres Lot 3, Section 1, Township 4, Range 15; Lots 31 & 34, Section 2, Township 2,
Range 14, 100 acres each. Heirs: Clarissa wife of Samuel Bancroft; Samantha wife
of William Stedman; Louisa wife of Oliver C. Dickinson; Lydia, dec'd, late wife of
William Clemens--her heirs (not named) who are all minors by William Clemons their
father as guardian; Timothy W. Rose; Samuel W. Rose; and Almena Rose; the last two
being minors by Samuel Bancroft their guardian. (62)

12-18-1822 - Thomas EDGAR and Anna EDGAR vs. Benjamin A. BROWN and others.
Filed 5-10-1822. (note: See page 55, essentially same as this entry; also see pages
97 and 124 for further record). (66)

8-19-1823 - Ann Lee PECK, et al vs. Heirs of Benjamin PECK, dec'd. Filed 5-2-1823.
Benjamin Peck, late of Licking Co., dec'd, died intestate April 1879. Widow, Mary
Peck. Land, 108.09 acres Lot 25, 3rd quarter, Township 1, Range 15 U.S. Military
tract; 60 acres Lot 6, Section 3, Township 5, Range 3; also lots in Johnstown. Heirs:
Anna Lee Peck, Benjamin Peck, Sarah Peck wife of Archibald Cornell, Clarissa Harlow
wife of Henry Fassett, Israel Harding Peck, Samuel Peck, Mary Eliza Peck, Sabra Jane
Peck, Harris Peck, Juliet Peck and George Peck; the last seven named being minors.
(70)

3-8-1824 William SYMMES vs. David CLARKSON, et al. Filed Aug. 1823. William Symmes,
late of Butler Co., Ohio, dec'd, died in 1809. Land, 400 acres, Section (not given),
Township 3, Range 14, U. S. Military tract. Widow, Rebecca Symmes of Butler Co.,
Ohio entitled to ¼ part. Children: William Symmes of Butler Co., Ohio; Esther
Symmes wife of James Davis; Phebe Symmes aged 19 yrs.; Timothy Symmes aged 15 yrs.;
the last two being minors by David C. Clarkson their guardian. (74)

6-15-1824 - Mathew HOPKINS vs. William Augustus HOPKINS and others. Filed 8-20-1823.
Mathew Hopkins, dec'd, died Oct. 1820. Land, 50 and 3/4 acres off east end Lot 3,
Section 2, Township 4, Range 13, U.S. Military land. Children: Mathew Hopkins,
William Augustus Hopkins, Mercy Hopkins wife of Silas Mott, Jeduthan Hopkins, Simon
Wright Hopkins, Lucy Hopkins, Rachel Hopkins, Caleb Hopkins and Dewitt Clinton Hop-
kins; the last seven named not of age. (77)

10-8-1824 - William BELL vs. Heirs of Nathan FAY, dec'd. Filed 4-11-1824. Nathan
Fay of Chautaugua Co., New York, dec'd, died 6-10-1810 at that place. Land, two
tracts, one containing 93 and 3/4 acres, the other 469 acres both in 4th quarter,
Township 1, Range 14, U.S. Military district in Licking Co. Seven Heirs: John,
Hetty wife of Simeon Guile, Nathan, Culling, Esther, Willard and Betsy. That John
Fay sold his interest to Esther (also given as Elisha) Fay (also given as Gray) who
died in the fall of 1823 (also stated that it was spring of 1820). leaving heirs whose
residence is unknown. That Culling Fay resides in Ohio, that Willard and Betsy Fay
resides in Chautaugua Co., N. Y. (80)

3-10-1826 - David MENTZER vs. John HOLTZBERRY. Filed 10-21-1825. Nicholas Holts=
berry, late of Licking Co., dec'd. Widow, Catharine, entitled to 24 acres dower.
Land, 90 acres N pt. S½ Section 11, Township 19, Range 17 of Refugee tract. Eleven
heirs: Jacob Holtsberry; Samuel Holtzberry; Ann Holtzberry now Ann Kenney; Richard
Holtzberry; Conrad Holtzberry; Sally wife of Isaac Harter; Polly wife of John
Woolard; Elizabeth Green, a widow, late Holtsberry; Susanna wife of John Wertsbaugh;
John Holtsberry of Randolph Co., Va.; James Holtsberry of Licking Co. Several of
heirs sold their interest to Mentzer. (83)

3-10-1826 - Nathan F. PIERSON and others vs. Firman PIERSON. Filled 12-17-1825. George Pierson, late of Licking Co., dec'd. died 1824 intestate. Land 124 acres Lo 1 and 63 acres Lot 5, 1st quarter, Township 3, Range 13. Children: John Pierson, dec'd, his only son-Firman Pierson; Eliza Howell, dec'd, her children-- George P., Phebe Y. and Mary Ann Howell; Phebe late Pierson wife of Harvey Jones; Nathan F. Pierson of Battlehill, New Jersey; Moses Pierson, Sally Pierson and Andrew D. Pierson, the last three of Licking Co. and the last four named being joint heirs to 1/7th part.   (85)

8-15-1826 - George TRACY and Basil TRACY vs. William TRACY and others.   Filed 10-21-1825. Basil Tracy Sr., dec'd. Land. 96 acres W pt. SE¼ Section 18 Township 1, Range 11 U. S. Military tract. That Basil Tracy Sr. by deed dated 11-22-1822 sold the 96 acres to: William Tracy of Belmont Co., Ohio; Knacky Kelly; Heirs of Sarah Bouring, dec'd, residence unknown; Heirs of Joshua Fry, dec'd of Belmont co., Ohio; Peggy wife of Thomas Downey, residence unknown; and Elizabeth wife of Caleb Bouring of Licking Co. (89)

8-19-1826 - David WILSON and others. Filed 8-15-1826. Archibald Wilson, late of Licking Co., dec'd, departed in March 18¼4. Land, 389 acres center corner Section 1, Township 2, Range 12. That Archibald Wilson made a will and disposed of said tract of land as follows: 100 acres to son Abraham C. Wilson; 100 acres to sons, Benjamin and George Wilson. Widow, Nancy Wilson to receive part of tract and at her decease to divided between David, William B., John N. and Enoch Wilson, sons and heirs of said Archibald, dec'd; Enoch being a minor.   (93)

10-6-1826 - John HUGHS and Thomas HUGHS vs. Willard FAY, Betsey FAY and Heirs of Elisha Fay, dec'd. Filed 6-27-1826. Nathan Fay, late of Chautaqua Co., N.Y., dec'd, died 6-6-1810. Land, two tracts of 93 acres and 169 and 1/4 acres totaling 314 acres in 4th quarter, Township 1, Range 14, U.S. Military tract. Heirs; John, Hetty, Nathan, Cutting, Esther, Willard and Betsy. That Esther Fay died in spring of 1820 intestate without issue leaving remaining six heirs as her heirs. That Elisha Gray (also given as Fay) purchased John Fay's share. Hughs interest by purchase also.(95) (note: see page 80, some information conflicts with above, believe information given above is probably the most accurate).

6-14-1827 - William STANBERY and Amos H. CAFFEE vs. Benjamin A. BROWN. Filed 8-11-1826. Daniel March, dec'd. (97) (note see pages 55,66 & 124)

6-15-1827 - Lucius D. MOWER vs. Heirs of Jesse MUNSON. Filed 3-15-1826. Jesse Munson, dec'd, died in 1823 intestate. Land, 200 acres lots 25 & 26, Section 3, Township 2, Range 13; 59.33 acres S pt. Lot 23, S3 T2 R13; 28 acres S pt. lot 1, S2, T2, R13; 160 acres lots 13 & 14, S1, T1, R14; and other land descriptions. Heirs: Jasper Munson, Lucy wife of Lucius D. Mower and Clarissa wife of Elizin Abbott. (102

6-15-1827 - Thomas ATKINSON vs. C. HERWOOD, etal. Filed 4-21-1827. Samuel HERRON, dec'd, died without issue. Land, in-lot 114 in Newark. Brothers and Sister: David Herron, John Herron, Cook Herron and Catharine Sherwood, late Herron, a widow all of Licking Co.; David and John by deed dated 4-7-1827 sold their interest at Atkinson. (105)

Feb. 1829 - Smith ALLEN and wife vs. Catharine SHERWOOD, etal. Filed 10-7-1828.
Robert Sherwood, dec'd. Widow Catherine Sherwood of Licking Co. Land, 102.65 acres
pt. NE corner Lot 4, 1st quarter, Township 1, Range 12, Children: Allen Sherwood of
Licking Co., Ohio; Nancy (wife of Smith Allen??); James Sherwood of Knox Co., Ohio;
each entitled to 1/3rd part. (121)

2-26-1829 - Benjamin A. BROWN and Heirs of Ralph MARSH, dec'd vs. Samuel PURDY, et al.
Filed 6-7-1828. Land, (see description of land given on page 35); that Daniel Marsh
and wife Esther deeded part of said land to Ralph Marsh by deed dated 6-2-1800. That
Ralph Marsh, died Oct. 1800 in Rahway, Essex Co., New Jersey, leaving 10 children:
Lewis R. Marsh of Richmond Co., New York; Sidney Marsh of Gettysburgh, Pa.; John
Marsh of Gettysburgh, Pa.; George Marsh of Gettysburg, Pa.; Rebecca Frame, late
Marsh of Baltimore, Md.; Mary Decamp formerly Marsh, wife of Aaron Decamp of Haver-
straw, New York; Catharine formerly Marsh, wife of Ephraim Gillmore of New Garden,
Pa.; Ann formerly Marsh, wife of Cornelius E. Price of Essex Co., N. J.; Elizabeth
Marsh of Rahway, Essex Co., N. J.; and Letitia Marsh, dec'd, her six children--Fanny
Thompson formerly Marsh, Caroline Moore formerly Marsh, John Marsh, Nathan Marsh,
Joseph Marsh and Solomon Marsh, all of Middlesex and Essex Cos., N. J. That Daniel
Marsh died in 1802 intestate leaving widow, Esther Marsh and 6 children: Mary widow
of Job DeCamp, dec'd; Ann wife of Thomas Edgar; Sarah wife of Robert Clarkson; Eliz-
abeth, late Marsh wife of Jacob Marsh, both dec'd, their four children--Mary wife of
Samuel Purdy of New York City, Anna Eliza wife of John Payne of Middlesex Co. N. J.,
Esther wife of Lewis Prall-Esther since died leaving 3 children Charlotte, Isaac and
Hester Pral of Essex Co. N. J., Noah Warren Marrah-Noah since died intestate leaving
2 children George D. and Jacob S. Marsh of New York City; Daniel Marsh Jr., died
intestate leaving 3 children--Elias Marsh, George Taylor Marsh, and Rachel Barnet
Marsh wife of Thomas D. Smith of New York City; William Ralph Marsh, dec'd, died
intestate leaving 4 children--Ann Marsh, John Ralph Marsh, Noah Marsh and Daniel
Marsh. (124) (note: see pages 55, 66 & 97)

2-27-1829 - David Campbell, etal. vs. John McELWIE, etal. Filed Aug. 1828. Land, pt
lot 2, 3rd quarter, Township 3, Range 13, U. S. Military tract as devised at May
Term 1819 Licking Co. t o Samuel and David Campbell, their being co-partners with
each having an one-half interest. That David CAMPBELL, dec'd, died in 1821 intestate
leaving heirs: David Campbell of Licking Co.; James Campbell; William Campbell; and
Eleanor late Campbell wife of Thomas Stalley; the last three of New Castle Co.,
Delaware. That Samuel CAMPBELL, dec'd, died in 1820 leaving heirs: Margaret late
Campbell wife of John Mc Elwie; James Campbell; William Campbell; Mary Campbell;
Elizabeth Campbell; Ann Campbell; Sary Campbell; and Daniel Campbell; all of New
Castle Co., Delaware. (129)

2-27-1829 - Norton CASE vs. William LEWIS, et al. Filed 2-17-1829. (note: mame of
deceased not given). Land, pt. SW corner 1st quarter, Township 2, Range 13, U. S.
Military tract. Partition 4/9th part, Norton Case, by purchase from heirs; 1/9th
part, William Lewis; 1/9th part, David Lewis; 1/9th part, Sarah Lewis; 1/9th part,
Morgan Lewis; 1/9th part, Lucretia Lewis; the last two named being minors by Samuel
Bancroft their guardian. (132)

6-5-1829 - Regnal GREEN vs. Heirs of Charles GREEN, dec'd. Filed 1-12-1829. Land, two tracts--160 acres SW corner Lot 33, Section 1, Township 3, Range 15 U. S. Military tract deeded by George Green to Charles Green on 2-15-1810 and recorded in Deed Book D, page 300; also NW¼ Section 4, Township 3, Range 15 U. S. Military tract. Children: Rebecca late Green wife of Jesse Hile, Regnal Green, George Green, Am mon Green, Clarinda Green, William Green, Sarah Green and Elihu Green; the last named being a minor. (134)

6-5-1829 - John S. CONINE vs. Heirs of Jacob CONINE. Filed 8-12-1828. Jacob Conine, dec'd. Widow Sarah Conine. Land 916 acres Section 4, Township 1, Range 15, U. S. Military District; lines--Richard Conine, Refugee tract; said land being granted to Jacob Conine, dec'd by his father, Jacob Conine, Sr. Children: Jacob Conine, Peter D. Conine, John S. Conine; Fanny wife of Isaac Vandorn, Mary wife of Ralph Vandorn, Jacob C. Donine (sic), Richard Conine, Daniel Conine, Harrison Conine and Elizabeth Conine, Jacob C., Richard, Daniel, Harrison and Elizabeth being minorsd. (137)

6-29-1829 - Samuel H. JOSEPH et al. vs. Elizabeth HORN, et al. Filed 1-16-1829. Henry HORN(E), dec'd, late of Licking Co., died in 1816 intestate. Widow, Hannah Horn. Land, 195.07 acres pt. Section 1, Township 1, Range 13, U. S. Military tract. Children: Mary late Horn wife of Allen H. Ingram, Margaret late Horn wife of Samuel H. Joseph, Elizabeth Horn, and Eleanor Horn; the last two named being minors. (142)

10-10-1829 - William PARR vs. Heirs of Thomas PARR. Filed 1-6-1829. Thomas Parr, dec'd, died in 1816. Widow (not named), is now deceased. Land, in-lot 49 in Newark. Children: William Parr, Mary Parr, Henry Parr, Thomas Parr and Samuel Parr; the last four named are all minors. (146)

Oct. 1829 - Francis JACKSON vs. William L. SULLIVANT, et al. Abram DEARDUFF, dec'd. Land 320 acres half Section 16, Township 17, Range 19 of Refugee tract. Abram had seven children but only names David Dearduff and his wife Rachel; and John Dearduff. That by deed dated 3-13-1827 David and wife Rachel sold their interest to Francis Jackson. Other persons listed in petition, relationship if any, not stated:-- William L. Sullivant, Michael Sullivant and Joseph Sullivant all of Franklin Co. Ohio, John Dearduff, Charles Hunter and wife, John Stone and Jacob Riley all of Licking Co. (150)

2-23-1830 - James MOORE adms. of William MOORE, dec'd vs. Heirs of William MOORE. filed 10-8-1828. William Moore of Huntinton Co., Pa. Land 12½ acres north side town of Newark being in 4th quarter, Township 2, Range 12, U.S. Military District. Heirs: (note; not named, but inferred that they are named in Huntington Co. Pa. court records). (153)

3-1-1830 - Alexander HOLMES vs. CHANNEL Heirs. Filed 2-25-1829. Land, 100 acres Lot 10, 1st quarter, Township 2, Range 11, U.S. Military tract. Alexander Holmes is entitled to 1/2 undivided interest and is joint tennet with Mary Ann, Jeremiah and Joseph A. Channel, all minors of Licking Co., who hold jointly and undivided 1/2 interest. (153)

6-2-1830 - Alfred GALE vs. Heirs of Joseph GALE, dec'd. Filed 7-23-1829. Joseph Gale, dec'd. Widow, Rebecca late Gale, now wife of ____(left blank) Campbell. Land, 160 acres NW¼ Section 9, Township 3, Range 10 of unapportioned lands in U. S. Military District. Children: Alfred Gale, Christiana wife of James Tunis, Cornelius Gale, Catherine Gale, Effa Gale, William H. Gale, Joseph Gale, Elinas Gale and Harrison Gale; the last six named being minors. (155)

June 1830 - Hiram WRIGHT and Elizabeth his wife vs. Nancy BLOOD, et al. Filed 12-23-1829. Land, Lot 21, Section 2, Township 2, Range 14, U. S. Military tract, Frederick L. Blood, dec'd, died in 1827 leaving a will in which he devised said tract of land as follows: 1/6th part to daughter, Elizabeth wife of Hiram Wright of Licking Co.; 1/6th part to Nancy Blood; 1/3rd part to Rufus F. Blood and 1/3rd part to his widow, Mary Blood; all of Licking Co. (158)

10-8-1830 - James H. HALL and wife vs. Heirs of Nathan and Abel JEWITT, dec'd. Filed 7-27-1829. Land, lot 10 and part Lot 5, in R(ow?) 2 of house lots in Johnstown being 1 acre. Nathan Jewett, dec'd. Brothers and Sisters: Sarah late Jewett, wife of James H. Hall; Daniel Jewett; David Jewett; Hannah late Jewett wife of Samuel Russell; William Jewett; and Abel Jewett, dec'd, his widow, Sarah and children--Nathan, Nabba, Timothy and Sarah Ann Jewett, all minors. (162)

Oct. 1830 - Barbara Smith vs. John Taylor, et al. Filed 4-16-1830. Land, pt. NE corner Section 4, Township 1, Range 14. David LOINBERGER, dec'd, left child, en-- John Loinberger, Isaac Loinberger, Barbara wife of Mann Almond and Nancy wife of Jacob Lincoln. That said David Loinberger, dec'd was co-partner in land with Isabell Symmes. That John Loinbarger purchased share of Mann Almond and wife Barbara and Isaac Loinbarger and that on 8-1-1828 said John being owner of 3/5ths part conveyed said 3/5ths part to John W. SMITH of Shenandoah Co., Virginia, now dec'd, former husband of Barbara Smith--their children--Sarah Ann, William D., Ambrose B. and Mary Catherine Smith, That John Taylor purchased interest of Jacob Lincoln and wife.(168)

732

The following records are from Partition Record B. Pages on which record may be found are given in parenthesis.

March 1831 - Allen FORSYTHE vs Betsey FORSYTHE, et al. Filed 4-21-1830. William Forsythe, dec'd. Widow Elizabeth, now the wife of James Kerr. Land, 6 acres part Lot 4, Section 2, Township 4, Range 12, U.S. Military district; lots 19 & 20 in town of Utica. Children: Allen Forsythe; Betsey Forsythe; William Forsythe; the last two of Licking Co., both minors by Allen Robinson their guardian; Patterson Forsythe, of Logan Co., Ohio, a minor by Thomas Scott his guardian; Jonathan Forsythe, of Logan Co., Ohio, a minor; Lucinda Forsythe, of Knox Co., Ohio, a minor by Patrick Moore her guardian. (1)

March 1831 - James SMART, et al. vs. James RANKINS, et al. Filed 4-7-1830. James Rankins Jr., late of Licking Co., dec'd, died in Sept. 1828. Widow, Nancy, now the wife of David   mart. Land, NW½ Section 14, Township 3, Range 10 in Zanesville land district, except 60 acres of north side conveyed by James Sr. in his life time to son, David Rankins. Children: James Rankins; David Rankins; Thomas Rankins; Abraham Rankins; William Rankins; Elizabeth wife of Thomas McCulloch; Margaret Rankins; Evaline Rankins; Rachel Rankins; and Jane Rankins; the last four named being minors by James Smart their guardian. (4)

March 1832 - Amasa VAN HORN vs. Heirs of Wm. B. VAN HORN, dec'd. Filed 8-29-1831. William B. Van Horn, late of Newark, Licking Co., dec'd, died in Oct. 1830. Widow, Mary H. Van Horn, That Amasa Van Horn and William B. Van Horn were equal co-owners in N½ in-lot #104 and also north side half lot #97; both in Newark. Children: Cornelius Van Horn, Henry Irwin Van Horn and Theodore Van Horn. (8)

March 1833 - James McLAURINE executor of Richard P. JAMES, dec'd vs. Heirs of Robert STOCKTON, dec'd. Filed 8-23-1831. That Richard P. James of Cumberland Co., Virginia died in the year 1826 leaving a widow. That under his will, James McLaurine was authorized to sell land in Ohio. That Francis J. James the immediate ancestor of Richard P. James in the year 1800 being in full life purchased from the executors of Robert Stockton, viz.--Ebenezer Stockton, Job Stockton and Thomas P. Johnson, one-third part of 600 acres in Licking Co. being part of a 4000 acre survey in the 2nd quarter, Township 1, Range 14. That Francis J. James died leaving Richard P. James as his only heir, seized of one-third interest in said land. That the heirs of Robert Stockton are unknown. (11)

6-23-1834 - David DOUD and Nancy DOUD vs. Mary BLOOD and Rufus F. BLOOD. Filed 12-7-1833. Land, lot 21, Section 2, Township 2, Range 14, U.S. Military tract, purchased from James Coe a resident of Fairfield Co., Ohio and recorded in Book C, page 70. Frederick Blood, dec'd, late of Licing Co., dec'd, left a will in which he devised 1/6th part of land to daughter, Nancy now wife of David Doud; 1/6th part to Eliza Blood now wife of Hiram Wright; 1/3rd part to Rufus F. Blood and 1/3rd part to his widow, Mary Blood. (16)

733

June 1834 - William R. ALEXANDER vs. Joseph SHAW, et al. Filed 4-23-1833.
Land, pt. lot 11, 2nd quarter, Township 4, Range 12 U.S. Military district.
Said land deeded by Allen Robinson and wife by deed dated 4-20-1824 to Martha
Stewart and Samuel Laughead. That Joseph Laughead was also possessed of an
equitable interest in above described land and by his will devised same to
daughter, Martha Stewart and to Samuel Laughead. That Samuel Laughead and
his wife deeded his interest to Martha Stewart. That since the making of the
deed, Martha Stewart married Hatfield Clark, then after living with him a
few years, she died about two years since, leaving no issue. That said Martha's
interest is to be inherited by her brothers and sisters, vix:--Brother, John
Laughead, his son--Allen Laughead of Knox Co., Ohio; Sister, Susan Shaw, dec'd,
her children--Joseph Shaw, residence unknown, Jane late Shaw wife of James
Alexander of Pa. and Ann Neely; Brother, William Laughead, reported to have
drowned 2 years ago, never married and leaving no issue; Sister, Rebecca Burnrides,
dec'd, her heirs, names and residence unknown; Sister, Mary wife of William
Gibson of Beaver Co., Pennsylvania; Sister, Margaret Clark, dec'd, her children--
Elizabeth, Margaret and Ann Clark, all of Alleghany Co., Pennsylvania; Sister,
Hannah Walker of Hamilton Co., Ohio; Sister, Mary Alexander wife of John
Alexander. (18)

June 1834 - John and Elizabeth WAGY vs Ary PUMPHREY, etal. Filed 6-15-1833.
Joshua Pumphrey, late of Licking Co., dec'd. Widow, Ary Pumphrey. Land,
SE pt. Section 3, Township 1, Range 13, U.S. Military lands, sold by John
Van Buskirk to Joshua Pumphrey on 11-18-1817 and recorded in Deed Book F,
page 620. Heirs: Elizabeth wife of John Wagy, Caleb Pumphrey, Jemina Pumphrey,
Henry Pumphrey, Editha Pumphrey, Reason Pumphrey, Ezra Pumphrey, Nicholas
Pumphrey and Eleanor Pumphrey; the last five named being minors. (24)

June 1834 - Edward BULL and wife vs. Thomas ASHTON and wife and Samantha SWAN.
Filed 6-6-1832. Aaron Swan, late of Licking Co., dec'd, died intestate in 1825.
Widow, Laura, now wife of Thomas Ashton of Violet twp., Fairfield Co., Ohio.
Land, 106 acres SW part Section 15, Township 16, Range 20. Children: Sophronia
wife of Edward Bull and Samantha Swan of Violet twp., Fairfield Co., Ohio.(28&30)

June 1834 - Andrew CAMPBELL, et al. vs. John S. CAMPBELL and James CAMPBELL.
Filed 7-21-1833. Joseph Campbell, late of Licking Co., dec'd, died in Aug. 1824.
Children: Andrew Campbell, Mary Campbell, Jane Campbell, John Campbell, Sarah
Campbell, Joseph Campbell, Rebecca Campbell, Samuel Campbell, Elizabeth Campbell
and Caleb Campbell; the last six named being minors by Nathan Conrad their guardian.
That John Campbell, dec'd, father of said Joseph, dec'd, named above and grand-
father of petitioner, died intestate in 1822 and that in his lifetime he purchased
from Elias Stanbery, Samuel H. Smith and Erkurius Beaty 312½ acres, lot 9,
3rd quarter, Township 4, Range 12, U.S. Military District as recorded in Licking
Co. in Deed Book D, page 225. That said John Campbell left children, viz.:
James Campbell of Licking Co.; John S. Campbell of Licking Co.; Joseph Campbell,
dec'd, of Licking Co. (his heirs as named above); and Margaret wife of Thomas
Green of Huntington Co., Pennsylvania. (32)

7-13-1835 - William SMITH and Sarah wife vs. Emely Jane HURSEY. Filed 4-11-1835.
Land, 140 acres SW¼ Section 22, Township 1, Range 10 in unappropriated lands of
Military District. William Hursey, dec'd. Widow, Sarah Hursey. Partition:
4/7th part, William Smith and Sarah wife of Delaware Co., Ohio; and 3/7th part,
Emely Jane Hursey of Muskingum Co., Ohio. (38)

7-13-1835 - Corrington W. SEARLE vs. Joseph WARTHAN, et al. Filed 2-20-1835.
That Corrington W. Searle and Alban Warthan were tenents in common in 176.14
acres NE¼ Section 12, Township 17, Range 18 of Refugee tract by virtue of patent
from United States. Alban Warthan, dec'd, died intestate. Widow, Elizabeth
Warthan of Licking Co., Ohio. Heirs: Joseph Warthan, residence unknown;
Margaret wife of Burgess Wright of Licking Co.; Louisa wife of Robert Mitchell
of Licking Co.; Elijah B. Mervin Warthan; Albert Warthan; Theoroderick Warthan Jr.;
Isabella Warthan; Harriet Warthan; Oliver H. Perry Warthan; Phebe Warthan;
and William Spencer Warthan; the last eight named being minors and all of Licking
Co. (40)

7-13-1835 - Andalutia PIER, etal vs. Robert DAVISON. Filed 12-11-1834. Andalutia
Pier of Newark, Licking Co. and Jonathan Child of Rochester, Monroe Co., New
York each are invested jointly in a one half interest in lot 102 in Newark.
That Robert Davidson is the owner of the other undivided one half interest.
Petition for Partition of same. (43)

7-13-1835 - John HANNA, et al. vs. James HANNA, et al. Filed 10-21-1834.
James Hanna, late of Fairfield Co., Ohio, dec'd. 150.82 acres SW¼ Section 12,
Township 16, Range 2 of Refugee tract. Heirs: John Hanna; Matild Hanna;
Amelia Hanna; Henry Hanna; William Hanna; Reuben Hanna; James Hanna, a minor
by John Hanna guardian; Hezekiah Hanna; Nathaniel Hanna, Hezekiah and Nathaniel
both minors by David Wintermute their guardian; Pheta Hanna; and Isaac Hanna;
Phetta and Isaac both minors by Jonathan Coulson their guardian; all of Fairfield
Co., Ohio. (47)

10-12-1835 - Alvin L. STURGESS vs. Widow and Heirs of Isaac STURGESS, dec'd.
Filed 4-20-1835. Isaac Sturgess, dec'd. Widow, Catharine Sturgess of Licking
Co. Land, 100 acres Lot 10, 1st Range lots, Section 3, Township 2, Range 13,
U. S. Military District. Heirs, each with a 1/11th interest: Alvin L. Sturgess,
Mary Ann late Sturgess wife of Peter Higby, Emely late Sturgess wife of Levi
Hughson, Lucinda late Sturgess wife of Lucius Cook, Maria Sturgess, Charles
M. Sturgess, George S. Sturgess, Albert A. Sturgess, Matilda S. Sturgess, Isaac
A Sturgess, all of Licking Co., and David S. Sturgess of Indiana. (56)

10-12-1835 - David WOOD vs. Leonard WOOD, et al. Filed 5-2-1835. Luther Wood,
dec'd. Widow, Harriet Wood of Licking Co. Land, in-lots 2,3, & 4 and E½ lots
9 & 10, block 9, Granville. Partition: 1/9th part, David Woods; 1/9th part,
Leonard Woods; 1/9th part, Calvin Woods; 1/9th part, John Wood; 1/9th part,
Harriet Wood; 1/9th part, Gardner Woods; 1/9th part, Laury Woods; 1/9th part,
Clarissa Woods; 1/9th part jointly or 1/18th part each, Charles H. and Irvin
Sawyer. (59)

735

10-12-1835 - William W. GAULT vs. Catharine HOLMES, et al. Filed 6-1-1835.
Land, 105 acres, lot 13, Township 17, Range 18 in Refugee tract, formerly owned
by Thomas Holmes in his lifetime and devised to Joshua Holmes and others as
recorded in Will of Thomas Holmes; that by Will of Joshua Holmes, portion of
land devised and conveyed same by deed to petitioner. Joshua Holmes, dec'd.
Widow, Catharine Holmes, entitled to dower of 205 acres she resides on in
Fayette Co. Partition: 1/4th part, Thomas Holmes of Licking Co.; 1/4th part,
Baraleel Holmes, residence unknown; 1/4th part, Alexander Holmes of Hamilton Co.,
Ohio; 1/4th part, William W. Gault. (62)

April 1836 - Thomas W. WILSON vs. Augustus or Gustavius HOLLER, et al. Filed
2-27-1836. John and Henry Holler were tenents in common, each owning one half,
in NE corner of 4000 acres in 2nd quarter, Township 2, Range 1, U. S. Military
District, said land granted to them by George Jackson by deed dated 1-8-1817.
John HOLLER, dec'd. Widow, Barbara Sparks, late Holler. Heirs: Lear Hollar;
Rebecca Hollar; Catharine wife of Daniel Benner; Sarah Holler; Gustavius Holler;
and Eliza Holler; the last two named being minors and the first three named having
conveyed their interest to Thomas W. Wilson. Henry HOLLER, dec'd. Widow,
Catharine Holler. Heirs: Henry Holler, Joseph Holler, Peter Holler, Absalom
Holler, Ellis Holler, Mary Holler, Elizabeth Holler and Moses Holler; the first
named having sold his interest to Wilson. (70)

4-11-1836 - John J. BRICE vs. Benjamin TURNER's Heirs. Filed 7-8-1836. Land
187 acres Section 2, Township 2, Range 12. Benjamin Turner, dec'd. Widow, Jane
Turner. Heirs: Benjamin Turner; George Turner, a minor; Jane late Turner wife
of William Barrick; Polly Turner, a minor; Eliza late Turner wife of John Colville;
all of Licking Co.; Levin Turner of Indiana; James Turner of Pike Co., Ohio;
Matilda Henderson, dec'd, late Matilda Turner, her heirs--Elizabeth Jane
and Benjamin Henderson of Indiana. That Samuel Turner sold his interest to Brice
which entitles said Brice to 1/5th interest in land. (73)

4-11-1836 - Justus HILLIER vs. Truman FRENCH, et al. Filed 5-9-1835. Land,
being nor side near tail race of Saw Mill formerly belonging to Capt. John
Phelps, being 6 and 2/4th acres on which mill is erected (note: no section,
township or range given). William PAGE, dec'd, late of Licking Co. Widow,
Rosetta M. Page. Tenents in common: Rositta Marilla wife of Truman French;
Lucinda Maria wife of Henry Taylor; Harriett Eliza Page; Mary Jane Page; Homer
Clayton Page; and William F. Paige; all of Licking Co., Ohio. That Justus
Hillier Jr. of Licking Co. is entitled to 1/3rd part (note: does not say if
Hiller's interest is by purchase or inheritance.) (78)

7-25-1836 - John MOODY, et al. vs. Mary MOODY, et al. Filed 3-29-1836. Land,
400 acres, 1st wuarter, Township 2, Range 22, U. S. Military district except
50 acres previously conveyed to Thomas Moody; 131 acres part lot 3, Section 4,
Township 2, Range 11; and 18 acres part lot 5, 1st quarter, Township 2, Range 11.
William Moody, late of Licking Co., dec'd. Widow, Mary Moody. Children: John
Moody of Richland Co., Ohio; Thomas Moody of Licking Co.; William Moody of
Licking Co.; Margarette wife of John J. Strother of Licking Co.; Rachel Reed;
Sarah Hoyt; Mary Bryant; Elizabeth Taggert, dec'd, late wife of Jonathan Taggert,
her children--Lucy and William Taggart of Licking Co. (90)

736

April 1836 - James R. STANBERRY vs. Sarah PUGH and Hananiah PUGH. Filed
8-5-1836. Land, W½ out-lots #1-10 in Newark and 8 acres addition to town of
Newark. Hananiah Pugh, dec'd. Widow, Sarah Pugh, entitled to dower. Partition:
2/3rds part, James R. Stanberry and 1/3 part, Hananiah Pugh. (82)

7-25-1836 - John W. BROWN, guardian vs. Jemima BROWN. Filed 8-28-1835. John
Brown, dec'd. Widow, Jemima Brown of Licking Co. Land, John Brown's estate
of inheritance in 66 and 2/3 acres part S quarter, Township 1, Range 13, of U.S.
Military tract, also lot 48 in Hebron. Heirs: Alfred, Mary Ann. Isaac, Angeline,
Caroline and John Brown; all minors by John W. Brown their guardian; all of
Licking Co. (98)

10-17-1836 - Martin BROOKS and David DEVINNEY vs. John WALES and Ann his wife.
Filed 2-29-1836. Land, 320 acres part 3rd quarter, Township 3, Range 13, U.S.
Military tract. Partition: 1/2 part, Martin Brooks and David Devenney; 1/2 part,
John Wales and Ann his wife, formerly Ann Pitten of Wilmington, New Castle Co.,
Delaware. (102)

10-17-1836 - James WELLS and wife vs. Perry RANDALL, et al. Filed 6-6-1836.
Land, 100 acres W 3nd of one-half Section 2, Township 17, Range 19 of Refugee
tract appropriated for Refugees from Canada and Nova Scotia; except 50 acres
sold by Levin Randall in his lifetime to Caleb Randal by deed dated 1-3-1815.
Levin Randal, late of Licking Co., dec'd. Children and Heirs: Persis late
Randal wife of James Wells, Perry Randal, Harriet Randal, William Randal and
Levin Randal; the last two named being minors. (106)

LICKING COUNTY, OHIO - PARTITION RECORDS 1837-1844

The following records are taken from "Partition Record B" located in the Common
Pleas Court (Clerk of Court's Office) at the court house in Newark. Page on which
record may be found in the original book is given in parenthesis. See October 1972
and January 1974 issues of "GATEWAY TO THE WEST" for Partition Records for the
period 1816-1836.

5-22-1837 - E.T. SMITH, etal. vs. E.T.S. SCHENCK. In Partition. Filed 3-4-1837.
William C. Schenck of Warren Co., Ohio died intestate 1-15-1821. Widow, Elizabeth
Schenck. Children and heirs: Sarah B. wife of Egbert T. Smith; James F. Schenck;
Robert C. Schenck; Woodhul S. Schenck; all of Warren and Montgomery Counties, Ohio;
and Edmund Schenck, dec'd, who died without issue. Land, 200 acres Quarter 4,
Township 2, Range 12 U.S.M. being tract 2 patented to Wm. C. Schenck; 193 acres
Quarter 4, Township 2, Range 12 U.S.M. being tract 11 set off to Wm. C. Schenck;
187 acres Quarter 4, Township 2, Range 12 U.S.M. being tract 12 set off to Wm. C.
Schenck; 187 acres Quarter 4, Township 2, Range 12 U.S.M. being tract 12; also
36 acres Quarter 4, Township 2, Range 12 U.S.M. being tract 17 set off to Schenck;
and parts of Tract 14, Quarter 4, Township 2, Range 12 U.S.M.; 260 acres lot 14,
50 acres lot 9 Holms subdivision, 131 acres lot 16; also in-lot 2 in Newark;
lots 4 & 6 SW of Newark; lot 39, Quarter 2, Township 1, Range 10, U.S.M. being
100 acres.   (112)

5-22-1837 - James YOUNG, etal vs. Daniel YOUNG. Petition for Partition. Filed
1-26-1837. Uzal Young, dec'd. Widow, Sarah Young of Licking Co. Partition:
1/4th part, James Young; 1/4th part, Eliza wife of John Wolf; 1/4th part, Mary
wife of Stephen Jaggers; all of Licking Co.; 1/4th part, Daniel Young. Land,
part Section 1, Township 2, Range 12 U.S.M., lines--land formerly owned by John
J. Brice and by Thomas Dickenson, Isaac Wilson, road leading from Newark to Mt.
Vernon being same tract conveyed by Isaac Wilson and Mae his wife to Uzal Young
by deed dated 7-22-1835 recorded in Book J, pages 5,10,11,12; also part Section 1,
Township 2, Range 12 U.S.M., lines--corner Wm Wilson as mentioned in amicable
partition by heirs of Archibald Wilson, dec'd, and recorded in Book A, pages 99,93
&c.(?) being same land deeded to Uzel Young by B.W. Brice and others dated 1-27-1832
recorded in Book P, page 296,297; also tract part of Quarter 4, Township 2, Range
12 U.S.M., lines--B.W. Brice, Newark and Old Mt. Vernon Rd., Meredith Darlington
(now out-lot "G") being 3.68 acres; also lots 16 & 17 in Young's addition to
Newark.   (118)

5-22-1837 - George DITTER vs. Peter RUDEBOUGH, etal. In Partition. Filed
3-26-1837. Land, in-lot 41 town of Brownsville. Partition: 1/10th part, George
Ditter of Licking Co.; 1/10th part, Elizabeth wife of Peter Rudebough of Putnam
Co., Ohio; 1/10th part, Faithful wife of Thomas McClure of Putnam Co., Ohio;
1/10th part, Elizabeth Ditter; 1/10th part, Mary Ditter; 1/10th part, James Ditter;
1/10th part, John Ditter; 1/10th part, Philander Ditter; 1/10th part, Jane Ditter;
1/10th part, Calendre Ditter; the last seven named all being minors by John Boner
their guardian and all of Muskingum Co., Ohio.   (126)

9-9-1837 - John SPENCER and John SMITH vs. Grace MICHAEL, et al. In Chancery,
Petition for Partition. Filed 7-11-1837. Land, 41 acres 4th Quarter, Township 3,
Range 12 U.S.M., lines--twp. line at SW corner of land lately owned by John Spencer,
dec'd, land of John Evans(?). Simon MICHAEL, dec'd, late of Licking Co. Widow,
Grace Michael entitled to dower. Heirs: Phebe late Michael wife of Joseph Miller,
Mary late Michael wife of Samuel Gibson, Harriet Michael, all of Licking Co., Ohio.
That John Spencer and John Smith of Licking Co. are jointly seized of one undivided
half part (note: apparently by purchase).   (134)

9-1-1837 - Caroline HAND by her guardian vs. Nancy BLACK, etal. Petition for
Partition. Filed 4-6-1837. Mathew BLACK, dec'd. Widow, Nancy Black of Licking
Co. entitled to dower. Partition: 1/4th part, Caroline Hand a minor by Wm. G.
Hand her guardian both of Licking Co.; 1/4th part, James Black; 1/4th part, David
Black; 1/4th part, Henry Black; all of Licking Co. and the last two named being
minors. Land, 3rd quarter, Township 1, Range 12 U.S.M., lines--NW corner of tract
of John Beam, land of Mathew Black and James Taylor; being 313½ acres except 50
acres conveyed by Mathew Black in his lifetime to James Peddicord.   (139)

4-21-1838 - James R. STANBERRY vs. Persons unknown. Petition for Partition.
Filed 1-2-1837. Land: 500 acres 3rd quarter, Township 3, Range 12 U.S.M., lines--
NE corner of section 3, west line of section, land of heirs of Benj. Elliott,
dec'd, lands belonging to children of John Keim, ·division line of Sections 3 & 4,
being same land conveyed by Benjamin Elliott, dec'd, to James Hamilton by deed
dated 2-9-1821. Partition: 1/2 part, James R. Stanbery; 1/2 part, owned by Heirs
of one Van Brant McGaw (names unknown) who reside in state of New York.   (148)

4-23-1838 - Thomas PRICE vs. John PRICE etal. Petition for Partition. Filed
7-11-1837. Land, 59 acres lot 6, Section 2, Township 1, Range 12, lines--Wm.
Young's lot, south fork of Licking. Joseph Price, dec'd. Widow, Mary now the
wife of John Price, entitled to dower (note: in one place widow is called Nancy,
but called Mary in all others). Partition: 1/3rd part, Thomas Price; 1/3rd part,
John Price; 1/3rd part, Samuel Price; all of Licking Co., the last two named being
minors.   (150)

4-20-1838 - Peter HIVELY vs. Mary HIVELY, widow, etal. Petition for Partition.
Filed 3-26-1837. Land, W½ NW¼ Section 9, Township 17, Range 19 in Refugee tract
sold at Chillicothe. Michael Hively, dec'd. Widow, Mary Hively entitled to dower.
Partition: 1/5th part, Peter Hively; 1/5th part, John Hively; 1/5th part, Catharine
Hively; 1/5th part, Ann Hively; 1/5th part, Michael Hively; all of Licking Co.,
the last four named being minors.   (155)

10-15-1838 - Caleb PUMPHREY vs. Ezra PUMPHREY, etal. In Partition. Filed
5-31-1838. Land, 200 acres part Section 3, Township 1, Range 13 U.S.M., part
of tract lately owned by Joshua Pumphrey late of Licking Co., dec'd, as described
in deed from John Van Buskirk to said Joshua Pumphrey dated 11-18-1817, lines--
John Van Buskirk's land, John Atkinson's land, land sold to Jesse Price, land of
George Calahan, military line. Subject to life estate of Ary Pumphrey ·reference
to previous case wherein John Wagy and wife were petitioners and Ary Pumphry, etal.,
defts. Partition: 4/7th part, Caleb Pumphrey of Licking Co.; 1/7th part, Ezra
Pumphrey; 1/7th part, Nicholas Pumphrey; 1/7th part, Ealeanor Pumphrey; the last
three named being minors.   (161)

5-20-1839 - Abraham WRIGHT vs. Joseph TAGGART, Edward GREY and Robert TAYLOR.
In Partition. Filed 2-4-1839. Land, NW corner Section 4, Township 2, Range 10,
U.S.M., 1300 acres same land conveyed by Jonathan Dayton and wife to Joseph Taggart,
Alexander McLaughlan, E. Gray and Robert Taylor by deed dated 2-13-1809. Partition:.
1/3rd part, Abram Wright; 1/3 part, Joseph Taggert of Pennsylvania; 1/3rd part
jointly, Edward Grey and Robert Taylor of Pennsylvania.   (164)

5-20-1839 - Edwin ADAMS vs. William SMITH, etal. Petition for Partition. Filed
1-10-1838. Land, NE¼ Section 7, Township 17, Range 18. Partition: 1/4th part,
Edwin Adams of Licking Co.; 1/4th part, Nancy wife of Wm. Smith of Fairfield Co.,
Ohio; 1/8th part each, Mary Adams, Emily Adams, Harriet Adams, James Foster Adams
and Caloline Delia Adams all of Licking Co. by Abraham Bruner guardian of James
Foster Adams and Nancy Smith guardian of Harriet and Caroline Delia Adams, minors.
(167)

5-20-1839 - Wm. D. WILSON, etal. vs. Rachel ENGLISH, widow, etal. Petition for
Partition. Filed 4-6-1839. Land, 200 acres part Section 1, Township 2, Range 12,
U.S.M., lines--Aaron Baker. John ENGLISH, dec'd, late of Licking Co. Widow,
Rachel English entitled to dower. Partition: 2/9ths part, William D. Wilson and
Rufus Wing; 3/9ths part, Daniel English and Nathaniel English; 1/9th part, Job
English; 1/9th part, Benjamin English; 1/9th part, Rachel English; 1/9th part,
Mary Jane English. (note; part of shares may be by purchase. although not specif-
ically stated).   (170)

5-14-1839 - William McCLARY and James DUCKWORTH and wire vs. George FRY and Ludwick
FRY. In Partition. Filed 1-24-1839. Land, 90 acres SE corner and 60 acres out
of SE¼ Section 9, Township 1, Range 11. Partition: 1/3rd part, William McClary;
1/3rd part, Rebecca late McClary wife of James Duckworth; 1/3rd part, Mary Fry,
dec'd, late Mary McClary and late wife of Ludwick Fry, her son--George Fry a minor;
all of Licking Co.   (175)

9-7-1839 - Jacob MILLER vs. Ruth EVANS and Rebecca EVANS. In Partition. Filed
9-3-1838. Land, W½ SE¼ Section 16, township 3, Range 15. Partition: 1/2 part,
Jacob Miller of Delaware Co., Ohio; 1/2 part, Ruth Evans and Rebecca Evans, both
minors of Delaware Co., Ohio.   (180)

11-5-1839 - Daniel BLOSSER, etal. vs. Mary BLOSSER. In Partition. Filed 5-20-
1839. Partition: 1/6th part, Daniel Blosser of Fairfield Co., Ohio; 1/6th part,
Anna formerly Blosser wife of Abraham Berry of Hocking Co., Ohio; 1/6th part, John
Blosser of Fairfield Co., Ohio; 1/6th part, Joseph Blosser of Fairfield Co., Ohio;
1/6th part, Abraham Blosser of Fairfield Co., Ohio; 1/6th part, Mary Blosser of
Licking Co., Ohio. Land 79.30 acres W½ NE¼ Section 11, 87.74 acres S½ SE¼ and
78.88 acres E½ NW¼ Section 11. all in Township 16. Range 20 of Refugee tract sold
at Chillicothe.   (184)

11-15-1839 - J.A.W. McCADDEN vs. Margaret McCADDEN, etal. In Partition. Filed
5-24-1839. Land, out-lot 9 in Newark. Partition: 1/5th part, Josiah A.W. McCadden;
1/5th part, Margaret McCadden; 1/5th part, Ellen McCadden; all of Licking Co.;
1/5th part, Amasa wife of Lorenzo Vanhorn of Muskingum Co., Ohio; 1/5th part,
John Moore a minor who resides with his father, John Moore in Jefferson Co.,
Ohio by James Parker his guardian.   (188)

6-6-1840 - Giles HOBERT, etal. vs. Charles H. WARDEN, etal. In Partition. Filed
6-16-1839. Land, Section 2, Township 2, Range 13 U.S.M. being lots 2 & 3 in 6th
Range of lots in Licking Land Company Purchase (so called)being 200 acres also
Section 2, Township 2, Range 13 U.S.M., W½ lot 2 in 5th Range of lots in Licking
Land Co. (so called) being 50 acres. Gabriel WARDEN, dec'd. Widow, Mary Warden
of Licking Co. Partition: 1/13th part, Mary Ann wife of Giles Hobert; 1/13th
part, Mariah Humphrey; 1/13th part, Homer Warden; 4/13th parts, William S. Warden;
1/13th part, Hiram S. Warden; 1/13th part, Lucius M. Warden; 1/13th part, Lewis
Warden; 1/13th part, Horation M. Warden; 1/13th part, Silas W. Warden; all of Licking Co., the last four named being minors by Ziba Woods their guardian; 1/13th part
jointly, Charles H. Warden and Harriet E. Warden, both minors of Licking Co. by
Marrilla C. Warden their guardian.   (196)

11-25-1840 - James STONE and Lucinda P. his wife vs. Huldah R. CHAPMAN, etal.
In Partition. Filed 11-15-1839. Land, 2nd quarter, Township 4, Range 13 U.S.M,
part lot 31 in town of Homer, lines--Methodist Meetinghouse lot, being 126½ rods
of land. Partition: 1/5th part, Lucinda P. wife of James Stone; 1/5th part,
Huldah R. Chapman; 1/5th part, Julia A. Chapman; 1/5th part, Henry C. Chapman;
1/5th part, Fanny L.Chapman; the last three named being minors.   (208)

8-29-1840 - Harriet CARTER, etal, vs. Thomas JONES, etal. In Chancery. Filed
7-1-1839. Land, two tracts--one 150 acres and one 60 acres totaling 150 acres,
part Section 1, Township 2, Range 10 U.S.M. Partition: 1/11th part, Harriet
Carter a minor by Troyless Carter her guardian, both of Licking Co.; 1/11th part,
Thomas Jones of Muskingum Co., Ohio; 1/11th part, Levi Jones of Hancock Co., Ohio;
1/11th part, Samuel Jones; 1/11th part, Stephen Jones; 1/11th part, Phebe wife
of Benson Mitchell; 1/11th part, Ezekiel Jones; 1/11th part, Helly Jones; 1/11th
part, Sally Jones; all of Licking Co., the last three named being minors; 1/11th
part, Mary Ann Jones; 1/11th part, Wesly Jones; the last two named being minors
of Licking Co. by Mason McVey their guardian. Thomas Jones and Levi Jones sold
their shares to Abram Wright.   (212)

11-25-1840 - William C. SMITH vs. Jacob HOLLER. In Partition. Filed 9-23-1839.
Land, 37 acres NW corner Section 1, Township 17, Range 18 in the Refugee tract.
Partition: 5/8ths part, William C.; 1/8th part, Harriet late Rice wife of Jacob Holler of Licking Co.; 1/8th part, Elizabeth Rice; 1/8th
part, Lousena (Louisa) Rice; the last two being minors with their residents
unknown.   (222)

5-29-1841 - John SHIPS vs. Samuel RODGERS, etal. In Partition. Filed 4-5-1841.
Land, 160 acres NW¼ Section 9, Township 1, Range 11 of unappropriated lands in
Military District sold at Zanesville. William Rodgers, dec'd. Widow, Sophia
now wife of Charles Hall of Licking Co. entitled to dower. Partition: 3/5ths
part, John Ships of Licking Co.; 1/5th part, Samuel Rodgers; 1/5th part, Charlotte
Rodgers; the last two named being minors of Licking Co. by Joshua Armstrong their
guardian.   (228)

5-29-1841 - James GAMBLE and Clarrissa GAMBLE vs. Millissa ALLEN, etal. Petition
for Partition. Filed 9-3-1840 with ammended petition filed Nov. 1840. Land,
122 acres Section 3, Township 1, Range 13 U.S.M. Simon ALLEN, dec'd. Widow,
Sophia Allen entitled to dower. Partition: 1/5th part, Clarrissa wife of James
Gamble; 1/5th part, Melissa Allen; 1/5th part, Sophia Allen; 1/5th part, Emily Allen
1/5th part, Franklin Allen; all of Licking Co.   (231)

5-29-1841 - Andrew J. McMULLIN, etal. vs. Alexander McMULLIN, etal. Partition.
Filed 3-14-1840. Land, 78 acres N½ NW¼ Section 8, Township 4 Range 1 of unappropriated lands in Military district sold at Zanesville. Andrew McMullin, dec'd.
Widow, Mary McMullin entitled to dower. Partition: 1/7th part, Andrew J. McMullin;
1/7th part, Alexander McMullin; 1/7th part, Francis Calvin McMullin; 1/7th part,
Alender McMullin; 1/7th part, Burr Newton McMullin; 1/7th part, Margaret McMullin;
1/7th part, Mary Jane McMullin; all of Licking Co., Ohio, several of the last
named being minors by Peter S. Mills their guardian.   (235)

9-3-1841 - Franklin FULLERTON vs. Phebe MAGAW, etal. In Partition. Filed
2-19-1841. Land, part of Section 3, Township 3, Range 12 U.S.M. with reference to
suit at August Term 1840 of Lawrence V. Magaw vs. Benjamin Elliott, etal. (Book O,
page 480) part of 500 acres belonging to James R. Stanberry as a remote (cont'd)

741

(cont'd) assignee of Elizabeth Magaw who was seized of inheritance of undivided one
half of said 500 acres as tenant in common with Van Brunt Magaw, who were heirs of
Robert Magaw, dec'd, said tract of 500 acres in same conveyed by Benjamin Elliott
who held same in trust for use of Robert Magaw and his heirs to James Hamilton
in trust for use of the heirs and devisees of said Robert Magaw by deed recorded
Licking Co. in Book K, page 232, this portion being 244 acres and 125 perches.
4/7ths part, Franklin Fullerton of Licking Co.; 3/7ths part jointly, Phebe Magaw,
Catharine Magaw and Abraham L. Magaw, minors and heirs of Van Brunt Magaw, dec'd,
of Kings in state of New York.   (242)

8-9-1841 - William PARR vs. Silas CONKLIN, etal. In Partition. Filed 5-19-1841.
Land, lots 5 & 6 in 1st quarter, Township 4, Range 14 U.S.M. being 228.75 acres
being same land deeded from W. Stanberry and A. Holmes to Silas WINCHEL as recorded
in Book C, pages 327,328,329. Partition: 1/4th part, William Parr of Licking Co.;
1/4th part, Sabra late Parr, wife of Silas Conklin; 1/4th part, Alvira Parr; 1/4th
part, Leonard Parr; the last two named being minors by John C. Conklin their
guardian.   (246)

11-8-1841 - William W. LOGAN vs. Samuel DEWEES, Petition for Partition. Filed
1-24-1838. Land part of lots 2,3,6,&7 NE corner Section 4, Township 2, Range 11
U.S.M. which lies on north bank of Main Licking Creek and south of the Bowling-
green subdivision. Partition: William W. Logan of Licking County entitled to
one undivided moiety. Samuel Deweese tenent in common.   (252)

11-8-1841 - William DODD vs. David HALL guardian of Hannah HALL. In Partition.
Filed 8-14-1841. Land, SW¼ Section 9 containing 140 acres and SE¼ Section 8
containing 77 acres, both in Township 1, Range 11 the first in unappropriated
lands in the Military district and the second (77 acres) in the appropriated lands
sold at Zanesville. Partition: 9/10ths part, William Dodd of Licking Co., Ohio;
1/10th part, Hannah Hall a minor by David Hall her guardian.   (256)

5-16-1842 - Alva SWITZER, etal. vs. John EMERY, etal. In Partition. Filed
6-25-1841. Land, 2nd quarter, Township 1, Range 11, U.S.M. being lot 13, lines--
land of Geo. Armstrong, John Wilkins and land formerly of Jacob Hockman, being
66 acres. Partition: 1/3rd of 8/9ths jointly, Alva Switzer a minor by Simon(?)
Switzer his guardian and David Switzer and Mary Ann Switzer, minors by Jacob
Swisher their guardian, all of Licking Co., Ohio; 1/9th part, Hannah wife of John
Emery, said Hannah as widow of_____(left blank) Switzer, dec'd, late of Licking
Co.   (260)

5-16-1842 - Mary Ann PRESLY vs. Martha Elizabeth PRESLY. Partition. Filed
9-10-1841. Land, 24 acres part lot 20 Section 3, Township 1, Range 15, U.S.M.
Partition: 1/2 part, Mary Ann Presly of Licking Co. 1/2 part, Martha Elizabeth
Presly of Licking Co., Ohio, a minor.   (264)

8-15-1842 - Francis H. NASH vs. Polly NASH, etal. In Partition. Filed 10-23-1841.
Land, 50 acres east end lot 36, of 4th quarter, Township 3, Range 10, U.S.M. being
land conveyed by Robert Parker and Hannah his wife to John Marvin NASH, dec'd,
(orators father) by deed dated 8-5-1817 as recorded in Book F, page 515; also part
lot 36 in same being 50 acres conveyed from Thomas Nash and wife to John Marvin
NASH, dec'd (orators father) by deed dated 8-4-1837 and recorded in Book F, page
493. Polly Nash holds dower in said land. Partition: 2/3rds part, Francis H. Nash
of Licking Co., Ohio; 1/3rd part, Rodney S. Nash and Susan M. Nash, minors, children
of John Marvin Nash, dec'd, of Licking Co.   (268)

8-15-1842 - William KANE vs. Melissa ALLEN, etal. In Partition. Filed 6-14-1842.
Land, one tract of tract of 20 acres and one tract of 102 acres both in Section 3,
Township 1, Range 13, U.S.M, lines--Jesse Haynes. Partition: 1/5th part, William
Kane; 1/5th part, Melissa Allyn; 1/5th part, Clarissa wife of James Gamble; 1/5th
part, Sophia wife of John Allen; 1/5th part, Emily Allyn; 1/5th part, Franklin Allyn;
all of Licking Co., Ohio.   (273)

11-14-1842 - William BROOKOVER vs. Simon THOMAS, etal. In Partition. Filed
9-21-1842. Land, S½ SE¼ Section 20, Township 1, Range 10, of unappropriated
lands sold at Zanesville, Edward HURSEY, dec'd. Widow, Elizabeth Hursey of
Licking Co. Partition: 1/2 part, William Brookover of Licking Co. 1/2 part
jointly, Simon Thomas, Abraham Hursey, Sarah Ann Hursey, Eve Hursey and Nancy
Hursey all of Licking Co., Ohio, the last four names being minors.   (284)

(note: no records are recorded for the year 1843, the jump from the above Nov.
Court 1842 to the Court of May 1844 mentioned below.)

5-27-1844 - Farling B. PARKER vs. John DORMAN, etal. In Partition. Filed 4-16-1844.
Land, NW¼ Section 14, Township 3, Range 11, 60 acres south side being premises
devised by Hugh DORMAN to Elizabeth and John DORMAN. Partition: undivided 1/2
part, Farling B. Parker, Licking Co. 1/2 part, John Dorman of Licking Co. and
insane person by John Evans his guardian.   (290)

5-27-1844 - David E. THOMAS and wife vs. Barbara REES and others. In Partition.
Filed 4-16-1844. John Rees, dec'd. Widow, Barbara Rees of Licking Co. entitled
to dower. Children entitled to 1/7th part each: Catharine wife of David E. Thomas
of Knox Co., Ohio; Theophilus Rees; Elizabeth Rees; John Rees; Mary Rees; Israel
Rees; and Jane Rees; all of Licking Co. That John Rees, dec'd, died seized of all
tracts of land described hereafter: 314 acres part Section 4, Township 1, Range 13,
U.S.ML., lines--John Myers, land formerly owned by Jacob Trigg and conveyed to John
Rees by deed dated 8-20-1834; 50 acres part S4 T1 R13, USM, lines--Philip Smith,
John K. Myers, Samuel Hand, Jr., as surveyed by James Holmes; 73.20 acres pt NW¼ S4
T1 R13, U.S.M., lines--land conveyed by Thomas and Mariah Ewing to Preston Coulter,
land conveyed by Ewings to John Rees; 65 acres pat NW¼ S4 T1 R13, U.S.M., lines--
Alexander Holmes; 218 3/4 acres pt S4 T1 R13, U.S.M., lines--John Ruffner; 9 acres
and 16 perches pt S4 T1 R13, U.S.M., lines--John Ruffner; 252.22 acres W½ NW¼ S14
and NE¼ S15, T17 R18 in Refugee Tract sold at Chillicothe; 66 2/3 acres pt. NE
corner of half section 20, T17, Refugee tract, lines--Amos Wilson, land formerly
owned by Aquilla Davis, conveyed by Gabriel Critten to John Thompson 8-31-1818 and
by Thompson to Jacob Claypool 8-3-1819; 11 3/4 acres part of lots 13,4, & 15, T17 R18,
Refugee tract sold at Chillicothe, lines--Joseph Carper's 200 acre tract bought from
heirs of Henry Wells, dec'd, Ohio Canal; 220 acres S1 T2 R13, U.S.M., lines--road
from Granville to McKean twp., south line of section, road from Granville to Utica,
Mc Kean road.   (291)

5-27-1844.- Joseph W. HOUGHTON vs. Rosetta M. HOUGHTON, etal. In Partition.
Filed 4-12-1844.. Land, lots 7 & 8 Section 4, Township 2, Range 13, U.S.M.(Licking
Land Company Purchase, so-called) except 11 acres off lot 7 sold to Elias Passett
& Co.; also 17 acres of north end lot 8 conveyed to P. W. Taylor, Knowles Linnel,
Justin Hillyer, Jr. and Joseph W. Houghton and except 30 acres set off to Mahal
Thrall in lot 8 as dower estate. Partition: 3/5ths part, Joseph W. Houghton of
Licking Co.;1/5th part, Mary Jane Paige; 1/5th part, Homer C. Paige; both of Licking
Co. Mary Jane and Homer C. Paige being minors heirs of William PAIGE, dec'ed.
Rosetta M. Houghton formerly Rosetta W. Paige of Licking Co., Ohio widow of William
Paige, dec'd entitled to dower.   (305)

743

5-16-1842 - George CHARLES vs. Presley CHARLES, etal. Petition for Partition.
Filed 3-14-1840. James CHARLES, dec'd. Widow, Elizabeth Charles of Licking Co.
entitled to dower. Partition: 7/9ths part, George Charles of Licking Co.; 1/9th
part, Presly Charles a minor by James M. Dorsey his guardian; 1/9th part, Polly
wife of Charles Evans. Land, Section 4, Township 1, Range 14, U.S.M. being land
conveyed to James Charles by Henry D. Ward; lines--Refugee line, land formerly
owned by Heirs of Nathan Farv and Henry D. Ward.   (316)

In using the following records it should be remembered that date of index indicates date land grant was recorded and that many grants were not recorded until quite a number of years after they were originally granted and received. Abbreviations used: R=Range; T=Township; Q-S=Quarter or Section; A=Acres; Bk=Book; Pg=Page

INDEX 1808-1836

Name	R	T	Q-S	A	Bk.	Pg.
WATSON, John	11	2	1	3614	ABC	29
BALDWIN, Abraham	13	4	3	4000	ABC	120
MOYER, Elizabeth	10	3	4	100	ABC	155
DANKS, Isaac	19	17	5	370	D	58
DANKS, Isaac	19	17	6	352	D	59
GARDNER, Ebenezer	17	19	12	321	D	70
ROGERS, Samuel	17	19	3	338	D	94
HARDING, Seth	17	19	6	345	D	122
DELESDERMIER, Lewis F.	17	19	4	355	D	197
BOGART, Martha	14	1	1	4000	D	307
PASKELL, John	16	18	1	366	E	47
SYMMONS, Van Jr.	13	4	2	70	E	107
SYMMONS, Tehnan	13	4	-	75	E	107
HOIT, Joseph	15	2	2	100	E	123
STEELE, Wm.	13	4	4	3882	E	194
STEELE, Wm.	-	-	-	4000	E	195
STEELE, Wm.	-	-	-	400	E	195
ROGERS, Samuel	16	18	19	326	E	306
ROGERS, Samuel	16	18	20	323	E	307
CUMMINGS, Jno. N.etal	12	2	4	4220	F	1
BARRACK, Philip	10	3	25	—	F	33
SIGLAR, John	11	1	8	—	F	186
GREEN, George	15	3	7	—	F	280
GREEN, George	15	3	8	—	F	283
WILKIN, Henry	11	3	17	—	F	360
DILLON, Jno. assn. of						
J. FROST	10	3	12	—	F	472
COOPER, Stephen Sr.	10	3	11	—	F	472
COOMES, John	10	1	1	—	F	515
SIGLER, John	11	1	12	—	F	611
MARIOTT, Homewood	11	4	2	—	F	636
MARIOTT, Homewood	11	4	9	—	F	636
MARIOTT, Homewood	11	4	2	—	F	637
TARCY, Basil	11	1	12	—	F	644
HILLS, Caleb	15	3	4	—	G	63
TRACY, Basil	11	1	18	—	G	183
CRAWFORD, P.L. assn.						
of Wm. SAIN	11	1	2	156	H	125
DAVIS, Sanford	10	2	1	3196	H	169
BOWMAN, D. & J. BASIL	10	1	23	—	H	208
IRWIN, Sam'l	11	1	3	—	H	216
IRWIN, Jas.	11	1	3	—	H	229
TAYLOR, John assn.						
of E. WESTOVER	10	4	11	160	H	229
ERWIN, Wm. assn. of						
John HULL	11	1	2	—	H	262
WHITEHEAD, Abner	15	2	19	—	H	391
WHITEHEAD, Abner	15	2	24	—	H	391
EDGERLY, Amos M.	15	2	23	—	H	498
SKEEL, Truman	10	1	2	—	H	550
WOLF, George	11	1	1	—	H	575
CARVER, Seth	11	3	15	—	I	37
STATELER, Michael	10	2	23	160	I	72
DRAKE, Thomas	10	4	20	160	I	90
REED, Hugh	18	17	13	—	I	215
OTMIN, John	10	2	17	160	I	267
NICHOLSON, Andrew	10	2	17	—	I	308
CRAWFORD, James	13	3	3	—	I	311
HAUGHEY, Jacob	—	—	—	—	I	322
TROUT, Henry	17	19	2	173	I	356
VARNER, Jno. assn.						
of J. LEVINGSTON	10	3	24	—	I	411
SCOTT, William	10	4	7	—	I	419
YOUNG, Charles	15	3	24	80	I	471
CLARK, George	11	1	22	—	I	481
CALHOON, John	10	1	20	—	I	513
BROWN, Simeon	11	4	4	106	I	536
JACKSON, Isaac	10	1	2	100	I	21
WAGER, James	18	17	18	164	J	130
STONER, Samuel	19	17	17	80	J	396
ENGLISH, Job	19	17	13	80	J	396
STOVER, Samuel	18	17	2	169	J	397
WATSON, Isaac	11	3	4	139	J	480
CALLAHAN, G. & J.						
ROADS	15	2	1	160	J	500
TRUMBO, Jacob	17	19	16	163	J	521
BRICE, John J.	15	3	25	160	J	604
BARRECK, Philip	10	3	17	160	J	666
SOTHARD, Francis	10	3	17	80	K	78
CRUM, Thos.	15	3	24	80	K	326
MORTON, Levi	14	4	3	50	K	486
COOPER, Geo.	11	4	5	—	L	6

Name	R	T	Q-S	A	Bk.Pg.
EVANS, Joseph	11	4	3	108	L 66
HULL, James	20	16	15	159	L 95
COOPER, George	11	4	5	—	L 183
LEE, John	14	3	14	80	L 188
ROWLEY, Tilman	10	3	2	78	L 230
MOATS, Jacob	11	4	15	160	L 361
HARDING, Abraham	10	3	18	—	L 375
ORR, James	16	18	—	105	M 44
POWELL, Thomas	17	19	11	159	M 103
HAZELTON, Joseph	14	3	8	80	M 104
RHODES, John	15	2	14	178	M 105
HARRINGTON, Hezekiah	10	2	25	151	M 105
JOHNSTON, Edward	10	2	16	—	M 281
STORER, Ebenezer	10	3	4	200	M 344
BROWN, James	11	1	20	—	M 388
McMULLEN, Joseph	16	18	9	160	M 434
STUMP, Joseph	10	1	1	—	M 535
STUMP, Joseph	—	1	1	—	M 536
COFFEY, Harmon	17	19	17	159	M 599
ARNOLD, Frederick	17	19	10	—	M 632
ARNOLD, Frederick	17	19	10	—	M 632
PITZER, Wm.	15	1	7	80	M 661
NOE, Aaron	15	2	22	160	M 669
MORRIS, Chas.	17	19	7	78	N 141
MENTZER, Jepheth	17	19	16	80	N 154
MENTZER, Japhet	17	19	16	161	N 193
RANKIN, L. D.	10	3	15	80	N 247
SHAW, W. & J. ARMSTRONG	20	16	11	157	N 257
LANGFORD, Chas.	—	—	—	—	N 302
MOORE, David	10	3	15	149	N 442
MOORE, David	10	3	16	150	N 443
MOORE, David	10	3	6	148	N 443
STEWART, Robert	11	3	24	80	N 444
MOORE, David	10	3	15	150	N 445
MOORE, David	10	3	16	151	N 446
MOORE, David	10	3	6	126	N 446
MOORE, David	10	3	16	160	N 447
BARRACK, Philip	10	3	17	80	0 38
PINCKNEY, Chas. C.	14	4	2	4000	0 86
FARMER, Isaac	10	1	2	—	0 114
LONG, R.&Wm. BURGE	10	1	2	—	0 115
MOWER, L. D. & E. FASSETT	11	3	18	80	0 165
HARRIS, Edward	11	1	23	—	0 260
HULL, Wm.	11	1	10	80	0 397

Name	R	T	Q-S	A	Bk.Pg.
TWIGG, Charles	15	3	14	81	P 3
SOUTHARD, Isaiah	10	3	18	80	P 109
SYMMES, John C.	13	1	4	2000	P 284
SMITH, Jacob	11	1	22	—	P 319
HOSKINSON, Jas.	11	1	22	—	P 320
HOSKINSON, Jas.	11	1	22	—	P 321
STANBERRY, Jonas	10	1	2	100	P 321
CHAMBERS, David	10	1	2	100	P 322
BODLE, Michael	11	4	14	160	P 340
CUSICK, Nicholas	15	2	2	200	P 588
DAY, John	11	4	20	80	Q 63
McMULLEN, Silas	11	1	19	80	Q 180
BROWN, Ephraim	11	1	1	158	Q 212
STEWART, Jno.	11	3	16	152	Q 229
LEE, Wm.	14	4	11	—	Q 224
WHITTEMORE, Nathan M.	10	4	2	100	Q 410
STEWART, Geo.	11	3	15	80	Q 510
HOLMES, Alex	10	1	2	—	R 1
DRUMM, Wm.	10	2	24	80	R 5
MORGAN, Dan'l Heirs	11	1	20	80	R 311
LATTA, John	20	16	9	155	R 415
LATTA, John	20	16	2	87	R 416
LATTA, John	20	16	10	157	R 416
ARMSTRONG, Jeremiah	18	17	17	80	R 444
ELLIOTT, John	11	4	3	112	R 496
O'BRIEN, Patrick	20	16	12	77	R 519
DAYMADE, Daniel	10	3	25	—	S 153
FLAGG, David	—	—	—	—	S 207
FALIER, Henry	17	19	11	—	S 384
MILLER, Abraham F.	19	17	17	80	T 44
MIERS, Andrew	10	1	—	50	T 116
MIERS, Andrew Jr.	11	1	10	80	T 184
BAKER, Jacob	11	4	11	80	T 245
MITCHELL, Wm.	11	4	8	80	T 265
JOHN, John	10	3	8	80	T 293
DAVIS, James	17	19	9	161	T 459
PATTERSON, Jas. R.	10	4	6	157	T 470
DAY, A. & R. CURTIS	10	1	2	200	T 473
WILKIN, Daniel	11	3	16	—	T 641
PLUMMER, John	10	2	25	80	T 649
NICHOLS, Elijah	11	1	18	156	T 652
ERWIN, James	11	4	16	—	T 679
STEWART, Robert	11	3	7	80	T 693
BONHAM, Samuel	20	16	15	40	U 269
ROBINSON, Wm.	10	1	2	200	U 49
SCOTT, James	14	3	6	80	U 387

Name	R	T	Q-S	A	Bk.Pg.
GUTRIDGE, Peter	11	1	21	160	U 514
FREY, Jesse	10	4	5	65	U 633
CAREY, Wm.	19	17	13	80	V 61
DEWEESE, Wm.	18	17	17	80	V 101
FIDLER, John	17	19	10	159	V 435
BARKLEY, George	15	2	22	160	V 561
LOCKARD, Robert	20	16	1	88	W 420
GLANCY, David M	11	3	3	69	W 537
SMITH, John	11	3	3	34	W 538
BUCKINGHAM, Alva	10	3	6	40	W 420
GIFFIN, John	11	3	14	160	X 110
CHAPMAN, Nathaniel	10	1	2	100	X 129
SMITH, John W. assn. of J. EDWARDS	18	17	2	169	X 130
CHANCELOR, Jas.	11	4	17	160	X 131
DAVIDSON, Richard	10	2	16	80	X 156
GROUT, Enos	15	2	—	160	X 168
PAYNE, Wm.	14	3	6	76	X 188
PAYNE, Wm.	14	3	6	—	X 188
OARD, Peter	11	1	13	75	X 189
OARD, Peter	11	1	13	—	X 189
PLUMMER, John	10	2	16	40	X 641
MEEKER, E. & D. PEFFERS	15	2	23	—	X 670
WOOD, Richard	10	3	13	90	Y 147
PRIEST, Wm.	10	3	8	80	Y 194
PRIEST, Wm.	10	3	8	80	Y 196
BRUSH, Daniel	10	3	3	39	Y 208

Name	R	T	Q-S	A	Bks.Pg.
HUSTON, Thomas	11	4	3	108	Y 279
GARVER, Seth	11	3	6	40	Y 360
BLANSER, Mary	20	16	11	79	V 457
STANBERY, Jonas	10	3	8	80	Z 11
BLANSER, Mary	15	1	6	89	Z 23
BROWN, Aaron	11	1	10	80	Z 184
EDGAR, John	17	19	9	313	U 616
TRIPPER, John	11	3	15	80	Z 236
GEIGER, Andrew	17	19	—	80	Z 421
GANDY, Isaiah	10	2	18	80	Z 426
McQUEEN, Minor	10	4	14	80	Z 463
BODLE, Michael	11	4	18	40	Z 508
PALMER, John	11	3	23	40	Z 669
CHINN, Edward	16	18	—	300	AA 28
ROMAINE, Minor	10	3	15	80	AA 295
ANDERSON, Wm.	10	3	7	80	AA 296
ROBINSON, Benj.	11	1	10	80	AA 325
PALMER, John	11	3	23	40	AA 328
DUNLAP, Robert	10	3	15	40	AA 328
BAKER, Aaron	11	4	11	160	AA 329
CALDWELL, John	18	17	8	41	AA 468
DEWEESE, Wm.	18	17	17	161	AA 476
PARKER, Farling B.	11	3	14	40	AA 584
PARKER, Farling B.	11	3	14	80	AA 585
WALKER, Cornelius	15	3	6	84	AA 734
BRHSH, Daniel	10	3	8	40	AA 816
ELLIOTT, Benj.	12	3	3	4000	BB 78
STANBERRY, Jonas	10	4	24	40	BB 100

INDEX 1836-1848

Name	R	T	Q-S	A	Bk.Pg.
STURGES, Solomon	10	2	17	80	BB 101
MATHENEY, John	11	4	25	80	BB 427
CALDWELL, Eleanor	18	17	15	163	CC 419
STURGES, Solomon	10	3	8	—	CC 420
McCARTER, Nathan	10	4	24	80	CC 483
TAGGART, Arthur	11	1	19	80	CC 493
LEVINGSTON, Jacob	10	3	15	40	DD 90
STANBERY, Jonas	10	3	6	37	DD 137
GLANCY, David M.	11	3	8	40	DD 229
CALDWELL, James D.	18	17	7	40	DD 282
LATTA, James	10	3	13	90	DD 415
HULL, Uriah	11	1	10	80	DD 416
HART, Joseph	15	2	2	—	DD 463
HART, Joseph	15	2	2	—	DD 464
HAINES, John	11	4	23	80	EE 65
UMBENHOWER, Abraham	10	3	3	39	EE 123

Name	R	T	Q-S	A	Bks.Pg.
HULL, Wm.	10	3	3	79	EE 290
GARDNER, Ebenezer	17	19	19	322	EE 360
ARNOLD, John	10	4	13	80	EE 366
BEBOUT, Ebenezer	10	4	13	40	EE 367
BUCKINGHAM, Alvah	11	3	24	40	EE 367
COOPER, Presley	10	3	4	300	EE 469
GEARHART, Mary	10	4	21	40	EE 540
McCARTY, Wm.	11	4	9	80	EE 557
HUGHES, Abraham	10	3	2	39	EE 565
HUGHES, Marshall	10	3	2	39	EE 567
CONNARD, Nathan	14	3	7	160	EE 632
McCARTY, Wm.	11	4	9	40	EE 208
CLOUD, Daniel	10	2	16	—	FF 217
BEARDSLEY, Charles	15	2	25	97	FF 284
BOYD, James's Heirs	18	17	16	—	FF 390
FOWLER, John	10	4	18	40	GG 30

Name	R	T	Q-S	A	Bk.	Pg.	Name	R	T	Q-S	A	Bk.	Pg.
OATMAN, John	10	2	17	80	56	154	HINTZE, Frederick	15	2	2	100	63	568
CONARD, Nathan	14	3	8	80	57	90	HOLMES, Alexander	10	1	2	100	63	599
McQUEEN, Minor	10	4	18	80	57	531	WHITE, John Jr.	15	1	3	153	64	125
LEACH, Thos. for							EDWARDS, Capt.						
Jas. NEIGHBARGER	10	3	8	—	58	477	THOMAS' Heirs	10	3	—	300	64	512
MOORE, John	10	3	7	80	58	478	PEFFERS, Jacob	15	2	19	80	64	561
DILLON, John	10	3	9	80	59	212	TALBOTT, Wm. W.	17	19	16	40	64	565
PRIEST & NORMAN	10	4	16	150	59	274	HULL, Samuel	11	1	8	—	65	295
FRY, Thomas	11	3	6	38	59	296	BARTHOLONEW, John	10	1	21	160	65	348
HOLTSBERRY, James	18	17	13	43	59	329	WILLS, Robert	10	2	23	160	65	363
RAMBO, Wm.	11	3	7	80	59	513	HULL, Samuel	11	1	2	156	66	182
RAMBO, Wm.	11	3	7	80	59	514	MARTIN, Lewis	15	2	24	—	66	229
McCLELLAND, Cary	15	3	4	152	59	515	MARTIN, Lewis	15	2	24	160	66	182
LIVINGSTON, Geo.	11	1	1	160	59	533	BALL, Sam'l D.	15	1	5	87	66	490
PARSONS & SMITH	18	17	11	178	61	164	IRWIN, Elijah	11	1	2	125	67	95
MERCER, John	10	3	4	—	61	465	RUBY, Arthur	15	3	6	80	67	176
EVANS, Wm.	10	3	24	160	62	148	STUMP, Daniel	10	1	—	160	67	248
EVANS, Wm.	10	3	24	80	62	149	WALMSLEY, Wm.	15	2	2	100	67	475
JOHNSON, James	10	4	25	80	62	207	STANBERY, Jonas	10	4	19	80	68	28
EDMUNDS, Thos. Heirs	10	3	4	—	62	260	CARPENTER, James	15	1	3	100	68	51
HILL, Tilbon	15	3	7	160	62	306	McALLISTER, John	15	1	3	100	68	129
HARRIS, John	11	3	4	69	62	353	PAINTER, Jesse	10	4	15	40	68	235
WEEKLY, Elias	10	4	16	40	62	355	CLABAUGH, Thos.	10	4	17	40	69	59
HOPPER, Baptist	11	4	18	160	62	422	CLABAUGH, N.	10	4	17	40	69	59
PADGETT, Elias	17	19	17	40	63	475							

INDEX 1855-1864

Name	R	T	Q-S	A	Bk.	Pg.	Name	R	T	Q-S	A	Bk.	Pg.
POGUE, Samuel	10	1	20	—	69	249	MARTIN, John	10	4	19	40	74	396
GEIGER, Jacob	15	2	15	108	69	375	MARTIN, John	10	4	19	40	74	397
FICKLE, Alfred	17	19	15	40	70	485	MYERS, John	15	2	15	40	75	259
BUCK, William	10	4	22	160	70	565	TAYLOR, James	15	1	3	200	78	596
DEWEES, Wm.	18	17	7	40	71	52	HAZEN, Charlotte	16	18	6	350	79	457
FERVER, Henry	15	2	2	100	72	366	POTTS, George	10	1	2	300	79	506
PRIEST, Moses	10	4	13	80	72	390	DEAMUDE, Sam'l	10	3	16	40	80	159
TAYLOR, James	15	1	3	100	73	370	BUCHANAN, Thos.	17	19	11	149	81	603
STEWART, Joseph	20	16	14	157	74	274	PRIEST, Moses	10	4	15	40	82	92
STEWART, Joseph	10	16	14	157	74	275	SMITH, James	10	2	16	40	83	189
STANBERRY, Jonas	10	1	2	100	74	282	SMITH, James	10	2	16	80	83	190
COULTER, J. &							GLOVER, Minor	11	3	13	40	84	615
Jas. HULL	11	1	11	80	74	297							

Name	R	T	Q-S	A	Bk.	Pg.	Name	R	T	Q-S	A	Bk.	Pg.
PRIEST, Mansfield	10	3	3	38	86	290	WARD, Josaiah L.	15	2	18	—	101	213
PRIEST, Mansfield	10	3	3	38	86	291	ARNOLD, John F.	10	3	9	—	101	598
BEEM, Daniel	15	2	25	160	87	617	HICKERSON, Sam'l	19	3	9	—	101	599
HUMMELL, Thos.	10	1	22	—	88	494	BROWN, Wm.	10	1	18	—	106	185
HILLERY, Benjamin	11	4	21	160	96	339	MOORE, Daniel	11	3	6	160	106	504
HALL, Allen	11	4	20	80	96	623	PARKHURST, Benj.	15	2	22	—	108	219
HALL, Jordan	10	4	16	78	96	623	THOMAS, Robinson	12	3	2	—	108	426
HALL, Jordan	11	4	20	80	96	624	DEMAN, Mathias	13	3	2	4000	108	534
HALL, Jordan	11	4	20	40	96	624	THOMPSON, Thos. M.	13	3	3	5040	108	534
LEWIS, Jones	10	4	16	40	100	196	DENMAN, Mathias	11	2	3	4000	108	561

750

LICKING COUNTY, OHIO- COMMON PLEAS COURT RECORDS 1819-1822 (JOURNAL)

The following records are taken from "Journal 1819-1823" found in the Common Pleas Court (Clerk of Court's Office) at the court house in Newark. Page on which record may be found is given in parenthesis.

8-23--1819 - Samuel WRIGHT granted license to vend merchandise in town of Granville. (1)

8-23-1819 - Will of Samuel OLIVER proved on oath of Charles Marstella and Jonathan Daniels, witnesses. Executrix, Lydia Oliver. (1)

8-23-1819 - John V. DOUSTON granted license to keep tavern in Newark. (2)

8-23--1819 - Chrisly VANCE granted license to keep tavern on road to Mt. Vernon. (2)

8-24--1819 - Frederick BLOOD granted license to keep tavern on road to Delaware in Saint Alban twp. (4)

8-24-1819 - Ralph GRANGER license to keep tavern in Granville. (4)

8-24-1819 - John HOGG an alien subject of Great Britain now residing in Licking Co. Naturalization. (6)

8-27-1819 - Adam CONNELL and Martha CONNEL minors over 14 years, heirs of John Connell, dec'd chose Daniel Forey as their guardian. (18)

8-27-1819 - Martha CONNEL a minor over 12 years, chose John Connell as her guardian and John Connel appointed to also serve as guardian for Peggy Connel under 12 years of age. (18)

8-28-1819 - Margaret BEARD's Petition. Court fully satisfied of the truth of facts set forth in petition of said Margaret BEARD and being fully satisfied that the said John Huffner in the petition mentioned is entitled to a deed for the land in the petition mentioned as aforesaid so here by appoint and authorize the said Margaret Beard executrix of John Beard, dec'd to convey to the said John Ruffner by deed on behalf of said heirs of John Beard, dec'd, land in petition mentioned as the said John Beard in his lifetime might have conveyed same. (2)

8-28-1819 - Will of Naomi CARPENTER, dec'd proved by Daniel Baker and Jerusha Baker, witnesses. Alexander Holmes, executor. (22)

8-28-1819 - Charlotte CONNELL and Ruth CONNELL, minor daughters and heirs of Naomi CARPENTER chose Alexander Homes as their guardian. (22)

8-28-1819 - Sarah PRICE and James PRICE appointed adms. of estate of John PRICE, dec'd. (22)

11-23-1819 - Mary JACKSON and Samuel HAND appointed adms. of estate of Joseph JACKSON, dec'd. (23)

12-27-1819 - Will of Richard PITZER proven by Alexander Holden and Wilson Holden, witnesses. Jacob Swisher and Anna Pitzer, executors. (24)

12-27-1819 - John CULLY granted license to keep tavern in Newark. (24)

12-27-1819 - John J. CRAWFORD granted license to keep tavern in Johnstown. (25)

12-28-1819 - Emanuel HOOVER appointed guardian of Reason VIOLET and Justin VIOLET minors under 14 yrs. (26)

12-28-1819 - Rev. Linion AVERY granted license to solemnize marriages. (34)

12-29-1819 - William TRINDLE granted license to keep tavern in Newark. (36)

12-29-1819 - William SCARDOROUGH born in Great Brittain in County of Yorkshirve in month of November 1799, migrated from same in month of June 1818 and landed United States August of same year at Baltimore, thence came to Ohio where he intends to become a resident and citizen filed declaration of intention to become citizen. (37)

751

12-29-1819 - Henry Strong of Norwich, Connecticut, adms of estate of James BACKUS late of Norwich, dec'd, petitions to sell lands in Licking Co. being 180 acres belonging to Backus at time of his death and set off to James Backus in a division of the estate of Mathew Backus, dec'd late of Marietta, (Ohio), being 102 acres Section 4, Township 1, Range 14 of United States Military lands and also 78 acres at east end of said tract, owned by Heirs of Mathew Backus, dec'd. (37)

12-30-1819 - Executor of Estate of Nathaniel CUNNINGHAM, dec'd allowed further time to file account. (40)

12-31-1819 - P. M. WEDDELL license to vend merchandize in Newark. (42)

12-31-1819 - Daniel JESTUS (no age given) chose John Cunningham as his guardian.(43)

12-31-1819 - On petition of William TRINDLE son of dec'd ordered that Alexander Holmes and Noah Harris appointed adms. of estate of William TRINDLE, dec'd. (43)

12-31-1810 - Settlement filed in estate of Jacob OILS. (43)

12-31-1819 - Settlement filed in estate of Jacob WILKINS. (44)

1-1-1820 - Ruth TRIMBLE and Anna TRINDLE minors over 12 yrs., children of William TRINDLE, dec'd chose David Moore as their guardian. Alexander Holmes appointed guardian of Eliza, Matilda and Rebecca TRINDLE, children of W. TRINDLE, dec'd, under age of 12 yrs. (45)

5-8-1820 - Will of Adam DUSH proved by Samuel Davidson and Stephen Mills, witnesses. John Dush and Susannah Dush, executors. (48)

5-8-1820 - Will of William DEBOLT proved by Alexander Holden and Jacob White, witnesses. Rhoda Debolt, executrix. (48)

5-8-1820 - Phillip DARRACK granted license to keep tavern on road leading to Zanesville. (50)

5-8-1820 - Will of Simon OVERTURF proved by William Carpenter and Samuel Carpenter, witnesses. John Waggoner and Mary Overturf, executors. (51)

5-8-1820 - John WAGGONER granted license to keep tavern on road to Mt. Vernon. (51)

5-9-1820 - Alpheus CHAPMAN granted license to keep tavern in town of Darlington. (52)

5-9-1820 - Samuel BOARDMAN and Lucus BOARDMAN, minors over 14 yrs. chose Samuel Bankroft as their guardian. (52)

5-9-1820 - Joseph Fassett and Hiram Boardman adms. of estate of Moses BOARDMAN late of Licking County who died leaving children, several who are minors, set forth that said Moses in his lifetime on 9-22-1815 gave bond to Heral Williams on warantte deed to lot 16 and 100 acres in 4th quarter, Township 2, Range 14 of U.S.M. (52)

5-9-1820 - Petition of Eliha BIGELOW adms. of estate of Oliver BIGELOW, dec'd saith that on 3-27-1815 said Oliver contracted to sell Bartholomew Anderson lot 2 in 1st Range and fractional part lot 4 in 4th Quarter, Township 3, Range 15 of U.S.M., also lot 3 of 1st range of out lots in town of Johnstown all Licking County. That Oliver Bigelow died leaving heirs under 21 years of age. (53)

5-10-1820 - James Dunlap adms. of estate of Samuel DUNLAP filed final settlement. (54)

5-10-1820 - John Day appointed adms. of estate of James SPENNY (orSPERRY?), Lydia SPENNY, dec'd. (note; does not say "and" but seems to infer that there are two dec'd persons--James and Lydia). (55)

752

5-10-1820 - Jane Maria BOARDMAN (no age given) chose Joseph Tassett as her guardian. (55)

5-10-1820 - Application of Trefosa THRALL widow of Samuel THRALL, dec'd, to set off her one third part to her as mentioned in the will of the deceased. (57)

5-11-1820 - Doctor AGARD license to vend merchandise in Granville. (63)

5-11-1820 - Leonard HUMPHREY and Lewis HUMPHREY minors over 14 yrs. chose Timothy Spellman as their guardian. (63)

5-11-1820 - Wm SCOTT and other heirs at law of Matthew Scott vs Samuel W. LEEPER and others, heirs of Wm LEEPER, dec'd. Matthew Scott in his lifetime possessed and owned in his own right a war office certificate issued under the United States entitling him to 300 acres land in U. S. Military land. That said warrant was placed by Elizabeth Scott, executrix by hands of Samuel Kirk to be located, that Kirk placed warrant in hands of William Leeper who agreed to locate land in Section 3, Township 2, Range 12 in Licking Co, Leeper entering total of 915 acres including warrants aforesaid. That William Leaper died sometime since leaving the following heirs: Mary wife of Joseph Arthur, Samuel W. Leaper, William Leaper, Elizabeth Leaper and Jane Leaper, who have legal title to 300 acres. Samuel KIRK is dead leaving heirs: Joseph Kirk, Jane wife of Samuel Dunlap, Mary wife of James Pollock and Martha wife of Enoch Rush. (66)

8-29-1820 - Elizabeth CHEDWICK and Ebenezer CHEDWICK appointed adms. of estate of Samuel CHECWICK, late of Licking Co., dec'd. (75)

10-16-1820 - Hugh Allison appointed adms. of estate of John McKIBBEN, late of Licking Co., dec'd. (75)

10-23-1820 - James KING appointed adms. of estate of William KING, dec'd. (76)

10-23-1820 - Will of William WILLS proven by Samuel Tarmer and Robert Wills. William Wills, executor. (76)

10-23-1820 - This day Samuel BALL appeared in Court, exhibited a declaration and schedule of his property, in order to procure a renewal of his pension conformable to the laws of Congress on that subject whereupon the Court estimated the property of said Samuel Ball to be one dollar and thereupon it is ordered by the Court that the said declaration be filed and remain of record in this Court and that a copy thereof be certified and sent to the Secretart if War aggreably to the aforesaid Act of Congress. (79)

10-24-1820 - Phineas PRATT a Soldier of the revolution appeared in open Court produced a declaration and exhibited a schedule of his property in order to obtain a renewal of his pension, and being sworn, and having subscribed the same are ordered to be filed and to remain of record in this Court and that a certified copy of said declaration and schedule be sent to the Secretary of War agreably to the said Act of Congress, The property of said Pratt being estimated to be worth the sum of $18.96. (80)

10-24-1820 - Also Squire BURNET, same as above, property estimated to be worth ninety one dollars and forty three cents. Same order as above. (80) (note: this is how the record appears in the original.)

10-24-1820 - Christopher Niberger appointed adms. of estate of Benjamin WILLIAMS, late of Licking Co., dec'd. (82)

10-24-1820 - This day Zerah CURTIS a revolutionary soldier personally appeared in open Court and produced a schedule of his property which the Court estimates to be worth the sum of $____ (note: left blank) And also produced a declaration

753

(Zerah Curtis, cont.) in order to obtain the provisions made by the Acts of Congress of 18th March 1818 and 1st of May 1820 to which he was duly sworn and the same ordered to be filed and remain of record in this court. (84)

10-24-1820 - Also Jacob HUMPHREY, as above, same order as above. $16.00. (84)

10-24-1820 - Also John McQUOWEN, same as above, property $92.64. (84)

10-24-1820 - Also Maxmiltian ROBESON, same as above, $147.50. (84)

10-24-1820 - Also George HILL, same as above, property valued at____(left blank). (84)

(note: above four records are given as found in original. They are not written out in complete form.)

10-25-1820 - David Thomas appointed guardian of Thomas EDWARDS and Nancy EDWARDS who are idiots. (92)

10-26-1820 - James JOHNSTON Jr. appointed adms. of the estate of James JOHNSTON late of Licking Co., dec'd. (94)

10-26-1820 - Saloma SQUIRES appointed guardian of Zeri SQUIRES under age of 14 yrs. and also Niron SQUIRES under aae of 14 yrs. and also Clarissa SQUIRES under age of 12 yrs., children of ____(note: left blank) SQUIRES, dec'd.(94)

10-26-1820 - Lucy Hopkins and Calvin Pratt appointed adms. of estate of Mathew HOPKINS, dec'd. (95)

10-28-1820 - James BELL granted license (note: type of license not stated).(102)

10-28-1820 - WARNER and TASSETT granted license to keep tavern in Granville. (102)

10-28-1820 - Henry MONTGOMERY granted license to keep tavern on road leading to Coshocton. (102)

10-28-1820 - GRANGER and PRITCHERD granted license to keep store in Granville.(102)

2-6-1821 - Ruth STEPHENSON granted license to keep tavern in Newark. (105

2-6-1821 - Isaac STADDEN granted license to keep tavern on the Zanesville road.(105)

2-6-1821 - GRANGER and VICTOR granted license to keep tavern in Granville. (105

2-6-1821 - John CULLY granted license to keep tavern in Newark. (105)

2-7-1821 - John HOUSTON granted license to keep tavern in Newark. (115)

2-7-1821 - Petition of Lucy HOPKINS widow of Mathew HOPKINS, dec'd to set off dower. (116)

2-8-1821 - Will of John KEAR (KEAN) proved by George Butler and Henry Beckell, witnesses. (119)

2-9-1821 - WOODS and GILLMORE granted license to ven merchandize in Newark. (122)

2-9-1821 - Will of Daniel THOMPSON proven by Wm Stanbery and Jonas Stanber, witnesses. (123)

3-13-1821 - Alexander Holmes and Henry Shurtz appointed adms. of estate of Andrew SHURTZ, late of Newark twp., dec'd, widow (not named) relinquishes her right to adms. estate. (127)

5-28-1821 - William TOWER a minor over 14 yrs. chose Benjamin Pratt as his guardian. (130)

5-28-1821 - Will of David LEWIS proven by David Thomas and Theophelus R. Thomas, witnesses. Martha Lewis, executrix. (130)

5-28-1821 - Samuel Bancroft appointed guarian of David LEWIS, Morgan LEWIS and William LEWIS, minors under 14 yrs. and Sally LEWIS and Lucretia LEWIS, minors under 12 yrs., children and heirs of David LEWIS, late of Licking Co., dec'd. (131)

5-28-1821 - Christian ROKHOL granted license to vend merchandize as a traveling merchang. (132)

5-28-1821 - Christian BURGE having credentials of the Christian Church grated
license to solemnize marriages. (132)

5-29-1821 - Petition of Sarah ANDERSON, late sarah GLAZE, widow of Henry GLAZE,
late of Licking Co., dec'd, to have dower in lands set off as agreable
to will of dec'd. (133)

5-29-1821 - William FORSYTHE granted license to keep tavern in town of Wilmington.
(134)

5-29-1821 - Alpneus CHAPMAN granted license to keep tavern in town of Burlington.
(124)

5-29-1821 - Rebecca BILLINGSLY a minor over 12 yrs. chose Josiah Ewing asher
guardian. (134)

5-29-1821 - Hannah BILLINGSLY a minor over 12 yrs. chose John Johnston as her
guardian. (134)

5-29-1821 - John Jonston appointed guardian of Sarah and Elizabeth BILLINGSLY
minors under 12 yrs. and Josias Ewing appointed guardian of Lach BILLINGSLY
a minor under 14 yrs. (135)

5-30-1821 - Almena ROSE a minor over 12 yrs. chose Samuel Bancroft as his guardian.
Samuel W. ROSE a minor over 14 yrs. chose Samuel Bancroft as his guardian.(142)

5-31-1821 - Cyrus BILLINGSLY a minor over 14 yrs. chose Josias Ewing as his
guardian. (151)

6-1-1821 - Solomon TYHURST a subject of Great Britain exhibited proof of his
having resided in United States for term of 5 yrs. and in Ohio for one
year. Naturalization. (154)

6-1-1821 - On motion of Jacob Swisher security of Sarah ANDERSON late Sarah GLAZE
a citation issued for Ephrain ANDERSON and his wife Sarah Anderson late
Sarah Glaze who is guardian of Benjamin and John GLAZE to give account of
property of said minors. (155)

7-27-1821 - Samuel Bancroft and Alexander Holmes appointed adms. of estate of Lewis
TWINING late of Licking Co., dec'd. Widow (not named) relinquishes right to
adms. estate. (156)

8-13-1821 - Abel Perrin appointed adms. of estate of Ezra PERRIN, dec'd. Widow
(not named) relinquishes right to adms. estate. (157)

8-13-1821 - Samuel Parr and Elizabeth Parr appointed adms. of estate of Richard
PARR, dec'd. (157)

8-13-1821 - Thomas S. Purdy a minor over 14 yrs. chose Anthony Pitzer as his
guardian. (158)

8-14-1821 - Judith HOLDEN widow of dec'd appointed adms. of estate of Lewis HOLDEN
late of Licing Co., dec'd. (167)

8-14-1821 - Albert Jewit Jr. appointed adms. of estate of Nathan JEWIT, dec'd/
(170)

8-14-1821 - Abel Jewett appointed adms. of estate of Nathan JEWET late of Licking
Co., dec'd. (170)
(note: records are found as above, with it being indicated that there are
two deceased persons by the name of Nathan Jewet or Jewit.)

8-15-1821 - Elizabeth OWENS, widow of dec'd and Pamach (or Parnach) Owens appointed
adms. of estate of Noah OWEN late of Licking Co., dec'd. (171)

8-15-1821 - Petition of James Holmes surviving adms of estate of John CONNELL,
dec'd to sell real estate. (172)

8-16-1821 - William Frost appointed adms. of estate of John FROST, dec'd. (175)

9-29-1821 - Mary Shanklin and Charles Marsteller appointed adms. of estate of Robert S. SHANKLIN, dec'd. (176)

9-29-1821 - Abel JEWET appointed adms. of estate of Nathan JEWET Jr late of Licking Co., dec'd, in the room of Abel Jewet Jr. who was appointed and qualified as adms. of said estate at the august term last and who has since deceased. (176)

9-29-1821 - Abel Jewett and Susannah Jewit, widow, appointed adms. of estate of Abel Jewet Jr., late of Licking Co., dec'd. (176)

11-14-1821 - Rev. Solomon S. MILES a minister of the Presbyterian church granted license to solemnize marriages. (177)

2-2-1822 - Will of Mary SHURTZ, dec'd proven by Hugh Scott and Rufus Blackmore, witnesses. (177)

2-14-1822 - Mathena CRAWFORD, widow and Noble Landon appointed adms. of estate of James T. CRAWFORD, late of Licking Co., dec'd. (178)

2-14-1822 - Hannah Bigelow and Clement D. Wolf appointed adms. of estate of Eliha BIGELOW, dec'd. (178)

2-14-1822 - Althea GRANGER, widow and Samuel Bankroft, Esq. appointed adms. of estate of Oun GRANGER, late of Licking Co., dec'd. (178)

2-14-1822 - Nesbet and John Alden appointed adms. of estate of Ambrose ALDEN, dec'd. Widow (not named) relinquishes right to adms. estate. (178)

2-14-1822 - Moses Critchel appointed adms. of estate of Benjamin CRITCHARD, dec'd. (178)

2-14-1822 - John Hill and James H. Hall appointed adms. de bonis non of estate of Nathan JEWETT, dec'd. (179)

2-14-1822 - Will of Doct: Oliver BIGELOW proven in Thompkins Co. New York and produced in this court and admitted to record on motion of Elisha Harding an executor of said will. (179)

5-6-1822 - Adms of estate of James CARPENTER granted further time to file account. (181)

5-6-1822 - William McLARY a minor over 14 yrs. and Rebecca McLARY a minor over 12 yrs. chose Deliliah McLarey as their guardian. (182)

5-6-1822 - Lucius MOORE granted license to vend merchandise in Granville. (182

5-6-1822 - Will of Samuel EVERETT, dec'd proven on oath of Clarissa Bancroft, continued for further proof. (182)!

5-6-1822 - John Hill appointed adms. of estate of Abel Jewet, dec'd. (183)

5-6-1822 - Robert John adms. of W. C. DREW, dec'd petitions to sell land. It appearing to court by a certificate authenticated that Robert Johns has been appointed adms. in Franklin County, Indiana of estate of William C. DREW, dec'd who died seized of undivided one half of south end lot 5, Section 4, Township 3, Range 13 in Licking Co., Ohio. (183 & 189)

5-6-1822 - William W. GAULT granted license to keep tavern in Newark. (184)

5-6-1822 - John CULLY granted license to keep tavern in Newark. (184).

5-6-1822 - Willard WARNER granted license to keep tavern in Granville. (184)

5-6-1822 - Messers WING and TASSETT license to keep tavern in Granville. (184)

5-6-1822 - Philip BARACK granted license to keep tavern on road to Zanesville.(184)

5-6-1822 - Robert John appointed executor of will of Mary G. DREW in Franklin County, Indiana petitions to sell land being south end of lot 5, Section 4, Township 3, Range 13 U.S.M. in Licking Co., Ohio, petitions to sell undivided one half interest in said tract. (188 & 189)

5-7-1822 - Vincent BOYD a minor over 14 yrs. chose John Evans as his guardian.(190)
5-7-1822 - This day John LARABER a revolutionary soldier personally appeared in
open Court and produced a schedule of his property which the Court esteemed to
be worth the sum of $110.37 and also produced a declaration in order to obtain
the provisions made by the Act of Congress of the 18 of March 1818 and 1st
of May 1820 to which he was duly sworn, and the same is ordered to be filed
and remain of Record in this Court. (190)
5-8-1822 - Elmira TWINING a minor over 12 years and Merrick S. TWINING and
Lavingston TWINING minors over 14 yrs. chose Jennet Twining as their guardian
with Jenet TWINING also appointed to serve as guardian of Edward W. TWINING
under 14 yrs. of age. (195)
5-8-1822 - Petition of John Dush executor and John SHANNON and Susanna his wife
executrix of will of Adam DUSH, dec'd set forth that Adam Dush Junr. in his
lifetime on 12-24-1818 contracted to sell Stephen Miles as soon as he received
patent 30 acres north and SW¼ Section 21, Township 4, Range 1 in unappropriated lands in Military District sold at Zanesville and that Adam Dush died
without making deed leaving minor children and heirs Eliza aged about 6 yrs.
and Rachel aged about 4 yrs. and that court now authorizes that deed be made
to said Miles. (195)
5-9-1822 - Estate of Abraham RUBLE, dec'd appraisal includes 100 acres of land.(202)
5-9-1822 - Samuel Elliott and Hugh Scott appointed adms. of estate of Mary SHURTZ,
1   dec'd, late of Licking Co. (202)
5-10-1822 - Joseph THARP a minister of the Methodist Episcopal Church presented
license grated in Muskingum Co., Ohio 3-21-1812 to the Licking County court
and it ordered received so he can solemnize marriages in said county. (208
5-10-1822 - Sill of Thomas BOUNDS Sr., dec'd proven by James S. Taylor Sr. and
Henry Clemon, witnesses. William Bounds, executor. (208)
8-10-1822 - Rev. Ahab JENKS residing in Granville produced a license issued
in Montgomery County, Ohio authorizing him to solemnize marriages and
said license is recorded this county. (209)
8-21-1822 - Shadrack RUARK produced a license to Licking County court issued
in Knox Co., Ohio authorizing him to solemnize marriages, dated 12-20-1816.
as minister of Methodist Episcopal Church, license recorded this county. (209)
9-2-18 22 - Grove Ore and Hiram Case appointed adms. of estate of John CASE, dec'd
(210)
9-2-1822 - Will of Timothy HARRIS proved by Abiathar Jenks and Samuel Bancroft,
witnesses. Bethia Harris and Joseph Lennel Jr., executors. (210)
9-2-1822 - Nicholas Brown and John Hook appointed adms. of estate of Isaac SMITH,
dec'd late of Licking Co., widow (not named) relinquishes right to adms.
estate. (210)
9-2-1822 - Will of Elisha S. GILLMAN proven by R. Grovenor and Ralph Granger,
witnesses. A. P. Prichard, executor. (210)
9-2-1822 - Will of William REED proven by Hugh Scott and John sain(?), witnesses.
Executor, James Winters. (217)
9-2-1822 - Rev. Samuel MONTGOMERY, minister of the Methodist Episcopal Church
granted license to solemnize marriages. (217)
9-2-1822 - G. A. and G. W. DARLINGTON granted license to vend merchandize in
Newark. (217)
9-3-1822 - Will of John FRY proven by Isaiah Hoskinson and Alexander McLelland,
witnesses. Jacob Fry, executor. (218)

757

9-3-1822 - Mary Winn and Lewis Myers appointed adms. of estate of William WINN, dec'd. (218)

9-3-1822 - Wm FORSYTHE granted license to keep tavern in Utica. (218)

9-3-1822 - Will of James LEE proven by James Smith and Joseph Connard, witnesses. John Lee and Adam Patterson, executors. (218)

9-3-1822 - Coroner made return this day on an inquest held on body of Jeremiah R. MUNSON, dec'd. (223)

9-3-1822 - Mrs. Mary Ann Nelson, widow appointed admsrx. of estate of Annanias NELSON, dec'd. (223)

9-3-1822 - Jesse Thompson appointed adms. of estate of John THOMPSON, dec'd, late of Licking Co. (224)

9-4-1822 - Albert GIER a minor over 14 yrs. chose John Phelps his guardian. (227) (Editor's Note: A fire in April of 1874 complete destroyed the Probate Court records--exception being the adms.-exec. docket for the early years which may have been kept in the Common Pleas. Thus, for the early period the records found in the Common Pleas Court (Clerk of Court's office) are all that are available to the researcher. They consist of Journals and Partition records. Partition Records for ther period of 1816 through 1836 have been previously published in Oct. 1972 and Jan. 1974 issues of GATEWAY TO THE WEST.)

Adby, Hannah 520
Adcox, Richard 644
Addison, William 452
Ades, Lenna 308
Ades, Luisa 311
Adgate, James 50
Adison, William 452
Adkins, Delfy 703
Adkins, Littlebay 703
Adkins, Martha 589
Adkinson, Frances 478
Adney, Sarah M. 100
Adset, Palmer 274
Adsit, Palmer 259
Aerl, Isaac 1, 200
Aery, John 269
Agan, James 358
Agard, --- (Dr.) 753
Agin, William 518
Agleshire, Esther B. 416
Agne, Elizabeth 351
Agne, Gertrude 351
Agne, Jacob 351
Ahles, Henry 356
Aikins, Almira 644
Aikins, Charles 644
Aikins, Daniel 644
Aikins, Eli 644
Aikins, George W. 644
Aikins, Israel 198
Aikins, Jane Lydia 644
Aikins, John 644
Aikins, Nancy 644
Aikins, Samuel 644
Aikins, Sarah Jane 644
Aikins, William 644
Aikins, William H. 644
Aimesworth, John 517
Airhart, Catharine 292
Airhart, Margaret 298
Airy, John 269
Airy, Mary 533
Aker, Catharine 419
Akert, Abraham 404
Akin, Anna 216
Akin, Betsy 216
Akin, David 269
Akin, Emaline 279
Akin, Harman L. 269
Akin, Harmon L. 279
Akin, Herman L. 454
Akin, James 216
Akin, John 216
Akin, Martha 216
Akin, Polly 216
Akins, Gabriel 234
Akins, James 523
Akins, Sarah 222
Alaways, Alexander 668
Alaways, Ann Florence 668
Albans, Alban 666
Albaugh, Alice 529
Albaugh, John 523
Albers, Wm. (Dr.) 638
Albert, Elias D. 323
Albert, Frederick
    William 370
Albert, William 678
Albertson, Mary 334

Albertson, Mary Ann 579
Albertson, William 168
Albin, Ann 214
Albin, Gabriel 214
Albin, John 214
Albin, Joseph 214
Albin, Mary 214
Albin, Samuel 214
Albin, William 214
Albrand, Mina 53
Albright, Daniel 333,
    335
Albright, E. 335
Albright, John 611
Albright, John H. 335
Albright, Sarah 611
Albright, T. 335
Alden, Ambrose 756
Alden, John 756
Alden, Nesbet 756
Alden, R. 23
Alderman, Jane 82
Alderman, Lucy 80
Aldoffer, Elizabeth 303
Aldoffer, George 288
Aldric, Henry 40
Aldrich, J. K. 398
Aldrich, John 398
Aldrich, Martin 549
Aldrich, P. 398
Aldrich, Thomas 471
Aldridge, Alfred 42
Aldridge, Anna 657
Aldridge, Azel 460
Aldridge, Edward 132,
    168
Aldridge, Littlebury 529
Aldrige, Ezekiel 708
Aleshire, David 474
Aleshire, Elizabeth 476
Aleshire, Ephrain 478
Aleshire, John 478
Aleshire, Peter 666
Alexander, A. J. 668
Alexander, Agnes 514
Alexander, Alonza Jane
    668
Alexander, Alphenon
    Americas 668
Alexander, Amelia 290
Alexander, An Jane 723
Alexander, Andrew 6, 625
Alexander, Arba 62, 63
Alexander, Athelbert 668
Alexander, Augustine M.
    721
Alexander, Eliza 58
Alexander, Eliza Matilda
    58
Alexander, Elizabeth
    145, 484
Alexander, Elvira
    Isabella 668
Alexander, Elvy May 668
Alexander, Ethelbert
    Janus 668
Alexander, Fanny 678
Alexander, George 501
Alexander, Hamilton 6

Alexander, James 734
Alexander, James Nichols
    514
Alexander, James Wilson
    668
Alexander, Jeremiah 678
Alexander, John 50,
    267, 274, 288, 313,
    331, 668, 734
Alexander, John (Jr.)
    49, 57
Alexander, John A. 535
Alexander, John Nicholas
    355
Alexander, Joseph 356
Alexander, Josephine
    Catherine 668
Alexander, Lerard 445
Alexander, Lucinda
    Adalade 668
Alexander, Martha
    Melissa 668
Alexander, Mary 734
Alexander, Mary Margaret
    514
Alexander, Matilda 587
Alexander, Matthew 515
Alexander, Nancy 295,
    668
Alexander, Nathaniel 512
Alexander, Peter 668
Alexander, Priscilla 501
Alexander, Rachel 63,
    668
Alexander, Rachel Ann
    668
Alexander, Revanda
    Austin 668
Alexander, Richard 222
Alexander, Robert 267,
    482, 487
Alexander, Ruehema 514
Alexander, Samuel 145,
    168, 625
Alexander, Smiley Ross
    668
Alexander, Thomas 482,
    484, 668
Alexander, William 145,
    163, 331, 514, 638
Alexander, William
    Humphrey 668
Alexander, William R.
    734
Aley, Abraham 508
Aley, Catharina 507
Aley, Elizabeth 507
Aley, Fanney 535
Aley, Fanny 75
Aley, Isaac 507, 508
Aley, Jacob 507, 508
Aley, John 507
Aley, Mary 507
Aley, Susannah 507
Alferd, Roy 478
Alford, James 703
Alford, Margret 482
Alfred, Ames 50
Alfred, George 246

Amentz, Phillip 95
Ames, Ambrose 654
Ames, C. 398
Ames, William 518, 724
Amiden, Abel 569
Amiden, Abner 569
Amiden, Aseal 569
Amiden, Caleb 569
Amiden, Cheney 569
Amidon, Abner 570
Amidon, Caleb 570
Amon, James 288
Amons, Elizabeth 299
Amons, Mary 299
Amory, George 317
Amos, Margaret 723
Amrine, Esther Maria 668
Amrine, Henry 668
Amrine, Henry Hosak 668
Amrine, Mary Angeline 668
Amrine, Nancy Isobel 668
Amrine, Nannee Loretta 668
Amrine, Robert 668
Amrine, Robert Frederic 668
Amrine, Robits 668
Amy, Charles 587
Andereck, Mary 418
Anders, Adam 249
Anders, Elizabeth 249
Anders, Ellen 251
Anders, G. W. 251
Anders, George W. 251
Anders, Jacob 249
Anders, Mar . . . iet J. 249
Anders, Ollie 251
Anders, Rebecca 251
Anders, Sarah 249
Anderson, --- (Capt.) 364
Anderson, Abigail 365
Anderson, Abigel 293
Anderson, Ache 12
Anderson, Agnes 230
Anderson, Alexander 88
Anderson, Archibald P. 230
Anderson, Bartholomew 752
Anderson, Bartolomew 198
Anderson, Benjamin 365, 573, 574
Anderson, Betsey 462
Anderson, Catharine 583
Anderson, Daniel 265, 529, 678
Anderson, David 518, 655
Anderson, Elias 198
Anderson, Elijah 214, 218
Anderson, Elijah R. 579
Anderson, Elizabeth 480, 589
Anderson, Ephrain 755
Anderson, Esamiah 230
Anderson, Franky 632

Anderson, George 662
Anderson, Harriet 172
Anderson, Isaac 553
Anderson, James 43, 48, 70, 168, 198, 365, 400, 507, 514, 518
Anderson, James A. 61, 65
Anderson, Jane 265
Anderson, John 2, 4, 50, 154, 234, 288, 507, 514, 587, 620, 625, 638
Anderson, John H. 507
Anderson, John Horney 518
Anderson, Joseph 625
Anderson, Lucinda 626
Anderson, Lucinthia 127
Anderson, Margaret 629, 678
Anderson, Margery 169
Anderson, Martha 678
Anderson, Mary 223, 678
Anderson, Mary C. 202
Anderson, Mathew 573, 574
Anderson, Matthew 219
Anderson, Miriam 198
Anderson, Molly 438
Anderson, Nancy 198
Anderson, Philip 108
Anderson, Polly 520
Anderson, Rhody 519
Anderson, Richard C. 573, 574
Anderson, Richard H. 1
Anderson, Robert 43, 158, 202, 230, 464, 686
Anderson, Sally 76
Anderson, Samuel 154
Anderson, Sarah 526, 755
Anderson, Sarah Ann 88, 365
Anderson, Seth 518
Anderson, Thomas 132, 263
Anderson, Thomas R. 198
Anderson, Verner 382
Anderson, W. 45
Anderson, William 1, 502, 597
Anderson, Wm. 502, 747
Andlemir, Mary Ann 603
Andrake, Frederic 441
Andrew, Aman B. 601
Andrew, Elizabeth 150, 525, 530
Andrew, Hannah 169
Andrew, Hugh 516
Andrew, James (Sr.) 510
Andrew, John (Dr.) 150
Andrew, Margaret 161
Andrew, Mary 170
Andrew, Polly 164
Andrews, A. V. 402
Andrews, Amos 195
Andrews, David 210, 313

Andrews, Dorcas 172
Andrews, Elis 579
Andrews, Elizabeth 511
Andrews, Felty 559
Andrews, Henry 148, 575
Andrews, Horace 402
Andrews, Hugh 511
Andrews, Jacques 355
Andrews, James 288, 576, 662, 666
Andrews, Jane 288, 464
Andrews, John 148, 509
Andrews, John (Dr.) 375
Andrews, Margaret 362
Andrews, Mary 333, 604
Andrews, Mary E. 127
Andrews, Samuel 286
Andrews, Sarah A. 472
Andrews, Thomas S. 333
Andrews, William 288
Andrews, Wm. E. 402
Androm, Aaron 631
Aneshensel, Aaron 427
Aneshensel, Phebe Ann 427
Angel, David 365
Angle, Catherine 441
Angle, Joseph 422
Anguish, David 684
Anguish, James 684
Anguish, Margaret 684
Ankeny, Henry 529, 536
Ankrane, John 702
Ankrim, Nancy 705
Annet, Archd. 546
Annis, David 362
Anshutze, Elizabeth 242
Anspaugh, Andrew 407
Anthony, C. 228
Anthony, Charles 228
Anthony, Charles McDonald 228
Anthony, Elizabeth 666
Anthony, Elizabeth E. 228
Anthony, George 666
Anthony, Jacob 666
Anthony, Joseph 228, 264
Anthony, Mary 658
Anthony, Oliver Benton 228
Anthony, Phillip 655
Anthony, Rebecca Sarah 228
Antisdale, Martin 579
Antran, Aden 263
Antran, John 258
Antran, Mary 263
Antrim, Adan 269
Antrim, Adin 251
Antrim, Alonza 251
Antrim, H. 251
Antrim, Justena 265
Antrim, Mary 251
Antrim, Robert 265
Antrim, T. 251
Antrim, William 269
Apple, Andrew (Sr.) 239
Apple, Hanery 239

Apple, Mary 305
Applegate, Adams 127
Applegate, Harrison 418
Applegate, John P. 620
Applegate, Vincent 123
Apt, Henry B. 422
Arbacast, Michael 205
Arbagast, Barbary 205
Arbagast, George 205
Arbogart, Enos 222
Arbogart, Otho 222
Arbogast, Priscilla 226
Arbuckel, Polly 476
Arbuckle, Minerva 243
Arbuckle, Ulrana 588
Archer, Aaron 443
Archer, George 4
Archer, Henry 548
Archer, James (Jr.) 542
Archer, John 464
Archer, Joseph 542
Archer, Margaret 582
Archer, Mary 4
Archer, Nancy 580
Archer, Sarah 463
Archer, Simon 168
Archer, William 460
Archibald, David 518
Archibald, James 542
Arentz, Philip K. 95
Arick, John 111
Arlington, Bazzava 81
Arming, Miner 373
Armitage, John 72
Armitage, Nancy 72,76
Armon, Elizabeth 466
Armon, George 460
Armstrong, --- (Col.) 362
Armstrong, Aaron 9
Armstrong, Alexander 513
Armstrong, Amelia 301
Armstrong, Andrew 288
Armstrong, Ann 726
Armstrong, Bennet 288
Armstrong, Catharine 726
Armstrong, Catherine 377
Armstrong, David 389
Armstrong, Edward 207
Armstrong, Eliza 726
Armstrong, Elizabeth 165
Armstrong, Elizabeth C.
  265
Armstrong, Elizabeth
  Jane 603
Armstrong, Geo. 742
Armstrong, George 265
Armstrong, Henry 655
Armstrong, J. 746
Armstrong, James 15,
  20, 140, 163, 288,
  363, 443, 554, 567
Armstrong, Jane 2, 309
Armstrong, Janie 289
Armstrong, Jeremiah 746
Armstrong, John 6, 24,
  41, 192, 288, 362, 364,
  443, 459, 460, 555,
  558, 567, 570, 572,
  573, 576, 689, 726

Armstrong, John H. 726
Armstrong, Jos. 546
Armstrong, Joseph 107
Armstrong, Joshua 741
Armstrong, Maria 107
Armstrong, Mary 6, 170,
  310
Armstrong, Mary G. 726
Armstrong, Moses 148
Armstrong, Nathaniel
  Shepherd 557
Armstrong, Phebe 299
Armstrong, Polly 140
Armstrong, Priscellar
  513
Armstrong, Priscilla 107
Armstrong, Rachel 12,
  363
Armstrong, Samuel 552,
  554, 576
Armstrong, Sarah 172
Armstrong, Silas 333
Armstrong, Tabitha 726
Armstrong, Thomas 222
Armstrong, Thomas Pool
  726
Armstrong, Viola Jane
  726
Armstrong, William G.
  726
Armstrong, Wm. 6, 546
Arnatt, Eve 57
Arnel, Catharine 376
Arnel, Daniel 376
Arnel, Nathaniel 376
Arnel, Susan 376
Arnell, John 543
Arner, Elizabeth 272
Arnest, John 529
Arnet, Jacob 59, 372
Arnett, Jacob 57
Arnett, James 222
Arnett, John 97
Arnett, Mary 617
Arnett, William 222
Arney, Joanna M. 431
Arney, Mary 430
Arnold, Aaron 365
Arnold, Anthony 539
Arnold, Betsy 80
Arnold, Caleb 641
Arnold, Cynthiann 83
Arnold, Daniel 451
Arnold, David 361
Arnold, Edna 365
Arnold, Eleanor 451
Arnold, Eleanor L. 451
Arnold, Elias 689
Arnold, Elijah 464
Arnold, Eliza 417
Arnold, Frederick 746
Arnold, George 365
Arnold, Henry 365, 366,
  368
Arnold, Jacob 407
Arnold, Jesse 259, 280
Arnold, John 259, 322,
  464, 689, 698, 747
Arnold, John Andrew 358

Arnold, John F. 750
Arnold, Kitty 412
Arnold, Luke 274
Arnold, Maria 419
Arnold, Nancy 78
Arnold, Rachel 689
Arnold, Thomas 392
Arnold, Welcome 81
Arnold, William 269,
  362, 364, 365, 369,
  539
Arnold, Wm. (Jr.) 365
Arrowsmith, Westley 199
Art, Nancy 10
Arter, Mary 302
Artes, Nancy 647
Arther, Jechonias 703
Arthur, Amos 655
Arthur, Benjamin 655
Arthur, Chas. R. 23
Arthur, Jennet 227
Arthur, Joseph 725, 753
Arthur, Mary 753
Arthur, Michael 288
Arthur, Pleasant 606,
  607
Ary, John 535
Asbaugh, Patsey 412
Asbel, John 168
Asberry, Lowery 523
Asberry, Rachel 192
Asberry, Thomas 192
Ash, Adam 210, 518
Ash, Ann Elizabeth 680
Ash, David 378
Ash, Eleanor 680
Ash, Harriet 680
Ash, James 680
Ash, Jane 532
Ash, Julia Ann 680
Ash, Louisa Caroline 680
Ash, Martha Eleanor 680
Ash, Phineas 680
Ash, Phinias Washington
  680
Ash, Rachel 680
Ashback, John 471
Ashbaugh, Catharine 404
Ashbaugh, Mary 412
Ashbrook, Adeline 424
Ashbrook, Eli 424
Ashburn, Sarah 99
Ashby, Bladen 139, 147,
  174
Ashby, Bladon 137
Ashby, Elizabeth 161
Ashby, Milton 147
Ashcraft, Jane 169
Ashel, John 168
Asher, Abraham 549
Asher, John 434
Asher, Sarah 434
Ashford, Elizabeth 301
Ashford, George 288
Ashford, Susannah 290
Ashfow, Nancy 299
Ashing, John 190
Ashing, Samuel 56
Ashing, Sarah Jane 53

Baker, Alexander 587
Baker, Alfred 50
Baker, Amos 692
Baker, Andrew 69, 378
Baker, Bazil 332
Baker, Betsey 466
Baker, Cassia 332
Baker, Catharine 301, 705
Baker, Catherine 275, 421
Baker, Charles 65
Baker, Christena 221
Baker, Conrad 358
Baker, Daniel 141, 175, 206, 213, 529, 751
Baker, David 133, 221
Baker, Elisha 579
Baker, Eliza 590
Baker, Elizabeth 54, 77, 133, 221, 222, 412, 579
Baker, Francis 589
Baker, Franeena 417
Baker, George 694
Baker, Henry 54, 186, 215, 221, 407
Baker, Jacob 211, 215, 703, 746
Baker, Jacob (Sr.) 215
Baker, Jacob L. 56
Baker, James 455, 456
Baker, Jemima 102
Baker, Jerusha 751
Baker, Jesse 523, 615
Baker, John 99, 215, 221, 419, 451, 547, 587, 601, 614
Baker, Jos. 460
Baker, Joseph 4, 701
Baker, Lavina 220
Baker, Levi 579, 748
Baker, Louisa 346
Baker, Magdalane 215
Baker, Magdalena 225
Baker, Mahlon 137
Baker, Margaret 12, 579
Baker, Martha 533
Baker, Martin 215
Baker, Mary 221, 332, 652
Baker, Mary Ann 332
Baker, Mary D. 535
Baker, Mary Jane 650
Baker, Melyn 501, 565
Baker, Melyn D. 222
Baker, Miller 220
Baker, Nancy 462, 580, 615
Baker, Nancy Catharine 332
Baker, Nathan 605
Baker, Nicholas (Jr.) 81
Baker, Obigjah 652
Baker, Peggy 412
Baker, Philip 288
Baker, Phoebe 51
Baker, Polly 421
Baker, Samuel 215, 221

Baker, Sarah 533
Baker, Squire 703
Baker, Stephen A. 529
Baker, Thomas 509
Baker, Varonica 221
Baker, William 449, 579
Baker, Williams 652
Baker, Zechariah 332
Balch, Israel 587
Balden, John 46
Balding, John 557
Baldridge, A. P. 229, 230
Baldridge, Adeline 230
Baldridge, Alleniah 44
Baldridge, Flora D. 229
Baldridge, James S. 229
Baldridge, John (Jr.) 44
Baldridge, Mary J. 229
Baldridge, Sam A. 229
Baldridge, Samuel 33
Baldridge, T. W. 47
Balduff, E. B. 346
Baldwen, John 561
Baldwin, . . . A. 382
Baldwin, Abraham 140, 745
Baldwin, Adeline H. 394
Baldwin, Amos P. 364
Baldwin, Ann 172, 692
Baldwin, Benjamin 460
Baldwin, Charles 394
Baldwin, Christena 8
Baldwin, David (Jr.) 523
Baldwin, David P. 506
Baldwin, Eli 120
Baldwin, Elias 140
Baldwin, Elijah 2
Baldwin, Elizabeth 382
Baldwin, Ellis 686
Baldwin, Enoch 222
Baldwin, Esther 382, 394
Baldwin, Floyd 382
Baldwin, James 19
Baldwin, Jeremiah 183, 184
Baldwin, John 31, 562
Baldwin, Jonah 197, 222
Baldwin, Jonathan 264
Baldwin, Joseph 394
Baldwin, Joseph G. 5
Baldwin, Joseph H. 394
Baldwin, Josiah 209
Baldwin, Julia A. 506
Baldwin, Kezua 11
Baldwin, Lucas 382
Baldwin, Margaret 465
Baldwin, Martha 461
Baldwin, Mary 686
Baldwin, Mary A. 120
Baldwin, May E. 394
Baldwin, Poley 12
Baldwin, Rogers S. 692
Baldwin, Sally 636
Baldwin, Saml. 19
Baldwin, Sarah M. 394
Baldwin, Sharp D. 360
Baldwin, Stephen 5, 31
Baldwin, Thomas 168, 175, 394

Baldwin, Thomis 382
Baldwin, Willard K. 8
Baldwin, William 160, 188, 211, 692
Baldwin, William (Jr.) 211
Baldwin, William A. 394
Baldwin, William H. 579
Baldwin, Wm. 186
Bale, Hiram 690
Bale, William 378
Balenger, Mizel 168
Bales, Jacob 529
Bales, Thomas 587
Baley, Jane O. 198
Baley, Stephen 39
Baley, Thomas 198
Balgenort, Wilhelm 99
Balgenort, William 99
Baliff, Joshua 269
Balin, Nancy 295
Balinger, Thomas 205
Balis, Martha 591
Balis, Nathin 288
Ball, --- (Dr.) 168
Ball, Abel 160
Ball, Abigail 166
Ball, Abner 163, 177
Ball, Benjamin J. 206
Ball, Betsey 690
Ball, Cornelius 564
Ball, Cyrus 690
Ball, Daniel 124
Ball, David 690, 717
Ball, Dennis 131, 154, 155, 160
Ball, Eliza J. 393
Ball, Elizabeth 690, 717
Ball, Enoch 688
Ball, Esther 131, 155
Ball, Ezekiel 140, 145, 150, 156, 157, 176
Ball, Hannah 293
Ball, Hiram 690
Ball, Isaac 131
Ball, Isaiah 154, 155, 163
Ball, James 579
Ball, Joanna 688
Ball, John 564, 717
Ball, John (Jr.) 717
Ball, Joshua 160
Ball, Lenas 690
Ball, Margaret 131, 155
Ball, Mary K. 717
Ball, Moses 543
Ball, Nancy 131, 155
Ball, Phebe 154
Ball, Robert 703
Ball, Sally 690
Ball, Saml. D. 749
Ball, Samuel 753
Ball, Sarah 131, 165, 167, 690
Ball, Solomon 131, 155
Ball, Stephen 163
Ball, Timothy 690
Ball, Topher 131
Ball, Zepher 155

Ball, Zopher 160
Ballantine, David 541
Ballard, Ann 272
Ballard, Anna 282
Ballard, Asa 282
Ballard, David 282
Ballard, Dinah 278
Ballard, Edith 282
Ballard, Harris 474
Ballard, Jesse (Jr.) 76
Ballard, John 278, 282
Ballard, Joseph 278, 282
Ballard, Lydia 282
Ballard, Martha 282
Ballard, Mary 282
Ballard, Nathan 282
Ballard, Phebe 77
Ballard, Rhoda 282
Ballard, Roxanna 78
Ballard, William 282
Ballard, Wm. 278
Ballentine, James 579
Ballinger, Ann 187
Ballinger, Caleb 183, 187, 205
Ballinger, Elizabeth 183, 187
Ballinger, Henry 183
Ballinger, Hope 183
Ballinger, Joshua 183, 211
Ballinger, Patience 187
Ballinger, Rachel 183, 187
Ballinger, Samuel 183, 187
Ballinger, Sarah 183, 187, 205
Ballinger, Thomas 183, 187
Balsigner, Elizabeth 51
Balsor, Henry 561
Balsor, Henry (Jr.) 575
Balsor, Margaret 561
Balston, Robert 36
Balsure, David 288
Baltzell, --- 498
Baltzell, John C. 587
Balwick, Peter 649
Balwig, Peter 649
Balyard, Charles Wesly 345
Balyard, Samuel 345
Bamborough, Allen 666
Bamfield, John 365
Bamfield, Martha 365
Bancroft, Clarissa 727, 756
Bancroft, John 229
Bancroft, Richard 222
Bancroft, Samuel 407, 727, 730, 754, 755, 757
Bane, Evan (Dr.) 554, 573
Bane, Mary 597
Banes, Evan 573
Banes, Gabrie 222
Banes, Jane 524

Bankroft, Samuel 752, 756
Banks, Anna 335
Banks, Cuthbert 28
Banks, Henry 378
Banks, Samuel 724
Bannan, William 464
Banning, Rachel 588
Bannon, John O. 28
Bannum, Sarah Jane 101
Banta, Albert 365
Banta, Daniel 365
Banta, Elizabeth 365
Banta, Jacob 365
Banta, Jain 365
Banta, Leah 162
Banta, Mary 365
Banta, Rachel 365
Bara, Vincent 488, 497
Barack, Philip 756
Barahart, Betsy 650
Barahart, Henry 650
Barbage, Wm. 378
Barbar, Weiler 472
Barbee, Benjamin 154
Barbee, Mary 154
Barbee, Thomas 29
Barber, Abraham 288
Barber, Elizabeth 167
Barber, Esquire D. 378
Barber, George W. 398
Barber, Henry 168
Barber, John 529
Barber, Larence 12
Barber, Margaret 533
Barber, Mary 407
Barber, Maryann 306
Barber, Nancy 462
Barber, Rebecca 306
Barber, Robert 288, 309
Barcalow, Deborah 128
Barcalow, Derick 128
Barcalow, Eleanor 128
Barcalow, Elizabeth 128
Barcalow, James 128
Barcalow, John 128
Barcalow, Lydia 128
Barcalow, Rachel 128
Barcalow, Rebecca 128
Barcalow, Tobias 128
Barcalow, William 128
Barclay, Elizabeth 163
Bard, Archibald 232
Bard, Eliza 232
Bard, Richard 236
Bard, Zebulan 205
Bardin, Samuel 585
Bardsley, Bartemus 714, 718, 720
Bardsley, Rebecca 705
Bardwell, Seth 222
Bare, David 125
Bare, John 437, 536
Bare, Mary 648
Bareau, John Peter Romain 483
Bareter, Jane 52
Bareth, John 200
Barfield, Betsy 610

Barfield, Jonathan 610
Bargdoll, Cloe 531
Barger, Anna Maria 99
Barger, Barbara 647
Barger, Christian 446, 455
Barger, John 446, 455
Barger, Lewis 446, 455
Barger, Peter 325
Barger, Philip 446, 455, 464
Barger, Susanna 292
Barger, Valentine 597
Barhelder, Daniel 76
Bark, Jacob 407
Barkalow, Benjamin 140
Barkalow, Derick 140
Barkalow, Eleanor 140, 173
Barkalow, Elizabeth 170
Barkalow, Lydia 135
Barkalow, Thomas 135
Barkalow, William 140
Barkalow, William P. 143
Barkalow, Zebulon 140, 168
Barkdull, John 288
Barkelow, Tobias 128
Barker, Achsah 474
Barker, Amos 478, 485
Barker, Betsy 444
Barker, Charles A. 426
Barker, Daniel 485
Barker, Eleazar 485
Barker, Eleazer 485
Barker, Eleazer (Jr.) 474, 486, 487
Barker, Eleazer Owen 487
Barker, Eli 438
Barker, Elizabeth 77
Barker, Gideon 487
Barker, Hiram 458
Barker, Isabella 462
Barker, James 460, 464
Barker, Jesse 615, 616
Barker, John 445, 464
Barker, Joseph 523
Barker, Mehetable 485
Barker, Michael 85
Barker, Nancy 616
Barker, Permilla 485
Barker, Sally 487
Barker, Sarah 615
Barker, Sarah Elizabeth 426
Barker, Theresa Owen 486, 487
Barker, Thomas 17
Barker, Thos. 462
Barker, Timothy 81
Barkhurst, Lewis 597
Barkless, William 319
Barkley, Elenor 269
Barkley, George 747
Barkley, John 240, 267, 269, 277
Barkley, Margaret 240
Barkley, Moses 267, 274
Barkley, Nathan 561

Barkshire, Susan 410
Barlett, Henry 84
Barlow, Ann 486
Barlow, Anne 481
Barlow, Bradford 601
Barlow, Edward 523
Barlow, Elnathan 486
Barlow, Thompkins 563
Barnard, John 135
Barnard, Mary 286
Barneby, Stephen 390
Barnes, Andrew C. 587
Barnes, Charlton 259
Barnes, Elizabeth 518
Barnes, F. A. 400
Barnes, Ford 542
Barnes, Hannah 545
Barnes, Huldy 224
Barnes, John 501
Barnes, Joseph 587
Barnes, Merandy 274
Barnes, Peter 108, 692
Barnes, Reese W. 606
Barnes, Salome 589
Barnes, Sarah 589
Barnes, Stephen 640
Barnet, Andrew 117
Barnet, David 117
Barnet, Elizabeth 109, 117
Barnet, Hiram 464
Barnet, James 117, 175
Barnet, John 117, 563
Barnet, Margaret 117
Barnet, Martha 109, 117
Barnet, Robert 360
Barnet, Susannah 625
Barnett, Andrew 109
Barnett, David 109
Barnett, Geo. 196
Barnett, James 109
Barnett, John 109
Barnett, Margaret 109
Barnett, Susanna 518
Barney, Benj. 697
Barney, Benjamin 690
Barney, James 523
Barney, John 690
Barney, Laura 334
Barnhart, David 407
Barnhart, George 67
Barnhart, Martha E. 381
Barnhart, Rachel R. 380
Barnhart, Sarah 420
Barnhart, Simon 407
Barnheart, James 373
Barnheart, Lu 373
Barnheart, Luisa 373
Barnhill, Margaret 597
Barnhill, Nancy 631
Barns, Betsy E. 400
Barns, Thomas 366
Barnum, Ebenezer M. 649
Barnum, Harriet M. 380
Barny, Ellen M. 381
Baroel, Cynthia 591
Barr, Andrew 442
Barr, Anna 223
Barr, Elnora 124

Barr, James 442
Barr, John 282, 442
Barr, Joseph D. 700
Barr, Mary 11
Barr, Nancy 438, 442
Barr, Phebe 189
Barr, Rachel 438
Barr, Robert 189
Barr, Robert D. 700
Barr, Thomas 407, 442
Barr, Wilkeson 438
Barr, William 442, 597
Barr, Wm. 509
Barrack, Philip 745, 746
Barrack, Phillip 752
Barrack, William 404
Barreck, Philip 745
Barrere, George W. 614
Barret, George 587
Barret, James 9, 514, 563
Barret, Jno. 26
Barret, John 139
Barret, Permelia 216
Barret, William 267, 269
Barrett, Abner 191
Barrett, David 269
Barrett, Dickison 222
Barrett, Eleanor 520
Barrett, Elizabeth 268, 275, 465
Barrett, Jacob 267, 274
Barrett, James 518
Barrett, Mahala 534
Barrett, Philip 518
Barrett, Polley 655
Barrett, Richard 605, 607
Barrett, Sarah 271
Barrett, William 268
Barrick, William 736
Barrier, George W. 262
Barringer, Jacklen 219
Barrington, John 99
Barrington, Martha 99
Barrington, Mary Agnes 100
Barrington, Mary Ann 102
Barrington, Richard R. 91
Barrington, Richd. R. 55
Barritt, John 18
Barrows, F. A. 401, 402
Barrows, Frank 403
Barrows, George 84
Barrows, Hannah 78
Barrows, Jacob 76
Barrows, Miranda 79
Barrows, Orange 75
Barrows, Parker 81
Barrows, Sally 79
Barrows, Susannah 77
Barrows, Wm. (Jr.) 76
Barry, Benjamin 544
Barsman, William 9
Bartan, Eve 57
Barten, Jesse 457
Barter, Enoch 625
Barters, Alexander 9

Bartholemew, Anthony 20
Bartholonew, A. W. 401
Bartholonew, John 749
Bartier, Stephen 482
Bartleson, Peter 460
Bartless, Perina 445
Bartlett, Anna C. 632
Bartlett, Betsey C. 79
Bartlett, Calvin 471
Bartlett, Catharine 626
Bartlett, Cephas 81
Bartlett, Elizabeth 696
Bartlett, Francis 72
Bartlett, Geo. 400
Bartlett, George H. 401
Bartlett, George W. 401
Bartlett, Henry 84
Bartlett, Hugh 85
Bartlett, Maria 631
Bartlett, Martha 633
Bartlett, Polly M. 78
Bartlett, Rachael 101
Bartlett, Therisa M. 79
Bartlett, W. B. 401
Bartlett, William 696
Bartlett, William H. 401
Bartlett, William N. 400
Bartlett, Wm. 400, 696
Bartley, Alexander 616
Bartlow, Polly 468
Barto, Enos 326
Barton, Anne 522
Barton, David 641
Barton, Eli 28, 29
Barton, George 662
Barton, Hutchins 30
Barton, Jacob 404
Barton, Jno. 30
Barton, John 30, 515, 518
Barton, John B. 641
Barton, K. 12
Barton, Kimber 9, 10, 24, 33
Barton, M. 33
Barton, Martha 139, 460
Barton, Nancy 125
Barton, Polly 480
Barton, Robert 30, 321
Barton, Sarah Jane 472
Barton, Sharp 666
Barton, Thomas 518
Barton, Thos. 655
Barton, William 53, 407
Bartsch, Christoph 337
Bartsch, Magdalena 337
Bartsch, Margaretha Magdalena 337
Bascom, Linus 360, 363, 364, 368
Basehore, Barnet 257
Basehore, John 65, 257
Baser, Elizabeth 270
Bash, Catharine 334
Bashore, Barnet 274
Bashore, David 432
Bashore, Elizabeth 413
Basil, J. 745
Basinger, Peter 222

Belote, Caroline 418
Belt, John S. 543
Belugar, John 594
Bemelton, Richard 655
Bemis, Jonathan 361
Benbower, J. W. 403
Bence, Daniel 625
Bender, Eli 350
Bender, Elizabeth 470
Bender, Jacob 350, 352
Bender, Jno. 470
Bender, Margaret 470
Bender, Nelly 350, 352
Bendure, Elizabeth 214
Bendure, William 214
Benedict, Aaron 384, 386, 389
Benedict, Aaron L. 389
Benedict, Allen 384
Benedict, Amos 384
Benedict, Cyrus 384
Benedict, Daniel 389
Benedict, Elizabeth 389
Benedict, Esther 389
Benedict, Esther L. 389
Benedict, Gidson 384
Benedict, Ira 384
Benedict, Jane 384
Benedict, John Brown 643
Benedict, Martha 384
Benedict, Mary 384
Benedict, Reuben 384
Benedict, Sarah 389
Benedict, Sylvester 384
Benedict, William 384, 386
Benedict, Wm. 384
Benedict, Ziba 691
Benedum, Wm. 418
Benefield, James 514
Benegar, Sarah 463
Benet, Margaret 12
Bengaman, Lydia 526
Benget, Emanuel 163
Benham, Richard 553
Benham, Robert 140, 576
Benit, Macy 307
Benjamin, Betsey 79
Benjamin, Elisha 631
Benjamin, Elizabeth 72
Benjamin, Gemima 407
Benjamin, James 502
Benjamin, Jared 456
Benjamin, Mary 72
Benjamin, Nancy 127
Benjamin, Nathan 72
Benjamin, Rebecca 78
Benjamin, Sophia 590
Benn, John 625
Bennard, Rebecca 380
Benner, Catharine 298, 736
Benner, Chloe Ann 381
Benner, Daniel 736
Benner, Frederick 585
Benner, Hester Ann 99
Benner, Nancy 297, 310
Benner, Susan 380
Bennet, Amos S. 57

Bennet, Amy 267, 274
Bennet, Anna 225
Bennet, Elizabeth 83, 264
Bennet, Gilbert 478
Bennet, Harriet 668
Bennet, James 554
Bennet, Maria 436
Bennet, Marinda 591
Bennet, Mary 209
Bennet, Michael 256
Bennet, Peter 289
Bennet, Reynolds 209
Bennet, Samuel S. 436
Bennet, Sarah 57
Bennet, Susannah 385
Bennet, Timothy 264, 267
Bennett, Amy 286
Bennett, Ann 252
Bennett, Betsy 286
Bennett, Catharine 610
Bennett, Caty 270, 286
Bennett, Elener 407
Bennett, Elizabeth 286
Bennett, James 239
Bennett, Jane 252
Bennett, Jesse 252
Bennett, Jesse K. 252
Bennett, John 225, 239, 655
Bennett, Joseph 252
Bennett, Kizih 286
Bennett, Margaret 267, 274, 463
Bennett, Mary 286
Bennett, Michael 286
Bennett, Milly 286
Bennett, Nathaniel 286
Bennett, Peggy 286
Bennett, Phebe 286
Bennett, Polly 413
Bennett, Sally 81
Bennett, Samantha 633
Bennett, Samuel 131
Bennett, Sarah 286
Bennett, Timoth 286
Bennett, Timothy 286
Bennett, Unice 286
Bennett, William 407, 579
Benney, Rachel 192
Benney, Spencer 192
Benning, James 327
Bennington, John 42
Bennington, Sarah 654
Bennit, Mary 271
Benny, Ann 192
Benny, Rebecca 192
Benny, Spencer 192
Bense, Jacob 328
Bensman, John Wilhelm 99
Bensmann, Hennamnus 99
Benson, Chancy 587
Benson, George 184
Benson, Hiram 642
Benson, Joel 420
Benson, Margrit 467
Benson, Mary 518
Benter, Elizabeth 441

Bentley, Alexander 616
Bentley, Anna 398
Bentley, Benj. 398
Bentley, Benjamin 257, 274, 398
Bentley, C. L. 653
Bentley, Caleb 464
Bentley, Catharine 616
Bentley, Frederick 316
Bentley, Hesse P. 653
Bentley, John 6, 398
Bentley, Joseph 616
Bentley, Lydia 398
Bentley, Margaret 398
Bentley, W. 653
Bentley, William 398
Bentley, Wm. 398
Bentley, Wm. I. U. 398
Bently, Darcus 271
Bently, Elizabeth 726
Bently, John 726
Benton, Jacob 441
Benton, Maria 421
Benz, Wm. 619
Benzly, John 149
Benzly, William 149
Beoucher, Benjamin 637
Beoucher, Daniel 637
Beoucher, Elizabeth 637
Beoucher, Henry 637
Beougher, Benjamin C. 644
Berbick, Arthur 289
Berch, Nancy 628
Berden, James 52
Berger, J. S. 402
Berigher, Benjamin 637
Berkshire, Susan 410
Berlene, Mary 333
Berlene, Nancy 333
Bernard, Polly 613
Bernard, Thomas 613
Bernbower, J. W. 403
Bernhart, Elizabeth 294
Bernhill, David 625
Beroel, Cynthia 591
Berrice, Christipher 358
Berriger, Mary 468
Berringer, William 478
Berrnett, Margaret 523
Berry, Abraham 412, 740
Berry, Achory 194, 196, 197
Berry, Alice 230
Berry, Anna 197
Berry, Arminda 472
Berry, Daniel 108, 118, 324, 478
Berry, David 196, 197, 199
Berry, Delilah 118
Berry, Elijah 194, 197
Berry, Elisha D. 192
Berry, Elizabeth 118, 161, 197, 529
Berry, Enoch 108, 118
Berry, Hannah 410
Berry, Henry 54
Berry, Isaac 108, 118

Berry, Isabella 511
Berry, Jacob 108, 118
Berry, James B. 222
Berry, John 108, 460,
  511, 516
Berry, John (Jr.) 118
Berry, John (Sr.) 118
Berry, Joseph 197
Berry, Margaret 647
Berry, Mary 118
Berry, Matilda 56
Berry, Millie 123
Berry, Rebecca 118
Berry, Sarah 72, 449
Berry, Thomas 108, 118,
  647
Berry, William 511
Berryhill, Sidney 534
Berryman, Adaline 52
Berryman, Anna Marie 54
Berryman, Eliza 50
Berryman, Jinkey 96
Berryman, Russell 53
Berryman, William 62
Berryman, Wm. 49, 50, 52
Berson, Jesse 289
Berthe, Antonette 476,
  481
Berthe, Lewis 483
Berthelot, Claudius 24,
  491
Berthelot, Mathew 491,
  497
Berting, Joseph 99
Berton, Charlott 401
Bertoon, Magdalene 333
Bertrand, John Baptist
  21, 24, 494
Bertrone, John Baptist 9
Berwind, George 64
Beson, Ammasia 214
Bess, Hannah 117
Bess, Samuel 117
Besse, Alden 98
Besse, Alden (Rev.) 53
Best, David 215
Best, Elizabeth 215
Best, Francis 215
Best, George 529
Best, Isabella 215
Best, Jane 215, 231
Best, John 215, 529
Best, Joseph 215
Best, Polly 215
Best, Rosanna 215
Best, Samuel 572
Best, Susannah 525
Best, T. 231
Best, Thomas 215, 572
Best, William 215
Bethel, Nancy 74
Bett, Apela 404
Betterton, Joshua 256,
  261
Betterton, William 269
Bettester, Joshua 261
Betts, Jane 477
Betts, John 559
Betts, William 573

Betz, George 289
Betz, Joredia 303
Bevenington, Mary 302
Beveridge, John L. 126
Beverly, Catharine 166
Beverly, Malinda 251
Bevington, Henry (Jr.)
  289
Bevington, Mary 461
Bevington, Pegay 468
Bevington, Sarah 460
Bevington, William 333
Beymer, Anna 294
Beymer, George 543
Bibbee, Mary 479
Bibbs, Barbara 416
Bibby, Abraham 9
Bibler, Abraham 440
Bibler, Anna 440
Bibler, Barbara 412, 440
Bibler, Catharine 440
Bibler, Catherine 440
Bibler, Elizabeth 333,
  406, 440
Bibler, Francis 440
Bibler, Jacob 440
Bibler, John 422, 440
Bibler, Joseph 440
Bibler, Mary 440, 583
Bibler, Nancy 333
Bibler, Susanna 414
Bice, Catharine 321
Bice, Henry 315, 321
Bice, Jacob 316
Bice, John 321
Bice, Joseph 321
Bice, Samuel 315, 321
Bice, William 321
Bichard, Daniel 540
Bichard, Nicholas 543
Bichtel, Andrew 419
Bickle, Henry 655
Bickle, Mary 479
Biddle, Clement 500
Biddle, Martha 68
Biddle, Sophia 230
Biddon, Augustus 494
Bidinger, Susanna 297
Biehler, Adam 341
Biehler, Barnhardt 341
Biehler, Margaretha 341
Bier, John 346
Bierce, Wm. W. 76
Bierley, John 44
Bierly, Catharine 639
Bierly, James W. 44
Bierly, Mary 639
Bierly, Mathias 639
Biesner, Conrad 359
Bigelow, Aaron 153, 159
Bigelow, Alpheus 391
Bigelow, Eliha 752, 756
Bigelow, Eliphaz 194
Bigelow, Hannah 153, 756
Bigelow, Hiram 464
Bigelow, Oliver 752
Bigelow, Oliver (Dr.)
  756
Bigelow, Russell 346

Biggart, Samuel 597
Bigger, John 141, 157
Bigger, John (Jr.) 176
Bigger, Thomas 523
Bigger, William 504
Biggerstaf, Wm. (II) 81
Biggerstaff, Jean 82
Biggerstaff, Rachel 82
Biggott, Moses 114
Biggs, Alfred 287
Biggs, Charlotte 258,
  287
Biggs, Daniel 274, 287
Biggs, Davis 692
Biggs, Eleazer 692
Biggs, Ephraim 692
Biggs, Ira 81
Biggs, Jemima 700
Biggs, Jeremiah 692
Biggs, John 686
Biggs, Mary 692
Biggs, Mehaley 278
Biggs, Nancy 258, 287
Biggs, Noah 692
Biggs, Racheal 700
Biggs, Rebeccah 287
Biggs, Rezin 692
Biggs, Robert 287
Biggs, Sarah 269, 692
Biggs, William 259, 287
Biggs, William B. 267,
  274
Biggs, Zaccheus 543, 544
Biggs, Zacheus 567
Bigham, David 130, 157
Bigham, George R. 157
Bigham, James 157
Bigham, Margaret 449
Bigham, Mary 172
Bigham, William 157
Bighill, J. 448
Bigler, John 99
Biglow, A. C. 377
Biglow, Laura 380
Bignell, Zimrod 76
Bigonville, John P. 247
Bilbe, Peter 9
Bilby, Mary 10
Bilieu, Phebe Ann 378
Billger, Catareena 298
Billing, Sally 420
Billinger, Hannah 647
Billinger, Jacob 647
Billings, J. K. 45
Billings, Polly 390
Billingsly, Cyrus 755
Billingsly, Elizabeth
  755
Billingsly, Hannah 755
Billingsly, Lach 755
Billingsly, Rebecca 755
Billingsly, Sarah 755
Billman, Andrew 315
Billman, Christena 315
Bills, Elijah 649
Bills, Sarah 166
Billups, Cynthia 704
Billups, Edward 478, 703
Billups, John 703

773

Blackford, John Hosac
  668
Blackford, Joseph 289,
  668
Blackford, Joseph
  Anderson 668
Blackford, Price 585
Blackford, Robert Allin
  668
Blackford, W. H. 668
Blackford, William Paden
  668
Blackledge, Joseph 289
Blackledge, Margaret 309
Blackledge, Robert 289
Blackman, Frederick 354
Blackman, N. 76
Blackman, Nathaniel 76
Blackman, Simeon 211
Blackmer, Rachael 387
Blackmer, Rufus 387
Blackmon, Joseph 460
Blackmore, Rufus 756
Blackmore, Susan 444
Blackshire, Benezer 544
Blagg, Elizabeth 478
Blagg, Saml. W. 487
Blagg, Samuel W. 486
Blagg, William 487
Blain, Barbara 87
Blain, Catherine 12
Blair, Adam 129
Blair, Archibald 20
Blair, Catherine 12
Blair, Daniel 333
Blair, Dinah 617
Blair, Eliza 528
Blair, Elizabeth 700
Blair, George 5
Blair, James 546, 617,
  700
Blair, Jane 580
Blair, John 545, 546,
  700
Blair, Joseph 668
Blair, Margaret 591
Blair, Maria 126
Blair, Mary Ann 536
Blair, Peter 378
Blair, Robert 668
Blair, Runnell 597
Blair, S. M. 127
Blair, Thomas 147, 148,
  163, 460, 617
Blair, William 127,
  541, 551
Blair, Wm. 129
Blake, Ann Elizabeth 102
Blake, Henry B. 403
Blake, Jenny 657
Blake, Richard 691
Blake, Statira 403
Blake, William 691
Blakeley, Atcheson 57
Blakeley, Samuel 57
Blakely, John 500
Blakely, Samuel 59
Blakemore, Wm. H. 447
Blakeslee, Lorin 625

Blaleck, Vacheal 187
Blanchard, Elizabeth
  223, 235
Blanchard, John 235
Bland, Cynthia 588
Blane, Joseph 625
Blane, Nancy 286
Blank, Jacob 99
Blank, Mary 627
Blank, Michael 419
Blanke, Anna Maria 102
Blankenship, Andrew 478
Blankenship, Elizabeth
  706
Blankenship, Isam 703
Blankenship, Isam (Sr.)
  703
Blankenship, Isham 703
Blankenship, Isom 485
Blankenship, Lodewick
  478
Blankenship, Lodwick 485
Blankenship, Margaret
  485
Blankenship, Mary 477
Blankenship, Nancy 481
Blankenship, Polly 474
Blankenship, Rhoda 480
Blankenship, Richard 485
Blankenship, Richard R.
  485
Blankenship, Saney 481
Blanknell, Jacqu Eetter
  Theadore 703
Blanser, Mary 747
Blasor, Elizabeth 417
Blasor, Isaac 417
Blaylock, Anne 520
Blaylock, Brewer 518
Blaylock, George 518
Blazer, Dolly 475
Blazer, Dorotha 486
Blazer, Elizabeth 486
Blazer, Jacob 486
Blazer, John 486
Blazer, Peter 478, 486
Blazer, Philip 486
Blazier, Susan 74
Blazure, David 309
Bleakley, Hugh 701
Bleakley, Samuel 52, 53
Bleasdale, John 330
Blecher, John 289
Blecher, Mary 301
Bleecher, Magdalina 291
Blergg, Samuel W. 486
Bletter, John 601
Blew, Benjamin 464
Blew, Peggy 460
Blieth, William 236
Blin, Franket 482
Bliss, Lester 58
Bliss, Washington 549
Blizzard, Jonathan 607
Blizzard, Wesley 579
Blocher, Matthias 460
Blocker, Susannah 372
Blocksan, Mary 527
Blood, Eliza 733

Blood, Elizabeth 732
Blood, Frederick 733,
  751
Blood, Frederick L. 732
Blood, Mary 732, 733
Blood, Nancy 732, 733
Blood, Rufus F. 732, 733
Blooke, Neathan 523
Bloom, Frederick 579
Bloom, Joseph 367
Bloomer, Benjamin 454
Bloomer, Catharine 453
Bloomer, Catherine 454
Bloomer, Gilbert 269
Bloomer, Jesse 460
Bloomer, Joseph 456,
  457, 464
Bloomer, Seely (Rev.)
  328
Bloomhuff, J. P. 6
Blore, Joseph 289
Blosser, Abraham 740
Blosser, Anna 740
Blosser, Daniel 740
Blosser, Isaac 420
Blosser, John 740
Blosser, Joseph 740
Blosser, Mary 740
Blosser, Salome 419
Blount, Ambrose 195, 215
Blowers, Pairpoint 703
Blowers, Refus L. 333
Blowers, Zibia 704
Bloxon, Ann 220
Bloxon, Catharine 220
Bloxon, Christian 220
Bloxon, Eliza 220
Bloxon, George 220
Bloxon, Gideon 220
Bloxon, James 220
Bloxon, Mary 220
Bloxon, Nancy 220
Bloxon, Richard 220
Bloxsom, Ann 217
Bloxsom, Anne 217
Bloxsom, Charles 217
Bloxsom, Elizabeth 217
Bloxsom, Gedion 217
Bloxsom, Gregory 217
Bloxsom, Mary 217
Bloxsom, Richard 217,
  220
Bloxsom, Richd. 217
Bloxsom, Sarah 217
Bloxsom, William 217
Bloxum, Nancy 531
Blue, Abraham 457
Blue, Alys 463
Blue, Andrew 222
Blue, Ann 443, 523
Blue, Barnabus D. 378
Blue, Benjamin 464
Blue, Betsey 172
Blue, Daniel 443
Blue, David 464
Blue, Elizabeth 443
Blue, Garret 443
Blue, Garret M. 456, 459
Blue, Henry 208

775

Blue, Isaac 443
Blue, Isabella 530
Blue, John 443, 508
Blue, Kiziah 443
Blue, Mary 443, 466
Blue, Michael 443, 453, 456, 459
Blue, Nancy 468
Blue, Sarah 464
Blue, Susannah 463
Blue, Uriah 443, 459, 464
Blue, William 464
Bluest, Catharine 95
Bluest, John 95, 97
Blunt, Wilson 748
Bly, Anna 122
Bly, John 407
Blythe, John 43
Boadman, Ann 306
Boals, Francis 156, 158
Boals, Margery 158
Boals, Mary 156
Boals, N. C. 690
Boane, Susannah 518
Boardman, Abigail 727
Boardman, Emily 727
Boardman, Hiram 727, 752
Boardman, Jane 727
Boardman, Jane Maria 753
Boardman, John 209
Boardman, John Clinton 209
Boardman, Lewis 727
Boardman, Lucus 752
Boardman, Mercy 727
Boardman, Moses 727, 752
Boardman, Rachel 209
Boardman, Samuel 752
Boardman, T. 391
Boarman, Moses 727
Boatman, William 262, 614
Bob, Charles 53
Bob, Elizabeth 96
Bob, John 96
Bob, Simon (Sr.) 94
Bobb, Anna 52
Bobo, Betsey 76
Bobo, Jemima 76
Bobo, Joshua 76
Bobo, Polly 77
Bobo, Ruth 82
Bobp, Michael 94
Bobst, Martin 98
Bochart, Kitty 414
Bock, Eunice 601
Bock, Lucy 601
Bock, William 601
Bockshire, Teboias 460
Boda, Henry 99
Bodat, --- 498
Bodey, Lewis 178
Bodey, Margaret 178
Bodfish, Charles H. 394
Bodkin, Anna 224
Bodkin, Eleanor 469
Bodkin, George 54
Bodkin, Lewis 99

Bodkin, William 53
Bodle, Michael 746, 747
Bodley, Thomas 14
Bodwell, Enoch 74
Bodwell, Jno. 81
Boerger, Agnes 90
Boerger, Elizabeth 90
Boerger, Henry 90
Boetwick, Adoriran 464
Bogard, Gasper 655
Bogart, Martha 745
Boggis, Elisha 474
Boggs, --- 455
Boggs, Alexander 113
Boggs, Alice 113
Boggs, Alse 657
Boggs, Andrew 230, 486, 553
Boggs, Anthony 655
Boggs, Catharine 450
Boggs, David 478, 485, 487
Boggs, Elizabeth 113, 479, 485
Boggs, Ezekiel 113, 478, 662
Boggs, Francis 113
Boggs, Hannah 113
Boggs, James 483, 485
Boggs, James (Rev.) 98
Boggs, James R. 113
Boggs, Jane 113, 633, 657
Boggs, John Johnston 230
Boggs, Joseph 450
Boggs, Lucinda 113
Boggs, Margaret 113, 679
Boggs, Martha E. 658
Boggs, Mary 475
Boggs, Rebecca 230
Boggs, Reuben 113
Boggs, Rice 113, 542
Boggs, Robert J. 679
Boggs, Sarah 450
Boggs, Sarah Biddle 230
Boggs, William 113, 450
Boggs, William (Sr.) 116
Bogle, John 546, 547
Bogle, Samuel 547
Bogue, Job 114
Bogue, John 114
Bogue, Jonathan 114
Bogue, Mark 114
Bogue, Mary Ann 114
Bogue, Ruth 114
Bogue, Sarah 114
Bohart, Delilah 582
Bohl, M. Elizabeth 126
Bohmer, Daniel 343
Bohmer, Gottlieb 343
Bohrer, Catharine 121
Bohrer, Fred 402
Bohrer, Jacob 402
Bohrer, Peter 464
Bohrer, Zelpah 464
Boiles, Rebecca 484
Boils, Rebecca 482
Bokrath, Henry 99
Boland, Clara 300

Boland, James 289
Bolander, Stephen 236
Boldon, Susanna 602
Bole, Wm. 81
Bolenbarrgh, Peter 421
Bolenbaugh, Catharine 587
Bolenbaugh, John 593
Bolenbaugh, Philip 579
Boley, Jane 169
Bolin, Wm. 43
Boling, Jane Frances 422
Boling, Susan 422
Bolinger, John W. 547
Bollenbach, Abraham 441
Bollenbach, Anna Maria 441
Bollenbach, Elizabeth 441
Bollenbach, Gertraud 441
Bollenbach, Johannes 441
Bollenbach, Katrina 441
Bollenbach, Magareta 441
Bollenbach, Nichlaus 441
Bolles, David C. 662, 666
Bollie, Henrietta 601
Bollman, Charles 289
Bolsinger, George 52
Bolt, Charles 623
Bolt, John 623
Bolt, William 623
Boltin, William 371
Bolton, John 116
Bolton, Joseph 142
Bolton, Patty 173
Bolton, Samuel 147
Bolts, George 238
Bolyard, Daniel 346
Bolyard, John 346
Bolyard, John Wesly 346
Bolyard, Mary Jane 346
Bolyard, Samuel 346
Boman, Alexander S. C. 51
Boman, Polly 72
Boman, Sarah R. 53
Boman, Thomas 579
Bomer, John 722
Bomgarner, Margaret 628
Bond, Edward 222
Bond, George 28
Bond, Hannah 225
Bond, Jemina 375
Bond, Joseph 407, 529
Bond, Samuel 616
Bond, Sarah 413
Bond, Stephen 651
Bondinot, Elias 554
Bone, George 518
Bone, Henry 523
Bone, Jacob 514
Bone, Martha 514
Bone, Nathaniel 176
Bone, Samuel 518
Bone, Thomas 523
Bone, Valentine 514
Bonebright, Mariah D. 67
Bonebright, Wm. 67

Bonecutter, A. T. 251
Bonecutter, Charlotte 250
Bonecutter, Christopher 250
Bonecutter, F. 250
Bonecutter, Ferdinand 250
Bonecutter, J. 250
Bonecutter, Job 250
Bonecutter, John 250
Bonecutter, John H. 250
Bonecutter, Lizzie M. 251
Bonecutter, Sarah 251
Bonecutter, Sophia 250
Bonem, Obed A. 260
Boner, John 289, 738
Boner, Martha 521
Boner, Matthew 239
Bongarner, Rodolph 329
Bonham, Levina 417
Bonham, Robert 579
Bonham, Samuel 746
Bonnel, David 153
Bonnel, Hannah 153
Bonnel, Moses 153
Bonnell, Abigail 161
Bonnell, Johannah 161
Bonner, Chappell H. 518
Bonner, Clory 465
Bonner, David 182
Bonner, David G. 182
Bonner, Elizabeth 182
Bonner, Nancy 521
Bonner, Nathaniel 371, 460
Bonnett, Isaac 687
Bonney, Margaret 133
Bonnoront, George 356
Bons, Geo. 400
Bonsall, Edward 289
Bonsbarger, George 176
Bonson, Nathaniel 55
Bonum, Obed A. 260
Booco, Susannah 475
Booes, Elisa 333
Booker, John 523
Booker, Wm. 117
Bookman, Anna 649
Boon, An 11
Boon, Daniel 69
Booth, Elizabeth 288
Booth, Fred 403
Booth, Hannah 297
Booth, Sarah 306
Boothe, Parmlia 163
Booton, John 474
Boots, Barbary 460, 533
Boots, Elizabeth 465
Boots, Jemima 461
Boots, John 460
Boots, Margaret 531
Boots, Mary 295
Boots, Rosannah 469
Booyce, Susanna 302
Bop, John 95
Bopp, Susanna 52
Borden, Bradford 320

Borden, John 698
Borden, Margaret Ann 270
Borden, Peter 256
Borden, Samuel 567
Borders, Catharine 532
Borders, Henry 529
Borders, John W. 364
Borders, Margaret 521
Borders, Nancy 593
Borders, Ruth 524
Borders, Sally 521
Bordner, Gersham 621
Boreman, Henry 289
Borer, Peter 655
Boret, Andrews 596
Borhens, H. (Rev.) 98
Borier, Peter 666
Borland, Charles 662
Borman, Christena 308
Borman, John 401
Bormat, Elizabeth 231
Bormat, John 231
Bormat, Terrance 231
Born, Elizabeth 596
Born, Jacob 417
Borrough, Thomas W. 550
Bortel, Sarah 602
Borten, Berthard 587
Borten, John 587
Borton, Elizabeth 94
Borton, George 94
Borton, Henry 94
Borton, Isaac 94
Borton, Jane 94
Borton, Job 94
Borton, John 94
Borton, Joshua 98
Borton, Josiah 94, 96, 99
Borton, Lydia 94
Borton, Mahson 94
Borton, Margaret 94
Borton, Mary 94
Borton, Phebe 94
Borton, Pheby 94
Borton, Rachel 94
Borton, Rachel Ann 94
Borton, Rebecca 94
Bortz, Margret 103
Borum, Obed A. 260
Bosche, John F. 86
Bosche, Sophia D. F. 86
Bosche, Sophia F. D. 86
Bosert, Frederick 595
Boshong, Mary 304
Bosserman, Samuel 587
Bost, Elizabeth 308
Bost, Jacob 289
Bostian, Anne 378
Boston, Michael 631
Bostoph, --- 470
Bostwick, Adley 456
Bostwick, Adoniram 456
Bostwick, Oliver 456
Bostwick, Sarah 467
Bostwick, William 446, 464
Bostwick, Wm. 456
Boswell, James H. 185

Boswell, John L. 185
Bosworth, Benajah 235
Botenheifer, Henry 353
Bothel, Benjamin 416
Bothel, William 190
Bothell, William 190
Bothwell, Anna 190
Bothwell, James 84
Botkin, Charles 269
Botkin, Deziah 224
Bottleman, C. 47
Bottleman, Chrisley 27
Bottleman, Christian 2
Bottleman, Cristian 37
Botts, George 239
Botts, John 547, 551
Botts, Williamson J. 274
Boucher, William 631
Boudinot, Elias 573
Bough, Elizabeth 289
Bough, George W. 625
Boughan, Susana J. 464
Boughan, Zachariah 464
Bougher, Henry 407
Bougher, Sarah 632
Bouhan, Sarah 460
Boulin, Margaret 298
Boulton, Levi 289
Bounds, Thomas (Sr.) 757
Bounds, William 757
Bounsaville, Ricd. 21
Bourdon, Marguerite 483
Bourer, Jacob C. 420
Bouring, Caleb 729
Bouring, Elizabeth 729
Bouring, Sarah 729
Bourton, Darling H. 378
Bousey, Charlotta 438
Bousey, Christian 438
Bousey, John 438
Bousey, Lucwick 438
Bousey, Ludwick 438
Bousey, Mary 438
Bousey, Mary Christiana 438
Bousey, Mary Elizabeth 438
Bousey, Williamena 438
Boush, Abby 392
Boush, James 392
Boush, John 392
Bousman, William 9
Boutdeville, Marie Madelaine Angeline 485
Bouteville, Mary Madelaine Angeline 486
Bouton, Henry C. 378
Bouton, Josiah 274
Boves, Elisa 333
Bow, Albert 662
Bowan, Catherine 591
Bowdel, Henry 407
Bowdle, Jesse 98
Bowdle, Jesse (Rev.) 53, 54
Bowdle, Jesse L. 56
Bowdle, Mirian 56
Bowdle, Rebecca 590
Bowdle, Samuel P. 587

Braugher, Allen G. 610
Braugher, Christopher 610
Braugher, Frederick 610
Braugher, Frederick Cary Trimble 610
Braugher, Hester Ann 610
Braugher, Isaac 610
Braugher, Margaret 610
Braugher, Mary Ann 610
Braugher, Nancy 610
Braugher, Sarah Ann 610
Brawcles, Frederick 9
Brawley, Margt. C. 77
Bray, Alicc 260
Bray, Charles 260
Bray, Daniel 421
Bray, Dinah 260
Bray, Harry 260
Bray, Jenny 260
Bray, Joseph 260
Bray, Mary 260
Bray, Matilda 260
Bray, Milo 260
Bray, Peter 260
Bray, Sarah 521
Bray, Venus 260
Brayden, Polley 206
Brayton, Lucy 333
Breakbile, Elizabeth 407
Brearley, Lewis 529
Brearly, Margaret 532
Brechbill, --- 376
Brechbill, Elizabeth 381
Brechbill, John 376
Brechbill, Susan 376
Breckenbridge, Jane 237
Breckenridge, Geo. W. 653
Breckenridge, James 653
Breckenridge, Jane 237
Breckenridge, John 240
Breckenridge, Lovina 653
Breden, David 597
Breeding, Docia 707
Breer, John 701
Brees, John 163
Breese, Phebe 163
Breeze, James 541
Brelsford, John 150, 151, 156
Brelsford, Sally 170
Bremer, Elizabeth 381
Bremer, Peter 378
Brems, Mary 479
Brener, Rebecca 102
Brenneman, Adam 653
Brenneman, Christian 725
Brenneman, John 653
Brenneman, Mary 653
Brennon, Thomas 523
Breno, Mary 479
Brentlinger, Sarah 99
Brentlinger, Susanna 52
Breslar, Rebecca 335
Bresler, Elizabeth 49
Bresler, Lydia A. 54
Bresler, Peter 99
Bretch, Philip 378

Brethers, Francis 208
Brett, Joseph 641
Bretton, Charles 563
Bretz, Anthony 441
Bretz, Catarina 441
Bretz, Christina 441
Bretz, Conras 441
Bretz, Elizabeth 441
Bretz, Heinrich 441
Bretz, Jacob 441
Bretz, Johannes 441
Bretz, Johannes (Jr.) 441
Bretz, Magtalena 441
Bretz, Margret 441
Bretz, Martin 441
Bretz, Philip 441
Bretz, Valentine 441
Brevard, Zebulon 222
Brewer, Alexr. 76
Brewer, Ann 241
Brewer, Isaac 241, 631
Brewer, Jemermiah 268
Brewer, Joseph 5
Brewer, Mary 656
Brewer, Mary Ann 101
Brewer, Nathan 631
Brewer, Siner 268, 276
Brewer, William 625
Brewer, Willis 655
Brewin, Luther 518
Briant, Elizabeth 133
Briant, Jacob 565
Briant, Nathaniel 560
Brice, B. W. 738
Brice, John J. 736, 738, 745
Brichman, Michael 438
Bricker, Adam 239
Bricker, Catharine 304, 690
Bricker, Elizabeth 690, 693
Bricker, George 690, 693
Bricker, George (Jr.) 690
Bricker, Hannah 690
Bricker, Jacob 690, 693
Bricker, John 289, 690, 693
Bricker, Kit 373
Bricker, Lewis 328
Bricker, Lodowick 693
Bricker, Lucinda 328
Bricker, M. 373
Bricker, Magdalena 306
Bricker, Margaret 690
Bricker, Peter 693
Bricker, Rachel 304
Bricker, Sarah 690
Bricker, Solomon 690
Bricker, Susanna 296
Bricket, Jacob 579
Brickler, Hannah 378
Bricklew, Hannah 378
Bricklin, Harriet 602
Bricklin, Osman 601
Bricourt, David 554
Bridge, Bazelul 81

Bridge, John 140
Bridge, John Townsend 563
Bridge, Nancy 173
Bridge, Pamelia 162
Bridge, William 163, 188
Bridges, John 404
Bridges, William 523
Bridget, Polly 172
Bridvill, Caroline 418
Brien, John 289
Brient, Benjamin 464
Brigdman, Mary 520
Brigger, Catherine 602
Briggs, Amniel 369
Briggs, Amville 369
Briggs, David 362
Briggs, Francis 289
Briggs, Israel 289
Briggs, John 9, 30, 40
Briggs, Levi 529
Briggs, Phebe 526
Briggs, Polly 631
Briggs, Roger 15
Briggs, Samuel 222
Briggs, Sibbel 633
Bright, Amela 583
Bright, Charity 408
Bright, David 700
Bright, John 407
Bright, Joseph 417
Bright, Lourenna 583
Bright, Mary 421
Bright, Nancy 700
Bright, Nicholas 700
Bright, Samuel S. 639
Bright, Sarah 419
Brightbill, Benjamin 407
Brikback, Rhoda 523
Briley, John 464
Brill, George 662
Brine, Jonathan 76
Briney, John 554, 563
Briney, Mark 168
Brinker, Caty 306
Brinker, Elisabeth 294
Brinker, Margaret 307
Brinker, Mary 289
Brinker, Peter 289
Brinklinger, William 99
Brinnig, Johann 554
Brison, Edward 105
Brison, James 553
Britigham, Christiana 417
Britin, Archibold 290
Britingham, Joseph 42
Briton, Elijah 625
Briton, Joseph 464
Brittain, Eliza 63
Brittain, Joseph 63
Brittenham, John 42
Brittenham, Solomon 408
Brittenham, Joseph 45
Brittingham, P. 45
Britton, Charles 563
Britton, Finley 378
Britton, John 547
Britton, Matilda 378

Brown, Isabella 540
Brown, J. 393, 452
Brown, J. P. W. 452
Brown, Jacob 119, 193
Brown, James 19, 108,
139, 177, 263, 286,
452, 540, 554, 746
Brown, James (Jr.) 138,
407
Brown, Jane 466, 666
Brown, Jean 384
Brown, Jefferson 108
Brown, Jemima 737
Brown, Jemimah 466
Brown, Jeremiah 702
Brown, Jesse 119, 542,
606
Brown, Jno. 35, 38
Brown, Joanna 380
Brown, Joel 606
Brown, John 21, 28, 35,
84, 105, 108, 134,
160, 193, 235, 236,
271, 393, 400, 421,
451, 452, 546, 551,
553, 554, 555, 625,
643, 644, 737
Brown, John M. 241
Brown, John W. 568, 737
Brown, Jonathan 506, 518
Brown, Joseph 57, 145,
193, 540
Brown, Joshua 407
Brown, Launcelot 108
Brown, Leathe 408
Brown, Liva 393
Brown, Lucy 408
Brown, Mahala 393
Brown, Manassa 567
Brown, Margaret 121, 627
Brown, Margaretta 451
Brown, Mariah 587
Brown, Mary 303, 506,
580, 626, 702
Brown, Mary Ann 737
Brown, Mary E. 74
Brown, Mason 451, 452
Brown, Mason Preston 452
Brown, Moriah 299
Brown, Moses 384
Brown, Nancy 108, 119,
420, 452, 644
Brown, Nathan 193, 290,
309, 666
Brown, Nelly 77
Brown, Nicholas 757
Brown, Olive 631
Brown, Orlando 451, 452
Brown, Pearley 662
Brown, Pearly 76
Brown, Peggy 194
Brown, Phillip 662
Brown, Polly 74, 627
Brown, Presachey Tiding
583
Brown, R. 177
Brown, Reuben 655
Brown, Rhoda 190
Brown, Richard 95, 121

Brown, Richard J. 587
Brown, Robert 134, 154,
157, 474, 539, 540,
541, 545, 555
Brown, Robert (Sr.) 666
Brown, S. 393
Brown, Sally 108, 384,
414, 613
Brown, Sally Nye 393
Brown, Samuel 108, 119,
163, 193, 290, 332,
539, 641
Brown, Sapa 373
Brown, Sarah 72, 669
Brown, Sarah Root 393
Brown, Silas 702
Brown, Simeon 745
Brown, Simon (Jr.) 669
Brown, Sofa 373
Brown, Solomon 655
Brown, Soverighn H. 613
Brown, Stephen 393
Brown, Thomas 9, 121,
148, 233, 235, 662
Brown, Thomas (Dr.) 146
Brown, Turner G. 538,
545
Brown, Wesley 378
Brown, William 72, 104,
108, 119, 129, 168,
190, 240, 290, 316,
322, 330, 370, 518,
523, 540, 597
Brown, Wilson 662
Brown, Wm. 108, 655, 750
Brown, Wm. G. 431
Brown, Zedekiah 418
Browne, Jno. W. 570
Browne, John 566
Browne, John W. 558,
566, 569, 574
Browne, Manassa 559
Browne, Mary 559
Browne, Mary Ann 575
Browne, Samuel 570
Browne, Sarah 575
Brownell, Phebe 603
Brownfield, Anna 11
Brownfield, John 474
Brownfield, Robert 313
Brownfield, Robert (Jr.)
322
Brownfield, Robert (Sr.)
322
Brownfield, Sarah 465
Brownfield, Tamson 313,
322
Brownlee, Moffit 508
Brownlie, Betsey 378
Brubacker, Benjamin 222
Brubaker, David 716
Brubaker, John 69
Bruce, Anna L. 125
Bruce, Charles 46, 138,
139
Bruce, Geo. 283
Bruce, James 518
Bruce, John 290
Bruck, Elisabeth 343

Bruck, F. Elisabetha 345
Brudage, Geo. 403
Brueck, Elisabeth 343
Brueck, F. Elisabetha
345
Bruey, Celeste 356
Bruganshimid, John
Bernard 99
Brugenschmid, Clara 99
Bruget, Emanuel 163
Bruggaman, Mary Engel 89
Bruggerman, Adam H. 89
Bruggerman, Henry 89
Bruin, Martin 464
Brukitt, Henry 116
Brumback, Jacob 441
Brumfield, Barbary 705
Brumfield, John 703
Brumfield, Polly 705
Brumgardner, Elizabeth
704
Brumigem, Simon 523
Brumlett, Reuben 711
Brundage, A. 652
Brundage, George 401
Brundage, James 401
Brundage, Louisa 652
Brundage, M. 652
Brundage, Samuel O. 333
Brundige, Anna 389
Brundige, Elizabeth 389
Brundige, John 389
Brundige, Mary 389
Brundige, Nathaniel 389
Brundige, Sarah 389
Brundige, Stephen 389
Brundige, Thomas 389
Brundige, William 389
Brundridge, John 391
Brundrige, John 390
Bruner, Abraham 739
Bruner, Michael 529
Bruner, Peter 210
Brunier, Francis 491
Brunk, Joseph 241
Brunner, Anna 125
Brunner, Henry 422
Brunners, Magdoline 420
Brunsman, Mary Elizabeth
99
Brunson, Catherine 385
Brunton, James 570
Brusenbark, Elizabeth
169
Brush, Daniel 548, 549,
550, 551, 747, 748
Bryan, Aaron 541
Bryan, Amos 541
Bryan, Conrad 637
Bryan, Cornelius 108,
541
Bryan, Daniel 235
Bryan, Daniel M. 3
Bryan, David 407, 523
Bryan, David C. 241
Bryan, Elizabeth 541
Bryan, Garner 529
Bryan, George S. 241
Bryan, Hannah 241

Burnet, Harriet 725
Burnet, Henry 464
Burnet, Jacob 235, 553,
563, 564, 571, 573,
576
Burnet, James 456
Burnet, James W. 725
Burnet, John 725
Burnet, Joshua 613
Burnet, Robert 458, 460
Burnet, Robert L. 456
Burnet, Robert S. 456
Burnet, Squire 753
Burnet, Steven 564
Burnett, Elizabeth 467
Burnett, Hiram 3
Burnett, Jacob 130, 509
Burnett, John S. 451
Burnett, Mary 176
Burnett, Nathan 478
Burnett, Rachel 176
Burnett, Robert 443
Burnett, Sarah 222
Burnett, Thomas 460
Burnett, William 407,
620
Burnham, Asa 652
Burnham, Phebe 79
Burnham, William A. 222
Burnie, Alexander 647
Burnie, Esther 647
Burnie, George M. 647
Burnie, Holmes 647
Burnie, John 647
Burnie, Mary 647
Burnie, Rachel 647
Burnie, Robert 647
Burnie, Samuel 647
Burnie, William 647
Burns, Agnes 105
Burns, Andrew 679
Burns, Barnebas 363
Burns, D. (Rev.) 52
Burns, David 51, 105
Burns, David (Rev.) 51
Burns, Denny 105
Burns, Elizabeth 656,
679
Burns, George 290, 392
Burns, James 2, 105
Burns, John 13, 679
Burns, Joseph 315, 317,
327, 332
Burns, Lettice 679
Burns, Margery 105
Burns, Mary 167, 169,
288, 363, 679
Burns, Nancy 165
Burns, Robert 679
Burns, Samuel 105
Burns, Susanna 295, 310
Burns, Thomas 679
Burns, William 679
Burnside, Alexander 9
Burnside, John 4
Burnside, William 546
Burnsides, Magdalena 434
Burnsides, Mary 658
Burnsides, Nicholas 434

Burnsides, Rebecca 734
Buroker, A. 178
Buroker, Adam 178
Buroker, Elizabeth 178
Burr, --- (Col.) 576
Burr, Aaron 576
Burr, Charles 470
Burr, Elijah 470
Burr, Hannah 270, 277
Burr, Olive 470
Burr, Peter 277
Burr, Sarah 275
Burrage, Benjamin 474,
485
Burrel, Charity 375
Burrel, Mary Marshal 480
Burrell, Charles 748
Burrell, Henry A. 421
Burrell, John 518
Burrell, Nathan 478
Burrell, Silas 378, 601
Burres, Joseph 316
Burril, George 474
Burrill, Abigail 85
Burris, Ann 525
Burris, Elisha 317
Burris, Geo. 662
Burris, George 662
Burris, Jeremiah 104
Burris, Nancy 480
Burris, Patsey 655
Burris, Rachel 273
Burris, Susannah 475
Burris, William 273, 662
Burris, William (Jr.)
655
Burris, William A. 529
Burris, Wm. 662
Burroker, M. 178
Burroker, Martin 178
Burroker, Molly 178
Burroughs, Hannah 269
Burroughs, John W. 392
Burroughs, Margaret 392
Burroughs, Rebecca 392
Burroughs, Stephen G.
392
Burroughs, Thomas 392
Burroughs, Thomas H. 392
Burrow, Harriet 647
Burrows, Benjamin 597
Burrows, Eden 568
Burrows, Elizabeth 267,
274
Burrows, F. A. 401
Burrows, Isaac 267
Burrows, John 536
Burrows, Joseph 508, 516
Burson, David 290
Burson, Fanny 465
Burson, James 18, 290
Burson, James C. 74
Burson, Laben 290
Burt, Andrew 572, 575
Burt, Daniel 550
Burt, David (Jr.) 547
Burt, John 546, 662
Burt, Samuel B. 662
Burt, Thos. 9

Burt, William 512
Burtch, Emily 49
Burtch, Sanford 49
Burtnett, Mary 324
Burtnott, John 324
Burton, Andrew W. 70
Burton, David 650
Burton, Jacob 70
Burton, John 30, 401,
402
Burton, Joshua U. 99
Burton, Lydia 650
Burton, Mary 291
Burton, Thomas 185
Burton, Wm. 650
Buruss, John 378
Bury, Ann Maria 425
Bury, Isaac (Rev.) 425
Busby, Edith 597
Busby, Elizabeth 168
Busby, Saml. S. 419
Busch, Charlotte 338
Busch, Joseph 56
Busch, Margaretha 338
Busch, Sophia 338
Busch, Wilhelm 338
Busch, Wilhelmina 338
Bush, Abraham 443
Bush, Christian 408
Bush, Daniel 464
Bush, David 625
Bush, Elizabeth 57,
463, 466, 637
Bush, George 408
Bush, Hannah 521
Bush, Horace M. 637
Bush, Isaac 565
Bush, Jacob 446, 460
Bush, Jane 408
Bush, Jemimah 468
Bush, John 389
Bush, Joseph 53, 57, 333
Bush, Joseph (Sr.) 57
Bush, Leonard (Sr.) 443
Bush, Magdalene 464
Bush, Michael 57
Bush, Nancy 404
Bush, Nelson 450
Bush, Peter 57
Bush, Philip 464
Bush, Platt 389
Bush, Rachel 460
Bush, Rebecca 409, 464
Bush, Richard 408
Bush, Samuel M. 637
Bush, Susan 460
Bush, Susanna 57
Bush, William 57
Bushaw, Edith 292
Bushell, Samuel 518
Bushman, George 290
Bushong, Augusteen 290
Bushong, Benjamin 448
Bushong, Betsy 448
Bushong, Catherine 297
Bushong, Elizabeth 295,
308, 310
Bushong, Esther 448
Bushong, George 290

785

Bushong, Jacob 448, 579
Bushong, James 448
Bushong, Margaret 448
Bushong, Mary 304
Bushong, Rachel 448
Busick, Mary 464
Busk, James 290
Busk, Joseph 333
Busker, Margaret 526
Bussard, Elizabeth 626
Bussard, Katharine 626
Bussard, Mary 646
Butcher, Alfred 587
Butcher, Ann 613
Butcher, Catharine 477
Butcher, David 205
Butcher, Jacob 587
Butcher, John G. 587
Butcher, Joseph 205, 518
Butcher, Lettice 210
Butenbaugh, Eliza Ann 379
Butin, Anthanas 625
Butin, Anthonias 625
Butin, Joanna 631
Butler, Anne 485
Butler, Asaph 216
Butler, Benj. 686, 687, 688, 689
Butler, Benjamin 686, 701
Butler, Betsey 701
Butler, Byanca 222
Butler, C. W. 397
Butler, Catharine E. 136
Butler, Charles 397
Butler, Charles S. 701
Butler, Daniel 384
Butler, Delila 701
Butler, Eleanor 485
Butler, Euebia 397
Butler, George 168, 754
Butler, George W. 290
Butler, Henry 660
Butler, Isaac 478, 483, 485, 486, 701
Butler, James 485, 516, 701
Butler, Joel 222
Butler, John 290, 485, 690, 701
Butler, Juliana 526
Butler, Lawrence 40, 41
Butler, Leah 686, 687, 688, 689
Butler, Levy 701
Butler, Malissa 135
Butler, Martha 531
Butler, Mary 471, 486
Butler, Mary Ann 602
Butler, Nancy Jane 603
Butler, Nathaniel 384
Butler, Prudence 701
Butler, Rebecca 332
Butler, Reuben T. 136
Butler, Sims 485
Butler, Syms 474
Butler, Thomas 332, 485, 523

Butler, William 129, 136, 222, 278, 279, 282, 485
Butler, Willie 397
Butler, Zimri F. 216
Butt, --- 132
Butt, Mary 352
Butt, Samuel 124, 523
Butter, Joseph 701
Butter, Thomas 701
Butterfield, Jeremiah 558
Butterfield, Polly 558
Butters, John 46
Butts, Susannah 293
Butts, William 290
Butz, William 309
Buxh, Amy 467
Buyers, Betsey 475
Buyers, David 484
Buyers, Edward 474, 482, 484
Buyers, Elizabeth 484
Buyers, George 484
Buyers, Isaac 484
Buyers, John 482, 484
Buyers, Sarah 484
Buyers, William 484
Buzzard, --- 80
Buzzard, Amy 421
Buzzard, Christian 631
Buzzard, Eliza 77, 80
Buzzard, Michael 446, 458
Buzzard, Nancy 407
Buzzard, Sarah 446
Buzzard, William 631
Byal, Absolem 585
Byal, Amy 585
Byal, Ann 585
Byal, Charles 585
Byal, Delia 585
Byal, Henrietta 581, 585
Byal, Jane 585
Byal, John 585
Byal, Martha 585
Byal, Peter 585
Byal, Samuel A. 585
Byal, Sarah Jane 585
Byal, William 585
Byal, Wm. 585
Byar, Jane 9
Byars, Wm. James 554
Bye, Jonathan 551
Bye, Lydia 308
Byerly, Frederick 453
Byerly, Jacob (Jr.) 625
Byerly, Nancy 628
Byerly, Samuel 329
Byers, Elizabeth 303
Byers, George 474
Byers, Margaret 467
Byers, Sarah 476
Byerstaffer, John 57
Byram, Ebenezer 365, 366, 369, 371
Byram, Elizabeth 150
Byram, H. J. M. 366
Byram, James 366

Byram, John 150
Byram, Mary 366
Byram, Nancy Ann 366
Byram, Nathl. L. 366
Byram, Polly 365
Byram, Sarah 475
Byram, Silas 366
Byram, Silas C. 366
Byram, Susan 366
Byram, Wm. 366
Byrd, John T. 631
Byrd, S. O. 619
Byres, John 701
Byrns, Rachel 299
Byrod, Sally 414
Byrson, John 112
Byxby, Willis 290

--- C ---

Cable, James 153
Cable, Rachel 78
Cadbury, H. 571
Cadbury, Henry 571
Cadey, Elias 655
Cadot, Claudius 482, 491, 496
Cadwalader, Elizabeth 523
Cadwalader, Isaac 597
Cadwallader, David 392
Cadwell, Aaron 555
Cady, Joseph 372
Caffee, Amos H. 729
Cagey, Christian 440
Cagg, John 75
Cahal, Sarah 126
Cahal, Thomas (Sr.) 126
Cahill, Abraham 168
Cahill, Isaac 464
Cahill, John 655
Cahill, Joseph 464
Cahl (?), Margaret 594
Caile, Jane 591
Cain, Aaron 115, 320
Cain, Abner 529
Cain, Daniel 523
Cain, John B. 99
Cain, Samuel 523
Cain, Sarah 320
Cain, William 575
Calaghan, Hannah 125
Calahan, Ann 122
Calahan, George 739
Calahan, Mary A. 122
Calahan, Samuel 163
Calahan, William 122
Calandine, Nancy 415
Calder, Emily 320, 332
Calder, James 320
Calder, James Taylor 332
Calder, Sophronia 320
Caldwell, Abraham R. 207
Caldwell, Alexander 104
Caldwell, Alexr. 76
Caldwell, Andrew 245
Caldwell, Charles 76

Candler, Martha Jane 52
Candles, Sarah 307
Cane, Christian 521
Cane, Thomas 44
Canegies, Cornelius M. 192
Caner, Corrinna 654
Caner, Daniel 654
Caner, Eunice 654
Caney, John 385, 387
Canfield, Elizabeth 149
Canfield, Israel 689
Canfield, Nathan 149
Canfield, Rachel 689
Canfield, Wm. 75
Cannan, Catharine 587
Cannen, Casse Ann 47
Cannen, J. A. B. 47
Canney, E. W. 253
Canney, H. J. 253
Canney, Mary 253
Cannon, Byas N. 43
Cannon, E. C. 43
Cannon, Edward C. 4
Cannon, Erasmus 597
Cannon, Esther 50
Cannon, Isaac 575
Cannon, J. A. B. 43
Cannon, Jeremiah A. M. 4
Cannon, Leah 224
Cannon, Levin M. 43
Cannon, Martha 43
Cannon, Mary 43, 748
Cannon, Nancy 49, 520
Cannon, Sarah 290
Cannon, Thomas Methias 43
Cannon, Westley 587
Canny, George 72
Canny, John 72
Canoll, Margery 308
Canon, Byard 464
Canon, John 290
Canter, Anny 703
Canter, Catherine 254
Canter, Henry 655, 662
Canter, Isaac 659
Canter, J. C. 254
Canter, John 254
Canter, Joseph 254
Canter, Mary 254
Canter, Rebecca 655
Canter, Thomas (Jr.) 703
Cantrall, John 208
Cantrill, John 197
Cantwell, John 714
Cantwell, Sally 714
Canyell, Rachel 526
Cappel, John 1
Car, Hannah 468
Car, Jane 267, 274
Caraway, George 212
Caraway, John 6, 184
Carback, W. M. 49
Card, Richard 52
Carder, Charity 460
Carder, Elizabeth 461
Carder, Nancy 463
Carder, Polly 465

Carder, Saray 462
Carder, Thomas 222
Carel, Rene 498
Caren, Thomas 597
Carey, Ann 614
Carey, Betsey 625
Carey, Christr. 559
Carey, David E. 378
Carey, John 547, 625
Carey, Margaret 263
Carey, Maurice 631
Carey, Nancy 536
Carey, Peter 40, 41
Carey, S. T. 37
Carey, Samuel 614
Carey, Stephen 27
Carey, Wm. 747
Cargdoll, George 529
Carick, George 309
Carick, Hana 311
Carl, Andrew B. 2
Carl, Charles 290
Carl, Dorothy 222
Carl, Joseph 2
Carl (?), Margaret 594
Carl, Sanford 9
Carle, Richard 290
Carlenter, Samuel 439
Carleron, Francis 494, 497
Carleton, Amos P. 222
Carlile, Nancy 304
Carlile, William 543
Carlin, James 579
Carlin, Parlee 579
Carlisle, Ellen M. 425
Carlisle, George 425
Carlisle, Hector 50
Carlisle, James 163
Carlisle, Jno. 33
Carlisle, John 239, 240, 562
Carlisle, Mary 425
Carlisle, Nancy 419
Carlock, Jacob 362
Carmack, Ephraim 147
Carman, Benjamin 221
Carman, Jason A. 378
Carman, Jenny 518
Carman, Rachael 520
Carmay, Chas. 21
Carmeal, Thomas 237
Carmerar, John 235
Carmichael, Eleanor 163
Carmichael, John 168, 702
Carmichal, John 702
Carmichel, Anne 702
Carmichel, Elizabeth 702
Carmichel, Hannah 702
Carmichel, Jacob 702
Carmichel, John 702
Carmichel, Mary 702
Carmichel, Meribah 702
Carmichel, Pheby 702
Carmichel, Rody 702
Carmichel, Sarah 702
Carmichel, Stephen 702
Carmin, Anna 221

Carmin, Elijah 221
Carmin, Eliza 221
Carmin, Elizabeth 221
Carmin, Jane 221
Carmin, John 221
Carmin, Lewis 221
Carmin, Mary 221
Carmin, Nancy 221
Carmin, Rhoda 221
Carmin, Sally 225
Carmin, Samuel 221
Carmin, Sarah 221
Carmin, Sootha 221
Carmin, William 221
Carmon, James 269
Carmy, James 190
Carnahan, Adam 316
Carnahan, James 316
Carnahan, John 316, 366
Carnahan, Sarah 366
Carnahan, William T. 366, 367
Carneal, Thomas 565
Carnes, Daniel 105
Carnes, Hannah 105
Carnes, Nancy 168
Carney, Sherm 523
Caron, Achsah A. 649
Caron, Henry 356
Caron, Mary F. 657
Caron, Polly 518
Carothers, Archibald 1
Carothers, Barbara A. 683
Carothers, E. J. 669
Carothers, Hannah 683
Carothers, Hugh W. 683
Carothers, James 232
Carothers, Jane C. 683
Carothers, John 683
Carothers, Johnson C. 683
Carothers, Mary 683
Carothers, Minerva 669
Carothers, Samuel 597, 683
Carothers, Samuel Y. 683
Carothers, Sarah A. 683
Carothers, William F. 683
Carothers, Wm. 235
Carp, Adam 316
Carp, Wilson 316
Carpenter, Abbey 651
Carpenter, Alfred 383
Carpenter, Amelia 434
Carpenter, B. 389, 391
Carpenter, Benjamin 385
Carpenter, Benjamin (Jr.) 386
Carpenter, Betsey 384
Carpenter, Betsy 463, 654
Carpenter, Catharine 531
Carpenter, Charles 385
Carpenter, David 601
Carpenter, Edwd. 544
Carpenter, Elisha M. 464
Carpenter, Eliza 384

Carpenter, Elizabeth 74, 385
Carpenter, Emily 80
Carpenter, Esther 384
Carpenter, Fredrick 654
Carpenter, Gabriel 415
Carpenter, George 408
Carpenter, George T. 376
Carpenter, Giles 654
Carpenter, Harriet 83, 384
Carpenter, Ira 383
Carpenter, Irena 383
Carpenter, Isaac 287
Carpenter, Israel 392
Carpenter, Jacob 625
Carpenter, James 383, 384, 385, 749, 756
Carpenter, Jno. 516
Carpenter, John 384, 543, 587
Carpenter, Jos. B. 471
Carpenter, Joseph 74
Carpenter, Lolla 385
Carpenter, Lorry 383
Carpenter, Lucy 383
Carpenter, Mary 384, 385
Carpenter, Moses 386
Carpenter, Nancy 582
Carpenter, Naoma 383
Carpenter, Naomi 751
Carpenter, Nathan 383
Carpenter, Orinda L. 82
Carpenter, Peggy 413
Carpenter, Peter 625
Carpenter, Peter A. (Rev.) 98
Carpenter, Polla 385
Carpenter, Reuben 378
Carpenter, Richard 470
Carpenter, Robert 385
Carpenter, Sabesten 408
Carpenter, Sally 383
Carpenter, Saml. 437
Carpenter, Sampson 625
Carpenter, Samuel 434, 752
Carpenter, Sarah 74
Carpenter, Solomon 408
Carpenter, Thomas 547, 703
Carpenter, Thos. 545
Carpenter, William 752
Carpenter, Wm. 416, 432
Carpenter, Wm. W. 2, 5
Carper, Joseph 743
Carr, David 2
Carr, Elizabeth 447, 468
Carr, Francis 574
Carr, Jacob 464
Carr, James 539
Carr, Jane 136
Carr, John 136, 422
Carr, Margaret 461
Carr, Nancy 126
Carr, Phebe 466
Carr, Robert 679
Carr, Samuel 290
Carr, Sarah 469

Carr, Solomon 465
Carr, Susan 50
Carr, William 18
Carrall, Amalthe 241
Carrall, David R. 241
Carrall, Elizabeth 241
Carrall, John W. 241
Carrel, Harriet 678
Carrel, James M. 678
Carrel, Judith 678
Carrel, Rachel 678
Carrel, Robert 678
Carrel, Thomas 678
Carrel, William 678
Carrell, John 486
Carrell, Mary Ann 627
Carrick, Frederick 638
Carrick, Ilana 301
Carrick, Jane 161
Carrick, John (Jr.) 638
Carrick, Robert 152
Carrick, Ruth 152
Carrico, John C. 84
Carrigain, Mark 9
Carrigan, Andrew 1
Carrington, Edward 284
Carrington, Edward C. 284
Carrington, Eliza J. 284
Carrington, Henry 284
Carrington, Jesse 9
Carrington, Lettice 284
Carrington, Mayo 16, 20, 21, 28, 33
Carrington, P. 284
Carrington, Paul 284
Carrington, Robert 284
Carrol, Andrew 327
Carrol, Deborah 475
Carrol, Thomas 163
Carroll, Elizabeth 606
Carroll, Joseph 290
Carroll, Margery 308
Carroll, Mathew 402
Carroll, Sally 308
Carron, Jane 411
Carruthers, John 534
Carson, A. W. 44
Carson, Abraham 523
Carson, Ambrose 189
Carson, Betsey 189
Carson, David 120
Carson, David G. 120
Carson, Elizabeth 532
Carson, Emelia M. 120
Carson, James 2, 29, 125, 189, 274, 316
Carson, Jane A. 120
Carson, Jinny 189
Carson, John 137, 141, 290
Carson, Mary A. 120
Carson, Nancy 189
Carson, Peggy 189
Carson, Polly 189
Carson, Rebecca B. 120
Carson, Robert 189
Carson, Samuel 168
Carson, Samuel G. 120

Carson, Valentine L. 120
Carson, Valentine S. 120
Carson, William 160, 530
Carson, Wm. 2
Carson, Wm. G. 120
Cart, Ezekiel 281
Cart, Sabrath 267, 274
Carter, A. B. 134
Carter, Alexander 631
Carter, Andrew 550
Carter, Becca 478
Carter, Belinda 662
Carter, Benjamin F. 659
Carter, Caleb 194
Carter, David 257, 259, 261, 262, 385
Carter, Elizabeth 118, 461
Carter, Emanuel 110
Carter, George 282, 283, 284, 286, 287
Carter, Hannah 606
Carter, Harley 76
Carter, Harriet 741
Carter, Israel 209
Carter, J. D. 188
Carter, James 606, 634, 703
Carter, John 76, 474
Carter, Levi 194
Carter, Margt. H. 134
Carter, Margt. L. 134
Carter, Mary 194
Carter, Nancy 603
Carter, Nathaniel 282
Carter, Nichlas 160
Carter, Philip 537
Carter, Rachel 51
Carter, Samuel 99, 530
Carter, Sarah 102
Carter, Susanna 472
Carter, Thomas 560
Carter, Troyless 741
Carter, William 376, 473
Carter, William A. 548
Cartlick, Elijah 631
Cartlick, Lucy 631
Cartmill, Ann 217
Cartmill, Elizabeth 217
Cartmill, Ellen 217
Cartmill, Jacob P. 217
Cartmill, James P. 217
Cartmill, John 217
Cartmill, Joseph 208, 217
Cartmill, Nathaniel 217
Cartmill, Rachel 217
Cartmill, Rebecha 217
Cartmill, Sarah 217
Cartmill, Thomas 217
Carto, Franklin 123
Carton, Mary D. 125
Cartor, Isaac 460
Cartright, Abraham 317
Cartright, Mary 317
Cartwell, Jane 161
Carty, Lydia 416
Carty, Mehaly M. 629
Carugher, Thomas 473

Carver, Jacob 518
Carver, James 605
Carver, Levinia 630
Carver, Seth 745, 748
Cary, Abel 545
Cary, Abraham 211
Cary, Calvin (Sr.) 190
Cary, Christopher 559
Cary, Ezra 190
Cary, Isaac 378
Cary, James 625
Cary, Jane 190
Cary, John 263
Cary, Liddy 190
Cary, Margaret 190
Cary, Mary 190
Cary, Samuel 190, 211, 614
Cary, Stephen 607
Carzatt, Mary Ann 376
Case, A. 395
Case, Abraham 569
Case, Albert 638, 644
Case, Almera W. 395
Case, Amanda 638
Case, Amaza 383
Case, Ambrose 638
Case, Bethea 170
Case, Betsey 482
Case, Chester 638
Case, David 163
Case, Electa 638
Case, Elisa 482, 483
Case, Elizabeth 475, 569
Case, Emerette 638
Case, Emiraetta 644
Case, Esther 638, 644
Case, Flavias 644
Case, Flavious 644
Case, Flavius 638
Case, Grove 725
Case, H. 395
Case, Hiram 757
Case, Isaac 385
Case, Jacob 138
Case, John 482, 483, 757
Case, Julia 638
Case, Lucius 638, 644
Case, Mary 164
Case, Norton 730
Case, Oakley 644
Case, Oakly 638
Case, Philadelphia 76
Case, Rebeckah 523
Case, Richard 638
Case, Sally Ann 638, 644
Case, Samuel S. 378
Case, Solon 638
Case, Ursula 638
Case, William 163
Case, Willie W. 395
Casebolt, Sally 462
Casebolt, William 50
Casel, Henry 655
Caseldine, John M. 244
Casenberry, Nancy 409
Casey, Cornelies 408
Casey, Effy 528
Casey, Peter 41

Casey, Rachel 524
Cashad, Anna Mariah 198
Cashat, John 478
Cashman, Cornelious 354
Cashman, John 353
Cashner, Leonard 649
Casner, John 550
Caspelman, William 722
Casper, Deborah 81
Casper, Mary 587
Cassada, John 283
Cassaday, Henry 117
Cassaday, James 117
Cassaday, Jane 117
Cassaday, Margaret 117
Cassaday, William Henry 117
Cassady, Asa F. 662
Cassady, Hugh 106
Cassady, John 283
Cassat, Dennis 537
Cassel, John 365
Cassell, Isaac 504, 506
Cassell, Lydia 504, 506
Cassidiy, John 141
Cassidy, Hugh 323
Cassidy, John 148, 555, 556
Cassidy, Patrick 141, 150, 158
Cassidy, Sally 148, 150, 556
Cassill, Henry (Sr.) 666
Cassill, Susanna 658
Cassingham, Thomas 331
Cast, Aquila 259
Cast, Elizabeth 269
Cast, Ezekiel 258, 267
Cast, Horatio 274, 284
Cast, Richard 268, 285
Cast, William 259
Castator, John 155
Casteel, Amos 748
Casteel, Shadrack 322
Caster, Elizabeth 270
Caster, Hezekiah 478
Caster, Thomas 270
Castle, Ellice 481
Castman, Emma 660
Casto, Andrew 700
Casto, Elizabeth 51
Casto, George 130
Casto, Phebe 333
Casto, Rachel 333
Casto, William 130, 558, 567
Castor, Anna 71
Castor, Elizabeth 587
Castor, Paul 587
Castor, Rebecca 162
Castor, Sarah 160
Castor, Solomon 160
Casty, Amos W. 290
Casy, Effy 510
Casy, Jacob 510
Casy, Rebecca 510
Casy, William 280
Cately, John 472
Caterlon, Joseph 566

Catio, Peter 160
Catlin, Daniel 76
Catlin, Hannah 82
Catlin, Huldah 82
Catlin, William 76
Catt, Elizabeth 298
Catt, George 290
Catt, John (Jr.) 290
Cattell, Ann 299
Cattell, Elizabeth 293
Catterlin, Charlotte 162
Catterlin, Ephraim 160
Catterlin, Joseph 554
Catterlin, Polly 226
Catterlin, Rachel 136
Catterlin, Regiah 136
Catterlin, Wm. 136
Catzenberger, Adam 57
Caulfield, John 357
Caunlee, Joseph 408
Cauter, Catharine 660
Cauter, Nancy 660
Cavalier, Edmund B. 195
Cave, Benjamin E. 631
Cave, Emanuel 635
Cave, Ezekiel 631
Cave, John 625
Cave, Matilda 626
Caveau, Claudius 485
Caveau, John Claudius 485
Cavenaugh, Laurence 160
Cavender, Thomas Steel 235
Cavenger, Elizabeth 224
Cavin, Alexander 44
Cavin, Alexander W. 42
Cavin, Calvin H. 207
Cavit, Unice 270
Cawley, Anne 194
Cay, Joseph M. 46
Caylor, Anna 469
Caylor, Jacob 449, 460
Cayton, Eaton 586
Cayton, Hannah 581
Cayton, Thomas 517
Cayton, Wm. 517
Caywood, James T. 585
Cazad, William 95
Cazier, Abraham 586
Cazier, Murry 586
Cecil, Joshua (Sr.) 597
Ceiese, Catharena 101
Cellar, George 383
Cellar, Hannah 383
Cellar, James 383
Cellar, Jane 383
Cellar, John Flanigan 383
Cellar, Joseph 383
Cellar, Margaret 383
Cellar, Robert McCoy 383
Cellar, Sarah 383
Cellar, Thomas 383
Cent, Betsey 409
Center, Ashley, W. 625
Center, Roderick 222
Ceohegan, Silas Smith (Dr.) 426

790

Ceperson, Zacariah 99
Cessna, Charles 322
Cessna, Cosh 595
Cessna, Elizabeth 322, 323
Cessna, Hannah 322
Cessna, John 322
Cessna, John (Jr.) 322
Cessna, Jonathan 322, 593
Cessna, Mary 322
Cessna, Nancy 322
Cessna, Oliver 322
Cessna, Rachel 322
Cessna, Rebecca 322, 589
Cessna, Stephen 322, 323
Cessna, William 322
Cessnco, Mary 588
Ceut, Betsey 409
Chabeau, Peter 490
Chadwick, Eliza M. 704
Chadwick, Polly 78
Chaffee, Wm. 49, 50
Chaffee, Wm. (Rev.) 50, 51, 52, 54
Chaffin, John H. 703, 708
Chainy, Sarah 279
Chalfant, Mordicai 315
Chalfant, William 606
Chalmers, Isabell 501
Chalmers, John 501
Chamberlain, Cleressa 591
Chamberlain, Elizia 654
Chamberlain, George 559
Chamberlain, Isaac 290
Chamberlain, Jno. D. 76
Chamberlain, John 290
Chamberland, Samuel 290
Chamberlane, Rachel 408
Chamberlin, James 143
Chamberlin, Job 579
Chamberlin, John 140, 143, 144
Chamberlin, Lucy 143
Chamberlin, Nancy 140
Chamberlin, Norman 579
Chamberlin, Thomas T. 99
Chamberlin, Vesta 582
Chambers, Aby 442
Chambers, Adam 523
Chambers, Agness 442
Chambers, Alexander 442
Chambers, Alexander (Sr.) 442
Chambers, Ann 518
Chambers, B. 567
Chambers, Benjamin 377
Chambers, Benjamine 9
Chambers, Catharine 166, 377
Chambers, Catherine Ann 669
Chambers, Charlotte 558
Chambers, David 163, 530, 746
Chambers, Elijah 518
Chambers, Elizabeth K. 669

Chambers, Isabella 521
Chambers, James 442
Chambers, John 442, 523, 636, 669
Chambers, John H. 685
Chambers, Joseph 129, 163, 685
Chambers, Margaret 527
Chambers, Mary 519
Chambers, Mary Ann 442
Chambers, Nancy 168
Chambers, Nathan 269
Chambers, Perry 48
Chambers, Rachel 52, 685
Chambers, Rebecca 442
Chambers, Robert W. 669
Chambers, Samuel 163
Chambers, Sarah 442
Chambers, William 442, 523
Chambers, Wm. 116
Champer, R. 401
Champion, Sarah Ann 334
Champlin, Martin 470
Chance, Benjamin 314, 316, 320
Chance, Elizabeth 303
Chance, Peter 290
Chanceller, Jesse 222
Chancelor, Jas. 747
Chandivert, Mary Magdalean LeBrun 497
Chandivert, Peter Mathew 497
Chandivert, Stephen 497
Chandler, E. 401
Chandler, E. H. 401, 402
Chandler, Elias 29
Chandler, Ellis 28, 33
Chandler, Hannah 334
Chandler, Isaac 551
Chandler, Jno. 76
Chandler, Mary 49
Chandler, Richard 286
Chandler, Robert 286
Chandler, Thomas 662
Chandwick, Thomas 76
Chane, Adam 121
Chaney, Benjamin 205
Chaney, Druzella 602
Chaney, John 290
Chaney, Jonston 290
Chaney, Levi 611
Chaney, Lydia 611
Chaney, Samuel 319
Chaney, Thos. 535
Chaney, William 551
Channel, Elizabeth 413
Channel, Jeremiah 731
Channel, Joseph A. 731
Channel, Mary Ann 731
Channell, Alpheus 420
Chanterell, Michael 497
Chanterelle, Michael 483
Chantrell, Michael 490
Chantrelle, Michael 498
Chapdu, --- 498
Chapdu, Peter Francis 478

Chapin, Geo. 400
Chapin, L. B. 402
Chapin, Leonidas 402
Chapin, Leonidis 402
Chaplin, Jona E. 194
Chaplin, Mary 117
Chaplin, William 117
Chaplin, Wm. 111
Chapman, Abraham 642
Chapman, Alpheus 752
Chapman, Alpneus 755
Chapman, Amasa 569
Chapman, Casper 625
Chapman, Clara R. 397
Chapman, Clark 601
Chapman, Corwin C. 397
Chapman, E. P. 397
Chapman, Emma 397
Chapman, Ephrain 638
Chapman, Fanny L. 741
Chapman, Hannah 569
Chapman, Hannah J. 379
Chapman, Henry 237
Chapman, Henry C. 741
Chapman, Huldah R. 741
Chapman, John 460, 548, 689
Chapman, Julia A. 741
Chapman, Lyman 378
Chapman, Mary 478
Chapman, Nathaniel 158, 747
Chapman, Peggy 158
Chapman, Phebe 707
Chapman, Polly 519, 688
Chapman, Rachel 397
Chapman, Samuel 397
Chapman, Stepehen 686
Chapman, Stephen 688, 700, 702
Chapman, T. C. 397, 401, 402
Chapman, Tal S. 397
Chapman, William 408
Chapman, Wm. 237
Chappius, Francis H. 355
Chard, James 222
Charles, Elizabeth 744
Charles, George 373, 744
Charles, James 744
Charles, John 238, 239, 535
Charles, Presley 744
Charles, Presly 744
Charlton, Henry 587
Charlton, John 708
Charpenter, Antoine Louis 36
Charpenter, Lewis Anthony 36
Charpentier, Duduit L. 35
Charte, Ally 11
Chartens, John 505
Chartens, Margaret 505
Chase, Abraham 560
Chase, Elizabeth 156, 157
Chase, L. Homedial 157

791

Clark, George D. 389
Clark, George Rogers 236
Clark, Hannah 82, 390
Clark, Hannah Mariah 101
Clark, Hatfield 734
Clark, Henry 13, 460, 625
Clark, Horatio 438
Clark, Isaac 158, 163, 168, 625
Clark, Isabella 445
Clark, Isaiah 662
Clark, Jackson 390
Clark, James 32, 47, 130, 160, 177, 445, 631
Clark, James R. 390
Clark, Jamime 629
Clark, Jane 177, 582, 625
Clark, Jas. 224
Clark, Joanah 177
Clark, Joannah 142, 177
Clark, John 1, 105, 163, 175, 315, 362, 446, 505, 547, 666, 709
Clark, Johnston 168
Clark, Jonas 177
Clark, Jonathan 389
Clark, Jos. 460
Clark, Joseph 234, 236, 559
Clark, Joshua 456
Clark, Katharine 718
Clark, Latitia 161
Clark, Lucy B. 77
Clark, Margaret 625, 734
Clark, Mary 584, 632
Clark, Mary Ann 69
Clark, Mary Clarissa 390
Clark, Matilda 581
Clark, Matthew 748
Clark, Miram 389
Clark, Nancy 390, 461
Clark, P. J. 401
Clark, Polly 171, 226, 302, 704
Clark, Polly C. 384
Clark, Priscilla 421
Clark, Rachel 420, 633
Clark, Rebecca 224, 381, 704
Clark, Reubin 699
Clark, Richard 179
Clark, Robert 179, 530
Clark, Robert M. 179
Clark, Robt. 625
Clark, Sally 158, 268, 275, 389
Clark, Samuel 1, 478, 550
Clark, Samuel B. 99
Clark, Sarah 460, 625
Clark, Sarah Ann 579
Clark, Stephen 142, 177
Clark, Steven 48
Clark, Syvester 701
Clark, Thos. 415, 460
Clark, William 168, 549, 625

Clark, William Hamilton 99
Clark, Wm. 42, 235, 553
Clark, Wm. H. 549
Clarke, Anthony 710
Clarke, Elizabeth 703
Clarke, Hugh 291
Clarke, James 703
Clarke, John 274
Clarke, Reuben 552
Clarke, Robert 427
Clarkson, David 728
Clarkson, David C. 728
Clarkson, Robert 727, 730
Clarridge, Edmund 457, 458
Clarrin, Margaret M. 295
Clary, Daveirn 367
Clary, Henry 542
Clary, Nathaniel 546
Claton, Elizabeth 500
Claton, John 500
Claton, Jonathan 500
Claton, Lewis 500
Claton, Margaret 500
Claton, Phebe 500
Claton, Reuben 500
Claton, Sarah 500
Claton, Thomas (Sr.) 500
Claton, Wm. 500
Clavenger, Hannah 463
Clawson, Isaih 99
Clawson, Josiah 49
Clawson, Lydia Minerva 135
Clawson, Maria 53
Clawson, Rachel 225
Claxton, Mary Ann 625
Claxton, Mary Jane 635
Claxton, Matilda 633
Claxton, Susan E. 628
Clay, Coonrod 601
Clay, Eliza 133
Clay, Green 237, 238
Clay, Isaac 291
Clay, Jacob 402
Claypool, Anna 80
Claypool, Eleanor 485
Claypool, Elizabeth 476
Claypool, Isabel 590
Claypool, Jacob 743
Claypool, Jane 628
Claypool, Jas. 80
Claypool, Leah 657
Claypool, Margaret 480
Clayton, Catharine 507
Clayton, Cynthia 507
Clayton, David 507
Clayton, Drusilla 500
Clayton, E. 179
Clayton, Elizabeth 500, 507
Clayton, George 507
Clayton, George Washington 198
Clayton, Harriet 589
Clayton, J. 179
Clayton, John 179, 198, 500

Clayton, Jonathan 198, 507
Clayton, Joseph 198
Clayton, Lewis 500
Clayton, Margaret 500
Clayton, Mary 500
Clayton, Mary Ann 507
Clayton, Maxom 512
Clayton, Maxon 517
Clayton, Menon 523
Clayton, Reuben 500
Clayton, Ruhama 179
Clayton, Ruhanna 198
Clayton, S. B. 179
Clayton, Samuel 198, 639
Clayton, Sarah 500
Clayton, Susannah Elizabeth 198
Clayton, William 483, 500, 512
Clayton, Wm. 500
Clear, Conrod 662
Clear, George (Jr.) 662
Clear, Samuel 662
Clegg, Matthew 548
Cleiner, Anna 441
Cleiner, Charles 441
Cleiner, Charles F. 441
Cleiner, Francis 441
Cleiner, John 441
Cleiner, Masse 441
Cleiner, Nancy 441
Cleiner, Sally 441
Cleiner, Susanna 441
Cleland, John 262
Clem, Barbara 173
Clem, George 163
Clem, John 143
Clem, John (Jr.) 168
Clemens, Benjamin 333
Clemens, Lydia 727
Clemens, Susan 536
Clemens, William 727
Clement, David 595
Clement, Hubert 247
Clement, James 247
Clement, Jane 247
Clement, Lizzie 247
Clement, Louis 247
Clement, Mary 247
Clement, Victoria 247
Clements, Alexander 553
Clements, Elizabeth 553, 573
Clements, Forgerson 553
Clements, Grier 553
Clements, Isaac 553
Clements, James 539, 553
Clements, Jesse 553
Clements, John 553
Clements, Joseph 553
Clements, Mace 32, 34
Clemmers, Eva 47
Clemmers, Henry 47
Clemmers, Henry W. 47
Clemmers, Laura V. 47
Clemmers, Lucinda 47
Clemmers, Nancy 47
Clemmers, Rebecca 47

Clemmers, Wm. S. 47
Clemming, Mary 467
Clemmons, Abigail 462
Clemmons, John (Jr.) 655
Clemmons, Josiah C. 662
Clemon, Henry 757
Clemons, Deborah 657
Clemonts, Thomas 631
Clendenan, Robert 408
Clendenen, Anderson 645
Clendenen, Andrew 645
Clendenen, Andrew (Jr.) 645
Clendenen, David 645
Clendenen, Elenor 645
Clendenen, James 645
Clendenen, Mary 645
Clendenen, Mary Margaret 645
Clendenen, William 645
Clendening, Jane 682
Clendening, Joseph D. 682
Clendening, Margaret 682
Clendening, Sarah 682
Clenn, Henry 168
Clensey, James 508
Clesson, Eve 413
Clester, Samuel N. 73
Clets, Frederick 291, 309
Cleveland, Asahel 76
Cleveland, Polly 90
Clevenger, Eden 455
Clevenger, Enos 518
Clevenger, Hannah 270
Clevenger, Polly 461
Clevenger, William 277
Clever, David 268
Clever, James 268, 274
Clever, Phebe 269
Clevinger, Anna Mariah 198
Clevinger, Jane 198
Clevinger, Joseph 198
Clevinger, Kizziah 198
Clevinger, Margaret 198
Clevinger, Nancy 198
Clevinger, William 198
Clevsey, Jane 524
Click, Delila 420
Click, John 686, 687, 689
Click, Michael 687, 689
Click, Sally 687
Clifford, Catherine 51
Clifford, John 722
Clifford, Thomas 523
Clifton, Pheynetty 247
Climons, Sarah 655
Clin, John 333
Cline, A. 250
Cline, Alfred 250
Cline, Alice 250
Cline, Anna 250
Cline, Annie 250
Cline, Armilda 250
Cline, Arminta R. 250
Cline, C. 250

Cline, Catharine 640
Cline, Charles 256, 262
Cline, D. 250
Cline, David 250, 421
Cline, Delila 250
Cline, Doris Marie 250
Cline, Eli 250
Cline, Eve 250
Cline, H. 250
Cline, Harison 250
Cline, Harrison 250
Cline, Ida 250
Cline, John 45
Cline, John H. 250
Cline, John J. 250
Cline, John M. 250
Cline, Laura E. 250
Cline, Lillie 250
Cline, Lillie M. 250
Cline, Louisa 250
Cline, Mary 524, 640
Cline, Mary E. 250
Cline, Ollie 250
Cline, Ona 250
Cline, P. 250
Cline, Philip 250
Cline, S. 250
Cline, W. H. 250
Cliner, Nancy 407
Clingamon, Hirom 99
Clinger, Benjamin 638
Clinger, Malena 373
Clinker, John 291
Clinton, Abel 678
Clinton, Edward 678
Clinton, Eve 678
Clinton, John 678
Clinton, Peter 678
Clinton, Priscilla 678
Clinton, Thomas 230
Cliphant, Perry 635
Clippinger, Catharine 415
Clippinger, Solamon 420
Cliveton, W. P. 45
Cloae, Adam 408
Clomens, Margaret 299
Clopp, John 625
Close, Geo. W. 403
Close, Margaret 596
Close, Wm. 596
Closser, Jacob 530
Cloud, Daniel 747
Cloud, Henry 274
Cloud, Prudence 274
Cloud, Thomas (Jr.) 263
Clough, Amilia Catherine 601
Clough, C. 398
Clough, L. 398
Clough, William 398
Clouse, Polly 410
Clow, Martha 381
Cloyd, James 104, 362, 364
Cluar, Lydia 660
Cluar, Mary 660
Clum, Geo. 420
Clum, Rosanna 421

Cluster, Mary 276
Cluster, Sophia 272
Clutter, Benjamin 436
Clutter, Betsey 411
Clutter, John V. 645
Clutter, Mary Ann 436
Clutter, Priscilla 632
Clutter, Rachel 698
Cluxton, Margaret 43
Cly, Anna 421
Cly, Jacob 421
Cly, Mary 420
Clyburn, Charles D. 618
Clymer, Fountain 417
Clymer, Mary 410, 532
Clymer, Nancy 579
Clymer, Sarah 581
Clyner, Anna 441
Clyner, Charles 441
Clyner, Charles F. 441
Clyner, Francis 441
Clyner, John 441
Clyner, Masse 441
Clyner, Masse (Sr.) 441
Clyner, Nancy 441
Clyner, Sally 441
Clyner, Susanna 441
Coakley, Barbara 637
Coakley, Daniel 637
Coakley, Isaac 637
Coakley, Jacob 637
Coakley, John 637
Coakley, Solomon 637
Coakley, William 637
Coal, Sarah 705
Coaltrap, William 597
Coapland, William 408
Coapstick, Elizabeth 177
Coapstick, Jean 177
Coapstick, John 177
Coapstick, Ruth 177
Coapstick, Samuel 143, 144, 177
Coapstick, Sarah 143
Coapstick, Sarrah 177
Coapstick, Thomas 143, 152, 168, 177
Coates, Hannah 282
Coates, Mary Ann 82
Coates, Nelson 421
Coats, Aquila 269
Coats, Arthur 85
Coats, Charles 547
Coats, James 579
Coats, William 269
Cobb, Eunice 396
Cobb, Foster 577
Cobb, Mary Ann 577
Cobbin, Nancy 627
Cobbs, Abigail 305
Cobbs, Elizabeth 305
Cobbs, Mary 311
Cobbs, Rebecca 291
Cobbs, Rhody 305
Cobean, John 62
Cobean, Samuel 62
Cobell, Calvin 391
Coberly, George 389
Coberly, Joseph 389

794

Coble, Lemuel 690
Coblentz, Samuel 365
Coblin, James 625
Coburn, David 291
Coburn, Elizabeth 290
Coburn, James 291
Coburn, John 27
Coburn, Margaret 293
Coburn, Rachel 297
Coburn, Samuel 291
Coc, Anna Maria 419
Cochran, Alexander 548
Cochran, Benj. 52
Cochran, Benj. F. 50,
51, 52, 53
Cochran, Daniel 248
Cochran, Elizabeth 10
Cochran, Fanny 287
Cochran, George W. 51
Cochran, George
Washington 195
Cochran, Hugh 14, 17,
195
Cochran, J. 248
Cochran, Jackson 195
Cochran, James 248
Cochran, John 248, 559,
567
Cochran, Lydia Ann 99
Cochran, Mary 287, 620
Cochran, Phebe 554
Cochran, Rebecca 195
Cochran, S. 248
Cochran, Samuel 552
Cochran, Simeon 50
Cochran, Simon (Rev.)
50, 51
Cochran, Solomon 687
Cochran, Thomas 552, 554
Cochran, Thos. 222
Cochran, William 96,
256, 287, 545, 688
Cochran, William
Harrison 195
Cochran, William S. 274
Cochrane, Andrew 49
Cochrane, Daniel K. 721
Cochrane, David K. 715
Cochrane, Hester R. 656
Cochrane, Joshua 313
Cochrane, Wm. 49
Cochrin, Mary 273
Cochron, Elizabeth 533
Cochron, R. H. (Dr.) 696
Cochrun, Benjamin L. 64
Cochrun, Josiah C. 64
Cochrun, Leah Jane 64
Cock, George 274
Cockaril, Elizabeth 465
Cockerell, J. P. 47
Cockerelle, J. R. 48
Cockerill, Daniel 44
Cockerill, William S.
465
Cockran, William 287
Cockrane, Joshua 313
Cockrell, Robert 662
Coddington, Asa 662
Coddington, William 97

Codner, Emily 76
Coe, Artenesia 650
Coe, Beach 76
Coe, Betsey 650
Coe, Edwr. H. 635
Coe, Eunice 81
Coe, Israel 650
Coe, James 81, 733
Coe, Jno. 76
Coe, Josiah 76
Coe, Mary 83
Coen, Ann 583
Coen, Edward 558, 559
Coen, Edward (Jr.) 176
Coen, James 140, 176
Coen, Jane 176, 225
Coen, John 465
Coen, Margaret 176, 558
Coen, William 662
Coffee, Wm. 109
Coffenberry, Sally 409
Coffenleny, Polly 405
Coffey, Harmon 746
Coffey, John 19
Coffin, Deborah 520
Coffin, J. B. 68
Coffin, James Parker 68
Coffin, Margaret 519
Coffin, Priscilla 518
Coffinberry, J. W. 625
Coffman, Daniel 112, 120
Coffman, Elizabeth 532
Coffman, John 70, 112,
120, 408, 417
Coffman, Martin 415
Coffman, Nathan 451
Coffman, Sarah 112, 120
Coffman, Sarah C. 451
Coffman, Zachary 378
Coffy, Joseph (Jr.) 222
Cogan, Rachel 301
Cogle, Hannah 269
Cogswell, Solomon F. 77
Cohagan, Sarah 527
Cohagen, John 530
Cohen, Wm. 46
Cohey, James 291
Cohran, Sally 466
Coil, Andrew 465
Coil, Anna 100
Coil, Elizabeth 468
Coil, George 460
Coil, Henry 443
Coil, Isaac 465
Coil, Peter 465
Coil, Thomas 457
Coile, James 192
Coke, Martha Ann 420
Cokeley, Jacob 418
Cokely, William 625
Colbert, Anny 188
Colbert, Catharine 188
Colbert, Joshua 188
Colbert, Mary 188
Colbert, Rachel 593
Colbert, Susana 188
Colbert, Thomas 188
Colby, Hannah 147
Colby, Joseph 163, 560

Colby, Martha 166
Colclo, Ann 585
Colclo, Ann Mariah 580
Colclo, Betsey 585
Colclo, Emily 585
Colclo, Hiram S. 585
Colclo, James H. 585
Colclo, Jeremiah 585
Colclo, Polly 585
Colclo, Sally 579, 585
Colclo, William 585
Colclo, Wm. M. 579
Cold, Sarah 585
Coldwell, Lodices 592
Cole, Abner 543
Cole, Abraham (Sr.) 586
Cole, Andrew J. 399
Cole, Athaliah 586
Cole, B. 654
Cole, Betsy 408
Cole, Calista 582
Cole, Clarisa 654
Cole, Cyrus 399
Cole, David 361, 362,
364
Cole, Elisha 438
Cole, Elizabeth 73, 407
Cole, Elizabeth A. 602
Cole, H. N. 48
Cole, Hamilton 28
Cole, James 2, 438
Cole, John 408
Cole, John W. 579
Cole, Joseph 366
Cole, Joshua 408, 586
Cole, Leonard 6
Cole, Mary E. 594
Cole, Melinda 586
Cole, P. 654
Cole, Polly 405, 579
Cole, Rebecca 399
Cole, Sally 407
Cole, Samuel 284, 361,
362, 586
Cole, Sarah 414, 586
Cole, Solomon 284
Cole, Stella 382
Cole, Susannah 587
Cole, Thomas 579, 586
Cole, Verlinda 586
Cole, William 586, 639
Cole, William R. 284,
523
Cole, Wm. R. 287
Coleman, --- 210
Coleman, Albert 400
Coleman, Ann Christena
444
Coleman, Anne 168
Coleman, Asa (Dr.) 222
Coleman, Ellen I. 381
Coleman, Genne 707
Coleman, Hartwell 631
Coleman, Henry 51
Coleman, Henry P. 444
Coleman, J. B. 186
Coleman, J. H. 52
Coleman, James H. 51,
52, 58, 99

795

797

Cool, Daniel 610
Cool, Elizabeth 610
Cool, Emanuel 610
Cool, Malinda 610
Cool, Mary 610
Cool, Peter 610
Cool, William 610
Coole, J. 188
Cooley, Abigail 224
Cooley, C. E. 393
Cooley, Elizabeth 656
Cooley, Eunice 194
Cooley, J. 188, 195
Cooley, James 194
Cooley, Jennett 194
Cooley, Jennie E. Morse 393
Cooley, Wm. H. 695
Coolman, Frederick Wilhelm 601
Cooly, Abigail 73
Cooly, Jacob 73
Cooly, William 587
Coombacher, Susana 306
Coombs, Henry 354
Coomes, John 745
Coon, Adam 460
Coon, Alexander 51, 65
Coon, Asa 51
Coon, Catherine 50
Coon, Charles 554
Coon, Christian 150
Coon, Elizabeth 58
Coon, George 65, 150
Coon, George W. 51
Coon, Hannah 51
Coon, James 554
Coon, Jesse 715
Coon, Maria 51
Coon, Michael 460
Coon, Nathan 65
Coon, Samuel 100
Cooney, Asa 195
Cooney, Frederick 641
Cooney, Nancy 596
Coonrad, Sophia 422
Coonrad, Woolery 631
Coonrod, A. 636
Coonrod, Catharine 628
Coonrod, Elizabeth 628
Coonrod, Rebecca 632
Coonrod, Wollery 626
Coons, Anne 420
Coonse, Catharine 559
Coonse, Frederick 559
Coonts, Henry 486
Coontz, Catharine 109
Coontz, Henry 109
Coontz, Jacob 109
Coontz, Peter 109
Coontz, Sarah 109
Cooper, Adam 384
Cooper, Alexander 100
Cooper, Amos 579
Cooper, Caleb 545
Cooper, Charles 125
Cooper, Charles (Jr.) 721
Cooper, Charles (Sr.) 721
Cooper, Cornelius 77

Cooper, Daniel C. 553, 561, 567, 568
Cooper, Elizabeth 334, 630
Cooper, Geo. 745
Cooper, George 698, 746
Cooper, Henry 579
Cooper, Henry C. 321
Cooper, Isaac 465
Cooper, Jacob 168
Cooper, Jacob G. 579
Cooper, James 502
Cooper, Jane 698
Cooper, John 587, 683, 698
Cooper, Joseph 508
Cooper, Joshua 291
Cooper, Justice 278
Cooper, Levi 408
Cooper, Margaret 101
Cooper, Margarett 124
Cooper, Mary 226, 321
Cooper, Mary Ann 582
Cooper, Mary M. 321
Cooper, Noah 321
Cooper, Presley 747
Cooper, Ralph 168
Cooper, Ralph A. 366
Cooper, Samuel 383, 384, 388
Cooper, Sarah 582
Cooper, Stephen (Sr.) 745
Cooper, Thos. 704
Cooper, William 698
Cooper, William M. 221
Cooper, Wm. 465
Coover, J. 135
Coover, P. 135
Coover, Prudence 135
Cope, Abigail 114
Cope, Caleb (Jr.) 291
Cope, George 114
Cope, Grace 114
Cope, Hannah 588
Cope, Israel 291
Cope, John 114, 291
Cope, Joshua 114, 291
Cope, Samuel 114
Cope, Sarah 114
Copeland, --- 44
Copeland, Abigail 298
Copeland, Abner 269
Copeland, Charlotte 590
Copeland, Eleazer 387
Copeland, Elijah 111
Copeland, George 291
Copeland, Isaac 478
Copeland, J. R. 45
Copeland, John 98
Copeland, Jonathan R. 662
Copeland, Joseph 270, 530
Copeland, Minor A. 659
Copeland, Rebecca 270
Copeland, Sally 525
Copeland, William 594
Copeland, Wm. 593

Copenhaven, John 704
Copes, William 196
Copestick, James 162
Copey, Philip G. 100
Copland, John 439
Coplin, Robert 579
Copner, Elizabeth 95
Copner, John D. 95
Copner, Justice D. 52
Copp, Mary D. 82
Copp, Nancy 80
Copp, Susanna 422
Coppess, Adam 370
Coppess, Devaul 530
Coppock, Jehu 291
Coppock, Rachel 301
Coppock, Samuel 291
Coppress, Devaul 530
Copsay, Philip G. 100
Copsey, Richard 100
Copsy, Hannah 92
Copsy, Nancy 535
Copus, Aaron 291
Copus, John 45, 269
Copus, Thomas 45
Copus, Wilson 42
Corah, John 269
Corben, Charlotte 583
Corbet, Samuel 111
Corbin, Alvin 691
Corbin, Artimas 691
Corbin, Calvin 691
Corbin, Clarissa 691
Corbin, Hester 580
Corbin, Jedediah 691
Corbin, Jeremiah 534
Corbin, Lucretia 691
Corbin, Lyman 691
Corbin, Schuyler 691
Corbin, Schyler 691
Corbin, William 580
Corbley, John 232
Corbly, Elizabeth 556
Corbly, John 556
Corburn, John 30
Corder, Elias 50
Corder, John 53
Corder, Nancy Jane 100
Corder, Susan C. R. 102
Cordrey, Hosea 46
Cordrey, James 46
Cordrey, Sarah 46
Cordry, Hosea 4
Core, Christian 454, 456, 457, 465
Core, Christian (Jr.) 446
Core, Doly 190
Core, Henry 454, 456, 457
Coregtie, --- 208
Corey, David 160
Corey, Elizabeth 225
Corey, Enos Ayres 587
Corey, Eunice 79
Corey, Naomy 333
Corgin, James 403
Corn, Henry H. 724
Corn, Jesse 655

Critchfield, Catharine
697
Critchfield, Margaret
697
Critchley, David 557
Critten, Gabriel 743
Crochran, Hugh 18
Crocker, Calvin 378
Crocker, Samuel S. 77
Crocket, Andrew 408
Crocket, James 169
Crocket, Leroy 600
Crocket, Milton 599, 600
Crocket, Nathaniel 439
Crocket, Nelson 599, 600
Crocket, Sarah 439, 599
Crocket, Sarah A. 599
Crockett, Benjamin A.
601
Crockett, Elizabeth N.
223
Crockett, Emily 599
Crockett, Frank 599
Crockett, George 601
Crockett, Laura 599
Crockett, Mary E. 603
Crockett, Milton 599
Crockett, Nelson 599,
601
Crockett, Oliver A. 599
Croft, Elizabeth 225
Croft, George 329
Croft, Henry 292
Croft, John 325
Croghan, William 236
Cromwell, John 518
Crone, Susanna 191
Cronice, Ann 504
Cronice, Anna 506
Cronice, Frederick 504,
506
Croninger, Mary 471
Cronkleton, Ann 193, 388
Cronkleton, Elizabeth
193, 388
Cronkleton, Elizabeth
Craig 383
Cronkleton, Jane 388
Cronkleton, John 193,
388
Cronkleton, Joseph 193,
386, 388
Cronkleton, Joseph (Jr.)
383
Cronkleton, Joseph (Sr.)
383
Cronkleton, Margaret 388
Cronkleton, Margarette
193
Cronkleton, Mary 193,
388
Cronkleton, Robert 193,
388
Cronkleton, Samuel 193,
388
Cronkleton, William 193,
388
Crook, John 408
Crook, Martha 631

Crook, William J. 636
Crook, Wm. 439
Crookham, John 662
Crooks, --- 243
Crooks, Amy 160
Crooks, Delilah 172
Crooks, Elizabeth 163
Crooks, Henry 544, 547
Crooks, Johmas 58
Crooks, Margaret 166
Crooks, Maria 452
Crooks, Mary 160
Crooks, William 142, 153
Crookshanks, Elizabeth
391
Croper, Isaac 596
Cropper, Hancy 5
Cropper, Handy 42
Cropper, John 5
Cropper, Major V. 5
Crosby, Cynthia 77
Crosby, E. 447
Crosby, G. P. 601
Crosby, John 644
Crosby, John C. 601
Crosby, Juenia E. 133
Crosby, Julia 334
Crosby, William 9
Croser, Susannah 302
Crosier, Christopher 615
Crosley, Cynthia 77
Crosley, John (Jr.) 513
Crosley, Joseph 65, 571
Crosley, Polly 571
Crosly, Mary 184
Cross, Alphews 84
Cross, Ann 437
Cross, Anna 588
Cross, Catharine 133
Cross, Catherine 290
Cross, Daniel D. 81
Cross, David 219
Cross, Deborah 590
Cross, Eleanor 290
Cross, Experience 82
Cross, John 292
Cross, Jos. 133
Cross, Martha 133
Cross, Mary 303
Cross, Matilda 534
Cross, Philinda 590
Cross, Rhoda W. 219
Cross, Sarah 292, 590
Cross, Thomas 292
Crossan, Mary Ann 590
Crossan, Polly 408
Crossen, Edward 262
Crosser, Adam 292
Crosser, Daniel 580
Crosser, James 292
Crossin, Wm. R. 408
Crossland, Cyrus 378
Crossley, Huldah 50
Crossley, Robert 182
Crosson, Edward (Jr.)
269
Crothers, Catharine 626
Crothers, James 443,
444, 626

Crothers, John 631
Crouch, Amy 666
Crouch, Daniel M. 328
Crouch, Joseph 666
Crouch, Robert 328
Crouse, Jacob 542
Crouse, John 269
Crouse, Leah 288
Crouser, John 268
Crouser, Margaret 268,
275
Crow, Abraham 292
Crow, Butler 486
Crow, Daniel 320
Crow, Elizabeth 320,
610, 657, 682
Crow, Frederick 320
Crow, Irial 610
Crow, Isaac 655
Crow, Jacob 587
Crow, James 292
Crow, John 474, 682
Crow, Joseph 189
Crow, Margaret 610
Crow, Mary 487
Crow, Mary R. 189
Crow, Mathias 559
Crow, Matthias 508
Crow, Richard 100
Crow, Robert 682
Crow, Samuel 682
Crow, Sarah 189, 320,
590, 682
Crow, Susanah 189
Crow, Thomas 610
Crow, William 328, 483,
682
Crowder, Elizabeth 195
Crowder, Harbert 195
Crowder, John 195
Crowder, Mark 195
Crowder, Martha 195
Crowder, Mary 195
Crowder, Nancy 195
Crowder, Nathaniel 195
Crowder, Thomas 503
Crowder, William 195
Crowell, John 530
Crowell, Joseph 366
Crowl, Elizabeth 532
Crowl, George 292
Crowl, Jacob 292
Crowl, Peggy 294
Crowl, Rosana 297
Crowley, John 315, 316
Crowser, Elizabeth 276
Croy, Benjamin 118
Croy, Jacob 530
Croy, John 542
Croy, Mary 310
Croy, Richard 542
Croy, Sarah 309
Crozer, Anne 114
Crozer, Joshua 114
Crozer, Samuel 114
Crozer, Sarah 114
Crozer, Susannah 310
Crozer, Thomas 114
Crozier, James 97, 114

Davis, Catharine 213, 417, 530, 560
Davis, Charity 655
Davis, Charles 461
Davis, Charles M. 395
Davis, Christena 682
Davis, Cornelius 73
Davis, Daniel 138, 140, 141, 157, 169, 371, 443, 450, 580, 652
Davis, Daniel R. 368
Davis, David 682, 724
Davis, David D. 659
Davis, Dorcas 630
Davis, Edward 465
Davis, Eleanor 166
Davis, Eli 164, 292
Davis, Elijah 587
Davis, Eliza 618
Davis, Elizabeth 165, 278, 291, 296, 299, 460, 521, 522, 581, 590, 625
Davis, Elnor E. 74
Davis, Esther 140, 444
Davis, Evan J. 660
Davis, Fanny 609
Davis, George 688
Davis, Gitta 182
Davis, Hannah 276, 302, 462, 466, 505, 521
Davis, Harmen 614
Davis, Harriett J. 473
Davis, Henry 278, 284, 401, 461
Davis, Hiram 378
Davis, Isaac 309
Davis, Isabella 519
Davis, J. 73
Davis, Jabez 550
Davis, Jacob 444, 457, 524
Davis, James 29, 141, 210, 258, 278, 367, 387, 465, 580, 662, 728, 746
Davis, James L. 134
Davis, James N. 454
Davis, Jane 526
Davis, Jane D. 666
Davis, Japheth 530
Davis, Jehu 292
Davis, Joana 468
Davis, John 4, 7, 9, 27, 105, 164, 194, 278, 292, 322, 326, 408, 415, 428, 444, 461, 524, 605, 662, 666
Davis, John B. 660
Davis, John F. 597
Davis, John G. 587, 661
Davis, John M. 503
Davis, John W. 378
Davis, Jonathan 217, 504
Davis, Jos. G. 551
Davis, Joseph 292, 318, 530, 704
Davis, Joshua 238
Davis, Josiah 4

Davis, Katherine 467
Davis, Lettia 213
Davis, Lewis 213, 609, 666
Davis, Lucy 165, 629
Davis, Luther 656
Davis, Malinda 450
Davis, Margaret 73, 138, 141, 274, 292, 650, 656
Davis, Martha 614
Davis, Martha P. 620
Davis, Mary 73, 134, 392, 415, 469, 527, 592, 666
Davis, Mary C. 660
Davis, Mary E. 401
Davis, Matilda 78, 171
Davis, Mercy 213
Davis, Mesheck 134
Davis, Michael 156
Davis, Mildred 454
Davis, Modaline 626
Davis, Morgan 660
Davis, Moses 114, 626
Davis, Nancy 136, 226, 465, 475, 626
Davis, Nathan 292
Davis, Nehemiah 84
Davis, Nelly 407
Davis, Nicholas 597
Davis, Owen 213, 662
Davis, Peggy 194
Davis, Peter 560
Davis, Phebe 197, 527
Davis, Pheby 308
Davis, Polly 278, 518
Davis, Rachel 173
Davis, Rachell 156
Davis, Rebeca Ann 100
Davis, Rebecca 194
Davis, Rebecca B. 587
Davis, Rhoda 475
Davis, Robert 292, 572
Davis, Robert F. 714
Davis, Ruana 194
Davis, Sally 156
Davis, Samuel 138, 140, 141, 157, 164, 194, 278, 659, 660, 666
Davis, Samuel (Jr.) 149
Davis, Samuel W. 569, 572
Davis, Sanford 745
Davis, Sarah 125, 163, 270, 278, 464, 524, 603, 650, 660
Davis, Sarah Ann 632
Davis, Seth L. 631
Davis, Sidney 518
Davis, Solomon 650
Davis, Stephen 556, 559
Davis, Susan 136
Davis, Susanna 105
Davis, Tarlton 609
Davis, Thomas 125, 137, 324, 327, 524, 626
Davis, Thornton 618
Davis, Thos. 415

Davis, Turner 9
Davis, Vincent 164
Davis, William 156, 194, 278, 292, 327, 333, 597, 626, 656
Davis, William W. (Rev.) 616
Davis, Wilson A. 450
Davis, Wm. 38, 447
Davis, Wm. L. 422
Davis, Youphamy 4
Davis, Zacariah 704
Davis, Zachariah 712, 713
Davis, Zarobabee 457
Davis, Zorababel 444
Davison, Abednego 211
Davison, Ann 266
Davison, Benjamin 61
Davison, Carahnis 197
Davison, Charity 197
Davison, David 636
Davison, Elizabeth 636
Davison, Frances 636
Davison, Francis 636
Davison, Hamilton 95
Davison, Hannah 462
Davison, Isaac 185
Davison, Jacob C. 197
Davison, James 185, 238
Davison, John 535
Davison, Levi 636, 638
Davison, Mary 185
Davison, Nancy 390
Davison, Perry 636
Davison, Rachel 381
Davison, Robert 735
Davison, Samuel 197
Davison, Thomas 185
Davison, William 636
Davison, Zachariah 636
Davison, Zachariah (Jr.) 636
Davisson, Andrew 519
Davisson, Elizabeth 208
Davisson, Isaac 709
Davisson, James 55, 85, 458
Davisson, John 709
Davisson, Joseph 709
Davisson, Josiah 504
Davisson, Margaret 458
Davisson, Mary 458, 533
Davisson, William W. 718
Davoius, Francis 489, 494
Davors, Francis 482
Davouis, Francis 497
Dawes, William 81
Dawkins, William 662
Dawley, Anna 77, 81
Dawley, Nathan 77, 81
Dawson, Ann 444
Dawson, Bendaa 462
Dawson, Benjamin 453
Dawson, Charoline A. 453
Dawson, Cinderilla 631
Dawson, David 644
Dawson, Delilah 81

806

Delong, Columbus S. 601
Delong, Isaac 666, 717
Delong, James 543
Delong, James (Jr.) 548
Delong, John 309, 421, 424, 545, 546
Delong, John (Jr.) 547
Delong, Josiah 63
Delong, Thomas 547
Delow, Elizabeth 554
Delow, Fredereck 554
Delp, Rebecca 348
Delrein, J. H. 44
Delsover, George 405
Delsover, John 410
Delsover, Mary Ann 405, 410
Deman, Mathias 750
Demas, Rachael 630
Dement, James 48
Demest, Henry 106
Demick, Ebenezer 108
Demint, James 209
Demint, Jesse 209
Demint, Nancy 224
Demintt, James 569
Demmick, Daniel 697
Demming, Job 39
Demos, John 239
Demoss, Martha 162
Demoss, Mary 630
Demoss, Peter F. 95
Demoss, Rebecca 627
Demoss, Sarah 626
Demp, Barbera 135
Dempsey, Andrew 717, 721
Deneen, Ann 164
Deneen, Betsey 168
Deneen, Elizabeth 133
Deneen, Esther 133
Deneen, Jas. 133
Deneen, John 164
Denham, Elizabeth 464
Denham, James 223, 239
Denham, Mary 238
Denham, Obed 238, 239
Denham, Sally 481
Denham, William 238
Denison, Agnis 56
Denison, James 56
Denison, James (Jr.) 56
Denison, Margaret 610
Denison, Martha 56
Denison, Thomas 610
Deniston, Alexander 442
Denlap, John 315
Denman, Betsey 167
Denman, David 555
Denman, Electa 698
Denman, Elizabeth 158
Denman, Jonathan 698
Denman, Joseph 697, 698
Denman, Lydia 698
Denman, Margaret 698
Denman, Mathias 566, 573, 750
Denman, Matthias 564, 567, 568
Denman, Moses 158

Denman, Nathl. 558, 559
Denman, Phebe 698
Denman, Prudence 698
Denman, Rachel 168, 698
Denman, Samuel 568
Denman, Sarah 698
Denman, Susanna 558
Denman, Uriah 697
Denman, William 698
Denman, Wm. 158
Denmann, Matthias 561
Denmann, Phebe 561
Denner, Elizabeth 352
Denney, John 100
Dennick, Daniel 408
Dennis, Becky 9
Dennis, C. 135
Dennis, Elizabeth 129
Dennis, John 129
Dennis, Joseph 81, 547
Dennis, Margaret 135
Dennis, Nancy 11
Dennis, Samuel 547
Dennison, Aurelia 99
Dennison, Henry 547, 551
Dennison, Julia 100
Denny, Emily 269
Denny, Heathy 526
Denny, James 203
Denny, Jorden 100
Denny, Margaret 519
Denny, Mary 150
Denny, Priscilla 464
Denny, Robert 150
Denny, Susanna 476
Denny, Walter 13
Denquinn, Elizabeth 408
Dent, Isaiah 624
Denton, John 73
Denwedie, Margaret 588
Denwidie, Sarah Ann 591
Deny, Elizabeth 226
Deorth, Randolph 422
Depery, Isaac 452
Depew, James 547
Depew, Nancy 468
Deph, Sarah 579
Dephenbaugh, Katherine 585
Deppore, August 356
Derbin, Baptist 117
Derbin, Samuel 408
Derby, Nancy 656
Derby, Rosewell 402
Derickson, Mary Ann 419
Derough, Blancy 520
Derr, Mary 305
Derren, John 221
Derringer, Catharine 591
Derrow, Sarah 154
Derrow, William 154
Deryimer, Christiana 604
Desavour, John 408
Deshler, Christopher 77
Dessel, Gertrude 669
DesNoyers, Peter John 490, 491
Deterecht, Anna Margaret 291

Deterly, Jacob 575
Detty, Elsy 656
Deu, Anthony Bartholomew 492
Deuy, Sally 476
Devacht, F. J. W. 489
Devacht, Fran. Jos. Win. 488
Devacht, Francis Joseph Winox 488, 489, 490, 492, 497
Devacht, Jeanne Francoise 488, 489, 493, 497
Devacht, Joseph W. 498
Devacht, W. 485
Devall, Elizabeth 411
Devalt, Abraham 626
Devault, Nicholas 458
Devault, Noah 465
Devault, Rebecca 631
Develer, Susanna 439
Devenney, David 737
Dever, Abraham 55, 113
Dever, Alexander 113
Dever, David 113
Dever, David H. 55
Dever, Elizabeth 55
Dever, Evan 55
Dever, George 113
Dever, James 113, 666
Dever, James B. 55
Dever, Jane 113
Dever, John 113
Dever, John (Sr.) 113
Dever, John J. 55
Dever, Jonathan 113
Dever, Jonathan T. 55
Dever, Louisa 55
Dever, Lucinda 55
Dever, Mariah 55
Dever, Mary 55
Dever, Polly 656
Dever, William 113
Dever, William S. 55
Deverbaugh, Susannah 289
Devere, Peggy 657
Devilbis, Levi 506
Devilbis, Sarah 506
Devilbliss, Levi 504
Devilbliss, Sarah 504
Devin, Jessa 374
Devinney, David 737
Devinney, Jane 479
Devolt, Nancy 53
Devor, James 363, 366
Devor, John 361, 362, 363, 368
Devore, Benjamin 77
Devore, Elizabeth 164
Devore, Eve 519
Devore, Felix 49, 52
Devore, James 182
Devore, Mary 521
Dew, Anna 76
Dew, David 549
Dew, Samuel 443
Dewees, Samuel 742
Dewees, Wm. 749
Deweese, Henry 87

Deweese, Mary 167
Deweese, Rachel 87
Deweese, Samuel 87, 742
Deweese, Wm. 747
Dewerge, Francis 20
Dewey, Elizabeth 54
Dewey, Justin 390
Dewit, Daniel 514
Dewit, Elasha 499
Dewit, Elisha 514, 524
Dewit, Elizabeth 514,
582
Dewit, Fields 514
Dewit, Isaac 514
Dewit, Jacob 152
Dewit, Joseph 579, 582
Dewit, Mercer 514
Dewit, Mercy 514
Dewit, Nancy 499, 514
Dewit, Peter 514
Dewit, Pracella 514
Dewit, Rachael 514
Dewit, Sarah 579
Dewit, Squire 514
Dewit, Zachariah P. 152
Dewitt, Adaline 580
Dewitt, Barney 698
Dewitt, Daniel 530
Dewitt, Elizabeth 133
Dewitt, Henry 445
Dewitt, James 77
Dewitt, John 445
Dewitt, Mary A. 133
Dewitt, Peter 238, 508
Dewitt, W. R. 133
Dexter, Betsey 559, 561
Dexter, Eliza 643
Dexter, Ellen Evans 643
Dexter, John L. 643
Dexter, John Luiger 643
Dexter, John P. 643
Dexter, John Pearce 643
DeCamp, Job 361, 562,
727, 730
DeCamp, Mary 562
DeFestard, Adrun 478
DeHoff, George 292
DeHoff, John 292
DeKuyper, Atto 153
DeLong, John 292
DeLong, Samuel D. 628
DeWalt, Catharine 693
DeWalt, Christiann 693
DeWalt, George 693
DeWalt, Philip 693
DeWitt, Ruth 222
D'Hebbercourt, Francis
496
D'Hebecourt, --- 489,
490
D'Hebecourt, Francis 28,
29, 32, 488, 491, 497
D'Hebercourt, Francis
496
D'Herbecourt, Francis 31
Dick, Betsey 173
Dick, Campbell G. 6
Dick, Charles 408
Dick, S. 132

Dick, Samuel 132, 138,
139, 142, 145, 146,
553, 557, 572
Dick, Samuel (Jr.) 128
Dick, Thomas 15
Dickenson, Elisha 223
Dickenson, Thomas 738
Dicker, Mathilda Sophia
102
Dickerson, Archer 569
Dickerson, Catherine 464
Dickerson, Frederick 541
Dickerson, John 105
Dickerson, Lydia 659
Dickerson, William 566,
569
Dickey, D. L. 669
Dickey, Ebenezer 146
Dickey, George 146
Dickey, Hugh 510
Dickey, Isaac 146, 155
Dickey, James 146, 147
Dickey, John 56, 77
Dickey, Kezia 146
Dickey, M. M. 669
Dickey, Margaret 146
Dickey, Margaret J. 669
Dickey, Mary 78, 146,
152
Dickey, Nancy 146
Dickey, Patrick 558, 559
Dickey, Peggy 559
Dickey, Robt. 236
Dickey, Samuel 139,
140, 146, 152, 155
Dickey, Sarah 146
Dickey, William (Rev.)
449
Dickey, Wm. Patrick 554
Dickins, Tabitha 466
Dickinson, Elenor 460
Dickinson, Harlon 727
Dickinson, Louisa 727
Dickinson, Lydia 727
Dickinson, Mary 288
Dickinson, Oliver 727
Dickinson, Oliver C. 727
Dickinson, Sarah A. 381
Dicks, John 597
Dicks, Sarah 288
Dickson, Abraham 662
Dickson, Betsy 185
Dickson, David 431
Dickson, Elizabeth 100
Dickson, Jane 185
Dickson, John 142, 185
Dickson, Maria 101
Dickson, Mary 101
Dickson, Platt B. 175
Dickson, Polly 185
Dickson, Robert 185
Dickson, Thompson 185
Dickson, William 185
Didot, John Nicholas 356
Diduit, W. 28
Diebl, Charles 292
Diegeldeyn, Elisabeth
347
Diesinger, Gottleib 359

Dieter, F. 346
Diether, Barnhardt 340
Diether, Carolina 341
Diether, Christina 340
Diether, Friedrich 341
Diether, Friedrika 344
Diether, Karl Franz 340
Diether, Regina
Christina Lidia 341
Diggin, Basel 474
Dill, Andrew 666
Dill, Elisabeth 529
Dill, Elizabeth 641
Dill, John 560, 565,
575, 641
Dille, Cephas 588
Dille, Deborah 594
Dille, Martha 590
Dille, Sarah 536
Dillen, Elizabeth 295
Dilley, Abraham 547
Dilley, Anny 705
Dilley, Elizabeth 703
Dilley, Peninah 704
Dilley, Robert 546
Dillihan, John 292
Dilling, Jacob 47
Dillinger, Mathias 73
Dillinger, Thomas 73
Dillon, Abigail 283
Dillon, Absalom 278
Dillon, Achsah 283
Dillon, Andrew 137
Dillon, Anna 324
Dillon, Betty 281
Dillon, Daniel 278, 281
Dillon, Elizabeth 137,
168, 308, 311
Dillon, Hannah 278, 283
Dillon, Hn. 278
Dillon, Israel 692
Dillon, James 278, 292,
683
Dillon, Jane 274
Dillon, Jesse 283
Dillon, Jno. 745
Dillon, John 278, 324,
379, 749
Dillon, Jonathan 283
Dillon, Josiah 105, 113
Dillon, Luke 283
Dillon, Lydia 278
Dillon, Malon 278
Dillon, Martha 283
Dillon, Mary 278, 324,
692
Dillon, Micajah 716
Dillon, Phebe 278
Dillon, Samuel 137
Dillon, Sarah 283
Dillon, Simon 324
Dillon, Susanna 307
Dillon, Susannah 283,
307
Dillon, Thomas 137,
324, 420
Dillon, William 256,
274, 278, 281
Dillow, Frederick 52

Donavan, Martha 192
Donavan, Robert 192, 203
Donavan, Sarah 192
Donavan, William 192
Donaven, Thomas 204
Done, Ann 407
Done, Phebe 286
Doner, Abreham 98
Donham, Abel 238
Donham, John 236
Donham, Nathl. 233
Donham, Robert 236
Donhan, Abel 236
Donine, Jacob C. 731
Donley, Catharine 134
Donley, Eliza 626
Donley, Levi 379
Donley, Michl. 134
Donley, Ruth 379
Donley, Steven 134
Donly, Ann 630
Donnallan, Ann Mariah 195
Donnallan, Benjamin 195
Donnallan, Edmund 195
Donnallan, Edward 195
Donnallan, Elizabeth 195
Donnallan, Hester 195
Donnallan, John 195
Donnallan, Mary 195
Donnallan, Nelson 195
Donnallan, Thomas 195
Donnallan, William 195
Donnally, Andrew 486, 666
Donnally, Hugh 662
Donnally, John 486
Donnehue, Nance 11
Donnel, Jonathan 519
Donnell, James 217
Donnesburg, Catharine 89
Donovan, Sarah 226
Donoven, Solomon 55
Doolittle, Benjamin 207
Doolittle, Cynthia 707
Doolittle, Jas. 691
Doolittle, Thos. 691
Dooly, Thomas 355
Dooney, Jacob 438
Door, Alesander 37
Door, Valentine 71
Dooup, Jacob (Rev.) 263
Dorakon, Elizabeth 603
Doran, Leuira 245
Doran, M. J. 245
Doran, T. W. 245
Doremus, Lydia C. 602
Dorman, Elias 636
Dorman, Elizabeth 626
Dorman, Hugh 743
Dorman, James D. 626
Dorman, John 609, 636, 743
Dorman, Leanah 636
Dorman, Milley 631
Dorman, William 636
Doron, Mary Jane 448
Dorr, Alexander 39
Dorr, Edmond 85
Dorr, Edmund 85

Dorr, Elizabeth 134
Dorr, Elizabetha 340
Dorr, Jacob 340
Dorr, Ruban Homart 340
Dorrel, Mary 242
Dorrel, William 242
Dorris, Mary 73
Dorsey, David 585, 586
Dorsey, James M. 744
Dorsey, William 580
Dorsten, Mariah Anna Franzisca 102
Dorston, John Henry 100
Doster, Lewis 465
Dotson, Pillettia 589
Dotson, Potite 589
Doty, Abraham 700
Doty, Ann 698
Doty, Betsy 135
Doty, Daniel 135, 140, 141, 175
Doty, Elizabeth 698
Doty, Esther 698
Doty, Frazy 367
Doty, Jemima 518
Doty, Jeremiah 698
Doty, John 698
Doty, Joseph 135
Doty, Margaret 149
Doty, Mary 169
Doty, Polly 698
Doty, Reuben 160
Doty, Saml. 638
Doty, Samuel 698
Doty, Sarah 698
Doty, William 149
Dotz, Maria 343
Doud, David 733
Doud, Nancy 733
Doudney, John 104, 119
Dougan, Mariah 464
Dougherty, --- (Capt.) 362
Dougherty, A. 109
Dougherty, Alexander 109
Dougherty, Andrew 109
Dougherty, Andrew (Jr.) 109
Dougherty, Barnard 217
Dougherty, Catherine 217
Dougherty, Daniel 217
Dougherty, Danl. 223
Dougherty, Elizabeth 217, 472
Dougherty, George 109
Dougherty, Hannah 272
Dougherty, Henry 115
Dougherty, James 217
Dougherty, Jane 109, 217
Dougherty, John 109, 185, 217, 577
Dougherty, Margaret 109
Dougherty, Mary 217
Dougherty, Michael 217
Dougherty, Nancy 217
Dougherty, Patrick 217
Dougherty, Rebecca 109
Dougherty, William 185, 217

Dougherty, Young 109
Doughlas, Preston 194
Doughman, Stephen 333
Douglas, Charles 230
Douglas, David 524, 548, 549
Douglas, Diana 681
Douglas, Hester 579
Douglas, James 401
Douglas, Jane 82
Douglas, Samuel 547, 575, 681
Douglas, Scott 616
Douglas, William 546
Douglas, Wm. H. 422
Douglass, Aaron (Capt.) 687
Douglass, Absalom 256
Douglass, Adam 22
Douglass, Ann 136
Douglass, Catharine 194
Douglass, David 194, 503, 504, 548
Douglass, Elihu 194
Douglass, Elizabeth 194
Douglass, J. S. 400
Douglass, James 189, 364, 400, 401
Douglass, Jas. S. 136
Douglass, Margaret 300
Douglass, Mary 194
Douglass, Samuel 549
Douglass, Sarah 194
Douglass, William 687
Dougless, Wm. 130, 136
Dougless, William 185
Douss, Jacob (Rev.) 263
Douston, John V. 751
Douston, Rebecca 469
Doute, Levina 99
Douthet, Harriet 657
Douvemire, Peter 420
Dove, Elijah 415
Dovenberger, Jacob 115
Dovenberger, John 115
Dovenberger, Margaret 115
Dovenberger, Mary 115
Dover, Mary 94
Dow, James 642
Dow, N. T. 643
Dow, Virgil M. 692
Dowas, Sarah 275
Dowd, Alexander 626
Dowd, Jesse 81
Dowden, Archibald 192
Dowenn, Jacob 601
Dowler, Thomas 372
Dowling, Susan 50
Downand, Latrenna 290
Downard, John 293
Downey, Andrew 524
Downey, James 514
Downey, John 530
Downey, Nancy 531
Downey, Peggy 729
Downey, Thomas 729
Downey, Walter 545
Downing, J. B. 45
Downing, Jane 602

811

Downing, Polly 278
Downing, Sally 173
Downing, Susannah 307
Downs, Benjamin 211
Downs, Daniel 196
Downs, Joseph 201
Downs, Nancy 295
Downy, Polly 525
Dowty, Margaret 148
Dowty, Reuben 148
Doyal, Sophia 185
Doyl, James 1
Doyle, James 48
Doyle, John G. 640
Doyle, Margaret 559
Doyle, Thomas 185, 206, 553, 559
Dozer, James 33, 47
Drace, Peter 454
Draganfuller, Wilhelmine 102
Draggue, Andrew 9
Dragoo, Andrew 248
Dragoo, B. 42
Dragoo, Belteshazer 29
Dragoo, Polly 248
Draher, Catharine 300
Drahman, John Henry 100
Drais, Henry 448
Drake, Belinda 629
Drake, Catharine 221
Drake, Daniel 73
Drake, David 548, 549
Drake, Elisha F. 473
Drake, Ellen 225
Drake, Hannay 124
Drake, Jacob 221, 383
Drake, Joel 169
Drake, John 174
Drake, Joseph 580
Drake, Lemuel F. 642
Drake, Lovina 581
Drake, Lucy 480
Drake, Mary 174
Drake, Peter 556
Drake, Rachel 531
Drake, Richard 524
Drake, Thed. 640
Drake, Thomas 530, 745
Drake, William 160, 565
Drake, Wm. 408, 420
Draper, Catharine 83
Draper, Clarisa 654
Draper, Edward 530
Draper, Hannah 268, 276
Draper, Isaac 588, 702
Draper, J. 250
Draper, Jacob 698, 700
Draper, Jean 460
Draper, John 465
Draper, R. 250
Draper, Rebecca A. 250
Draper, Sarah 592
Draper, Simson 465
Draper, Thomas 268, 270, 285
Drees, John Michael 100
Drennen, Eugene James Alex. 669

Drennen, Genetta Ezilbella 669
Drennen, Isabella 669
Drennen, J. H. 669
Drennen, James 669
Drennen, James H. 669
Drennen, Jane 669
Drennen, Lycurgas John Clark 669
Drennen, Margaritta 669
Drennen, Mary 669
Drennen, Miney Lawretta 669
Drennen, Peter Ross Jefferson 669
Drenning, Elizabeth 382
Dresse, Richard 100
Drew, Abner 223
Drew, Mary G. 756
Drew, W. C. 756
Drew, William 726
Drew, William C. 756
Drewyer, Simon 704
Driggs, George 81
Driggs, Seth 81
Driscal, Margaret 523
Driscal, Rachel 523, 529
Driscol, John 223
Driscoll, Clara Belle 251
Driscoll, E. 251
Driscoll, Eliza Ann 251
Driscoll, J. B. 251
Driscoll, John 251
Driscoll, Joseph William 251
Driskall, John 524
Driskell, William 293
Driskil, Ann 526
Driskill, Catherine 613
Driskill, Denis 293
Driskill, Elizabeth 295
Driskill, John 613
Dritre, John 374
Driver, Catharine 149
Driver, Emarilla 401
Driver, James E. 401
Driver, Joshua 400
Driver, William 149
Drollinger, Hannah 169
Drollinger, Philip 147
Dromgoole, Edward 519
Droudt, Maria 345
Drouillard, Joseph 704
Droz, Peter 483, 489, 496
Droz, Sophia 483
Drum, Chas. D. 423
Drum, Jane Wilson 423
Drum, Mary 411
Drumm, Wm. 746
Drummond, Sarah 226
Druna, Margaret 418
Drury, Isaiah 404
Drury, James H. 724
Drury, Jemima 679
Drury, Marshall 679
Drury, Sallie 649
Drury, Samuel 408

Drury, Sarah 405
Drybread, Hannah 163
Drybread, Joseph 164
Drybread, Margaret 161
Drybread, Sarah 160
Dryden, Isaac 5, 45
Dryden, Isaac N. 43
Dryden, Lemuel 43
Dryden, Martha 43
Dryden, Nancy Jane 43
Dryden, Samuel 1
Dryden, Thos. G. 42, 45
Dryden, W. H. 42
Dryden, William 1
Dryden, Wm. 42
Dryden, Wm. H. 45
Dryden, Wm. H. C. 45
Drydin, Wm. 5
Dryer, James 132
Dubal, William 580
Dubble, Henry 421, 426
Dubble, Margaret M. 426
Dubler, Mary 407
Dubois, Daniel 140
Dubois, Frances Maria 53
Duc, Anthony Bartholomew 489, 490, 492, 497
Ducenbury, Nathaniel 626
Duck, Elizabeth 292
Ducker, Samuel 333
Ducks, George 293
Duckwall, Frederick 270
Duckwall, Lewis 620
Duckwall, Sally 617
Duckwall, Samuel 620
Duckwall, Susan 620
Duckworth, James 740
Dudder, Jane 77
Duddleston, Catharin 333
Dudiet, William 488
Dudleson, James 580
Dudley, Elizabeth 661
Dudley, William S. 624
Duduit, William 488
Due, Charity 408
Duer, Joh 203
Duff, David 547
Duff, David (Jr.) 549
Duff, James 548
Duff, John 549
Duff, Oliver 550
Duffee, James 164
Duffie, Daniel 552
Duffy, Daniel 81, 553
Duffy, James 293
Duffy, Leuis 521
Dufler, Barbara 344
Dugalles, John 293
Dugan, James 364, 542
Dugan, Jane 364, 404
Dugan, Polly 215
Dugan, Ross 364
Dugan, Thomas 572
Dugan, William 364
Dugbee, Andrew G. 207
Duggin, Joseph 236
Dugles, Sectoque 9
Duhurst, Mary Ann 633
Duke, Bazil 27

Dukeman, Stephen 333
Dukes, John 580
Dulcher, Freelove 83
Dulin, Sanford 580
Dull, David 551
Dulty, John 542
Dum, J. I. 127
Dum, Lydia 127
Dumbroff, Michael 59, 65
Dument, James 569
Dun, Sarah 700
Dunbar, Charles D. 429
Dunbar, George 465
Dunbar, Isabella 6
Dunbar, James 6
Dunbar, Mary Ann 583
Dunbar, W. F. 44
Dun Barr, James 700
Dunbaugh, Jacob 77, 85
Dunbaugh, Polly 82, 85
Duncan, Amos 519
Duncan, David 572
Duncan, Elizabeth 319
Duncan, Isabella 319
Duncan, James 175, 423
Duncan, John 333, 389
Duncan, Mariah 470
Duncan, Mary 75, 389
Duncan, Mary Jane 319
Duncan, Matthew 319
Duncan, Samuel 319
Dungan, Benjamin 141, 164
Dungan, James 423
Dungan, John 141
Dungan, Sarah 463
Dunham, Abel 238
Dunham, Amos 223
Dunham, John 239
Dunham, Jonathan 588
Dunham, Stephen 662
Dunkel, Elizabeth 421
Dunkel, William 704
Dunkelberger, Daniel 379
Dunkell, Catharine 78
Dunkell, Mary 80
Dunket, Margaret 78
Dunkin, Amos 5
Dunkin, Hercules 43
Dunkle, George 448, 641
Dunkle, K. H. 641
Dunkle, Leah 629
Dunkle, Phebe 633
Dunkle, Polly 82
Dunkle, Rachael 628
Dunkle, Saville 632
Dunkreeg, Elizabeth 270
Dunlap, Adam 597
Dunlap, Alexander 29, 201
Dunlap, Catharine 325
Dunlap, Emely 265
Dunlap, George 45
Dunlap, Henry 325
Dunlap, James 184, 186, 524, 687, 752
Dunlap, Jane 753
Dunlap, Jane Maria 535
Dunlap, John 315, 325, 715

Dunlap, John F. 384
Dunlap, John R. 265
Dunlap, Joseph 363
Dunlap, Lewis 325
Dunlap, Milly 190
Dunlap, Rachael 289
Dunlap, Robert 747
Dunlap, Samuel 687, 752, 753
Dunlap, Sarah 475
Dunlap, Sarah Ann 325
Dunlap, William 9, 39, 46, 186, 325
Dunlap, Wm. 35, 38, 45, 46
Dunlavay, Jno. 10
Dunlavey, Antony 35
Dunlavy, Francis 240
Dunlavy, Jno. 10, 11, 12
Dunlavy, John 9, 10, 12
Dunleavy, Francis 564
Dunleavy, Jno. 9, 11
Dunmire, Katherine 385
Dunn, A. 654
Dunn, Abner N. 23
Dunn, Ann 407
Dunn, Armstrong 704
Dunn, Dennis 519
Dunn, Emilim 333
Dunn, George 265
Dunn, Henry 121
Dunn, James 127, 137, 139, 147, 164
Dunn, John 130, 156, 160, 511, 516
Dunn, M. 654
Dunn, Margaret 654
Dunn, Mary 127
Dunn, Milley 123
Dunn, Simeon 500, 511, 524
Dunn, Sophia 500
Dunn, Thomas (Rev.) 322
Dunn, Walter 203
Dunn Barr, James 700
Dunreth, David 5
Dunreth, James W. 5
Dunreth, Robert 5
Dunseth, Andrew 561
Dunwiddie, Polly 519
Dunwiddy, Nancy 522
Dunwitt, Ezekiel 239
Dunwoody, William 169
Duple, Catharine 625
Dupler, Elizabeth 626, 629
Dupler, John 626
Dupont, Guy Soussigne Marin 483
Duport, Marin 490, 497
Duport, Marion 496
Durbin, James 699
Durbin, John 699
Durbin, Rebecca 699
Durbin, Samuel 699
Durbin, Sarah 602
Durbin, Scott 699
Durbin, Thomas 699
Durbin, Thomas W. (Jr.) 601

Durbin, Thos. 686
Durbin, William 601
Durden, Polly 165
Durgman, Anny 190
Durgman, Margery 190
Durham, Jane 241
Durham, Joseph 241
Durham, Rachael 602
Durlin, Mary 224
Durnbaugh, Elizabeth 507
Durnbaugh, Samuel 507
Durrant, John 680
Durrant, Nathan 680
Durst, Benjamin 478
Durst, Christina 481
Dusenberry, Nathan 626
Duserge, Francis 20
Dush, Adam 752, 757
Dush, Adam (Jr.) 757
Dush, Eliza 757
Dush, John 752, 757
Dush, Rachel 757
Dush, Susannah 752
Duskey, Dennis 561
Duskey, Elis 561
Duskey, Rachel 561
Dusouchet, Francis 540
Dustin, Nathan 386
Dustine, Catherine 377
Dustman, Salome 431
Dutchell, --- 722
Dutcher, Elias 632
Dutchos, Oswald 293
Dutiel, Francis Charles 491
Dutr . . . , Dan 373
Dutre, G. 373
Dutre, M . . . 374
Dutri, Be . . . 374
Dutro, Be . . . 374
Dutro, John 374
Dutro, M . . . 374
Dutro, Mary 296
Dutton, Jonathan 64
Dutton, Kinsman 81
Dutton, Margaret 415
Dutton, Mary Lizzie 669
Dutton, Samuel 81
Dutwiler, E. A. 425
Dutwiler, Eli 425
Duty, Zina 169
Duvall, Eleanor 168
Duvall, John 613
Duvall, Josiah M. 612
Duvall, Polly 167
Duvall, Prissella 408
Duvall, Rebeckah 183
Duvarge, Francis 28
Duzan, Abraham 3
Dwiggins, James 544
Dwiggins, Joseph 461
Dwiggins, Robert 279, 285
Dwiggins, Sarah 283
Dwire, John 691
Dwire, Sarah 691
Dwyer, Mary 617
Dye, Achsa 299
Dye, Harrison 465

Ekert, Heinrich 337
Ekert, Katharina 337
Elam, Josiah 515
Elam, Susannah 523
Elanson, Elizabeth 530
Elbert, John D. (Jr.) 197
Elder, Ann 527
Elder, Charles F. 216
Elder, Jeremiah 580
Elder, John 324, 602, 690
Elder, John W. 584
Elder, Leve Maria 344
Elder, Margaret 690
Elder, Margret 405
Elder, Mary Ann 584
Elder, Mathew 293
Elder, Robert 666
Elder, Samuel 344
Elder, Sarah 584
Elder, Susannah 216
Elder, Thomas 223, 690
Elder, Thos. (Jr.) 690
Elder, Thos. (Sr.) 690
Eldredge, Polly 638
Eldridge, Benjamin 106
Eldridge, Elizabeth 106
Eldridge, Patty 106
Eldridge, Thomas 106
Eldridge, Walter 626, 634
Elemsing, Charles 595
Elengton, William 408
Eley, Catharine 524
Eley, Elizabeth 507
Eley, Isaac 507
Eley, Jacob 507
Eley, Sarah 507
Elifretze, Elizabeth 529
Elik, John 636
Eliot, George 580
Elis, Martha 469
Elkin, William F. 524
Elkins, Alfred 379
Elkins, Lucy 704
Ellander, John 293
Ellenworth, David 530
Eller, Elizabeth 169
Elleson, Lydia 633
Ellick, Catharine 644
Ellick, Christopher 644
Ellick, Christopher Frederick 644
Ellick, Jacob 644
Ellick, Sarah 644
Ellinger, Mary 434
Ellington, Pleasant 713, 714, 715, 716, 717
Ellington, William 408
Elliot, Alex 215
Elliot, Eliza 44
Elliot, Fuller 482
Elliot, James 205
Elliot, John 386
Elliot, Patience 536
Elliott, Alexander 100, 223
Elliott, Alexr. 699

Elliott, Allen 134
Elliott, Anna A. 655
Elliott, Arthur W. 158
Elliott, Benj. 739, 747
Elliott, Benjamin 251, 255, 739, 741, 742
Elliott, Catharine 255
Elliott, Catherine W. 386
Elliott, Charles 681
Elliott, Corn. 408
Elliott, David 384, 386
Elliott, David Wilson 386
Elliott, Ebenezer 524
Elliott, Edmund 270
Elliott, Elizabeth 386
Elliott, Elizabeth S. 386
Elliott, Ellen 56
Elliott, G. 133
Elliott, James 51, 53, 54, 95, 145, 255, 270, 656
Elliott, James S. 386
Elliott, Jane 386
Elliott, John 73, 320, 384, 386, 542, 661, 746
Elliott, Joseph 386
Elliott, Joshua 158
Elliott, Louise 255
Elliott, Margaret 386
Elliott, Martin 251
Elliott, Mary 251, 405, 657
Elliott, Mary A. 255
Elliott, Micajah 169
Elliott, Moses 317
Elliott, Patience 251
Elliott, Richard 111, 116
Elliott, Ruby 134
Elliott, Samuel 134, 317, 404, 757
Elliott, Sarah 171, 534
Elliott, Sarah E. 255
Elliott, Thomas 681
Elliott, William 158, 662
Ellis, A. 244
Ellis, Aaron H. 244
Ellis, Abraham 262, 263, 524
Ellis, Anny 467
Ellis, Catherine 270
Ellis, Christopher 244
Ellis, Cornelius 397
Ellis, David 100
Ellis, E. 244, 397
Ellis, Elenour 463
Ellis, Elijah 502
Ellis, Elizabeth 290, 397, 536, 719
Ellis, Ency Beardsley 100
Ellis, Francis 325
Ellis, Gainer 293
Ellis, Hannah 287

Ellis, Harrison 719
Ellis, Henry 461
Ellis, Isaac 270, 274
Ellis, James 127
Ellis, Jehu 285
Ellis, Jehue 285
Ellis, Joel 524
Ellis, John 38, 46, 97, 530
Ellis, John H. 220
Ellis, Katharine 526
Ellis, Mary 462
Ellis, Mary Ann 16, 38, 40
Ellis, Michael 104
Ellis, Monanda 397
Ellis, Nathan 16, 19, 25, 30, 33, 36, 40, 236
Ellis, Nathl. 38
Ellis, Phebe 220
Ellis, Robert 285
Ellis, Rosanna 269
Ellis, Samuel 2, 126
Ellis, Sarah 287
Ellis, Sarah A. 244
Ellis, William 233, 474
Ellison, Andrew 29, 32, 34, 36, 270, 713, 714, 715
Ellison, Andrew (Jr.) 2
Ellison, Andrew Jackson 715
Ellison, Andw. 33
Ellison, Archibald B. 715
Ellison, Arthur 2
Ellison, Isaac 293
Ellison, James 39, 47
Ellison, Jane G. 2, 713, 714
Ellison, Jno. 34, 35
Ellison, John 2, 30, 38, 710
Ellison, John A. 715
Ellison, Johnson 46
Ellison, Marcissa P. 715
Ellison, Mary 29, 32, 34, 36
Ellison, Mary Jane 715
Ellison, Moris 1
Ellison, Robert 1, 9, 36, 48
Ellison, W. S. 6
Ellison, William 2, 3
Ellison, Wm. 5
Ells, Sarah 649
Ellsworth, George 100
Ellsworth, Joseph C. 51
Elmore, John 257
Elmore, Mahala 280
Elmore, Providence 530
Elmore, William 280
Elmss, --- 567
Elred, Ann 74
Elrick, Bernard 116
Elsasser, Eva 590
Elsberry, William 524
Elsey, Mary 271

Elsey, Nancy 270
Elson, Joseph 397
Elson, Julia A. 397
Elson, Lutecia 397
Elson, Margaret 397
Elson, Maria Angelan 100
Elston, Levi 362
Elstun, Ralph 570
Elsworth, David 52
Elwaine, John M. 274
Elwell, Daniel 690
Elwell, Isaac 218
Elwell, John 164
Elwood, Robert 55
Ely, Abraham 507
Ely, Elizabeth 524
Ely, Isaac 515
Ely, James 132
Ely, John 132
Ely, Joseph 132, 174
Ely, Mary 132
Ely, Sarah 132
Ely, William 132
Elzey, James 274
Elzey, Rachel 276
Emans, James 169
Emberling, Catherine 461
Embree, Hannah 114
Embree, John 363
Embree, Samuel 114
Embree, Sarah 519
Emerick, Catherine 467
Emerick, Christian 293
Emerick, Elisabeth 311
Emerick, Elizabeth 300
Emerick, Peter 293
Emerling, George 465
Emerson, Adams 100
Emerson, John 551
Emerson, John Prat 160
Emerson, Timothy (Sr.) 330
Emert, Mary 587
Emerts, Barbary 592
Emerts, Mary Ann 592
Emery, Betsy 286
Emery, Catharine 171
Emery, Ellis 588
Emery, Hannah 742
Emery, Harriet N. 601
Emery, John 742
Emler, Margaret 661
Emmens, Margaret 288
Emmerson, James 164
Emmerson, Rhoda 164
Emmons, --- 373
Emmons, Elijah 624
Emmons, Jacob 624
Emory, Judson 602
Enb, Charles 134
Enb, Mary 134
Enb, Rebecca 134
Enbree, Mary 363
Endorff, Frederick 353
Ene, Nancy 477
Engel, Maria 87
Enginton, Isaac 34
England, Amos 415
England, Asa 408

England, Enoch L. 580
England, Esa 440
England, Isaac 179, 409, 440
England, Mary Ann 179
England, Polly 628
England, Thomas 645
England, Titus 626
Engle, Axsha 273
Engle, Elizabeth 631, 632
Engle, Exsha 273
Engle, George 408
Engle, Job 551
Engle, Joseph 631
Engle, Martin 700
Engle, Mary Ann 627
Engle, Peter 448
Engle, William 626, 631
Engler, Henry 409
English, Benjamin 740
English, Daniel 740
English, Job 740, 745
English, John 740
English, Mary Jane 740
English, Nathaniel 740
English, Rachel 740
Engman, Edmond 404
Engman, Edwd. 404
Ennis, Elizabeth 522
Ennis, Forey 403
Ennis, Mary 533
Ennis, Samuel 519, 530
Enoch, Abigail 162
Enoch, Abner 137
Enoch, Alexander Campbell 669
Enoch, Eliza 223
Enoch, Henry 223
Enoch, Nancy 166, 226
Enochs, Hannah 629
Enocks, Elisha 542
Enocks, Margaret 632
Enos, Margaret 527
Enos, Sarah 182
Enos, William E. 379
Enrig, Mary 301
Ensign, Wm. O. 377
Enslen, Abraham 49
Enslen, Mary 49
Ensly, Aaron 274
Ensminger, Andrew W. 270
Ensminger, Caroline 582
Ensworth, David A. A. 75
Ensworth, Jediah 75
Ensworth, Jediah 75
Ensworth, Lucy 75
Ensworth, Lucy A. 75
Ensworth, Sophia F. 75
Entricks, Frederick 409
Entsminger, Betsey 479
Entsminger, John 474, 478, 484
Entsminger, John Henry 484
Entsminger, Margaret 477
Entsminger, Martha 474
Entsminger, Mary 475
Entsminger, Michael 484

Entsminger, Polly 479
Enyart, Ann 129
Enyart, Catharine 129
Enyart, Charlotte 129
Enyart, James 129, 164
Enyart, John 129
Enyart, Lewis 169
Enyart, Nancy 129
Enyart, Polly 129, 163, 168
Enyart, Sarah 129
Enyart, Susannah 161
Enyart, Thompson 129
Enyart, William 129, 156
Eppes, Sarah 187
Eppes, William 187
Erakes, William 626
Erenfight, Christopher 562
Erls, Nancy 9
Ernast, Elizabeth 590
Ernest, George (Jr.) 588
Ernst, Carolina 343
Ernst, Godfrey 719
Erret, John 333
Erskin, Betsy 165
Ertes, Nancy 703
Ertill, Sophia 557
Ertill, Valentine 557
Ervin, James 666
Ervin, Rachel Jones 271
Ervin, Thomas 666
Erwin, Ann E. 136
Erwin, Chas. R. 136
Erwin, Dolly 474
Erwin, J. W. 136
Erwin, James 746
Erwin, John 474, 704
Erwin, Joseph 293
Erwin, Polly 78
Erwin, Rebeckiah 291
Erwin, Robert 474
Erwin, Samuel 556
Erwin, Sebschi 601
Erwin, Wm. 745
Eshelman, Samuel 618
Eskridge, K. L. 600
Eskridge, Kendell 602
Eskridge, Rosanna 600
Espy, George 293
Espy, Josiah 524
Essea, Maria 601
Essex, Mary 581
Este, John K. 142
Estep, Catharine 297
Estep, George 293
Estep, Henry 293
Estep, Sarah 304
Estep, William 293
Esterly, Catharine 303
Esterly, George 293
Esterly, Jacob 293
Estes, Mary 301
Estil, Levi 560
Estill, Levy 560
Etamore, Christopher 483
Etienne, C. 36, 482
Etienne, Christopher 483, 485, 489, 493, 497

817

Ettenton, George 626
Ettion, Catharine 629
Ettles, Betsey 168
Eubank, James 26
Eubanks, Fanky 655
Eubanks, Joseph 656
Eubanks, Josiah 662
Eugh, Sofiah 627
Eutsler, C. 77
Eutsler, Elizabeth 77
Eutsler, George 656
Eutsler, Henry 77
Eutsler, Jno. (Jr.) 77
Eutsler, Sarah 77
Evans, A. 249
Evans, A. G. 375
Evans, Abraham 16, 38, 40, 44, 124
Evans, Ailsey 182
Evans, Aldrige 474
Evans, Alexander 597
Evans, Alice 205
Evans, Allan 249
Evans, Almeda 587
Evans, Amos 126
Evans, Ann Eliza Ellen 378
Evans, Anna 531
Evans, Benjamin 264, 285, 718
Evans, Benjamine 9
Evans, Burwell 110
Evans, Carey 375
Evans, Catharine 110
Evans, Charles 744
Evans, Clark 249
Evans, David 249, 549
Evans, E. P. 48
Evans, Edward 182, 184, 286, 392, 702
Evans, Eleanor 392
Evans, Eli B. 379
Evans, Elias 110
Evans, Elijah 661
Evans, Eliza 375
Evans, Elizabeth 126, 164, 319, 588, 659
Evans, Elizabeth E. 228
Evans, Emily 249
Evans, George 182, 184, 319
Evans, George W. 316, 319
Evans, Griffeth 44
Evans, Harvey 249
Evans, Henry 316, 319
Evans, Henry H. 546
Evans, Isaac 110, 182, 184, 205, 316, 318, 319
Evans, Isaac (Sr.) 182
Evans, James 182, 184, 205
Evans, Jas. M. (Dr.) 126
Evans, Jeremiah 182
Evans, John 36, 202, 375, 738, 743, 757
Evans, John C. 551
Evans, Joseph 228, 319, 746

Evans, Joshua 82
Evans, Margaret 182, 184, 249
Evans, Margaret H. 660
Evans, Martha 249, 319
Evans, Mary 182, 184, 249, 285, 319, 407, 597, 724
Evans, Mary A. 381
Evans, Mary Ann 124, 415, 610
Evans, Mary B. 249
Evans, Merica 375
Evans, Mevirel 110
Evans, Moses 160
Evans, Nancy 110, 182, 184, 205, 275
Evans, Nelly 481
Evans, Noah 454
Evans, Pearce 375
Evans, Peirce 610
Evans, Pierce 375
Evans, Polly 437, 744
Evans, Rache 10
Evans, Rachel 228
Evans, Rebecca 740
Evans, Reece 659
Evans, Rees 666
Evans, Richard 474
Evans, Rush 375, 740
Evans, S. 249
Evans, Samuel 285
Evans, Samuel Goodall 285
Evans, Sarah 12, 249
Evans, Sarah A. 249
Evans, Solomon 418
Evans, Stephen 249
Evans, Susannah 285
Evans, Thomas 42, 110, 392
Evans, Townsend 110
Evans, William 100, 164, 169
Evans, William C. 262
Evans, William Clarke 285
Evans, William H. 379
Evans, Wm. 749
Evans, Wm. W. 702
Eve, Nancy 477
Everet, Moses 487
Everett, Joseph (Jr.) 197
Everett, Moses 487
Everett, Mosses 485
Everett, Samuel 478, 487, 756
Everhart, Jacob 293
Everheart, Nancy 241
Everheart, Titus 241
Everitt, Isaac 188
Everle, William 230
Everly, Jos. 722
Everman, Sally 10
Eversole, George 428
Eversole, Henry 435
Eversole, John 691
Eversole, Sarah J. 428

Eversole, Susan 435
Everston, Jamima 467
Everton, Relief 478
Everts, Ambrose 77
Everts, Amelia 77
Everts, Eheelock 77
Everts, Louisa 81
Everts, Milo 82
Evertson, Caleb 465
Every, Mary 625
Evet, John 333
Evick, Absalom 50
Evins, Elizth. 408
Evins, Sarah 409
Evmer, John 74
Ewens, James 626
Ewens, Rufus 713
Ewin, Peggy 527
Ewing, Andrew 474, 552
Ewing, David 427
Ewing, Eliza 428
Ewing, Elizabeth 480
Ewing, Hannah 427
Ewing, Hugh 555
Ewing, James 293, 575
Ewing, James H. 423
Ewing, Jane 475
Ewing, John 484, 554, 702
Ewing, Joseph 150
Ewing, Josiah 755
Ewing, Josias 755
Ewing, Lavina 589
Ewing, Lyddia 669
Ewing, Lydia 474
Ewing, Margaret 137
Ewing, Mariah 743
Ewing, Nancy 476
Ewing, Rachel 531
Ewing, Samuel 137, 139, 150, 293, 428, 524
Ewing, Sarah 702
Ewing, Susannah 531
Ewing, Terese Ellen 427
Ewing, Thomas 122, 743
Ewing, Thomas E. 417
Extol, Thomas 699
Eyler, Aaron R. 47
Eyler, Charles E. 47
Eyler, Elizabeth 47
Eyler, Elizabeth V. 47
Eyler, Emaline A. 47
Eyler, Henry 123
Eyler, James M. 47
Eyler, Joseph (Sr.) 47
Eyler, Madison F. 47
Eyler, Samuel H. 47
Eyman, Catherine 460
Eyre, Robert 465, 597
Eyre, Samuel 465
Eyrs, Ann 468
Eyster, Anna 289
Eyster, Barbary 290, 309
Eyster, Elizabeth 310
Eyster, Esther 295
Eyster, Mary 290
Eyster, William 293

818

Ferris, Zena 635
Ferris, Zina 82, 635
Ferver, Henry 749
Fessel, James 293
Fessel, Sarah 307
Fester, Margaret 76
Fetherolf, Samuel 636
Fetherston, Margaret 74
Fetherston, Thomas 74
Fetter, Henry 409
Fetter, Rachel 419
Fetterly, Jacob 434
Fetterly, Mary 434
Fetterow, Elias L. 417
Fetters, Philip 425
Fetters, Thos. 419
Fettsgerald, Johanna 404
Feurt, Benjamin 27
Feurt, Gabriel 27
Feurt, Joseph 27
Feut, James 465
Feutinhoft, Cornelia 135
Feutinhoft, Magdelana
  135
Feutinhoft, Roger 135
Fewell, Henry 457
Fewell, James 457
Fezel, James 310
Fezel, Sarah 311
Fickle, Alfred 749
Fidler, John 607, 747
Fidler, Sarah 472
Fieiermood, Christina
  224
Field, Arthur 90
Field, George W. 564
Field, Henry A. 90
Field, John 293, 564
Field, John (Jr.) 564
Field, Mehitable 79
Field, Reuben 547
Field, Richard M. 641
Field, Roswell 385
Fielder, Mary R. 189
Fielder, Susanah 189
Fielding, Margaret 135
Fields, Allison 524
Fields, Anson 379
Fields, Elizabeth 530
Fields, Gilbert 465
Fields, Hannah Lucina
  379
Fields, J. A. 245
Fields, John 118, 524,
  556
Fields, P. C. B. 245
Fields, Sarah 118
Fields, Susan 594
Fields, Thomas 530
Fields, Walter 223
Fierbaugh, Phillip 409
Fierce, Nancy 78
Fierec, Fanny 82
Fife, David 310
Fife, Elizabeth 291, 519
Fife, James 274, 283,
  293
Fife, John 293
Fife, Joseph 293

Fife, Samuel 293
Fife, William 293
Fifer, John 524
Fifer, John K. 474
Figley, Nancy 68
Figley, Sarah M. 380
Fike, Elizabeth 68
Filbley, Hannaw 10
Filkey, Grace 389
Fill, Henry 409
Filman, Sally 481
Filo, Jacob 127
Filson, John 564
Filson, Mary 625
Filson, Polly 288
Finch, Ann 109
Finch, Elizabeth 392
Finch, Gertrude 403
Finch, Hannah 109
Finch, Isaac 392
Finch, Jane 109
Finch, Jesse 109
Finch, Jesse (Jr.) 109
Finch, John 109
Finch, Nathaniel 109
Finch, William 109
Findlay, James 237, 509,
  561, 563, 564, 567
Findley, Elisabeth 41
Findley, Sarah 656
Fine, Sally 626
Finey, Sylvenus 631
Fink, Allen Adleine 343
Fink, Frederick 720
Fink, Heinrich Franz 342
Fink, James C. 48
Fink, James Eli 346
Fink, John Albert 346
Fink, Maria Katharina
  342
Fink, Samuel 342, 343,
  346
Fink, William 89
Finkbone, Nancy 419
Finke, William 91, 100
Finkham, Abel 390
Finkham, Elizabeth 390
Finkham, Hannah 390
Finkham, Isaac 390
Finkham, Noah 390
Finkle, John P. 132
Finley, B. 402
Finley, Celestina
  Caroline 669
Finley, D. D. 43
Finley, Ebenezer 543
Finley, Elizabeth P. 52
Finley, James 1, 4
Finley, James W. (Rev.)
  50
Finley, Jehu 537
Finley, John 237, 238
Finley, Joseph 548
Finley, Joseph S. 4
Finley, Margaret 618
Finley, Robt. 18
Finley, Samuel S. 2
Finly, Glasgow 44
Finn, Mary Jane 343

Finnell, Elijah 422
Finney, Alvan 642
Finney, Caleb M. 631
Finney, Harvey 631, 642
Finney, James 597
Finney, Joseph W. 642
Finney, Phebe 597
Finney, Silvanus 642
Finney, Solomon 626, 642
Finney, Solomon (Jr.)
  642
Finney, Solomon (Sr.)
  642
Finney, Sylvanus 631
Fires, James 524
Fires, Lucy 520
Firestone, Catherine 291
Firestone, Mary 290, 291
Firestone, Peter 294
Firing, Katharina 100
First, Nancy 79
Fisbach, Michael 100
Fisback, Samuel D. 623
Fish, Angeline 333
Fish, Nathaniel 77
Fish, Nathl. 77
Fish, Rebekah 82
Fishbach, Jacob 613
Fishbach, John 613
Fishbach, Rosanah 613
Fishback, Freeman 697
Fishback, Mary 697
Fishback, Michael 100
Fishback, Richard 690,
  697
Fishback, William Parker
  697
Fishel, John 580
Fishel, Michael 333
Fishell, John 294
Fisher, Adam 235, 409
Fisher, Amy 286
Fisher, Andrew 50, 56
Fisher, Anna 296
Fisher, Barbara 56
Fisher, Betty 383
Fisher, Blasius 53
Fisher, Catharine 164,
  310, 639
Fisher, Catherine 294
Fisher, Christena 101
Fisher, Daniel 267, 274
Fisher, David 140, 142,
  154, 270
Fisher, E. P. 400
Fisher, Edwin 588
Fisher, Eliza 582
Fisher, Elizabeth 168,
  296, 597, 682
Fisher, Francis 719
Fisher, Frederick 294,
  565
Fisher, George 389, 597
Fisher, H. D. 403
Fisher, Henry 294
Fisher, Isaac 267, 274
Fisher, Isear P. 265
Fisher, Iseear P. 265
Fisher, J. D. 402

Foster, Sarah 72, 579
Foster, Seth 39
Foster, Theodore 727
Foster, Thomas 2, 10,
  119, 663
Foster, William 441
Foster, Wm. 663
Fouch, Ruth 647
Fought, Anthony 663
Fought, Eliza Ann 587
Fought, Eve 420
Fought, James 588
Fought, Mary Ann 588
Fought, Preston 588
Foulke, Joseph 118
Foulks, Charles 294
Foulks, William 294
Fountain, Mary M. 420
Fountain, Stephen 363
Fourney, William 294
Foust, Anthony 586
Foust, Catharine 586
Foust, Daniel 586
Foust, John 586
Foust, Margaret 586
Foust, Philip 294
Foust, Rebecca 586
Fout, Ann 716
Fout, Philip 716, 717
Fout, Rachel 302
Fout, Sherman 716, 717
Foutch, Jonathan 420
Fouts, Elizabeth 95
Fouts, John 95
Fouts, Mary 307
Fouts, Philip 294
Foutz, Lena 421
Fowble, Jacob 572
Fowler, James 164, 679
Fowler, John 747
Fowler, Richard 315, 318
Fowler, Robert 602
Fowler, Sarah 629, 679
Fowler, Thomas 294
Fowler, William 580
Fowler, Zadich 421
Fowley, John 666
Fowlis, A. 246
Fowlis, Biddy 624
Fowlis, Jane 246
Fowlis, Martha 624
Fowlis, Mary 624
Fowlis, Millie J. 246
Fowlis, Paul 246
Fowlis, S. 246
Fowlis, Winston 624
Fox, Aaron 217
Fox, Abraham 294
Fox, Absalom 191
Fox, Andrew H. 612
Fox, Arthur 27
Fox, Asher 217
Fox, Betsey 520
Fox, Catharine 291, 309
Fox, Catherine 217
Fox, Dan 400
Fox, Daniel 217, 401
Fox, David 217
Fox, Eliza 580

Fox, Elizabeth 507
Fox, Emily Eliza 612
Fox, Hannah 612
Fox, Henry 294
Fox, Jacob 294, 507, 524
Fox, James 77
Fox, John 26, 37, 217,
  294, 401, 409, 530,
  612, 654
Fox, John (Jr.) 217
Fox, John O. 602
Fox, Joseph 217
Fox, Margaret 579
Fox, Mary 217, 294,
  295, 408
Fox, Matilda 589
Fox, Mickiel 72
Fox, Nancy 217
Fox, Nathl. 17
Fox, Philip 294
Fox, Polly 305
Fox, Rebecca 295
Fox, Roger 727
Fox, Samuel 217
Fox, Sarah 217, 352
Fox, Stephen 563
Fox, Susanna 612
Fox, Susannah 612
Fox, Uzal Bates 561
Fox, William 580, 612
Foy, Jacob (Jr.) 333
Foy, Judith 124
Foy, Mary 632
Fr . . . p, Frank 373
Frad, John 704
Frailey, Jane 611
Frailey, W. R. 403
Fraizer, Alexander 285
Fraizer, Jonah 285
Fraizer, Mary 285
Fraizer, Moses 285
Fraker, John 409
Fraker, Rebecca 471
Frakes, Hannah 169
Frakes, Nathan 530
Frakes, Robert 519
Fraley, James 611
Fraley, Jeremiah 354
Fralick, Mary 599
Frame, David (Jr.) 547
Frame, James 544
Frame, John 551
Frame, Nath. 93
Frame, Rebecca 730
Frame, Thomas 544
Frame, William 543
Frame, Wm. (Sr.) 544
Frampton, --- 723
Frampton, Elijah 704
Frampton, Hugh 370
Frampton, Sally 705
France, Christopher 211
France, John 238, 597
France, Mary 50
Franceska, William 626
Francesko, Abraham 626
Franch, Rachel 223
Franch, Sally 479
Francis, Anna 707

Francis, Charity 628
Francis, Daniel 77
Francis, Delila 633
Francis, Edward 124
Francis, Elihu 704
Francis, Francis John
  355
Francis, George 367
Francis, John 597
Francis, Jule 355
Francis, Mary 165
Francis, Nancy 625
Francis, Nicholas 77
Francis, Peggy 486
Francis, Polly 625
Francis, Thomas 77
Francis, Unis 126
Francis, William 626
Francisco, Aaron 626
Francisco, Ann 627
Francisco, Catharine 633
Francisco, Sally 628
Francisco, William 636
Franciscoe, Ann 434
Francisko, Hannah 627
Frank, Catharine 419
Frank, Martin 191
Frank, Michael 595
Frank, Peter 100
Frank, Sara 303
Frankelberger, Joel 194
Frankelberger, Margaret
  189
Frankerberger, Margaret
  191
Frankforter, Caty 304
Franklin, Elizabeth 222
Franklin, George 10
Franklin, James 50
Franklin, Melinda 226
Franklin, Nelly 56
Franklin, Nelson 616
Franklin, Sarah 56
Franks, Ann 293
Franks, Elizabeth 297
Franks, Henry 294
Franks, Michael 294, 580
Franks, Peter 379
Frants, John 238
Frantz, Anna 224
Frantz, Daniel 223
Frantz, David 223
Frantz, George 70
Frantz, John 223
Frantz, Michael 223
Frantzman, Jacob 639
Frantzman, Mary 639
Frantzman, Nicholas 639
Frantzman, Peter 639
Frantzman, Susannah 639
Franz, Michael 59
Frasair, Thomas 513
Fraser, Daniel 294
Fraser, Louisa 416
Fraser, William 294
Frasier, Sarah 417
Frausdalee, Ann 9
Frautwain, T. F. 100
Frazea, Thomas 576

Fry, Jane 271
Fry, John 255, 593, 757
Fry, Joseph 45
Fry, Joshua 729
Fry, Ludwick 740
Fry, Margaret 124, 126
Fry, Martha 255
Fry, Mary 588, 740
Fry, Michael 284
Fry, Michael C. 255
Fry, Peter A. 255
Fry, Susan 255
Fry, Thomas 749
Fry, William 690
Fry, Williamena 438
Frybarger, Valentine 503
Fryberger, George 517
Fryberger, Lewis 235
Fryberger, Peter 242
Frye, Elizabeth 409
Fryer, Alex 43
Fryer, William 43
Fryer, Wm. 43
Fryman, Catharine 125
Fryman, John George 55
Fryman, Philip 125
Frymore, Catherin 101
Fuchs, Elinora 347
Fudge, Jacob 704
Fudge, John 704
Fudge, Sarah 707
Fudge, Steny 706
Fuel, Bartholomew 456
Fuel, Henry 456
Fuel, James 456
Fuel, Jeruch 456
Fuel, Lewis 456
Fuel, Lucy 456
Fuhrer, Anna Maria 338
Fuhrer, August 338
Fuhrer, Elizabethe 338
Fuhrman, Phillip 133
Fuhter, Catharine 121
Fulcorson, Mary 301
Fuleton, John 607
Fuleton, Julianna 607
Fuleton, Nancy 607
Fulk, Nancy 294
Fulks, Charles 310
Fulks, Daniel 294
Fulks, John 107
Full, Katherine 50
Full, Magdalene 50
Fullens, Hannah 505
Fullenwider, Elizabeth
156
Fullenwider, John 144,
156
Fuller, Abel 551
Fuller, Adaline Augusta
707
Fuller, Amos 392
Fuller, David 72
Fuller, Debby 72
Fuller, Ephraim B. 67
Fuller, Fanny 78
Fuller, G. 373
Fuller, Gideon 256, 281

Fuller, James 77, 164,
524, 530
Fuller, Jedadiah 72
Fuller, Joel 97
Fuller, John 558
Fuller, Joseph 84
Fuller, Luther 294
Fuller, Mary 79
Fuller, Nancy 75
Fuller, Resolve 84
Fuller, Sally 479
Fuller, Samuel 82
Fuller, Sanford W. 602
Fuller, Sarah Ann 601
Fuller, Thomas 540
Fuller, Thos. R. 547
Fuller, William 275
Fullerton, Franklin 741,
742
Fullerton, Geo. S. 447
Fullerton, Jane 656
Fullerton, Nancy 705
Fullerton, Robert 447
Fullet, William 656
Fullor, Thomas 543
Fulmer, John 69
Fulton, Alexander 85
Fulton, Betsey 82
Fulton, Carnes 108
Fulton, David 1, 48, 117
Fulton, Elijah 18
Fulton, James 597
Fulton, John 77, 122,
597
Fulton, Loammi 77
Fulton, Mahlon 42, 44
Fulton, Mahon 44
Fulton, Malon 44
Fulton, Nancy 474
Fulton, Peggy 83
Fulton, Polly 77
Fulton, Rachel 1, 76, 85
Fulton, Robert 20
Fulton, Samuel 77, 332
Fulton, William 392,
461, 509
Fultz, Anna 595
Fultz, Barbary 463
Funderburg, Daniel 519
Funderburgh, Daniel 508
Funderburgh, John 524
Funk, Abraham 631
Funk, Adam 74
Funk, Daniel 409
Funk, Dorathy 468
Funk, Elizabeth 641
Funk, Jacob 404, 461
Funk, John 461
Funk, Joseph E. 470
Funk, Sally 629
Funk, Sarah 463
Funk, Tabitha 468
Funkhous, Elizabeth 407
Funkhouser, Elizabeth
407
Funston, Elizabeth 657
Funston, Rosanna 656
Funston, William 223
Furgason, Mary 652

Furgersen, Nelson 602
Furgeson, Elizabeth 654
Furgeson, James 654
Furgeson, Mary 654
Furgeson, Polly 501
Furgeson, Zachariah 501
Furguson, Daniel R. 259
Furguson, James 17
Furguson, John 704
Furman, Samuel 198
Furmann, Catarina 441
Furness, Thomas D. 53
Furney, Emanuel 370
Furnier, David 2
Furnier, Henry 2
Furniss, John 698
Furr, Sinci 40
Furrow, Mary 222
Furrow, William 223
Furst, Jno. 78
Furst, Peggy 78
Fuson, James 199
Fuson, Wm. 199
Fyers, James 363
Fyers, James 364
Fyffe, W. H. 189

--- G ---

Gabill, Bazel 82
Gabill, Dorcas 81
Gabriel, William 200
Gadberry, Samuel 619
Gaddis, John 258
Gaddis, Margaret 258
Gaddis, Thomas 258
Gadner, Christina 344
Gadner, Jacob 344
Gaehr, Henry 91
Gaevels, Gertrude 101
Gaff, David M. 448
Gaff, Hannah 452
Gaff, James H. 452
Gaff, Joanna 452
Gaff, John S. 530
Gaff, Maria 533
Gaff, Sarah Jane 452
Gaffield, Benjamin 223
Gaffin, Mary 45
Gaggin, William 45
Gahn, Christian 346
Gahn, Conrad 341
Gahn, Luisa 341
Gahn, Margaretha 341
Gain, Soloman 619
Gaines, Alexander 223
Gains, Benjamin P. 215,
216
Gains, Ludwell G. 242
Galaspy, Jane 481
Galaspy, Mary 10
Galaspy, Robert 478
Galbraith, Work 423, 424
Galbreath, --- 567
Galbreath, Robert 241
Galbreath, Thomas 294
Gale, Alfred 732

826

Griffeth, Sarah 724
Griffey, Elizabeth 526
Griffin, Abraham 479
Griffin, Andrew 121
Griffin, Daniel 74, 519
Griffin, David 160
Griffin, James 270,
277, 550
Griffin, John J. 31
Griffin, John Taylor 23
Griffin, Phebe 137
Griffin, Rachael 634
Griffin, Robert 277
Griffin, Sally 521
Griffin, Sarah 269, 277
Griffin, Thos. W. 549
Griffin, Zebulon 84
Griffing, Daniel 563
Griffing, Rachel 525
Griffith, Adam 475
Griffith, Azel 223
Griffith, E. 253
Griffith, Edward 660
Griffith, Elias D. 552
Griffith, Elizabeth 692
Griffith, Elizabeth W.
253
Griffith, Hannah 659
Griffith, Henry 253
Griffith, Israel P. 195
Griffith, James 430, 692
Griffith, John 111,
164, 280, 416
Griffith, Josiah 360
Griffith, Lucinda 478
Griffith, Martha 430
Griffith, Nancy 166
Griffith, Robert 111
Griffith, Sarah 111
Griffith, Sarah Ann 111
Griffith, Standsbery 253
Griffith, Thomas (Rev.)
98
Griffith, W. 253
Griffith, William 548
Griffith, Wrightsle 253
Griffiths, Elisabeth 660
Griffman, Ann 416
Griffy, John 362
Griffy, Nancy 703
Grigsby, Wm. 416
Grill, H. 346
Grim, Elizabeth 306
Grim, George 295, 310
Grim, Henry 313, 315,
627
Grim, Peter 602
Grim, Polly 467
Grimary, Ann 271
Grimblebeck, John 588
Grimes, Betsey 517
Grimes, Elizabeth 169
Grimes, Ephraim 627
Grimes, Geo. 135
Grimes, George 295
Grimes, James 295, 372
Grimes, John 136, 164,
295, 517
Grimes, Margaret 136

Grimes, Mary 29
Grimes, Nancy 557
Grimes, Noble 9, 10,
11, 12, 27, 28, 29,
33, 34
Grimes, Rebecca 163, 165
Grimes, Richard 27, 29
Grimes, Richd. 30, 33,
34
Grimes, Samuel 295,
310, 512, 517
Grimes, Sarah 11, 552
Grimes, Susan 136
Grimes, Thomas 10, 27,
29, 34, 536, 552
Grimes, William 627
Grimes, Wm. 557
Grimm, John 295
Grimm, Nicholas 295
Griner, Elizabeth 536
Grinnett, Geo. 641
Grinshaw, William 724
Grinson, Frank 722
Grisol, Samuel 295
Griss, Crescentia 649
Grissel, Rachel 289
Grissell, Ann 308
Grissell, Joseph 295
Grist, John B. 389
Griswald, Esther 706
Griswold, E. 390
Griswold, Eva 388
Grizzle, Margaret 416
Groce, Lewis (Sr.) 72
Grof, Nietoria 102
Grogg, Mary 304
Grogg, Sarah 293
Grohs, Barbara 341
Grohs, Friedrich 341
Grohs, Susanna Dortha
341
Grooms, Abraham 5
Grooms, Eli 3
Grooms, John 5, 47
Grooms, Lorenzo 45
Grooms, Zachariah 3, 5
Grooms, Zachariah (Jr.)
5
Groshauts, Catherin 99
Gross, Abraham 639
Gross, Barbara 639
Gross, Elizabeth 639
Gross, John 625
Gross, Susan 639
Grosscup, Paul 68
Grossell, Joseph 376
Grossman, John 47
Grote, William 355
Grout, Enos 747
Grove, Albra. 253
Grove, Andrew 419
Grove, Ann 252
Grove, Catherine 253
Grove, Daniel 169
Grove, David 253
Grove, Elizabeth 253
Grove, George 253
Grove, Henry 252
Grove, Irvine 252

Grove, J. 253
Grove, Jacob 253
Grove, John 253
Grove, Kelly 411
Grove, Kitty 411
Grove, Lewis 416
Grove, Louisa 253
Grove, M. 253
Grove, Margaret Ann 252
Grove, Martha 253
Grove, Mary 253
Grove, Nancy 253
Grove, Susan M. 253
Grove, Tabithe 630
Grovenor, R. 757
Grover, Curtis T. 396
Grover, Frank B. 396
Grover, Maria M. 396
Grover, Mary 394
Grover, Mary Anderson 518
Grover, S. B. 394
Grover, Sally Griffin 521
Grover, Saml. 593
Grover, Sarah I. 394
Grover, Shepherd 394
Groves, --- 199
Groves, Barnet 112
Groves, David 416
Groves, Eley 381
Groves, James 108
Groves, John 112
Groves, Joseph 112
Groves, Lavina 112
Groves, Nancy 112, 628
Groves, Rosanna 112
Groves, William 106, 112
Groves, Wm. 112
Grow, Augusta 124
Grow, Isaac 654
Grow, Peter 85
Grow, Sarah 654
Grow, Thirza 76
Grub, Mary 430
Grubb, Curtis 114
Grubb, George 195
Grubb, James 466
Grubb, John 645
Grubb, Stephen 466
Grubb, William 585
Grubb, William Byal 585
Grubb, Winne 460
Grubb, Wm. 585
Grubbs, Mary 411
Grubbs, Sarah 411
Gruber, Susanna 52
Grubli, Elizabetha 102
Grumman, David 564
Grummon, David 570
Grummore, David 559
Grummore, Rachel 559
Grundy, Emily 379
Grunzelbauch, Coon 403
Grunzelbauch, Neil 403
Guant, John 310
Guartmann, Maria
Elizabeth 99
Guartmann, Maria
Elizabetha 100
Gudiman, Sophia 603

Guenther, Anna Maria 346
Guenther, Elisabetha 346
Guess, Joseph 364
Guest, Mary 168
Guffey, Isabella 522
Guffy, Mary 518
Gugler, Anna Maria 345
Gugler, L. 345
Gugler, Louisa 345
Guieler, Augustus 594
Guile, Benjamin 84
Guile, Benjamin (Jr.) 84
Guile, Hannah 84
Guile, Hetty 728
Guile, James 84
Guile, Lucy 84
Guile, Polly 84
Guile, Simeon 728
Guilford, Phoebe 471
Guille, V. R. 663
Guimer, Jane 460
Guir, David 482
Guisinger, Rebecca 333
Guiter, John S. 379
Guithen, Elijah 448
Gukidge, John (Sr.) 191
Gulick, Samuel 568
Gullenlin, Eliza 207
Gullick, Tunis 568
Gulliford, Allen 615
Gum, John 588
Gume, Isabel 596
Gunckel, Michael 507
Gunckel, Sarah 507
Gunder, Barbara 409
Gunder, Killy 407
Gunder, Kitty 407
Gundy, Joseph 597
Guner, Polly 408
Gunn, Edward M. 379
Gunn, Eunice L. 601
Gunn, Isabelle 391
Gunn, J. W. 401
Gunn, John (Jr.) 391
Gunn, John M. 401
Gunn, Maria 391
Gunn, Nelson 602
Gunn, Robert 391
Gunning, James 443
Gunning, John 466
Gunther, Abraham 344
Gunther, Anna Maria 346
Gunther, Catharina 344, 346
Gunther, Elisabeth 346
Gunther, Rosina 344
Gunyon, Alice 170
Gunyon, Susanna 170
Gurley, Jane 649
Gurnes, Rachel 334
Guseman, Adam W. 427
Guseman, Wm. 428
Gustin, Amos 29
Gustin, John 4
Gustin, Margaret 628
Guston, Samuel 169
Gutcher, Gottleeb 295
Gutharie, Joseph 84
Gutherie, Esther 169

Gutherie, Hannah 304
Gutherie, Richard 295
Guthery, Margaret 291
Guthrie, Albert Lewis 424
Guthrie, C. B. 640
Guthrie, Elizabeth 4
Guthrie, Henry 4
Guthrie, James 525, 656
Guthrie, Joseph 84
Guthrie, Lyman H. 424
Guthrie, Nancy 656
Guthrie, Robert 10
Guthrie, Sarah M. 424
Guthrie, Stephen 77
Guthrie, Thomas 59
Guthrie, William 479
Guthry, John 514
Gutridge, Aaron 191
Gutridge, Andrew 3
Gutridge, Catharine 191
Gutridge, Elizabeth 191
Gutridge, James 39, 191, 192
Gutridge, Jane 191
Gutridge, Jesse 191
Gutridge, Jno. 10
Gutridge, John 9, 10, 11, 12, 16, 41, 42, 191
Gutridge, John (Sr.) 41, 191
Gutridge, Moses 39, 191
Gutridge, Peter 747
Gutridge, Richard 191
Gutridge, Sarah 191
Gutridge, William 191
Guttery, Robert 597
Guttery, Samuel 295
Guy, Abbey Jane 651
Guy, Ambrose 651
Guy, Andrew 479
Guy, Elizabeth 292
Guy, Jesse 295
Guy, Peggy 481
Guy, Polly 651
Guy, William 295
Guyer, George 64
Guyer, Mary 67
Guynne, E. 207
Guynne, E. W. 207, 210
Guynne, W. 210
Gwalteney, Josiah 566
Gwaltney, Josiah 558
Gwandt, Friedrich Jacob 339
Gwandt, Ludwig 339
Gwandt, Maria 339
Gwilly, Morgan 164
Gwynne, Eli W. 192
Gwynne, Jane 192
Gwynne, Thomas 192
Gygar, David 409

--- H ---

Haarlos, Jacob 370
Haas, John I. 650

Haas, Rebecca 587
Haber, Adam 336
Haber, Margaratha 336
Haber, Maria Ava 336
Haber, Rudolf 336
Habig, Philip 359
Hackathorn, John 296
Hacker, John 532
Hackhart, Nich. 296
Hackley, Edward S. 238
Hadden, Catharine 529
Hadden, Jacob 517
Haddix, Enoch 580
Haddix, John 532
Haddix, Philip 532
Haddox, Enoch 585
Haden, Alfred 709
Haden, Malinda 709
Hadin, Isaac 100
Hadix, Nimrod 516
Hadley, Ann 265
Hadley, James 285
Hadley, John 282
Hadley, Smith 697
Hadley, William 259, 260, 265
Haefner, C. H. 346
Hael, John 525
Haeutrauck, John F. 687
Haffner, Anny 649
Hafily, Christiana 293
Hagaman, John 653
Hagaman, Margaret 137
Hagaman, Michael 137
Hagaman, Nelley 653
Hagaman, Thomas 653
Hagdorn, Conrad 359
Hageman, Abigail 142
Hageman, Jane 166
Hageman, Margaret 142
Hageman, Michael 142
Hagene, Edward 669
Hager, Kelion 546
Hagerly, Jacob Frederick 627
Hagerman, John 82
Hagerman, Margaret 586
Hagerman, Mary J. 473
Hagerman, Mary Jane 586
Hagerman, Richard 580
Hagg, Johnny 373
Haggard, David Rice 187
Haggard, Elizabeth 187
Haggard, J. 249
Haggard, James 187
Haggard, John 249
Haggard, Levy 187
Haggard, Nancy 187
Haggard, Okelly 187
Haggard, Rice 187
Haggard, S. 249
Haggard, Samuel 249
Haggard, Sarah Jane 249
Haggerty, John P. 602
Hagler, George 455, 466
Hagler, Isaac 446
Hagler, John 421
Hagler, Susannah 456, 531

Halterman, John 458, 663
Haman, Sinah 477
Hambelton, Blewford 580
Hambelton, Elizabeth 582
Hambelton, Zebella 582
Hamble, James 296
Hambleman, Geo. 222
Hambleton, Benjamin 296
Hambleton, James 10
Hambleton, Sussan 306
Hamblin, Alfred 694
Hamblin, Ann 583
Hamblin, Don Alonzo 580
Hamblin, Elizabeth 694
Hamblin, Lorrain 580
Hamblin, Mary Elizabeth
694
Hamblin, Reuben 588
Hamer, George 554
Hamer, John (Sr.) 661
Hamersley, Isaac 548
Hamill, Hugh 499
Hamill, Joseph 500, 502
Hamilton, Alexander 123
Hamilton, Allen 375
Hamilton, Amanda Jane
207
Hamilton, Betsy 467
Hamilton, Catharine 293
Hamilton, Cinthia 224
Hamilton, Daniel 17, 18
Hamilton, David J. 100
Hamilton, Eliza 183
Hamilton, Eliza
Catherine 207
Hamilton, Elizabeth 225
Hamilton, G. W. 366
Hamilton, George 150
Hamilton, Hannah 125
Hamilton, Harriett 417
Hamilton, Henry 296
Hamilton, Israel 197
Hamilton, James 36, 137,
317, 325, 561, 562,
588, 669, 739, 742
Hamilton, John 6, 43,
125, 138, 183, 202
Hamilton, John (Jr.) 160
Hamilton, Joseph 296,
549
Hamilton, Margaret 464
Hamilton, Mary 292, 325
Hamilton, Nancy 299
Hamilton, Polly 476
Hamilton, Richard 588
Hamilton, Rosanna 632
Hamilton, Ruthy Eleanor
207
Hamilton, Samuel 100
Hamilton, Sarah 125,
170, 183, 289, 325
Hamilton, Sarah Ann 207
Hamilton, Sary 636
Hamilton, Susan 325
Hamilton, Susanah 293
Hamilton, Thomas 669
Hamilton, William 46,
150, 296, 442, 514,
666

Hamilton, Wm. 24, 442,
688
Hamlin, William 296
Hammel, Eleanor Jane 88
Hammel, Eve 418
Hammel, Joseph 88
Hammel, Peter 88
Hammell, Peter 60
Hammen, Nathan (Jr.) 215
Hammer, Catherine 379
Hammer, Polly 170
Hammer, Rachel 166
Hammersly, Isaac 551
Hammil, Joseph 516
Hammock, Alanda 99
Hammon, Margaret Ann 101
Hammond, Charles 537
Hammond, David P. 551
Hammond, Elizabeth. 544
Hammond, Joe 129
Hammond, John 683
Hammond, Mordecai 584
Hammond, Nathan 223
Hammond, Rachel 581
Hamond, John 683
Hamphill, Mathew 44
Hampshire, Joseph 473
Hampson, James 110
Hampson, John 437, 440
Hampson, Leah 431
Hampson, Martha 110
Hampton, Abraham 275
Hampton, Ephraim 223
Hampton, Margaret 224
Hampton, Maria 632
Hamrich, David 262
Hamrich, John 261
Hana, Peter 479
Hanah, David 208
Hanbey, Elisha 519
Hanbrich, John 261
Hance, Thomas 387, 390
Hancock, Betsey 385
Hancock, Derusia 583
Hancock, Emily 584
Hancock, George 385
Hancock, Isabell 168
Hancock, Nancy 165
Hancock, Van R. 580
Hancock, Warren 580
Hancock, William 580
Hancock, Wm. 584
Hancuker, Samuel 632
Hand, Benjamin 532
Hand, Caroline 739
Hand, Elizabeth 172
Hand, Enoch 149
Hand, Joanah 465
Hand, Joseph 169
Hand, Martha 149
Hand, Mary 171
Hand, Robert O. 466
Hand, Samuel 751
Hand, Samuel (Jr.) 743
Hand, Wm. G. 739
Handback, Barbara 196
Handback, David 196
Handback, Hannah 196
Handback, Lewis 196

Handley, Elizabeth 533
Handley, Mary 467
Handley, Obadiah E. 223
Handman, Catherine 121
Handshaw, John 479
Haneby, John 223
Hanel, Jesse 169
Haneline, George 223
Haner, John (Jr.) 466
Hanes, Ann 468
Hanes, Benjamin Mitchell
669
Hanes, Catharine 460
Hanes, Ebenezer 48
Hanes, Elizabeth 629
Hanes, Harriet Luisa 669
Hanes, Jacob 515
Hanes, James Clark 669
Hanes, Jemima Angaline
669
Hanes, Joab 270
Hanes, John 597
Hanes, John Thomas
Bracken 670
Hanes, Mary 269, 465
Hanes, Nathan 532
Hanes, Rebecca 670
Hanes, Samuel 669, 670
Haneson, Kitty 404
Haney, Elenor 468
Hanford, Thaddeus 576
Hanger, D. G. 179
Hanger, Elizabeth 179
Hanger, Georg 340
Hanger, Jacob 698, 702
Hanger, Johannes 340
Hanger, Katharina 340
Haniman, Betsy 216
Haning, Isaac 78
Hank, Thomas P. 666
Hankin, Mary 460
Hankins, Amos 277, 455,
461
Hankins, Anne 163
Hankins, David 451
Hankins, Hannah 464
Hankins, John 451
Hankins, Nancy 706
Hankins, Rameth 285
Hankins, Rhoda 462
Hankins, Rolen 718
Hankinson, Charles 94
Hankinson, Eleanor 94
Hankinson, James 639
Hankinson, Rebecca 94
Hanley, Cornelius 716
Hanley, Martha Ellen 670
Hanley, Oliver C. 716
Hanlin, John D. 602
Hanlon, Benjamin 680
Hanlon, Daniel 680
Hanlon, Elizabeth 680
Hanlon, James 680
Hanlon, John 679, 680
Hanlon, Moses 680
Hanlon, Nancy 680
Hanlon, Sarah 680
Hanlon, Thomas 680
Hanlon, Wabrantz 680

Hanlon, William 680
Hanmon, Uley 655
Hanna, Amelia 735
Hanna, Andw. (Jr.) 547
Hanna, Anna 296
Hanna, Benjamin 296
Hanna, Christopher 656
Hanna, David 208, 211
Hanna, Elizabeth 658
Hanna, Esther 297
Hanna, Henry 415, 735
Hanna, Hezekiah 735
Hanna, Isaac 735
Hanna, Jacob 296
Hanna, James 422, 545, 547, 597, 661, 735
Hanna, Jane 658
Hanna, John 544, 735
Hanna, Joseph W. 663
Hanna, Matild 735
Hanna, Nathaniel 735
Hanna, Pheta 735
Hanna, Reuben 735
Hanna, Robert 543
Hanna, Thomas 547
Hanna, William 597, 735
Hannah, Aaron 44
Hannah, Barbara 692
Hannah, David 296
Hannah, George W. 595
Hannah, James 113, 133
Hannah, John 6, 111, 133
Hannah, Margaret 161
Hannah, Mary 173, 308, 587
Hannah, Rebecca 111
Hannah, Sarah 6, 10, 133
Hannah, William 44, 692
Hannaman, Elizabeth 462
Hannaman, George 461
Hannaman, Polly 461
Hannon, Anna E. 604
Hanond, Anne 160
Hansacker, John 642
Hansel, Jacob 640
Hansel, John 409
Hansford, Squires 534
Hanshew, Kitty 410
Hanson, Ann 466
Hanson, Benjamin 55
Hanson, Hollis 54
Hanson, James A. 50
Hanson, Mahala 49
Hanson, Mary 51
Hanson, Sabra 657
Hanson, Samuel C. 632
Hanson, Wm. 232, 233
Hanthorn, Eliza 49
Hanthorn, Martha 49
Hanthorn, Sarah 50
Hanthorn, Thomas 49
Hanzel, Francis 122
Hapkirk, Ann 670
Hapkirk, William 670
Happin, Benj. 641
Happin, Frederick Street 641
Happin, Thomas 641
Happin, Thomas Coles 641

Happin, William W. 641
Haragan, Daniel 572
Harbaugh, Wm. 416
Harbert, John 203
Harbert, Jonathan 189
Harbert, Robert 224
Harbin, Samuel 256, 258, 259
Harbison, Joseph 504
Harbour, Elijah 444
Harbour, Elisha 205
Harbour, Joel 205
Harbour, Noah 201
Harden, Catharine 161
Harden, James 636, 638
Harden, Jemima 162
Harden, John 169
Harden, Peter 164
Harden, Samuel 270
Harden, Thomas 546
Hardeste, Mary 9
Hardesty, Ann 38
Hardesty, Benjamin 224
Hardesty, Catharine 119
Hardesty, Elizabeth 119
Hardesty, George 440
Hardesty, Joshua 248
Hardesty, Lewis 119, 548
Hardesty, Lydia 171
Hardesty, Mary 51, 119
Hardesty, Nancy 407
Hardesty, Obediah 119
Hardesty, Polly 160
Hardesty, Ralph 119
Hardesty, Rebecca 119
Hardesty, Sarah 119, 161
Hardesty, Solomon 119
Hardesty, Urias 119
Hardey, Jacob 228
Hardey, Jane 228
Hardin, Elizabeth 588
Hardin, James 556
Hardin, Matilda 601
Hardin, Thomas 260, 267, 541
Hardin, Thompson 267, 275
Hardin, William 275
Harding, Abraham 746
Harding, Elisha 756
Harding, Esther 166
Harding, Henry 121
Harding, Seth 745
Hardisty, Elizabeth 698
Hardisty, Francis 698
Hardisty, Hannah 698
Hardisty, Hugh 698
Hardisty, Mary 698
Hardisty, Rachel 698
Hardisty, Ruth 698
Hardisty, Sarah 698
Hardman, Catherine 121
Hardman, F. P. 133
Hardman, Leah 311
Hardman, Mariah 507
Hardman, Michael 588
Hardman, Nancy 133
Hardman, Peter E. 507
Hardman, Sarah 530
Hardman, Simeon 311

Hardon, Sary 276
Hardsock, Benj. 748
Hardwick, William 270, 519
Hardy, C. A. 400
Hardy, Fristram 403
Hardy, James 270, 404
Hardy, Joseph 585, 586
Hardy, Tristram 403
Hare, Christena 530
Hare, Daniel 532
Hare, John Pollock 240
Hare, Mary 384
Hare, Nancy 384
Harell, Philip 169
Harell, Thomas 237
Haren, Catherine F. 126
Haren, Peter 126
Harford, Allen 683
Harford, Ann 683
Harford, Hiram 683
Harford, John 683
Harford, Joseph 683
Harford, Louiza 683
Harford, Sena 683
Haring, Mary Ann 422
Haris, Bambo 233
Haris, Emor 701
Harison, Benjamin Mitchell 670
Harison, William 670
Harkless, Aaron 666
Harlan, Edward 169
Harlan, Eli 532
Harlan, George 139, 144
Harlan, Ishmael 144
Harlan, Margaret 276
Harlan, Samuel 3
Harland, Margaret 182
Harland, Mary 309
Harley, David 602
Harlin, Margaret 184
Harlin, Rebecca 275
Harlow, Clarissa 728
Harlow, Francis 126
Harlstrom, Thomas Coles 641
Harman, Frederick 296, 438
Harman, John 597
Harman, Jonas 296
Harman, Joseph 355
Harman, William 296
Harmar, William 532
Harmer, Josiah 560
Harmon, Chas. 417
Harmon, Elizabeth 10
Harmon, John 417, 428
Harmon, Margaret 304
Harmstrong, Andrew 475
Harnan, Sinah 477
Harnden, Jeduthan 275
Harnell, John 372
Harner, Benj. 516
Harner, Doratha 93
Harner, F. 93
Harner, Francis 93
Harner, I. 93
Harner, Isabell 93

838

Hart, William 164
Harten, Edward 508
Harter, Charles 50, 296
Harter, Conrad 363, 364
Harter, Daniel 363
Harter, Elias 52
Harter, Henry 49, 693
Harter, Isaac 693, 728
Harter, Jacob 362
Harter, Jane 388
Harter, Jinkey 96
Harter, Sally 728
Harter, Sarah 52
Harter, William 96
Hartle, Ester 588
Hartley, Mary 10, 579
Hartley, Thomas 656
Hartly, Benjamin 580
Hartman, Christopher 235
Hartman, Elizabeth 49
Hartman, Elizabeth C. 379
Hartman, Ganer 284
Hartman, George 284
Hartman, Isaac 461
Hartman, James 284
Hartman, Maryann 303
Hartsborn, Edward 64
Hartsborn, Elmer 65
Hartsell, Frederick 170
Hartshorn, Julia Ann Ellis 637
Hartshorn, Thomas C. 641
Hartsill, Abraham 296
Harus, Ana Catherin Mary 102
Harvey, Alice 266
Harvey, Andrew 224
Harvey, Ann 282, 284, 589
Harvey, Asa 559, 560, 569
Harvey, Caleb 257, 282
Harvey, Catharine 417
Harvey, Catherine 305
Harvey, Christopher 560
Harvey, Cynthee 282
Harvey, Cynthia 261, 265
Harvey, D. 697
Harvey, Eli 265, 282
Harvey, Elizabeth 258, 265, 282, 706
Harvey, Ephraim 588
Harvey, Esther 560
Harvey, H. 284
Harvey, Harlan 266
Harvey, Isaac 258, 277
Harvey, James 588
Harvey, Jesse 258
Harvey, John 588
Harvey, Joshua 258, 261, 266
Harvey, Lydia 282
Harvey, Marth 282
Harvey, Martha 269
Harvey, Mary 265, 267, 274, 282
Harvey, Mibar 474
Harvey, Nancy 162

Harvey, Ogden 131
Harvey, Rebecca 258
Harvey, Ruth 266, 273
Harvey, Samuel 267, 285, 716
Harvey, Sarah 258
Harvey, Thos. 417
Harvey, William 149, 164, 265, 282, 570
Harvey, Wm. 483
Harvie, John 30
Haseltin, Nancy 133
Haseneyer, Henry 65
Hases, Mara 602
Hases, Marah 602
Hashberger, Delila 580
Hashberger, Samuel 580
Haskell, James 713, 721
Haskell, Samuel 713
Haskins, Maria S. 651
Haskins, Rachel 703
Hasler, Mary 627
Haslet, Eliza 688
Haslet, Henry 688
Hass, Jacob 479
Hassett, Har. B. 20
Hassey, Minerva 588
Hastings, Malinda 711
Hastings, Mary 587
Hastings, Rosannah 590
Hastler, Isaac 627
Hastler, Jacob 627
Hastler, Lydia 627
Hatch, Abigal 387
Hatch, Alfred 387
Hatch, Betsey 77
Hatch, Harriet 82
Hatch, Horatio 426, 627
Hatch, Jonathan 387
Hatch, Joseph 387
Hatch, Nathaniel 387
Hatch, Waterman 387
Hatcher, Charles 704, 708
Hatcher, Farley 708
Hatcher, John 119, 296
Hatcher, Lydia 300
Hatcher, Priscilla 476
Hatcher, Rachel 296
Hatcher, Sally 474
Hatcher, Sarah 296
Hatcher, Thomas 296
Haten, Alexander 581
Hatfield, Barbara 711
Hatfield, Catherine 468
Hatfield, Edward 379
Hatfield, Isaac 704
Hatfield, Magdelene 216
Hatfield, Mary 703
Hatfield, Moses 519
Hatfield, Nancy 703
Hatfield, Nathan 564
Hatfield, Nelson 588
Hatfield, Noah 588
Hatfield, Thomas 708, 714
Hathaway, Daniel F. 52
Hathaway, Eleazer 96
Hathaway, Electa 698

Hathaway, Elijah 702
Hathaway, Elizabeth 471
Hathaway, Jane 191, 635
Hathaway, John 702
Hathaway, Joseph 278
Hathaway, Nimrod 627
Hathaway, Phebe 465, 698
Hathaway, Ruth 702
Hathaway, Sally 96
Hathaway, Samuel 702
Hathaway, Sarah 702
Hathaway, Simeon 702
Hathaway, Thomas 362, 364
Hathaway, Uriah 702
Hatinger, Annis 398
Hatinger, William 398
Hatinger, Wm. 398
Hattery, David 588
Hattfield, Eve 216
Hauck, Peter (Rev.) 98
Haughey, Jacob 745
Hauker, Polly 534
Haulk, Elizabeth 466
Haun, Elizabeth 296
Haun, John 597
Haus, Ann Margaretha 340
Haus, Anna Margaretha 337
Haus, George 348
Haus, Johan Heinrich 340
Haus, Johann Georg 337
Haus, Peter 337, 340, 348
Hausenfoes, John 351
Hausenfoes, Margaret 351
Hausenfoes, Mary Ann 351
Hauser, Josiah 416
Hautey, Abijah 663
Havel, Jesse 169
Havenrback, Anthony 92
Havens, Christina 417
Havens, Emily 422
Havens, James 546
Havens, Sarah 660
Havenstock, John H. 377
Hawes, Mara 602
Hawes, Marah 602
Hawes, Sally 443
Hawes, Wells 550
Hawk, Christiana 82
Hawk, Conrad 78
Hawk, John 53, 475
Hawk, Joseph 475
Hawk, Lewis 42
Hawk, Mary 50
Hawk, Sarah 79
Hawk, Susan E. 74
Hawker, Abraham 536
Hawkins, Amos 175
Hawkins, Ann 280
Hawkins, Anne 175
Hawkins, Benjamin 156, 175
Hawkins, Eleaser 654
Hawkins, Henry 175
Hawkins, James 170, 175
Hawkins, Jane 453
Hawkins, Jehu 270

Hawkins, John 40, 175, 224
Hawkins, Joseph 148, 156
Hawkins, Levi 175
Hawkins, Lewis 121
Hawkins, Mary 175
Hawkins, Nancy 453
Hawkins, Nathan 139, 175
Hawkins, Nathen 175
Hawkins, Olive 156
Hawkins, Philip 698
Hawkins, Polly 654
Hawkins, Rebecca 175, 453
Hawkins, Reuben 535
Hawkins, Samuel 654
Hawkins, Tamer 166
Hawkins, Thomas 453
Hawks, John 651
Hawley, --- 243
Hawley, David 296
Hawley, Isaac 78
Hawley, Mercy 223
Haworth, Ezekiel 283
Haworth, George 281
Haworth, George D. 259, 283
Haworth, James 275, 281
Haworth, Malon 256, 283
Haworth, Ruth 281
Haws, Abraham 279
Haws, Conrad 279
Haws, David 279
Haws, Fanne 279
Haws, Jacob 279
Haws, James 264
Haws, John 264, 279
Haws, Lavina Jane 264
Haws, Lieulla J. 245
Haws, Mary 269
Haws, Polly 279
Haws, S. E. 245
Haws, T. J. 245
Haws, Tabitha 706
Haws, Thomas 264
Hawthorn, James 546
Hawthorn, John 100
Hawthorn, John Mc. 551
Hawthorn, Margaret 103
Hawthorne, Mary Ann 670
Hawthornthwait, Mary Isabell 670
Hawthornthwait, Smithson 670
Hawthornthwait, William Alex. 670
Hay, Alexander 320, 332
Hay, Nicholas 448
Hay, Peter 418, 422
Hay, Robert 331
Hay, William 275
Haycock, Jacob 296
Hayden, Christopher 562
Hayes, James 379
Hayes, Jehu 296
Hayes, Kelly 413
Hayes, Kitty 413
Hayes, Mary 297
Hayes, Mordecai 296

Hayes, Nathaniel 651
Hayes, Orlando 588
Hayes, Phebe 651
Hayes, Sturges 651
Hayford, James H. 379
Haymaker, Cyntha 379
Haymaker, Eliza Ann 380
Haymaker, Frederick 379
Haymaker, John 224
Haymaker, Joseph 461
Haymaker, William D. 379
Hayman, Elizabeth 477
Hayman, Jacob 409
Hayman, James 479
Hayman, John (Jr.) 479
Haynes, Allen 197
Haynes, Archibald 279
Haynes, Asa 650, 651
Haynes, Elizabeth 197, 651, 679
Haynes, Emaline 279
Haynes, Hannah 270
Haynes, Harriatt 269
Haynes, Jane Lina 279
Haynes, Jefferson 253
Haynes, Jesse 743
Haynes, Job 197
Haynes, Jonathan 197
Haynes, Joseph 197, 270
Haynes, Lewis Harmon 279
Haynes, Margaret 631
Haynes, Mary 695
Haynes, Milly 253
Haynes, Nancy 253
Haynes, Nathaniel 651
Haynes, P. 253
Haynes, Samuel 197, 270
Haynes, Sarah 253
Haynes, Thomas 679
Haynes, William 275, 279
Haynes, William H. 258
Haynes, Wm. 253
Haynie, Geo. W. 416
Hays, Adam 296
Hays, Alexander 365
Hays, Ann 282
Hays, Betsy 461, 529
Hays, David 263, 296, 461
Hays, George R. 260
Hays, Hannah 461
Hays, Harriet 587
Hays, Jacob 270
Hays, James 18, 19, 224, 363, 369, 451, 515
Hays, James (Rev.) 321
Hays, Jane 451
Hays, John 270, 277, 451
Hays, Jonathan 409
Hays, Mary 451
Hays, Nancy 532
Hays, Nehemiah 41
Hays, Sarah 464
Hays, Thomas 216, 542, 543
Hays, William 170, 369, 371, 451
Hays, William O. 588
Hayse, James 170
Hayse, William 140

Hayslip, John 6
Hayslit, Thomas K. 534
Hayward, Ezekiel 122
Hayward, Solomon 479
Hayworth, Absalom 273
Hayworth, Daniel 614
Hayworth, Elizabeth 273
Hayworth, George 614
Hayworth, Hannah 272
Hayworth, Jonathan 614
Hayworth, Mary 614
Hayworth, Phebe 281
Hayworth, Rachel 281
Hayworth, Sarah 272
Hazard, John 266, 270
Hazard, Phebe 269
Hazelet, Martha 476
Hazelton, Joseph 746
Hazen, Charlotte 749
Hazlett, Cunningham 104
Hazlett, Isaac 104
Hazlett, James 104
Hazlett, Margaret 104
Hazlett, Mary 104
Hazlett, Moses 487
Hazlett, Nancy 479
Hazlett, Sarah 104
Hazlett, William 104
Hazlette, Mary 70
Heacock, Jonathan 296
Head, Bula 271
Headly, John 296
Heady, Stilwell 164
Heagler, George 447
Heagler, Isaac 451
Heald, Anna 289
Heald, C. A. 401
Heald, Elizabeth 301
Heald, James 296
Heald, Joseph 296
Heald, Mary 288
Heald, Rachel 302, 304
Hearst, John 67
Heaston, Catharine 583
Heaston, William 284
Heath, Abraham 137, 138
Heath, Ann 463
Heath, Deborah 468
Heath, Elizabeth 462
Heath, George 466
Heath, Hervy 32
Heath, John 16, 20, 33
Heath, John T. 602
Heath, Margaret 33
Heath, Mary 33
Heath, Nancy 523
Heath, Peter 29, 33
Heath, Polly 468
Heath, Rebecca 32
Heath, Sarah 469
Heath, Vincey J. 529
Heath, William 441
Heatly, Clarissa 378
Heatly, Mary 379
Heaton, Aaron 315
Heaton, Daniel 129, 160
Heaton, David 129
Heaton, Elizabeth 223, 529

Henderson, F. 585
Henderson, George L. 118
Henderson, James 118,
    184, 296, 441, 701
Henderson, John 118,
    441, 537, 663
Henderson, John (Jr.)
    544
Henderson, Joseph 315,
    441, 532
Henderson, Levina 469
Henderson, Margaret 110,
    118, 681
Henderson, Maria 330
Henderson, Mary 307,
    441, 616
Henderson, Mary Jane 330
Henderson, Matilda 736
Henderson, Matty 441
Henderson, Nancy 330,
    441
Henderson, Nathan 616
Henderson, Robert 118
Henderson, Samuel 17,
    438, 441
Henderson, Sarah 441
Henderson, Sarah Ann 330
Henderson, Susan 616
Henderson, Thomas 681
Henderson, Thompson 616
Henderson, William 296,
    314, 315, 317, 330
Henderson, William L.
    170, 585
Henderson, William
    Taggart 118
Henderson, Wm. 316,
    319, 332
Hendrake, Sarah 286
Hendrick, Byrd 36
Hendrick, James 200
Hendricks, John (Sr.)
    597
Hendrickson, Cornelius
    268
Hendrickson, Eli 170
Hendrickson, Harvy 588
Hendrickson, Rhoda 268,
    275
Hendrickson, Wm. 748
Hendrix, Elizabeth 461
Hendrix, Mary 302
Hendrixson, Elizabeth 124
Hendshue, Kitty 413
Heneck, Friederich 340
Heneck, Rosina 340
Henefelt, Maria
    Margaretta 89
Hening, Abagail W. 685
Hening, Thomas G. 46
Henise, T. G. 46
Henkle, Elen 466
Henkle, Jacob 466
Henkle, Nelson M. 251
Henkle, Peneny 465
Henkle, Regana 465
Henkle, Salem 466
Henkle, Saml. 213, 214,
    215

Henkle, Samuel 217
Henkle, Tena 468
Hennack, Friederich 340
Hennack, Herman 340
Hennack, Rosina 340
Henner, Ebenezer H. 279
Henning, Barbara 351
Henning, Catharina 351
Henning, Christina 351
Henning, Isaac 351
Henning, Jacob 351
Henning, Johannes 351
Hennings, Easter 439
Hennington, Stephen 384
Hennuh, Jacob 296
Henor, David 517
Henry, Abraham 663
Henry, Barbary 96
Henry, Betsy R. 96
Henry, Catharine 156
Henry, David 96, 663
Henry, Elizabeth 190,
    334
Henry, Isabel 96
Henry, Isabella 577
Henry, J. 577
Henry, James 126, 233,
    296, 555, 557
Henry, Jane 77, 96, 577
Henry, Jno. 13
Henry, Jno. Jos. 27
Henry, John 263, 666
Henry, John B. 356
Henry, John H. 96, 588
Henry, John Joseph 556
Henry, John N. 355
Henry, Joseph 96, 156,
    175
Henry, Maria 381
Henry, Morris 724
Henry, Nancy 81, 134
Henry, R. 577
Henry, Robert 96, 692
Henry, Robinson 58, 96
Henry, Rodia Ann 134
Henry, Sally 77
Henry, William 96, 296,
    525, 577
Henry, Wm. 577
Henry, Wm. J. 134
Hensel, Charles 420
Hensel, Christine 420
Hensel, Elizabeth 629
Hensel, Geo. 420
Hensel, George 409,
    437, 627
Hensel, Mary 408, 631
Hensel, Michal 439
Henshour, Polly 413
Hensley, Samuel 704
Henson, John 479
Henson, Lydia 657
Henthorn, James 104
Henthorn, John 104
Henthorn, Rabecca 404
Henton, Benjamin 444,
    456, 466
Henton, James 444
Henton, Nancy 413

Henwood, Joshua 704
Heolethneel, Andrew 98
Hephner, Dolly 293
Hephner, Elizabeth 302
Hepler, Jacob 475
Hepner, Henry 310
Hepner, John 296, 310
Hepner, Sarah 300
Hepp, Rosa 651
Herbelet, Peter 355
Herbert, Noblett 283
Herbert, Peter 354
Herbert, Thomas 659
Herbstrait, George 370
Herd, Ann 206
Herd, Stephen 206
Herd, Thomas 200
Herd, William 6
Herdman, Peter 525
Herger, Christena 339
Herger, Gottlieb 339
Herger, Karoliene 339
Herger, Karolina 339
Herger, Luisa Matilda
    339
Hering, Lewis 51
Hering, Philip 49
Herkimer, Orintha 604
Hermal, John 565
Herman, Christian 296
Herman, Elizabeth 336
Herman, Elizabeth Ana
    336
Herman, Henry 296
Herman, Johann 336
Herman, John 627
Hermann, Elizabeth 337
Hernden, Susannah
    Beverly 196
Hernden, Thomas 196
Herod, Mary 410
Herold, Mina 379
Heron, Andrew 499
Heron, Eve 405
Heron, James 237
Heron, Nancy 441
Herren, David 404
Herrick, Hughey 471
Herrick, Samuel 697
Herrick, William D. 470
Herring, Barbarra 406
Herring, Elizabeth 520
Herring, Harriet 419
Herring, Mary Jane 53
Herring, Phebe H. R. 603
Herringdon, Squire 211
Herriot, Ephraim 443
Herrmann, Christina 337
Herrmann, John 337
Herrod, Elizabeth 700
Herrod, James 700
Herrod, Jemima 700
Herrod, Levi 700
Herrod, Michael 700
Herrod, Racheal 700
Herrod, Rachel 700
Herrod, Samuel 700
Herrod, Sarah 700
Herrod, William 700

Herrold, Barbara 72
Herrold, Catharine 72
Herrold, Daniel 72, 78
Herrold, Daniel (Jr.) 82
Herrold, David 297
Herrold, Jno. 82
Herron, Catharine 729
Herron, Cook 409, 729
Herron, David 409, 729
Herron, Jane 588
Herron, John 130, 410,
725, 729
Herron, Mary 441
Herron, Polly 409
Herron, Samuel 729
Hersh, Peggy 405
Hershey, Jacob B. 367
Hershfield, George 100
Hershman, John 509
Hershman, Polly 525
Herson, Maria V. F.
Vintroux 709
Herson, Maria Viryile
Fanny Vintroux 709
Herst, Aaron 550
Herter, Elizabeth 653
Herter, John 653
Herter, Martin 653
Hervey, John 554, 556
Herwood, C. 729
Herzer, Emma Emilie 345
Herzer, L. G. 345
Hesler, Barbara 409
Hesler, Catherine 24
Hesler, Cathrina 25
Hesler, Cathrine 25
Hesler, John 10, 24, 25
Heslet, Samuel 134
Heslip, Thomas 316
Hess, Ann 682
Hess, Charity 70, 71
Hess, Elisabeth 347
Hess, Elizabeth 136
Hess, John 136, 682
Hess, John M. 136
Hess, Lydia 381
Hess, Margaret 682
Hess, Mary Marce 582
Hess, Peter 682
Hesser, Betsy 465
Hesser, Catharine 465
Hesser, Kittury 333
Hessker, Margaret 378
Hessler, Jacob 475
Hester, Abigail 272
Hester, David 100, 275
Hester, Elizabeth 53,
273
Hester, Henry 270
Hester, Henry A. 51
Hester, John 297
Hester, Martin 270, 277
Hester, Peter 285
Hester, Susanna 270
Hestin, Magtalena 441
Hestler, John 22
Heston, Amos 284
Heston, Martin 297
Heston, Mercy 284

Heston, Phineas 284
Heston, Phinius 514
Heston, Tacy 305
Heston, William 284
Heston, William (Sr.)
284
Hetfield, Abel 131
Hetfield, Elihu 131
Hetfield, Elizabeth 131
Hetfield, George 131
Hetfield, Jacob 131
Hetfield, John 131
Hetfield, Mary 131
Hetfield, Nancy 131
Hetfield, Rachel 131
Hetfield, Sarah 131
Heth, Mary Ann 241
Heth, William 241
Heuize, Eliza 126
Heull, L. S. 390
Heus, Ruth 406
Heuton, Jas. 448
Hevbaugh, Elizabeth 592
Heviston, William 519
Hewel, N. S. 45
Hewett, Ira 705
Hewett, Thomas 203
Hewey, Catharine 589
Hewey, Lenday 30
Hewey, Lendy 30
Hewit, Susannah 303
Hewitt, Aaron 78, 84
Hewitt, Betsy 83
Hewitt, Ephraim 84
Hewitt, Ephram 84
Hewitt, G. 447
Hewitt, George 84
Hewitt, John 84
Hewitt, Joseph 78, 84
Hewitt, L. M. 395
Hewitt, Leeds M. 395
Hewitt, Moses 84
Hewitt, Moses (II) 78
Hewitt, Pardon 84
Hewitt, S. L. 395
Hewitt, Sally 83
Hewitt, Sally L. 395
Hewitt, Tryphena 77
Hewitt, William E. 395
Hewlings, Abel 199
Hewlings, Joseph 199,
201
Heylin, Isaah 192
Heylin, Jane 192
Heylin, Marcus 192, 210
Heyne, William 466
Heys, A. 403
Heys, J. A. 403
Heys, Polly 460
Hezeker, Arolina Louisa
101
Hezeker, Charles A. 100
Hfley, Polly 519
Hiamman, George 595
Hiatt, Eleasor 278
Hiatt, Gideon 275
Hiatt, Hezekiah 278
Hiatt, Reuben 270
Hiatt, Samuel 262, 264

Hibbard, Jane Eliza 472
Hibbard, Julia Ann 222
Hibben, James 536
Hibben, John 263
Hibben, Mary 263
Hibben, Thomas 263
Hibben, William 256
Hibbens, Sophia 524
Hibbin, Thomas 275
Hibbit, James 297
Hibbs, Valentine 543
Hibbs, William 543
Hibel, Catherine 306
Hickerson, Saml. 750
Hickle, Mary Ann 479
Hickman, Dolly 529
Hickman, Jeremiah 297,
310
Hickman, John 297
Hickman, Mary 299
Hickman, Sarah 169
Hickox, James 627
Hicks, Henrietta Hone
670
Hicks, Josephine 670
Hicks, Saml. 82
Hicks, William 575
Hide, John 538
Hide, Thomas 538
Hide, William 475
Hidelbach, Peter 409
Hidy, William 466
Hielbear, Mary 603
Hiers, Abraham 532
Hiers, Anthony 525
Hiersted, Emily 391
Hierz, Elizabetha Maria
340
Hierz, Eva 340
Hierz, John Georg 340
Hiesler, John 663
Hiestand, Joseph 439,
440
Hiestand, Samuel 439
Hiestend, Samuel 438
Higby, Isaac 239
Higby, Peter 735
Higgins, Andrew 75
Higgins, Edward 670
Higgins, Elizabeth 706
Higgins, John 670, 715
Higgins, Joseph 700
Higgins, Maria 670
Higgins, Mary 41
Higgins, Michael 75, 78
Higgins, Nancy 706
Higgins, Patrick 38
Higgins, Rachel 174
Higgins, Robert 41
Higgins, Ruth 463
Higgins, Salvina 398
Higgins, Sarah 75, 311
Higgins, Susanna 670
Higgins, William 506
Higgins, Willis 270
Higgonbottom, John 656
Highby, Isaac 239
Higher, Elizabeth 49
Higher, Nancy 52

Highland, Anthony 558
Hight, George 363
Hight, George W. 362, 363, 364
Highway, John 509
Highway, Samuel 563
Higingbottom, Delia 479
Higins, Samuel 297
Higley, Laura 480
Hilards, Shadrick 415
Hilberg, Mary 603
Hilbert, Peter 597
Hilbert, Samuel 379
Hildebrand, Elias 663
Hildebrand, Jacob 400
Hildenbrant, Andrew 354
Hilditch, Saml. 558
Hilditch, Samuel 558, 568, 569, 572, 576
Hildreth, Jefferson 694
Hildreth, Miner 694
Hildreth, Samuel 694
Hile, Elizabeth 413
Hile, Jesse 731
Hile, Sarah 590
Hiler, Jacob 127
Hiles, Christopher 638
Hiles, Nicholas 297
Hiliday, John 422
Hill, Aaron 384
Hill, Adnne 196
Hill, Amanda 583
Hill, Anny 469
Hill, Asa 461
Hill, Austin 394
Hill, Betsey 393
Hill, Calvin 317
Hill, Caty 224
Hill, Conrad 65
Hill, D. 252
Hill, Delilia 420
Hill, Druzilla 196
Hill, E. 252
Hill, Elias 691
Hill, Eliza 375
Hill, Eliza M. 252
Hill, Elizabeth 467, 626
Hill, Elmina A. 228
Hill, George 19, 754
Hill, Henry 393
Hill, James 239, 663
Hill, Jemima 655
Hill, John 443, 446, 691, 756
Hill, John (Jr.) 130
Hill, John (Sr.) 130
Hill, John C. 376
Hill, John J. 659
Hill, Jonathan 78
Hill, Joseph 211
Hill, Joseph Henry 196
Hill, Joseph M. 333
Hill, Josiah 691
Hill, Juli Ann 445
Hill, Kisiah 629
Hill, Louisa 394
Hill, Margaret 376
Hill, Martha 130
Hill, Mary 196, 302, 590

Hill, Nancy 130, 467
Hill, Nathan 189, 196
Hill, Nathen 184
Hill, Rachael 602
Hill, Rebecca 210
Hill, Rebeckah 196
Hill, Richard 547
Hill, Roxana 393
Hill, Samuel 82, 589
Hill, Sarah 590
Hill, Stephen 691
Hill, Thomas 130
Hill, Thomas P. 691
Hill, Tilbon 749
Hill, William 445, 466, 538
Hill, William R. 210
Hill, Wm. 373
Hillard, Elizabeth 466
Hillard, Joseph Thomas 424
Hillebrecht, Andy 136
Hiller, Aaron 365, 366
Hiller, Henry 366, 415
Hiller, John 360
Hiller, John S. 366
Hiller, Justus 736
Hiller, Samuel 640
Hillery, Benjamin 750
Hillier, Ann 697
Hillier, Anthony 697
Hillier, Franklin 697
Hillier, John 697
Hillier, Justus 736
Hillier, Justus (Jr.) 736
Hillier, Richard 697
Hillier, Thomas 697
Hillier, William 697
Hilling, Mary A. 122
Hillis, Thos. 415
Hillis, William 297
Hillman, . . . rena 422
Hills, Caleb 745
Hills, J. H. (Dr.) 391
Hills, James H. 390
Hills, Reuben 391
Hillwer, Aaron 365
Hillyer, Justin (Jr.) 743
Hilnner, William 561
Hilsamer, David 257
Hilt, Moses 415
Himes, Betsey 628
Hin, Joshua 297
Hinchsman, Hannah 305
Hinckle, George W. 602
Hincle, Mary 463
Hincle, Phebe 461
Hindbaugh, Sarah Ann 589
Hinde, Edward 401
Hinde, John W. 26
Hinders, Anna Maria 102
Hindman, David 39
Hindman, Hannah 39
Hindman, John 39
Hindman, Robert 589
Hine, Henry 401
Hinelin, Almira Jane 588

Hineman, Ruth 11
Hines, Catharine 628
Hines, Jesse 258
Hines, Mary Christiana 438
Hines, Rudolph 597
Hines, Sarah 307
Hines, Susanah 102
Hingood, Isaac 321
Hinhsley, John 94
Hinkle, Asa 554
Hinkle, Barbary 466
Hinkle, Enan 466
Hinkle, George W. 602
Hinkle, Sarah 333
Hinkley, Hannah 650
Hinkley, Horace 650
Hinkley, Joshua 650
Hinkson, Benjamin 261
Hinkson, John 461
Hinkston, Mary 273
Hinkston, Polly Lually 273
Hinneman, Sarah 723
Hins, Henry 525
Hintene, William 589
Hinterlich, Jacob 419
Hinton, Ellenor 587
Hinton, George 698
Hinton, John 698
Hinton, Levi (Jr.) 391
Hinton, Malinda 698
Hinton, Mary 698
Hinton, Thomas 698
Hintze, Frederick 749
Hipes, Nancy 532
Hipner, Caty 290
Hipner, Henry 297
Hipperds, Elizabeth 57
Hipshear, Christian 421
Hire, Catherine 49
Hire, Jacob 377
Hires, Keziah 99
Hirn, Adam 339
Hirn, Christoph 339
Hirn, Veronica 339
Hirschberger, Anna 338
Hirschberger, Eva 336
Hirschberger, Jacob 336, 338
Hirschberger, Lidia 336
Hirschberger, Susanna 336
Hisel, Catherine 477
Hisey, Mary 703
Hisle, Elizabeth 475
Hitchcock, Elisha 654
Hitchcock, Erastus 589
Hitchcock, Sarah 432
Hitchcock, Thomas 333, 597
Hite, Abrm. 409
Hite, Adam 410
Hite, Andrew 538
Hite, Barbary 407
Hite, Conrad 409
Hite, Delilia 417
Hite, Elizabeth 529
Hite, George 189

Hite, Henry 538
Hite, Isaac 410
Hite, Jacob D. 428
Hite, John 209, 404
Hite, Jonas 429
Hite, Joseph 415
Hite, Lewis 419
Hite, Maryann 524
Hite, Rachael 418
Hite, Sarah 527
Hite, Silas W. 429
Hites, John 589
Hites, Susan 588
Hitsman, H. 402
Hitsman, Henry 402
Hitsman, Lant 401
Hitt, Caleb 196
Hitt, John Wesley 197
Hitt, Peter R. 632
Hitt, Samuel 206
Hittle, Christian 532
Hittle, Hannah 531
Hittle, Solomon 164
Hively, Adam 376
Hively, Ann 739
Hively, Catharine 739
Hively, Christopher 297
Hively, Gracy A. 379
Hively, Harriet 378
Hively, Isaac 376
Hively, John 376, 739
Hively, Mary 739
Hively, Michael 297, 739
Hively, Mottlena 289
Hively, Paul 440
Hively, Peter 739
Hively, Polly 420
Hively, Thomas 376
Hivling, John 516
Hivling, Margaret 532
Hix, John 656
Hixon, Elijah 445, 449
Hixon, Enoch 532
Hixon, Rachel 445
Hixon, Rebecca McClure 617
Hixon, Reuben 532
Hixon, Reubin 445
Hixon, William 445
Hiy, Amanda M. 602
Hizer, Richard 466
Hoak, Daniel 53, 54
Hoard, Eliza 422
Hobbs, Ephergn 705
Hobbs, Nancy 524, 581
Hobbs, Polly 476
Hoberger, John Kilian 379
Hobert, Giles 740
Hobert, Mary Ann 740
Hoblet, Jane 527
Hoblett, William 258, 261
Hoblit, A. W. 244
Hoblit, Elizabeth 244
Hoblit, Margaret 245
Hoblit, William 245
Hoblit, William (Dea.) 245

Hoblitt, Mary W. 245
Hobson, Anna 273
Hobson, Arksie 274
Hobson, Cornelius 270
Hobson, Deborah 279
Hobson, George 279
Hobson, Jane 633
Hobson, John 279, 280
Hobson, Joseph 279
Hobson, Mary 270
Hobson, Samuel 279
Hobson, Sarah 279
Hobson, William 279
Hobsugh, Caty 462
Hock, George 297
Hocke, Elizabeth 419
Hocker, Margaret 418
Hocker, Margretha 344
Hocker, Richard 410
Hocket, Hannah 275
Hocket, Nathan 257
Hocket, Rachel 275
Hocket, Seth 277
Hockett, Anna 271
Hockett, Anne 270
Hockett, Elizabeth 271
Hockett, Jos. 271
Hockett, Seth 270
Hockman, Abraham 639
Hockman, Ann Mary 639
Hockman, Elizabeth 419
Hockman, Henry 438
Hockman, Jacob 742
Hodge, Andrew 204, 209, 211
Hodge, Catherine 441
Hodge, Charity 441
Hodge, Elenor 441
Hodge, Elizabeth 441
Hodge, Isaac 441
Hodge, John 441
Hodge, Joseph 441
Hodge, Levi 441
Hodge, Mary 441
Hodge, Palina 209
Hodge, Robert 597
Hodge, Sarah 334
Hodge, Sarah 441
Hodge, William 224
Hodgson, Achsah 283
Hodgson, Amos 279
Hodgson, Daniel 279
Hodgson, Elizabeth 279
Hodgson, Enos 279
Hodgson, George Hur 279
Hodgson, James 122
Hodgson, Joel 270, 279
Hodgson, John 279
Hodgson, Jonathan 279
Hodgson, Joseph 279
Hodgson, Levisa 270
Hodgson, Mary 270, 273, 279
Hodgson, Matthew 279
Hodgson, Ruth 279
Hodgson, Sarah 279
Hodgson, Solomon 279
Hodgson, Susanna 270
Hodson, Hiram 612

Hodson, Lydia 271
Hodson, Maria 612
Hodson, Ruben 286
Hoemaker, Elias 110
Hoey, Mary 293
Hofacker, Martin 357
Hofer, Jacob 432
Hoff, Elizabeth 169
Hoff, Isaac 146, 150
Hoff, James 224
Hoff, John 120
Hoff, Lewis 147
Hoff, Sally 147
Hoffert, Samuel 642
Hoffman, Anson 401
Hoffman, Caroline 602
Hoffman, Catharine 655
Hoffman, Delilah 148, 153
Hoffman, Elizabeth 381
Hoffman, Geo. M. 49
Hoffman, George 549
Hoffman, Isaac 697
Hoffman, Jacob 297
Hoffman, John 401, 402, 420
Hoffman, John (Jr.) 65
Hoffman, Louisa 378
Hoffman, Margaret 658
Hoffman, Peter 148, 153
Hoffman, Robert 170
Hoffman, Rosanna 422
Hoffman, Sampson 153
Hoffman, Samuel 690
Hoffman, Sarah Ann 601
Hoffman, Susannah 294
Hoffmann, Louis 359
Hoffmire, Johanna 471
Hofstatter, Jacob 344
Hofstatter, Johnnes 344
Hogan, James 401
Hoge, Alivia 268, 275
Hoge, James 297, 310
Hoge, Robert 479
Hogen, James 356
Hogg, John 751
Hogg, Miriam 670
Hoghen, Elizabeth 644
Hogset, Dafney 553
Hogue, Esther 296
Hogue, James 297, 310
Hogue, William 264
Hoisington, Betsy 584
Hoisington, Elizabeth 584
Hoisington, Elvira 584
Hoisington, John S. 584
Hoisington, Lucy 584
Hoisington, Polly 584
Hoisington, Rhoda 584
Hoisington, Saniel 584
Hoisington, Smith 584
Hoisington, Triphene 584
Hoit, Joseph 745
Hoit, Ruth 79
Hoke, Alice Ann 422
Hoke, Catharine 69
Holaday, Andrew 705
Holben, Catharine 473

Horner, Edward 147
Horner, Elias 56
Horner, Elijah 147
Horner, Isam 595
Horner, John 170, 371, 571
Horner, Joshua 708
Horner, Kelly 520
Horner, Mary 170, 530
Horner, Moses 708
Horner, Nathan 152, 532
Horner, Phebe 532
Horner, Sarah 708
Hornet, Elijah 209
Hornet, Elizabeth 404
Hornet, Mary 412
Hornet, Polly 412
Horney, Anderson 511
Horney, Daniel 519
Horney, Deborah 511, 514
Horney, Elizabeth 462
Horney, Esther 511, 514
Horney, Hannah 521
Horney, Lida 514
Horney, Lyda 514
Horney, Lydia 520, 521
Horney, Paris 514
Horney, Parris 514
Horney, Paul 511
Horney, Rhoda 511
Horney, Rody 514
Horney, Sarah 530
Horney, William 519
Horniday, Rachel 169
Hornish, John (Jr.) 379
Hornning, Gustav 357
Horr, Francis 392
Horstman, J. W. (Rev.) 53
Horton, Isaac C. 656
Horton, Jacob 55, 607
Horton, James 661
Horton, John 660
Horton, Louisa 581
Horton, William 724
Hosbrook, Archibald 560
Hoschar, Barbary 531
Hoseman, Mary Ann 592
Hoseman, Rachel 589
Hosenfooes, Margaret 352
Hosier, Elizabeth 506
Hosier, Frederick 506
Hosier, Gilbert 639
Hosier, Jacob 525
Hosier, John 535
Hoskings, George 270
Hoskins, Elizabeth 723
Hoskins, Hannah 267, 274
Hoskins, John 270
Hoskins, Jonathan 271
Hoskins, Margaret 469
Hoskins, Marie S. 650
Hoskins, Moses 267
Hoskinson, Isaiah 757
Hoskinson, Jas. 746
Hosner, John 651
Hoss, Abraham 627
Hoss, Barbara 631
Hoss, Jacob 627

Hosse, Susannah 625
Hossenfoois, John 352
Hossenfoose, John 352
Hossenfoose, Marg. 352
Hossrod, Rebecca 419
Hostetter, David 297
Hostetter, Henry 635
Hostetter, John 632
Hostetter, Rachel 626
Hostiller, John 170
Hoteman, Jesse 466
Hottle, Clarisey B. 417
Hotts, Easter 105
Houch, Jane 580
Houck, James 410, 698
Houdesel, Ann 434
Houdesel, John 434
Hough, Benjamin 139
Hough, Gustavus 297
Hough, Joseph 139, 148, 152, 158, 170
Hough, Phebe 579
Hough, Sarah 304
Hough, Thomas 139
Hougham, David 170
Hougham, Polly 172
Houghan, Aaron C. 589
Houghman, Aaron 164
Houghman, Sarah 170
Houghton, Joseph W. 743
Houghton, Rosetta M. 743
Hougland, Alvina 379
Houk, Catharine 130, 522
Houk, Felix 515
Houk, Jacob 405
Houk, John 515
Houk, William 130
Houke, Mary 517
Houlette, Lizzie S. 311
Houlette, N. B. 311
Houlette, Nicholas B. 311
Houlette, Nicholas B. (Jr.) 311
Houlette, S. 311
Houlton, Howard 640
House, Abraham 368
House, Caty 626
House, Elizabeth 83, 301
House, Henry (Jr.) 368
House, Isaac 368, 369
House, Jacob 458
House, Jemima 172
House, John 546
House, Mary 468
House, Mercy 305
House, Nathan 691
House, Richard 691
Houselman, Crestina 304
Houseman, Peggy 610
Houseman, Peter 610
Houser, Anny 589
Houser, Ellen 589
Houser, George H. 589
Houser, Isaac 589
Houser, Jacob 67
Houser, John H. 589
Houser, Katharine 591
Houser, Sarah 67

Housman, Barbara 627
Houstan, Robert 88
Houstan, William 88
Houston, John 88, 754
Houston, Nancy 590
Houston, Polly 288
Houston, Priscilla 224
Houston, Robert 224
Houston, Wm. A. 88
Hout, Adam 678
Hout, Catherine 678
Hout, Elizabeth 678
Hout, George 678
Hout, Henry 678
Hout, Jacob 678
Hout, John 678
Hout, Margaret 678
Hout, Mary 678
Hout, Peter 678
Hout, Sarah 678
Houton, Hannah 295
Houts, Philip 297
Houty, William 297
Hoveler, Catharine 292
Hover, Caroline 58
Hover, Cyrus H. 58
Hover, Eliza 58
Hover, Eliza M. 50
Hover, Eliza Matilda 58
Hover, James A. 58
Hover, John 410
Hover, John B. 594
Hover, Joseph 58
Hover, Joseph O. 58
Hover, Joshua B. 58
Hover, Julius A. 58
Hover, Manuel 58
Hover, Maria B. 53
Hover, Sarah A. 50
Hover, William U. 58
Hover, William Ulysses 58
How, Elizabeth 272
How, Jacob 466
How, James 271, 405, 410
How, Jane 465
How, John 275, 443, 461, 666
How, Lelden 589
How, Margret 460
How, Nancy 469
How, Susanah 467
How, Tacy 655
Howald, John 120
Howan, Thomas 715
Howan, William 714
Howard, Betsey 476
Howard, Burr 284
Howard, Frances 704
Howard, George 165, 515, 556, 559
Howard, Hannah 10
Howard, Henrietta 705
Howard, J. 648
Howard, James 170, 618
Howard, Jane 525
Howard, John 532
Howard, Joseph 257, 284
Howard, Martha 705, 714

Howard, Mary Hannah 284
Howard, Polly 171
Howard, Rebecca 375
Howard, Robert 202
Howard, Sophia 12
Howard, Susanna 525, 532
Howard, Sylvia 81
Howard, W. S. 402
Howard, William 571, 656
Howard, William (Jr.) 708
Howard, William (Sr.) 708
Howd, George W. 231
Howd, Rerec I. 231
Howdeshall, Fanny 631
Howdeshall, John 627
Howdeshall, Michael 632
Howdeshall, Sarah 632
Howdeshelt, Absalom 663
Howe, Ann 32
Howe, David 410
Howe, Edward 32
Howe, Jennie 8
Howe, Joel 713
Howe, Polly 404
Howe, Rebeckah 12
Howel, Isreal 211
Howel, Samuel Jackson 100
Howell, A. 93
Howell, Abigail 93
Howell, Adin 205
Howell, Benjamin 275
Howell, Charles 271
Howell, Daniel 560
Howell, Deborah 308
Howell, Eleanor 50
Howell, Eliza 729
Howell, George P. 729
Howell, George W. 93
Howell, J. M. 93, 93
Howell, James P. 93
Howell, John M. 50, 93
Howell, John T. 417
Howell, Lemira Lee 229
Howell, Levi 475
Howell, Martha 301
Howell, Martha Ann 416
Howell, Mary Ann 729
Howell, Mary J. 93
Howell, Moses A. 659
Howell, Nancy 276
Howell, Phebe Y. 729
Howell, Rebecca 51
Howell, Ruth 273
Howell, Samuel 220, 501
Howell, Sarah 93, 272
Howell, Silas 554
Howell, Thankful 7
Howell, William 7
Hower, Henry 178
Hower, John 178
Hower, Sarah 178
Howey, Catharine 589
Howey, John 589
Howey, Samuel 170
Howland, Beam 48
Howland, Benjamin 259

Howland, Clarinda 275
Howryhouser, Wm. 418
Howser, Sarah Ann 588
Hoy, Ann 302
Hoy, Charles 67
Hoy, Dawson 67
Hoy, Sarah 288, 309
Hoyle, Elizabeth 307
Hoyle, Jane E. 473
Hoyt, Sarah 736
Hoyt, Susan 54
Hozier, Anna Barbery 506
Hozier, John 506
Huahes, C. 382
Huahes, Emma 382
Huahes, W. H. 382
Hual, James 208
Hubball, Abijah (Jr.) 475
Hubbard, Aley 460
Hubbard, Ephraim B. 297
Hubbard, Levin 252, 253
Hubbard, Margaret 589
Hubbard, Nancy 588
Hubbard, William 170
Hubbel, Sarah 477
Hubbell, Abijah 475
Hubbell, Elizabeth A. W. 228
Hubbell, Jesse 479
Hubbell, R. H. 228
Hubbell, Sampson 215
Hubben, William 282
Hubble, Jacob 516
Hubble, Sampson 185, 519
Hubeigh, Peter 461
Hubel, Ruthy 657
Huber, Anne Elizabeth 637
Huber, Anthony 125
Huber, Catharine 636
Huber, Elijah 627
Huber, Henry 416
Huber, John 410
Huber, Martin 418
Huber, William 637
Huchtscheiper, Clara Elizabeth 100
Huckman, Nicholas 297
Huckriede, Henry W. 100
Hucks, Benjamin 479
Huddle, Henry 414
Huddleston, Agnes 705
Huddlestun, Elizabeth 192
Huddlestun, Henry 192
Huddlestun, John 192
Huddlestun, Lithe 192
Huddlestun, Patcey 192
Huddlestun, Rachel 192
Huddlestun, Sally 192
Huddlestun, William 192
Huddlestun, William (Jr.) 192
Hudgel, Joseph 160
Hudson, Elijah 100, 663
Hudson, Harriett 603
Hudson, Jacob 379
Hudson, James 82

Hudson, Jesse J. 62
Hudson, John 45, 127
Hudson, Mary 62
Hudson, Mary F. 380
Hueston, Jane 161, 589
Hueston, John 170
Hueston, Matthew 137, 138, 139, 140, 141, 142, 157
Huey, Catherine 121
Huey, John 597
Hufer, Michael 416
Huff, Abraham 141, 584
Huff, Catharine 162
Huff, Isaac 141
Huff, John 548
Huff, Lewis 160
Huff, Nancy 123
Huff, Samuel 708
Huff, Thomas 581
Huffman, Abraham 147, 157, 186, 197
Huffman, Ambrose 200
Huffman, Ann 186
Huffman, Anna 177, 225
Huffman, Barbary 186
Huffman, Betsy 170
Huffman, Christana 186
Huffman, Daniel 656
Huffman, David 202
Huffman, Elizabeth 156, 186
Huffman, Eve 412
Huffman, George 142, 143, 147, 156, 157, 177
Huffman, Isaac 142, 156, 177
Huffman, Jacob 165, 545
Huffman, Jeremiah 191
Huffman, Jesse 65
Huffman, Joanna 602
Huffman, Levi 134
Huffman, Lewis 186, 200
Huffman, Lily 177
Huffman, Margaret 133
Huffman, Mary 172, 186
Huffman, Mathias 186, 224
Huffman, Moses 186, 224
Huffman, Peggy 161
Huffman, Peter 142, 177
Huffman, Polly 177
Huffman, Robt. F. 551
Huffman, Sally 177
Huffman, Sampson 177
Huffman, Sarah 186
Huffman, William 186
Huffner, John 751
Hufford, Dorcas 419
Huffstutter, Mary 605
Huffstutter, William 605
Hufman, Andrew 632
Hufman, Mary 409
Hufman, Rebecca 415
Hugchins, Hannah 171
Hughbanks, Fanky 655
Hughes, Abraham 183, 747
Hughes, Ada M. 382

Hughes, Ariel 647
Hughes, Barnabas 623
Hughes, C. 382
Hughes, David 228
Hughes, Delilah 270
Hughes, E. W. 402
Hughes, Elijah 129
Hughes, Elizabeth 308, 659
Hughes, Emily 228
Hughes, Emma 382
Hughes, Ezekiel 561, 569
Hughes, Hannah 183, 276
Hughes, Hathander 658
Hughes, Ida A. 382
Hughes, Idela A. 382
Hughes, Isaac 183
Hughes, J. C. (Dr.) 695
Hughes, James 461
Hughes, James M. 695
Hughes, Jesse 382
Hughes, Jn. 624
Hughes, John 267, 624
Hughes, Jonas M. 382
Hughes, Jonathan 1, 475
Hughes, Lydia 183
Hughes, Margaret 410
Hughes, Marshall 747
Hughes, Mary 183, 404, 624
Hughes, Nancy E. 382
Hughes, Polly 267, 274
Hughes, Rebecka 476
Hughes, Rosabell 382
Hughes, Sarah 183
Hughes, Sarah G. 53
Hughes, Silas 479
Hughes, Stephen 45
Hughes, Thomas B. 623
Hughes, W. H. 382
Hughes, William 238, 238
Hughett, Jacob 454
Hughett, Nancy 454
Hughey, Catherine C. 620
Hughey, Isaac 620
Hughey, Isabella 532
Hughey, Kate 620
Hughey, Nancy A. 587
Hughs, Abraham 183
Hughs, Absalum 722
Hughs, Asa 705
Hughs, David 466
Hughs, Elizabeth 293, 655
Hughs, Isaac 183
Hughs, J. 45
Hughs, J. R. 187
Hughs, James 206
Hughs, John 729
Hughs, Jonathan 45, 46
Hughs, Katherine 708
Hughs, Margaret 183, 585
Hughs, Patrick 602
Hughs, Rebeckah 183
Hughs, Rosana 604
Hughs, Ruth 183
Hughs, Sarah 183
Hughs, Silas 708
Hughs, Thomas 729

Hughs, Wesley 183
Hughson, Levi 735
Hughy, Isabella 59
Hughy, Margaret 525
Hughy, William 525
Hugt, Rebecca 78
Hukel, Hiram 466
Hukill, David 445
Hukill, Elizabeth 681
Hukill, Elsy 445
Hukill, Hiram 445
Hukill, Isaac 681
Hukill, James 681
Hukill, Nancy 445
Hukill, Nathan 445
Hukill, Noah 445
Hukill, Polly 445
Hukill, Richard 445
Hukill, Samuel 445
Hukill, Seth 445
Hukill, Stephen 445
Hukill, Zebulon 445, 461
Hukle, Letticia 445
Hukle, Niomi 445
Hukle, Polly 445
Hukle, Richard 445
Hukle, Stephen 466
Hukrom, Aaron 638
Hukrom, Elizabeth 638
Hukrom, Nancy 638
Hukrom, Polly 638
Hukrom, William 638
Hulbert, Catharine 81
Hulbert, Elisha 84
Hulbert, Eliza 76
Hulburt, Marcia 379
Hulet, Lewis 224
Hulett, Martha 224
Hulinger, Mary 591
Hull, Aaron 297
Hull, David 186, 188
Hull, David McL. 717
Hull, Edy 111
Hull, Elizabeth 413, 602
Hull, Ezra 78
Hull, Henry 297, 402
Hull, Hiram 581
Hull, Hiram D. 717
Hull, James 746
Hull, Jas. 749
Hull, Jesse 297
Hull, John 3, 297, 410, 745
Hull, Josiah 43
Hull, Louisa 214
Hull, Lydia 224
Hull, Martin 482
Hull, Rachel 83
Hull, Saml. B. 748
Hull, Samuel 297, 310, 749
Hull, Trustram 214
Hull, Uriah 747
Hull, Wm. 746, 747, 748
Hullenbarger, John 55, 63
Hullenbarger, Mary 55
Huller, Warden 410
Hullinger, Elizabeth 101

Hullinger, George 461
Hulpruner, Susannah 303
Hulse, Albert P. 586
Hulse, Ambrose 586
Hulse, Aristeus 586
Hulse, Elizabeth 225
Hulse, Israel 586
Hulse, Joseph 118
Hulse, Mary 586
Hulse, William 105
Hulsey, Asahel 282
Hulson, Sarah 53
Hultz, Joseph 200
Hum, Adam 312
Hum, Adam C. 311
Hum, David 311
Hum, E. 311
Hum, Elizabeth 311, 312
Hum, J. 311
Hum, J. W. 311
Hum, Jacob 311
Hum, John 312, 647
Hum, Lucinda 311
Hum, M. M. 311
Hum, Margaret 311
Hum, Martha 312
Hum, Mary 311
Hum, Robert 403
Hum, Sarah 647
Hum, Ulysses C. 311
Humberson, Thomas 10
Hume, John 410
Hume, Robert 519
Humes, John 555, 556, 558, 564, 566, 572
Humes, Margaret 558
Humfill, Valentine 211
Humfreville, David 516
Humlong, George 239
Hummel, C. 245
Hummel, Charles (Rev.) 245
Hummel, Lucy Ann 245
Hummel, Thomas 405
Hummell, Thos. 750
Humond, Anna 333
Humphreville, Julianna 670
Humphreville, Susana 670
Humphrey, Aaron C. 385
Humphrey, Arminda M. C. 385
Humphrey, David 685
Humphrey, Dorcas 385
Humphrey, Eber 385
Humphrey, Eliza 385
Humphrey, Elizabeth 685
Humphrey, George 685
Humphrey, Henry 475
Humphrey, Isaac 78
Humphrey, Jacob 84, 754
Humphrey, James 597, 615
Humphrey, John (Jr.) 685
Humphrey, John (Sr.) 685
Humphrey, Laura 385
Humphrey, Lemuel 385
Humphrey, Lemuel G. 385
Humphrey, Leonard 753
Humphrey, Lewis 753

Huston, Abraham 499, 501
Huston, Amanda 589
Huston, Andrew 417, 748
Huston, Austin 448
Huston, Austin C. 448
Huston, Benjamin 297
Huston, David 110, 499, 501, 502, 503, 507, 510, 511
Huston, Elizabeth 560
Huston, Hannah 292
Huston, Isabella 683
Huston, Israel 501
Huston, James 683
Huston, Jane 683
Huston, John 297, 617, 683
Huston, John R. 379
Huston, Mary 617
Huston, Mordecia 110
Huston, Moses 78
Huston, Peggy 189
Huston, Saml. 517
Huston, Samuel 297, 560
Huston, Sarah 502, 503
Huston, Thomas 3, 589, 617, 747
Huston, Tyrantus R. 448
Huston, William 110, 297, 589
Hutchason, Sarah 11
Hutchens, Bradberry 405
Hutchenson, William 40
Hutcheson, James 645
Hutcheson, Lydia 222
Hutchin, Thomas 170
Hutchin, William 150, 158
Hutchings, Benjamin 532
Hutchings, Moses 560
Hutchings, Sarah 560
Hutchins, William 424
Hutchinson, Andrew 320
Hutchinson, Elizabeth 560
Hutchinson, Ezekiel 238, 560, 562
Hutchinson, George 532
Hutchinson, Henry 570
Hutchinson, Jonathan 560, 562, 565
Hutchinson, Joseph 243
Hutchinson, Robert 329
Hutchinson, Silas 234
Hutchinson, Sylvanus 570
Hutchinson, Sylvester 238
Hutchinson, William H. 243
Hutchison, Catherine 663
Hutchison, John 125
Hutchison, Peter 663
Hutchman, Lant 401
Hutson, Henry 6, 42
Hutson, John 42, 150
Hutson, Sarah 529
Hutson, Smith 42
Hutson, Solomon 100
Hutt, Wm. T. 52

Huttenlocker, Fred 401
Huttenlocker, Fredrick 401
Hutton, James 10
Hutton, Ruth 12
Hutton, William 297
Hutzen, John 91
Hutzman, David 472
Hyatt, Jesse 110
Hyatt, Kissiah 625
Hyatt, Mahala 110
Hyde, Jarred 637
Hyde, Joseph 402
Hyde, Lemuel 56
Hyde, Oliver (Jr.) 82
Hyde, Wm. 78
Hyels, Joseph 297
Hyeth, David 297
Hyles, Levi 297
Hyndman, Saml. 176
Hyndman, Samuel 152
Hynes, Mary 405
Hyre, Susannah 389
Hyres, Anthony 508
Hyres, Mary 508
Hysel, Anthony 479
Hysel, Edward 475
Hysel, Elizabeth 480
Hysel, Jemima 475
Hysel, Margaret 479
Hysel, Rhody 478
Hysell, Francis 479
Hysell, Hedgeman 475
Hysey, Hannah 705

--- I ---

Ice, Elizabeth 55
Ice, Mary Ellen 55
Ice, Samuel 55
Ice, Solomon 55
Iddings, Joseph 298
Ide, Lemuel H. 95
Ide, Mary 95
Ienpia, --- 422
Ierich, Beatha Margarete 439
Ierich, Catharina 439
Ierich, Catherina 439
Ierich, Eve 439
Ierich, George 439
Ierich, Jacob 439
Ierich, Magdaline 439
Ihle, Francis C. 359
Ijams, Mary 406
Ijams, Wm. 405
Ilear, Joseph 34
Iler, Jacob 627
Iler, John 632
Iler, Sally 580
Iles, David 645
Iles, Elizabeth 411
Iles, George 645
Iles, Henry 645
Iles, Jacob 646
Iles, John 636, 646
Iles, Margaret 645

Iles, Sarah 645
Iles, William 646
Iles, William McKendrie 645
Iliff, Joshua 581
Iligan, William 357
Illick, Frederick 627
Iman, Abraham 466
Imerot, Geo. 416
Immell, Sarah 378
Imnsell, Sarah 378
Inbody, Betcy 632
Inbody, Daniel 627
Inbody, George 627
Inbody, John 627
Inbody, Margaret 625
Inbody, Polly 625
Indicott, Jesse 519
Ingave, Permelia 225
Ingland, Delila 581
Ingle, Betsey 499
Ingle, Isaac 499, 519
Inglehart, Adam 550
Ingles, Martha 326
Ingles, Rufus 326
Ingman, George P. 589
Ingman, Ruth 593
Ingram, Allen H. 731
Ingram, Andrew W. 362
Ingram, John 555, 589
Ingrun, Anne 184
Inhoff, John 70
Inkens, Susanah 191
Inks, John 404
Inks, Rebecca 408
Inks, Sarah 414
Inloes, Daniel 156
Inloes, William 156
Inlow, Abraham 525
Inlow, James 230
Inlow, Rebecca 531
Inman, Dulin 417
Inman, Elijah 560, 569
Inman, Rachael 602
Inman, Rosina 603
Inmun, John 520
Innis, Francis 363
Inscho, Mary 404
Inskeep, John 598
Insley, Zard 532
Inston, Nancy 413
Inyard, Benjamin 563
Ionbarger, Peter 715
Iray, John 298
Irdour, Drydent 231
Irdour, Keturah Ann 231
Irelan, Aaron 571
Irelan, Dayton 571
Ireland, Aaron 571
Ireland, Dayton 571
Ireland, Elenor 276
Ireland, John 49, 53
Ireland, Samuel 87
Ireland, Sarah 276
Irey, Hannah 303
Irey, Isaac 298
Irey, Margaret 298
Irey, Martha 290
Irey, Phineas 298

John, Nancy 186
John, Rachael 638
John, Rebecca 501, 535
John, Robert 756
John, Samuel 271, 287
John, Sarah 287
John, Shedrick 638
John, Thomas 10, 152
John, William 501
Johns, George 410
Johns, Israel 284
Johns, Jane 592
Johns, Martha 589
Johns, Robert 756
Johnson, A. 244
Johnson, Aaron 453,
 454, 455, 457
Johnson, Abraham 78
Johnson, Achillis C. 275
Johnson, Adams 332
Johnson, Alexander 613
Johnson, Anderson 332
Johnson, Andrew 486
Johnson, Ann 286
Johnson, Ashla 271
Johnson, Ashley 245,
 261, 285
Johnson, Benjamin 589,
 638
Johnson, Betsy T. 378
Johnson, C. C. 403
Johnson, Caleb 77
Johnson, Charles 34
Johnson, Charles E. 379
Johnson, Charles H. 332
Johnson, Chas. 35
Johnson, Chas. K. 415
Johnson, Christopher 614
Johnson, Court 475
Johnson, David 359,
 538, 643
Johnson, Delila E. 591
Johnson, Dianna 468
Johnson, E. 244
Johnson, Edith 617
Johnson, Edmund 547
Johnson, Edw. 443
Johnson, Eleanor 331
Johnson, Elisha 617
Johnson, Eliza 580
Johnson, Elizabeth 52,
 245, 306, 379, 418,
 435, 465, 526
Johnson, Esther 275
Johnson, Fanny 625
Johnson, Francis 321,
 325, 330
Johnson, Gavin 525
Johnson, George W. 332,
 663
Johnson, Hannah 332, 422
Johnson, Harriet 631
Johnson, Harriett 614
Johnson, Henry 78
Johnson, Isaac 280,
 285, 461, 580
Johnson, James 45, 70,
 71, 78, 237, 237,
 282, 332, 379, 520,

Johnson, James (cont.)
 525, 532, 543, 608,
 627, 666, 749
Johnson, James C. 499
Johnson, James E. 55
Johnson, Jane 76, 286,
 533
Johnson, Jas. 237
Johnson, Jeptha 217
Johnson, John 217, 298,
 379, 388, 435, 547,
 572, 613, 663
Johnson, John H. 298
Johnson, Jonathan 183,
 575
Johnson, Joseph 525, 581
Johnson, Levi 84, 331
Johnson, Louisa 393
Johnson, Lucinda 55, 589
Johnson, Lydia 580
Johnson, Margaret 307,
 613
Johnson, Martha 613
Johnson, Mary 124, 222,
 292, 332, 388, 404,
 579, 589, 607, 613,
 726
Johnson, Mary A. 373
Johnson, Mary C. 535
Johnson, Matthew 332
Johnson, Meribah 592
Johnson, Mildred 523
Johnson, Mille A. 332
Johnson, Miller 581
Johnson, Milly 474
Johnson, Nancy 658
Johnson, Oakly 726
Johnson, Obadiah 217
Johnson, Peter 78
Johnson, Polly 164,
 398, 464
Johnson, Rebecca 332
Johnson, Rhoda 273, 466
Johnson, Richard 217,
 331
Johnson, Robert 613
Johnson, S. M. 373
Johnson, Sabra 625
Johnson, Sally 76, 83
Johnson, Sam 373
Johnson, Samuel 82
Johnson, Samuel R. 656
Johnson, Sara 373
Johnson, Sarah 126,
 135, 217, 244, 531
Johnson, Susan 332, 395
Johnson, T. C. 403
Johnson, Thomas 135,
 332, 444, 466, 644
Johnson, Thomas (Jr.)
 135
Johnson, Thomas P. 733
Johnson, Virginia 613
Johnson, Walter 78
Johnson, William 17,
 124, 130, 188, 332,
 403, 444, 520, 608
Johnson, William (Jr.)
 331

Johnson, William J. 659
Johnson, William K. 321
Johnson, Wm. 126, 313
Johnson, Wm. H. 318
Johnston, Abigail 636
Johnston, Abraham 686
Johnston, Adam 322, 327
Johnston, Alexander
 190, 206, 333
Johnston, Alfred 190
Johnston, Amanda 315
Johnston, Andrew 228,
 644
Johnston, Ann 188, 706
Johnston, Arthur 535
Johnston, Ashly 271
Johnston, Barnabas 410
Johnston, Barnet 188
Johnston, Barney 205
Johnston, Beers 628
Johnston, Benjamin 636,
 638, 712
Johnston, Burs 628
Johnston, Caroline 192
Johnston, Catharine 638
Johnston, Catherine 405
Johnston, Charles 26, 35
Johnston, Charles H.
 322, 327
Johnston, Chas. 32, 37
Johnston, Daniel 697
Johnston, David 39, 170
Johnston, Delila 190
Johnston, Edward 184,
 190, 746
Johnston, Edward (Jr.)
 190
Johnston, Edward (Sr.)
 190
Johnston, Eleanor 161
Johnston, Elenor 224
Johnston, Elizabeth 170,
 188, 190, 192, 207,
 219, 228, 657, 706
Johnston, Ellen 51, 188
Johnston, Emsley 697
Johnston, Ephraim 681
Johnston, Evan 404
Johnston, Gavin 209
Johnston, George 10
Johnston, George W.
 322, 327, 642
Johnston, Gideon 165,
 220
Johnston, Hannah 188,
 322, 327
Johnston, Hugh 682
Johnston, Jacob 188
Johnston, James 105, 190,
 192, 207, 313, 546,
 644, 705, 726, 754
Johnston, James (Jr.) 754
Johnston, Jean 188
Johnston, Jesse 190
Johnston, Jno. W. 28
Johnston, John 105,
 160, 220, 277, 405,
 410, 510, 516, 542,
 686, 716, 755

Johnston, John (Sr.) 510
Johnston, John B. 410
Johnston, John Waller 28
Johnston, Joseph 188
Johnston, Lewis 602, 705
Johnston, Lidia 188
Johnston, Lucinda 589
Johnston, Lucy 686
Johnston, Luisy 192
Johnston, Macajah 466
Johnston, Mahela 166
Johnston, Margaret 168,
  209, 520, 644, 657
Johnston, Maria 220
Johnston, Martha 190
Johnston, Mary 190,
  441, 530, 644, 682
Johnston, Mathew 322
Johnston, Matthew W. 327
Johnston, Michael 713
Johnston, Milly 190
Johnston, Nancy 190,
  192, 220, 644
Johnston, Nicholas 555
Johnston, Noel 190
Johnston, Othia 207
Johnston, Otho 188, 205
Johnston, Parmela 220
Johnston, Patsey 190
Johnston, Paul F. 228
Johnston, Peggy 192
Johnston, Polly 523, 528
Johnston, Rachel 302
Johnston, Rebecca 313,
  315, 317
Johnston, Richard 220
Johnston, Robert 666
Johnston, Ruth 634
Johnston, Samuel 158,
  165
Johnston, Sarah 206,
  327, 535, 656
Johnston, Sterling 105
Johnston, Susan 322
Johnston, Thomas 170,
  219, 277, 537, 644
Johnston, Unity 220
Johnston, Washington 313
Johnston, Washington B.
  317
Johnston, William 105,
  130, 188, 190, 192,
  240, 298, 322, 327,
  479, 589, 697, 717
Johnston, William C. 712
Johnston, William H. 220
Joiner, Charles 198
Joiner, Fanny 223
Joler, M. A. 121
Joler, Robert 121
Jolly, Maria 300
Jolly, Samuel 298
Jone, John 387
Jone, Margaret 387
Jone, Polly 387
Jone, Susannah 387
Jones, A. Ream 421
Jones, Abraham 160, 175
Jones, Alexander 170

Jones, Ambrose 256
Jones, Amilia 528
Jones, Amos 466, 670
Jones, Andrew 6
Jones, Ann 237, 659
Jones, Ann Elizabeth 602
Jones, Anna 122
Jones, Anthony 692
Jones, Asbury 551
Jones, Betsy 690
Jones, C. W. 636
Jones, Casander 85
Jones, Catharine 446,
  453, 454
Jones, Charles M. 59
Jones, Christiana 526,
  692
Jones, Churchill 20,
  21, 28, 29, 509
Jones, Daniel 175, 271,
  385, 610
Jones, David 186, 198,
  210, 224, 510, 705
Jones, David Evans 391
Jones, Edith 581
Jones, Edward 137, 175,
  211
Jones, Eleanor 692
Jones, Elias 479
Jones, Eliline 317
Jones, Elisha 271
Jones, Elizabeth 52,
  133, 270, 271, 581,
  582, 610, 692, 703
Jones, Elizabeth A. 59
Jones, Elvira 584
Jones, Enoch 545
Jones, Enos 690
Jones, Ephriam 45
Jones, Esther 175, 211
Jones, Ezekiel 741
Jones, Flavel B. 59
Jones, Frankey 272
Jones, George 692, 708
Jones, Hannah 460, 481
Jones, Hariet 670
Jones, Harvey 729
Jones, Helly 741
Jones, Henry 149, 183
Jones, Hiram 6
Jones, Hudson 363
Jones, Isabella 474
Jones, Isaiah 220, 581,
  589
Jones, J. M. 93
Jones, Jacob 73, 236
Jones, James 316, 479,
  575, 609, 637, 705
Jones, Jane 175, 271, 659
Jones, Jane Seymore 631
Jones, Jarret 85
Jones, Jean 468
Jones, Jemima 520
Jones, Jesse 589
Jones, John 10, 43, 170,
  224, 237, 263, 267,
  271, 279, 298, 316,
  387, 454, 564, 567,
  571, 572, 627, 726

Jones, John L. 551
Jones, John M. 45
Jones, John M. (Rev.)
  539
Jones, John W. 257, 282
Jones, Jonas 149, 165
Jones, Jonathan 149
Jones, Joseph 520, 589
Jones, Jurdan 298
Jones, Justus 175
Jones, Kezia 163
Jones, Lawrence 298
Jones, Leah 226
Jones, Leander 670
Jones, Levi 741
Jones, Lewis 237, 454
Jones, Lucinda 136
Jones, Lucy 59
Jones, Lucy Ann 59
Jones, Magy E. 59
Jones, Mahala 454
Jones, Margaret 726
Jones, Martha 291
Jones, Martha Jane 670
Jones, Mary 85, 165,
  220, 223, 276, 518,
  524, 658, 692
Jones, Mary Ann 741
Jones, Mary Anne 670
Jones, Mathus 461
Jones, Melanchloe S. 59
Jones, Melesa 579
Jones, Mirriam 271
Jones, Nancy 49, 164,
  175, 222, 224, 455
Jones, Nathan 690, 692
Jones, Nathaniel 446,
  453, 454, 455
Jones, Ned 165
Jones, Nicholas 129
Jones, Norman F. 453,
  454, 455, 466
Jones, Norman J. 445
Jones, Oliver 6, 701
Jones, Owen 663, 666
Jones, P. 59, 93
Jones, Patience 59
Jones, Patty 481
Jones, Philip 475
Jones, Polly 83
Jones, Rachel 454
Jones, Rebeccah 270
Jones, Robert 129, 197,
  392
Jones, Robert W. 117
Jones, Robert Wiley 670
Jones, Robt. C. 2
Jones, Rosand 582
Jones, Rosetta 211
Jones, Roxy Ann 45
Jones, Ruth 273, 629,
  658
Jones, S. M. 59
Jones, Sabina 692
Jones, Sally 274, 741
Jones, Samuel 298, 410,
  581, 642, 644, 741
Jones, Samuel Woodmancy
  670

Karnaghan, George 598
Karnek, Amanuel 594
Karnes, Stephen D. 663
Karns, Harry 589
Karr, George 234
Karr, John 437
Karr, Martha 234
Karr, Sarah 472
Karr, William 410
Karshner, Jacob (Jr.) 638
Karshner, Martha Jane 601
Karsner, Isaac 602
Karsner, John 602
Karson, Sarah 466
Katharenam, Josephus Tabbens 101
Katts, Caroline M. 102
Katzenberger, Francis M. 353
Kauffman, Mary 420
Kaufman, Catharine 229
Kaufman, J. E. 229
Kaufman, John 408
Kaufman, Michael 229
Kavanaugh, Thomas 534
Kavangh, James 179
Kavangh, Rachel 179
Kay, Wm. 330
Kayle, Philip 298
Kaylor, David 371
Kaylor, Samuel 54
Keahy, Nancy 628
Kealofer, Henry (Jr.) 500
Kean, John 754
Kear, John 754
Kearines, Henry 663
Kearines, James 663
Kearnes, David 78
Kearns, Azariah 466
Kearns, William 101
Keasey, Christian 627
Keasly, Delzil 569
Keasy, Joseph 627
Keasy, Kitty 628
Keath, Catherin 102
Keath, Christian 656
Keath, Nancy 441
Keath, William 60
Keaton, Jno. 82
Keck, Christian 310
Keck, Daniel 298, 310
Keck, John 51
Keck, Magdalena 305
Keckley, Benj. 547
Kecler, Katy 479
Kee, Mary 469
Kee, Samuel 466
Keedy, Hannah 581
Keefer, Elizabeth 291
Keefer, George 183, 217
Keeffer, Martin 473
Keegan, Anna 133
Keegan, Barney 133
Keegan, Peter 133
Keeky, Jane 284
Keel, Sofia 305

Keeler, Rebecca 650
Keelor, Joseph 642
Keely, Betsy 461
Keen, Abiah Ann 388
Keen, Exra 388
Keen, Ezra 388
Keen, Hannah 388
Keen, Jesse 550
Keen, Joseph 388
Keen, Nancy 388
Keen, Peter 388
Keen, Sanford 388
Keenan, Beverly 663
Keenan, Caty 413
Keenan, Lydia 271
Keenan, Martha 663
Keenan, Peter 271
Keene, Peter 561, 574
Keeney, Moody 703
Keeney, William H. C. 724
Keenon, Betsy 271
Keer, John 689
Keer, Sally 689
Kees, Thomas 660
Keeton, Andrew 663
Keeton, John 637, 663
Keeton, Martin 627
Keeton, William 656
Keeton, Zeletty 480
Keffer, Jacob 525
Kehl, Martin 298
Keifer, Benedict 589
Keifer, George 186
Keifer, Michael 64
Keifer, Polly 222
Keigler, George 637
Keilbride, John 403
Keim, John 739
Keister, Samuel 69
Keiterson, Peggy 83
Keith, Agness 438
Keith, Edmon 438
Keith, Elizabeth 55, 60, 438
Keith, Hannah 438
Keith, James T. 59
Keith, Jane 438
Keith, Margret 438
Keith, Nancy 9, 441
Keith, Sarah 55, 291, 441
Keith, William 55, 59, 63, 438
Keith, Wm. 56, 59
Keith, Zachariah 438
Keithler, Daniel 615
Keithler, Mary 615
Kell, John 545, 551
Kell, Robert 550
Kellam, George H. 694
Kellam, James A. (Rev.) 53
Kellar, Absalom 106
Kellar, Benjamin 106
Kellar, Comfort 106
Kellar, George 106
Kellar, Isaac 106
Kellar, John 106

Kellar, Levi 106
Kellar, Sarah 470
Kellar, Thomas 106
Kellen, Nathaniel 170
Keller, Barbara 290
Keller, Betsey 481
Keller, Catherine 101
Keller, Catherine F. 126
Keller, David 422
Keller, Elizabeth 290, 468, 470
Keller, Fanny 290, 293
Keller, Georg 337
Keller, George 107, 357
Keller, Gristian 337
Keller, Hortensia 421
Keller, Jacob 160, 298, 421 632
Keller, John 50, 61, 298
Keller, Joseph 60, 65
Keller, M. 48
Keller, Margaret 62
Keller, Margaretha Barbara 337
Keller, Mary 656
Keller, Nancy 468
Keller, Nathaniel 170
Keller, Peter 663
Keller, Sam 373
Keller, Sarah 707
Keller, Seley 463
Kellerhaus, John U. 593
Kelley, Alexander 298
Kelley, Amey 707
Kelley, Aramatha 722
Kelley, Catharine 230
Kelley, Charles 708, 710
Kelley, Clarissa 162
Kelley, David 298
Kelley, Frances 230
Kelley, Isaac 298
Kelley, Isam 724
Kelley, James 230, 722
Kelley, John 421
Kelley, Nathan 271
Kelley, Reuben 711
Kelley, Rhody 706
Kelley, Robert 196
Kelley, Sarah 308
Kelley, William 298, 663
Kellington, Ann 381
Kellog, William 589
Kellogg, Asher Porter 653
Kellogg, C. C. 396
Kellogg, Caroline 396
Kellogg, Chester 396
Kellogg, L. O. 396
Kellogg, Martha 396
Kellogg, Rebecca 653
Kellogg, Solomon 653
Kellough, Martha Ann 589
Kellough, William 589
Kellum, Jas. A. 127
Kelly, Alexander 160
Kelly, Charles L. 263
Kelly, Daniel 598
Kelly, Daniel R. 581
Kelly, Elizabeth 232

Kelly, George 146, 155
Kelly, James 10, 438
Kelly, John 210, 263, 401, 520, 666, 705
Kelly, Joseph 705
Kelly, Joshua 581
Kelly, Knacky 729
Kelly, Martha 595
Kelly, Mary 521, 531
Kelly, Mena 405
Kelly, Moses 581
Kelly, Nancy 232
Kelly, Rebecca 194
Kelly, Reuben 708, 709
Kelly, Ruth 588
Kelly, Whitfield 718
Kelly, William 310, 720
Kelsby, Ann 603
Kelsey, David 271
Kelsey, William 271
Kelso, George 543
Kelso, John 525
Kelso, Juliann 605
Kelso, Robert 224
Kelso, Samuel 360, 361
Kelson, Ann 605
Keltner, Anderson 417
Kemerer, Eve 412
Kemmerer, John 700
Kemmerer, Nancy 700
Kemmerer, Samuel 700
Kemp, Daniel 135
Kemp, Henry 432
Kemp, John N. 718
Kemp, Lucinda 417
Kemp, Polly 166
Kemper, James 611
Kemplin, Andrew 98
Kempson, Mathew 10
Kempt, Joseph 520
Kenady, Jane 618
Kenaga, Christopher 182
Kendall, Catharine 502
Kendall, Elizabeth 500
Kendall, Francis 424, 500, 501
Kendall, James 500
Kendall, Jane 500
Kendall, John 2, 500, 502
Kendall, John (Sr.) 500
Kendall, Jos. 461
Kendall, Joseph W. 500
Kendall, Robert 500
Kendall, Robert (Jr.) 500
Kendall, Samuel 2
Kendall, Sarah 500
Kendall, Thomas 500
Kendall, Thomas L. 500
Kendall, Thos. L. 500
Kendall, Vrancis 500
Kendall, Wilson 500
Kendall, Wm. 500
Kendle, Lucy 461
Kendle, Valentine 687
Kendle, Wm. 462
Kendles, Catharine 305
Kendrick, Elizabeth 80

Keneday, James 362
Kenedy, Jane 303
Kenedy, Robert 690
Kengrey, Michael 520
Kennady, Ambrose 666
Kennady, Ezekiel 666
Kennady, James 520
Kennady, John 525
Kennady, Massey 281
Kennand, Rebecca 415
Kennard, John 165
Kenneday, James C. 362
Kennedy, Alexander 236
Kennedy, Ann 301
Kennedy, Elizabeth 518
Kennedy, James 160
Kennedy, Jannet 294
Kennedy, Joel 155
Kennedy, Loren 64
Kennedy, Martha 53
Kennedy, Mary 408
Kennedy, Wm. A. 663
Kennell, Isaac 705
Kenney, Ann 728
Kenney, John 231
Kenney, Katharine 231
Kenney, Martha 228
Kennon, John 119
Kenny, Laughlin 217
Kenny, Michal 217
Kensey, Elinora 595
Kenson, Christopher 420
Kensser, Catharine 626
Kensy, Balser 608
Kent, Asfor 298
Kent, Asford 298
Kent, Ira 643
Kent, Jonathan 105
Kent, Joseph 598
Kent, Orabel M. 80
Kent, Sophrona 99
Kentner, Emanuel 52
Kenton, Phebe 504
Kenton, Simon 504, 552
Kenworthy, Thomas 131
Keogh, Patrick 354
Kephart, Catharine 62
Kephart, George 62
Kephart, Susan 49
Keplar, Andrew 645
Keplar, Andrew (Jr.) 645
Keplar, Barnet 645
Keplar, David 645
Keplar, John 645
Keplar, Nelly 645
Keplar, Peggy 645
Keplar, Polly 645
Keplar, Samuel 645
Kepler, Andrew (Jr.) 645
Kepler, Barnet 639, 645
Kepler, Benjamin 405, 413
Kepler, David 645
Kepler, Elizabeth 405, 413
Kepler, John 645
Kepler, Margaretha 345
Kepler, Nancy 378
Kepler, Samuel 645

Ker, --- 460
Ker, Henry 561, 570
Ker, Sarah 689
Keran, Nathaniel 324
Keran, Rebecca 464
Kerby, Benjamin 279
Kerby, Mary 279
Kerchavel, Benjamin 160
Kercheval, Reuben 161
Kerct, Jacob 595
Kercue, Joseph 702
Kerey, John Jacob 410
Kerkendall, Sarah 531
Kerkindall, Richard H. 663
Kerkley, Mary 189
Kerkpatrick, John 466
Kerlin, Robert 683
Kermmer, Frederick 355
Kern, George 298
Kern, Rachael 100
Kerns, Elizabeth 416
Kerns, William 310
Kerr, Alexander 170, 200
Kerr, David 426
Kerr, Eleanor 289
Kerr, George 113, 234
Kerr, Jacob 170
Kerr, James 733
Kerr, James (Sr.) 598
Kerr, John 384, 389, 475, 686, 687, 688, 689
Kerr, Jos. 26, 30, 31
Kerr, Joseph 12, 15, 24, 29, 30, 31, 32, 34, 239
Kerr, Judith 378
Kerr, Letticia 291
Kerr, Lewis 571
Kerr, Martha 234
Kerr, Mary 293
Kerr, Nancy 32
Kerr, Polly 167
Kerr, Robert 660
Kerr, Sally 478
Kerr, Sarah 687, 688
Kerr, William 298, 310, 466, 683
Kerran, John 462
Kerregan, --- 81
Kerrnard, Wm. L. 416
Kersay, Thomas 279
Kerscher, John 298
Kersey, David 271
Kersey, John 271
Kersey, Thomas 284
Kershaw, Mitchel 543
Kershner, Daniel 525, 532, 637
Kershner, Eleoner 629
Kershner, Elijah 637
Kershner, Elizabeth 533
Kershner, Martin 504
Kershner, Susan 632
Kervan, Sarah 461
Keslar, John 356
Kesler, Barbara 200
Kesler, Henry 200

Kesler, Niomi 445
Kessler, Nancy 378
Kester, Barbara 412
Kester, Catharin Maria 349
Kester, Eliz. C. 352
Kester, Elizabeth 350, 352
Kester, Elizabeth C. 349, 352
Kester, Elizabeth Catharina 351
Kester, Eve 350, 351
Kester, George 350, 351
Kester, John 264
Kester, John A. 349
Kester, Lucetta Ann 351
Kester, Mary 350
Kester, Paul 351
Kester, Peter 24
Kester, Releran 11
Kester, Sarah 349
Kester, Solomon 350
Kester, William 351, 352
Kester, William W. 349
Kester, Wm. 352
Kester, Wm. W. 350, 352
Kesterson, Meredy 78
Ketcham, Andrew J. 380
Ketchum, Susan 295
Ketring, Barbara 352
Ketring, Catharine 352
Ketring, David 349, 352
Ketring, Ellen 352
Ketring, Johannes 352
Ketring, John 352
Ketring, Jonethan 349
Ketring, Katharine 352
Ketring, Sarah 352
Kettenack, Issabella 305
Key, Amos 410
Key, Caleb 216
Key, James 525
Key, Martin 466
Key, Moses 410
Keys, John 3
Keyse, Elizabeth 627
Keyser, John F. 101
Keyt, Ann Eliza 129
Keyt, Daniel 129, 153
Keyt, David R. 129, 159
Keyt, Eleanor 129
Keyt, James 129
Keyton, William 656
Keyzar, Jacob R. 602
Keyzer, Eliza Ann 603
Keyzer, Eliza Jane 603
Khan, Arthur 298
Kibbey, Ephraim 573
Kibbey, Ephrain 568, 574
Kibble, Eliza Ann 379
Kibble, Margaret 381
Kibby, Eph. 576
Kibby, Ephrain 575
Kibby, Moses 10
Kibler, Adam 67
Kibler, George 67
Kibles, Susanna 472
Kiblinger, Daniel 213

Kiblinger, Danl. 206
Kiblinger, Jacob 206
Kiblinger, Peter 224
Kiblinger, Philip 58
Kidd, David 238
Kidd, John 153, 555
Kidd, Joseh 241
Kidd, Nancy 238
Kidd, Nathaniel G. 52
Kidd, Sarah 241
Kiger, Margaret 418
Kiger, William 632
Kight, Amilla 663
Kikendall, Elsy 466
Kilboum, Stephen 470
Kilbourn, Alexander 391
Kilbourn, Benjamin 313
Kilbourn, Eunice 391
Kilbourn, Susan 391
Kilbourne, Stephen 470
Kilbride, John 403
Kilbride, Michael 551
Kilby, Ephraim 560
Kile, James 748
Kile, Oliver 443
Kilgore, George 10
Kilgore, Jeremiah 705
Kilgore, John C. 462
Kilgore, Nancy 467
Kill, Mary 51
Killen, John 10, 30, 33, 39
Killen, Rachel 39
Killey, Eli 316
Killey, Ephraim 560
Killgore, Elizabeth 462
Killin, William 48
Killy, Joseph 316
Kim, Peter 298
Kimball, Amherish S. 711
Kimball, Asa 708, 711, 713
Kimball, James M. 380
Kimball, Mary 391
Kimbell, Daniel 216
Kimberling, Nancy 475
Kimble, Asa 713
Kimble, Barbary 468
Kimble, Christina 629
Kimble, Jacob 632
Kimble, John 627
Kimble, Johnathan 639
Kimble, Jonathan 635
Kimble, Lydia 698
Kimble, Maria 632
Kimble, Maris Martha 461
Kimble, Mary 628
Kimble, Oliver 639
Kimble, Solomon 627
Kimble, Titan 709
Kimble, William 298, 310, 627
Kimbrough, Elizabeth 268, 275
Kimbrough, Jeremiah 268, 283
Kimbrough, Sarah 283
Kimerling, Catharine 350, 352

Kimerling, George 352
Kimerling, Henry 350
Kimerling, Lewis 350
Kimmel, George 370
Kimmel, Henry 598
Kimmel, John 581
Kimmel, Lenard 598
Kimmel, Timothy 380
Kimmering, Katharine 349
Kimmering, Lewis 349
Kimmering, William 349
Kimmerling, Abraham 349, 350, 352
Kimmerling, Catharine 352
Kimmerling, George 352
Kimmerling, Ka. 349
Kimmerling, Katharine 350, 352
Kimmerling, Katherine 350, 352
Kimmerling, Susannah 349
Kincade, Samuel 190
Kincaid, George 475
Kincaid, James 663
Kincaid, Jeaney 9
Kincaid, John 6, 10
Kincaid, John H. 5
Kincaid, Joseph 111
Kincaid, Margaret J. 43
Kincaid, Margaret Jane 5
Kincaid, Matthew 125
Kincaid, Robert 125
Kincaid, Thomas 5, 43
Kincais, John H. 7
Kindeheut, Catharine 298
Kindel, Wm. 466
Kinder, Elizabeth 280
Kinder, Jacob 280
Kinder, Nancy 291
Kine, Peter 310
Kineer, Robert 748
King, Aaron 101
King, Alexander 117, 560, 569
King, Andrew 117
King, Ann 260, 308
King, Catharine 117
King, Charles Rufus 670
King, Charles W. 395
King, Chester 395
King, David 202, 260
King, David B. 333
King, Deborah 167
King, Elizabeth 74, 220, 260, 395, 441, 463
King, George W. 117
King, Henrietta 703
King, Hiram 395
King, Jacob 134, 148
King, James 117, 593, 753
King, Jemina 395
King, John 115, 117, 138, 141, 148, 220, 224, 258, 260, 444, 450, 705
King, Joseph 621
King, Joseph S. 395

861

Kirkpatrick, Robert 220
Kirkpatrick, Saml. 517
Kirkpatrick, Samuel 520,
541, 647
Kirkpatrick, Samuel D.
502, 512
Kirkpatrick, Sarah 216,
219
Kirkpatrick, Sarah J. 43
Kirkpatrick, Susan 220
Kirkpatrick, Susanna 529
Kirkpatrick, Thomas 540
Kirkpatrick, Thomas C.
6, 43
Kirkpatrick, Thos. 542
Kirkpatrick, William
170, 219, 505
Kirkton, Jane 70
Kirkwood, D. 132
Kirkwood, David 132, 179
Kirkwood, Elizabeth 179,
523
Kirkwood, J. 179
Kirkwood, John 190
Kirkwood, Joseph 132
Kirkwood, Margaret 179
Kirkwood, Mariah E. 179
Kirkwood, Martha 132
Kirkwood, Martha J. 179
Kirkwood, Mary 132,
179, 523
Kirkwood, Moses 517
Kirkwood, N. 179
Kirkwood, Robert 536
Kirkwood, S. 179
Kirkwood, Sarah 179
Kirkwood, Thomas J. 179
Kirkwood, William 532
Kirkwood, Wm. 179
Kirkwood, Wm. H. 179
Kirler, Fred 536
Kirrans, Kitty 411
Kirtland, Matilda 589
Kirtz, Law 410
Kisaman, Ellen 101
Kiser, Abraham 499
Kiser, Benjamin 499
Kiser, Catherine 499
Kiser, Daniel 499
Kiser, John 138, 139,
499
Kiser, Lewis 499
Kiser, Mary 499
Kiser, Philip 275
Kiser, Samuel 499
Kiser, Sarah 499
Kisler, Saml. 416
Kisling, Barbary 378
Kisling, Wm. 2
Kistler, David 419
Kistler, Elizabeth 409,
435
Kistler, Lizza 435
Kistler, Peter 410
Kitch, Solomon 380
Kitchel, Abigail 175
Kitchel, Alurah 175
Kitchel, Ashbell 175
Kitchel, Johannah 175

Kitchel, John 138, 175
Kitchel, Matildah 175
Kitchel, Mildan 175
Kitchel, Phebe 564
Kitchel, Polly 175
Kitchel, Rachel 564
Kitchel, Rosalindah 175
Kitchel, Samuel 564
Kitchell, Calvin 560
Kitchell, John 562
Kitchell, Margaret 558
Kitchell, Mary 560
Kitchell, Piercy 560
Kitchell, Samuel 558
Kitchen, Allice 602
Kitchen, John 627
Kitchen, Phebe 632
Kite, Adam 191, 410
Kite, Elisabeth 39
Kite, John 31, 39
Kithcart, Anna Catherine
670
Kithcart, Catherine 670
Kithcart, Elizabeth 670
Kithcart, Elizabeth Ann
670
Kithcart, Elizabeth Jane
670
Kithcart, Henry Comings
670
Kithcart, Jessie Bertha
670
Kithcart, Joseph 670,
671
Kithcart, Joseph A. 670
Kithcart, Kate 670
Kithcart, Martha Ellen
671
Kithcart, Martha Hellen
671
Kithcart, Mary 670
Kithcart, Mary Althiza
671
Kithcart, Mary Elizabeth
670
Kithcart, Rebecca 670
Kithcart, Robert
Sherrard 670
Kithcart, Sara Louisa
671
Kithcart, Sarah K. 671
Kithcart, William Smiley
671
Kitsmiller, Benj. 422
Kitsmiller, Elijah 422
Kitt, George 205
Kitt, Peter 205
Kitteman, Jonathan 532
Kitterow, Catharine 161
Kitts, Mary 225
Kittsmiller, Susana 410
Kittsmiller, Wm. 410
Kizer, Ann 226
Kizer, Anna 213
Kizer, Caty 213
Kizer, Danl. 226
Kizer, David 213
Kizer, Elizabeth 213,
217, 222

Kizer, George 213
Kizer, Jesse 525
Kizer, John 213
Kizer, Joseph 101
Kizer, Margaret 225
Kizer, Mary 213
Kizer, Michael 213
Kizer, Peggy 213
Kizer, Philip 213
Kizer, Sarah 213
Kizer, William 213, 520
Klaneroth, Wm. 416
Klefoth, Catharine 89
Klefoth, Maria 89
Klickard, Barbara 54
Klikhammer, Catharine
102
Kliman, M. 400
Kline, Catharine 640
Kline, Coonrad 413
Kline, Elizabeth 413
Kline, Henry 627
Kline, Jacob 640
Kline, Joseph 602
Kline, Mary 640
Klingamann, Elizabeth 89
Klingamann, George 89
Klingamann, Mary 89
Klingmann, Elizabeth 89
Klingmann, Geo. 89
Klinker, Isaac 298
Klisner, Sebastian 651
Kloph, Barbary 64
Kloph, Martin 64
Kloppenstine, Peter 472
Knapp, Amelia 294
Knapp, Christian 473
Knapp, Cyrus 78
Knapp, Eliza 603
Knapp, Elizabeth 601,
603
Knapp, Eunice 477
Knapp, Henry 473
Knapp, Rheda 650
Knapp, Sally 78
Knapp, Sarah 604
Knapp, Sarah Ann 601
Knappenberger, Elizabeth
339
Knappenberger, Georg 339
Knappenberger, Johann
Georg 337
Knappenberger, Katharina
337
Knappenberger, Rosina
337, 339
Knause, Henry 37
Knave, Catharine 527
Kneese, Peter 165
Kneff, Elizabeth 704
Knepely, Ann 229
Knepely, Lawrence 229
Knepely, Thomas
Jefferson 229
Knepper, Sally 419
Knerr, Adam 53
Knieriehmen, Jacob 431
Kniffin, Salley 653
Knight, Anna 704

Kruse, Katharine Mary 87
Kruse, Mary Agnes 99
Kruse, Sophia Eliza 87
Krusen, Mary 458
Krutsch, Elizabeth 416
Kruzan, Ruanna 526
Kruzen, Joseph 499
Kucherbarger, Geo. 415
Kuder, Elizabeth 632
Kuenzel, Catherin 100
Kugler, Jacob 520
Kuhendall, Geo. 513
Kuhlhorst, Frederick 89
Kuhn, Andrew (Rev.) 613
Kuhn, Christian 347
Kuhn, Helena Sophia 347
Kuhn, John 725
Kuhn, John Julius 380
Kuhns, David 420
Kukemiller, Fritz 92
Kukenmiller, Caroline 92
Kukenmiller, Henry 92
Kukenmiller, Henryietta 92
Kukenmiller, Maria C. 92
Kukns, John 417
Kull, Carolina Philippina 415
Kuncel, Henry 89
Kuns, William 298
Kunsi, Christian 343
Kunsi, Heinrich 343
Kuntz, George J. 124
Kuntz, John 298
Kuntz, Salome 420
Kuntz, Sophia 289
Kunzel, Catherin 100
Kusey, Henry 298
Kusman, Frederick 375
Kusnack, Francis 358
Kutzly, Elizabeth 470
Kuyckemdal, Rosannah 518
Kyger, Bennet 416
Kyger, Betsey 163
Kyger, Catharine 171
Kyger, John 152
Kyle, Ann 148
Kyle, Dorcas 589
Kyle, Elizabeth 520
Kyle, Henry L. 589
Kyle, John 716
Kyle, John G. 534
Kyle, Joseph 502, 525
Kyle, Joseph (Jr.) 502
Kyle, Joseph (Sr.) 502
Kyle, Robert 573
Kyle, Samuel 502, 525
Kyle, William 148, 716, 718
Kyzer, Sally 411

--- L ---

Labaker, John 411
Laban, Eliz. 748
LaCaisse, Mary Margaret 494, 495, 496
Lacey, Claraissa 631
LaCirer, Ambrose 490
Lackey, James 666
Lacock, Joseph 236
Lacock, Silruce 236
Lacock, Wm. 233, 236
LaCour, Ambrose 490
Lacy, Amos 416
Ladd, William 637
Laeber, Conrad 359
Laeo, John 206
Laer, John 206
Laferty, Polly 223
Lafetra, Robert E. 371
Lafferty, Catharine 189
Lafferty, David 189
Lafferty, Hester Ann 189
Lafferty, J. W. 48
Lafferty, Jane 189
Lafferty, John 182, 189, 205, 206
Lafferty, Joseph W. 3, 5, 48
Lafferty, Lydia 198
Lafferty, Molly 189
Lafferty, Sally 189
Lafferty, Saml. 214
Lafferty, Samuel 214
Lafferty, Sarah 189
Lafferty, Thomas 189
Lafferty, Wesley 189
Lafferty, William 189
Laffillard, Peter 497
Laforge, Peter Anthony 489, 490, 491, 492, 497
Lager, Heinrich 343
Lager, Jacob 343
Lahman, Henry 380
Lahman, Jacob 380
Laier, Johan Heinrich 344
Laier, Sara Regina 344
Lain, Hulda R. 590
Lain, Margaret 691
Lain, Polly 521
Laing, Claresy 560
Laing, Lewis 560, 565
Laird, David 663
Laird, Mathew 536
Lake, Cornelius 325
Lake, Eveline 325
Lake, Florentine 325
Lake, John 548, 549
Lake, Joseph 325
Lake, Lydia 583
Lake, Martha 582
Lake, Phasris 388
Lake, Silas 656
Lake, Thomas 10
Laken, Daniel 435
Laken, Julian 435
Laken, Lewis 435
Lakin, I. O. 422
Lalance, Peter 482, 483
Laman, John 219
Laman, Rachel 219
Lamb, Abner 210
Lamb, Adelene 210
Lamb, David 210
Lamb, Elizabeth 409, 621
Lamb, George 210, 405, 411
Lamb, Jacob 411
Lamb, John 210
Lamb, Joseph 210
Lamb, Louisa 621
Lamb, Moses 210
Lamb, Nancy 72
Lamb, Phillip 411
Lamb, Reuben 383, 388
Lamb, Samuel 360
Lamb, Sarah 210, 418
Lamb, Thomas 621
Lamb, Washington 418
Lamb, Winney 621
Lambaugh, Joseph 705, 717
Lambaugh, Lydia 717
Lambert, Aaron 520, 525
Lambert, Amos 214, 505
Lambert, Anna 505, 703
Lambert, Betsey 706
Lambert, Elizabeth 711
Lambert, Hannah 505, 579
Lambert, Harvey 694
Lambert, Harvey Clark 694
Lambert, Isaac 589, 705
Lambert, Jeanette 694
Lambert, John 505, 525
Lambert, Joseph 718
Lambert, Josiah 705
Lambert, Kiziah 443
Lambert, Leandra 703
Lambert, Lucina 505
Lambert, Lydia 478
Lambert, Martha 703
Lambert, Mary 723
Lambert, Nicholas 490
Lambert, Rebecca 703
Lambert, Richard 711
Lambert, William 214, 217, 505, 714
Lambeson, Richard 724
Lambough, Joseph 720
Lambs, Joseph 420
Lamdal, Thomas L. 182
Lamme, Alonzo 536
Lamme, Betsey Chambers 207
Lamme, George Chambers 207
Lamme, James 184, 185
Lamme, James W. 185
Lamme, John 184, 185, 208
Lamme, Joseph 208
Lamme, Josiah 520
Lamme, Nancy G. 185
Lamme, Nathan 513
Lamme, Samuel 525
Lamme, William 184, 211, 520
Lammonton, Hiram 380
Lamon, Joseph 14
Lampher, Nancy 79
Lamphire, Aaron 602

LeClerqc, F. 28
Leclerq, Francis 709
LeCour, Ambrose 497
Ledwell, John 170
Lee, Abraham 175
Lee, Adam 567
Lee, Alfred 246
Lee, Allen 10
Lee, Ann 273
Lee, Anna 642
Lee, Benjamin 183, 184
Lee, Bessie 246
Lee, Boss 642
Lee, Charlotte 381
Lee, Edward 605
Lee, Elijah 642
Lee, Elisibeth 704
Lee, George 627, 635, 642
Lee, Grethel 246
Lee, Hanna 311
Lee, Harriet Amanda 256
Lee, Henry 246
Lee, Hugh 387
Lee, James 46, 642, 758
Lee, James (Sr.) 642
Lee, John 161, 170, 462, 598, 746, 758
Lee, John Westley 605
Lee, Julian 642
Lee, Laura 246
Lee, Levi 653
Lee, Lydia 165
Lee, Margaret 183
Lee, Mary 231, 518, 531, 649
Lee, Nancy 12, 169, 525, 628, 642
Lee, Peggy 184
Lee, Peter 23
Lee, Rachel 582
Lee, Rebecca 272
Lee, Richd. 20
Lee, Rosannah 642
Lee, Sabina 246
Lee, Samuel 175, 314, 318, 642
Lee, Sarah 274, 305, 411, 653
Lee, Susannah 480
Lee, Thomas 403
Lee, Washington 642
Lee, Wesley 6
Lee, William 268, 275
Lee, Wm. 746
Leece, Jacob 726
Leece, Sarah 726
Leech, Archibald 3
Leech, David 3, 5, 6
Leech, James 3
Leech, Jane 6
Leech, Matthew 546
Leech, Thomas 550
Leech, Wm. 6
Leederman, Peter 602
Leederman, Sophia 602
Leedom, Asa 6
Leedom, Eligah 45
Leedom, Elijah 3

Leedom, Elizabeth 39
Leedom, Nathan 711
Leedom, Will 34
Leedom, William 34, 39
Leedom, Wm. 34
Leedon, T. R. 45
Leeka, Christian 265
Leeka, Elizabeth 265
Leeka, George 265
Leeka, Henry 265
Leeka, John 265
Leeka, Justena 265
Leeka, Lydia 265
Leeka, Philip 265
Leeliger, Elisabat 437
Leeliger, John 437
Leeper, Elizabeth 725
Leeper, George 725
Leeper, James 544
Leeper, Jane 725
Leeper, John 547
Leeper, Mary 725
Leeper, Samuel W. 725, 753
Leeper, William 725, 753
Leeper, Wm. 753
Leeport, George 598
Lees, George 443
Lees, William 443
Leese, Robert 165
Leever, A. A. 243
Leever, Adam 242
Leever, Benjamin 242
Leever, Elizabeth 242
Leever, George 242
Leever, Joseph 242
Leever, Lewis 242
Leever, Lizzie A. 243
Leever, Margaret 242
Leever, Maria 100
Leever, Mary 242
Leever, Nancy 242
Leever, Peter 242
Leever, Sally 242
Leever, Samuel 242
Lefebvre, Emil 482
Lefever, Emulus 498
Lefever, Jacob 431
Lefever, Rebecca 431
Lefever, William 431
Leffel, Anthony 215
Leffel, Elizabeth 221
Leffel, James 215, 221, 224
Leffel, Michael 221
Lefferson, Arthur 128
Lefferton, Arthur 170
Leffler, John 639
Leflar, Margaret 136
Lefler, Magdelena 412
Lefler, Susanna 272
Leftridge, Katharine 704
Leftwich, Nancy 704
Legg, Clarissa 163
Legg, Owen 165
Legg, William 140
Legget, Aseneth 135
Legget, Jas. 135
Legget, Lydia Minerva 135

Leggett, Betsey 268, 276
Lehman, Jonathan 224
Lehman, Mary 380
Lehster, Catharine Elizabeth 101
Leib, Elises 420
Leib, Josef 440
Leiberman, Elizabeth 126
Leibert, John 573
Leibert, John Stapler 573
Leibert, Jos. B. 572
Leibert, Joseph B. 571
Leibert, Joseph Bowman 573
Leibert, Sidney 573
Leids, Robert 238
Leis, Robt. 417
Leist, Elias 51
Leist, John 441
Leith, James 421
Leitpf, Anna Christina 338
Leitpf, Georg 336
Leitpf, Georg Heinrich 338
Leitpf, Greorg 336
Leitpf, Johannes Ludwig 338
Leitpf, Katharina 336
Leitpr, Georg Friedrich 339
Leland, Rebecca 415, 417
LeLeivre, John 543
Leman, William 362
Lemar, Charles 441
Lemart, Abner 599
Lement, Lyod 322
Lement, William 322
Lemert, Thaddeus 748
Lemkuhl, Albert 91
Lemkuhl, Fredericka 91
Lemmler, Esa 344
Lemmler, Peter 344
Lemmon, David 561
Lemmon, M. B. 400
Lemmon, Mary 204
Lemmon, S. N. 400
Lemmon, Sayres N. 400
Lemmon, William 573
Lemmond, William 573
Lemon, Elizabeth 158
Lemon, Jane 210
Lemon, John R. 210, 217
Lemon, Jonathan 139, 156, 158
Lemon, Joseph 206
Lemon, Joseph O. 186
Lemon, Mary 206
Lemon, Nancy 139, 165
Lemon, Simon Kenton 210
Lemon, Vandiver 210
Lemon, William 206, 546
LeMoyne, John 495
LeMoyne, John Julius 490, 494, 495, 496
LeMoyne, Julia 480
Lenbarger, Sarah 410
Lendenberger, John 384

868

Linton, William B. 257
Lintz, Eve 381
Linzee, Rachel 82
Linzee, Robert 82
Lipley, Christian 294
Lippert, William 101
Lippincott, Elizabeth 60
Lippincott, George 60
Lippincott, Hariet Ann 49
Lippincott, Henrietta 60
Lippincott, Mary Jane 60
Lippincott, Samiramis 60
Lippincott, Samuel 60
Lippincott, Samuel B. 60
Lippincott, William 60
Lippincott, Wm. 49
Lippingcott, Rebecca 527
Lippingcutt, Sarah 533
Lisby, Maria 676
Lisby, Solomon 676
Lish, Angeline 333
Lisk, James 316, 325
Lisle, Robert 551
List, Robert 1
Lister, Eliphas 165
Lister, Mary 173
Liston, Betsey 165
Liston, Charles 165
Liston, Sarah 160
Liston, William 170
Listor, William 170
Litsenberger, Henry 581
Litsenberger, Isaac 581
Litsenberger, Sarah 579
Littel, Squire 142
Litten, Abram 679
Litten, Elizabeth 679
Littil, Sarah 298
Little John, Aaron 10
Little, Caroline 416
Little, Catharine 291
Little, Charity 269
Little, David 325
Little, Fanny 65
Little, George 65, 475
Little, Jacob 224
Little, James (Col.) 362
Little, John 46, 170, 411, 534, 627
Little, John N. 418
Little, Mary 165
Little, Nicholas 543
Little, Squire 147, 175, 177
Little, William 25, 317, 389
Littler, Elizabeth 426
Littler, Henry 426
Littler, Seth 467
Littleton, Elizabeth Ann 592
Litz, Caterina 413
Litzenberger, George 585
Litzenberger, Henry 585
Litzenberger, Isaac 585
Litzenberger, Katherine 585
Litzenberger, Mary 585

Litzenberger, Sarah 585
Litzenberger, Susan 585
Livengood, Henry 372
Livengood, Isabella 366
Livengood, Jacob 366
Livengood, Peter 366
Livengood, William 366
Livermore, Polly 305
Livery, Joseph 250
Livery, Sarah 250
Livesay, Thomas 484
Livesay, Winnefield 484
Liveston, John 411
Livesy, Sterling 666
Livingston, Andrew 41
Livingston, Geo. 749
Livingston, Jacob 748
Livingston, John 82, 411
Lloyd, Abel 443
Lloyd, Edward 666
Lloyd, Mary D. 661
Loar, Sarah 705
Loathers, John 411
Loce, George (Jr.) 318
Locey, William 712
Lochard, Thalia 427
Lochart, Jacob 419
Lock, Mary 461
Lockard, Elizabeth 102
Lockard, James 101
Lockard, John 323
Lockard, Joseph 657
Lockard, Robert 747
Lockart, John 321
Lockhart, Josiah 4
Lockhart, Mercy 705
Lockhart, Rebeca 9
Lockhart, Robert 4
Lockhart, Thomas 427
Lockridge, William 467
Lockwood, Alvah 654
Lockwood, M. W. 402
Lockwood, Mary W. 402
Lockwood, Peter 581
Lockwood, T. 654
Lockwood, U. 654
Loclercq, Ft. 21
Loder, John 161
Lodge, Catherine 307
Lodge, Mary 307
Lodge, Susanna 301
Lodwick, John 10, 39
Lodwig, Elenor 383
Loffland, Branston 141
Loffland, William 141
Lofland, Thomas 411
Logan, Alexander 170
Logan, Alfred 52
Logan, Benjamin 284
Logan, Catharine 165
Logan, Charles 170
Logan, David 140, 176
Logan, Eli 58
Logan, James 687
Logan, Jane 12
Logan, John 176, 224
Logan, Keziah Ann 53
Logan, Lydia 51
Logan, Orpha 530

Logan, Samuel 205
Logan, William W. 742
Logue, Mary 151
Logue, Samuel 151, 475, 484
Lohman, Bernard H. 90
Lohman, Bernard Henry 90
Lohman, Henry 101
Lohnes, Catharine 230
Lohnes, Peter 230
Lohr, George W. 220
Lohr, Sarah F. 220
Loinberger, Barbara 732
Loinberger, David 732
Loinberger, Isaac 732
Loinberger, John 732
Loinberger, Nancy 732
Loloway, Elizabeth 410
Loman, Elizabeth 436
Loman, Joseph 436
Loman, Robert 280
Loman, Thomas 581
Lombard, Eli 589
Lombert, James 392
Lonabagh, Jacob 411
Lonas, John 54
Loncor, Leonard 82
Loncor, Margaret 77
Loncor, Nancy 83
Londing, John 96
Long, Abigail 568
Long, Abigal 568
Long, Abraham 55, 65
Long, Alex V. 663
Long, Andrew 660
Long, Barton S. 42
Long, C. W. 578
Long, Catharine 77, 306
Long, Charles 548
Long, Daniel 568
Long, David D. 421
Long, Earl 64
Long, Eleanor 172
Long, Eli 154
Long, Elisha 663
Long, Elizabeth 55, 221, 223, 306
Long, Ester 411
Long, Eva 481
Long, Frances 656
Long, Frederick 431, 542
Long, George 310
Long, George W. 578
Long, Harman 575
Long, Henry 111, 221
Long, Herman 574
Long, Hugh 333
Long, Isaac M. 660
Long, Jacob 55, 65
Long, James 170, 194, 657
Long, Jane 194
Long, Jarrett 609
Long, Jemima 152
Long, Joel 657, 663
Long, John 170, 194, 202, 581, 584, 619
Long, John G. 150
Long, Jonathan 194

Low, Wm. 500, 504
Low, Wm. J. 42
Lowden, Joseph 598
Lowderman, Henry 467
Lowe, --- 408
Lowe, Derick 554, 557
Lowe, Edin 632
Lowe, Elijah 6
Lowe, George W. 42
Lowe, Jacob 554, 557
Lowe, Jacob D. 557
Lowe, John 211, 299, 513
Lowe, Liddy 636
Lowe, Mary 513
Lowe, Sarah 530
Lowe, Thomas 42, 512, 517
Lower, A. J. 312
Lower, Adam 628
Lower, Catherine 591
Lower, Charles 64
Lower, Cora A. 312
Lower, E. 312
Lower, Elizabeth 9, 312
Lower, Ella Louada 312
Lower, F. P. 312
Lower, George 312
Lower, Henry 312
Lower, Jacob 312
Lower, John 299
Lower, M. 312
Lower, R. 312
Lower, S. 312
Lower, Samuel (Jr.) 312
Lower, Sarah Ann 312
Lowerie, William 185
Lowery, Abraham 176
Lowery, Catherine 604
Lowery, David 185
Lowery, Eliza 176, 601
Lowery, Elizabeth 176
Lowery, Fleming 176
Lowery, James 86, 192, 201
Lowery, John 58, 86, 176, 192, 628
Lowery, Margaret 86
Lowery, Martha 176
Lowery, Miles B. 86
Lowery, Nancy 86
Lowery, Samuel 86
Lowery, Sarah 176
Lowes, Benjamin 421
Lowes, James 554, 574
Lowes, James A. 170
Lowes, William 555
Lowman, Abraham 611
Lowman, George 206
Lowman, Joseph 206
Lowmaster, Eleanor 419
Lowmaster, John 416
Lowrey, Almira 377
Lowrey, Bloomy 377
Lowrey, Chancey P. 377
Lowrey, Henry C. 377
Lowrey, Isaac 377
Lowrey, Levina C. 377
Lowrey, Lydia 377
Lowrey, Martha C. 377

Lowrey, Oscar 377
Lowrey, Peter 5
Lowrey, Sarah 515
Lowrey, Talman 377
Lowry, Abigail 80
Lowry, Ann 501
Lowry, Archabald 513
Lowry, Archd. 513
Lowry, Archibald 204, 212
Lowry, Catharine 137, 192
Lowry, D. 204
Lowry, Daniel 82, 642
Lowry, David 513
Lowry, Elizabeth 140, 152, 157, 192, 204, 513
Lowry, Elmira 642
Lowry, Fleming 153
Lowry, J. C. 396
Lowry, J. S. 396
Lowry, James 39, 78, 192, 224, 513
Lowry, Jane 185
Lowry, John 55, 58, 60, 84, 137, 152, 153, 192
Lowry, Joseph 58, 192
Lowry, Joseph S. 396
Lowry, Justice 192
Lowry, Lettis 513
Lowry, Lucinda 192
Lowry, Martha 152
Lowry, Mary 78, 533
Lowry, Mary Ann 192
Lowry, Nancy 192
Lowry, Pallt J. 396
Lowry, Queen 513
Lowry, Rebecca Phillips 396
Lowry, Samuel 549
Lowry, Sara 192
Lowry, Sarah 77
Lowry, Sarah L. 396
Lowry, Thomas 204, 513
Lowry, William 85, 396, 543, 546
Lowsey, Nancy 706
Lowther, Delilah 81
Lowther, Sally 83
Loy, Adam 137, 174
Loy, Christianna 160
Loy, Mary 161
Loy, Sarah 632
Loyd, Elizabeth 408
Loyd, James 525
Loyd, John 525
Loyd, Masse 518
Luallen, Francis 540
Luallen, James 540
Luallen, Zadock 540
Lucas, Burton 705
Lucas, Caleb 267
Lucas, Daniel 452
Lucas, David 360
Lucas, Drusilla 126
Lucas, Ebenezer 53
Lucas, Elisha 107

Lucas, Elizabeth 33, 35, 533
Lucas, Elizabeth Ann 114
Lucas, H. 397
Lucas, Hannah 107
Lucas, Hiram G. 397
Lucas, Ira 397
Lucas, Isaac 52
Lucas, John 68, 174
Lucas, John Nelson 114
Lucas, Joseph 39
Lucas, M. 397
Lucas, Mary 273
Lucas, Mary Ellen 114
Lucas, Mary Trumble 397
Lucas, Massey 161
Lucas, Nathaniel 238
Lucas, Phebe 276
Lucas, Rhoda 276
Lucas, Robinson 125
Lucas, Ruth 114
Lucas, Samuel 114
Lucas, Sarah Anne 114
Lucas, Simon 532
Lucas, Temperance 114
Lucas, William 14, 33, 35, 114
Lucas, Wm. 35
Luccock, Nephtali 551
Luce, Abner G. 504
Luce, Freeman 581
Luce, Hayes G. 380
Luce, Zephimieh 182
Luckenbell, John 389
Luckey, --- (Dr.) 426
Luclow, Israel 555
Lucus, Elizabeth 171
Lucus, Hiram 401
Lucus, Robert 666
Lucus, Sally 523
Lucus, William 114
Ludeman, Sophia 603
Luderman, Peter 602
Luderman, Sophia 602
Luderman, William 602
Ludlow, Charlotte Chambers 567
Ludlow, Cooper 215
Ludlow, Elizabeth 558
Ludlow, Henry 562
Ludlow, Israel 552, 555, 558, 559, 565, 566, 567, 568, 569, 726
Ludlow, John 559, 565, 567, 574
Ludlow, Joseph 78, 635
Ludlow, Wm. 558
Ludwick, Magdaline 417
Ludwig, Anna Maria 347
Ludwig, Catherine 335
Ludwig, Charles 335
Ludwig, Elenor 383
Ludwig, Hannah 335
Ludwig, Hannah P. 335
Ludwig, Isaac 335
Ludwig, Johann 347
Ludwig, John 383
Ludwig, Lettice 383
Ludwig, Thomas 383

Ludwig, Wm. 335
Luhman, Bermardina 99
Luis, Hetty 628
Luitz, Eli 380
Luka, Henry 271
Lukus, Sarah 267, 274
Lum, Jonas 310
Lumb, Reuben 383
Lumbaugh, Joseph 710
Lumbert, James 384
Lunbeck, Mary Jane 450
Lunday, James 105
Lunday, James (Sr.) 105
Lundy, Abigail 263
Lundy, Charlotte 260, 263
Lundy, Enoch 260
Lundy, James 260, 285
Lundy, Jesse 263
Lundy, Mary 286
Lundy, Nathan 278
Lunn, Esquier 607
Lunn, James 607
Lunsford, Polly 705
Lupee, Kurnhopeth 590
Lupton, Anna 265
Lupton, Jonathan 271
Lupton, Mercy 333
Lupton, William 265
Lurey, James 444
Luse, John 186
Luse, Robert 165
Luse, Zepheniah 186
Lush, Charles C. 352
Lush, Juliana 352
Lusk, Charles 52
Lusk, Elizabeth 53, 54
Lusk, Isaac 53
Lusk, Joseph 51
Lusk, Margaret 404
Lust, David 341
Lust, Jacob 341
Lust, Katharina 341
Luttrell, Barbara J. 253
Luttrell, Fanny 253
Luttrell, John L. 101
Luttrell, Mary 253
Luttrell, Polly 253
Luttrell, Richard 253
Luttrell, Robert 253
Luttrell, Ruth 253
Lutz, Catharine 422
Lutz, Geo. 420
Lutz, S. 641
Lutz, Samuel 640
Luzader, Abraham 542
Luze, Elizabeth 521
Lybarger, George 687
Lyberger, Caty 689
Lyberger, George 687, 689
Lybolt, Mary Ann 67
Lydy, Daniel 441
Lydy, John 441
Lyle, Alfred 671
Lyle, Elizabeth 671
Lyle, Finley 619
Lyle, Frances 671
Lyle, Hannah 671

Lyle, Jacob 671
Lyle, John 188, 671
Lyle, Katherine 671
Lyle, Mary Ann 671
Lyle, Robert 548
Lyle, Sarah Jane 671
Lyle, William 671
Lyles, Lucretia 587
Lyman, Edward 602
Lyman, Elizabeth 641
Lyman, Mary 632
Lyman, Samuel 479
Lyman, Sarah Coles 641
Lyman, Thomas C. 641
Lynch, A. M. 251
Lynch, Aaron 324
Lynch, Bezaleel Wells 678
Lynch, Cornelius 324
Lynch, Cynthia 324
Lynch, Eliza 324
Lynch, Elizabeth 251, 324, 592
Lynch, F. 251
Lynch, Fanny 678
Lynch, George H. 251
Lynch, Hannah 590
Lynch, James 327, 353
Lynch, James F. 101
Lynch, James Westley 678
Lynch, John 595
Lynch, Joseph 251
Lynch, Letty 324
Lynch, Maria 678
Lynch, Mary 588
Lynch, Mary Elizabeth 678
Lynch, Mathus 324
Lynch, Nancy 324
Lynch, Samuel 65
Lynch, Sarah C. 251
Lynch, Solomon 678
Lynch, W. H. 251
Lynch, William 313, 315
Lynd, John 475
Lyne, Betty 486
Lyne, Edmond 26
Lyne, Edward 32
Lyne, Nancy Ann 589
Lyne, William 32
Lynes, Absalom 224
Lynn, Adam 144
Lynn, Barbara 411
Lynn, John 144, 598
Lyon, Abraham 299
Lyon, James 131
Lyon, John 565
Lyon, Jonathan 299
Lyon, Jonham 161
Lyon, Mary 588
Lyon, Phebe 81
Lyon, Richard 369
Lyon, Sarah 226
Lyons, Anna 77
Lyons, Arabella 330
Lyons, Arbuthnot 330
Lyons, Arbuthnott H. 330
Lyons, Betsey 650
Lyons, Catherine 123

Lyons, Eleanor 330
Lyons, Elizabeth 274, 418
Lyons, Hugh 330
Lyons, Hugh Robert 330
Lyons, Jane 330
Lyons, John 271, 330, 632
Lyons, Joseph 650
Lyons, Lois 650
Lyons, Mary 330
Lyons, Rachel 419
Lyons, Robert 330, 550
Lyons, Sylvester 576
Lyons, Thomas 330
Lyons, Washington 101
Lyons, William 330
Lytle, Eliza 238, 239
Lytle, Eliza N. 36, 232, 233, 234, 235, 236, 237, 238
Lytle, Elizabeth 581
Lytle, James (Col.) 362
Lytle, Jane 165
Lytle, John 10, 237, 271, 278, 284, 422
Lytle, Margaret 163
Lytle, Margt. 136
Lytle, R. 175, 177
Lytle, Rachel 165
Lytle, Robt. 136
Lytle, Sarah 136
Lytle, William 36, 232, 237, 239, 552
Lytle, Wm. 232, 233, 234, 235, 236, 237, 238, 239
Lytle, Wm. (Col.) 239

--- M ---

Macbeath, William 224
Mace, Esther 615
Mace, Job 615
Macey, Reuben 134
Macey, Sarah 134
Macher, Jno. 38
Macherman, Catharine 306
Machetauz, Gotleip 101
Machir, James 558
Machir, Rebecca 558
Machir, W. W. 663
Machirs, --- 20
Mack, Betty 560
Mack, John 547
Mack, Richard 560
Mackelroy, Hugh 299
Mackerel, Thomas W. 720
Mackey, Elizabeth 74
Mackey, James 225
Mackey, Mary 529
Mackey, Robert 548
Mackey, William 544
Mackley, John (Sr.) 667
Macklin, Catharine 57
Macklin, Elizabeth 640
Macklin, Jacob 411, 640
Macklin, John 628, 640

Malone, Elizabeth 171
Malone, John 705
Malone, Leslie 525
Malot, Tene 466
Malott, David 124
Malott, Joseph 124
Malott, Susan 124
Maloy, Alford 549
Maltbie, Harrison 50
Maltby, Amos 520
Man, Abel 85
Man, Ann 220
Man, Charles 520
Man, John 220, 467, 557
Man, Mahitabel 557
Man, Rhody 460
Man, Warner 467
Manage, Claudius R. 28
Manager, C. 24
Manary, James 19
Maneger, C. 24
Manes, James M. 277
Manger, John 59
Mangin, Lewis 356
Manier, Charity 54
Manker, Ruth 274
Mankin, Isaac 299
Mankins, George 299
Mankins, Thomas 299
Manley, Catherine 10
Manley, Samuel 411
Manly, --- 9
Mann, Alexander 377
Mann, Allen 130
Mann, Archibald 377
Mann, David 82, 271
Mann, Elizabeth 416
Mann, George 377
Mann, Isaac 82
Mann, John 721
Mann, Joseph 377
Mann, Lydia Ann 653
Mann, Mary 335
Mann, Nancy 79
Mann, Phillip (Jr.) 299
Mann, Rebecca 514
Mann, Richard 444
Mann, Robert 377
Mann, Thomas 377
Mann, William 377, 380
Mannen, Hanna 408
Mannen, Moses 706
Mannen, Nancy 706
Mannen, Polly 706
Mannen, Sinthy 706
Mannen, Wilson 706
Manning, --- 373
Manning, Elisha 240
Manning, Elishua 232
Manning, Nathan 232
Manning, Sophia 296
Mannon, Andrew J. 43
Mannon, Henry 712, 717,
718
Mannon, James 723
Mannon, Lucy 717
Mannon, Mary 43
Mannon, Robert 43
Mannon, Samuel 632

Mannon, William 43
Manor, Persatia 78
Manring, Elizabeth 476
Manring, Mary Ann 476
Manring, Masquil 485
Mans, George 52
Mansfield, Anna 79
Mansfield, Charles 137
Mansfield, Elizabeth 77
Mansfield, Esther 76
Mansfield, John 137,161
Mansfield, Katherine 602
Mansfield, Margaret 165
Mansfield, Mary Ann 603
Mansfield, Rebecca 164
Mansfield, Rebeccah 137
Mansfield, Sarah 77
Mansfield, Simeon 78
Mansfield, Thomas (Jr.)
78
Mantle, George 454
Mantle, Mary 465
Manuel, Philip 367
Manypenny, Geo. W. 549
Mapen, Emeline 262
Maple, Abraham 549
Maple, Elizabeth 299
Maple, Isaac 546, 548
Maple, William 549
Mapler, Asa Spencer 479
Maples, Asa Spencer 479
Mapples, Fanny 478
Maque, Mary 411
Maranda, James 574
Marbel, Mary 631
Marble, Isaiah 640
March, Daniel 729
Marchant, Susan 617
Mares, Nicholas D. 55
Maret, Peter 29
Maret, Peter (Sr.) 29
Margandall, Gasper 50
Marguarsten, Jacob 602
Marien, Francis 27
Marietta, Hannah 295
Maring, Peter 109
Marion, Clavin 479
Marion, Francis 488,
493, 495, 497, 498
Mariott, Homewood 745
Mark, Amanda 367
Mark, Amanda M. 367
Mark, David 213, 383
Mark, Elijah 213
Mark, James 213
Mark, Jesse 367
Mark, John 367
Mark, John N. 367
Mark, Jonathan 456
Mark, Joseph 213, 467
Mark, Lavina 367
Mark, Margaret 367
Mark, Nicholas 367
Mark, Peter 411
Mark, Polly 213
Mark, Sarah 213
Mark, Susanah 465
Mark, William 213
Markel, Effa Ann 470

Markel, Geo. 470
Marker, Jacob 271, 281
Marker, John 2
Marker, Jonathan 271
Markham, Sally 78
Markham, Sarah 722
Markim, Thomas 706
Markims, Charles 706
Markin, Charles 712
Markin, Lucinda D. 712
Markland, Eleanor 157
Markland, Joshua 156
Markland, Matthew 156,
157
Markland, Wm. 32
Markley, Catharine 473
Markley, Emma 473
Markley, John 470
Markly, Rachael 101
Marks, Betsy Ann 588
Marks, Daniel 199
Marks, Dolly 405
Marks, Elizabeth 165,
469
Marks, Hastings 26
Marks, Jacob 442
Marks, James 139
Marks, Jane 166
Marks, John 26, 139,
142, 442, 612
Marks, Jonathan 467
Marks, Joseph 453
Marks, Nathaniel 142
Markworth, Henry 602
Marlatt, Abraham 551
Marlatt, F. 48
Marlatt, Field 4
Marlatt, Fields 3
Marlatt, Silas 47
Marlow, Isaac 663
Marlow, Judson 590
Marman, Martin 595
Marmon, David 282
Marmon, Edmund 210
Marmon, Martha 282
Marmot, Stephen 36
Maronkey, Archd. M. 214
Marple, Prudence 468
Marple, Thomas 447
Marpole, Prudence 468
Marquand, John 546, 549
Marquart, David 225
Marquart, Elizabeth 224
Marquat, John 411
Marquis, Joseph 1
Marquis, Ruth 333
Marrah, Noah Warren 730
Marret, Basil 482
Marret, Basil Joseph 493
Marret, Isaac 271
Marret, Marieannie R. 476
Marret, Mary Madelane
Ferrand 489
Marret, Peter 476, 486,
487, 489
Marret, Peter (Jr.)
482, 483, 492, 493
Marret, Peter (Sr.) 492,
493

Marret, Petit P. 32
Marring, Elizabeth 120
Marring, Jacob 120
Marring, John 120
Marring, Lavina 120
Marring, Margaret 120
Marring, Moses 120
Marring, Peter 120
Marring, Rachel 120
Marring, Rhoda 120
Marring, Sarah 120
Marriott, Homewood 748
Marrs, William 191
Mars, Elizabeth 197
Mars, Mary 51
Marsh, Ann 730
Marsh, Anna 727
Marsh, Anna Eliza 727,
730
Marsh, Caroline 730
Marsh, Catharine 730
Marsh, Daniel 727, 730
Marsh, Daniel (Jr.) 727,
730
Marsh, David 651
Marsh, Edward 110, 119
Marsh, Eliakim 171
Marsh, Elias 299, 727,
730
Marsh, Elisabeth 590
Marsh, Eliza 221
Marsh, Elizabeth 706,
727, 730
Marsh, Enoch 543
Marsh, Ester 727
Marsh, Esther 727, 730
Marsh, Fanny 730
Marsh, G. F. 403
Marsh, Geo. F. 403
Marsh, George 47, 730
Marsh, George D. 730
Marsh, George Taylor
727, 730
Marsh, George W. 44
Marsh, Henry 543
Marsh, Israel 214, 221
Marsh, Jacob 727, 730
Marsh, Jacob S. 730
Marsh, Jane 304
Marsh, John 730
Marsh, John Ralph 727,
730
Marsh, Jonathan 299
Marsh, Joseph 299, 545,
730
Marsh, Julius N. 470
Marsh, Letitia 730
Marsh, Lewis R. 730
Marsh, Lydia 167
Marsh, M. 651
Marsh, Marvin M. 651
Marsh, Mary 591, 727,
730
Marsh, Nathan 730
Marsh, Noah 221, 727,
730
Marsh, Noah Warren 730
Marsh, Rachael 110
Marsh, Rachel 590

Marsh, Rachel Barnet
727, 730
Marsh, Ralph 727, 730
Marsh, Rebecca 730
Marsh, Roswell 682, 685
Marsh, S. M. 403
Marsh, Samuel 221
Marsh, Sarah 110, 226,
727, 730
Marsh, Sidney 730
Marsh, Solomon 730
Marsh, Susannah 221
Marsh, W. R. 403
Marsh, William 605
Marsh, William Ralph
727, 730
Marsh, Zachariah 110
Marsh, Zachariah H. 119
Marshal, Joseph 325
Marshall, Andrew 104
Marshall, Ann 516
Marshall, Benjamin 299
Marshall, Benuel 419
Marshall, Catharine 325
Marshall, Catherine 419
Marshall, Charles Albert
229
Marshall, Charles C. 96
Marshall, Cinthia 222
Marshall, David 299
Marshall, Deborah 521
Marshall, Elenor 325,
518, 533
Marshall, Elinor 325
Marshall, Eliza 125
Marshall, Elizabeth 548
Marshall, George 325
Marshall, Hannah 527
Marshall, Ichabod 690,
697
Marshall, Isabella 325
Marshall, Jacob 598
Marshall, James 176,
225, 275, 359, 377,
525
Marshall, Jane 325, 526
Marshall, John 104,
132, 506, 513, 516,
520, 532
Marshall, Joseph 104,
299
Marshall, Laura Louisa
229
Marshall, Louisa 229
Marshall, Mary 10, 290,
526, 527, 546
Marshall, Michael 229
Marshall, Polly 411
Marshall, Robert 515,
516, 532
Marshall, Saml. 462
Marshall, Samuel 97, 104
Marshall, Sarah Ann 229
Marshall, Susan 96
Marshall, Thomas 365
Marshall, William 237,
598
Marshall, Wm. 325
Marshallon, Lany 521

Marstella, Charles 751
Marsteller, Charles 756
Marstiller, Charles 726
Mart, Elizabeth 275
Martain, Eloner 297
Martain, John 706
Marten, Margaret 529
Marten, Samuel 78
Martin, Abigail 166
Martin, Absalom 31, 32,
104
Martin, Abslom 29
Martin, Alexander 233,
562
Martin, Andrew 299
Martin, Ann 130, 143,
151, 195, 691
Martin, Anna 251, 596
Martin, Anne 160, 163
Martin, Annie 251
Martin, Archelaus 49
Martin, Archelias 96
Martin, Asahel 505
Martin, Benj. 386
Martin, Benjamin 385
Martin, Benjamin (Jr.)
480
Martin, Betsey 130,
145, 151, 172
Martin, Burman 447
Martin, Catharine 96,
297
Martin, Charity 195
Martin, Charles 57, 90,
255, 275, 462
Martin, Christopher
366, 367, 969
Martin, Christopher
(Jr.) 367
Martin, Christopher
(Sr.) 367
Martin, Cornelius 82
Martin, D. 255
Martin, Dan 49
Martin, David 480
Martin, David E. 255
Martin, Dorcas 389
Martin, E. 255, 638
Martin, Edward 16
Martin, Eleaser 450
Martin, Eli 251, 254,
571
Martin, Eli P. 195
Martin, Elijah 251
Martin, Elisabeth 10
Martin, Elizabeth 79,
120, 130, 172, 255,
272, 525, 691, 706
Martin, Eunice 196
Martin, Evi 575
Martin, Ezekiel 196
Martin, Fanny 520
Martin, Frank 251
Martin, Frederick 358
Martin, George 196,
483, 557, 691
Martin, Gilbert 652
Martin, Hannah 275,
475, 652

Mathews, Henry 586
Mathews, Isaac 299
Mathews, Jacob 594
Mathews, James 332, 480
Mathews, James J. 586
Mathews, John 686, 687, 688, 689
Mathews, John J. 586
Mathews, John K. 586
Mathews, Joseph 586
Mathews, Lizz 374
Mathews, Mahala 687
Mathews, Mariah 586
Mathews, Mary 525
Mathews, Mary J. 586
Mathews, Nancy 595
Mathews, Nathan N. 586
Mathews, Nathaniel 480
Mathews, Peter 271
Mathews, Rebecca 307
Mathews, Sally 686, 689
Mathews, Samuel 590
Mathews, Sarah T. 586
Mathews, Thomas 476
Mathews, William 586
Matheys, John 280
Mathias, Eve 629
Mathias, Jacob 418
Mathias, Levi 645
Mathias, Peter 637
Mathis, James 576
Matle, Jesse 454
Matley, Henry 412
Matlock, Sarah 466
Matrie, Peter 21
Matry, Peter 21, 24, 495, 496, 498
Matson, James 247
Matson, John 269
Matson, Mary 247
Matson, Mary J. 247
Matson, Rhoda 269
Matta, Elizabeth 412
Mattas, Henry 412
Mattes, Mary 412
Matthews, Angeline 417
Matthews, Betsy 272
Matthews, Catherine 276
Matthews, David W. 317
Matthews, Edwin 208
Matthews, James 156
Matthews, John 520, 567
Matthews, Paul 542
Matthews, Rebecca 274
Matthews, Susannah 272
Matthews, Thomas 571, 572
Matthias, Abraham 628, 632
Matthias, Polly 628
Matthias, Sarah 630
Mattiell, Christian 616
Mattocks, Harriet 647
Mattocks, Samuel 647
Mattox, David 153
Mattox, Moses 51
Mattox, William 153
Matz, John 310
Matz, Mary 298
Matz, Matilda 298

Mauger, George 470
Mauk, George 644
Mauker, Zimri 608, 609
Maus, Philipina 344
Mauzey, Polly 531
Mauzy, Joseph 202
Mavis, Abraham 380
Max, Ele 373
Maxan, Mary 409
Maxen, Lydia 529
Maxey, Bennet 516
Maxey, Elizabeth 703
Maxey, Polley 525
Maxfield, Fanny 699
Maxon, Ephraim 225
Maxson, Elizabeth 223
Maxson, Jesse 223
Maxson, Jonathan 598
Maxwell, Absalom 117
Maxwell, Boswell 117
Maxwell, David 117, 526, 551
Maxwell, Eliza 117
Maxwell, Elizabeth 378, 526
Maxwell, Ephraim 462
Maxwell, Franklin Collins 672
Maxwell, James 117, 165, 404
Maxwell, Jane 117
Maxwell, John 117, 141
Maxwell, Joseph 551
Maxwell, Julia 117
Maxwell, Lucinda 117
Maxwell, Maria 117
Maxwell, Mary 117, 409
Maxwell, Morgan 117
Maxwell, Nancy 117, 308, 510, 516
Maxwell, Senah 117
Maxwell, Thomas 117, 598
Maxwell, Thompson 165
Maxwell, William 117, 510, 516, 526
May, Allena 246
May, Anna 303
May, Benjamin 480
May, Chesum 411
May, Elizabeth 298, 310
May, Iazam 411
May, John 299,373
May, Sarah 294
May, William 299
Maybeery, Mary 469
Mayberry, Elizabeth 53
Mayberry, Mary 531
Mayberry, William 49
Mayers, Mary Catharine 102
Mayes, George 645
Mayhew, Richard 545
Maynard, James 590
Maynard, Luther 667
Mays, Jonathan 722
Mays, Joseph 480
Mayse, Wm. H. 405
Mc . . . , Elizabeth S. 230

Mc . . . , Sareph 230
Mc . . . , William 230
Mc . . . ain, R. 179
McAdam, John 207, 748
McAdams, Ann 232
McAdams, Ephraim 232, 233
McAdams, Isaac 444
McAdams, John 187, 192, 197, 205, 236, 444, 559, 576
McAdams, Nancy 444
McAdams, Patrick 299
McAdams, Samuel 197
McAdams, Thomas 153, 161
McAfarty, Thos. 280
McAfee, Mark 78
McAfee, Robert W. 589
McAfee, Sally 80
McAfee, Sophia 80
McAffee, Sarah 531
McAlester, Joseph 532
McAllister, John 749
McAlpin, Alexander 354
McAmbus, Benjamin 705
McAnally, Elizabeth 379
McAnally, Moses 581
McAnless, William 532
McArdle, John P. 697
McArthur, Duncan 18, 612
McArthur, Mary 464, 510
McArthur, Peter 510
McBafferty, Almira 417
McBean, Jane 479
McBeth, Alexander 207
McBeth, Alexr. 182
McBeth, Elizabeth 223
McBeth, John 179
McBeth, John W. 505
McBeth, William 206
McBeth, Wm. 179
McBrating, Alexander 110
McBrattney, Samuel 329
McBride, Charles 698, 701
McBride, Elizabeth 701
McBride, Hannah 298
McBride, Henry 520
McBride, Hugh 701
McBride, James 129
McBride, Jane 701
McBride, Letty 411
McBride, Margaret 589
McBride, Mary 308, 701
McBride, Nancy 589, 701
McBride, Ruth 701
McBride, Saley 11
McBride, Sarah 577, 701
McBride, Stephen (Jr.) 299
McBride, Thomas 701
McBride, Thos. 687, 688
McBride, William 411, 701
McBride, Wm. 577, 687
McBroom, John K. 646
McBroom, Joseph C. 643
McBroom, Nancy V. 645
McBroom, Robert 637, 645, 646

McBurney, John 547
McCabe, Armstrong 520
McCabe, Isaiah 422
McCabe, Jane 629
McCabe, Jostenus 411
McCadden, J. A. W. 740
McCaddenx, Ellen 740
McCaddenx, Josiah A. W. 740
McCaddenx, Margaret 740
McCafferty, David 458, 467
McCafferty, Eliza 458
McCafferty, Jonathan 455
McCafferty, Sarah 453
McCafferty, William 446, 453, 455, 458, 467
McCaily, Michael 197
McCain, Susanna 171
McCaleb, Mary 468
McCaleman, Robert 37
McCaless, Elizabeth 466
McCaless, Wm. 462, 467
McCaliss, Elizabeath 462
McCall, Margaret 124
McCall, Mary 438
McCall, Matthew 116
McCall, Nancy 116
McCalla, Andrew 405
McCalla, Edward 405
McCalla, Polly 404
McCalley, John 210
McCallister, Heiter 299
McCallister, Walter 299
McCallum, Cornelius 239
McCalmont, Mary 301
McCalny, George 299
McCamber, Charles 590
McCamp, Silas C. 389
McCance, David 175
McCandles, Hugh 462
McCane, John 709
McCane, Miomi 707
McCane, William 717
McCanles, James (Jr.) 371
McCanless, James 46
McCann, George 249
McCann, J. J. 249
McCann, Thomas 551
McCanny, Peter 204
McCardle, Mary 700
McCardle, May 700
McCardle, Nancy 700
McCardle, Peter 700
McCarhen, Sally 434
McCarley, Elizabeth 487
McCarley, John 479, 487
McCarley, Margaret 487
McCarley, Moses 487
McCarley, Samuel 487
McCarley, Sibby 476
McCarley, William 475, 487
McCarley, Zebiah 487
McCarran, Barnabus 560
McCarran, Barney 560
McCarren, Barnabas 161
McCarroll, Rebecca 118

McCarron, John 299
McCart, Henry 404
McCarter, Nathan 747
McCarthy, James 620
McCartney, Andrew 705
McCartney, Mary 61
McCartney, Sally 707
McCartney, William 61, 97
McCartny, Isaac 462
McCartor, Jonathan 748
McCarty, Alice 8
McCarty, Alta Pearl 8
McCarty, Amos 310
McCarty, Andrew 467
McCarty, David 479
McCarty, E. C. 8
McCarty, George 479
McCarty, J. A. 8
McCarty, Jared 602
McCarty, Louella Rader 8
McCarty, Mattie 8
McCarty, Mehaly 629
McCarty, Michael 358
McCarty, Paul Forest 8
McCarty, Rebecca 298
McCarty, Robert L. 8
McCarty, Rosanna 625
McCarty, Van R. 5
McCarty, Wesley 8
McCarty, Wm. 747
McCash, David 562, 563
McCashon, Elizabeth 526
McCaskey, Catharine 165
McCaskey, Elizabeth 176, 313
McCaskey, George 58, 315
McCaskey, Henry 176
McCaskey, Hugh 313
McCaskey, Isabella 176
McCaskey, James 176
McCaskey, Jane 292
McCaskey, John 176
McCaskey, Joseph 176
McCaskey, Letty 176
McCaskey, Polly 176
McCaskey, Wm. 313
McCaughey, Cyrus 679
McCaughey, Elizabeth 679
McCaughey, Jackson 679
McCaughey, James 679
McCaughey, Jemima 679
McCaughey, Joseph 679
McCaughey, Margaret 679
McCaughey, Mary Ann 679
McCaughey, Thomas 679
McCaughey, William 679
McCauley, Mary Ann 380
McCaull, Jane 485
McCauly, Jane 518
McCauly, Philip 380
McCawley, Sarah 404
McCay, Ann 444
McCay, Job 444
McCay, Robert 467
McChesney, John 554
McChristy, Jesse 506
McChristy, Nancy 506
McClain, Catherina 702

McClain, Charles 234
McClain, Elizabeth 610
McClain, James 195
McClain, Jeremiah 18
McClain, Thomas 610
McClain, William 568
McClalland, Elizabeth 404
McClanahan, John 4
McClanahan, Samuel 4
McClanahan, Thomas 43
McClanahan, Wm. 5
McClane, Jane 523
McClane, Jno. 515
McClane, Margery 303
McClaran, Richard 299
McClaran, Robert 299
McClaren, Robert 472
McClarran, William 32
McClarren, Polly 288
McClarrin, Margaret 310
McClary, Mary 740
McClary, Rebecca 740
McClary, Silas C. 392
McClary, William 740
McClaskey, Henry 176
McClay, Charles 189
McClean, William 144
McCleary, Andrew 149
McCleary, Darcus 598
McCleary, Mary 149
McCleary, Sally 149
McCleary, Samuel 149
McCleland, Polley 520
McCleland, Sarah 410
McClelend, Thomas 192
McClellan, Abraham 513
McClellan, Alexander 585
McClellan, David 585
McClellan, Eleanor 525
McClellan, Eliz. 524
McClellan, Forges 585
McClellan, George 585
McClellan, James 143, 558, 576, 585
McClellan, John 128, 152, 513, 585
McClellan, Margaret 585
McClellan, Nancy 585
McClellan, Peggy 513
McClellan, Polly 170, 513
McClellan, Robert 525, 554, 585
McClellan, Thomas 585
McClellan, William 137, 138, 139, 140, 141, 142, 145
McClellan, Wm. 128, 152
McClelland, --- 128
McClelland, Abraham 515
McClelland, Cary 749
McClelland, Catharine 529
McClelland, Isabel 82
McClelland, James 442, 556, 560, 573
McClelland, James B. 2
McClelland, Joseph 525

McClelland, Nancy 532
McClelland, Peggy 515
McClelland, Polly 515,
523
McClelland, Samuel 2
McClelland, Sarah 515
McClelland, T. J. 45
McClelland, Thomas 2
McClelland, Wm. 154,
177, 517
McClenahan, Robt. 39
McClennaham, Elizabeth
323
McClennaham, James 323
McClennaham, John 323
McClennaham, Mary 323
McClennaham, Susannah
323
McClennahan, John 546
McClennanham, Andrew 323
McClentick, Polly 78
McCloskey, Elizabeth 161
McCloskey, John 170
McClosky, Henry 140, 146
McClosky, John 146
McClosky, Joseph 146
McClosky, Lettice 160
McCloud, Elizabeth 270
McCloud, Jane 475
McCloud, Mary 480
McCloud, William 590
McCluer, Moses 63
McCluer, Nathaniel S.
363
McCluer, Samuel 363
McCluer, Sarah Ann 51
McCluney, William 562
McClung, Alice 660
McClung, James 130
McClung, Sally 476
McClure, Ann 170
McClure, Elizabeth 213
McClure, Faithful 738
McClure, Henry 462
McClure, Holbert 3
McClure, James 467, 673
McClure, Jane 154, 213,
296
McClure, Janet 154
McClure, John 154
McClure, Lewis 673
McClure, Louisena 673
McClure, Margaret 213,
222
McClure, Martha 658
McClure, Martha Lewellen
673
McClure, Mary 154, 213,
533
McClure, Mary E. Brown
673
McClure, Matthew 213
McClure, Nancy 213
McClure, Rebecca 213
McClure, Robert 213
McClure, Robt. 175
McClure, Samuel 3, 46,
150, 161, 213, 666
McClure, Samuel Lewis 673

McClure, Sarah 673
McClure, Thomas 738
McClure, W. 175
McClure, W. T. 46
McClure, William 154,
165, 175, 213, 520
McClure, William
Mitchell 673
McClure, Wm. 154
McCollester, Abram 638
McCollester, John 299
McCollister, Hector 310
McCollister, John 657
McCollister, Walter 310
McCollock, N. Z. 500
McCollock, Sol. 500
McCollom, Cornelius 575
McCollough, Robt. 544
McCollum, Isaac 546
McColough, Hannah 521
McComas, Mary A. 723
McComas, Mary Ann 722
McComb, Hugh 544, 546
McComb, Mary 635
McConahey, Margaret
McCune 673
McConahey, Nancy Clark
673
McConahey, Samuel 673
McConahey, Thomas
Mitchell 673
McConaughty, John 237
McConaughy, Jas. 550
McConaughy, Wm. 550
McConeighy, Mary 309
McConell, Rosanna 102
McConesshey, Mary 289
McConn, Thomas 546
McConnal, Jesse 299
McConnel, Ann 525
McConnel, Catharine 179
McConnel, Edward 299
McConnel, Ezekiel 130,
147
McConnel, Harriet 286
McConnel, James 673
McConnel, Jane 532
McConnel, Levi 299
McConnel, Nancy 525
McConnel, Patsey 525
McConnel, Polly 519
McConnel, Robert 116
McConnel, William 520
McConnel, William Thomas
673
McConnell, Adam 515
McConnell, Alexander 685
McConnell, Ann 504
McConnell, Arthur 10
McConnell, Dorcehus 286
McConnell, Elizabeth 286
McConnell, Isabell 235
McConnell, Isaiah 504
McConnell, James T. 586
McConnell, John 97,
467, 598, 663
McConnell, John D. 286
McConnell, Joseph 684
McConnell, Joseph M. 286

McConnell, June Eliza
416
McConnell, Katharine 705
McConnell, Lydia 416
McConnell, Mary 286, 594
McConnell, Nancy 523
McConnell, Reason 286
McConnell, Samuel 605
McConnell, Sarah 286
McConnell, Thomas 233,
286
McConnell, William 586
McConnelly, G. R. 400,
401
McConner, Samuel 299
McCook, Daniel 299
McCook, Hannah 265
McCool, Thomas 265
McCool, Thomas P. 265
McCoonsy, Adam 3
McCoprty, Charles 7
McCord, Celia 230
McCord, Celia W. 230
McCord, Elizabeth 230
McCord, Isabella 233
McCord, John 230, 233
McCord, Joseph 520
McCord, Louisa 652
McCord, Nancy 230
McCord, Sam. 186
McCord, Saml. 186, 192
McCord, Samuel 195,
198, 202
McCord, Samuel M. 380
McCorkle, Andrew 660,
714
McCorkle, Betsey 714
McCorkle, Catharine 714
McCorkle, Daniel 714
McCorkle, Jacob 714
McCorkle, James 714
McCorkle, Joel 714
McCorkle, John 708, 714
McCorkle, Joseph 545
McCorkle, Polley 714
McCorkle, Robert 708,
710, 711, 712, 714
McCorkle, Robert F. 714
McCorkle, Robert F.
Davis 714
McCorkle, Sally 714
McCorkle, Samuel 705,
714
McCormack, Hugh 411
McCormack, James 475
McCormack, John 138, 446
McCormack, John (Jr.)
170
McCormack, William 476
McCormas, Catharine 705
McCormeck, Rachael 518
McCormek, Wm. 663
McCormick, Adam 48
McCormick, Calvin 454
McCormick, Catharine 499
McCormick, Elizabeth
454, 679
McCormick, Hanah Maria
673

McCormick, Hannah 673
McCormick, James 679
McCormick, James (Sr.) 679
McCormick, Jas. 48
McCormick, John 454, 456, 499, 555, 679
McCormick, Louis 454
McCormick, Martha 679
McCormick, Mary Jane 679
McCormick, Nancy 461
McCormick, Philey 499
McCormick, Priscilla 679
McCormick, Robt. 547
McCormick, Samuel 47
McCormick, William 2, 454
McCormick, Wm. 4, 456
McCormick, Wright 454
McCormus, George 705
McCormus, Sartin 705
McCornas, Ammon 705
McCornic, E. 373
McCouran, George 408
McCourtney, Comfort 486
McCoveny, Adam 48
McCowan, Alexander 320
McCowen, James 165
McCowmes, Elizabeth 12
McCown, Wm. H. 443
McCoy, Abigail 506
McCoy, Alex M. 444
McCoy, Alexander 6, 299, 506
McCoy, Amelia 506
McCoy, Andrew 56, 63
McCoy, Ann 486
McCoy, Benjamin 480
McCoy, Catharine 480
McCoy, Daniel 74
McCoy, David 56, 486, 506, 515, 520
McCoy, Eleanore 480
McCoy, Elijah 56
McCoy, Elisha 56
McCoy, Elizabeth 56, 294, 520, 595, 704
McCoy, Ephraim 387
McCoy, Epraim 387
McCoy, George 6
McCoy, Harriet Ann 449
McCoy, James 320, 506, 544, 679
McCoy, Jane 56, 707
McCoy, Jesse 462
McCoy, Job 444
McCoy, John 17, 300, 324, 462, 506, 598, 705
McCoy, Joseph 17
McCoy, Letitia 56
McCoy, Malinda 56, 102
McCoy, Margaret 474
McCoy, Mary 387, 533, 591
McCoy, Mary Elizabeth 61
McCoy, Mary Violet 703
McCoy, Mary W. 56
McCoy, Matilda 54, 56, 592

McCoy, Michael 660
McCoy, Miram 53
McCoy, Mirian 56
McCoy, Moses 55, 56, 590
McCoy, Nancy 49, 506
McCoy, Polly 480, 506, 515
McCoy, Rachel 290
McCoy, Rebecca 121, 446, 453, 456
McCoy, Robert 193, 388
McCoy, Sally 478
McCoy, Saml. 595
McCoy, Sarah 50, 56, 303, 387, 533
McCoy, Susanna 476
McCoy, Thomas 279
McCoy, Thos. 17
McCoy, William 506
McCracken, Charles 392
McCracken, Clara 382
McCracken, Eliza B. 426
McCracken, Isabel 587
McCracken, James 333
McCracken, Jane 309
McCracken, John 426
McCracken, John B. 426
McCracken, Margaret 530
McCracken, Robert 590
McCraken, Thomas 300
McCraren, Christr. 543
McCrary, James 15
McCray, Margaret 656
McCray, Patsy Ann 655
McCray, Samuel 171
McCray, Sarah 173, 656
McCray, Shaphet 516
McCrea, Catharine 168
McCrea, David 545
McCrea, Gilbert 128
McCrea, James 128
McCrea, John 128
McCrea, Mary 128, 418
McCready, Daniel 300
McCreary, Archibald 556
McCreight, David 46, 47
McCreight, Elizabeth 46
McCreight, James 44, 46
McCreight, James S. 46
McCreight, Jesse 42, 46
McCreight, John 46
McCreight, John M. 46
McCreight, Jonathan 46
McCreight, Joseph 44, 46
McCreight, William 46
McCreight, Wm. 46
McCreight, Wm. O. 42
McCreight, Wm. R. 42
McCright, David 44
McCright, Joseph 44
McCristy, Charles 506
McCristy, Phebe 506
McCritton, John 420
McCrory, James 436
McCrory, Mary Ann 436
McCue, James A. 612
McCugh, Jane 268, 276
McCul, John 206
McCulgan, William 659

McCullah, George 220
McCulley, Matthew 551
McCulloch, David 107
McCulloch, Harriet 185
McCulloch, Hugh 375
McCulloch, Isaac 107
McCulloch, John 107, 185, 326
McCulloch, Robert 598
McCulloch, Samuel 205
McCulloch, Thomas 733
McCullock, Daniel 327
McCullock, John 106, 206
McCullock, Robert 327
McCullock, Sampson 176
McCulloh, Alexander 321
McCullon, John 316
McCullough, A. B. 42
McCullough, Addison 4, 5
McCullough, Adison 47
McCullough, Archibald 42, 44, 46
McCullough, Eliza A. 722
McCullough, George 323
McCullough, Hugh 4
McCullough, James 65
McCullough, John 1, 4, 6, 7, 44, 512, 525
McCullough, Lawson 233
McCullough, Margat 704
McCullough, Samson 553
McCullough, Samuel 42
McCullough, Thomas 139, 145
McCullough, William 598
McCully, James 520
McCully, Philip 380
McCully, Solomon 509
McCumsey, Alexander 193
McCumsey, Barbara 193
McCumsey, Carter 193
McCumsey, Davison 193
McCumsey, Henry 193
McCumsey, Joseph 193
McCumsey, Josina White 193
McCumsey, Mary 193
McCumsey, Matthias 193
McCumsey, Thomas 193
McCumsy, Alexander 193
McCun, Thomas 367
McCune, Adam 673
McCune, Agness Adeline 673
McCune, Albert Elsworth 673
McCune, Caroline McCormick 673
McCune, Catherine Ann 673
McCune, Elizabeth 673
McCune, Emiline Whitely 673
McCune, George Gillespie 673
McCune, Henry Russel 673
McCune, James 549, 673, 674, 679, 685
McCune, Jane 685

884

McIlyar, William 547, 548
McIlyar, Wm. 547
McIntire, Alexander 29, 616
McIntire, Amariah 219
McIntire, Andrew 2, 7
McIntire, Daniel 616
McIntire, Elizabeth 222, 705
McIntire, Esther 219
McIntire, James W. 219
McIntire, Jane 657
McIntire, John 42, 44, 219, 256, 258, 263, 264, 268, 616, 748
McIntire, John S. 219
McIntire, Joseph 219, 532, 705
McIntire, Joseph A. 42
McIntire, Joseph C. 590
McIntire, Margaret 219
McIntire, Maria 219
McIntire, Mary 219, 290
McIntire, Polly 268, 276
McIntire, Rachel 304
McIntire, Robert S. 4
McIntire, Samuel 219
McIntire, William 616
McIntire, William T. 219
McIntire, Wm. 2, 5, 6, 42, 43, 44, 46, 47
McIntosh, --- 288
McIntosh, Elizabeth 366
McIntosh, Issabella 305
McIntosh, James M. 366
McIntosh, John J. 366
McIntosh, Melinda 366
McIntosh, Nancy 309
McIntosh, Rue 366
McIntosh, William 300
McIntyre, John 44
McKaby, Thomas 300
McKaig, Isabella 288
McKaig, James 525
McKaig, Jno. 516
McKain, William (Sr.) 598
McKan, John 300
McKay, A. M. 252
McKay, David M. 252
McKay, Ephraim 55
McKay, Isaac 55
McKay, J. 252
McKay, Jesse 252
McKay, Jessie 557
McKay, Jessie R. 252
McKay, Jno. 516
McKay, Mary 252, 264
McKay, Moses 264
McKay, Patience 460
McKay, Robert 252, 462
McKea, John 711
McKean, Alexander 300
McKean, Elizabeth 173
McKean, James 138
McKean, John 147, 153
McKean, Peggy 166
McKean, Richard 145, 150

McKean, Robert 147
McKearn, --- 558
McKearnan, Peter 570
McKebbin, Margaret 269
McKechin, Brice 300
McKee, Albin 628
McKee, Alexander 560
McKee, Allice 161
McKee, Andrew 321, 325
McKee, Arthur 628
McKee, Daniel 300, 330
McKee, David 78
McKee, Dennis 433
McKee, Elizabeth 524, 626
McKee, Gilbert 319
McKee, James 326, 332, 467
McKee, John 705
McKee, Joseph 46
McKee, Mary 634
McKee, Nancy 330
McKee, Patrick 320
McKee, Robert 78, 300
McKee, Samuel 82, 332
McKee, Sarah 486
McKee, Thomas 234, 363, 687
McKee, William 715
McKee, William (Jr.) 715
McKeel, Moree 657
McKenney, Elizabeth 518
McKenney, Samuel 183
McKenney, Sarah 183
McKenney, William 520
McKennie, Gerrard 190
McKenny, Benjamin F. 265
McKenny, Charity 520
McKentiffer, Jacob 310
McKenzie, Andrew 171
McKenzie, Donald 82
McKhan, William 365
McKibban, Mary 273
McKibben, Hugh B. 69
McKibben, Hugh Baird 69
McKibben, John 753
McKibben, Robt. 69
McKibbian, Gideon 280
McKibbian, James 280
McKibbian, John 280
McKibbian, Margaret 280
McKibbian, Martha 280
McKibbian, Polly 280
McKibbin, A. M. 365
McKibbin, John 557
McKibbins, Gideon 271
McKibbon, David 24
McKibbon, John 280
McKibbon, Joseph 280
McKilip, John 448
McKillip, Nancy 466
McKim, Elizabeth 649
McKim, James 649
McKim, Sarah 674
McKim, Thomas 674
McKindley, Sarah 310
McKinley, Benj. 67
McKinley, David 300

McKinley, John 201, 586
McKinley, Samuel 67
McKinley, Sarah 294
McKinley, Thomas 201
McKinly, Esther 302
McKinly, John 42, 47
McKinnes, Hiram 663
McKinney, Anthony 525
McKinney, Easter 521
McKinney, John 573
McKinney, Lewis 268
McKinney, Saml. F. 548
McKinney, Stephen 268
McKinney, William 476
McKinnie, Joseph 388
McKinnie, Josiah 390
McKinnie, Saml. F. 545
McKinnis, --- 664
McKinnis, Charles 663, 667
McKinnis, Eliza 581
McKinnis, James 581, 663
McKinnis, James S. 663
McKinnis, Joseph 657
McKinnis, Robert 581, 663
McKinnis, Sarah 580
McKinnis, William 663
McKinnon, Daniel 204, 212
McKinnon, Elizabeth 219
McKinnon, James B. 219
McKinnon, John M. 590
McKinnon, Joseph 300
McKinnon, Sally 222
McKinnon, Theophilus 224
McKinnon, William 206
McKinny, Joel 268, 275
McKinny, Lewis 275
McKinny, Samuel 185
McKinny, Stephen 268
McKinny, Thomas 476
McKinsey, Alexander 476
McKinsey, Elizabeth 707
McKinsey, Jane 163
McKinsey, Mary 627
McKinstry, James 171
McKinstry, Jane 169
McKinstry, John 171
McKinstry, Robert 85
McKinstry, Sally 160
McKinstry, William 85
McKinzee, Duncan 45
McKitterick, Thomas 661
McKlean, Robert 165
McKlean, Samuel 165
McKnight, Ann 527
McKnight, Daniel 532
McKnight, Elizabeth 527
McKnight, John 176, 300, 516
McKnight, Joseph 152, 176
McKnight, Lydia 300
McKnight, Polley 522
McKnight, Samuel 550
McKonkey, Archibald 220
McKonkey, Lydia 220
McKown, John 680

McLain, Betsy 197
McLain, James 197
McLain, James A. 197
McLain, Jane Polly 197
McLain, John R. 197
McLain, Joseph 197
McLain, Sarah 197
McLain, Stephen 197
McLain, William 197
McLanahan, Andrew 315
McLanahan, Elizabeth 315
McLanahan, Jane 315
McLanahan, John 315
McLanahan, John L. 315
McLanahan, Mary 315
McLanahan, Susannah 315
McLane, Eleanor 300
McLane, Hugh 234
McLane, Jno. 515
McLane, John 300
McLane, Nalky 636
McLarey, Deliliah 756
McLary, Rebecca 756
McLary, William 756
McLaskey, Mary 164
McLasky, Henry 176
McLaughen, David 712
McLaughlan, Alexander 739
McLaughlin, Alex. 688
McLaughlin, Alexander 236, 553, 688
McLaughlin, Catharine 294
McLaughlin, Elizabeth 292
McLaughlin, Hannah 690
McLaughlin, James 300
McLaughlin, Jane 303
McLaughlin, Joseph 300
McLaughlin, Laughlin 112
McLaughlin, Patk. 547
McLaughlin, Rebecca 304
McLaughlin, Robert 370
McLaughlin, Sarah 112
McLaughlin, Thomas 300
McLaughlin, William 462
McLaurine, James 733
McLean, Alexander 389
McLean, Allen 389
McLean, Amy 389
McLean, Betsey 389
McLean, Daniel 445
McLean, Eunice 389
McLean, Forgus 38
McLean, Joseph 206
McLean, Lauchlin 389
McLean, Mary 389
McLean, Mordock 389
McLean, Polly 466
McLean, Susan 389
McLelland, Alexander 757
McLemm, Annie 126
McLennahan, Andrew 319
McLennahan, Elizabeth Susannah 319
McLennahan, John 319
McLennahan, John L. 319
McLennahan, Mary Jane 319

McLillery, Margaret 294
McLilley, Margaret 310
McLin, Mary 278
McLish, Jacob 300
McLish, Robert 300
McLoud, Elizabeth 608
McLughlin, Elenor 523
McMahan, George 467
McMahan, James 705
McMahan, John 451
McMahan, Joseph 4, 84, 140
McMahan, Robert 4, 42
McMahan, Stephen 705
McMahon, Joseph 137, 561
McMahon, William 361
McMaken, Joseph H. 157
McMaken, Mark 132
McMan, John 705
McManis, Elizabeth 275
McManis, George 263, 263, 458
McManis, James 272
McManis, John 458
McManis, Margaret 272
McManis, Rachael 276
McMannis, Jacob 674
McMannis, Margaret Jane 674
McMannis, Sarah 674
McManorey, Mary 227
McManus, Charles 171
McManus, Henry 628
McManus, Robert 165
McManus, William 165
McMasters, Starr 680
McMasters, William 680
McMean, Elizabeth 405
McMeekin, Moris 1
McMichael, Elizabeth 532
McMichael, Mary 334
McMichael, Mary (Jr.) 333
McMillan, David 280
McMillan, Deborah 280
McMillan, Edith 280
McMillan, Jane 280
McMillan, John 44, 300
McMillan, Matilda 535
McMillan, Thomas 280
McMillan, William 130, 258, 561, 563, 564, 566, 573, 574
McMillen, Archibald 556
McMillen, Eliza 316
McMillen, John 45, 316
McMillen, Robert 590
McMillen, Susannah 700
McMiller, William 224
McMillice, Ann Sophia 220
McMillice, James 220
McMillin, James 556
McMillion, Jane 475
McMillon, Gideon 384
McMorris, Joseph 314
McMullen, Barbara 301, 310
McMullen, David 61

McMullen, Joseph 404, 746
McMullen, Silas 746
McMullen, William 467
McMullin, Alender 741
McMullin, Alexander 741
McMullin, Andrew 741
McMullin, Andrew J. 741
McMullin, Burr Newton 741
McMullin, Francis Calvin 741
McMullin, Jane 479
McMullin, Margaret 741
McMullin, Mary 741
McMullin, Mary Jane 741
McMullin, Ruth 476
McMurty, Elsey 487
McMurty, Samuel 476
McNabb, Dorothy 144
McNabb, John 139, 144, 145
McNabb, Mary 144
McNabb, Sarah 167
McNaighton, Neil 197
McNamee, John 520
McNames, Amos 387
McNamor, Mary 567
McNamor, Morris 567
McNary, Alexander 108
McNary, Eleanor 108
McNary, James 108
McNary, John 4, 108
McNary, Joseph 108
McNary, Margaret 108
McNary, Samuel 108
McNary, William 108
McNeal, John 286
McNeal, Joseph 29
McNeale, Abraham 185
McNear, Mary 534
McNeel, John 364
McNeel, Pamillia 480
McNeelance, George 300
McNeil, James 3, 4, 46
McNeil, John 687
McNeil, Jonathan 47
McNeil, Joseph 47
McNeil, Saml. 415
McNeill, James 48
McNeill, Joseph 47
McNichol P. 559
McNicoll, Peter 573
McNigh, Elizabeth 475
McNight, Anna 476
McNight, Charles 709
McNight, James 512
McNight, Joseph 709, 717
McNutt, Feeby 657
McNutt, James 195
McNutt, James (Sr.) 598
McOlray, James 208
McPeek, Daniel 544
McPeek, John 543
McPeek, Richard 545
McPheaters, Moses 300, 310
McPheoin, George 209
McPheron, Wm. 51

Melker, Ann 699
Melker, Barbara 699
Melker, Charlotte 699
Melker, Elizabeth 699
Melker, Mary 699
Melker, Molly 699
Melker, Philip 699
Melker, Wendal 699
Mellerarned, Gertrude 99
Mellhouse, C. 373
Mellinger, Catharine 297
Mellinger, Colin 88
Mellinger, Elizabeth 302
Mellinger, Florence 88
Mellinger, Jacob 300
Mellinger, Jasper 88
Mellinger, John 88
Mellinger, Leonora 88
Mellinger, Martha 88
Melton, William 598
Melvin, Charles 526
Melvin, Nathan 706
Melvin, Sally 704
Melzer, John 402
Menage, C. 21
Menager, Claud Romain
    491
Menager, Claude R. 498
Menager, Claude Romain
    491, 494, 497, 498
Menan, Michael 161
Menas, Hugh 1
Mench, Adam 565
Mench, Elizabeth 171
Mendenhall, Aaron 300,
    511, 531
Mendenhall, Elcy 530
Mendenhall, Eley 530
Mendenhall, Eli 283
Mendenhall, Elizabeth
    283
Mendenhall, Hannah 283
Mendenhall, Isaac 283
Mendenhall, James 283
Mendenhall, John 283,
    520
Mendenhall, Joseph 531
Mendenhall, Mordecai 283
Mendenhall, Nathan 283
Mendenhall, Rachel 283
Mendenhall, Ruth 533
Mendenhall, Samuel 283
Mendenhall, Sarah 283
Mendenhall, Stephen 282,
    283, 526
Mendenhall, Thomas 283
Mendenhall, William 531
Mendinghall, Aaron 520
Mendinghall, Martin 516
Mendinghall, Sarah 521
Mendinghall, Sophia 462
Menessier, Francis 575
Menexs, James 11
Menke, Elizabeth 90
Menke, Gertrude 90
Menke, John W. 90
Menke, John William 90
Menke, William 90
Menn, William 377

Mennessier, --- 573
Menser, Elizabeth 296
Menthow, Ephraigm 512
Menton, Nancy 518
Mentzer, David 728
Mentzer, Japhet 746
Mentzer, Jepheth 746
Mentzer, Samuel 590
Meosker, Susan 618
Merandy, James 568
Mercer, Aaron 514
Mercer, Daniel 300
Mercer, Edward 520
Mercer, Henry 514
Mercer, Huldah 507
Mercer, Jane 289
Mercer, John 47, 553,
    563, 749
Mercer, Jonathan 512,
    514
Mercer, Joseph 667
Mercer, Mary 514
Mercer, Moses 514
Mercer, Olive 297
Mercer, Rebecca 297
Mercer, Robert 512,
    514, 667
Mercer, Sabrann 657
Mercer, Susan 593
Mercer, Susanna 553, 563
Mercer, Thomas 300, 657
Mercer, Thomason 514
Mercer, Wm. 507
Merchant, Isaac 411
Merchant, Rachel 440
Merchant, Samuel 197
Merchant, William 467
Mere, Philip 300
Meredith, Anne 194
Meredith, Benjamin H.
    106
Meredith, David 106, 322
Meredith, Elizabeth 106,
    194
Meredith, George 542
Meredith, Israwl 106
Meredith, John 194
Meredith, Josiah 106
Meredith, Margaret 106
Meredith, Mary 106
Meredith, Sarah 106
Mereness, A. D. 228
Mereness, Abraham D. 225
Mereness, Margaret 228
Mergan, Joseph 441
Mergenthal, Ana Maria 59
Mergenthal, Casper 59
Meriahan, Ann 379
Merica, D. 178
Merica, Daniel 178
Merica, H. 178
Meriden, Lettitia 527
Merideth, Caleb 161
Merifield, James 476
Merihue, Gideon 380
Merphey, John 467
Merredeth, John 194
Merrel, --- 456
Merrel, Abel 310

Merrel, Ann 288
Merret, Levi 405
Merrie, R. 559
Merrie, Robert 573
Merrifield, James 183
Merrifield, John 476
Merrill, Clarissa 655
Merrill, Lucretia 475
Merrill, Samuel S. 471
Merrill, Susannah 687
Merrill, Thomas 687
Merrit, Jane 407
Merrit, Mathew 697
Merritt, Hetty 78
Merritt, William 117
Merriweather, Rachel 219
Merriweather, Reuben 219
Merryman, Caleb 598
Merryman, Kesiah 519
Merryman, Ruth 466
Merser, Mary 518
Merter, Margaret 602
Mertz, Casper 101
Mervin, Elijah B. 411
Messer, Edward 515
Messinger, Elizabeth 474
Metcalf, Daniel 333
Metcalf, George 539
Metcalf, John 238
Metcalf, Sarah 70, 539
Metcalf, Thomas 539
Metham, Caroline 331
Metham, Charlotte Louisa
    331
Metham, Eliza 331
Metham, Eliza Ann 331
Metham, Emily 331
Metham, Henry 331
Metham, Josephine 331
Metham, Margaret 331
Metham, Mary 331
Metham, Pren 331
Metham, William 331
Metheany, Richard 52, 53
Methers, Sarah 121
Metsker, John 225
Metts, John 415
Metz, Casper 101
Metz, Christina 341
Metz, Friedrich 341
Metz, Jacob 325, 329
Metz, Maria Luisa 341
Metz, Phillips 101
Metz, T. 45
Metz, William 101
Metz, Wm. 4, 45, 47
Meuch, Adam 565
Mewhorter, Nancy 88
Meyer, John N. 376
Meyer, William 359
Meyers, Francis 370
Meyers, Frederich 418
Meyers, George 51
Meyers, Jacob 441
Meyers, Nancy 9
Meyrose, Agnes 90
Meyrose, Henry 90
MGree, Mary 633
Michael, Adam 225

888

Mitchell, Ross Andrews 673
Mitchell, Ruth 77
Mitchell, Samuel 363, 367
Mitchell, Samuel (Sr.) 367
Mitchell, Samuel C. 500
Mitchell, Samuel Martin 673
Mitchell, Sanford 235
Mitchell, Susanna 673
Mitchell, Susannah 500
Mitchell, Sylvanus 725
Mitchell, Thomas 122, 672, 699
Mitchell, Thomas Jefferson 673
Mitchell, Vincent 672, 673
Mitchell, William 19, 673, 689
Mitchell, Wm. 500, 649, 690, 746
Mite, Elizabeth 311
Mite, George 310
Mite, Mary 306, 311
Mitetry, Elizabeth 307
Mits, David 301
Mits, George 301
Mitten, Lovey 527
Mittendorf, Frederick 65
Miveut, Francois 484
Mix, Lucinda 52
Mix, Mary 333
Mix, Uri 53
Moats, Jacob 746
Mobley, Mary 467
Mochimer, Elizabeth 377
Mochimer, George 377
Mochimer, John 377
Mochimer, Lydian 377
Mochimer, Mary 377
Mochimer, Nancy 377
Mochimer, Rachel 377
Mochimer, Sarah 377
Mochimer, William 377
Mochmar, Lydia 378
Mock, Daniel 520
Mock, Eliza Ann 420
Mock, Phebe 526
Moenkwith, Wilhelm 101
Moffat, T. D. 400
Moffet, John 141, 578, 598
Moffett, Frances C. 231
Moffett, Sarah 231
Moffett, William 231
Moffitt, Catharine 634
Moffitt, Charles 581
Mohler, David 603
Mohler, Lucy Ann 603
Mohrenhaut, Johann 347
Mohrenhaut, Johann Jacob 347
Mohrenhaut, Louise 347
Moiser, Henry 417
Molder, Polly 480
Moler, Isaac 615

Moler, Jacob 664
Moler, John 213
Moler, Stephen 121
Mollenhower, John 628
Moller, John 615
Moller, Joseph 615
Moller, Lewis 615
Molonsbury, Elizabeth 289
Molten, Esibela 297
Moman, Elizabeth 705
Monahon, Elizabeth 705
Mones, Abraham 230
Mones, Elizabeth 230
Mones, Mary Ann 230
Moneysmith, Susanna 301
Monfort, Henry 361
Mong, Jacob 130
Monger, Margaret 50
Monger, Polly 223
Mongold, Henry 411
Moninger, Mahlon 435
Moninger, Sophia 435
Monkwith, Wilhelm 101
Monley, Judy 299
Monohan, Gershom 225
Monohon, Samuel 462
Monot, Stephen 28
Monroe, --- 544
Monroe, Barbary 505
Monroe, David 505
Monroe, Elizabeth 481
Monroe, George 505
Monroe, Henrietta 505
Monroe, Isaac 590
Monroe, James B. 505
Monroe, John 94, 317, 319
Monroe, Joseph F. 331
Monroe, Martha 505
Monroe, Mary 94
Monroe, Moses 657
Monson, Submit 223
Montague, D. 45
Montgomery James 47
Montgomery, Aeloner 308
Montgomery, Boone 2
Montgomery, David 101, 145, 153
Montgomery, Eleanor 418
Montgomery, Elizabeth 50, 153, 172, 220, 691
Montgomery, Ellen 418
Montgomery, Henry 171, 754
Montgomery, J. T. 47
Montgomery, James 199, 208, 313, 691
Montgomery, Jane 313
Montgomery, John 313
Montgomery, Joshua 421
Montgomery, Margaret 166
Montgomery, Mitchell 550
Montgomery, Nancy 313
Montgomery, Samuel 46, 220
Montgomery, Samuel (Rev.) 757
Montgomery, Thomas 153

Montgomery, Thos. 78
Montgomery, William 18, 158, 628
Montgomery, Wm. 42
Montjar, Francis A. 126
Mood, Richard 320
Mood, Sarah 590
Moodle, Anney 529
Moodle, Samuel 526
Moody, Elizabeth 736
Moody, John 736
Moody, Margarette 736
Moody, Mary 736
Moody, Rachel 736
Moody, Sarah 736
Moody, Thomas 736
Moody, William 185, 205, 736
Mooma, Tena 579
Moon, Aaron 467
Moon, Christian 443
Moon, Daniel 277
Moon, David 443, 462
Moon, Elizabeth 284, 525
Moon, George B. 262
Moon, Harriet 456
Moon, Henry 271
Moon, Jacob 443
Moon, James 268, 271, 277, 287
Moon, Jane 443
Moon, Jesse 277
Moon, John 467, 594
Moon, Jonathan 467
Moon, Jos. 462
Moon, Joseph 275, 277
Moon, Joseph R. 285
Moon, Lydia 265
Moon, Margaret 292, 443, 463
Moon, Martha 465
Moon, Sarah 274
Moon, Simon 265
Moon, Thomas 271, 443, 450, 451, 453, 467
Moon, William 268, 275, 443, 456
Moona, Barbara 581
Moone, William 520
Mooney, George 664
Mooney, Phebe 465
Mooney, Rebeckah 520
Mooney, William 445
Mooney, Wm. 450
Mooninger, Alexander 380
Moor, Andrew 673
Moor, Betsy 625
Moor, David 317
Moor, Elizabeth 20
Moor, Forgus 20
Moor, Jane 462
Moor, John McCormick 673
Moor, Joseph 238
Moor, Mary 177
Moor, Reuben 75
Moor, Samuel Alexander 673
Moorcraft, Elizabeth 100
Moore, Aaron 39

Moore, Abner 684
Moore, Adam 571
Moore, Alexander 115, 165
Moore, Alice C. 529
Moore, Alvin 47
Moore, Amos 25, 27
Moore, Andrew 25, 27, 58, 104, 545
Moore, Ann 292
Moore, Anna 79
Moore, Anthony 457, 467
Moore, Aron 35, 581
Moore, Benjamin 590
Moore, Bridget 722
Moore, Bustard 565
Moore, Caroline 730
Moore, Charles 565
Moore, Curtis 211
Moore, Cynthia 254
Moore, Daniel 750
Moore, David 542, 643, 686, 691, 746, 752
Moore, Edward 2
Moore, Edward S. 3
Moore, Elizabeth 49, 133, 170, 589, 637, 691
Moore, Ephraim R. 467
Moore, Esther 291
Moore, Forgus 15, 20
Moore, George 130
Moore, George B. 262
Moore, George G. 101, 590
Moore, Gerusha 153
Moore, Henry 38, 301
Moore, Hose 13
Moore, Hosea 2, 43
Moore, Hugh 560, 562
Moore, Jacob 572, 574
Moore, James 48, 118, 130, 171, 185, 268, 275, 554, 581, 731
Moore, James B. 121
Moore, James B. 581
Moore, James Thompson 130
Moore, Jane 164
Moore, Jeremiah 61
Moore, Jesse 266
Moore, Jesse W. 161
Moore, Jno. 43
Moore, Jo. 11
Moore, John 4, 6, 22, 25, 79, 206, 358, 505, 740, 748, 749
Moore, John A. 531
Moore, John B. 454
Moore, Johnathan Limerick 643
Moore, Jos. 9, 10, 11, 12, 29, 271
Moore, Joseph 12, 24, 238, 301, 546, 689
Moore, Josiah H. 641
Moore, Katherine 457
Moore, Kinder 301
Moore, Levi 125, 487

Moore, Lewis 152, 161
Moore, Lucinda 42
Moore, Lucius 756
Moore, Lydia 126, 165, 169, 592, 641
Moore, Margaret 309, 487
Moore, Margery 303
Moore, Martha 170
Moore, Mary 125, 210, 211, 405, 637
Moore, Mary Ann 505
Moore, Mary Jane 592
Moore, Mary Magdalene 319
Moore, Matthew 79
Moore, Micajah H. 275, 287
Moore, Michael 125
Moore, Mordecai 683
Moore, Mordica 74
Moore, Moses 25, 27
Moore, Nancy 643
Moore, Nicholas 219
Moore, P. 23
Moore, Patrick 138, 143, 200, 565, 568, 733
Moore, Peggy 11
Moore, Penelope 309
Moore, Phebe 166
Moore, Philip 22, 37, 457
Moore, Polly 130, 463, 723
Moore, Preston 709, 711
Moore, Rebecca 582
Moore, Reuben 75, 165
Moore, Robert 50, 206, 210
Moore, Robert B. 545
Moore, Rodie 641
Moore, Rozella 580
Moore, Ruth 289
Moore, Saml. 207
Moore, Samuel 85, 210, 301, 476, 531, 637
Moore, Samuel A. 380
Moore, Sarah 61, 163, 169, 207, 223, 637, 703
Moore, Solomon 153
Moore, Susannah 300
Moore, Thomas 182, 204, 206, 207, 271
Moore, Thomas J. 61
Moore, Thos. 42
Moore, William 206, 207, 233, 301, 327, 537, 546, 643, 731
Moore, William (Jr.) 638
Moore, William Camm 526
Moore, William White 130
Moore, Wm. 577
Moorehead, Thomas 154, 165
Mooreman, Sarah 523
Moorhead, John 192
Moorhead, Thomas 632
Moorhead, William 581
Moorland, Elizabeth 524

Moorland, Margaret 523
Moorland, Mary 524
Moorman, Charles 531
Moorman, Childs 535
Moorman, James 526
Moorman, Manson 534
Moorman, Matilda 535
Moorman, Polly 525
Moorman, Thomas 517
Moorman, Thos. (Jr.) 516
Moorman, William 450
Moorman, Zachariah 526
Moot, Aaron 657
Mooters, L. 398
Mooters, P. 398
Mooters, William S. 398
Mor, Solomon G. 697
Moran, Johanna 535
Moran, Magdalena 293
More, Casander 85
More, Ezekiel 462
More, George W. 590
More, James 15
More, Jarret 85
More, John 405
More, Joseph 480
More, Mary 309
More, Nancy 462
More, Parthenia 591
More, Samuel 590
Morecraft, Esther 49
Morecraft, John 50, 237
Moredock, Eliza 658
Morehart, Adam 421
Morehart, Betsey 413
Morehart, Elizabeth 434
Morehart, John 434
Morehead, Alexander 411
Morehead, Amanda 377
Morehead, Calvin 678
Morehead, Catherine 377
Morehead, Elizabeth 377
Morehead, Emeline 377
Morehead, James 377
Morehead, John 377
Morehead, Justina 94
Morehead, Lincoln G. 94
Morehead, Maria 377
Morehead, Robert 147, 153
Morehead, Sarah 678
Morehouse, Abner S. 387
Morehouse, Abraham 387
Morehouse, Charles R. 387
Morehouse, Ebenezer 387
Morehouse, Ebenezer E. 387
Morehouse, Joanna B. 387
Morehouse, John 390
Morehouse, Mary 387
Morehouse, Matilda 390
Morehouse, Seth 387
Morehouse, Stephen 387, 390
Morehouse, Thomas 225
Morelan, Elizabeth 292
Moreland, Jonah 301
Moreland, Martha 532

Moreland, Mary 291
Moreland, William 531
Moreman, Hannah 283
Morey, David 725
Morey, Hariet 725
Morey, Jonathan 79
Morfoot, Onuro Elinor 301
Morford, Kennard 1
Morgan, --- 257
Morgan, Ann S. 220
Morgan, Asa 706
Morgan, B . . . ger 411
Morgan, Benjamine 75
Morgan, Calvin 590
Morgan, Daniel 240, 241, 368
Morgan, Danl. 746
Morgan, David 60, 543, 561
Morgan, David D. 659
Morgan, E. J. 397
Morgan, E. L. 187
Morgan, Edward L. 212
Morgan, Edward S. 194
Morgan, Elisa 308
Morgan, Elizabeth 465
Morgan, Emma Chapman 397
Morgan, Evan 510
Morgan, Evin 515
Morgan, F. W. 397
Morgan, George 101
Morgan, Jacob 214
Morgan, Jane 333, 523, 530
Morgan, Jean 11
Morgan, John 510, 515
Morgan, Jonathan 220, 510, 515, 526, 531
Morgan, Joseph 581
Morgan, Martha 515
Morgan, Mary 660
Morgan, Michael 598
Morgan, Morgan 667
Morgan, Moris 317
Morgan, Moses 317, 322
Morgan, Nancy 419, 515, 526
Morgan, Naomi 420
Morgan, Nathan 239
Morgan, Patsy 526
Morgan, Peggy 269, 515
Morgan, Rachel 460
Morgan, Ruth 518
Morgan, Sallie 515
Morgan, Sally 515
Morgan, Sarah 518
Morgan, Stafford 171
Morgan, Stryker 318
Morgan, Styker 314
Morgan, Thomas 269, 526
Morgan, Thomas C. 301
Morgan, William 510, 515, 520
Morgans, Peter 659
Moring, Christopher 421
Morison, Albert 198
Morison, William 447
Morit, Michael 416

Moritz, S. M. 251
Morlan, Elizabeth 299
Morlan, Isaac 301
Morlan, Jonah 301
Morland, Stephen 301
Morledge, John 301
Morlen, Judy 299
Morley, Charlotte 658
Morlock, Jacob 430
Morningstar, Elizabeth 527
Morningstart, Elizabeth 166
Moroman, Thomas (Jr.) 4
Moroman, Thomas (Sr.) 4
Morot, Stephen 28
Morran, James 259
Morrell, Calvin 563
Morrell, Lovina 580
Morrer, Sarah 69
Morres, Thomas 412
Morris, Anna 645
Morris, Benjamin 545
Morris, Betsy 640
Morris, Calvary 79
Morris, Chas. 746
Morris, Deborah 251
Morris, Eastin 361, 364, 369
Morris, Easton 361
Morris, Elaseph 9
Morris, Elizabeth 130
Morris, Elwood 251
Morris, Isaac 255, 436, 542, 559, 645
Morris, Isaiah 252
Morris, J. 724
Morris, Jain 467
Morris, James 301, 412, 549, 556, 640
Morris, Jane 255
Morris, John 50, 51, 52, 53, 54, 57, 58, 613
Morris, Jonathan 545
Morris, Jonathan J. 550
Morris, Joseph 301
Morris, Joseph H. 421
Morris, Joshua 301, 613
Morris, L. 252
Morris, Leah 307
Morris, Lorenzo 251
Morris, M. C. 252
Morris, Maria 436
Morris, Michael 353
Morris, Morris 667, 702
Morris, Moses 645
Morris, Nancy 222, 613
Morris, Osco 252
Morris, Owin 271
Morris, Polly 643
Morris, Rebecca 559
Morris, Richard 380
Morris, Robert 23
Morris, Roliff 613
Morris, Rollif 613
Morris, Samuel 462
Morris, Sarah 11, 170, 217
Morris, Stephen 314

Morris, Tamer 252
Morris, Thomas 613
Morris, William 154, 225, 467
Morris, William (Jr.) 613
Morris, William (Sr.) 613
Morris, Willie 252
Morrison, Abrahm. 543
Morrison, Affia 447
Morrison, Albinah 106
Morrison, Alex. 551
Morrison, Alexander 48
Morrison, Andrew 42, 691
Morrison, Anna Jane 447
Morrison, Archibald 21
Morrison, Archibald F. 1
Morrison, Calvin 79
Morrison, Carolina 436
Morrison, David 91
Morrison, Elizabeth 625
Morrison, Ellen 436
Morrison, Ephraim 182, 520
Morrison, Ester 293
Morrison, Gaven 268
Morrison, Harriet 91
Morrison, Isabel 9
Morrison, James 15, 21, 106, 156, 310, 628, 632
Morrison, James E. 1
Morrison, Jane 707
Morrison, John 5, 46, 301, 628, 714
Morrison, Joseph 301, 706
Morrison, Lettice 182, 210
Morrison, Letty 182
Morrison, Mary Ann 112
Morrison, Nancy 182, 268, 276
Morrison, Nancy Jane 586
Morrison, Patty 629
Morrison, Poley 12
Morrison, Polley 714
Morrison, Richard 721
Morrison, Robert 1, 113
Morrison, Samuel 156
Morrison, Samuel F. 225
Morrison, Sarah 156, 303
Morrison, Thomas 691
Morrison, William 43, 447, 542
Morrison, Wm. 43, 47
Morriss, Isaac 467
Morrow, Almira 268, 275
Morrow, Benjamin 146, 434
Morrow, Charlotte 680
Morrow, Elizabeth 618
Morrow, James 137, 257, 268, 502, 510, 515, 551
Morrow, Jas. 78
Morrow, John 434, 526, 605

Morrow, Katherine 411
Morrow, Kitty 411
Morrow, Lewis 137
Morrow, Mary 146
Morrow, Mary Ann 434
Morrow, Polly 480
Morrow, Rebecca 748
Morrow, Richard 680
Morrow, Robert 257
Morrow, Susanna 78
Morrow, William 275,
551, 605, 678
Morse, A. 393
Morse, Alma 82
Morse, Betsy 384
Morse, Clarinda 603
Morse, E. 393
Morse, Edward 393, 714
Morse, Eliza J. Ball 393
Morse, Emily 378
Morse, Emma 393
Morse, George 380
Morse, George B. 393
Morse, George C. 393
Morse, George T. 393
Morse, J. R. 393
Morse, James 79
Morse, James R. 393
Morse, Jennie E. 393
Morse, Joseph 561
Morse, M. 393
Morse, Mahala Brown 393
Morse, Mary Elgiva 393
Morse, Matilda 378
Morse, Ora 76
Morse, Orrin D. 603
Morse, William B. 377
Mortemore, William 467
Morten, James 209
Mortimor, Sarah Ann 378
Mortimore, Adam 380
Morton, Alexr. 218
Morton, Ann 525
Morton, Charles A. 402
Morton, George 301
Morton, Henry 726
Morton, Hezekiah 200,
203
Morton, Israel 301
Morton, James T. 161
Morton, Joseph 726
Morton, Kennedy 553
Morton, Levi 745
Morton, Samuel 301
Mory, Nancy 80
Moser, Conrad 544
Moser, John 520
Moses, John (Jr.) 387
Moses, William 391
Mosher, Wealthy 51
Mosher, Wm. 375
Mosholder, Adam 700
Mosman, Jemima 46
Mosman, Silas 46
Moss, Bethany 658
Moss, Bythama 658
Moss, Charles A. 526
Moss, Hugh 37
Moss, Jane D. 592

Moss, John 635
Moss, Joseph 377, 557
Moss, Mary 126
Moss, Matilda 74
Moss, Tency 12
Moss, Thomas 79
Mosser, Susanna 288
Mosses, Margaret M. 589
Mot, Abe 374
Mote, Timothy 363, 364
Motes, Abraham 657
Motring, Jane 417
Motsinger, Felix 243
Motsinger, Mary 243
Mott, Gideon 702
Mott, Samuel 229
Mott, Sarah 112
Mott, Silas 728
Mott, Wm. 112
Motz, John 657
Mouen, Elizabeth 288
Moulton, Earl 584
Moultrip, --- 68
Moultrip, Rosannah 71
Mount, Elizabeth 284
Mount, Jane 267, 274
Mount, John 284
Mount, Thomas 284
Mount, William 275, 284
Mount, Wm. 241, 267
Mountjoy, --- 36
Mounts, Humphrey 384
Mounts, Scina 271
Mounts, Wm. 570
Mountz, Abner 412
Mountz, Catharine 308
Mountz, Mari 292
Mourey, Charity 588
Mourning, Rodham 236
Mourse, Michael 686
Mourtz, Abner 412
Moury, George 590
Moury, Jacob 590
Moury, John 590
Moury, John A. 628
Moury, Joseph 590
Mouser, Benjamin 446,
453
Mouser, George 467
Mouser, Susannah 453,
469
Mouter, Andrias 64
Moutz, Peter 430
Mowen, Jacob 301
Mowen, Peter 301
Mower, L. D. 746
Mower, Lucius D. 729
Mower, Lucy 729
Mowey, Jenks 473
Mowrer, Alfred 43
Mowrer, Christian 43
Mowrey, Alexander 326
Mowrey, Andrew 326
Mowrey, Betsey 326
Mowrey, Catharine 326
Mowrey, Conrad 326
Mowrey, Elizabeth 326
Mowrey, Henry 326
Mowrey, John 326

Mowrey, Martin 326
Mowrey, Polly 326
Mowrey, Susan 326
Moxey, Bennett 516
Moxley, Christopher 616
Moxley, John 616
Moxley, William 616
Moyer, Abraham 405
Moyer, Daniel 441
Moyer, Elizabeth 380,
745
Moyer, Jacob 377
Moyer, Jane 412
Moyer, Mari Magdalena
308
Moyer, Mariah 421
Moyer, Mary 307
Moyer, Polly 410
Moyer, Rakina 333
Mozier, L. D. 702
Muchmore, Samuel 563
Mueller, Franz Johann
Melchoir 356
Mueller, Hana 297
Mufit, John 301
Muhlenberg, Peter 611
Muhlenberg, Peter (Gen.)
261
Muir, Francis 509
Muirell, Esther 121
Mulern, W. 48
Mulford, Benjamin 571
Mulford, Daniel 85
Mulford, David 132,
149, 154
Mulford, Eupheme 132
Mulford, Hannah 149
Mulford, Harriet 132
Mulford, Hugh 85
Mulford, Jane 132, 168
Mulford, Joab 405
Mulford, Job 132
Mulford, John 132, 149,
171
Mulford, Polly 85
Mull, Elizabeth 581
Mull, Margaret 580
Mullen, Elizabeth 416
Mullen, Isaac 547
Mullen, Thomas 582
Mullenix, John 526
Mullenix, Nancy 518
Mullenix, Thomas 606
Muller, Wilhelmine 101
Mulligan, James 722
Mulligan, Josiah J. 380
Mullin, Charles 11
Mullin, William 526
Mullins, Daniel 26
Mullon, John 536
Muma, Lena 294
Mumahan, Edward 710
Mumey, Sarah 346
Mumma, Catherine 412
Mundle, Catharine 560
Mundle, Jonathan 560
Munford, Ismay 42
Munford, Wm. 240
Munger, Mary E. 100

895

Nichols, --- 192
Nichols, C. 395
Nichols, Clara A. 395
Nichols, Curtis 395, 403
Nichols, Cynthia 591
Nichols, Daniel 196
Nichols, David 559, 572
Nichols, Edward 116
Nichols, Elias N. 83
Nichols, Elijah 746
Nichols, Elizabeth 196
Nichols, Enos 45
Nichols, Hannah 49
Nichols, Humphry 166
Nichols, John 111, 430, 431
Nichols, John M. 582
Nichols, M. 395
Nichols, Maria 395
Nichols, Mary 53, 395
Nichols, Myrtle 395
Nichols, Priscilla 49
Nichols, Sarah 420
Nichols, Thornton 259, 264
Nichols, William 156, 514
Nichols, William (Capt.) 485
Nichols, William H. 101
Nicholson, Andrew 745
Nicholson, Daniel 280
Nicholson, Elizabeth 280
Nicholson, James 657
Nicholson, John 116
Nicholson, Robt. 547
Nickel, John 664
Nickels, Rebecca 655
Nickerson, Arteunas 272
Nickerson, David 272
Nickerson, Susanah 275
Nickles, Elizabeth 52
Nickleson, Thomas 11
Nickols, A. J. 400
Nickols, Arthur 403
Nickols, Curtiss 400, 403
Nicodemus, Andrew 504, 506
Nicodemus, Ann Mariah 504, 506
Nicodemus, Catharine 504, 506
Nicodemus, Hana 504
Nicodemus, Hannah 506
Nicodemus, Henry 504, 506
Nicodemus, John 504, 506, 509
Nicodemus, Rachel 504, 506
Nicolson, George 554
Nida, Henry 748
Niebarger, Mary 460
Nieland, Mary A. 249
Nieman, John B. 101
Nierle, Elizabeth 339
Nierle, Elizabetha 339
Nierle, Gottlieb 339

Niersted, Jane 391
Nieserauer, Barbara 470
Nieter, Sophia 101
Nietert, Gottlieb 97
Nigh, Elizabeth 418
Nigh, Jacob 415
Nigh, Sarah 582
Nigh, Sophia 435
Night, Ebee 706
Nightengale, Eliza 643
Nightengale, George Edward 643
Nightengale, Mary Dexter 643
Nihiser, Jacob 632
Nile, Laurence 520
Niles, Amanda M. 180
Niles, F. 180
Niles, L. 180
Niles, Rebecca J. 180
Niles, Thomas J. 180
Niles, W. H. 179
Nimerich, Peter 526
Nimerick, John 526
Nimmo, John 561, 566, 569, 570, 571
Nimmo, Mary 561
Nimmo, Mathew 566
Nimmo, Matthew 561, 566, 569, 571
Nimmo, Matthias 562
Nimmo, Sarah 561
Nimo, John 573
Nimrod, George 585
Ninnegar, Martha 73
Nipgen, Casper 97
Nipgen, John 97
Nipgen, Michael 97
Nippichen, Margarethree 102
Niscewonger, Charles Buck 483
Niscwonger, John 476
Nisewonger, Charles Buck 483
Nisewonger, John 483
Nisewonger, John (Jr.) 483
Nisewonger, Rachel 475
Nisewonger, Winnifield 483
Nisewonger, Winny 483
Niswanger, Chestena 475
Nixon, --- 470
Nixon, Andrew 111, 117, 679
Nixon, Cillian 679
Nixon, Fanny 679
Nixon, Francis 301
Nixon, George 263
Nixon, Jasper 628
Nixon, John 679
Nixon, Margaret 111, 117
Nixon, Maria 679
Nixon, Mary 679
Nixon, Nancy 679
Nixon, William 301, 621, 706, 714
Nixon, Wm. 622

Noacre, John 333
Nobbs, John 471
Noble, Agness 137
Noble, Alfred B. 444
Noble, Benjamin 256, 272
Noble, Catharine 271
Noble, Charles 674
Noble, Daniel 171
Noble, Elizabeth 135, 161
Noble, Isabella 425
Noble, James 153
Noble, Joshua 256, 265, 272
Noble, Leander C. 380
Noble, Mary 256
Noble, Nancy 704
Noble, Peggy 275
Noble, Polly 169
Noble, Priscilla 268, 275
Noble, Robert 137
Noble, Robert A. 425
Noble, Sarah 163
Noble, Susan 253
Noble, William 137, 253, 268
Noble, Wm. 271
Nodna, Elizabeth Hukenburg 99
Noe, Aaron 746
Noe, David 380
Noel, Peter 33
Noffsinger, Hannah 377
Noffsinger, John 360
Noftsinger, Matthias 105
Noggle, Esther 259
Noggle, George 259
Noggle, Heprpha 259
Noggle, Isaac 412
Noggle, J. 648
Noggle, Jacob 371
Noggle, Mahala 99
Noggle, Perry 259
Noggle, Polly 259
Noggle, Susanna 410
Noggle, Ursula 259
Nogle, G. C. 101
Nogle, Isaac 412
Nogle, Mary Ann 603
Nogle, Michael 318
Nogle, Samuel 352
Nolan, Sallie 472
Noland, Julia Ann 467
Noland, William 332
Nolas, George 11
Nolas, John 11
Nolas, Memcy 9
Noleman, Richard 1
Noler, Wm. 36
Noll, Louise 347
Noorhees, Abraham (Sr.) 562
Nordyke, Abraham 265, 285
Nordyke, Aden 285
Nordyke, Ann 265
Nordyke, Benajah 265, 285

Oglesbee, Jacob 267
Oglesby, Asa 526
Oglesby, Sarah 524
Oglevee, John 598
O'Hara, George 553
O'Hare, Hugh 645
O'Harra, Elizabeth 51
O'Harrow, Mary 67
O'Heare, Rebecca 108
O'Heare, Thomas 108
Ohlwine, Chas. 501
Ohmart, --- 217
Ohmert, Adam 217
Ohmert, Barbary 226
Oiler, Henry 193
Oils, Jacob 752
Okley, Abraham 301
Olam, Peter 628
O'Laughlin, Dennis 286
O'Laughlin, Martha
   Matilda 286
Olbers, Mary 103
Oldeges, Catharine 92
Oldeges, Detrick 92
Oldeges, Theodore 92
Oldfield, Mary 412
Oldham, Asa 623
Oldham, Elizabeth 87
Oldham, James 539
Oldham, Jerry 623
Oldham, Joseph B. 87
Oldham, Margaret Ann 87
Oldiger, Wilhelm 101
Oldsen, James R. 47
Oldshoe, John 598
Oldson, Samuel 3
Oler, Peter 598
Olinger, Mary 226, 467
Oliphant, Ann 289
Oliphant, Ephraim 301
Oliphant, Perry 55, 60
Oliphant, Rachel 291
Oliphant, Rebeccah 288
Oliphant, Samuel 302
Oliver, Alexander (Col.)
   562
Oliver, Andrew 468
Oliver, Anna 285
Oliver, Electra 562
Oliver, Elizabeth 655
Oliver, George 370
Oliver, John 3, 6, 44,
   48
Oliver, Joseph F. 327,
   332
Oliver, Lydia 751
Oliver, Nancy 480
Oliver, Polly 225
Oliver, Reuben 585
Oliver, Samuel 751
Oliver, Susan 327
Oliver, Thomas 551, 667
Oliver, William 370, 657
Ollifant, William 171
Olmstead, Austres 470
Olney, Nancy 81
Olverholser, Jacob 367
Olverholser, Jno. 367
Omerman, Mary 302

Omit, Anna 223
Ommerman, Henry 526
O'Nail, Ellen 380
O'Neal, Anna Maria 102
O'Neal, James 679
O'Neil, Charles 635
O'Neil, Elenor 658
O'Neil, Henry 635
O'Neil, James 635
O'Neil, James (Jr.) 642
O'Neil, Jane 635
O'Neil, John 635
O'Neil, Laura 635
Oneil, Margaret 626
O'Neil, Martha 635
O'Neil, Nancy 635
O'Neil, Peggy 635
O'Neil, Stiles 635
O'Neil, Thomas 635, 642
O'Neill, Catharine 644
O'Neill, Charles 635,
   644
O'Neill, Henry 635
O'Neill, James 635
O'Neill, Jane 627
O'Neill, John 635
O'Neill, Laura 635
O'Neill, Margaret 635
O'Neill, Martha 627, 635
O'Neill, Nancy 635
O'Neill, Thomas 628, 635
O'Niel, Charlotta 411
Onspough, Mary 166
Opdyche, Henry C. 49
Opfer, Elizabeth 394
Opfer, Jacob 394
Opperman, M. 394
Opperman, Mary E. 394
Opperman, P. 394
Oppy, David 11
Orbison, Catharine 177
Orbison, Elizabeth 171,
   177
Orbison, Ellanor 177
Orbison, John 161, 177
Orbison, Margaret 177
Orbison, Mary 165, 177
Orbison, Matthew 142,
   177
Orbison, Robert 142, 177
Orbough, Nancy 479
Orcutt, Darius C. 556
Ordway, John 197
Ore, Grove 757
Oren, Joseph 272
Ormsby, Oliver 553, 554
Orndorf, Perry 171
Orney, Athony 276
Orpurd, Mary 225
Orr, --- 384
Orr, A. D. 38
Orr, Alesander D. 37
Orr, Arthur 152
Orr, Eleanor 463
Orr, Elizabeth 631
Orr, Isaiah 158, 166
Orr, Jackson 636
Orr, James 746
Orr, Jane 636

Orr, Jane Ruth 134
Orr, John 101, 302,
   543, 636
Orr, John (Sr.) 636
Orr, Margaret 519, 636
Orr, Mary 630
Orr, Nancy 633
Orr, Sanders 243
Orr, Sarah 243, 636
Orr, William 243, 543,
   635, 636
Orre, Thomas 412
Orson, Joseph 166
Orth, Adam 595
Orth, Margaret 589
Orton, Olive S. 102
Orwick, Henry 585
Orwick, Samuel 310
Orwig, Daniel 152
Orwig, Samuel 585
Osbern, Samuel 590
Osborn, Aaron 77
Osborn, Alexander 675
Osborn, Arabella 675
Osborn, Azar 392
Osborn, Barzilla 49
Osborn, Charles 392
Osborn, Clorinda 652
Osborn, Daniel 386,
   389, 392
Osborn, Daniel W. 695
Osborn, David 190
Osborn, Dorcas 392
Osborn, Ebenezer 49, 652
Osborn, Elij. 121
Osborn, Elizabeth 49
Osborn, Emeline 378
Osborn, Esther 392
Osborn, Henry 392
Osborn, Jabid (Jr.) 392
Osborn, James 190
Osborn, Jeremiah 190
Osborn, John 198
Osborn, John F. 101
Osborn, Joseph 190
Osborn, L. D. 225
Osborn, Levi 190
Osborn, Mary 190, 269
Osborn, Nancy 190
Osborn, Patsey 190
Osborn, Rhoda 51
Osborn, Thomas 272
Osborn, Wilson S. 121
Osborne, Alexander 675
Osborne, Amos James 675
Osborne, Cyrus 140, 141
Osborne, Daniel 141
Osborne, David 141
Osborne, Elias James 675
Osborne, Esther 140, 141
Osborne, George 675
Osborne, Henry 675
Osborne, James 675, 696
Osborne, Joseph 171
Osborne, Martha 675
Osborne, Martha Ann 675
Osborne, Mary Elizabeth
   675
Osborne, Oliver 141

Plotner, Eve 413
Plotner, George 582
Plotner, Maria 626
Plum, Lorinda 385
Plum, Marques L. 390
Plum, Mary 222
Plum, Rachel 225
Plumb, Catherine 227
Plumb, Jared 448
Plumer, Caroline 639
Plumer, Gottleib 639
Plumer, John 590
Plumer, Mary 639
Plumer, Reuben 613
Plummer, Ann 683
Plummer, Calahan 53
Plummer, Caleb 683
Plummer, Deborah 683
Plummer, Eli 251
Plummer, George 412
Plummer, Henry 421
Plummer, Hiram 210
Plummer, James 210
Plummer, John 683, 746, 747
Plummer, Joseph 683
Plummer, Joseph W. 683
Plummer, Lucinda 210
Plummer, Mahala 683
Plummer, Margaret A. 127
Plummer, Mary 683
Plummer, Mary P. 127
Plummer, Mason 210
Plummer, Mathew 127
Plummer, Nathan 127
Plummer, Rachel 52, 683
Plummer, Sally 210
Plummer, Sarah 683
Plummer, Thomas 104, 206, 210, 664, 683
Plummer, Tilman 210
Plummer, Washington 225
Plunk, Fanny 629
Pluns, Bernard 86
Pluns, Elizabeth 86
Plyly, Casper 424
Poage, G. G. 58
Poage, James A. 706
Poage, Malinda 52
Poage, Samuel 207
Poague, Geo. B. (Rev.) 53
Poague, Geo. D. (Rev.) 53
Poague, Geo. G. (Rev.) 53
Poals, Maetalan 410
Poals, Valentine 410
Pobenmire, George 101
Pocock, Anner 375
Pocock, Charity 375
Pocock, Eli 375
Pocock, Israel 375
Pocock, James 375
Pocock, Jemina 375
Pocock, Jesse 375
Pocock, Jesse P. 375
Pocock, Mary 375
Pocock, Thirza 375

Poe, Andrew 302, 590
Poe, Elizabeth 579
Poe, Isaac 302
Poe, John 302
Poe, Mary 273
Poe, Polly 590
Poe, Rebecca 587
Poe, Sarah 298
Poe, Thomas 302
Poff, Samuel 272
Pogue, John 171
Pogue, Robert 237
Pogue, Samuel 749
Pointer, Susannah 292
Poister, Elisabeth 348
Polan, Peter 526
Poland, Pete 415
Poland, Wm. H. 547
Polander, Stephen 234
Polen, Daniel 499
Polen, Peter 499
Polen, Rebeckah 499
Polen, William 499
Poling, John 418
Poling, Rachel 409
Poling, Robert 412
Polish, Netta 603
Pollack, Isaac 354
Pollard, George 286
Pollard, Jael 563
Pollard, Joel 37
Pollard, Robert 23, 37, 265, 286, 563
Poller, Frederick 354
Pollock, Anna 240
Pollock, James 240, 456, 564, 698, 753
Pollock, Jno. 23
Pollock, John 240, 326
Pollock, John (Jr.) 235
Pollock, John (Sr.) 598
Pollock, Joseph 456
Pollock, Mary 295, 535, 753
Pollock, Nancy 456
Pollock, Oliver 235
Pollock, Rachael 240
Pollock, Sarah 598
Pollock, Thomas 302
Pollock, William 302
Polly, Amos 79
Polly, George 723
Polly, James 368
Pomeroy, Ralph 637
Pommert, Adam 345
Pommert, Charles Levieth 345
Pommert, John Joseph 345
Pommert, Josephine Rosella 345
Pond, Mabel 651
Ponday, Mary 322
Ponsious, Elizabeth 627
Ponsler, John 628
Pontious, Elizabeth 306
Pontious, Polly 294
Pontius, George 412, 632
Pontius, John 642
Pontius, Margaret 642

Pontius, Mary 627
Pool, Catharine 300
Pool, Elizabeth 297, 377
Pool, Frederick 377
Pool, Ginney 410
Pool, Jemima 382
Pool, Lois 226
Pool, Mary 467
Pool, Mary Ann 377, 378
Pool, Nancy 606
Pool, Thomas 302
Pool, Wm. S. 8
Pool, Wm. W. 8
Pool, Zebadiah 377
Poor, Alexander 480
Poor, George 476, 486
Poor, Hugh 664
Poor, Martin 480, 664
Poor, Sarah 656
Pop, Barbary Jane 91
Pop, Catharine 91
Pop, George 91
Pop, John 91
Pop, Mary Ann 91
Pope, Catharine 417
Popejoy, Nathan 171, 362, 364, 371
Popejoy, Polly 463, 464
Popejoy, Susannah 461
Popejoy, William 462
Popence, James 213
Popenoe, James 225, 516, 517
Poppleton, Samuel 690
Portee, William 380
Porter, Andrew 209
Porter, Betsy 309
Porter, David 191
Porter, Edward 333
Porter, Elias 278
Porter, Eliza 688
Porter, Elizabeth 651
Porter, George 14, 16, 553
Porter, Hannah 688, 702
Porter, Horace 651
Porter, James 405, 681, 702
Porter, Jane 405, 688
Porter, John 11, 121, 276, 543, 598
Porter, Joshua (Jr.) 553
Porter, Lucia 79
Porter, Margaret 688
Porter, Mary 533, 688
Porter, Moses 546, 688
Porter, Nicholas 272
Porter, Prescilla 704
Porter, Samuel 210
Porter, Solomon 79
Porter, Sophia 688
Porter, William 380, 688
Porter, Wm. C. 375
Porter, Zipporah 79
Portleman, Christian 22
Posey, Thomas 503
Post, Abraham 449
Post, Andrew 449
Post, Barbary Ann 449

909

Prentiss, Turner 651
Presly, Martha Elizabeth 742
Presly, Mary Ann 742
Pressler, D. 178
Pressler, Daniel 178
Pressler, E. 178
Pressler, Elizabeth 178
Pressler, George 582
Prestley, Joseph 551
Preston, Amos 302
Preston, Barbara 584
Preston, Elizabeth 603
Preston, George 563
Preston, John 590
Preston, Moses 706
Preston, Patrick 563
Preston, Paul 107
Preston, Samith 69
Preston, Sarah 333
Preston, Silas 543
Preston, William 584, 590
Previtt, Byrd 200
Prewe, Mary Elizabeth 438
Preweth, Bayll 265
Preweth, Levi 265
Preweth, Peggy 265
Price, Atha Ann 583
Price, Catherine 243
Price, Cornelius E. 730
Price, David 104, 161, 510, 513
Price, Easter 513
Price, Elizabeth 520, 522, 645
Price, Enme 373
Price, George 526
Price, George B. 586
Price, Hannah 405
Price, Hezekiah 558
Price, Isaac H. 2
Price, James 751
Price, Jesse 739
Price, Jno. 83
Price, Joel 544
Price, John 104, 186, 462, 510, 513, 521, 739, 751
Price, John S. 243
Price, Joseph 405, 513, 739
Price, Margaret 104
Price, Mary 534, 739
Price, Nancy 172, 739
Price, Nancy N. 601
Price, Peter 104, 510, 513, 521
Price, Philip 572
Price, Polly 587, 705
Price, Pugh 236
Price, Rebecca 465
Price, Samuel 104, 422, 645, 739
Price, Sarah 463, 751
Price, Seth 603
Price, Susanna 166, 513
Price, Thomas 171, 739

Price, William 166, 171, 513
Price, Wm. 380
Price, Wm. H. 664
Price, Wm. M. 644
Prichard, A. P. 757
Prichet, Luis 706
Prickard, Nathaniel 184
Pricket, Chas. H. 392
Pricket, Isaac 182
Pricket, Isaiah 239
Pricket, Japheth 94
Pricket, John 182
Pricket, Mary 226
Pricket, Nicholas 182, 239
Prickett, --- 125
Prickett, John 225
Priddy, Daniel 171
Priddy, George 468
Priddy, John 444
Priddy, Thomas 171
Priedle, Thomas 122
Prier, Abigail 653
Priest, Cassa 223
Priest, Jeremiah 221, 225
Priest, Mansfield 750
Priest, Moses 749
Priest, Sarah 221
Priest, Wm. 225, 747
Priggin, Henry 603
Primmer, Henry 628
Prince, Joseph 556
Prince, Martin 203
Princehouse, Sally 53
Prindle, Daniel 72
Prindle, David 72
Prindle, Deliverance Chaffar 385
Prindle, Jemima 72
Prine, Daniel 561
Pringle, John 664
Pringle, Robert 526
Pringle, William 664
Priome, P. 28
Prior, Abagail 685
Prior, Abner 685
Prioux, Nicholas 492, 493
Priss, Isaac H. 2
Pritchard, Benjamin 302
Pritchard, John 97
Pritchard, Nathaniel 710
Pritchard, Tabitha 291, 309
Pritcherd, --- 754
Procter, Jesse 687
Proctor, Jacob 720
Proctor, Jesse 687, 688
Proctor, Mary G. 720
Prosser, Nancy 50
Prother, Wilson 48
Proudfoot, Andrew 440
Prough, Betsy 626
Prough, George 412
Prough, Hannah 413
Prough, John 504, 506, 632

Prough, Kitty 412
Prough, Rebecca 504, 506
Prough, Samuel 632
Prouse, Leah 288
Provines, Matthew 598
Provinmire, Sarah 51
Pruckard, Nathan 184
Pruddy, John 161
Pruden, Mary A. 535
Pruden, Polly B. 82
Pruden, Rebecca C. 420
Pruden, S. R. 83
Pruity, Jonathan 192
Pruton, John 240
Pryne, Daniel 561
Pryor, Amos 107
Pryor, Isaac 107
Pryor, James 107
Pryor, John 107
Pryor, John (Sr.) 107
Pryor, John B. 107
Pryor, Joshua 107
Pryor, Levi 107
Pryor, Luther 107
Pryor, Margaret 107
Pryor, Nathan 107
Pryor, Robert 107
Pryor, Samuel 107
Pryor, Surete 107
Pryor, Thomas 107
Pryor, William 107
Pucket, James (Jr.) 276
Puckett, Benj. 285
Puckett, Elizabeth 269
Puckett, John 266
Pue, Phebe 160
Pugh, Charity 302
Pugh, David 388
Pugh, Elizabeth W. 428
Pugh, Ellis 259
Pugh, Hanahiah 737
Pugh, Hugh 590
Pugh, Hulet 171
Pugh, John H. 432
Pugh, Lanough 588
Pugh, Margaret 281
Pugh, Marshell (Sr.) 439
Pugh, Mary 281
Pugh, Sarah 737
Pugh, Thomas 591
Pugsley, Abram 85
Pugsley, Anna 81
Pugsley, Comfort 78
Pugsley, Francis 83
Pugsley, Ruth 617
Pully, Henson 548
Pumphrey, Ary 734, 739
Pumphrey, Caleb 734, 739
Pumphrey, Ealeanor 739
Pumphrey, Editha 734
Pumphrey, Eleanor 734
Pumphrey, Ezra 734, 739
Pumphrey, Henry 734
Pumphrey, Jamina 734
Pumphrey, Joshua 734, 739
Pumphrey, Nicholas 734, 739
Pumphrey, Reason 734

Ralph, John 487
Ralph, Stephen 480
Ralphenider, Magdalena
  299
Ralphsnider, Anna 308
Ralphsnider, John 302
Ralphsnider, Mary 308
Ralphsnider, Sarah 307
Ralphsnyder, Hannah 307
Ralston, Andrew 476,
  484, 486
Ralston, Jonathan 5, 42
Ralston, Joseph 108
Ralston, McCoy 486
Ralston, Rebecca 44
Ralston, Rebecca M. 44
Ralston, Robert 6, 36,
  44
Ralston, Thomas 6, 44
Ralstone, Robert 11
Rambaugh, William 657
Rambler, John 302
Rambo, French 195
Rambo, Peter 315
Rambo, William 699
Rambo, Wm. 749
Ramey, David 52
Ramgee, Lewis 593
Ramsay, Mary 533
Ramsay, Samuel 126
Ramsby, Elizabeth 635
Ramsby, John 635
Ramsby, Mehela 632
Ramsey, Alexander 468
Ramsey, Andrew 468
Ramsey, Betsey 629
Ramsey, Betsy 634
Ramsey, Catherine 243
Ramsey, Charity 634
Ramsey, David 302
Ramsey, Dorotha 590
Ramsey, Henry 315, 319
Ramsey, Isabella 243
Ramsey, James 243, 302,
  513
Ramsey, James B. 634,
  640
Ramsey, Jane 640, 641
Ramsey, Jean 634
Ramsey, John 243, 302,
  634, 640, 641, 645
Ramsey, John (Jr.) 560
Ramsey, Letty 47
Ramsey, Lloyd 678
Ramsey, Lucy 560
Ramsey, Margaret 260
Ramsey, Maria 678
Ramsey, Mary 292, 513,
  634, 640, 641
Ramsey, Minerva Arbuckle
  243
Ramsey, Nancy 634
Ramsey, Nelson 645
Ramsey, Rebecca 645
Ramsey, Robert 47, 634,
  641
Ramsey, Rosella Jane 260
Ramsey, Samuel H. 634
Ramsey, Samuel L. 641

Ramsey, Samuel M. 634
Ramsey, Samuel Mc. 640
Ramsey, William 47, 634
Ramsey, Wm. 47
Ramsy, Jane 641
Rand, Horace W. 402
Randal, Anna 387
Randal, Caleb 737
Randal, Harriet 737
Randal, Levin 737
Randal, Perry 737
Randal, Persis 737
Randal, Thomas Wright
  387
Randal, William 737
Randale, Catharine 102
Randall, Ann Celia 72
Randall, Annanias 542
Randall, Edw. S. 391
Randall, Levin 737
Randall, Louisa 161
Randall, Perry 737
Randall, Richard H. 387
Randel, Abigail 590
Randle, Mary 481
Randle, Sarah 590
Randle, Susanna 171
Randles, Oliver B. 314
Randolph, Drake 166
Randolph, Elizabeth 307
Randolph, James B. F.
  225
Randolph, Jonas 302
Randolph, Joseph T. 141
Randolph, Mary 76
Randolph, Nathan 40
Randolph, Rachel 289
Randolph, Ruth 307
Randolph, William 302
Randolph, Wm. 421
Range, George 591
Ranger, Lewis 593
Rank, Barbara 421
Rank, Philip 420
Ranken, James 412
Rankin, --- 29
Rankin, Jacob 443, 455,
  468
Rankin, James 548, 549
Rankin, John 454, 462
Rankin, L. D. 746
Rankin, Mary 469
Rankin, Moddy 469
Rankin, Robert 39
Rankin, Robt. 34
Rankin, Thomas 463, 598
Rankins, Abraham 733
Rankins, Daniel 58
Rankins, David 733
Rankins, Elizabeth 242,
  733
Rankins, Evaline 733
Rankins, James 733
Rankins, James (Jr.) 733
Rankins, James (Sr.) 733
Rankins, Jane 733
Rankins, Margaret 733
Rankins, Nancy 733
Rankins, Peggy 34

Rankins, Rachel 733
Rankins, Robert 34, 36
Rankins, Robt. 34
Rankins, Thomas 733
Rankins, William 733
Ranklin, David 316
Ranklin, William 316
Rannelle, Charles S. 221
Rannelle, Mary 221
Rannells, David 551
Rannels, William 542
Ranolds, Abigail 590
Ransbottom, Diana 583
Ransbottom, Eveline 581
Ransbottom, Simeon 582
Rape, Henry 1, 2
Rape, Lewis 42
Rapp, Eliza 592
Rapp, John 723
Rardon, Jonathan 149
Rarick, Daniel 368
Rarick, Jacob 417
Rarick, Philip 368
Rarick, Sarah 368
Rarrick, Sarah 368
Ratcliff, Elias 632
Ratcliff, Ezekiel 628
Ratcliff, John 276, 634
Ratcliff, Miles 628
Ratcliff, Priscilla 479
Ratcliff, Ruth 632
Ratcliff, Thomas 628
Rath, Elizabeth 378
Rathbone, John (Jr.) 330
Rathbun, Nancy L. 396
Rathbun, Thomas 214
Rathburn, Daniel (Jr.)
  480
Rathburn, Dwight 400
Rathburn, John W. 657
Rathburn, Polly 224
Rathburn, Roanna 657
Rathburn, Thos. 224
Rathmal, Martha 381
Rathwer, Anna Maria 100
Ratlif, John 404
Ratliff, Edam 272
Ratliff, John 276, 634
Rauch, Jacob 441
Rauch, Matthias 347
Rauch, Peter 441
Rauch, Sarah 422
Raudebaugh, Nicholas 412
Rauderbaugh, Nicholas
  632
Raugh, Frederick 639
Raugh, Margaret 209
Raugh, Mary Ann 639
Raugh, Peter 639
Rausch, Johann George
  347
Rauzen, John 303
Ravencraft, William 314
Ravenscraft, James 322
Ravenscraft, Rebecca 314
Ravenscraft, William 314
Ravenscraft, Wm. 314
Raver, Mary 435
Raver, Sophia 422

Reid, James Lafayette 675
Reid, Jane 601
Reid, John 213, 231, 536
Reid, John Washington 675
Reid, Joseph 213
Reid, Lafe Catherine 675
Reid, Lawson P. 456
Reid, Lucinda Mitchell 675
Reid, Lyman 676
Reid, Margaret 219
Reid, Mary Alma 676
Reid, Michal Mag. 596
Reid, Rachel 675, 676
Reid, Sally 213
Reid, Thomas 213
Reid, Thomas (Jr.) 380
Reid, William 213, 535
Reid, William Henry 676
Reier, Adam 57
Reier, Elizabeth 57
Reier, Falleathine 57
Reier, Joseph 57
Reier, Margaret 57
Reier, Philip 57
Reier, Phillip 57
Reily, Hugh 657
Reily, John 166, 176, 235
Reimenschnider, Engehart 98
Reimer, Susan 311
Reimers, William 312
Reinacher, Chi 100
Reinhardt, Geo. 415
Reinhart, Charles 353
Reinhart, John G. 71
Reitter, R. 400
Relker, Catharina 301
Relsa, John 628
Remck, Robert 183
Remley, Christian 566
Remly, Christian 555
Renaga, Christopher 182
Renard, Julia 478
Renard, Mitchel 498
Rency, William S. 628
Rendesil, Jacob 225
Rendick, Robert 207
Renebold, Mathias 438
Renebolt, Mathias 441
Renerd, Adam 31
Renfrew, James 316, 543
Renfrow, William 331
Renglespaugh, Abraham 439
Renglespaugh, Barbara 439
Renglespaugh, Christian 439
Renglespaugh, Easter 439
Renglespaugh, Susanna 439
Renick, Robert 204, 209, 210
Renkenberger, George 303
Renly, Jane 231

Renly, John 231
Rennels, Catharine 102
Rennisnider, John J. (Rev.) 616
Reno, Polly 164
Renshaw, E. C. 229
Renshaw, John 635
Renshaw, T. S. 229
Renshaw, Thomas 229
Renshaw, Thomas S. 229
Renshe, William S. 628
Rentz, Conrad 359
Rentzler, Mathias 359
Rep, Margaret 374
Replogel, Adam 217
Replogel, Catharine 217
Replogel, David 217
Replogle, Elizabeth 533
Replogle, J. 373
Replogle, Margaret 374
Reppetoe, Mary A. 380
Reproghe, J. 373
Rese, Archibald 706
Resler, Niomi 445
Resoner, Calvin 331
Restor, Elizabeth 652
Reubel, Owen 526
Reuter, G. A. 346
Reuter, Georg A. 346
Reves, Catharine 524
Rex, Lucretia S. 611
Rex, Samuel S. 611
Rey, Catharien 431
Reyburn, James 206
Reyburn, Jemima Katherine 500
Reyburn, William M. 206, 210
Reynalds, John 458
Reynalds, Joseph 458
Reynalds, Mary 458
Reynalds, Nancy 458
Reynalds, William 458
Reynearson, Jacob 568
Reynolds, Abigale 436
Reynolds, Ann 408
Reynolds, Benjamin 437
Reynolds, Bertha E. 394
Reynolds, Daniel 396
Reynolds, Deckison 437
Reynolds, Edward 79
Reynolds, Electa 79, 82
Reynolds, Elizabeth 182
Reynolds, Enox 725
Reynolds, Isaac 182
Reynolds, Isabella 274
Reynolds, Jas. 182
Reynolds, Jeremiah 283
Reynolds, John 46, 150, 182, 185, 204, 205, 206, 208, 211
Reynolds, John D. 46
Reynolds, Joseph 117, 182, 412, 453
Reynolds, Joseph S. 182
Reynolds, Joseph Smith 182
Reynolds, Laurey 725
Reynolds, Lee 412

Reynolds, Martin 182
Reynolds, Mary 54, 117, 182, 224
Reynolds, Phebe 396
Reynolds, Prusella 404
Reynolds, Rebecca 394
Reynolds, Robt. 182
Reynolds, Rufus 394
Reynolds, S. M. 394
Reynolds, Sally 76
Reynolds, Samuel 182
Reynolds, Sarah 150, 182
Reynolds, Sherman M. 394
Reynolds, Theodose 725
Reynolds, Thomas 437
Reynolds, Thos. 182
Reynolds, W. T. 45
Reynolds, William 23, 405, 543, 725
Reynolds, William Thompson 458
Reynolds, Wm. 34
Reynolds, Wm. T. 2
Rhamy, George 582
Rhamy, Mary 69
Rhay, Mary 411
Rhea, Easter 407
Rhea, Eliza 128
Rhea, Elizabeth 128
Rhea, Henry 128, 145
Rhea, James 208
Rhea, John 128
Rhea, Juliann 128
Rhea, Thomas Lyon 128
Rhea, William 145
Rhinehart, Catharine 172
Rhinehart, Jacob 172
Rhinehart, Martin 141
Rhinehartt, Phillip 317
Rhoads, Frances 296
Rhoads, Samuel 2
Rhoads, Thomas 2
Rhode, Jonathan 172
Rhodes, ---- 431
Rhodes, Anna Maria 290
Rhodes, Elizabeth 602
Rhodes, Frederick 303
Rhodes, Harriet 51
Rhodes, James 664
Rhodes, Jane 531
Rhodes, Jno. 185
Rhodes, John 746
Rhodes, Moses 303
Rhodes, Rebecca 300
Rhodes, Sandford 303
Rhodes, Sarah 191
Rhodes, William 303
Rhods, ---- 210
Rhonemous, Jacob 272
Rhonemus, Andrew 257
Rhonemus, Jesse 261
Rhonemus, William 257
Rhoods, Elizabeth 123
Rian, Polly 462
Ribht, Jonathan 468
Riblet, Henry 69
Riblet, Levi 69
Ribsaman, Adam 303
Ricby, William 22

917

Riddle, Abner 463
Riddle, James 207, 509, 572
Riddle, Jane 205
Riddle, John 561, 706
Riddle, Mary 561
Riddle, Samuel 553
Riddle, William 141
Ridenhour, John 412
Ridenhour, Lewis 412
Ridenour, Eliza 49
Ridenour, Hannah 49, 64
Ridenour, Michael 64
Ridenour, P. 49
Ridenour, Peter 49, 50, 51
Ridenour, Phoebe 53
Ridenour, Rebecca 51
Ridenour, Samuel 64
Ridenour, Sarah 52
Rider, Christiana 586
Rider, Christina 586
Rider, Isaac 693
Rider, Marinda P. 586
Rider, Mathew 657
Rider, Reuben 586
Rider, Sarah H. 586
Rider, Silas H. 586
Ridgley, Sarah 333
Ridinger, Celia 268, 276
Ridinger, Sarah 272
Ridley, Abigail 87
Ridley, Amanda 87
Ridley, Barbra 99
Ridley, Benjamin 87
Ridley, Eliza 87
Ridley, Ester 100
Ridley, Esther 87
Ridley, John 87
Ridley, Juda 87
Ridley, Mary 87
Ridley, Matthias 87
Ridley, Sarah 87, 99
Ridley, Sarah (Jr.) 87
Ridonhour, Jacob 412
Ridwell, Bransan 46
Ridwell, T. B. 46
Riel, Isaac 712
Riel, Nelly 463
Rife, Catharine 474
Rife, Jacob 476
Rife, Joseph 476
Riffe, Margaret 478
Riffle, David 363
Riffle, Jacob 363
Riffner, Michael 420
Rigbey, Hannah 299
Rigby, Aaron 303
Rigby, Amelia 411
Rigby, James 303
Rigdon, Elizabeth 207
Rigdon, John 207, 209
Rigdon, Lewis 207, 209
Rigel, Abraham 272
Rigel, Barbara Ann 382
Rigg, Thomas 476
Riggs, --- 243
Riggs, Charles 709, 711
Riggs, Isaac 272

Riggs, Joseph 2, 4, 713
Riggs, Malinda 711
Riggs, Sally 481
Riggs, Thomas 709, 711
Right, Jonathan 468
Right, Peggey 467
Right, Robert 42
Rightmire, James 700
Rigle, Peter 315
Riglet, Comfort 636
Rigly, Emelia 411
Rike, Jacob 507
Riker, Jacob 172
Rilea, John 468
Riley, Bridget 618
Riley, Henry 383
Riley, Jacob 731
Riley, John 383, 403, 598
Riley, John F. 591
Riley, Joseph 389
Riley, Levi 69
Riley, Margaret 292, 383
Riley, Mary 383
Riley, Methenia 63
Riley, Nathan 63
Riley, Richard 113
Riley, William 383
Riley, Wm. 42
Rinard, Jeremiah 272, 277
Rinard, Margaret 272
Rinard, Nancy 272
Rinard, Solomon 272
Rine, George 591
Rinehard, Catharine 291
Rinehart, Betsy 309
Rinehart, John 423, 424
Rinehart, Jonas 412
Ringiser, Jacob 639
Ringland, Elizabeth 164
Ringland, Isabella 161
Ringland, Joseph 172
Rinker, --- 56
Rinnerman, Frederick 664
Rinolds, Milley 626
Rintzel, Jacob 455
Rion, Elizabeth 479
Rion, Sarah 474
Ripley, David 706
Rippey, John 575
Rippy, John 573
Rise, Rebecca 629
Rish, Hannah 298
Rish, Mary 305
Risher, Catharine 290
Rishforth, Joseph 126
Rising, Benjamin 582
Rising, John 646
Rising, Polly 409
Risley, David 421
Risley, Julia 704
Rismiller, William 359
Ritchey, Eliza 333
Ritchey, Jacob 303
Ritchey, Jeptha 591
Ritchey, John 154
Ritchey, Samuel 591
Ritchie, George 543

Ritchie, Margaret 300
Ritchie, Mary 293, 660
Ritchie, Thomas 543
Ritchy, Sally 79
Rithelbach, Andre 440
Rithelbach, Dorothea 440
Rithelbach, Fridrich 440
Rithelbach, Johannes 440
Rithelbach, Maria 440
Ritsman, Abigail 285
Ritsman, James Eli 285
Ritsman, John 285
Ritsman, Lucretia 285
Ritsman, Lydia L. V. 285
Ritsman, Mary 285
Ritsman, Peter 285
Ritsman, Phenia 285
Ritsman, Rebecca 285
Ritsman, Sarah 285
Rittenhouse, H. S. 471
Rittenhouse, Mary 471
Rittenhouse, Richard 463
Ritter, Abraham 93
Ritter, Benjamin 303
Ritter, Nicholas 719
Ritter, Tobias 517
Rittgers, Daniel 420
Rittgers, John 419
Ritz, Polly 297
River, Mariah 603
Rnearson, Elizabeth 160
Roa . . ., Neville 240
Roab, Peter 303
Roach, Ann M. 292
Roach, Caty 310
Roach, Elizabeth 298, 311
Roach, John 225
Roach, Margaret 292
Roach, Rebecca 222
Roadamer, George 480
Roadamer, John 476
Roadarmer, Jacob 486
Roads, Abraham 610, 628
Roads, Catharine 616
Roads, Caty 610
Roads, David 618
Roads, Elizabeth 296, 422, 432, 610, 627
Roads, George 610
Roads, J. 745
Roads, Jacob 609, 610, 628
Roads, John 628
Roads, Joseph 610
Roads, Julian 289
Roads, Mary 610
Roads, Matthias 632
Roads, Peggy 610
Roads, Polly 626
Roads, Rachel 610
Roads, Sarah 632
Roads, Susannah 610
Roads, William (Jr.) 303
Roat, Hugh (Jr.) 439
Robb, Alexander 238
Robb, Andrew 584
Robb, Jacob 702
Robb, James 546

919

Rose, Timothy 727
Rose, Timothy W. 727
Rose, William 238
Roseboom, Gilbert 172
Roseboom, Maria 170
Rosebrook, John 468, 591
Rosebrook, Sarah 466
Rosecrans, Crandall 388
Rosecrans, Jacob 390
Rosecrans, Jemima 388
Rosecrans, Joseph 388
Rosecrans, Thankful 388
Rosegrant, Polly 519
Rosel, Elizabeth 460
Rosenbarger, Joseph 191
Rosenberger, Joseph 210
Rosigrant, Eliza 222
Rositer, Thomas 550
Rosman, Peter 582
Ross, --- 210
Ross, Abner 702
Ross, Alexander E. 526
Ross, Ann 231
Ross, Anna 702
Ross, Austin 161
Ross, Calvin 83
Ross, Catherine 601
Ross, Charlotte 655
Ross, Conard 748
Ross, Conyngham 320
Ross, Cyrus Presty 231
Ross, Deborah 702
Ross, Elenor 702
Ross, Elizabeth 82
Ross, Esther 531
Ross, Hannah 463, 702,
  704
Ross, Ignatius 234, 236
Ross, Isnatius 235
Ross, Isnatius (Capt.)
  234
Ross, Jacob 166
Ross, James 11, 723
Ross, Jane E. 368
Ross, John 128, 216,
  318, 319, 526, 702
Ross, Jonathan 208
Ross, Joseph 368, 706
Ross, Joseph W. 487
Ross, Levin 446, 454
Ross, Martha 702
Ross, Mary 216, 235, 702
Ross, Misouri 123
Ross, Moses 56
Ross, Nancy 481
Ross, Phebe 702
Ross, Polly 79
Ross, Rachel 702
Ross, Robert 564
Ross, Robt. A. 546
Ross, Samuel 46, 702
Ross, Sarah 169, 702
Ross, William 216, 231,
  702
Ross, William N. 198
Ross, Wm. 450
Rossell, Caleb 303
Roth, Adam 416
Roth, Conrad 95

Roth, George Frederick
  64
Roth, Mary 472
Rothaas, August 91
Rothaas, Caroline 91
Rothaas, Louisa 91
Rothaas, Philip 91
Rothass, Johan Philip 91
Rothause, Henrich 102
Rothschulling, Joseph
  Herr 102
Rothwell, Hester A. 312
Rothwell, Jared B. 312
Rothwell, Joseph O.
  (Dr.) 312
Rotrock, Benjamin 443
Rotrock, Daniel 443,
  453, 455
Rott, Antonie 63
Rouch, Revel 215
Roudebush, Daniel 235
Roudebush, David 242
Rough, George 405
Rough, John 303
Rough, Margret 186
Rough, Peter 639
Rough, Sarah 639
Rough, Susanna 407
Roult, Martha 625
Round, Daniel 150
Round, Diana 160
Round, Jacob (Jr.) 172
Round, Martin 161
Round, Polly 162
Rounsaville, Richard 37
Rounsbury, Cathrine 596
Rourke, Coonrod 376
Rousbarg, George 358
Rousch, Elizabeth 477
Rouse, Catherine 389
Rouse, George 545
Rouse, James 199
Rouse, John 389, 391
Roush, Abraham 480
Roush, Absolem 42
Roush, Betsy Ann 42
Roush, Catharine 42
Roush, Catherine 480
Roush, Dobbins 1
Roush, Dolly 479
Roush, Ellen 619
Roush, Eve 476
Roush, George 629
Roush, Henry (Jr.) 476
Roush, Jacob 470
Roush, John 42
Roush, Mary Sevilla 42
Roush, Michael 42, 480
Roush, Michael (Jr.) 42
Roush, Moses 42
Roush, Nathan 42
Roush, Parmunius 1
Roush, Permenius 42
Roush, Philip 42
Roush, Robert 42
Roush, Samuel 42
Roush, Susannah 480
Roush, William 614
Roush, Wm. 42, 45

Rout, Eliza Jane 101
Routh, Susanna 631
Routsan, Mary Ann 588
Routson, Polly 310
Routson, Susannah 294
Rouze, Abigail 204
Rouze, Rebeckah 204
Rouzer, Daniel 216
Rouzer, John 216
Rouzer, Margaret 216
Row, Esther 444
Row, Mary 464
Rowe, Abraham 172
Rowe, Isaiah 449
Rowe, Jane 461
Rowe, Jonathan 468
Rowe, Polly 461
Rowe, Sally 466
Rowe, Sarah 464
Rowe, Susannah 463
Rowe, Thos. 468
Roweboth, Polly 461
Rowell, Elijah 84
Rowell, Hannah 81
Rowell, William 79, 83
Rowen, Edward 521
Rowen, John P. 603
Rowen, Susanna 168
Rowin, Katharine 188
Rowin, Peter 188
Rowland, David 55
Rowland, Henry 55
Rowland, Joshua 130, 161
Rowland, Lydia 55
Rowland, Margaret 55
Rowland, Philip 55
Rowland, Rebecca Jane 601
Rowland, Samuel 55
Rowler, Rachel 293
Rowley, Alpeus 463
Rowley, Isham 706
Rowley, Joseph 713
Rowley, Joseph L. 713
Rowley, Tilman 746
Rowlison, Halron 198
Rowze, Wilden 204
Rox, Nehemiah 480
Roy, William 68
Royer, James 582
Roys, Sarah 9
Rozencrantz, Jacob 158
Rozett, James 463
Ruark, Shadrack 757
Rubel, Walter 277
Rubert, Catherine 304
Rubert, Margaretta 305
Rubert, Rachel 294
Rubert, Vincent 545
Ruble, Abraham 757
Ruble, David 105
Ruble, George 439
Ruble, Henry 531
Ruble, Jane 439
Ruble, Jesse 439
Ruble, John 439
Ruble, Rachel 268, 276
Ruble, Samuel 272
Ruble, Samuel (Jr.) 277
Ruble, Samuel (Sr.) 277

Ruble, Walter 268, 272
Ruble, William 285
Ruble, William (Rev.)
 260
Rubon, Elizabeth 276
Ruby, Arthur 749
Rucker, Adaline 724
Rucker, Elizabeth 723
Rucker, Georg 345
Rucker, Robert 480
Rucker, Wilhelm Heinrich
 345
Ruckert, Anna Katharina
 337
Ruckert, George 337
Ruckert, Maria Elizabeth
 337
Ruddlebaugh, Polly 407
Rude, James 463
Rude, Pheby 463
Rudebaugh, Nicholas 412
Rudebeauch, M. 9
Rudebough, Elizabeth 738
Rudebough, Peter 738
Rudicilly, Elizabeth 225
Rudicilly, Michael 225
Rudisell, Elizabeth 304
Rudisill, Daniel 303
Rudisill, Lena 288
Rudisill, Mary 298
Rudolph, Elizabeth 421
Rudolph, John 427, 545
Rudolph, Mary Jane 427
Rudy, Aaron 102
Rudy, Frederick 56, 63
Rudy, Isaac 372
Rue, Christianna 574
Rue, Henry 79
Rue, Joseph W. 313, 332
Rue, Lewis 574
Rue, Margaret 524
Rue, Mary 519
Rue, Nancy 531
Rue, Russell 79
Rue, Thomas 574
Rue, Thomas L. 317
Ruecker, Georg 345
Ruecker, Wilhelm
 Heinrich 345
Rues, Rachel 411
Ruf, M. 346
Ruff, Christopher 303
Ruff, Isabella 303
Ruff, Issabella 311
Ruff, Jacob 419
Ruff, John Martin 422
Ruff, John P. 415
Ruff, Margaret 525
Ruff, Sarah 303
Ruffin, William 556
Ruffner, Catharine A.
 423, 425
Ruffner, David 423
Ruffner, Dorothy 419
Ruffner, Jacob 412
Ruffner, John 743, 751
Ruffner, Magdaline 422
Rufner, Catherine 405
Ruford, --- (Col.) 314

Rugh, Christian 416
Rugles, Thomas 11
Ruhe, Anna Mary Clara 99
Ruhlen, John 417
Rukart, Anna Katharina
 336
Rukart, Georg 336
Rukart, Peter 336
Rule, John Henry 649
Rull, Nancy 596
Rulon, Caleb 257
Rulon, Elizabeth 276
Rulon, Joseph 257
Rulon, Rebecca 257
Rulon, Samuel H. 257
Rumbaugh, George 63
Rumbaugh, Hannah 52
Rumbaugh, Jane 52
Rumbaugh, John D. 413
Rumbaugh, Morris 51
Rumbough, Katharine 527
Rumel, Henry 303
Rumer, Isaac 582
Rummel, Frances 582
Rummell, Jacob 303
Rumple, Daniel 128
Runamus, Jacob 287
Runamus, Rachel 287
Runamus, William 287
Runcle, Peter 191
Runcle, William 191
Rundel, Lydia 326
Rundel, Margaret 326
Rundel, Mary Ann 326
Rundel, Susan 326
Rungen, Doratea
 Elizabeth 604
Runkel, William 194
Runkle, Danl. 413
Runkle, Elizabeth 407
Runkle, Jacob 413
Runkle, John 419, 420
Runkle, Mary 191
Runkle, Ralph E. 591
Runkle, William 188, 193
Runnells, I. 254
Runnells, Joseph 303
Runnells, Nancy 475
Runnells, Polly 477
Runnells, R. 254
Runnels, Joseph 446
Runnels, Nancy 446
Runnels, William 279
Runner, Emeline 645
Runner, Frelin Alexander
 644
Runner, Isaac 480
Runner, Margarette Ann
 645
Runner, Mary Ann 645
Runner, Michael 644,
 645, 696
Runner, Milton 645
Runner, Rheuben 645
Runner, Sarah 644
Runyan, Abraham 220
Runyan, Andrew B. 220
Runyan, George
 Washington 691

Runyan, Henry 220
Runyan, Hill 691
Runyan, Hiram 220
Runyan, Hiram L. 220
Runyan, John W. 220
Runyan, Mary 220
Runyan, Matilda 220
Runyan, Peter L. 220
Runyan, Rachel 220
Runyan, Sophia 220
Runyon, Abraham 220
Runyon, Andrew B. 219
Runyon, Richard 197
Ruoff, Daniel 136
Ruoff, Ludwig 136
Ruoff, Mary 136
Rupart, Rachel 466
Rupe, Catharine 474
Rupe, David 11
Rupel, James 314
Rupel, John 368
Rupel, Joshua 314, 316
Rupel, Martin 368
Ruperd, John 310
Rupert, Adam 69
Rupert, Catherine 304
Rupert, Christian 303
Rupert, Eva 309
Rupert, Henry 472
Rupert, John 50, 303
Rupert, John Adam 69
Rupert, Leah 290
Rupert, Rachel 294
Ruple, A. H. 401
Rupp, Frederick 664
Rupp, Peter 472
Ruppert, Jacob 303, 310
Ruppert, John 63
Rureh, Phillip 315
Rus, David 281
Rus, Elizabeth 281
Rus, Jacob 502
Rus, Lewis 281
Rus, Margaret 281
Rus, Mary 281
Rus, Rachel 281
Rus, Robert 281
Rus, Robert (Sr.) 281
Rus, Sidney 281
Rus, Thomas 281
Rusbaugh, Jacob 413
Ruse, Henry 377
Ruse, William 403
Ruseh, Maria 67
Rusel, James 314
Rusel, Joshua 314
Rusel, Wm. 31
Rush, Abel 368
Rush, Able 368
Rush, Andrew 360
Rush, Barbara 369
Rush, Betsey 160
Rush, Christopher 369
Rush, Cynthia 360
Rush, Enoch 753
Rush, Isaac 368
Rush, Isabella 360
Rush, Jacob 172, 368,
 501, 501

927

Sellers, John 500
Sellers, Jos. 133
Sellers, Lydia 500
Sellers, Permelia 133
Selley, Ralph 413
Sellinger, Mary 381
Sellinger, Michael 102
Sellinger, Sophia 376
Sellinger, Volentine 376
Sellman, John (Dr.) 552
Sellman, Peter 141, 142, 155
Selsover, George 410
Selvey, Leonard 166
Selvy, Benjamin 699
Sennet, Elizabeth 725
Sennet, Isham 725
Sensbary, Elizabeth 311
Senter, Asa 687, 688
Senter, Lucy 408
Septon, Elizabeth 134
Septon, Henry 134
Serfis, John 226
Sergeant, John 571
Sergeant, Prudence 571
Sergencourt, George 629
Serl, John 438
Serlott, Mary 532
Serring, Samuel 141, 556
Serrot, Peter 489, 490, 495
Server, Jacob 521
Sessions, Aurel 378
Sessions, H. 376
Sest, Peggy 519
Setlamd, Robert 712
Setland, Robert 712
Settings, Ason 116
Seuy, Abraham 413
Sevelier, Andrew 517
Sever, George 51
Sever, Hannah 422
Severly, John 79
Severn, Abigail 701
Severn, Absolom 701
Severn, Daniel 701
Severn, Daniel (Jr.) 701
Severn, Daniel (Sr.) 701
Severn, Elizabeth 701
Severn, John 701
Severn, Joseph 701
Severn, Mary 701
Severn, Rebeca 701
Severn, Sarah 701
Severn, Stephen 701
Severns, John 701
Severs, Casper 326
Severs, Charity A. 252
Severs, James 252
Seving, George 237
Seward, Caleb 141, 153
Seward, Canfield 199
Seward, Daniel 129, 141, 153
Seward, Hannah 199
Seward, James 141, 153
Seward, John 555
Seward, John (Rev.) 564
Seward, Margaret 590

Seward, Nancy 171
Seward, Rachel 171
Seward, Samuel 137, 172, 563
Seward, Susanna 171
Sewart, John 38
Sewel, David 281
Sewel, Mary 281
Sewell, Aaron 258, 272
Sewell, Amos 176
Sewell, Amos T. 166
Sewell, David 166, 176, 280
Sewell, Elizabeth 267, 272, 275
Sewell, Hannah 268, 276
Sewell, Hester 176
Sewell, Jane 176
Sewell, Jno. 267
Sewell, John 267, 268
Sewell, John R. 176
Sewell, Mary 176, 268, 276
Sewell, Mirian 258
Sewell, Nancy 169, 176
Sewell, Peter 176, 186
Sewell, Rebecca 268, 275
Sewell, Sarah 176, 267, 274
Sewell, Susannah 176
Sewell, Timothy 139, 176
Sexton, D. 246
Sexton, Dempsey 246
Sexton, L. M. 246
Sexton, Lavina M. 246
Sexton, Mary 163
Sexton, Zadock 166
Seybold, Sally 164
Seydel, Michael 304
Seymore, Adam 413
Seymour, Effa Ann 470
Seymour, Hart 650
Seymour, William 632
Sgafferm, Henry 304
Shaal, Diana 342
Shaal, Georg Wesley 342
Shaal, Gottlieb 342
Shackleford, William 468
Shad, Elizabeth 308
Shad, Mary 628
Shadd, Ann 628
Shadd, John 632
Shadley, Kath. 410
Shadley, Sarah 404
Shaeffer, Charlotte 100
Shaeffer, Frederick A. 426
Shaeffer, Henry Clinton 426
Shaeffer, Mary 426
Shaeffer, Samuel 421
Shafer, Alexander 115
Shafer, Catharine 115
Shafer, Daniel 172
Shafer, David 226
Shafer, Elizabeth 115, 298, 410
Shafer, Hetty 301
Shafer, John 115, 692

Shafer, Mary 305
Shafer, Michael 304
Shafer, Otillia 421
Shafer, Peter 115
Shafer, Susan 115
Shafer, Susannah 304
Shafer, William 172
Shaffer, Abraham 632
Shaffer, Catharine 632
Shaffer, Christopher 549
Shaffer, Elizabeth 594
Shaffer, George 549
Shaffer, Henry 304
Shaffer, Isaac 422
Shaffer, Joseph 416
Shaffer, Line 633
Shaffer, Margaret 629
Shaffer, Mary 625
Shaffer, Oscula 136
Shaffer, Peter 183
Shaffer, Polly 380
Shaffer, Rachel 53
Shaffer, Sally 471
Shaffer, Samuel 549
Shaffner, Martin 334
Shaffner, Samuel 334
Shagler, Malinda 629
Shahan, John 304
Shaik, Johanna 166
Shain, Thomas 29
Shalds, James 258
Shall, Mary 517
Shallenberger, Barbary 412
Shallingberger, Isaac 226
Shan, Arthur 311
Shanahan, George 93
Shanahan, J. 93
Shanahan, Mary A. 93
Shane, Thomas 29
Shaner, Elizabeth 533
Shaner, Peter 463
Shang, John M. (Jr.) 422
Shank, Henry 506
Shankland, Rhoads 36
Shanklin, Addison 198
Shanklin, Mary 756
Shanklin, Robert 316
Shanklin, Robert S. 756
Shanks, Catharine 596
Shanks, Henry 591
Shanks, Hiram 582
Shanks, Samuel 591
Shanks, Thomas 596
Shanks, William 596
Shannahan, H. 93
Shannahan, J. 93
Shannahan, Mary 93
Shannahan, Robert M. 93
Shannon, Alexander B. (Jr.) 234
Shannon, Charles 73
Shannon, Delilah 682
Shannon, Elizabeth 682
Shannon, H. J. 403
Shannon, Hannah 49
Shannon, Hugh 39, 40
Shannon, James 682

Shannon, James W. 682
Shannon, Jane 173
Shannon, John 11, 502, 757
Shannon, Joseph 582
Shannon, Polly 226
Shannon, Samuel 676
Shannon, Sarah 520
Shannon, Susanna 757
Shannon, Wilson 110
Shanon, Caroline 676
Shanon, Nuton 72
Shanuon, Barbery 303
Shappell, George 166
Shardleman, John Henry 88
Sharer, James 304
Shares, Rebecca 295
Sharon, Joseph 676
Sharon, Juliet 676
Sharon, Martha Ellen 676
Sharon, Sarah J. 676
Sharp, A. B. 251
Sharp, Agness 116
Sharp, Andrew G. 447
Sharp, Benjamin W. 591
Sharp, Betsey 389, 478
Sharp, Burt 251
Sharp, David Henry 250
Sharp, Dorrity 300
Sharp, Elizabeth 265
Sharp, Esther 619
Sharp, George 116, 447, 512
Sharp, Henry 1
Sharp, Horatio 172
Sharp, J. 250, 251
Sharp, Jacob 418, 582
Sharp, James 251
Sharp, James C. 447
Sharp, Jno. 17
Sharp, Job 187
Sharp, John 17, 194, 389, 481, 629, 658, 723
Sharp, Joseph 116, 447
Sharp, K. 250, 251
Sharp, Kesiah 269
Sharp, Kizzirh 251
Sharp, Lewis R. 250
Sharp, Louisa 722
Sharp, Lucinda 251
Sharp, M. 251
Sharp, M. J. 250
Sharp, Margaret 421
Sharp, Mary 269, 389
Sharp, Mary Ann 447
Sharp, Mary E. 250
Sharp, Nancy 116
Sharp, Nancy Jane 447
Sharp, Oner 646
Sharp, Peter 50, 51
Sharp, Peter (Rev.) 51
Sharp, Phebe 187
Sharp, R. R. 250
Sharp, Rachel 250, 280
Sharp, Rhoda 481
Sharp, Richard 481, 486
Sharp, Sally 389

Sharp, Sarah 269
Sharp, Solomon 272, 280, 512
Sharp, Thomas 598
Sharp, Thomas K. 447
Sharp, William 116, 194, 265, 272, 387, 447
Sharpe, John 13
Sharr, Robt. 68
Shartle, --- 454
Shasteen, Elizabeth 381
Shasteen, Jackson 603
Shasteen, James M. 603
Shasteen, John 481
Shastzer, Rosina 602
Shattreck, Samuel 79
Shattuck, Esther 721
Shattuck, John H. 721
Shaub, Conrad 125
Shaub, John 125
Shaul, Aaron 531
Shaver, Alexander 113
Shaver, Catharine 113
Shaver, Elizabeth 113
Shaver, J. Calvin 113
Shaver, John 113
Shaver, Peter 113
Shaw, A . . . 231
Shaw, Albin 558, 559, 560
Shaw, Amos 516
Shaw, Andrew 700
Shaw, Ann 520, 734
Shaw, Antony 124
Shaw, B. L. 403
Shaw, Beverley 94
Shaw, Cusing 477
Shaw, David 700
Shaw, Elijah 314
Shaw, Elizabeth 285, 414
Shaw, Eunice 558, 559
Shaw, Geo. W. 124
Shaw, George 531
Shaw, Hester 176
Shaw, Hezekiah (Rev.) 172
Shaw, Jane 734
Shaw, Jenner 700
Shaw, Jno. 386
Shaw, John 304, 413, 414, 555, 560, 646, 699
Shaw, John M. 57, 94
Shaw, Jonathan 304, 311, 608
Shaw, Joseph 34, 734, 734
Shaw, Joseph S. 419
Shaw, Julian 94
Shaw, Knoles 142
Shaw, Knowles 558, 560
Shaw, Louisa 231
Shaw, Margaret 299, 307, 700
Shaw, Mary 231, 516, 532, 700
Shaw, Mary E. 649
Shaw, Mary M. 99
Shaw, May 700

Shaw, Nancy E. 101
Shaw, Patty 169
Shaw, Peter 481
Shaw, Peter T. 259
Shaw, Philip 304
Shaw, Rachel 296, 682
Shaw, Rhoda 584
Shaw, Robert 700
Shaw, Ruth 383
Shaw, Salla 560
Shaw, Samuel 304, 700
Shaw, Sanuel 11
Shaw, Sarah 54, 124, 231
Shaw, Sindy 166
Shaw, Sophia 560
Shaw, Susan 734
Shaw, Susannah 305
Shaw, Thomas 304, 582
Shaw, W. 746
Shaw, William 57, 231, 700
Shaw, William (Sr.) 700
Shaw, William H. 53
Shawk, Henry 304
Shawke, Jacob 304, 311
Shawke, Rachel 296
Shawver, Christopher 598
Shay, Abraham 115
Shay, Ann 115
Shay, Barby 115
Shay, Catharine 115
Shay, David 334
Shay, Elizabeth 115
Shay, Israel David 115
Shay, John 115, 136
Shay, Margaret 136
Shay, Mary 115
Shay, Peter 188
Shay, Rebecca 115
Shay, Sarah 115
Shayes, Elizabeth 651
Shea, Michael 354
Sheaf, Elizabeth 588
Sheafer, Elizabeth 161
Sheafer, Raehel 167
Sheaffer, John 413
Sheakler, J. 304
Sheapard, Mary 700
Shear, Christine Elizabeth 100
Shearer, Louisa 657
Shearer, Patrick 667
Shearer, William 304
Sheath, Thomas 526
Sheck, Job 205
Sheckler, D. J. 335
Sheckler, John 335
Sheckler, S. A. 335
Shederly, David 242
Sheehan, Cornelius 304
Sheehan, Elizabeth 308
Sheehan, Isabel 292
Sheehan, Nelly 297
Sheeler, Jacob 558
Sheels, David (Jr.) 385
Sheely, Henry 16
Sheely, William B. 535
Sheere, John 405
Sheets, Ann 301

929

Sheets, Elizabeth 292, 299
Sheets, Jacob 304
Sheets, John 304
Sheets, Mariah 308
Sheetz, Mariah 311
Sheff, John 57
Sheffield, Edward 603
Sheffield, Margaret E. 473
Shegley, Adam 521
Shegley, Barbary 508
Shegley, Frederick 521
Shegley, George 508
Sheldenberger, Nicholas 603
Sheldon, Geo. (Rev.) 50
Sheldon, George 50
Sheldon, Myrtle O. 395
Shelenberger, Elizabeth 297
Shelenger, Elizabeth 524
Sheley, Benjamin 527
Sheley, Michael 521
Sheley, Regiah 136
Shell, John 304
Shellabarger, Elizabeth 219
Shellabarger, Ephraim 219
Shellabarger, Martin 219
Shellabarger, Reuben 219
Shellenbarger, Jonas 432
Shellenbarger, Jos. 49
Shellenbarger, Sarah 410
Shellenberger, John 413
Shellenberger, Kitty 408
Shellenberger, Nelly 408
Shellenberger, Sarah 409
Sheller, Polly 478
Shelley, Alexander 683
Shellhouse, Margaret 168
Shellinberger, Nancy 292
Shellingberger, Aaron 603
Shellingberger, Solomon 603
Shelly, David 18
Shelly, Evan 32
Shelly, James 356
Shelton, Alex 43, 45
Shelton, Aley 45
Shelton, Cicely A. 202
Shelton, Clough 202
Shelton, Henly 481
Shelton, Jeremiah 4
Shelton, Maria C. 202
Shelton, Nelson F. 202
Shelton, Polly 306
Shelton, Robert 4, 42, 43, 45
Shelton, Robert (Sr.) 42
Shelton, Tabitha 480
Shelton, Thomas 4, 48, 124
Shelton, Thompson 42
Shelton, Thornton 42, 48
Shelton, William A. 202
Shely, Henry 13

Shely, John 542
Shemshimer, Jacob 68
Shenard, Anne 169
Shenbarger, Baltzer 70
Shendecker, Nathl. 536
Shenk, Henry 55
Shennabarger, Elizabeth 296
Shepard, Albert 196
Shepard, Daniel 85
Shepard, Luther 477
Shepard, William 196
Sheperd, Abraham 25
Shephard, Emily 580
Shephard, William 166
Shepherd, Abraham 11, 24, 25, 27, 32, 35, 38, 39, 41, 208
Shepherd, Abraham (Sr.) 41
Shepherd, Calvin 686
Shepherd, Celia 530
Shepherd, Eliah 11
Shepherd, Eliak 11
Shepherd, Emily 584
Shepherd, Esther 83
Shepherd, Frederick 166
Shepherd, Icabe 11
Shepherd, Isaac 11, 25, 27, 38, 39
Shepherd, Jacob 25, 27, 38, 39, 584
Shepherd, John 25, 35, 38, 39
Shepherd, Mahala 686
Shepherd, Margaret 41
Shepherd, Martha 38
Shepherd, Mary 536, 690, 692
Shepherd, Moses 272, 276
Shepherd, Nathan 110
Shepherd, Nathan (Jr.) 110
Shepherd, Polly 332
Shepherd, Rhoda 275
Shepherd, Sarah 9, 41
Shepherd, Susannah 529
Shepherd, Thomas H. 584
Shepherd, Thomas M. 582
Shepherd, Thomas N. 584
Shepherd, William 262, 541
Shepherd, Wm. 2
Shepler, Elizabeth 417
Shepperd, Isaac 35
Sheppler, Catharine 294
Sherb, Elizabeth 183
Sherewood, Samuel 38
Sherick, John 415
Sheridan, James M. 249
Sheridan, M. 722
Sheridan, Margaret 249
Sheridan, Mary E. 249
Sheridan, Nancy 75
Sheridan, Patrick 249
Sherk, Jacob 629
Sherlock, James 546
Sherman, --- (Gen.) 428
Sherman, Charles R. 437

Sherman, James G. 706
Sherman, William 381
Shermer, John Leonard 60
Shermer, John Leonhard 50
Sherraden, Abram 79
Sherrard, Robt. A. 542
Sherrard, William 550
Sherren, John 642
Sherrick, Henry 415
Sherrod, Daniel 14
Sherwood, Allen 730
Sherwood, Catharine 729, 730
Sherwood, Catherine 730
Sherwood, James 172, 664, 730
Sherwood, Nancy 730
Sherwood, Robert 730
Sheward, Nathan 658
Sheward, Theresa 475
Shibeler, Henry 472
Shidementle, A. 596
Shidler, Maria 79
Shield, John 405
Shields, Alexander 682
Shields, Anne 682
Shields, D. 179, 244
Shields, D. S. 244
Shields, David 244, 261
Shields, Deborah 244
Shields, Eliza 257
Shields, Elizabeth 271, 682
Shields, George 272
Shields, Henry E. 244
Shields, Hetty 165
Shields, James 139, 145, 161, 176, 244, 658
Shields, Jane 682
Shields, Jehu 257
Shields, John 276, 278, 682
Shields, John A. 244
Shields, John M. 102
Shields, Kesiah 535
Shields, Leah 682, 709
Shields, Margaret 303
Shields, Martha 171
Shields, Mary E. 244
Shields, Patrick 132
Shields, Rebecca 165
Shields, Robert 682
Shields, Samuel 304, 682
Shields, William 257, 271, 272, 682, 709
Shigley, Elizabeth 52
Shigley, Sarah 51
Shillebarger, Anny 528
Shillibarger, Eprian 527
Shilt, John 603
Shilt, Peter 536
Shimmel, Conrad 50
Shimp, Polly 420
Shinaman, John 603
Shinberry, Ruth 700
Shineberger, Catharine 303
Shingle, John Phlip 238

Smith, Vallantine 305
Smith, Vom 701
Smith, Waide 311
Smith, Walter B. 653
Smith, Ward 305
Smith, Washington 718
Smith, William 50, 72,
140, 142, 166, 260,
272, 276, 285, 305,
370, 452, 481, 527,
538, 598, 610, 691,
706, 718, 724, 735,
739
Smith, William C. 741
Smith, William D. 732
Smith, William R. 594
Smith, Williard M. 367
Smith, Wm. 43, 268,
272, 420, 689, 739
Smith, Wm. C. 545
Smith, Wm. T. 1, 6, 42
Smith, Zirah 388
Smithby, Casper 633
Smithson, Drummond D. 276
Smives, Catharine 421
Smoot, Solomon 598
Smure, John 653
Smyers, Elizabeth 627
Smyers, John 629
Smylie, --- 695
Smyth, Reuben 43
Smyth, William 230
Smythe, William 551
Snap, Daniel 197
Snavely, Christina 503
Snavely, Jacob 503
Snavely, John 503
Snavely, Margaret 503
Snavely, Samuel 503
Snedaker, John 598
Snedeker, Christian 214
Snediker, Anna 214
Snediker, Christian 214
Snediker, Gabrial 214
Snediker, Isaac 214
Snediker, John 214
Snediker, Rebecca 214
Sneider, George 63
Sneider, Matilda 50
Snell, Albert 723
Snell, John 360, 364
Snell, Katharine 706
Snell, Pleasant 121
Snell, Sylvania 602
Snell, William 15
Snelling, John 591
Snethen, George W. 272
Snider, Adam 238, 616
Snider, Adam George 616
Snider, Benjamin 238
Snider, Catherine 460
Snider, Daniel 438,
441, 616
Snider, David 616
Snider, Elizabeth 616
Snider, George 616
Snider, Hannah 703
Snider, Henry 305, 527,
616

Snider, Hewy 450
Snider, Jacob 450, 484,
616
Snider, James 616
Snider, Jefferson 450
Snider, John 450, 468
Snider, Lavina 592
Snider, Martin 305
Snider, Peter 614, 616
Snider, Rachel 616
Snider, Samuel E. 616
Snider, Sarah 450
Snider, Susanna 419
Snider, Susannah 475
Snider, Thomas 616
Snider, William 305,
450, 616
Snip, Daniel 201
Snip, John (Jr.) 201
Snip, Solomon 201
Snitch, George 664
Snively, Ann Elizabeth
230
Snively, David 230
Snively, Hannah 230
Snively, Hannah E. 230
Snively, William H. 230
Snivly, Rachel 466
Snoddy, John 591
Snodgradd, John 216, 218
Snodgrass, Abigal 535
Snodgrass, Ann 12
Snodgrass, James 516,
521, 550
Snodgrass, Jane 657
Snodgrass, John 209
Snodgrass, Joseph 226,
527
Snodgrass, Nancy 529
Snodgrass, Robert 527
Snodgrass, Sarah 9
Snodgrass, William 451,
508
Snook, Henry 658
Snook, John 658, 664
Snook, John (Jr.) 664
Snook, Matthias 658
Snook, Peter 376, 381
Snook, Rebecca 310
Snook, Susannah 381
Snow, Arminta 254
Snow, D. G. 254
Snow, E. 254
Snow, F. 254
Snow, F. L. 254
Snow, Frances E. 253
Snow, Frances Ellen 253
Snow, Ice & 254
Snow, Lovil 83
Snow, Martha J. 253
Snow, Mary 254
Snow, Mary C. 254
Snow, Robert 83, 253
Snow, Sarah M. R. 253
Snow, Thomas 254
Snow, Thomas J. 254
Snowden, Hannah 523
Snowden, James 515
Snowdon, Benjamin 521

Snowdon, Sally 76
Snuff, Jacob 161
Snyder, Abraham 305
Snyder, Adam 62
Snyder, All . . . 374
Snyder, Benjamin 650
Snyder, Dan 373, 374
Snyder, Daniel 52
Snyder, George 305
Snyder, Henry 305
Snyder, Jacob 638
Snyder, John 334, 422
Snyder, Laruw 293
Snyder, Lovina 471
Snyder, Lydia 70
Snyder, Mary 68
Snyder, Rebecca 134
Snyder, Rosana 536
Snyder, Sally 335
Snyder, Samuel 335
Snyder, Sarah 301
Sockridger, David 334
Soles, Mary 421
Solida, Jacob 421
Soliday, Samuel 417
Sollars, Isaac 456, 457
Sollars, John 456
Sollars, Julia Ann 457
Sollars, Lucy Ann 457
Sollars, Ruth Jane 457
Sollars, Samuel 457
Sollers, Samuel 455
Solman, Love 592
Solomon, Beth 391
Somer, David 305
Somerville, Catharine 591
Sommer, Daniel 338
Sommer, Gottlieb
Friedrich 338
Sommer, Rosina 338
Sonard, Melly 463
Song, George 305
Sook, Henry M. 683
Sooy, Elizabeth 289
Sooy, Mary 288
Sorrick, Levi 604
Sortman, Benjamin 154
Sothard, Francis 745
Sothers, Mary 272
Sougrain, Anthony 498
Souter, Barbara 470
South, David 614
South, James 238
South, John B. 477
South, Martha 75
South, Mary 614
South, Nancy 657
South, William 238
Southard, Isaiah 746
Southard, Vincent 658,
664
Southrell, Edward 148
Southwich, Samuel 262
Souverain, Francis 481
Sovern, Jane 701
Sovern, Joseph 701
Soverns, Daniel 314
Soverns, Mary Margarett
314

Soward, Abigail 460
Soward, Biram 172
Soward, Daniel 463
Soward, Mahlon 527
Soward, Melly 463
Soward, Rhoda 465
Sowards, Griffin 707
Sowards, Harriet 461
Sowards, James 707
Sowards, Thomas 707
Sowartz, Juliana 462
Sowerman, Margaret 603
Sowers, Joseph 121
Sowers, Moses 438
Sowers, Paul 582
Spacey, Nancy 77
Spacht, Sally 79
Spafford, Amexicus M. 604
Spafford, Amos 186, 188
Spafford, Aurora 188
Spafford, Ausora 186
Spafford, Cloe 188
Spafford, Oliver 186
Spafford, Samuel 186, 188
Spahr, Matthias 531
Spaid, Michael 548
Spain, Abraham 187
Spain, Daniel 183, 187, 194
Spain, Edward 194
Spain, Edwin 195
Spain, Elizabeth 187
Spain, Hezekiah 194
Spain, J. H. 198
Spain, James 183, 187, 513
Spain, John Peterson 187
Spain, Joshua 183, 194
Spain, Martha 194
Spain, Mary 187
Spain, Mary M. 194
Spain, Robert 197
Spain, Sally 197
Spain, Sarah 187
Spain, Theo. 513
Spain, Theodorick 189
Spain, Thomas 183, 194, 195, 197
Spain, Thos. 513
Spain, William 187
Spain, Willis 194
Spalding, Noah 383, 387
Spanger, Phillip W. 605
Spangler, Betsey 409
Spangler, Daniel 582
Spangler, Eve 429
Spangler, Jacob 429
Spangler, Margaret 473
Spangler, Samuel 413
Spar, Benjamin 584
Sparger, John 619
Sparger, Marie 619
Spargur, Anthony W. 619
Spark, John 7
Sparks, Amos 104
Sparks, Andrew 527
Sparks, Barbara 736

Sparks, Cassander 526
Sparks, Elias M. 451
Sparks, George 2, 3, 4
Sparks, J. O. 44
Sparks, James 3, 48
Sparks, John 1, 2, 4, 5, 6, 7, 46
Sparks, Margaret 4
Sparks, Mark 104
Sparks, Mary T. 4
Sparks, Salethial 39
Sparks, Simon 527
Sparks, Solomon 3
Sparling, Elizabeth 707, 717
Sparling, George 712
Sparling, Lettie 713
Sparling, Stephen 717
Sparrow, Rebecca 223
Spaulding, Henry C. 403
Spaulding, J. J. 403
Speaker, Barbara 378
Speakes, Aaron 323
Speakes, Catharine 323
Speakes, Charles 323
Speakes, Delia 323
Speakes, Elisa 318
Speakes, Elizabeth 323
Speakes, Francis 323
Speakes, Harriett 323
Speakes, John 318, 323
Speakes, Lucinda 318, 323
Speakes, Margaret 323
Speakes, Maria 323
Speakes, Mary 323
Speakes, Namott 318
Speakes, William 323
Speakman, Ebenezer 629
Speakman, Jacob 629
Speakman, James 698, 699
Speaks, William 317
Spear, Catharine 422
Spear, W. 701
Spears, Andrew 559
Spears, Charles 723
Spears, Jacob 554
Spears, Rosannah 707
Spears, Susannah 704
Speed, George 79
Speer, Elizabeth 300
Speer, John 598
Speer, Robert 542
Speer, Stewart 542
Speer, Stuart 539
Speers, Peter 545
Spees, Andrew 57
Spees, Daniel 57
Spees, Eve 57
Spees, George 127
Spees, John 57
Spees, Mathias E. 50
Spees, Matthias 57
Spees, Matthias E. 57, 97
Spees, Samuel 57
Speirer, A . . . 421
Spellman, Timothy 753
Spelman, Mary 725

Spelman, Thomas 226
Spelman, Timothy 413, 725
Spence, Hannah 296
Spence, James 676
Spence, James Alexander 676
Spence, Oliver 567
Spence, Sarah 300
Spence, Sarah Jane 676
Spence, Thomas Pickens 676
Spencer, Abigail 80
Spencer, Abraham 185
Spencer, Alice 323
Spencer, Alvan 79
Spencer, Anderson 140, 158, 176
Spencer, Anne 552
Spencer, Asa 361, 364, 527
Spencer, Ben 574
Spencer, Betsy 627
Spencer, C. M. 576
Spencer, Catharine 272, 318
Spencer, Catherine 323
Spencer, Charles W. 629
Spencer, Clover 576
Spencer, Delilah 518
Spencer, Edmund 318, 323
Spencer, Eleanor 639
Spencer, Elias 85
Spencer, Elisa 318
Spencer, Eliza 323
Spencer, George 591
Spencer, James 260, 263, 629, 637, 639
Spencer, Jeny 185
Spencer, John 273, 738
Spencer, John C. 264, 285
Spencer, John W. 544
Spencer, Joseph 142, 161
Spencer, Joshua Osburn 318
Spencer, Josiah 229
Spencer, Margaret 323
Spencer, Margarite 318
Spencer, Mary 165, 323
Spencer, Mary Ann 229
Spencer, Nancy 318, 323
Spencer, Nathan 318, 323
Spencer, O. M. 576
Spencer, Oliver 552, 556, 562, 563
Spencer, Osburn 323
Spencer, Phineas 323
Spencer, Polly 76, 158
Spencer, Samuel 318
Spencer, Sarah 318, 323, 472, 630
Spencer, Thomas 285, 536
Spencer, W. 375
Spencer, Watson 591
Spencer, William 138, 318, 323
Spencer, William (Sr.) 268

Stahl, Adam 69
Stahl, Catharine 70
Stahl, Danl. 70
Stahl, Ellen 403
Stahl, J. M. 401
Stahl, S. M. 403
Stahl, Spencer M. 403
Stain, John 620
Stainbring, Elizabeth 411
Stainbrook, Henry 305
Stakehouse, James 369
Staldut, Rosanna 80
Staler, Mahala 81
Staley, Catharine 507
Staley, Catharine (Jr.) 507
Staley, Daniel 507
Staley, Daniel (Jr.) 507
Staley, Easter 519
Staley, Jacob 162, 533
Staley, Jonathan 507
Staley, Mahala 50
Staley, Mary 507
Staley, Peter 507
Staley, Samuel 507
Staley, Sophiah 507
Stall, Edward H. 560
Stall, Geo. 419
Stall, Hugh 633
Stalley, Thomas 730
Stamler, Rachel A. 396
Stanber, Jonas 754
Stanberry, Ann Lucy 687
Stanberry, Elizabeth 405
Stanberry, Howard 550
Stanberry, James 273
Stanberry, James R. 737, 739, 741
Stanberry, Jonas 549, 550, 687, 746, 747, 749
Stanberry, Nehemiah 273
Stanberry, W. 742
Stanbery, Elias 734
Stanbery, Howard 551
Stanbery, James R. 739
Stanbery, Jonas 549, 550, 551, 747, 748, 749
Stanbery, Juliann 420
Stanbery, William 729
Stanbery, Wm. 754
Stanbrough, Solomon 260
Stanbury, Josiah H. 36
Stanbury, Mary 523
Stanbury, Rebekah 527
Stanchak, Phoeb 650
Stancliff, Anna 656
Stancliff, David 80
Stancliff, Hannah 78
Stancliff, Lucina 78
Stanclift, E. C. 91
Standcliff, David 629
Standeford, E. 57
Stander, Mary 125
Standerford, Elijah 204
Standford, James 264
Standiford, Elijah 57

Standiford, Provy 57
Standiford, Rebecca 57
Standish, Thomas H. 59
Standley, Abraham 521
Standly, Joseph 305
Stanfer, Abraham 70
Stanferd, James E. 447
Stanfield, Jane 524
Stanfield, John 533
Stanfield, Mary 533
Stanfield, William 514
Stanfield, Wm. 512
Stanford, Hector 521
Stanford, James 405
Stanford, Nancy 533
Stang, Frank 400
Stanley, Abraham 305
Stanley, Archelaus 80
Stanley, Benjamin 305
Stanley, Betsey 78
Stanley, Delia 585
Stanley, Elizabeth 309
Stanley, Garland 305
Stanley, James 305
Stanley, James (Jr.) 305
Stanley, John 305, 311
Stanley, John H. 486
Stanley, Joshua 305
Stanley, Judith 291
Stanley, Milley 292
Stanley, Moses 305
Stanley, Nancy 272
Stanley, Nathaniel J. 305
Stanley, Rachel 225
Stanley, Sally 558, 562
Stanley, Solomon 311
Stanley, William 527, 556, 558, 562, 571
Stanly, Isaac 137, 141
Stansberry, Recompence 276
Stansbery, Jonas 551
Stansbury, Henry 636
Stansell, Zady P. 593
Stant, Jane 631
Stanton, Benjamin 305
Stanton, Elizabeth 471, 472
Stanton, Sarah Coles 641
Stanup, Gracy 204
Stanup, Richard 204
Stapf, John G. 353
Staples, Jno. 37
Stapleton, John 521
Star, Elizabeth 271
Star, John 658
Star, Nancy 271
Star, Olovia 294
Star, Richard 276
Star, William 273
Starbuck, Hannah 275
Starbuck, Hezekiah 257
Starbuck, Susannah 283
Stare, Abraham 533
Stare, Jane 529
Starey, Mary 412
Stark, Almon 390
Stark, Amy 413

Stark, Archibald 141
Stark, Franklin 342
Stark, Heinrich Franklin 342
Stark, John 16
Stark, Juliana 342
Stark, Lucy 474
Stark, Philip 381
Starkey, James 687
Starkey, Rachel 625
Starkey, Rhoda 629
Starkey, Sarah 626
Starks, Betsey E. 398
Starks, Jemamiah 398
Starky, Pheaby 629
Starlin, Manul 72
Starlin, Martha 72
Starling, Susanna 32
Starling, William 32
Starling, Wm. (Jr.) 32
Starner, Susan 415
Starns, John E. 610
Starr, Anna Matilda 683
Starr, Barbara 380
Starr, Betsey 634
Starr, Hugh 683
Starr, James (Jr.) 172
Starr, John W. 52, 53
Starr, John Westly 108
Starr, Mary 302
Starr, Nancy 276
Starr, Naoma 683
Starr, Richard 305
Starr, Sally 76
Starr, William 683
Starret, Samuel 29
Starrett, Daniel 45
Starrett, E. 45
Starrett, Ellen C. 229
Starrett, J. A. 229
Starrett, John 45
Starrett, Samuel 45
Starrit, Elijah 42
Stateler, Michael 745
Staten, David 544
Stater, Mahala 81
States, Sarintha 472
Statker, Nathan 286
Statler, Mahal 413
Statler, Nancy 65
Statler, Samuel 65
Statten, Hannah 404
Statts, Jacob 481
Staufer, Barbara 70
Stauffer, David 305
Stauffer, Elizabeth 302
Stauffer, Jacob 305, 313
Stauffer, John 305
Stauffer, Nancy 288
Staunt, John 633
Staunton, Bordon 114
Stawser, David 629
Stead, Harriet 723
Stead, Margaret 561
Stead, Thomas 561, 562
Steadman, Alexander 85
Steamer, Rebecca 415
Steapleton, Samuel 306
Stearns, Achsah 262

940

Stephenson, Samuel 658, 664
Stephenson, Sarah 168
Stephenson, William 527, 658
Stepleton, Rebecca 417
Stepney, Hannah 451
Stepney, James 451
Stepney, Mary 451
Stepney, Miles 451
Stepney, Mourning 451
Sterett, Joseph 527
Sterit, Charles 468
Sterling, James 664
Sterling, Michael 640
Stermen, Charles 394
Stermen, G. M. 394
Stermen, S. A. 394
Stern, John 591
Stern, Peter 431
Stern, Salome 431
Sterner, Caroline 335
Sterner, Daniel 335
Sterner, Dianna 335
Sterner, Francis 335
Sterner, Rosina 335
Sterns, Cynthia 270
Sterns, David 270
Sterns, John W. 707
Sterns, Joseph 192
Sterns, Lysander Francis 192
Sterret, Alexander 137, 139
Sterret, Isaac 568
Sterret, John 527
Sterret, Mary 516
Sterret, R. B. 46
Sterrett, Ann 530
Sterrett, Elizabeth 501
Sterrett, John 515
Sterrett, Joseph 501, 510, 516
Sterrett, Mary 510
Sterrett, Peggy 515
Sterrett, Robert E. 533
Sterrett, Sally 515, 531
Sterrett, William 533
Sterris, Joseph 192
Sterritt, John 513
Sterritt, Peggy 513
Stevanson, John 52
Stevems, Chas. A. 546
Stevens, Amiza 691
Stevens, Anna 478
Stevens, Benjamin 306
Stevens, Edward (Gen.) 286
Stevens, Elizabeth 52
Stevens, Gelly 286
Stevens, Jacob G. 604
Stevens, James 521, 550
Stevens, John 521, 550, 613, 691
Stevens, Justin 593
Stevens, Laura 691
Stevens, Nancy 407
Stevens, Polly 286
Stevens, Sarah 505

Stevens, Sisson 296
Stevens, Sophia 649
Stevens, Thomas 72
Stevens, William 182, 505
Stevenson, Ann 10
Stevenson, Anna 184
Stevenson, Arthur 184
Stevenson, Charles 5, 6, 184
Stevenson, Daniel D. 699
Stevenson, David 184
Stevenson, Edward 326
Stevenson, Eli 56, 63, 591
Stevenson, Elias 51
Stevenson, Elizabeth 526
Stevenson, Enoch G. 604
Stevenson, George 413
Stevenson, Henry 422
Stevenson, Homer P. 591
Stevenson, James 24, 38, 40, 422, 517, 521
Stevenson, Jane 184
Stevenson, Jenny 519
Stevenson, Jesse Leo 49
Stevenson, John 184, 521
Stevenson, Joseph F. 51
Stevenson, Margaret 289
Stevenson, Margaret A. 590
Stevenson, Martha 184
Stevenson, Mary 219
Stevenson, Mary W. 56
Stevenson, Rebeckah 413
Stevenson, Robert 6, 527
Stevenson, Samuel 535
Stevenson, Sarah 125, 291
Stevenson, Thomas 219, 413
Stevenson, William 521
Stevenson, Wm. 4, 5, 6, 7
Steveson, Isaac 106
Stevins, Catharine Belinda 601
Steward, Ann 525
Steward, John 273
Steward, Keturah 391
Steward, Lillie 8
Steward, Mahlan 306
Steward, Russell 8
Steward, Sarah 391
Steware, John 484
Stewart, Abigal 518
Stewart, Abram S. 191
Stewart, Adam 229
Stewart, Alexander 558, 572
Stewart, Ann 191
Stewart, Ann W. 191
Stewart, Archd. 447
Stewart, Archibald 189, 196, 447
Stewart, Asa 226
Stewart, Barbary 191
Stewart, Barnet 566
Stewart, Charles 191, 548, 549, 583

Stewart, Daniel 75, 84, 664
Stewart, Edward 707, 717
Stewart, Elizabeth 123, 191, 213, 535
Stewart, Galbreath 544
Stewart, Geo. 746
Stewart, Gerrett 80
Stewart, H. 396
Stewart, H. C. 447, 450
Stewart, Harlon 403
Stewart, Henry 191
Stewart, Hugh 447
Stewart, I. M. 46
Stewart, Jacob 552, 554
Stewart, James 46, 62, 185, 191, 213, 306, 447, 448, 450, 468, 516, 521, 551
Stewart, Jane 271, 717
Stewart, Jane C. 448
Stewart, Jno. 83, 746
Stewart, John 185, 191, 241, 246, 527, 544, 629, 707
Stewart, John T. 213
Stewart, Joseph 213, 306, 749
Stewart, Levi 80
Stewart, M. 396
Stewart, Margaret 447
Stewart, Maria 396
Stewart, Martha 734
Stewart, Mary 191, 213, 229, 241, 301, 447, 521, 703
Stewart, Matthew 205
Stewart, Mercy 213
Stewart, Nancy 280
Stewart, O. J. 126
Stewart, O. M. 45
Stewart, Pallas P. 574
Stewart, Rachel 191, 413, 544, 545, 547, 607, 634, 746
Stewart, Robert Peeble 229
Stewart, Saml. 213, 514
Stewart, Samuel 216, 273, 306, 748
Stewart, Sarah 270, 271, 447, 559, 593, 634
Stewart, Stephen 213, 709
Stewart, Thomas 187, 191, 192
Stewart, Timothy 276
Stewart, William 372, 544, 545, 559
Stibbins, E. 133
Stibbins, Rebecca 133
Stibbs, Joseph 306
Stich, Peter 722
Stickell, John 49
Stickle, Christian 359
Stiff, Elizabeth 441
Stiles, Asahel 505
Stiles, Benjamin 558
Stiles, Byrd 148, 175

Stiles, Elizabeth 148, 175, 647
Stiles, Hannah 558
Stiles, John 148, 175
Stiles, Jonathan W. 647
Stiles, Kesiah 523
Stiles, Mary 532
Stiles, Newell B. 53
Stiles, Raney 505
Stiles, Rebecca 163
Stiles, Richard 139, 148, 175
Stiles, Saml. 516
Stiles, Thomas 549
Still, Alexander 162
Stillway, Philip 97
Stillwell, Obadiah 699
Stilt, Thomas 277
Stilwell, James 172
Stilwell, John 172
Stilwell, Rachel 172
Stimpes, Thomas 220
Stinchcomb, Ann 428
Stinchcomb, Elizabeth W. 428
Stinchcomb, George 428
Stinchcomb, George F. 428
Stinchcomb, James 428
Stinchcomb, Susan H. 428
Stine, Catharine 472
Stine, Daniel 149
Stine, Godlip 325
Stine, Jacob 633
Stine, John 167
Stine, Josiah C. 619
Stine, Lewis 102
Stine, Martin 149
Stine, Mary 334
Stinehelfer, Christoph 342
Stinehelfer, Elizabetha 342
Stineman, J. H. 91
Stiner, Nicholas 547
Stinger, Mary 299
Stininger, A. 578
Stininger, Amos 578
Stininger, E. 578
Stininger, Eleanor 578
Stininger, George 306
Stininger, Leannah J. 578
Stininger, Samuel W. 578
Stinnbrin, Elizabeth 411
Stinor, Margaret 655
Stinson, David 468
Stinson, Lewe 461
Stinson, Rachel 466
Stinson, Thos. 463
Stip, David 533
Stip, Frederick 527
Stipy, Katharine 527
Stiss, David 533
Stites, B. 576
Stites, Benjamin 559, 560, 568, 569, 574
Stites, Benjamin (Maj.) 552

Stites, Benjamin (Sr.) 552
Stites, Hannah 559, 560
Stites, Henry N. 381
Stites, Hezekiah 559
Stites, Jonathan 559
Stites, Martha 574
Stites, Saml. 516
Stites, Samuel 574
Stith, Elizabeth 705
Stith, John 417
Stitt, Lavinia 466
Stitt, Moses 450
Stitt, Samuel 559
Stitth, Elizabeth 705
Stivason, Christina 627
Stiver, Anna Mary 588
Stivers, Jane 126
Stiverson, Barney 629
Stiverson, John 629
Stnavely, John 503
Stnier, Magdalena 298
Stoakes, John 681, 684
Stoakes, William 684
Stoat, Elizabeth 168
Stock, Elizabeth 289
Stockam, John 12
Stockdale, --- 51
Stockdale, Ellen 56
Stockdale, George 56, 95
Stockdale, Jane 56
Stockdale, Joseph 56, 64, 95
Stockdale, Mary 56
Stockdale, Melissa E. 95
Stockdale, William 56, 60, 95, 458
Stockdale, Wm. 445
Stockham, Anne 655
Stockham, Mary 11
Stockham, William 664
Stockley, R. 373
Stockman, George 381
Stockman, John H. 172
Stockman, Sarah 68
Stocksdale, George 93
Stocksdale, George (Sr.) 93
Stocksdale, William 64
Stocksdale, William (Sr.) 93
Stockton, Aron 510
Stockton, Catherine 573
Stockton, Ebenezer 733
Stockton, Elizabeth 510
Stockton, Job 733
Stockton, Philip 573
Stockton, Robert 733
Stodard, --- 456
Stodard, Julia 601
Stodard, L. L. 402
Stoddard, Henry 60, 360
Stoddard, James 640
Stoetzel, George Heinrich 347
Stoffer, Abraham 306
Stokeley, Joseph 544
Stokely, Samuel 679
Stoker, Kitty 409

Stokes, Edward 203
Stokes, John 511, 616
Stokes, John R. 511
Stokes, Stephen 226
Stokesbury, Rebecca 272
Stoksbury, David 280
Stollen, Helena Sophia 347
Stolts, Patty 409
Stomb, Jacob 306
Stomer, Zac 373
Stone, Abigail 560
Stone, Abigail M. 559
Stone, Anster 477
Stone, Arvilla 380
Stone, Dan 198
Stone, Ethan 558, 559, 560, 572
Stone, George 413
Stone, Horace 629, 639, 641
Stone, James 741
Stone, James Horace 640
Stone, Jane 379, 641
Stone, John 731
Stone, Joseph 52
Stone, Lewis E. 583
Stone, Lucinda P. 741
Stone, Mary 641
Stone, Nelson 381
Stone, Noyce 544
Stone, Sarah 641
Stone, Thomas 172
Stone, W. 400
Stoneberger, Elizabeth 191
Stonebreaker, Catharine 164
Stonebreaker, John 167
Stonebreaker, Sebastian 146
Stonebreaker, Susanna 164
Stoneburner, Christiana 642
Stoneburner, Elizabeth 642
Stoneburner, John 425
Stoneburner, Malinda 425
Stoneburner, Philip 642
Stonemit, Casper 574
Stoner, Samuel 745
Stonerspring, Henry 405
Stonewit, Casper 574
Stookery, Barbara 413
Stookey, Anny 405
Stookey, John 413
Stookey, Kitty 409
Stookey, Peter 405
Stooksbury, David 280
Stoop, Jacob 620
Stoop, Rebecca 618
Stoop, Robert 277
Stoops, Robert 257
Stoors, Louisa H. 602
Stopes, John 664
Storer, David 12
Storer, Ebenezer 746
Storer, Henry H. 6

Storer, James 6
Storer, William 609
Storey, Robert 3
Storres, Sebastian 472
Storts, Abraham 481
Story, James 422
Story, Sarah 723
Stothart, William 552
Stott, Teagle 583
Stotts, Abraham 441
Stotts, Arthur 441
Stotts, Betsey 441
Stotts, Hiram 441
Stotts, John 441
Stotts, Margaret 441
Stotts, Margret 441
Stotts, Maria 441
Stotts, Polly 441
Stotts, Rebecca 441
Stotts, Uria 441
Stotzel, George Heinrich 347
Stough, John (Rev.) 334
Stough, Mary 297
Stoughton, William 162
Stount, Susannah 269
Stout, Ann 563
Stout, Benj. 84
Stout, Benjamin 433
Stout, Charles 167, 281
Stout, Cordelia 599
Stout, Cynthia 241
Stout, Daniel 563, 566
Stout, David 281
Stout, Dinah 273
Stout, Elizabeth 168, 465
Stout, Elvina 73
Stout, Ephraim 273
Stout, George 80
Stout, Hannah 505
Stout, Henry 535
Stout, Hezekiah 207, 209
Stout, Isaac 12, 286, 505
Stout, James 3
Stout, John 259
Stout, John R. 46
Stout, Joseph 381
Stout, Joseph A. 599
Stout, Lety 477
Stout, Mary 213, 270, 271
Stout, McCalla 241
Stout, Obediah 34
Stout, Peter 468
Stout, Polly 79
Stout, Robert B. 46
Stout, Sally 275
Stout, Susan S. I. 603
Stout, William 463
Stout, Wm. 12
Stout, Wm. (Jr.) 5
Stout, Wm. (Sr.) 3, 5
Stouter, David 419
Stouts, Elizabeth 474
Stover, Barbara 711
Stover, Elizabeth 711
Stover, Harriet 709, 711

Stover, Joel 711
Stover, John 714, 715
Stover, Mary 705
Stover, Samuel 714, 715, 745
Stover, Susanna 715
Stow, Edward 49
Stow, Solomon 381
Stoy, Joseph 381
Straas, Thomas Alfred 344
Straas, Wilhelm 344
Strack, Lidia 342, 344
Strader, Albert 422
Strader, Ellen 421
Stradley, Daniel 583
Stradley, Mary Ann G. 583
Stradley, Thomas 583
Strahl, John 120
Strahl, Mary 289
Straight, Jno. 80
Strain, Elihu W. 667
Strain, Elizabeth 229, 524
Strain, Isaac 229
Strain, Isaac (Lt.) 229
Strain, John R. 605
Strain, Mary 229
Strain, Robert 229
Strain, Robert Montgomery 229
Strain, Robt. 229
Strain, Sarah 308
Strait, John 157
Strait, Peter 629
Straley, Joseph 450
Strander, Fany 133
Strane, Polly 526
Strange, John 172
Straton, Stephen 216
Straton, Timothy 216
Strattan, Jacob 188
Strattan, Rebecca 291
Stratton, Albert 617
Stratton, Amy 290
Stratton, Ann 291
Stratton, Anne Humphreys 474
Stratton, Anny 309
Stratton, David 282, 306
Stratton, Edward 258
Stratton, Esther 276
Stratton, James 653
Stratton, Joseph 257, 258, 282, 306
Stratton, Josiah 306
Stratton, Margaret 301
Stratton, Mary 295
Stratton, Minard F. 102
Stratton, Rebecca 258
Stratton, Richard 653
Stratton, Stephen 226
Stratton, Thomas 583
Stratton, William 574
Straughan, Margaret 306
Straughn, Isaiah 306
Straughn, Jacob 306
Straughn, Merriman 276

Strauss, Daniel 226
Strawbridge, Thos. 213
Strawn, Sarah 308
Strayer, Lawrence 429
Streach, William 188
Streaet, William 182
Street, Anna 294
Street, Betsey 171
Street, E. N. 400
Street, Jesse 306
Street, Wm. 182
Streets, Mary 419
Strench, Christian 353
Stretch, Andrew 186, 188
Stretch, Jemima 186, 188
Stretch, Sarah 467
Stretch, Thomas 186, 188
Stretch, William 186, 188
Strickford, Joseph 402
Strickland, Joshua 664
Strickle, Jacob 287
Strickle, John P. 61
Strickle, Susannah 61
Strickler, Barbara 412
Strickler, John 58, 345
Strickler, Margaretha Lucinda 345
Strickler, Mary Ann 345
Strickley, Jacob 12
Strieby, Christopher H. 306
Strienz, Jacob 355
Stringer, Daniel 83
Stringer, George Marion 118
Stringer, Jane 118
Stringer, Jenny 118
Stringer, John 118
Stringer, Malcom 118
Stringer, Maria 118
Stringer, William 118
Stringer, William (Jr.) 118
Stringer, William (Sr.) 118
Strobredge, Jane 439
Strode, Betsy 437
Strode, Edward 437
Strode, Margaret 437
Strode, Nancy 437
Strode, Polly 437
Strode, William 437
Stroll, Nicholas 418
Strong, Arvin C. 699
Strong, Benjamin 527
Strong, Cynthia Adelia 699
Strong, Daniel 477
Strong, Darius 699
Strong, David 557
Strong, David (Lt. Col.) 556
Strong, David G. 664
Strong, Emily Caroline 722
Strong, Geo. Washington 521
Strong, George 306

944

Sunderland, Cornelius 172
Sunderland, Daniel 53
Sunderland, Eleanor 49
Sunderland, James 102
Sunderland, John 564
Sunderland, Mary 51
Sunderland, Wm. 52
Sunderlin, John 413
Sunnafrank, Jacob 551
Suppinger, Alexander P. 533
Supton, John 217
Surber, John 445
Surlock, George 664
Sutennisler, Jacob 593
Sutherland, A. 375
Sutherland, Alexander 375
Sutherland, Jane 375
Sutherland, John 128, 139, 140, 141, 145
Sutherland, John H. 375
Sutherland, John R. 680
Sutherland, Mary Jane 375
Sutherland, Rebecca Elizabeth 375
Sutherland, Robert 463
Sutherland, William 375
Sutterfield, James 45
Sutton, Amos 533
Sutton, Asenith 522
Sutton, Edward 148, 155, 156
Sutton, Elenor 527
Sutton, Elisha 162
Sutton, Eliza 49
Sutton, Elizabeth 164, 532
Sutton, Ezra 527
Sutton, Hannah 171
Sutton, Isaiah 533
Sutton, Jane 148, 155
Sutton, Jesse 527
Sutton, John Shaw 155
Sutton, Matthew 155
Sutton, Rachael 520
Sutton, Thomas 49, 155
Sutton, Thomas H. 102
Sutton, William 521, 527
Sutton, Wm. 194
Swaartz, Nathaniel 416
Swafford, Isaac 172
Swaggart, Mary 583
Swaim, Jno. Alexr. 80
Swaim, Sarah 52
Swain, David 621
Swain, John 357, 664
Swain, Rachel 52
Swain, Vesti 590
Swairy, Sarah 411
Swala, Rachel 10
Swallow, Garret 172
Swallow, Salome 272
Swan, Aaron 734
Swan, Catherine 226
Swan, Laura 734
Swan, Samantha 734

Swan, Sophronia 734
Swan, Theodore 471
Swaney, John 667
Swaney, Robert 468
Swanger, Jacob 68
Swank, Sally 378
Swann, R. G. 193
Swann, Richard 226
Swanson, Dennis 664
Swartout, Amy 473
Swarts, George 440
Swartz, Andrew 416
Swartz, Elizabeth 594
Swartz, Henry 385
Swartz, J. 413
Swartz, John 421
Swartz, John J. 384
Swartz, John S. 385
Swartz, Sarah 333
Swartz, Sebastian 359
Swartz, Susannah 384
Swasick, James 71
Swayer, Amos 420
Swayne, Barnett 120
Swayne, Caleb 120
Swayne, Eli 120
Swayne, Evans 120
Swayne, Jane 120
Swayne, Joseph 120
Swayne, Joshua 598
Swayne, Mary 120
Swayne, Thomas 120
Swayze, Daniel 417
Swayze, Margaret 417
Swazy, Mary 625
Sweadler, Jacob 533
Sweany, Mary 580, 625
Sweany, Nancy 81
Swearingen, Henry 306
Swearingen, Isaac 137, 139
Swearingen, John 44
Swearingen, Katthran 11
Swearingen, Mary 306
Swearingen, Thomas 550
Swearingen, Thos. V. 413
Swearingen, Wm. 42
Sweasey, Henry 633
Sweasey, Johannah 626
Sweasey, Sophia Jane 629
Sweasy, Elizabeth 629
Sweatt, Sally 83
Sweesey, Christeen 632
Sweet, Armillia 480
Sweet, Asael 187
Sweet, Benjamin D. 215
Sweet, Eliza 591
Sweet, Elvira 380
Sweet, Joseph 463
Sweet, Rebecah 241
Sweet, Robert 241
Sweet, Sarah B. 333
Sweney, Mary 603
Sweny, George 507
Sweny, Margaret 536
Sweny, Margery Jane 507
Swesy, Henry 629
Swett, Keziah 77
Sweyer, John 422

Sweyer, Mary 416
Swickard, George 97
Swift, James 543
Swift, Jedediah 157
Swift, Mary 164
Swift, Thomas 629
Swigart, Susanna 519
Swigert, John 329
Swigert, Michael 511
Swihart, Aaron 583
Swihart, Mathias 583
Swim, Jesse 43
Swim, Katy 628
Swim, Rinear 306
Swim, Samuel 12
Swim, Susanna 630
Swinebarger, Catharine 68
Swineford, Peter 441
Swinehart, Adam 306
Swinehart, Elizabeth 632
Swing, Hannah 208
Swinger, Jacob 372
Swinhart, Anthony 636
Swinhart, Rebecca 625
Swinhart, S. 630
Swinny, Thos. W. 9, 12
Swirck, Elizabeth 417
Swisher, Elizabeth 11, 226
Swisher, George 40
Swisher, Jacob 742, 751, 755
Swisher, Liddy 412
Swisher, Susan 582
Swisser, Jacob 405
Switser, George 306
Switser, Jacob 306
Switser, John 306
Switzer, Alva 742
Switzer, David 742
Switzer, Dolly 475
Switzer, Elizabeth 478
Switzer, Fr . . . ack 413
Switzer, Hannah 742
Switzer, Jacob 693
Switzer, Jerusha 334
Switzer, Mary Ann 742
Switzer, Polly 703
Switzer, Rebecka 475
Switzer, Sarrah 479
Switzer, Simon 742
Swords, Mary 154
Swords, William 154
Syford, Eliza 421
Syler, Barbara 476
Syler, Margaret 476
Symes, John C. 553, 554, 555, 556, 559, 560
Symes, John Cleves 573
Symmes, Celadon 141
Symmes, Daniel 562, 563, 564, 570
Symmes, Eliza 562
Symmes, Esther 728
Symmes, Jeremiah 205
Symmes, John (Jr.) 559
Symmes, John C. 552, 746

Taylor, Nathan 390
Taylor, Noble 110
Taylor, Obed 594
Taylor, Ober 391
Taylor, P. W. 743
Taylor, Persifo 306
Taylor, Peter 207, 527
Taylor, Philo 80
Taylor, Pinem 306
Taylor, Polly 162, 390
Taylor, R. S. 180
Taylor, Rachael 584
Taylor, Reubin 232
Taylor, Richard 236, 327
Taylor, Robert 145,
172, 688, 739
Taylor, Rosanna 214
Taylor, Ruhanna 192
Taylor, S. 180
Taylor, Samuel 80
Taylor, Sarah 257, 390,
410
Taylor, Sarah Ann 680
Taylor, Siles 390
Taylor, Sophia 391
Taylor, Susanna 49, 413
Taylor, Susannah 257,
680
Taylor, Tempe 272
Taylor, Theresa 398
Taylor, Thomas 192,
214, 639
Taylor, William 46, 54,
102, 192, 367, 468
Taylor, William H. 680
Taylor, Wm. 452
Taynor, Saray 469
Teagard, Abraham 162
Teagarden, Daniel 233,
238
Teagardin, Elizabeth 430
Teague, Conrad 560, 561
Teague, Elijah 273
Teague, Eve 560, 561
Teal, Edward 404
Teal, Eli M. 422
Teal, Jacob 233, 236
Teal, Nathaniel 413
Teal, Sarah 422
Teal, Walter 406
Teaman, F. 44
Teaquis, Neddy 463
Teas, Hugh 598
Teats, George 629
Teatsorth, Ann Elizabeth
583
Ted, William 102
Tedron, Naomi 619
Tedrow, George 598
Teebles, Reuben 80
Teel, Alexander 549
Teeman, Caroline 100
Teeples, Henry 683
Teetees, John 43
Teeters, A. 45
Teeters, A. S. 43
Teeters, Abraham 42
Teeters, Agnes 303
Teeters, Elisha 306

Teeters, John 306
Teeters, William 306
Teets, Rosanna 78
Teford, Aaron 349
Teford, Daniel 351
Teford, Elicabeth 352
Teford, Elizabeth 349,
351
Teford, George 349
Teford, Jacob 349, 351,
352
Teford, Jain 351
Teford, Ludwick 349
Teford, Molly 349
Teford, Susanna 349
Tegarden, George Jacob
172
Telafero, William 692
Teller, Edwin S. 591
Teller, Isaac 226
Tellman, Wilhelm 102
Tembelton, Mary 523
Temple, Francis 723
Temple, Michael (Jr.)
150
Temple, Peter 150
Temple, Rachel 150
Temple, William 306
Templer, James 172
Templeton, Betsey 714
Templeton, Catharine 527
Templeton, Daniel Gooden
98
Templeton, James 707
Templeton, Jane 527
Templeton, John 516, 540
Templeton, Margaret 164
Templeton, Thomas 714
Tenary, Thomas 273
Tence, Elizabeth 618
Tence, Teneror 618
Tenel, John 266
Tener, Jonathan 44, 45
Tenft, Polly 405
Tenner, Catarina 309
Tennerbill, Eliza 638
Tennery, Zepheniah B.
210
Tenney, Eligah 369
Tenny, H. G. 643
Tennyon, Richard 189
Tenor, Jacob 45
Tepton, Thomas 113
Ter Boss, Sarah 389
Tergue, Conrad 576
Terrel, John 461, 468
Terrell, David 606, 607
Terrell, John 263
Terry, Enos 360, 369,
570, 574
Terry, Nathan 361
Terry, Rebecca 558
Terry, Robert 56
Terry, Sarah 80
Terry, William 233,
570, 574, 575
Terry, Wm. 403, 558
Terwillegar, Ann 558
Terwillegar, Nathl. 558

Terwilleger, Nathaniel
561, 562
Test, Benjamin 306
Test, Isaac 306
Test, Richard Johnson
286
Test, Samuel 306
Test, Sarah 306
Tester, Conrod 1
Tester, Margaret 628
Tester, Mary Ann 99
Teter, Benjamin 614
Teter, Catherine 614
Teter, Thomas E. 614
Teterick, Jacob 542
Teterick, Michael 543
Teters, Catherine 105
Teters, Francis 105
Tethero, Michael 277
Tethero, Rachel 277
Tetirick, Danl. 542
Tetirick, William 546
Tetrack, Jacob (Jr.) 542
Tetrack, John (Jr.) 544
Tetrick, Daniel 543
Tetrick, Michael 543
Tetter, Susannah 588
Thacker, John 381
Thacker, Reuben 723
Thaker, John 381
Thannihill, Ruth 627
Tharp, Abner 184
Tharp, Alexander 591
Tharp, Eli W. 377, 381
Tharp, Elizabeth E. 380
Tharp, Hannah 184
Tharp, Isaac L. 377
Tharp, James 548
Tharp, John 556
Tharp, Joseph 757
Tharp, Nathan 184
Tharp, Sarah Ann 380
Tharpe, Robert 216
Thatcher, Esther 276,
300
Thatcher, Jesse 261
Thatcher, Joseph 282
Thatcher, Mary 268, 275
Thatcher, Ruth 256
Thatcher, Susannah 282
Thatcher, Thomas 268,
277, 282, 283
Thatcher, Thomas (Jr.)
277
Thatcher, Thomas (Sr.)
282
Thatcher, William 283
Thayer, Ephraim 315
Thayer, Naomi 651
Theaker, George 676
Theaker, George Albert
Parks 676
Theaker, George M. 676
Theaker, George
Whitfield 676
Theaker, Hugh Albert 676
Theaker, John 676
Theaker, Mary Elizabeth
676

Tipton, Samuel 598
Tipton, Thomas 118
Tipton, William 307
Tish, John 326
Tish, Sarah 326
Tissue, Edward 58
Tissue, Esther 58
Tissue, Isaac 58
Tissue, Jackson 58
Titerick, Jacob 542
Titsworth, Elizabeth 610
Titsworth, Joseph 58
Titsworth, William 451,
610
Tittle, Elizabeth 375
Tittle, Jacob 375
Tittle, James 375
Tittle, James M. 381
Tittle, Jonas 375
Tittle, Peter 375
Tittle, Polly 375
Tittle, Rachael 375
Tittle, Rachel 375
Tittle, Thomas I. 381
Titus, Philip 264
Titus, Priscilla 264
Titus, William (Sr.) 264
Tobias, Elizabeth 53
Tobin, Elijah 427
Tobin, James 419
Tod, John 521
Tod, Samuel 307
Todd, A. S. 197
Todd, Betsey 520
Todd, Catherine 301
Todd, Elizabeth 216
Todd, James 216
Todd, Joseph 719
Todd, Levi 235
Todd, Lot 307
Todd, Martin H. 592
Todd, Owen 36, 236, 553
Todd, Rebeckah 519
Todd, Robert 238, 570
Todd, Robt. 552
Todd, Sarah 309
Todhunter, Jacob 469
Todhunter, Margaret 463
Todhunter, Mary 467
Tolbert, Sampson 211
Tolbot, Wm. 11
Toler, Lucy 706
Toles, John 162
Toll, Jefferson 43
Tolman, Sally 438
Tolman, Samuel 438
Tom, Jacob 645
Tombleson, Leah 414
Tomlin, Elizabeth 273
Tomlin, Hannah 274
Tomlin, Peter 277
Tomlinson, Jesse 469
Tompkins, Benjamin 109
Tompkins, Bennet 235,
553
Tompkins, Daniel C. 64
Tompkins, Edward 109
Tompkins, Henry 510
Tompkins, James 510

Tompkins, John 510
Tompkins, Lewis 109
Tompkins, Margaret 109
Tompkins, Polly 77
Tompkins, Sarah 109, 510
Tompkins, William 510
Tompkins, Wm. 510
Tomplin, Esther 10
Tompson, William 102
Tomson, John 413
Tomson, Matthew 556
Tone, Bennet 642
Tone, Catharine 642
Tone, Henry 642
Tone, Jacob (Jr.) 642
Tone, Jacob (Sr.) 642
Tone, Josiah 642
Tone, Mary Ann 642
Tone, Susan 642
Tong, George 438
Tong, William 406
Tonkinson, Mary 225
Tonner, George 30
Tonner, Hannah 30
Tool, Mary 421
Toothaker, Clarisa 468
Toothaker, Mary 462
Topkins, Malvina 51
Torbet, Ambrose 453
Torbet, John 453
Torbet, William S. 453
Torence, James 186
Torode, Hannah 540
Torode, John 550
Torode, Mary 540
Torode, Peter 540
Torrence, Albert 572
Torrence, Emma 140, 167
Torrence, Geo. P. 509
Torrence, George P. 508
Torrence, Jane 519
Torrence, John 137, 138,
139, 140, 141, 162
Torrence, Mary 533
Torrence, Samuel H. 572
Torrence, Sophia 572
Torrence, William 527,
572
Torrence, William B. 572
Tossh, William 572
Totherow, Katherine 271
Totten, Jane 302
Totten, Rachel 475
Towel, Frances 304
Towell, Henry 273
Towell, Martha 284
Tower, William 754
Towers, James 638
Town, Delecta 221
Town, Elizabeth 216
Town, James 221
Town, Lucinda 221
Town, Nathan 221
Town, Ruth 221
Town, Sally 221
Townly, Robert 573
Townsend, Abigail 259
Townsend, Catharine 723
Townsend, Catherine 521

Townsend, Diana 163
Townsend, Edith 299
Townsend, Elizabeth 269,
303
Townsend, Eunice 487
Townsend, Hannah 699
Townsend, Isaac 307
Townsend, James 699
Townsend, Joseph 487,
259
Townsend, Judith 302
Townsend, Levy 521
Townsend, Lewis 307
Townsend, Lydia 299
Townsend, Martha 305
Townsend, Rebeckah 521
Townsend, Reed 417
Townsend, Ruth 299
Townsend, Talbot 307
Townsend, Thomas 699
Townsend, Unice 526
Townsend, William 699
Townsley, Alexander
515, 521, 527
Townsley, George 515,
521, 533
Townsley, Joanna 522
Townsley, John 527
Townsley, Jonanna 524
Townsley, Patsey 519
Townsley, Robert 235
Townsley, Sarah 515
Townsley, Thomas 533
Townsley, William 533
Traber, Joel 48
Tracey, John 469
Tracht, Adam 347
Tracy, Basil 729, 745
Tracy, Basil (Sr.) 729
Tracy, Daniel 645
Tracy, George 729
Tracy, Julis 45
Tracy, Mary 115
Tracy, Stephen 29
Tracy, William 729
Trader, Arthur 276
Trader, Moses 522
Tradfield, Susannah 298
Traebing, Henry 65
Traichler, Daniel 12
Transkoph, Elisabeth 348
Transkoph, Elizabeth 348
Trasey, Esther 238
Trasey, John 238
Trask, Orville C. 471
Trask, Sophronea 583
Travis, Asa 12
Travis, Assenth 390
Travis, F. M. 102
Travis, John 583
Travis, Permelia 381
Travis, Rebecca 530
Traxler, Emanuel 22
Trebein, William 50
Treber, Jefferson 43
Treeborn, John 68
Treece, Henry 585
Treene, Rebecca 163
Tremain, Susan 73

Trenany, Mary 463
Trenary, Jane 275
Trenary, Thomas 273
Trene, William 140
Tresse, Deborah 282
Tressler, Catherine 603
Trevenin, Nicholas 28
Trever, Jacob 6
Trevinin, Nicholas 490
Trexler, Emanuel 664
Trexler, Samuel 664
Tribbey, Asahel 258, 283
Tribbey, Ashahel 260
Trickler, Elizabeth 136
Trickler, Henry 136
Trieboldt, Henry 359
Trieschman, John 357
Trigg, Jacob 743
Triggott, William 613
Triggs, Salley 703
Trimble, Allen 612
Trimble, Carry A. 612
Trimble, Cyrus 612
Trimble, James 612, 695
Trimble, James A. 607, 608, 612
Trimble, John 316, 685, 699
Trimble, John A. 612
Trimble, Jonathan 278
Trimble, Margaret C. 612
Trimble, Mary 685
Trimble, Mathew 320
Trimble, Polly L. 612
Trimble, Ruth 752
Trimble, Sarah 695
Trimble, Virginny 278
Trimble, William 326, 437, 439
Trimble, Wm. A. 612
Trimmer, David B. 230
Trimmer, Mary Ann 230
Trimmer, Matthias 230
Trindle, Ann 726
Trindle, Anna 752
Trindle, Eliza 752
Trindle, Elizabeth 726
Trindle, Hannah 726
Trindle, Matilda 726, 752
Trindle, Peggy 726
Trindle, Rebecca 726, 752
Trindle, Ruth 726
Trindle, Sally 726
Trindle, W. 752
Trindle, William 725, 726, 751, 752
Triplett, Christopher C. 616
Triplett, Elizabeth 616
Triplett, James 616
Triplett, John 608, 616
Triplett, John (Jr.) 616
Triplett, John (Sr.) 616
Triplett, John M. 608
Triplett, Wm. M. 616
Tripp, Calvin T. 415
Tripp, Ira 355

Tripp, Russ 80
Tripp, William 629
Tripper, John 747
Trippy, George 307
Trisler, Catherine 603
Tritt, Harriett 305
Tritt, Rachel 293
Trivet, Esther 605
Trivet, Joseph 605
Trobridge, Nathaniel 720
Trollinger, Jacob 535
Tropf, Catharina 344
Tropf, Georg Friedrich 346
Tropf, Heinrich 344
Tropf, Jacob Friedrich 344, 346
Tropf, Louisa 344
Tropf, Reinhardt 344
Tropf, Reinhart 346
Trostel, Carl 348
Trothergill, Eliziah 463
Trott, John 329, 549
Trotter, Christian 459
Trotter, Patsy 459
Trotter, Polly 459
Trotter, William R. 276
Trout, Abraham 219
Trout, Abrm. 413
Trout, Catharine L. 219
Trout, Eliza 579
Trout, Henry 745
Trout, Noah 418
Troutman, Elizabeth 136
Troutman, John 136
Troutman, Peter 136
Trovinger, Sarah 419
Trowbridge, Abner 698
Troxel, Elijah 381
Troxel, Polly 530
Troxell, Frederick 167
Troxell, Nancy 163
Truasdale, Ann 9
Truax, Rachel 466
Trubee, Catharine 523
Trubee, John 527
Trubey, Mary 533
Truby, Elizabeth 520
Truby, Jacob 522
Truby, John 604
Trude, Rachael 581
True, Betsey 518
True, Josiah 85
True, Polly B. 519
True, Sarah 530
Truit, James 42, 43
Truitt, --- 36
Truitt, James 1, 45
Truitt, Joshua 7
Truitt, Parker 46
Truitt, Robert 24
Trumble, Mary 397
Trumbo, Jacob 745
Trumbull, George W. 95
Trumbull, James 375
Trump, Andrew Jackson 592
Trump, P. Van 419
Truxell, Jacob 59

Truxell, Rebecca 59
Tryon, Elijah 80
Tubbs, Laura 72, 73
Tucker, Anna 300
Tucker, Clementy 308
Tucker, Drusilla 80
Tucker, Elizabeth 199
Tucker, George W. 609
Tucker, Isaac 199
Tucker, J. W. 624
Tucker, Jno. (II) 80
Tucker, John 199
Tucker, Lydia 519
Tucker, Michael 210
Tucker, Polly 481
Tucker, Sarah 290
Tucker, Thomas R. 4
Tukle, Mathus 307
Tull, William 707
Tulling, William 102
Tullis, John 583
Tulter, David 540
Tumble, Daniel 399
Tumble, Isaac 399
Tumblson, Bolly 404
Tumbly, Elizabeth 133
Tumelston, Polly 11
Tumelston, Prisela 11
Tumelston, Samuel 12
Tumlinson, James 714
Tunget, Mary 51
Tunget, Peter 55
Tunis, Christiana 732
Tunis, Nehemiah 556
Tunnell, Lovey W. 704
Tupper, Anselem 28
Tupper, Benj. 27
Tupper, Benjamin 688
Tupper, Edward White 487
Tupper, G. W. 485
Turdall, William 563
Turk, John 117
Turman, Margaret 226
Turman, Rhoda 226
Turnbaugh, Samuel 527
Turnbell, James 221
Turnbull, Alexander 501, 506, 533
Turnbull, David 501
Turnbull, Elizabeth 501
Turnbull, Gilbert 501
Turnbull, James 501
Turnbull, John 501
Turnbull, Margaret 501
Turnbull, Mary Ann 501
Turnbull, Nancy 501
Turnbull, Sarah 501, 506
Turnbull, Susanah 501
Turnbull, Thomas 501
Turnbull, William 501
Turnbull, Wm. 501, 502
Turner, . . . enna 654
Turner, Andrew 469
Turner, Anne 523
Turner, Aquila 226
Turner, Benjamin 736
Turner, Caleb 658
Turner, Caroline 397
Turner, Charles 173

Turner, Chloe 701
Turner, Cyrus 654
Turner, Eleanor 523
Turner, Eliza 736
Turner, Elizabeth 275,
415, 536, 633
Turner, F. B. M. 397
Turner, George 571, 736
Turner, George
Washington 633
Turner, Hannah 521
Turner, Ienpia 422
Turner, James 189, 736
Turner, James (Sr.) 192
Turner, James C. 404
Turner, James E. 192
Turner, Jane 736
Turner, Jesse 123
Turner, John 63, 273,
307, 311, 538
Turner, Jos. 413
Turner, Kesiah 523
Turner, Lee 63
Turner, Levi 536
Turner, Levin 736
Turner, Margaret 269
Turner, Maria 415
Turner, Mary 300, 520,
526
Turner, Mary P. 654
Turner, Matilda 736
Turner, Matthias 162
Turner, McPherson 422
Turner, Nancy 63, 410,
525
Turner, Polly 736
Turner, Robert 533
Turner, Samuel 226,
664, 736
Turner, Sarah 523
Turner, Thomas 701
Turner, Thos. 596
Turner, Walter 269, 326
Turner, William 226, 658
Turner, William M. 192
Turnett, Thomas 443
Turnipseed, Benjamin 469
Turnipseed, Cathareine
301
Turnipseed, Christian
458
Turnipseed, Elizabeth
457
Turnipseed, George 457
Turnipseed, Henry 457
Turnipseed, Jackson 458
Turnipseed, Morgan 457
Turnipseed, Susannah 293
Turpin, Philip 238
Turton, Elizabeth 53
Tury, Lewis 307
Tuttle, Caleb 226
Tuttle, Chandler 451
Tuttle, Cyrus 83
Tuttle, David 226
Tuttle, Joel (Rev.) 328
Tuttle, Thadius 205
Tuttor, Amos 527
Tutweiler, Thos. 416

Twaddle, John 678
Twaddle, Joseph 191
Tway, John 455
Tway, Nathaniel 469
Tweed, Jane 121
Tweed, Samuel 12
Tweedy, John 684
Tweedy, Margaret 684
Tweedy, Sarah 684
Tweedy, William 684
Tweezey, Abel 115
Twezey, Abel 115
Twigg, Charles 746
Twining, Edward W. 757
Twining, Elmira 757
Twining, Jacob 583
Twining, Jenet 757
Twining, Jennet 757
Twining, Lavingston 757
Twining, Lewis 755
Twining, Merrick S. 757
Twinmon, Laura 649
Twitchel, Mary 466
Twitchel, Sarah 77
Tyhurst, Solomon 755
Tyler, Drusella 136
Tyler, Elenor 523
Tyler, Isaac 477
Tyler, Margaret 233
Tyler, Prudence 11
Tyler, Robert 233

--- U ---

Ulet, Thomas 12
Ulin, Eliza 582
Ulin, John 592
Ulin, John P. 592
Ulmer, Adam 336, 338
Ulmer, Israel 338
Ulmer, Katharina 336,
338
Ulmer, Wilhelm 336
Ulmer, Wilhelmia 336
Ulmsted, Aaron 650
Ulmsted, Elizabeth 650
Ulmsted, John 650
Ulry, Jacob 233
Umbenhower, Abraham 747
Umphries, Elizabeth 660
Umphries, Joseph 307
Umstatte, John 366
Umstot, Peter 544
Undersood, Elizabeth 292
Underwood, Hannah 307
Underwood, James 198
Underwood, John 307, 664
Underwood, Mary 664
Underwood, Maryon 198
Underwood, Nancy 306
Underwood, Robert 58
Underwood, Ruth 306
Underwood, Sarah 296
Underwood, Stephen 173
Underwood, Susannah 296
Underwood, Thomas 639
Underwood, William 276

Unger, Henry 722
Unkefer, John 307
Untiet, Casper 89
Untiet, Clara 89
Untiet, Maria 89
Untiet, Mary 89
Updegraff, J. S. 60
Updegraff, James 680
Updegraff, Josiah 114
Updike, Mary 193
Upp, Lydia 463
Upson, Jane 11
Uptoon, Hannah 412
Urmston, Mary 171
Urmston, Samuel 173
Urnestand, David 177
Urnsted, Emanuel 102
Urquehart, Alexander 598
Urwell, George 664
Ustick, Abner 700
Ustick, W. A. 447
Utley, Amos 389
Utsler, Henry 633
Utts, Henry 22
Utzler, Fanny 414

--- V ---

Vaber, Frederica 601
Vail, Aaron 140, 141, 176
Vail, Catharine 176
Vail, Emma 168
Vail, Henry 162
Vail, Hugh 176
Vail, Isaac 175
Vail, Jessie 403
Vail, Mary 176
Vail, Moses 140, 176
Vail, Phobal 141
Vail, Randal 176
Vail, Randolph 167
Vail, Sally 165
Vail, Samuel 176
Vail, Sarah 176
Vail, Shobal 176
Vail, Shubal 141
Vail, Stephen 141, 176
Vail, Thomas 173
Vail, William 173
Valentine, Amos 141
Valentine, Crain 61, 63
Valentine, Cram 50
Valentine, David 205
Valentine, Hannah 55
Valentine, John 583
Valentine, Jonathan 226
Valentine, Lana 591
Valentine, Mary 160
Valentine, Sarah 205
Valentine, William H. 59
Vallen, Francis 491
Vallentine, Amos 140
Valling, Stephen 64
Vallon, Francis 491
Valodin, Francis 25,
489, 491, 496, 497,
498

952

Wagner, Mary 102, 352, 579
Wagner, Maryan Julyan 350
Wagner, Samuel 102, 592
Wagner, Stephan 350
Wagoner, --- 374
Wagoner, Anthony 592
Wagoner, Barbary 582
Wagoner, Elizabeth 407
Wagoner, George 352
Wagoner, John 44, 319
Wagoner, Kitty 412
Wagoner, Maria 352
Wagoner, Mary 319, 411
Wagoner, Ruth 125
Wagstaff, James 550
Wagstaff, John 547
Wagy, Elizabeth 734
Wagy, John 734
Wahl, Winebald 359
Waide, Elizabeth 697
Wait, Caroline 604
Wait, Tracy L. 381
Waite, Charles 235
Waite, Isabella 48
Waite, John 55
Waite, Jonathan 5, 48
Waite, Sarah 6
Waites, Joseph 722
Waits, Rachel 127
Wakefield, Auratha 713
Wakefield, E. W. 711
Wakefield, Elnathan W. 708
Wakefield, Harriet 713
Wakefield, Marinda 708, 713
Wakefield, Peter 710, 717
Wakefield, Rebecca 713
Wakefield, Sarah 713
Wakefield, Thomas L. 713
Wakefield, Thomas W. 713
Wakefield, Timothy 708, 711, 713
Wakeman, Gideon 279
Wakeman, Jane 257
Walace, Reuben 209
Walbridge, Caulina 704
Walburn, Catherine 223
Waldean, George 658
Walden, Francis 72
Walden, J. M. 42
Walden, John O. 72
Walden, Joseph M. 6
Walden, Mary 72
Waldo, Carlton 173
Waldoe, Albert 135
Waldoe, Carlton 135
Waldoe, Rhoda 135
Waldren, Elizabeth 656
Waldren, Phillip 658
Waldren, Solomon 658
Waldron, Cynthia 654
Waldron, Elijah 43
Waldron, Garret 162
Wales, Ann 737
Wales, Barbara 474

Wales, John 737
Walfenbarger, Betsey 481
Walfinbarger, John 481
Walgamot, David 549
Walin, Elias 139
Walk, John 96
Walke, Anthony 203
Walker, Alexander 3, 686, 697
Walker, Amelia 289
Walker, Ann 83, 581
Walker, Anna 538
Walker, Azel 278
Walker, B. B. 402
Walker, Benjain 307
Walker, Benjamin 684
Walker, Catherine 270, 386
Walker, Christina Elizabeth 417
Walker, Cintha 505
Walker, Cornelius 747
Walker, David 397, 684
Walker, Elizabeth 660, 684
Walker, Elizabeth C. 505
Walker, Emily 684
Walker, Evelina 80
Walker, Frances Ann 397
Walker, Geo. L. B. 545
Walker, George 307, 538
Walker, George L. B. 545
Walker, Hannah 124, 397, 697, 734
Walker, Henry 458
Walker, Horation 458
Walker, Isaac 386, 684
Walker, James 3, 688, 697
Walker, James (Jr.) 686, 697
Walker, Jeremiah 614
Walker, Jesse 697
Walker, Joel 386
Walker, John 38, 307, 386, 684, 697
Walker, John R. 386
Walker, John W. 505
Walker, Jonathan 684
Walker, Jos. 687, 688, 689
Walker, Joseph 3, 4, 139, 149, 686, 687, 689, 697
Walker, Lucinda 593
Walker, Lydia 288, 378
Walker, Madison 684
Walker, Margaret 593
Walker, Maria 77, 386
Walker, Martha Ann 684
Walker, Mary 74, 302, 434, 641
Walker, Mary Ann 684
Walker, Mary P. 505
Walker, Mathew 386
Walker, Mordecai 256
Walker, Nancy 386, 581, 686, 687, 688, 689
Walker, Perry G. 397

Walker, Philip 697
Walker, Polly 697
Walker, Rebecca 131, 418
Walker, Robert 238, 697
Walker, Robert (Jr.) 276
Walker, Robt. 687
Walker, Samuel 239
Walker, Samuel L. 505
Walker, Sarah 302, 697
Walker, Sarah Ann 641
Walker, Thomas 80, 195
Walker, W. John 564
Walker, William 323, 386, 684
Walker, William H. 505
Walker, Zacariah 505
Walkup, Samuel 6
Wall, Azariah 260
Wall, Daniel 179
Wall, Elizabeth 667
Wall, Frank 374
Wall, John 571, 572
Wall, Susannah E. 179
Wallace, Brice W. 639
Wallace, Cadwalader 444
Wallace, Cadwallader 202
Wallace, David 459
Wallace, Deborah 183, 560
Wallace, E. S. 230
Wallace, Elaner 183
Wallace, Elizabeth S. 230
Wallace, Ellen 125
Wallace, Eloner 183
Wallace, Hugh M. 182, 215
Wallace, Isaac 125
Wallace, James 183, 230, 681
Wallace, Jane 404
Wallace, John 5, 183, 185, 194, 459, 555
Wallace, Jonathan 512
Wallace, Jonathan H. 522
Wallace, Joseph 183
Wallace, Levi 459
Wallace, Maria 532
Wallace, Mary E. R. 230
Wallace, Matthew G. 560
Wallace, Moses 183
Wallace, Nancy 183
Wallace, Patience 687
Wallace, Rachel 183
Wallace, Reuben 186, 207, 208
Wallace, Reubin 185
Wallace, Robert 107
Wallace, Ross 183
Wallace, Rueben 184
Wallace, Ruth 444
Wallace, Sarah 519
Wallace, Tallaferro 718, 720
Wallace, Thomas 183, 459
Wallace, Tuften 459
Wallace, W. 634, 636
Wallace, William 142, 183, 459, 552, 566, 592, 686

Weir, Susannah 79
Weir, Thomas 550
Weirts, John 414
Weis, Atalia 342
Weis, Emanual 342
Weis, Israel 342
Weis, Maria Catharina 343
Weis, Mary 346
Weis, Samuel 342
Weisbrod, Cecelia 578
Weisbrod, Clement L. 578
Weisbrod, J. C. 578
Weisbrod, M. 578
Weisbrod, Mary 578
Weisbrod, Minerva 578
Weiser, Catharine 136
Weiser, George 136
Weiser, Jacob 136
Weisleder, Magdalena 296
Weiss, Jacob 80
Weitzel, Henry 353
Welch, Aaron 383
Welch, Abbey Jane 651
Welch, Abigail 302
Welch, Andrew 533
Welch, Asahel 392
Welch, Catharine 264, 296
Welch, Content 383
Welch, Daniel 264, 598
Welch, David 385
Welch, Henry 256, 264, 264
Welch, Jacob 307
Welch, Jane 295, 653
Welch, John 689
Welch, Joseph 317, 320
Welch, Lewis 307
Welch, Lorenzo C. 264
Welch, Loretta 383
Welch, Luther 383
Welch, Mary 296
Welch, Philina 383
Welch, Ruth 383
Welch, Samuel 653
Welch, Susanna 383
Welch, T. 287
Welch, Turner 276
Welch, William 162, 173, 383
Weld, Alfred 80
Weldon, Christopher 322
Weldon, Elizabeth 229
Weldon, Frederick 322
Weldon, George 322
Weldon, George Henry 229
Weldon, Jacob 322
Weldon, James 477
Weldon, John 322, 638
Weldon, Joseph 229
Weldon, Michael 322
Weldon, Richard 80
Weldon, Ruhannah 638
Weldon, Susannah 638
Weli, Johannes 440
Weliner, Francis 57
Welker, Cahriot 307
Welker, Henry 429

Welker, John 307
Welker, Joseph 418
Welker, Philip 688
Welker, Sariah 310
Welker, William 307, 311
Well, Haldy 519
Well, Jacob G. 665
Wellbarger, Mary 479
Weller, Henry 418
Weller, Margaret 52
Weller, Sarah 180
Weller, Susanna 57
Weller, William 64
Wellerding, Mary Cath. 100
Welling, John (Sr.) 598
Wellman, Henrietta 88
Wellman, Herman F. 88
Wellman, Herman Frederick 88
Wellman, James 658
Wellman, Sophia Margaret 88
Wells, Alexander 677
Wells, Alice 677
Wells, Ann 677
Wells, Barshaba 706
Wells, Cadwalader 677
Wells, Cadwalider 677
Wells, Calvin 647
Wells, Charles 506
Wells, Delila 601
Wells, Delilah 108
Wells, Eleanor 677
Wells, Elizabeth 133, 601, 722
Wells, Farries 102
Wells, Genny 706
Wells, George 438
Wells, George Mitchell 677
Wells, Harris 97
Wells, Henry 381, 743
Wells, Honor 438
Wells, Hugh 414
Wells, Isaac 307
Wells, James 438, 737
Wells, John 438, 667, 677
Wells, Joseph 604
Wells, Levi 547, 677
Wells, Margaret Jane 677
Wells, Maria 677
Wells, Mary 307, 438, 603
Wells, Merca Cass Ander 677
Wells, N. 108
Wells, Nancy 379, 702
Wells, Nichols 118
Wells, Oliver 133
Wells, Perequin 533
Wells, Prudencia 477
Wells, Rachel 410, 438
Wells, Robert T. 544
Wells, Sally 438
Wells, Sanford 665
Wells, Sue W. 133
Wells, Susan 647

Wells, Thomas 438
Wells, William 567, 686, 726
Wells, Wm. 469, 686
Wells, Zemariah 481
Welsh, Crawford 119
Welsh, Elizabeth 108
Welsh, George 414
Welsh, Hannah 532, 723
Welsh, James 357
Welsh, Jas. 108
Welsh, Joseph 318
Welsh, Lamy 134
Welsh, Marcissa A. 51
Welsh, Mary 134
Welsted, David F. 604
Weltner, John 643
Welty, Saloman 642
Weltz, Christian 419
Wendelin, B. A. 89
Wenger, George 357
Wenner, Christopher 356
Wentermote, Judy 531
Wenzell, Ann 106
Wenzell, Lewis 106
Werden, William 195
Werman, Henry 307
Werner, Susana 422
Werse, Leonard 481
Werst, Andrew 57
Werstenberger, Susanna 404
Wert, Anna M. 74
Wertsbaugh, John 728
Wertwine, Henry 404
Wertz, George 229
Wertz, John 418
Wese, Leonard 481
Wese, Peter 665
Wessler, Mary 380
Wessler, Solomon 381
West, Abner 213
West, Amillia 275
West, Amos 665
West, Benjamin 213, 621, 645
West, Catherine 213
West, Deborah 213
West, Edward 124
West, Elenor 40
West, Eli (Sr.) 449
West, Eliza 213
West, Elizabeth 620, 645
West, Eppe 463
West, Henry 167
West, Isaac 80
West, James 276
West, Jane 526
West, John 40, 187, 193, 645, 667
West, Joseph 226
West, Julian 213
West, Mary 645
West, Nancy 511, 525
West, Owen 256
West, Owen (Jr.) 278
West, Polly 213
West, Robert 40
West, Rose Ann 645

960

West, Sarah   124
West, Susan   645
West, Thomas   213
West, William   276, 278,
   528, 645, 665
Westbay, Matthias   102
Westbrook, Joseph   12
Westbrook, Lucinda   589
Westcoat, Simanthey   82
Westcott, Betsey   704
Westcott, Rhodes   716
Westenberger, John (Jr.)
   419
Westerfield, John H.   346
Western, John   381
Westfall, Absalom   369
Westfall, Absolem   371
Westfall, Andrew   369
Westfall, Ann   510, 522
Westfall, Celista   511
Westfall, Cynthia   511
Westfall, Elbert   511
Westfall, Eli   369, 658
Westfall, Elizabeth
   369, 525
Westfall, George   361
Westfall, Hannah   301
Westfall, Harvey   653
Westfall, Jacob   363,
   369, 371
Westfall, James   511
Westfall, Job   369
Westfall, Job (Sr.)   361
Westfall, Joel   369, 512
Westfall, John   369,
   369, 370, 371, 502,
   528, 533
Westfall, Jonathan   512,
   528
Westfall, Lavinia   531
Westfall, Levi   308, 369
Westfall, Margaret   369
Westfall, Marybe   366
Westfall, Merba   366
Westfall, Orepenia   526
Westfall, Pegey   369
Westfall, Simpson   369
Westfall, Tabitha   657
Westfall, W.   371
Westfall, William   369
Westhaver, John   630
Westlake, William   457
Weston, Mary C.   59
Westover, E.   745
Weterect, Anna Margaret
   309
Wetherill, Ada   727
Wetherill, Amelia   727
Wetherill, Calvin   727
Wetherill, Clement   727
Wetherill, Comfort   727
Wetherill, Daniel   727
Wetherill, Hannah   727
Wetherill, Luther   727
Wetherill, Marquis   727
Wetherill, Phebe   727
Wetherill, Polly   727
Wetsel, Peggy   658
Wetson, Robert   592

Wettsbough, Judith   414
Wetzle, Gust   401
Wever, John   12
Weyant, Susannah   591
Weyra . . . ch,
   Margaretha   347
Whaley, Arden   83
Whaley, David   83
Whaley, David W.   80
Whaley, Hannah   81
Whaley, Mary   657
Whaley, Silas   665
Whalley, Sarah   9
Whan, William   308
Wharton, George
   Washington   121
Wharton, John   547
Whealin, Frederick   308
Wheally, Thomas   414
Wheals, Mary   12
Wheatley, Brayeda   421
Wheatley, Henry (Jr.)
   665
Wheatley, Rosan   657
Wheaton, Ephriam   44
Wheelan, George   331
Wheeler, Amos   594
Wheeler, Anna   692
Wheeler, H. N.   592
Wheeler, Horatio N.   712
Wheeler, Irena   81
Wheeler, Jacob   558,
   567, 568, 574
Wheeler, Joanna   558
Wheeler, John   690
Wheeler, Joseph   592,
   714, 720
Wheeler, Martha   411
Wheeler, Mary Ann   381
Wheeler, Minerva   78
Wheeler, P.   594
Wheeler, Rezin   549
Wheeler, Samuel   692
Wheeler, Sarah   69
Wheeler, Stephen   560,
   564
Wheeler, William   481
Whetsel, Catharine   657
Whetsel, John   658
Whetsel, Sarah   594
Whetsell, John   667
Whetstone, Abijah   241
Whetstone, Abraham   50
Whetstone, Caroline   381
Whetstone, Cynthia   241
Whetstone, Elizabeth
   57, 333
Whetstone, Elnathan   241
Whetstone, Frances   241
Whetstone, George   414
Whetstone, Henry   57
Whetstone, Jacob   241
Whetstone, James   57
Whetstone, Jasper   241
Whetstone, John   57, 102,
   237, 241, 560, 667
Whetstone, Lucinda   241
Whetstone, Margaret   57
Whetstone, Mary Jane   101

Whetstone, Michael   57
Whetstone, Nancy   241
Whetstone, Peter   334
Whetstone, Rhoda   241
Whetstone, Samuel   54,
   102, 334
Whetstone, Sarah   57
Whetstone, William   57
Whetzel, Margary   656
Whickar, Matthew   522
Whicker, John   528
Whicker, Sarah   527
Whilesy, Maria Finetta
   422
Whinery, John   281
Whinery, Joseph   273
Whinery, Patsey   281
Whinery, Solomon   281
Whinery, William   308
Whinery, Zinni   308
Whinnery, James   308
Whinnery, James Arthur
   259
Whinnery, Jane   290
Whinnery, John   259, 308
Whipple, Eliza   643
Whipple, J.   639, 641
Whipple, John G.   643
Whipple, Joseph   637
Whisker, Isaac   665
Whisler, Jacob   574
Whitacre, Aaron   308, 311
Whitacre, Ann   305
Whitacre, Asa   308
Whitacre, Catharine   292
Whitacre, Cornelius   308,
   311
Whitacre, Daniel   308
Whitacre, Elizabeth   288,
   300
Whitacre, Hannah   293
Whitacre, Isaac   308
Whitacre, J.   373
Whitacre, J. A.   373
Whitacre, J. J.   373
Whitacre, John   308,
   360, 362, 364
Whitacre, Kesiah   306
Whitacre, Leticia   295
Whitacre, Lizza   373
Whitacre, Martha   298
Whitacre, Nancy   295
Whitacre, Patrience   288
Whitacre, Phebe   292, 293
Whitacre, Sarah   309
Whitacre, Stephen   308
Whitaker, Catharine   577
Whitaker, Deacon   665
Whitaker, Eli   440
Whitaker, Elisha   268
Whitaker, Elizabeth   262
Whitaker, Jonathan   173
Whitaker, Oliver   259,
   262, 287
Whitaker, Peter S.   577
Whitaker, William   258
Whitam, Morris   240
Whitcomb, Catherine   378
Whitcraft, Thomas   640

White, --- 609
White, A. 642, 645
White, Adam 51, 52, 53, 54, 55
White, Adams 54
White, Alexander 12, 638
White, Andrew 469
White, Bartlet 621
White, Betsey 626
White, Catharine 532
White, Charles 375
White, Clarinda 81
White, Clarissa 651
White, Daniel 622
White, David 238, 599, 621, 622, 623, 633, 707
White, Eliza 422
White, Elizabeth 455, 535, 621
White, George 128, 414
White, Harriet 333
White, Horace 83
White, Isaac 80, 681
White, Jacob 570, 571, 574, 752
White, Jacob (Jr.) 565
White, James 137, 138, 174, 432, 555, 556, 565, 633, 658, 707, 717
White, Jane 621
White, Jas. 12
White, Jemima 268, 275
White, Johannah 574
White, John 33, 173, 414, 533, 621, 658, 667, 723, 748
White, John (Jr.) 749
White, Jonathan 48, 622
White, Joseph 12, 528
White, Joshua 268
White, Josiah 435
White, Louisa 525, 621
White, Margaret 700
White, Mary 142, 168, 534, 622
White, Melinda 521
White, Nancy 622, 625, 628, 657, 706
White, Noah 384
White, Orream 599
White, Osmond 623
White, Patience 622
White, Peter 622
White, Robert 470
White, Sally 455, 630
White, Samuel 420, 469, 623
White, Sarah 164, 435
White, Smith 621, 622
White, Solomon 42
White, Tabitha 137
White, Tabithey 174
White, Thaddeus 621, 622
White, Thomas 118, 142, 143
White, Triphene 584
White, Wiley 622

White, William 455, 533, 592, 681
Whitecraft, Thomas 645
Whiteharts, John 592
Whitehead, Abner 745
Whitehead, Edward 665
Whitehead, Gerusha 151
Whitehead, Stout 151
Whitehead, Thomas 144
Whitehill, Thos. (Jr.) 545
Whitehouse, Hannah 432
Whitehunt, John 416
Whitehurst, John 416
Whiteleather, Christian 308
Whiteleather, Elizabeth 309
Whiteleather, John 308
Whiteleather, Mary 308
Whiteley, Christiany 215
Whiteley, John 215, 216
Whiteman, Benj. 516
Whiteman, Catharine 213
Whiteman, Eliza 590
Whiteman, Letticia 526
Whiteney, Geo. 396
Whitham, Hannah 239
Whitham, Morris 239
Whitham, Perry 110
Whithartt, John 592
Whitinger, Deborah 142, 145
Whitinger, Francis 143, 167
Whitinger, Francis (Jr.) 142, 145
Whitinger, Henry 142
Whitinger, Jacob 130, 131, 142
Whitinger, James 143
Whitinger, Joel 130
Whitinger, Mary 143, 169
Whitinger, Nicholas 143
Whitingin, Nicholas 383
Whitlock, J. 45
Whitman, Henry 418
Whitman, Julia Ann 582
Whitmore, John (Rev.) 98
Whitmore, Miles 162
Whitney, A. M. 651
Whitney, Clarissa 396
Whitney, Elisha 638
Whitney, Eliza 396
Whitney, Eunice 638
Whitney, George 396
Whitney, Maranda S. 653
Whitney, Margaret 652
Whitney, Margaret H. 631
Whitring, Frances 506
Whitrow, William 308
Whitsel, Henry 406, 414
Whitsel, Margary 656
Whitsell, Emily 466
Whitsell, Jacob 665
Whitson, John 173, 286
Whitson, Samil 280
Whitson, Samuel 281
Whitstone, Abraham 463

Whitstone, John 238
Whittaker, Rhoda 274
Whittemore, Nathan M. 746
Whitten, Eliza 315
Whitten, Hanna 481
Whitten, Joanna 315
Whitten, Nanlua 315
Whitten, Ranson 481
Whitten, Robert 315
Whitten, Thomas 540
Whitten, Walter 714
Whitten, William 315
Whittesey, Susanna 628
Whittlesey, Charles 665
Whittlesy, Roger Newton 640
Whitworth, John 568
Wians, George 583
Wibright, William 455
Wichers, Maria 601
Wick, John 463
Wickams, Peter 29
Wickart, Mary 296
Wickel, Catherine 413
Wicker, Tally 665
Wickerham, Peter 7
Wickerhan, Peter 14
Wickersham, Catharine 536
Wickersham, Ellis 308
Wickersham, Enoch 285
Wickersham, George 308
Wickersham, Jacob 4, 7, 44, 552
Wickersham, John 4, 42, 44
Wickersham, Margaret 285
Wickersham, Peter 44
Wickersham, Thomas 308
Wickham, Emiline 580
Wickham, J. E. 584
Wickham, Lucy 581
Wickham, Polly 80
Wickham, Seth (Rev.) 321
Wickham, William 586
Wickiel, Rebecca 531
Wickisson, Abagail 582
Wickizer, Elizabeth 416
Wickoff, Anna 214
Wicks, Joseph 68
Wicks, Wm. 463
Wickwine, William 599
Wicoff, Elleanor 94
Wicoff, Jacob 549
Widener, Jacob 149, 158
Widener, Jacob (Jr.) 173
Wider, Henry 690
Widericht, Elizabeth 306
Widner, John G. 659
Wiechens, Maria 601
Wiemann, Anna Marie 53
Wiemann, Maria A. 470
Wiemeyer, Adelheit 89
Wiemeyer, Christopher H. 89
Wiemeyer, John W. 89
Wiemeyer, John William 89

963

967

Wolford, Catharine 582
Wolford, Elizabeth Elen 584
Wolford, George W. 584
Wolford, Gideon 592
Wolford, Jeremiah 583, 584
Wolford, John 584
Wolford, Mary Ann 584
Wolford, Mary S. 584
Wolford, Massy 580
Wolford, Sarah 584
Wolford, Washington 583
Wollard, --- 246
Wollard, Rachel 274
Wollery, Henry G. 604
Wollet, Catharine 55
Wollet, Daniel 55
Wollet, Elizabeth 55
Wollet, George 60
Wollet, Lydia 55
Wollet, Mary 55
Wollet, Michael 55
Wollet, Nancy 55
Wollet, Philip 55, 60
Wollet, Samuel 53, 55
Wollet, Solomon 51, 55
Wollett, Ann Eliza 73
Wollett, Catherine 603
Wollihan, Sarah 288
Wollivus, Anne 280
Wollman, Kesiah 307
Wollman, Mary Ann 305
Wollman, Susanna 299
Wollum, Sally 304
Wolsey, John T. 103
Wolters, Saml. 416
Woltz, Silas 633
Wolum, Sally 311
Wolvy, Anne 280
Womble, Edward 528
Womble, Silvia 526
Womelsdorff, Michael 481
Wone, Mary 225
Woocock, Sarah 86
Woocs, Hetty 113
Wood, Aaron 198
Wood, Abraham H. 543
Wood, Albert G. 49
Wood, Andrew 227
Wood, Anna M. 723
Wood, Anthony S. 155
Wood, Benjamin 152, 154, 155, 238
Wood, Charles 143, 145
Wood, Christopher 60
Wood, Daniel 384, 398
Wood, David 12, 234, 384, 735
Wood, Desire 392
Wood, Dianah 143, 145
Wood, Elijah 113
Wood, Elizabeth 381
Wood, Enoch 198
Wood, F. H. 398
Wood, Gilbert 420
Wood, Harriet 735
Wood, Hetty 113
Wood, Isaac 227

Wood, Isaac S. 592
Wood, Isabella 155
Wood, Israel 167
Wood, James 173, 398
Wood, James C. 365
Wood, Jane 152
Wood, Jesse 198
Wood, Joel 463
Wood, John 735
Wood, Jonathan (Jr.) 392
Wood, Joseph 155
Wood, Judith 579
Wood, Leonard 735
Wood, Luther 735
Wood, Lydia 198
Wood, Margaret 415
Wood, Mary 170, 198, 305, 311
Wood, Maryon 198
Wood, Mathew 477
Wood, Minnie J. 398
Wood, Mose 415
Wood, Moses 198
Wood, Nancy 168
Wood, Orpha 381
Wood, Paulus Emelius 707
Wood, Phebe 398
Wood, Rachel 198
Wood, Rebecca 154, 630
Wood, Richard 37, 39, 747
Wood, Samiramas 49
Wood, Saml. R. 45
Wood, Samuel R. 4, 6
Wood, Sarah 227
Wood, Solomon 276
Wood, William 173, 198, 598
Wood, Wm. 145, 198, 594
Wood, Zachariah 598
Woodard, Ichabord (Sr.) 72
Woodard, Isaac M. 469
Woodard, Joseph 534
Woodard, Martha 72
Woodard, Polly 519
Woodard, William 72
Woodbridge, Dudley (Jr.) 31
Woodbridge, John 31
Woodbridge, Wm. (Rev.) 84
Woodburn, John 70, 308
Woodburn, Robert 686
Woodburn, Sarah 686
Woodbury, Nathan 56, 85, 97
Woodbury, Polly 80
Woodcox, A. M. 376
Woodcox, Sarah J. 379
Wooden, James 364
Wooden, Samuel 658
Wooderd, Isaac W. 463
Woodley, Robert 53
Woodman, Rachel 222
Woodmansee, Lydia 135
Woodmansee, Samuel H. 287
Woodmansee, Thomas 287

Woodmeyer, Mary Engel Louisa 100
Woodred, John 70
Woodring, Kitty 409
Woodrow, Alexander 2
Woodrow, Alexr. 48
Woodrow, Henry 547
Woodrow, Joseph 607
Woodrow, Zlexr. 3
Woodruff, Chauncey 654
Woodruff, Daniel 135
Woodruff, Elijah 583
Woodruff, Eliza 135
Woodruff, Elizabeth 417
Woodruff, Eunice 654
Woodruff, Geo. H. 654
Woodruff, Hannah 582
Woodruff, Isaac 437
Woodruff, Israel 144
Woodruff, Jesse 173
Woodruff, Joel 277
Woodruff, Mary 165
Woodruff, Mary Ann 580
Woodruff, Parmelia 165
Woodruff, Sarah 166, 169
Woodruff, Stephen 135
Woodruff, Weald 748
Woodruff, William 640
Woods, --- 754
Woods, Albirda 312
Woods, Alexander 205
Woods, Amos J. 639
Woods, Anna 216
Woods, Arvine 312
Woods, Arvine W. 312
Woods, Calvin 735
Woods, Caroline 312
Woods, Catharine 419, 684
Woods, Catherine 216
Woods, Clarissa 735
Woods, Daniel 113
Woods, David 735
Woods, Ebenezer Zane 113
Woods, Elijah 113
Woods, Elizabeth 50, 216, 288, 639, 684
Woods, Enos 308
Woods, Frederick 308
Woods, Gardner 735
Woods, George 639
Woods, H. 312
Woods, Hannah 312, 639
Woods, Hetty 113
Woods, Isabella 639
Woods, J. F. (Sgt.) 312
Woods, J. P. 312
Woods, James 312, 457
Woods, James (Jr.) 457
Woods, James H. 312, 639
Woods, James P. 312
Woods, Jane 106
Woods, Jesse 132
Woods, John 113, 216, 684
Woods, Joseph 312
Woods, Joseph H. 198
Woods, Joshua 308
Woods, Laury 735

Woods, Leonard 735
Woods, Lonidas H. 639
Woods, Margaret 684
Woods, Mary 216, 684
Woods, Mary A. 312
Woods, Mathew 213
Woods, Moses 414
Woods, Nancy 639
Woods, Polly 704
Woods, Rebecca 113, 684
Woods, Robert 113
Woods, Sally 684
Woods, Samuel 563
Woods, Sarah 296, 312
Woods, Sarah Ann 50, 113
Woods, Sary 704
Woods, Simon 718
Woods, Thomas 113, 216
Woods, W. R. 312
Woods, William 104,
   230, 457, 667, 684
Woods, Wm. 106
Woodside, John 542
Woodside, Robert 308
Woodson, Alex 46, 47
Woodward, Elooman 80
Woodward, Eunice 83
Woodward, Isaac 630
Woodward, Isaac M. 444
Woodward, John 309
Woodward, John C. 381
Woodward, Levi 567
Woodward, Oliver A. 80
Woodward, Samuel 500
Woodward, William 140,
   444, 558, 569, 572
Woodworth, Daniel 575
Woodyard, Matilda 83
Woolard, Catherine 254
Woolard, Elizabeth 253
Woolard, Isaac 254
Woolard, John 261, 728
Woolard, John Odel 429
Woolard, Joseph M. 253
Woolard, Polly 728
Woolard, Walter 253
Woolery, William G. 65
Wooley, John 572
Wooley, Martha 572
Woolf, Conrod 503
Woolf, George 509
Woolf, John 309
Woolf, Nancy 627
Woolfe, John 637
Woolis, John 606
Woolman, Abraham 534
Woolman, John 514
Woolman, Louisa 55
Woolman, Mary 224
Woolman, Mary Ann 311
Woolman, Ruth 534
Woolmen, Elizabeth 532
Woolrey, Rachael 100
Woolsey, Elizabeth 334
Woolsey, Jos. 32
Woolsey, Joseph 12, 18,
   21, 32
Woolsey, Sarah Jane 333
Woolsy, Betsey 625

Woolverton, Thomas 162
Wooster, Maria 417
Wooten, Sally 478
Wooten, Thomas 477
Wootring, Peter 414
Worch, Sebastian 354
Word, Benjamin 420
Wordley, El. 10
Wordner, Thomas 406
Work, Ann 432
Work, John 423
Work, Joseph (Sr.) 425
Work, Nancy 425
Work, Robert 414
Workman, --- 208
Workman, Abigail 702
Workman, Abraham 702
Workman, Daniel 210
Workman, Elizabeth 702
Workman, Eve 702
Workman, Hannah 702
Workman, Isaac 106, 702
Workman, Jane 702
Workman, John 104, 702
Workman, Joseph 469, 702
Workman, Levi 702
Workman, Lucinda 582
Workman, Lydia 702
Workman, Margaret 702
Workman, Mary 702
Workman, Nancy 702
Workman, Rachel 619
Workman, Rebecca 702
Workman, Sarah 702
Workman, Solomon 702
Workman, Stephen 702
Workman, Susannah 702
Worley, Caleb 369
Worley, John 36, 369
Worley, Nathan 369
Worline, John 384
Worll, Richard 309
Worman, David 312
Worman, Henry 312
Worman, Joshua 311
Worman, Noah 312
Worrel, Mary 295
Worrel, Nancy 587
Worriner, Ann 217
Worriner, Mary 217
Worshell, David 38
Worst, Robert 18
Worstell, David 38
Worstell, Joseph 12
Worth, John A. 604
Worth, Joseph 154, 167
Worth, Massy 168
Worthington, Albert 635
Worthington, Albert G.
   635
Worthington, Eleanor 635
Worthington, Elizabeth
   635
Worthington, Francis 635
Worthington, James 635
Worthington, James T.
   635
Worthington, Jane 465
Worthington, Joseph 609

Worthington, Margaret
   635
Worthington, Mary 635
Worthington, Nancy 226
Worthington, Sarah 126,
   635
Worthington, T. 13, 14,
   15, 16, 17, 18, 19,
   20, 22, 635
Worthington, Thomas 13,
   635
Worthington, Thos. 482
Worthington, William 635
Worthman, Sary 422
Wost, Florence May 229
Wost, G. S. 229
Wost, J. M. 229
Wray, James 149
Wray, Rebecca 303
Wray, Samuel 309
Wreff, Rebecca 68
Wren, Thomas 227
Wresler, Henry 123
Wright, A. C. 402
Wright, Abel 277, 282
Wright, Abigail 283
Wright, Abraham 273, 739
Wright, Abram 739, 741
Wright, Albert 328
Wright, Alice 524
Wright, Allen 444
Wright, Amos 273, 444
Wright, Ann 277, 444, 683
Wright, Anthony 444
Wright, Asa 51, 53, 56,
   64
Wright, Barbara 643, 646
Wright, Benjamin 309
Wright, Betty 281
Wright, Burgess 735
Wright, Charity 281, 299
Wright, Charles 323,
   328, 636
Wright, Charles H. 646
Wright, Charlotte 269
Wright, Clarissa 299
Wright, Daniel 328, 334
Wright, David 277, 633
Wright, Edward 328
Wright, Elias 50
Wright, Eliza Ann 225
Wright, Elizabeth 12,
   281, 732
Wright, Elizabeth Mary
   259
Wright, Elwood 328
Wright, Emson 276
Wright, Esther 220
Wright, Evelina 444
Wright, Gilbert 309
Wright, H. S. 646
Wright, Hannah 283
Wright, Henry 643
Wright, Hiram 732, 733
Wright, Hiram (Rev.) 321
Wright, Hosea 469
Wright, I. W. 401, 402
Wright, Isaac 276, 281,
   402, 694

Wright, Isaac W. 402, 403
Wright, Isabella 444
Wright, Issaac W. 402
Wright, Jacob 469, 684
Wright, James 281
Wright, Jane 56, 64
Wright, Jehu 324
Wright, John 3, 4, 12, 44, 45, 227, 256, 258, 259, 281, 309, 444, 449
Wright, John (Capt.) 44
Wright, John (III) 630
Wright, John D. 620
Wright, John T. 42
Wright, Joseph 315, 316, 630, 635
Wright, Joshua 262
Wright, Josiah 469
Wright, Judith 308
Wright, Julian 643
Wright, Lewis 328
Wright, Lucy 168
Wright, Margaret 444, 735
Wright, Martha 226, 301, 474, 684
Wright, Martin 328
Wright, Mary 106, 172, 328, 387, 453, 461
Wright, Nancy 636
Wright, Nathan 313
Wright, Patsy 328
Wright, Patty 474
Wright, Phebe 281
Wright, Rachel 281, 444
Wright, Robert 641
Wright, Ruel 309
Wright, Ruth 281
Wright, Sampson 259
Wright, Samuel 6, 29, 208, 220, 751
Wright, Sarah 52, 272, 281, 684
Wright, Selvinv 694
Wright, Snythia 271
Wright, Sophia 525
Wright, Stephen 42
Wright, Susanna 281, 412
Wright, Susanna James 530
Wright, Susannah 275, 444
Wright, Thomas 109, 120, 277, 683
Wright, Thomas C. 535
Wright, W. C. 402
Wright, W. W. 699
Wright, William 109, 281, 328, 472, 630, 684
Wright, Wm. 106
Wright, Wm. W. 695
Wrightsman, Jacob 277
Wrightsman, Nancy 272, 277
Write, Mary 225
Write, Polly 225

Writehouse, Thos. 19
Wroten, Westly 594
Wunderlich, E. 346
Wyant, Mary 590
Wyath, Joseph (Col.) 623
Wyatt, Achsah 78
Wyatt, Anna 389
Wyatt, Charlotte 390
Wyatt, Ezra 390
Wyatt, John 80
Wyatt, Joshua 84
Wyatt, Leonard 390
Wyatt, Mary Ann 390
Wyatt, Nathaniel 390
Wyatt, Polly 82
Wyatt, Sarah 390
Wyatt, T. D. 390
Wyckiff, John 80
Wyckoff, Sarah 628
Wycloff, Matthew 419
Wycoff, Elisabeth 9
Wycoff, John 630
Wycoff, Samuel 630
Wycuff, Francia 625
Wyeth, Fanny 222
Wykle, Jacob 652
Wykoff, Elizabeth 631
Wykoff, John 12
Wykoff, Samuel 634, 639
Wyland, Elizabeth 524
Wyland, Jonathan 227
Wyland, Susannah 519
Wylde, Benj. 394
Wylde, Benjamin 394
Wylde, Elizabeth 394
Wylde, Hannah Worcester 394
Wylde, Sarah H. 394
Wylde, Sarah June 394
Wylde, William 394
Wylde, Wm. 394
Wyley, David 309
Wylie, David 317
Wylie, Elizabeth 723
Wylie, John 425
Wylie, Mary Ann 425
Wylie, Samuel 317
Wyllis, Mary W. 637
Wyllis, Oliver St.John 637
Wyllis, Samuel 637
Wyllis, William 637
Wyllis, William Alfred 637
Wyllys, Samuel 637
Wyman, John 658
Wymer, Sally 472
Wymott, Catherine 51
Wyrick, Peter (Jr.) 551
Wysong, Joseph 259, 264

--- Y ---

Yacobe, John 51
Yancy, Joel 445
Yankey, Jonathan 6
Yants, Catharine 528

Yaple, Alfred 665
Yarden, Margery 11
Yarian, Conrad 309
Yarnal, Thomas 604
Yarnall, Abraham 309
Yarnall, Amos J. 186
Yarrian, Matthias 309
Yasell, Sarah 50
Yates, Aquitiah 629
Yates, Benjamin 309, 707
Yates, Easter 513
Yates, Elizabeth 625
Yates, Jamima 290
Yates, Joseph 68
Yates, Lydia 116
Yates, Mary 627
Yates, William 522
Yatts, Mary 294
Yauger, Sarah Ann 603
Yawky, Sarah 333
Yeager, Philip 667
Yeakle, Michael 147, 148, 154, 155
Yeaman, Ann 68
Yearger, James 74
Yearger, John 381
Yearnal, Jane 182
Yeater, Samuel 71
Yeates, Mary 294
Yeatman, Griffin 563, 567
Yeazel, Solomon 53
Yeichner, Jacob 343
Yeichner, Martin 343
Yenge, Maria 343
Yengling, Elizabeth 304
Yeoman, Abigail 443, 464
Yeoman, Alva 456
Yeoman, Assenath 702
Yeoman, Benjamin S. 449
Yeoman, James 456
Yeoman, Jared 456
Yeoman, Lydia 456
Yeoman, Minerva 456
Yeoman, Samantha 456
Yeoman, Samuel F. 456
Yeoman, Stephen 443, 449, 450
Yeoman, Walter 456
Yergen, Margaret 136
Yetzel, Ester 343
Yingling, Franey 706
Yingling, Polly 703
Yoakam, Absalom 700
Yoakam, Drusilla 700
Yoakam, Elizabeth 700
Yoakam, Jacob 700
Yoakam, John 700
Yoakam, Michael 700
Yoakam, Michael (Jr.) 700
Yoakam, Morgan Diether 700
Yoakam, Ruth 700
Yoakam, William 700
Yoesting, Ferd. (Rev.) 50
Yoesting, Ferdinand (Rev.) 50